THE SWORD OF ST. MICHAEL

THE SWORD OF ST. MICHAEL

THE 82ND AIRBORNE DIVISION IN WORLD WAR II

GUY LoFARO

DA CAPO PRESS
A Member of the Perseus Books Group

 Printed in the United States of America. For information, address Da Capo Press, 11 Cambridge Center, Cambridge, MA 02142.

Designed by Trish Wilkinson
Set in 10.75 point Adobe Garamond Pro by the Perseus Books Group

Library of Congress Cataloging-in-Publication Data

LoFaro, Guy.
The Sword of St. Michael : the 82nd Airborne Division in World War II / Guy LoFaro.
p. cm.
Includes bibliographical references and index.
ISBN 978-0-306-82023-6 (hardcover : alk. paper)—ISBN 978-0-306-82024-3 (e-book) 1. United States. Army. Airborne Division, 82nd. 2. World War, 1939–1945—Regimental histories—United States. 3. World War, 1939–1945—Campaigns—Western Front. 4. World War, 1939–1945—Aerial operations, American. 5. World War, 1939–1945—Personal narratives, American. I. Title. II. Title: Sword of Saint Michael.
D769.34682nd .L64 2011
940.54'1273—dc22 2011013352

Published by Da Capo Press
A Member of the Perseus Books Group
www.dacapopress.com

10 9 8 7 6 5 4 3 2 1

To the troopers of "The Division," past, present, future

. . . but the sword
Of Michael from the Armorie of God
Was giv'n him tempered so, that neither keen
Nor solid might resist that edge: it met
The sword of Satan with steep force to smite
Descending, and in half cut sheere, nor staid,
But with swift wheele reverse, deep entering shar'd
All his right side; then Satan first knew pain . . .

JOHN MILTON, *PARADISE LOST*

CONTENTS

ACKNOWLEDGMENTS

MORE THAN ANYONE, I owe a debt that I will never be able to repay to Starlyn Jorgensen. I met Star many years ago through a mutual friend who, when he learned I was working on a history of the 82nd Airborne Division, told me that I had to get in touch with Star because she knew more about the division than anyone he'd ever met. He was right. Star provided me with counsel, contacts, and, most important, comfort over the course of this project. She and her husband, Al (to whom I owe the title), have been the best of friends. Though I have dedicated this book to the troopers of the division, it is also here dedicated to Star.

I also want to thank my professors at Stony Brook University, in particular Professor Michael Barnhart, my adviser, who hung with me and this project well beyond the point when most would have abandoned a foundering student, and Professors Herman Lebovics and Ian Roxborough, who agreed to read a much larger (and poorer) version of this work. Thanks also go to Professor John Shy of the University of Michigan, who taught me how to read and write history, and Professor Dennis Showalter of Colorado College, who took the time while he was a visiting professor at West Point to help me hone my message.

I had the great fortune to have been afforded the opportunity to teach at West Point on two separate occasions and while there was mentored by two outstanding soldier-scholars, Colonels Jim Johnson, PhD, and Cole Kingseed, PhD. They not only afforded me the time I needed to get this project off the ground, they also provided encouragement, friendship, and leadership.

For getting this project to someone who would take the time to look at it I owe my agent, Gayle Wurst at Princeton International Agency for the Arts, a huge debt of gratitude. I also want to thank Bob Pigeon, Annie Lenth, and Annette Wenda of Perseus/Da Capo for guiding me through the publication process and making this work much better than the one I submitted. Thanks go to Chris Robinson, as well, for the beautiful maps.

One of the great pleasures of doing history like this is the opportunity it affords to meet some wonderful persons, not last of whom were the veterans who took the time to tell me their stories and take phone calls from an unknown would-be author. Without exception they were wonderful men and exemplars of America's Greatest Generation. Their names are listed in the bibliography. Others I met along the way who were both kind and helpful were the staffs of the Alden Library at Ohio University; the U.S. Military History Institute at Carlisle Barracks, Pennsylvania; and the National Archives and Records Administration at College Park, Maryland.

Then there is the great list of persons who helped me in ways large and small, by either providing me with information, pictures, or advice or by offering their support and encouragement. They are, in alphabetical order: Doug Bekke, Nick Benne, Mike Bigalke, Carolynn Cavanaugh, Laurier Fish, Barbara Gavin Fauntleroy, Larry Junek, Al Larson, Len Lebenson, John Lee, J. J. Marzullo, Emily Norman, Don Patton, Jason Pogacnik, Cary Russell, Dave Schmitt, Les Schwarm, Bill Solis, Tristan To, Chris Turner, Marilyn Wasleski, and Cheryl Weissman.

I want to thank my parents, Tony and Judy, for their love and encouragement, not only with this project, but in life; my daughter, Beth, who endured years of grumbling from a distracted father but who never failed to happily read parts of the manuscript aloud so I could make sure that what I wrote made sense; and Max and Jake, for keeping their friends out of the house when I was struggling over some particularly difficult sentences and for providing humor and a sense of proportion.

Finally, I could not have done this without my wife, Diane. Not only did she read several drafts of this book, she also endured hours of my "thinking aloud" as I tried to work out just what it was I wanted to say. She never wavered in her faith in me and this project, even when subjected to days on end of tromping through battlefields in France, Belgium, and Holland. Through it all she loved me, and because of it all I love her more.

TABLE OF EQUIVALENT RANKS

U.S. ARMY	GERMAN ARMY	WAFFEN SS
General of the Army	Generalfeldmarschall	Reichsführer SS
General	Generaloberst	Oberstgruppenführer
Lieutenant General	General der Infanterie (or Artillerie, Panzertruppen, etc.)	Obergruppenführer
Major General	Generalleutnant	Gruppenführer
Brigadier General	Generalmajor	Brigadeführer
(None)	(None)	Oberführer
Colonel	Oberst	Standartenführer
Lieutenant Colonel	Oberstleutnant	Obersturmbannführer
Major	Major	Sturmbannführer
Captain	Hauptmann	Hauptsturmführer
First Lieutenant	Oberleutnant	Obersturmführer
Second Lieutenant	Leutnant	Untersturmführer

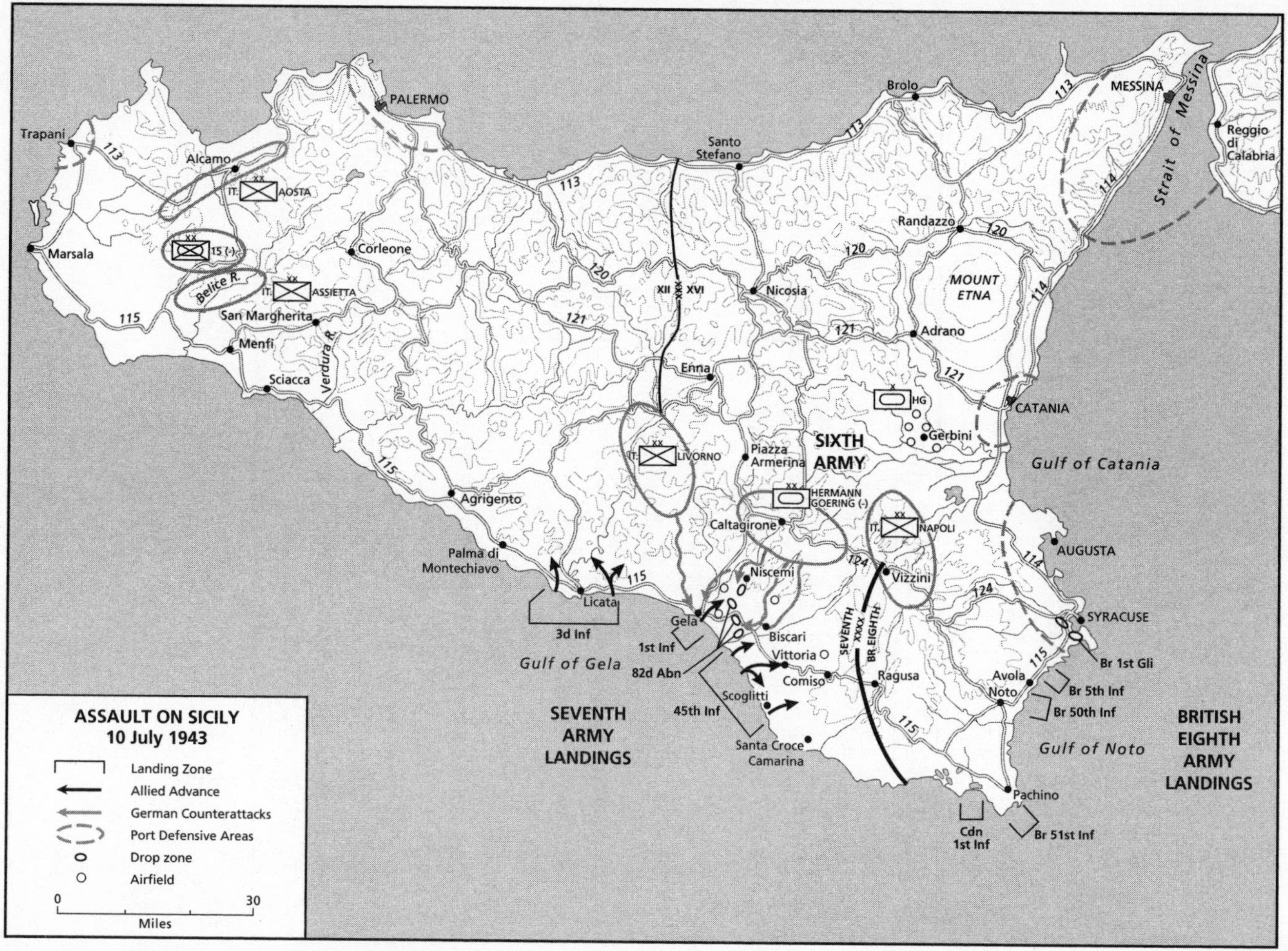
ASSAULT ON SICILY
10 July 1943
Landing Zone
Allied Advance
German Counterattacks
Port Defensive Areas
Drop zone
Airfield
0
30
Miles
PALERMO
Trapani
Alcamo
Marsala
AOSTA
15 (-)
Belice R.
ASSIETTA
Corleone
San Margherita
Menfi
Sciacca
Verdura R.
Santo Stefano
XII
XVI
Nicosia
Enna
LIVORNO
Agrigento
Palma di Montechiavo
Licata
3d Inf
Gela
1st Inf
82d Abn
45th Inf
Gulf of Gela
SEVENTH ARMY LANDINGS
Piazza Armerina
SIXTH ARMY
HERMANN GOERING (-)
Caltagirone
Niscemi
Biscari
Vittoria
Comiso
Scoglitti
Santa Croce Camarina
NAPOLI
Vizzini
SEVENTH
XXXX
BR EIGHTH
Ragusa
HG
Gerbini
Adrano
MOUNT ETNA
Randazzo
Brolo
MESSINA
Strait of Messina
Reggio di Calabria
CATANIA
Gulf of Catania
AUGUSTA
SYRACUSE
Br 1st Gli
Avola
Noto
Br 5th Inf
Br 50th Inf
Gulf of Noto
Pachino
Cdn 1st Inf
Br 51st Inf
BRITISH EIGHTH ARMY LANDINGS

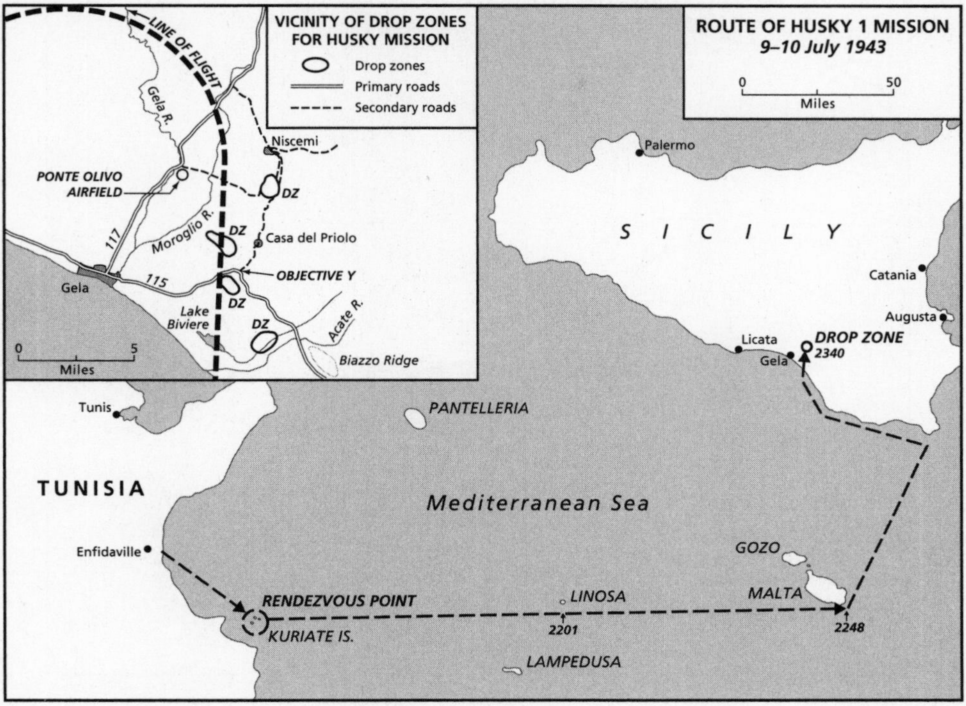
VICINITY OF DROP ZONES FOR HUSKY MISSION
Drop zones
Primary roads
Secondary roads
LINE OF FLIGHT
Gela R.
Niscemi
PONTE OLIVO AIRFIELD
DZ
Moroglio R.
DZ
Casa del Priolo
117
OBJECTIVE Y
Gela
115
DZ
Lake Biviere
DZ
Acate R.
Biazzo Ridge
0
5
Miles
ROUTE OF HUSKY 1 MISSION
9–10 July 1943
0
50
Miles
Palermo
SICILY
Catania
Augusta
Licata
Gela
DROP ZONE
2340
Tunis
PANTELLERIA
TUNISIA
Mediterranean Sea
Enfidaville
GOZO
MALTA
RENDEZVOUS POINT
LINOSA
KURIATE IS.
2201
2248
LAMPEDUSA

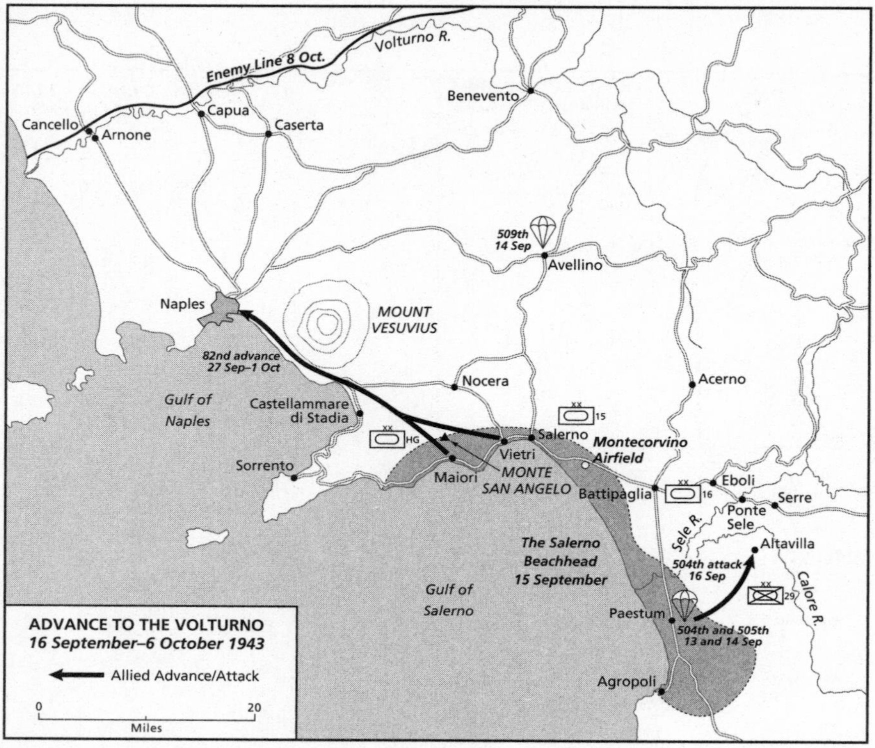
ADVANCE TO THE VOLTURNO
16 September–6 October 1943
Allied Advance/Attack
0
20
Miles
Enemy Line 8 Oct.
Volturno R.
Benevento
Capua
Cancello
Arnone
Caserta
509th
14 Sep
Avellino
Naples
MOUNT
VESUVIUS
82nd advance
27 Sep–1 Oct
Nocera
Acerno
Gulf of
Naples
Castellammare
di Stadia
HG
15
Salerno
Montecorvino
Airfield
Vietri
Sorrento
Maiori
MONTE
SAN ANGELO
Battipaglia
16
Eboli
Serre
Ponte
Sele
Sele R.
The Salerno
Beachhead
15 September
Altavilla
504th attack
16 Sep
29
Calore R.
Gulf of
Salerno
Paestum
504th and 505th
13 and 14 Sep
Agropoli

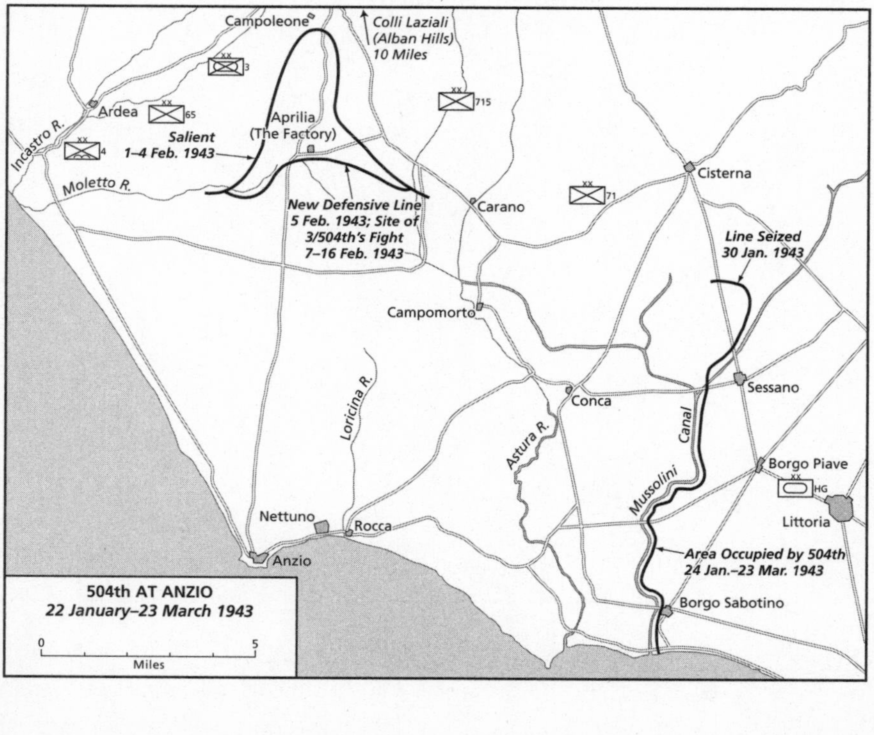
504th AT ANZIO
22 January–23 March 1943
0
5
Miles
Campoleone
Colli Laziali
(Alban Hills)
10 Miles
3
Ardea
65
715
Incastro R.
Aprilia
(The Factory)
4
Salient
1–4 Feb. 1943
Cisterna
Moletto R.
71
New Defensive Line
5 Feb. 1943; Site of
3/504th's Fight
7–16 Feb. 1943
Carano
Line Seized
30 Jan. 1943
Campomorto
Loricina R.
Sessano
Conca
Canal
Astura R.
Borgo Piave
HG
Mussolini
Littoria
Nettuno
Rocca
Area Occupied by 504th
24 Jan.–23 Mar. 1943
Anzio
Borgo Sabotino

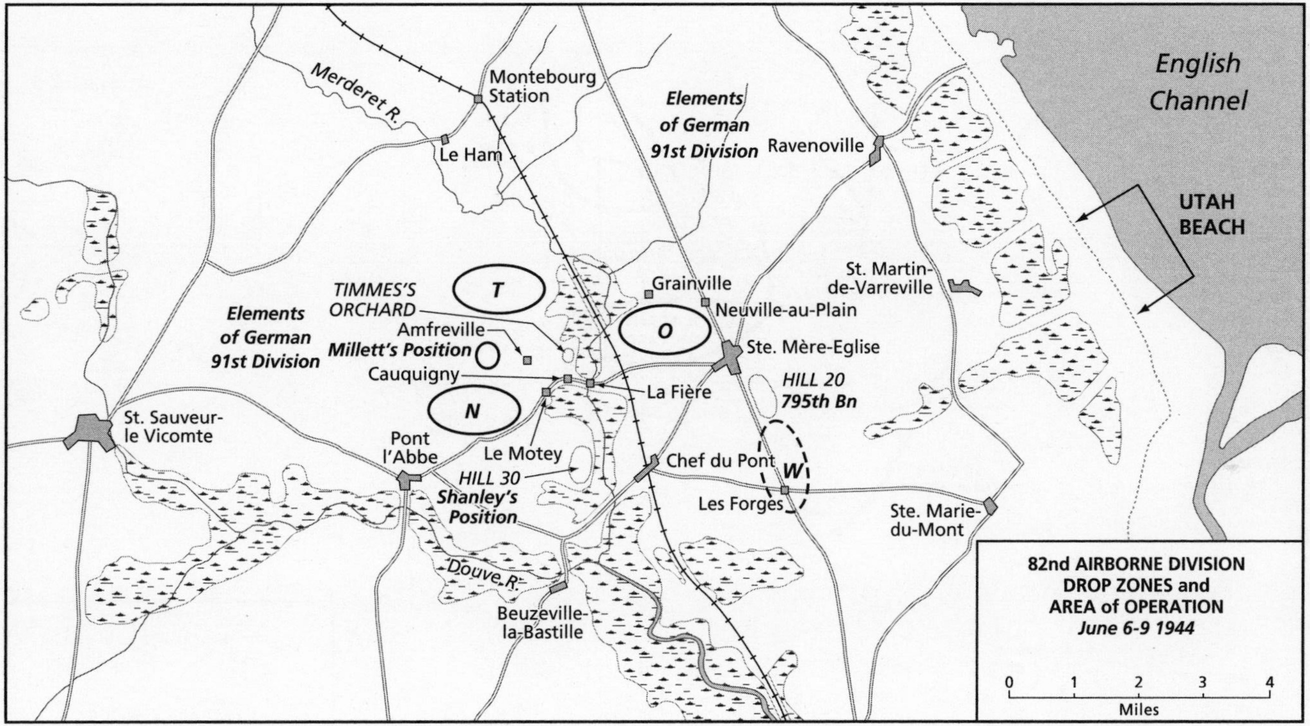

English Channel
UTAH BEACH
Montebourg Station
Merderet R.
Le Ham
Elements of German 91st Division
Ravenoville
St. Martin-de-Varreville
Grainville
Neuville-au-Plain
Ste. Mère-Eglise
T
O
N
W
TIMMES'S ORCHARD
Amfreville
Millett's Position
Elements of German 91st Division
Cauquigny
La Fière
HILL 20
795th Bn
St. Sauveur-le Vicomte
Pont l'Abbe
Le Motey
HILL 30
Shanley's Position
Chef du Pont
Les Forges
Ste. Marie-du-Mont
Douve R.
Beuzeville-la-Bastille
82nd AIRBORNE DIVISION
DROP ZONES and
AREA of OPERATION
June 6-9 1944
0 1 2 3 4
Miles

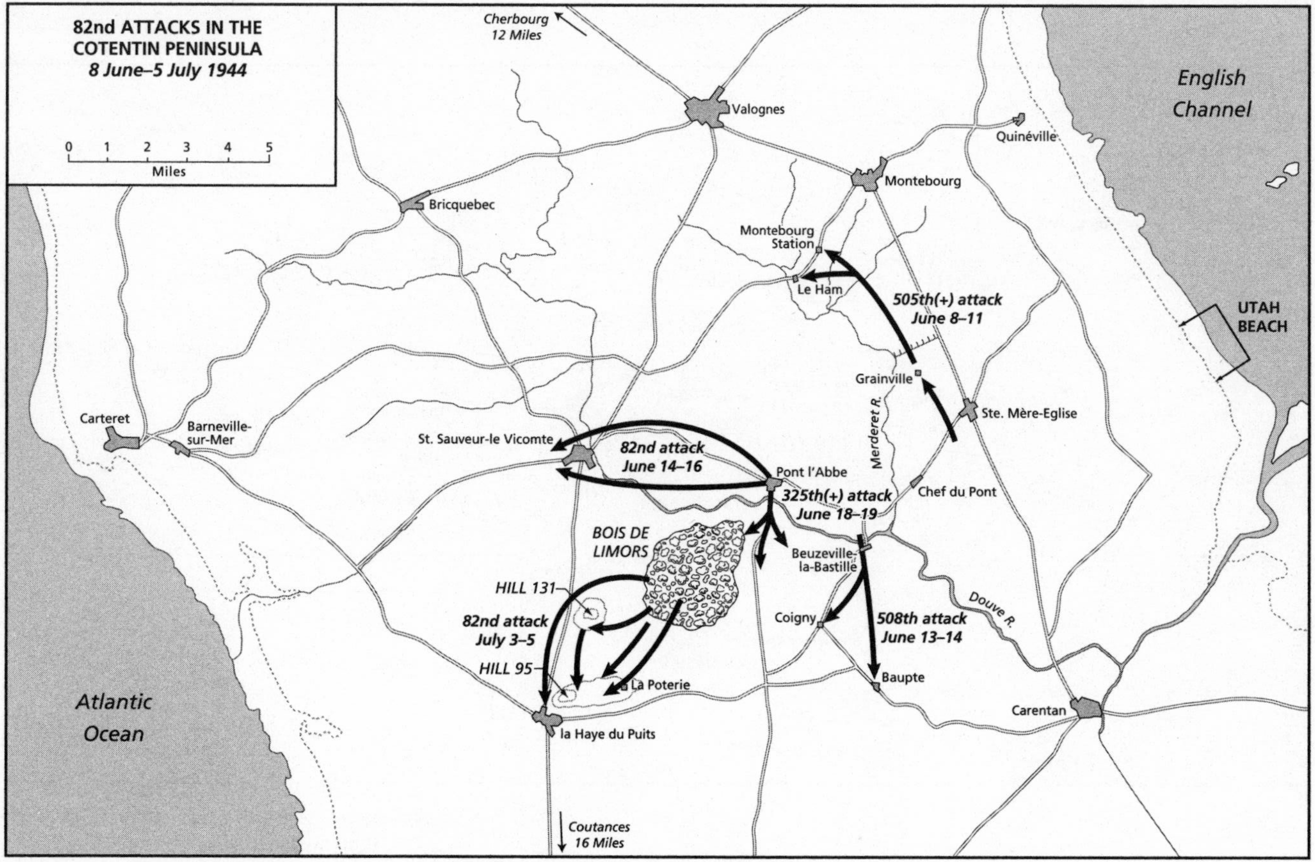
82nd ATTACKS IN THE
COTENTIN PENINSULA
8 June–5 July 1944
0 1 2 3 4 5
Miles
Cherbourg
12 Miles
English
Channel
Valognes
Quinéville
Montebourg
Bricquebec
Montebourg
Station
Le Ham
505th(+) attack
June 8–11
UTAH
BEACH
Grainville
Ste. Mère-Eglise
Merderet R.
Carteret
Barneville-
sur-Mer
St. Sauveur-le Vicomte
82nd attack
June 14–16
Pont l'Abbe
Chef du Pont
325th(+) attack
June 18–19
BOIS DE
LIMORS
Beuzeville-
la-Bastille
HILL 131
82nd attack
July 3–5
Coigny
508th attack
June 13–14
Douve R.
HILL 95
La Poterie
Baupte
Carentan
Atlantic
Ocean
la Haye du Puits
Coutances
16 Miles

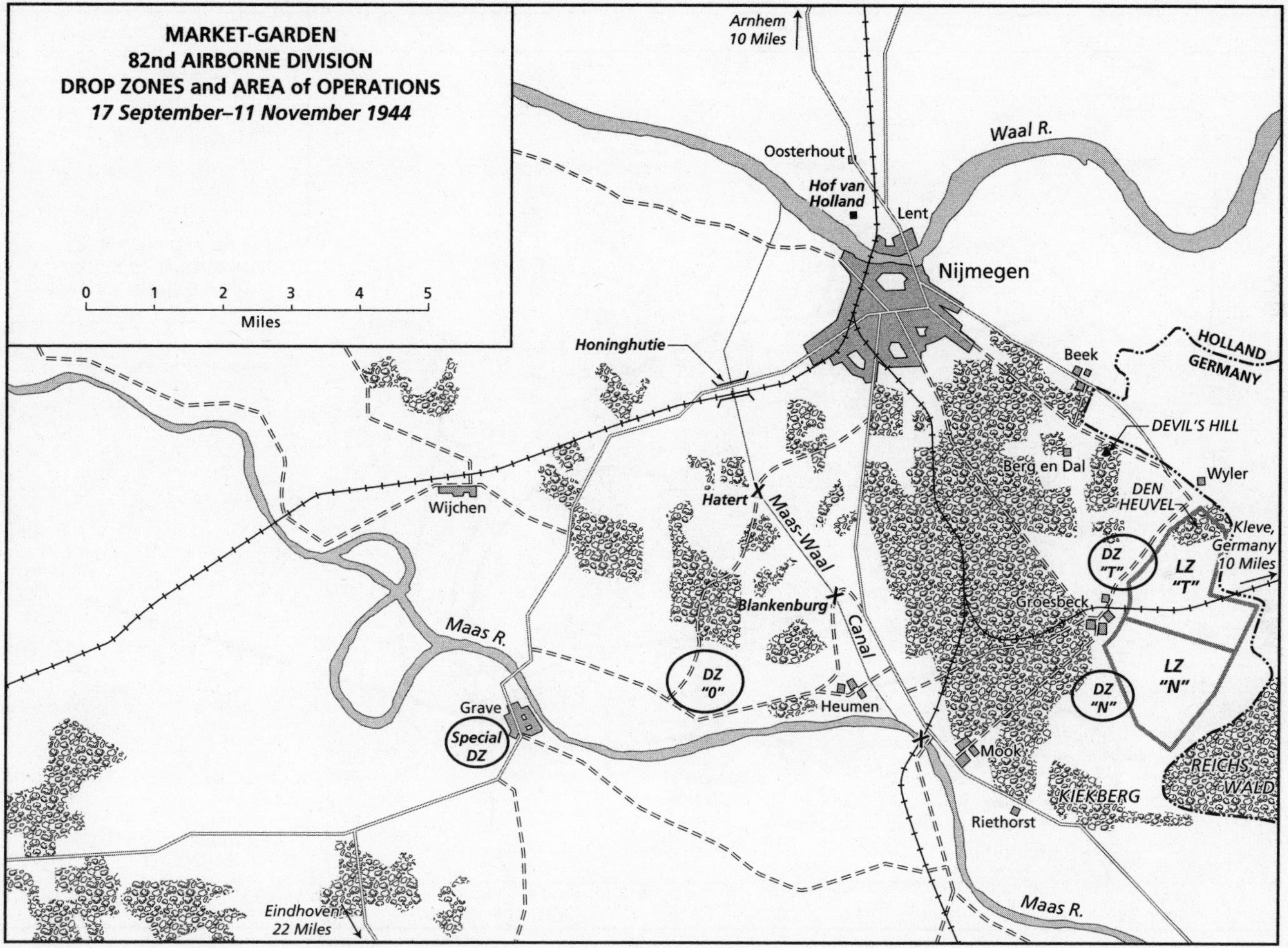
MARKET-GARDEN
82nd AIRBORNE DIVISION
DROP ZONES and AREA of OPERATIONS
17 September–11 November 1944
0 1 2 3 4 5
Miles
Arnhem
10 Miles
Waal R.
Oosterhout
Hof van Holland
Lent
Nijmegen
Honinghutie
Beek
HOLLAND
GERMANY
DEVIL'S HILL
Berg en Dal
Wyler
DEN HEUVEL
Kleve, Germany
10 Miles
Wijchen
Hatert
Maas-Waal
Canal
Blankenburg
DZ "T"
LZ "T"
Groesbeck
Maas R.
DZ "0"
Heumen
DZ "N"
LZ "N"
Grave
Special DZ
Mook
REICHSWALD
KIEKBERG
Riethorst
Eindhoven
22 Miles
Maas R.

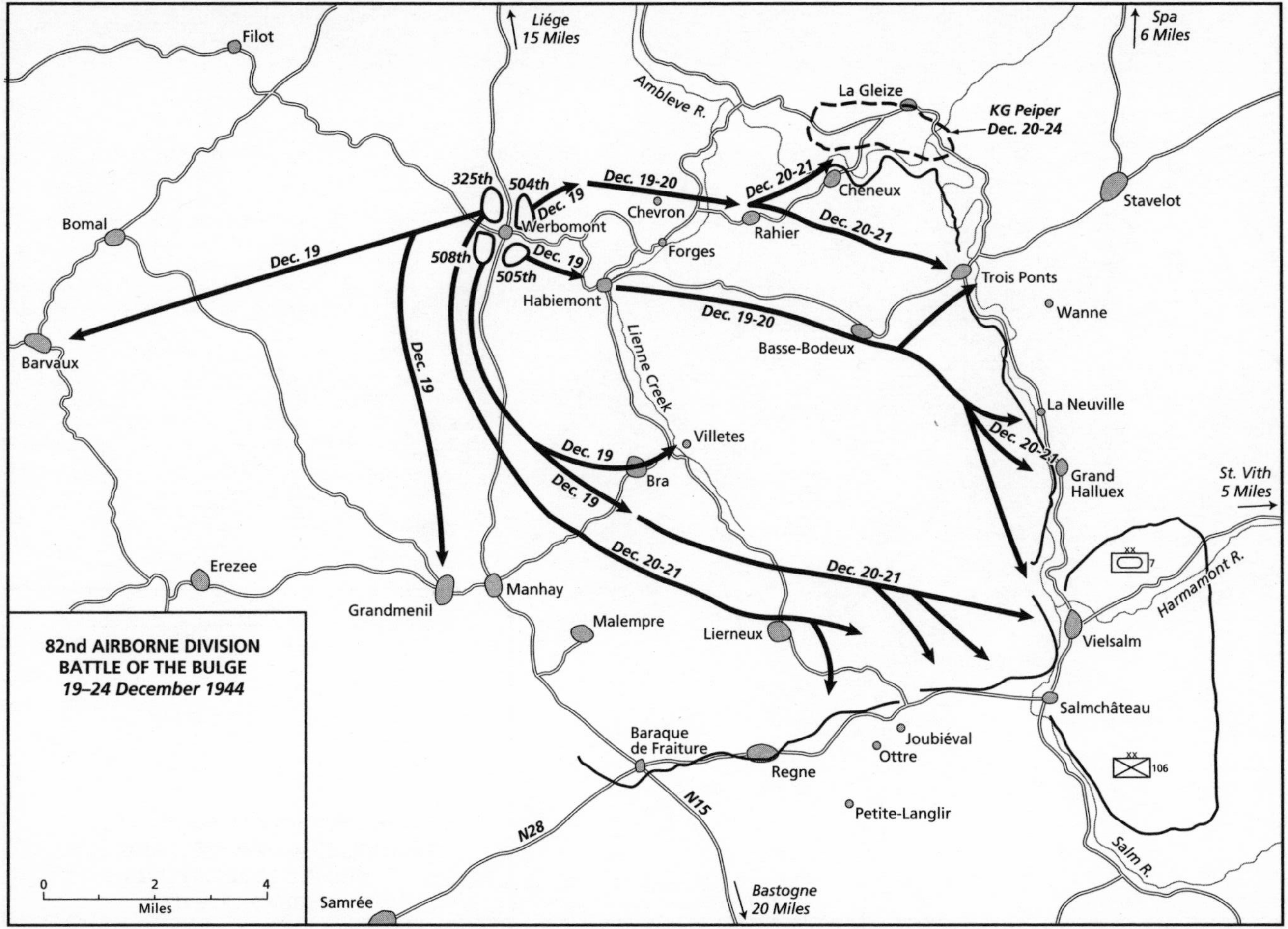

82nd AIRBORNE DIVISION
BATTLE OF THE BULGE
19–24 December 1944

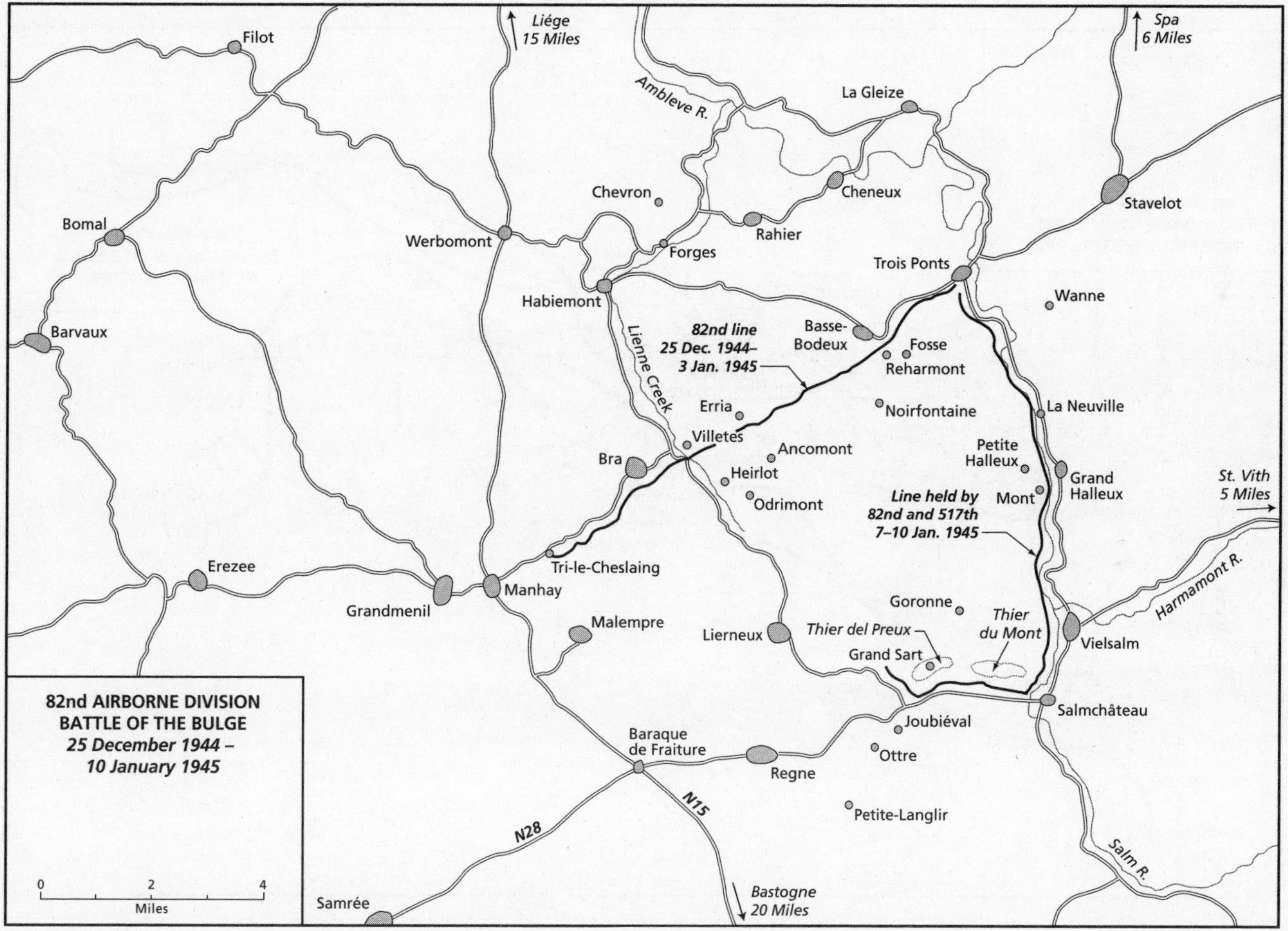
82nd AIRBORNE DIVISION
BATTLE OF THE BULGE
25 December 1944 –
10 January 1945
0
2
4
Miles
Liége
15 Miles
Spa
6 Miles
St. Vith
5 Miles
Bastogne
20 Miles
Filot
Ambleve R.
La Gleize
Chevron
Cheneux
Stavelot
Bomal
Werbomont
Forges
Rahier
Trois Ponts
Habiemont
Wanne
Barvaux
Lienne Creek
Basse-
Bodeux
Fosse
Reharmont
82nd line
25 Dec. 1944–
3 Jan. 1945
Erria
Noirfontaine
La Neuville
Villetes
Ancomont
Petite
Halleux
Bra
Heirlot
Grand
Halleux
Odrimont
Line held by
82nd and 517th
7–10 Jan. 1945
Mont
Tri-le-Cheslaing
Erezee
Grandmenil
Manhay
Goronne
Thier
du Mont
Harmamont R.
Malempre
Lierneux
Thier del Preux
Grand Sart
Vielsalm
Salmchâteau
Joubiéval
Baraque
de Fraiture
Ottre
Regne
N15
Petite-Langlir
N28
Salm R.
Samrée

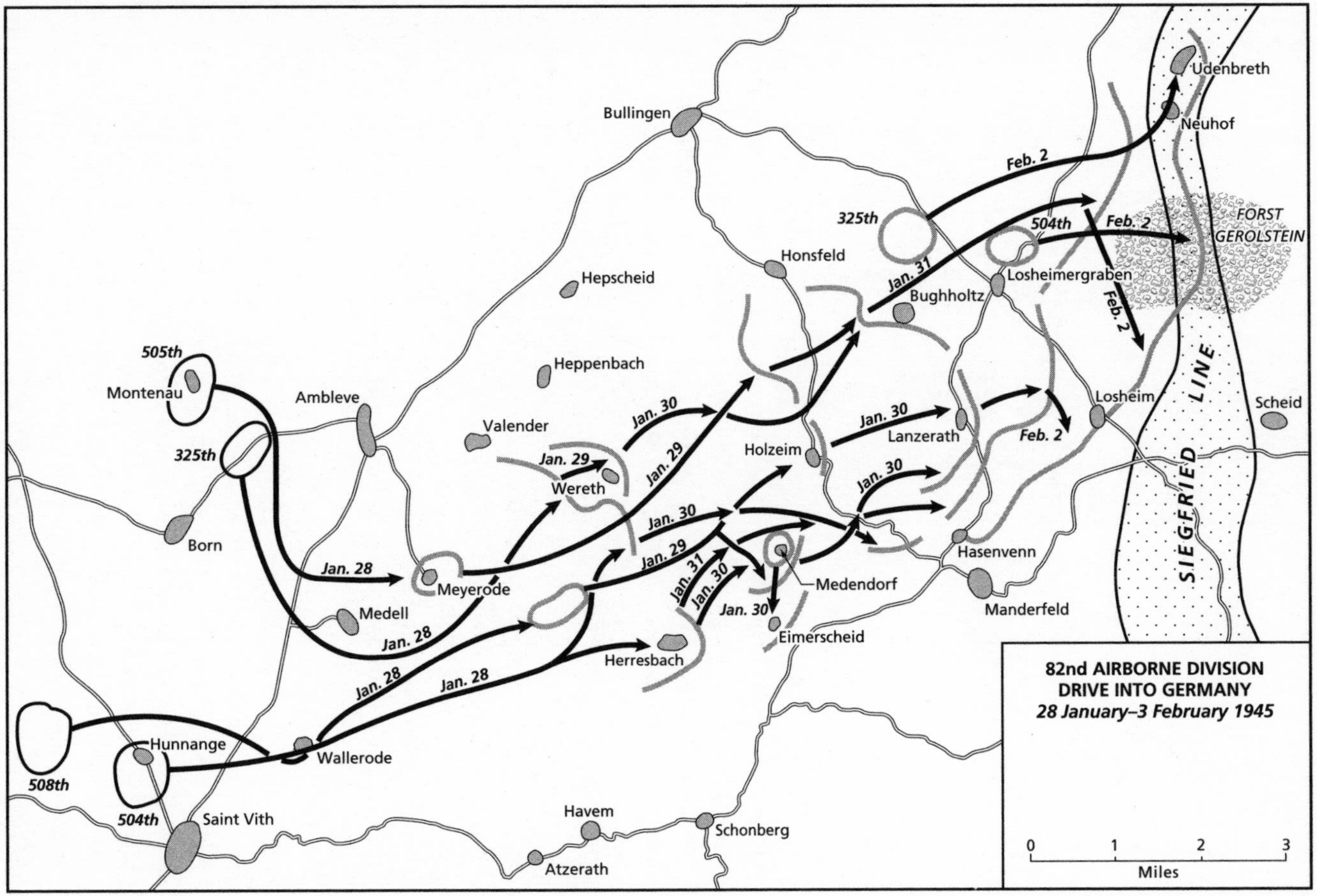

82nd AIRBORNE DIVISION
DRIVE INTO GERMANY
28 January–3 February 1945
0
1
2
3
Miles
Udenbreth
Neuhof
FORST GEROLSTEIN
Scheid
SIEGFRIED LINE
Bullingen
Honsfeld
Hepscheid
Heppenbach
Valender
Montenau
505th
325th
Ambleve
Born
Wereth
Meyerode
Medell
Holzeim
Lanzerath
Bughholtz
Losheimergraben
Losheim
Hasenvenn
Manderfeld
Medendorf
Eimerscheid
Herresbach
Wallerode
Hunnange
508th
504th
Saint Vith
Havem
Atzerath
Schonberg
Jan. 28
Jan. 29
Jan. 30
Jan. 31
Feb. 2

INTRODUCTION

However vague and indefinable the reasons may be—racial stock, training, leadership, motivation, or more likely a blend of these—the US paratroopers were in the forefront of the fight and their combat effectiveness was outstanding.

GENERAL DER PANZERTRUPPEN LEO FREIHERR GEYR VON SCHWEPPENBURG, "GLIMPSES OF THE US SOLDIER"

DURING A CONFERENCE held in 1994 to commemorate the fiftieth anniversary of the Normandy invasion, Stephen Ambrose posited that "man-for-man the American soldier in the campaign in Northwest Europe was way better than his German counterpart." Moreover, continued Ambrose, "The American best, the rangers and the airborne, were way better than the German best."[1] Given the outcome of the Second World War, Ambrose's claims would appear to be nothing more than a statement of the obvious. Yet for many years following the war, through the 1980s, this was not the prevailing orthodoxy. Instead, a spate of historians, political scientists, and sociologists published several influential books, monographs, and journal articles in which they denigrated the battlefield performance of the American army as a whole and claimed that, when compared to the German army of World War II, it was relatively ineffective.

The opening salvo of this postwar discussion on combat effectiveness came from an unlikely source: U.S. Army historian S. L. A. Marshall, who, not more than two years after the war, questioned the battlefield performance of the American army in his influential book *Men Against Fire: The Problem of Battle Command in Future War*. A pioneer in the use of after-action interviews as a means of gathering historical data, Marshall criticized the battlefield performance of American soldiers in both the Pacific and Europe. The battlefield, wrote Marshall, is "the epitome of war" and the place where "the issues of war are decided." The key to success on the battlefield, he continued, is fire superiority, but his interviews revealed that not more than 25 percent of American soldiers actually shot their weapons.[2] According to Marshall, the primary reason for this was the American army's personnel management policies. Marshall maintained that a soldier in combat "is sustained by his fellows," and hence, in order to build effective combat units, it is imperative to foment cohesiveness among the soldiers in a unit, something he claimed the American army did not do during World War II. Instead, U.S. Army personnel managers "moved men around as if they were pegs and nothing counted but a specialist classification number." These managers had become, in Marshall's eyes, "fillers-of-holes rather than architects of the human spirit."[3]

Men Against Fire set the stage for another influential work published the following year by two sociologists, Edward A. Shils and Morris Janowitz, titled "Cohesion and Disintegration in the Wehrmacht in World War II." Whereas Marshall excoriated the American army for failing to nurture cohesiveness within its ranks and pointed to this lack of cohesion as the reason its soldiers performed poorly in combat, Shils and Janowitz posited that it was because the German army actively promoted unit cohesion that its soldiers fought so well. According to them, "The unity of the German Army was in fact sustained only to a very slight extent by the National Socialist political convictions of its members." Instead, what was "more important in the motivation of the determined resistance of the German soldier was the steady satisfaction of certain *primary* personality demands afforded by the social organization of the army."[4] Central to this thesis is the importance of "primary groups," which Shils and Janowitz defined as small groups "characterized by intimate face-to-face association and cooperation."[5] The primary groups of the Germany army of World War II were its squads, platoons, and companies. Recognizing this and the importance of primary group cohesion to combat effectiveness, Germany army personnel managers fashioned a recruiting and replacement system that promoted their formation and sustenance. The result was an organizational structure that satisfied the individual's basic needs for affection, esteem, and power and regulated his personal behavior. Even in the waning days of the war, declared the authors, despite the odds arrayed against them, it was this primary group loyalty and the cohesiveness born of that loyalty that kept German soldiers in the field.

These two works set the tone for much of the postwar analysis about combat effectiveness, especially when that analysis compared the German and American armies, and what eventually developed was "a virtual cult of the Wehrmacht" by which historians accepted a sanitized version of German history that not only separated the German army from its Nazi masters but also heralded the German army of World War Two as a standard to be emulated.[6] This cult also formed the basis of what was, for years, the standard historical interpretation of the war against Nazi Germany. Simply put, this interpretation assumed the superior fighting mettle of the German army and explained its defeat through either the incompetence of its Nazi masters or its inability to withstand the weight of men and materiel aligned against it or a combination of both. Some, like John Keegan, took the notion of German martial prowess to fanciful lengths, comparing German soldiers on the Eastern Front to "the warriors of the Teutonic tribes of old." Others, such as Russell F. Weigley, offered a more sober yet still damning indictment of the American army compared to its German adversary. In his highly regarded *Eisenhower's Lieutenants: The Campaign of France and Germany, 1944–1945*, Weigley wrote that "the United States Army suffered long from a relative absence of the finely honed professional skill of the Germans, officers and men, in every aspect of tactics and operations." As a result, "the German army remained qualitatively superior to the American army, formation for formation, throughout far too many months of the American army's greatest campaign." Victory, he concluded unequivocally, resulted from the Allies' "preponderance of materiel resources" and not battlefield prowess.[7]

As Ambrose's comments indicate, however, there have been recent challenges to the claims of German military superiority. One of the first was from Omer Bartov in *The Eastern Front, 1941–45: German Troops and the Barbarisation of Warfare*. In this work, Bartov tested the Shils and Janowitz thesis by examining three German divisions that fought extensively on the Eastern Front and concluded that "it is difficult to speak of a more or less stable 'primary group' in divisions which suffered between 200 and 300 per cent casualties within the space of about three years of fighting." Having thereby demonstrated that, on the Eastern Front at least, the primary group thesis as a basis for explaining combat motivation could not be sustained, Bartov asked "whether it was possible to fight for years in a foreign and hostile land, with the imminent danger of death lurking behind every tree and hill and to endure the most terrible physical and mental hardship, without believing that all this was necessary for the achievement of some 'higher cause,' however confused and nonsensical, let alone inhuman, it may seem to us today." According to Bartov, the answer to this question lay with the influence exercised by junior officers, "the backbone" of the German army. Bartov's analysis demonstrated that these officers were generally young men who grew up under National Socialism and hailed from the same social classes that supported Hitler's regime. As translators of orders to the rank and file, these young men infused those in their charge with National Socialist ardor. Their impact, combined with the political indoctrination to which German soldiers were subjected, ensured that "by and large, the German soldier on the Eastern Front felt he was fighting for the cause of National Socialism and was motivated by an unquestioning belief in Hitler."[8]

Bartov expanded his thesis in *Hitler's Army: Soldiers, Nazis, and War in the Third Reich*, writing that with the destruction of primary groups in the German army, other factors came to bear to keep German soldiers in the fight. One was an incredibly harsh disciplinary system. The second was that "as the fortunes of the *Ostheer* [German army in the east] rapidly deteriorated, the troops' 'belief' in Hitler did not falter, but rather increased in direct proportion to the hopelessness of the situation." In fact, claimed Bartov, even as the war on the Eastern Front became ever more brutal and inhumane, the troops at the front remained "the firmest of Hitler's followers, and the least cynical about his ideology."[9] Thus, Bartov laid bare the notion of small group cohesion as the primary motivating force for German soldiers on the Eastern Front and exposed what others had taken pains to avoid—the influence of National Socialist ideology on the German army. In addition, by challenging the main pillar upon which the altar of German military prowess had been built, Bartov set the stage for others to look again at prevailing notions of German combat effectiveness and, by extension, American combat effectiveness during the Second World War.

H. P. Willmott took up the challenge in *The Great Crusade: A New Complete History of the Second World War*, in which he wrote of his "contempt for that popularly accepted but pernicious myth of German military excellence." According to Willmott, the blame for Germany's defeat in the Second World War lay squarely at the feet of the German military. "The German military genius," wrote Willmott, "was in fighting, not in war, [and] . . . indeed Germany's failure stemmed from her inability to understand the nature of war."[10]

In *Why the Allies Won*, Richard Overy furthered Willmott's indictment of German military excellence, labeling the preponderance-of-materiel explanation for Allied victory "at best an unsophisticated argument":

> The material balance also tells us little about *how* the weapons were used once the forces got them. This was not a question of economic power or technical ingenuity, but of fighting skills. During the war there were plenty of instances of poorly-armed troops fighting superbly; a super-abundance of weapons and equipment was no guarantee that forces could use them effectively. Fighting power was determined not just by weapons, but by training, organisation, morale and military elan.

Moreover, explained Overy, as the war progressed, Axis forces stagnated, while the Allies learned their lessons and "were forced by the nature of their enemy to stretch their strategic imaginations to embrace ways of warfare that were more ingenious and effective."[11] The result was that, by the end of the war, Allied combat formations were qualitatively every bit as good as those of their enemies.

In separate works, Michael D. Doubler and Peter R. Mansoor further refined the historical debate about German-versus-American military competence, although whereas Willmott and Overy took a comparative approach, Doubler and Mansoor focused mainly on the performance of the American army, thereby bringing full circle the discussion begun by Marshall in 1947. In *Closing with the Enemy: How GIs Fought the War in Europe, 1944–1945*, Doubler offered a detailed assessment of the tactical performance of American army divisions during the war. According to Doubler, it was "the army's ability to learn on the battlefield and to implement improved methods of combined arms warfare [that] contributed significantly to the American success in World War II." American army divisions, he continued, "were more effective instruments of national policy than is generally believed" and were "powerful, cohesive combined arms formations capable of generating awesome firepower and effective ground maneuver." In *The GI Offensive in Europe: The Triumph of American Infantry Divisions, 1941–1945*, Peter R. Mansoor echoed Doubler, writing that one of the main failings of the German army was "its inability to adapt to the changing tactics and operations of its foes as World War II progressed." Conversely, the strength of the American army was "its ability to adapt to changing conditions on battlefields across the globe, its use of intelligence, outstanding fire support, the ability to execute joint operations, and, most important, its endurance."[12]

This work seeks to further the conversation about the combat effectiveness of the American army of World War II by approaching the topic from a micro level. In a manner similar to Bartov's examination of three German army divisions on the Eastern Front, the focus here is on one American army division during its campaigns in Sicily, on the Italian mainland, and in northwest Europe. Notwithstanding the fact that the 82nd Airborne Division was not a typical U.S. Army division of the Second World War, in many respects the 82nd's story mirrors quite closely that of the larger American army of which it was a part. For example, both grew from humble origins. In the summer of 1940, when Germany, France, Britain, and Russia each had millions of men under arms, the U.S. Army as a whole was comparatively minuscule, counting no more than 270,000 soldiers, only 50 of whom constituted its entire airborne contingent.[13] Moreover, in the same manner that the War Department reorganized and reequipped the Army to form armored and mechanized infantry divisions, so too did a small group of airborne enthusiasts bring about the reorganization and reequipping of the 82nd Infantry Division into an airborne division. And finally, when by war's end the American armored and mechanized infantry force could proudly boast that it had bested the Germans at their own game, so could the 82nd Airborne Division boast that it, too, had achieved what Germany's airborne pioneers only dreamed of.

But an examination of America's premier airborne division of World War II offers several unique insights as well. One, of course, is the story of the development and evolution of U.S. Army parachute and glider units, a story that is an integral part of that of the 82nd Airborne Division itself. A second is the multiplicative effect that a relatively small unit can have on operations when its unique capabilities are properly employed and exploited. Third is the power of initiative and innovation at all levels of the chain of command, both in combat and in training. And finally, there is the impact of leadership on morale, unit cohesiveness, esprit, and combat effectiveness, especially the special brand of leadership by example that the division's two wartime commanders both embodied and demanded of their subordinates.

CHAPTER 1

OUR WHOLE FUTURE IS IN THE AIR

But what would be the security of the good, if the bad could at pleasure invade them from the sky? Against an army sailing through the clouds neither walls, nor mountains, nor seas, could afford any security.

—SAMUEL JOHNSON, *THE HISTORY OF RASSELAS, PRINCE OF ABISSINIA*

FIVE DAYS BEFORE the final German surrender of World War II the Supreme Commander of all Allied forces in Europe, General Dwight D. Eisenhower, gathered with his staff for dinner at his headquarters in Rheims, France. Musing aloud about the impending end of the war, Eisenhower commented that he wanted "to seal the Allied victory so completely that no one in Germany, civilian, soldier, airman, or sailor, will fail to appreciate the fact that the 'superrace' has had the hell beaten out of it."[1]

That same day, four hundred miles to the northeast, the troopers of the 82nd Airborne Division were witnessing Eisenhower's desire made manifest. Having "had the hell beaten out of it," an entire German army was making its way into captivity. A report by the division's 319th Glider Field Artillery Battalion captured the poignancy of the scene:

> Along five miles of Highway 191, over which we traveled, was a sight which climaxed two years of warfare for the veterans of this battalion. A whole German Army had laid down its arms and was marching in to surrender. The endless column composed of soldiers on foot, bicycle, motorcycle, automobiles, trucks, tanks, horses and covered wagons crowded the highway as they

> shuffled along westward. Rifles, guns, ammunition and supplies were haphazardly scattered along the route. . . . Wrecked vehicles lying by the road, horses which faltered due to fatigue, and once arrogant field officers side by side with lowly privates sitting on the side of the road doctoring their corns and bunions accentuated the fact that the will to resist in this army had definitely been broken. . . . No one bothered to take prisoners. Like cattle they were herded on to the road and directed toward the stockade.[2]

It was a fitting climax for those wearing the "AA" patch of the 82nd Airborne Division. Not only had they demonstrated the potency of a new form of warfare—vertical envelopment by parachute and glider troops—they did so while serving at the forefront of the Allied effort in Europe. Spearheading invasions, repulsing Axis offensives, and defeating the best that Nazi Germany had to offer, the 82nd's troopers saw some of the most ferocious fighting of the war. Only once did they give up ground and then only after being ordered to do so. They later took back that ground. They accomplished every mission assigned, sometimes at the cost of tremendous casualties, yet they remained doggedly determined to close with and destroy the foe, testament to which is the fact that by war's end, the 82nd Airborne Division participated in more airborne operations than any airborne unit, Axis or Allied, and had more days in combat than almost any American army division. It might be averred that this rings a bit hagiographic. It is, however, true.

Ironically, the U.S. Army was late in coming to accept the idea of airborne troops. Even more ironic, it was an Army man, Brigadier General William L. "Billy" Mitchell, who was one of the first to see the great potential of such a force. In October 1918, he met with General John J. Pershing, the commander of the American Expeditionary Force in France during World War One, to propose his novel idea:

> I . . . proposed to him that in the spring of 1919, when I would have a great force of bombardment airplanes, he should assign one of the infantry divisions permanently to the Air Service, preferably the 1st Division; that we should arm the men with a great number of machine guns and train them to go over the front in our large airplanes, which would carry ten or fifteen of these soldiers. We could equip each man with a parachute, so that when we desired to make a rear attack on the enemy, we could carry these men over the lines and drop them off in parachutes behind the German position. They could assemble at a prearranged strong point, fortify it and we could supply them by aircraft with food and ammunition. Our low[-]flying attack aviation would then cover every road in their vicinity, both day and night, so as

> to prevent the Germans falling on them before they could thoroughly organize the position. Then we could attack the Germans from the rear, aided by an attack from our army on the front and support the whole maneuver with our great air force. This was a perfectly feasible proposition.[3]

But the war ended before Mitchell could carry out his plan, and the idea of forming an American parachute division died, overcome by victory celebrations and the attendant rush to demobilize.

During the ensuing interwar period, the American response to the idea of parachute troops was episodic and fleeting. It was not until 1927, when twelve Marines jumped over Anacostia in Washington, D.C., that the U.S. military conducted its first experiment with parachute troops, although the attitude of the Marine Corps brass about the experiment, and parachuting in general, was that it was "a sideshow, [and] a carnival attraction."[4] The Army's reaction to the concept was similarly ephemeral. It was not until 1928 that it staged its first experiment with parachute troops when it dropped three men and a machine gun from four two-man observation planes at Brooks Field, Texas. After that, the Army did not drop another parachutist until 1940.[5]

The American military's interest in gliders was equally meager, despite a strong civilian gliding program in the United States. In 1922, U.S. Air Service experiments with gliders for use as aerial targets came to naught. Seven years later, the U.S. Navy considered using gliders as escape modules for airship crews, but this too went nowhere. In 1933, the Navy again turned its attention to gliders, going so far as to establish a glider pilot training school at Pensacola, Florida, but abruptly ended the program in 1936 when it got too expensive for the sparse budgets with which it had to operate. In the small interwar Army, meanwhile, gliding became a popular off-duty sport, and in 1931 the Army could even boast a distance soaring champion in Second Lieutenant John C. Crain, who soared for sixteen hours and thirty-eight minutes over Hawaii. Nonetheless, the next year Secretary of War Patrick J. Hurley prohibited soldiers from participating in the sport because of the many injuries they sustained.[6]

In the main, the U.S. Army's interest in wedding aerial transport with ground combat formations during the interwar years was confined to the relatively unimaginative concept of moving troops and equipment from point to point by airplane. The first large-scale test of this means of military transportation occurred on 20 March 1931 when "a heterogeneous group of transport planes" flew the troops and howitzers of B Battery, 2nd Field Artillery Battalion, from France Field in the Panama Canal Zone to a ranch some seventy-six miles away. Upon landing, B Battery "proceeded to go into position and fire a few rounds of blanks to celebrate the advent of a new means of transportation for the field artillery," after which the exercise promptly ended.[7] Two years later, the entire 2nd Field Artillery Battalion replicated this feat when it moved by air from Bejucca to Chorrera in the Panama Canal Zone, a distance of thirty-five miles, an event that prompted the Army to conduct similar experiments with infantry battalions in 1934.[8] Captain George C. Kenney provided a glimpse of the tactical possibilities envisioned by Billy Mitchell when he air-landed a small infantry detachment behind "enemy" lines during maneuvers at Fort DePont, Delaware, in 1933, surprising not only his opponents but the umpires and observers as well.[9] Yet despite these achievements, the U.S. Army was, as an institution, unimpressed with parachutes, gliders, or air-landed troops, and it was not until prompted by events overseas that it again explored their use.

Conversely, as so often happens following a major conflict, it was the defeated that were most avidly driven to innovation, and after World War One it was in Germany and Russia that the potentialities of airborne forces were most thoroughly explored. Shackled by the provisions of the Versailles Treaty, which denied Germany a military air force and severely limited its civilian aviation industry, German flying enthusiasts turned to gliding.[10] The military potential of gliding was not lost on those who rankled over the restrictions placed on Germany's armed forces and who saw the nation's glider clubs as surrogate military pilot training centers in anticipation of a day when the restrictions of Versailles were lifted. In 1922, American ace Eddie Rickenbacker came face-to-face with this sentiment. Traveling through Germany on his honeymoon, Rickenbacker met with a group of his former aerial opponents, who laid out for him their disgust with the provisions of Versailles and the means by which they sought to skirt its restrictions. Speaking with particular vehemence was Hermann Göring, who proclaimed: "Our whole future is in the air. And it is by air power that we are going to recapture the German empire. To accomplish this we will do three things. First, we will teach gliding *as a sport* to all our young men. Then we will build up commercial aviation. Finally, we will create the skeleton of a military air force. When the time comes, we will put all three together—and the German empire will be reborn."[11]

Göring's proclamation proved no false bluster. Not long after coming to power in 1933 the Nazis began an aggressive program to grow a new generation of German aviators by subsidizing glider clubs that, in turn, provided young boys of the Hitler Youth free access to their facilities, training, and certification.[12] Shortly thereafter, the Nazis dropped all pretense of the peaceful pursuit of gliding by subsuming the glider clubs into the Air Ministry. But the Nazis' interest in gliders extended beyond the simple expedient of using them as a means to train pilots; they were also interested in turning gliders into weapons of war and in this vein subsidized research and experimentation toward that end. By 1939 their investment paid off with the development of the DFS-230, a 37.5-foot glider that weighed 1,800 pounds and had a wingspan of 72 feet. It carried a single pilot plus nine combat-equipped soldiers or 2,800 pounds of equipment and could be towed by a JU-52 aircraft, the Luftwaffe's primary transport plane.[13] Sturdy, reliable, easy to manufacture, and cheap (each glider cost but 7,500 deutsche marks, the equivalent cost of ten parachutes), the DFS-230 became Germany's primary military glider during the Second World War.[14]

The Germans also turned to external sources for help in rebuilding their war machine. A secret covenant of the 1922 Russo-German Treaty of Rapallo allowed Germany to conduct military training in Russia beyond the watchful eyes of the Allied Control Commission. This arrangement proved a boon for the German military, and it was in the Soviet Union that they were introduced to the theory and practice of parachute troops.

Led by the brilliant Marshal Mikhail Tukhachevsky, the Red Army was holding theoretical discussions about airborne warfare as early as 1929. Two small yet highly successful tests of this new mode of warfare in 1930 led to the formation in March 1931 of a 164-man experimental parachute unit. From that point, Soviet experimentation with parachute troops picked up considerable momentum; by 1932 the Red Army had conducted more than 550 airborne exercises; by 1933 it had twenty-nine parachute battalions. The Soviets were so convinced of the value of parachute forces that it became the first major military power to incorporate their use in doctrine. In the Red Army's 1936 field regulations, a publication one leading scholar called "the epitome of Soviet pre–World War II doctrinal development," the role of parachute troops was discussed in detail: "Parachute landing units are the effective means . . . [of] disorganizing the command and rear services structure of the enemy. In coordination with forces attacking along the front, parachute landing units can go a long way toward producing a complete rout of the enemy on a given axis."[15] Complementing the development of its parachute force, the Red Army also developed a robust glider force, and by 1934 the Soviets could boast ten glider manufacturing plants, 230 gliding stations, and 57,000 trained glider pilots.[16]

Despite having forged a commanding lead in the organization, equipping, and theoretical employment of parachute and glider troops, the Soviets were unable to exploit this advantage and never dropped more than a brigade at any one time during World War II. By 1943 the Soviets had abandoned large-scale airborne operations altogether and relegated their highly trained paratroopers to partisan and diversionary roles. After the war, a Russian paratroop colonel was asked about this. He replied, "We just couldn't make sense out of all those men and airplanes."[17]

Another who could not make sense of it all was future British field marshal Archibald P. Wavell, who, in 1935, observed a Soviet airborne exercise during which the Red Army flew two parachute regiments totaling more than 1,100 men from airfields 280 kilometers away and dropped them onto a landing zone that they then seized and held against a notional enemy attack until reinforcements could be landed in the airhead. It was, wrote Wavell, "a most spectacular performance," but of "doubtful" tactical value.[18] German military observers, who were also on hand for this and other Red Army demonstrations, disagreed.

One man, in particular, who could not have thought Wavell more wrong was Oberst Kurt Student of Germany's resurgent Luftwaffe. Enthralled by what he saw developing in Russia, Student proselytized for the organization of German parachute and glider units. In this he had a powerful ally and patron, Chief of the Luftwaffe Hermann Göring, who was likewise enamored of parachute and glider forces. In 1933, while Prussian minister of the interior, Göring sponsored the development of a small paramilitary parachute unit in the Prussian police force. When he took command of the Luftwaffe, he used this unit's personnel as cadre to form paratroop units for the German air force.[19] Finding in Student a like-minded protégé, Göring promoted him and appointed him to command Germany's first airborne division. Student took full advantage of Göring's patronage and by war's end had raised eleven paratroop divisions, two paratroop corps, and one paratroop army (which he commanded).[20]

Drawing on what they had observed in Russia, Student and his acolytes revealed in stunning fashion the deadly potential of airborne forces during the opening campaigns of the Second World War. Having made sense of all those men and airplanes, the Germans successfully used airborne forces during the invasions of Denmark and Norway (April 1940), Holland and Belgium (May 1940), and Greece (April 1941). Watching from afar, like-minded American airborne enthusiasts were impressed and began pressing for a similar capability in the U.S. Army. But it was the German invasion of Crete in May 1941, an invasion conducted totally from the air by parachute, glider, and air-landed forces, that proved "the greatest single impetus to airborne development and expansion" in the American army.[21] In an article published in *Military Review* shortly after the war, Lieutenant Colonel Jack G. Cornett, an instructor at the U.S. Army's prestigious Command and General Staff College at Fort Leavenworth, Kansas, characterized the invasion of Crete as "a definite shock to many of those who had scoffed at this new weapon. It was startling. . . . It was thought-compelling. . . . It was new. . . . And most important of all, it was successful! Almost immediately the wheels began to turn in various circles, including our U.S. Army, and although nebulous at that time and opposed by many authorities on war in positions both high and low, its place in modern warfare was assured."[22]

One of those enamored of Germany's use of airborne forces was James M. Gavin, who recalled that as early as 1940, while assigned as a tactics instructor at West Point, he felt that "the most promising area of all was airborne warfare, bringing parachute troops and glider troops to the battlefield in masses." To study this new type of warfare, Gavin obtained from the War Department "copies of the German orders for the invasion of Holland and later, copies of the detailed orders for the invasion of Crete [from which he gleaned] . . . [t]he German method of organizing after landing, the equipment they used in assault and follow-up, and their means of control and command."[23]

Another early student of airborne warfare was William C. Lee, the man who would come to be known as the father of American paratroopers. In January 1941, Lee published an article in *Infantry Journal* in which he cited Germany's use of paratroopers and air-landed infantry in Holland as an example from which the U.S. Army could learn much. In a follow-up article published in April 1941, Lee declared that, based on the German example, "By now, even the most skeptical agree on the feasibility of using airborne troops."[24] Shortly after the end of the war, the official historian of the American Airborne Command and Center further underscored the effect Germany's use of airborne troops had on the development of like organizations in the U.S. Army:

> Not only was attention directed to the accomplishments of the comparatively small German airborne forces employed, but the relative bearing of their achievements in the attainment of the main objective provided a concrete example of the capabilities of airborne troops, when properly employed. The tactics of employment of these German airborne troops furnished an initial guide, which for a time at least, was to influence the development of the doctrine of employment of airborne troops in the United States Army.[25]

Yet Gavin, Lee, and others felt "it would not be enough to copy the Germans, that would never provide a margin sufficient for victory." Recognizing that the U.S. Army was well behind in the race to develop and organize airborne forces, they forcefully promoted their ideas so that they could gain "a quantum jump on the Germans."[26] And by war's end, despite its late start, the U.S. Army organized, trained, and equipped an airborne force that far surpassed anything the Germans, or any nation, could match. Based, at first, on the example set by their enemy and then increasingly on their own experience, American army airborne forces, and the 82nd Airborne Division in particular, ensured that "the German was to reap a sorry harvest from the seeds he had so powerfully sown."[27]

CHAPTER 2

A BREED APART

They walk as if they know how good they are, and they walk like individual men. All combat troops have a special pride and style. All combat troops despise garrison life and garrison soldiers, and all combat troops look like something very rare and would shock anyone with stern ideas about uniforms and compartment [sic]. But these airbornes seem to me even more remarkable than most and, seeing them now, you notice every face, for every face is that of an entire man, and you notice that each man wears his soiled and baggy clothing as if it had been designed for him alone and was not Army issue at all.

—MARTHA GELLHORN, "ROUGH AND TUMBLE"

IT BEGAN WITH a memo. On 1 May 1939 there landed on the desk of the U.S. Army's chief of infantry, Major General George A. Lynch, a War Department memo requesting that he "make a study for the purpose of determining the desirability of organizing, training, and conducting tests of a small detachment of air infantry with a view to ascertaining whether or not our Army should contain a unit or units of this nature." Unlike the air-landed units with which the Army had experimented in the 1930s, however, the memo directed Lynch to study the efficacy of a unit whose role would be, "after being transported in airplanes, to parachute to the ground a small detachment to seize a small vitally important area, primarily an air field, upon which additional troops will later be landed by transport aircraft."[1]

Lynch's preliminary findings, submitted five days later, suggested four possible ways to employ parachute units. First, small detachments could be deposited "within enemy territory for special specific missions where the possible accomplishments of the detachment warrant the risk of possible loss of the entire detachment." These "suicide missions" would be aimed at the destruction of vital communications centers or special industrial plants. Second, parachute units could conduct reconnaissance "to gain information not otherwise obtainable." Third, parachute units of battalion or regimental size could be inserted behind enemy lines "to hold a key point, area, or bridgehead" until relieved. Finally, parachute units could "work in conjunction with a mechanized force at a considerable distance from the main body."[2]

There the matter stood for some eight months, the project put on hold while other matters took priority as America fitfully mobilized for war. But when, in January 1940, Lynch appointed Major William C. Lee to oversee and breathe new life into the project, there began a chain of events that saw the idea of an airborne force become reality. Lee's new task was a daunting one. According to one of his assistants at the time, when Lee took over the project, "the entire file on what we knew about parachute troops was contained in a small manila folder."[3]

William Lee was a native of North Carolina who, after attending Wake Forest University and North Carolina State University, joined the Army, was commissioned in the infantry, and saw combat in France during World War One as a platoon leader and company commander. Electing to remain in uniform after the war, he was subsequently posted to a variety of assignments that, unknown to him at the time, would later serve him well while he played midwife to the Army's embryonic airborne force. In particular were assignments during the 1930s to the French tank school and a French tank regiment, followed by instructor duty at the U.S. Army's Tank and Infantry Schools, during which he experienced the trials and frustration of introducing a new concept of warfare to militaries that, bound by tradition, were inherently resistant to change. Yet Lee persevered and in 1938, after graduating from the Army's Command and General Staff College, served for a time as the executive officer of the 2nd Brigade of the 1st Infantry Division before being posted to Lynch's staff in Washington, D.C.[4] According to Gavin, who for a time served under Lee, "there couldn't have been a better man" for the job of shepherding the Army's fledgling airborne force through its first years because Lee "knew Washington quite well. . . . So when he wanted something, he could pick up the phone and get it." Still more important, at least in Gavin's eyes, was Lee's character. He was "the most tolerant, kind, considerate, intelligent man I've ever dealt with in a situation like that," recalled Gavin. Doubtless influenced by the frustration he experienced earlier in his career, when charged with forming an American airborne force Lee was open-minded to the extreme. According to Gavin, "He let us try anything we wanted to do. And we did."[5]

It was well that Lee was a tolerant man, for immediately upon being handed his new assignment, he found himself at the center of a conflict over which branch of the Army should lead the development of an airborne force. Angling to take over the project were, in particular, the Engineers and the Army Air Corps. The chief of engineers proposed that since airborne troops would be employed primarily for demolition and sabotage missions, their training and development should fall under his direction. The Air Corps staff argued that since they would be supplying the means to get airborne troops to the battle, they should have the lead. Lynch maintained that since airplanes were but a means of transport, and that once on the ground the airborne troops would be expected to fight as infantry regardless of their mission, his branch should be lead proponent for the project. This discussion, which began in the fall of 1939, remained unresolved until August 1940 when it was finally decided that the development of airborne units would remain under the control of the infantry.[6]

Undeterred by these turf wars, Lee forged ahead and in April 1940 obtained War Department approval to organize a parachute test platoon.[7] Two months later the commandant of the Infantry School at Fort Benning, Georgia, received a War Department memorandum ordering him to designate personnel for the test platoon from Benning's 29th Infantry Regiment. The memo also stated, "The test platoon will be a composite of specially selected men rather than a regular platoon" and that "service with the test platoon will be voluntary," thereby setting the parameters for parachute duty that remained throughout the war.[8]

While volunteers for the test platoon were interviewed and vetted, the Infantry Board established an eight-week training regimen for the platoon that looked very much like what British Commandos or U.S. Army Rangers underwent, reflecting what had become the dominant strain of thinking about how parachutists would be employed—in relatively small formations against high-risk targets. There was heavy emphasis on physical training, night fighting, use of explosives, and hand-to-hand combat as well as instruction in parachute packing and parachute manipulation. At the conclusion of the eight-week program, which was also to serve as a laboratory to test parachuting tactics, techniques, and procedures, recommendations were to be made on the organization, training, uniform, and equipment of parachute units as well as the best methods to land troops and equipment by parachute and the "practicability and feasibility of employment of the platoons under the assumed conditions."[9]

Command of the test platoon went to Lieutenant William T. Ryder, just four years out of West Point. His platoon comprised an assistant platoon leader, Lieutenant James A. Bassett, and forty-eight enlisted men, all of whom were volunteers, seasoned soldiers, and outstanding physical specimens.[10] The training they endured was, to say the least, challenging. According to test platoon member Thad P. Selman, each day began with a six-mile run, followed by breakfast and then additional physical training during which the platoon "did pull-ups, chin-ups, that sort of thing. And we worked out with medicine balls. We'd stand in a circle and you'd throw a ball and you [were] supposed to hit [your buddy] in the stomach. And you'd try to catch a fellow unprepared. And it got so, you know, it could knock you down. We were tough. We thought we could whip anything with hair or a bark . . . and almost could. But they encouraged that in us. They wanted to build it; they wanted us to feel like we were superior individuals."[11]

The platoon made its first jump onto Lawson Field at Fort Benning from a C-33 transport plane on 16 August 1940. Lieutenant Ryder, the first man to jump, became the U.S. Army's first official paratrooper. Unfortunately, the second man scheduled to jump (who would have become the Army's first enlisted paratrooper) froze in the door. Thad Selman, who was on the plane, described what happened. The platoon had a 180-pound dummy nicknamed "Oscar" that it used to check wind drift so the jumpers could gauge where they should exit the plane. Ryder had released "Oscar" just before he jumped, and things worked perfectly. Ryder then had the plane circle around, land, and pick him up along with a second "Oscar." By that time "a certain amount of tension was building up. And we got ready to circle around and drop the dummy to check the wind drift again and the sucker didn't open. It augured in. Well, we all saw that of course. So the first man [after Ryder] got to the door. And he just . . . he was willing, but he just wouldn't go. As I recall we circled the drop zone two or three times to give him an opportunity to change his mind but he went back and set down."[12] Fortunately, the second "Oscar's" untimely accident did not affect the rest of the platoon, and by the end of the day the U.S. Army had its first forty-nine paratroopers.

The platoon's final jump was its first mass jump. Staged before an assemblage of high-ranking officials, including Major General Lynch (accompanied by Major Lee), Army Chief of Staff General George C. Marshall, and Secretary of War Henry L. Stimson, the members of the platoon jumped from three planes, hit the ground, recovered their weapons and equipment, and attacked a mock enemy position. Afterward, a duly impressed Marshall talked to the members of the platoon, complimented them on their achievements, and announced that he was going to activate whole battalions of parachute troops.[13] True to his word, on 16 September 1940 Marshall had the War Department issue a memorandum announcing, "The 1st Parachute Battalion is constituted and will be activated at the earliest practicable date at Fort Benning, Georgia."[14]

Command of the 1st Parachute Battalion (later renamed the 501st Parachute Infantry Battalion) went to Major William M. "Bud" Miley. An Army-wide call for volunteers to fill the 501st met with an overwhelming response, and by November 1940 the battalion was assembled at Fort Benning, ready to begin parachute training under the direction of Lieutenant Ryder and several members of the test platoon, who formed the nucleus around which the 501st was organized.[15] According to Lieutenant William P. Yarborough of the 501st, its training was "more in line of [a] combination of Ranger–Special Forces" than of mere "straight leg infantry arriving by air," reflecting the still predominant thought that parachute units would remain small commando-type organizations. Brigadier General Omar N. Bradley, who arrived at Benning shortly after the 501st assembled, inspected the unit and called Miley's men "a breed apart—the toughest best-trained infantry I had ever seen."[16]

In order to demonstrate to others and to his men that they were, in fact, a breed apart, Miley instituted a number of uniform changes that clearly differentiated paratroopers from the rest of the "straight leg" Army.[17] The first significant change was replacing the standard-issue ankle-high boots and leggings with specially designed jump boots, which Miley authorized his men to wear with their dress uniforms and into which they bloused (tucked) their pants. He also authorized them to wear a circular cloth patch depicting a white parachute on a blue field on their overseas caps. To Lieutenant Yarborough he assigned the task of designing a badge that could be awarded to all those who successfully completed the parachute course. Working closely with Lee, who was still overseeing the program from Washington, D.C., Yarborough designed what became—and has remained—the U.S. Army's parachute qualification badge, or "wings," the first group of which was struck by Bailey, Banks and Biddle of Philadelphia.[18] A few months later, the innovative Yarborough also designed a special combat uniform for paratroopers with oversized pockets on the blouse and pants for carrying all the items that would be required for battle.[19]

These uniform items quickly became jealously guarded symbols of distinction among the Army's growing ranks of paratroopers, symbols that they believed marked them as members of an elite fraternity. Sergeant John D. McKenzie, an 82nd trooper who passed through parachute school relatively late in the war, described the moment he entered this fraternity: "I hobbled up to receive my silver parachute wings . . . in a very impressive ceremony. I was far more proud of this accomplishment than either of my two college graduation ceremonies." Another college man, Princeton graduate Richard

Mott Janney, who enlisted in the Army, volunteered for the paratroopers, and later served as an officer in the 82nd, highlighted the importance those who had earned them attached to their distinctive uniform items, especially their jump boots: "The paratroopers take a great deal of pride in their boots. When they are new, the leather is orange tan, but they ripen with age and proper treatment, like a meerschaum pipe, until the leather is the color of a horse chestnut. It is not remarkable to see a lad, who never bothered to kick mud off his shoes, spend three hours bent over his boots with a cloth and a dozen different kinds of lotions and ointments."[20]

Occasionally, the intensely proud paratroopers discovered straight-leg soldiers wearing their regalia. When that happened, trouble followed. Sergeant Richard L. Blank recalled that just before leaving for North Africa, he and his mates were restricted to camp and told to remove anything that identified them as members of the 82nd, including their jump boots. But, explained Blank, "some of the troopers . . . did get outside the restricted area and found that an engineering outfit at the camp had been issued jump boots. This was resented by the troopers since they thought this was our special equipment and our badge of distinction. That resulted in fights and in some the offending boots were cut down to GI shoe size."[21]

A reflection of the importance that paratroopers attached to their totems is a letter Major General Matthew B. Ridgway, the first commander of the 82nd Airborne Division, wrote to General Marshall on 12 June 1944, just six days after the Normandy landings. Although the 82nd was still "in the midst of the world's greatest battle," Ridgway made time to address a matter he felt had "deep significance." He had learned that manufacture of the paratrooper combat dress uniform was to be discontinued and wrote to request that this decision be reversed, for, in his eyes, the "parachutist combat dress is distinctive and now represents, in the eyes of all our combat forces in all theaters, fighting spirit second to no troops in the world."[22]

Even before Miley's 501st completed training, the War Department announced its intention to form three more parachute battalions in 1941. But personnel shortages and a lack of transport aircraft with which to train subsequently delayed the activation of a second parachute battalion for some seven months. The shortage of transport aircraft, both for training and for combat, would dog the Army's airborne force throughout the war. In 1941 it was particularly acute; by midyear there were but ninety-four transports in the entire U.S. Army Air Force, only twelve of which were available for parachute training, and no additional transports were projected to be available until February 1942.[23]

Despite the manpower and aircraft shortages, on Miley's recommendation a new organization was formed so that, once the shortages abated, the expansion of the Army's parachute force could continue apace. Activated in March 1941 at Fort Benning, the Provisional Parachute Group assumed responsibility for all future parachute training, to include the further development and refinement of the tactics, techniques, and procedures for the employment of parachute troops. Command of the group went to the newly minted Colonel Lee.[24]

Staffed largely by cadre drawn from the 501st, the Provisional Parachute Group established a training regimen that maintained, if not exceeded, the demanding physical requirements experienced by members of the test platoon. The distance runs, which began every morning around four o'clock, were particularly memorable. Lieutenant Bernard McKearney recalled "running around Lawson Field until someone dropped." Sergeant Joe Stolmeier recalled that if you fell out of a run, "the meat wagon [a truck that trailed the formation] would pick you up and . . . take you to the office, and they'd transfer you back to where you came from." The runs were followed by two hours of calisthenics and then a day filled with instruction on parachute jumping, landing, and assembling, both during day and night, as well as classes on how to pack parachutes and equipment bundles. According to Sergeant McKenzie, the program "weeded out some of the volunteers who might have been weaker than those who succeeded and who might later have failed in their duties." The sheer physical brutality of the course had two added benefits, the first being the strong sense of camaraderie that developed among the men who survived its rigors. According to McKenzie, "Whether these men succeeded because of what they individually brought to the program or because the program brought out the best in them, I do not know. I tend to believe it was a combination of these two factors, and perhaps others. I do know that I would rather have died than fail the men for whom I was responsible or my commanders and peers. I believe the majority of the men . . . shared that feeling, and it was a powerful contributor to the [unit's] success in combat."[25] Second, it became a data point against which troopers later compared their experiences in combat—and many preferred the unpredictable hazards of combat to the known hazards of parachute training. In thinking back on his parachute training, Joe Stolmeier stated:

> Later on I realized that no matter how much combat, no matter how much mud, no matter how many shells came in, no matter how much machine gun fire, or anything that the Germans could throw, it was never as bad as those instructors at Fort Benning. So we all said that. We said, "Would you rather be here, or would you rather have those guys at Fort Benning working you over?" And we always agreed we'd rather take . . . combat. And that's, I've always felt, how you make superior soldiers.[26]

In retrospect, the creation of the Provisional Parachute Group proved a crucial step on the way to establishing an American airborne force. Had there been no training organization ready to quickly expand the ranks of paratroopers once the manpower and aircraft shortages had been overcome (albeit only temporarily for the latter), it is quite possible, given the widespread resistance to the very concept of parachute troops in the Army, especially large formations of them, that the program would have been stillborn. As it was, in mid-1941, when the men and planes were made available, Lee's Provisional Parachute Group provided the momentum the program needed to remain viable by overseeing the creation, by October 1941, of three additional parachute battalions: the 502nd, 503rd, and 504th. And although there remained the "general supposition . . . that such troops would be used principally, in small detachments, for demolition work in enemy rear areas," given the quantity of paratroopers on hand, as well as the proven potential of Lee's group to train more, there emerged a competing notion, based on the German example, of using parachute troops en masse.[27]

According to Lieutenant Melvin Zais, an original member of the 501st Parachute Battalion, "The big thing that convinced us to go ahead and expand our parachute troops was the Germans. It was the German invasion of Crete." Omar Bradley concurred, writing in his memoirs that "after the German operations on Crete . . . Lee, Miley, Gavin and others began to think in much larger terms: airborne regiments, airborne divisions," and "I shared their enthusiasm." Finally, the most influential member of the fledgling airborne community at the time, William Lee, wrote, "After these successful operations [on Crete], I think it would indeed be dull of us to say that parachute troops will seldom be employed in units larger than a battalion."[28]

Heeding the call of the Army's parachute pioneers, the War Department G-3, Brigadier General Harry L. Twaddle, submitted a memorandum on 11 December 1941 to the chief of staff of Army General Headquarters, Lieutenant General Lesley J. McNair, the man General Marshall had charged with creating and training the Army's ground forces, in which Twaddle observed that "experience in Europe, and in the November maneuvers, showed that in the future parachute troops would be employed in larger numbers."[29] To that end, Twaddle recommended that the four existing parachute battalions be grouped under a single headquarters. McNair concurred with Twaddle's assessment, but preferred instead to use the existing parachute battalions as core units around which to form parachute regiments of three parachute battalions apiece. On 24 February 1942, therefore, the War Department issued a directive constituting four parachute regiments, each of which received one of the existing parachute battalions. Hence, the 501st Parachute Infantry Battalion became the 1st Battalion of the 501st Parachute Infantry Regiment (or

1/501st), the 502nd Parachute Infantry Battalion became the 1/502nd, and so on.[30] Furthermore, in order to facilitate the increased training burden this expansion portended, in March 1942 the Provisional Parachute Group was disbanded in favor of a more robust Airborne Command at Fort Bragg, North Carolina.[31]

Meanwhile, the Army was experimenting with two other programs for delivering combat forces to battle by air. The first, which focused on the development of air-landing units, resulted in the formation of two air-landing battalions, the 550th and 88th Infantry Airborne Battalions, by October 1941. Shortly thereafter General McNair squelched the air-landing program, seeing no need for special air-landing units since, to his mind, there was really nothing special about riding to battle in an airplane, a perspective that was subsequently promulgated by an April 1942 War Department directive that all "infantry divisions . . . will so far as practicable be trained for airborne [air-landing] operations prior to departure of the unit to an overseas theater of operations."[32] The second experiment involved the landing of combat troops and their equipment by glider.

When in February 1941 Major General Henry H. "Hap" Arnold, the chief of the U.S. Army Air Force, announced that "in view of certain information received from abroad, a study should be initiated on developing a glider that could be towed by an aircraft," he set in train events that would eventually lead to the development of the world's largest glider force.[33] The first of these events was the opening of glider pilot training centers in Elmira, New York, and Lockport, Illinois, where, at first, the goal was to qualify 150 glider pilots. But following Pearl Harbor, the quota was increased dramatically, first to 1,000 pilots, then to 4,200 pilots, and ultimately to 6,000 pilots, all of whom were to be trained by December 1942.[34] Simultaneously, the need for powered pilots was also growing, and hence the glider pilot program suffered from insufficient qualified volunteers, even after standards for acceptance into the program were lowered. Moreover, the glider pilot training program was hampered by a lack of gliders with which to train. In fact, what would become America's standard combat glider for the war, the CG-4A Waco, was not successfully test flown until some sixteen months *after* the glider pilot training program began. Constructed of wood, steel tubing, and canvas, the CG-4A had a wingspan of 83.6 feet, was 48 feet long, and had a cargo capacity of 4,060 pounds. It could carry thirteen combat troops plus a pilot and copilot or a jeep, trailer, or small artillery or antitank piece with crew. By the end of the war, approximately 14,000 Wacos had been manufactured by firms as varied as the Heinz Pickle Company, Steinway Pianos, and Anheuser-Busch, making it the fourth most produced combat aircraft of World War II.[35]

Despite the challenges besetting the glider development and pilot training programs, in May 1942 General McNair agreed to stand up the Army's first combat unit specifically designed for transport by glider. Although in retrospect this proved a significant step toward the development of a much larger gliderborne combat force, the manner by which this unit was activated—McNair simply redesignated the 88th Infantry Airborne Battalion as the 88th Glider Infantry Battalion—set several unfortunate precedents, the most significant of which was the feeling that there was nothing special about glider troopers.[36] There were, of course, some organizational and equipment changes made to ensure that the 88th and its weaponry could be transported in gliders, but the 88th's troopers were given no choice. Moreover, since they were not volunteers like their parachuting brethren, they were given no special insignia. Nor were they awarded flight pay like the glider pilots with whom they would be flying into combat or hazardous duty pay like that received by paratroopers (enlisted paratroopers received an extra fifty dollars per month, while officers received an extra one hundred dollars per month) until July 1944, when they also earned the right to wear a glider badge.[37] The mind-set behind this state of affairs was outlined in a War Department communiqué in response to a request to obtain for glider troopers hazardous duty pay. In coldly bureaucratic fashion, the War Department ruled that parachutists received extra pay because they were individually trained and "VOLUNTEER FOR THIS DUTY WHICH IS CONSIDERED EXTRA HAZARDOUS . . . WHILE GLIDER TROOPS ARE UNIT TRAINED [A]ND ARE NOT VOLUNTEERS. . . . IT IS THEREFORE FELT THAT NO REPEAT NO INCREASE IN PAY SHOULD BE PROVIDED FOR GLIDER PERSONNEL WHO MERELY RISE [*sic*] IN AIRPLANES OR GLIDERS."[38] This differentiation between glider and parachute troops, in terms of both pay and status, later resulted in considerable tension between the two groups when they began working together, especially when the units were in garrison. Yet an unintended consequence of this rivalry was also heightened battlefield performance by both parachute and glider units, as members of the former sought to uphold their elite status while those in the latter sought to earn a similar distinction for themselves.

By mid-1942, the Army was well on its way to developing a significant airborne force. Moreover, the newness and danger, especially of parachuting, attracted mavericks who saw in the paratroopers an opportunity to carve a niche for themselves and potentially transform warfare. According to one veteran paratrooper, what distinguished him and his comrades from other soldiers was a "willingness to take chances and risks in a branch of the army that provided a great, new, almost unexplored frontier." They were the same type of men, he continued, who in other days would have sailed with Columbus or been among "the first to seek out the West and fight the Indians." Additionally, because of the premium placed on physical fitness, parachuting was a young man's game, and thus relatively young officers with new ideas commanded a measure of influence not found in other branches of the Army, a point Lieutenant Ryder made in a letter to an aspiring parachute officer: "I know that you will like the [parachute] service, because there is nothing to this jumping out of an airplane, and there is a great need for ideas. We are still suffering from growing pains, and if there was ever a place in the Army where people are willing to listen to your ideas—this is it! The older officers are always willing to listen to the jumping officers [*sic*] point of view."[39]

The man to whom Ryder addressed his letter was a thirty-four-year-old captain serving in the Department of Tactics at the United States Military Academy at West Point. That man, Captain James M. Gavin, had volunteered for parachute duty but had had his request disapproved by both the commandant and the superintendent of West Point, with the latter adding that "in order to replace [Captain Gavin], it would be necessary to have an officer of equal ability ordered to this station," and "so far as I know, he is not particularly fitted for this type of duty."[40] Undeterred, Gavin traveled to Washington, secured a list of officers who had been previously considered for duty at West Point, verified their availability, and with this information convinced both the commandant and the superintendent to release him.[41] Upon graduating from jump school in August 1941, Gavin took command of C Company, 503rd Parachute Battalion. His drive and intellect did not go long unnoticed, however, so when Lee formed the Provisional Parachute Group, Gavin became the group's training and doctrine officer. While in this position, Gavin quickly made a name for himself by literally writing the book on airborne warfare, U.S. Army Field Manual 31-30, *Tactics and Technique of Air-Borne Troops*.[42]

James Gavin epitomized the men who flocked to the paratroopers—young, tough, adventurous men, full of ideas about how to employ parachute and glider units—men who, because of their youth, were not beholden to "old-army" norms of social decorum, discipline, or training methods.[43] These men were led by officers, almost all as young as the troopers themselves, with novel ideas about how to mold their roughnecks into a finely honed fighting force. As Gavin wrote, despite the advent of "machine weapons . . . between World War I and World War II countless hours were spent on wheeling about and moving squads to the right and to the left, as though they were preparing to fight the wars of a century ago." Discarding these outmoded notions, young officers like Gavin promoted a revolutionary idea—that their troopers should think for themselves—for given the nature of parachute and glider operations, they would very likely be isolated in small pockets, without officer leadership, and still be expected to perform their assigned missions. "In this respect, we decided that the old method of forcing individuals into a mold, while at the same time removing their personal identities as far as possible, had to be done away with. From the moment they joined the parachute units, we tried to impress upon them what outstanding individual soldiers they were. We wanted to do everything we could to enhance their pride, and we sought to do so. At the same time, we wanted to train them as thoroughly as we . . . could."[44]

It was not only training with which Gavin, Lee, and others in the nascent airborne community concerned themselves but also size. In order to make a significant impact, the disparate parachute and glider regiments had to be combined into larger formations. After the German invasion of Crete, this idea gained increasing impetus. So in the spring of 1942, William C. Lee traveled to Washington in company with his expert on training and doctrine, James Gavin, and as the latter later related, "We were talking then about a division."[45]

CHAPTER 3

MEN OF A PARTICULARLY HIGH ORDER

The fine men I met and served with in the old 82d were not all paragons of virtue, but a goodly number of them demonstrated traits of character and a manliness which make one proud to have served with them.

—CHARLES A. HARRINGTON TO JAMES M. GAVIN, 14 OCTOBER 1982

ON 7 DECEMBER 1941, after more than three years of fitful mobilization, the United States Army comprised 36 combat divisions, a paltry force when compared with the hundreds of divisions the Axis powers could boast.[1] The War Department was fully aware of this disparity; it had completed a strategic assessment—the Victory Plan—two months earlier that emphasized that Germany, Italy, and their European allies had among them "approximately 300 divisions fully equipped and splendidly trained" and estimated that by 1943, this number would grow to "a total of 400 divisions available in the European Theater." Given those numbers, and taking into consideration the forces of the United Kingdom and the Soviet Union, the Victory Plan concluded that defeating the Axis would require the United States to raise and equip at least 215 divisions.[2]

Expanding from 36 to more than 200 divisions would be no mean feat. The War Department had already activated all 18 National Guard divisions and of the 36 divisions on the rolls, only 1 was at a full wartime footing, with the rest being woefully ill-equipped and undermanned.[3] Yet victory's price had been established, and the War Department was committed to making payment.

Following the Japanese attack on Pearl Harbor and the German declaration of war on the United States, the drive to mobilization picked up considerable momentum. Gone were the political and social constraints that had curbed the prewar program, and within three months of America's entry into the war, the War Department instituted an accelerated program designed to activate 3 to 4 divisions per month.[4] Among the first contingent activated under this program was the 82nd Infantry Division, on 25 March 1942, at Camp Claiborne, Louisiana, a brand-new post on the banks of the Red River, near Alexandria.[5]

The 82nd Infantry Division had a pedigree that began with its service in World War I. Originally activated as a "National Army" division at Camp Gordon, Georgia, on 25 August 1917, it was formed from draftees that hailed predominately from Alabama, Georgia, and Florida. By the time it arrived in France in May 1918, however, it had experienced so much personnel turbulence that its ranks included soldiers from across the United States, a good many of whom were recent immigrants who could not speak English.[6] Seeking to turn this potentially fractious makeup into something around which his soldiers could rally, the 82nd's commander, Major General William P. Burnham, issued an order in which he christened the 82nd the All American Division since "the Eighty-second Division represents the best men from every state in the union."[7]

Once in France, the 82nd trained under British tutelage and was then posted to the front under the operational command of a French corps for two months to get "blooded" before it was pulled out, rested, and then put back in the line to participate in the two major American actions of the war, the Saint Mihiel and Meuse-Argonne offensives. All told, the 82nd suffered more than 7,300 casualties in the war (this from an authorized strength of 28,105, a 25 percent casualty rate) and earned a reputation as a solid, if not spectacular, division.[8] Two of its members, Lieutenant Colonel Emory J. Pike and Sergeant Alvin C. York, earned the Medal of Honor.

Following the cessation of hostilities, the 82nd remained in France until February 1919, when it started redeploying to the United States in stages. By 1 June 1919, the last of the division colors had been furled, and the 82nd was placed on the inactive list.[9] In summing up his service with the 82nd, the division's most famous and perhaps most colorful character, Alvin York, opined providentially that the heart of the 82nd was the troopers who, despite coming from every state in the Union as well as numerous foreign countries, were "all of them most awful hard fightin' men and most awful tough soldiers. Most of them were always causing a lot of trouble; but they bothered the Germans a heap more than they bothered anybody else."[10]

The man who issued the orders reactivating the 82nd for service in World War II was its newest commander, Major General Omar N. Bradley. Before assuming command of the division, Bradley had been commandant of the Infantry School at Fort Benning, Georgia, where his performance and innovative training methods caught General Marshall's eye. Based on this performance, Marshall nominated Bradley for a second star, gave him command of the 82nd, and charged him with preparing it for combat as quickly as possible. It was a daunting task.[11]

In order to meet its mobilization quota of three to four divisions per month, the War Department drastically modified its training and organizing paradigms. Formerly, recruits received thirteen weeks of basic training at a training center before they were shipped to their units, which were already formed and waiting to receive them. In the charged atmosphere of early 1942, however, the challenge was to simultaneously train recruits and form the units to which they would be assigned. To make that happen, trained personnel from extant "parent" divisions were reassigned as cadre to divisions still in the process of being organized in order to provide a "nucleus" around which the new division's recruits could then be "poured, like concrete around a form."[12] There were obvious shortcomings to this, not least of which was the loss of trained soldiers by the "parent" division, which wreaked havoc with unit readiness, especially in those divisions that were tapped as "parents" more than once. Moreover, those selected as cadre faced a difficult, some thought near-impossible, task: Not only were they charged with forming new units, but they had to do so while teaching raw recruits everything from facing movements to the intricacies of combined arms warfare. And they had but seventeen weeks to do it.[13]

The 82nd's cadre—approximately 700 officers and 1,200 enlisted men—came predominately from the 9th Infantry Division at Fort Bragg, North Carolina. Arriving at Camp Claiborne in early 1942, they had little time to organize themselves before they were inundated by 16,000 men who knew not the first thing about soldiering. According to Bradley, the challenge before him and his cadre "was large; the danger of failure, or even disaster, lay everywhere."[14]

Of particular concern to Bradley was how his soldiers would be greeted when they arrived at Camp Claiborne. He felt strongly that acclimating them to the "strange, impersonal and wholly unfamiliar world" of the Army as quickly and painlessly as possible was essential. Otherwise, there was the "real danger that we might experience devastating morale problems, delaying our training and readiness, and generating the usual flood of accusatory letters to Congress, Drew Pearson and other columnists, and even to Marshall himself."

Displaying the innovativeness that had brought him to Marshall's attention and earned him his command, Bradley instituted a plan, considered "radical at the time," to make "the draftees feel they were coming to a 'home' where people really cared about their welfare." To make this happen, Bradley sent a team from the division's G-1 (personnel) section to the reception centers to "greet, interview, classify and assign each draftee to a specific paper unit and duty, according to his civilian background." Hence, rather than arriving at Claiborne an inchoate mass, draftees assigned to the 82nd knew not only what they would be doing once they arrived but with whom they would be doing it. Then, to further develop his soldiers' sense of belonging to an organization that cared for them, Bradley welcomed the recruits at Claiborne's train depot with a brass band that played while the cadre shepherded them off the trains, formed them into the units to which they had been assigned, and marched them to their tents, where they found their equipment waiting for them on a cot. They were then fed a hot meal while their travel uniforms were laundered in preparation for the next day's events.[15]

Bradley's reception scheme was part and parcel of his training philosophy, which demanded that his cadre be "tough as hell on [the recruits], but in an intelligent, humane, understanding way." According to one of Bradley's soldiers, "the officers conducting basic training . . . were patient and understanding," and "there was no shouting and profanity as men learned to be citizen-soldiers." What shocked Bradley, however, was his "discovery that [the recruits], the prime youth of America, were generally in appallingly bad physical condition." The first few weeks of training, therefore, were devoted to whipping the men into trim and building physical toughness. To this end Bradley designed a training regimen that included daily calisthenics, foot marches, organized sporting events, and the frequent negotiation of a demanding obstacle course.[16]

Word of Bradley's methods soon spread, and a mere two weeks after the division's activation, McNair and his chief of staff, Brigadier General Mark W. Clark, paid the 82nd a visit to see firsthand how things were proceeding. Afterward, Clark reported that his boss "was certainly well pleased" and suggested that the example the 82nd was setting for the rest of the Army's new divisions "should certainly whip [them] into shape in rapid fashion." According to Bradley, "General McNair gave us a hearty pat on the back" and soon thereafter "recommended that all new divisions adopt" similar methods.[17]

Bradley's methods also kept him in Marshall's sights. He had worked miracles with the 82nd, "adhering closely or exceeding McNair's seventeen-week training schedule," and he looked forward to "leading it into battle whenever and wherever it might be sent." But success precluded him this opportunity. The 28th Infantry Division, a National Guard unit at nearby Camp Livingston, had not made comparable progress despite having been mobilized a full year before the 82nd, so to save the foundering guardsmen, Marshall relieved its commander and reassigned Bradley to command of the 28th. Assuming command of the 82nd would be Bradley's assistant division commander, Brigadier General Matthew B. Ridgway. It was a propitious choice, both for Ridgway and for the 82nd.[18]

Like Bradley, Matthew Bunker Ridgway was a Marshall protégé. Having graduated West Point two years behind Bradley, at the time of Pearl Harbor Ridgway was a lieutenant colonel assigned to the War Department, albeit on temporary duty at Fort Benning, where he was attending a course to prepare him for regimental command. But news of the Japanese attack sent him rushing back to Washington, where he resumed his staff duties, his plans for command on indefinite hold. It was a command Ridgway never got. Instead, in January 1942, Marshall called Ridgway into his office, told him he was to be promoted to brigadier general (after only six weeks as a full colonel), and then sent him to Camp Claiborne as Bradley's second in command.[19]

Bradley felt "lucky to get" Ridgway and rated him "first and foremost one of the most charismatic and able young infantrymen in the Army." Likewise, Ridgway praised Bradley's "great warmth of nature" and admired his commander's "quiet, soft-spoken" demeanor and "great athletic ability." The two hit it off immediately (they had served together before but had never been close) and began a friendship and mutual admiration that lasted the war. During their time together in the 82nd, Bradley entrusted his assistant with "complete" latitude in training the division's three infantry regiments, a task Ridgway called "a full time job every waking hour of the day." Consequently, when Marshall announced Ridgway as Bradley's successor to command the 82nd, the latter felt this "the best possible choice," and though sad at leaving the division he had had so large a part in creating, he was content to see command of his "pride and joy" go to Matt Ridgway.[20]

Ridgway was an impressive man. John S. D. Eisenhower recalled that as a second lieutenant fresh out of West Point he had the unique opportunity to accompany his father, the Supreme Allied Commander, during some of the toughest fighting of the Normandy campaign. Enjoying the view from his lofty perch without the attendant responsibilities, he spent his time observing the men who did the fighting. "Ridgway," he wrote, "was by any yardstick a strong commander" and a man who "prided himself on being a soldier's soldier." According to another observer, Ridgway's "powerful presence made him no stranger in a crowd" because his "image, profile and reputation projected more than his 5-foot-10-inch frame indicated." A third commented on

Ridgway's "mature leadership," which "made a lasting impression."[21] And a fourth, who came to know Ridgway quite well during the war while serving as his bodyguard, commented:

> The General was a type of man who could make you feel at ease. He could talk to you on your own level. At the same time, you read about him and he was conversing with the biggest men in the country.
>
> I would not know how to compare the general with those other generals. . . . He was a great commander and after all, he looked the part of the warrior and I fully believe I would prefer being with him more than, well, a lot of others.[22]

Matt Ridgway was the son of a soldier, Thomas Ridgway, an 1883 West Point graduate who retired as a colonel in 1919.[23] Though "a soldier to the core," Thomas did not pressure his son to follow in his footsteps, nor did the younger Ridgway "recall feeling any strong inner compulsion to take up the trade of arms as a career." But Matt did sense that his father would approve were he to do so, and it was "as much an effort to please him as it was any burning desire . . . to become a soldier" that led Matt Ridgway to apply to West Point. Failing to gain admission on his first attempt (he failed the geometry portion of the entrance exams), Matt applied again, was accepted, and graduated four years later in the top third of his class of 1917 with a commission in the infantry.[24]

According to one biographer, Ridgway possessed "decisiveness, self-confidence, and single-mindedness of purpose . . . in abundance," and "even as a young officer, Ridgway was an overly serious and perhaps somewhat humorless workaholic."[25] On one occasion, for example, following a relapse of streptococcal throat that sent Ridgway to the hospital, Marshall upbraided him for the relentlessness with which he drove himself and chastened him to take it a little easier. Despite the insouciance with which he entered the Army, no one ever doubted that Matt Ridgway took his calling seriously, and even during the professionally stifling atmosphere of the interwar years, when there seemed little prospect of advancement, he zealously devoted himself to what many would have considered mundane tasks best left to others. A fellow officer who served under then Captain Ridgway at Fort Sam Houston, Texas, in 1926 related the following illustrative anecdote:

> I easily remember one very hot August afternoon when I went by the company to find Capt. Ridgeway [*sic*] in the supply room. He was very carefully inspecting the bore of each rifle to make sure the lans [*sic*] and grooves were

> not eroded or gummed up so that the rifle would be able to fire accurately and not with a too great amount of dispersion.
>
> I don't really know how he felt in his heart about doing this—but to me he seemed to be seeking perfection in the company preparations for the coming rifle qualification program at Camp Bullis, Texas. I might add that such detailed extra work that could have been delegated was not common in the peacetime army of the 20's where there was little thought of impending conflict. Capt. Ridgeway [*sic*] himself qualified as an Expert Rifleman, the highest award, over a then quite difficult course.[26]

Intelligent without the mien of an intellectual, Ridgway was suspicious "of purely technological solutions to military problems," and as "a serious reader of [Carl von] Clausewitz he understood moral superiority as the underpinning of *morale* superiority, an absolutely necessary ingredient for overcoming the friction of war." As he told a gathering of chaplains, good morale was vital because all war was a "moral struggle," with victory going "to the side which refuses to become discouraged."[27] In turn good morale was the product of "charismatic leadership" exercised "by men who were deserving because of their strength and spiritual power as well as their technical expertise."[28] In Ridgway's mind, therefore, the effectiveness of any military organization "is dependent on primarily its officer corps and secondarily on its noncommissioned officer corps." With effective leadership, he contended, soldiers "will rise to any height," and without it "they won't, and that's the key to the whole thing—leadership."[29]

Leadership was Ridgway's "eternally fascinating question," the answer to which he felt was more art than science.[30] He defined leadership as "the art of imposing one's will upon others in such a manner as to command their implicit obedience, their utmost confidence, their profound respect, and their wholehearted cooperation." It was, he believed, indispensable to effective military organizations not only because it was essential for good morale but also because it undergirded discipline, albeit "not the discipline of the martinet or the guard house" but discipline based on a feeling of "mutual confidence between the leader and his men."[31] In Ridgway's eyes the "action of any military organization, from a squad to an army group, is merely the reflection of the qualities of leadership possessed by its commander."[32]

Ridgway worked hard to translate his thoughts on leadership into action, pushing himself to set the example and expecting "all his officers to devote the same time, energy and attention to duty that he demonstrated." Desiring always to be where the action was, Ridgway spent most of each day in the field alongside his soldiers. He was everywhere, enforcing standards, inspecting training, and inspiring through his presence. According to Colonel Maxwell D. Taylor, who at the time was also in the 82nd, "We worked in the field from morning till night, seven days a week in sizzling Louisiana temperatures—which were an excellent preparation for our later service in the desert of North Africa. Matt was a stickler for physical condition and drove his men hard to reach that level of fitness necessary for combat. I often accompanied him to inspect troop training in the field, the two of us jogging briskly from site to site under the midday sun to the wonderment of the troops."[33] A junior officer who served in the division through Normandy recalled:

> The officers and soldiers of Company E welcomed [Ridgway's] unannounced visits during which he would offer constructive criticism, but would always end up with some sort of compliment. He never talked down to us, but spoke as though we were on his level. He never used a profane or vulgar word and his tone was always conversational. He could be ruthless, but never cruel. His knowledge of Infantry weapons was phenomenal, he knew each part and its function. He gained the respect of my people by pointing out our mistakes in a gentlemanly, but firm, manner and he, therefore, secured instant compliance.[34]

And another junior officer wrote: "I can truthfully say that [Ridgway's] image and stature projected down to the troops where, basically, everything happens. We saw him on occasion and just assumed that he knew what he was doing and never questioned his directives and commands."[35]

As division commander, Ridgway carried on Bradley's firm but caring training philosophy. Eschewing the hours of mindless drills that had been the norm in the interwar Army, Ridgway demanded that the "enthusiasm [and] imagination of [the] instructor must preclude all boredom," that "all instructors must stress 'the reasons why,'" and finally that "supervision must be constant and effective." Accordingly, Ridgway required that his officers and noncommissioned officers enunciate "in clear positive language . . . [standards] which each individual or unit must reach in order to be considered satisfactorily proficient" and that progress charts be kept "which will indicate to the unit commander . . . the status of training of the unit or individual concerned."[36]

In short, Ridgway believed fervently in the power of leadership to transform a group of strangers into a cohesive fighting force. Of course, technical and tactical competence were also important to him, but it was leadership that, in his eyes, made the difference between victory and defeat on the battlefield. Unbeknownst to Ridgway at the time, events were in train that would put him at the head of an organization that required just the sort of leadership he personified.

Far removed from the training grounds of Camp Claiborne, War Department planners were engaged in a dialogue that would have a significant impact on both Ridgway and the 82nd. In March 1941, American and British planners inaugurated a series of secret "staff conversations" in Washington, D.C., aimed at fashioning a grand strategy should the United States be drawn into the war. As a result of these conversations, all agreed that the "early defeat of Germany, the predominant member of the Axis," should be their primary focus, and therefore "the principal military effort of the United States . . . [would be] in the Atlantic and European area, the decisive theater."[37] How to achieve that end, however, was a contentious issue, for while the British preferred a peripheral approach aimed at weakening Germany through blockade, aerial bombardment, and ground operations in North Africa and the Mediterranean, the Americans wanted to engage and defeat the Nazi war machine in northwest Europe as soon as possible. To give substance to their argument, on 27 March 1942, War Department planners published a document—subsequently known as the Marshall Memorandum—which called for the buildup of American forces in the British Isles with the goal of launching a cross-Channel invasion by April 1943. As part of the invasion force, the memorandum envisioned one U.S. airborne division plus an unspecified number of U.S. parachute units that could be dropped inland astride key transportation arteries in order to impede the advance of German reinforcements.[38]

The Marshall Memorandum had far-ranging ramifications, not least of which was the direction it provided to those responsible for ensuring the Army could accomplish what would be required of it. Chief among them was General McNair, whose new command, Army Ground Forces, assumed responsibility for training and organizing ground combat forces from the defunct Army General Headquarters.[39] It had long been McNair's policy that "special-type units and excessively specialized personnel, useful on certain occasions only, should be discouraged."[40] But the Marshall Memorandum's requirement for at least one U.S. airborne division for use in a cross-Channel invasion compelled McNair to rethink his policy, and so, in early summer 1942, he sent Bill Lee, now a brigadier general, to London to discuss with Britain's airborne commanders how to organize and equip one.[41] When he returned and briefed McNair on what he learned, Lee discovered that the Army Ground Forces commander had done a complete turnabout in his thinking. According to Lee, McNair "not only approved the organization of one division but of two, in order to provide an additional division for the Mediterranean area." To effect this, McNair proposed that the Army "should inaugurate studies without delay looking to the organization of whatever airborne divisions can be formed from one triangular division, plus the available parachute regiments."[42] With Marshall's approval, this task fell to Lee's Airborne Command.

Lee's first order of business was to determine which of the Army's regular infantry divisions were likely candidates for conversion. According to Gavin, who was a member of the study group, "The division had to be one that had already completed basic training, and it could not be a Regular Army or National Guard division; the States would not want the National Guard made airborne. It was also stipulated that the division should be one that was then stationed where flying weather was generally good and near one or more airfields."[43] Only one division met these criteria—Ridgway's 82nd.

Having selected a division to convert, the next step was to determine how the airborne divisions it would give rise to would be organized. It had always been assumed that airborne divisions would contain both parachute and glider units (as were British airborne divisions), but beyond that not much thought had been given to the matter. Now that the idea was to become reality, more specific planning was called for. Underlying that planning was the "concept of employment envisioned by General McNair, General Lee, and other airborne authorities" that airborne divisions would be used only "for definite missions" for which "sustained ground action beyond a period of six to ten days was not contemplated." With no need, therefore, for the robust logistical and administrative structure found in standard infantry divisions, Lee's Airborne Command and McNair's Army Ground Forces designed an airborne division structure of one parachute and two glider regiments that contained, in McNair's words, "a stinginess in overhead and in transportation which has absolutely no counterpart thus far in our military organization."[44]

Once the organization had been settled, McNair moved swiftly to stand up America's first airborne divisions. To that end, on 6 July 1942 he recommended that the 82nd be split in half, with its infantry regiments reorganized as glider regiments, and that each half be paired with an existing parachute regiment. Proceeding in this manner, he emphasized, would result in the creation of two trained and ready airborne divisions, one for the contemplated cross-Channel invasion of April 1943 and a second for employment in the Mediterranean. After referring his recommendation to the War Department, where it was accepted without delay, he dispatched his new chief of staff, Brigadier General Floyd Parks, to Camp Claiborne to deliver the news.[45]

Ridgway was wholly unaware of the decision that had been made about his division when Parks visited him at Camp Claiborne, "wearing an air of mystery." Parks "came into my office," recalled Ridgway, "shut the door, looked about him cautiously, and then in a voice that was almost a whisper asked me how I'd like to command an airborne division." Ridgway responded that he "didn't know what an airborne division was," to which Parks replied, "Nobody else knew much about it either." However, continued Parks, "a new form of warfare was coming into being and the 82nd, as the best of the divisions then in training, had been chosen to develop its tactics."[46] But there was a downside to the opportunity, explained Parks. Ridgway had to release half the 82nd to form a second airborne division, the 101st, command of which would go to Bill Lee. How to split the 82nd equitably was left to the two airborne commanders. According to Ridgway:

> Bill came to me and said, "Now, you and I are old Army people. You know if you get ordered to transfer some men, all the jailbirds and guard house [*sic*] lawyers are going to be the first on the list. How are we going to divide this thing, the 82nd?" I said, "'Bill, I'll tell you what I'll do. I'll make two lists of the 82nd as nearly equal as possible in rank, experience and everything else. We will put them in two different posts [pots] and we'll flip a coin. If you win the coin [flip], you take whichever half you want." It couldn't have been better and that's the way we did it.[47]

For several weeks following Parks's visit the 82nd's fate was held in strictest secrecy. Then, on 15 August 1942, Ridgway held a division review during which he announced that effective immediately, the 82nd had been redesignated as an airborne division and that furthermore half the soldiers standing on the parade field would be transferred out in order to form a second airborne division.[48] "There were sixteen thousand men [the figure was closer to 14,000] standing there," recalled an eyewitness, "and you could have heard a pin drop. And when Ridgway explained that four *glider* regiments would be formed from the ranks of the regular infantry, I saw a lot of faces go white."[49] Yet, according to another witness, despite the shock and predictions "that casualties would be high" in the glider ranks, only a "very few requested a transfer."[50]

Forming the nucleus of the two airborne divisions were the nine battalions of the 82nd's three infantry regiments, which were reorganized into four two-battalion glider infantry regiments: the 325th and 326th, which remained with the 82nd, and the 327th, and 401st, which became part of the 101st. Each division was also assigned a parachute infantry regiment, the 82nd getting the 504th and the 101st the 502nd. The rest of the 82nd's units were likewise redesignated either glider or parachute units and split among the two new airborne divisions accordingly.[51]

In compliance with McNair's dictum that airborne divisions be lean, personnel rosters were pared significantly; when recast as glider units, rifle companies went from having more than 200 men to 5 officers and 150 men, and formations that were standard in regular infantry battalions, such as heavy weapons companies, were not included in a glider battalion's organizational structure. Given these and other cuts, glider regiments contained just 1,605 men, lean indeed when compared with each regiment's preconversion strength of 3,000.[52]

The parachute regiments assigned to the divisions were a bit larger. Instead of two battalions, each parachute regiment contained three battalions and had an aggregate strength of 1,958 men.[53] However, instead of the standard three-squad platoons, parachute rifle platoons had only two squads, each with a light machine gun (a Browning automatic rifle, or BAR) and a 60mm mortar.[54] To make up for this shortfall, parachute units had a higher density of automatic weapons than conventional infantry units, especially .45-caliber Thompson submachine guns, and almost every paratrooper carried an additional weapon by his side.[55] The end result of this personnel economy was airborne divisions of 8,520 men, a little more than half the authorized strength of standard infantry divisions, which counted 14,248 men.[56]

Equipment tables were also modified. Since an airborne division's equipment had to be deliverable by either parachute or glider, the tanks, half-tracks, and trucks of a standard division were replaced by smaller antitank guns, jeeps, and trailers. The most significant modification, however, was to the artillery. Instead of the 105mm and 155mm howitzers found in the artillery battalions of standard infantry divisions, airborne divisions were organized with three artillery battalions (two glider and one parachute) armed with thirty-six 75mm pack howitzers.[57] Pack howitzers were short-barreled guns that would easily fit inside a glider or, if needed, disassembled, put in parachute bundles and attached to "para-racks" on the underside of transport planes. (Pack howitzers, originally designed for mountain fighting, were purposefully designed in component parts that could be disassembled for transport by mules.) During a drop the bundles were released just ahead of the paratroopers, gathered up on the ground, and the guns reassembled for immediate use. Although a 75mm howitzer did not deliver as heavy a punch as a 105mm or 155mm gun and had a shorter range, they could be manhandled if necessary, a critical characteristic in a division with so little transport (instead of the more than 2,000 vehicles and trailers found in standard infantry divisions, airborne divisions had approximately 400 vehicles, mostly jeeps, and about 240 trailers).[58]

The organizational and materiel structure of airborne divisions was a point of contention for Ridgway and other airborne commanders. At the lowest level, the two-squad parachute infantry platoons contravened doctrine, which taught junior officers and noncommissioned officers to fight with three squads per platoon and therefore required paratroop leaders to improvise new tactics. This same problem held true, on a larger scale, for the two-battalion glider regiments. Moreover, the paucity of transportation assets and the lack of heavy-caliber weapons, especially in the artillery, meant that an airborne division, once committed, was relatively immobile and often outmanned and outgunned. After the war, a board of general officers convened to consider the value of airborne divisions in light of the experience of combat in Europe. Without exception, they agreed:

> The fighting qualities of the airborne soldier have proven to be of the highest order and the best, but as a unit the airborne division has worked under several handicaps which limited the missions to which it could be assigned with expectation of complete success. It has very little transportation and is in effect a foot division once on the ground, its artillery is light and engineer construction equipment is practically nil. . . . The airborne divisions, however, have never faltered or failed and have played an important part in the winning of the war.[59]

That the airborne divisions contained "men of the highest order" that "never faltered or failed" was due in no small measure to Ridgway and Lee. Shortly after taking command of their respective airborne divisions, they addressed a joint letter to General McNair in which they wrote, "In the type of combat in which airborne divisions are likely to engage, control will be decentralized to leaders of small units among whom casualties will be high." Because of this, they contended that "airborne divisions will require an unusually large number of junior officers and enlisted men of a particularly high order of intelligence, leadership, and physical condition." They requested, therefore, the authority to get rid of unsuitable officers and enlisted men in the lowest Army General Classification Test (AGCT) categories, as well as troopers who were prone to airsickness, possessed a lack of physical stamina or strength, were too old, or demonstrated a temperament unsuitable for the airborne. Finally, they also requested a 20 percent overage in first and second lieutenants to fill their expected combat losses.[60]

Although unintended, the Ridgway-Lee letter proved amazingly prescient about the impact the War Department's personnel policies would have on the Army's ground combat formations. It also flew in the face of the War Department's paradigm for allocating manpower that reserved for the technical and support services, especially the U.S. Air Corps, the largest percentage of high-quality draftees (Categories I and II) while burdening ground combat formations with a larger share of lesser-quality men (Categories IV and V). Quality was measured by several criteria, the most important of which was an individual's AGCT score, and there was direct correlation between a high AGCT score and leadership potential.[61] By about mid-1943, when Army formations were committed to combat in increasing numbers, it became glaringly apparent that the manpower allocation paradigm had had a deleterious impact on the performance of ground combat units by denying them a pool of potential junior leaders. An observer with the U.S. Fifth Army fighting in Italy noted that "squad leaders and patrol leaders with initiative were scarce. . . . The assignment of Grade [Category] V intelligence men to infantry is murder." The U.S. XIV Corps surgeon rendered a similar report after the fighting in New Georgia in the Pacific, attributing a high rate of combat neurosis to a dearth of quality junior leaders. Another medical officer noted, "I saw one whole platoon of an infantry company go out because the platoon sergeant went 'wacky.' It is very important to select strong leaders, men with strong minds, especially during training periods in the States."[62]

Taken in this light, the Ridgway-Lee letter was of singular importance, for McNair acceded to the request (with the exception of the 20 percent overage in junior officers) by allowing the airborne commanders to transfer low-scoring AGCT men until the percentage of Category IV and V men in the divisions approximated the Army average (21.6 percent and 8.9 percent, respectively).[63] However, since "the Army average was better than the average for the ground arms, this policy constituted preferential treatment for the airborne divisions." Moreover, McNair also allowed the airborne divisions the latitude to get rid of anyone deemed "unsuitable for airborne duty," which, in practice, gave Ridgway and Lee the leeway to get rid of anyone they deemed substandard. According to Ridgway, "I had the authority to wash out anybody who had any qualms about the airborne business, and in the next few months we got rid of thousands on the grounds that they were not temperamentally suited for airborne training."[64] As a result the airborne divisions did not lack for men capable of stepping into leadership positions and taking charge, which later proved crucial to their success in battle.

What the newly minted 82nd Airborne Division did lack was stability. Shortly after the reorganization was complete, Ridgway received orders to move that part of the division still at Camp Claiborne to Fort Bragg, North Carolina, where it could link up with its parachute elements and begin airborne training in concert with Colonel Harold L. "Hal" Clark's 52nd Troop Carrier Wing stationed at nearby Pope Field. The move, which was completed by mid-October 1942, was immediately followed by a call for the 82nd to supply a large contingent of trained soldiers as cadre around which another new division, the 98th Infantry, would be formed. In their place the 82nd received raw recruits, all of whom required basic training, which set back airborne training commensurately.[65]

The division's officer ranks were likewise in turmoil. Soon after the 82nd arrived at Fort Bragg Ridgway lost his assistant division commander, Brigadier General "Bud" Miley, and his division artillery commander, Brigadier General Joseph M. Swing, both of whom had been earmarked to take command of two additional airborne divisions then being organized: the 11th, which went to Swing, and the 17th, which went to Miley. To replace Miley, Colonel Charles L. "Bull" Keerans was promoted and transferred to the 82nd from the 101st. It would prove an ill-fated move. Swing's replacement was Colonel Maxwell Taylor, an artilleryman by training who was promoted out of his job as the 82nd's chief of staff. To everyone's surprise, Ridgway made Lieutenant Colonel Ralph P. "Doc" Eaton, an adjutant general corps officer who was formerly the division's G-1 his new chief of staff, a position usually reserved for combat arms officers.[66] But Ridgway and Eaton were old friends, and, as Ridgway later related, Eaton could "get as much out of coordination of a General Staff as anybody I have ever seen." This was important to Ridgway. "Doc ran the staff and kept house at home, and I spent all the days out with the troops—where I wanted to be anyway."[67]

There were also several changes in regimental command. The 325th's commander, Colonel Claudius Easley, was promoted and transferred to the 96th Infantry Division as its assistant division commander. To replace Easley, Ridgway made another surprising selection when he gave command of the 325th to Colonel Harry L. Lewis, a man quite old for the airborne (he had been in the Army four years longer than Ridgway).[68] There were mixed feelings about Lewis. Some found him to be "an energetic type of fellow" who, though "small in stature . . . was tall in ability." Others felt that though old, Lewis was "young of spirit . . . quick and a bundle of energy," even "hyper," and a man who was "fair and loyal to those who were performing, but perhaps impatient with others." Conversely, there were some who thought Lewis "too old to lead an airborne regiment," a man that not only "looked old" but "acted old." And then there were the much more damning who saw Lewis as a "weak officer" who "looked like a Mr. Milquetoast—short, slim, steel-rim glasses, sharp little face, humorless expression," a man for whom "bank teller would be a better description." Yet Lewis had Ridgway's confidence and remained in command of the 325th until after the invasion of Normandy, where he proved, in Ridgway's estimation, to be "a very gallant little fighting man."[69]

Ridgway also replaced the 504th's commander, Colonel Theodore L. "Ted" Dunn. Ridgway first met Dunn while undergoing parachute training and was not impressed. Dunn drank too much and jumped too seldom for Ridgway's liking, and when he did jump, he used a specially designed oversized parachute to slow his descent, soften his landing, and save his knees, which were bad from his football days at West Point. Furthermore, Dunn was an incompetent trainer, which was made painfully obvious during a parachute exercise he staged for Ridgway that consisted of nothing more than a mass drop after which Dunn's troopers simply recovered their parachutes and moved back to the barracks. There was no tactical maneuver at all. "There was this definite feeling that the job ended with the jump," stated one of Ridgway's staff officers who also attended the exercise. "They made the jump; they were all heroes and they went home." Dunn's failures as a leader and trainer would not stand, especially after Ridgway learned that two of the regiment's three battalions failed their precombat tests, so Ridgway relieved Dunn "for inability to secure results" and elevated Lieutenant Colonel Reuben H. "Rube" Tucker III, the 504th's executive officer, to replace him.[70]

Tucker was an inspired choice, but one that Ridgway feared would be overruled by Army personnel managers because, at the time, "there were several hundred surplus [full] Colonels" looking for commands. To allay this possibility, Ridgway wrote preemptively to the Army G-1. "Under Tucker's leadership there was an immediate improvement, which has continued steadily," emphasized Ridgway. "He has force, determination, and common sense to a high degree, and is determined to get the results I want. . . . I should regret very much having an outsider brought in, regardless of his ability, as I am convinced that Colonel Tucker will lead this regiment in action as well or better than he has during the training period."[71] Ultimately, Ridgway was able to protect Tucker, who was quickly promoted and remained in command of the 504th throughout the war. He proved to be an outstanding combat leader.

By January 1943, it appeared that the turbulence that had gripped the 82nd since the previous August had subsided. The organization was set, the command team was in place, and the ranks were filled with troopers who had been around long enough to learn at least the basics of soldiering. It was time to begin the airborne training and large-scale unit exercises that would complete the 82nd's transformation. But before that started, an unexpected logistical dilemma compelled another significant organizational change.

Unlike powered planes, which could be either flown or ferried aboard aircraft carriers to forward areas, the fragile gliders had to be disassembled and packed in five large shipping crates for movement overseas and then reassembled at the port of debarkation.[72] So packaged, one glider weighed 20,000 pounds and took up considerable cargo space. This presented shipping managers with a significant challenge—how to get enough gliders overseas in time for the next planned operation given their disproportionate weight and bulk and relatively low shipping priority? The answer was simple—they couldn't.

It had already been determined that the 82nd would be the first airborne division to ship out. At the time all that was known was that it would be going to the Mediterranean; the specifics of when and where it would be employed had yet to be determined. But without sufficient gliders, *how* it would be employed, which spoke to the very reason it was created, was seriously undermined since roughly two-thirds of the division was gliderborne. Faced with this conundrum, the War Department's solution was to change the organization.[73] Consequently, in February 1943 Ridgway received a directive to release one of his glider regiments in place of which he would receive a second parachute regiment. Ridgway elected to retain Harry Lewis's 325th Glider Infantry Regiment. Its sister regiment, the 326th, was transferred to Alliance, Nebraska, where it became part of the 1st Independent Glider Brigade. In return, Ridgway received Colonel Jim Gavin's 505th Parachute Infantry Regiment as well as a second parachute field artillery battalion, the 456th (Ridgway also retained both glider field artillery battalions, giving him four artillery battalions).[74]

Meanwhile, the Casablanca Conference of January 1943 had clarified when and where the 82nd would first see combat. It would be Sicily, in July. Planning for the operation, code-named HUSKY, was already in train, so in early March, Marshall summoned Ridgway to Washington and told him to report immediately to Eisenhower's Allied Force Headquarters in North Africa so that he and a small planning staff he was to bring with him could participate in the HUSKY planning effort. When Ridgway arrived in Algeria on 8 March, Eisenhower was too focused on finishing off the *Afrika Korps* to spend much time discussing the Sicily invasion with him. But to ensure the trip was not a complete waste, Eisenhower suggested that Ridgway shadow his old boss, Omar Bradley, at the front so that he could get a feel for the foe. Ridgway leaped at the chance.

At the time, Bradley was the deputy commanding general of the U.S. II Corps, serving under one of the Army's most flamboyant combat commanders, Lieutenant General George S. Patton Jr. Bradley and Ridgway spent a week together visiting the forward echelons of the U.S. 1st and 9th Infantry Divisions, both of which were in daily contact with German forces. Ridgway even accompanied relatively small American units on patrol. Having never been in combat, Ridgway saw for the first time "the loneliest and most ominous of all landscapes, a battlefield," and contemplated "that strange exhilaration that grips a man when he knows that somewhere out there in the distance, hostile eyes are watching him and that at any moment a bullet he may never hear, fired by an enemy he cannot see, may strike him."[75]

By the time he returned to Fort Bragg on 24 March, Ridgway's exhilaration had been replaced with foreboding. Having seen the enemy and taken his measure, and knowing, at least in outline, what the 82nd would be called upon to do against that enemy, he was hit by the sober realization that he had little time to prepare.

CHAPTER 4

A WHOLE NEW DIMENSION TO SOLDIERING

It might be interesting . . . to describe how an airborne division is committed to battle, compared to a standard unit in the Army. The infantry unit goes into battle with its communications and its command structure at its best. The radios are all functioning, the command chain is intact. The commander knows where all his people are, and what's happening to them, and he can exercise an excellent degree of control. The exact opposite is true of an airborne division. When its people hit the ground they are individuals, and a two-star general and a Pfc. are on exactly the same basis.

—MATTHEW B. RIDGWAY,
SOLDIER: THE MEMOIRS OF MATTHEW B. RIDGWAY

WHILE RIDGWAY WAS away, the 82nd's regimental and battalion commanders, under the direction of "Bull" Keerans, began the training that would forge the division into an airborne team. Generally, this type of training is guided by doctrine, which outlines how an army fights and how its various elements should work together. In 1943, however, no such doctrine existed for America's airborne divisions. In fact, the only manual in existence that addressed airborne operations was Field Manual (FM) 31-30, *Tactics and Technique of Air-Borne Troops,* which focused almost exclusively on parachute operations. Its principal author was Jim Gavin, whose 505th Parachute Infantry Regiment officially joined the division the day after Ridgway left for North Africa.

Airborne Command published FM 31-30 in May 1942. Gavin was still a relatively junior officer when he wrote it and later admitted that he "didn't know anymore [*sic*] about it [airborne operations] than anybody else" but simply "wanted to do it" and in "doing it" read everything he could on the subject, including captured German documents. He was aided in his endeavor by another young airborne pioneer, William P. Yarborough, who served with Gavin on the Airborne Command staff and who contributed additional reference material in the form of translated Soviet manuals, which proved to be "some of the best training material we had in the early days on the techniques of parachuting."[1]

Armed with this material, Gavin and Yarborough produced a manual that covered in detail everything they had learned about parachuting and parachute operations, from the proper way to pack a parachute to the foreign phrases paratroopers should know when they jumped into combat. But the two bright, young officers were not content with producing a simple "how-to" handbook. They wanted to produce something more substantial, so they included in FM 31–30 some principles on the employment of parachute troops.

Parachute troops, they wrote, "may be considered the spearhead of a vertical envelopment or the advance guard element of air landing troops or other forces" and therefore "must seek decisive action immediately upon landing." In this vein they should be "assigned specific missions and limited objectives" and "should not be used for missions that can be performed by other troops." Accordingly, suitable missions for parachute troops were: "Seizing and holding terrain suitable for the landing of troop carrying airplanes or gliders"; "Seizing and holding river and canal crossings, and defiles"; "Establishing bridgeheads"; "Assisting ground offensives by means of vertical envelopment"; and "Creating confusion and acting as a diversion to the operations of the main force."[2] In 1943, these principles were the only thing that even approximated doctrine for the employment of airborne divisions, but in FM 31–30 they were more suggestive and theoretical than directive. For most of the Army's senior officers—the men who would ultimately decide when, where, and how to employ airborne divisions—the attitude was "that some airborne troops would be 'handy to have around.'"[3]

The absence of an airborne doctrine would later haunt the division, but in early 1943 Ridgway had more pressing matters at hand, the foremost of which was preparing his troopers for their deployment overseas. With no specific set of doctrinal tasks on which to concentrate, Ridgway focused on preparing his troopers for "the weariness, the long marches, the loss of sleep, the tremendous exertion that men in combat must undergo." There were two key elements to this preparation. One was physical conditioning; he wanted each trooper "to be as finely trained as a champion boxer."[4] The second was realistic training that emphasized tactical fundamentals, stretched troopers to the limit, and nurtured initiative in junior leaders. If they were tough, smart, and tactically proficient, figured Ridgway, his troopers could undertake any mission.

Gavin shared Ridgway's training philosophy and as the 82nd's ranking parachute regiment commander designed a training regimen for the division's paratroopers that accomplished all that Ridgway desired. Under Gavin's tutelage, a typical training exercise began with "a 25- or 30-mile forced march" followed by "two-sided maneuvers" during which Gavin sought to "grind . . . [junior leaders] down to where the leaders would make mistakes because they were tired" so that he could "teach 'em how to overcome the fatigue factor."[5] According to 505th veteran Private Allen Langdon, "Every facet of this training was directed toward the accomplishment of the two-fold goal: . . . to have a skilled, aggressive body of men that could fight as a combat team or lead and fight as individuals in small unit actions." Furthermore, continued Langdon, an unstated goal of the training was "to eliminate misfits, and a daily run of at least four or five miles and a weekly march of twenty to thirty miles assured this. The rule was, 'if you fall out, you ship out,' and there were seldom second chances."[6] One particularly grueling exercise, related by Gavin himself, underscores this dictum:

> I remember taking the 505 out on a night march one time. We walked from the training area down to Cottonton, 23 miles and we got there about seven–eight in the morning. We maneuvered all day and then I moved them at night on the way back by a different route and went into bivouac at around nine–ten o'clock and let them sleep for two hours and then got them up, and it was as black as could be, and moved them to Bragg. We were marching all night, and they had then walked about 50–55 miles. And one or two of them bitched and complained. They began to bitch and complain and we yanked them right out, right there in the field, "OK, back! Get your stuff out! You're out of the regiment!"[7]

Though not considered elite soldiers like their parachuting brethren, the 82nd's glider troopers experienced equally rigorous training. After returning from his consultations with British airborne commanders in England, Bill Lee wrote a memo stressing that "it is the experience of the British that it is highly wasteful to attempt to carry ordinary troops in gliders, as thirty percent must be eliminated due to air sickness." Because of this he recommended that "the selection, physical standards and special training for glider troops must approximate that prescribed for parachute troops." Ridgway adopted Lee's recommendation and to this end sent several of his glider officers to an Army Ranger training camp to learn their techniques for training and conditioning. When they returned, they initiated a training program for the 82nd's glider troopers that was every bit as demanding as the paratroopers'. In one typical four-day training period, for example, the 325th completed a five-mile march in fifty-eight minutes, a ten-mile march in four inches of snow, and a twenty-five-mile march in just over seven hours. As a result of this strenuous program, "the older men began to fall out, not being able to keep up with the speed marches, incessant night-training exercises, and live-fire combat course." Inevitably, "this brought to the fore the younger, more physically fit men" who "lived in the field" and, like wolves, eventually "became inured to sleet, rain and snow."[8]

Because they lived and trained side by side, there developed an intense rivalry between the 82nd's glider troopers and paratroopers. "The paratroopers always looked down their noses on glider troops, and they would run around, with their arms spread out, tilting their bodies at an angle right and left, yelling, 'Look, Herman, no motor; look Herman, no motor.'" The paratroopers also had a tendency to "beat their breasts a little bit" because they viewed themselves as specially selected soldiers who, having endured a difficult rite of passage to earn their airborne wings and jump boots, were not enamored of the idea of having to share the same divisional shoulder patch with "legs."[9] Lieutenant Wayne Pierce of the 325th had the impression that the troopers of the 505th "did not care for their assignment to the 82nd Airborne, maybe because they felt that they would not receive full credit for their accomplishments, or perhaps because they would be associated with the Glider Troops whom they openly despised." There were, to say the least, "frequent fights, some quite serious, almost amounting to riots."[10]

To be certain, the paratroopers' boastfulness, unique uniforms and badges, and disdain for anyone not a part of their fraternity earned the enmity of much of the Army, to say nothing of the tension these things created between the paratroopers and glider troopers of the division. But in Ridgway's eyes a more serious problem was the pay disparity. The fact that paratroopers received hazardous duty pay rankled the glider troopers who felt that they, too, were performing hazardous duty for which they should be compensated. When it became known that glider pilots also received extra pay but were not expected to fight once on the ground, the glider troopers became especially resentful.[11] Fearing that this issue would undermine morale and combat effectiveness, Ridgway fought hard to get his glider troopers what he felt they rightfully deserved. In a particularly forceful memorandum to the War Department, he wrote, "The existing discrimination in pay between the parachute and glider personnel of the Airborne Division perpetuates a fundamental injustice." The troopers train together, enter combat together "under similar and equal hazards," and the "work of one supplements and is essential to that of the other." Both glider troopers and paratroopers, he asserted, "are subject to much greater risks than other troops," and "to maintain that [a glider trooper] is subject in his training to no greater hazards than those incident to casual air transportation is a refusal to recognize facts." Yet despite Ridgway's repeated entreaties, glider troopers were not granted extra pay until July 1944.[12]

Since there was little more he could do about pay, Ridgway devised other means to close the status gap between his paratroopers and glider troopers. He authorized the wearing of a glider cap patch much like that worn by the paratroopers, an "oval, about two and one half inches across with a white glider on a blue background." When he saw that this did little to bring his troopers together, he authorized anyone who made a parachute jump to wear jump boots and the parachute cap badge. This, too, fell flat, as evidenced by a sarcastic memorandum found on the 505th's bulletin board, which stated: "Any man in the 505 who makes one glider ride shall be entitled to wear shoes and canvas leggings."[13]

Yet, remarkably, this competition within the ranks, potentially so destructive, did not tear the division apart. Nor did it affect its performance. In fact, it had the opposite effect. The glider troopers fatalistically accepted, and even mocked, their situation. A popular poster depicting burned and crashed gliders on which was emblazoned "Join the Glider Troops! No Flight Pay. No Jump Pay. But—Never a Dull Moment" hung on most of their barrack walls.[14] And though there was always the opportunity for glider troopers to volunteer for parachute duty, very few did. Instead, they trained as hard if not harder than their parachuting brethren in anticipation of the day they could prove their mettle in combat. Seeing this, the paratroopers also upped their game; they had, after all, to live up to their own high standards. The end result was a rivalry, played out in training (as well as a few bars), in which each side sought to outrun, outshoot, outmarch, and otherwise outperform the other. In the process, both glidermen and paratroopers got faster and tougher and became more proficient soldiers.

There was another reason the 82nd did not self-destruct. That reason was the division commander, one of the few men in the 82nd who was both parachute and glider qualified and therefore knew the hazards of each.[15] But it was not Ridgway's qualifications that kept the division working together. It was his presence. Almost without exception the officers and men of the division held him in awe. Many likened him to a steadying, competent father figure. In their eyes he was above the conflict in the ranks and instead was a figure around which they could all rally and to whom all appealed for approval. Describing the effect Ridgway had on others, Captain Arthur Kroos, his onetime aide, stated:

> He was brilliant. He was a military man in every way. I never, ever saw him cross his legs. Unbelievable! He always would sit up straight. There was never any slouching. No matter how soft the chair was, somehow the goddamn chair stiffened up when he sat in it.
>
> He would walk in a room and he would create a presence by being in that room. He didn't have to say anything. Just the way he walked, the way he looked. When his eyes would go over a room, everyone was instantly drawn to him, just like that. He didn't have to say a word. . . .
>
> He was intense. I think he slept that way. He was a very determined person. He knew what he wanted. He wouldn't tolerate anything that was not right up to perfection. When things went not to his liking, just his look told you everything. He didn't have to say anything. . . . His appearance in itself, his facial expressions, his use of eyes, perhaps his raising his eyebrows, said one hell of a lot more than any words that he could have come out with. He was just a remarkable person.[16]

Even the most battle-hardened troopers found themselves at a loss for words when describing Ridgway. One legendary paratroop commander, Lieutenant Colonel Benjamin H. Vandervoort, stated categorically "I love the man and an attempt by me to analize [*sic*] him feels presumptious [*sic*]."[17] Lieutenant Colonel Al Ireland, an original member of Gavin's tough 505th, wrote that his impression of Ridgway was "one of awe and admiration for the appearance of this man—his countenance, posture (warlike); his manner; gentle and most gracious." He concluded, "I knew we were in good hands under the generalship of this person."[18]

Ridgway was a soldier in the mold of his mentor, George Marshall, who, in turn, emulated his mentor, John J. Pershing. Both Pershing and Marshall were stoic, aloof, and unapproachable yet set an example that influenced strongly the generation of Army officers who came to maturity during the interwar years. Officership for them was a vocation, defining not only what a man did but who he was, and having come of age in the First World War (Marshall served under Pershing in France), they were grounded in the ideals of two epochs: the nineteenth-century ideal of officer as heroic symbol and the twentieth-century view of officer as technician. This paradigm required that officers be technically and tactically competent and inspirational leaders. Ridgway was its very embodiment. He had, without question, mastered the skills of his profession. He was an expert shot and proficient with every infantry weapon in the American arsenal, and while stalking the ranges he was not above demonstrating the proper way to sight a machine gun or anchor a mortar. When confronted with a new weapon or technological development, as he was with the introduction of gliders and parachutes, he made it a priority to immediately become familiar with the intricacies and nuances of the thing by experiencing it firsthand. Yet despite the physical proximity with his troopers that ensued from this hands-on approach, Ridgway remained a distant figure, someone the troopers admired from afar in much the same way that Pershing and Marshall were admired. Lieutenant Colonel Bob Piper, another original member of the 505th, recalled that few people really knew Ridgway and that "a lot of people more or less ran . . . scared of him" because he was the division commander, and the thought was to "leave him the hell alone." Gavin, who felt he knew his commander as well as anyone, stated that Ridgway's extreme integrity made him appear "flinty" and "hard to get along with."[19] But both Piper and Gavin, like so many others, admired the man immensely, with the latter commenting that under Ridgway's leadership the 82nd developed "attributes that would serve it well for the remainder of the war."[20]

One of those attributes was what one author called a "military corporatist ideology" that prized both individual initiative and teamwork, with the former enhancing the effectiveness of the latter. According to Gavin, who shared Ridgway's vision, achieving this end required "a whole new dimension to soldiering" that did not seek to destroy a soldier's individuality but integrated myriad individuals into cohesive fighting teams and the teams into an unstoppable division. Eschewing the mind-set of the interwar Army that held unquestionably to "the need for close order drill and the need for imposing on the soldier a sort of templet [*sic*] to make him fit into the platoon, fit into the squad," Ridgway and Gavin encouraged and even celebrated their troopers' individuality. To this end they introduced name tags, highlighting the fact that each 82nd trooper "wasn't just another soldier" but was, in fact, something different, "a special kind of animal." Their goal was to form units comprising soldiers who, knowing the larger mission and its intent, could seize the initiative on a chaotic battlefield and, even in the absence of higher direction, accomplish the mission. Corollary to this unique and, for the time at least, heretical emphasis on individuality was the idea that there was "nothing too good for [their troopers]; no bed too soft, no food too good; no conditions too good for them to live" with the payoff being that when the time came, much would be asked of them, and they would be expected to deliver.[21]

Ridgway returned to Fort Bragg from North Africa on 24 March, just in time to greet a coterie of dignitaries who wanted to see if the 82nd was ready to fight. This was an important test, not simply because Generals Marshall and Arnold, British Foreign Secretary Anthony Eden, and Britain's liaison officer to the American chiefs of staff, Field Marshal Sir John Dill, were watching, but because by that time the draft plans for the invasion of Sicily had been published, and those plans called for the extensive use of airborne troops. Ridgway was anxious to prove that his troopers were up to the task, especially since there were grumblings in the American airborne community that he had stolen a march on his friend Bill Lee and the 101st. According to Gavin, there were many who felt that "if one of the divisions went into combat right away it should be [Lee's] division because he was senior." But Ridgway had done "some jockeying in Washington for the honor of being the first airborne division into combat," and this was his chance to demonstrate for Marshall, who had selected the 82nd for the assignment, that he had made the right decision.[22]

To highlight both his troopers' capabilities and their level of training, Ridgway staged a demonstration for the dignitaries at nearby Pope Field that began with a simulated combat jump followed by the insertion of twenty-six Waco gliders carrying Lieutenant Colonel Paul Turner's 2/325th. The jump went off without incident, and, on cue, the gliders cut loose from their tow planes and made precision landings right in front of the reviewing stands, after which Turner's troopers performed a mock assault. To Ridgway's surprise, both Marshall and Arnold came away disappointed. Arnold, in particular, was piqued because the gliders did not, upon landing, taxi toward the cover of a nearby stand of trees before disgorging the glider troopers, as they would in a real combat situation. When apprised of this Ridgway became a little "irked." Of course, he was aware that the demonstration "bore little resemblance" to what would be done in actual combat. As he explained in a subsequent letter to Brigadier General Elbridge G. Chapman, who as Lee's replacement as the chief of Airborne Command was the man in whom Marshall had entrusted the authority to validate each airborne division's readiness for combat, "Only the compelling necessity of conserving material in order that training might continue, induced us to bring these gliders in over open ground and land them carefully on a good airport."[23]

Fortunately for Ridgway, six days later he had a chance to redeem himself and put to rest any reservations about the 82nd's readiness. Taking off from Pope Field in approximately 130 C-47 transports, Gavin's 505th jumped on three separate drop zones near Camden, South Carolina, the Army's largest parachute operation to date. Though marred by the death of three troopers who were killed when one of the planes lost power and plowed through the descending parachutists, the exercise was an "unbelievable, uncanny watershed" because it proved that Ridgway's 82nd could plan, organize, and execute large airborne operations over long distances.[24] Moreover, both General Marshall and Field Marshal Dill were again on hand to witness the drop and were favorably impressed, as was Prime Minister Winston Churchill, who accompanied them.[25]

The Camden drop was the last significant Stateside training event for the 82nd. The division had been alerted for movement, and though where it was going was a closely guarded secret, it was obvious that it was going to a combat zone when arrangements were made for the troopers to make out wills, allotments, and insurance papers, after which they were confined to the division area. But security was not tight enough to keep quite a number of Ridgway's high-spirited individualists from going AWOL in search of a last hot time on the town. Fortunately, the vast majority reported back in time to board the troop trains, albeit a stripe lighter.[26] Before boarding the trains, however, the troopers had to undergo one last "great ordeal." Operational security dictated that the "cocky troopers" were to "pretend they were just ordinary doughboys and be on good behavior and to profess ignorance of the identity of their units."[27] Paratroopers had to hide their jump boots and don infantry leggings, and everyone was required to sew another patch over the 82nd insignia on his left shoulder.[28]

The lead element departed Fort Bragg on 18 April. Twenty-six hours later it arrived at Camp Edwards, on Cape Cod, Massachusetts, where the entire division closed by 23 April. While at Camp Edwards, the troopers kept fit with daily distance marches, zeroed their weapons, received the necessary inoculations, attended classes on security and hygiene, and were issued additional equipment. On 28 April, the troopers again boarded trains, this time for the ports of Staten Island, New York, and Hoboken, New Jersey, where awaiting them were the transports that would carry them off to war. Early on the morning of 29 April 1943, the troopers of the 82nd Airborne Division, at least those awake and topside, saw the American shore recede from sight. For many, it would be the last time they saw their homeland.[29]

Thirteen years later Ridgway recounted the uncertainty he felt that morning. "Looking back on it now," he wrote, "I am convinced that no division that left the States for battle, either in Europe or the Pacific, had been torn up and put back together again so frequently or so drastically as had the 82nd," and as a result his division sailed with "about a third the amount of training that the [other] infantry divisions had had." Yet others felt much more assured and confident. Gavin, for one, was convinced that his troopers would fight and that "there have never been soldiers like them." He knew he had a highly spirited regiment in a highly spirited division and remarked in his diary that "if they fight as well in Africa as they fight in Fayetteville [North Carolina] we have nothing to worry about."[30]

CHAPTER 5

A SMALL PHALANX IN A VAST, STRANGE LAND

We sleep on the ground, give up most of our blood to the insects, march long hours in the dust, eat no better than you would expect, and occasionally gaze at the stars and dream of home. It is the life of the Foreign Legion, the land of no return, the school of forgetfulness, and gradually the men are acquiring the habits and thoughts of a professional soldier.

—RICHARD MOTT JANNEY, *RICHARD MOTT JANNEY, 1ST LT. 505 REG. 82 A.B. DIV. KILLED IN ACTION VILLA LITERNO, ITALY, OCTOBER 5, 1943*

IN JANUARY 1943, Roosevelt, Churchill, and their military chiefs came together at Casablanca, French Morocco, for a ten-day conference to discuss strategy. High on the agenda was what to do next in the war against Germany and Italy. Operation TORCH, the Allied invasion of North Africa of the previous November, forced the American Joint Chiefs of Staff to reconsider their strategic precepts, outlined in the Marshall Memorandum, because it had resulted in "such an investment of resources that a cross-Channel operation became improbable in 1943." On the other hand, TORCH's success had bolstered British calls to continue operations in the Mediterranean. The strike at North Africa had compelled Hitler to shift eleven divisions from northern to southern France, noted the British. Another undertaking in the Mediterranean would likely force a shift of additional divisions, thereby weakening the Nazi grip on northwest Europe, or in Russia, or both.[1]

Opening on 14 January, the Casablanca Conference was a rancorous affair that pitted each nation's principal military spokesman against the other.

For the United States this was General Marshall, who still wanted to mount a cross-Channel invasion as quickly as possible and avoid getting sidetracked by "interminable operations in the Mediterranean." He was opposed by Field Marshal Alan Brooke, the chief of the Imperial General Staff, who emphasized that the Allies should capitalize on their success in the Mediterranean, knock Italy out of the war, force Germany to further disperse its forces, and thereby lend immediate relief to the Russians who, at the time, were fighting for their lives in front of Moscow.[2] After days of stalemate, during which Brooke became so despondent that he penned in his diary, "We are further from obtaining agreement than we ever were," Marshall largely acceded to the British plan.[3]

In return for British concessions to limited offensive operations in the Pacific, Marshall agreed to "an invasion of Sicily [with a target date of 25 July 1943] because of the large number of troops which would become available in North Africa, the great economy in shipping tonnage to be obtained (the major consideration), and the possibility of eliminating Italy from the war and thereby forcing Germany to assume responsibility for Italian commitments."[4] Roosevelt and Churchill, in the full flush of Allied comity, congratulated the military chiefs for producing "the most complete strategic plan for a world-wide war that had ever been conceived, and far exceeding the accomplishments of the last war."[5] Brooke and Marshall, however, were not as comfortable with the Casablanca agreements. Although the outcome had been a win for Brooke, he realized that left uncertain was the question of what to do after Sicily, and, for his part, Marshall was determined to exploit that uncertainty.

After deciding to invade Sicily the Combined Chiefs of Staff (the name given to the Anglo-American committee comprising the American Joint Chiefs and the Chiefs of the British Imperial General Staff) addressed the question of command. Brooke felt that it had become "clear that centralised command was essential" to coordinate Allied actions in the Mediterranean. Marshall agreed and nominated Eisenhower to head a theater headquarters. Brooke was uneasy with Marshall's choice. "From many points of view," wrote Brooke, "it was desirable to hand this Command over to the Americans, but unfortunately up to now Eisenhower . . . had neither the tactical nor strategical experience required for such a task." Nonetheless, left without a credible alternative the British acquiesced to Eisenhower's elevation "into the stratosphere and rarefied atmosphere of a Supreme Commander" (his official title was commander in chief, Allied Forces in North Africa).[6] However, to ensure that the conduct of operations remained in British hands (and, according to some, conformed to British strategy), Brooke maneuvered to emplace a trio of British officers as Eisenhower's principal deputies. Hence, General Sir Harold R. L. G. Alexander became Eisenhower's deputy and the overall ground force commander, while command of the theater's naval and air forces was vested in Admiral Sir Andrew B. Cunningham and Air Chief Marshal Sir Arthur Tedder, respectively. It was this team, a bastardized version of the British committee system of command, that the Combined Chiefs charged with finishing the fight in North Africa and planning and executing the invasion of Sicily. And as is true of most committee-led projects, both the process and the product suffered commensurably.[7]

Upon being named to his new post, Eisenhower established a special planning cell—dubbed Force 141 after the room in the St. George's Hotel in Algiers where it first met—to formulate a plan for Operation HUSKY, the invasion of Sicily.[8] He and his deputies, meanwhile, focused their attention on completing the destruction of Axis forces in North Africa, which at the time were cornered in Tunisia and appeared ripe for defeat. But in February 1943, things changed drastically. The Germans ambushed an American force at Kasserine Pass, demonstrating that, though cornered, they were far from beaten. In the wake of Kasserine Pass, finalizing the plan for HUSKY became "a nuisance that—like it or not—would simply have to wait."[9]

The object of the nuisance, the island of Sicily, lies approximately ninety miles from the tip of Cape Bon, Tunisia. Triangular in shape with sides measuring 180 miles in the north, 125 miles in the east, and 170 miles in the south, it comprises an area of approximately 10,000 square miles, about the same size as Vermont. The island's most prominent feature, the 10,000-foot-high Mount Etna, lies on Sicily's eastern shore and dominates that part of the island. But the features that most interested Force 141 were Sicily's ports and airfields. There were four major ports on the island, Messina, Catania, Syracuse, and Palermo, and two minor ones, Augusta (on the eastern coast about halfway between Syracuse and Catania) and Licata (on the southern coast). Each major port had an estimated daily capacity of more than 1,000 tons, and Force 141 deemed it essential to seize at least one of them early in the operation for use as a supply hub. Force 141 was likewise focused on quickly capturing as many airfields as possible. With these in hand Allied pilots could provide sustained and responsive air cover to both the fleet and the ground forces.[10]

So while everyone else at Eisenhower's newly established theater headquarters was preoccupied with the ongoing fight in North Africa, Force 141 drafted a plan that called for sequential landings around Sicily's periphery over a period of three to five days. The initial landings were to occur in the east, followed by landings in the south and then in the north. Although each landing site was selected for its proximity to ports and airfields, the overall intent of the landing scheme was to leverage the Allies' command of the sea by separating the invading forces in time and space, which would compel the enemy to defend in multiple directions and, in turn, dilute his combat power and hasten his defeat. When briefed on the plan in late February 1943, Alexander accepted it as tentative and preliminary simply because he did not have the time to devote to its more thorough study.[11] However, when General Bernard Law Montgomery, whose British Eighth Army had been selected as one of the two major ground forces for the invasion, was briefed on the plan in mid-March, he rejected it out of hand. "In my opinion the operation breaks every common-sense rule of practical battle fighting and is completely theoretical," stormed Montgomery in a cable to Alexander. "It has no hope of success and should be completely recast."[12]

Montgomery's reaction to the Force 141 plan heralded several weeks of bitter wrangling. To anyone who would listen, but especially to Alexander whom he browbeat into submission (the forceful Montgomery completely overshadowed the reserved and gentlemanly Alexander and in so doing became, de facto, the primary ground force commander for HUSKY), Montgomery railed against the Force 141 plan because it was "based on the assumption that the opposition will be slight and that Sicily will be captured rather easily." This assumption, he continued, was wrong. "The Germans and also the Italians are fighting desperately now in Tunisia," Montgomery countered, "and will do so in Italy."[13] He proposed instead that the Allies mass the largest invasion force possible and hurl it ashore at a single place and time. He saw Sicily's southeastern tip as the most favorable location because, once ashore, this force could drive north to Messina, cut off Axis forces on the island, and destroy them.

Tedder and Cunningham howled at Montgomery's proposal. Tedder declared that without the early capture of sufficient airfields, "the operation is impossible," while Cunningham maintained that "from a naval point of view, the massing of so many ships in [one] area is to invite disaster, and besides, the chief merit of amphibious attack is to do so on a broad front and disperse the enemy effort."[14] Meanwhile, the man who should have decided the issue—Eisenhower—was too consumed with ending the fight in North Africa and relied on his Force 141 team to referee. But devoid of command authority, Force 141 became nothing but a sounding board or, for Montgomery, a whipping boy.

Montgomery's objections, Alexander's vacuity, and Eisenhower's inattention threw the whole HUSKY planning effort into disarray, a point that did not escape Ridgway when he visited North Africa. More troubling was his discovery that some were taking advantage of the chaos to craft for themselves larger roles in the upcoming invasion. He thought this particularly true of the "dapper, handsome, [and] charming" British major general Frederick Arthur Montague "Boy" Browning, the senior Allied airborne officer and Eisenhower's principal airborne adviser.[15] Ridgway felt that Browning was "a bit patronizing in his manner toward those who had had considerably less airborne experience than he" and feared that "from his post at Supreme Headquarters, [Browning] was in a position to exert an undue influence."[16] Ridgway became especially concerned about Browning's machinations when he compared the Force 141 plan to Montgomery's plan and saw how the differences impacted the employment of Allied airborne forces.

The Force 141 plan called for airborne insertions in support of each of the amphibious landings.[17] Since these were to occur sequentially, both the British and the American airborne contingents would have access to all the available transport aircraft in theater. Montgomery's plan, on the other hand, called for only one amphibious landing and one airborne insertion to support that landing. Ridgway feared that were Montgomery's plan accepted, there would not be sufficient aircraft "to fill the minimum combat needs of both the U.S. and British airborne forces who were to jump into Sicily [on D day]," and "every plane allotted the British, therefore, meant less combat strength [the 82nd] could take into battle."[18] Ridgway was also convinced that Browning would exert his influence to secure for the British the lion's share of the available transport aircraft, the vast majority of which were American planes with American crews that, to Ridgway's thinking, should be used primarily to transport American airborne forces.[19]

To counter Browning, Ridgway enlisted the aid of General Patton, whose Seventh Army was slated to be the other major ground force for HUSKY. As Ridgway saw things Patton was a natural and formidable ally. The 82nd would be attached to Seventh Army regardless of which plan was adopted, and Patton was in a fight of his own with Montgomery because, like Ridgway, he was certain that the British were trying to take advantage of the chaos surrounding the HUSKY planning to maneuver themselves into starring roles, leaving second billing to their less experienced American cousins.[20] Hence, as soon as he returned to the United States, Ridgway sent General Taylor and a small planning staff back to North Africa in order to lend Patton's Seventh Army staff some airborne expertise and look after the 82nd's interests.[21]

The final plan for the invasion of Sicily, adopted in mid-May, was very much what Montgomery proposed in that it called for simultaneous, not sequential, amphibious landings in the east, southeast, and south. It also recognized the importance of securing Sicily's ports and airfields. In broad outline, the plan envisioned a five-phase operation. Phase one, which called for "preparatory measures by Naval and Air Forces to neutralize enemy naval efforts, and to gain air supremacy," had already been partially accomplished.[22] Cunningham's Allied naval forces had savaged the Italian fleet, and although the threat of Axis naval action remained a concern, it was not likely. Tedder's Allied air forces had likewise gained air superiority in the Mediterranean, but until Allied fighters could operate from air bases on Sicily itself, the probability of Axis aircraft making periodic appearances over the battlefield remained high.[23]

Phases two, three, and four of the HUSKY plan, therefore, were devoted to seizing Sicily's airfields, along with several ports through which the Allies would receive supplies once they were established ashore. Phase two called for "pre-dawn airborne [parachute] assaults, assisted by airborne [glider] landings with the object of seizing airfields and the ports of SIRACUSA and LICATA"; phase three, "the establishment of a firm base from which to conduct operations for the capture of the ports of AUGUSTA and CATANIA, and the GERBINI group of airfields"; and phase four, "the capture of the ports and airfields outlined in Phase 3." With the ports and airfields in hand, phase five of the plan—"the reduction of the island"—could proceed apace, although how the reduction would occur was not addressed in detail, an oversight that would later cause even more friction between Patton and Montgomery.[24]

Given the lack of detail devoted to phase five, the central, almost exclusive, focus of the HUSKY plan was the massive D-day amphibious assault by seven British, Canadian, and U.S. divisions on Sicily's eastern, southeastern, and southern shores. For this there were more than enough landing craft and amphibious assault ships to go around. The same could not be said of the resources required for the phase-two airborne assaults. As Ridgway had predicted, the paucity of transport aircraft gave rise to a conflict within the Allied ranks over which airborne contingent would receive the largest share on D day. All told there were about 366 C-47s available for the invasion, and in one of the few decisions Eisenhower made during the planning for HUSKY, he apportioned them between the armies more with an eye to achieving peace among his subordinates than to the attainment of specific objectives, assigning 144 of the available aircraft to Montgomery and the remaining 222 to Patton (conversely, Montgomery received more than 200 more landing craft and amphibious assault ships than did Patton). Given this apportionment, and the attendant limits it placed on the size of the airborne force each army commander could insert on D day, selecting objectives for them that would achieve the maximum effect was critical.[25]

The manner by which the airborne forces would be inserted was affected by another resource constraint—gliders. A consignment of 500 Wacos, disassembled and packed in their shipping crates, had been haphazardly unloaded at several North African ports in late April. Reassembling them was the task of 105 U.S. glider pilots who, it was assumed, knew not only how to fly them but how to put them together. It was a poor assumption. Plagued by their mission's low priority and a lack of parts and tools, it took the pilots thirty days to assemble four gliders. For General Taylor and his airborne planners, the lack of gliders reinforced a tendency, already strong in the American airborne community, to lead assaults with parachute troops. (This tendency was due primarily to the leading role played by paratroopers in the formation of American airborne units combined with the lack of any doctrinal template that addressed the sequence by which glider and parachute forces should be inserted.)[26] Therefore, it was decided that the D-day drops in support of Seventh Army would be carried out solely by paratroopers. Conversely, in late May Montgomery decided to insert his D-day airborne force by glider. Like the Americans, he had initially planned to lead with paratroopers, but became convinced that the enemy armor threat was too great for them to handle, so he decided instead to use his glider troops because they could bring with them antitank guns. This decision, in turn, energized the glider assembly program, and within days, under the watchful eyes of trained mechanics who were rushed to the ports to oversee things, 346 gliders were ready, all of which were earmarked for British use. Having already decided to lead with paratroopers and now with no gliders at all available for their use, Taylor and his planners simply assumed that the 82nd's glider contingent would be air-landed on Sicily sometime after D day.[27]

A final consideration with which Taylor and his airborne planners had to contend was the state of training of the transport crews. Colonel Hal Clark's 52nd Troop Carrier Wing was slated to carry the 82nd's paratroopers to Sicily. The two units had trained together at Fort Bragg, and based on that training neither Ridgway nor Clark was confident that the pilots and navigators could locate drop zones at night. "The 52d [Troop Carrier] Wing was not, at date of departure [from Fort Bragg], capable of conducting night operations," wrote Ridgway in a letter to Taylor, and Colonel Clark was "in full agreement . . . that with present training levels operations in darkness of the scope contemplated are not practicable."[28] Taylor, therefore, was to try to set the D-day drop times so that Clark's crews would have some daylight by which to navigate. A dawn drop was Ridgway's preferred solution. But the HUSKY amphibious forces were sequenced to hit the beaches during darkness, with H hour set for 0245 hours (H hour was the time the main attack, in this case the amphibious assault, would commence). This meant that the only way the initial drop could both precede the amphibious assault and be carried out during daylight was if it were conducted, at the latest, during dusk on the previous day. When Taylor suggested this, Eisenhower overruled him. However, based in part on the requirement for some light by which to navigate, D day was moved up to 10 July during which there would be a second-quarter moon, enough, it was hoped, for Clark's pilots to find the drop zones.[29]

Once the overarching HUSKY plan had been approved, the resources apportioned, and specific dates and times set, it fell to the two army commanders to finalize their tactical plans to accomplish the tasks highlighted in phases two, three, and four of the operation. Montgomery's plan was to land elements of three divisions and an independent brigade in the Gulf of Noto on Sicily's eastern shore in order to seize Syracuse and its port, while a fourth division landed on either side of the Pachino Peninsula at the southeastern tip of the island to secure an airfield located there.

To aid in the taking of Syracuse and its port, Montgomery planned a complementary operation, code-named LADBROKE, by which the 1st Airlanding Brigade of the British 1st Airborne Division would conduct a glider assault to seize the Ponte Grande Bridge over the Anapo River, just south of Syracuse; secure Syracuse's western outskirts; and then hold both so that British troops landing in the Gulf of Noto could pass over the bridge and through the city to the port.[30]

Patton planned to land his Seventh Army along a seventy-mile front in the Gulf of Gela on Sicily's southern shore in order to seize four airfields in the area, the port at Licata, and a smaller port at Gela. To do this he had the U.S. 1st and 45th Infantry Divisions of Omar Bradley's II Corps landing on the army's eastern flank at Gela and Scoglitti, respectively, while the U.S. 3rd Infantry Division, under direct army control, landed on the western flank at Licata. To protect his amphibious forces from enemy counterattack while they were getting established ashore, he wanted Ridgway to drop as many paratroopers as possible on some high ground several miles inland from the invasion beaches.[31] With this in mind he assigned the 82nd four tasks:

> (1) Land during night D-1/D in area N and E of GELA, capture and secure high ground in that area.
>
> (2) Disrupt communications and movement of reserves during night.
>
> (3) Be attached to 1st Infantry Division effective H/1 hours on D-Day.
>
> (4) Assist 1st Infantry Division in capturing and securing landing field at PONTE OLIVO.[32]

The details of how he would accomplish these tasks were left to Ridgway, his commanders, and his staff to work out in coordination with Clark's 52nd Troop Carrier Wing (Taylor, acting as part of the Seventh Army staff, did not have the authority to approve a tactical plan for the 82nd). But when Patton issued his order Ridgway was at sea along with the rest of his division, the vast majority of whom were not even aware where they were headed when they climbed the gangplanks of their troop ships. Only after they had sailed and were out of sight of land was the secret revealed—Casablanca.[33]

The convoy in which the 82nd sailed comprised twenty-three transports, eight destroyers, one aircraft carrier, and the battleship *Texas*.[34] The division occupied three of the transports: Gavin's 505th was on the *Monterey*, Lewis's 325th was on the *Santa Rosa*, and Ridgway, his staff, and Tucker's 504th were on the *George Washington* (other divisional units were spread among the three transports). Zigzagging in order to confuse German U-boats, it took the convoy twelve days to reach Casablanca, during which the troopers learned to speak a smattering of Arabic—"Which way is north?" "I am wounded," and "Where is the railway station?"—held wrestling and boxing matches, and watched each ship's limited repertoire of movies. For the troopers of the 325th, this meant seeing *The Bank Dick* and, appropriately, *Casablanca* over and over again. Otherwise, the troopers spent most of their time aboard the crowded transports conforming to a routine that was dictated by a colored card system. Since the transports were not large enough to sleep everyone aboard simultaneously, shifts were set up. Those with white cards were to be below deck at night, while those with yellow cards were to be below during the day, an arrangement that was reversed every three days.[35]

Life at sea, though uncomfortable, was relatively benign. The only event of any significance involved Ridgway's transport, the *George Washington*, which kept breaking down, a problem that came to a head a few hundred miles off the coast of Africa when Ridgway awoke in the middle of the night to "discover that the old tub had stopped again, and that the convoy had already disappeared over the horizon." Distraught that his division would arrive in North Africa without him, Ridgway "sent a message to . . . the convoy commander, and told him if we weren't under way by morning, [he] was going to jump overboard." Ridgway's threat "seemed to provide all hands with some amusement," but, said Ridgway, "I wasn't joking."[36] Eventually, the *George Washington* was repaired and on 10 May 1943 sailed with the rest of the convoy into Casablanca's port, where the troopers saw for the first time war's devastation in the form of the French battleship *Jean Bart*, beached, burned, gutted, and lying on its side.[37]

It did not take long to get the troopers off the ships. Most were anxious to escape the crowded confines of the transports, so by late afternoon the entire division was ashore, standing silent retreat in the setting sun. "Brushed and polished we stood," recalled one trooper, "a small phalanx of men in a vast, strange land."[38] Then, though still wearing the long johns, wool shirts, and trousers that had kept them warm at sea, the troopers shouldered their packs and weapons and began a march that "soon turned to pure misery as shipboard muscles complained about full packs, bed rolls, and weapons, and the sweat poured down."[39] Their destination was a temporary bivouac site, Camp Don B. Passage, which was nothing more than a patch of desert five miles outside Casablanca. Reaching Camp Passage well after dark, most of the troopers erected pup tents, crawled inside, and fell into a stupor.[40] But for those unable to sleep there was a surprise. Despite the stringent security measures taken to hide the 82nd's movement overseas, its arrival in North Africa was being trumpeted on the radio. According to Lieutenant Joe Lyons of the 456th Parachute Field Artillery Battalion, "On the radio were the German propaganda duo, Axis Sally and George. The propaganda was rather crude but the music was great and the gags corny. Their news of the moment was 'Welcome 82nd Airborne to Casablanca.' Ben Wright [another 456th trooper] made a classic remark, 'American Top Secret Equals the British Most Ridiculous.' The Great Secret was out of the bag."[41]

While in North Africa, the 82nd was attached to Lieutenant General Mark Clark's U.S. Fifth Army, which had assigned the 82nd to more permanent billets near the airfields where the 52nd Troop Carrier Wing was housed (the 52nd had arrived about two weeks before the 82nd). So after two days at barren Camp Passage the troopers were again on the move with Ridgway, the division headquarters, and the two parachute regiments bound for Oujda, Morocco, while General Keerans, the bulk of the division's support units, Lewis's 325th, the 80th Airborne Antiaircraft Battalion, and the 320th Glider Field Artillery Battalion made for Marnia, a small village some twelve miles from Oujda, just across the border in Algeria.[42] A "fortunate few" made the four-hundred-mile journey by truck, but the bulk of the troopers traveled for several days by train in World War I–era "forty and eight" rail cars.[43] Although otherwise uneventful, it was during this trip that the troopers got their first glimpse of their German foe.

> At some point in the desert the train stopped on a siding directly opposite a train load of big, blonde, bronzed Afrika Korps prisoners of war. Riding on top of each of the box cars was an equally big, inky-black Senegalese soldier with a tommy gun. One German who spoke good English began talking to the troopers and the following conversation took place:
>
> Afrika Korps POW: "Where do you Americans think you are going?"
>
> Paratrooper: "We're going to Berlin."
>
> Afrika Korps POW: "Well, that's fair enough. We're headed for New York."[44]

When the troopers finally clambered out of their boxcars and took a look at their new homes, there was unanimous agreement: Marnia and Oujda were hellholes. The former was "no more than a railroad siding with one or two buildings." The slightly larger Oujda was where troopers fortunate enough to have some free time went "if there was nothing else to do and if life had become so unbearable that one didn't care what happened to him."[45]

While at Oujda and Marnia the troopers slept in two-man pup tents, arranged with parade-ground precision. But the neatness of the tent cities belied the reality of life in the desert, a life made almost unbearable by a potent combination of extreme heat, wind, sand, and flies. The water, which "was so heavily chlorinated it burned the troopers' throats," offered scant relief, and the meals were anything but relaxing repasts.[46] While "going through every mess line with our mess kit," recalled Arthur Kroos, "one ha[n]d was constantly fanning the flies off," so troopers had to eat "in a sort of circular motion—if you let them land, then you had to pick them off and ten more would land while you were doing that." According to Lieutenant Kenneth R. Shaker, the swarms of flies were so thick, "When we drank coffee, we learned to clench our teeth to strain out the dead flies, and then we would spit them out." In the estimation of Lieutenant Richard Mott Janney, "All agree that the greatest blessing would be to be able to live without the necessity of eating."[47]

Besides the flies, the troopers had also to contend with the fine sand, which was "richly mixed with sheep dung" and got into everything. The result was mass dysentery.[48] "Every morning we got up, we took [a] pill to stop [the diarrhea]. It sealed us off for about 8 hours during the day. . . . Everyone in the division had dysentery. You'd be lying on your bunk with your butt on one end and your head at the other and you just [shot] both ways. Unbelievable." Training while so afflicted required that the troopers keep their entrenching tools readily at hand so that they could quickly carve out a hole in which to relieve themselves. "This malady was so universal and struck so suddenly it became commonplace to see someone break ranks and tear off to some unoccupied part of the desert, with no explanation needed or demanded. Toilet paper [became] more valuable than French franc notes." Gavin joked that during this plague the height of individual achievement was the ability "to travel 100 y[ar]ds removin[g] a pair of coveralls enroute."[49] According to the 505th's regimental surgeon, even the medics had to adjust their protocols. "If you had 10 stools a day, you pulled fully [*sic*] duty; 20 stools a day you were on quarters, and 30 a day you were sent to the hospital."[50]

Yet despite the dysentery training continued unabated, although Ridgway did make one change—the extreme daytime heat forced him to train the division at night. This paid huge dividends in Sicily because the troopers grew accustomed to operating in the dark, but in North Africa it only added to the their discomfort, for there was nowhere to sleep comfortably during the day and the bit of shade provided by the pup tents was not enough to offset the stifling heat.

The training was hard, realistic, and for the most part conducted with live ammunition. It began with weapons training during which the troopers learned to use every weapon in the division arsenal and most of those of the enemy. It then progressed to tactical training with squads, platoons, and companies. To measure progress, Ridgway organized a series of "fire control problems" that every unit had to successfully pass; failure meant going through again until a satisfactory level of competence was attained. As a result, "At the conclusion of its two month training period . . . the 82d [Airborne] Division was in superb physical condition, well qualified in the use of its armament except in the case of the Field Artillery, well advanced in combined ground operations and had adopted a workable SOP for equipment and personnel drops."[51]

About the only training that suffered was glider and parachute training, the former because of the dearth of gliders, the latter because of unpredictable winds and the rough terrain. "Even on the rare calm days, jumping was a hazard," recalled Ridgway, "for the ground was hard, and covered with loose boulders, from the size of a man's fist to the size of his head."[52] These hazards took their toll. During one jump twenty-two troopers were hospitalized for injuries they sustained while landing; a few days later fifty-three more suffered the same fate.[53] Faced with these casualties Ridgway curtailed parachute training, especially for key leaders. (Gavin did not like asking his troopers to do what he would not, so during the next jump he sneaked aboard one of the aircraft, but just as his plane was "loaded and all set to take off . . . the control tower called and said that Gen[eral] Ridgway ordered [Gavin] not to jump.")[54]

All told, the division conducted only two regimental-size jumps while in North Africa, but these were designed primarily as training exercises for Hal Clark's aircrews so very few paratroopers actually exited the aircraft, and then only to gauge the accuracy with which Clark's crews were able to find the drop zones and deliver their loads. In the first Clark's pilots "scattered [Gavin's 505th] at every turn," while the second exercise, carrying Tucker's 504th, "proved deceptively successful."[55] Yet the lack of parachute and glider training did not worry Ridgway. He realized these were but means of delivery and that what mattered more was the troopers' tactical proficiency once they were on the ground, so it was on this that he and his subordinate commanders focused the bulk of their training time. But given the mixed results of the regimental drops, Ridgway was not as sanguine about the ability of the 52nd to accomplish its HUSKY mission.

By any measure, the mission assigned the 52nd was daunting. After flying an extended route in formation at night over water, Clark's crews would have to find specific drop zones in unfamiliar and enemy-held terrain while, presumably, being shot at. When the 52nd Trooper Carrier Wing arrived in North Africa it was far from adequately trained for any part of this task, with an official rating as "qualified for daylight operations over familiar terrain, but unqualified for night operations."[56] Clark and his crews, therefore, had much to learn but little time—about two months—in which to learn it.

Clark began his training regimen by focusing on the basics of formation flying at night. Unlike modern aircraft, the C-47s of the era did not have radar to help a pilot see in the dark. Everything was line-of-sight, which made flying in formation at night difficult and mentally taxing, especially during course changes. It also took some time to master, time that was not otherwise available for training on two other critical tasks: night navigation over water and the pinpointing of drop zones. Like Ridgway, Gavin was also concerned with the 52nd's state of training, presciently noting in his diary that "there is reason to believe that some of the [parachute combat team] will miss their [drop zones] by a great deal."[57]

Despite the need to devote as much time to training as possible, a need that Ridgway and Clark felt keenly, they had to contend with an unexpected distraction that consumed significant chunks of training time—visiting dignitaries. In the words of one trooper, "Suddenly it seemed as if every General Officer in North Africa wanted to see what this new-fangled outfit was all about."[58] Each time one arrived there would be an inspection, a parade, a demonstration, or all three, which ate up not only the time it took to stage them but even more precious time preparing for them, to say nothing of how they affected training schedules, since the dignitaries arrived during the day and the troopers and aircrews trained at night. The first to visit was Lieutenant General Mark Clark, who stopped by less than a week after the 82nd settled in at Oujda and Marnia. He was followed the next day by Lieutenant General Carl A. Spaatz, the commander of the Northwest African Air Force. Four days after Spaatz's visit General Browning arrived. Then, on 3 June, Generals Eisenhower, Clark, and Patton visited with several French and Spanish generals in tow. According to Gavin, the extravaganza staged for this visit, for which significant preparation time was devoted, was designed to impress the Spanish, whose hold on Spanish Morocco and friendship with Germany posed a potential threat to Allied lines of communication.[59] Of course, Ridgway's troopers and Hal Clark's aircrews trained around these events as best they could, but the visits had a decidedly adverse impact on readiness, especially for the 52nd, which by D day "was still insufficiently trained on formation flying, navigation, and drop-zone location at night."[60]

Gavin was particularly concerned about the 52nd's navigational skills because his regiment, reinforced by one of Tucker's battalions, would lead the American airborne assault, a decision Ridgway made two days after the 82nd arrived in North Africa and learned that the Seventh Army had been allocated just enough aircraft to drop one reinforced parachute regimental combat team.[61] Although Ridgway felt both his parachute regiment commanders were "splendid officers and very gallant fellows" he selected Gavin because "he was the older and more experienced commander of the two parachute regiments."[62] Moreover, as one of the Army's leading theorists on airborne operations, Gavin was the best choice to work with Patton's Seventh Army to hammer out the details of the largest airborne assault the U.S. Army had yet attempted.

But Gavin was much more than a woolly-headed theorist. He was also a tough yet revered leader of men whose youthful appearance—though four years older than Tucker, Gavin "looked like a leggy young lieutenant fresh out of college"—belied his depth of character. He was, according to Arthur Kroos, "a frontline soldier's soldier all the way through. He was never warm, he's not a warm person. But he's a person who's close to his troops. He was the sort who had no hesitation of helping a private, or kicking a private in the butt if he deserved kicking. When you'd see him stand, he'd look like a statue. . . . He was a tremendously hard worker. He was out in the field, he was all over. When he said something, you listened because it was very meaningful, there was nothing trite about anything he said." According to another veteran, Gavin "assumed that you were better than you were, and you worked so hard to receive his approbation that all of a sudden you discovered you were better than you thought you were."[63] This desire to please Gavin was a feeling that permeated the 505th. Several troopers recalled that a few days before taking off for Sicily, "We were having a beer party when Colonel Jim Gavin . . . climbed on a beer keg and talked—as only [he] can. . . . As he talked we drank our beer and listened. And we wondered if this would be our last beer for a long time—or just our last beer. We looked at the Colonel, and liked what we saw. We'd follow him straight to Hell, if he asked us, and plant our color[s] over Satan's C.P. ahead of schedule."[64] Writing to Gavin after the war, 505th veteran Edwin Sayre summed up Gavin's achievements as regimental commander as succinctly as anyone:

> You built an esprit de corps that made all of us feel that we were unbeatable. You also lead [*sic*] us in a training program that toughened our minds and

bodies to the extent that we all knew that we could fight forty-eight hours without rest and still be on our feet and combat ready.

When we landed in Sicily and saw ourselves outnumbered, surrounded and faced with tanks . . . it never even occured [*sic*] to us that we should retreat. You had imbued us with only one concept—attack! In my opinion this was the secret to the 505's success. When the Germans and Italians found themselves being attacked on all sides it was impossible for them to believe that it was by a numerically inferior force.[65]

After informing him that he was to command the American airborne spearhead, Ridgway had Gavin report to Seventh Army headquarters to lead the 82nd's planning effort. Given that Patton wanted the paratroopers to protect the invasion beaches, particularly those of Bradley's II Corps, Gavin sought to fashion a plan that would enable his relatively small force to do this, even against enemy armor. The key was to use Sicily's rugged terrain to advantage. Taking into account intelligence about enemy positions, Gavin selected as the central focus of his defensive scheme a road junction about seven miles east of Gela and four miles inland, code-named Objective "Y." With "Y" in hand, Gavin's troopers would seal off the II Corps beaches from attacks from the east and northeast. In addition, holding Y would cut one of Sicily's few major thoroughfares, Highway 115, which paralleled the island's southern coast. Without Highway 115, the enemy would have a difficult time shifting forces from the western part of the island to meet the Allied invasion in the east.

Objective Y was also easily identifiable from the air and adjacent to two prominent landmarks, the Acate River and Lake Biviere, so therefore the drop plan was predicated on the pilots' finding these landmarks and then guiding off them to deliver their loads to four separate drop zones around Objective Y. Slated to jump just north of Y was Gavin's regimental headquarters, the 1/505th, the 2/505th, and A and B Batteries of the 456th Parachute Field Artillery Battalion. Jumping just south of Y would be the 3/505th and C Battery of the 456th. Dropping farthest inland, about six miles north of Y and just south of the small town of Niscemi, would be the 3/504th, on loan from Tucker's regiment. Its mission was to cut the road running south from Niscemi to Y. Finally, a small demolition detachment was to drop just west of the Acate River and prepare two bridges there for demolition, thereby cutting access to Y from the east.[66]

Following the initial drops, the rest of the division was to remain ready to "concentrate rapidly in the zone of action of the Seventh Army and assist in the assault of SICILY."[67] How, when, and where would be determined by conditions on the ground and the availability of aircraft. This did not sit well with the troopers who would be left behind. They, too, wanted a chance to prove themselves in combat or, for the troopers of one battalion, to test themselves again.

When the 82nd arrived in North Africa it received, as an attachment, the independent 509th Parachute Infantry Battalion, which had participated in Operation TORCH and already had three combat jumps to its credit.[68] Because of its veteran status, the 509th's troopers felt strongly that their battalion should have rounded out Gavin's combat team. But Ridgway was not enamored of the 509th's commander, Lieutenant Colonel Doyle R. Yardley, nor of its former commander, Colonel Edson D. Raff, who at the time was serving under Browning on Eisenhower's staff. But what really compelled Ridgway to leave the 509th behind (and the evidence suggests that he had no intention of using the 509th) was his belief that Browning was using it as a pawn in his gambit to gain control of all Allied airborne forces.

Ridgway's concern was not without foundation. While in England preparing for Operation TORCH, the 509th had been under the operational control of British Airborne Forces, and before the 82nd arrived in North Africa it was under the de facto command of Browning.[69] Ridgway knew this, but keen to assert his independence he rejected Browning's attempts to assert control over the 82nd or any American airborne contingent. Ridgway made this clear in a heated conversation with Browning during which the latter indicated that he was "in a command status since his recommendations on basic decisions effecting [*sic*] Airborne troops are very likely to be accepted without change by [Eisenhower]." Ridgway rejected Browning's claim of "command status," countering that since the 82nd was assigned to the Seventh Army, the only commander from whom Ridgway would take orders was Patton.[70] There the issue lay for several weeks. Then Ridgway learned that Browning was communicating with Yardley behind his back. In a letter sent directly to Yardley and not, as protocol dictated, through 82nd command channels, Browning informed the 509th commander that his troopers had been made honorary members of British Airborne Forces and that, as such, Browning was attempting to secure for them maroon berets worn by British paratroopers. Additionally, Browning indicated that he would soon stop by to inspect the newest addition to British Airborne Forces.[71] This would not stand for Ridgway, who squelched the inspection and the unauthorized berets, thus igniting a simmering feud between the two airborne commanders that would last the war. For the 509th, it meant banishment to Ridgway's doghouse.

Yet as heated as were the Anglo-American squabbles, they did not begin to approach the distrust fermenting in the Axis camp. The seemingly invincible Pact of Steel was crumbling in the face of setbacks at Moscow, Stalingrad, and North Africa. Threatened by Allied successes in the Mediterranean, as early as December 1942 Italian prime minister Benito Mussolini was urging Hitler to make a separate peace with the Soviet Union so that Germany could turn its full military might against the British and Americans. Hitler dismissed Mussolini's entreaties and instead sought to bolster his flagging ally with German aid. To this end he assigned Luftwaffe Feldmarschall Albert Kesselring as *Oberbefehlshaber Sued* (commander in chief South). He could not have made a better choice. Kesselring was "a gifted, thoroughly trained, and experienced officer [who] had a strong sense of duty as well as considerable personal charm and tact" and was one of the few German generals who held the Italians in high regard.[72] But for all his charm and tact, Kesselring knew what he was about. As long as Italy remained an ally, he would work with the *Comando Supremo* (the Italian High Command). If the alliance failed, he was prepared to use the German units under his command to defend Italy and its possessions alone.

Where to defend was a question that vexed the Axis partners. Even before the fall of North Africa, Axis intelligence officers were attempting to predict the Allies' next move. An Allied deception operation indicating that Sicily was nothing more than a cover operation for landings in Sardinia and Greece was moderately successful and resulted in the diversion of thousands of German troops.[73] Kesselring was convinced that the next battle in the Mediterranean would be for Sicily. For Generale d'Armata Alfredo Guzzoni, the man charged with defending the island, there was never any doubt.

The sixty-six-year-old Guzzoni, who was called out of retirement to take command of the *Italian Sixth Army* on Sicily, had a tough task before him.[74] He had practically no naval support: Most German submarines had been withdrawn from the Mediterranean, and Italy's surface fleet was holed up at La Spezia, on the mainland. For air support he had 1,000 aircraft of all types, but many were obsolete, and almost all were based on the mainland. Moreover, German and Italian pilots were being bested by the Americans and British, a circumstance that so inflamed Göring that he warned that if "improvement is not forthcoming, [German] flying personnel from the commander down must expect to be remanded to the ranks and transferred to the Eastern front to serve on the ground."[75] Finally, Guzzoni's ground forces were, with two exceptions, incapable of sustained combat.

Approximately 200,000 Italian soldiers, organized into four mobile divisions and numerous coastal units of varying size, composed the bulk of Guzzoni's ground force. Overall they were of poor quality, especially the overextended coastal units, which were armed with antiquated weapons and were, in the eyes of Generalleutnant Frido von Senger und Etterlin, the German liaison officer to Guzzoni's headquarters, "incapable of effective defense, and at best could provide only a security service."[76] The Italian mobile divisions were not much better. The *Aosta* and *Napoli Divisions*, composed largely of disaffected Sicilian conscripts, were understrength, ill-trained, and poorly led. Although of somewhat higher caliber, the *Assietta Division* was also understrength and equipped with outdated equipment, especially artillery. Only the *Livorno Division* was at anywhere near its full complement of men and materiel. Regardless of their relative readiness, however, all of the Italian mobile divisions lacked sufficient quantities of artillery ammunition and were handicapped by nonexistent or unreliable communications equipment.[77]

Given the state of his Italian formations, Guzzoni had to rely on the two German ground combat units in Sicily, the *15th Panzer Grenadier Division* and the *Hermann Göring Division*, to supply the backbone for his defense. The *15th Panzer Grenadier Division*, commanded by Generalmajor Eberhard Rodt, had been on the island longer and was at a high state of readiness. It had stockpiled twenty days of supplies and, though not completely mobile, was still capable of swift action. The *Hermann Göring Division*, a Luftwaffe panzer division commanded by Generalmajor Paul Conrath, arrived in late June. Though well trained and equipped, it was deficient in infantry.[78]

Guzzoni used the two Italian corps headquarters at his disposal, the *XVI* and *XII Corps*, to effect tactical control of the units in the eastern and western halves of the island, respectively. Anticipating that the Allies would land at the southeastern tip of Sicily, Guzzoni weighted that part of the island with his best Italian division, *Livorno*, along with the much less effective *Napoli Division*. In consultation with Kesselring, he also placed the *Hermann Göring Division* in the east, with its headquarters at Caltagirone, twenty miles northeast of Gela, and a combat command from the *15th Panzer Grenadier Division* near Catania. Securing the western part of Sicily were the *Aosta* and *Assietta Divisions* along with the rump of the *15th Panzer Grenadiers*.[79]

The placement of the German divisions caused quite a stir in German command channels, especially with Generalleutnant Senger, who heartily disagreed with the arrangement. The *15th Panzer Grenadier Division*, he wrote, "had been on the island for a considerable time and was familiar with local conditions. It had well-organised coastal reconnaissance and possessed sufficient infantry and armour at least to fight a delaying battle with some prospect of success. . . . General Roth [*sic*], the commander of this division, was an experienced leader with a General Staff background. The division should therefore have been given the main task of defending the eastern part of the island." Conversely, the *Hermann Göring Division* "had some notable weaknesses," not least of which was its "inconsiderable" infantry strength. In addition, "Two of its principal commanding officers were unfit to lead in action. The first, commander of an infantry regiment, was removed by the divisional commander, while the second, commanding the armoured regiment, was replaced . . . immediately after the fighting had started. Similar shortcomings appeared among other officers. The division enjoyed an unmerited prestige on all sides and especially among our Italian allies." Senger attributed the *Hermann Göring Division*'s "unmerited prestige" to "the predominance of personal over professional motives." Whether because of Göring's intervention or Kesselring's desire to "comply with the wishes of his superior officer in the Luftwaffe" he could not ascertain, but he was certain that German dispositions on Sicily had been "arranged behind the scenes." But to be fair, Kesselring may have been attracted by Conrath's aggressiveness, who stated during a discussion the two had about the possibility of an Allied invasion: "If you mean to go for them, Field-Marshal, then I'm your man."[80]

Guzzoni's plan was predicated on a coordinated defense aimed at defeating the Allies at the shore. Relying on his coastal units and local reserves to pinpoint the invasion beaches and harass the initial landings, Guzzoni would then follow up with his Italian mobile divisions to hold the Allies on the beaches so that the German divisions could come in for the kill.[81] Kesselring agreed with Guzzoni's plan, but had little faith in his ability to execute it. Therefore, Kesselring secretly issued an order to Rodt and Conrath that would later sow confusion in the Axis ranks and undermine the coordination upon which Guzzoni's plan depended. "It makes no difference . . . whether or not you get orders from the Italian [Sixth] Army," Kesselring told them. "You must go into immediate action against the enemy the moment you ascertain the objective of the invasion fleet."[82]

While Axis forces on Sicily spent the last half of June finalizing their plans for the defense of the island, across the Mediterranean Allied forces were repositioning for the invasion. For the troopers of the 82nd and the crews of the 52nd Troop Carrier Wing, this meant moving to staging areas and airfields near Kairouan, Tunisia. This huge logistical undertaking, which started on 16 June and was not complete until 4 July, not only ate up even more training time but also had a deleterious effect on the 52nd's equipment readiness.[83] According to a Fifth Army report, "group by group, the [aircraft] of the 52d Wing were deadlined as the division employed the [aircraft] in continuous shuttle movements between the Oujda Airfield and the advanced take-off airfield and dispersal area of Khairouan [*sic*]."[84] This tug-of-war between those who wanted to use troop carrier units as transportation assets versus those who wanted them for training and operations was a problem that would plague the 82nd and troop carrier units throughout the war. As Ridgway noted:

> They [the pilots and navigators] had the skill and the guts all right. All they needed was training. Throughout the war, the 82nd and the 52nd were handicapped by the fact that they didn't get much chance to train together. As soon as a combat operation was over, everybody from Supreme Headquarters on down started grabbing these troop carrier wings for other purposes. They'd put them on a milk run somewhere, hauling cargo, and they never got sufficient practice in the precise formation flying that was so essential to the success of an airborne operation.[85]

During HUSKY, this lack of training time would have disastrous results.

While at Kairouan, the troopers spent their time preparing their equipment and studying air photos, maps, and sand tables of the objective area. They also slept better, having set up bivouac in olive groves that offered shade while temperate winds off the Mediterranean kept the nights tolerably cool. But their new home offered its own brand of unpleasantness, for surrounding the bivouac site was a Muslim cemetery.[86] "Bodies were interned [*sic*] only two feet below the surface of the ground and each tomb featured an air-conditioning vent that was to serve as an escape route for evil spirits that might have inhabited bodies of the faithful. Unfortunately, and much to the discomfort of those nearby, evil spirits weren't the only elements to escape through the vents and the air constantly reeked with the odor of departed Moslems."[87]

As D day neared, there was a palpable increase in tension. Ridgway felt that "by take-off time for Sicily, the men were so lean and tough, so mean and mad, that they would have jumped into the fires of torment just to get out of Africa." For the man leading the division into combat for the first time, emotions were mixed. "We are in for one hell of a fight," wrote Gavin in his diary. "I love the prospects but feel as scared as I did on my first jump. It is going to be exciting."[88] One of those Gavin would be leading, Sergeant John McNally, perhaps best described the surreal sensations experienced in the last days before the first fight. The beauty of his prose is worth quoting at length.

> It was in Africa that our division held its last review before combat. For us, there never will be another review quite like it. We knew instinctively that it was to be our great day.

Picture a great, empty, dusty stretch of land in the desert. At one side was the reviewing stand, brilliant with the blues and reds and greens of the massed colors—flags of America, France and England. Before it the long lines of paratroopers stood motionless in the shimmering heat, in that awe-inspiring silence of an entire division standing at attention. The great silence was broken only by the drone of the fighter planes overhead, circling back and forth, spreading their protecting wings over the field.

Then came a burst of martial music and down the long field they marched, rank after rank, battalion after battalion strong in their pride and youth—boots gleaming in the sun, flat-waisted, sure of themselves. The dust boiled around their marching feet and the guidons swooped forward as they passed the stand. The line of generals receiving the review stood motionless—Eisenhower, Patton, Giraud, de Gaulle, Ridgway. The drums beat out the march and the cymbals crashed as the trumpets rose to a climax. There was no cheering crowd, no waving handkerchiefs—just the Division, almost lost in the empty expanse. It was our greatest moment. Sometimes I think the men who marched there for the last time that day are the real winners, with this, their brief, bittersweet moment of glory.

Experiences like these are contained in the word "Africa" for me.[89]

Hardened by Africa's heat, the 82nd Airborne Division stood ready for its first test of fire.

CHAPTER 6

A SELF-ADJUSTING FOUL-UP

Regardless of anything that may go wrong on an operation, if the small unit commander knows his job, his mission, and the missions of other units in the operation, and has the physical and mental courage to try to accomplish the mission, regardless of the obstacles that may confront him, the over-all operation will be a success.

—Edwin M. Sayre, *The Operations of Company "A" 505th Parachute Infantry (82d Airborne Division), Airborne Landings in Sicily, 9–24 July 1943 (Sicily Campaign) (Personal Experience of a Company Commander)*

Friday, 9 July 1943, D-minus-one (D-1), began an hour earlier than usual for Gavin's combat team, although it felt like any other day—the men crawled from their pup tents, washed, shaved, and filed through chow lines for breakfast. Following breakfast the day took on a decidedly different tenor as the troopers began their last-minute preparations: drawing equipment and ammunition, dismantling their tents, turning in items for storage, preparing equipment bundles, ensuring each plane's "para-racks" functioned properly, cleaning weapons, sharpening knives, packing musette bags, and then, if possible, resting. Dinner was served at 1600 hours, after which the troopers piled aboard trucks for the ride to the airfield where they drew their parachutes and lounged beside their assigned aircraft. They also received the password for D day—a challenge of "George" was to be answered with "Marshall"—and a mimeographed message from Colonel Gavin.[1]

> Soldiers of the 505th Combat Team
>
> Tonight you embark upon a combat mission for which our people and the free people of the world have been waiting for two years.
>
> You will spearhead the landing of an American Force upon the island of SICILY. Every preparation has been made to eliminate the element of chance. You have been given the means to do the job and you are backed by the largest assemblage of air power in the world's history.
>
> The eyes of the world are upon you. The hopes and prayers of every American go with you.
>
> Since it is our first fight at night you must use the countersign and avoid firing on each other. The bayonet is the night fighter's best weapon. Conserve your water and ammunition.
>
> The term American Parachutist has become synonymous with courage of a high order. Let us carry the fight to the enemy and make the American Parachutist feared and respected through all his ranks. Attack violently. Destroy him wherever found.
>
> I know you will do your job
>
> Good landing, good fight, and good luck.[2]

Despite his assurance that "every preparation has been made," privately Gavin was not so certain.

Before leaving the States, Ridgway told his subordinate commanders that the division would have about six weeks in North Africa to train. When he heard this Gavin felt, on the one hand, that the division "could use considerably more time before combat," but on the other hand he mused that perhaps the best thing would be to experience "the real thing" followed by "a lull to absorb the lessons and lick our wounds."[3] By the evening of 9 July, Gavin's ambivalence had vanished. Time had gone by too quickly. He complained about this in his diary, but since there was little he could do about it, he turned his attention to other things—details, seemingly minor, that in their totality might provide the advantage his troopers would need in combat. He wrote about these details in his diary, no doubt so he could remember them for the next mission, but also, its seems, to exorcise his dread.

He wrote of obtaining cork so that his troopers could blacken their faces, of procuring the metallic crickets he had been told would facilitate night assembly, of ensuring that everyone had one of the new trench knives that could be used for close-quarters combat, and of somehow getting enough olive-drab patches to cover the red, white, and blue divisional insignia each trooper wore on his left shoulder. To lessen the chances of fratricide he sent troopers, in full combat regalia, to the 1st and 45th Infantry Division encampments to familiarize those soldiers with American paratroopers' distinctively different uniforms.[4] Luminous tape to mark equipment bundles so that they could be quickly found on the drop zone suddenly became important. There was a concern that not every trooper had an entrenching tool, so more were acquired and distributed, one per man. Commanders were to ensure that every soldier was wearing a set of two dog tags. No explanation for this requirement was necessary.[5] A last-minute idea by Lieutenant Colonel Arthur F. "Hard Nose" Gorham, the 1/505th's commander, was that each trooper should sew a strip of luminous tape on the cuff of his jumpsuit so that they could more easily find and identify one another in the dark. In the attack the tape could be easily covered up. Gavin ordered that it happen.[6]

In his last entry before D day, made two days before the jump, Gavin wrote about a unit picnic, held the previous afternoon, during which he spoke with his troopers, both en masse and in smaller groups. He came away from these talks confident in their ability to accomplish the mission. They were "enthusiastic and keen," he noted. Yet there remained the one looming question: Had he done everything he could to prepare them for the upcoming fight?[7]

Gavin was not the only one suffering anxiety. Aboard the USS *Monrovia* was an equally anxious Patton.[8] "It is a moving sight," wrote the Seventh Army commander in his diary shortly after getting under way, "but over all is the feeling that only God and the Navy can do anything until we hit the shore. I hope God and Navy do their stuff."[9] The devout Ridgway, just a few cabins away, would have added solicitations for the U.S. Army Air Force.

At the departure airfields the reverie was broken about thirty minutes before takeoff when the aircrews began their preflight checks. This was the signal for the paratroopers to board, a feat that could be accomplished only by pushing and pulling one another through the narrow fuselage door on the plane's port side.[10] At 2010 hours, 9 July, the planes revved their engines, taxied to their designated spots, and started taking off three at a time at thirty-second intervals. In the air they formed up in V-of-V formations with three planes in each V. Although the prop wash from so many planes created a dust storm "so thick it could be seen five miles away and [caused] many pilots . . . to take off [*sic*] on instruments," the departure went without incident.[11] "The planning for the final takeoff had been complete and thorough," and its execution "went off like clock-work," noted a Fifth Army observer.[12] It was the last event of that evening, and for several days thereafter, about which that claim would be made.

It took little more than an hour for all 226 C-47s of the 52nd Troop Carrier Wing carrying Gavin's 3,405 paratroopers to take off, form up, and head out to sea. A modified version of the Douglas DC-3, the C-47 was a sturdy aircraft. It could take off from a dirt airstrip less than 3,000 feet long with a maximum cargo load of 5,000 to 6,000 pounds or fourteen to eighteen paratroopers, had a range of 1,500 miles, could cruise at 150 miles per hour, and could slow down to a drop speed of 110 miles per hour without sacrificing stability. It could also fly shot full of holes and on one of its two engines for up to 100 miles. It was the principal Allied troop carrier plane of the war, during which more than 10,000 were put into service.[13]

Early weather reports for the invasion were foreboding. Meteorologists reported winds of gale intensity off Sicily's southern coast; they eventually subsided but remained high throughout the night.[14] Nonetheless, it was too late to cancel the drop; Patton was depending on the paratroopers to repel enemy counterattacks against his invasion beaches. Still there was cause for concern, a concern heightened for Gavin as he was sitting aboard his plane as it revved for takeoff. A harried airman stuck his head in the door and yelled that "the wind [was] going to be thirty-five miles an hour, east to west." Gavin nodded and prepared himself for a hard landing.[15]

Once aloft, the pilots were to observe radio silence and maintain formation while flying no higher than 500 feet along a strictly circumscribed route that began at the Kuriate Islands, about forty miles southwest of the departure airfields. From the Kuriates, the route ran almost due east for approximately 200 miles, past the small island of Linosa and on to Malta, where beacons were to be lit as navigation aids. At Malta, the route doglegged northeast for 62 miles to a point just southwest of Cape Passero, a prominent peninsula at the eastern end of Sicily where the pilots were to turn left and parallel Sicily's southern shore until they reached the mouth of the Acate River, where they were to turn inland, locate Lake Biviere, their last checkpoint, and then head for their drop zones.[16]

The complex route was the direct result of an argument between airborne and troop carrier planners, on one side, and naval planners, on the other. The argument arose because naval commanders could not promise that all their vessels would hold their fire if they saw planes approaching them at night. "While fire from men-of-war could be controlled," they maintained, "fire from the many miscellaneous merchant vessels and small craft included in the various convoys was impossible to control."[17] Consequently, the air route to Sicily had to avoid friendly naval convoys. What planners came up with was a route that required flying and navigational skills that the 52nd Troop Carrier Wing's crews did not possess and for which they had had no time to train. As

Ridgway saw it, the route was so difficult that even "at war's end we still could not have executed [the] first SICILY mission, AS LAID ON, at night and under like conditions."[18]

At the outset all 226 planes, forming an air column about 100 miles long, were on time and on target. But when the sun set the formations disintegrated. Since a pilot could see the dim wingtip lights on the surrounding planes only if he maintained his ship's place in formation, even the tiniest deviation was cause for concern lest there be a midair collision (remarkably, there were none). Were a pilot to suddenly discover that he could no longer see the lights on the planes around him, he had two options: He could try a blind correction to regain his place in formation, or he could take the safer alternative and fly on alone. Most chose the latter. Adding to the pilots' difficulties were rough air currents at the prescribed low altitudes and a constant spray of saltwater that clouded windshields and obscured vision. Finally, the stiff wind Gavin was informed of just before takeoff wreaked havoc with the navigators' time-distance calculations. Consequently, well before Sicily had been reached, "a large part of the expedition was off route and off schedule."[19]

The 52nd's air column was composed of five subordinate troop carrier groups, which were, in order of flight, the 61st, the 314th, the 313th, the 316th, and the 64th.[20] The 61st Group, carrying Lieutenant Colonel Charles W. Kouns's 3/504th, hit Malta twelve minutes ahead of schedule, although by that time several planes were already straggling (two of the stragglers got so lost they missed Sicily altogether and made landfall on the toe of Italy). By the time the 61st neared Sicily, only the group commander was still on course; his formation of nine planes dropped its paratroopers about a mile east of the intended drop zone; the rest of the 61st Group was so disoriented that it scattered Kouns's battalion over a 50-mile swath of southeastern Sicily.[21]

The second group in the column, the 314th, carrying Major Edward C. "Cannonball" Krause's 3/505th, did the best job of navigation that night, hitting all of its checkpoints until reaching the Acate River, where it turned inland and promptly got lost. Only one flight of planes, carrying I Company, dropped on its designated drop zone. The rest of the 314th turned back out to sea to line up for a second pass. But the second pass was no better than the first, and as a result most of Krause's troopers landed 10 to 15 miles east of their intended drop zone.[22]

The third and fourth groups in the air column fared the worst, having lost all semblance of integrity well out to sea. In the ensuing chaos small, scattered groups of planes somehow formed up in the air and flew blindly toward Sicily with most never even sighting Malta. According to Captain Edwin Sayre, the

A Company, 1/505th, commander, who was aboard a plane from the 313th Troop Carrier Group:

> The first thought that all was not going just as planned came when the Island of MALTA was not sighted on schedule. At about the time the planes should have passed over MALTA, the formation ran into heavy headwinds and then began breaking up into small groups. The nine-plane formation carrying the Battalion Commander's group and the first and second platoons and Company Headquarters of Company "A" managed to stay together. At the time when the planes were supposed to be nearing the Drop Zone, anti-aircraft fire could be seen coming up on the left side of the planes. This could mean only one thing: the planes were coming in on the wrong [eastern] side of the Island.[23]

Twenty-three of the 313th's planes made landfall on Sicily's eastern shore and dropped their paratroopers in the British zone, more than 50 miles from the designated drop zone.[24] But Sayre's group of nine planes continued on:

> The Flight Commander realized this [that he was on Sicily's eastern shore] and the formation was turned back out to sea in order to make another attempt to find the correct Drop Zone. After about an hour, a lake [Lake Biviere] which was the final check point was sighted. The planes turned over the lake in the direction to bring them over the Drop Zone in about two minutes. After proceeding about one minute and a half, the formation met heavy anti-aircraft fire and began breaking up. One minute later the green "go" light was given and the parachutists left the planes.[25]

As things turned out, this was a most fortuitous drop.

The fourth group in the order of flight, the 316th Troop Carrier Group, carrying the regimental headquarters, the 456th Parachute Field Artillery Battalion, and the engineers and signal and medical personnel, fared the worst of all.[26] According to Gavin, who was flying with the 316th's commander, "I had memorized the route and times and knew we should pass the island of Linosa at 2230. But 2230 came with no sign of Linosa. I thought perhaps we were slightly off course and [a] correction would be made before reaching Malta. Malta was a big target and certainly would not be missed. The lights would be on, so I expected no difficulty in recognizing it." But at 2300 hours there was still no sign of Malta, so the lead navigator ordered a left-hand turn to compensate. This brought the planes over some ships bound for Sicily, which provided "an anxious moment, since we knew that we would probably draw fire if we flew over any ships [they did not draw fire]."[27] Finally, around midnight, Gavin saw land.

> We turned and flew parallel to the coast for some time. All troops prepared to jump and we turned in toward the coast. I had memorized all the terrain surrounding the landfall we should have passed. We were supposed to fly over a large lake [Lake Biviere], the one I had already flown over a month before [Gavin and two of his battalion commanders had accompanied a bombing raid bound for Sicily in order to get a glimpse of the objective area under moonlight conditions similar to that expected during the drop]. But we saw none of the recognizable landmarks. It was almost time to jump. Finally the green light in the plane came on and out we went.[28]

By this time Gavin's plane was all alone, and since they had not seen any of the landmarks or checkpoints, they had no idea where they were. They were not even certain that the ground below was Sicily.

Though it, too, was hopelessly lost, the last group in the air column, the 64th Troop Carrier Group carrying Major Mark Alexander's 2/505th, remained together. Before departing, Alexander made the 64th's commander, Lieutenant Colonel John Cerny, promise that "if they didn't do anything else, they'd drop us all together."[29] Cerny kept his promise—the 64th maintained its formation and dropped Alexander's battalion en masse, albeit on a plateau approximately 25 miles from its drop zone.[30]

Gavin's orders were that everyone was to jump, that no one, unless wounded or dead, was to return to North Africa. Reed Satterstrom of the 456th took desperate measures to comply with those orders: "When it came time to hook up, my snap wouldn't open on my static line. Gavin had said that everyone had to jump—no one could return. I handed my static line to the plane crew chief and told him to HANG ON TO IT—he braced himself against the bulkhead—and out I went. But my hand was on my reserve! Later, they came looking for me—to hear the story—they wanted to give that air force guy a medal!"[31] Enemy antiaircraft fire, or "flak," also convinced many paratroopers that jumping was a much safer prospect than staying aboard. Though flak was generally not a problem for the lead groups, as the enemy recovered from the surprise and realized that the planes overhead were transports disgorging paratroopers and not bombers on their way to the Italian mainland, succeeding groups encountered increasingly heavy enemy fire. Captain Ireland remembered: "Standing at the door with Jim [Gavin], and the flak was starting to come up all around us. The pilot asked us if we needed to make another pass. I said, 'If we go around again we may not make it.' He said, 'I think you are right.' We got the green light and we got out." According to John H. "Beaver" Thompson, a war correspondent from the *Chicago Tribune* who jumped in with Gavin's combat team, as soon as he exited, "the sky . . . broke out in a brilliant white, just like it was high noon under a blazing sun. A C-47 had apparently been struck by shellfire, bursting into a fiery ball. How many of our boys had gone to their deaths? I wondered. The sight sickened me."[32] The 52nd lost 8 planes that night, all after having dropped their paratroopers, while 10 more sustained some sort of damage. Despite Gavin's orders, 3 planes, which had become hopelessly lost, returned to North Africa without dropping.[33]

The first planes returned to their North African bases at 0125 hours, 10 July (the last did not stagger in until 0620 hours). Initial reports were optimistic with estimates as high as 80 percent drop accuracy. But the truth was far different. Of the 3,405 men who enplaned the night before, 50 did not jump, and the rest were spread throughout the width and breadth of southeastern Sicily. Thirty-three planes had dropped inside the British sector, while another 127 dropped in front of the U.S. 45th Infantry Division, well to the east of the objective area. Only 53 planes dropped in the vicinity of Objective Y, and of those only 9 dropped on the correct drop zone.[34]

Years after the war Gavin overheard someone call the Sicily drop "the best executed Snafu in the history of military operations," a characterization with which he demurred. Rather than "Snafu," he countered, a better acronym would be "Safu," for "Self-Adjusting Foul Up," for in the face of their predicament, his troopers adjusted and improvised and, in so doing, accomplished the mission they had been assigned.[35]

Trained to take the initiative and act aggressively to keep the enemy off balance, once they were on the ground Gavin's troopers formed in groups large and small and attacked the enemy wherever they found him. According to Lieutenant T. Moffatt Burriss, a platoon leader in the 3/504th:

> Despite the fact that many of us landed many miles from the drop zone, the invasion proved the wisdom of our paratrooper training. From the beginning, we were taught to fight in small groups and behind enemy lines. Our purpose was to disrupt communication lines, divert the enemy's attention, and create general havoc in areas where we were least expected to be. When we were isolated from the main force, we didn't panic. We regrouped in twos and threes, then proceeded to seek out and attack the enemy. Avoiding superior forces that might have overwhelmed us, we nonetheless fought aggressively and killed many times our own numbers. We didn't fight by the book or wait to receive orders from headquarters. In an atypical situation, we improvised, as we had been taught to do.[36]

The result was fear and frustration in the Axis ranks and chaos and confusion in their headquarters. Italian and German soldiers alike could not or would not leave the safety of their bases at night because they believed they were surrounded by paratroopers who would ambush them if they did. And there were a great many ambushes. Kesselring's headquarters reported that "paratroops have greatly delayed the advance of our own troops and have inflicted considerable casualties on our troops. Small groups of parachutists who had jumped into overgrown country made themselves noticed in a particularly unpleasant manner." Or as one frustrated German officer proclaimed after being captured, "Our people will cut the throats of these parachutists if they capture them. . . . It has been unsafe to use the roads for the past forty-eight hours."[37]

Other paratroopers, dropped far from their assigned objectives, simply secured or helped secure other objectives that ultimately proved just as important to the Allies' success on D day. For example, the British 50th Infantry Division's assault objective was Avola, a city of some 22,000 on Sicily's eastern shore. Expecting a hard fight, the British were surprised to find that when they entered the city's outskirts, the enemy was gone. They discovered the reason for this when they got to the city square, which was already in the possession of some 75 misdropped American paratroopers under the command of Lieutenant Charles E. "Pinkie" Sammon, the 2/505th's intelligence officer, who had attacked into Avola from the inland side, diverted the defenders' attention, and thereby cleared the way for the British entering the city from the opposite direction.[38] Likewise, another group of paratroopers, dropped near Pachino on Sicily's southeastern tip, assembled under the command of Major William R. Beall, the 3/504th's executive officer, and fought for two days alongside the Canadian 1st Division to help secure its D-day objectives.[39]

Those dropped too far inland to link up with the amphibious forces effected a different tack—they seized key terrain or set up blocking positions and held until relieved. Captain James P. McGinity, the G Company, 3/505th, commander, and the 80 troopers with him defended a concrete slab spanning the Acate River for two days against Axis counterattacks before being relieved by elements of the 45th Division.[40] A group of about 50 troopers under Lieutenant Peter J. Eaton, a platoon leader in the 3/504th, ambushed an Italian detachment transporting two antitank guns, and then set up a roadblock and used the guns to destroy an Italian infantry battalion.[41] Lieutenant H. H. Swingler, the 505th Regimental Headquarters Company commander, led a band of 40 troopers in an attack against a pillbox complex located astride a key thoroughfare that led right to the 45th Division's beaches. After taking the pillboxes, Swingler and his troopers used them to defend the intersection until relieved the next day by elements of the 45th, to which they also turned over their haul of prisoners: 4 officers and about 100 enlisted men from an Italian field artillery battalion who, when they encountered the American paratroopers, surrendered en masse.[42]

Perhaps the greatest swath of destruction by a group of misdropped paratroopers was that wreaked by Major Alexander's 2/505th, the only battalion of Gavin's combat team that was dropped intact, albeit well off course and right on top of occupied pillboxes. Following a stiff firefight during which the troopers destroyed the pillboxes and killed or drove off the defenders, Alexander found that he had with him some 475 men, which accounted for most of his battalion, along with some 456th Parachute Field Artillery Battalion troopers who had with them one of their howitzers. Moreover, unlike many who dropped into Sicily that night, Alexander knew where he was, and that was too far away from his assault objective to get there on time to accomplish his assigned mission. So instead Alexander opted to march toward the coast with the intent of destroying any enemy positions that could interfere with the amphibious landings. He got all the way to the seaside village of Marina di Ragusa before encountering any enemy positions—more pillboxes. Wanting to avoid another wild shoot-out, especially in the light of day when advantage rested with the ensconced defenders, Alexander turned to his artillerymen. Led by Lieutenant Colonel Harrison B. Harden Jr., the 456th's commander, who personally directed the fire of the group's lone 75mm howitzer, the artillerymen fired several rounds into the pillboxes with uncanny accuracy (it was well that they were accurate, for they had but thirty rounds of ammunition) and thereby compelled the wholesale surrender of the Italian naval contingent manning them.

Alexander next moved his force, and his prisoners, toward some high ground north of the village. He hoped to be able to observe and disrupt enemy movement along the coastal road from the high ground, but when he got there he and his troopers got pinned down by snipers hidden in some nearby cliffs. Alexander tried making radio contact with a British cruiser he could see just off the coast to request fire support. When that proved unsuccessful, Alexander told a lieutenant to flash the cruiser a request for help using Morse code. According to Alexander, he knew his request got through when several rounds passed overhead sounding like "a bunch of freight cars" and exploded against the cliffs. "We didn't have a peep out of that hillside the rest of the night," recalled Alexander.[43]

The next day, 11 July, Alexander again moved his force, this time north and west toward Santa Croce Camerina, one of the 45th Infantry Division's initial objectives. His troopers, who had captured enough arms and ammunition at Marina di Ragusa to outfit another battalion, had also procured a mélange of donkeys, donkey carts, and wheelbarrows in which to transport their haul. Moving along in what must have looked like a heavily armed gypsy caravan, Alexander's force reached Santa Croce Camerina, which was still in enemy hands, later on that morning. Without halt Alexander ordered an attack and, in conjunction with a battalion from the 45th moving in from the coast, reduced the town by midmorning. With so much combat power at his disposal and more than enough arms and ammunition, Alexander next marched on Vittoria, one of the larger towns in the 45th Division's sector, which fell to Alexander's gypsies later on that day. All told, in its first two days of combat Alexander's force cleared a significant portion of the area fronting the 45th's invasion beaches and took two of that division's major assault objectives. As a result the 45th got ashore with fewer casualties than expected.[44]

The aggressiveness and initiative of Gavin's troopers, exemplified by Sammon, Beall, McGinity, Eaton, Swingler, Alexander, and the troopers they led, threw Guzzoni's plans into disarray, even though Guzzoni knew that the Allies were coming. Sometime on 9 July, Axis reconnaissance planes spotted the invasion convoys and got word back to *Sixth Army* headquarters, which, in turn, put its forces on full alert. But in the wake of the scattered airborne drop the reports of enemy contact coming in from seemingly everywhere so confused Guzzoni that he held his forces in check, hoping to obtain a clearer picture of Allied intentions before releasing them. When he did so it was too late; the Allied invasion fleet was offshore, firing its preparatory bombardment, and the amphibious forces were making their way to the landing beaches.[45]

Although Guzzoni always felt that the Allies would land in the southeast, he was taken aback by the size of the invasion fleet and the length of coast it covered. With nowhere enough combat power to counterattack everywhere, he focused on those locations he deemed most critical: Syracuse in the east and Gela and Licata in the south. Syracuse's defenses, he felt, were strong enough to hold. Moreover, the *Napoli Division* and elements of the *Hermann Göring Division* and the *15th Panzer Grenadier Division* were nearby. The landings along the southern coast were another matter. Although he did not have many mobile forces in the immediate area of those landings, Guzzoni figured that if he could gather enough combat power to mount a coordinated attack on the southern beaches before the invaders were firmly ashore, he could push them back into the sea. To this end he issued his first offensive order of the campaign. The Italian *XVI Corps* was to take operational control of the *Livorno Division*, the bulk of the *Hermann Göring Division*, and two Italian mobile airfield defense groups in the area and mount a coordinated attack on the American invasion beaches east of Gela. So complete, however, was the devastation wrought on Axis communications—Gavin's troopers were trained to cut every wire they came across—that Conrath's *Hermann Göring Division* never received this order. In fact, Conrath never received word of the invasion from *Sixth Army* or *XVI Corps* at all; it was via a wireless transmission from Kesselring's headquarters on the Italian mainland that Conrath learned that the invasion was on.[46]

But even with no word from Guzzoni, Conrath was intent on making good his boast about going after the Allies, so he spent the night of 9–10 July putting in train his own plan to attack the American beaches. His concept was relatively straightforward—he would move the bulk of the *Hermann Göring Division* from its positions around Caltagirone along two parallel routes to attack the American beaches east of Gela from the northeast and northwest simultaneously. Dividing his force into two reinforced regimental combat teams, he sent an infantry-heavy force comprising two truck-mounted infantry battalions, an armored artillery battalion, and seventeen Mark VI Tiger tanks southward along an eastern route to the beaches by way of Biscari. His tank-heavy force, comprising two tank battalions (with a total of ninety Mark III and Mark IV tanks), two armored artillery battalions, and armored reconnaissance and engineer troops, was to advance to the beaches along a western route by way of Niscemi. To facilitate coordination between the two forces he designated attack positions—one for each column—just north of the beaches, where they could halt and synchronize their actions before jumping off for the final assault. Although he did not know it, Conrath had aimed his columns at the center of the American sector. If successful, he would cut it in half and be in position to flank the American divisions landing to the east and west of his point of aim.

Both columns jumped off shortly after 0400 hours, 10 July, with a planned attack time of 0900 hours, but as soon as they started moving they became targets for Allied fighter-bombers and paratroopers lying in ambush. As a result, the scheduled 0900 attack time came and went while both columns were still some distance from their attack positions.[47]

Meanwhile, the Italian attacks on Gela moved forward as well, but because the *XVI Corps* commander was unable to contact Conrath, what was supposed to be an attack by two divisions devolved into an uncoordinated and tentative advance. Yet despite this failure of communication and coordination, there was still a chance that one of the Axis columns would get to the beaches with enough combat power to attack the initial assault waves with devastating effect, perhaps even forcing them back into the sea. This did not occur, primarily because of the actions of a group of paratroopers under the command of Lieutenant Colonel "Hard Nose" Gorham and Captain Edwin Sayre.

The saga of the Gorham-Sayre group began in a vineyard about four miles south of Niscemi, where six planeloads of paratroopers from Captain Sayre's A Company, 1/505th, landed.[48] Taken under fire immediately upon landing by machine guns located near a large villa and hampered by the dark and vegetation, the troopers were slow to assemble. Seeing that he would be unable to gather his company until he silenced the enemy guns, Sayre grabbed twelve troopers and told them to follow. They were going to crawl as close as possible to the enemy guns, throw their grenades, wait for the explosions, and then assault through the enemy positions. If things went awry, if the enemy force was too big to handle, they were to break contact and withdraw. "With the pop of the fuze [*sic*] on the first grenade," wrote Sayre, "the teams threw their grenades. By the light of the grenades thrown and by about twenty which the enemy threw back, it could be seen that the troops were attacking not dug-in machine guns as supposed, but heavy concrete and stone pill boxes. A very hasty withdrawal to the rendezvous point was made. One man was slightly wounded, but none were lost."[49] Sayre waited until daybreak before mounting a second attack; he wanted to get a better look at what he was up against. What he saw was a formidable strongpoint consisting of a ring of pillboxes surrounding a two-story stone farmhouse. There was no way to determine how many enemy soldiers it held. Since the first attack, however, he had gathered more troopers, and now had some forty-five in all, along with two 60mm mortars, 50 rounds of mortar ammunition, and two machine guns. With this added firepower, Sayre tried a more conventional attack, setting half his force, the mortars, and the two machine guns in positions from which they could suppress the enemy defenses while he led the other half in the assault. At precisely 0530 hours, Sayre was again leading a charge, this time "carrying one hand grenade in his teeth and another in his left hand, and with his carbine in his right hand."[50] By 0600 hours the strongpoint was his, as were forty Italian and ten German prisoners, at a cost of four wounded Americans.

Identified as Casa del Priolo on maps, the strongpoint dominated the road running south from Niscemi toward the invasion beaches. Its location as well as its strength made it key terrain, so Sayre decided to occupy it and hold it as long as possible. Not long after settling in he was joined by Lieutenant Colonel Gorham and thirty more paratroopers. Gorham, too, liked what he saw, especially the cache of twenty machine guns and more than 50,000 rounds of ammunition that Sayre and his troopers had captured. Gorham took command of the strongpoint and settled down to wait.

Casa del Priolo was indeed key terrain, for it blocked the road that both Conrath and the *XVI Corps* commander, independent of one another, designated as an attack route for their respective forces. So while Gorham and his troopers were settling down to defend the strongpoint, there were two Axis forces moving toward it: Conrath's tank-heavy column and *Mobile Airfield Defense Group E*, one of the two Italian mobile airfield groups under *XVI Corps*'s control. The Italians got there first.

The advance guard of *Mobile Airfield Defense Group E* appeared on the road north of Casa del Priolo at about 0700 hours, 10 July. Several hundred yards behind was the main body, about a battalion in strength. By the way they were moving—in column formation on the road—they were obviously unaware that the strongpoint was in American hands. Playing on that ignorance, Gorham had his troopers hold their fire until the last possible moment. Only when the scout element actually drove into Casa del Priolo did they open up. This alerted the main body of *Mobile Airfield Defense Group E*, which halted and sent two infantry companies forward to investigate. As they had with the scouts, Gorham's troopers held their fire until the Italians were practically on top of them and then opened up with devastating effect, killing or wounding most of the Italians in the initial fusillade. Only the appearance of a heavy assault gun that started systematically shelling Casa del Priolo forced the paratroopers to cease fire and take cover.[51]

It was about this time that a reconnaissance patrol Sayre had sent out earlier returned to report that Objective Y was about a mile and a half to the south and that it was being defended by about twenty Italians from inside several pillboxes. With their present position untenable and the combat team's main objective still in enemy hands, Gorham decided to withdraw from Casa del Priolo and move on Objective Y. Unwilling to leave his wounded behind, he enlisted several prisoners as stretcher bearers. When told to pick up the stretchers, however, the German prisoners balked. They "just popped their heels together [and shouted] '*nein, nein,*'" recalled Sayre, who was in no mood to debate, so he turned to one of his sergeants and, pointing to who he thought was the ranking German, said, "Would you convince that son of a bitch that we really need for him to pick up those stretchers?" Without hesitation, the sergeant "just jabbed [the German] in the ass with his bayonet, a pretty good jab, about two inches [in, and] everybody laid hand and picked up the stretchers real quick."[52]

Having solved the problem of the uncooperative prisoners, Gorham and his troopers were met with another challenge—six Italian tanks that appeared suddenly on their flank. With nothing heavy enough with which to engage them, it appeared the Italians would win the day after all, but then the lead tank burst into flames. Seconds later another tank blew up, and the four remaining tanks withdrew. A wandering band of paratroopers armed with bazookas and marching to the sound of the guns sneaked up on the tanks just as Gorham and his troopers were pulling out of Casa del Priolo and won for them just enough time to get away. When the other tanks returned, the second group of paratroopers held their ground, expended all their ammunition, and were eventually forced to surrender.[53]

Meanwhile, Gorham and his troopers escaped to some high ground overlooking Objective Y. From their position they could see that an American spotter plane was directing naval gunfire against the objective, although that ceased when a passing German fighter shot the spotter down. Given the lay of the land, it was obvious that there was no way the naval guns would hit the objective anyway, but betting that the Italians defending Y did not know that, Gorham decided on a ruse. Turning to one of his Italian prisoners, Gorham told him to move to the pillboxes around Y and deliver a message to his comrades: Surrender or the Americans would recommence the bombardment (a false promise since Gorham had no way to communicate with the ships). According to Sayre, "The prisoner was evidently an eloquent speaker for in a very few minutes after he entered the first pill box, all occupants of the three pill boxes in the area came out with their hands up."[54] So it was that at 1045 hours, 10 July, the primary assault objective of Gavin's combat team was in American hands. Shortly thereafter, scouts from the 1st Battalion, 16th Infantry Regiment, of the U.S. 1st Infantry Division linked up with Gorham's group at Objective Y. Since he had no contact with Gavin, Gorham attached himself and his troopers to the 1/16th, which fell in around the crossroads and dug in.[55]

Oblivious to what had happened to *Mobile Airfield Defense Group E*, Conrath was still struggling to get his attack back on track. Already well behind schedule, it was not until 1400 hours that his columns reached their attack positions where, following a short pause, they moved out for the beaches. This brought the tank-heavy column down the same road taken earlier by *Mobile Airfield Defense Group E.* Harassed by artillery and naval gunfire though impervious to anything but a direct hit, the tanks moved through Casa del Priolo and on toward Objective Y slowly yet steadily. Just north of Y the column halted and deployed scouts and engineers to secure the surrounding high ground. Gorham's paratroopers and the soldiers from the 1/16th, lying in wait, annihilated them. Without control of the high ground the column commander balked, attempted a halfhearted advance, then withdrew.[56]

Meanwhile, a few miles to the east Conrath's infantry-heavy column was barely crawling along. Harassed by roving bands of paratroopers that were taking advantage of the terrain, the column was continually halting and deploying its infantry in pursuit only to find the troopers had melted away into the hills or vineyards. When Conrath learned of this he relieved the column commander and ordered his replacement to push forward without regard to the paratroopers. Although initially successful—it overran an American infantry battalion and captured the battalion commander—this column, too, was halted when it ran headlong into elements of the 45th Infantry Division pushing inland. In the ensuing firefight, the German broke and ran.[57]

Hence, by midafternoon on D day the Axis attacks on the American beaches had been turned back, and the key intersection at Objective Y was firmly in American hands. This was fortuitous, for although the 1st and 45th Divisions had established footholds on their respective beaches, the scene on those beachheads was one of clutter and confusion. Minefields in the 1st Division's sector had forced the first wave to hold on the beach until paths could be cleared through them, and even after they were cleared the tanks had problems traversing the fine sand, leaving the infantry to push inland without armor support. Meanwhile, follow-on waves landed, and the congestion mounted. The scene was worse on the 45th Division beaches. Having landed among soft sand dunes through which there were few usable exits, its assault beaches "were cluttered with masses of stranded landing craft and milling groups of men and vehicles."[58] Although beach masters worked throughout the night to get the mess cleaned up, with daybreak on 11 July the beaches were still cluttered and vulnerable to attack.

That night (10–11 July), after regrouping his division, Conrath traveled to *XVI Corps* headquarters. Only then did he learn that he was under the operational control of *XVI Corps* and that he was to have coordinated his attack with his Italian allies. Having failed to achieve that on 10 July, the Axis partners agreed to try again on 11 July and worked out a plan to conduct a converging attack on the American beaches east of Gela beginning at 0600 hours, with the *Livorno Division* advancing from the northwest while Conrath's *Hermann Göring Division* moved in from the northeast. To facilitate movement, Conrath split his division into three columns, two of which, both tank heavy, were to advance west of the Acate River, while the third, infantry-heavy column advanced along the river's east bank. The point of aim for all three columns was the road intersection, Objective Y, where they would re-form before jumping off for the final assault.[59]

Back at Objective Y the 1/16th had moved on, replaced by Lieutenant Joseph Crawford's 2/16th. Gorham's troopers remained in place. Major General Terry de la Mesa Allen, the 1st Division commander, had ordered all the units under his command to advance inland to provide a buffer between the front lines and the overcrowded beaches.[60] For Crawford this meant a brief stop at Y before moving farther north along the same road down which

Gorham and his troopers had fought, so, since they were familiar with the terrain, Crawford enlisted Gorham's troopers as his lead element. Moving out at dusk on 10 July, the paratroopers advanced about a mile before darkness set in and Crawford ordered a halt. They were back at Casa del Priolo.[61]

During the paratroopers' earlier fight at Casa del Priolo they lost one of their group, a brand-new second lieutenant who had been leading the reconnaissance patrol that found Objective Y. Sayre was convinced the lieutenant was somewhere in the vicinity of the villa, so he persuaded Gorham to let him look for him. Setting out with eight other paratroopers, Sayre had not gone far before finding the lieutenant's body. "His [the lieutenant's] gun was still in his holster so evidently he was caught totally by surprise. And I thought well I'll just take that gun with me, might need it a little later. I took the gun out and just as I got it out evidently the same machinegun that got him opened up on me. They missed me by about two feet and I started running for some cover." Sayre and his troopers withdrew to a dry streambed and were preparing to return to Casa del Priolo when a German patrol unwittingly entered the streambed, touching off a close-quarters melee during which Sayre fought with the dead lieutenant's .45 in one hand and his own .45 in the other. The Germans eventually withdrew, leaving three dead behind. There were no American casualties. Later, witnesses recounted Sayre's exploits, the details of which no doubt got more extravagant with time. For his part, Sayre laughed off his reputation as a quick-drawing cowboy from Texas, but the image of the 82nd as a bunch of cowboys persisted and in time would draw ire from a most unexpected quarter—the Allied high command.[62]

The next morning, 11 July, Crawford gave word to continue the advance northward. Gorham's troopers, still in the lead, took a small hill about a half mile to their front against slight resistance. They were consolidating on their new position when, suddenly, they came face-to-face with Conrath's tanks.

Conrath's attack had jumped off at 0615 hours. Unlike the previous day's advance, this one met with immediate success when the westernmost tank-heavy column overran another battalion from the 1st Division and with nary a pause turned east to link up with the other columns near the intersection at Objective Y. Meanwhile, Conrath's middle tank-heavy column was advancing south down the Niscemi road. As a result, both columns converged on the small hill north of Casa del Priolo shortly after Gorham's troopers got there.[63]

As Sayre remembered it, six tanks came straight down the road, while another twenty hit the American positions in their left rear. Some of the infantrymen from the 2/16th broke and ran, but the rest, "about one third of the [infantry] battalion and all of the parachutists stuck to their positions" and fought back "desperately with rocket launchers, rifle grenades, machine guns, rifles, pistols and even throwing hand grenades." Two officers from the 2/16th got the battalion's lone antitank gun into position and knocked out one German tank, while Gorham single-handedly took out a second tank with a bazooka. But the Americans were hopelessly outgunned. There was no way they could stop Conrath's tanks; the most they could do was delay them long enough to allow others time to react. In this they were successful. Word of the fight near Casa del Priolo got back to General Allen, who hurriedly assembled a force of artillery, infantry, and armor just north of the beaches that turned back the German tanks. With no hope of breaking through and casualties mounting, the panzers turned tail and retreated back up the Niscemi road. As they pulled back, however, they lost four more tanks, a parting gift from Gorham's paratroopers through whom they passed a second time.[64]

This action eliminated the German threat west of the Acate River. East of the river, however, on a slight rise known as Biazzo Ridge, Conrath's infantry-heavy column ran into another group of paratroopers under the command of the indomitable Jim Gavin, whose own Sicilian odyssey began somewhat ingloriously.

Gavin had no idea where he was when he landed and had with him but six troopers, including Captains Al Ireland and Benjamin Vandervoort. It was, to say the least, an inauspicious start for the commander of the largest airborne force the United States had ever committed to combat. Undeterred, Gavin led his tiny band west, toward the sound and flash of battle. It was a full hour before they saw another human being—a magnificently drunk Italian soldier whistling, singing, and staggering down a darkened road. Wanting to take the Italian prisoner so they could interrogate him and get a fix on their location, Gavin and his troopers hid behind a stone wall until he drew near, at which Gavin yelled, "*Alto*," while "Vandervoort rushed through an opening in the wall with a .45 in one hand and a knife in the other."[65] The Italian surrendered without a fight. Questioning their captive proved futile, however; none of the Americans spoke Italian and the Italian spoke no English, so they brusquely forced the Italian under a shelter half where Vandervoort, flashlight in hand, attempted to "work the guy over to get more information."[66] This, too, proved unsuccessful. Anxious to push on, Gavin told Vandervoort to take charge of the prisoner, whom they would bring with them. Vandervoort had taken an intelligence course and supposedly knew something about securing prisoners.

> The idea was to take the belt out of the prisoner's trousers and cut the buttons off his fly so that he would have to hold up his trousers when he walked.

> Van[dervoort] put his .45 in its holster, pressed his knife against the Italian's chest, and said "I'll take care of the bastard."
>
> The Italian was muttering, "*Mamma mia, Mamma mia,*" over and over again. His concern was understandable. The moonlight was shining on the knife blade, and it looked as though it were a foot long. He took off his belt and dropped it. Then Van[dervoort] went into Phase Two of the operation and reached for his fly with one hand, bringing the knife down with the other.[67]

The frightened Italian grabbed the knife, and a struggle ensued during which the prisoner escaped, blood dripping from his hand and emitting a scream "that could be heard all the way to Rome." Gavin was "madder than hell" and asked a sheepish Vandervoort, "What in the hell did you think you were doing?" Before Vandervoort could answer, Gavin turned on his heel and continued on his way, fearful that the struggle, the screams, and the manic Italian would attract forces his small band could not handle.[68]

Oriented on the bursting shells on the horizon, Gavin set a blistering pace. According to Ireland, "Gavin was the kind of person . . . he had one thing on his mind and that was to get to his objective. Anything that was going on was done to try to get to that point. He wanted to speed it up, so we took off and we cut communications [wires] wherever we could find them; we were all working on it."[69] Traveling all night and most of the next day, Gavin and his charge finally made contact with a 45th Division outpost at 0230 hours, 11 July. It was not until then that he learned where he was—about five miles southwest of Vittoria, which, he also discovered, was in American hands. Hoping to find there someone who could provide him an overall picture of the battle, Gavin raced to town. What he found instead were more misdropped paratroopers, most likely Alexander's 2/505th and Harden's 456th, which now had three guns. Gavin told them to start moving toward Gela, where he hoped to find the rest of his combat team. He then commandeered a jeep and with Vandervoort and Ireland in tow sped west on the coastal road.[70]

Gavin came across more paratroopers just outside of Vittoria, some 250 in all, mostly from the 3/505th, who were bivouacked "in foxholes in a tomato field and [were] just awakening."[71] With them was Major "Cannonball" Krause, the 3/505th commander, whom Gavin found "sitting on the side of a foxhole dangling his lower legs into the hole, no equipment, no security out." When asked what he was doing Krause replied that "there were a lot of Germans 'up that way' toward where [the regimental] objectives were."[72] Gavin was dumbstruck. He could not believe what he was seeing from Krause, who was always so "gung ho" in training. Gavin's first thought was to relieve Krause, but he reconsidered. Instead, he told Krause to get his men organized and start moving west. Gavin then jumped back in his jeep and continued on his way.

Two miles down the road Gavin came across some 40 soldiers from the 45th Infantry Division and 20 engineers from B Company, 307th Airborne Engineer Battalion, under the command of Lieutenant Benjamin L. Wechsler, who also just arrived on the scene.[73] The 45th Division soldiers told Gavin that there was a sizable German force on some high ground to the west, though they were none too anxious to go meet the threat. Gavin, therefore, took his engineers and, with Ireland and Vandervoort still with him, continued west on foot. About a mile farther on they came upon a railroad station where, without warning, a motorcycle with a sidecar careered into their midst. The two Germans it carried surrendered immediately and "appeared to be quite disgusted with the lack of resistance being offered by the Italian troops, but refused to give any information regarding their own troops."[74] One of the Germans, pointing to his insignia that identified him as a medical officer, demanded to be released, but Gavin would not have it.[75] He had spotted some grenades in the sidecar and, "reasoning that an armed medic should not be let loose, . . . took the motorcycle and sidecar from him and started him to the rear on foot, disarming the driver also."[76]

Capturing the German officer underscored what the 45th Division soldiers told Gavin earlier—there were obviously enemy troops in the area. How many was still uncertain. Nonetheless, the high ground on which the Germans were supposedly located was key terrain, and Gavin was bent on taking it. With so few troopers with which to do so, and no knowledge of the size of the enemy force atop the high ground, Gavin's only recourse was to attack aggressively to surprise whoever was up there and take the ground before they knew what hit them. Holding that ground was another matter, especially were the enemy to realize that Gavin's force was so small, so he sent Vandervoort back both to hurry Krause's paratroopers along and to find the 45th Division command post to inform the division commander, Major General Troy H. Middleton, of their situation and request reinforcements. He then formed Wechsler's engineers into a skirmish line and, leading from the front, pressed on toward the high ground. A few hundred yards from the crest they began taking scattered small arms fire. Gavin urged his troopers forward and told them to maintain a steady stream of return fire "because it [gave] the impression of a unit in strength coming at [the Germans]."[77] The closer they got to the crest, the more intense the enemy fire became, creating "a rain of leaves and branches as bullets tore through the trees, and there was a buzzing like the sound of swarms of bees."[78] Several paratroopers were hit, including Lieutenant Wechsler, but those who remained fought on, following Gavin's lead, and dislodged the German defenders to gain the crest, where they dug in and prepared to defend. The name of the place, Gavin later learned, was Biazzo Ridge, and he was determined to keep it.

The Germans Gavin's attack dislodged were most likely a flank guard from Conrath's infantry-heavy column, which, at the time, was skirting Biazzo Ridge on its way to Objective Y. But with the unexpected appearance of American paratroopers on Biazzo Ridge threatening his flank and rear, the column commander elected to take back the ridge before continuing on, touching off one of the bloodiest fights of the entire campaign.

Gavin knew the Germans would try to take back the ridge, but rather than wait for the counterattack to develop, he wanted to break it up before it could gain any momentum, and within twenty minutes of taking the ridge he had the resources to do so. Vandervoort had done as ordered; he had contacted Krause's 3/505th and sped it along. In the lead was the battalion executive officer, Captain William H. Hagan. Krause, reported Hagan, "went to the Headquarters of the 45th Infantry Division to tell them what was going on." Gavin "just couldn't believe it," but with no time to waste he told the 3/505th troopers to drop their packs and prepare to advance. When they were ready, sometime between 1030 and 1100 hours, Gavin told them to move out.[79]

The 3/505th troopers moved up and over the ridge, through the engineers, and down the other side. At first they encountered nothing but small arms fire until, about a mile beyond the ridge, they ran into a sizable contingent of German infantry and six Mark VI tanks. Back on the ridge Gavin knew the 3/505th was in a fight, but the dust, smoke, and vegetation obscured his vision and he had no idea how big a fight it was. He found out when wounded paratroopers, including Hagan, started drifting back. "They all told the same story," wrote Gavin. "They fired their bazookas at the front plate of [the] German tanks, and then the tanks swiveled their huge 88 mm. guns at them and fired at the individual infantrymen."[80]

With his bid to break up the German counterattack in ruins, Gavin looked around to see what he had left with which to defend the ridge. It was a scant force: the remains of Wechsler's platoon, a few wounded 3/505th troopers, and some infantrymen he had dragooned from the 45th Division. Yet Gavin was determined to keep the ridge, even at the risk of being overrun. Moving from foxhole to foxhole while the sound of German tank treads grew louder, Gavin checked his troopers' fields of fire and prepared them to defend in place. At one point he was caught in the open "lying on the ground bouncing from the concussion" of a mortar and rocket barrage, a sure prelude to a final assault.[81] When it lifted, he ran to his foxhole and readied himself for the fight. Peering over its lip, he saw a German tank inching clear of some buildings to the front of the ridge, swiveling its barrel in his direction. Fortunately for him, there were others who saw the same thing.

Unbeknownst to Gavin, one of the 75mm howitzers he had discovered earlier that day in Vittoria had arrived. Lieutenant Ray Grossman was one of the artillerymen manning the gun. "Word came that the Germans had a Tiger tank across the ridge, and they were kicking hell out of our boys," so Grossman and his mates manhandled their gun to the top of the ridge with the intent of using it as an antitank weapon. Their first shot at the tank fell short. Watching from his foxhole, Gavin next saw

> a tremendous explosion in front of the gun. The tank had fired and hit the ground just in front of the gun, knocking the troopers like tenpins in all directions. . . . The troopers got up and ran off like startled quail. A second later they realized, to their embarrassment, what they were doing, and they ran back to the gun. They fired one round that hit the tank, or the corner of the building. In the smoke and dust the tank backed out of sight.
>
> That was the last we saw of it.

Grossman and his fellow artillerymen cheered "like we had just scored a touchdown."[82]

It was a short-lived celebration, for though they had chased away one tank, others appeared on their left flank. In the face of this threat two other artillerymen, in an apparent attempt to effect a ruse that would stay the German advance by fooling them into thinking there was American armor in the area, rode up and over the ridge in a captured Italian personnel carrier. A direct hit from one of the German tanks destroyed the personnel carrier, killing both men instantly. The German tanks also destroyed an Italian truck, clearly marked with a red cross, that a 505th surgeon and two medics had commandeered for use as an ambulance. Although all three escaped relatively unharmed, it was obvious that any movement forward of or on top of the ridge was suicide. Hence, Gavin ordered a withdrawal.[83]

Yet it was not to be a wholesale withdrawal. Rather, Gavin arranged his troopers in a new defensive line on the reverse slope of Biazzo Ridge. The advantage of defending from the reverse (or friendly) side of the ridge was that it shielded the troopers from German tank fire. The disadvantage was that it relegated them to a close-in fight once the enemy crested the ridge. Gavin felt that if his troopers engaged "the less heavily armored underbellies of the tanks when they first appeared at the top of the rise," they might have a chance of knocking a few of them out, and, if not, they were to remain in place anyway to kill or drive off the accompanying German infantry.[84] It was a risky proposition. Vandervoort, who had arrived back at the ridge with Hagan, suggested that Gavin at least move the command group back to a large culvert that afforded a bit more protection. Gavin refused because of his "belief that the commander's presence was an inspiration to the troops." According to Ireland, Gavin simply would not accept defeat. "We are staying on this goddamned ridge," he shouted at one point, "no matter what happens!"[85]

"They drove up five or six tanks and infantry, they were coming at us," recalled Ireland. "They looked like they were the biggest tanks ever invented. I thought we had it when the Germans got up within fifty or sixty yards of the C[ommand] P[ost], but we held them off with a lot of heavy firing, and we used pack 75-mm howitzers to kind of slow them down." Through it all Gavin was everywhere, shifting reserves, checking on his heavier weapons (by the end of the day all three of the howitzers from Vittoria were in the battle along with two antitank guns the paratroopers had somehow scrounged), and encouraging his men to hold on. At one point a shaken Major Krause, who had rejoined his battalion on the ridge, told Gavin that "all of his battalion was killed, wounded, or pinned down and ineffective." Gavin angrily replied that they "were going to stay at the top of the ridge with what [they] had and fight the German infantry that came with the tanks." Muttering that they "didn't have a chance" and would be finished if they stayed there, Krause drifted to the rear.[86] But Krause was an exception that day. Other groups of paratroopers, marching to the sound of the guns, rushed forward into the fight on Biazzo Ridge. Gavin used them, along with anyone else in the area—clerks, cooks, truck drivers, as well as troops from the 45th Infantry Division—to form ad hoc squads to plug holes in his lines. Lieutenant Richard Janney, a communications officer in the 505th, wrote that since none of his radios worked, his "radio operators were in the front lines, firing bazookas."[87] In this manner, Gavin and his troopers held off three separate assaults.

Sometime during the fight Gavin also sent Ireland to the rear to find reinforcements. Riding furiously toward the beach on a bicycle he had liberated from a local civilian, Ireland came upon some soldiers from the 45th Infantry Division who directed him to the division command post (Vandervoort never got there), where he found both Middleton and Bradley. After listening to Ireland's report, Bradley instructed Middleton to give Ireland whatever he wanted, which was heavy artillery support, armor support, and a jeep with which to return to Biazzo Ridge. Since it would take some time to round up the tanks and knowing that Gavin needed help quickly, Ireland loaded a three-man forward observer team in the jeep and returned to the fight. He arrived back at the ridge at about 1500 hours. The fighting was even more intense than when he left. Immediately the artillery observers went into action, bringing 155mm and naval gunfire to bear to the attacking Germans. According to Ireland, one of the observers was "a fat guy who had never been under fire. But the shelling never fazed him. He leaped up, grabbed the radio transmitter from his operator, and gave coordinates to his guns back near the beach. I heard the big guy shout into the mouthpiece, 'To hell with zeroing in! There's so goddamned many targets out there you can't miss! Fire for effect!'"[88] Fire from the big guns broke the back of the German assault. What remained of their infantry and armor withdrew, and the position was never again threatened. Gavin and the hodgepodge of paratroopers and infantrymen he had gathered about him had beaten back Conrath's last column in one of the most desperate and one-sided fights of the entire campaign.

But Gavin was not content with simply driving off the Germans. He wanted to destroy them. So when he learned that Lieutenant Swingler's group of paratroopers and a company of Sherman tanks were headed his way, he readied a counterattack. Using Ireland's forward observers to keep the Germans pinned down with artillery and naval gunfire, Gavin improvised an infantry-armor task force that, at 2045 hours, he led up and over the ridge and through the enemy positions on the other side. Those Germans not killed, wounded, or captured broke and ran. Lieutenant Swingler also accounted for the division's first captured enemy tank when he single-handedly crawled up to one and killed the crew—who were inexplicably standing outside the tank—with a hand grenade. All told, American losses at Biazzo Ridge were forty-three killed and one hundred wounded. Besides Swingler's tank, the paratroopers captured twelve 120mm mortars and two half-tracks and took fifty prisoners. They found fifty more Germans dead on the field.[89]

By early evening on 11 July, all three of Conrath's columns were retreating north, their bid to drive the Americans back into the sea unrealized. Yet even retreat brought them no respite. In one of the last major actions of the day some one hundred paratroopers, ensconced in a hilltop chateau known as Castel Nocera, three miles southwest of Niscemi, ambushed a force at least twice its size from one of Conrath's tank columns. The action, which began in the early afternoon, did not end until well after dark. Under the command of Lieutenants Willis J. Ferrill and George J. Watts the paratroopers, most of whom were from the 3/504th, inflicted more than one hundred enemy casualties at the cost of five of their own killed, and despite reinforcement from at least two tanks, it was the Germans who eventually broke contact and fled. At one point during the fight the American fire was so devastating that the Germans considered surrender. "There was a break in the battle [and] a German lieutenant, bearing a white flag, came up the hill to arrange a surrender, but when he saw he was fighting American parachutists he refused to surrender and returned to his position."[90]

In one day of fighting the *Hermann Göring Division*, the unit Guzzoni had counted on to form the backbone of his counterattack force, had been mauled, having lost more than one-third of its tanks.[91] More important, the cumulative effect of the defeats suffered throughout the day broke the will of the Axis commanders. Guzzoni was the first to break. When he learned that Conrath's tanks had been turned back, he ordered Conrath to withdraw his division to Caltagirone. Yet Conrath and Senger still held out hope that the infantry-heavy column could break through to the U.S. beaches and deliver a killing blow. When they received news of the defeat at Biazzo Ridge, they, too, despaired and withdrew the *Hermann Göring Division*, as Guzzoni had ordered.[92]

Gavin was also despondent at day's end 11 July. Conrath at least knew where the elements of his division were, in what strength, and where they were headed. The only elements of his combat team that Gavin had positive control over were those that were with him on the ridge, a mere handful compared to the size of the force that had jumped in with him. As for the rest, he knew neither where they were nor what they had suffered. What he did know was that wherever they were, they were facing an enemy for which they were wholly unprepared. There were "supposed to be no Germans (except a few technicians) on the island," recalled Gavin, and there was certainly not supposed to be any German armor, especially Tiger tanks.[93] The only antitank weapon the paratroopers had were bazookas, which, they found out, fired rockets with warheads that did not penetrate the panzers' frontal armor, a point driven home to Gavin the next day when, while burying his dead, he discovered that "many of them had had pieces of bazookas ground up in them by tanks as they were crushed."[94] Killing a German tank with a bazooka meant angling for a flank or rear shot, a tactic that required a lot of skill, guts, and luck. Even the bravest were not always successful. The day after the fight at Biazzo Ridge, Colonel Gorham went tank hunting again, looking to bag another Tiger. His luck did not hold out. Before he could get a round off, the Tiger targeted him with its main gun and fired, killing Gorham instantly.[95]

Back in North Africa, the rest of the 82nd hung on reports from the battlefield and prepared for employment as needed. The call came on the morning of 11 July. General Patton wanted Colonel Tucker's two remaining parachute infantry battalions (and their supporting elements) dropped near Gela as reinforcements.[96] It was a decision that, in retrospect, had far-ranging and tragic consequences.

CHAPTER 7

A VERY RUGGED DELIVERY

Deplorable as is the loss of life which occurred, I believe that the lessons now learned could have been driven home in no other way, and that these lessons provide a sound basis for the belief that recurrences can be avoided.

The losses are part of the inevitable price of war in human life.

—MATTHEW B. RIDGWAY, MEMORANDUM, HEADQUARTERS, 82D AIRBORNE DIVISION, "REPORTED LOSS OF TRANSPORT PLANES AND PERSONNEL"

AT FIRST LIGHT on D day, General Ridgway and his aide-de-camp, Captain Don C. Faith Jr., boarded one of the many landing craft headed toward the invasion beaches.[1] As soon as he landed Ridgway made for the 1st Infantry Division's command post to see what news General Allen had of his paratroopers. It was not good. Allen told him that he "hadn't seen hide nor hair of them, and hadn't heard a peep out of them on the radio," and based on reports from his forces inland there was "one thing he was sure of, . . . they weren't out in front of him."[2]

But Ridgway wanted to see for himself, so he and Faith headed inland. What they found was a landscape as "ominously still and empty, as silent and forbidding as the surface of the moon." They saw no one until they reached what Ridgway described as a "main road" (most likely Highway 115), where Ridgway flagged down a jeep containing the 1st Division's assistant division commander, Brigadier General Theodore R. Roosevelt Jr. Ridgway and Roosevelt were friends, so they stopped to talk. Ridgway asked

Roosevelt if he had seen any paratroopers. When Roosevelt replied that he had not, Ridgway thanked his friend and moved on. Ridgway and Faith continued inland for quite a while without seeing another soul—enemy, friendly, or civilian—until they came upon Captain Willard R. Follmer, the I Company, 3/505th, commander, who was sitting beneath a tree nursing a broken ankle. Follmer told Ridgway that although several small groups of paratroopers had crisscrossed the area, to his knowledge there was no substantial airborne force anywhere nearby. After ensuring that Follmer was comfortable (Follmer refused Ridgway's offer of assistance, preferring to await medical attention where he was), Ridgway and Faith moved on, and though they eventually spied other paratroopers, it was never more than two or three at a time. It was, for Ridgway, unnerving.[3]

Later that morning Ridgway returned to the 1st Division command post, reported what he had seen (or, more appropriately, not seen), and tried, unsuccessfully, to raise Gavin on the radio. He then returned to the *Monrovia* and convinced Patton to postpone the drop scheduled for later that night. Patton wanted to use Tucker's paratroopers as reinforcements by dropping them on the Gela-Farello landing area, an abandoned airfield approximately three miles east of Gela and a mile inland. Ridgway demurred. Having not yet accounted for Gavin's troopers, Ridgway was chary of risking Tucker's, especially given that the Gela-Farello area was not totally secure. Patton agreed, and the drop was postponed.[4]

Patton changed his mind the next morning. He wanted Tucker's 504th dropped as soon as possible. The congestion on the beachheads was preventing him from pushing inland; a parachute drop was a way to bypass the congestion and get more troops into the fight quickly. If all went according to plan, Hal Clark's 52nd Troop Carrier Wing could deliver more than 2,000 paratroopers in approximately forty minutes (the time it would take the air column to pass over the drop zone). In Patton's eyes it was an option too good to pass up.

Ridgway had worked out an elaborate code system by which he could alert those elements of the division still in North Africa to any number of on-call missions. Accordingly, the obscure message Ridgway sent back to North Africa at 0839 hours on 11 July—"Mackall tonight, wear white [pa]jamas"—signaled Tucker that he and his troopers were to fly in to Sicily that night ("Mackall"), that the drop zone was the Gela-Farello landing area, and that Tucker was to "be prepared for ground action as ordered" ("white").[5] For some reason Ridgway's message was delayed, but it did not matter; Clark's aircrews and Tucker's paratroopers were standing by. They had but to chute up and take off.[6]

Nine hours later 144 aircraft were headed for Sicily carrying 2,304 troopers of Tucker's combat team, which consisted of the 1st and 2nd Battalions of the 504th, the 376th Parachute Field Artillery Battalion, and C Company, 307th Airborne Engineer Battalion. The route was essentially the same as that flown for the first drop except that once they rounded Malta, the pilots were to head for Sampieri, a point about thirty miles east of Gela, where they were to turn west and fly a corridor two miles wide and roughly two miles inland at an altitude of 1,000 feet, all of which would be over friendly lines, to the Gela-Farello landing field.[7]

The planes assembled in their familiar nine-ship V-of-V formations with the 313th Troop Carrier Group leading, followed at ten-minute intervals by the 61st, 314th, and 316th groups, respectively. Because they departed an hour earlier than they had for the first drop, the pilots had the advantage of daylight as far as Linosa.[8] Moreover, the night was clear and calm, without the strong winds that had affected navigation two nights previously, and the moon was bright. As a result, the planes rounded Malta on course, on time, and in formation. The pilots were convinced that this would be a "milk run." Most of the paratroopers dozed in the cargo holds. One notable exception was the combat team commander, Colonel Reuben Tucker.[9]

Chagrined that Ridgway had selected Gavin to lead the first drop, Tucker wanted to get in the fight and prove that his 504th was every bit as good as the 505th. So when he received word that his drop was on, Tucker made his way through the ranks of his combat team and personally challenged his troopers "to be the kind of soldiers you were trained to be, and I know you will be."[10] The epitome of the tough, relentless paratroop officer, Tucker would prove to be "a combat leader of extraordinary ability."[11] Much to the annoyance of Ridgway, he paid scant attention to administrative, logistical, and disciplinary matters, and because of this Ridgway could never bring himself to promote Tucker beyond colonel, but "Rube couldn't care less. He wanted to fight. And the troops all knew that."[12]

Whereas Tucker was keen to get to Sicily, Ridgway was fretful. This was because Allied naval commanders refused to accept the strict fire-control measures that Ridgway and others felt were necessary to ensure the safety of friendly aircraft. During the first drop, the planes followed a route that steered well clear of the invasion convoys, but any follow-on drops in or around the beachheads would inevitably bring the transport aircraft over or near the hundreds of vessels lying offshore and expose the vulnerable C-47s to friendly fire at the time when they were most vulnerable—after they had descended to drop altitude and slowed to drop speed. Despite Ridgway's and others' arguments, naval commanders would not agree to measures they felt would undermine their self-defense. This intransigence so exasperated Ridgway that he took the unusual step of jumping the chain of command to take his concerns directly to the top. The occasion was a visit to Kairouan by Eisenhower and Spaatz a week before D day during which Ridgway cornered the theater commander and made his case. Eisenhower listened intently and "made instant reply that he thought the desired action could be taken."[13] Much to Ridgway's disappointment, the only action Eisenhower took was to send a message on 5 July reminding Allied naval commanders of something they already knew: "THERE WILL BE ADDITIONAL PASSAGES OF AIRBORNE TROOPS AFTER [THE] INITIAL ASSAULT AND INFORMATION CONCERNING THEM WILL BE FORWARDED WHEN AVAILABLE. ACTION ADDRESSEES [WILL] GIVE WIDE DISTRIBUTION TO VESSELS UNDER THEIR COMMAND SO AS TO PREVENT SHOOTING DOWN THESE PLANES."[14] On 6 July, Eisenhower issued a similar message to the ground commanders, warning them "to expect flights of friendly troops" at any time from D day to D+6 that "will pass between 2230 and 2400 hours," will be overhead for about forty minutes, and will either "drop parachutists or release gliders." In a message to his subordinates, Patton echoed Eisenhower's warning but also ordered them to "advise respective naval commanders."[15] But beyond this flurry of message traffic, Eisenhower did nothing to ensure the safety of follow-on airborne echelons, although he was the *only* person with the *unquestioned* authority to demand and enforce compliance with *any measures* among all Allied air, ground, and naval forces.

When Patton changed his mind about inserting Tucker's combat team, Ridgway still had had no contact with Gavin and, fearing the worst, was understandably reluctant to hazard the rest of the 82nd's paratroopers. Yet he had his orders, so he did the only thing he could—he returned to Sicily several hours before drop time to personally pass the word to as many units as he could that the 504th was inbound. He focused his effort on the antiaircraft batteries near the Gela-Farello landing area.[16]

Notwithstanding Ridgway's efforts, Patton's orders, and Eisenhower's messages, there occurred that day in and around the American beaches events that would have sorely tested even the most stringent fire-control measures, for it was that day that the Axis mounted some of the heaviest aerial attacks to date in the Mediterranean. They began shortly after first light and continued throughout the morning and early afternoon, with each attack seemingly more violent than the one before. At 1540 hours, during an attack by approximately thirty German bombers, the Liberty Ship *Robert Rowan*, filled with ammunition, took a bomb in its hold, caught fire, exploded, and sank in shallow water, and for the rest of the day its exposed bow spewed fire and smoke, further complicating landing operations. It also served as a beacon for other enemy aircraft and precipitated the largest and last attack of the day at 2150 hours when 381 enemy aircraft converged on the invasion area, setting off an hourlong surface-to-air and air-to-air melee during which more ships were damaged and the vulnerable transports were forced to weigh anchor and disperse.[17] All told, there were twenty-four air raids on and around the invasion beaches on 11 July.[18] As a result the troops ashore, sailors at sea, and most especially the antiaircraft gunners were operating with frayed nerves and hair triggers.

Even Patton was unnerved. Having been caught in one of the attacks while ashore, he returned to the *Monrovia* to try to call off the jump. He was too late. He could do nothing but wait and hope. Alone in his wardroom, he confided to his diary: "Went to the office at 2000 to see if we could stop the 82d Airborne lift, as enemy air attacks were heavy [during the day] and inaccurate Army and Navy anti-air[craft gunners] were jumpy. Found we could not get contact by radio. Am terribly worried."[19]

By early evening scattered cumulous clouds blanketed Sicily, which compelled the transport pilots to gain altitude. This change in altitude, combined with the resultant smoke and haze from the Axis bombing raids, had two effects: It obscured landmarks, which made aerial navigation difficult, and, for the forces on the ground and at sea, made identification of the incoming aircraft problematic.[20]

The first planes of the lead group arrived over Gela-Farello at 2240 hours and dropped their paratroopers five minutes ahead of schedule. Then, according to Captain Willard E. Harrison of the 1/504th, "one gun open[ed] fire on the formation, and that . . . seemed to be the signal for many others to open fire, both from the beach and from ships offshore."[21] Within minutes the sky was ablaze with tracers as nervous antiaircraft gunners, and seemingly anyone else who had a weapon at hand, opened fire at what they thought were more enemy bombers.

The contagion spread rapidly, even to ships well out to sea. The second troop carrier group in formation, the 61st, was some five to ten miles offshore when it took fire, and, according to its pilots, "no amount of recognition signals [from the aircraft] had the least effect."[22] Yet the pilots flew on, albeit after taking evasive action to avoid the wall of steel being thrown at them. Many dove for the deck, using high-speed, low-level maneuver to defeat the antiaircraft gunners' aim and, hopefully, provide them a better view of their markings and silhouette. It was to no avail. The fire never abated. Instead, it grew more intense as succeeding flights approached the drop zone. Testament to this was the experience of the last troop carrier group in the armada, the 316th, which took the heaviest losses: twelve aircraft and thirty-seven crew casualties.[23]

One particularly harrowing account by an unnamed pilot who flew this mission provides a poignant picture of the intensity of the antiaircraft fire, the ruggedness of the C-47, and the bravery of the aircrews and paratroopers alike:

> A few minutes before reaching the drop point with the paratroopers, a shell smashed into the starboard side of the fuselage and knocked out a hole four by six feet while a fragment from the shell slit the aluminum and every rib from hole to rudder. Passing through the plane the fragment ripped off a door as a second ack-ack blast carried away a portion of the left stabilizer. The explosion also blew away a large piece of equipment, and the impact was so great that it felt like a motor crash in the pilot's cabin.
>
> The airplane spun at a right angle and nearly pulled the controls from my grasp. For a second I didn't realize what had happened, then finding myself out of formation I began a violent evasive action. I saw three planes burning on the ground and red tracers everywhere as machine gunners sprayed us as if potting a flight of ducks.
>
> Meanwhile I had cut into a less dangerous spot to give the parachutists a fighting chance to reach ground. But I've got to hand it to those boys; one, who had been pretty badly hit by shrapnel, insisted on leaping with the others although he had been ordered to remain in the plane.[24]

In all twenty-three transports were shot down, thirty-seven more were badly damaged, and the 52nd Troop Carrier Wing lost seven dead, thirty wounded, and fifty-three missing.[25] After returning to base a pilot and copilot from the hard-hit 316th Group claimed somewhat bitterly, "Evidently, the safest place for us tonight while over SICILY would have been over enemy territory." For some time thereafter, "the legend of a navy which shot from the hip without distinguishing friend from foe spread widely and lingered long among the troop carrier units."[26]

Six planes were shot down with paratroopers still aboard. Lieutenant John P. O'Malley of the 2/504th saw one of them go down: "Riding in the plane on our left wing was half of my platoon. In its frenzy to escape the lethal inferno, their C-47 veered sharply to its right and almost struck our plane. I watched in horror as their C-47 then tilted and plunged to earth, where it exploded in a huge ball of fire. Those were my boys. That was the most anguishing experience of my life; one that I would never forget."[27]

Captain Adam A. Komosa, the 504th Headquarters Company commander, recalled planes dropping out of formation and crashing into the sea, while "others, like clumsy whales, wheeled and attempted to get beyond the flak which rose in fountains of fire, lighting the stricken faces of men as they stared through the windows." According to Chaplain Delbert Kuehl, the air was so full of tracers "it looked like a mammoth Fourth of July celebration." He saw "plane after plane go down in flames. Some exploded in the air; others crash-landed in the sea. Tragically, some that were on planes that crashed in the sea, a few of them were alive and they [naval antiaircraft gunners] shot them in the water. One of our medics, who later survived, was shot in the water." Later investigations revealed that it was not uncommon that night for naval gunners to continue firing on downed planes in the water. According to the army's official history, "it is probable that a majority of the troop carriers shot down . . . were given the *coup de grace* by naval guns."[28]

Even those troopers who made it out of the aircraft and landed among friendly soldiers were not safe. Lieutenant Charles A. Drew of the 2/504th reported that of the four men killed and four men wounded from his platoon, three were hit while descending in their parachutes, and "one was killed on the ground because he had the wrong pass word."[29] Tucker's paratroopers had been told that the challenge and password were "Ulysses—Grant," but after being shot at by soldiers from the 45th Infantry Division with whom they attempted to make contact, it quickly became apparent that they had been misinformed. Even Ridgway had this problem. While standing at the edge of the drop zone, he saw several soldiers from the 45th firing on his paratroopers. When he ran forward to order them to cease fire, he discovered that that he, too, had the wrong password.[30]

It took several days to determine the extent of the tragedy, but what was immediately apparent was that Tucker's 504th was as badly scattered as Gavin's 505th. Only the first few planes dropped their paratroopers on target. Once the firing began, the evasive action taken by the pilots combined with the intense desire of the paratroopers to exit as quickly as possible resulted in the rest being scattered from the Acate River in the west to Vittoria in the east. Patton's plan to have Tucker's paratroopers immediately at his disposal had been thwarted.[31]

Not as immediately apparent was the casualty toll among the paratroopers. Days later the count was put at 81 dead, 132 wounded, and 16 missing, approximately 10 percent of Tucker's combat team.[32] Maxwell Taylor, who oversaw the evacuation of the dead and wounded paratroopers back in North Africa, recalled talking with one of the wounded. The trooper had an American bullet in his shoulder, and Taylor remarked "awkwardly that it must have been pretty hot over the beachhead in all that fire." The trooper replied, "Yes, it was . . . but I was glad to see that our fellows could shoot so good."[33]

Taylor was supervising the evacuation of the dead and wounded because the assistant division commander, Brigadier General "Bull" Keerans, was among the missing. Ridgway had ordered Keerans to remain in North Africa, but Keerans sneaked aboard one of the transports as an observer. Long thought to have been lost at sea, others reported seeing Keerans alive onshore, although his body has never been found. His loss, though tragic, cleared the way for the rise of other, more able, officers.[34]

In the wake of the friendly-fire disaster Eisenhower canceled plans for the glider insertion of the 325th, which therefore never got to Sicily.[35] Ridgway, however, remained in Sicily to take command of his paratroopers, although it took him until midnight 17 July to get them assembled near Gela in any appreciable strength. Meanwhile, other plans had changed as well, compelled by Montgomery's unilateral decision to adjust the boundaries between his Eighth Army and Patton's Seventh Army so that he could use a highway that had been previously reserved for the Americans. This decision, which Bradley called "the most arrogant, egotistical, selfish and dangerous move in the whole of combined operations in World War II," cut Seventh Army out of the advance on Messina and relegated to it the rather unglamorous role of flank guard for the British Eighth Army.[36]

Patton was uncharacteristically docile when informed of Alexander's decision to approve Montgomery's boundary adjustment; his only request was that he be allowed to advance west to seize Agrigento and Porto Empedocle, for "by so doing [Seventh Army] can obviate the necessity of using Siracusa as a [supply] base, thus saving a turn around of 140 miles [by trucks] over bad roads, and also obviating the necessity of using a port in conjunction with the Eighth Army." Alexander replied that "if this could be done through the use of limited forces, in the nature of a reconnaissance in force, he had no objection."[37] Patton agreed, although never did he intend to limit his advance to a reconnaissance.

Since taking Messina was out of the question, Patton had switched his attention to Palermo, which drew him "like a lode star."[38] Securing Agrigento and Porto Empedocle was simply the first step toward that end. He took the second step two days later when, on 15 July, he reorganized and reoriented Seventh Army. Patton assigned what was ostensibly his primary mission, the security of Montgomery's left flank, to Bradley's II Corps, still composed of the U.S. 1st and 45th Infantry Divisions. He then grouped the 3rd Infantry and 82nd Airborne Divisions under a "provisional" corps headed by his deputy, Major General Geoffrey Keyes, and tasked Keyes with attacking west and northwest toward Palermo with all due speed.[39]

Concurrently, Ridgway received orders to move the 82nd to Palma di Montechiaro, a town on the southern coastal highway approximately thirteen miles east of Agrigento. Assigned a zone of action abutting the southern coast and extending five to ten miles inland, the 82nd was to advance twenty-five miles to the Verdura River and keep pace with Major General Lucian K. Truscott Jr.'s 3rd Infantry Division advancing on its right. Once both divisions reached the Verdura, the 3rd Division would veer sharply north toward Palermo, while the 82nd secured its left and cleared the westernmost part of the island.[40]

On the evening of 18 July, with the advance set to begin at 0500 hours the next morning, Keyes gathered his division commanders for a last conference. Stressing the importance of remaining in their respective zones, Keyes enjoined Ridgway and Truscott to move fast and not stop unless ordered to do so by him or Patton.[41]

Ridgway selected the 504th combat team to lead the division attack. The impetuous Tucker, having finally assembled the bulk of his regiment (to include the 3/504th, which was returned to his control), jumped off two hours ahead of time. Intelligence had reported "no known organized fighting forces . . . located to the immediate west on the route of advance," so Tucker's troopers moved fast, easily overrunning any enemy forces they did encounter, and reached the Verdura by nightfall, having bagged more than 500 prisoners along the way.[42] According to Gavin, whose 505th followed Tucker's 504th, "The usual action of the Italians was to fire a few shots, rifle and [machine gun], cause the [advance guard] to deploy, and then surrender as soon as pressure was brought to bear on them."[43]

The second day of the advance was a repeat of the first. Tucker's 504th, still in the van, jumped off at 0600. By 0925 it had taken the coastal town of Sciacca and by nightfall was in Menfi, twenty miles beyond Sciacca, with an additional 745 prisoners at the cost of only 1 killed and 1 wounded.[44]

The unanticipated speed of the advance forced a change of plan. Keyes had at his disposal a third division, the U.S. 2nd Armored. Because enemy resistance had been so sparse, and the 82nd's advance so swift, Patton and Keyes felt the time right to unleash the 2nd Armored for the final thrust to Palermo. This, in turn, compelled a change to the 82nd's mission. Instead of continuing westward, Ridgway was to secure the line of the Belice River and, in so doing, secure the 2nd Armored's assembly area.[45]

Ridgway assigned the mission to Gavin's 505th, for although the 504th had advanced swiftly and sustained hardly any casualties, it "had lost 2/3rds of its effective strength from stragglers." Tucker had directed his troopers to live off the land, and faced with a relatively benign enemy, his troopers' penchant for plunder increased commensurately. As Gavin observed, "All along the roads they were bumming under trees around houses and in fields. On the march officers and men alike would leave ranks to pick grapes, melons, and get water." But what contributed most to the straggling, continued Gavin, was the troopers' desire to "capture" vehicles:

> Every wreck and abandoned vehicle that had not the slightest chance of ever operating again was the center of a group of from three to six parachutists who upon being questioned said that they were getting it ready to run to use for the reg[iment]. This had the sanction of the reg[iment] in its desperation to get transportation. Our experience was that even the good servic[e]able vehicles soon broke down and became much more of an automotive liability than asset. Orders were accordingly issued forbidding troops from leaving ranks to capture vehicles.[46]

Of course, Gavin's troopers also liberated arms and equipment from enemy and civilian sources alike, most notably Alexander's 2/505th. The division's training regimen stressed that if they needed water, food, arms, ammunition, or transportation to accomplish a mission, they were expected to take it. In their first taste of combat, however, Tucker's troopers took this to extremes, and although they procured a fleet of "Italian light tanks, motorcycles, horses, bicycles, mules, trucks, and even wheelbarrows for transportation," in doing so they had dissipated their combat strength.[47] This proved a valuable lesson. Throughout the rest of the war, division troopers would use their wiles to obtain what they needed, especially transportation, but never again would this lead to a situation wherein they were too scattered to fight.

Yet Tucker did have one battalion that was still relatively intact: Major William P. Yarborough's 2/504th. In order to maintain the momentum of the advance, Ridgway wanted the 2/504th to take San Margherita, a small town just short of the Belice River. With San Margherita secure, Gavin's combat team could then pass through the 504th and move on to secure the river line. What ensued, quite unexpectedly, was the most spirited fight of the westward march at a place called Tuminello Pass.

Yarborough's troopers moved out shortly after first light on 21 July with no enemy in sight, but this changed suddenly once they approached Tuminello Pass, a passage through a chain of hills a few miles southeast of San Margherita. Atop the hills was an Italian artillery battery protected by camouflaged machine-gun emplacements. Once the paratroopers got within range, the Italians opened up with uncharacteristically accurate artillery and machine-gun fire that pinned Yarborough's battalion in place for thirty minutes before friendly mortars and artillery could be brought up to respond in kind. This freed up Lieutenant Charles Drew's F Company platoon to maneuver onto the Italian flank, where they fixed bayonets and charged. The shock so discomfited the Italians that they surrendered en masse. At a cost of 6 killed and 8 wounded, Yarborough's troopers killed more than 100 Italians, wounded 35 more, and captured 1 Italian colonel, 13 officers, and more than 1,500 enlisted men. Shortly thereafter, Gavin's combat team passed through the 2/504th and secured the Belice River line by nightfall.[48]

The division's stay along the Belice was short-lived. On the morning of 23 July Ridgway received orders to "move without delay to seize TRAPANI," a fairly large city on Sicily's westernmost tip. Since speed was imperative, Gavin's troopers, leading the way, boarded trucks for the 45-mile ride to the city. Encountering nothing more than mined roads at two points along the way, both of which were quickly cleared, the bulk of the journey seemed more parade than combat operation. "All along the route . . . the local population competed with each other in their expressions of good will," for as the troopers passed through the small towns, "the roads were lined with people who not only shouted their approval and showed in one place a prepared sign: 'Welcome Liberators,' but who also showered the vehicles with fruit, bread and chocolate, much of which had been pilfered from abandoned Italian military stores."[49]

In fact, it was not until they approached Trapani's outskirts that the 505th troopers even saw any enemy soldiers, most of whom surrendered without much resistance. One group of about 50 Italian soldiers hiding in a railroad tunnel surrendered to a squad of paratroopers. Another, larger, group traded fire with the 505th's point element, but when the paratroopers assaulted they, too, surrendered, adding another 110 prisoners to the division's total.[50]

The most determined resistance of the day occurred when Gavin's troopers appeared on some hills above Trapani, where roadblocks and minefields slowed their advance and Italian artillery positioned on adjacent hills opened up on them. The 376th Parachute Field Artillery Battalion responded in kind, as did the 34th Field Artillery and 83rd Chemical (4.2-inch mortar) Battalions, which had been attached to the 82nd for the advance. A two- to three-hour artillery duel ensued, during which Gavin's troopers maneuvered on the Italian positions and took them one by one. Once the guns were silent and Trapani surrounded, Ridgway sent an envoy into the city with his terms of surrender. The Italian commander accepted without delay and, as agreed, ceased all resistance, preserved his stores of supplies, and posted guards on all military and naval equipment until Gavin's troopers arrived to relieve them. The net result, besides an "uncounted amount of guns and other military and naval material and stores," was an additional 2,639 prisoners of war.[51]

While the 505th was securing Trapani, Tucker's 504th took Alcamo, 22 miles to the east, and completed the occupation of western Sicily the next day by taking Castellammare del Golfo. With the mainland of western Sicily in hand, the only enemy force remaining in the 82nd's area was a contingent of approximately 1,000 Italian soldiers and sailors on the Edagi Islands, roughly 10 to 12 miles off the coast of Sicily at Trapani. On 29 July, two officers from the division staff sailed to the main island of Favignana to parlay with the local commander who, after a short discussion, surrendered his force without a fight.[52]

In ten days, the 82nd advanced 158 miles, secured approximately 1,550 square miles of Sicily, and captured 18,836 enemy personnel.[53] For the remainder of its time in Sicily, the 82nd conducted police and occupation duties, ensured that the local population was fed, maintained order, and rounded up local fascists. The troopers were justifiably proud of their achievements. These feelings, however, were not universal.

Well before the Sicilian campaign ended investigations were under way to determine what went wrong with the airborne operations. An obvious deficiency was the inability of troop carrier pilots to find the drop and landing zones, but aerial navigation was a problem with Allied air forces in general; bomber pilots, for example, had a hard time finding targets as large as cities. Hence, although airborne commanders, especially Ridgway, were concerned about this shortcoming, it was not, by itself, adequate to explain what occurred in Sicily.

The foremost concern was the lack of interservice coordination, a deficiency that demanded hasty redress if future invasions, already being planned, were not to be likewise marred by catastrophe. Although Ridgway had been loud and clear about his concerns in this area, it took two separate but eerily similar friendly-fire incidents to drive this point home. The first, of course, was the 504th's ill-fated jump on 11 July. The second occurred the next day in the British zone. Operation FUSTIAN was a parachute and glider assault by the British 1st Parachute Brigade aimed at seizing a bridge over the Simeto River, roughly five miles south of Catania. Of the 135 transports involved, 14 were shot down and 34 severely damaged by fire from Allied ships off Sicily's east coast.[54]

Hal Clark, the 52nd Troop Carrier Wing commander, submitted a preliminary report on the 504th drop the day after it happened. Inconclusive at best, Clark's report offered nothing more than initial observations gleaned from his pilots, although it did claim (incorrectly) that "all group elements reached [the] designated [drop zone] on schedule."[55] The next day, U.S. Brigadier General Paul L. Williams, commander of the North Africa Air Force Troop Carrier Command, the 52nd's higher headquarters, forwarded his report of the incident. Addressed to Eisenhower, Williams's report stated unequivocally that air planners had done everything in their power to coordinate with naval and ground force commanders beforehand to guard against just such an accident and, in summary, posited several explanations for the fratricide, including the obvious—that enemy air attacks coincident with the drop confused friendly antiaircraft gunners.[56]

Reports were not enough to mollify Eisenhower, especially after FUSTIAN. Furious at what he assumed were unforgivable failures, he wanted the culprits discovered and disciplined. Cabling Patton, he demanded "an investigation [of the 504th incident] and statement of punishments for those guilty of firing on them." He also appointed his own investigatory body, headed by Major General Joseph Swing, his American airborne adviser. Swing's report, submitted on 16 July, cited five contributory causes for the mishap: insufficient planning "with respect to successive lifts of the 82nd Airborne Division [that] resulted in lack of coordination between Army, Air, and Navy," the inability of the pilots to adhere to prescribed routes, the "unalterable" position of Allied naval planners that ships at sea would fire on all targets within range at night, the "unfortunate circumstance of an enemy bombing raid coinciding with the arrival of the Troop Carrier element," and negligence by some ground commanders who failed to warn their units that friendly aircraft were inbound.[57]

Eisenhower was not convinced by Swing's assessment. He was still looking for culprits. In a cable to General Marshall the next day he acknowledged (incorrectly) that "some German night bombers came in at the same moment that our troop-carrying planes did and the dropping of bombs and flares made all the ground troops open up a maximum fire" but stated that he still found it "odd" that "even in the daytime we have great trouble in preventing our own naval and land forces from firing on friendly planes," especially in an operation "where we have such great air superiority that the presumption is that any plane flying in a straight and level course is friendly."[58]

Eisenhower's insistence that those responsible be found and punished impelled the services to close ranks and engendered an atmosphere of defensiveness and recrimination. A primary example of this was a cable Admiral Cunningham sent to Eisenhower after he learned that Eisenhower was appointing a second board of officers to look into the fratricides. Cunningham averred that by emphasizing the supposed indiscipline of naval antiaircraft gunners, the board would be prejudiced. Cunningham stressed that it was a given that "all ships fire at once at any aeroplane particularly low flying ones which approach them" and that "nothing less is acceptable without incurring grave risk of the loss or damage to valuable merchant vessels or fleet units." He also reminded Eisenhower that during planning, this had been "constantly kept in the foreground and pointed out" by his naval staff. To Cunningham any fault, therefore, lay with the Allied air forces, a result of either "bad routing or bad navigation on the part of the aircraft pilots."[59]

The board to which Cunningham referred convened on 24 July. Composed of Brigadier General H. A. Craig of the U.S. Army Air Corps, Brigadier General W. C. Crane of the U.S. Army, Rear Admiral Philip Vian of the Royal Navy, and Colonel Fay Ross, an American infantryman, the board began its investigation by hosting a conference that was attended by high-ranking British and American army, air force, and airborne representatives. Also in attendance was Air Chief Marshal Tedder, Eisenhower's theater air commander. Major General Browning facilitated the discussion. Colonel Harry Lewis represented the 82nd.[60]

The diplomatic Browning opened the conference by stating that in his opinion the difficulties encountered during HUSKY were not the result of any one service in particular. He concluded by saying that despite the scattered drops, the operations were a success because they caused "abject confusion in the Axis General Headquarters and undoubtedly contributed materially to the decision of the Axis to withdraw the[ir] troops so rapidly, apparently not knowing just how many paratroopers had been dropped and where." Following Browning's introduction ways to improve aerial navigation were discussed and approved, and then, according to Lewis, the conference turned rancorous. Since Admiral Vian was absent, the only other naval representative present was a Captain Barnard of the Royal Navy from Cunningham's staff. Barnard had obviously been instructed to repeat a prepared line and no other, a line that echoed Cunningham's cable to Eisenhower. Just as Cunningham had attempted to shift focus away from naval antiaircraft gunners, so did Barnard whenever he was asked why the ships fired on friendly aircraft. For example, when asked why the transports were fired on by Allied ships at least twenty miles out to sea, Barnard "studiously, laboriously and perspiringly [*sic*] avoided any direct replies" and instead repeated the same prepared response: "Is it not possible for the Air Corps to fly a course well removed from the naval operations and then at a point change directions and hit the [drop zone] from some direction other than that covered by the Navy?" This went on for some time, much to the malevolent delight of Tedder and Browning, who mercilessly badgered Barnard and "made life utterly miserable for him." Eventually, his shirt wet with perspiration, Barnard broke with his prepared statement and in exasperation proclaimed, "Will you gentlemen please remember that up to the present any airship over our naval craft in the Mediterranean has been an enemy ship, and while the Navy is now in the transition period, it was extremely difficult to impress upon all 'light-fingered gentry' that there were such things as friendly planes flying over our craft."[61]

The board met seven more times between 24 and 31 July before rendering its report. Not once did it call the airborne division commanders to testify. The board's findings included a list of conclusions about the cause of the incident, none of which differed significantly from those of Swing and Williams. As far as the touchy subject of fault was concerned, the board was circumspect and vague, concluding that "there was a lack of a well understood, uniform definition of the responsibilities of the several authorities concerned in all stages of airborne operations and of command in the various stages."[62] Finally, the board made some recommendations and suggested that these recommendations be codified in a training memorandum, a draft of which was included in the report. The resultant two-and-a-half-page Training Memorandum Number 43, *Employment of Airborne Forces*, was a predictable product of a process undermined from the outset by Eisenhower's desire to find fault rather than solutions. Filled with vacuous statements of the obvious such as "full coordination of all elements involved is paramount to the success of airborne operations," it failed to delineate which organization or service was ultimately responsible for ensuring that this occurred, thereby prolonging the faulty system it was meant to improve.[63]

Three days later Ridgway submitted his report on the incident involving the 504th. Summarizing in detail the events that led to the incident and the coordination that had been conducted beforehand, as well as the resistance he encountered from naval authorities, he refused in the end to implicate any one service or organization for the tragedy. Furthermore, with eloquence unequaled on any of the hundreds of pages of documents devoted to examining the Sicily fratricides, Ridgway put the matter to rest with one sentence: "The responsibility for loss of life and materiel resulting from this operation is so divided, so difficult to fix with impartial justice, and so questionable of ultimate value to the service because of the acrimonious debates which would follow efforts to hold responsible persons or services to account, that disciplinary action is of doubtful wisdom."[64] This, it appeared, was the last word, for no person, organization, or service was ever found to be ultimately responsible.

In his 1947 book *Airborne Warfare*, Gavin called American airborne forces "the toddling tot that . . . was born in Sicily and survived a very rugged delivery."[65] He was correct in more than one respect; not only did American paratroopers experience two disastrous drops, but because of these disasters, they also had to face a movement, led by Eisenhower, to disband American airborne divisions.

The movement to disband airborne divisions was sparked by observers from the War Department and Eisenhower's headquarters, who reported "from the experience of this campaign and from numerous conversations with [unnamed] participants in airborne operations therein, that the organization of Airborne troops into divisions is unsound." According to Gavin, the observers based their logic on the premise that "if a regiment could not be delivered more effectively than had occurred in Sicily, what chance would a division have?" Although those involved in the fight maintained otherwise—Patton insisted that "his swift and successful landings followed by a rapid advance inland would not have been achieved at such a light cost or at such speed without the action of his Airborne Division," and Bradley wrote that "in spite of the foul-ups, Gavin's scattered force had caused great confusion and distraction among the enemy on D-day"—in the wake of the friendly-fire incidents, condemnation drowned out commendation.[66]

The matter came to a head in September 1943 when, in a letter to Marshall, Eisenhower stated categorically, "I do not believe in the Airborne *Division*." He continued:

> I believe that airborne troops should be organized in self-contained units comprising infantry, artillery, and special services, all of about the strength of a regimental combat team. Even if one had all of the air transport he could possibly use, the fact is that at any given time and at any given spot, only a reasonable number of air transports can be operated because of technical difficulties. To employ at any time and place a whole division would require dropping over such an extended area that I seriously doubt that a division commander could regain control and operate the scattered forces as one unit. In any event, if these troops were organized in smaller, self-contained units, a senior commander with a small staff and radio communications could always be dropped in the area to insure necessary coordination.[67]

Spurred by Eisenhower's letter, Marshall convened two boards of his own to examine the airborne division concept. The first, headed by Brigadier General Albert Pierson of the 11th Airborne Division, came to naught, for although the board concluded that the "division organization for airborne troops could be supported in combat and recommended that the division be retained," Pierson himself felt the support for this finding was "sketchy."[68]

The second board, chaired by Major General Swing—the same Swing who had already reported once to Eisenhower—comprised paratroop, glider, and troop carrier officers, including glider and transport pilots, who met for several weeks at Camp Mackall, North Carolina, to study every airborne operation, Allied and Axis, of the war to date. Based on that study the board concluded unequivocally that "airborne divisions are tactically sound" and, as stated in Training Memorandum Number 43, emphasized that the "successful employment [of airborne divisions] requires careful and exact planning and coordination with the major ground effort."[69] The most important thing to come out of the Swing Board, however, was Training Circular 113, *Employment of Airborne and Troop Carrier Forces*, which superseded Training Memorandum Number 43 and became the accepted doctrine for all Allied airborne forces for the remainder of the war.

Published in October 1943, and later modified slightly to accommodate changing circumstances, Training Circular 113 not only codified procedures for the planning, coordination, and execution of airborne operations in detail, but also clearly placed the onus for ensuring that this occurred on the theater commander, the *only* one who had the "authority to direct the necessary coordinated action of all land, sea, and air forces in the areas involved." In addition, it mandated that airborne units remain under the theater commander's "direct control" until such time as they were deployed in a subordinate ground commander's area of operations, thereby making them, in effect, strategic and operational assets.[70] In other words, a theater commander was not to divide up his airborne assets among his subordinates, as Eisenhower had done for HUSKY. Instead, theater commanders were to employ them against operational or strategic objectives that would facilitate the successful termination of the campaign or war. This shift of focus would, in the future, have a significant impact on the missions for which airborne divisions were selected and the resources that would be available to support them.

Before validating the Swing Board's recommendations Marshall wanted proof, so he had General Lesley McNair design an exercise to test the principles and procedures set forth in Training Circular 113. Known as the Knollwood Maneuvers, the exercise involved the capture of Knollwood Airport in North Carolina by Swing's 11th Airborne Division (who better to demonstrate the validity of Training Circular 113 than its principal author?). Its goal was "to test the feasibility of loading up an airborne division in its jump transports and gliders, flying a four-hour triangular course—for the most part over water—hitting the drop and landing zones at night under blacked-out conditions, assembling the units into combat formations speedily, and then attacking the defending forces aggressively" and thereby answer once and for all the overarching question of the practicability of airborne divisions.[71] Conducted in December 1943, the six-day exercise was a resounding success. Even McNair, who had opposed the formation of "specialty units" and who had therefore acted as chief umpire of the exercise so that he could observe the results firsthand, had a change of heart. In a letter to Swing, McNair wrote:

> I congratulate you on the splendid performance of your division in the Knollwood Maneuver. After the airborne operations in Africa and Sicily, my staff and I had become convinced of the impracticality of handling large airborne units. I was prepared to recommend to the War Department that airborne divisions be abandoned in our scheme of organization and that the airborne effort be restricted to parachute units of battalion size or smaller. The successful performance of your division has convinced me that we were wrong, and I shall now recommend that we continue our present schedule of activating, training, and committing airborne divisions.[72]

So ended the U.S. Army's debate about the efficacy of airborne divisions, a debate that, ironically, advanced airborne doctrine more than any single event of the war.[73] Now that they were defined as operational and strategic assets, commanders looked to employ them in new ways and in larger numbers. Even Eisenhower changed course and started contemplating ever-larger formations of paratroopers and glider troops—a trend that after Normandy became irresistible.

With the exception of Ridgway, Taylor, and a few others on the division staff, most 82nd troopers were oblivious to the debate raging for and against the retention of airborne divisions. Instead, they concerned themselves with what they had learned in their first experience of combat. A particular point of emphasis was their weapons and equipment.

"Sicily had been a sobering experience," recalled Gavin. "For years [the troopers] had been told that [their] weapons were superior to any [they] would encounter," yet this had not proved true.[74] The bazooka was a noteworthy failure. Too many rockets had bounced off German tanks for the troopers to think otherwise, and to prove their point they conducted tests of their own on captured German vehicles. They concluded that "a larger bore bazooka that could penetrate the front armor of the German Mark VI tank" was the division's most needed weapon."[75] It would be some time before they had one, at least one of U.S. manufacture. The troopers also thought that the M-1 carbine was "unsatisfactory, both from mechanical malfunctioning and ineffectiveness at mid ranges." Conversely, they judged the M-1 Garand "the best weapon in the hands of any troops on either side" and recommended the replacement of all carbines with Garands (most were replaced, including Gavin's that had jammed during his first firefight in Sicily; for the remainder of the war, Gavin carried a Garand). Troopers also thought the .30-caliber machine gun unwieldy; these were replaced with BARs. The 75mm pack howitzer, although not given a thorough test as an indirect-fire weapon, "proved very valuable as an antitank gun," and these, too, were retained, at least in the parachute field artillery battalions (sometime later, the division's glider field artillery battalions replaced their 75mm howitzers with 105mm howitzers).[76]

Packing lists were also modified. Toiletry, extra clothing, and blankets were, in the future, left behind to make room for additional ammunition, mines, grenades, and socks, the last not only because they were essential for foot care, but also because the troopers found that they made great improvised plastic explosive satchels.[77] Because so many equipment containers were lost during the drops, parachute harnesses were adapted so that troopers could jump with their weapons on their body.[78] Finally, mechanical assembly devices (the crickets) were abandoned in favor of simple passwords, which, it was emphasized, had to be the same for all friendly forces.[79]

Operations in western Sicily convinced Ridgway that he needed more vehicles. "The statement that airborne troops are highly specialized, should be reserved for airborne roles, and withdrawn from ground action as early as possible is fallacious," said Ridgway, because he was certain that when ground commanders got control of airborne troopers, they would be reluctant to give them up. Therefore, in order to keep pace with armor and mechanized infantry divisions, and to ensure against the straggling that had plagued the 504th, Ridgway recommended that the airborne division's equipment tables be changed to include two truck companies and more jeeps and trailers.[80] This recommendation was denied, but future operations proved the truth of Ridgway's prediction, while transportation remained a major shortcoming for airborne divisions throughout the war.

On his own authority, Ridgway did make one change as a result of lessons learned in Sicily. He authorized the formation of pathfinder teams. British Bomber Command had already demonstrated the success of its pathfinder units, which it formed specifically to improve navigational and bombing accuracy, and every board that looked into the Sicily drops recommended that similar units be formed in airborne and troop carrier units. Ridgway assigned Captain John Norton the task of working with Lieutenant Colonel Joel Crouch of the 52nd Troop Carrier Command to adapt Bomber Command's pathfinder concept to airborne operations. The two began their work while the division was still on occupation duty in Sicily. Crouch selected the most experienced and proficient transport pilots and navigators in North Africa to form the 1st Pathfinder Group, the air component of the joint team. Norton formed three pathfinder teams, one for each regiment, composed of one officer and five enlisted men. Training with special "halophane" lamps, radio transmitters, radars, smoke grenades, and brightly colored ground panels, Norton's pathfinders and Crouch's aircrews developed techniques and procedures that would be used for the remainder of the war. The concept was simple: The 1st Pathfinder Group would drop the division's pathfinder teams on the planned drop or landing zones about twenty minutes ahead of the main body. The pathfinders would then set up homing and recognition signals on which the follow-on aircraft could orient. If all went well, troopers would be delivered to the correct drop or landing zones, which would facilitate assembly and the quick seizure of assault objectives.[81]

One thing that, in Ridgway's eyes, did not have to be changed as a result of lessons learned in Sicily was the manner by which he trained his troopers. Though outgunned, outnumbered, and scattered throughout the island, his paratroopers had, almost without exception, proved up to the task of combat. Ridgway attributed this to the division's emphasis on small unit training, which compelled junior leaders to display the initiative and leadership that underwrote success on the battlefield. Gavin agreed, writing that if junior leaders "have learned their missions and those of other units working with them and if they have the initiative and moral and physical courage to do something about it, everything will turn out all right."[82]

This emphasis on initiative accrued other benefits as well. Not only did the troopers adapt to the unexpected situations in which they found themselves, but their penchant for action also gained them the upper hand, which was critical given their light armament. "Most people become somewhat mesmerized by the holocaust and the danger to be promptly and energetically ag[g]ressive in a fight," observed Gavin. "That moment, the initial moment of indecision, should be made the most of." Even the more heavily armed Germans, who were "good fighters," could "be beaten badly especially if outsmarted and attacked when they least expect it. Surprise is costly to them always whereas a paratrooper will fight anytime."[83]

Forging a unit in which initiative, aggressiveness, and toughness were so highly valued placed a great deal of responsibility on the higher-ranking officers of that unit to measure up to the same standards. Given what was demanded of them, the 82nd's troopers would not have tolerated officers who remained in the rear when battle was joined. As Ridgway later described the demands he placed on himself and his officers, commanders should be "where the crisis of action is going to happen." Accordingly, once combat is joined, the commander "doesn't belong back at his command post" but should be "where the going is the toughest," and although a senior leader should not "trespass on the sphere of his subordinates," he should be up front to assess the situation, "to drink in, by his senses and all his experience, the actual situation and the human element above all else."[84] In that manner leaders could get a feel for the fight, lend support and reinforcements if necessary, and inspire their troopers by their presence.

In Sicily, Ridgway, Gavin, and Tucker demonstrated beyond doubt that they were tough, aggressive, and competent combat commanders. They led from the front, exposed to enemy fire as much as anyone. Their actions not only earned the troopers' respect but also inspired them with their courage. The effect was electric, especially in a division as small as the 82nd. This was no mass organization; it was an intimate brotherhood. Tales upon which reputations were forged passed quickly through its ranks.

The reputation Ridgway earned in Sicily was that of the intense commander for whom the war was a Manichaean crusade. Although outwardly cool, before a fight Ridgway would get very tense, "almost grinding his teeth" like a police dog straining at its tether.[85] He also personalized the war. According to Gavin, "It was always Ridgway versus the Wehrmacht in my mind. He'd come up to the front and go around the road bend and stand and urinate in the middle of the road. I'd say, 'Matt, get the hell out of there. You'll get shot.' No, he was defiant. Even with his penis he was defiant."[86]

Tucker was a fighter who cared little for anything else. His regiment reflected his personality and during lulls in combat tended to bend the rules. Illustrative of these proclivities is an incident that occurred while Tucker was presiding at a court-martial. According to Gavin, "A soldier got caught driving a stolen jeep. Tucker sat on his court martial. Acquitted him. I said, 'How the hell can you acquit him? He was driving the stolen jeep?' Tucker said, 'He's a good combat soldier; we need him.'"[87]

Gavin was the steely-eyed, soft-spoken commander destined for higher station. Though young, he was too talented, too smart, and too innovative to remain a regimental commander. Many of the tactics and techniques that were employed during the Sicilian campaign were a direct result of his thoughts, theories, and experimentation. But for Gavin, Sicily was more than a test of his theories; it was also a personal test. He wanted to know if he was smart enough, and brave enough, to lead paratroopers in combat. After Sicily, no one doubted that he was. During the fight on Biazzo Ridge, Gavin earned his first Distinguished Service Cross for "cool courageous leadership of the highest order throughout the day's fighting, encouraging and inspiring his men, and by his heroic example achieved decisive success in the face of greatly superior odds."[88] He was that rare commander who is not only respected but worshiped by his men, a sentiment best summed up by Stephen Ambrose (who was writing of Gavin after he took command of the 82nd):

> To indulge in a generalization, one based on four decades of interviewing former GIs but supported by no statistical data, Jim Gavin was the most beloved division commander in the [European theater of operations]. Some veterans can't remember their division commanders' names because there were so many of them, or because they never saw them; others don't want to remember. But veterans of the 82nd get tongue-tied when I ask them how they feel about General Gavin, then burst into a torrent of words—bold, courageous, fair, smart as hell, a man's man, trusted, a leader, beloved.[89]

Sicily had been a good proving ground for the 82nd, and although some in the Allied camp questioned its efficacy, the enemy was decidedly impressed with its performance. Kesselring recognized that although Gavin's combat team had been widely scattered, "Operating as nuisance teams, they considerably impeded the advance of the *Hermann Göring Panzer Division* and helped to prevent it from attacking the enemy promptly after the landings at Gela and elsewhere." The German airborne pioneer Kurt Student echoed Kesselring, calling Allied airborne operations in Sicily decisive "despite the widely scattered drops which must be expected in a night landing," for had it not been for the delay imposed on the *Hermann Göring Division* by American paratroopers, "that Division would have driven the initial seaborne forces back into the sea."[90]

Much had gone wrong during the Allies' first attempt at mass airborne warfare, but once battle was joined, the troopers of the 82nd proved fearsome fighters. This reputation for fearsomeness, worn as a badge of honor, would also prove an albatross. Higher commanders, vaguely familiar with the division's capabilities but knowing beyond a doubt that the troopers were superb fighters, would in the future design plans just so they could use the 82nd. Many of those plans would have assuredly resulted in its destruction. Ironically, the next time the 82nd was committed to combat it was not as a result of a plan. Rather, it was as a result of an emergency that *only* the 82nd could answer.

CHAPTER 8

TAKING OFF FOR THE GATES OF HELL

And it seems to me, too, that the hard decisions are not the ones you make in the heat of battle. Far harder to make are those involved in speaking your mind about some hare-brained scheme which proposes to commit troops to action under conditions where failure is almost certain, and the only results will be the needless sacrifice of priceless lives. When all is said and done, the most precious asset any nation has is its youth, and for a battle commander ever to condone the needless sacrifice of his men is absolutely inexcusable. In any action, you must balance the inevitable cost in lives against the objectives you seek to attain. Unless, beyond any reasonable doubt, the results reasonably to be expected can justify the estimated loss of life the action involves, then for my part I want none of it.

On the other hand, there are occasions in which daring and risky operations, boldly executed, can pay great dividends. One such plan, hastily conceived and carried out with great daring, probably turned the tide in the early days of the Battle of Italy. With only the briefest preparation the 82nd was sent in as a fire brigade and stopped a German drive that was threatening to split the Allied beachhead and drive our attacking forces into the sea.

—MATTHEW B. RIDGWAY,
SOLDIER: THE MEMOIRS OF MATTHEW B. RIDGWAY

THE AMERICAN CHIEFS of Staff had been soundly outmaneuvered by their British colleagues during the Casablanca Conference. So when Churchill and Roosevelt agreed to meet again to discuss post-HUSKY operations, General Marshall, in particular, saw it as an opportunity to professionally redeem himself and, more important, focus the war effort where he felt it ought to be—on a cross-Channel invasion. The resultant conference, code-named TRIDENT, was held in Washington, D.C., from 12 to 25 May 1943.[1]

In reality the American and British positions were not that far apart. The American Chiefs' focus on a cross-Channel invasion, for instance, did not blind them to the possibility of continuing operations in the Mediterranean, which the British proposed; a position paper published by the War Department's joint planning staff conceded that "there were certain merits in operations in the western Mediterranean immediately after HUSKY—to maintain the momentum of HUSKY, utilize resources in the area, furnish support to the USSR, and threaten southern France and Italy." And as Churchill made clear in his opening remarks at TRIDENT, "His Majesty's Government earnestly desired to undertake a full-scale invasion of the Continent from the United Kingdom as soon as a plan offering reasonable prospects of success could be made."[2] But to Churchill and the British Chiefs, the "reasonable prospects of success" could be best secured by expanding operations in the Mediterranean, which, they contended, would force Italy to surrender and Germany to divert more divisions from Western Europe. The Americans, on the other hand, eschewed expanding operations in the Mediterranean because it would divert resources needed for a cross-Channel invasion.

Since the Americans were better prepared than they were at Casablanca, TRIDENT resulted in a decision with which both sides were reasonably comfortable: The British agreed to a 1 May 1944 target date for a cross-Channel invasion (Operation OVERLORD), while the Americans accepted "such operations to follow the conquest of Sicily as were best calculated to eliminate Italy from the war and to contain the greatest number of German forces." At Marshall's insistence, it was also agreed that any post-HUSKY operation would first have to get the unanimous approval of the Combined Chiefs of Staff, thereby allowing him to veto any scheme he felt would detract from preparations for the cross-Channel invasion.[3] Finally, it was left to Eisenhower to propose the post-HUSKY operations, since all agreed that as commander in chief in the Mediterranean, he was best placed to do so.

Desirous of influencing post-HUSKY Mediterranean strategy, Churchill, Brooke, and Lieutenant General Hastings L. "Pug" Ismay, Churchill's chief of staff, left Washington immediately following TRIDENT for Eisenhower's headquarters in Algiers. At Churchill's request, Marshall traveled with them so that it would not appear that the British were attempting to undermine the TRIDENT agreements.[4] Arriving in Algiers in late May—five weeks before HUSKY—Churchill, Brooke, and Ismay tried persuading Eisenhower that landings on the Italian peninsula would be the best course of action following victory in Sicily. But Eisenhower refused to be pinned to any specific operation, feeling that

> he would be able to determine early in the campaign for Sicily the attitude and defensive strength of the Italians on the mainland. If Sicily proved to be relatively easy, this would be an index which would dictate an immediate follow-up of a bridgehead on the toe of Italy across the Messina Strait. If the Italians fought stubbornly in Sicily, . . . then [the Allies] would be confronted with a long campaign, fighting for each hilltop. This would tie down [Allied] forces. It was simply too early, he emphasized, to make a firm commitment now, but, like the P[rime] M[inister], he didn't want to lose any opportunity for exploitation that presented itself.[5]

By way of compromise, Marshall suggested that Eisenhower set up two planning staffs, each of which would prepare plans for a different post-HUSKY operation: one against Sardinia and Corsica (the American preference) and one against southern Italy. In this way, without committing to any specific course of action, Eisenhower would at least have two post-HUSKY plans ready. Then, in light of the Axis reaction to HUSKY, Eisenhower could gauge which plan would be most advantageous and, following concurrence by the Combined Chiefs, execute it with minimal delay. When all agreed to Marshall's proposal, Eisenhower assigned the Italian plan to the British and the Sardinia-Corsica plan to Mark Clark's Fifth Army (the Corsica operation subsequently evolved into a wholly French affair, planned and executed by Free French forces in North Africa).[6]

By 15 July, five days into HUSKY, it had become glaringly apparent that, in the words of Major General George V. Strong, Marshall's intelligence chief, "Italian combat power had deteriorated to the point where the Allies could assume calculated risks in dealing with Italy." To that end, Strong recommended "prompt action against the Italian mainland," citing Naples as the most lucrative target. A landing at Naples, Strong felt, would avoid protracted land operations in Calabria (the Italian toe), rule out an Axis defensive stand anchored on Naples, give the Allies a major port, and provide aid to the Soviets, who, at the time, were battling the Germans at Kursk. Impressed with Strong's presentation, Marshall brought it to the attention of the Combined Chiefs the next day. The British were stunned, believing that their arguments had finally borne fruit. In reality, Marshall saw the Naples option as a "device to gain all the advantages of a position in Italy—as far north as Rome—as quickly and as cheaply as possible, thereby ensuring rather than impeding the success of OVERLORD."[7] Regardless, the misunderstanding smoothed the way for quick and unanimous agreement among the Combined Chiefs, who then forwarded it to Eisenhower for study.[8]

Eisenhower met with his subordinate commanders to discuss Strong's recommendation on 17 July. Although unable to gain a consensus for or against the Naples scheme, they agreed that if they were going to attack the Italian mainland, they should do so as soon as possible after securing Sicily to keep the enemy off balance and deny him the chance to recover.[9] Accordingly, Eisenhower requested that he be granted the authority to decide where and when to invade the Italian mainland without having to seek the approval of the Combined Chiefs. He received this permission two days later.[10]

The fall of Mussolini on 25 July lent further impetus to an invasion of the Italian mainland, especially for the Combined Chiefs, who sent another message to Eisenhower urging him to seriously consider landing a force near Naples at the earliest possible date in anticipation of Italy's collapse. To sweeten the deal, they offered Eisenhower one light and four escort carriers previously earmarked for the cross-Channel invasion. They also sent him a staff study on the feasibility of and possible options for an amphibious assault in the vicinity of Naples.[11]

Riding this wave of support for a landing at Naples, Eisenhower told Clark to quit work on Sardinia and start drawing up plans based on the staff study. The operation would be known as AVALANCHE. According to that study the best place for an amphibious assault was south of Naples in the Gulf of Salerno. The advantages of landing there were the underwater gradients, which would allow large warships to come in close to support the landings; the two small ports in the area, one at Salerno and the other at Amalfi, that would facilitate the unloading of supplies; and the fairly robust road network running inland from the ports over which supplies could be transshipped to the front. Moreover, the gulf was within range of Allied fighters based in Sicily, though just barely, but as the study pointed out, this risk could be mitigated by the capture of Montecorvino airfield, a few miles inland of the beaches, for use as a forward operating base.[12]

Of course, landing in the Gulf of Salerno was not without its disadvantages, three of which were fairly significant. A steep-banked river, the Sele, bisected the proposed landing area, making lateral movement within the beachhead difficult. Mountains inland of the beaches would also limit the initial depth of penetration and give the defenders a positional advantage. Finally, the mountainous Sorrento Peninsula, just north of the proposed invasion area, cut the gulf off from Naples, the ultimate prize.[13] But as Eisenhower saw things, if anyone could overcome these disadvantages, it was Mark Clark.

In a letter to Marshall, Eisenhower called Clark "the best organizer, planner and trainer of troops I have met" who was superb at "preparing the minute details of requisitions, landing craft, training of troops and so on, [and] he has no equal in our Army." Eisenhower also thought highly of Clark's Fifth Army staff, which many thought "a collection of very brilliant men, exceptionally so."[14] Yet neither Clark nor his staff could foresee the effect events beyond their control would have on the landings at Salerno, events that, taken together, would turn AVALANCHE from an opportunity into a near disaster.

Clark's overall concept for AVALANCHE was to get overwhelming combat power ashore as quickly as possible, establish a firm beachhead by taking control of the surrounding mountains, capture Montecorvino airfield, and then rush north to take Naples. With Naples and its port in hand, he could then debark the rest of his army and continue the attack toward Rome. To accomplish this the Fifth Army staff fashioned a plan for the simultaneous landing of two corps—the British X and U.S. VI Corps—in the Gulf of Salerno. Landing on the left with two divisions abreast (the British 46th Infantry Division in the north and the British 56th Infantry Division in the south), the British X Corps, under Lieutenant General Sir Richard L. McCreery, was to be Clark's main effort. Its tasks were to land north of the Sele River, secure the bridges spanning the river, seize the port of Salerno, capture Montecorvino airfield, take the rail and road center of Battipaglia (located about six miles inland), and gain possession of the mountainous passes on the Sorrento Peninsula leading to Naples. The U.S. VI Corps, under Major General Ernest J. Dawley, was to land south of the Sele River with one division in the lead, the Texas National Guard's 36th Infantry, and protect the army's right flank by seizing the high ground to the east and south of the Salerno Plain.[15]

Eisenhower also allocated the 82nd to AVALANCHE, although, remarkably, neither Eisenhower's nor Clark's headquarters bothered to tell Ridgway. Nor had anyone at either headquarters given any thought to regrouping and reconstituting the 82nd so that it could prepare. Meanwhile, the division's paratroopers, spread all over western Sicily, were in dire need of resupply. Having been provided nothing but food, water, and ammunition since jumping in, they were wearing the same uniforms they arrived with, and many of their weapons required repair or replacement.[16] In addition, the two parachute regiments required about a thousand replacements, all of which were located at the division's base camp in Kairouan, Tunisia, along with the rest of the 82nd.[17] Anxious to integrate his replacements and refit the division so that it would be ready when next called, Ridgway crisscrossed the Mediterranean, speaking with anyone who would listen, pleading for transportation so he could get his paratroopers back to Kairouan. It was while on one of these trips that he learned about AVALANCHE and, much to his surprise, that plans to use the 82nd in the invasion were already well advanced.

What Ridgway found was that although the Fifth Army staff had done nothing to prepare the 82nd for AVALANCHE, they were keen "to prove to the world . . . that they were bold thinkers, quick to seize upon and utilize a new and dramatic weapon." And because they were "new" and "dramatic," wrote Ridgway, "airborne divisions were particularly vulnerable to these noble experiments."[18] As a result, Fifth Army engaged in "a fantasia of planning," working feverishly to somehow "fit" the 82nd into its scheme of maneuver. This, in turn, forced the 82nd to rub "Aladdin's magical lamp and [turn] out detailed plans for mission after mission as fast as Fifth Army revised its plans for the invasion."[19] So hectic was this planning effort that the division's staff officers quipped that what the code name for the operation really described was "the avalanche of airborne plans and papers that engulfed them."[20]

The first plan the Fifth Army conjured for the 82nd envisioned both an airborne and an amphibious assault on the Sorrento Peninsula to facilitate the debouchment of the British X Corps onto the Plain of Naples. Ridgway objected to this plan because it called for a night drop, and he would "not recommend a night parachute operation until I can be shown by actual demonstration in training that the Air Corps can put down in a selected area units of the size of battalions."[21] Air planners also maintained that "it would be extremely difficult if not impossible to land paratroopers effectively in that area because of treacherous air currents sweeping around Mount Vesuvius [a few miles northwest of the intended drop area], the limited space in which transport planes could be brought to a low altitude, and the intense enemy anti-aircraft concentrations nearby."[22] Hence, on 12 August, the Sorrento Peninsula operation was canceled.[23] In its place a second operation was tabled, code-named GIANT.

As originally conceived, Operation GIANT (later renamed GIANT I) called for an even bolder use of the 82nd—an airborne and amphibious operation along the Volturno River, some forty miles north of the invasion beaches, in order to "prevent movement of hostile forces south across the VOLTURNO towards the NAPLES Area, [and] to assist the Fifth Army's attack of the NAPLES Area from the Southeast."[24] To accomplish this both parachute regiments and their supporting troops, one gliderborne field artillery battalion, and two gliderborne antitank batteries would drop on the night of D-1/D day along the length of the Volturno from Triflisco to the sea. Simultaneously, a seaborne task force formed around the 325th would land at the mouth of the Volturno and fight its way inland. Once united, the division was to destroy all crossings over the Volturno from Triflisco to the coast, a straight-line distance of approximately nineteen miles but more than double that when measured along the flow of the meandering river. If successful, GIANT I would seal off southern Italy from the bulk of the German forces then on the peninsula, which were still north of Rome.[25] It was anticipated that linkup with the British X Corps would occur within five days, but if not, the division would either hold along the river, fall back on Naples, or disappear into the rugged interior.

GIANT I was a fantastic proposal and given what eventually transpired would almost certainly have resulted in the destruction of the 82nd Airborne Division. Fortunately, the plan began to disintegrate almost as soon as it was put on paper. First, naval planners announced that sandbars at the mouth of the Volturno prohibited the landing of a large force, so the seaborne effort was reduced, first to a battalion, then to a company, until finally the amphibious landings were canceled altogether and a heavy naval bombardment substituted. This, in turn, presented a problem for the airborne task force because it was to have been resupplied by sea. Without a seaborne line of communication the airborne task force would require the aerial delivery of some 175 tons of supplies per day for as long as it was out of contact with Fifth Army. When faced with this requirement, the air planners blanched. An aerial resupply effort of this magnitude would require the daily commitment of 90 to 145 planes, or 30 percent to 45 percent of all the C-47s in the Mediterranean. Additionally, the planes would have to fly unescorted since the Volturno was well beyond the range of the Sicily-based fighters. Hence, the magnitude of the resupply mission forced a reduction of the size of the airborne force to two battalions and a scaling back of the mission to one of simply destroying the Volturno bridges at Capua, located fifteen miles inland.[26]

Ridgway was appalled at the prospect of GIANT I in any size and said so, but his protests fell on deaf ears, as did his pleas to get his paratroopers back to North Africa in sufficient time to prepare. Although he insisted that the 82nd needed at least three weeks to complete the detailed planning and coordination necessary to avoid a repeat of the Sicily fiasco, it was not until after the end of the Sicilian campaign (Messina, the last major city, fell on 17 August) that Ridgway obtained the aircraft needed to move his paratroopers back to Kairouan, a move that was not completed until 21 August.[27] With D day for AVALANCHE (and GIANT I) set for the evening of 8–9 September, there was little time to lose.

Immediately upon returning to North Africa, the paratroopers began a crash program of refitting, reorganizing, and integrating replacements that Ridgway placed in Gavin's charge, who, with the death of Keerans, became the 82nd's de facto assistant division commander. The program centered on a tough training regimen designed "to imbue the replacements with the high degree of morale and esprit de corps" of the division, including a week of joint training with the troop carrier command, although competing demands on the transport aircraft limited the size of the drops.[28] Meanwhile, the 1/325th, 2/325th, and 3/504th plus supporting elements moved to Bizerte, Tunisia, under the command of Colonel Lewis to prepare for the amphibious landings called for in the initial draft of GIANT I. When the amphibious landings were subsequently canceled, Lewis's mission was changed—he was to constitute Fifth Army's reserve and be prepared for employment as needed.[29]

But before Clark could implement GIANT I, even in its much reduced form, the operation was canceled and the 82nd was stripped from Fifth Army control. The reason was not immediately clear. Then, on the morning of 2 September, there arrived at Kairouan a cryptic message instructing General Taylor to report to Alexander's 15th Army Group headquarters in Sicily immediately. Later on that day Ridgway received a similar order: He was to meet General Spaatz at La Marsa, Tunisia. When Ridgway arrived, Spaatz told him that secret negotiations for an Italian surrender were under way, that this may portend a new mission for the 82nd, and that Ridgway, too, was to report to Alexander's headquarters. What he learned when he arrived was startling.[30]

Following the fall of Mussolini, conspirators in Italy's *Comando Supremo* began pushing the new head of the Italian government, Maresciallo d'Italia Pietro Badoglio, and the country's aging monarch, King Victor Emmanuel III, to conclude a separate peace with the Allies. Following weeks of equivocation the lead conspirator, Generale di Brigata Giuseppe Castellano, received approval to open secret preliminary discussions with the Allies. To do so, he traveled in disguise to neutral Portugal, where, on 17 August, he met with the British ambassador in Lisbon and divulged his purpose. Two days later, General Walter Bedell "Beetle" Smith and British Brigadier Kenneth Strong, Eisenhower's intelligence chief, arrived in Lisbon to see what Castellano had to say and table Eisenhower's surrender terms, which Castellano brought back with him to Rome.

After more wrangling in the Italian high command, Castellano traveled to Alexander's headquarters to continue the negotiations. Meeting again with Smith and Strong, along with Alexander and a host of other military and diplomatic representatives, Castellano made it clear that "one of the conditions of the armistice . . . [was] that Allied military support be given the Italians at Rome to protect their capital city and the Vatican from the Germans when and if the armistice is announced."[31] Castellano added that a minimum of one armored and one airborne division would be required for this task.

After conferring with Eisenhower, Smith countered that the Allies could provide only the airborne division to protect Rome, but it would be dropped in concert with a larger amphibious operation (AVALANCHE) somewhere else in Italy. Again Castellano returned to Rome, and again he encountered squabbling. Finally, Victor Emmanuel summoned the courage to make a decision and ordered Castellano to return to Sicily to sign the terms of surrender, which Castellano did on 3 September, although by mutual agreement the surrender was not to be made public until 8 September, just before the first troops waded ashore at Salerno.[32]

When Taylor, Ridgway, and a small group of 82nd staff officers arrived at 15th Army Group Headquarters on the evening of 2 September, they were told nothing more than that the Italians were prepared to surrender. How and why this required their involvement was a mystery. Only after the negotiations were almost complete did Alexander and his deputy chief of staff, U.S. Brigadier General Lyman L. Lemnitzer, brief them about a tentative drop on Rome. The next day, with the surrender signed, Lemnitzer codified the concept for the drop in writing. Under Alexander's direct command and "in cooperation with Italian forces and not subordinate thereto," the 82nd Airborne Division was:

> a. On the night of D-1–D-day, and on subsequent nights as required, to land the maximum force in the ROME Area, either by dropping or in air transports, or both, as the situation dictates.
>
> b. To provide moral and physical reinforcement for the Italian forces located in the Rome Area.
>
> c. In cooperation with these Italian forces, secure the City of Rome and adjacent airfields and prevent their occupation by German forces.[33]

With this mission in hand Ridgway, Taylor, and the division planners, along with Lemnitzer and representatives from Eisenhower's air staff, met with Castellano and his delegation to work out the details of the drop, codenamed GIANT II. According to Castellano, the Italians had four divisions in and around Rome and did not lack men. What they did lack was firepower, especially antitank guns and artillery. The Germans, he continued, had two divisions in the immediate vicinity of Rome and four more within a few days' march. The Germans had also emplaced a number of antiaircraft batteries along the Tiber River, but Castellano promised that the Italians would silence the batteries before the drop, which would be on six Italian-held airfields around Rome. Castellano also promised that a high-ranking Italian military officer would be present at each of the airfields and would be prepared to offer whatever assistance the Americans required, from trucks to shovels. There would also be a five-hundred-man labor force to aid the Americans in setting up a defense of Rome.[34]

Ridgway was skeptical. This scheme was even more far-fetched than GIANT I. But what really disturbed Ridgway was his feeling that the Italians were promising more than they could deliver. He became even more suspicious when, after a short break, the Italians changed their story, saying that they could not guarantee they could silence all the antiaircraft defenses along the Tiber and that therefore the initial drops would have to occur on airfields some twenty-five miles north of Rome, with follow-on insertions at three airfields nearer to the center of the city once the initial force secured them.[35] Increasingly anxious and leery of Italian promises, Ridgway sought an audience with General Smith. According to Ridgway:

> I stated that I felt it my responsibility as Division Commander to express my views frankly on the contemplated mission; that within the past few days the Division had been assigned two different missions in a distant area; and that now with only four full days for preparation, two of which would have to be employed for air movement of the Division from TUNISIA to SICILY [in order to get the transport planes within range of Rome], I was about to receive a mission involving the employment of over three hundred aircraft in a new area. I stated that in my opinion this mission, under these conditions, violated every sound principle we had developed in our training, and that my conscience compelled me to state my strong objections. General SMITH supported this view and directed me to restate these opinions to General ALEXANDER.[36]

When Ridgway met with Alexander, the latter "treated the whole matter in a cavalier fashion, making light of the enemy situation, apparently giving full faith to the Italian guarantees of full military support, and exhibiting startling ignorance of the logistics of airborne operations."[37] From Alexander's perspective, the Italians would not have surrendered had not the Allies promised a drop on Rome, and it was therefore imperative that GIANT II happen. However, because of Castellano's equivocation about the antiaircraft batteries along the Tiber, which were especially worrisome in light of what had occurred in Sicily, Alexander agreed to scale back the initial assault force to just two parachute battalions. The remainder of the 82nd would be inserted as the situation permitted, including Lewis's amphibious forces at Bizerte, which were to be prepared to land at the mouth of the Tiber.[38]

Following his audience with Alexander, Ridgway briefed his staff on the changes to the plan and sent them back to Kairouan to work out the final details and prepare the division for combat (which included moving the bulk of the division back to Sicily, where it would stage for Rome). He then cloistered himself with Taylor. Castellano's hedging had both men worried; he seemed too willing to make promises, anything to get the Allies committed to the defense of Rome. They also sensed that Castellano's ardor was not shared by everyone in the Italian government and agreed that someone ought to get to Rome to ascertain the truth. Alexander had already vetoed a scheme to do so, but, using "Beetle" Smith as an intermediary, Ridgway floated the idea by Alexander a second time. Taylor, a linguist who spoke French and "could get along all right in Italian," had "very gallantly offered to go in personally," as did Colonel William T. Gardiner of the Troop Carrier Command.[39] This time Alexander approved.[40]

Taylor and Gardiner left Sicily aboard a British PT boat early in the morning on 7 September, disguised as airmen who had ditched their plane at sea. The British transported them to Ustica, a small island approximately forty miles north of Palermo, where they transferred to an Italian corvette that took them to Gaeta, Italy. When they arrived at 1950 hours, they were bundled into a military sedan and taken to the outskirts of town, where they transferred to an ambulance for the final ride to Rome. They arrived at the Pallazzo Caprara, opposite the Italian War Office, at nightfall and were met by a delegation of military officers led by Colonel Giorgio Salvi, chief of staff to General di Corpo d'Armata Giacomo Carboni, commander of the Italian corps manning Rome's outer defenses. The Italians insisted that their guests eat, clean up, rest, and begin negotiations in the morning. "It appeared," recalled Gardiner, "that they were attempting to stall, and later it was evident that they did not expect us to move so fast: it was stated that they had expected our operation September tenth to fifteenth, but nearer the fifteenth." Taylor insisted that time was of the essence, so Salvi contacted his boss, Carboni, who arrived at 2130 hours.[41]

Carboni "immediately launched upon an expose [*sic*] of his views of the military situation in the Rome area." He began by outlining the disposition of German forces around Rome, which was not news to Taylor or Gardiner, who had been well briefed on the German situation in Italy. What did surprise them was Carboni's opinion about GIANT II. Unlike Castellano, who declared the drop on Rome a prerequisite for Italy's surrender, Carboni insisted it would be a disaster.[42] According to Gardiner, Carboni stated:

> If the Italians declare an armistice, the Germans will occupy Rome, and the Italians can do little to prevent it. The simultaneous arrival of U.S. airborne troops would only provoke the Germans to more drastic action. Furthermore the Italians would be unable to secure the airfields, cover the assembly

> and provide the desired logistical aid to the airborne troops. If it must be assumed that an Allied seaborne landing is impossible North of Rome, then the only hope of saving the capital is to avoid overt acts against the Germans and await the effect of the Allied attacks in the South. He stated that he knew that the Allied landings would be at Salerno [which surprised Taylor and Gardiner], which was too far [a]way to aid directly in the defense of Rome. He stated that General [Mario] Roatta [chief of the Army staff], shared his views.[43]

Because of Carboni's "alarming pessimism," which the Americans felt not only colored his views but might also affect his conduct were GIANT II launched, Taylor suggested that the matter be brought to the head of state. Carboni agreed and arranged to have the Americans meet Badoglio at his residence.[44]

Carboni, Taylor, and Gardiner arrived at Badoglio's villa around midnight. Carboni first saw Badoglio alone, after which Taylor and Gardiner were ushered in. Standing before the Americans in his pajamas, Badoglio echoed Carboni's views: The Italians were too weak to resist the Germans, an airborne drop on Rome would unnecessarily provoke the Germans, and therefore GIANT II must be canceled. Taylor asked Badoglio "if he realized how deeply his government was committed by the agreements entered into by the Castellano mission." Badoglio replied "that the situation had changed and that General Castellano had not known all the facts." Stunned by this backpedaling, Taylor asked Badoglio if he would draft a message to Eisenhower that reflected this change of heart. Badoglio agreed, writing, "Due to changes in the situation brought about by the disposition and strength of the German forces in the Rome area, it is no longer possible to accept an immediate armistice as this could provoke the occupation of the capital and the violent assumption of the government by the Germans." Taylor, too, wrote a message for Eisenhower, stating that since Carboni could not provide what Castellano had promised, GIANT II was impossible.[45]

Carboni, Taylor, and Gardiner then returned to the Pallazzo Caprara, where both messages were transmitted to the waiting Allies in Sicily and North Africa. At 0800 hours, 8 September, Taylor received word that Allied Force Headquarters in Algiers had received the message, although nothing was said about GIANT II. Concerned that the drop was still on, takeoff for which was slated for 1745 hours that day, Taylor sent a second message at 0820 hours, emphasizing that American airborne forces were not wanted, "as their arrival would bring an immediate attack on Rome." By 1135 hours, having still received no positive assurance that GIANT II had been canceled, Taylor sent a third message: "Situation innocuous" (*innocuous* was the code word Taylor was to use to cancel the operation). Then, having done all they could, Taylor and Gardiner were again trundled into an ambulance and taken to Centocelle airfield, where they boarded an Italian bomber for their return trip to North Africa, where they arrived at 1905 hours, 8 September.[46]

Somehow, despite Taylor's three messages, Tucker's 504th (the 1/504th and 2/504th; the 3/504th was still at Bizerte, less one company), which was to lead the drop on Rome, did not get the word until after several planes had taken off. Fortunately, they were easily recalled, and although the fiery Tucker may have been disappointed, the news met with general approval in the ranks.[47] Few, if any, troopers were enamored of the idea of fighting alongside the Italians. As Captain Edwin Sayre said, "Well, having captured three thousand of them in the last two weeks, I really wasn't very confident that the Italians were going to be all that much help."[48] Based on what he had learned during his trip to Rome, Taylor, too, was relieved:

> In light of what we know today, had we decided to go ahead with Giant II in spite of the refusal of the Italians to cooperate with us, we could never have introduced more than the first night's increment of about 2,500 troops, fewer than a full regimental combat [team]. They would have landed twenty-five miles from Rome with no trucks, few supplies, and limited ammunition. With surprise lost after the first night's landing, and no Italian antiaircraft defense of the airfields, the German air force would never have allowed further reinforcements to arrive from Sicily by air, and our men on the ground would have been on their own with no assurance that the Italian forces would be even friendly to them. What they could have accomplished under these circumstances I certainly do not know, but I have never regretted the decision which spared these elite troops to serve their country with distinction at Salerno, Anzio, Normandy, and elsewhere rather than end their useful days in Italian graves or German prisons.[49]

Gavin concurred. After the war he visited the airfields on which his regiment would have dropped on day two of the operation and concluded that "the decision to cancel was the proper one."[50] For him this was especially poignant following "the soul cleansing experience of seeing what flak can do to C-47's in Sicily."[51] Yet no one was more relieved when GIANT II was canceled than Ridgway, who saw the whole affair in moral terms. How far should he go in speaking his mind about a "hare-brained scheme" certain to fail and end with the needless sacrifice of his troopers? After the war, he wrote, "And when the time comes that I must meet my Maker, the source of most humble pride to me will not be accomplishments in battle, but the fact that I was guided to make the decision to oppose this thing, at the risk of my career, right up to the top. There were other operations which I opposed, on similar grounds, but this was the one of greatest magnitude, and I deeply and sincerely believe that by taking the stand I took we saved the lives of thousands of brave men."[52]

Because of the last-minute cancellation of GIANT II, when Clark's Fifth Army hit the Salerno beaches on 9 September, the 82nd was without a mission; although Alexander returned the division to Fifth Army control when the Rome drop was called off, there was not enough time to turn GIANT I back on.[53] Scattered among ten airfields on Sicily, the troopers stood by and listened to news from the front.[54] Gavin was certain that Clark would eventually have a mission for them, "but very likely not [for] the entire division."[55] As it turned out Gavin was incorrect; in due course the entire division would be fighting at Salerno, although not under Ridgway's command. There was, in fact, one division element that had already sailed for Italy.

Task Force Bertsch was an amphibious task force under the command of Lieutenant Colonel William H. Bertsch, the 319th Glider Field Artillery commander, consisting of the 319th; A, B, and C Batteries of the 80th Airborne Antiaircraft Battalion; H Company of the 3/504th; some signal and engineer troopers; and several platoons of tank destroyers. It had been formed from Lewis's force, which was still at Bizerte, for the purpose of landing at the mouth of the Tiber River in support of a drop on Rome and had already set sail when GIANT II was canceled, after which Bertsch received orders to alter his course for the Gulf of Salerno. When he arrived Clark told him to sail to Maiori on the Sorrento Peninsula, disembark, and attach himself and his task force to Lieutenant Colonel William O. Darby's Ranger Force, which was fighting to open the passes leading to Naples. Task Force Bertsch remained under Darby's control and fought alongside the Rangers until 30 September, when it again reverted to Ridgway's control.[56]

Ridgway's temporary loss of Task Force Bertsch was but precursor to the wholesale parceling out of the 82nd to other headquarters, leaving Ridgway, at one point, a division commander without a division to command. This, of course, bothered Ridgway to no end, but since Alexander had given the 82nd to Clark, it was Clark's to do with as he wished. Moreover, it was about this time that Eisenhower became convinced that airborne divisions should be broken up into smaller, more manageable formations (Eisenhower sent his infamous "I do not believe in the Airborne *Division*" letter on 20 September). Hence, Ridgway got no succor from the theater commander when, on 11 September, Clark took from Ridgway the rest of Lewis's force.

By that time the situation on the Salerno beachhead was critical, so Clark ordered Ridgway to send over as much infantry as could be packed aboard nine landing craft that Alexander had recently released for Fifth Army's use.[57] Ridgway complied by embarking his troopers stranded at Bizerte under

Lewis's command. Sailing on 13 September, Lewis's hodgepodge force waded ashore at Salerno on 15 September to find, surprisingly, that the division's paratroopers were already there.[58]

The presence of the 82nd's paratroopers at Salerno was the direct result of two strategic miscalculations by the Allied high command. The first was that the Italian surrender would compel a German withdrawal to northern Italy. The second was that Montgomery's Eighth Army, advancing from the south, would tie down any remaining German forces and, by the time AVALANCHE was launched, would be within supporting distance of Clark's Fifth Army.[59]

At first it appeared that the strategic calculations were correct. Nine hours before Clark's Fifth Army hit the beaches at Salerno, Eisenhower made a radio address from his headquarters in Algiers announcing the Italian surrender. The news prompted "scenes of sheer joy" among Tommies and GIs aboard the assault vessels who, in light of the announcement, fully expected to "dock in Naples harbor unopposed, with an olive branch in one hand and an opera ticket in the other."[60] And when they landed, it seemed their hopes had been borne out. Enemy resistance at Salerno was slight. The few Germans in the area were easily driven off, and by nightfall both of Clark's corps were firmly established ashore. Montgomery's Eighth Army, which had landed on the toe of Italy on 3 September, was also advancing against scant German resistance.[61] Consequently, it seemed that the Germans had withdrawn and the Eighth and Fifth Armies would soon be joined.

But the Germans had not withdrawn and, though surprised by the Italian surrender, were not unprepared. They had long been infiltrating units into Italy in anticipation of either an Italian collapse or its surrender, and when combined with the forces they already had in place and those they had evacuated from Sicily, they had more than enough strength to take over the defense of the peninsula themselves.[62] Additionally, immediately following Eisenhower's announcement Kesselring broadcast the signal "bring in the harvest," which activated *Operation Achse* (Axis), a contingency plan he had drawn up just in case this were to occur. Upon receipt of the signal, German units throughout Italy disarmed their former allies. Italian commanders, on the other hand, told their soldiers not to fight anyone, German, British, or American, and "simply to pretend that the war had gone away."[63] In fact, so submissive were the Italians to German demands that the only casualty incurred as a result of *Operation Achse* was one Italian general, who, when pressed to surrender, "indignantly refused and was shot out of hand."[64]

Kesselring next put in train his plans for the defense of Italy, which called not for a withdrawal but rather a defense in depth across the length and breadth of Italy with the intent of exploiting the difficult Italian terrain to keep

Clark bottled up on the Salerno beachhead and Montgomery's Eighth Army from coming to his aid. Kesselring also took advantage of Montgomery's tentativeness by committing no more than the minimal combat power needed to keep the Eighth Army from advancing with alacrity. This, in turn, freed up other German units to respond to the Salerno landings, which, in German eyes, "represent[ed] the main danger to the whole of the German forces in Southern Italy."[65]

What this spelled for Clark was near disaster. Not only had the Germans not reacted to the Italian surrender as predicted, but because they no longer had to coordinate their actions with the Italians, they responded to the Salerno landings with unanticipated speed. Kesselring's principal ground force commander, General der Panzertruppen Heinrich von Vietinghoff, the commander of the German *Tenth Army*, anticipated an Allied landing in the Naples-Salerno area and had positioned the *16th Panzer Division* along the heights surrounding the beachhead.[66] Although the *16th Panzer* was spread too thin to make a vigorous defense of the initial landings, which accounted for the sparse resistance the Allies encountered on D day, within four days Vietinghoff had reinforced his Salerno defenses with three more divisions—the *15th Panzer*, *29th Panzer Grenadier*, and the *Hermann Göring*—while Kesselring kept the slow-moving Montgomery at bay and out of supporting distance with a hodgepodge of lesser units.[67]

Once reinforced, Vietinghoff attacked all along the periphery of the Salerno beachhead and, aided by temporary Luftwaffe air superiority, successfully contained the Allies on the beaches, thereby thwarting Clark's plans for a quick thrust to Naples. Clark reacted by shifting his corps boundaries and shuttling forces from the southern American sector to the hard-hit British in the north. In doing so, he widened a gap between his two corps that had existed since D day (before retreating, the few Germans encountered on D day blew the bridges over the Sele River, which was what created the gap in the first place). One lone engineer battalion was all he could spare to cover the gap because the U.S. 36th Infantry Division, Clark's southernmost unit, was stretched thin covering some thirty-five miles of mountainous terrain.[68]

By 13 September, Vietinghoff sensed that the Allies were contemplating a withdrawal from Salerno. The arrival of additional ships off the coast, the heavy use of smoke in the British sector, and the gap he discovered in the Allied lines all pointed to this possibility. He decided therefore to attack to destroy them before they could escape. Massing elements of the *16th Panzer* and the *29th Panzer Grenadier Divisions*, he thrust into the Sele River corridor. The defending Americans broke and ran. More than five hundred U.S. soldiers were lost. By 1830 hours, having fought their way well inside the gap, the only thing facing the Germans was two American artillery battalions and behind that the Fifth Army Command Post itself, established in the ruins of the sixth-century B.C. Greek colony at Paestum.[69]

That night, a German *Tenth Army* war diarist wrote, "The battle for Salerno . . . appears to be over." Many in Fifth Army felt likewise. So when Clark assembled his commanders and staff that evening, the discussion inevitably turned to evacuation.[70] But first Clark tabled three other options.

The best course of action would have been to spur on the Eighth Army, but Montgomery's deliberateness and the masterful fighting withdrawal by German forces to his front left him too far away to impact events at Salerno.[71]

A second option was to increase naval and air support to the beleaguered Fifth Army. Admiral Cunningham had already ordered the battleships *Valiant* and *Warspite* to Salerno, but they would not arrive until 15 September. Eisenhower also diverted some heavy bombers from their long-range bombing missions to targets nearer the Salerno beachhead, but this, too, was insufficient, especially given the close proximity of the opposing ground forces. Moreover, Allied carrier-based fighters had expended almost all their fuel and ammunition while Allied fighters flying from Sicily were at the extreme limit of their range and largely ineffective. The British had seized Montecorvino airfield on day two of the battle, but it remained under German artillery fire and was unusable. On the other hand, the Luftwaffe had been massing as many as 120 aircraft over the beachhead, wreaking havoc with the forces on the beach and the ships offshore.[72]

The last option was to bring in reinforcements. At the time there were four uncommitted divisions in the Mediterranean—the 82nd Airborne (less its glider forces and one parachute battalion) and U.S. 3rd Infantry Division in Sicily and the U.S. 1st Armored and 34th Infantry Divisions in North Africa—but a paucity of landing craft ruled out the quick movement of the armored and infantry divisions. Hence, "the only hope for quick help appeared to rest with the 82d Airborne Division." According to Major Yarborough (formerly of the 2/504th), who was serving as Clark's airborne adviser and was with him at Paestum, at the height of the crisis, "when the going was really tough, when the whole 5th Army headquarters was in the weeds no higher than your waist and crawling around on their hands and knees, the four stars and the three stars and everybody else all together," Clark turned to Yarborough "to see what could be done about bringing some parachute reinforcements in."[73]

Yarborough put together a hasty plan to get the 82nd's paratroopers into the bridgehead to shore up the lines. Captain Jacob R. Hamilton, a fighter pilot who had made an emergency landing on the beachhead, volunteered to deliver the plan, along with a personal letter from Clark to Ridgway. Following a harrowing flight out of Salerno, Hamilton arrived at Licata field in Sicily at 1330 hours, 13 September, where he was greeted by Eaton and Gavin; Ridgway had just departed by plane to inspect the division's far-flung bivouac sites. Recalled by the airfield tower, Ridgway returned to receive Yarborough's rough plan and Clark's letter. "I want you to accept this letter as an order, [wrote Clark]. I realize the time normally needed to prepare for a drop, but this is an exception. I want you to drop within our lines on the beachhead and I want you to make it tonight. This is a must." Two hours later, Hamilton was on his way back to Salerno with Ridgway's response: "Can do."[74]

Yarborough's plan called for regimental drops on successive nights onto a 1,200-by-800-foot drop zone located just behind the front lines. Taking off from multiple airfields at 2040 hours that evening, the 52nd Troop Carrier Wing's transports would rendezvous at Cape Rasocolmo, just north of Messina, then fly up the west coast of Italy to the Salerno beachhead. Once they were within range, Yarborough would illuminate the drop zone with flaming five-gallon cans of gasoline-soaked sand arranged in a giant *T*. Additional navigational guidance would be provided by the division's pathfinders, who would drop three minutes ahead of the main body and set up their homing and radar equipment. For the first night's drop, Ridgway selected Tucker's 504th Parachute Regiment (less the 3rd Battalion, which was sailing to Salerno with Lewis's 325th Glider Infantry Regiment), reinforced with C Company, 307th Airborne Engineer Battalion. Gavin's 505th and the independent 509th Parachute Infantry Battalion, which was still under Ridgway's control, would follow the next night.[75]

In Sicily, all was frantic action. With no time for the normal orders process, pilots and paratroopers were briefed planeside. According to one observer, "Some [Troop Carrier Command] groups and Airborne units had less than two hours to load their men and equipment, give their planes a final servicing and arrange their take-off plans." Typical of the hurried preparations was the experience of F Company of the 2/504th, which had just completed a conditioning march up a mountain road near Trapani. According to Private Joe Watts, "We had just arrived at the top of the hill, it must have been about noon, and were looking forward to melons and rest, maybe beer and wine when a jeep screamed up the road with an officer from our battalion . . . standing and holding on to the windshield frame, shouting for us to return to the airfield immediately. We were to load for a drop that night." Jogging back down the mountain, Watts saw dozens of C-47s over the airfield, "circling to land like buzzards around roadkill." Tucker's briefing to his troopers was to the point: "The Krauts are kicking the shit out of our boys over at Salerno. We're going to jump into the beachhead tonight and rescue them. Put on your parachutes and get on the plane—we're taking off in a few minutes for the gates of hell."[76]

Tucker's pathfinders hit the drop zone at 2314 hours, 13 September, and within three minutes had their "Eureka" transmitting device operating. This first use of pathfinders in combat proved spectacularly successful. Pilots in following groups received the Eureka signals anywhere from seven to thirteen miles out, well before they spotted Yarborough's flaming *T*. Twelve minutes behind the pathfinders, thirty-four C-47s of the 313th Troop Carrier Group carrying the 2/504th arrived and dropped most of the troopers within two hundred yards of the drop zone. Mechanical problems delayed the departure of the rest of Tucker's troopers for several hours, but by 0430 hours, 14 September, Clark had at his disposal 1,300 paratroopers. All but one group of planes, which dropped B Company, 1/504th, eight to ten miles off target because of a mistake by the operator of a "Rebecca" receiver, delivered their loads within one mile of the drop zone. Jump injuries numbered but seventy-three.[77]

Less than an hour after the last trooper dropped Clark found Tucker and directed, "As soon as assembled you are to be placed in the front lines." Tucker replied, "Sir, we are assembled and ready now." By daylight, Tucker's paratroopers were dug in and holding the center of the VI Corps zone.[78]

The drop was repeated the next night, although on a slightly larger scale, with Gavin's 505th. As had Tucker, Gavin led with his pathfinders (although the 504th pathfinders were on the drop zone already manning the Eureka device, and Yarborough again lit the drop zone with gasoline cans), who dropped dead center on the drop zone at 2338 hours, 14 September. Like the night before, mechanical difficulties vexed the takeoff, so it was another ninety minutes before the lead planes of the main body appeared. After that the planes carrying the 505th along with B Company, 307th Airborne Engineer Battalion, arrived in a steady stream. By 0300 hours, 15 September, 123 planes of the 52nd Troop Carrier Wing had dropped an additional 1,900 paratroopers all within a mile and a half of the drop zone; by 0345 hours they were assembled and on their way to the front lines.[79]

The second night also saw another, separate, drop, by the 509th Parachute Infantry Battalion reinforced by a 40-man demolition section from the 82nd. Led by Lieutenant Colonel Doyle R. Yardley, the 509th's task was to drop near Avellino, a small crossroads nestled among mountain peaks more than 4,000 feet high and some fifteen miles behind enemy lines in order to "block all roads leading to and from that area" and stem the flow of German reinforcements to the beachhead.[80] Although a gamble, given the situation at Salerno many in Fifth Army, including Major Yarborough (who had previously served in the 509th), thought it worth the risk. "It seemed to me," Yarborough recounted, "that since we were fighting for our lives on the beachhead, that anything that would stop that jugular, even temporarily, would react [*sic*] to our advantage."[81] But the drop was a disaster. The pilots had little hard intelligence with which to plan a flight route, and aerial photographs were of practically no value. In addition, none of the planes were equipped with Rebecca receivers; hence, the only things the pathfinders could use to guide in the main body were lights and orange panels. But when the pathfinders were dropped over a mile south of the selected drop zone, the planes of the main body, flying practically blind, dropped their loads anywhere from four to twenty-five miles from the drop zone. One group of paratroopers landed inside a German tank park and were either captured or scattered before they could organize. Others assembled in groups large and small and caused as much damage as they could, but generally the men spent their time hiding, and running, from German patrols. Of the 640 troopers who jumped, 510 eventually made it back to friendly lines, although many went missing for as long as three weeks. Colonel Yardley was wounded and taken prisoner.[82]

Opinion varies about the Avellino drop. Gavin wrote that "it is doubtful that it had any decisive bearing on the outcome of the Battle of Salerno," although he qualified his remarks by adding that it caused "the enemy to keep units on antiparachute missions that otherwise could have been used at the point of his main effort at Salerno." Clark maintained that Yardley's paratroopers "seriously disrupted the German communications," and "considering the hazards of merely existing on the Salerno beachhead at the time, the mission of the 509th paid off in big dividends."[83] The most significant damage caused by the 509th troopers, however, was the blowing of a hole in a single-span concrete bridge. This did not occur until the night of 18–19 September, well after the crisis at the beachhead was over.[84] The bravery of the troopers notwithstanding, the force was too small and too dispersed to be more than "a minor nuisance" to the German defenders.[85]

There is less doubt about the value accrued from the drops onto the Salerno beachhead. Brigadier General Lauris Norstad of the Mediterranean Allied Air Force called them the only "essential" airborne operations conducted in the theater.[86] Others saw in them "history's greatest example of the mobility of airborne troops." Gavin, of course, felt the drops "had a decisive influence on the final outcome of the Salerno operation as a whole." On the other hand, the Army's official history of the campaign was ambivalent about the operation, calling it "a brilliant expedient," but then qualifying that praise by adding that "the value of the reinforcement stemmed less from the actual number of troops than from its psychological lift to the commanders and men in the beachhead who were beginning to feel uneasy; they had no way of knowing that the worst had passed."[87] But had it?

At 0800 hours, 14 September, just after Tucker's troopers moved into the front lines, Vietinghoff renewed his push in the Sele River corridor with a battalion of infantry and eight tanks. Unlike the day before, this attack met resolute resistance. Seven of the eight tanks were destroyed, the eighth was immobilized, and the accompanying infantry withdrew. Surprised by this sudden change of events, Vietinghoff ordered three more attacks that day at various points along the VI Corps perimeter. All were blunted. This was the high-water mark of the German assault on the beachhead. It had been made possible by the addition of Tucker's two battalions, which allowed Clark to adjust his lines and solidify what had previously been a porous front. Furthermore, aggressive patrolling by Tucker's paratroopers discovered German attacks before they began and thereby gave other American units advance warning of what was coming and where. All told, the Germans lost almost thirty tanks during the day's fighting, while the VI Corps lines held firm. That evening Kesselring ordered Vietinghoff to disengage and make preparations for a fighting withdrawal to Rome.[88]

Consequently, when Lewis's seaborne contingent arrived the next day, Clark felt strong enough to go over to the offensive. In this vein, he ordered Major General Fred L. Walker, commander of the 36th Infantry Division, to attack Altavilla, the highest point in the VI Corps sector, in order to deny the Germans observation of the beachhead. To lead the attack Clark gave Walker control of Tucker's First and Second Battalions.[89]

Tucker's advance on Altavilla, "a collection of light-colored houses etched on the top of a mountain," began with a difficult march under artillery fire followed by an attack, almost straight up hill, against stiff resistance.[90] After seizing two hilltops overlooking Altavilla, and thereby effectively negating it as an enemy observation post, Tucker's troopers dug in and for three days thereafter held out against repeated counterattacks while under incessant artillery fire. The fighting was brutal, a fact reflected even in the normally staid unit journals:

> 17 September: [Captain] WIGHT has been killed. . . . A piece of shrapnel hit him in the back. . . . [S]evere 88 fire. . . . [M]en jumpy. Water and food are scarce. Pvt Stokes . . . killed. . . . 88 shell. He was buried in his foxhole. Sgt Warner got it this afternoon. . . . As yet he hasn't been buried.
>
> 18 September: Continued 88 fire during the night and throughout the day. There are no rations. . . . [M]en are hungry and tired.[91]

Fearing that Tucker's two battalions might be destroyed—they were at one point completely surrounded—on 18 September Walker conferred with Ridgway about ordering Tucker to withdraw (at the time Ridgway was acting as the Deputy VI Corps commander, a posting that was "in part a reflection of General Clark's growing dissatisfaction with General Dawley, in part a practical matter designed to give Ridgway a 'home' on the beachhead" since his units had been temporarily parceled out to other commands).[92] When informed of Walker's proposal, Tucker responded, "Retreat, Hell!—Send me my other battalion!"[93] Ridgway assented and pushed the 3/504th up the mountain, which Tucker used to fight his way into Altavilla and break the German hold on the high ground.[94] When two days later the 504th was relieved, the troopers returned to the beachhead proud that they had "done something the army field manuals often talked about: infiltrated into enemy territory, chased out the enemy, and taken over his positions."[95]

Salerno was "a touch-and-go affair" that "came very close to being a disaster."[96] When the Germans did not respond as expected to the Italian surrender and Montgomery failed to advance as rapidly as hoped, Clark was faced with a crisis. Ironically, he was saved by a unit that, had Eisenhower had his way, would have been disbanded because it was thought to be too cumbersome.

CHAPTER 9

A FORCE UPON WHICH THE FIFTH ARMY COULD DEPEND

American parachutists—devils in baggy pants—are less than 100 meters from my outpost line. I can't sleep at night; they pop up from nowhere and we never know when or how they will strike next. Seems like the black-hearted devils are everywhere.

—EXCERPT FROM DIARY OF ANONYMOUS GERMAN OFFICER AT ANZIO, QUOTED IN WILLIAM D. MANDLE AND DAVID H. WHITTIER, *COMBAT RECORD OF THE 504TH PARACHUTE INFANTRY REGIMENT: APRIL 1943–JULY 1945*

WITH FIFTH ARMY out of danger General Alexander turned his attention to Naples. German pressure around the Salerno beachhead had slackened, and he felt certain that indicated that the Germans were about to withdraw to more defensible terrain north of Naples. He wanted to turn that withdrawal into a rout by pressing the Germans hard, breaking them, and then unleashing Fifth and Eighth Armies in pursuit. But pursuits require a lot of logistical support, and for that he needed Naples and its port.[1]

Clark needed no reminder of the importance of Naples. Darby's Ranger Force had been trying to break through the mountainous Sorrento Peninsula and onto the Naples Plain since D-Day. Fighting alongside the Rangers since its arrival on 11 September was Task Force Bertsch. But even with Bertsch's task force, it was a slow, rough slog, so on 16 September Clark reinforced

Darby again, this time with the 2/325th (less G Company, which was on detached service elsewhere).[2]

Darby used the 2/325th to plug a prominent gap in his line, assigning it to positions on two mountains that commanded a critical pass. For the glidermen, it was the first chance to prove their mettle. They did not disappoint, defending their positions for several days against repeated German attacks. One of the more intense fights occurred atop the 3,000-foot-high Monte San Angelo di Cava, where E Company, 2/325th, skirmished for five days with German forces bent on taking this critical point because of the unobstructed view it provided to both sides' rear area. The skirmishing culminated on 20 September in a ferocious battle.[3]

A light fog enshrouded the San Angelo heights that morning. Peering out of their foxholes, the glider troopers could barely discern a herd of sheep approaching their positions, a sight to which they had grown accustomed. But Staff Sergeant Donald T. Harmon noticed something unsettling—the bells on the sheep's necks were not ringing in consonance with their movement. Sensing that there might be German wolves hidden among the sheep, Harmon spread the alarm. His hunch proved correct. Fifty yards from the E Company positions, German infantrymen emerged from the herd and charged. The glider troopers fought back, firing so furiously that they burned out two machine-gun barrels, and the German attack receded. Minutes later the Germans attacked another part of the E Company line. Again the glider troopers stood their ground. Several hours passed before the Germans attempted a third assault. In the interim they plastered E Company's positions with mortar fire. Then, at 1400 hours, behind a crescendo of mortar rounds, the Germans came on again. By that time E Company had taken some forty casualties and expended all its machine-gun ammunition, so Captain Robert Dickerson, the E Company commander, called for help. First Lieutenant Wade M. Meintzer's platoon responded. Counterattacking across open ground, Meintzer and his troopers hit the German attackers head-on, forced them back, and then pursued them into the gullies and ditches to which they retreated to finish them off.[4] Ridgway was impressed and commended E Company in writing: "When a bold and aggressive enemy repeatedly attacked the positions of Company 'E' with intense machine gun, mortar and artillery fire, it stood fast and repelled every hostile effort for more than eight hours. Outnumbered and out-gunned, every element of this command . . . displayed high courage, spirit and devotion to duty to make possible the successful accomplishment of their assigned mission."[5]

The fight on Monte San Angelo came as a result of a shift in German strategy. Having failed to turn back the landings at Salerno, Kesselring wanted to withdraw to a succession of fortified positions north of Naples, but he needed time to prepare those positions, which he designated the *Barbara*, *Reinhard*, and *Gustav Lines*, before falling back on them. Vietinghoff, therefore, was to conduct a fighting withdrawal to gain that time. Accordingly, Vietinghoff shifted his strength to seal off the Sorrento Peninsula and keep Fifth Army bottled up in the Salerno beachhead for as long as possible. Tactically, this meant mounting local counterattacks—like those against E Company—to keep Fifth Army off balance.[6]

Clark was bent on breaking through the peninsula. Notwithstanding the defensive stand of the Rangers and glider troopers, Clark wanted them to act *offensively* to seize the passes through the mountains and open the way to the Naples Plain and the city itself. When it became apparent that Ranger Force was too small for this mission, it was reinforced, and then reinforced again. Ultimately, Darby's ad hoc command comprised more than 8,500 soldiers from three Ranger battalions, Task Force Bertsch, the 2/325th, another infantry battalion from the 36th Infantry Division, and the entire British 23rd Armored Brigade. Yet given the difficult terrain and Vietinghoff's determination to hold as long as possible, Ranger Force was still not strong enough to effect a breakthrough, so Clark assigned the mission to McCreery's X Corps, which subsumed Ranger Force. Furthermore, to ensure he was poised to exploit a breakthrough, Clark assembled an unusually large reserve of two divisions, the 82nd Airborne and the U.S. 36th Infantry.[7]

Happily for Ridgway, being put in reserve brought with it the chance to reassemble the 82nd, elements of which were scattered all over the beachhead. To this end he congregated the 82nd just south of the Sorrento Peninsula. This not only positioned the division for a rapid move on Naples but also brought it closer to those elements of the 82nd already fighting on the peninsula.

On 23 September, McCreery tried bulling his way though the mountain passes by attacking with two divisions abreast. The attack went nowhere. Clark then gave McCreery control of the 82nd for another go. McCreery, in turn, put Ridgway in command of all forces on the peninsula, including Ranger Force and the British 23rd Armored Brigade.[8] Ridgway's orders were to "seize and secure the dominating ground in the EGIDIO-SALA area [at the northern terminus of the Chiunzi Pass] for debouchment of the 23d Arm[ore]d Brig[ade]" and to "get out on [the] plain before full light." He was to attack "at the earliest practicable date," if possible on the night of 27–28 September but no later than 28–29 September.[9]

With Gavin and the 505th concentrated in the western portion of the peninsula and the Rangers, 325th, and 504th concentrated in the east under Darby, Ridgway attacked the night of 27 September. Everywhere his troopers hit thin air—the Germans had already withdrawn—so by dawn the next day Ridgway was through the passes and descending on the Naples Plain. By 30 September he had assembled his force on the coastal road just south of Mount Vesuvius.[10]

Anxious to make a rush on Naples, McCreery told Ridgway to thrust up the coastal road and make for the city along the most direct route.[11] Jumping off the early morning of 1 October, Ridgway led with the 23rd Armored Brigade, followed by Gavin's 505th in column.[12] According to Gavin, "The day began, as often happened during the early period of the battle for Italy, with the Germans completely out of sight, and our first attacks were blows into the air. The situation stiffened a bit; then late in the afternoon all resistance seemed to disappear. Soon there were throngs of people in the streets of the small villages along the main road to Naples. I wondered what would happen if the Germans were to counterattack."[13] Upon reaching the southern outskirts of Naples, Ridgway ordered the 23rd Armored Brigade to bypass the city to the east and continue on to the Volturno River.[14] Strangely, he also ordered the 505th, following behind, to halt, despite reports that Naples was undefended. Up front with his lead elements, Gavin soon learned the reason for the halt when his operations officer, Major John Norton, walked up and declared, "Colonel . . . we are to wait until a triumphant entry is organized."[15]

Norton had received orders "saying wait for General Clark who is going to have a triumphant cortege into Naples where [he would] address the assembled multitudes."[16] It was, after all, the first major European city to fall to the Anglo-Americans. Gavin and Norton drew up a hasty plan so that Clark could realize his grandiose vision. Their first concern was security. Their second was that, as everyone knew, an appropriately glorious entry would require the participation of the Neapolitans. They could do something about security. Waving throngs of Neapolitans were left to chance.

Clark wanted his victory procession to end at Garibaldi Square. Norton and Gavin were to lead the procession in a jeep, navigating as they went, since there had been no time to send reconnaissance elements ahead. Generals Clark and Ridgway would follow in a British armored vehicle, while the 3/505th, mounted in trucks, provided security.[17]

> The plan was to move directly into Garibaldi Square, and as General Clark's vehicle entered the square, the vehicles of the 3rd Battalion of the 505th would make a complete circle around the square and thus seal it off. The troopers would then jump from the trucks and clear all of the people out of the square. Then, if General Clark wanted to make the customary conqueror's speech, he could do it from one of the trucks, or he might find some arrangement in the square more suitable.

When Clark's procession entered Naples, "the streets were ominously empty."[18] Then, after "wandering around town looking for the multitudes," the procession finally made it to Garibaldi Square, where it was greeted with silence. "Every door and window was shuttered," Ridgway wrote, "and not a living soul moved in the streets except our own men." According to Gavin and Norton, Clark's triumph had been aimed at the wrong place; the expected crowds were about a mile away, in the Plaza Plebescito, where "the conquerors traditionally had been received" and hence the location where the Neapolitans expected their liberators to appear.[19]

Clark's celebratory moment, a real "flopo-flopo" in Norton's eyes, passed quickly, and Ridgway set about taking control of the city.[20] After clearing some pockets of German resistance, he turned his attention to the Neapolitans, who were exploiting their liberation to settle old scores at gunpoint, "accusing friends and foes alike of being fascists or tedeshi [*sic*, German]."[21] His approach to restoring order was simple: His regimental commanders were "to get in touch with the city authorities [in each of their assigned areas] and tell them that if those people kept on firing, we would kill them."[22] In compliance with these orders, Gavin grabbed a local police chief and told him:

> Any Italian, regardless of his sympathies, who possessed a weapon in the vicinity of where a weapon had been fired would be shot at once. [The police chief] seemed startled and gulped a bit as we explained exactly what we meant; then off he went. A few minutes later a weapon was fired in a side street. I took a platoon of troopers and went right out to get anyone with a weapon. The men had orders to shoot. No one with a weapon could be found. Almost at once quiet descended on the city.[23]

With order restored, the troopers started cleaning up the devastation the Germans left in their wake. Before leaving, the Germans had wrecked the city's transportation infrastructure, water and sewage systems, and electrical generating facilities, to say nothing of the port, which was mined and blocked by sunken ships. They also left behind hundreds of booby traps and delayed-action high-explosive bombs. The first of these exploded on 7 October, destroying the city's post office and causing scores of military and civilian casualties.[24] Three days later a second bomb demolished an Italian army barracks where B Company, 307th Airborne Engineer Battalion, was billeted. Twenty-three troopers were killed and another twenty-one wounded.[25] Yet in spite of the damage, explosions, intermittent artillery fire, and German bombing raids, the 82nd kept order while engineers and technicians from the Fifth Army restored the city and its harbor to working order. On 4 October the first Liberty Ship docked in Naples Harbor. By the end of the month, an average of 7,000 tons was being unloaded at the port each day, only 1,000 tons short of the prewar average.[26]

Meanwhile, the rest of McCreery's X Corps, to which the 82nd remained attached, was advancing beyond Naples to the Volturno River, which Clark wanted to get across before winter set in. Specifically, Clark wanted X Corps to attempt the quick seizure of one of two crossing sites: a highway bridge approximately six miles inland of the coast linking the twin villages of Cancello (on the northern bank of the Volturno) and Arnone (on the southern bank) or an unimproved crossing located near the mouth of the river.[27] Because he lacked sufficient infantry to get the job done, McCreery turned to the 82nd. Ridgway passed the mission to Gavin's 505th.

Gavin sent McCreery two battalions: Lieutenant Colonel Mark Alexander's 2/505th and Major Walter F. Winton Jr.'s 1/505th. Working under the tactical command of Brigadier R. H. E. Arkwright's 23rd Armored Brigade, the paratroopers were to clear the way by seizing five canal bridges south of the Volturno. If possible, they were also to take Arnone and its highway bridge.

Once unleashed, the paratroopers moved fast. Alexander's troopers took the first canal bridge by nightfall on 4 October, the same day they left Naples. They took the other four the next day and advanced to the southern outskirts of Arnone, where they paused so that Arkwright's brigade could catch up (it never did).[28] On 6 October Alexander sent a platoon into Arnone that drove the Germans across the river into Cancello, although not before they damaged one of the bridge spans in an attempt to make the highway bridge unusable. Despite the damage, Alexander thought the bridge still sturdy enough for dismounted infantry, so he moved F Company and his mortars into Arnone and then radioed Arkwright for permission to attack across the river to clear Cancello. Arkwright denied the request, "as he had not been able to keep pace with his armor and said that he could not support me."[29] Not wanting to pull back, Alexander left F Company inside Arnone to guard the southern end of the bridge and positioned the rest of the 2/505th outside the village.[30]

Shortly thereafter, the Germans counterattacked. Following a heavy artillery barrage, a battalion of German infantry charged across the highway bridge, while a company-sized force hit Arnone from the west. The Germans also brought up several 88mm guns to support the attack and used them like large-caliber sniper rifles. Alexander's paratroopers held firm. Inside Arnone, F Company drove the Germans back across the highway bridge, while Alexander led a charge by E Company that wiped out the enemy force moving in from the west. By late afternoon the fight was over, although the Germans continued to shell Arnone, which compelled Alexander to move his forces completely out of the village, where, along with Winton's 1/505th, they remained in position along the south bank of the Volturno, still waiting for Arkwright's tankers to arrive. They never did, so two days later the paratroopers returned to Naples. Because Arkwright's armored brigade had not been able to keep up and exploit the paratroopers' success, it would be another week before the Fifth Army got a toehold on the northern bank of the Volturno. Though a relatively minor affair when set against other actions in Italy, Arnone had cost dearly, some sixty casualties, most of whom were dead.[31]

On 10 October, Gavin learned that he had been promoted to brigadier general and that he was now, officially, the 82nd's assistant division commander.[32] At thirty-six, he was the youngest general officer in the Army.[33] Taken aback by his meteoric rise—only three years before he had been a captain—and a bit unsettled by the stars on his collar, he confided in his diary, "I do not believe that I wear them particularly well, I may in time." Command of the 505th went to his executive officer, Lieutenant Colonel Herbert F. Batchellor.[34] Mark Alexander became Batchellor's executive officer, and Major Ben Vandervoort took command of the 2/505th.[35]

Concentrated in Naples with a respite from combat in the offing, the 82nd was able to refit and receive replacements while it continued its none-too-demanding police duties (the only divisional unit not in Naples was the 456th Parachute Field Artillery Battalion, which was in Ridgway's doghouse and had been left behind in Sicily).[36] Concerned that such a lax assignment would play havoc with combat readiness, Ridgway assigned his newest general the task of keeping the troopers sharp. Gavin, in turn, designed a training regimen that focused on basic combat skills and lessons learned in combat. He also rotated each battalion through a short, intense exercise to test how well those lessons had been disseminated.[37]

Gavin also continued experimenting with pathfinder techniques. Salerno had been a "proof of concept" for the pathfinders. Now was the time to expand on what had been learned. For this Gavin again turned to John Norton, who, with a handpicked group of officers and noncommissioned officers from across the 82nd, returned to Sicily to conduct experiments with the 1st Pathfinder Group of the 52nd Troop Carrier Wing. For three weeks they worked "out all the experiments that you can think of: how to get in, with and without pathfinders; jumping out of airplanes like we'd been doing; or jumping out of tugs towing gliders; or jumping out of gliders; or jumping at 200 feet; or at nighttime; and landing gliders on the roads at nighttime; and how should the equipment be distributed; what lights should we use; what should the patterns be; how soon should they go in." What emerged from this frenzied experimentation (during which, Norton dryly commented, "we didn't kill anybody, but we came awfully close") was a more thoroughgoing understanding of the capabilities and limitations of parachuting and gliders and a more sophisticated pathfinder doctrine, to include complete tables of organization and equipment for pathfinder teams that became standard for all U.S. airborne divisions and troop carrier units for the remainder of the war.[38] It was a three-week investment that paid great dividends in France and Holland later on.

While Gavin concentrated on training, Ridgway waged his continuing battle against those wanting to employ pieces and parts of the 82nd in operations with little strategic value. According to Ridgway, the 82nd's airborne capability and proven fighting ability made it "a tremendous temptation to all higher tactical commanders," who, lacking enough aircraft to employ it as a whole, looked constantly to employ it piecemeal. "It was not unnatural . . . to find senior commanders reaching for this magic key which would open many tactical doors, whenever an assault operation was planned," and the first thing the planning staffs invariably thought of, "when pondering how to overcome some enemy strongpoint, was to drop some airborne troops on top of it."[39] Typical of this was a Fifth Army plan to drop a battalion near the small town of Sessa, almost thirteen miles behind enemy lines and seven miles inland from Italy's west coast, in order to deliver a "left-hook" from the sea and air that would isolate the right wing of the German *Tenth Army*, which was still firmly entrenched on the north bank of the Volturno River. Much to Ridgway's relief the operation was canceled when intelligence revealed the presence of strong German reserves around Sessa.[40]

Ridgway was also concerned with another matter; the 82nd's impending departure for the United Kingdom as part of the buildup for OVERLORD. Scheduled to leave Italy in mid-November, as the time grew near Ridgway became increasingly reticent about committing his units to combat lest they become so engaged that they could not be pulled from the line. He told Gavin, whose duties included analyzing the various plans that Fifth Army churned out, to guard against anything too extravagant because he did not want to be forced into leaving elements behind when the 82nd departed.[41] Ridgway's most significant fight in this regard was with Eisenhower, who, in early October, began canvassing Marshall about "the possibility of retaining one combat team out of the 82nd (U.S.) Airborne Division when we ship troops to the U.K."[42]

Though still convinced that an airborne division was "too large to use as an entity and that the proper organization is in strong regimental combat teams," Eisenhower hoped to retain at least one American and one British parachute regiment to "carry out airborne operations during the winter in conjunction with amphibious landings behind the enemy's lines."[43] When he heard about this, Ridgway appealed to Eisenhower, through Clark, for reconsideration. In a passage he drafted for inclusion in a letter from Clark to

Eisenhower, Ridgway stressed that breaking up the 82nd "runs counter to every sound principle of organization and training." He continued:

> One of the prime objectives in the building of an Army is to weld the elements of a Division together into one fighting team embued [*sic*] with pride of membership based on the Division's accomplishments. This is a long and laborious process to which the devotion of officers and men must be given over a long period of time. It has been accomplished in high degree in the 82d Airborne Division. While it takes much time and effort to build this spirit, it takes a very brief time to destroy it. To remove a Combat Team is one of the most effective ways I can think of to destroy this spirit into which a year and a half of painstaking effort has gone.[44]

Eisenhower's feelings about airborne divisions were, in part, a reflection of the paucity of resources in the Mediterranean theater, especially transport aircraft. Having lived with this limitation since taking command in the Mediterranean, Eisenhower was against airborne *divisions* because he could not conceive of ever having enough aircraft to employ one *as a division.* He did, however, have enough for a regiment, especially a parachute regiment, and since the only place to get one was from the 82nd, he had to make his case before the division left. But there was another aspect to Eisenhower's argument against airborne divisions, and it was this aspect that Ridgway found most threatening. Based on what had occurred in Sicily and, on a smaller scale, Avellino, Eisenhower remained convinced that even were there enough transports to drop an entire division at once, it would be so scattered that command and control would be impossible and for this reason the very notion of an airborne *division* was, in Eisenhower's mind, flawed.

At the time the efficacy of the airborne division was still being hotly debated. The Knollwood Maneuvers, which ultimately convinced Marshall and McNair that airborne divisions were viable entities, were still weeks away. In the interim Ridgway wanted to ensure that Eisenhower's was not the only voice they heard, so, as he had done before, he jumped the chain of command and wrote a memorandum directly to the chief of the Operations and Plans Division of the War Department. Knowing that his memo would eventually get to Marshall and McNair, Ridgway used "strong but temperate language" to ensure that the situation, "so far as it pertains to the ability of the 82d Airborne Division to carry out airborne missions of the kind the Service expects it to conduct," was presented "as accurately as possible."[45] Acknowledging that "grave deficiencies exist in the present training for *airborne* operations of this Division and its associated Troop Carrier Command units," Ridgway maintained that the deficiencies arose from causes "beyond the control of both [the airborne division and troop carrier] Commanders." There was "only one reason" for these deficiencies, he continued, which was that "the opportunity to conduct such training has been denied."[46]

Ridgway's spirited defense of airborne divisions was propitious. Were the 82nd to leave Italy stripped of one of its regiments, it would have been an easy matter to disband it and form separate parachute and glider regiments in its stead. That this did not occur can be attributed, in large measure, to the weight accorded Ridgway's memo. This was not the first time, and would not be the last, that Ridgway appealed to Marshall, whom he knew to be an advocate of airborne divisions. (Marshall once told a group of officers, including Eisenhower, that "in the proper development of airborne operations lies one field in which we have real opportunity and capability to get ahead of the enemy.")[47] At the very least Ridgway's memo, dated 6 November, staved off a decision until after the Knollwood Maneuvers. Ironically, by that time Eisenhower had been announced as the overall commander of the pending, and much more lavishly resourced, cross-Channel invasion, and his opinion about airborne divisions underwent a sea change. For example, less than three weeks after being named to his new position, Eisenhower denied a request by Alexander to retain one of the 82nd's parachute regiments in the Mediterranean![48]

Ultimately, Ridgway did not leave Italy with his entire division, the result not of theoretical wrangling over the organization of airborne forces but the hard reality of the fight in Italy. Through ULTRA, the Allies learned of Kesselring's strategy to defend from a series of fortified positions south of Rome. They also learned that Hitler had approved this strategy and had sent Kesselring additional construction personnel and materiel. Based on this intelligence Alexander enjoined Clark to get Fifth Army moving in order to breach the German defenses before Kesselring had a chance to organize and consolidate them. Lacking sufficient light infantry capable of operating in the mountainous Italian interior Clark, in turn, asked Ridgway for a regimental combat team. Ridgway sent him Tucker.[49]

Alerted on 27 October, Tucker's 504th, along with C Company, 307th Airborne Engineers, attacked two days later. Advancing twenty-two miles over terrain "so difficult that it was necessary often to communicate by carrier pigeon and sometimes to send food and ammunition by overhead trolley strung across deep mountain gorges," the 504th crossed the Volturno, captured the road and rail center at Isernia, pushed on to the town of Colli, and took Hill 1017, the primary Fifth Army objective in the sector.[50] The swiftness of Tucker's advance so surprised the Germans that many did not know there were any Americans in their area until too late. Lieutenant Wesley D. Harris of the 307th Engineers, for example, captured two Germans who "were reading a book when he walked in on their cozy little machine gun nest."[51]

Gavin, too, was impressed, noting that Tucker was "doing well on his front" and that because of the 504th's performance, "Parachute troops are making a name for themselves with the Germans. [The] 504 captured five [G]ermans from a seven[-]man patrol the other day, they killed the other two. One of the [G]ermans told the 504 that their company commander had gathered the company together and asked for volunteers, he told them that the troops to their front were special troops and barbarians." There was some truth to the German company commander's comment, added Gavin, for so ferocious were the 504th troopers in combat that the regimental intelligence officer "says that if he does not go out and plead with the men he does not get any prisoners."[52]

Because the 504th had acquitted itself so well, the situation Ridgway feared came to pass; the 504th was decisively engaged and could not be extracted in time to join the division when it set sail for the United Kingdom. Moreover, since Clark was unable to get the rest of Fifth Army to advance with the 504th's alacrity, Alexander began contemplating other ways to get around Kesselring's defenses. Since an airborne operation might be an integral part of any such operation, Alexander requested that the 504th Combat Team remain in theater (which would include the 376th Parachute Field Artillery Battalion as well as the 504th and C Company, 307th Airborne Engineers).[53]

Ridgway did not oppose this as vigorously as he did Eisenhower's request. Given the evidence, the most likely explanation for this is that Ridgway simply trusted Clark. They were West Point classmates, and Clark was having a rough go of it. Clark needed Tucker's troopers to help him break the deadlock on his front and promised to return them once that was done (as opposed to Eisenhower's request, which was open-ended). Additionally, unlike Eisenhower, Clark had no problem with airborne divisions; Clark, in fact, had long championed the airborne concept and had even adopted the style of tucking his trousers into paratrooper boots, although he never made a parachute jump.[54]

The decision to leave the 504th Combat Team behind was made about a week before the 82nd left Italy. On that day, Ridgway wrote Clark a personal letter. "Within the next few days the situation which has happily placed me under your personal command will change," he began. "There is nothing I can add to what I have so often told you. Your continued and expanding success will remain very close to my heart. Thirty years of admiration and affection have gone into the building of that feeling." Yet despite this expression of affection for his friend (the only other soldier to whom he expressed himself in this manner was Marshall; he never used this type of language when corresponding with Eisenhower), Ridgway reminded Clark that he wanted the 504th back. The division's "officers and men view this separation, temporary as it is promised to be, with live concern," wrote Ridgway, adding, "I know I can count, as you have assured me I may, upon your assistance in securing the prompt return of these troops to Division control as soon as the temporary need for their services in your ARMY shall have ceased."[55]

Clark's response, written two days later, was equally warm, although in it he made promises that he ultimately was not able to keep:

> I have always appreciated, as you know, your wonderful support and feel the same admiration and affection for you. It is a source of great regret to me that we are not to be permitted to fight together, for I have found your Division, under your magnificent leadership, to be a force upon which the Fifth Army could always depend. The wonderful discipline, morale and fighting ability of your command speaks well of their [*sic*] leader.
>
> I have worried about keeping your combat team, for I know what it means to you, and I would fight to keep my Division together the same way you have done. I, of course, must look at it from the Fifth Army point of view, and I needed to have done the splendid work that team has just completed. My troops are tired. I do not have the strength I need for this show; hence, your Regimental Combat Team is indispensable at the present moment. I will get it out in time for any airborne mission, and I will return it to you in the best shape I can, commensurate with any job they have to do. You know I have your interests at heart, and I will protect them as though they were mine, and I will see that my staff does likewise.[56]

The rest of the 82nd boarded transports on 18 and 19 November and soon thereafter set sail for Britain.[57] Although casualties to date had been relatively light, the troopers, tired and worn out, were looking forward to the rest.[58] Among the ranks were a number of troopers who, not wanting to be left behind, went AWOL from their hospital beds to rejoin their units before they departed.[59]

Rumors about the division's destination ran rampant; only a select few knew for certain, yet almost everyone surmised that the 82nd would have some part to play in the cross-Channel invasion. One rumor, perhaps the result of the zigzag route the convoy followed to avoid German submarines, held that the transports would run far out in the Atlantic, as if headed for New York, to make the Germans think that the division was rotating home.[60] As it turned out the German high command was confused, but not because of the convoy route. Leaving the 504th behind fooled the Germans into thinking that the entire division was in Italy and therefore unavailable for use elsewhere, a point underscored by the confusion later expressed by German intelligence officers in Normandy who could not account for the fact that some of their prisoners were wearing 82nd patches.[61]

Tucker's troopers were still at the front when the division departed; it would be 22 November before they were withdrawn.[62] By that time Clark's offensive had ground to a halt, his units exhausted from the heavy fighting. As a result Alexander posited a three-phased plan to unhinge Kesselring's three lines of defense. Phase one called for the British Eighth Army to attack to gain control of the main road to Rome from the east, which Alexander hoped would force Kesselring to withdraw. To hasten that withdrawal, phase two called for Clark to secure the Liri Valley south of Rome so he could unleash the U.S. 1st Armored Division for a dash to Frosinone, a city well north in the valley. With Frosinone in hand, Clark could then initiate phase three of Alexander's plan, an amphibious end run around the *Gustav Line*, the last of Kesselring's defensive belts south of Rome.[63]

The Eighth Army's attack jumped off on 20 November, but heavy rains and tough resistance from German reinforcements halted the attack well short of the road to Rome. Regardless, Alexander had Clark launch phase two on 1 December, which opened with an attack by Major General Geoffrey Keyes's U.S. II Corps "up the dark and forbidding slope of Monte Sammucro" that controlled access to the Liri Valley. After three days of heavy fighting, elements of the U.S. 36th Infantry Division, assisted by Darby's Rangers, seized the heights, but in the wake of persistent and ferocious German counterattacks Keyes asked for reinforcements. Clark sent him Tucker's combat team.[64]

The fighting on and around Monte Sammucro would be some of the toughest Tucker's troopers ever experienced. It began on 10 December with an agonizing seven-hour trek, entirely uphill, under incessant enemy artillery fire. According to Lieutenant James Megellas, the terrain they traversed was "more suited for goats and donkeys than for men."[65] Another trooper called Monte Sammucro and its surrounding heights "terrain that God must have made when He was mad at somebody and forgot to improve after He made it." The Germans, this same trooper wrote, "were hidden in the caves, grottoes, camouflaged pillboxes, foxholes and behind the rocks" with artillery "leashed like giant dogs awaiting the signal to tear us to death."[66] The experience of I Company, 3/504th, on the first day was typical of what the combat team would see in the coming days. Sent to relieve some Rangers on an adjacent hilltop, I Company fought its way through German positions, linked up with the Rangers, took over their defensive positions, and then endured seven counterattacks in the succeeding twelve hours that cost I Company forty-six casualties, almost 50 percent of its assigned strength.[67] A little more than two weeks later, when Tucker's troopers were finally relieved, these casualty rates had become the norm. The largest company in the 2/504th, for example, had two officers and twenty-eight enlisted troopers still standing; the smallest, four officers and ten enlisted troopers.[68]

Even when not under attack the 504th suffered horribly because the weather had turned cold and damp, and the troopers were still wearing summer fatigues. In addition, because of the difficult terrain and German artillery and sniper fire, Italian mule skinners employed by Fifth Army to keep the troopers supplied balked at proceeding too far forward. The troopers often went days without food, water, and ammunition.[69]

It was tough, redoubtable leadership that held the combat team together during those nineteen days of fighting above the clouds (at one point, noted one 2/504th officer, the battalion was "situated so high up that one has to look down to watch the air raids taking place").[70] It began at the top. At one juncture several troopers were hugging the ground to escape German fire when, to their surprise, they looked up to find "the little colonel [Tucker] with one man as a bodyguard" in their midst "wanting to know why in the hell the attack had failed." When they responded that a German pillbox was blocking the way, "the little colonel took two men, walked to the pillbox, caught the Nazis cleaning the machine gun and took eleven prisoners without firing a shot."[71] On another occasion, the troopers of C Company, 1/504th, who were dug in so close to German guns that even the smallest movement "immediately drew heavy fire," saw their battalion commander, Lieutenant Colonel Warren Williams, walking toward their position "as though he were on a Sunday outing in the park." Upon reaching a cave in which several troopers were seeking cover, Williams stooped down, "ostensibly to tie his boot lace, and rolled a bottle of Old Grandad into the cave entrance," wished his troopers holiday cheer, and then moved off to visit the remainder of his battalion. "We will never forget those long days and nights, week after week, in the rain and snow, not enough to eat and the constant shelling in the Italian mountains," recalled Chaplain Delbert Kuehl, who, in a story about one sergeant, underscored the type of leadership that was commonplace in the 504th: "One day during that terrible winter fighting in the mountains of Italy, I was standing by a rocky trail and a sergeant came by with no boots on, as his feet were too swollen. He had his feet bound up with cloth and rags. I said, 'Sergeant, you can't go up this rugged trail like this, you need medical attention.' He replied, 'Chaplain, I can't go back [down], my men need me.'"[72]

By the time the 504th Combat Team was relieved on 27 December, 54 troopers had been killed, another 226 had been wounded, and 2 went missing.[73] According to the regimental after-action report, "The combat efficiency and physical condition of the personnel available for duty upon relief was poor and impaired by mental and physical exhaustion and a deficiency of basic equipment and ordnance," and "the adviseability [*sic*] of sending the Combat Team into another mission so closely following one of the type just finished might have been questionable."[74] Yet this was exactly what Alexander and Clark had in mind.

Phase three of Alexander's plan called for an amphibious assault at Anzio, just thirty-five miles south of Rome.[75] Anzio itself offered a sheltered anchorage, while the surrounding beaches, suitable for amphibious landings, fronted a wide, level coastal plain onto which the Allies could quickly debouch and maneuver. Furthermore, twenty miles inland lay "the last barrier the Germans could use to bar an Allied entry to Rome," the Alban Hills.[76] Lying astride two north-south highways, possession of the Alban Hills would give the Allies a dominating position in the rear of Kesselring's *Gustav Line* to the south and provide an excellent jumping-off point for a push to Rome.[77] As originally envisaged, the amphibious operation at Anzio, code-named SHINGLE, was to be a supporting effort to Fifth Army's attack up the Liri Valley, and when Clark's attack up the valley stalled, both he and Alexander recommended that SHINGLE be canceled. Churchill, however, would not be deterred. He was bent on taking Rome and would entertain no talk of cancellation. Furthermore, he was well positioned, both physically and politically, to have his way.[78]

Following their conference with Stalin at Teheran (28 November–1 December 1943), Roosevelt and Churchill stopped by Cairo, Egypt, before returning to their respective capitals. While at Teheran, Stalin had pressed them for information about the promised cross-Channel invasion and at one point turned to Roosevelt and asked who would command OVERLORD. When Roosevelt responded that this had not been decided, Stalin was dismissive: "Then nothing will come out of these operations." Stung by Stalin's comment, Roosevelt promised a decision soon and while in Cairo made good on that promise—it would be Eisenhower. This left Churchill free to name General Sir Henry Maitland Wilson to succeed Eisenhower in the Mediterranean, and with the assumption of overall command in the theater by a British officer, strategic direction in the theater passed from American to British hands. This opened the way for Churchill to make his play for SHINGLE. So after seeing Roosevelt off, Churchill flew to Tunis for a series of conferences on future operations in the Mediterranean. "The stagnation of the whole campaign on the Italian Front is becoming scandalous," wrote Churchill, and he was going to do something about it.[79] That he did. Employing his considerable powers of persuasion, he reanimated SHINGLE and convinced those present (to include Alexander, who reversed his previous position; Clark did not attend) that SHINGLE should go ahead, with the promise that sufficient landing craft would be made available (a promise to which Roosevelt later agreed).[80]

Faced with this turn of events, Clark issued the order for SHINGLE on 12 January 1944. Major General John P. Lucas's U.S. VI Corps—composed of the U.S. 3rd Infantry Division, the British 1st Division, the 509th Parachute Infantry Battalion, two battalions of British Commandos, and three battalions of Rangers—was to "seize and secure a beachhead in the vicinity of Anzio" and "advance on Colli Laziali [on the Alban Hills]."[81] As part of the initial assault, Lucas also received permission to insert the 504th Combat Team by parachute and glider on two drop zones approximately eight miles north of Anzio so it could block the roads and rail lines from Rome and thereby impede the flow of German reinforcements to the beachhead. This airborne operation, code-named SUN ASSAULT, was canceled just three days before D day. Fears that the troopers would be cut up by German armor, that the assault would prematurely tip the Allies' hand, and that the difficulties of coordinating amphibious and airborne assaults would result in another friendly-fire fiasco all contributed to this decision.[82]

The cancellation of SUN ASSAULT should have resulted in the 504th's being released so that it could rejoin the 82nd in Britain. Alexander had specifically requested the retention an airborne formation *for use in airborne operations*. With none in the offing, there was no reason to keep the paratroopers in the Mediterranean. But Lucas did not want to release a proven combat unit, so he found a way to integrate it into his amphibious plan. Hence it was that at 1357 hours, 21 January 1944, twelve landing craft carrying the 504th Combat Team left Pozzuoli, on the northern coast of the Gulf of Naples, for Anzio. Hastily inserted into the D day landing scheme, Tucker's troopers had the vaguest of missions: to land near the small seaside town of Nettuno (about two miles northeast of Anzio) "as soon after daylight as possible" and then move to an assembly area inland, where it would become the VI Corps reserve.[83] What followed was approximately two months of some of the toughest fighting of the war during which the 504th would consistently battle enemy forces that were larger, more mobile, and had considerably more firepower.

Leading the landings were elements of the British 1st Division on the left, Darby's Rangers and the 509th in the center, and the U.S. 3rd Infantry Division on the right. Since surprise was paramount, a prolonged prelanding naval bombardment was canceled. Instead, two landing craft, each carrying 798 five-inch rockets, unleashed a barrage to shock enemy defenders, explode minefields, and destroy defenses ten minutes before the first wave hit the beach at 0200 hours, 22 January.[84] It was a waste of rockets.

The Germans were completely surprised. A major amphibious operation in his rear was the last thing Kesselring expected. In early January, Admiral Wilhelm Canaris, chief of the Office of Intelligence in Berlin, visited Kesselring's headquarters and reported, "There is not the slightest sign that a new landing will be undertaken in the near future." On 15 January, therefore, Kesselring's chief of staff, Generalmajor Siegfried Westphal, announced, "I consider a large-scale [Allied] landing operation as being out of the question for the next four to six weeks."[85] Based on this analysis, on 18 January Kesselring committed his last remaining reserves, the *I Parachute Corps* consisting of the *29th* and *90th Panzer Grenadier Divisions*, to the defense of the Liri Valley.[86] As a result, when the Allies hit the beaches at Anzio, German resistance was so sparse, unorganized, and scattered that by midnight of D day, VI Corps had pushed ashore some 36,000 men, 3,200 vehicles, and large quantities of supplies—some 90 percent of the equipment and personnel in the assault convoy—at a cost of only 13 killed, 97 wounded, and 44 missing (227 dazed German prisoners were also taken).[87]

Some of the Allied casualties were from the 504th. Approaching the beach in their landing craft between 1030 and 1130 hours on D day, Tucker's troopers were the targets of one of the day's few German aerial attacks. One of the craft, carrying a portion of G Company, 3/504th, sustained a direct hit resulting in 14 casualties.[88] The battalion medical officer, Captain Hyman Shapiro, who was himself wounded in the blast, swam ashore and administered first aid to his comrades before accepting evacuation himself, an act that earned him the Silver Star, the first of what would be many awards for valor Tucker's troopers earned during the hell of Anzio.[89]

Despite the tough landing, Tucker gathered his force in its assigned assembly area by midafternoon and then reported to the 3rd Infantry Division command post for orders. German forces to the east had repulsed the division's advance. Tucker was to attack with his entire combat team, drive off the Germans, and secure the line of the Mussolini Canal.[90] Constructed as part of a massive land-reclamation project, the Mussolini Canal was, in places, 120 feet across with steep sloping sides, a perfect antitank ditch and strong position on which to anchor the VI Corps right flank.[91]

Tucker's attack jumped off the next day, 23 January, at about 1300 hours, but the beachhead was so congested that, although the canal was less than ten miles from the assembly area, it was not until 0400 hours, 24 January, that the combat team made first contact. Advancing on the combat team's left, Lieutenant Colonel Warren Williams's 1/504th ran into about 30 Germans and two half-tracks that took four hours to drive off. Lieutenant Colonel Leslie G. Freeman's 3/504th, advancing on the right, ran into a much larger enemy force, touching off a back-and-forth fight that lasted well into the morning. The most significant action occurred at about 0600 hours when I Company was attacked by some 200 infantry and four tanks. It was, for the Germans, an ill-fated attack. Infuriated at the death of their company commander, who had been killed earlier in the day, and in no mood for another drubbing, I Company's troopers counterattacked, broke up the German attack, and then pursued the broken enemy across the canal, exacting a fierce revenge along the way.[92] By 1130 hours, having given vent to their bloodlust, Freeman ordered the troopers back to the canal. They left no fewer than 150 dead Germans in their wake.[93]

Tucker's troopers had run into the first wave of German reinforcements at Anzio, soldiers from their old nemesis, the *Hermann Göring Division*. Despite his misleading intelligence, it did not take Kesselring long to size up the Allied landings at Anzio, and once he did he acted swiftly. He had to. Were the Allies to push inland, there was little to stop them from overrunning his lines of communication and opening the back door to the Liri Valley and the *Gustav Line*. According to Generalmajor Westphal, so too was "the road to Rome . . . open, and an audacious flying column could have penetrated to the city." But Lucas did not drive inland; his foremost concern was building up his strength. Clark visited the beachhead on D day and confirmed this course when, just before leaving, he told Lucas not to stick his neck out as he (Clark) had done at Salerno.[94] Kesselring was thereby given a respite, one of which he took full advantage. By nightfall of the first day elements of twelve German divisions were rushing toward the Anzio beachhead where the *I Parachute Corps* was on hand to receive them and organize the defense.[95]

By securing the Mussolini Canal, the 504th also secured the positions it would occupy (with some slight adjustments) for most of its stay at Anzio and from which it would repel countless German attacks, counterattack in turn, and endure deadly artillery bombardments directed by German observers atop the surrounding Alban Hills. According to Corporal Fred J. Baldino of the 1/504th, the thought at first was that the Allies would take Rome "within a week, so we dug only shallow slit trenches." But as time passed and enemy resistance stiffened, "Our foxholes along the Mussolini Canal got deeper and deeper. We were like moles. Because we had to stay down in our holes constantly [to avoid German artillery fire], the wax boxes that the K rations came in were very useful. They served as urinals, and if you tore them up into small strips and put a match to it [*sic*], it made just enough heat to warm up a canteen cup of water to be used for coffee or bullion."[96]

At times the 504th's front exceeded 5,000 yards.[97] To cover this expanse Tucker built his defenses around outposts and strongpoints backed by reserve forces ready to respond to any enemy penetration:

> Our front line outposts being as much as two hundred yards apart, the Krautheads, armed with machine pistols, easily passed through our lines at night and prowled unmolested for hours. Our front line positions were so

> well camouflaged that they ran into them only by accident. If the two or three men on an outpost detected a twenty-man patrol, they let them pass but telephoned the information to a small reserve of tommy gunners located back a few hundred yards, who would sally forth to shoot it out.
>
> It must have been very disconcerting and was certainly misleading to the enemy to prowl behind our lines for an hour and find nobody. When enemy patrols returned to their company commander and reported that the line was weakly held, a counterattack took place at the presumed weak spot. They came storming over almost every day and were always surprised when the boys rose out of their gopher-hole hiding places and scattered the ground with them.[98]

But the aggressive Tucker was not content to just sit back and take it, so each night he sent out patrols to probe enemy positions, conduct reconnaissance, or take prisoners. At first, the troopers ranged far behind enemy lines and kept "the enemy in a constant state of bewilderment." Over time both sides laid so many mines that the patrols became "more than ordinarily hazardous," and their effectiveness and frequency dropped off, although there was one trooper that neither mines nor Germans could stop.[99]

Private Ted Bachenheimer of the 1/504th was born in Germany and had immigrated with his family to the United States when he was twelve years old. He spoke flawless English and German. According to Gavin,

> At Anzio [Bachenheimer] developed considerable facility in moving around among the German units. On one occasion he joined a chow line and, having finished a meal of wieners and potatoes, captured the German troops that had been eating with him and took them back to the 504th. When the 504th left Anzio . . . Bachenheimer knew most of the German command posts as well as their supply points and medical stations. According to veterans of the 504th, he even knew the officers and their reputations among the German troops.[100]

Lieutenant Colonel Williams once approached Bachenheimer as he was readying for another solo mission behind enemy lines. Williams asked Bachenheimer if he was scared when he went out. Bachenheimer replied, "Well, I'm a little nervous when I leave friendly lines, and have to piss a few times, out in no-man's land. But after that, I'm not bothered."[101] Miraculously, Bachenheimer survived Anzio and next saw combat in Holland, where he continued his personal war against the German army.

By far the most debilitating aspect of life on the beachhead was the constant rain of German artillery and mortar shells interspersed with sniper, small arms, and machine-gun fire; shelling from self-propelled guns and tanks; and periodic strafing and bombing runs by German aircraft. The beachhead was so crowded that just by lobbing a few shells in the general direction of Anzio the Germans were sure to hit something. Much worse, however, was the fire directed by enemy observers on the high ground surrounding the beachhead. They could see everything, and everything they could see they could hit. There was no "rear area" to which units could retire for a few days' rest. For example, on 29 February the 1/504th rotated off the line to a supposed rest area near the 376th's gun positions, but found that enemy counterbattery fire was so intense that the rest area "proved to be practically an 'impact area.'"[102] An excerpt from the 2/504th's combat journal reeks with numb futility as it recounts what the troopers endured:

> 2 February: Lt. Richardson hit by shrapnel.
>
> 3 February: Rear CP abandoned. . . . Several casualties. . . . 2 [Headquarters Company] men cracked under strain—sent to rear.
>
> 4 February: Had first experience with German "screaming mimis."
>
> 5 February: Extremely noisy night. Large exchange of artillery fire—rounds landing in close vicinity to B[attalio]n CP.
>
> 6 February: Artillery fire has its constant effect (one to two men per day). . . . During afternoon enemy artillery zeroed in on B[attalio]n CP (felt like 105 or larger), made several shell holes in area—also E Co[mpany] CP (wounded one man and hit a jeep belonging to artillery officer).
>
> 7 February: Enemy fire coming into area of CP fairly constant all morning—mortar, artillery and at noon a tank or T[ank] D[estroyer] which concentrated on F Co[mpany] CP (killed two, wounded nine). Roof of E Co[mpany] CP also knocked off and one wounded. . . . Machine gun fire directed on B[attalio]n CP front door kept personnel traffic to a minimum. Also machine gun fire on crossroads kept road traffic down. Every time a jeep went by it, it would be fired on but so far nobody hit.
>
> 8 February: Enemy rounds came in more rapidly in afternoon. Zeroed in on house used for supply opposite E Co[mpany]—killed 2 litter bearers, wounded 3 more and 1 E Co[mpany] man. . . . Our whole position is under observation by Germans in mountains to our front—our terrain is flat.[103]

Although the 504th's fight at Anzio was mostly a defensive one, the troopers participated in some fairly large attacks as well. The first was a supporting attack on Borgo Piave, a road junction a little more than a mile beyond the Mussolini Canal, to thwart the movement of German reinforcements to Cisterna, where General Truscott's 3rd Infantry Division was making the main attack.[104] To make his supporting attack credible, Tucker advanced with three battalions abreast, with the 2/504th in the center moving on Borgo Piave, while the other two battalions seized objectives to its north and south. Jumping off at 1330 hours, 25 January, the combat team met stiff resistance but fought through it and gained its objectives. At Borgo Piave, however, D Company, which led the 2/504th advance, was ambushed while establishing a security perimeter some two hundred yards beyond the town. Hit in the front and flank by five German tanks, eight flak wagons mounting 20mm and 40mm guns that the Germans employed like machine guns, and 20mm cannons, the troopers took to the roadside ditches. For the next several hours they played a deadly game of hide-and-seek with German tanks ranging the roads, their main guns pointed downward, firing point blank at anything that moved. Tucker finally ordered a withdrawal at 2030 hours; the main attack on Cisterna had failed, so there was no reason to keep the Germans occupied at Borgo Piave. Fortunately, D Company's losses were not as heavy as feared: three troopers killed and twenty-nine missing.[105]

Five days later the 504th attacked again. Clark and Alexander had been pressuring Lucas to push inland. In response, Lucas planned a massive two-pronged offensive for 30 January. The main effort was to be conducted by the British 1st Division attacking north toward the Alban Hills, while the U.S. 1st Armored Division followed. To support the main effort Truscott's 3rd Infantry Division was to again attack Cisterna. This time, however, Truscott wanted to try something different. He wanted to infiltrate two Ranger battalions into Cisterna during the night of 29–30 January and then, at daybreak, attack in a rush up the road to Cisterna with a third Ranger battalion supported by tanks and mounted infantry.[106] Meanwhile, the 504th Combat Team, minus the 3/504th, which had been attached to the U.S. 1st Armored Division, was to make a diversionary attack by blowing two bridges over the Mussolini Canal and then advancing to a creek bed beyond the canal, where it was to dig in to seal off the 3rd Division's right flank. To make up for the loss of the 3/504th, Tucker was reinforced with a platoon of three tanks and two tank destroyers.[107]

The 504th moved out at 0100 hours, 30 January, with A and C Companies, 1/504th in the lead, each of which was to blow one of the canal bridges, followed by the remainder of the 1/504th, the regimental headquarters section, and the 2/504th in order. Under cover of darkness, the troopers made slow yet steady progress, but at dawn things changed. Pockets of enemy soldiers bypassed during the night attacked Tucker's combat team from all sides. German flak wagons and 20mm cannons also joined the fight. When the advance began to stall, Lieutenant Colonel Williams climbed aboard one of the accompanying tanks, which at the time was too far in the rear to be of any use, and directed it forward. While standing outside the turret, he directed the tank's fire against the enemy guns, ignoring the ricochet of 20mm rounds all round him, and either destroyed or drove off the menacing flak wagons and cannons. Williams then ordered the rest of the tanks forward and, with his A and C Companies following, blasted his way through to the bridges. In each case the defending Germans did their work for them by blowing the bridges before the Americans arrived.

Once the bridges were blown the 2/504th leapfrogged forward and continued the advance to the creek bed, where it dug in, drove off several counterattacks, and sent out patrols to clear the rear of any remaining pockets of resistance. Although Tucker's troopers inflicted heavy casualties, taking more than 150 prisoners alone, the attack on Cisterna ended in disaster. The two infiltrating Ranger battalions were ambushed at daybreak by German armor and annihilated—767 Rangers departed on the attack, but only 6 returned.[108]

The 504th's attack of 30 January carved out a small but important salient that was, for some time, the deepest penetration into the German ring surrounding the Allies at Anzio. Moreover, it bisected a road the Germans had been using to shift forces around the periphery of the beachhead. Because of this the salient became the focus of some heavy counterattacks.

The 2/504th repulsed the first significant counterattack against the salient on 7 February made by a German infantry company that assaulted "with seeming disregard for the casualties sustained" and left 20 dead and 3 prisoners behind. Three days later the 1/504th repulsed another company-size attack, this one supported by flak wagons. The Germans launched a third major attack on 14 February, switching their effort back to the 2/504th's sector, only to be turned back again. On 16 February, the entire salient was ablaze. A regiment supported by numerous flak wagons advanced behind a rolling barrage up to the edge of the American positions, only to be met with murderous small arms and machine-gun fire from the paratroopers and deadly accurate artillery fire from the 376th's guns that stopped it cold. So heavy were the German casualties from this attack that Tucker granted the German commander a two-hour truce to remove his dead and wounded, which "were literally stacked up" in front of the American positions, after which the Germans melted away. The last major attack came on 4 March when the 3/504th, returned from detached duty, held off two infantry companies, two flak wagons, and two self-propelled guns. Thenceforward, there were no other large-scale attacks on the salient, although fire from German artillery and mortars continued unabated. During one particularly heavy barrage, more than a hundred rounds landed on the 1/504th's command post. According to the 504th's after action report, enemy shelling was so persistent that "enemy counterattacks were almost welcomed as an opportunity for the men on the line to 'blow off steam' as contrasted to sitting under an artillery barrage with no means of self[-]defense."[109]

There was one other significant action on Anzio in which an element of the 504th distinguished itself. When the 3/504th was attached to the U.S. 1st Armored Division for Lucas's 30 January offensive, it moved into an assembly area behind the British 1st Division. Its mission was to be prepared to assist the 1st Armored to exploit the British 1st Division's expected breakthrough. But the breakthrough never occurred. Instead, the 1st Division's attack ground to a halt near Campoleone, a small village fourteen miles due north of Anzio, creating a salient on both sides of the main road connecting Anzio with Campoleone that was seven miles wide at its base, narrowed to less than a mile at its tip, and extended five miles into German lines. Encompassing a frontage of more than ten miles, the salient was too vast for the 1st Division to hold, yet Lucas was unwilling to give it up, for at its tip it cut a major rail line the Germans had been using to supply their forces in the *Gustav Line*. In order to strengthen the salient Lucas attached the 3/504th to the 1st Division, which, in turn, immediately thrust the paratroopers into positions along the left (west) face of the salient. Although in place by 1 February, it would be several days before the troopers saw any action. When they did it was some of the most intense fighting experienced anywhere on the beachhead.[110]

Generaloberst Eberhard von Mackensen, whose *Fourteenth Army* headquarters took command of all German forces around the beachhead on 25 January, had one object in mind—to drive the Allies into the sea. He had, in fact, been preparing to attack in the very area the British 1st Division mounted its drive, but the British beat him to the mark. Ironically, this accrued for Mackensen unexpected advantages. First, because he had already massed five of his divisions on either side of the Anzio-Campoleone road for his attack, Mackensen easily stopped the British drive. Then, with the British contained in an exposed salient, he found that his forces were well positioned to counterattack, cut the British off, and destroy them. Finally, by erasing the salient he hoped to create a hole in the Allied lines that he could exploit to destroy the rest of VI Corps.[111]

Mackensen opened his counterattack on 3 February, which was aimed at cutting off and destroying British forces in the tip of the salient and regaining control of the rail line. The attack began with an artillery barrage just before midnight that kept the British pinned down, disrupted communications, and covered teams of German infantry as they infiltrated between British positions to attack them from the rear while Panther tanks attacked from the front.[112]

Mackensen's counterattack shook Lucas. Though the Tommies stubbornly refused to quit their positions and were still holding the tip of the salient by day's end, 4 February, the German attack had taken a toll—the British 1st Division had already lost more than 1,400 men—and Mackensen almost achieved his aim. Moreover, the appearance of so many German tanks was ominous. And then there were Clark and Alexander. Both had recently visited the beachhead, whispering a message quite different from the one they trumpeted earlier: instead of advance inland, it was get ready, many Germans, prepare to defend. (Clark and Alexander had access to ULTRA intelligence while Lucas did not, so they knew how formidable a force Mackensen had as well as his plan to use it.) Consequently, once the fighting died down, Lucas ordered Major General W. R. C. Penney, the British 1st Division commander, to withdraw to a new line that was considerably shorter and less vulnerable to attack on the flanks. Penney completed this move on the night of 4–5 February.[113]

Following the withdrawal the front remained relatively quiet for three days. Penney used that time to replace some of his worn-out troops with those of the 168th Brigade, attached to him from the newly arrived British 56th Division. Penney placed the 168th in the middle of his line. Behind the 168th was the 3/504th, occupying positions astride the Anzio-Campoleone road.[114]

Mackensen renewed his attack at 2100 hours, 7 February, as he did before, with an artillery bombardment behind which German infantry infiltrated through gaps in the British line. His objective was a cluster of three- and four-story brick buildings the Allies called "the Factory" and the small hamlet of Carroceto, five hundred yards to its southwest. Built in 1936 as a model Fascist farming community (and properly called Aprilia), the Factory sat atop the only high ground in the area. Taking it and Carroceto would allow the Germans to dominate the surrounding low, wet, boggy ground and give them possession of several important road intersections. With these in hand, Mackensen could build up forces and continue his attack in any of several directions, with the ultimate aim of breaking through to the coast with armor and annihilating VI Corps.[115]

The German *65th Division*, which led the attack down the west side of the Anzio-Campoleone road, successfully infiltrated the 168th's positions and overran several of its strongpoints.[116] As a consequence at 2120 hours Lieutenant Colonel Freeman, the 3/504th commander, received an urgent call for help—the front was in danger of collapse and needed reinforcement. In response Freemen sent H Company, which had but twenty-seven troopers present for duty, to restore the 168th's line, which had been along an embankment several hundred yards to their front.[117] While moving forward, the paratroopers passed a number of retreating Tommies, but once they reached the embankment, they discovered that "the Germans were everywhere, and the British were nowhere to be found." It was not long, therefore, before H Company was embroiled in a fierce fight of its own.[118] Sometime during the fight Corporal John C. Granado was taken prisoner. While being marched to the rear, he bore witness to the devastation wreaked by the German attackers: "We were taken back through the attacking forces and the German lines. We passed through what had been the British lines where we saw a lot of dead British soldiers. A lot of them were killed in their foxholes."[119]

Early the next morning Freeman ordered I and G Companies to attack to relieve H Company, which by that time was surrounded, but the attack stalled when it ran headlong into intense German small arms and machine-gun fire, so Freeman consolidated his position and waited for dark before continuing.[120] Commanding I Company was the Lieutenant Roy Hanna. Jumping off at 1900 hours, Hanna

> was leading his men in an assault against well-entrenched forces with greatly superior firepower when a bullet tore through his rib cage and lung and exited from his lower back.
>
> Nevertheless, he continued leading the attack until he lapsed into unconsciousness. When he came to his senses, he got up and continued the attack. He collapsed three more times and got up each time until his unit had driven the Germans from their seemingly impregnable position. Only then was he evacuated to a hospital and later sent back to the United States for thirty days. Afterward, he rejoined his unit for the remainder of the war. He received the Distinguished Service Cross for this action.[121]

Eventually, I and G Companies broke through to H Company, but the 3/504th's attack was not enough to stem the German advance, and later that day the Germans took the Factory, which forced Penney to again adjust his positions rearward. Freeman's 3/504th, down to about 25 men per company and fewer than 100 total, abandoned the embankment and moved back as well.[122]

With the Factory in hand Mackensen opened his heaviest attack yet with a push down the Anzio-Campoleone road that began at 0430 hours, 10 February, thus precipitating another bloody brawl during which Freeman's paratroopers often found themselves fighting in three directions at once. Yet they refused to budge, fighting back furiously, firing as fast as their weapons would allow (the battalion's 81mm mortars actually wore out their barrels during the fight, averaging 1,200 rounds fired each day) and held out for six days, a bulwark against a German tide trying to break through to the beachhead. Finally, down to less than one-third strength in each company, the 3/504th was relieved. Two days later, 18 February, Mackensen called off his offensive altogether. His units had suffered debilitating casualties, and he had insufficient combat power remaining to continue the attack. He had failed to break through to the coast, and although this was not the last time he attacked the beachhead, it marked the German high-water mark at Anzio.[123]

For its actions along the Anzio-Campoleone road the 3rd Battalion, 504th Parachute Infantry Regiment, received the division's first Presidential Unit Citation, the highest award a unit can earn. As is true of most award citations, the accompanying narrative is replete with platitudes about holding ground "courageously and stubbornly" against "continuous and determined hostile attacks" and attacking "with fighting determination" until "all objectives were regained." But toward the end of the narrative there is a sentence that, more than any other, bespeaks not only what carried the 3/504th through the terrible fight, but what marked it, as well as the rest of the 82nd Airborne Division, as a fighting force to be reckoned with: "Officers and men . . . consistently distinguished themselves by aggressive patrolling, exceptional initiative, and great individual courage."[124]

The 504th Combat Team did not see the end of the fight at Anzio. It was relieved of frontline duty on 23 March (VI Corps did not break out until 23 May) and the next day sailed for Pozzuoli, Italy, the same port it left sixty-two days earlier. Anzio had cost the combat team 120 dead, 410 wounded, and 60 missing, 35 percent of the strength with which it had arrived.[125] Many of the troopers were wounded twice, and a not insignificant number had returned to the beachhead after having been evacuated to safer and manifestly more comfortable conditions. According to Corporal Robert Kinney, who had been shot in the buttocks early in the campaign,

> We were taken off the beachhead and sent to a hospital in Naples and got sewed up. Several weeks later we were all down the hospital—lots of us down there in Naples. One of the officers of the 504th came down and said, "Anyone from the 504th who can stand up, can walk, meet me down here at the end of the hall." We all went down, about forty of us in casts, bandages, arms in slings and everything. He said, "Your buddies up there are catching hell and we've got to go back if we can. You don't have to, we're not going to order you, but we're looking for volunteers." We said, "Hell, we'll go."
>
> We just had the best-spirited bunch of scrappers you ever saw. I was wearing a kind of diaper, and the nurse gave me a bottle of boric acid to keep it [my wound] clean with. We went; only one guy didn't go.[126]

Tucker and his troopers remained at Pozzuoli for eighteen days. They rested, did some minimal training, and, when possible, visited Naples. On 10 April they boarded the HMS *Capetown Castle* for transport to the United Kingdom, where they would join their comrades who were preparing for the great cross-Channel invasion.[127] But the troopers were too beat up to participate in OVERLORD, so the 504th was scratched from the invasion. Anzio had taken a lot out of them.[128]

But it had not taken everything. The character of the regiment remained. Also aboard the HMS *Capetown Castle* were some British Guardsmen who regarded the paratroopers as undisciplined pirates. Inspired by this haughtiness, one trooper penned what he would say to a Guards officer if asked about Tucker and the regiment:

> Hell, yes, Colonel Tucker and I get along fine. He is just one of the boys. When Old Rube tells us to go out and kill off some Krautheads, we go out and kill 'em off for him. He tells us to kill some: He don't say how. He leaves the way of doing it up to us and we go out and do it. He is a hard old joker to get along with, but he stands up for our rights and we fight like hell for him. Yeah, we salute our officers cause we're in the dam' army, but most officers in the [504th] don't give a damn whether they're saluted or not. Discipline, hell yes, we got it, but not the lady-laced kind! We'd obey Old Reuben if he told us to jump into hell. What you mean . . . we ain't got discipline? We got more discipline than we need![129]

Though certainly not Guardsmen, the battlefield performance of the 504th helped earn for the 82nd a very similar title—America's Guard of Honor.

CHAPTER 10

A TERRIBLE AND HANDSOME SIGHT

Finally, bulky and shapeless with guns, knives, rations, ropes, maps and food, we climbed into the waiting plane. The sunset glowed red and a cold wind started to blow. We smelled again the old familiar scent of high octane gasoline, hot metal and airplane fabric. We sat down and tightened our straps as the motors roared and the plane vibrated. The crew chief came through and slammed the door shut. We knew that the next time we went through it would be over France. I wouldn't trade those moments for anything in the world. With pride and tenseness we sat side by side, the common loneliness of men dissolved in the white heat of the coming hours. We knew that we were going in ahead of everyone else and would be alone, behind the German lines for hours, and upon our efforts depended in a large measure the success of the storming of the beach.

—JOHN V. MCNALLY, *AS EVER, JOHN: THE LETTERS OF COL. JOHN V. MCNALLY TO HIS SISTER, MARGARET MCNALLY BIERBAUM, 1941–1946*

NONE OF THE 82nd's general officers accompanied the division when it sailed from Italy. Gavin had already departed, called to Britain to participate in the airborne planning effort for the cross-Channel invasion. Taylor remained behind as the liaison officer to the Italian government; he would not again serve with the 82nd. Ridgway headed for the United States, where the debate over airborne divisions was reaching its denouement.[1]

Ridgway also wanted to be heard. Disgusted with the piecemeal manner by which the 82nd had been employed in the Mediterranean, he wanted those in Washington who still questioned airborne *divisions* to understand that they had yet to witness their potential. He outlined his views in a memorandum he carried with him. It began succinctly: "Airborne troops are weapons of opportunity." They should not, therefore, be used for tactical ends, and commanders should "refrain from assigning airborne missions merely because airborne troops are available." Rather, airborne troops should be used only against operational or strategic targets. And when used in this manner, they should be employed en masse, *as divisions*.[2]

Of course, the Swing Board had come to the same conclusion and stated as much in Training Circular 113. But coming from the Army's only airborne division commander with combat experience, Ridgway's memo lent the argument added weight. Moreover, it captured exactly the views of Marshall and Arnold, who would eventually use its argument and Training Circular 113 to push Eisenhower to use his airborne forces boldly.

While in the United States Ridgway also pressed the War Department on several other matters. Foremost among them were the issues of pay and organization, both of which he had raised in the past without success. The pay discrepancy between glider troopers and paratroopers was, he contended, a "fundamental injustice," especially since, based on his "personal observation and experience . . . there is no essential difference between the hazards of parachute and glider duty."[3] Ridgway also asserted that the experience of two campaigns had demonstrated that airborne divisions were not robust enough because, once committed, they were "almost certain to be used for sustained mobile ground operations." He recommended, therefore, increasing the number of squads in parachute rifle platoons from two to three, the number of battalions in the glider regiment from two to three, and the inclusion of a second glider field artillery battalion in the division artillery array (although Ridgway already had two glider field artillery battalions in the 82nd, the 319th, and 320th, he was only authorized one). He also recommended strength increases for the military police, engineer, signal, medical, quartermaster, and ordnance units of the division as well as substantially more wheeled vehicles and heavier antitank weapons.[4]

Ridgway's requests were denied, but his entreaties were not in vain. The War Department told him it could do nothing about the pay discrepancy, but Marshall promised that he would seek congressional help to rectify the matter.[5] McNair replied that though the Knollwood Maneuvers had convinced him that airborne divisions were worthwhile, he was not similarly compelled to admit that they required substantial increases in personnel and equipment. Ridgway, however, was convinced he was right, and when the opportunity presented itself he made many of his proposed organizational changes on his own authority.

While Ridgway was fighting the bureaucracy in Washington, Gavin was in London, a posting that resulted from an urgent call from Marshall for "AN ABLE OFFICER WITH VISION AND COMBAT EXPERIENCE FOR THE STAFF IN ENGLAND . . . WHO COULD GIVE US THE BEST OF THE EXPERIENCE IN AIRBORNE OPERATIONS AND COULD WORK WITH OTHER PEOPLE IN A BRITISH SETTING." Ridgway sent Gavin because, as he told Marshall, "He more than any other I know in my Division or out, has vision, combat experience, professional knowledge and personality, for this assignment." When Gavin arrived in London on 19 November, however, it appeared that the urgency had passed. "No one seems to know just what in the hell I am supposed to be doing here except that I am on the COSSAC staff."[6]

COSSAC was the Anglo-American staff that had been established to plan for "a full scale assault against the Continent in 1944, as early as possible."[7] Its name derived from the title of its chief, British lieutenant general Frederick E. Morgan, the chief of staff to the Supreme Allied Commander, whom Gavin thought "a quiet, scholarly type of officer and an excellent chief of staff."[8] For the immediate future Morgan would be Gavin's boss, but protocol demanded that Gavin also check in with the highest-ranking American officer in England. Hence, within hours of arriving in London, Gavin was at Omar Bradley's First Army headquarters.

Although plans for the invasion had not been finalized, Bradley's First Army had been designated the command and control headquarters for American forces in the invasion. It was, therefore, not only protocol that compelled Gavin's visit; he wanted to get the measure of the man for whom the 82nd would be fighting. The two talked for an hour after which Gavin noted that Bradley had "some sound ideas." Additionally, Bradley came across as an "enthusiastic supporter of airborne operations" who was keen to use them in the upcoming operation, although he warned Gavin that "some senior officers, particularly those in the R.A.F. [Royal Air Force], believed that the airborne operation would be too costly."[9] Both buoyed and forewarned by his visit with Bradley, Gavin went to see Morgan the next day.

When Gavin arrived at Morgan's office he found there—whether coincidentally or not is unknown—General "Boy" Browning, who was "as smooth as ever and quite generally distrusted by American high commanders."[10] Leading the list of distrustful Americans was Ridgway, who had warned Gavin about Browning's "machinations." He was "intelligent, charming, and very close to Mr. Churchill," said Ridgway, but he was also "unprincipled and ruthless in his efforts to align every operation and every piece of equipment to the complete benefit of the British Empire at our expense." Furthermore,

Browning had convinced Major General Bill Lee, whose 101st Airborne Division was already in England, that "his word was law." Gavin, therefore, was to handle Browning "cautiously but firmly."[11] But Gavin quickly discovered that Browning was not the bugaboo Ridgway portrayed (at least not yet). That epithet fell to Air Chief Marshal Sir Trafford Leigh-Mallory, OVERLORD's air commander in chief, the RAF officer about whom Bradley had warned Gavin. Formerly chief of Britain's Fighter Command, Leigh-Mallory had but a tenuous grasp on the capabilities and requirements of airborne forces and exacerbated his ignorance by disregarding those who did, a trait that complicated the already difficult task of planning airborne operations for OVERLORD.

Gavin made two other office calls before beginning his COSSAC duties. The first was to Lieutenant General Lewis H. Brereton, commander of the U.S. 9th Air Force and, as such, commander of all American troop carrier units in Britain. Brereton wrote that he was impressed with Gavin, whose "experience in airborne operations" made him "invaluable as an adviser" and that he wished to use Gavin "to the utmost to direct our planning and training," granting him full authority "to deal directly with both the Troop Carrier Command and the airborne divisions in order to get the best results." Gavin's impression of Brereton was not as favorable. He found him "a most difficult man to deal with" and felt that "his attitude and plans make the picture look very very black." To be fair, the situation was bleak. At the time Brereton had insufficient airlift and green crews, although when Gavin suggested that he request the transfer of the experienced 52nd Troop Carrier Wing from the Mediterranean, Brereton turned resentful and jealous. Gavin left the meeting uncharacteristically depressed about what lay ahead.[12]

Gavin's last visit was to his old boss Bill Lee. Surprisingly, Gavin recorded little about the meeting, writing only that Lee asked him to wring from COSSAC a clear statement on airborne policy. Lee had tried and failed. Now that Gavin was in England, Lee would leave it to him to wrestle with COSSAC while he concentrated on preparing the 101st for its first taste of combat.[13]

When Gavin finally settled down to the staff work for which he had been summoned, he quickly became acquainted with the frustrations Lee told him about. For an American, COSSAC was Byzantine. When organizing COSSAC, Morgan instinctively adopted the British planning system with which he was familiar. In the British system myriad committees, or syndicates, were formed to analyze and prepare plans for every aspect of an operation. Americans, on the other hand, relied on their staffs for planning. Morgan later admitted that "to the American mind the committee system appeared just exactly what was not needed if we were after positive results and rapid action" and that "to the shrewd American observer it seemed that one of the safest ways of ensuring that positive action is postponed indefinitely . . . is to refer the question to a properly constituted committee."[14] Gavin could not have agreed more. "Before an order is published," complained Gavin in his diary, "everyone must be queried on their attitude toward its publication. It makes for an intolerable situation since in some measure, large or small, depending upon the circumstances, squabbling, jealousies, politics and self-aggrandizement are rampant."[15]

It was no wonder that Lee had been stymied in his quest to obtain a clear statement of airborne policy. What perplexed Gavin was why such a thing was needed. Training Circular 113 "fully meets our needs," he wrote, so all that was required was interpreting it in light of conditions in the theater. "But specifically interpreting anything around this headquarters," Gavin railed, "is asking for trouble."[16] Nevertheless, Gavin and his British counterpart, RAF wing commander Dugald MacPherson, spearheaded the effort and after six weeks of haggling produced a document that satisfied everyone.[17] The final product, a SHAEF (Supreme Headquarters, Allied Expeditionary Force) memorandum titled "Employment of Airborne Forces," was in essence a plagiarism of Training Circular 113 and the memo Ridgway had carried with him to Washington.[18] Its significance, however, lay not in establishing a *new* doctrine but in establishing a *common* doctrine that would govern airborne forces from both nations. It was also a giant leap toward the realization of an Allied airborne command.

The reason Gavin was debating policy and not, as he expected, completing detailed plans for airborne operations was that the final form the invasion would take had not yet been decided. Granted, COSSAC had completed a conceptual outline for the invasion, which was misleadingly called the COSSAC plan, but until a Supreme Commander took the reins, it remained nothing more than an abstract product born of an intellectual exercise to match an invasion scheme to available resources. It was predicated on the early seizure of Caen in Normandy, France, which Morgan called the "objective of supreme importance" because it commanded roads the Allies would need to break out into the open terrain to the east and thrust toward Germany.[19] To do this, it envisioned an assault from the sea by three divisions supported by an airborne drop of one division.[20]

Morgan briefed the COSSAC plan to Roosevelt, Churchill, and the Combined Chiefs at the August 1943 QUADRANT Conference in Quebec, Canada. The plan, he told them, was generally within resource constraints with one exception, transport aircraft. Estimates were that it would take an entire airborne division to take Caen, but OVERLORD had been allotted enough transports to lift but two-thirds of a division. Neither Marshall nor

Arnold thought this insurmountable and immediately took steps to alleviate the shortfall. As a result, the Americans eventually amassed thirteen and a half troop carrier groups in England (to include the 52nd Troop Carrier Wing, which was, as Gavin suggested, transferred from the Mediterranean). When added to the two British groups, this accounted for more than 1,100 aircraft and crews.[21]

Eisenhower, too, received a briefing on the COSSAC plan. His initial impression was that the assault frontage was too narrow and the assault force lacked punch, but he kept this to himself. Like everyone else, Eisenhower assumed that Marshall—the odds-on favorite for Supreme Commander—would be the one executing the plan. But when in early December Roosevelt picked Eisenhower for the slot, he revisited the COSSAC plan's shortcomings.[22] To assist with this he called on General Montgomery, who himself had just been appointed the 21st Army Group commander and, as such, Eisenhower's principal ground force commander for the invasion.

At the time both men were wrapping up their affairs in the Mediterranean, so they met in Algiers. According to Montgomery, Eisenhower told him that "he had only a sketchy idea of the [COSSAC] plan and that it did not look too good," so he asked Montgomery, who was departing straightaway for England (Eisenhower was returning to the United States for a short rest before assuming his new post), to "act as his representative in London until he himself could get there" and, in the meantime, "analyse and revise the plan and have it ready for him on his arrival in England about the middle of January." Montgomery was only too happy to comply. Hence, when Eisenhower convened his first meeting as Supreme Commander on 21 January 1944, Montgomery had ready for him a much-revised concept for the cross-Channel attack.[23]

Assembled at Norfolk House in London for the meeting were all of Eisenhower's key deputies: Montgomery; Leigh-Mallory; Air Chief Marshal Sir Arthur W. Tedder, Eisenhower's deputy; and Admiral Sir Bertram Ramsey, the Allied naval commander in chief. Also in attendance were Bradley; Major General Sir Francis "Freddie" de Guingand, Montgomery's deputy; Lieutenant General "Beetle" Smith, whom Eisenhower had brought with him to serve as SHAEF's chief of staff; Morgan, who became Smith's deputy; and Rear Admiral Alan G. Kirk, commander of the naval task force that would carry Bradley's First Army to Normandy. Montgomery opened the meeting by stating that after studying the COSSAC plan, he was in total agreement with Eisenhower: The envisioned three-division assault was insufficient. In its stead, he proposed a five-division assault by two American and three British or Canadian divisions over a much wider front (although in the same general area), to include the landing of one U.S. division on the Cotentin Peninsula.

This would position the Americans closer to Cherbourg, the port city at the tip of the Cotentin. It was Cherbourg, Montgomery stressed, that was the key to success, not Caen, for by taking Cherbourg the Allies would free themselves from their dependence on the two prefabricated harbors (code-named MULBERRIES) that would be installed shortly after D-Day and that everyone agreed would be insufficient to sustain Allied forces once they started driving inland. Because of this, he also recommended that the focus of the airborne effort be switched from Caen to the Cotentin in order to protect the U.S. right flank and help secure the ground from which Bradley's First Army could launch its drive on Cherbourg. After some debate, most prominently a remark by Ramsey that a five-division assault necessitated the postponement of D-Day from 1 May to 1 June in order to obtain sufficient landing craft for the two additional divisions, Montgomery's concept was accepted (as was the new target date for D-Day).[24]

A few days later Montgomery's concept was codified in the NEPTUNE Initial Joint Plan, which replaced the COSSAC plan as the fundamental planning document for the invasion (*NEPTUNE* referred to the assault phase of the operation, while *OVERLORD* referred to the overarching plan for the invasion of Europe).[25] In it, Bradley was allocated one American airborne division, which he intended to drop behind the U.S. beach on the Cotentin, code-named UTAH. Intelligence had shown that the Germans had flooded the area behind UTAH beach, turning it into a swampy marsh traversed by but four causeways. The airborne division was to seize the causeways and hold them open long enough for Bradley to amass his tanks and mechanized infantry on the beach, drive through the causeways, and attack toward Cherbourg.[26]

The Initial Joint Plan made vague reference to subsequent airborne missions as well, but where and when these might occur were left open. Thanks to Marshall and Arnold, however, by mid-February 1944 it was clear that there would be sufficient troop carrier aircraft on hand to drop one and two-thirds divisions on D-Day. As a result, the Initial Joint Plan was revised to include D-Day drops astride the Orne River, on the left flank of the British beaches. In addition, with so many aircraft available it was envisioned that another division-size drop would be possible after D-Day, so Bradley was told that he could plan for a second drop in his sector as early as the morning of D+1.[27]

Once the revisions to the Initial Joint Plan were finalized, detailed airborne planning could finally commence, with the first order of business being the assignment of units against objectives. Bradley selected the 101st to make the D-Day drop behind UTAH beach; two brigades from the British 6th Airborne Division would make the D-Day drop on the Orne. Bradley assigned the D+1 mission to the 82nd. Dropping near La Haye du Puits, a small town on the west coast of the Cotentin Peninsula, its mission was to "throw a barricade across the [Cotentin] peninsula at its neck" by seizing a narrow strip of dry land centered on La Haye du Puits that was the only passable thoroughfare to Cherbourg from outside the Cotentin.[28] With this in American hands, German reinforcements to Cherbourg would be stopped. Bradley selected the 82nd for this mission because, in his mind, it was the more hazardous of the two drops; the objective area was more than twenty miles from UTAH beach, so the division would have to fight isolated until link up could be made. It was, he thought, a job for a battle-tested unit.[29]

Watching from afar, Marshall and Arnold were disappointed with the airborne plans. Having made so many transports available for the invasion, they felt that Eisenhower was frittering away his airborne forces for limited tactical gains. In an attempt to change his mind they sent him a proposal called Plan C, a scheme to drop two or three airborne divisions into the Orléans Gap, some eighty-five miles inland from the proposed invasion beaches, where they would seize four airfields suitable for flying in reinforcements. Backed by Allied airpower this force could, they believed, threaten enemy lines of communication, block reinforcement by enemy units in northern France and Germany, and ultimately force a German withdrawal from Normandy. It would also win for the Allies a position much closer to the Seine and Paris, a line that the Initial Joint Plan did not envision the Allies reaching until D+90. For Marshall and Arnold, Plan C represented Training Circular 113, Ridgway's memo, and SHAEF's "Employment of Airborne Forces" made manifest.[30]

Brigadier General Frederick W. Evans, commander of the I Troop Carrier Command in the United States, and Colonel Bruce W. Bidwell of the War Department Operations Division were the two selected to fly to England to brief Eisenhower and his commanders on Plan C.[31] Preceding them was a personal letter from Marshall to Eisenhower in which the Army chief of staff asked the Supreme Commander "to give the young men an opportunity to present the matter to you personally before your Staff tears it to ribbons." Marshall also explained his reasoning behind Plan C:

> Up to the present time I have not felt that we have properly exploited air power as regards its combination with ground troops. We have lacked planes, of course, in which to transport men and supplies, but our most serious deficiency I think has been a lack of conception. Our procedure has been a piecemeal proposition with each commander grabbing at a piece to assist his particular phase of the operation, very much as they did with tanks and as they tried to do with the airplane itself. It is my opinion that we now pos-

> sess the means to give a proper application to this phase of air power in a combined operation.
>
> I might say that it was my determination in the event I went to England [as the Supreme Commander] to do this, even to the extent that should the British be in opposition I would carry it out exclusively with American troops. I am not mentioning this as pressure on you but merely to give you some idea of my own conclusions in the matter. . . .
>
> This plan appeals to me because I feel that it is a true vertical envelopment and would create such a strategic threat to the Germans that it would call for a major revision of their defensive plans. It should be a complete surprise, an invaluable asset of any such plan. It would directly threaten the crossings of the Seine as well as the city of Paris. It should serve as a rallying point for considerable elements of the French underground.
>
> In effect, we would be opening another front in France and your build-up would be tremendously increased in rapidity.
>
> The trouble with this plan is that we have never done anything like this before, and frankly, that reaction makes me tired.[32]

Eisenhower dutifully complied with Marshall's request. When Evans and Bidwell arrived in England in mid-February, he granted them a private audience but reserved judgment until he could hear from his subordinates. Next he had Evans and Bidwell brief his staff officers, whom he ordered to hold their comments as well. Finally, he had them brief the three commanders whose opinions on the matter carried the most weight: Montgomery, Bradley, and Ridgway.[33] At this last meeting, held 18 February, Bradley strenuously objected. "Cherbourg had to be secured as soon as possible," he insisted, "and nothing should be allowed to deflect from that aim." Bradley "also felt that the Germans could destroy the [Orléans Gap] airhead before it became an effective threat." Ridgway seconded Bradley, although why is unclear, while Montgomery, with uncharacteristic tact, stated that although he agreed that "Allied airborne potential should be developed to the maximum," he felt that "initially it should be used only to win the *main* battle, i.e., the beach landing."[34] The next day, Eisenhower summarized the objections to Plan C in a letter to Marshall: "My initial reaction to the specific proposal is that I agree thoroughly with the conception but disagree with the timing. Mass in vertical envelopments is sound—but since this kind of an enveloping force is *immobile on the ground*, the collaborating force must be strategically and tactically mobile. So the time for the mass vertical envelopment is *after* the beach-head has been gained and a striking force built up!" Eisenhower added that because his primary focus was to secure Cherbourg as quickly as possible in order to alleviate the "anxiety concerning Mulberries, Gooseberries, and other forms of artificial aids in landing supplies and troops," he intended to "devote [to that end] everything that can be profitably used, including airborne troops." He also reminded Marshall of "the enemy's highly efficient facilities for concentration of ground forces at any particular point" despite Allied air supremacy, something the Germans had demonstrated in Italy. Finally, using Anzio as his example, he posited that an immobile force deep behind enemy lines was more of a liability for the attacker than the defender.[35]

Ironically, though SHAEF planners had agreed to reject Plan C, they were in disagreement about their own airborne plans. The crux of the disagreement was gliders. Both Ridgway and Taylor, who took command of the 101st in mid-March after Bill Lee suffered a heart attack, wanted large glider insertions immediately following their nighttime parachute assaults in order to bring in antitank weapons, artillery, and additional infantry. When presented with this, the troop carrier commanders balked. Landing a glider in combat was tricky, but landing a mass of them at night was suicide given the inexperience of most of the glider pilots. When the issue was elevated to Leigh-Mallory, he sided with his pilots and canceled night glider operations altogether. This compelled Ridgway and Taylor to rework their ground tactical plans. Accordingly, several days later they forwarded a new proposal calling for glider insertions at dawn. Leigh-Mallory vetoed this scheme too, based on the proposition that since the paratroopers would have been on the ground for several hours before dawn, the element of surprise would be lost, making the ungainly gliders and their tow planes easy targets for alert German antiaircraft gunners. At this, the usually mild-mannered Bradley weighed in with a blistering reply. If glider pilots could not carry out missions when and where they were needed, Bradley countered, then they were irrelevant, which implied, of course, that they should be disbanded. Wanting to avoid this outcome, a chastened Leigh-Mallory sought a compromise. It took until the end of April to find one.[36]

To appease air force planners, it was agreed that no glider missions would be flown with the initial U.S. parachute assault; instead, all available aircraft would be used to carry paratroopers, thereby making possible the simultaneous drop of all three airborne divisions on D-Day (this was possible because a C-47 could not both tow a glider and drop paratroopers; hence, those originally scheduled to be tow planes were now available to conduct parachute drops). The drops would then be followed by a small force of gliders that would be inserted just before dawn on D-Day. A second, larger, insertion would follow at dusk on D-Day, and on D+1 two more insertions would deliver what remained. So matters stood until a change in German dispositions on the Cotentin Peninsula forced yet another adjustment to the airborne plans, but that was weeks away.[37]

With the exception of a select few "bigoted" individuals, those whose fate would be determined by these great debates were wholly unaware they were occurring.[38] They knew, of course, they were going to participate in the invasion in some manner, but when and where were secrets not revealed to them until the last moment. Instead, their concern was to ready themselves for anything, and for that they trained and trained hard. For the troopers of the 82nd, this began immediately following their disembarkation at Belfast, Northern Ireland, on 9 December 1943.

By the time the 82nd arrived there were already more than 750,000 U.S. and a comparable number of British Commonwealth and other Allied soldiers occupying the British Isles, all of whom were competing for limited space.[39] Because of this the 82nd remained in Northern Ireland for two and a half months, occupying a string of camps just northwest of Belfast. Ridgway was not pleased. The area afforded neither sufficient maneuver space nor training facilities, and there was nowhere to conduct airborne operations. Gavin tried procuring a different location for the 82nd, but Bradley squelched this, telling him that the 82nd would have to make do until about sixty days before the invasion, at which time the division would be moved nearer its departure airfields (as it turned out the division was moved earlier than that, about ninety days before D-Day).[40] While in Northern Ireland, therefore, the division's focus was on integrating replacements, conducting physical training, and individual and small unit proficiency.[41] By far the most significant event that occurred in Ireland was the integration of the green 507th and 508th Parachute Infantry Regiments and the 2/401st Glider Infantry Battalion into the 82nd.[42]

When Ridgway arrived in Britain he was, by date of rank, the senior American airborne officer in the European theater of operations (the senior Allied airborne officer in theater was Browning, who had been promoted to lieutenant general in December).[43] As such, he had administrative authority over all U.S. airborne units in Britain, and quite a disparate collection that was. Besides the 82nd and 101st, this included the independent 501st Parachute Infantry Regiment and, with its arrival in January, the U.S. 2nd Airborne Brigade, which was composed of two more parachute regiments, the 507th and 508th. Moreover, for some reason the 101st was still organized in accordance with the old scheme—one parachute regiment, the 502nd, and two glider regiments, the 327th and 401st—although it also had a second attached parachute regiment, the 506th. The first thing on Ridgway's agenda, therefore, was to create organizational coherence, so with the backing of Bradley and Eisenhower he reconfigured and combined units to form two robust and identical airborne divisions. To accomplish this he disbanded the 2nd Airborne Brigade and attached both its parachute regiments to the 82nd (and assigned the brigade commander, Brigadier General George P. Howell, as a second assistant division commander for the 82nd) and the independent 501st to the 101st, thereby giving each division three parachute regiments (the 82nd had the 505th, 507th, and 508th; the 101st had the 501st, 502nd, and 506th). To even out the glider forces he disbanded the 401st and used its two battalions to give the remaining glider regiments a third battalion (the 1/401st went to the 327th; the 2/401st went to the 325th), thereby effecting an organizational change that he had recommended and McNair denied just weeks before.[44]

Ridgway also took advantage of the resource-rich environment in Britain to make other equipment and organizational adjustments. This included reconstituting the 456th Parachute Field Artillery Battalion, which arrived in England with only two batteries, and forming a division reconnaissance platoon, a parachute maintenance company, and a fourth parachute engineer company in the engineer battalion. He also bolstered the division's antitank capability by converting another of the 80th Airborne Antiaircraft Battalion's antiaircraft batteries into an antitank battery, giving it a total of four antitank and two antiaircraft batteries. He also had the 80th swap its U.S. 57mm antitank guns for British 6-pounders, which had narrower wheelbases and were thus easier to get on a glider.[45]

In mid-February, the reorganized 82nd moved from Northern Ireland to the English Midlands, where the training intensity increased and the comparatively spacious surroundings allowed for larger and more complex exercises, to include battalion-size parachute drops and glider insertions employing both U.S. Waco and British Horsa gliders.[46] As always, long conditioning marches and live-fire exercises were standard, but added to the regimen were courses on operating armored vehicles; Ridgway and Gavin left little to chance.[47]

The hard training produced results. Gavin, who kept an especially sharp eye on the division's two new parachute regiments, was pleased, noting that it was "refreshing to work with troops fresh from America" because they were "enthusiastic" and "anxious" and "listen and hang on to every word and . . . try to do exactly as they are told." What they lack in experience, he added, "they more than make up for in their zeal and interest in doing the correct thing." He was particularly impressed with the 508th, which, he wrote, "looks as good as any new outfit that I have ever seen, if they cannot do it it cannot be done by green troops."[48]

Although quite parochial in his attitude toward paratroopers, Gavin was also pleased with the division's glider troopers. "This afternoon visited the 325 training," he noted in his diary. "Coming along OK. A steady appearing regiment, probably never will fight with the élan and dash of the parachute regiments but it can be counted upon for a steady fight."[49] Ridgway, too, was impressed with Colonel Lewis's glider troopers. For example, after observing a tactical exercise by the 1/325th, he wrote to Lewis to commend him on the battalion's performance, stating that it was "without exception the best of such exercises I have observed during two years on duty with this Division."[50] Even Leigh-Mallory was impressed. According to Brereton, the air chief marshal became so enthusiastic after watching a glider exercise that he was moved to opine that "airborne forces are one of the most powerful weapons in modern warfare, and they will become increasingly important with each new operation."[51]

Since the 82nd was to be dropped so far behind German lines, and therefore have no recourse to heavy artillery or naval gunfire support, Ridgway and his new division artillery officer, Colonel Francis "Andy" March III (March assumed the position after Taylor went to the 101st), designed a particularly rigorous artillery training program. They started by honing basic artillery handling skills like preparing and camouflaging firing positions and rapidly displacing from one position to another both during day and night. Once these had been mastered the artillerymen moved to a firing range in Wales, where March put them through a six-day live-fire exercise during which they fired every conceivable scenario, beginning at the battery level and progressing through battalion and division fire missions. The training paid off, as the 456th demonstrated one afternoon when Ridgway, Gavin, and March suddenly appeared in the battalion's fire direction center. Spotting some sheep in the distance, Ridgway turned to Major Wagner J. D'Alessio, the 456th's commander and told him to "scatter those sheep—don't kill." D'Alessio, in turn, directed Lieutenant Clarence McKelvey to adjust the fire of the guns. Though he was working with an untrained observer from the Air Corps—who, instead of repeating the artillery command "On the way!" disconcertingly shouted into the phone "Bombs away!"—McKelvey remained calm and scattered the sheep as ordered. According to McKelvey, "D'Alessio looked like he had just pee'd his pants," but both Gavin and Ridgway grinned.[52]

A final parachute training exercise was held on 12 May, a full-dress rehearsal for the D-Day drop. Code-named Exercise EAGLE, it involved 432 aircraft from the 50th and 53rd Troop Carrier Wings carrying the 101st and 369 aircraft from the 52nd Wing carrying the 82nd. The air route was more than 260 miles long, half over water, and required the pilots to navigate using the same light and radar aids that would be used during the invasion. The results were mixed, as were opinions about what EAGLE demonstrated. Despite a midair collision involving two C-47s that killed all aboard, fortunately after they had dropped their paratroopers, Brereton wrote Arnold that "the dress rehearsal indicated to my satisfaction that the plan of employment is practicable from a flight and navigational point of view, and that we have reached an effective state of readiness to carry out the plan." Gavin was not as sanguine. He was still not impressed with the pilots' ability to locate and deliver paratroopers to the correct drop zones (one serial from the 52nd had delivered only sixteen of forty-two loads accurately), and when he pointed this out there followed a heated discussion. It was, he wrote, "the damndest touchy problem, how to get them to fly better and show more concern for our aspects of the operation without becoming too critical of their technique. They are quick to resent it if we do."[53] But by that time there was little more that could be done. No more drops were scheduled for fear that jump injuries could not be replaced by D-Day. Moreover, by late May training had ceased altogether so the airborne divisions could move to the airfields, where they were locked down.[54]

Awaiting them across the Channel was a mixed lot of defenders under the command of Generalfeldmarschall Gerd von Rundstedt who, as *Oberbefehlshaber West* (commander in chief West, hereafter *OB West*), had at his disposal fifty-eight divisions with which to defend France and the Low Countries.[55] Thirty-three of the divisions were of poor quality and suitable only for defensive duties. They were also significantly weaker than standard German infantry divisions and almost bereft of transportation; according to one observer, some of them were so immobile that "they were hardly able to resupply themselves."[56] In addition, the manpower in these divisions was suspect. Many of the soldiers were old, averaging thirty-five years, and sick, having been declared unfit for duty elsewhere. Moreover, in an attempt to reduce the impact of troop transfers to the east, in 1943 the Germans began raising *Ost* (East) battalions to fill them out. Composed mainly of Eastern European volunteers who wanted to avoid forced labor, by summer 1944 there were more than forty-five *Ost* battalions in *OB West*; in the German *Seventh Army* sector—a subordinate command to *OB West* responsible for the area in which the Allies would land—there were twenty-one *Ost* battalions, which amounted to more than a quarter of the total number of battalions in *Seventh Army*. But offsetting these weaknesses were the strength and experience of Rundstedt's other twenty-five divisions, some of Germany's best: thirteen army infantry divisions, two parachute divisions, six army panzer divisions, and four Waffen SS panzer or panzer grenadier divisions. In addition, the Germans had one great advantage—they owned the ground—and since November 1943 they had been working to turn that ground into one of the most heavily fortified areas in the world.[57]

Although the Germans had had some three and a half years to fortify the Atlantic coast, little was done until Hitler issued Führer Directive No. 51 on 3 November 1943: "For the last two and one-half years the bitter and costly struggle against Bolshevism has made the utmost demands upon the bulk of our military resources and energies" it began, but "the situation has since changed." The threat from the east remained,

> but an even greater danger looms in the West: the Anglo-American landing! In the East, the vastness of the space will, as a last resort, permit a loss of territory even on a major scale, without suffering a mortal blow to Germany's chance for survival.
>
> Not so in the West! If the enemy here succeeds in penetrating our defenses on a wide front, consequences of staggering proportions will follow within a short time. All signs point to an offensive against the Western Front of Europe no later than spring, and perhaps earlier.[58]

The reason for this sudden change was elementary: Hitler and his generals could read a map. Though they did not know where the Allies would land, they did know that if the Allies gained a foothold in the west, they could soon be in the Ruhr, Germany's industrial heart. In fact, the Anglo-American forces in southeastern England were *closer* to the industrial cities of Cologne, Düsseldorf, and Essen than was Hitler in Berlin. They were also closer to Berlin than were the leading Russian units by more than 1,000 kilometers.[59] "For that reason," Hitler ordered, "I can no longer justify the further weakening of the West in favor of other theaters of war. I have therefore decided to strengthen the defenses in the West."[60]

Two days after issuing his directive Hitler gave it teeth by appointing Generalfeldmarschall Erwin Rommel inspector of coastal defenses and then, a month later, commander of *Army Group B*, the subordinate headquarters to *OB West* responsible for everything north of the Loire River.[61] Rommel had not been in the west since 1940, but he had heard of the vaunted Atlantic Wall, the name Nazi propagandists had given to a supposedly impregnable network of 15,000 interconnected concrete strongpoints manned by 300,000 men.[62] Upon being named to his new position he set off on an inspection tour. Starting in Copenhagen, Denmark, and working his way south, traveling hundreds of miles a day, Rommel discovered that the Atlantic Wall was a "figment of Hitler's *Wolkenkuckkucksheim* [cloud cuckoo land]."[63] There were some areas that were heavily fortified, especially port cities, river mouths, U-boat pens, and the areas defending the V-1 rocket launching sites, but for the most part the fortifications were, at best, partially complete. So with Hitler's backing, he instituted a vigorous fortification program of his own design.[64]

Eschewing elaborate concrete positions that took too much time and effort to construct, Rommel had his commanders build with whatever materials were available. They were to focus their efforts on routes leading inland from the coast. They were to lay mines by the thousands and emplace metal tetrahedrons that were designed to rip the bottoms from landing craft on every open beach. They were to cover landing sites with camouflaged primary, secondary, and tertiary defensive positions connected by trenches and carefully sighted to ensure interlocking fields of fire. The result was that by D-Day there were some 4,200,000 mines and more than 500,000 offshore obstacles along the Channel coast, behind which was an interconnected web of strongpoints. The intent was not to stop an amphibious attack cold; it was to slow, stall, and break it up long enough for armored reserves to be brought up for a killing blow.[65]

Rommel took an equally strong interest in defeating an Allied airborne assault. Almost without exception German commanders expected that large-scale airborne drops would precede the amphibious assault. Some estimated as many as eight to ten airborne divisions would be dropped. To meet this threat, Rommel ordered the emplacement of antiairborne obstacles in every open field. Nicknamed *Rommelspargel* (Rommel's asparagus), the obstacles consisted of eight- to twelve-foot poles driven upright into the ground at irregular intervals that were then wired together and topped with mines.[66] In addition, he ordered the flooding of several rivers, turning potential landing areas into vast marshlands unsuitable for parachute or glider landings. He also held frequent map exercises and maneuvers to train his commanders to counter an airborne assault.[67]

While Germany's soldiers dug where the Allies could land, Germany's leaders tried to determine where they would land. After a time this became something of an analytical parlor game among German generals. According to Generalleutnant Günther Blumentritt, Rundstedt's chief of staff, the German high command "expected invasion on a different front each month. Invasion was expected first in Norway, then in Denmark and the North Sea, in the OB West area, in Spain and Portugal, in Genoa and upper Italy, in the Adriatic, and in Greece and Turkey. Expectations changed continually."[68] In late April 1944 Admiral Theodor Krancke's *Naval Group West* posited another possibility. Based on a study of Allied bombing and minesweeping patterns and aerial reconnaissance photos of Allied camps in Britain, Krancke and his staff believed that Normandy and the Brittany Peninsula were the most likely landing places.[69] Coincidentally, Hitler had recently received reports from a trusted spy working in the British Embassy in Turkey that also indicated Normandy as the invasion area. This induced him, in early May, to order the reinforcement of Normandy.[70] Before long a parachute regiment, two separate parachute battalions, a crack machine-gun battalion, a rocket-launcher regiment, and the *Seventh Army Sturm Battalion*, an unusually large combined arms unit designed for shock action, were all moved to the Cotentin Peninsula. Also diverted to the Cotentin was the *91st Division*, a veteran unit that had been en route to Nantes.[71]

According to Allied intelligence, the *91st* took up positions centered on La Haye du Puits, the same area into which the 82nd was to be dropped. When Bradley saw this he immediately summoned Ridgway and Taylor to his headquarters, where they all agreed that the 82nd's drop on La Haye du Puits had to be scrapped. But Bradley wanted the 82nd in the fight, so he ordered the two airborne generals to find someplace else to drop the division. Several hours later they had their answer, which Bradley accepted without delay. Instead of dropping on the other side of the Cotentin, the 82nd would drop just north of the 101st to seize the important road center at Ste.-Mère-Église, located some six miles west of UTAH beach; secure several crossings over the nearby Merderet River; destroy other crossings on the Douve River; and protect the northwest flank of U.S. VII Corps landing on UTAH beach.[72]

Once the new missions and drop zones were determined it was a relatively simple matter to adapt the original movement scheme to the new area of operations. The 82nd had already been broken down into three echelons. Force A, the parachute echelon comprising all three parachute regiments along with signal, engineer, and artillery assets, would jump onto three drop zones around Ste.-Mère-Église and the Merderet River in the early morning hours of D-Day. Force B, the glider echelon, would follow in four increments, landing both north and south of Ste.-Mère-Église, on D-Day and D+1. Finally, Force C, the division's seaborne echelon under the command of Brigadier General Howell (also known as Howell Force) would come in over UTAH beach. It, too, was divided into increments. Leading Howell Force would be a small task force under Colonel Edson D. Raff composed of F Company, 2/401st, and some tanks and armored cars. Its mission was to land on D-Day and fight its way to Ste.-Mère-Église. Two days later (D+2) Howell would land with the remainder of Howell Force, an assortment of artillery, tank destroyer, truck, and support units and move to link up with the division wherever it may be.[73]

Because Bradley had effected such a major change, Eisenhower's deputy, Air Chief Marshal Tedder, chaired a meeting to ensure that the new airborne plan did not conflict with other established plans. Present at the meeting was Leigh-Mallory, who, when he heard Bradley's new plan, was aghast. Despite the changes to the plan, he was certain that the new German dispositions spelled disaster and estimated between 50 percent and 70 percent casualties for the two American airborne divisions. In light of these estimates, he insisted that the drops be canceled. Though no one was certain how Leigh-Mallory came to his conclusion, he remained convinced that he was correct and immediately following Tedder's meeting called Eisenhower to express his firm refusal to sanction Bradley's new plan.[74]

Leigh-Mallory's histrionics was the last thing Eisenhower needed. He was already on edge about the American airborne operation. In fact, even *before* he learned about the German reinforcements he had expressed concerns about the 82nd's drop in a secret memorandum for his diary:

> In contemplating Airborne operations, which I had originally thought would present very little difficulty because of our tremendous preponderance in fighters, we have run into a great deal of difficulty because of the almost universal coverage of the European continent by strong flak. When going into areas where gliders cannot land at night we run into most appalling difficulties and obstacles due to this fire. This is one phase of the operation that still worries me and I am somewhat concerned that the 82nd Airborne Division will have a most sticky time of it. I am going to see whether or not special support by fighter bombers cannot be given them.[75]

Hence, Leigh-Mallory's protest could not have but redoubled Eisenhower's worry. But it was not enough to compel him to cancel the drops without first seeking other counsel. The first person Eisenhower called was Bradley, who told him that if Eisenhower canceled the airborne operation he would cancel the landings on UTAH beach. He could not do one without the other. Eisenhower then called Ridgway, who seconded Bradley. Consequently, Eisenhower called Leigh-Mallory back to tell him that the American drops were a go. He also told Leigh-Mallory that if he desired, he could put his objections in writing. The next day Leigh-Mallory sent Eisenhower a letter. The air chief marshal apologized for his stridence but maintained that he would be "failing in my duty to you if I did not let you know that I am very unhappy about the U.S. airborne operations as now planned." Then, after explaining why he thought the American paratroopers and glider troopers were in such danger, he expanded his argument by insisting that if success at UTAH was contingent upon the success of the airborne drops, then the entire operation on the Allied western flank was a flawed and hazardous proposition.[76]

After receiving Leigh-Mallory's note Eisenhower phoned him, acknowledged receipt of the letter, and told him that the drops were still a go. He also drafted a note in reply:

> Thank you very much for your letter of the 29th on the subject of airborne operations. You are quite right in communicating to me your convictions as to the hazards involved and I must say that I agree with you as to the charac-

ter of these risks. However, a strong airborne attack in the region indicated is essential to the whole operation and it must go on. Consequently, there is nothing for it but for you, the Army Commander and the Troop Carrier Commander to work out to the last detail every single thing that may diminish these hazards.

It is particularly important that air and ground troops involved in the operation be not needlessly depressed. Like all the rest of the soldiers, they must understand that they have a tough job to do but be fired with determination to get it done.

I am, of course, hopeful that our percentage losses will not approximate your estimates because it is quite true that I expect to need these forces very badly later in the campaign.[77]

Fortunately, the thousands of airborne troopers, glider pilots, and troop transport crewmen who were to carry out the operation were unaware of Leigh-Mallory's concerns. Spread among fourteen airfields and ports throughout England and Wales, surrounded by double rows of barbed-wire fences that were patrolled by military police, and strictly quarantined from access to the outside world, their sole focus was on readying themselves for the fight.[78] Generally, this consisted of studying elaborate sand tables of the invasion area. For most, this was the first time they knew for certain where they were going. According to *Times* correspondent Bill Walton, who jumped in with the 82nd, these were "extraordinary tables with—everything you know in Europe was photographed from the air—repeatedly every day. If there was anything new that appeared it was then added to the sand tables," even Rommel's asparagus, added Walton, which concerned the troopers more than anything else.[79]

When not studying sand tables the troopers spent their days playing baseball or lying on their cots reading and writing letters. Nights were spent listening to military bands or watching movies. The food was tremendous. The only discomfort, one that every soldier in the invasion experienced, came from the combat uniforms, which had been impregnated with a chemical that was supposed to make them resistant to gas. But the "treatment eliminated any airflow through the fabric and made the jumpsuits very hot and almost impossible to clean. They were also stiff, uncomfortable, and smelled bad," recalled Sergeant John McKenzie of the 456th. Of course, washing the uniforms was not an option since that would neutralize the treatment, so, by D-Day, the troopers were wearing uniforms soaked with more than two weeks of sweat, dirt, and a mysterious chemical compound. "We all smelled to high heaven," recalled another trooper.[80]

But this was a minor inconvenience to the men in the camps. For them, the most pressing issue was the wait and the constant tension, knowing that the "go" order could come at any time. Even the veterans were nervous. Before Sicily, life in North Africa had been so miserable that many were anxious to "escape" to combat, and the jump into Italy had been mounted in a matter of hours, leaving little time for reflection. But the troopers marshaled in camps throughout England and Wales had had six months in a friendly, livable environment, and once they were moved to the departure airfields the barbed wire and military police patrols were constant reminders of what was looming. According to Sergeant Bill Dunfee, a veteran of Sicily and Italy, "Everyone sweats it out in his own way. We all put on happy faces for appearance' sake. I saw one young replacement who was really down. I got the company barber kit and trimmed his hair. I told him I wanted him to look good when we entered Paris. I was able to talk him out of his funk. I assured him that every man in that hangar was as scared as he was, including myself. I feel I relieved him of some of his anxiety. I hope so; he was one of the first killed." For some reason getting a haircut was something many troopers did to relieve the tension. Many in the 101st took this to extremes, cutting their hair Mohawk-style, but most of the troopers in the 82nd, influenced no doubt by the combat-tested among them, simply wanted a close cut, compelled not by military regulations as much as by the feeling that it would have to last a while. Bill Walton recalled his experience at the hands of a trooper who "had the toughest looking mug you've ever seen in your life." This trooper, explained Walton, sat placidly on a chair in a hangar, and "if he saw you going by with more hair than he thought you should have [would say,] 'Buddy come on in,' which he did to me. He said, 'don't you want to get rid of that? It will be growing bugs in a few days.' And he mowed it off."[81]

Ridgway and Gavin sensed the growing tension, so they spent a lot of time traveling to each of the 82nd's camps, giving impromptu talks to reassure both officers and men. Ridgway inspired "enthusiasm by his presence and his impressive appearance," recalled Lieutenant Wayne Pierce of the 325th.[82] Bill Walton also noticed Ridgway's striking look. It was, he said, the ideal visage of a "Roman Emperor and very sharp . . . very sharp." Though not as regal, Gavin, too, left his mark. According to Captain Hubert Bass, "You could always expect him to pop up at the damdest [*sic*] places. He just didn't act like a general, more like one of us." Major Daniel McIlvoy Jr., the 505th's regimental surgeon, remembered standing with Captain Matthew Connelly, the regiment's Catholic chaplain, while listening to Gavin. "I turned to Fr. Connelly and said 'I hope he doesn't ask us to jump without parachutes, because I'm sure no man would refuse to go!'"[83] With his inimitable talent for description, Sergeant John McNally explained the effect Gavin, "the soldier's general," had on the troopers of the division:

> Picture, if you can, a general who, arriving a little ahead of time and seeing the waiting soldiers being entertained by a GI doing card tricks, would stand unnoticed and wait until the little act was over before coming out to speak. Then he started talking in his quiet way, punctuated once in a while by a slow, tentative smile. He has the intense eyes and lined mouth of a man who has fought the Nazis a long time and well. I watched the faces of the men as he talked. It was as though an electric shock had gone through the whole group. When he talked, every man felt drawn into the company of the elect who, for the space of a breath, risked their lives a thousand feet above the ground.
>
> When he had finished, he needed only to lift a finger and say "Follow me," and there wasn't a single man who wouldn't have followed him straight to hell.[84]

There was one false alarm. Eisenhower had decided several weeks earlier that D-Day would be 5 June, a fact known to but a small group of "bigoted" individuals.[85] For the paratroopers of the 82nd, 101st, and British 6th Airborne, this necessitated a takeoff time of about 2300 hours on 4 June. Thus, on the afternoon of 4 June, under even tighter security than usual and with little warning, the paratroopers were assembled in their "sticks" (a stick was a planeload of paratroopers), drew their ammunition, issued their parachutes, and moved to their planes. Then the invasion was postponed, so they stripped off their gear and moved back to their barracks and tried to relax. Few could. Many tuned their radios to a popular American-music station, which was ironically broadcast by the Germans and hosted by Mildred Elizabeth Gillars, affectionately known as "Axis Sally" or, as the troopers of the 82nd called her, the "Berlin Bitch." They were stunned by what they heard. As Sergeant Robert L. Bearden of the 507th remembered it, during a break in the music "the 'Berlin Bitch' . . . welcomed our virgin parachute regiment to the Division—and pointed out that a very warm reception had been planned for us on the 5th. She then advised her sorrow that the project had been called off, and that our reception would still be one to remember." Major Ben F. Pearson, also of the 507th, remembered her saying, "Hello, boys of the 82nd [Airborne] Division. We know you are coming. We'll be waiting for you."[86] Veterans like Private First Class Anthony "Tony" Joseph DeMayo were unimpressed. German claims that 82nd troopers "would never see or walk on French soil" were empty, wrote DeMayo; he had heard the same thing before Sicily and Italy.[87]

Early that evening Eisenhower assembled his principal subordinates at Southwick House, just north of Portsmouth, Admiral Ramsay's headquarters.

His meteorologists had forecast marginally favorable weather for the morning of 6 June. Eisenhower canvassed those present for their opinion. All agreed to go, but the decision was Eisenhower's alone. At 2145 hours he made that decision—D-Day would be 6 June 1944—and the great engine of invasion restarted.[88]

The troopers returned to their waiting planes in the afternoon of 5 June, where they methodically checked and rechecked their equipment, blackened their faces, caught catnaps, and dealt with their mounting anxiety. Many sought out priests, ministers, and rabbis for a final blessing. Others were almost giddy. Bill Walton remembered a British band pulling up in a truck next to the airstrip to play some popular dance tunes for the troopers nearby. "These GIs . . . many of them with black faces, you know . . . hung with knives . . . and everything else, homely guys, began jitter-bugging together. . . . Oh, they were so mad—it was the goddamdest thing, most fantastic thing I ever saw."[89]

As takeoff drew near the troopers donned their equipment, lounged near their planes, and awaited word to board. Jumpmasters were given a mimeographed copy of a message from Eisenhower to read to their sticks that reminded them that their task would "not be an easy one," that the "enemy is well trained, well equipped and battle hardened" and would "fight savagely." Following suit—for no one questioned the momentousness of the event—several officers also took the time to impart their feelings to their troopers. Lieutenant Colonel Ed Krause, commander of the 3/505th (the man Gavin had almost relieved in Sicily), put on the most flamboyant show. Hoisting an American flag over his head he declared, "This was the first flag to fly over Naples when we captured that city last October. I want all of you, no matter where you land in France tonight, to march on the town of Sainte-Mère-Église, where together, we're going to liberate the people and fly this flag from the tallest building in town!" A more reserved Homer Jones, a lieutenant in the 508th, recalled looking at his men and realizing "there were a lot I wasn't ever going to see again," but when he tried to say something he was overcome with emotion and sputtered, "Oh shit!" to which Private Japhet Alphonso responded, "That's okay, lieutenant. We know what you mean." Sergeant Bill Lord, another 508th trooper, recalled the words of his platoon leader, Lieutenant Neal Beaver. "Neal told me this was going to be the greatest thing I ever did in my life. If we survived, we would have something to talk about to our grandchildren. I told him that was pretty much word for word what Yale coach Ducky Pond used to tell his football players on the day of the Harvard game" (Lord had dropped out of Yale to join the paratroops).[90]

At 2300 hours, 378 C-47s of the 52nd Troop Carrier Wing began taking off from seven separate airfields, carrying the division's 6,420 paratroopers.

Each of the planes was newly painted with three white and two black two-foot-wide stripes on each wing and around the fuselage back of the jump door to facilitate recognition by friendly ground and naval units, a lesson from Sicily. In a little more than an hour every plane except one was in the air and moving toward aerial assembly point ATLANTA some twenty miles east of Birmingham. From there the nine-ship V-of-V serials flew a dogleg route of approximately 150 miles to departure point FLATBUSH at the tip of a sandy cape called Portland Bill, where they left England behind and headed out to the Channel en route for France.[91] All over southwestern England "people were awakened by the thunder of a great armada," wrote Sergeant McNally. "Not the familiar far-off roar of the bombers, but a sharper, lower throbbing—the C-47's. Hour after hour it went on and they lay wide-eyed in their beds. Aware that the men they had known for months were now helmeted and strained, sitting in those planes above their heads. They knew that in a few hours the assault would be made, that the greatest D-Day of a thousand years was at hand." For war reporter Martha Gellhorn, who was one of those looking skyward that evening, it was "a terrible and handsome sight."[92]

CHAPTER 11

ALLES KAPUTT! THE AMERICANS ARE KILLING EVERYBODY!

In the narrative to follow, the great names drop out. Even Eisenhower and Montgomery appear but seldom. In their place will be the corps and division commanders, the colonels, the lieutenants, and the privates. For the few will be substituted the many, as the battlefield, so long seen as a single conceptual problem, becomes a confused and disparate fact—a maze of unrelated orchards and strange roads, hedgerows, villages, streams and woods, each temporarily bounding for the soldier the whole horizon of the war.

—GORDON A. HARRISON, *CROSS-CHANNEL ATTACK*

WHILE ALLIED PLANES were taking off, German intelligence officers solved one of the two great secrets of the invasion—when it would come. But no one believed them.

Several days earlier German spies obtained twenty-eight seemingly innocuous phrases that the British Broadcasting Corporation would transmit no more than forty-eight hours before the invasion to alert Allied agents and Resistance fighters throughout France to be prepared to sabotage predetermined targets. When German listening posts intercepted several of these messages between 2200 and 2300 hours on 5 June, they immediately sent word up the chain of command that the invaders were coming. But no one believed them because other indicators did not corroborate their finding. German naval analysts had calculated that an invasion fleet could sail only in seas of less than intensity four (wave heights of five to eight feet), with surface visibility of at least three miles and with winds of less than twenty-four knots. None of these conditions held the night of 5–6 June.[1] In addition, reconnaissance flights over English ports indicated that the Allies had not assembled enough tonnage for a large-scale amphibious assault. Based on this analysis, on 4 June the Kriegsmarine announced that "at the present moment, no immediate major invasion is to be expected."[2] Moreover, the major Russian offensive that many posited would accompany the invasion had yet to break. Consequently, Generalleutnant Hans Speidel, the chief of staff of *Army Group B*, dismissed the radio intercepts and did not bother to inform his superior, Erwin Rommel, who was in Germany. At *OB West* headquarters a courier who pulled a gruff and somewhat tipsy Rundstedt away from his dinner to inform him of the news was upbraided. "Does anyone think the enemy is stupid enough to announce his arrival over the radio?" barked the man responsible for the defense of Western Europe before returning to his meal.[3] Perhaps the most auspicious and assuredly the most ironic disregard was that shown by Generaloberst Friedrich Dollmann, whose *Seventh Army* was responsible for the defense of Normandy. Because of the bad weather, Dollmann canceled an alert so his subordinate commanders could get an early start for Rennes, where they were to participate in a map exercise. The subject of the map exercise: defense against airborne attack.[4]

The first Americans to hit French soil were the pathfinders. Landing between 0025 and 0138 hours, 6 June, they were responsible for setting up Eureka beacons and lights in the form of giant *T*s on each of the division's three drop zones, designated "O," "N," and "T." Drop zone "O," located east of the Merderet and just north of Ste.-Mère-Église, was the 505th's drop zone. Drop zones "T" and "N," located west of the Merderet, were for the 507th and 508th, respectively. Landing about thirty minutes before the main body, the pathfinders were acutely aware that the accuracy of the drop rested in large part on their shoulders, and, as Gavin told them, "When you land in Normandy . . . you will have only one friend: God."[5]

The pathfinders met with mixed results. The 505th's landed squarely on drop zone "O," met no resistance, and within ten minutes had their Eureka beacon and lights set up. The 507th's pathfinders also dropped accurately onto drop zone "T," which was about one and a half miles northwest of the Merderet River crossing at La Fière, but they were under fire as soon as they exited their planes. Lieutenant Charles Ames, the 507th pathfinder team leader, eventually found a secure location on the drop zone where he set up the Eureka beacon, but with Germans all around him he could not risk setting up any lights. The 508th's pathfinders had the worst luck of all. Dropped about a mile southeast of drop zone "N," which was about a mile and a half south of drop zone "T," they quickly assembled and got their bearings but found the way to drop zone "N" barred by a substantial force of Germans. With no time to work their way around, they set up their Eureka beacon and two amber lights where they were and hoped for the best.[6]

The pathfinder aircraft had flown the same route that the main body would take, a route designed to avoid enemy antiaircraft and radar concentrations, achieve surprise, and facilitate navigation. Additionally, since the German defenses in Normandy were oriented north and east, their guns pointed toward the Channel, the route was designed to bring the paratroopers in from the west, or landward, side. Beginning at Portland Bill, where the route left British airspace, it continued southwest over water for fifty-seven miles to checkpoint HOBOKEN, marked by a Royal Navy vessel outfitted with radar and light beacons. At HOBOKEN the route turned left ninety degrees for a fifty-four-mile leg between the occupied islands of Alderney and Guernsey until it hit the west coast of the Cotentin Peninsula at initial point PEORIA. At PEORIA the route turned left again, albeit slightly, and continued overland for approximately twenty miles to the three drop zones. The route back was simple. The planes were to make a beeline for the coast and head back to England.[7]

For the most part the flight of the main body was flawless. Flying in temperate weather with no winds, scattered clouds, a bright moon, and excellent visibility, the aerial armada approached France on course, at or ahead of schedule, and in formation.[8] So smooth was the ride that many troopers slept. Those not sleeping passed the time in myriad ways. Quite a few prayed. Others, like Captain Lyle Britain Putnam, the 2/505th's surgeon, silently wrestled with fear, apprehension, and homesickness. Many thought of their girls; some joked openly of the "unfortunate females who were being deprived of [their] so outstanding and exceptional company." Private Ken Russell, who had begged an early release from the hospital so he would not miss the jump, spent his time thinking of his high school class, which was graduating that night in Tennessee. Those lucky enough to be near an open door watched the scene unfold around them. Private First Class Tony DeMayo recalled "looking out of the plane and seeing the [C]hannel spotted with all sorts of seacraft. It looked as if one could walk across the Channel." Captain Robert M. Piper of the 505th sat nonchalantly in the open door of his plane with his "feet in the breeze." Common to everyone making their way to France that night, whether they be praying, sleeping, or joking, was the strength each man drew from those around him. Other than the "very real concern for personal welfare," recalled Captain Putnam, the average trooper in the 82nd did not worry "about general environments as long as he was in contact with other members of his unit." "These men around me were the best friends I will ever know," thought Private Dwayne Burns, who worried only that he would not do anything to get any of them killed.[9]

There was another source of strength in the planes that night: leadership. On every plane there was a leader—a sergeant, lieutenant, captain, major, or colonel—who would be the first man out the door. The 82nd's leaders were expected to "jump first and eat last," a creed Gavin, who was aboard the lead plane of the 508th's serial, enforced by personal example.[10] "In all of our airborne drops, the first man out of the plane is always the General [Gavin] himself!" wrote Sergeant John McNally. "All of the thousands of men who crouch in the door of a plane, ready to leap into the roaring, flak-filled night know that someone else was down there before them. Imagine the terrific morale factor of the simple, stark facts: the General jumps first! If there is a mistake in picking the drop zone, the General is the first to pay the penalty."[11]

Gavin was not the only general flying in with the 82nd that night; Ridgway, too, was preparing himself for the drop, his first into combat. He had originally planned to go in with the lead glider serial but later changed his mind. According to Ridgway's aide, Captain Arthur Kroos, going in by glider "would have been an ego destroyer" for Ridgway and would not have conformed to the "symbol he was creating," a symbol that had been recently assailed by Ridgway's *bête noire* "Boy" Browning.[12]

Browning had made cutting remarks about how Ridgway handled the 82nd in Sicily and questioned his not having jumped in with his troopers, which was surprising given that Browning had never made a combat jump, either. Gavin defended his boss, asserting that Ridgway "had handled the division as it should have been handled, that he had had much more responsibility than just the parachute assault."[13] Nonetheless, Ridgway could not ignore Browning's jibe. The rivalry between the two was intense and, at times, vitriolic. Moreover, there was talk about establishing an Allied airborne command in Europe. By anyone's estimation, Ridgway and Browning were the two front-runners to command it. Jumping into Normandy would afford Ridgway a qualification Browning could not match.

Simply jumping was not enough for Ridgway, however. When he hit the ground he had to be in position to actually command his division. As Kroos put it, "No way did he want to land 200 miles out someplace when his troopers were winning the war over in this place."[14] So on the day of the jump Ridgway asked the 505th's executive officer, Lieutenant Colonel Mark Alexander, to "pick a plane and jump master where-by [*sic*] he had the best chance of landing in the chosen landing area." Alexander selected Lieutenant Dean Garber, an experienced jumpmaster whose plane would be on the right side of the formation and thus in the best spot to see the pathfinder lights.[15] It was a fortuitous choice.

Although their flight over the Channel had been uneventful, when the planes of the main body reached the coast of France they flew both figuratively and literally into the fog of war, entering a cloud bank so thick that many troopers mistook it for a German smoke screen. The first three of the 82nd's ten serials, carrying the 505th and Ridgway, climbed above the clouds without breaking formation. Encountering sporadic and generally ineffective fire en route to drop zone "O," the pilots homed in on the Eureka signal, which they picked up some fifteen to twenty-one miles out. Three to five miles out they saw the lighted *T*s—according to Lieutenant Colonel Krause, seeing the *T*'s "was a Godsend and I felt that I had found the Holy Grail"—made their final adjustments, and turned on the green jump lights.[16] Despite flying too high and too fast, the pilots were amazingly accurate; 80 of 118 planes dropped within two miles of the drop zone, including Ridgway's, which dropped "exactly where we were supposed to go."[17]

Next to arrive over France were four serials carrying the 508th and Gavin. They met with disaster. Not only did they scatter when they entered the clouds, they encountered heavier antiaircraft fire, and, because the 508th pathfinders had set up the Eureka beacon off course, most of the pilots received no homing signal at all. Flying blind through flak that grew more intense the nearer they got to the target area, the pilots resorted to the crudest form of navigation, time-distance calculations. They knew that after seven to eight minutes of straight and level flight after entering France they would be over drop zone "N." Few pilots, however, were able to keep their planes straight and level, and those that did searched for the drop zone lights in vain. Knowing also that twelve minutes into their flight over France they would be completely across the Cotentin Peninsula and over water, most pilots simply estimated their position and turned on the green jump lights when they thought they were near the drop zone. As a result, only 63 of the 508th's 132 planes dropped anywhere near drop zone "N," and many dropped over the marshlands created by Rommel's deliberate flooding of the Douve and Merderet Rivers. Twenty planeloads were still unaccounted for a month later.[18]

The last three serials, carrying the 507th, fared no better. They, too, scattered in the cloud bank and flew through the most intense antiaircraft fire of all, and although these pilots received a strong Eureka signal from drop zone "T," because the pathfinders there had not set up any lights they also used time-distance calculations to make best-guess drops (unlike modern radar, Eureka could only get pilots in the general vicinity of the drop zone, after which pilots required visual aids, like the lighted *T*s, to pinpoint their targets). All told, only 73 of the 507th's 117 planes dropped near drop zone "T," many of which also dropped over the marshlands.[19]

Altogether, in less than two hours about 6,400 paratroopers from the 82nd dropped into France that night (13,400 from both U.S. divisions). Only 8 men refused to jump. Thirty-six troopers are known to have drowned in the marsh, while another 223 sustained some sort of injury when landing (173 of these made it to friendly lines; the rest were taken prisoner). Only 1 plane was known to have been shot down before dropping. The crew and troopers of a second were never found. A third did not drop because flak wounded 7 troopers inside before they could exit. Seven planes were either shot down or ditched on the way home, and 111 returned to base with some sort of flak damage.[20]

As had been the case in Sicily, the scattered drop (the 101st was also widely dispersed) confused and paralyzed the enemy. Information gathering and analysis replaced aggressive action. Staff officers argued among themselves over the meaning of spotty, conflicting, and often quite wildly inaccurate information that flowed into their headquarters. Major Friedrich Hayn, intelligence officer of the *LXXXIV Corps* (of the *Seventh Army*), left a telling account of what it was like in his headquarters following the drops:

> The minutes were dragging on and the nervous strain became almost unendurable. Single reports arrived in rapid succession, contradicting or confirming each other. The Command Post of the Seventh Army as well as the Army Group Command [*Army Group B*, Rommel's headquarters] kept calling us. But our Staff could do nothing but wait! Wait until the confusing situation had become somewhat clearer; until the centers of attack of the paratroops and beach parties could be discerned; until we knew which of our strongpoints had been encircled or outflanked by the enemy; until our reconnoit[e]ring parties had brought in some prisoners.[21]

As a result it was not until well after daylight that the Germans attacked anywhere in the Cotentin, although two of their headquarters, *LXXXIV Corps* and *Seventh Army*, had correctly determined the foci of the drops by 0400 hours, 6 June, about an hour and fifteen minutes after the last paratrooper touched down.[22]

Ironically, the German force that was both well positioned and possessed enough firepower and mobility to wreak havoc on the 82nd's paratroopers was the *91st Division*, the same unit whose sudden appearance on the Cotentin forced the last-minute change to U.S. airborne plans and caused Leigh-Mallory so much angst. Allied intelligence had mistakenly placed the *91st* near

La Haye du Puits on the west side of the peninsula. In reality the *91st* was centered on the village of Picauville in the southwest portion of the 82nd's sector. So despite the frantic preassault machinations aimed at avoiding the *91st*, the 82nd ended up dropping right on top of it. But like its parent headquarters, *LXXXIV Corps*, the *91st* was incapacitated by the chaos precipitated by the parachute assault. In addition, the *91st*'s headquarters had poor communications with its subordinate units because paratroopers cut the communication wires, leaving the subordinate units isolated and without orders. The ensuing silence led to caution on the part of the *91st*'s regimental, battalion, and company commanders who elected to remain in their defensive positions rather than venture forth in search of marauding paratroopers.[23] A third contributing cause of the paralysis that gripped the *91st*—and one that reinforced the cautious attitude in its ranks—was the death of its commander, Generalleutnant Wilhelm Falley, at the hands of a small band of 508th troopers.

Falley had set out early that morning to attend the war game at Rennes. He was a few miles outside his headquarters at Picauville when four troopers under the command of Lieutenant Malcolm D. Brannen of the 3/508th put a burst of gunfire through the windshield of his sedan, causing it to swerve and crash into a ditch. Falley, who was not killed in the crash, either had opened his door and freed himself or was thrown free and was crawling toward his pistol when Brannen walked up and shot him (according to witnesses Falley was muttering "Don't shoot, don't shoot" in English, but his actions belied his protests).[24] News of Falley's death fueled rumors that an entire parachute battalion was outside Picauville preparing to attack, which compelled the *91st* headquarters to shut down operations—and thereby completely sever its links with its subordinate commands—and move to an alternate location several miles away.[25]

While German staff officers debated and German commanders awaited orders that never came, American paratroopers sought one another in the night. The best way to do this was to "roll up the stick." Once on the ground and free of his parachute harness the first jumper in each stick was supposed to move in the same direction as that flown by the plane from which he had jumped while the last jumper in the stick moved in the opposite direction. Theoretically, the first and last troopers would meet somewhere in the middle, having gathered the other troopers in the stick as they moved toward one another. In Normandy this technique proved worthless. Not only were most of the planes flying too high and too fast during the drop, which increased the dispersion between jumpers, but the Norman hedgerows so compartmentalized the terrain that moving in a straight line anywhere in the Cotentin was nearly impossible.[26] So formidable were the hedgerows that it was not uncommon for fairly large groups of soldiers to be on opposite sides of the same hedgerow, physically separated by only a few feet, yet remain oblivious to the presence of one another.[27] General Morgan, who had visited Normandy before the war and knew it well, perhaps best described this country, which the French called the *bocage*. It was, he wrote, "a tactical feature of major importance" that "consists of a series of minor undulations, well wooded and divided up into small enclosures, each one separated from the next by an earth bank some feet in height and some feet in thickness. In most cases these banks were topped by considerable quickset hedges and trees garnished on at least one side by a considerable ditch."[28]

Because they could not assemble in their sticks, the troopers instead moved to their objectives individually or in small groups, aided in no small measure by the terrain features they had memorized from maps, aerial photos, and sand tables. For many troopers from the 507th and 508th, however, this was problematic because the terrain where they landed looked nothing like expected. They expected seeing two rivers, the Merderet and the Douve, and had been reminded that the former was more akin to a stream, while the latter was approximately sixty feet wide.[29] But because the Germans had flooded both rivers, what these troopers saw gleaming in the moonlight as they descended in their parachutes were *two* large rivers, not one, and they became disoriented. Even savvy veterans like Gavin were stymied. When descending in his parachute he looked down and "estimated that we must be on the DOUVE because of the depth and width of the water. Our pre-operational photo interpretation had rather clearly established the fact that the MERDERET was a narrow stream, about 20 yards wide and several feet deep."[30] In reality, he landed near the Merderet. Likewise, Colonel Roy E. Lindquist, the 508th regimental commander, found himself in so much water he thought he had landed at the confluence of the two rivers when in fact he was at the upper reaches of the Merderet.[31] And some, like Private First Class Orville A. Amorose, were more concerned with survival than with pinpointing their location:

> Halfway down, I saw that I was over water. Before, I had been merely scared; now I was petrified—for I didn't know how to swim. I knew I was about to die, that I'd never get out of my harness and the 90 pounds of gear to even inflate the Mae West I was wearing. When I hit, I went clear under the water. That's the end, I thought. But my legs hit the muddy bottom and I stood up—in water up to my neck. Miraculously, I had beaten the odds, for many places in that swamp were ten feet or more deep. I thanked God.[32]

Eventually, the 82nd's troopers coalesced into five major groups, two to the east and three to the west of the Merderet River. The largest gathering was east of the river at Ste.-Mère-Église, where mostly 2/505th and 3/505th troopers congregated. The other group east of the river, and the second-largest gathering overall, was at La Fière, one of two crossings over the Merderet that the division was to secure. Of the three groups west of the Merderet, two were north of La Fière, while the third assembled on a prominent terrain feature, Hill 30, opposite Chef du Pont, the other Merderet crossing site the division was to secure.

Taking Ste.-Mère-Église was the 3/505th's mission, which for the most part landed accurately on drop zone "O." Hence, forty-five minutes after landing Lieutenant Colonel Krause had with him about 180 troopers and one drunk Frenchman who verified Krause's position and volunteered to guide the Americans along a trail that entered the town from the northwest. He also told Krause that the German garrison inside Ste.-Mère-Église was relatively small and that it was mainly situated on the outskirts of town and not inside the town itself. Reluctant to place too much faith in his inebriated scout, Krause put him on point along with a small security detachment and followed at a safe distance with the rest of his force. As it turned out, the Frenchman proved true, and thirty minutes after starting out Krause's force was on the outskirts of Ste.-Mère-Église. Buoyed by his success so far and gambling that the Frenchman's account of German dispositions was as accurate as his navigation, Krause elected to clear the town from the inside out. Leading his troopers in a rush to the town square, Krause then had them fan out in all directions, following the major roads that intersected at the square, clearing as they went. Using only their bayonets and grenades, the troopers fought their way to the edge of town, where they stopped and set up blocking positions. By 0430 hours, Krause owned Ste.-Mère-Église and the American flag he had carried with him was flying over the first town liberated in France.[33]

Although taking Ste.-Mère-Église was, for Krause and his men, a relatively bloodless affair during which they killed ten German stragglers, took thirty prisoners, and sustained no casualties of their own, they found indications that before they arrived the town had been witness to a vicious struggle. Near the town square, where a building had been set on fire by incendiary debris from German flak, were the charred remains of several troopers who had drifted into the fire, their bodies torn apart by the detonation of their grenades and ammunition. Other troopers were hanging from trees and buildings, their bodies riddled with bullet holes. Some had been bayoneted.[34] Even more disturbing were scenes like that described by Private Clarence Ollom, who saw "American paratroopers who were tied to a fence . . . with their throats cut." This angered the men, recalled Chaplain George Wood, "but I explained that this was what we could expect in our kind of an outfit."[35] But perhaps the best portent of what lay in store was captured in a scene recalled by Private John Fitzgerald of the 101st, who fought alongside the 3/505th at Ste.-Mère-Église:

> It was a picture story of the death of one 82nd Airborne trooper. He had occupied a German foxhole and made it his personal Alamo. In a half circle around the hole lay the bodies of nine German soldiers. The body closest to the hole was only three feet away, a potato masher [grenade] in its fist. The other distorted forms lay where they had fallen, testimony to the ferocity of the fight. His ammunition bandoliers were still on his shoulders, empty of M-1 clips. Cartridge cases littered the ground. His rifle stock was broken in two. He had fought alone and, like many others that night, had died alone.[36]

By daylight there were approximately 350 troopers in Ste.-Mère-Église along with one of the two 75mm howitzers that dropped in with the regiment.[37] Morning also saw the town's residents emerging from their hiding places. Most, like Andre Mace, had spent the night hiding but were overcome with joy at their long-awaited liberation. "The Americans are the only ones in the streets of the town. There are no more Germans," recorded Mace in his diary. "It is an indescrib[a]ble joy. I was never as happy in all my life." Others had yet to come to grips with what had occurred. In a letter to General Charles de Gaulle, the mayor of Ste.-Mère-Église wrote of several women who were crying and beseeching the paratroopers not to leave. One of the paratroopers, he continued, "made this reply with a big smile, 'We'll never leave, we're staying right here!'"[38]

Securing Ste.-Mère-Église was important for two reasons. First, it denied the Germans use of the only major highway in the eastern Cotentin, which diminished their ability to counterattack into the invasion area. Second, it provided the 82nd a base from which to defend in the event the amphibious invasion went awry. As late as noon on D-Day, six hours after the amphibious landings, Ridgway still had no information from the beaches, and rumors were rampant that the assault had been postponed due to weather. At one juncture he met with Gavin to discuss what to do if the rumors proved true. According to Gavin, "Matt and I decided right then that if the seaborne assault had been called off or beaten back, then we would continue to fight to the end."[39] Ste.-Mère-Église would be their battle position. They shared their thoughts with no one.

Just as Krause's men were securing Ste.-Mère-Église, the first glider insertion occurred. Code-named DETROIT, it involved fifty-two C-47s towing fifty-two Waco gliders bringing in sixteen antitank guns of the 80th Airborne Antiaircraft Battalion, twenty-two jeeps, five trailers, ten tons of supplies, and ammunition, signal equipment and 220 troopers, mostly from the division staff. Flying the same route as had been taken by the paratroopers, the formation reached the French coast intact (with the exception of one C-47 and glider, which had problems at the airfield and followed thirty minutes behind), but then it, too, hit the cloud bank and scattered. As a result seven gliders were either cut or broke loose early and landed in the western Cotentin. Seven more released west of the Merderet because their pilots saw the water and thought they were about to fly into the Channel. Of the rest, seventeen to twenty-three gliders landed on their objective, drop zone "O," between 0401 and 0410 hours. Nine others landed within a two-mile radius of Ste.-Mère-Église, to include two that landed inside the town, and three came down in the 101st area.[40] Most of the gliders were destroyed on impact.

Tony DeMayo was near drop zone "O" when the gliders came in and recalled "one crash after another as they hit the so[-]called hedgerows. It was just like crumbling wooden match-boxes in your hand." According to Lieutenant Jack Tallerday, when the gliders hit the hedgerows the "equipment in the rear of the glider was torn loose and pinned the crew members in the nose of the glider. . . . The moans of the dieing [*sic*] and injured men, lack of sufficient first aid men and the fact that the gliders were being attacked by the Germans as they landed makes this incident one that is hard to forget." Master Sergeant Charles W. Mason, who flew in with this contingent, remembered German antiaircraft fire tearing through his glider and ripping the groin out of an artillery captain sitting across from him.[41] Miraculously, only 3 troopers were killed and 23 injured in the landings, including the 82nd's chief of staff, Colonel Eaton. Eleven of the jeeps were damaged beyond repair, but, most welcome, six (or seven; accounts vary) of the antitank guns were salvaged and in action by noon.[42]

After taking Ste.-Mère-Église Krause sent a runner to find and inform his regimental commander, Colonel William E. Ekman. Ekman was new to the regiment, having taken over in late March from Batchellor, who had been relieved and sent to command the 1/508th. According to one of Ekman's troopers: "I doubt that any regimental commander took over a regiment under a greater handicap than he did. The 505, with two combat jumps and two campaigns to their [*sic*] credit, felt that they were combat hero[e]s and entitled to go home since we had already won the war so to speak. And then to be handed a noncombatant commander was the absolute pits [Normandy was Ekman's first combat]." But Ekman quickly earned the respect of his subordinates and superiors alike and remained in command of the 505th for the rest of the war. According to Lieutenant Colonel Alexander, Ekman became a "very good" regimental commander despite trying "so hard to prove himself the first days in Normandy that he was lucky he wasn't killed. He made mistakes in Normandy but it was because he was so aggressive and without the experience to back it up." The self-effacing Ekman, too, admitted to being a little shaky during his first hours in combat, but not because he was being overly aggressive. Rather, he explained, when he landed he "was knocked out and came to with everyone gone. It was dark, of course, and I found myself in the middle of a herd of cattle. Due to my difficulty in walking for the next several days, I am sure I landed astride a cow."[43] Ekman eventually found his operations officer, Major John Norton, and the two worked together to get a grip on the regiment, but they never received Krause's message that Ste.-Mère-Église had fallen, and as it grew light Ekman became concerned. By that time he had also found Lieutenant Colonel Benjamin H. Vandervoort, who was leading the 2/505th to its objective, Neuville-au-Plain, a hamlet about a mile northwest of Ste.-Mère-Église. Apparently still suffering the effects of his hard landing, Ekman issued Vandervoort a string of conflicting orders. First he ordered Vandervoort to stop, then proceed, and then stop again. Finally, at 0817 hours, having still not heard from Krause, Ekman told Vandervoort to proceed to Ste.-Mère-Église.[44]

Ridgway called Vandervoort "one of the bravest, toughest battle commanders I ever knew."[45] Vandervoort proved this true in Normandy. Although injured while landing, Vandervoort refused to leave the fight. Captain Putnam recalled meeting his commander about an hour after the jump near a small farmhouse:

> He was seated with a rain cape over him reading a map by flashlight—he recognized me and calling me close, quietly asked that I take a look at his ankle with as little demonstration as possible. His ankle was obviously broken; luckily a simple rather than compound fracture. He insisted on replacing his jump-boot, laced it tightly, formed a very makeshift crutch from a stick, and moved with the outfit as an equal and a leader without complaint. We were able to reduce the fracture and apply a walking cast some four days after D-day in a field hospital advance unit. The man did not lose two hours in our forty some days in Normandy [*sic*; actually the division fought for thirty-three days], covered rough ground and was personally very active in combat. He thoroughly convinced every man of his battalion of his merits and qualities.[46]

As it turned out Vandervoort's first major decision as a battalion commander in combat, although seemingly insignificant at the time, was one that would prove monumentally important. The decision was this: Instead of diverting his entire battalion to Ste.-Mère-Église, Vandervoort ordered Lieutenant Turner B. Turnbull to take Third Platoon, D Company, to Neuville-au-Plain in order to fulfill the 2/505th's original mission to stop anything north of Ste.-Mère-Église from getting into town.[47]

Turnbull and his forty-three troopers moved swiftly up the road linking Neuville-au-Plain with Ste.-Mère-Église without making contact, passed through Neuville-au-Plain, and dug in on a small rise about forty yards north of the hamlet. With fields of fire extending six hundred yards to the front, Turnbull was optimistic that he could hold the position against a much larger force for some time. Meanwhile, Vandervoort led the rest of the 2/505th to Ste.-Mère-Église, but as soon as he arrived he grabbed a jeep and an antitank gun and its crew, which arrived in the DETROIT gliders that morning, and took them to Turnbull.[48]

When Vandervoort arrived at Turnbull's position he learned that a Frenchman had informed Turnbull that a column of American paratroopers was approaching from the north and that they had with them a large number of German prisoners and some captured vehicles. Minutes later the column appeared. Soldiers that were clearly German were marching on either side of the road, while on the flanks were what appeared to be American paratroopers guarding them. The soldiers on the flanks were also waving orange panels, the same panels used by paratroopers to identify themselves to friendly aircraft, and interspersed throughout the column were several armored vehicles. It was just as the Frenchman foretold, yet something did not look right, so to be safe Vandervoort ordered the antitank gun crew to ready its weapon, and, when the column was about a hundred yards away, he told Turnbull to have one of his machine gunners fire a burst to the left of the column to see what would happen. The fire revealed the ruse, scattering the alleged prisoners and guards to both sides of the road, while the lead vehicle, a self-propelled gun, returned fire. Responding in kind, the antitank gun crew made quick work of the self-propelled gun along with the vehicle behind it; the third vehicle in the column fired smoke and backed away. Turning to Turnbull, Vandervoort told him to hold as long as possible and then jumped in his jeep and sped back to Ste.-Mère-Église to spread the word and get help.[49]

The unit advancing on Turnbull's position was a reinforced battalion from the *1058th Regiment* of the *91st Division*. It had been bivouacked about five miles north of Neuville-au-Plain, and, though ordered to move to Ste.-Mère-Église at 0130 hours, because of the confusion throughout the German command in Normandy its movement had been delayed until midmorning. It was approximately 1100 when it appeared on the road fronting Turnbull's position. Turnbull and his troopers beat it there by approximately thirty minutes.[50]

Back at Ste.-Mère-Église Vandervoort told his E Company commander, Captain Clyde Russell, to send a platoon to reinforce Turnbull. Russell sent Lieutenant Theodore Peterson's First Platoon. When Peterson reached Neuville-au-Plain, Turnbull told him that although he already had sixteen casualties, including six killed, and was low on ammunition, he and his troopers were determined to hold. Peterson could help out, however, by taking up position on the left and, if possible, silencing a troublesome enemy machine gun, a task Peterson's troopers accomplished by massing all their firepower on the gun. Ten minutes later Peterson's platoon eliminated another enemy threat, this one a large number of Germans who, remarkably, were moving across Peterson's front seemingly oblivious to the presence of American paratroopers on their flank. Waiting until the Germans were but a few feet away, Peterson had his troopers open up with another fusillade. The fire obliterated the German formation. Most of the enemy soldiers were killed outright. A few escaped. There were no wounded.[51]

The two platoons held out for the rest of the afternoon without giving ground. They endured several more attacks, most of which were aimed at Turnbull's platoon. As a result, by dusk Turnbull was down to twenty-three men, while Peterson's platoon was still at full strength. The Germans had also zeroed in on Turnbull's position with mortar and sniper fire. With his position fast becoming untenable, Turnbull told his troopers there was but one thing to do—charge. Private First Class Joseph Sebastian disagreed. "I think there's a chance we can still get out," offered Sebastian. "That's what we ought to do."[52] In a rare display of battlefield democracy Turnbull took a poll. All agreed with Sebastian. Turnbull relented but added that they would have to leave the wounded behind; there was no way any of them would get back if they had to carry them along. Sebastian spoke up again. Since the withdrawal was his idea, he would stay behind to cover his comrades. Sergeant Robert Niland and Corporal Raymond Smitson also volunteered to stay and fight alongside Sebastian while the platoon medic, Corporal James Kelly, volunteered to remain behind with the wounded. The decisions having been made, Niland made for a machine gun but was shot dead before he could reach it.[53] The others, totaling but sixteen, took off for the rear. Everyone got back to Ste.-Mère-Église. Turnbull was killed the next day. Shortly thereafter, Peterson's platoon also withdrew, still having lost no one.[54]

For all its fury, the action at Neuville-au-Plain involved an infinitesimally small number of the thousands of paratroopers that landed in Normandy that night. Yet what occurred there was of tremendous import, for although the paratroopers were forced to withdraw, it was not the ground gained or lost at Neuville-au-Plain that was critical; it was time. By holding off the German force advancing on Ste.-Mère-Église from the north, Peterson's and Turnbull's paratroopers gained the time Krause's 3/505th needed to defeat an enemy attack south of town.

When Vandervoort's 2/505th arrived at Ste.-Mère-Église, Krause was barely hanging on against an attack on the southern edge of town by two companies of infantry from the *795th Georgian Battalion* (an *Ost* battalion) supported by tanks and self-propelled guns. The arrival of the 2/505th, however, allowed him to mass his troopers at the southern edge of town while Vandervoort assumed responsibility for the northern half. With more troops at his disposal, Krause could also mount a spoiling attack. His outposts had reported truck movement to their front, signaling the arrival of enemy reinforcements, and he wanted to scatter them before another enemy attack got started. Krause assigned this mission to Captain Harold H. Swingler's I Company.[55]

Swingler led his eighty-four troopers along a zigzag course through a maze of hedgerows in an attempt to get astride the enemy flank. But Swingler miscalculated and instead hit the *Ost* battalion head-on about a mile south of Ste.-Mère-Église, precipitating a two-hour gunfight at point-blank range. With little hope of defeating his numerically superior foe by frontal assault, Swingler tried repeatedly to sideslip I Company onto the enemy flank, but since he was both outgunned and outnumbered, he could never get enough room between his force and the enemy's to make that happen. However, the aggressiveness of Swingler's troopers had an effect: The German officers commanding the *Ost* battalion became convinced that they were facing a superior force and ordered a withdrawal.

So ended the last serious attack on Ste.-Mère-Église from the south, but it had come at a high cost. Among the several troopers killed during the attack was Swingler, whose body, along with the other American dead, was borne back to Ste.-Mère-Église by a mournful I Company. Remembered by his troopers as "a superior officer in every way," Swingler was not supposed to have jumped into Normandy.[56] He had been in the hospital recovering from knee surgery but signed himself out so that he could be with his men.[57]

The *Ost* battalion joined a German antiaircraft unit that had previously fled Ste.-Mère-Église on a long, low ridge south of town known as Hill 20. Although it was not a formidable terrain feature, its vegetation provided cover, its height dominated the surrounding area, and it lay astride the roads leading to Ste.-Mère-Église from the south. Since the mixed bag of defenders atop the ridge possessed significant firepower, to include at least one 88mm gun, they could not be ignored. More important, the position constituted an undeniable threat to that evening's glider insertion, for it was in the flatlands just south of Hill 20 that the gliders were to land, an area known as landing zone "W."

Colonel Edson D. Raff, leading a task force from the 82nd's seaborne element, tried to clear Hill 20 before the gliders arrived. Composed of a platoon of armored cars, a company of Sherman tanks, and approximately ninety troopers from F Company, 2/401st, Task Force Raff landed at UTAH beach at 1530 hours, hurriedly dewaterproofed its vehicles, and made a dash for Ste.-Mère-Église. Following the 8th Infantry Regiment (U.S. 4th Infantry

Division), which also debarked at UTAH, Task Force Raff got all the way to Les Forges, a hamlet just over a mile south of Hill 20, when the 8th Infantry Regiment halted. Raff pleaded with its commander to keep going. He had much more firepower than Raff and stood a better chance of clearing the enemy from Hill 20 before the gliders arrived (there was no way to divert them to an alternate landing zone). It was to no avail. So Raff tried an attack of his own, a quick rush by his armored cars and tanks that he hoped would close on Hill 20 before its defenders could react. The rush ended almost as soon as it began. Three of Raff's Shermans and one armored car were destroyed before they had gone three hundred yards. Raff pulled the rest back and sent in his glider troopers. Supported by Raff's remaining Shermans firing from hull defilade, the troopers were within five hundred yards of Hill 20 when the first gliders appeared overhead.[58]

Scheduled to fly in to landing zone "W" were 26 Waco and 140 Horsa gliders carrying the 319th and 320th Field Artillery Battalions, the remainder of the 80th Airborne Antiaircraft Battalion, various division troops, jeeps, trailers, antitank guns, and tons of supplies and ammunition. Flying in from the east in two echelons of two serials each under heavy fighter escort, this second glider mission, code-named ELMIRA, was supposed to touch down beginning at 2100 hours, 6 June. The lead serial of the first echelon arrived but four minutes late.[59]

With Hill 20 still in German hands, those on the ground did everything possible to divert the gliders to an alternate, and safer, location. The 505th pathfinders cleared an alternate landing zone on drop zone "O," some two miles to the northwest, and marked it with a Eureka beacon, lights, and smoke in hopes of guiding the tow planes and gliders there. At the southern edge of landing zone "W" Raff's troopers used yellow flags and orange smoke to get the gliders' pilots to guide on them and away from Hill 20.[60] But, as Raff later observed, "Like watching a movie in which the full plot was known I realized that the smoking knocked-out tanks were appearing as LZ [landing zone] markers in the evening light to the pilots of the Troop Carriers, so unerringly did they release the gliders over the valley."[61]

Flying through a wall of flak emanating from Hill 20, all but a handful of gliders in both serials of the first echelon landed within two miles of landing zone "W." Miraculously, casualties were light: 5 pilots were killed, 4 went missing, and 17 were either injured or wounded, while their passengers sustained 5 killed and 18 injured or wounded.[62] Raff's troopers, meanwhile, swarmed the landing zone, corralled as many men as they could, and led them to safety at Les Forges. By the next morning they had gathered about 200 of the 437 troopers that had flown in with the echelon.[63] Others, like Private Gordon Adams, who silenced a German machine-gun position armed only with a knife, fought their way off the landing zone and into Ste.-Mère-Église individually or in small groups.[64]

The second ELMIRA echelon arrived at 2255 hours. It, too, was supposed to land on landing zone "W" but for some reason diverted to drop zone "O." Inexplicably, most of the gliders in the first serial drifted past the well-lit landing zone and landed behind enemy lines. Fortunately, the second landed right on target. All told 10 glider pilots of the second ELMIRA echelon were killed, 29 were wounded or injured, and 7 went missing. Of the 737 passengers, 28 were killed and 106 wounded or injured.[65]

There were twenty-four artillery pieces aboard the ELMIRA gliders (twelve 75mm and twelve 105mm howitzers). Fifteen of them survived the landing intact, but seven of the fifteen, from the 319th, were in the serial that landed behind enemy lines. Unwilling to abandon their guns, jeeps, ammunition, and equipment, yet unable to fight their way to Ste.-Mère-Église with them, the artillerymen aboard the errant gliders collected their gear and moved east, where they linked up with the 4th Infantry Division advancing from the sea; it was another two days before they returned to 82nd control. Meanwhile, the 320th collected only two of its guns, and although they made it to Ste.-Mère-Église by daybreak on 7 June, this brought Ridgway's artillery complement to but three tubes. For the next forty-eight hours his troopers had to rely almost exclusively on their mortars, which had neither the range nor the weight of ordnance to compete with the heavier German guns.[66]

At daybreak, 7 June, as Raff was organizing yet another attack on Hill 20, the last two of the 82nd's planned glider insertions commenced, code-named GALVESTON and HACKENSACK. The GALVESTON mission, composed of eighty-two Wacos and eighteen Horsas organized in two fifty-ship echelons, carried 968 troopers of the 325th Regimental Headquarters and the 1/325th along with additional division troops, supplies, and equipment. Because the enemy still occupied Hill 20, it had been decided to fly GALVESTON into landing zone "E," one of the 101st's landing zones a little more than three miles southeast of Ste.-Mère-Église. Flying in from the east, the first GALVESTON echelon arrived at 0655 hours, encountered almost no enemy fire, and for some reason released most of its gliders early, resulting in 17 glider troopers killed and 85 injured during landing. Ironically, the second GALVESTON echelon, which mysteriously made for landing zone "W," had fewer casualties and a more accurate drop. Appearing at 0701 hours, all but two of the second-echelon gliders landed within two miles of landing zone "W" and, although they were under fire as soon as they appeared, sustained but 13 injured in the landings.[67]

The first echelon of HACKENSACK arrived approximately two hours later at landing zone "W." Carrying 968 troopers of the 2/325th and 2/401st in thirty Wacos and twenty Horsas, the gliders flew through a dense cloud of flak and scattered. According to Lieutenant Richard B. Johnson of the 2/401st, the air "was filled with gliders, flying no pattern whatsoever, but all making for the nearest feasible landing area." Several gliders collided in midair. Others improvised quick stops after landing, necessitated by the debris littering the landing zone, "by flying between two trees and shearing off the wings."[68] Quite a few landed at the northern edge of landing zone "W," right under the guns of the enemy still entrenched atop Hill 20. Still, casualties were light: 2 pilots were killed and 10 or 11 injured, while 15 troopers were killed and 59 injured. The second HACKENSACK echelon, carrying 363 supply and service troopers along with mortars, ammunition, equipment, and supplies in fifty Wacos, had a more accurate and controlled drop and sustained but 1 pilot killed and 5 injured and 1 trooper killed and 15 injured. With HACKENSACK complete, Ridgway had most of his division in France, although it would be days before he gathered it all in one place.[69]

The Normandy glider missions marked a significant turning point in the attitude of the paratroopers toward the glider troopers. Almost every paratrooper that witnessed the glider insertions was awed by the courage of their gliderborne brethren. Sergeant Elmo Jones said, "There's never been a greater slaughter than what took place that night. It was the most horrible thing a person could see." Sergeant Ernest L. Gee of the 505th called the glider insertion "pitiful and ghostly," adding, "I always tip my hat to this day if a meet a glider man who hit Normandy because he is a fighting fool and alive by the Grace of God."[70] First Sergeant Howard Melvin of the 505th recounted that he and his fellow paratroopers felt somewhat guilty about their extra pay when witnessing what the "glider-riders" endured:

> These gliders guys had the worst of the worst. I'd rather jump any day in the week, make five jumps, than do a glider ride. . . . A paratrooper slogan was, a paratrooper should be on a DZ [drop zone] when gliders are coming in, with a stack of thousand-dollar bills, and anybody who walks out of a glider you would hand him a thousand-dollar bill. And that was because at that time we were getting jump pay and they were getting nothing—no hazardous-duty pay. And they weren't volunteers, either. A glider trooper didn't get anything extra.[71]

Those who flew in on Horsas were particularly unlucky; statistics compiled after Normandy revealed that a trooper was twice as likely to get injured in a Horsa than in a Waco.[72] This was because, although larger than the Waco, the Horsa's frame was made of wood as opposed to the tubular construction used in U.S. gliders and had a tendency to disintegrate on landing. Consequently, Ridgway insisted that "for the next operations of the 82d and 101st Airborne Divisions glider personnel and equipment will be carried in CG-4's only. No Horsas will be used." Taylor concurred.[73]

The paratroopers, meanwhile, accepted the glider troopers as equals and signified this in the best way they could, by agreeing to the issuance of jump boots to every glider trooper in the division. Henceforward, glider troopers, too, proudly wore their trousers bloused, especially after they returned to England, where they could make use of another dividend they earned in France—hazardous-duty pay.[74]

Hill 20 did not fall until late in the morning of 7 June. By that time the Germans among the mixed group of defenders had melted away. Urged on by a Russian-speaking American officer they had earlier taken prisoner who convinced them that continued resistance was futile, what remained of the *795th Georgian Battalion* surrendered. With Hill 20 in American hands, the way was open for Task Force Raff and the 8th Infantry Regiment to move to Ste.-Mère-Église, where they helped defeat the last and most significant German counterattack against the town yet.[75]

After their opening foray against Ste.-Mère-Église was blunted, the Germans north of town regrouped and prepared a much stronger attack to retake the town the next day. First they pounded Ste.-Mère-Église with artillery and mortar fire throughout the night of 6–7 June and used the cover of their fire to probe the American defenses. Next they gathered a more substantial force with which to make the attack: two battalions of German infantry—the *1st Battalion, 1058th Regiment* of the *91st Division*, and the *Seventh Army Sturm Battalion*—supported by three artillery battalions, an antitank gun company, and ten self-propelled guns. Poised just north of town astride the road linking Neuville-au-Plain and Ste.-Mère-Église, the plan was to mount a coordinated attack down both sides of the road on the morning of 7 June. But before it began the German attack was knocked off-kilter due to the actions, once again, of a relatively junior officer.[76]

That officer was Lieutenant Waverly W. Wray, the D Company, 2/505th, executive officer. Wray appeared at Vandervoort's command post around 0700 hours to report that his company's positions east of the road were being pressed hard and he feared they could not hold much longer. Vandervoort responded that there was little he could do since help had not arrived and that perhaps Wray should consider a limited counterattack to throw the Germans back a bit. A soft-spoken, devoutly religious Mississippian, Wray returned to his position, quietly collected all the grenades he could carry, along with his M-1, a .45-caliber semiautomatic pistol, and a silver-plated .38 revolver that he stuck in his boot and informed his company commander that he was going to take a look around. Picking his way cautiously through the hedgerows, Wray was some three hundred yards north of town when the sound of German voices froze him in his tracks. Snaking to the top of the hedgerow that separated him from the voices, his M-1 at the ready, Wray popped up and "in his best invasion German said, 'Handy-ho!' Seven Germans, in a sunken road and grouped around a radio transmitter, froze and turned their eyes toward him. One of them pulled a pistol and fired, tearing Waverly's cartridge belt half off his belly. Waverly reflexed with seven shots from his M1 rifle as two German Schmeisser machine pistols fired from the hedgerow . . . glanced bullets off his helmet and nicked two half-moon notches from his ear."[77] But Wray got the better of the exchange and killed the seven Germans who, it turned out, were the commander and staff of the *1st Battalion, 1058th Regiment*, which was lined up in a nearby sunken road awaiting orders, oblivious to what had befallen its leadership. Before they discovered what had happened, Wray rushed back to friendly lines, collected D Company, and led it forward into positions from which it had clear fields of fire. He then used the company's 60mm mortars to flush the Germans from the sunken road and into the sights of D Company's guns. It was a slaughter. The few Germans that survived did so only after a German medical officer appeared under a white flag asking for a truce to care for his wounded, in the process covering the escape of those Wray and his troopers had not yet gunned down.

Later that morning Vandervoort met Wray, minus part of his ear and with dried blood caked on his neck and shoulder. "They've been getting kind of close to you haven't they Waverly?" asked Vandervoort. In his heavy drawl Wray replied, "Not as close as ah've been gettin' to them, Suh." When D Company's first sergeant, John Rabig, saw Wray, he turned to Vandervoort and said, "Colonel, aren't you glad Waverly's on our side?"[78] Wray was later killed in Holland.[79]

The D Company attack erased the threat of a German attack down the east side of the Neuville-au-Plain–Ste.-Mère-Église road, but the *Seventh Army Sturm Battalion*'s attack down the west side of the road pressed forward. Supported by several armored vehicles, the *Sturm Battalion* pushed F Company, 2/505th, back to the edge of town. "By early afternoon we and the Germans were one hedgerow apart," recalled Vandervoort. "They kept driving their tanks and self-propelled guns south toward us. They would fire smoke shells to conceal the movement of their vehicles, then suddenly dart from the smoke . . . firing as they came."[80] Eventually, a fairly large group of German infantrymen broke through F Company's lines and got to within fifty yards of the 82nd's aid station. Captain Putnam saw them from inside and watched as the German infantrymen were coordinating their next move with a nearby assault gun when there suddenly appeared from nowhere three paratroopers who rushed into the fray without thought of numbers or relative firepower and drove them off. The first, an anonymous private from H Company, 3/505th, ran through a hail of fire to an abandoned antitank gun that he then used expertly to force the assault gun to reverse course and back away. Stunned by this unexpected loss, the German infantry froze. There then appeared two more troopers, a lieutenant and a sergeant, both armed with Thompson submachine guns who, standing "side by side, at the end of the road emptied clip after clip into the milling and disorganized crowd." Putnam was dumbfounded, but Colonel Ekman had come to expect this of his troopers. "Whenever a machine gun or other automatic weapon, including 88's, opened up, it seemed like everyone in the vicinity started to converge on it to knock it out."[81]

The penetration near the aid station was the closest the *Seventh Army Sturm Battalion* got to breaking into Ste.-Mère-Église. By that time it was about 1500 hours, and Task Force Raff, along with two battalions from the 8th Infantry Regiment, had arrived.[82] So before the Germans could regroup the Americans seized the moment and counterattacked, advancing elements of the 2/505th, supported by several tanks, up the west side of the road to Neuville-au-Plain, while the 2nd Battalion, 8th Infantry Regiment, advanced up the east side.

Leading the 2/505th's advance was its intelligence officer, Lieutenant Eugene A. Doerfleur, an unusually young-looking man without "two whiskers on his face."[83] Known as "the Creeper," Doerfleur spoke fluent German and, like Private Bachenheimer of the 1/504th, spent many a night behind enemy lines gathering intelligence. He told Vandervoort that during a foray the day before he discovered a sunken road, just wide enough for a tank, that he believed might lead to the *Sturm Battalion*'s right flank. Trusting Doerfleur's judgment, Vandervoort committed his reserve to the attack—approximately twenty E Company troopers under Lieutenant James Coyle—along with three of Raff's tanks. Jumping off at 1715 hours with Doerfleur in the lead, the tanks in column behind him, and Coyle's troopers behind the tanks, the small force advanced cautiously along the lane until Doerfleur turned a corner and found himself looking down the right flank of the *Sturm Battalion*, which was massed in the lane, preparing to renew its attack. Before the Germans could react the tanks following Doerfleur opened up, firing their main guns down the sunken lane while the E Company troopers fanned out atop the hedgerows to either side and fired down into the lane, picking off the startled Germans as they attempted to flee. "It was their death trap," recalled Sergeant Otis Sampson. "It was so easy I quit firing."[84] When the firing stopped some 160 Germans surrendered, many of whom were wounded. The rest were killed. Some, but not many, escaped.[85] One of the few American casualties was Lieutenant Coyle, who, though shot in both thighs, ignored his wounds and continued fighting until the firing stopped; only then did he allow Sampson to patch him up. "When he tried to stand up his legs would not hold him," Sampson recalled. "He had been going on pure spunk."[86]

E Company broke the back of the German attack; Ste.-Mère-Église was never again threatened, and what was left of the German attack force fell back on Neuville-au-Plain. In two days of fighting the troopers at Ste.-Mère-Église took more than 700 prisoners and inflicted untold casualties on their enemy; north of the town alone there were more than 400 German dead. An American lieutenant who was being held captive at the *1058th*'s command post (and later liberated as the Americans advanced north) reported that as the German survivors streamed past, one ran in and shouted "Allus kaput! [*sic*] The Americans are killing everybody." Surveying the area a few days later, even General Gavin was moved to comment on the slaughter inflicted by the 2/505th—"Van, don't kill them all. Save a few for interrogation."[87]

The 82nd's stand at the crossroads town astride the only highway in the eastern Cotentin also kept the Germans from massing against UTAH beach and allowed the amphibious forces landing there to get established ashore with relative ease (there were fewer than 200 casualties on UTAH during D-Day).[88] And with Ste.-Mère-Église in hand the division had a secure base from which to conduct attacks elsewhere in its zone, most notably along the banks of the Merderet, where two of the 82nd's D-Day objectives were still being hotly contested.

CHAPTER 12

YOU CROSSED THAT CAUSEWAY

Upon reading these accounts, one cannot fail to be impressed by the significant results achieved by the little groups of men . . . who advanced in the opening minutes of operation NEPTUNE against whatever enemy confronted them without asking whether they were outnumbered, and then held their ground waiting for the larger forces to come up. Without drawing any conclusions as to the merits of the tactical argument by either side, it is enough to point out that had these small fractions not acted so, much less would have been accomplished by the airborne forces.

—Anonymous SHAEF historical officer,
"Comment on 82nd Division Operation"

Since Allied intelligence had placed the main concentration of German mobile units farther west on the Cotentin, the prevailing attitude was that the Merderet crossings at La Fière and Chef du Pont would fall quickly (La Fière was about two miles due west and Chef du Pont two and a half miles southwest of Ste.-Mère-Église). As Vandervoort put it, "We don'[t] think that in our immediate area [there] are many enemy troops—we estimate about two companies."[1] In addition, since the 507th and 508th were dropping west of the river and the 505th east of it, both sites would be within the division's airhead. But when the intelligence proved wrong and the drops went awry, so did the plan, and once the Germans west of the Merderet recovered from their surprise they made a rush for the river with La Fière and Chef du Pont their points of aim.

The troopers in the marshes north of La Fière had also to recover from surprise, the surprise of being dropped in water that, in many places, was over their heads. Predominantly from the 507th and 508th, these troopers struggled from their parachute harnesses, joined in groups large and small, and waded and swam to the only recognizable, and dry, landmark in the area, a raised railroad embankment silhouetted against the sky. Running in a north-south direction, this embankment became both a rallying point and a thoroughfare the troopers used to get themselves back on track. From their sand tables, they knew that by following the railroad, they would eventually come to the La Fière–Ste.-Mère-Église road at a point approximately 1,000 yards east La Fière. From there they could move due west to La Fière or southwest to Chef du Pont, cross the Merderet, move to their assigned drop zones, and hopefully link up with their units.

So the scene was set for the clash of opposing forces bent on securing two innocuous bridges and the causeways on which they were situated. This was key terrain for both sides. For the Germans the causeways were thoroughfares through which they could pass reinforcements to shore up their defenses at UTAH beach. For the Americans they were holes to be plugged to keep the enemy away from the beaches and, when the time was right, sally ports through which would be launched the drive across the base of the Cotentin Peninsula.

The bridge at La Fière was "a smallish stone affair and little more than a large culvert." Securing it was the mission of Lieutenant John J. Dolan's A Company, 1/505th. Flying in a nine-plane serial that kept perfect formation, avoided flak, slowed to the correct drop speed, and descended to the correct drop altitude, A Company jumped squarely onto drop zone "O." "We hit our drop zone right on the nose," wrote Dolan, "because within twenty minutes to one-half hour I knew our exact location."[2] Yet assembly was slow, hampered by hedgerows, and Dolan waited until he had gathered more than 90 percent of his company before moving out. By that time it was an hour before dawn.[3]

Moving south off the drop zone with First Platoon in the lead, A Company saw its first German when it hit the La Fière–Ste.-Mère-Église road, a motorcyclist speeding by hell bent for Ste.-Mère-Église. This unexpected encounter created some confusion, for soon thereafter Dolan discovered that he had lost contact with a portion of First Platoon. Undeterred, he put Third Platoon in the lead, crossed to the south side of the road, and turned west. A combat veteran with a good eye for terrain, Dolan cautiously maneuvered A Company toward La Fière until, several hundred yards short of his objective, he halted at the edge of an open field. If there was an enemy force defending La Fière, and the motorcyclist certainly indicated there was, this would be a likely kill zone, thought Dolan, so he had one of his platoon leaders, Lieutenant Donald G. Coxon, send some scouts ahead to reconnoiter the far wood line. Leading the reconnaissance party himself, Coxon and the two troopers with him were just short of the wood line when they were killed by German machine-gun and sniper fire.[4]

Now that he knew the approximate location of the enemy, Dolan split his company, placing some of his troopers in positions from which they could pin the Germans in place by fire while he led the rest on a flanking movement. Major James P. McGinity, the 1/505th's executive officer, had joined A Company somewhere along the way and was near the point of Dolan's flanking force ready to pounce on the machine gun that killed Coxon and his scouts when a second machine gun opened up, killing McGinity instantly. Dolan and the rest of the flanking force went to ground and were pinned in place for more than an hour.[5]

Meanwhile, the lost troopers from Dolan's First Platoon moved along the north side of the La Fière–Ste.-Mère-Église road and made it all the way to the causeway. But when they broke from cover and moved on the bridge, they were fired on by Germans inside a stone manor adjacent to the span and driven back. Dolan's A Company, split into three groups, had come to an abrupt halt.

Unbeknownst to Dolan, help was nearby. Captain F. B. "Ben" Schwartzwalder and approximately 60 troopers from his G Company, 3/507th, were also maneuvering toward La Fière on the south side of the road. They, too, had taken fire and gone to ground, but in the mazelike terrain each company was oblivious to the presence of the other. But Schwartzwalder knew something Dolan did not. Because he had traveled the railroad embankment, Schwartzwalder knew that back where it intersected the La Fière–Ste.-Mère-Église road there were plenty of reinforcements, so he went in search of help. He found there Colonel Roy Lindquist, the 508th's commander, who had formed the troopers collecting at that point into three companies. When Schwartzwalder reported that his company was pinned down by Germans in the vicinity of La Fière, Lindquist organized a hasty attack. Schwartzwalder was to return to his company and renew his push south of the road, while Lindquist sent a second force, composed mostly of B Company, 1/508th, troopers, to attack La Fière from the north. The attack was set for 1200 hours.[6]

Lindquist's coordinated attack never came off. Instead, what occurred was a confused affair that saw paratroopers from three different regiments maneuvering toward the same objective. Attacking south of the road, Schwartzwalder's G Company, 3/507th, took out several German outposts and pushed all the way to the river. Simultaneously, several B Company, 1/508th troopers took the manor adjacent to the causeway by entering through the cellar and killing or wounding the Germans above by shooting through the floor. And while that fight was raging inside the manor, troopers from Dolan's lost First Platoon, aided by other 1/505th troopers who had wandered into the area, assaulted enemy positions in the manor's courtyard. Finally, Dolan regrouped that part of A Company he had with him and attacked toward La Fière as well. When the firing stopped, the manor and the east end of La Fière causeway were in American hands, the defending Germans either killed, wounded, or captured.[7]

The 1/505th troopers assisting Dolan's lost platoon during the fight in the courtyard were from a large group that arrived at the bridge under their battalion commander, Major Francis Caesar Augustus Kellam. As the ranking officer present, Kellam took charge and set about organizing a defense of the eastern end of the causeway. As he was doing so, Gavin arrived. Kellam told Gavin that he had the situation under control and that he would have both ends of the causeway firmly in hand in less than two hours.[8]

As was true for most troopers that morning, Gavin's journey to La Fière had been eventful. Having landed in the marsh north of La Fière and west of the Merderet, he was, at first, confused about his exact whereabouts but eventually got oriented while wandering around gathering troopers. Within two hours he had with him more than 150 troopers, mostly from the 507th, including Lieutenant Colonels Arthur A. Maloney, the 507th's executive officer, and Edwin J. Ostberg, the 1/507th commander. (Journalist Bill Walton was also part of this group. Finding Gavin, recalled Walton, "was like finding 'Daddy'—it really was.")[9] With gunfire emanating from the direction of Ste.-Mère-Église, Gavin sent his aide, Captain Hugo Olson, to find a route through the marsh to Ste.-Mère-Église. Olson returned to report that although deep in places, the marsh was passable and that the railroad embankment was not far off. With dawn approaching and German fire increasing, Gavin pushed his troopers through the marsh and eventually got all of them safely to the railroad embankment.[10] One member of the group, Lieutenant Thomas Graham, recalled the difficult journey: "I'm sure many of the others like me were both excited and scared. I had cramps in both my legs. I didn't know whether I could make the next step, and I believe others felt the same. The general was out in front, and when you have someone like that leading, you know you're going to make it. And we all did."[11]

After gaining the railroad embankment, Gavin led his troopers south to the La Fière–Ste.-Mère-Église road, where he ran into some 1/505th troopers making for La Fière. They told Gavin that there was a fight at the causeway, that Major Kellam was on the scene, and that Kellam wanted all his troopers to come up. By that time things had quieted down at Ste.-Mère-Église, so Gavin led his ad hoc force to La Fière. When he arrived the fight was over, and it was then that Kellam told him things were under control.

Satisfied with the situation at La Fière, Gavin led his ad hoc force south toward the other Merderet River crossing at Chef du Pont. A Frenchman he met along the way told him that although there were Germans on the west bank of the river, Chef du Pont, which was on the east bank, was unoccupied. Were a force rushed there, insisted the Frenchman, it could take the town and the adjacent bridge and causeway before the Germans could react. Gavin sent Ostberg and 75 troopers ahead to make the attempt.[12]

Whether the Frenchman's information was inaccurate or Ostberg's force was too late is unknown, but when Ostberg's troopers arrived at Chef du Pont, they ran into heavy sniper fire. Fearing that if he got bogged down his opportunity to take the causeway, which was on the western edge of town, would pass, Ostberg led his men in a charge.[13] Captain Roy Creek, the E Company, 2/507th commander, related what happened next: "Two officers reached the bridge [atop the causeway] and were both shot. One toppling off the bridge into the water. The other falling on the eastern approach. The officer toppling into the river was Col. Ostberg. He was rescued shortly afterward by two soldiers of the 507 and lived to fight again. (The other officer was dead)." Yet the troopers charged on until, suddenly, they found themselves in the midst of well-camouflaged foxholes where the fight turned into a kill-or-be-killed melee at point-blank range until, lacking the protection afforded the dug-in Germans, the paratroopers withdrew to cover inside Chef du Pont, having suffered 11 dead and 23 wounded. Afterward, some contended that the charge would have succeeded and the bridge and causeway taken had it not been for the killing of 2 German soldiers who stood up in their foxholes in an apparent attempt to surrender. Captain Creek, who took command at Chef du Pont after Ostberg was wounded, challenged this criticism:

> Having witnessed this action at close range, I would defy anyone to make a split[-]second judgment on what to do when an enemy soldier jumps out of a foxhole 5 to 20 feet from you in the heat of heavy firing on both sides and in your own very first fight for your life. I support the action taken by our troops under these conditions and circumstances and to this day, years later, I don't know if the enemy was trying to surrender or not. I observed this whole action at very close range, and in my opinion, any enemy shot during this attack as close and intense as it was at times had waited too long to surrender. He was committed, as the attacker was, to a fight for survival.[14]

Not long thereafter Lieutenant Colonel Maloney arrived with another 75 troopers and led a second charge on the bridge and causeway that got as far as the western end of the bridge before it, too, was stopped, after which the troopers again withdrew. They had, however, cleared the causeway up to the eastern edge of the bridge, where they dug in. At 1700 hours, a runner arrived with a message from Gavin: Maloney was to bring his troopers to La Fière immediately. Creek was to remain at Chef du Pont with what remained of Ostberg's contingent and hold as long as possible, but if the position became untenable, he, too, was to fall back on La Fière.[15]

Maloney's departure left Creek with 34 combat effective troopers, but by that time the fight at Chef du Pont had settled down into a desultory exchange of small arms fire, so Creek was confident he could hold. This confidence dissipated when the Germans on the opposite bank brought up a howitzer that blasted away at Creek's positions, further reducing his numbers to twenty. To make matters worse, there appeared on the east side of the river, a few hundred yards to Creek's rear, a substantial force of *Ostruppen*. Cut off, pinned down, and expecting an attack from two directions, Creek prepared his troopers for a fight to the last when salvation dropped literally from the heavens.

A few minutes after 2100 hours, during the insertion of the first ELMIRA echelon, there landed near Chef du Pont a lone glider from which emerged several troopers from C Battery, 80th Airborne Antiaircraft Battalion, who had with them an antitank gun that they quickly put into operation to silence the troublesome German howitzer. Sensing that with their artillery out of commission the German infantry across the river would sit tight, Creek adjusted his defenses to meet the threat to his rear. There then appeared a second salvation, albeit one less heavenly—a group of about 100 paratroopers, mostly from G Company, 3/508th, who joined with Creek's men to drive off the *Ostruppen*. With his rear secure and momentum, numbers, and luck on his side, Creek felt it propitious to take another shot at the western end of the bridge. Under devastating covering fire from some troopers he had positioned on a small rise, Creek led an attack across the bridge that gained and held the far end of the causeway. With the bridge and causeway in hand, but lacking enough combat power to continue the attack and encumbered by his dead and wounded, Creek settled his troopers into defensive positions at both ends of the causeway and waited.[16]

This did not end matters at Chef du Pont; there would be another battle there but not before Creek was reinforced. The significance of this first battle at Chef du Pont, however, was not what Creek and his troopers gained; it was that they denied the enemy use of the crossing, for, had they held Chef du

Pont's causeway, the Germans could have moved across it to attack Ste.-Mère-Église or La Fière, both of which, at the time, were being hotly contested.

Gavin had recalled Maloney and his troopers from Chef du Pont because of a major German counterattack at La Fière, the more critical of the two Merderet crossings since from there it was a straight shot into Ste.-Mère-Église. But when Maloney returned to La Fière, sometime around dusk on D-Day, the fight was over, at least for that day, although the bridge had yet to be secured and would not be until 9 June. In the interval there would rage three days of bloody, close-quarters combat back and forth across its span, combat comparable in every way to that experienced by those who stormed OMAHA beach. There would also be displayed "more gallantry per square foot . . . than probably in any other single action of the war."[17] Ironically, it was a battle that might never have occurred, for American paratroopers had occupied the west end of the La Fière causeway earlier in the day without a fight.

One of the three large groups of paratroopers that formed west of the Merderet after the drop consisted of approximately 50 troopers, mostly from the 507th, in an orchard just north of La Fière. Gathered under the command of Lieutenant Colonel Charles J. Timmes, the 2/507th commander, they moved out just before daylight on D-Day for Amfreville, a village about a mile and a half northwest of La Fière that was the 2/507th's primary objective, but heavy fire forced Timmes back to the orchard after which he sent out patrols in search of more men. One of those patrols consisted of 10 troopers under the command of Lieutenant Louis Levy, whom Timmes told to move south toward La Fière.

Levy and his patrol got to Cauquigny, a hamlet on the western end of the La Fière causeway, without incident. Along the way they were joined by several troopers under the command of Lieutenant Joseph Kormylo. From Cauquigny, Levy and Kormylo could clearly hear gunfire on the Merderet's east bank, but with such a small force at their disposal, they opted to take up position in a church courtyard to wait and see what developed. They had not been there long when they were joined by more paratroopers, some 40 in all, led by two officers, most likely from B Company, 1/508th, one of the three companies that had maneuvered on the La Fière manor. Now that he had a much larger force, Levy decided to make a personal reconnaissance of the far bank, where he could still hear scattered gunfire, to see if he might be able to help. When he moved out on the causeway and peered through his binoculars, what Levy saw was yet another group of American paratroopers walking toward him. On point was Lieutenant John W. Marr. Following behind was Captain Schwartzwalder's G Company, 3/507th.

After conferring with Marr, Levy walked across the bridge to the east bank, where he talked with a field grade officer, most likely Kellam. He then returned to Cauquigny, where with the addition of Schwartzwalder's G Company there were now some 150 to 200 paratroopers. Backed by Kellam's 1/505th troopers on the east bank, there was approximately 300 to 400 troopers on both ends of the crossing. But these numbers quickly dissipated when Schwartzwalder, who was bent on joining his regiment, decided to take G Company to Timmes's orchard. In a matter of minutes, what was a more than ample force to defend Cauquigny and the west end of the crossing site was reduced to little more than a platoon. It was then that the lead element of the *1057th Regiment* of the *91st Division*, a combined infantry-tank force, marched in from the west, setting off a short, sharp fight during which Levy's troopers destroyed one enemy tank before they, too, made for Timmes's orchard.[18]

Rolling through Cauquigny, the Germans continued their attack across the La Fière bridge (it was this attack that prompted Gavin's recall of Maloney from Chef du Pont). Fortunately for Kellam, the delay imposed on the Germans by Levy's paratroopers gave him enough time to organize a defense in depth. With Dolan's A Company dug in around the east end of the bridge comprising his forward line of resistance, Kellam positioned the rest of the 1/505th on a slight rise to the rear from which it could support Dolan's troopers with fire. In addition, Kellam had with him an engineer platoon from B Company, 307th Engineers, who had with them an antitank gun that he placed on the road about 150 yards behind Dolan's positions so that it could fire directly onto the bridge over the heads of the entrenched A Company.[19]

Dolan's troopers occupied a string of foxholes in a line approximately 75 yards long. Given so narrow a sector, Dolan placed two of his platoons forward and held one platoon in reserve ready to plug gaps in the line. Dolan also positioned two two-man bazooka teams in the marsh on either side of the bridge. He also barricaded the bridge with an abandoned truck his troopers found and surrounded the truck with antitank mines. In this manner Dolan and Kellam hoped to negate the enemy's numerical and materiel advantage. If the Germans led with tanks, they would be vulnerable to the mines, bazooka fire, and antitank gun fire. If the Germans led with infantry, they would run into small arms, machine-gun, and mortar fire. And, because of the width and depth of the marsh, there was only one way to get vehicles from Cauquigny to Ste.-Mère-Église—on the causeway, over the bridge, and through the 1/505th's defenses.[20]

At about 1700 hours the Germans presaged their assault on the bridge with a rolling artillery barrage that killed both Kellam and his operations officer, Captain Dale S. Roysden. Advancing behind the barrage were three tanks and behind the tanks were some 200 infantrymen who stopped on the causeway just short of the bridge. The tanks moved cautiously onto the span until, halted by Dolan's improvised barricade, the lead tank commander emerged from his hatch to get a better view. He was killed instantaneously, and in the ensuing confusion the A Company bazooka teams—Privates First Class John D. Bolderson and Lenold Peterson and Privates Gordon C. Pryne and Marcus Heim—went to work. Emerging from their hiding places in the marsh they fired shot after shot at the tanks. "I cannot understand why all four of them were not killed," recalled one eyewitness.

> They fired and reloaded with the precision of well-oiled machinery. I don't think that either team wasted a shot. The first tank received several direct hits. A tread was knocked off and within a matter of minutes it was on fire. . . .
>
> The bazooka-teams [*sic*] soon went to work on the second tank. Within 30 seconds it too was on fire. Peterson put another round into the tank's turret as it swung around to take a pot shot at him. As Peterson was running out of rockets he sent Marcus Heim over the other side of the bridge to get extra ammunition. Heim ran through a hail of enemy bullets only to find the Bolderson bazooka with a hole blown through it. He picked up a bag of rockets he found and ran back to Peterson's side. They then hit the second tank seven more times. As the panzer crew tried to back away, their tank burst into flames, incinerating the crew.[21]

The third tank, which was about fifty yards behind the others, was knocked out by the antitank gun.[22]

With no armor to cover their advance, the German infantry withdrew, although mortar and artillery fired continued to plaster the American positions. The Germans also brought up an 88mm gun, the most feared in the German arsenal. "The German technique," recalled Gavin, "was to fire [the 88s] directly at the infantry kicking up tons of dust and smoke" so thick that "weapons were frequently clogged and jammed." The 88s also had a "tremendous psychological effect" because the "interval between the scream of the incoming projectile and the tremendous impact and detonation was very small," and when they hit "fragments ricocheted with unusual velocity," producing many casualties. Lieutenant William R. Oakley was one such casualty. Oakley had been Gavin's junior aide prior to Normandy but had requested transfer to a line unit. At La Fière he was hit by shrapnel that produced a fist-size hole in his back. His platoon sergeant, William Dale Owens, found Oakley, bandaged him up, and administered morphine. Owens then called for a couple of men to carry the lieutenant to the rear, but Oakley refused and insisted on making it back on his own. Before leaving, he told Owens to hold the bridge at all costs and then, turning to his troopers, yelled, "Sergeant Owens is now in command, what ever you do, obey him and stick with him, good luck to all, I am very proud of every one, I'll see you in England." Oakley got as far as the aid station in Ste.-Mère-Église before he went into shock and died.[23]

When word reached the 505th command post at Ste.-Mère-Église that Kellam had been killed, Lieutenant Colonel Alexander, the regimental executive officer, rushed to La Fière to see what he could do. On the way he met Gavin, who told him to take command of the 1/505th and hold at all costs. Collecting troopers as he went, Alexander arrived at La Fière after the German attack had been repulsed. Dolan, who took over after Kellam was killed, was expecting another attack and had already repositioned the defenses to meet it. Alexander took over from Dolan, added his reinforcements to the line, and then walked around to see what else he could do. He found, laying in a ditch, the lone antitank gun at La Fière. It had two holes in its front armor and its sight was gone, but it could still shoot, so Alexander dragooned some nearby troopers and told them to get the gun back into position and aim it by sighting down the barrel.[24]

La Fière saw no further attacks on D-Day, although the Germans continued pounding the American positions with mortar and artillery fire. Then, at about 0200 hours, 7 June, a lone tank inched its way onto the bridge in an apparent attempt to drag away the burned-out hulls blocking the roadway. Alerted by the clank of treads, Sergeant Owens grabbed two Gammon grenades and crawled through the marsh to take it out. From a distance of about thirty to forty yards Owens rose, threw both grenades, and missed, but the resulting explosions convinced the tank commander to reverse course and flee.[25]

Dawn broke at La Fière on 7 June with shells still falling on the American positions, but with no sign of another ground attack. At about 1000 hours things changed. The shelling grew more intense, and it was not long before there appeared at the western end of the causeway two tanks followed by a battalion of German infantry. Advancing behind the falling artillery, the column got all the way onto the bridge when shots from the antitank gun Alexander had recovered the day before hit home and destroyed the lead tank. The German infantry then tried several times to rush the American positions, but each time they were beaten back by paratroopers who, braving a barrage of artillery that was "coming in like machine[-]gun fire," rose from their holes to lay down a withering fusillade. Through it all the ubiquitous Sergeant Owens, "one of the best fighting men in the division," ranged the front line, encouraging his troopers, redistributing ammunition, tending the wounded, and manning several different weapons. "The machine gun I had [wrote Owens] was so hot it quit firing. I took Pvt. McClatchy's BAR, he had been wounded earlier, and fired it until I ran out of ammo. I then had a machine gun that belonged to a couple of men that took a very near hit, they were killed and the gun had no tripod so I rested it across a pile of dirt and used it along with . . . one other machine gun and our 60 m.m. mortor [*sic*], we stopped them but they had got to within 25 yards of us."[26] The battle raged into the afternoon. Finally, after suffering some 200 casualties, the Germans requested a truce to evacuate their dead and wounded. Alexander agreed. During the thirty minutes of peace that subsequently enveloped La Fière, the Germans evacuated their casualties and withdrew to Cauquigny.

It had been a costly fight for the Americans as well. Dolan's company alone had 17 killed and three times that number wounded. Those who remained were tired and jumpy, having been denied sleep by the incessant artillery and mortar fire. Moreover, the intensity of the fighting was something none of the troopers had ever experienced, including the veterans. Even Gavin, who saw firsthand the beating Dolan's troopers were taking, questioned whether they could hold. Bill Walton was in the general's foxhole at the time. Gavin turned to him and said, "You know, you don't have to stay here." When Walton asked why, Gavin replied, "We can't hold . . . but we are not going to give up . . . we're going to keep at it." Privately, Sergeant Owens felt likewise. After enduring two German assaults, some troopers suggested that it might be time to withdraw. "No, we will wait for orders," Owens barked. "We haven't been told to withdraw." But with ammunition running low and casualties mounting, Owens was not sure he could hold, so he sent a runner to Dolan requesting guidance. "Stay where you are," Dolan replied and, in a handwritten note for Owens's eyes only, added, "I don't know a better place than this to die."[27] Fortunately for the weary paratroopers, the Germans did not make a third assault, and later that evening Gavin withdrew the 1/505th, replacing it with an ad hoc force composed mostly of stray 507th troopers.[28]

When things settled down around La Fière, at least temporarily, Gavin turned his attention once more to Chef du Pont. He had made radio contact earlier in the day with Lieutenant Colonel Thomas J. B. Shanley, the 2/508th commander, who told Gavin that he and about 300 troopers were in a strong defensive position on Hill 30, a small rise west of the Merderet and just north of the Chef du Pont causeway (this was the second of the three major groups of paratroopers west of the Merderet). Shanley and his troopers had been in almost constant combat, both defending their hilltop bastion and attacking to drive off any enemy forces that got too close, including a German howitzer battery and a reinforced infantry battalion. Without question these actions contributed significantly to the defense of Chef du Pont by breaking up

German attacks against it before they got going, but Shanley could not hold out indefinitely; as he told Gavin, he was low on ammunition, food, water, and, above all, plasma for his wounded.

But if Shanley could hold out a little longer, Gavin saw an opportunity. While Shanley provided cover, a large force might be able to get across the river at Chef du Pont and then turn north to attack the Germans at Cauquigny in their flank. Gavin turned to Lindquist, who had gathered a fairly large number of 508th troopers at La Fière, and told him to get to Chef du Pont, relieve Creek, force his way across the river, resupply Shanley, and then advance north along the west bank of the Merderet to Cauquigny.[29]

Sometime thereafter Lindquist received reports of a large enemy concentration east of the Merderet and south of Chef du Pont (which was true) and another large enemy concentration near the western end of the causeway (this was not true; although there were some Germans on the far bank, they were not present in large numbers). When he arrived at Chef du Pont early in the morning of 8 June, he found that Creek had withdrawn his troopers from the west bank of the river because he felt that his force was too small to defend both ends of the causeway, which confirmed for Lindquist the report about a strong enemy force on the opposite bank. Consequently, instead of crossing the river and moving on Cauquigny as Gavin wanted, Lindquist sent two companies under Captain Royal Taylor to find and destroy the enemy force south of Chef du Pont.

Taylor and his troopers were wildly successful. They drove off the Germans south of Chef du Pont, made contact with the 101st, and took 135 prisoners without a single loss. But in the meantime Shanley's situation had grown critical, and because Taylor did not return to Chef du Pont that night, Lindquist felt that he did not have enough combat power to break through to Hill 30. Lindquist radioed Shanley and told him that he would have to wait until Taylor returned unless Shanley wanted to try clearing the west end of the causeway. When Shanley said that he did, Lindquist promised artillery support.[30]

Shanley sent Lieutenants Woodrow W. Millsaps and Lloyd L. Polette with 30 men to accomplish the job. They moved out around midnight, 8 June. The plan was that they would use the cover of night to get as close to the bridge as possible. At 0230 hours, 9 June, Lindquist would lay down an artillery barrage against the west end of the causeway behind which Millsaps, Polette, and their troopers would attack. At first everything went well. The troopers crept into position, and, right on time, Lindquist's artillery opened up. But the artillery was woefully off target. Only three rounds landed anywhere near the causeway; the rest fell harmlessly in the marsh.

Alerted by the artillery miscue, the few Germans in the area popped flares, which revealed Millsaps, Polette, and their troopers advancing toward them. German machine guns then opened up, and the paratroopers, caught in the open and temporarily blinded by the flares, wavered and started falling back. Although Millsaps and Polette grabbed them and turned them around, it looked as though there was no way they were going to break through to the bridge. But then Millsaps noticed a flaw in the German defenses. The arc of the German tracers revealed that their machine guns were not mutually supporting. If he could get his troopers up and through the gap in the German fire in a fast, determined rush, it might be possible to overrun the enemy positions before they could react.

Working his way from trooper to trooper, Millsaps explained what he had discovered and told them that on his signal they were to follow him at a run, fire on the move, and not stop until they were on top of the German positions. But when Millsaps stood up, yelled, and charged, no one followed, so he returned to his men, explained his plan again, and readied them for another go. This time everyone followed. The Germans broke and ran.

Millsaps halted the charge near the western end of the causeway, organized a hasty defense, and then along with a Sergeant Kleinfelter moved atop the causeway to the opposite bank. Side by side the two men shot, grenaded, and bayoneted their way through any Germans in their path. Millsaps was knocked down four times during the advance, while Kleinfelter was shot six times. Still they continued on, each man supporting the other until they made it to the east end of the causeway, where Millsaps dropped Kleinfelter off for medical aid and reported to Lindquist. But Lindquist was chary of sending any supplies across the causeway. It was still under fire, albeit desultory, and the supplies were too precious to risk their loss. Hence, it was not until the next afternoon, after both Lindquist and Shanley sent out patrols to mop up the last Germans in the area, that the men on Hill 30 received their badly needed supplies. Once again both ends of the Chef du Pont causeway were in American hands, and would remain so. Lindquist did not continue his advance to Cauquigny, however, for by the time he got across the Merderet, the fight at La Fière was over.[31]

The third group of paratroopers west of the Merderet, no fewer than four hundred, was holed up about a mile west of Timmes's orchard under the command of Colonel George V. Millett, the 507th commander. Gavin had never been enamored of Millett and while still in England tried to get him relieved because he thought Millett "lazy, soft, indolent, [and] lacking leadership necessary for combat."[32] Gavin was overruled, but his characterization proved correct. Unlike Shanley and Timmes, Millett sat tight, kept his force hidden, and, except for minor clashes with German units that stumbled on his position, remained untouched. Ironically, one of the clashes was with a German supply column containing enough ammunition, water, and food to last a week, to say nothing of an ample supply of cigars and cognac, making Millett's not only the largest but the best supplied of any of the three forces west of the Merderet.[33]

Ridgway had had intermittent radio contact with Millett, so he knew roughly where he was. Conversely, neither Ridgway nor Gavin was aware of Timmes's position until the evening of 7 June, when Lieutenant Willard E. Chambers stumbled into the division command post. Timmes had sent Chambers to find a way through the marsh. The Germans had targeted Timmes's orchard with artillery, mortar, and automatic weapons fire, and casualties were mounting—there were already twenty-two dead and thirty wounded—and Timmes needed either reinforcement or relief soon.

Not long thereafter two more troopers from Timmes's position arrived at the command post: Lieutenant John Marr (the same Marr that Lieutenant Levy met on the La Fière causeway) and Private First Class Norman V. Carter. They explained that when the first patrol returned without Chambers, who had sent his troopers back when it seemed they were inexorably lost, Timmes sent Marr and Carter with the same mission: find a way through the marsh. Marr and Carter reported that they passed through the marsh atop a submerged roadway that a Frenchman they encountered along the way showed them. This decided Ridgway on a bold maneuver. Rather than extricate Timmes, Ridgway would use his position as a rallying point from which to mount an attack to clear Cauquigny and the western end of the La Fière crossing. To accomplish this, Ridgway told Millett to move his force that night (8–9 June) to Timmes's orchard, where he would find, in addition to Timmes's force, Major Teddy H. Sanford's 1/325th and nine antitank guns that Ridgway was sending back across the marsh via the submerged roadway. Millett was then to lead this force in an attack against Cauquigny.[34]

Moving out at about 2300 hours 8 June with Lieutenant Marr leading, Sanford's troopers made it across the marsh and linked up with Timmes without encountering anything heavier than scattered fire. While moving into position for the attack, however, C Company, 1/325th, stumbled into a German artillery position, which set off a firefight during which one of C Company's platoons got pinned down in a roadside ditch and was in danger of being overrun. The only avenue of escape was across the road, but crossing it meant running through heavy machine-gun fire. It was then that Private First Class Charles N. DeGlopper, armed with his BAR, jumped into action. "Scorning a concentration of enemy automatic weapons and rifle fire, [DeGlopper] walked from the ditch onto the road in full view of the Germans, and sprayed the hostile positions with assault fire. He was wounded, but he continued firing. Struck again, he started to fall. . . . Kneeling in the roadway, weakened by his grievous wounds, he leveled his heavy weapon against the enemy and fired burst after burst until killed outright."[35] DeGlopper's heroism saved the platoon, which withdrew under cover of his fire, and earned for him a posthumous Medal of Honor. But the fight in the artillery park alerted the Germans around Cauquigny to the threat on their flank, compelling Sanford to withdraw to the relative safety of Timmes's orchard.[36]

Sanford led the attack on Cauquigny because Millett had not arrived and never would. Millett set out from his position at 0300 hours, 9 June, his troopers strung out in a long column behind him. They had not gone far when they started taking fire. In the resultant confusion Millett lost control, and the column disintegrated; Millett himself was captured. A count taken twenty-four hours later revealed that fewer than half (155) of the more than 400 troopers with Millett made it back to friendly lines.[37]

When word reached Ridgway that his plan had failed, he turned to Gavin and told him to "get the Merderet crossing . . . [and] get it without delay." Time was running short. The causeway had to be seized so that the 90th Infantry Division could attack westward across the base of the Cotentin Peninsula in order to set the stage for the advance on Cherbourg. Four hours later Gavin was ready to go.[38]

Gavin's plan was straightforward. He would lead the attack with the division reserve, Lieutenant Colonel Charles Carrell's 2/401st, the only uncommitted infantry battalion in the 82nd, which was also relatively fresh since it had yet to see any substantive combat. Preparing the way for Carrell would be ten or twelve Sherman tanks (accounts differ) from Task Force Raff that Gavin positioned on the high ground overlooking the causeway, all of the division's howitzers, and a battalion of 155mm howitzers from the 90th Infantry Division. Starting at 1030 hours, 9 June, the tanks and artillery were to commence a fifteen-minute bombardment of enemy positions on and around the causeway after which the 2/401st was to conduct an assault down its length. Carrell arrived at La Fière at around 1000 hours with no idea what was in store. When Gavin briefed him on the plan Carrell turned white and later told his officers he thought the mission "impossible."[39] Yet the order stood.[40]

The bombardment opened right on schedule. It was devastating. "For about 15 minutes," related Gavin, "we poured everything we had right on top of the German positions. Dust, horses screeching and getting shot up—the Germans had all this horse-drawn stuff. Finally the Germans were coming up out of their foxholes with dust streaming down their faces and blood streaming out of their mouths and coming in surrendering." At 1045 hours, Gavin turned to Carrell and told him to go. "I don't think I can do it," came the reply. "I'm sick."[41] Gavin was floored, but with no time to waste he relieved Carrell and put Major Arthur Gardner in command.

Before being relieved Carrell had selected Captain John Sauls's G Company to lead the assault. Sauls had no need for Carrell's dire prediction; he knew the stakes and knew it was going to be bloody, but he was determined to do everything possible to better the odds and protect his troopers. To that end, under cover of the bombardment he moved his company into position directly behind one of the manor's stone walls, figuring that the chances of success, and of his troopers' survival, increased the closer they got to the bridge. In addition, after taking a look at his objective he concluded that this was no time for tactical finesse. He passed word back—once the charge started, everyone was to run as fast as he could across the causeway in a "bull-like rush."[42] Sauls would lead the way.[43] Still, the charge would be "500 yards, directly into the teeth of well-aimed, grazing machine[-]gun and rifle fire, interspersed with mortar and artillery fire. The causeway was little more than a one-lane road with water and marshland on both sides. There was no cover and the few bushes and small trees along the edge of the causeway offered very little concealment."[44]

When Sauls got the order to go, he jumped up and ran through a hole in the stone wall onto the causeway and over the bridge. On his heels was Second Platoon, most of which made it all the way to the other side with him. The rest of the company was nowhere to be seen. A trooper had been hit and killed as he was climbing through the hole in the wall, and his body had become wedged in the opening. Several minutes passed before the body could be removed. In the interim the Germans zeroed in on the opening, leaving Sauls and his Second Platoon alone on the far bank. It was another G Company officer, Lieutenant Frank E. Amino, who got the charge started again. Jumping to his feet, he shouted, "Let's get up and kill the sons of bitches" and then led the remainder of G Company across the bridge.[45]

Next in line was Captain Charles Murphy's E Company. While briefing his troopers on the plan Murphy got so choked up he could not continue. "All that [he] could say was 'God bless you,' while two big tears rolled down his cheeks."[46] But when it was time to attack, he was all business. Having positioned his company right behind Sauls's, Murphy led his troopers through the wall and onto the causeway as soon as G Company was clear. By that time the Germans were firing on the causeway from both flanks, mowing down the charging troopers "like wheat before a scythe."[47] They were also firing down the length of the causeway, turning the bridge into what Ridgway described as "a funnel" through which "the Germans were just pouring in the fire. . . . [W]e were losing a lot of men. . . . [T]he fire was so intense that men were just physically recoiling."[48] Yet E Company charged on.[49]

Captain James M. Harney's F Company was the next to hit the causeway. By that time it was so congested with dead and wounded from both sides that it was impossible to take it at a run. Adding to the congestion were dozens of dazed Germans who, having surrendered, were told to throw away their weapons and move to the American side of the river unescorted. And just as F Company was crossing the bridge a Sherman tank that had moved forward to clear away the wreckage on the roadway hit an antitank mine. The explosion all but wiped out Harney's Weapons Platoon. Nevertheless, Harney and his troopers pressed forward. To those observing from the American side, however, it appeared that the assault was losing momentum.[50]

"Something about the laws of physics applies to combat," said Gavin later when speaking of the assault. "A certain amount of inertia will bring [attacking soldiers] to a stop and a certain amount of inertia will make them go."[51] Gavin was prepared for this. Even before the first man set foot on the causeway he had alerted a company of 507th paratroopers under Captain R. D. Rae to be prepared to reinforce the 2/401st's assault if it bogged down. As Gavin described it, "I told Rae now once this thing starts, you watch me and I'll give you an arm signal if the glidermen look to me as though they are not going to make it. I want you to get those troopers up and go across that bridge and take them with you."[52] When Harney's F Company was staggered by the tank explosion Gavin gave that signal. With eighty to one hundred paratroopers in his wake, Rae charged onto the causeway and joined the assault.[53] Another 507th officer, Lieutenant James D. Orwin, gathered stragglers and led them across to the other side, albeit in a particularly memorable manner. Orwin's helmet had been blown apart earlier in the day, so when he ventured onto the causeway, he was wearing a knit cap that was incongruously adorned with several red roses. So attired, Orwin blithely strolled the causeway, gathering troopers who, for whatever reason, had temporarily halted and told them, "Now, fellows, we're all going to the other side. Things are good over there. Walk with me—for I'm a lucky bastard!"[54]

Incredible courage (though not all as peculiar as Orwin's) was common that day at La Fière. The mere effort to propel oneself into the maelstrom of fire that defined the bridge and causeway was, in itself, an act of heroism. Nevertheless, accounts of the battle are replete with acts of extraordinary valor that, when taken together, form the only coherent explanation for the success of the mad assault. One of the first men over, Lieutenant Donald B. Wason, was killed while single-handedly taking out a German machine-gun position. Nearby, Private First Class Frank Thurston silenced a second machine gun by calmly shooting the crew with his rifle one at a time. Lieutenant William H. Condon of F Company, already suffering from injuries he had sustained in the glider landing, was hit in the head and shoulder by shrapnel during the crossing but refused evacuation. Another lieutenant, Joseph H. Shealy, was also hit by shrapnel and refused evacuation; he remained at the head of his platoon until reaching the enemy side of the river, then dropped dead from loss of blood. Sergeant Albert Morrison, a signalman, was lying in the roadway repairing a break in the communication wire; he was lying because he could not stand, having been shot through both thighs. Lieutenant Bruce H. Booker, E Company's executive officer, made five trips back and forth across the bridge, urging men forward. Finally, hit in both legs, he propped himself on the roadway and continued his exhortations, stopping only long enough to crawl to other, more seriously wounded troopers to administer first aid. The medics, too, were everywhere, ignoring cover and "running up and down the causeway bandaging the wounded as rapidly as they could get to them." Captain Rae observed them at work during his dash across and stated that "the success of the Medical Corps in clearing the causeway of wounded . . . was nothing short of phenominal [*sic*]."[55] And in the midst of the bloody chaos, as much exposed to danger and imminent death as any man that day, were the two most recognizable figures in the division—Ridgway and Gavin.

Some years after the war, Gavin mused on the proper place of a general on the battlefield. "Historically, there has always been much discussion in the U.S. Army about the proper place of a general in battle. Although lip service is paid to the view that the general belongs as close to the scene of action as circumstances will allow, the fact is that very few generals behave this way." But for Gavin, there was "no question that the place for the general in battle is where he can see the battle and get the odor of it in his nostrils." Ridgway, likewise, held that a general should always be "where the crisis of action is, where the going is the toughest." That day at La Fière, both were in the thick of the fight, right on the fire-swept bridge, ensuring the attack did not slacken. "The physical force of that fire," recalled Ridgway, "was such that [troopers] just stopped and started back, not from cowardice at all. We just grabbed them by the shoulders and lead [*sic*] them . . . and pushed them."[56] When not urging their men forward, they were tending wounded, hooking up tow cables to the burned-out hulks so they could be pulled off the roadway, or clearing a lane for jeeps carrying ammunition. One trooper recalled seeing them organize the roadway so that it resembled "an escalator, two streams of men on the inside trying to run forward and on the outer side streams of wounded trickling back." "The presence of these senior officers," wrote another trooper, "helped a lot to encourage the men and get them better organized."[57]

River crossings involve two necessary steps. The first is to get across the river. The second is to establish a foothold on the far shore. To accomplish step two each of the 2/401st companies was to peel off in a different direction when it reached the German side of the Merderet; G Company was to veer left, E Company was to veer right, and F Company was to fill the gap in between in order to form a semicircular perimeter around the western end of the causeway. Once that was done they were to make contact with the troopers in Timmes's orchard. Then, with two of his battalions in hand Colonel Lewis was to expand the foothold to a depth of 1,000 yards.[58]

Although the plan for establishing the foothold was conceptually straightforward, executing it proved just as bloody as seizing the causeway, for having spanned the divide of river and marsh, Americans and Germans were now face-to-face, locked in close-quarters, no-quarter combat. Hence, the necessities inherent to creating a coherent perimeter—tying in flanks, coordinating fires, shifting units to cover holes—fell prey to the chaotic man-killing struggle that engulfed the far shore. In this frenzy there was no centralized, meticulous control. Once again it was junior leaders displaying initiative and aggressiveness that underwrote success.

When Captain Sauls's G Company reached the far bank and veered left, it ran headlong into a line of German entrenchments. By that time Lieutenant Wason, whose platoon was in the lead, was dead, killed during his assault on a machine-gun nest. Into the breach stepped Sergeant Wilfred L. Ericsson, Wason's platoon sergeant. Taking half his platoon with him, Ericsson attacked the German entrenchments and forced the defenders to withdraw right into the guns of the other half of his platoon, which he had positioned along the Germans' escape route. With the entrenchments cleared and the Germans manning them dead or wounded, the left shoulder of the foothold was secured.[59]

As directed Murphy's E Company, second across the bridge, veered slightly right and straight at Cauquigny. Already down by thirty troopers killed or wounded on the causeway, E Company's fight got even more intense as it neared the hamlet. Yet Murphy pressed the attack, and E Company eventually overran Cauquigny, where Murphy discovered the reason for the ferocious resistance—he and his troopers had captured the *1057th Regimental Headquarters* and the regimental mortars, taking some fifty-two prisoners in the process. With the fall of Cauquigny, not only was the right shoulder of the American foothold established, but so also was German command and control of the battle lost.[60]

Captain Harney arrived at the far shore with most of F Company intact (with the exception of Weapons Platoon) but in the confusion could find neither of the companies on his flanks. Nevertheless, he made for some high ground to his front, which carried F Company and a platoon of Rae's paratroopers into the village of Le Motey. There they ran into a wall of friendly artillery fire that had been shifted westward once the attack across the causeway got under way that drove them back. Isolated and about 800 yards from the nearest friendly unit, Harney formed his troopers into a defensive perimeter and returned to the western end of the causeway, seeking both reinforcement and a means to turn off the friendly artillery. Harney eventually found Major Gardner, who told him that he had no communications with the artillery and therefore could not call it off. What he would do was order Murphy's E Company forward to form up on Harney's right flank. But in the confusion Murphy moved past Harney's flank and right into a German ambush, which forced him back to Cauquigny. Harney, meanwhile, returned to his company and with his mixed bag of troopers fought for three hours against repeated counterattacks. Finally, weakened by casualties and in danger of being surrounded, Harney withdrew. Only then was he able to tie in with the rest of his battalion. Although a seemingly pointless action on its face, Harney's stand gained the time needed for the forces nearer the bridge, to include those of Timmes and Sanford, to consolidate, expand, and solidify the foothold around the western end of the causeway.[61]

The last act of the fight for the La Fière causeway commenced at around 1900 hours, announced by a heavy German artillery and mortar barrage. By that time Colonel Lewis had been evacuated due to exhaustion, and command of the forces defending the foothold had passed to his executive officer, Lieutenant Colonel Herbert G. Sitler.[62] When the barrage began, Sitler sent word to the 82nd command post that the tanks that had been supporting him had withdrawn and that some of his troopers had taken this as a sign to withdraw as well. The foothold, he continued, was in danger of collapse. To right things, Ridgway turned to Gavin.

Taking Lieutenant Colonel Maloney and Major Willard E. Harrison with him, Gavin rushed to Sitler's position to see things for himself (Harrison was one of the few 504th troopers to participate in the Normandy campaign). Along the way he dropped Maloney at the bridge with orders to stop anyone from moving to the rear. Maloney was a large man who had been wounded earlier in the day and still had blood caked on his face. Armed with a huge tree branch, he stood at the western end of the bridge and, through his presence alone, "convinced" several troopers that their proper place was at the front.

Gavin and Harrison continued on to Sitler's command post, where Sitler reiterated his feelings about not being able to hold. Gavin would have none of it. "After what we had been through for three days," wrote Gavin later, "we simply could not give up the causeway," so Gavin told Sitler to gather every trooper he could lay hands on, "including himself, regimental clerks, headquarters people, anyone . . . with a weapon," and prepare to launch a spoiling attack. Gavin then buttonholed the ubiquitous Captain Rae and told him, "Take your men and go forward. . . . Go to [Le Motey]." With Rae's troopers attacking on one axis and Sitler's troopers attacking on a second, Le Motey finally fell. The last significant threat to the La Fière causeway had been defeated.[63]

Taking the La Fière causeway was the last of the 82nd's assigned missions. With it secure Bradley's First Army was poised to attack to clear the Cotentin Peninsula and seize the ultimate prize, Cherbourg. The attack jumped off at 0300 hours, 10 June, with the U.S. 90th Infantry Division passing through the 325th's lines. The 82nd, less the 505th and the 2/325th, which were assisting the U.S. 4th Infantry Division clear the area north of Ste.-Mère-Église, went into reserve.[64]

No one has ever counted the cost of the La Fière causeway. The only reliable figures are from the 2/401st, which lost 40 troopers killed and another 180 wounded.[65] German figures have been forever lost, although it is certain that the fight destroyed the *1057th Regiment*, which ceased to exist as a cohesive fighting force. Yet even absent the numbers the ferocity of the battle made a lasting impression. Ridgway called it "as hot a single battle as any U.S. troops had, at any time, during the war in Europe." Gavin opined that "the shock of battle never has been greater than it was . . . in the causeway crossing," adding, "Probably the only thing that compared with it in raw courage was the crossing of the Waal River at Nijmegen [Holland]." The fight also changed his perception about glider troopers. "From then on," he wrote, "the 325th became one of the great regiments of the war."[66]

More than thirty years later Gavin accepted an invitation to speak to some veterans at a relatively small venue. By that time Gavin was well known. He had retired as a lieutenant general, authored five books, and been ambassador to France. Richard Brigham Johnson, who served with the 2/401st in Normandy and had been wounded on 9 June at La Fière, had arranged the event. While the two were alone setting up a projector in preparation for the talk, the general turned to Johnson and asked, "Do you know why I'm doing this?" When Johnson replied that he did not, Gavin said, "You crossed that causeway, and I can't say no to any man who did."[67]

SHAEF's "Employment of Airborne Forces" memorandum—the same memorandum Gavin had worked so hard on while with COSSAC—stated explicitly that airborne divisions were to be withdrawn as soon as ground forces relieved them. But Bradley found that his conventional infantrymen lacked aggressiveness, especially given the close fighting dictated by the *bocage*, and he was chary of releasing troopers that, though bloodied, had proved capable of offensive maneuver in restricted terrain. For the 82nd, Ste.-Mère-Église, Chef du Pont, and La Fière were but a beginning.

CHAPTER 13

CAN'T ANYTHING STOP THOSE MEN?

It is essential that infantry in training be imbued with a bold, aggressive attitude. Many units do not acquire this attitude until long after their entry into combat, and some never acquire it. On the other hand units containing specially selected personnel such as Airborne and Rangers exhibited an aggressive spirit from the start.

—U.S. First Army Report on Normandy, quoted in *Overlord: D-Day and the Battle for Normandy*, by Max Hastings

THE FIRST FEW days of fighting in Normandy took a tremendous toll on the 82nd, and although there exists no accurate accounting of the casualties sustained during this period (one estimate, however, puts the 82nd's casualty count at 1,259 for D-Day alone), a sampling of units suggests that losses were high across the board.[1] In addition to the 220 troopers killed or wounded from the 2/401st at La Fière, for example, were the more than 130 casualties sustained within Timmes's orchard; the more than 200 killed, wounded, or taken prisoner from Millett's column; and the 130 killed and wounded during the fight for Ste.-Mère-Église.[2] And since much of the combat occurred at close range, it was not the infantry alone that paid the Norman butcher; the division's combat support units were also hit hard. Two such units for which accurate records were kept, the 307th Airborne Engineer Battalion and the 319th Glider Field Artillery Battalion, sustained 20 and 30 percent casualties, respectively, in the first few days of combat.[3]

By necessity, the slightly wounded were patched up and sent back to their units. The more serious cases were treated at the division's aid station at Ste.-Mère-Église and subsequently evacuated to England. But it took several days for the evacuation pipeline to mature, so in the interim the 82nd's medics and doctors did their best with what they had. Chaplain George Wood saw the 505th's medical officer, Captain Lyle Putnam, perform major surgery, "even to amputations, all night long, with the few instruments he jumped in with on his person in a blacked-out room of the school-house which we were using as an aid station, to the music of a rain of shells which never ceased."[4] Journalist Bill Walton was forever haunted by the carnage he saw at that aid station:

> I went into the barn where all the wounded were and it looked like something out of the Crimean War. Because they were shot through the face, lying on their back . . . sitting here, his tongue half shot off . . . the lower part of his jaw missing . . . G. I. sitting up in his own blood . . . and people were just hunks of flesh and everything that could be done was being done . . . but it just meant walking wounded and a slight clean-up. This is about all there was. And all the broken legs were put in separate sections. While I was still there I found Phil Buckley of *Stars & Stripes* who had broken both legs. He laid in the field all day under machine gun fire . . . caught . . . unable to get out . . . and finally, I went out . . . tired . . . I was nearly dead. I decided to join some sleeping guys outside. They were wrapped up in parachutes so I pulled half the parachute cloth off one guy and rolled up with him. And about a half hour later some guard shook me on the shoulder, and said, "Come on, we've got to abandon this command post quick." I shook the guy behind me and found he was dead. He had been dead when I went to sleep with him. How innocent I was. . . . I didn't know that all troopers were always rolled in their chutes when they died.[5]

Replacements were available in England, but only 43 were brought forward, all of them junior officers whose ranks were especially hard hit. Overall, 71 percent of the 82nd's infantry first lieutenants (168 of 238 committed to combat) and 65 percent of its infantry second lieutenants (115 of 178 committed) became casualties in Normandy.[6] Enlisted replacements were not brought forward "possibly because it had not been expected that the Division would stay in action so long, possibly because it was felt that so many new men could not be advantageously absorbed."[7] As a result, when the division left France many units were down to less than 50 percent strength.[8] One outfit—G Company, 2/325th—returned to England with only 13 of its authorized complement of 155 officers and men.[9]

Early casualty returns were also misleading. Many listed as missing were actually misdropped troopers who returned to the division fold days and weeks after they jumped or glided in. Illustrative of this was the odyssey of Technical Sergeant Edward W. Shimko who, along with 12 troopers from the 2/325th and the pilot and copilot of the glider that delivered them to Normandy, did not return to division control until 14 June, and then only after traveling the entire length of the Allied beachhead in Normandy. They landed about three miles north of Caen, some forty-five miles from their designated landing zone, then spent the next few days dodging enemy and friendly fire, hiding from German patrols, and picking their way through minefields before finally reaching friendly lines, where they hitched a ride to Ste.-Mère-Église.[10]

The same day Shimko's group returned, so did a group of 3/507th troopers, the remnants of a force that barely escaped annihilation. They had been dropped ten miles southeast of their intended drop zone and assembled at the village of Graignes under the command of Major Charles D. Johnson, the battalion executive officer. For seven days Johnson and the approximately 180 officers and men with him defended Graignes against overwhelming odds. Finally, low on ammunition and with no succor in sight, Johnson ordered his troopers to split up and infiltrate toward friendly lines. A little more than half made it all the way. The rest were either killed or captured, and at least 24, along with several French civilians who had nursed Americans wounded during the fight at Graignes, were executed by the Germans.[11]

Perhaps the longest journey back to friendly lines was by a group of 508th paratroopers led by First Sergeant Leonard A. Funk. They landed forty miles from their drop zone. Funk told his troopers that "come hell or high water, I would never be taken prisoner, that we were going to fight our way back to friendly forces—even if it took us the rest of the war." Hiding by day and traveling by night, Funk and his troopers fought their way across Normandy. "When possible," Funk recalled, "we avoided enemy contact, but got mixed up in all sorts of shootouts and scrapes."

> Several times, we ambushed Kraut vehicles and small groups, and we blew up one panzer by putting a landmine in the road. Much of the time we were starving and thirsty—didn't dare to approach a house. Hardly ever took our boots off. The closer we got to American lines, the thicker were the Germans. Now it was touch-and-go every yard of the way, and we had several brushes with disaster. Finally, after 21 days, we reached an outpost of our 90th Infantry Division—and we were so filthy and disheveled that the straight-legs thought we were Krauts and damned near shot us.[12]

Most of the misdropped troopers were west of the Merderet, and once the division took the crossings at La Fière and Chef du Pont, they came streaming in. This allowed Ridgway and Gavin to disband the many ad hoc formations they had formed and reestablish the chain of command. By daybreak 10 June, the 82nd again resembled the organization that had left England five days before, albeit significantly smaller due to casualties. As already stated, it should have then moved back to England to refit and get ready for follow-on airborne missions. But instead the 82nd remained in France and participated in five major drives, even, at times, attacking in two different directions simultaneously. The first occurred even before the fighting at La Fière and Chef du Pont had died down.

At 1700 hours, 7 June, while Vandervoort's 2/505th was still beating back the attack by the *Seventh Army Sturm Battalion* on the northern outskirts of Ste.-Mère-Église, Major General J. Lawton "Lightning Joe" Collins, the VII Corps commander, arrived at the 82nd command post to outline a plan to clear out some long-range artillery that had UTAH beach under fire. Collins's plan called for an advance to the towns of Montebourg and Quinéville, some six miles to the northwest. The 505th—reinforced with the 2/325th—was to be the westernmost of the attacking units. Its mission was to seize the hamlet of Le Ham and the road and rail intersection at Montebourg Station (two miles southwest of Montebourg) while securing the flank of the 4th Infantry Division advancing on its right.[13]

Collins wanted to jump off early in the morning of 8 June but had to postpone the attack because the 4th Infantry Division was not ready. Although maddening for Collins, this was a welcome respite for Ekman's troopers, who had been in almost constant combat for some forty hours. Fatigue and exhaustion were beginning to take their toll, especially among the leaders. Colonel Ekman was so tired that he fell asleep while issuing his attack order. His operations officer, John Norton, took over the briefing after "unceremoniously" shoving the comatose Ekman under a table to sleep undisturbed.[14] Vandervoort, too, felt the effects of sleep deprivation:

> The most amusing incident I remember was when I thought I'd been killed and woke up in heaven. At the end of the third day of almost continuous fighting we were approaching exhaustion. It was just before sunset and my C. P. was being shelled by a German 88. I issued orders for the C. P. to move and fell asleep in my fox-hole [*sic*]. The next thing I knew I was waked by beautiful music. I looked up and saw beautiful blossoms above me. I knew I had been killed and was in heaven and thought "What a lovely place it is." When they moved the C.P. my troopers had been unable to wake me and poured me into a jeep and then a fox-hole [*sic*] under one of the Normandy

apple trees which was then in full blossom. The music was the BBC broadcasting over a small portable radio one of the troopers had carried in with him.[15]

The enemy also took advantage of the delay. Generalleutnant Karl-Wilhelm von Schlieben, commander of the *709th Division*, scooped up what remained of his division and two others—the *243rd*, which had been defending the western side of the Cotentin, and the hard-hit *91st*—as well as the remnants of the *Seventh Army Sturm Battalion*, formed them into three regimental *Kampfgruppen* (battle groups), and positioned them on ground that dominated likely avenues of approach to the north. Set in camouflaged field fortifications that made maximum use of the hedgerows and backed by more than three battalions of artillery, Schlieben's force was far from the broken host last seen retreating from the killing fields north of Ste.-Mère-Église.[16]

When, at midday, word finally came to move out, Ekman's troopers jumped off with the 2/505th and 3/505th in the lead, while the 1/505th, the 2/325th, and a platoon of tanks followed. Ekman told his troopers to advance aggressively and not get bogged down. They did not disappoint. When fired on by German artillery, they literally ran through the barrage and closed with the startled defenders so quickly that they did not have time to react. By 2300 hours Ekman's lead battalions had advanced more than two miles and taken the town of Grainville, where Collins ordered Ekman to halt, consolidate his force, form a defensive barrier to protect the American left flank, and remain poised for a continuation of the attack on the morrow.[17]

The advance to Grainville cracked the crust of Schlieben's defenses. Taking Le Ham and Montebourg Station would require breaking through his main line of resistance. Ekman could not have mistaken where that would be. A canal and two streams (tributaries of the Merderet) flowed perpendicularly across his front, and it was on those obstacles that Schlieben anchored a considerable defense in depth. To take their objectives, Ekman's troopers would have to first cross the canal and the lower stream. Then, Ekman would have to attack in two directions simultaneously: north toward Montebourg Station, near the banks of the upper stream, and west to Le Ham, situated on the Merderet itself. He would have to do this while restricted to a narrow attack corridor since Collins reserved for the 4th Infantry Division the majority of the maneuver room in the area. Ekman's advance, therefore, would be straight into the teeth of Schlieben's defenses.[18]

The advance recommenced at 0930 hours, 9 June. Because of his narrow attack corridor Ekman elected to advance in a column of battalions with the 2/325th leading, followed by the 2/505th and 1/505th, while the 3/505th remained at Grainville to protect their flank and rear. His plan was to breach the defenses on the canal and lower stream and then have the 2/325th turn west to attack Le Ham while the 2/505th continued north toward Montebourg Station and the 1/505th remained ready to support either. But when the 2/325th got pinned down short of the canal by heavy machine-gun and mortar fire and Ekman wanted to bring up another battalion to press the attack, he was again compelled to hold, this time until the next day because the 4th Infantry Division on his right, which was also heavily engaged, had elected to halt and regroup.[19]

When Ekman renewed the attack the next day he leapfrogged the 1/505th into the lead with orders to advance on Montebourg Station; the 2/505th followed and assumed the mission to take Le Ham, while the 2/325th remained in place to protect the left flank. Advancing behind a rolling barrage fired by the 320th Glider and 456th Parachute Field Artillery Battalions, the 1/505th got across the canal and lower stream and took Montebourg Station by early evening. Although the station fell with relative ease, the fight en route had been hedgerow-to-hedgerow against an enemy backed by plenty of artillery, to include 88mm guns. Casualties were heavy; by day's end the 1/505th could muster only 250 combat effective troopers. Additionally, since the Germans at Montebourg Station fled toward Le Ham and bolstered the defenders already there, when the 2/505th turned to take Le Ham, it ran into heavy resistance and had to halt for the night.[20]

The terrain leading to Le Ham was ideally suited for defense. The streams north and south of the town created a channel down which any attacker from the east would have to travel, and the hedgerow-partitioned fields in the area were much smaller and the hedgerows themselves much stouter than elsewhere in Normandy. Furthermore, Le Ham's eastern outskirts were inundated with small streams and swamps. To offset these defensive advantages, Ekman organized a two-battalion attack for 11 June: The 2/505th was to mount a feint northeast of Le Ham to draw off enemy defenders, while the 2/325th, which had moved forward, assaulted the village from the east.

Following a fifteen-minute artillery bombardment, Lieutenant Colonel John H. Swenson, the 2/325th commander, led his battalion in the attack. With all three rifle companies on line, the glider troopers advanced at a run with fixed bayonets, firing from the hip, supported by fire from the 456th. Not long into the attack Swenson was hit. When Lieutenant George Cockle, the G Company commander, stopped to render first aid, Swenson waved him off. "Attack, Cockle, forget me!" bellowed Swenson, who, though subsequently bandaged by a passing medic, refused to leave the fight and refused morphine because, as he told the medic, "it would knock me out and I want to be alert and know what is going on."[21] With Swenson down, Major Osmond Leahy, the 325th's operations officer, took command of the assault, which continued unabated to the eastern edge of Le Ham, where Leahy halted the troopers to reorganize before pushing into the village itself. Meanwhile, the Germans inside Le Ham started drifting out the opposite side of the village. Sensing this, Leahy sent his troopers after them. Within hours Le Ham was in American hands, as were about 100 Germans prisoners.[22]

Taking Le Ham ended the 82nd's role in Collins's push north. For the next two days the 505th and 2/325th remained in defensive positions protecting the 4th Infantry Division's left flank as it cleared out the last of the German long-range artillery. Although not a quiet sector by any means, remaining in one place for more than a few hours afforded the troopers the opportunity to reequip, reorganize, and rest. It was much needed. The 505th had been reduced to but 1,400 effectives (out of an authorized strength of just more than 2,000), and the 2/325th had lost 40 percent of its strength. As was the norm in the 82nd, the battalion's leaders suffered the most; besides a battalion commander, two company commanders, and a battalion intelligence officer, numerous junior officers and noncommissioned officers were also killed or wounded.[23]

Collins's thrust north eliminated one threat to UTAH beach, but a far more significant threat, at least in the eyes of Eisenhower, Montgomery, and Bradley, was the fact that Collins's VII Corps had yet to link up with Major General Leonard T. Gerow's V Corps, which landed on OMAHA beach. The NEPTUNE plan emphasized the importance of consolidating the beachheads before driving on Cherbourg. The Allies needed the room to bring in more forces and supplies; otherwise, they would be too weak to break out and in danger of defeat in detail.

Bradley told his deputy, Lieutenant General Courtney H. Hodges, to make the linkup happen. Hodges, in turn, called on the 82nd. The mission was to attack south across the Douve River at Beuzeville-la-Bastille, which lay on the south side of the river about two miles southwest of Chef du Pont, and then continue south for approximately three and a half miles to Baupte to link up with the 101st. Ridgway assigned the mission to Lindquist's 508th, which had consolidated around Chef du Pont, reinforced by A Battery, 80th Airborne Antiaircraft Battalion; a detachment from A Company, 307th Airborne Engineer Battalion; and a platoon of tanks. Supporting the 508th would be the guns of the 319th and 320th as well as 155mm howitzers from VII Corps.[24]

Lindquist's orders were to attack on the night of 12–13 June, but in order to gain a better picture of the enemy defenses south of the Douve, he tried slipping a reconnaissance patrol across the river the night before. Although the attempt failed—the patrol never got to the south side of the Douve because its boat foundered—leaving Lindquist with but the sketchiest idea of what was on the opposite bank, he eschewed a preassault bombardment. Hence, at one minute past midnight, 13 June, the troopers of F Company,

2/508th, loaded several small boats piloted by engineers from the 307th and paddled silently across the Douve. It was "a most eerie feeling," recalled Private Bill Giegold. "We couldn't see a thing or hear anything on the other side. It was like paddling into the JAWS OF HELL." But Lindquist's gamble paid off. Forty-five minutes later the entire company was on the south bank of the Douve. The crossing had been "effected so quietly and skillfully that not a shot was fired and the infantry company was enabled to take the enemy by complete surprise."[25]

After consolidating, F Company set out for Beuzeville-la-Bastille, which, in American hands, would open the way for an advance on the primary objective, Baupte. Creeping along in the dark, F Company got to a point just north of Beuzeville-la-Bastille before two German tanks took the company under fire. Lieutenant Lloyd Polette, an F Company platoon leader, sprang into action. "Polette knocked out one tank by dropping a Gammon grenade down a vent," recalled radioman Private Edward Chatoian. "He destroyed the other with a bazooka rocket." With the enemy alert and the element of surprise gone, the company commander, Lieutenant Hoyt T. Goodale, radioed the dormant artillery to fire a barrage to clear the way for a charge into town. For some reason the fire never came.

> We lined up in assault formation behind a fence, [recalled Chatoian]. We were supposed to attack after the artillery softened up the enemy for fifteen minutes. I kept looking at my watch—no artillery and 0115 was getting close. I radioed, "Where are the firecrackers?" No response. Goodale said, "We will go without the firecrackers." Exactly at 0115, Goodale ordered, "Run, yell and fire!" It was a long run across an open field—several hundred yards. I saw one trooper stop, take out his canteen, and take a long drink (probably Calvados), and start running again. . . . We took the town and didn't lose a man. It was the surprise that did it. We were better off without the artillery.[26]

Covered by F Company's attack, Lindquist's engineers constructed a hasty bridge across the Douve. So smoothly had Lindquist coordinated the operation (with the exception of the artillery miscue) that by 0500 hours, 13 June, his entire force was across the river. Lindquist then released his battalions so they could proceed to their respective objectives, unleashing what would become a rampaging horde of paratroopers whose actions would throw German forces in the area into complete disarray.[27]

The first battalion across was Major Shields Warren Jr.'s 1/508th (Warren took command of the battalion after Lieutenant Colonel Batchellor was killed on D-Day). Passing through Beuzeville-la-Bastille without incident, Warren's troopers moved on to their objective, the town of Coigny, some three miles distant. Along the way they destroyed seven tanks from the *100th Panzer Replacement Battalion*, a makeshift unit composed of a large number of foreign vehicles and personnel.[28] At 1600 hours, having taken Coigny without a fight, Warren sent A and B Companies, each of which was reinforced by one of the 80th's antitank guns, on search-and-destroy missions. Captain Jonathan E. Adams's A Company enjoyed especially good hunting; before returning to Coigny for the night Adams's troopers ambushed a German command post and destroyed five more tanks.

Lieutenant Colonel Louis G. Mendez's 3/508th was next across the Douve. Experiencing little resistance beyond an occasional sniper, Mendez's battalion occupied its objective, more than four miles from Beuzeville-la-Bastille, by early morning.

Last across the river was Lieutenant Colonel Thomas Shanley's 2/508th. Its mission was to take Baupte and link up with the 101st. Picking up F Company as it passed through Beuzeville-la-Bastille, Shanley's battalion proceeded south without incident until, about 2,500 yards northeast of Baupte, it ambushed and destroyed two more German tanks. Pressing on, Shanley and his troopers got to Baupte's outskirts before again making contact. Based on the volume and intensity of the fire, Shanley surmised that inside Baupte was a substantial force, although how substantial was a mystery, so he sent out reconnaissance patrols to find out. When they returned, they told Shanley that Baupte contained at least a battalion of infantry supported by tanks and artillery. According to doctrine, it would require at least a reinforced regiment to overcome such a force, but Shanley had no time for doctrinal solutions so, counting on the speed and aggressiveness of his troopers, he attacked. It was the right call. Following a two-hour, close-quarters fight, during which Shanley's troopers overran two enemy infantry companies, destroyed ten more tanks and four automatic cannons, and captured some fifty vehicles, Baupte was his. Linkup with the 101st was achieved shortly thereafter and the juncture of V and VII Corps cemented. To ensure he held this critical point, that evening Lindquist moved Warren's 1/508th to Baupte to bolster Shanley's defenses.[29]

The 508th's advance had been so swift and devastating that German intelligence mistook it for an American armor column. The fall of Baupte and destruction of the *100th Panzer Replacement Battalion* also tore a gaping hole in the German defenses and so threatened the effort to contain the Allied beachheads that a *Kampfgruppe* from the *265th Division*, originally slated to reinforce Cherbourg, was diverted to the area to counterattack. Thus it was that early the next morning Mendez radioed Lindquist to tell him that he had just repulsed an attack by a company-size element and that there appeared to be an even larger force moving toward Baupte.

Eager to stop the German attack before it started, Lindquist ordered Warren to mount a preemptive strike. Advancing with two companies abreast and one in reserve and supported by fire from the 319th, the 1/508th overran several German outposts before it was halted by heavy return fire from a nearby village, where the enemy column Mendez had warned about was preparing for its attack. Since he was too weak to assault the massing Germans, Warren organized a hasty defense and for three hours stymied every German attempt to kick off the attack, aided in no small measure by the 319th's supporting artillery fire. Chary of pulling more units from his thinly held sector to reinforce the 1/508th, Lindquist finally ordered Warren to fall back to Baupte, where, in concert with Shanley's 2/508th, he was to prepare to defend. But the attack on Baupte never materialized. The German *Kampfgruppe* had been shattered. And with the exception of a probe by fifty German bicyclists that D Company, 2/508th, ambushed early the next morning, there developed no further threats to the continuity of the Allied beachhead. Bradley and Collins were free to concentrate on cutting the Cotentin Peninsula.[30]

Collins had pegged the inexperienced U.S. 90th Infantry Division to lead the thrust across the base of the Cotentin. Sallying forth at 0400 hours, 10 June, through La Fière and Chef du Pont, the 90th advanced little more than a mile before stalling. Two days later the 90th was still creeping along, a far cry from the bold drive Collins had envisioned. On 13 June the 90th took its interim objective, the city of Pont l'Abbé, but only after leveling it with heavy artillery and bombers. Still, the 90th was less than three miles from the line of departure and more than five miles from its final objective, and every day that the Cotentin remained open was another day that the Germans could send reinforcements to Cherbourg. Convinced that the 90th would never move with alacrity, Collins relieved the division commander and two of its regimental commanders and revamped his scheme of maneuver by placing two veteran outfits in the van, the U.S. 9th Infantry and 82nd Airborne Divisions.[31]

On 14 June, with the 508th still holding Baupte and the 505th in a rest area, having just returned to division control, Ridgway passed the 82nd through the 90th Infantry Division's lines and attacked west with the 507th and 325th. The advance got off to a rocky start. Advancing astride the east-west Pont l'Abbé–St. Sauveur–le Vicomte road, both regiments had to unexpectedly fight for terrain the 90th claimed it had already cleared. This threw the timetable for the advance off, but despite the delay by nightfall the 507th, attacking north of the road, and the 325th, attacking south of it, had advanced more than a mile. It was a costly mile, especially for the 325th. Because of the 90th Infantry Division's miscalculations, the 325th ran into stiff resistance that cost the regiment fifty-eight wounded and an unknown number dead. Among the latter were two more battalion commanders: Major Gardner of the 2/401st and Major Roscoe Roy of the 2/325th (Roy replaced Leahy following the fight at Le Ham).[32]

The regiments continued their advance at 0500 hours the next morning, this time under conditions of their own making. Consequently, the attack went more smoothly, at least at the outset. South of the Pont l'Abbé–St. Sauveur–le Vicomte road Lewis's 325th, assisted by a platoon of tanks, smashed through hedgerow after hedgerow and by nightfall was within 1,000 yards of St. Sauveur–le Vicomte, the division objective (Lewis had recovered from his bout of exhaustion and was back in command of the regiment). North of the road the 507th, under Lieutenant Colonel Maloney, who took over after Millett was captured, was also making great progress until it discovered that its northern flank was exposed—the 9th Infantry Division had been unable to keep pace—and into the void left by the 9th there soon appeared German armor. Intent on maintaining the momentum of the advance, Ridgway had Maloney turn the 507th ninety degrees to the north to set up a defensive barrier and then called on Ekman's 505th to rush forward, pass behind the 507th, and continue the fight westward. Both regiments executed flawlessly, and by nightfall the 505th, reinforced by C Battery, 80th Airborne Antiaircraft Battalion, and a platoon of tanks had come on line with the 325th. By then it was apparent that the 82nd had pierced the German defenses guarding the base of the Cotentin, a fact confirmed later that night by a patrol from the 325th led by Lieutenant Scott Cole that crossed the Douve and reported that German vehicles were fleeing westward.[33]

The advance of 15 June pushed the 82nd farther west than any other unit on the peninsula. Because of this its flanks were exposed, but neither Ridgway nor Collins wanted to surrender momentum by having the 82nd wait for other units to catch up. Instead, they agreed that the division would continue advancing while the rest of VII Corps followed behind in echelon. Jumping off early the next morning (16 June), the 325th and 505th moved swiftly, overran a German rearguard, and occupied the bluffs overlooking St. Sauveur–le Vicomte, which was on the far, or west, bank, of the Douve. Looking down into the city from atop a tall château on the bluffs, an astonished Vandervoort excitedly radioed the regimental operations officer, Major John Norton: "From where I am standing I can see everything—the town is full of Germans. Our artillery is in position to give them Hell. I tell you, Norton, this is it. This is the place to cut off the Nazis and cut off the peninsula. If we don't take advantage of this, we are crazy. I am counting on you to get this information to Col[onel] Ekman and General Ridgeway [*sic*]. Tell them to come up here and see for themselves."[34] Although in his excitement Vandervoort forgot to give his location, the resourceful Norton deduced this and sent word through Ekman to Ridgway, who eventually arrived at Vandervoort's château with General Bradley in tow. Vandervoort was right. It was "an artilleryman's dream," a massive traffic jam that had bunched the fleeing Germans in the open. To take maximum advantage of this opportunity, the 82nd's forward observers coordinated for a "time-on-target" shoot, a barrage technique designed to deliver fire from as many guns as possible on the target at the same time. "The guns were far enough back so that those who were watching hardly heard a single gun fired, but suddenly there was a whispering sound that changed into a roar and two-thirds of [St. Sauveur–le Vicomte] blew up at once. The observer called a slight adjustment and a second barrage finished the rest. German soldiers, trucks, horses and wagons, all disappeared in a cloud of smoke, dust, and steel shrapnel." Although Collins's orders were to advance to the Douve and hold, as soon as the barrage lifted, Ridgway asked Bradley for permission to take St. Sauveur–le Vicomte. Without hesitation Bradley approved. Attacking through a hail of German artillery fire aimed at the bridge over which they passed en route to St. Sauveur–le Vicomte, the 1/505th and 2/505th were soon in complete control of the city and pushing outward from its northern and western fringes. Still observing from the high ground, Bradley turned to Ridgway and said, "My God, Matt, can't anything stop those men?" Ridgway replied, "Sir, I would rather have a platoon of those men than a battalion of regular infantry."[35] By 2230 hours, Ridgway had five battalions across the river (three from the 505th and two from the 508th, which had moved up from Baupte) holding a bridgehead some 2,000–3,000 yards in depth.[36]

The 82nd (less the 507th, which had switched places with the 508th and was holding Baupte) spent the next day clearing out pockets of resistance, while Collins exploited the 82nd's success by passing a motorized regiment from the 9th Infantry Division through the bridgehead. So devastating had been the 82nd's advance—in three days it had killed, wounded, or taken prisoner more than 1,000 of the enemy—that when the 9th Division passed through the 82nd's lines, it encountered "nothing more than straggler units of a completely disorganized enemy."[37] Consequently, the 9th took Barneville on the west coast of the Cotentin on 18 June without much of a fight, thereby severing all connection between the Cotentin and the rest of France. Cherbourg fell nine days later.[38]

On 19 June Bradley passed operational control of the 82nd to Major General Troy H. Middleton's newly activated VIII Corps. Although primarily charged with defending the base of the Cotentin Peninsula while VII Corps advanced on Cherbourg, Middleton was also to set the conditions for a breakout to the south. To that end Middleton ordered Ridgway to attack from Pont l'Abbé south across the Douve to carve out a lodgment from which a larger offensive could be launched once forces became available. Ridgway gave this task to the 325th, reinforced by the 3/508th, while the 507th, still at Baupte, conducted a supporting attack.[39]

Although a relatively limited action given the more sweeping maneuvers elsewhere in Normandy, the 82nd's attack south from Pont l'Abbé was a textbook example of tactical deftness and agility. Coordinating the actions of infantry, artillery, engineer, and support units, in one twenty-four-hour period the 82nd conducted a feint, a nighttime river crossing, a linkup of two separate fronts, and a passage of lines. Whereas the division's successes to date in France, though not lacking in tactical skill, were more the result of hard marching, aggressiveness, and initiative, the attack of 19 June was an exercise in finesse. That it played out almost flawlessly indicated that the division had attained a level of battlefield competence equaled by few and surpassed by none.

The attack opened with a ruse. Ten troopers from the 325th under the command of Sergeant Clarence A. Rohrbacher crossed the Douve by boat at a point well west of the main crossing site and, armed with automatic weapons, began firing wildly. Under cover of darkness, for more than three hours Rohrbacher's patrol scurried from point to point on the southern shore attempting to draw as much attention as possible. So convincing were Rohrbacher and his small band that prisoners later related that they believed a force of not less than two companies, and possibly as large as a battalion, had landed.

At 2350 hours, 18 June, with enemy attention focused on Rohrbacher's phantoms, the 2/325th under the command of Major Charles Major—Major replaced Roy upon the latter's death, the battalion's fourth commander since landing in Normandy—boarded twenty-five assault boats piloted by A Company, 307th Engineers, to begin the main assault crossing of the Douve. Sixty-five minutes later the entire battalion was across without a shot being fired and, with the aid of a French guide, had infiltrated behind the German defenders opposite the only bridge in the area. Major then called Lewis, who, in turn, unleashed an artillery barrage on the unsuspecting Germans. Under cover of the barrage, which counted more than five hundred rounds, a second contingent of 307th Engineers ran onto the partially destroyed bridge to make repairs. When the barrage lifted Major assaulted, drove the Germans away from the southern terminus of the bridge, and cleared the way for the rest of the 325th and the attached 3/508th to cross and join the attack. Meanwhile, the 1/507th launched a supporting attack that cleared the 325th's flank. By nightfall, the lodgment Middleton wanted was his.[40]

The attack of 19 June was the division's last major action for almost two weeks, for that day saw the onset of a Channel storm that raged for three days, destroyed the American artificial harbor at OMAHA beach, and thoroughly disrupted Allied lines of communication. Consequently, Middleton postponed an attack out of the 82nd's lodgment as the bulk of available supplies were diverted to the drive on Cherbourg. On his own initiative Ridgway mounted some limited attacks to expand his lodgment and deny the enemy favorable terrain, but combat actions during this period were mostly confined to patrols and artillery duels.[41]

The Channel storm of 19 June ushered in several weeks of rain and cold during which, for many troopers, being dry was of equal, if not greater, moment than being safe, especially since the latter meant standing in a foxhole or lying in a slit trench filled with several inches of frigid, muddy water. Lieutenant Colonel Alexander, whom Ridgway had transferred to the 508th to serve as Lindquist's executive officer (Ridgway relieved the previous executive officer, Harry J. Harrison, for countermanding an order), was so wet and tired after returning from an inspection of the lines one evening that he elected to savor a few moments of dry comfort in his pup tent rather than slither into a muddy slit trench during an enemy mortar barrage. It took a second barrage, which tore four holes in the canvas over Alexander's head, to convince him to move.[42]

Because conditions were so miserable, it was incumbent on the division's leaders to ensure the troopers remained vigilant and sharp. Alexander walked the lines every night, as did almost every commissioned and noncommissioned officer in the 82nd. Ridgway and Gavin demanded that they look after their troopers, and this meant leaving the safety of one's own foxhole to prowl the lines. To drive home their point, Ridgway and Gavin led by example. Major Warren was hunkered down behind a hedgerow observing the fall of artillery rounds he had called in to disperse some German tanks to his front when he suddenly heard someone address him from nearby:

> "Well, Shields, how are things going?" The voice sounded familiar, so I dropped the [field] glasses from my eyes and turned to the speaker, who turned out to be General Ridgway. . . . I recounted my experience with the 2.36" bazookas, and the 81mm mortars [both had failed to disperse the tanks], and then told him we had moved them out with 155mm howitzers. The General said: "Well, that's fine, but be careful how you use that heavy stuff, there's a storm in the Channel and we're having problems getting supplies ashore." And then as he turned to go, he said with a smile, "Besides, isn't that sorta like swatting a fly with a sledgehammer?" I had no rejoinder to the comment, since I had been quite aghast at the appearance of the division commander at my elbow where he could have been hit by some of the hot lead and steel flying around. The point of the story is that no one had to

tell General Ridgway what his assault troopers were doing—he knew from personal observation.[43]

Privates First Class John P. Lynn and Steve Minarcik of C Company, 1/505th, were manning a foxhole on the battalion's outpost line, trying to stay warm, dry, and alert, when they heard movement to their rear. Expecting that it was their sergeant, but not wanting to take chances, they issued the challenge. The reply came from a voice they did not recognize. When the figure emerged from the darkness, they were aghast. Standing over them was Gavin, who asked if he could climb into the foxhole with them to get out of the rain. Keeping watch with the two stunned troopers in their foxhole, Gavin asked how things were going. Minarcik's only complaint was that there was not enough coffee. At that Gavin reached into his pocket, pulled out a coffee packet, handed it over, and then stood guard with Lynn while Minarcik prepared the coffee, which the three of them passed around for the remainder of the watch. After the war Minarcik would tell this story to anyone willing to listen and always prefaced it with "General Gavin saved my life once."[44]

Once Cherbourg fell, Bradley tapped Middleton's VIII Corps to lead the breakout into the heart of France. At the time VIII Corps consisted of three divisions, the U.S. 79th Infantry, 82nd Airborne, and 90th Infantry, aligned west to east respectively across the base of the Cotentin. Facing south to defend against enemy forays during the drive on Cherbourg, they were ideally positioned to kick off Bradley's breakout, the opening act of which was to be an attack on Coutances, a major road and rail junction fifteen to twenty miles south of VIII Corps's lines. Taking Coutances was critical. With it in hand all of First Army could advance and, in turn, carve out enough room for Patton's Third Army to come ashore. To make this happen Bradley called on the 82nd for one last offensive effort.[45]

Fronting VIII Corps was a string of hills ringed around the town of La Haye-du-Puits, beyond which the terrain was flat and open, excellent maneuver space for armored and mechanized forces. In order to get south of La Haye-du-Puits and on to Coutances as quickly as possible, Middleton envisioned attacks by the 79th Division to the west and the 90th Division to the east along diagonal axes that converged south of La Haye-du-Puits, thereby bypassing the town and its protective line of hills altogether. Clearing the hills fell to the 82nd, attacking in the center. The attack was set for 0515 hours, 3 July, and would be announced by a massive fifteen-minute artillery bombardment.[46]

Prevailing opinion at VIII Corps was that the offensive would meet half-hearted resistance from a hodgepodge of enemy units with nowhere near the combat power Middleton commanded. Although partially true, this prediction proved monumentally misleading, especially as it concerned the enemy's ability to resist. From atop the hills around La Haye-du-Puits—one of which, Hill 131, was the highest point on the Cotentin Peninsula—the Germans had an unobstructed view all the way to the American invasion beaches. Generalleutnant Dietrich von Choltitz, whose *LXXXIV Corps* defended the area, was determined to defend those hills in order to keep the Americans bottled up in the Cotentin, and he used the time afforded by VIII Corps's offensive lull to organize a strong defense in depth. Choltitz's outpost line was manned by *Kampfgruppe Koenig* composed of the remnants of the *91st*, *243rd*, and *265th Divisions*, along with several detachments of *Ostruppen*. Behind *Kampfgruppe Koenig* Choltitz positioned the entire *353rd Division*, just arrived from Brittany, and a *Kampfgruppe* from the *77th Division*. Bolstering the defense was the entire artillery complement of the *243rd Division*; two cannon companies; five antitank companies; a tank destroyer battalion; miscellaneous howitzer, rocket launcher, and antiaircraft batteries; and a collection of French Renault tanks. Though a hodgepodge force, it was not one to be discounted.[47]

Ridgway did not share VIII Corps's opinion about the enemy forces to his front. Reports from reconnaissance patrols indicated that the enemy was present in much greater strength than intelligence from VIII Corps indicated. Faced, therefore, with what he believed was a substantial enemy force that had the advantage of high ground and had had several weeks to prepare, Ridgway's plan was to avoid a head-on clash by attacking diagonally through his zone, from northeast to southwest, with three regiments on line, the 505th on the right, the 508th in the center, and the 325th on the left, while the 507th followed in reserve. Ridgway focused the 505th and 508th on Hill 131, while the 325th, constituting the 82nd's main effort, attacked to seize the string of hills just north of La Haye-du-Puits known collectively as La Poterie Ridge. For the attack the division also had two tank platoons, a platoon of tank destroyers, and a battery of 4.2-inch mortars.[48]

At 0515 hours, 3 July, every howitzer and mortar in VIII Corps commenced a fifteen-minute preparatory barrage behind which the infantry regiments moved forward to their lines of departure. For the 505th and 508th this meant passing through the Bois de Limors. The 505th had occupied a portion of the Bois de Limors since 20 June. It had been its deadliest assignment yet. Situated just east of Hill 131, from which German artillery spotters looked down into the forest, the 505th endured almost two weeks of shelling and sustained 293 casualties, about half the total suffered by the regiment in France. When the 505th and 508th moved out on the morning of 3 July, however, few enemy shells fell; the friendly artillery barrage and a driving rainstorm that blew in that night drove most of the defenders to seek safety and shelter at the expense of security.[49]

Both regiments advanced with two battalions forward and one following in reserve. Moving silently and swiftly through the Bois de Limors, "which recent rain had rendered impassable to anything but infantry and ducks," the lead battalions were through and behind the German outposts before their occupants realized what happened.[50] By 0900 hours they had secured their initial objectives and were preparing for the final assault on Hill 131. By noon the 2/508th had secured the hill's southern slope, and the 2/505th, which had enveloped the hill from the north, was moving undetected toward its summit, thanks to the keen eyes and quick thinking of a private who spotted a strand of communication wire running up of the hill. Surmising that the wire led right where the 2/505th wanted to go, the private suggested that the battalion follow the wire—and, he added, it was a good bet that the area around the wire was free of mines and booby traps. Vandervoort and Ridgway, who was accompanying the 2/505th, agreed. By 1225 hours the 2/505th owned Hill 131. The 18 Germans manning an observation post there surrendered with hardly a fight, utterly surprised at the sudden appearance of American paratroopers in their midst.[51]

The only unit in the area that was not focused on Hill 131 was the 1/505th. Advancing on the extreme right of the division, the 1/505th's mission was to secure the St. Sauveur–le Vicomte–La Haye-du-Puits highway, the boundary between the 79th Infantry and 82nd Airborne Divisions. To do so without driving any Germans defending the road into the 79th's zone of attack, the 1/505th conducted a "hammer and anvil" attack, a stratagem based on information obtained from prisoners that indicated that the German defenses in the area were porous. To effect this the 1/505th infiltrated a reinforced rifle company through a gap in the enemy line, which then took up position behind the enemy defenses to form the anvil. The hammer was provided by the rest of the 1/505th, which flushed the German defenders from their positions right into the sights of the company to their rear. In this manner the 1/505th secured the road by 1400 hours and bagged 105 prisoners.[52]

Although taking Hill 131 and securing the St. Sauveur–le Vicomte–La Haye-du-Puits highway were relatively bloodless affairs, the 325th's attack on La Poterie Ridge was not as easy, or bloodless. Advancing in standard attack formation—two battalions forward and one following in reserve—the 325th started slowly, the troopers picking their way through extensive minefields, and then picked up speed until about noon when the pace again slowed. The 90th Division on the 325th's left was lagging behind, which exposed the glider troopers to devastating enfilading fire, and resistance in the 325th's sector was more resolute than elsewhere because, advancing at an oblique, it ran into Choltitz's main line of resistance. When he realized this, Ridgway told Lewis to limit his advance to the village of La Poterie at the eastern edge of the ridge until he could arrange for help. But despite support from five tanks and two tank destroyers, the 325th could get no closer than 600 yards of La Poterie before stalling. Enemy fire was simply too devastating. So thinned, in fact, were Lewis's ranks that he had had to bring up his third battalion to fill in the gaps.[53]

Ridgway renewed the attack on the ridge the next day, 4 July, with the 325th attacking from the east while the 505th and 508th, repositioned late the previous night, attacked from the north. Start time was 0800 hours. By noon the 325th was in La Poterie and the 505th owned the northern slope of Hill 95 on the opposite end of the ridge. But the 508th, which was to have attacked the center of the ridge with all three battalions on line, was held up due to some confusion over its axis of advance. Eventually, Captain Chester E. Graham, then in command of the 2/508th (Lieutenant Colonel Shanley was wounded on 3 July, and Lieutenant Colonel Alexander moved forward to take command of the battalion; Alexander was then wounded during the night of 3–4 July; both would be sorely missed by the division), shook his battalion free of the confusion and attacked toward the summit of Hill 95, which he and a handful of troopers reached shortly after noon. But Graham's casualties had been severe, and before he could be reinforced the Germans counterattacked and drove them back down the hill. The rest of the 508th remained pinned down at the base of the ridge.[54]

As darkness fell, with the exception of the 325th's positions around La Poterie village, the division's hold on the rest of the ridge bearing that name was, at best, tenuous. In the west, although the 505th and 2/508th had secured the base of Hill 95, the crest was still in enemy hands. In the center, where the Germans had amassed significant firepower behind well-prepared positions, the 3/508th and 2/401st had been stopped cold. But Ridgway was not done. He was certain that a concerted attack could secure the ridge, but he was equally certain that the division could not withstand another bloodbath; it was simply too weak across the board. So the attack had to be that night, before the Germans had time to make their already formidable defenses nearly impregnable. Attacking during darkness would also negate the enemy's positional advantage, especially his long-range fires, and give the troopers time to close with the enemy without suffering casualties on the approach march. Metaphorically, Ridgway wanted a knife fight, not a gun battle. Shock and surprise were the keys to success. To this end he threw just about everything he had into the attack: The 2/508th, with support from the 1/505th and 3/505th, was to regain the crest of Hill 95; the 1/507th and 2/507th were moved up from their reserve positions to attack the center of La Poterie Ridge; and the rest of the 508th would support the 507th with fires and be prepared to reinforce if needed, while the 325th mounted a supporting attack from its positions around La Poterie village.[55]

The attack was a stunning success. The troopers closed with the enemy before being detected and, after some brief clashes at close range, took their objectives. The enemy, unwilling to fight without the advantage of long-range fires, melted away. By 0500 hours, 5 July, Hill 95 and all of La Poterie Ridge were in 82nd hands. The only fight of any consequence occurred at daybreak when a reinforced company from the 2/507th, which had been pushed forward of the rest of the battalion, found itself in the middle of a German bivouac area. A firefight erupted that lasted until early afternoon, fought at point-blank range. Both sides sent in reinforcements, but in the end the paratroopers prevailed and won the ground. With the exception of mopping up bypassed enemy formations and repelling some limited counterattacks, this was the 82nd's last major action in Normandy.[56]

In three days the 82nd advanced four miles, killed or wounded about 500 enemy soldiers and took another 772 prisoner, and captured or destroyed five enemy field pieces.[57] An impressive achievement on its face, the fact that the division accomplished this against an enemy force entrenched in strength on high ground at a time when the strongest company in the 82nd was at only 50 percent strength and after almost thirty days of continuous combat makes this a truly remarkable feat. As if to punctuate the 82nd's Normandy saga, the last attack also saw an act of courage exclamatory of its performance.

During the fight at the German bivouac site, German tanks and infantry reinforcements strayed into the 325th's area. Private First Class James L. Geach grabbed a bazooka and used it to force the tanks to retire. Exchanging the bazooka for his rifle, he then charged the accompanying enemy infantry and killed four before driving the remainder away. Not long thereafter friendly tanks arrived, and Geach volunteered to lead them on foot to break up a second German counterattack. This, too, was successful. For his actions, Geach was awarded the Distinguished Service Cross.[58]

At 1000 hours, 7 July, Ridgway issued Operations Order No. 4 that outlined the division's move to the rear in preparation for its return to England. Early the next morning the U.S. 8th Infantry Division passed through the 82nd's lines, and the 82nd moved to assembly areas in the rear. On 11 July, having showered and received fresh uniforms, the troopers trucked to holding areas near UTAH beach. On 12 and 13 July they marched to UTAH beach and boarded LSTs for transport back to England. Debarking at Southhampton, the troopers then entrained for movement back to the same base camps from which they had departed some six weeks before.[59]

During its thirty-three days of combat (6 June–8 July) the 82nd battled five major enemy units (the *77th*, *91st*, *243rd*, *265th*, and *353rd Divisions*), killed an estimated 1,500 enemy soldiers, took another 2,200 prisoner, and destroyed sixty-two tanks, two light reconnaissance vehicles, three self-propelled guns, and forty-one artillery, antiaircraft, and antitank guns. It accomplished all missions assigned and on several occasions advanced with such alacrity that it outpaced friendly mechanized units on its flanks. It had come at a high cost. All told the division sustained 5,436 casualties out of a committed strength of 11,770. Of the casualties, 1,142 were killed in action or died of their wounds, while another 2,373 were wounded in action. The rest were listed as missing or known captured (840), evacuated sick (377), or evacuated injured (704). The parachute and glider infantry regiments were hit the hardest, with casualty rates ranging from a low of 51 percent in the 505th to 61 percent in the 507th.[60]

The entry for 7 June 1944 in the 505th's combat journal includes a telling quote penned by an anonymous paratrooper: "Two days ago I was 19 years old; now I feel like I am 40." At the time of the entry the 82nd had been engaged for only twenty-four hours. A little over a month later the survivors were all much considerably older men. Two things struck those that saw them: their look and their numbers. Lieutenant Sidney Eichen of the U.S. 30th Infantry Division recalled standing with his soldiers in silent awe as a group of 82nd troopers filed past. "We asked them: 'Where are your officers?', and they answered: 'All dead.' We asked, 'Who's in charge then?', and some sergeant said, 'I am.' I looked at the unshaven, red-eyed GIs, the dirty clothes and the droop in their walk, and I wondered: is this how we are going to look after a few days in combat?"[61]

CHAPTER 14

A LASTING AND FIRM FAITH IN THE AIRBORNE

From the realization of . . . necessity and because of the ever-increasing size of the Airborne–Troop Carrier contingent in the theater, it became self-evident that some organization must be activated to bring all the elements of such a force into one cohesive whole rather than permit them to remain echelons of various diversified major units of unrelated characteristics. Hence, upon direction of the Supreme Commander and with War Department concurrence from the U.S. and British approval for her units, there was formed the First (Allied) Airborne Army. . . . It was a major step in the right direction, and needless to say, placed airborne operations on the level at which they were suited to function best.

—JACK G. CORNETT, "DEVELOPMENT OF AIRBORNE FORCES"

THE REPLACEMENTS AWAITING the return of the 82nd from Normandy were stunned as they watched the thinned files march back into their English base camps. They had, of course, heard tales of the division's exploits in Sicily and Italy, but Normandy was "the stuff of instant legend," and the reports that had filtered across the Channel had given them no sense of the fighting.[1] Even the wounded who had been evacuated to England could relate only what they had seen from their very limited perspective; the enormity of the losses was something few below the rank of colonel grasped. The return of the bedraggled survivors changed all that. Companies looked like platoons, battalions like companies. The horror hit like a load of bricks. "When they told us the boys should be there any hour we were very interested," related

Private Louis Moon, one of the 325th's replacements. "When the men came, it was my first unpleasant feeling in a long time. Their clothes were dirty, long beards, their packs were shot up and worst of all, only 16 men out of 200 came in that day."[2] When eventually reorganized and replenished many units, especially the infantry battalions, contained more replacements than veterans by a wide margin.[3] For the first time since leaving the States, the 82nd had the look of a green outfit. Ridgway estimated that it would take at least seventy-five days for the division to regain its "full combat efficiency."[4]

The first two days back were devoted to cleaning equipment, repairing what could be repaired, and requisitioning what could not. More important, the men rested. They had lived outside for more than a month, enduring the heat, wind, rain, and cold of Normandy. Now more than ever they appreciated their English accommodations: neatly arrayed, graveled streets; five-man pyramidal tents; and latrines instead of slit trenches. Even the chow was to their liking. "We quickly learned to appreciate army food cooked from fresh ingredients more than anyone thought possible after a month of eating mostly field rations," recalled John Sergeant McKenzie of the 456th. "The reputation of army cooks reached an all-time high, at least for a week or two."[5] But soon the troopers grew restless. They had been promised week-long furloughs, and they were anxious to cut loose. Ridgway kept his word. Thirty-six hours after returning to their base camps, the Normandy veterans passed back through the gates sporting spit-shined jump boots and neatly pressed dress uniforms adorned with newly awarded ribbons.[6]

So began a second invasion, one for which the rear-echelon soldiers and military policemen throughout England were wholly unprepared (the 101st observed the same liberal furlough policy, hence veterans from both divisions were loosed on an unsuspecting England).

The troopers returned from Normandy heroes. After their ships docked at Southampton, cheering crowds swarmed them, military bands serenaded them, and Red Cross girls plied them with donuts and coffee as they marched down the gangplanks to waiting trains ready to take them to their camps in the Midlands. At the small towns bordering the camps, the homecoming celebration was even more exuberant. One 508th trooper recalled that the return of his regiment to Nottingham "was beyond comparison. Met at the [railroad] station by two bands . . . and most of the inhabitants of the city, the troopers were given a welcome second only to a return to the States. As the notes of 'Over There' filled the air, some of the girls looked for a familiar face in the crowd, and old women wept, mumbling little statements like, 'God bless you, son.'" So when the troopers got their furloughs they were primed to "unwind and forget the war for the moment."[7] Many headed for London, where the threat of death from Hitler's vengeance weapons encouraged a frenzied live-in-the-moment temperament that assuaged their pent-up tension. They also found rear-echelon services and supply soldiers and military policemen, two groups the cocky, hardened combat veterans held in high disdain. Inevitably, there was conflict, especially with the MPs, who tried to police unruly troopers and enforce dress standards that those recently returned from the mud and blood of France found hard to countenance. Within a week the situation had become so serious that Brigadier General Pleas B. Hodges, commander of Central Base Section (London), was moved to write the commanders of the airborne divisions requesting their help. His letter is worth quoting at length:

> We have just had a deluge of paratroopers in London, and they are the finest type of American soldier. They apparently think they can whip their weight in wild cats, and if they think it, they can do it. When they arrived there immediately showed up a very large number of uniform violations. I do not mean one pocket unbuttoned, but all buttons on their blouses unbuttoned, no coats worn, no hats worn, and no ties with two or three shirt buttons unbuttoned and the collar pulled open overlapping the lapel of the blouse. . . .
>
> We expect the men to have a good time when they come to London, and we have a very liberal policy on drunks, namely, if a man apparently has had about all he can handle, my Military Police go up to him and tell him that he had better get off the streets. If his attitude is one of cooperation we will tell him where a Red Cross Club is, or even take him to the nearest Club where we have arranged for beds to take care of them until they sober up. Conversely if he tries to tell us that he isn't drunk, or starts back about three generations telling the MP what kind of a family he comes from, he is arrested and tried for being drunk in a public place. He is either so drunk that the American uniform needs protection, or he is utterly undisciplined, and both positions are untenable.
>
> I suppose it is natural, but I think it will have to be broken up, but these men feel that now [that] they have been in combat they are beyond uniform regulations, and they should be given very special consideration. 24 hours after their arrival, the Commander of the Military Police Battalion wanted to change the patrols from 2 to 4 men as the paratroopers were inclined to gang up on our Military Police when they had to make arrests. Of course it is a serious matter when any soldier tries to restrain a Military Policeman in the execution of his duty, and the next step is a young riot.
>
> My Colonel Provost Marshal had to call the assistance of a Scotland Yard officer to arrest two of your paratroopers as they refused to get in his car and started to walk away. The troopers in question had their garrison caps stuck

> under their shoulder loop of the blouse, a la British, and had all the buttons on their coats unbuttoned. After they got in the car one of them who was a Corporal told my Provost Marshal that the last time he had seen his brother in Normandy he didn't have a blouse on [presumably because he was either dead or wounded].[8]

Ridgway neither denied nor condoned the mayhem. But he did understand it. "Combat mutually shared draws men together, but it sets them apart from other men who have not seen battle, or who have known war of a different kind," he wrote. Acknowledging that his troopers had "little enough respect for other soldiers . . . who have not experienced the peculiar joys and trials of jumping [or gliding] into battle," Ridgway recognized that surviving Normandy heightened their belief in their "God-given right to go around punching other soldiers in the nose." War correspondent Martha Gellhorn, albeit a great admirer of the 82nd, was more forgiving of the troopers' behavior: "If you take very young men and teach them to hold their own lives lightly and to kill, and then expect them to go out and kill on your behalf, you cannot be indignant in case they raise some hell outside the combat zone."[9] Ridgway later contended that he solved the problem by "stern lectures and sterner discipline," although it is more likely that the problem shrank to manageable levels because the furloughs expired and the troopers began another round of tough training.[10]

Not all Normandy veterans got furloughs. A significant number had to attend jump school. These men, mostly from the division's noninfantry parachute units, had entered France in gliders. When they returned they learned that if they desired to remain with the 82nd, they had to attend a parachute course at Rutlandshire Royal Air Force Base that was every bit as grueling as the course in the States. According to Sergeant John McKenzie, who was one of them, "To my knowledge, no one who had been in Normandy failed to sign up."[11] This is no small point. No one could be ordered to attend jump school. Paratroopers were volunteers. Any man who opted out would be sent to a replacement detachment where he could easily get lost for weeks before being assigned to another unit. That these troopers, recently returned from combat and fully cognizant of what was expected of the 82nd, volunteered to remain with the division in spite of the hard training they would have to undergo speaks volumes about the type of unit Ridgway, Gavin, and the other leaders of the 82nd had forged.

Another group that went to unusual lengths to remain with the division was the injured and wounded in hospital. Getting oneself declared unfit for combat duty was relatively easy and a sure path to spending the rest of the war in a rear-echelon job. Instead, they returned in droves, many going

AWOL from the hospitals, to make their way back to the 82nd's camps. Niches were found for all of them; none were transferred out except at their own request.[12] All told, 67 percent of the troopers injured or wounded in Normandy returned to the division (3,077 troopers were wounded or injured; 2,056 returned to duty).[13] More than anything it was this invaluable core of combat veterans that enabled the division to so quickly regain its fighting edge. And there was little time to lose.

On 25 July Bradley's First Army launched Operation COBRA, broke out of the Cotentin, and cleared the way for Patton's Third Army to race across France. It appeared the German Army in the west was in complete disarray. Talk turned to its quick defeat if only some way could be found to cut it off and kill it before it escaped.[14] In the eyes of SHAEF planners, the airborne was perfect for this job. Even the most pedestrian among them saw in the airborne a war-ending panacea, making the 82nd and 101st troopers "the most prestigious and sought-after troops in the history of the Army."[15] So prevalent was this thinking that, during the period 6 June to 17 September 1944, no fewer than twenty-five airborne operations were planned only to be canceled, postponed, or shelved for later use.[16]

There had doubtless occurred a sea change in the prevailing attitude about the airborne. Prior to Normandy many in the Allied high command viewed airborne forces, especially airborne divisions, as expensive luxuries. Much smaller than standard infantry divisions and packing much less firepower, airborne divisions not only required an inordinate amount of air transport to get to the battlefield, but their use also necessitated special plans, prohibitions, and control measures to prevent fratricide. Consequently, many felt that airborne divisions were simply more trouble than they were worth. But the airborne fight in Normandy changed everything.

Virtually without exception everyone in First Army, SHAEF, and the War Department was convinced that the invasion would not have succeeded but for the airborne divisions. Bradley trumpeted the fact that the "airborne operations back of Utah Beach . . . were essential for the success of the attack" (and in the process vindicated his insistence that the drops proceed).[17] Eisenhower echoed Bradley. Once an advocate of doing away with airborne divisions, Eisenhower readily admitted that "our good luck was largely represented in the degree of surprise that we achieved by landing on Utah Beach, . . . and by the effective action of the two airborne divisions." Even General Marshall's observer, Colonel Bruce Bidwell—one-half of the team Marshall sent to England prior to the invasion to convince Eisenhower to adopt a bolder airborne plan for NEPTUNE—reported that using the 82nd and 101st directly behind the beaches "was a success." It is important to note, however, what Bidwell wrote next. In a veiled swipe at Eisenhower's timidity, he attributed success not to any stunning operational foresight but to the airborne troopers themselves who "slugged it out with the defenders and had no thought other than to achieve eventual victory."[18] In so doing, Bidwell kept alive the notion of a bold war-ending airborne stroke, a notion that rang with increasing resonance in Allied headquarters.

Ridgway and Gavin pushed the troopers hard once they returned from furlough. The training regimen focused on physical conditioning, weapons proficiency, and small unit tactics. Ten-mile runs were not an uncommon way to begin the training day and road marches, beginning with five miles and culminating in forty-mile hikes, were the standard. Troopers were expected to become proficient with every weapon in the division's inventory, with special emphasis on those essential for close fighting—bayonets, hand grenades, and pistols. Junior leaders had to demonstrate their ability to navigate, scout, and patrol.[19] "Little by little," recalled one trooper, "as the summer wore on our bodies got tough in spite of drunks, women and ornery carousing." About the only respite from this grueling schedule came when the troopers had to prepare for visits by Eisenhower and other dignitaries, which necessitated hours of drill and ceremony. This gave rise to the loudest grumbling in the ranks. "The top brass felt that in England we had to demonstrate that we knew our left foot from the right and could drill as well as we could fight," wrote Lieutenant James Megellas. "I was never able to understand how hours and hours on end of close order drill contributed anything to combat readiness except perhaps to irritate the men."[20]

While the troopers conducted maneuvers in the fields around Leicester, Ridgway conducted maneuvers in the corridors of power around London, clearly intent on taking advantage of his post-Normandy cachet. Foremost on his agenda was a topic he had addressed several times before—the role and proper employment of airborne forces. Ridgway opened a memorandum to Bradley and Eisenhower on the subject with a flourish:

> Landing during darkness, beginning at H-4 Hours on D-Day, this Division participated in the initial operation of the Invasion of WESTERN EUROPE for thirty-three continuous days without relief and without replacement. It accomplished every assigned mission on or ahead of the time ordered [a statement not entirely accurate]. No ground gained was ever relinquished, and no advance ever halted except on the order of Corps or ARMY. It sustained an aggregate loss of 46% in killed, missing and evacuated wounded. Prior to launching its final offensive, its infantry had sustained a loss of 45%. At the conclusion of its operation it went into ARMY Reserve, with fighting spirit as high as the day it entered action.

Ridgway then explained that Normandy proved that the principles for employing airborne divisions articulated in Training Circular No. 113 were "sound, comprehensive, and if properly applied to any given future operation, may be expected to yield optimum results." But, he warned, there was "a growing optimism among some commanders which, if unchecked, can lead to dangerous conclusions and, if applied in subsequent operations, to heavy and unnecessary losses." This optimism, a result of the low loss rate for transport aircraft during NEPTUNE and the unexpectedly low casualty rate for personnel and equipment brought into Normandy by glider, could lead to "fallacious" conclusions. Transport aircraft were extremely vulnerable to even small arms fire, and the dispersion of the parachute and glider insertions "while representing a tremendous improvement over similar phases of the SICILIAN Operation, was still greater than what we may reasonably expect with continued intensive training." His conclusion was that any

> decision to employ airborne forces on subsequent missions should accord full consideration to anticipated losses, and if these are expected to be heavy, then the loss of so many superior troops must be carefully weighed against the anticipated probable gain. Commitment of airborne forces by air, merely because they are available, is basically unsound. Their subsequent large-scale commitment, in the face of an estimated heavy loss, should only be as part of a decisive effort, comparable in anticipated results, to the initial Invasion.[21]

Normandy proved what Ridgway had always believed: that airborne forces employed en masse could make a decisive contribution to the attainment of operational or strategic objectives. He was determined to squelch all talk of using airborne divisions to solve tactical problems, as Clark had done in Italy. Subsequent airborne operations should be massive affairs and the centerpiece of campaign- or war-winning efforts. In making these pronouncements Ridgway underscored concepts heralded by Generals Marshall and Arnold and, more recently, kept alive by Colonel Bidwell in his after-action report. He also presaged the manner in which airborne divisions would next be used, although, ironically, when they were, he would have no role to play.

To ensure that American airborne divisions packed the requisite punch such an effort would require, Ridgway renewed his pleas to change their official tables of organization to reflect the changes he made to the 82nd and 101st prior to OVERLORD. Ridgway assumed, as did everyone else, that these changes were temporary. Based on the experience of Normandy, he argued that they should be permanent. He made his case in a strident memorandum to Bradley that he wrote even before the 82nd quit France: "Thirty-three days' front line participation by this Division in operations on the continent of EUROPE demonstrate[s] once more, and with increasing emphasis, the need for . . . basic changes in the organization of the airborne division." His previous recommendations, he continued, had been disapproved "largely if not entirely on the basis of inadequate manpower." Now, he believed, "there are means available to the War Department for surmounting this obstacle" and that "it is far better to have a smaller number of airborne divisions soundly organized than to have a larger number basically defective in organization."[22]

Unlike Ridgway's previous endeavors, this one elicited no immediate response from the War Department, whose attentions were focused on manning and supplying the conventional armored and infantry divisions as they raced toward Germany. But Ridgway's efforts were not wasted. In the absence of a firm no, the 82nd and 101st retained the organization with which they fought in Normandy, and when the War Department finally tabled Ridgway's recommendations for consideration in December 1944, it agreed to most of them.[23]

There was one organizational decision that was wholly Ridgway's to make. Since the airborne divisions were going to continue operating with three parachute regiments until told otherwise, Ridgway had to decide which of the attached parachute regiments he took to Normandy he would keep. When it returned to England, the 82nd resumed control of Tucker's 504th (as well as C Company, 307th Airborne Engineer Battalion, and the 376th Parachute Field Artillery Battalion) giving it, temporarily, four parachute regiments. Since the 504th and 505th were organic elements of the division, Ridgway's decision came down to selecting either the 507th or the 508th. Ridgway chose Lindquist's 508th and sent the 507th, then under Edson Raff, to the 17th Airborne Division, which was forming in England. It was not an unexpected decision. According to Captain Chester McCoid, a company commander in the 507th, "Such logical considerations as unit strength and availability of key leaders aside, had I been in the boots of General Ridgeway [*sic*]—or of Gavin . . . —choosing Roy Lindquist and the 508, over Edson Raff and the 507 would have taken an instant. There are enough hair shirts to be worn in life without donning one willing[ly]."[24]

Raff was flashy, abrasive, and an insufferable egomaniac. During the invasion of North Africa, he led the first parachute assault in U.S. history as commander of the 509th Parachute Infantry Battalion. Praised for his innovativeness and daring—an image Raff did much to advance in *We Jumped to Fight*, an account of the operation he wrote while still in North Africa—he was immediately promoted to full colonel and became the principal American airborne adviser in North Africa before Ridgway arrived. Mark Clark was especially enamored of Raff and brought the brash colonel with him to the

States so that he could impart his wisdom to the 82nd before it deployed. Gavin was unimpressed and likened Raff to Orde Wingate, the eccentric British general whose unconventional exploits in Burma won Churchill's admiration (Churchill had likewise paraded Wingate before senior military and political leaders at the QUADRANT Conference).[25]

Raff was oblivious to the rancor he caused and fully expected that when the 82nd arrived in North Africa, he would be given command of one of the division's parachute regiments. When he was not, he became livid. "I was an experienced officer in combat," Raff wrote, "had made quite a reputation [and] he [Ridgway] had no interest in anyone like myself who was already famous and already had combat experience." With no place to go, Raff floated around, attached to various headquarters as an airborne expert. He eventually made his way to England, where he tried getting a regimental command in the 1st Infantry Division, but since he was a paratrooper, Bradley assigned him to the 82nd. It was, according to Raff, a transfer vehemently opposed by Ridgway whom Raff felt resented him.[26]

Ridgway's actions belie this, for while he was with the 82nd Ridgway gave Raff positions of increasing responsibility despite the availability of other, less caustic, officers who, by that time, had much more combat experience than Raff. For example, Raff's first assignment as commander of the task force that landed on UTAH beach on D-Day was unnecessary. Brigadier General George Howell, who was also temporarily attached to the 82nd, was in overall command of the division's seaborne element and could easily have led the task force himself. Ridgway then made Raff the division chief of staff after "Doc" Eaton was injured in the initial glider insertion. A few days later, in another surprising move, Ridgway gave Raff command of the 507th, a position Raff retained for the rest of the campaign, the very position he had been trumpeting as his right given his experience and rank.

Despite these plum assignments Raff had an unusually vitriolic opinion of Ridgway. In Raff's eyes, Ridgway was a poseur and a "man-killing bastard." He even accused Ridgway of being dismissive of him because of his (Raff's) talent and aggressiveness at deck tennis![27] Given the implacable and ill-disguised loathing Raff bore for Ridgway, few doubted that when the time came to cut a parachute regiment loose, it would be the 507th.

But, in reality, Raff *requested* the transfer of his regiment to the 17th Airborne Division, convinced that the 17th's commander, his friend Major General William M. "Bud" Miley, "would certainly listen to me once in a while."[28] Moreover, the transfer made sense. The 17th needed a veteran parachute regiment, and the 507th had performed well under Raff. Even Raff's harshest critics agreed that he was "a *terrific* combat leader" who "by any standard . . . was the class of the 17th [Airborne] Division."[29]

The Raff episode is interesting because many 507th veterans remained bitter about Ridgway's decision, feeling discarded because of one man. Ridgway may have unwittingly furthered this bitterness when in his wartime memoir he wrote that "one of the attributes of military leadership is knowing when to get rid of a sorehead, or a subordinate who is dragging his feet—the early recognition of those who can't, or won't respond, and their prompt elimination."[30] Although Ridgway did not mention Raff by name, many assumed that it was Raff about whom he was referring. But Ridgway never harbored any enmity for his difficult subordinate. In fact, in a personal letter he wrote after the war, with full knowledge of the attacks Raff continued to make on him, Ridgway characterized Raff as "a gallant [and] aggressive troop commander" for whom he had "the greatest respect."[31] And, as will be seen, even after Raff left the 82nd, as a result of Ridgway's next assignment Ridgway had the authority to relieve Raff at any time, but he did not, and Raff remained in command of the 507th for the rest of the war.

Ridgway also had to do something about the 325th, which needed a new commander. Normandy had been rough on Harry Lewis. Sometime in August he was relieved without prejudice and sent back to the United States, where it was discovered he had cancer. He died within a year. Ridgway replaced him with Tucker's executive officer, Colonel Charles Billingslea. Billingslea had proven himself in Sicily and Italy and was one of the few 504th troopers to jump into Normandy, where he went along as one of Ridgway's "spare" colonels.

Billingslea was an inspired choice, exactly what the 325th needed. Whereas Lewis had been melodramatic and, some would say, unbalanced, Billingslea was soft-spoken, "quiet and efficient," according to the regimental sergeant major. Billingslea's physical presence alone made an impression, for at six foot six he was unusually tall for a paratrooper, easily one of the tallest men in the division, and though he did not cultivate close relations with his subordinates, he earned their respect. "We knew that he had the stamina and the courage to stay with us," recalled a 325th veteran. "He could and would show up everywhere, night problems in training, asking straight questions and giving orders that had better be followed. In combat he was fearless."[32] As a paratrooper assigned to a glider regiment, he also represented a trend that, in time, blurred the distinction between the division's glider and parachute units, for by war's end a significant number of troopers assigned to glider outfits were also qualified paratroopers.

Ridgway made decisions about transferring key personnel, the assignment of parachute regiments, and recommendations about airborne doctrine and missions because, as the senior and most experienced American airborne division commander in theater, he was primus inter pares. He did so much more forcefully upon returning to England because of his knowledge about what the future held. Shortly after returning to England, Ridgway told Gavin that he (Ridgway) would soon be leaving the division to form an airborne corps, that this corps would become part of an even larger entity, and that Ridgway's recommendation was that Gavin take command of the 82nd.[33]

Notions about forming one organization to command all Allied airborne and troop carrier units in Europe had been bandied about for some time. General Arnold posited the idea as early as December 1943 in a letter to General Carl A. "Tooey" Spaatz, commander of U.S. Strategic Air Forces in Europe. Arnold suggested that the U.S. Ninth Air Force, which encompassed all U.S. troop carrier units in England, would be an appropriate headquarters upon which to build such an organization.[34] When tabled for discussion with the British, however, Arnold's idea met with stark rejection. British airborne commanders were especially vehement in their opposition, fearful of placing their parachute and glider formations under the command of an air force officer lest one day it be assumed that RAF officers command them.[35]

Interservice rivalry was not the only stumbling block; national pride stymied the idea as well. During a planning conference for OVERLORD, the British suggested a compromise to Arnold's suggestion: the realignment of all Allied troop carrier units under a single command. General Brereton, who was present at the conference, "agreed in principle provided the command is American." This, too, was unacceptable for the British, so the idea was shelved, and Leigh-Mallory ruled "that the policy would be for American control of American airborne operations and British control of British airborne operations."[36]

So it stood for several months until the idea was revived by an unlikely source, Eisenhower himself, who proposed an all-encompassing airborne command in a letter to Marshall in late June 1944. "Experience has proved that in preparing to utilize large airborne forces there is at present no suitable agency available to the High Command to assume responsibility for joint planning between Troop Carrier Command and the airborne forces." He wanted, therefore,

> an airborne commander directly under this [SHAEF] headquarters [and] give him these responsibilities. . . . He would not command troops actually fighting on the ground but would be responsible for providing them all logistical support until normal lines of communication could be established. Assuming that an airborne attack by two or three divisions took place within a single area, a temporary corps commander would be designated to conduct the fighting on the ground. He would operate under directives issued by this

> headquarters until his forces could join up with the nearest army, whereupon he would be taken over by the army commander both operationally and logistically.

Eisenhower also stated that he wanted an American (presumably from the U.S. Army Air Corps) to command the organization so that he could ensure that the troop carriers, the vast bulk of which were American, would receive adequate operational and training oversight. "This whole activity," he closed, "has been too loosely organized and I want to tighten it up under an energetic man who will do the job properly."[37]

Choosing the right man for the job was critical. In a subsequent cable to Arnold, to whom Marshall delegated the authority to select a commander for the new organization, Eisenhower explained that "there are questions of personality involved in this command which are difficult and delicate." Ridgway was "quite senior and . . . has commanded in combat with great distinction," while his British counterpart, Lieutenant General "Boy" Browning, "has long and varied experience both in the air and on the ground."[38] The man selected had to possess enough rank and operational experience to justify placing him above them. Major General John K. Cannon, commander of the U.S. Twelfth Air Force in the Mediterranean, was such a man and quickly emerged as the front-runner for the position. But with the invasion of southern France looming (Operation ANVIL, launched 15 August 1944), for which the Twelfth Air Force was to provide support, it was thought unwise to move Cannon. Next considered was Cannon's deputy, Brigadier General Hoyt S. Vandenberg. Eisenhower was satisfied that Vandenberg could do the job but pointed out that his selection would require that he be promoted two grades.[39] Although not uncommon in wartime, such an accelerated promotion would have proved problematic, so Vandenberg was dropped from consideration. In casting about for a third candidate, Marshall, Arnold, and Eisenhower eventually set their sights on a surprising choice, the staunch air power advocate Lewis H. Brereton.

Brereton had had something of a checkered career. He was a 1911 Annapolis graduate who subsequently transferred to the Army, won his wings in the nascent Air Corps, and served with distinction in World War I, during which he earned a Distinguished Service Cross during a dogfight in which he sustained grievous wounds. Assigned to Billy Mitchell's staff after his release from the hospital, Brereton remained with the Air Corps after the war and adopted his mentor's zealous belief in the revolutionary potential of airpower. So convinced was Brereton of the rightness of these views that he risked his career by serving on Mitchell's defense team during the latter's highly publicized 1926 court-martial. Yet Brereton continued to advance, and in November 1941, he was assigned to command MacArthur's U.S. Far East Air Force in the Philippines. It was a command he never led in combat. A month later the Japanese destroyed most of the Far East Air Force on the ground, an unpardonable sin for one so enamored of the offensive power of airplanes. But Brereton escaped censure and with what was left formed and commanded the tactical air force for the short-lived ABDACOM (American-British-Dutch-Australian Command) in Java. When ABDACOM was disbanded in February 1942, Brereton and the few bombers he had remaining were transferred to North Africa, where they played a minor role in support of Montgomery's El Alamein offensive. Eventually, Brereton's command grew in size, was renamed the U.S. Ninth Air Force, and supported the invasions of Sicily and Italy.

While in the Mediterranean Brereton also got the chance to put his views on strategic bombing to the test. On 1 August 1943, Ninth Air Force mounted Operation TIDAL WAVE, a massive bombing raid on the Axis oil fields at Ploiesti, Romania. Fifty-four of the 178 B-24s sent on the raid failed to return, while the damage to the oil refineries, although severe, was easily repaired. Despite this tragedy, two months later Brereton and the Ninth Air Force were earmarked for even greater responsibilities and transferred to England as part of the buildup for OVERLORD. By April 1944, Brereton had been awarded his third star, and the ranks of Ninth Air Force had swelled to some 170,000 airmen.[40] Steadfast in his views on the efficacy of strategic bombing, Brereton was somewhat taken aback when, on 16 July 1944, General Spaatz invited him to lunch and told him he had been selected to command an organization that contained not one bomber. "I 'took a dim view' of this new assignment," recorded Brereton in his diary, but it was an assignment he nonetheless accepted.[41]

On 2 August, Eisenhower's chief of staff, Lieutenant General "Beetle" Smith, handed Brereton a directive ordering him to form what was then known as Combined Airborne Forces. In the margin of the directive Eisenhower had penciled a reminder to Smith about what Brereton's initial focus should be: "In accordance with our conversation this morning, Brereton should be working on his new job instantly. Please inform him that I am particularly anxious about the navigational qualifications of the Transport Command Crews. He is to get on this in an intensive way. He is to keep me in touch with his progress. There is nothing we are undertaking about which I am more concerned than this job of his. I want him on the ball with all his might."[42] But before he could concentrate on training Brereton had to form his staff. General Arnold was only too pleased to help. Finally seeing his idea of a joint airborne–troop carrier command come to fruition, Arnold immediately assigned to it two of his brightest general officers: Brigadier General Floyd L. Parks, who became Brereton's chief of staff, and Brigadier General Ralph S. Strealey, who became the operations officer. To leaven the headquarters, Brereton also needed an officer with ground combat experience for his deputy, and since this was to be an Allied organization, it would be best if that person were British. Browning was the logical choice, but there was a problem—Browning was also a lieutenant general with four-months' seniority on Brereton and had been heavily campaigned for the top slot. But with no other airborne commands in the offing, Browning accepted the post.[43]

Combined Airborne Forces was officially announced 8 August 1944. Eight days later, at Brereton's prodding, its name was changed to First Allied Airborne Army. It encompassed all Allied airborne units in the European theater of operations, which were further organized into two corps-size elements: British Airborne Troops (which became British I Airborne Corps upon commitment to combat) and the U.S. XVIII Airborne Corps. The former, commanded by Browning (it was not unusual for a deputy commander to also command a subordinate unit in the organization for which he was deputy), comprised the British 1st and 6th Airborne Divisions, the British 52nd Lowland (Air Transportable) Division, and the 1st Polish Parachute Brigade. The XVIII Airborne Corps comprised the U.S. 17th, 82nd, and 101st Airborne Divisions. Also subordinate to First Allied Airborne Army was the U.S. IX Troop Carrier Command under Major General Paul L. Williams, as well as "such Royal Air Force troop carrier formations as might be allocated from time to time [generally RAF 38 and 46 Groups]."[44]

Command of XVIII Airborne Corps was never an issue. There was no one else but Ridgway. It took some time, however, to assemble the staff, including the sergeants, clerks, and everyone else that make a headquarters run, so it was not until 27 August that Ridgway formally took command of the corps.[45] As was his prerogative, Ridgway brought with him several key staff officers, all of whom assumed the same staff positions they had held in the 82nd: Colonel "Doc" Eaton became the corps chief of staff; Lieutenant Colonel Fred Schellhammer, corps G-1; Lieutenant Colonel Whitfield Jack, corps G-2; and Lieutenant Colonel Bill Moorman, corps G-4 (Ridgway also brought along the division surgeon, Lieutenant Colonel Wolcott Etienne; his aide, Captain Don Faith; his driver, Sergeant Frank Farmer; and his orderly, Sergeant Jim Casey).[46]

Normally, losing a commander and so many primary staff officers at the same time would devastate a division, but that was not the case with the 82nd when, on 16 August 1944, Ridgway handed Gavin the division's colors. "I had a lot of combat experience," recounted Gavin, "and I knew everybody in the division, all the commanders as well."[47] He also knew whom he wanted on his division staff, so on the same day that he became the 82nd's commander, Majors Al Ireland, John Norton, and Albert G. Marin assumed their duties as the new G-1, G-3, and G-4, respectively; Lieutenant Colonel Walter Winton became the new G-2; and the one man Ridgway left behind to provide some continuity, Lieutenant Colonel Bob Wienecke, moved from G-3 to become the new chief of staff. All of these men had proven their mettle in combat and had earned Gavin's trust and respect. Like their commander (who became, at thirty-seven, the youngest man to command a U.S. Army division since the Civil War), they were all extremely young, but they were also smart, reliable, and loyal.[48]

The one position left unfilled was that of assistant division commander. Ridgway and Gavin discussed several candidates. A logical choice was Brigadier General Howell, but not only was Howell irascible—"he didn't get along with anybody," recalled Maxwell Taylor—he was also six years Gavin's senior in rank.[49] Ridgway rejected Howell for his XVIII Airborne Corps staff as well. Another candidate was Brigadier General Stuart Cutler, whom Ridgway favored. Cutler had commanded the 82nd's 326th Glider Infantry Regiment before it had been cut loose and replaced by the 505th. He had already served as assistant division commander in the 13th Airborne Division and at the time was on Brereton's staff. But Gavin was not high on Cutler either, and, like Howell, he was also senior to Gavin. Gavin's preference was Reuben Tucker, but Ridgway vetoed this. As good a combat commander as was Tucker, he was not, in Ridgway's eyes, general officer material. Tucker "was famous for screwing up everything having to do with administration" and was notoriously lax when it came to matters of discipline, dress, and decorum. When finally released from duty with Mark Clark's Fifth Army in Italy, for example, Tucker reputedly threw an orange crate full of charge sheets preferred against his 504th troopers into Naples Harbor, an act the by-the-book Ridgway simply would not countenance. "Everybody in the paratroops wondered why we didn't name Rube," Gavin mused. "We just couldn't do it." As it turned out, Gavin was victim to his own startling success. Besides Tucker there was no one in the airborne community of requisite rank who had as much combat experience as he did. Until December 1944, when Colonel Ira P. Swift was assigned to the position, Gavin operated without an assistant division commander. "I sure could have used one," he later lamented.[50]

On the day he took command of the 82nd, Gavin wrote:

> I have a thousand ideas and I am going to carry them through, in combat and out, with zeal and determination come what may. Either this division will rise to heights of combat attainment in our service unprecedented or

> rush to oblivion. In either case I will be with it all of the way. To those of us who have had a lasting and firm faith in the efficacy of airborne troops as a means of waging war there is of course no doubt about the future of this or any other parachute division nor is there any doubt or concern really with what value posterity will place on what we do now. We are supremely confident of ourselves. I suppose that we would not be in the hazardous business we are in if we in the slightest degree lacked this confidence. . . . With this abiding confidence in our professional creed, and a determination to excel in combat unmatched in any army anywhere, all airborne soldiers look to the future certain that they have a rendezvous with greatness.[51]

Little did he know when penning these lines that in a month and a day, he and his troopers would be jumping into combat for the fourth time. Operation MARKET-GARDEN, the largest airborne operation in history, would finally put the airborne forces center stage. It was, most assuredly, a measure of how solidly "the firm faith in the efficacy of airborne troops as a means of waging war" had taken hold.

CHAPTER 15

WE'LL NEED TWO DIVISIONS TO DO THAT

General Eisenhower wants a plan prepared which would have as its purpose a maximum contribution to the destruction of the German armies in western Europe. He wants imagination and daring. . . . In parting, I told General Eisenhower that if he wanted plans with daring and imagination he would get them, but that I did not think his staff or the ground commanders would like it. My mind went back to October 1918, when Gen. Billy Mitchell dumped plans in my lap to work out details for what then was something unheard of—a parachute drop behind the enemy's lines. General Mitchell sold General Pershing on the feasibility of the operation and was proceeding with plans to take Metz from the rear by dropping an entire division by parachute from big bombers. The Armistice cut short General Mitchell's plans. Now, 26 years later, we had the same thing in mind. That's how far ahead Billy Mitchell was.

—LEWIS H. BRERETON, *THE BRERETON DIARIES: THE WAR IN THE AIR IN THE PACIFIC, MIDDLE EAST, AND EUROPE, 3 OCTOBER 1941–8 MAY 1945*

ONCE THE ALLIES established a firm foothold in France, Eisenhower turned his attention to the second part of his mission—to "undertake operations aimed at the heart of Germany and the destruction of her armed forces."[1] But where, exactly, the "heart of Germany" lay was a matter left to interpretation. Berlin was too far east to be of any immediate significance. Much closer were Germany's industrial centers, the Ruhr and Saar. Taking one or both of them would degrade Nazi war-making capabilities, while threatening them would force the German army to stand and fight, hastening its destruction as well. Eisenhower decided to go for both, initiating what has come to be known as the broad-front approach. Montgomery's 21st Army Group, composed of the Canadian First and British Second Armies, would advance in a northeasterly direction, pass north of the Ardennes Forest, and make for the Ruhr, while Bradley's newly activated 12th Army Group, composed of the U.S. First Army (which Bradley's former deputy Lieutenant General Courtney Hodges commanded) and Patton's Third Army, headed east, passed south of the Ardennes, and made for the Saar.[2] Although the drives were to occur simultaneously and be mutually supporting, it was understood that Montgomery's was the main effort since its objective, the Ruhr, was Germany's largest and most important industrial center.[3]

The Allies anticipated that Rundstedt would conduct a fighting withdrawal from a series of fallback positions anchored on defensible terrain. They therefore assumed that their advance would be methodical and punctuated by operational pauses during which they could move forward and build up needed supplies and materiel. Based on this assumption, Allied logisticians drew up a timetable upon which they predicated support requirements. According to this timetable the Allies would not reach Paris and the Seine until D+90 (4 September 1944), and, because of the formidable barrier a fortified Seine portended, they also assumed that there would be at least a month's pause before the advance continued beyond the Seine. What the Allies overlooked was Hitler's maniacal determination to fight for every inch of ground, a determination that changed the course of the war in Western Europe dramatically.[4]

Four days after the Normandy landings Hitler sent a message to his *Seventh Army* commander. "There can be no question of fighting a rearguard action nor of retiring to a new line of resistance," he ordered. "Every man shall fight or fall where he stands."[5] Following the fall of Cherbourg, he underscored his no-retreat dictum by ordering the commanders of all ports still in German hands to barricade their forces inside and fight "to the last man, to the last cartridge."[6] Finally, on 2 July Hitler sealed his resolve to yield nothing by firing Rundstedt who, despite Hitler's decrees, remained persistent in his desire to withdraw to more defensible ground.

Hitler replaced Rundstedt with Generalfeldmarschall Günther von Kluge, one of his favorites. But Kluge was unable to stop the Allied advance, and it was on his watch that the Allies broke out of Normandy. Hitler ordered Kluge to counterattack toward the Channel and reestablish the front in Normandy.[7]

Launched on 7 August, Kluge's counterattack failed miserably. Forewarned by ULTRA, the Americans beat back Kluge's counterattack and launched a counterattack of their own. The ensuing Battle of the Falaise Pocket resulted in some 60,000 German dead and captured.[8] By the end of August the German army in the west looked beaten. Since the landings at Normandy, it had lost approximately 240,000 men killed or wounded and another 210,000 captured, and of the fifty German divisions that had been so far thrown against the Allies, fewer than ten could be classified as "reasonable fighting divisions."[9] By 29 August, six days ahead of schedule, the Allies controlled all of France south of the Seine. All thoughts of a methodical advance were forgotten. It appeared a pursuit was in order.

Eisenhower was one of the first to contemplate changing the pace of the Allied advance. On the day Kluge launched his counterattack Eisenhower cabled Marshall to inform him that he was considering operations "to cross the Seine before the enemy has time to hold it in strength." The subsequent collapse of the German counterattack further emboldened Eisenhower, who posited in another cable to Marshall that the destruction of German forces encircled at Falaise set the stage for a "dash across the Seine," thereby turning the Allied advance into an all-out pursuit. On 19 August Eisenhower made his decision. Calling his two army group commanders to conference, he ordered them to leap the Seine without pausing and pursue the beaten foe into Germany, albeit along the same axes of advance they had already been prescribed.[10]

Eisenhower's decision to take the Seine in stride was one of "the most fateful tactical decisions of the war." Having before him a foe seemingly ripe for a killing blow, a pursuit was what doctrine called for. However, by unleashing Montgomery *and* Bradley in the pursuit, Eisenhower made a decision that "carried with [it] a supply task out of all proportion to planned capabilities."[11]

During the first seven weeks of the fight in France, the Allies had moved much more slowly than expected, which allowed time for the development of Cherbourg and other minor ports in Normandy and the stockpiling of supplies. But once the Allies broke out of Normandy, their stockpiles quickly dwindled. For example, at D+49 (25 July, the date Bradley launched Operation COBRA) the Allies were still at the line logisticians predicted they would reach by D+20. However, in the thirty days following COBRA the Allies advanced a distance that logisticians predicted would take them seventy days to traverse. Lines of communication from the Channel coast to forward supply depots could not be developed at that rate (the most efficient source of transportation, French railroads, had been ravaged by Allied airpower in the weeks leading up to the invasion), so when the Allied armies leapt the Seine in accordance with Eisenhower's directive, they did so after having used up most of their supplies. And once across the Seine the advance accelerated; by D+100 (14 September) Allied combat formations were at a point logisticians anticipated they would not reach until D+330 (2 May 1945). Inevitably, the pursuit slowed. Keeping both army groups supplied with enough ammunition, water, food, repair parts, and, above all fuel was simply not possible. This compelled Eisenhower to again adjust his strategy.[12]

Montgomery had always been dead set against a broad-front advance. In his mind, mounting two drives would dissipate combat power. He felt it would be far better to aim both army groups at the Ruhr in "a solid mass of some forty divisions which would be so strong that it need fear nothing."[13] Acting in his capacity as the overall ground force commander, Montgomery suggested this to Bradley on 17 August. Although it is unclear whether Bradley agreed with the plan at the time (Montgomery insisted that he did; Bradley contended that he did not), the point became moot on 1 September when, in accordance with a previously agreed protocol (albeit in the face of vehement opposition by Montgomery), overall command of the ground campaign passed from Montgomery to Eisenhower.[14]

Having failed to convince Eisenhower that "the Supreme Commander must sit on a very lofty perch in order to be able to take a detached view of the whole intricate problem" and that someone else (read: Montgomery) should run the ground battle for him, Montgomery campaigned aggressively to have his strategy accepted. Furthermore, felt Montgomery, the straitened supply situation made this imperative, so on 4 September he sent a message to Eisenhower to make his case. "I consider we have now reached a stage where one really powerful and full-blooded thrust towards Berlin is likely to get there and thus end the German war," he wrote. "We have not enough maintenance resources [supplies] for two full-blooded thrusts," and since "the thrust likely to give the best and quickest results is the northern one via the Ruhr," his 21st Army Group should get absolute priority on all supplies.[15]

Eisenhower, too, finally realized that sustaining two thrusts was problematic. "For a very considerable time," he informed Marshall, "I was of the belief that we could carry out the operation to the northeast simultaneously with [Bradley's] thrust east [toward the Saar], but later have concluded that due to the tremendous importance of the objectives in the northeast we must first concentrate on that movement."[16] Nevertheless, for political reasons Eisenhower could not and would not stop Bradley completely. What he did agree to do, during a series of tense and, at times, barely civil meetings with Montgomery, was give his drive *priority*.[17] Furthermore, he granted Montgomery permission to use the First Allied Airborne Army.

Eisenhower had been pestering his staff to come up with plans for using airborne troops to either cut off the German retreat or facilitate the advance of the Allied armies. One of the first to be considered was Operation TRANSFIGURE, a drop in the Paris–Orléans Gap to cut off German forces retreating from the Falaise Pocket. But TRANSFIGURE was canceled when Patton's Third Army overran the drop zones.[18] In the ensuing weeks, fourteen other airborne plans were prepared and subsequently canceled as well.[19] The reason given for the cancellations was that, as with TRANSFIGURE, the ground forces were moving so fast the drop zones were being overrun before the airborne operations could be mounted.

This was true: The Allied ground forces were moving fast. But while gaining ground they lost focus on the real objective—the destruction of the German army. Patton's spectacular drives, the liberation of Europe's leading cities (Paris fell on 25 August, Brussels on 3 September, Antwerp on 4 September), and the allure of being first across the Rhine were what captured the imagination and made headlines.[20] Accordingly, though the German army in the west suffered grievously, it was never decisively beaten. In the words of one historian, "If a battle of annihilation were being sought, then an airborne operation might have been the very instrument to bring it about."[21] Mounting such an operation, however, would have meant temporarily diverting hundreds of transport planes from the task that had accounted for the bulk of their flying time following the breakout: the ferrying of supplies to the front.

Eisenhower's American commanders were the most adamantly opposed to releasing the C-47s from their ferrying missions so that they could prepare for an airborne operation. According to Brereton, "George Patton has been exceedingly audible in his appreciation of the air supply assistance given him, and there is a definite and determined reluctance on the part of Bradley not to favor airborne operations in front of his armies at the expense of air supply."[22] After the war Eisenhower wrote of this reluctance to release the C-47s during the heady days of August and early September:

> Unfortunately this withdrawal of planes from other work [supply runs] had to precede an airborne operation by several days, to provide time for refitting equipment and for briefing and retraining of crews. In late August, with our supply situation growing constantly more desperate, and with all of us eagerly following combat progress in search for another prospect of cutting off great numbers of the enemy, the question of the Transport Command employment came up for daily discussion. On the average, allowing for all kinds of weather, our planes could deliver about 2000 tons a day to the front. While this was only a small percentage of our total deliveries, every ton was so valuable that the decision was a serious one.[23]

Indeed, it was a small percentage. A standard division in combat required 600–700 tons of supplies per day, and by the end of August the Allies had thirty-six divisions in combat (to say nothing of numerous independent regiments and battalions), with more arriving weekly. Various schemes were tried to keep the armies supplied, the most famous of which was the Red Ball Express, a hastily improvised ground convoy system comprising just shy of 6,000 trucks that ran nonstop from August to November 1944. Still, demand outpaced supply (at its most efficient the Red Ball Express could supply only about 7,000 tons per day to the 12th Army Group and 4,000 tons per day to the 21st Army Group). By adding Breretons's C-47s to the transportation chain it was thought that enough supplies could be delivered to give the Allies the edge needed against a German army that, by early September, intelligence reports characterized as "no longer a cohesive force but a number of fugitive battle groups, disorganized and even demoralized, short of equipment and arms."[24] Yet despite hundreds of C-47 sorties, the Allied armies were simply too far from the depots to be kept adequately supplied. Something had to be done to drastically shorten the overextended lines of communication. The liberation of Antwerp on 4 September carried with it that promise.[25]

Boasting a sheltered deepwater port, more than six hundred cranes, forty-two kilometers of quays, and "clearance facilities [that] included more than 800 kilometers of rails, extensive marshaling yards, and excellent linkage with the Belgian network of over 5,000 kilometers of railroads and 2,200 kilometers of navigable rivers," Antwerp ranked with New York as one of the world's largest seaports.[26] Hence, when Major General G. P. B. "Pip" Roberts's British 11th Armored Division entered the city, it made straight for the docks and, astonishingly, captured them "in full working order." As Roberts's immediate superior, Lieutenant General Brian Gwynne Horrocks, the British XXX Corps commander, related, "This was an almost unbelievable stroke of luck, for the sluice gates and the dockside equipment, all electrically operated, could easily have been put out of action." But capturing the docks was not enough because to reach the docks, ships had to traverse the sixty-mile Scheldt Estuary, both sides of which were still held by the *German Fifteenth Army*. "If I had ordered Roberts to bypass Antwerp," wrote the self-effacing Horrocks, "and advance for only fifteen miles north-west, . . . the whole of this [German] force, which played such a prominent part in the subsequent fighting, might have been destroyed or forced to surrender. Napoleon, no doubt, would have realized this, but I am afraid Horrocks didn't."[27] Nevertheless, Montgomery used the promise of Antwerp and the potential it held for solving Allied supply difficulties as leverage in his argument with Eisenhower over strategy. His message of 4 September was the opening salvo. What he needed to seal the deal was a plan that would force Eisenhower's hand.

Even before the fall of Antwerp Montgomery's staff and Brereton's staff had been seeking ways to use the airborne forces Eisenhower had put at 21st Army Group's disposal. The outcome of this planning effort was Operation COMET, which envisioned parachute, glider, and air-landing insertions into the area stretching from Arnhem, Holland, on the Neder Rijn (lower Rhine) through Nijmegen, Holland, in order to seize a series of bridges so that XXX Corps, advancing overland, could pass over them en route to the Ruhr. According to Montgomery, COMET would cut off the German forces surrounding the Scheldt Estuary, leaving them vulnerable to annihilation or surrender; open the sea-lanes to Antwerp; obtain a bridgehead over the lower Rhine in Holland; bypass the Siegfried Line, Germany's fortifications along its western border; and poise 21st Army Group for a strike into the Ruhr. Eisenhower bought it. Originally planned for 8 and 9 September, COMET was delayed twice, once because of bad weather and the second time because of a significant buildup of German forces fronting XXX Corps. On 10 September, COMET was canceled altogether.[28] Undeterred, Montgomery proposed a second plan, Operation INFATUATE, which called for a drop on Walcheren Island, the key to the German defenses around the Scheldt Estuary. But INFATUATE was too risky for Brereton, who vetoed the plan because of the heavy concentration of antiaircraft batteries in the area, terrain that was unsuitable for glider landings, and the expectation of excessive losses by drowning.[29]

Montgomery then prepared a third plan, Operation MARKET-GARDEN, a scheme so bold that according to Bradley, "Had the pious, teetotalling Montgomery wobbled into SHAEF with a hangover, I could not have been more astonished." Yet, for all its audacity, MARKET-GARDEN was more than just another proposal to use First Allied Airborne Army. It was, in fact, a gambit by Montgomery, who was still piqued about being replaced as the overall ground force commander, to obtain untrammeled access to Allied resources. As Bradley saw it, Montgomery "was desperately, obsessively determined to lead a single thrust to Berlin and this was about the only way left to do it. It was strategy by subterfuge, legerdemain." Adding to this was Montgomery's wounded ego. Although Montgomery "was wont to assert that he did not mind what anybody said about him," wrote Horrocks, he "deeply resented American suspicion that his handling of the Normandy battle showed evidence of caution and timidity, and that he would never be equal to the demands of exploitation and pursuit." "In his heart of hearts," continued Horrocks, "he knew that the moment had come, to use his own words, 'to throw his bonnet over the windmill and soar from the known to the unknown.'"[30]

MARKET-GARDEN was, in essence, COMET on a much larger scale. COMET had called for dropping one airborne division plus the Polish Parachute Brigade and air-landing the British 52nd Division. MARKET-GARDEN was to be a drop by an airborne corps composed of three Allied airborne divisions, the Polish Brigade, and the 52nd Division. It would, promised Montgomery, bring about the same results as had been promised for COMET, but in addition it would also eliminate the V-2 launching sites in the vicinity of Rotterdam and Amsterdam (the first of these new weapons fell on London on 8 September and caused quite a bit of consternation).[31]

Finally, and perhaps most persuasively, MARKET-GARDEN would satisfy Eisenhower's desire to use the airborne divisions, which, by that time, had become "coins burning holes in SHAEF's pocket."[32] According to Bradley, both Marshall and Arnold had been hounding Eisenhower to use the "valuable" and "expensive" airborne forces for some time, and "Monty's Arnhem plan offered Ike a golden opportunity to stage a splashy airborne spectacle."[33] It also satisfied Marshall's and Arnold's desire to use those forces in bolder ways.

Yet Montgomery almost blew his chances of getting MARKET-GARDEN approved. When Eisenhower replied to Montgomery's 4 September message, communication difficulties due to SHAEF's forward headquarters being so far from the front (it was in Granville, France, more than three hundred miles from Montgomery's command post) resulted in Montgomery receiving it in two parts, on 7 and 9 September, and in reverse order. The second half of Eisenhower's reply, which Montgomery received first, seemed to indicate Eisenhower's agreement to provide Montgomery absolute priority for his drive on the Ruhr. However, the first part of the reply, received two days later, stated that although Eisenhower agreed with Montgomery's "conception of a powerful and full-blooded thrust towards Berlin [he did] not agree that it should be initiated at this moment to the exclusion of all other maneuvers."[34]

This put Montgomery over the edge. Not only had he been supplanted as overall ground force commander, but he was receiving garbled directions from a headquarters far removed from the action. The only thing to do was to have it out with the Supreme Commander face-to-face, so he requested that Eisenhower meet with him at his headquarters near Brussels. Eisenhower agreed. The meeting took place aboard Eisenhower's plane at Brussels airport.[35]

When Eisenhower's plane landed, Montgomery met it in fighting trim. Eisenhower had with him Air Chief Marshal Tedder and his chief administrative officer, Lieutenant General Sir Humphrey Gale, neither of whom were great admirers of their difficult countryman. Immediately upon boarding the plane Montgomery soured the atmosphere by insisting that Gale leave and then started lecturing Eisenhower about the broad-front approach and its many flaws. Listening quietly, but with growing indignation, Eisenhower finally leaned forward, put both hands on Montgomery's knees and, staring him full in the eyes, said, "Steady, Monty! You can't speak to me like that. I'm your boss."[36] A chastened Montgomery mumbled an apology but continued to insist on his plan.

> I told him that enemy resistance was stiffening on the line of the Albert Canal; that there was a steady consumption of petrol and ammunition; and that we were outstripping our maintenance [supplies]. It was becoming clear

> that I would not be able to launch the large-scale operation towards Arnhem as soon as I had hoped and that this would give the enemy more time to recover. Since crossing the Seine my headquarters had moved northwards, and Bradley's eastwards. The land battle was becoming jerky and disjointed. I said that so long as he continued with two thrusts, with the maintenance split between the two, neither could succeed. . . . The quickest way to open up Antwerp was to back my plan of concentration on the left—which plan would not only help our logistic and maintenance situation but would also keep up the pressure on the stricken Germans in the area of greatest importance, thus helping to end the war quickly.[37]

Eisenhower was unimpressed. "Monty, you're nuts," he replied. "You can't do it. What the hell!"[38] Montgomery then played his ace card and outlined for Eisenhower Operation MARKET-GARDEN, which no one outside a select group of trusted officers knew anything about. Eisenhower instantly warmed to the plan, seeing it as a solution that promised results without his having to give absolute priority to Montgomery at the exclusion of Bradley, who had no interest in employing airborne forces anyway. Montgomery, on the other hand, saw MARKET-GARDEN as a means to obtain irreversible momentum, for having a force over the Rhine poised to advance on the Ruhr and, perhaps, on to Berlin would force Eisenhower to give outright primacy of supply to 21st Army Group. Patton called this the "rock soup" method of influencing strategy—start small, achieve success, and get so enmeshed in combat that those holding sway over supplies were forced to support your forces. It was, he wrote, "hell to wage war by inadvertence [and] to conquer by deceit," but it was the manner by which both Montgomery and, in his own way, Bradley secured resources.[39] In September 1944, Montgomery's recipe became the Allied soup du jour.

One of those who did have prior knowledge of MARKET-GARDEN was Browning, who for several days had been cloistered with the 21st Army Group staff exploring ways to use airborne forces to further Montgomery's ambitions.[40] Immediately following Eisenhower's approval of MARKET-GARDEN, Browning hopped a plane back to England where he told the First Allied Airborne Army chief of staff, Brigadier General Floyd Parks, to assemble the Airborne Army's principal commanders and their assistants. As Browning, but no one else in First Allied Airborne Army, knew, there was little time to lose; the earliest proposed drop date was five days away (15 September; it was later changed to 17 September). Furthermore, by hand-delivering the time-sensitive plan, Browning all but ensured that he would be named the airborne corps commander and salvage a career that, a few days previously, he had almost discarded in a fit of pique.[41]

The day before leaving for Montgomery's headquarters, Browning had submitted his resignation as First Allied Airborne Army deputy commander following a violent disagreement with Brereton over Operation LINNET II, a drop in the Liège-Maastricht Gap that Browning was to have commanded. Brereton conceived LINNET II after a previous operation in the Lille-Tournai area, code-named LINNET, was canceled on 2 September. Seeking to realize Eisenhower's desire to use his airborne forces somewhere soon, Brereton proposed simply switching the LINNET force package—the British 1st and U.S. 82nd and 101st Airborne Divisions, the Polish Parachute Brigade, a U.S. engineer group, and the British 52nd Division—to the Liège-Maastricht Gap in order to seize crossings over the Meuse River.

Inexplicably, especially in light of how quickly MARKET-GARDEN was mounted, Browning protested LINNET II, insisting that there was no way he could prepare an airborne operation in a new area on such short notice. He would not, therefore, command LINNET II unless given a direct order. Browning maintained his opposition to LINNET II during a meeting with Brereton on the evening of 3 September. When Brereton again ignored his protests, Browning became so upset that he stormed out, but not before telling Brereton that he would tender a written protest that would be backed by the division commanders who, he intimated, also had serious reservations about LINNET II. Shaken by his deputy's intransigence, Brereton turned to Ridgway, who was also at the meeting, and asked if he thought Gavin and Taylor would, in fact, back Browning. Ridgway replied that "he felt sure that the commanders of the 82nd and 101st Divisions would not protest the execution of any decisions handed down to them—that they would express an opinion in the formative stages before the decision was made, but that once the decision was made their determination to carry it out could not be questioned." Gavin and Taylor, continued Ridgway, "would do as ordered and make a 100 percent job of it."[42] With that assurance, Brereton relieved Browning as the LINNET II commander and replaced him with Ridgway. Not long thereafter, Browning left for 21st Army Group headquarters.

Later that evening Brereton received Browning's written protest and was stunned to read that Browning felt "that in view of our sharp difference of opinion he [Browning] felt that he could not continue as Deputy Commander of the First Allied Airborne Army and therefore tendered his resignation."[43] Ironically, just fifteen minutes before Browning's letter arrived, LINNET II was canceled. But the incident did Browning's standing grave harm. Subsequent First Allied Airborne Army plans all called for the use of XVIII Airborne Corps in lieu of British I Airborne Corps (Browning's field command) as the airborne command and control element. Brereton was not only keeping Browning on the sidelines but replacing him with his chief rival,

Ridgway. MARKET-GARDEN, therefore, had huge personal import for Browning. By keeping the plan close to his chest until *after* it had been approved by Eisenhower—no one at First Allied Airborne Army knew of the plan until Browning's briefing—and then flying back to England to personally lay it out for the assembled airborne and troop carrier commanders, he all but forced Brereton to appoint him the overall airborne force commander. Ridgway was stunned.

> I well remember my bitter disappointment when General Brereton announced that he was giving command of this operation to General Browning. I had not anticipated this. We had two divisions committed to the operation. The British had one. We had won our spurs in three battles already—Sicily, Italy, and France. I felt in my heart that we could do a better job of commanding that operation than could anyone else, and I imagine I expressed these views, in private, with some fervor. I made no official protest, however, for I could not justify such an action. General Browning was a brave and widely experienced soldier, and it was entirely Brereton's prerogative to appoint any commander he pleased.[44]

Gavin concurred. As he saw it, although "there was no better soldier than . . . General Browning," he was too much of a "theorist" and lacked the hard-driving persona that MARKET-GARDEN required.[45]

The conference Browning had requested opened at 1800 hours, 10 September, at First Allied Airborne Army headquarters in Sunnyhill Park, just west of London. All the airborne and troop carrier commanders and their principal planners were present with the exception of Ridgway, who was in France, and Taylor (representing the 101st was Brigadier General Anthony C. McAuliffe, the division artillery commander). Following some opening remarks, Brereton turned the conference over to Browning who, he announced, would be the overall airborne commander for the operation.

MARKET-GARDEN, Browning explained, was actually two interdependent operations. MARKET, the airborne part of the plan, was to be a drop by the British 1st Airborne Division (reinforced by the Polish Parachute Brigade) and the U.S. 82nd and 101st Airborne Divisions under the command of British I Airborne Corps along a corridor extending sixty-four miles northeastward from the British Second Army's front lines astride the Meuse-Escaut Canal to Arnhem, Holland. GARDEN, the complementary ground plan, referred to the advance that the British Second Army, spearheaded by Lieutenant General Horrocks's XXX Corps, would make through this corridor. The overarching concept was that the MARKET force would seize and hold a series of bridges to facilitate the rapid transit of the GARDEN force up the corridor to Arnhem, where it would cross the Neder Rijn and be in position for a subsequent advance to the Ruhr. Both the drop and the start of the ground advance would occur simultaneously; D day was tentatively set for no earlier than 15 September.[46]

Following Browning's briefing the troop carrier commanders made two recommendations, both of which were accepted without objection, and both of which would have significant import. The first concerned the objective areas. From south to north MARKET envisioned the taking of bridges in the general vicinity of three Dutch cities: Eindhoven, Nijmegen, and Arnhem. Browning's concept had the British and Poles jumping at Arnhem, the 101st at Nijmegen, and the 82nd at Eindhoven. The troop carrier commanders suggested that the objective areas for the 82nd and 101st be switched so that the planes carrying the 101st from southern England would not have to cross paths with those carrying the 82nd from the Midlands. This also ensured that the 101st, the division with the least combat experience of the three, would be the first with which XXX Corps would link up.[47] The second recommendation concerned the always contentious issue of aircraft allocation. To facilitate rapid planning Major General Paul Williams, whom Brereton had assigned as commander of all troop carrier units for MARKET, suggested that the aircraft be allocated essentially as they were for LINNET with the exception that instead of double tugs (one plane towing two gliders), which was to be the norm for LINNET, MARKET would be restricted to single tugs because of the greater distances the planes would have to fly to the target areas (LINNET's objectives were Lille, France, and Tournai, Belgium, cities much closer to the English departure airfields). This, in turn, meant that none of the airborne divisions could be dropped in its entirety on D day; instead, each of the divisions would have to plan for a phased insertion over several days. Moreover, because the bulk of the available aircraft would be dedicated to parachute and glider insertions for the first few days of MARKET, aerial resupply missions could not begin any earlier than D+2.[48]

Before breaking up, Brereton made one more decision—the drops would go in during the day. This surprised many of those present, although it was not unprecedented. The parachute and glider insertions of Operation ANVIL, the invasion of southern France, had occurred during daylight hours with negligible losses. Furthermore, Allied intelligence had determined that the Luftwaffe's daylight fighters had been savaged and posed no serious threat, while the night-fighter squadrons were relatively intact. And although intelligence also estimated that enemy antiaircraft concentrations in the objective area had recently increased by 35 percent, Brereton believed that "a proper employment of the supporting air forces available could knock out flak positions in advance and beat them down during the airborne operations themselves."[49] Additionally, 15 and 16 September were the last two days before a new moon. Flying at night with no lunar illumination meant that pilots would have to navigate by radar and direction finding, but the nearest Allied radar chain was more than two hundred miles away and all but useless. A night drop, therefore, would be well nigh blind. The large number of relatively inexperienced troop carrier pilots that would be flying the mission was the final element that persuaded Brereton to go during the day.[50] "Carrying out the operation in daylight would be much easier for them [the green pilots]," wrote Gavin, "and we all agreed that this was the way we wanted to go about it."[51]

The conference broke up at about 2100 hours so everyone could return to their headquarters to issue warning orders that would start precombat preparations. A second conference was scheduled for 0900 hours the next morning at IX Troop Carrier Command headquarters in Eastcote, during which air routes, drop and landing zones, and load plans would be finalized. Before returning to their headquarters in Leicester, Gavin and Major John Norton visited British I Airborne Corps headquarters at nearby Moor Park to pick up maps, aerial photographs, and terrain studies of the area around Nijmegen that Browning's planners had collected while preparing for COMET. While there the British planners also shared with Gavin and Norton their thoughts about dropping around Nijmegen, especially as they concerned two terrain features in the area. The first was the Reichswald, a heavily wooded area of approximately twenty-four square miles just inside the German border and about eight miles southeast of Nijmegen, which intelligence indicated housed a great deal of German armor. The second was a hill mass, just west of the Reichswald, atop which sat the small town of Groesbeek. These heights dominated the surrounding area. The British were convinced, and Gavin agreed, that "the retention and control of the high ground [around Groesbeek] would mean control of the flatlands and glider landing areas, and would prove to be the key to the success of the over-all Grave-Nijmegen operation."[52]

At Eastcote the next morning departure airfields were assigned, flight routes were laid out, drop and landing zones were pinpointed, and the insertion of parachute and glider elements was synchronized.[53] Armed with this information the airborne divisions could complete their insertion and ground tactical plans. The swiftness with which MARKET came together was due in no small measure to the very existence of the First Allied Airborne Army, which brought together, under one command, troop carrier and airborne forces and thereby enhanced cooperation and coordination and, in instances of disagreement, provided a clear chain of command for swift resolution. Furthermore, because First Allied Airborne Army and its subordinate elements had already prepared plans for other contingencies they were well apprised of the situation in Europe, had honed their planning skills, and possessed a wealth of information from which they could draw as needed.[54] Operation MARKET was, after all, simply a modification of Operations LINNET (from which the air movement plan was adopted) and COMET (for the selection of the objective area and drop zones).

Additionally, the airborne divisions were already at a high state of readiness. As Gavin pointed out, the experience of readying for missions, even when they were canceled, "was useful in training our new troopers and junior officers to cope with the problems of pre-drop preparation; ammunition, food, maps, and air photos all had to be distributed, all commands had to be prepared, and every conceivable operational detail anticipated and covered." According to the division G-4, "A great deal of planning for Operation 'MARKET' had been done prior to September 10, 1944. . . . All supplies required for the 'MARKET' Operation had actually been received and distributed prior to the actual receipt of the mission."[55] Consequently, just five days after they were alerted the troopers of the 82nd and 101st boarded buses for their departure airfields, ready to go (the Brits and Poles were already at theirs, having previously marshaled for Operation COMET).

On the morning of 16 September, Browning gathered his subordinate airborne commanders for a final coordination conference to ensure that, taken together, the divisional plans that constituted Operation MARKET formed a coherent whole and that, furthermore, Operation MARKET was synchronized with Operation GARDEN. Each division commander briefed his plan in turn.[56]

Major General Maxwell Taylor's 101st Airborne Division, Browning's southernmost unit, would drop just north of Eindhoven to seize several canal and river crossings after which it would attack into Eindhoven itself to seize the bridges there.[57]

Browning's northernmost unit, the British 1st Airborne Division, commanded by Major General Robert E. Urquhart and reinforced by Major General Stanislaw Sosabowski's Polish Parachute Brigade, would drop west and south of Arnhem, seize the road and railway bridges over the Neder Rijn, and hold until relieved by XXX Corps.[58]

The 82nd, along with Browning's corps headquarters, would drop between the 101st and 1st Airborne Divisions in the vicinity of Nijmegen, forming the vital middle linkage. Dropping onto drop zones south of the city, its mission was to "capture the bridges over the Maas at Grave, over the Waal at Nijmegen and over the Maas-Waal Canal between."[59]

During the conference Browning emphasized that Gavin was "not to attempt seizure of NIJMEGEN Bridge until all other missions had been successfully accomplished and the BERG-EN-DAL high ground [the Groesbeek

Heights] was firmly in [82nd] hands."[60] But Gavin needed no reminder. He had been convinced of the importance of the Groesbeek Heights ever since visiting British I Airborne Corps headquarters following the first briefing on MARKET-GARDEN.

> The Nijmegen-Groesbeek high ground was the only high ground in all of the Netherlands. With it in German hands, physical possession of the bridges would be absolutely worthless, since it completely dominated the bridges and all the terrain around it. . . . It is a basic concept of airborne tactics that an airhead must first be established from which further tactical operations can be conducted. This high ground provided ideally such an area. I personally considered it the key to the accomplishment of the entire mission and thought that even if we were driven off the low ground around the bridges, if the high ground could be held, ultimately the [British] Second Army could accomplish its mission.[61]

Following right behind the Groesbeek Heights in priority was the bridge over the Maas at Grave, the "other missions" Browning spoke of. A vital link in the main Eindhoven-Nijmegen highway up which XXX Corps would be racing, the Grave Bridge had to be taken intact lest the advance to Arnhem be thrown behind schedule. (The bridges over the Maas-Waal Canal, which lay between the Grave Bridge and the Groesbeek Heights, were of secondary importance because it was thought that, were they blown, the canal could be easily bridged.)[62]

Browning also had his commanders go over the air movement and insertion plans a final time. This had been MARKET's most vexing problem, for although General Williams's IX Troop Carrier Command had 1,544 planes and 491 gliders available for D day, when divided three ways this was barely enough to carry half of each division.[63] Furthermore, the length of the air corridors to and from England restricted the troop carriers to one lift per day. Given these conditions, it would take three days to insert all the parachute and glider forces into each objective area.

Both Gavin and Taylor opted to use the aircraft allotted them on D day to insert their parachute regiments followed by small gliderborne contingents, mostly antitank and artillery. Urquhart, on the other hand, would be leading with a glider-heavy force. His drop and landing zones were far from the Arnhem bridges so he needed to bring in many more vehicles with the initial assault wave. On D+1, when it was expected that XXX Corps would have already linked up with the 101st, the loads were arranged to provide the divisions what they thought they would need given the changed tactical situation. For the British 1st Airborne, this meant the remainder of the division. For the

82nd this was the division gliderborne artillery complement. For the 101st it was glider infantry; having linked up with XXX Corps it was assumed that the 101st would have recourse to corps artillery. On D+2, when it was thought XXX Corps would be at or beyond Nijmegen, the British 1st Airborne would be reinforced by the Polish Parachute Brigade dropping south of Arnhem. The 82nd would receive the 325th Glider Infantry Regiment, and the 101st would receive its glider artillery. Finally, once XXX Corps was across the Neder Rijn at Arnhem, the British 52nd Division would be air-landed on airfields north of the city.[64]

To make this happen IX Troop Carrier Command would employ two aerial highways, dubbed the Northern and Southern Routes. The Northern Route would be used to insert the 1st Airborne and 82nd. It had the advantage of being a fairly straight shot from England to Arnhem and Nijmegen, except that the last eighty miles was over enemy-held territory. Intelligence indicated, however, that it was territory relatively free of enemy antiaircraft guns. The Southern Route to Eindhoven had the advantage of spending the least amount of time over enemy territory, although it did cross the British Second Army's front lines, a thought that terrified many who fretted about the artillery that would be firing in support of XXX Corps's advance. Once planes had dropped or released their loads, they would turn 180 degrees and return the same way they came.

Because the pilots would be flying in daylight, each route was designed to act like a stacked three- and four-lane highway, with serials consisting of anywhere from twenty-seven to fifty aircraft flying above and below one another separated by one and a half miles of altitude. Moreover, the space between serials was reduced to four minutes between parachute and seven minutes between glider serials. In this way, more than 1,000 planeloads of paratroopers and some 470 gliders in the initial lift could be delivered to three separate objective areas within sixty-five minutes, "the same time it took to bring in 369 sticks of paratroops for the 82d Division in NEPTUNE." In addition, it was expected that the tighter serials would result in more concentrated drops, which would, in turn, speed assembly on the ground and facilitate the quick seizure of objectives.[65]

To keep this vast aerial armada oriented, navigational aids were emplaced along each of the routes. Starting in England, Eureka and radio compass beacons would guide the pilots to aerial lighthouses called "occults" that designated their departure points. From there they would home in on boats equipped with Eureka and green lights that marked the way across the Channel. Finally, pathfinders would be inserted fifteen minutes before the main bodies of the 82nd and 101st to set up Eureka and radio compass beacons, panels, and smoke to help pilots pinpoint the drop and landing zones.[66]

During the final coordination conference Browning told his commanders that "he was fully aware of the danger [of flying during daylight] and was prepared to loose [*sic*] 33% of his forces getting in."[67] Although there is no record of the reaction Browning's comment generated, his airborne division commanders must surely have been taken aback. Losing one-third of your force *before* combat was joined was not a recipe for success. Fortunately, Brereton and Leigh-Mallory did not share Browning's attitude and did everything possible to protect the troop carriers on the way in.

Calling on elements of RAF Bomber Command, a second RAF command called Air Defense of Great Britain, and the U.S. Eighth and Ninth Air Force, Leigh-Mallory assembled a powerful supporting air armada that Brereton put to good use. To soften up the German defenses, on the night preceding the drops 282 RAF bombers would drop more than 1,100 tons of bombs on suspected antiaircraft positions along both air routes. This would be followed the next morning with attacks by U.S. Eighth Air Force B-17s on 177 separate enemy locations while a mélange of British Lancaster bombers, Mosquito fighter-bombers, and Spitfires staged an aerial raid on Walcheren Island in order to deceive the Germans about the true location of the drops. Dummy paratroopers would also be dropped throughout Holland, as had been done during NEPTUNE, to further confuse the Germans. Further inland, Mosquitoes, B-25 bombers, and other attack planes were to bomb and strafe German barracks located at Arnhem, Nijmegen, and Ede, a village west of Arnhem. Finally, British and American fighter planes from the Air Defense of Great Britain and the U.S. Eighth and Ninth Air Force would escort the troop carriers to and from the objective areas to guard against Luftwaffe attacks and pounce on any remaining flak batteries. All told, some 550 American P-47s, P-38s, and P-51s along with 371 British Tempests, Spitfires, and Mosquitoes would fill the already crowded sky that day.[68]

Following the conference with Browning Gavin traveled to Cottesmore Airfield for his division's final "rehearsal of concept" drill.[69] "All commanders, regimental and battalion, are assembled in a conference room before a large-scale map of the operational area," wrote Gavin in describing how these drills were conducted.

> Each regimental and battalion commander, in turn, outlines to the assembled group his own mission and plan of operation upon landing. He is then questioned carefully on his plans for making contacts with other units, and on what he will do if his unit lands in a locality other than the one planned for, and what he considers the most important elements of his tactical objective and his plan. We found from experience that this was the only method to insure that every commander knows what every other commander is going to

> do. And—most important—what he should do in order to contribute to the common tactical effort if he should land with his own or any other unit in the wrong area.
>
> The importance of such a conference can be best judged when we realize that there never yet has been an airborne operation in which every unit has landed in its proper area. In an airborne operation every battalion commander must know the plan of *every other* battalion commander within the division. He must be prepared to undertake the execution of any of those plans immediately upon landing as well as his own plans.[70]

On D day, the 82nd's three parachute regiments were to drop on three drop zones—drop zones "N," "O," and "T." Drop zones "T" and "N," were situated north and south of the town of Groesbeek, respectively, to facilitate taking the heights of the same name and the formation of a defensive line facing east and fronting the Reichswald, the foreboding forest from which everyone expected the fiercest enemy resistance to emanate. Drop zone "O" was four miles west of the Groesbeek Heights and lay between the Maas River and the Maas-Waal Canal. From drop zone "O" troopers would move to seize the Grave Bridge as well as the bridges over the Maas-Waal Canal. A fourth drop zone, called "Special DZ," was about one-half mile west of the Grave Bridge (and therefore west of the Maas River as well). At Colonel Tucker's insistence, whose 504th was charged with taking the Grave Bridge, "Special DZ" was written into the 82nd's D-day insertion plan about thirty-six hours before drop time. Tucker's intent was to drop one parachute company on "Special DZ" so that he could assault the Grave Bridge from both ends simultaneously. Finally, between and overlapping drop zones "T" and "N" was an oblong area about three and a half miles north to south and one and a half miles east to west that was to serve as the 82nd's glider landing zone. Split into two, with the northern half labeled landing zone "T" and the southern half landing zone "N," estimates were that this area was large enough to hold nine hundred gliders, more than enough to bring in the division's glider echelon.[71]

Leading the division's D-day insertion would be a ten-man pathfinder team that would drop on drop zone "O" fifteen minutes ahead of the main body to set up navigational aids. Since the following aircraft would approach the target area from the west and overfly drop zone "O" en route to drop zones "N" and "T," both of which were easily identifiable from the air, there was no requirement to have a pathfinder team for each drop zone. Instead, the first paratroopers to hit the ground at drop zones "N" and "T" were to pop colored smoke and set up marker panels.[72]

The first three serials of the 82nd's main body would carry Ekman's 505th along with Gavin and his command group. Dropping on drop zone "N" (three separate serials were to drop on "N" on D day), the 505th was to clear, secure, and mark landing zone "N," seize and hold the high ground south and southwest of Groesbeek, and capture the town of Groesbeek itself. The next three serials, carrying Tucker's 504th, would drop on drop zone "O," with the exception of E Company, 2/504th, which would drop on "Special DZ." The 504th's primary mission was to seize the 640-foot bridge over the Maas at Grave and then any one of four bridges over the Maas-Waal Canal. The seventh serial, carrying B, C, and D Companies of the 307th Airborne Engineer Battalion as well as an element from the division artillery cell, would be the second serial to drop on drop zone "N." The engineers, of course, would provide their expertise as required, but in the meantime they were to provide security for Gavin's command post and be the division reserve. Serials eight, nine, and ten would carry Lindquist's 508th. Dropping on drop zone "T," it was to clear and secure landing zone "T" and set up defensive positions and roadblocks on the high ground north of Groesbeek. It was also to be prepared to conduct an assault on the five-span, 1,960-foot highway bridge in Nijmegen.

After adjourning, Gavin pulled Lindquist aside to discuss the Nijmegen highway bridge. "I told him," recalled Gavin, "that if, in his opinion, the situation along the Groesbeek high ground was quiet in the late afternoon of the day of our landing, he was to send a battalion against the Nijmegen bridge that night."[73] Furthermore, Gavin "pointed out that the way to get to the bridge was to go down into the flatland east of the city [Nijmegen] and approach it over the farms without going through the built-up area. We had had considerable fighting in towns in Sicily and Italy, and some in Normandy, and I cautioned him about the dangers of getting caught in streets. One Kraut with a machine gun can hold up a battalion under such circumstances, as we had learned earlier."[74]

The last of the 82nd's D-day parachute serials would carry the 376th Parachute Field Artillery Battalion. It would be the last element to drop on drop zone "N" so that Ekman's 505th would have enough time to clear the drop zone before the 376th released its heavy equipment bundles. Gavin risked jumping it in rather than inserting it by glider in order to conserve aircraft—a gliderborne field artillery battalion required ninety-five gliders and tugs while parachuting one in required but forty-eight planes. But conserving aircraft was not the only reason Gavin wanted some artillery jumping in with him: "It is an interesting aspect of an airborne operation that artillery is comparatively more effective than it is in any other type operation. The reason being that the type of units that are first committed against airborne landings are local police, militia, home guards, etc. A battalion concentration [i.e., all guns in a battalion firing simultaneously at the same target] will make them so ineffectual that they are not worth much for some time."[75]

Thirty minutes behind the last parachute serial fifty Waco gliders carrying elements of the division headquarters and various support elements; the division Reconnaissance Platoon; A Battery, 80th Airborne Antiaircraft Battalion (with eight antitank guns); and 24 jeeps with 7 trailers would land at landing zone "N." They would be followed by six more Wacos and thirty-two Horsas carrying Browning and his corps command group, which would set up within the 82nd's perimeter.[76]

On D+1, 454 C-47s towing an equal number of Waco gliders would insert the 319th and 320th Glider and the 456th Parachute Field Artillery Battalions; B Battery, 80th Airborne Antiaircraft Battalion; and sundry engineer, signal, and medical personnel. Set to arrive in eleven serials of anywhere from forty to fifty aircraft beginning at 1000 hours, 18 September, this lift counted 1,899 troopers, sixty howitzers (both 75mm and 105mm), 206 jeeps, and 133 trailers loaded with ammunition and supplies.[77]

At 1000 hours on D+2, the third and final lift, comprising 406 C-47s and Wacos, was to arrive at landing zone "T" carrying Billingslea's 325th Glider Infantry Regiment along with Batteries C, D, E, and F of the 80th Airborne Antiaircraft Battalion; Headquarters and A Company of the 307th Airborne Engineer Battalion; and the division Military Police Platoon, a total of 3,385 troopers, 104 jeeps, 59 trailers, and an additional twenty-five artillery pieces. After assembling, Billingslea's 325th was to become the division reserve and be prepared to assault into the city of Nijmegen.[78]

Although satisfied with his plan, Gavin was concerned about the size of his airhead. He recognized that, until being reinforced, there "would be huge gaps in the perimeter that I was to seize and defend," a perimeter that he estimated would be about twenty-five miles in diameter. He therefore had had to make some difficult decisions when allocating his troopers against particular objectives. His intent, in full light of the risks, was to take the objectives first and then deal with the gaps later.[79] When Gavin explained what the 82nd was to accomplish to his staff, they were stunned. His chief of staff, Colonel Wienecke, protested, "We'll need two divisions to do all that." "There it is," replied Gavin, "and we're going to do it with one."[80]

Gavin was also concerned with his veterans:

> They had been through many difficult battles, and many of them had been wounded, some several times. I knew practically all the survivors personally, and I knew what went on in their minds. They were well aware of our heavy losses in the past, and to ask them once again to jump into combat more than fifty miles behind the German lines in broad daylight was asking a great deal. I remembered Lord Moran's *The Anatomy of Courage*. His book was based on World War I experience, and from it he concluded that courage, for

> every man, is like a bank account—it can be overdrawn. The parachute veterans, although quite fatalistic, believed that the odds went up significantly with further exposure to combat, no matter how experienced or how careful you were.[81]

Gavin was right. The troopers were fatalistic, but not humorless. According to Private Philip H. Nadler of the 2/504th, while briefing the mission Nadler's platoon leader "grabbed the opportunity to be dramatic. With a pointer in his hand he threw back the cover of the sand table and said, 'Men, this is our destination,' and pointed to a sign on the table—'GRAVE.'" "Yeah, we know that," cracked Nadler, "but what country are we dropping into?"[82]

At 1630 hours, 16 September, Brereton met with his weather experts. A high-pressure area approaching from the southwest would bring early-morning fog, but the outlook was generally favorable through 20 September.[83] At 1900 hours, Brereton gave the go order: "Confirmed MARKET Sunday 17 Sept. . . . All informed. . . . Acknowledge."[84] The largest airborne operation in history was set to commence.

CHAPTER 16

A SUNDAY DRIVE IN AN AIRPLANE

At 1400 hours local time on 17 September 1944, Lieutenant Joseph Enthammer, a Wehrmacht artillery officer, was gazing in the direction of Oosterbeek [Holland, a suburb of Arnhem] when he detected what appeared to be white snowflakes hanging in the air. "That cannot be," he wondered; "it never snows in September! They must be parachutists!"

They were. It certainly does not snow in September. The war had reached the Reich. The blow, moreover, had come as a total surprise.

—ROBERT J. KERSHAW, *"IT NEVER SNOWS IN SEPTEMBER": THE GERMAN VIEW OF MARKET-GARDEN AND THE BATTLE OF ARNHEM, SEPTEMBER 1944*

ON THE DAY "Pip" Roberts's 11th Armored Division liberated Antwerp, Generaloberst Kurt Student received a phone call at his Berlin-Wannsee headquarters from a frantic Generaloberst Alfred Jodl, Hitler's chief of operations. Jodl told Student that his skeleton staff had been redesignated *First Parachute Army* (a "rather high[-]toned title," thought Student) and that he and this newly minted army were to proceed at once to Generalfeldmarschall Walter Model's *Army Group B* headquarters.[1] Student's mission, continued Jodl, was to "collect all available units together and build a new front at the Albert Canal," a new front that was "to be held at all costs!"[2]

Student met with Model the next day at the latter's headquarters. The situation, Model informed his new army commander, was grim. According to the official order of battle *Army Group B* had sixteen infantry and eleven panzer or panzer grenadier divisions. But in reality, warned Model, the army group's total infantry strength amounted to no more than four full-strength divisions, and many of the panzer and panzer grenadier divisions had been reorganized into smaller regimental-size *Kampfgruppen* with an average of only five to ten tanks apiece. Moreover, General der Infanterie Gustav von Zangen's *Fifteenth Army* defending the Scheldt Estuary was in danger of being cut off, while General der Panzertruppen Erich Brandenberger's *Seventh Army* was barely holding against the U.S. First Army's advance on Aachen. In between was a sixty-mile gap stretching from Antwerp to Maastricht. It was that gap that Student's *First Parachute Army* was to fill. And there was one more thing, concluded Model—his forces were in headlong retreat.[3]

The Dutch called 5 September, the day of the Model-Student conference, *Dolle Dinsdag*—"Mad Tuesday"—the day that the flight from Holland of Dutch Nazis and their German overseers reached its peak. A few days before Dr. Arthur Seyss-Inquart, the Reichskommissar for Holland, and Anton Mussert, the Dutch Nazi Party leader, issued orders to evacuate to the east. Almost immediately Holland's railway stations were jammed with some 65,000 Dutch Nazis clambering aboard anything heading toward Germany. The German occupiers, meanwhile, simply confiscated anything with wheels or hooves to carry them and their belongings back to the Fatherland. Panic spread like a contagion, infecting the military as well. German soldiers threw away their weapons and begged or coerced civilians to give them clothes so they could avoid military police checkpoints.[4] SS-Rottenführer (Corporal) Wolfgang Dombrowski of the *9th SS Panzer Division* recalled that the situation was so desperate that "it seemed impossible that a front could be built out of these disparate fleeing elements." Feldwebel (Sergeant) Erich Hensel, an Eastern Front veteran who was no stranger to defeat, was likewise taken aback. "The retreat from France was the first time I had ever seen demoralised German units," he recalled.[5]

For some time Allied intelligence reports had been indicating that the German army was on the verge of collapse. The 23 August SHAEF intelligence summary stated with categorical certainty that "the August battles have done it and the enemy in the West has had it. Two and a half months of bitter fighting have brought the end of the war in Europe within sight, almost within reach."[6] British I Airborne Corps intelligence reports echoed this view, holding that "once the crust of resistance in the front line had been broken, the German Army would be unable to concentrate any other troops in sufficient strength to stop the break-through," and British XXX Corps, racing up the airborne corridor, should be able to "reach the ZUIDER ZEE [ninety-nine miles away] between 2–5 days after crossing the BELGIAN-DUTCH frontier."[7] And just four days before the start of MARKET-GARDEN, British 1st Airborne Division intelligence calculated that German forces in Holland were nothing more than infantry reserves backed by not more than one hundred tanks. "It was thought," continued this intelligence report, that "the enemy must still be disorganized after his long and hasty retreat from south of the River Seine and that though there might be numerous small bodies of enemy in the area, he would not be capable of organized resistance to any great extent."[8] When Browning issued the order for MARKET-GARDEN, therefore, it was based on the premise that the airborne divisions would not encounter any significant or organized enemy forces.

There had been some opposing views in the Allied camp, but not only were they discounted, so was the evidence on which they were based. On 5 September ULTRA reported that on the previous day Model ordered the *2nd*, *116th*, *9th SS*, and *10th SS Panzer Divisions* to move to the Venlo-Arnhem-'s Hertogenbosch area to refit, which placed them squarely in the MARKET-GARDEN target area, and on 6 September ULTRA intercepted an order directing *II SS Panzer Corps* to move to the same general vicinity. Furthermore, Dutch resistance reported that German army and SS troops had moved into the Arnhem area and that they had tanks with them.[9] Based on these and other indicators, one of the first to challenge prevailing orthodoxy about an impending German collapse in the west was Patton's intelligence chief, the prescient Colonel Oscar W. Koch (Koch was one of the only intelligence officers to later predict the German counteroffensive through the Ardennes in December 1944). The German retreat "has not been a rout or mass collapse," he contended. Conversely, in his view the enemy "has been able to maintain a sufficiently cohesive front to exercise an overall control of his tactical situation. . . . Barring internal upheaval in the homeland and the remoter possibility of insurrection within the Wehrmacht, it can be expected that the German armies will continue to fight until destroyed or captured."[10] Koch, however, was not directly involved with the planning for MARKET-GARDEN, and so his views could and, in many circles were, chalked up to either insufficient information or a parochial attempt to undermine Montgomery's grand plan. Yet two others who were involved with the planning were equally pessimistic. They, too, were quieted.

The first was Eisenhower's chief of staff, Lieutenant General "Beetle" Smith. Privy to ULTRA intercepts as well as the Dutch Resistance reports, Smith became increasingly concerned about the prospects for MARKET-GARDEN's success, especially with regard to the fight he feared the British 1st Airborne Division would face, if, in fact, the *9th* and *10th SS Panzer Divisions* were where they were reported to be. So, with Eisenhower's permission, Smith flew to 21st Army Group headquarters to suggest that either a second airborne division be dropped near Arnhem or one of the U.S. divisions be redirected to Arnhem. According to Smith, Montgomery "ridiculed the idea" and "waved my objections airily aside."[11]

The second was Major Brian Urquhart (no relation to the British 1st Airborne Division commander), Browning's intelligence chief. He, too, saw the Dutch Resistance reports (although not the ULTRA intercepts) and approached both Browning and his chief of staff, Colonel Gordon Walch, with his concerns. According to Urquhart, "They seemed little concerned and became quite annoyed when I insisted on the danger. They said, as I remember, that I should not worry unduly, that the reports were probably wrong, and that in any case the German troops were refitting and not up to much fighting." But Urquhart persisted and ordered, with Browning's reluctant consent, low-level reconnaissance flights of the Arnhem area. The pictures confirmed Urquhart's worst fears. "There were German tanks and armoured vehicles parked under the trees within easy range of the 1st Airborne Division's main dropping zone. I rushed to General Browning with this new evidence, only to be treated once again as a nervous child suffering from a nightmare. Even in my overwrought state I got the message very clearly. I was a pain in the neck, and only our long association and his natural kindness prevented the general from saying so." Although he did not use the term, in Urquhart's mind Browning and the British I Airborne Corps staff were suffering from "victory disease." "There seemed to be a general assumption that the war was virtually over and that one last dashing stroke would finish it," said Urquhart. "The possibility of German opposition was scarcely considered worthy of discussion. The 'Market-Garden' operation was constantly referred to as 'the party.'"[12]

It was a party that Urquhart, because of his naysaying, would not be allowed to attend. Not long after delivering his news about tanks at Arnhem, Colonel Arthur Eagger, I Airborne Corps's chief medical officer, approached Urquhart and suggested that he go on sick leave. When Urquhart protested and requested that he be allowed to "go on the operation in any capacity," he was refused. When he asked "if there was no way of stopping, or at least reshaping, the operation," Eagger again said no.[13]

Doubtless, both Smith and Urquhart would have given anything to have been wrong. Unfortunately, they were not. Not only were there panzers near Arnhem, but following "Mad Tuesday" there occurred the near-miraculous regeneration of German forces throughout Holland.

"In every country that has been engaged in a long war there are half-forgotten formations which have come to exist almost in their own right," explained General Horrocks. In Holland, "the most important of them were the Parachutists, . . . [who were] mainly engaged in training recruits and scattered through the Netherlands and Western Germany," but also present were "considerable numbers of well-trained men in Luftwaffe and naval units, as well as the battle-hardened Panzer troops who had escaped from Normandy." These "not easily identifiable" yet "valuable assets" were what Model and Student used to fashion a force that would stymie XXX Corps every step of the way.[14]

From Student's perspective, the first thing to do was to get something into the gap for which he was responsible. To this end, following his meeting with Model, Student took control of the *LXXXVIII Corps* headquarters, which he used to organize the disparate mass of occupation, training, and antiaircraft units in the area into a coherent force, and the *719th Infantry Division*, a fortress unit with limited mobility that he placed in static positions along the Albert Canal. Student also took under wing a second division-size unit, *Kampfgruppe Chill*, a "crazy-quilt mob" pieced together by Generalleutnant Kurt Chill that Student found occupying positions along the eastern end of the Albert Canal.[15] Together, *Kampfgruppe Chill* and the *719th Division* contained a British bridgehead over the Albert Canal and gave Student enough time to bring forward a third division, albeit one composed primarily of convalescing soldiers, the *176th*. Hence, by 7 September, three days after he was told to form an army from scratch, Student had assembled the equivalent of three divisions that, though of dubious quality, proved just enough to hold the British in place while he formed a more formidable fighting force to their rear.[16]

The core of that force was German paratroopers. In his capacity as chief of German parachute troops, Student moved several independent battalions and regiments of German paratroopers, a parachute antitank battalion, and some 5,000 service troops to Holland. From this mass, he fashioned two more division-size combat units: *Kampfgruppe Walther* and the *7th Parachute Division*. This brought Student's fighting complement to five divisions, two of which were top quality, all of which were assembled in an area that, days before, was almost devoid of German combat formations.[17]

Model, too, had been hard at work, scratching together forces with which to back *First Parachute Army*. To do so he extricated most of *Fifteenth Army* from the area south of the Scheldt Estuary. Working day and night under a constant rain of Allied aerial and artillery bombardment, *Fifteenth Army* salvaged elements of nine infantry divisions comprising some 86,000 men, more than 600 artillery pieces, 6,000 vehicles, and 6,000 horses.[18] Model placed these forces, which ranged from "a collection of chaff that even a mild wind might blow away" to units with better-than-average combat power, behind the west wing of Student's army.[19] Model next tasked the German occupation headquarters, *Armed Forces Command Netherlands*, to organize the myriad service, logistics, regional defense, and training formations in the country into a rear-area security force, thereby freeing the *First Parachute* and *Fifteenth Armies* to concentrate on the Allied forces to their front. Finally, Model reorganized *Wehrkreis VI*—a regional headquarters responsible for that portion of Germany abutting Holland—into a whole new corps, which he named *Corps Feldt* (after its commander, General der Kavalerie Kurt Feldt) and another division, which he christened the *406th Landesschuetzen Division.*[20]

By 17 September, therefore, the conditions under which MARKET-GARDEN was conceived had changed significantly. No longer was Holland a transit point for broken German units fleeing one step ahead of 21st Army Group. In less than two weeks' time Student and Model had stopped the retreat, formed one entirely new army, extricated the bulk of a second army from almost certain encirclement, and fashioned a rear-area security force where none had before existed. And as luck would have it—and it was luck, not foreknowledge, as some have contended—Model also situated two SS panzer divisions and an SS panzer corps headquarters in the very area where the British 1st Airborne Division was to drop. As SS-Obergruppenführer Wilhelm Bittrich, commander of the *II SS Panzer Corps*, recounted, "There was no particular significance in Model choosing the Arnhem vicinity—except that it was a peaceful sector where nothing was happening."[21]

Allied intelligence was not blind to what had occurred in Holland, but the prevailing attitude was that although the retreat had stopped, stiff resistance was unlikely. The SHAEF intelligence summary of 16 September 1944, for example, recognized that "the sector between MAASTRICHT and ARNHEM, which looked at first as though it was going to be able to offer little resistance, did eventually, with the help of elements of Fifteenth Army from across the SCHELDT Estuary and of First Parachute Army from NANCY with a collection of tough oddities, manage to stiffen considerably, and is now more or less holding." The same summary then downplayed their combat effectiveness, reporting that although "First Parachute Army has energetically taken over the ANTWERP-HASSELT Sector from C-in-C NETHERLANDS, [it] has contributed little more than the glamour of its name, that little being the remnants of the two or three parachute divisions."[22]

In hindsight, it is difficult to reconcile the intelligence reports of panzers around Arnhem and stiffening German resistance throughout Holland with the myopia with which the Allies, in particular Montgomery and Browning, approached MARKET-GARDEN. According to Major Urquhart, "Browning's ambition to command in battle was a major factor both in the conception of 'Market-Garden' and in his refusal to take the latest news on German opposition seriously." Montgomery, on the other hand, simply downplayed the threat. "We knew it [*II SS Panzer Corps*] was there," he later wrote. "But we were wrong in supposing that it could not fight effectively; its battle state was far beyond our expectation."[23] On balance, however, neither Browning's ambition nor Montgomery's insouciance provides an adequate explanation for the "ahead at all costs" attitude they and so many others adopted in the days leading up to MARKET-GARDEN. Instead, it was the insightful Horrocks who perhaps best explained why the operation went ahead despite so much uncertainty.

According to Horrocks, it was simple. They—SHAEF, 21st Army Group, First Allied Airborne Army, and British I Airborne Corps—"were determined not to scrap once again the operation of the Airborne Army." There was a lot of pressure from Washington "to use this powerful force in one magnificent gesture to finish the war in 1944, and Montgomery eagerly grasped the chance of an advance at last on a narrow front, which had originally been turned down by Eisenhower."[24] By 16 September, therefore, Montgomery had achieved what he wanted, irreversible momentum. Only one thing could have stopped the operation—weather. It almost did.

Maddeningly for those who banked so much on MARKET-GARDEN, Sunday, 17 September 1944, dawned overcast and drizzly in England, but by 0900 hours, the sun had come out and burned off the haze to reveal a bright, almost cloudless sky. Visibility was anywhere from four to six miles with a cloud base of 2,500 feet. MARKET-GARDEN was a definite go.[25]

Arising at dawn, the troopers of the 82nd Airborne Division ate a breakfast-dinner mix of hot cakes and syrup, fried chicken with all the trimmings, coffee, and apple pie. "It was as if the condemned were being served a hearty meal," recalled Lieutenant James Megellas of the 504th.[26] After breakfast the troopers attended religious services, wrote letters, rested, or contemplated what lay ahead. Some, like Megellas, were "happy and anxious to return to action." "We recognized that a job had to be done . . . ," and "we accepted that fact that this was a fight to the finish and we were eager to get on with the job." Others, like Private Donald D. Lassen of the 2/505th, were a bit more subdued. "No one was anxious to get into combat . . . [but] we all knew we had a job to do," said Lassen. Furthermore, "we got ourselves into this outfit, we knew what was required and we did it because it had to be done." Captain Jack R. Isaacs of the 3/505th echoed Lassen's sentiments. "While we had approached previous assignments with a great deal of spirit and élan I think for this operation we had begun to develop a methodical, calculating cunning which came to full fruition a few weeks later in the Battle of the Bulge." Lieutenant James E. Baugh of the 80th Airborne Antiaircraft Battalion, felt that MARKET-GARDEN "was a show the Generals wanted." Having been in all the "hot spots" before, Baugh was "cynically fatalistic" and saw no end "to the missions for us until Tokyo had capitulated." Still, Baugh recognized in his troopers a "determination to excell [*sic*]," because "we truly felt we were the best soldiers in the world." Lieutenant Jack Tallerday of the 1/505th, who had already made three combat jumps and been wounded twice, was "not exactly over-eager," but he was certain that his unit was "combat ready" and was relieved that "the suspense of waiting was now over." Finally, there were the new troopers like Lieutenant Hanz Karl Druener of the 2/504th, who was "somewhat anxious not having been in combat before." "However," continued Druener, "training with my platoon which included many troopers and non-commissioned officers who had participated in prior combat jumps had the effect of [my] 'looking forward' to the operation."[27]

At about 0930 hours, the troopers boarded trucks and buses for the flight line. Once there, jumpmasters rechecked the "para racks" in which were contained the extra ammo, explosives, mortar tubes, and the disassembled 75mm howitzers to ensure that the loads were secure and that the release mechanisms functioned properly, while the rest of the paratroopers began their now familiar routine of turning themselves into human pack mules. Besides parachutes, helmets, and musette bags, each trooper carried his individual weapon and at least one sidearm, ammunition, grenades, antitank mines, at least one knife, first-aid packets, and two days' worth of rations. Each man was also issued two maps—one 1:50,000-scale map of the objective area and one 1:200,000-scale escape map of the Netherlands printed on silk—as well as partial pay in Dutch, Belgian, and German currency and an orange armband that would identify him as a friend of the Dutch Resistance.[28]

The great armada started taking to the air from scores of airfields throughout England shortly after 1000 hours. Ninety minutes later 1,534 troop carrier aircraft and 491 gliders were in the air headed toward the Continent.[29] Correspondent Martha Gellhorn, observing from below, remembered "the endless flying wedge of transport planes and the gliders with men crowded in those canvas cockleshells without parachutes moved through the sky like an enormous procession of clay pigeons."[30] Clay pigeons they were, but well-protected pigeons as swarms of British and American fighters and fighter-bombers rose to escort the lumbering transports from the coast of England all the way to the target areas and back.

The P-38s, P-47s, P-51s, Tempests, Spitfires, and Mosquitoes darted in and around the troop carrier columns, keeping a sharp lookout for any sign of the enemy both in the air and on the ground.[31] Seeing so many friendly fighters set Captain Hugo Olson's mind at ease. "They seemed to be all over. We had a lot flying top cover and there were others . . . sweeping in and out of our formations." The "fighters gave us excellent support," stated Lieutenant Colonel Charles H. Young, commander of the 439th Troop Carrier Group, the seventh of the 82nd's D-day parachute serials. "Four of them shot up a gun position on a docked ship at the east end of Schouwen [Island] right under our noses before they could fire a shot at us. Every direction we looked, up, down, sideways, we saw airplanes." Sergeant Albert A. Tarbell of the 3/504th recalled that when a battery opened up, "immediately a fighter plane swooped down on it like a hawk after a chicken and knocked it out." Olson said that the first indication that they were taking any fire at all was when "puffs of smoke" appeared below them, and just as suddenly "one of the fighters would peel off and dive on it." Many of the flak batteries had already been bombed and strafed both the night before and earlier that morning. What remained for the escorts was to mop up. Resistance was so slight that Lieutenant John A. Holabird of the 307th Airborne Engineers likened the flight to "a picnic, a Sunday drive in an airplane."[32]

The Luftwaffe made two forays against the aerial convoys that day, both along the Southern Route on which the 101st flew. None of the German interceptors got close to the troop transports.[33] German flak, on the other hand, accounted for 35 American transports, 13 gliders, and 22 fighters destroyed.[34]

The 82nd's D-day parachute echelon lost 10 aircraft.[35] In every case the paratroopers had already jumped or were able to jump before the plane crashed. Only one plane, carrying sixteen H Company, 3/504th, troopers, was shot down before reaching Grave. Lieutenant Virgil Carmichael saw it happen: "The pilot, although the aircraft was involved [*sic*] in flames, somehow kept the plane steady until the paratroopers jumped. . . . The Air Corps used white chutes, so I figured it had to be the crew chief. He was the last man out. Almost immediately the blazing plane nose-dived and, at full throttle, plowed into a flooded area . . . below. On impact, a white chute billowed from the plane, probably ejected by the force of the crash." Lieutenant Allen F. McClain III also saw the plane go down. Like Carmichael, he counted parachutes and recalled that "at the precise time the C-47 was hit, a P-47 Fighter plane came out of nowhere and knocked out the anti-aircraft gun emplacement."[36] Some of the troopers from this plane eventually made it to friendly lines with the help of the Dutch Resistance; others were taken prisoner, but all survived. Of the remaining planes lost in the 82nd's D-day echelon, 6 were shot down over the objective area, where the flak grew significantly more intense and the planes, flying at five hundred feet and slowed to drop speed, were easy targets. Two collided over Holland on their way back to England. The last ditched at sea, also on the way back to base. Besides these losses, 118 other planes carrying 82nd paratroopers were damaged, 20 so badly that they required salvage or lengthy repairs. Most of the damage was to planes that had dropped on drop zone "T" because they had to make their turn for home over the Reichswald, where hidden guns put up some of the most intense antiaircraft fire encountered anywhere that day.[37] Captain Donald M. Orcutt piloted one of the planes and remembered the flak being so heavy that

> it formed a veritable cloud layer of black smoke at our flight level. The lead airplanes in our serial disappeared from view as they flew into this black cloud. I thought they couldn't possibly survive this hail of enemy fire, and I tried to make myself as small as possible in the hope that I could pass through without being shot down.
>
> Amazingly, the lead airplanes emerged on the other side just as my squadron was entering the black cloud. My navigator, Lt. Michael Whitfill, shouted that he could hear hits being scored on us. Indeed he had. When we got back to England, we counted more than 100 bullet and shell-splinter holes in our C-47.[38]

Aircrews were told to take no evasive action en route to their drop zones. They were to remain on course, descend to jump altitude, slow to jump speed, and drop their paratroopers or release their gliders as planned. No one was to return with a full load.[39] That day Captain Orcutt and thousands of his fellow pilots completed their charge magnificently.

The first 82nd troopers to jump were pathfinders from the 504th flying in two C-47s from the IX Troop Carrier Command's Pathfinder Group. Unlike the main body, they approached the objective area by way of the Southern Route without incident. When the C-47s descended to drop altitude and slowed to drop speed, however, some antiaircraft guns near Grave opened up; just as quickly they were silenced by a flight of P-47s. Consequently, at 1247 hours the pathfinders landed squarely on drop zone "O" with no injuries. Three minutes later, despite sporadic sniper fire, their navigational aids were up and operating.[40]

The first three serials carrying the division command element and the 505th Parachute Infantry Regiment arrived approximately fifteen minutes later. The lead serial, carrying Ben Vandervoort's 2/505th and the regimental headquarters section, veered slightly north after passing drop zone "O" to avoid flak from some hitherto silent antiaircraft guns and made its drop one to three miles northeast of drop zone "N," the intended drop zone. "Hitler, count your men," shouted Private Earl W. Boling of E Company before exiting. "We are coming down."[41] And come down they did, right on top of six 20mm antiaircraft guns that opened up as soon as they started jumping. One trooper, Private Fred Hebein, actually landed in one of the gun positions, his chute draped over the gun tube.[42] Another, Private Edwin C. Raub, steered his bullet-riddled chute as close as he could to another gun position and, without removing his harness, killed one German, captured the rest of the crew, and disabled the gun.[43] According to Gavin, many troopers jumped with their pistols in hand or readily accessible so they could fire back at the Germans while drifting toward the ground. "Troopers talking about it later recalled it as being pretty silly because they were just as likely to shoot themselves as the Germans." It also seemed foolish to fire at such big guns with only a .45-caliber pistol, but "fortunately for the troopers, their mere arrival caused most of the Germans manning the antiaircraft batteries to scatter and disperse in the interest of survival." One lieutenant told Gavin that he saw a young German throw down his rifle and run toward the border at the sight of so many paratroopers; the lieutenant let him go, not having it in him to shoot an unarmed boy running for home. Captain Robert M. Piper had a similar experience. There were "three Germans manning a machine gun and they were firing at us as we came down," he recalled, "but seeing so many parachutists that were armed and would be landing on top of them they stopped firing and were standing outside their gun position with their hands in the air waiting to surrender as soon as we could get out of our chutes."[44] Despite the antiaircraft fire, the 2/505th sustained few casualties, and within thirty-five minutes the battalion was assembled and moving toward its objective, a wooded hill about one mile west of Groesbeek. Along the way a heady Vandervoort moved through the ranks dispatching praise for the manner in which the battalion had assembled so quickly until one hard-bitten trooper reminded him, "Hell, Colonel, everybody knows you can move a lot faster when you're being shot at."[45]

Next to arrive was Major James L. Kaiser's 3/505th. Landing squarely on drop zone "N," within thirty minutes it was moving toward its objective, the town of Groesbeek, which fell after G and H Companies (along with elements of Vandervoort's 2/505th) easily swept through the German defenders, some one hundred of whom were taken prisoner. Accompanying the 3/505th was the regimental surgeon, Major Daniel B. McIlvoy, who accounted for one of the prisoners taken that day. McIlvoy cracked his ankle on landing and while hobbling around collecting his medics took possession of a wood-burning ambulance and its German driver, "whom we had little or no difficulty in persuading to join us." Loading himself, his medics, and their equipment into the ambulance, their prisoner-driver at the wheel ("a very jovial German . . . who stuck with us a considerable part of this campaign until the higher echelon caused us to release him"), they joined Kaiser's column heading to Groesbeek. Along the way they witnessed another unusual capture. As the column approached a crossroads outside of town, "we noticed a Volkswagen coming down the column and it passed about three-fourths of the column before it finally dawned on someone that the American Army had no Volkswagens and those troops in the back stopped the vehicle and a German officer got out and surrendered."[46]

With Groesbeek secure, Kaiser turned his attention to manning his portion of the division perimeter, a two-mile arc that stretched generally northeast to southeast of Groesbeek, facing the German border. By dark, he had established a series of strongpoints and roadblocks on commanding terrain and astride major avenues of approach. Kaiser also sent a patrol under Lieutenant Cletus C. Asbra to reconnoiter the Reichswald; Asbra reported back that although he ran into stiff opposition, the woods were simply too thick to house armor.[47]

The third serial carried the 1/505th. It, too, had a perfect drop on drop zone "N," quickly assembled, and moved out toward its assault objectives. Specifically, the 1/505th was to man that portion of the division perimeter almost due south of Groesbeek and seize a railroad bridge over the Maas just north of Mook, a village about three miles southwest of Groesbeek. In carrying out these missions the 1/505th experienced the regiment's heaviest fighting on D day, in particular B Company, for it was to that company that Major Talton W. Long, the battalion commander, assigned the Mook bridge mission (Mook itself was also to be taken, but was of secondary importance to the bridge). The B Company commander, Lieutenant Harold E. Miller, sent his First and Third Platoons to the bridge; Second Platoon, meanwhile, was to establish a roadblock in the vicinity of Riethorst, an even smaller village about one and a half miles southeast of Mook, the southernmost point of the division's perimeter.[48]

Led by Lieutenant Stanley Weinberg, Second Platoon moved out at about 1400 hours. Just outside Riethorst, Dutch civilians informed him that some Germans were setting demolition charges in a nearby ammunition dump. Before Weinberg could react the dump exploded, so Weinberg led his troopers through what remained of the ammunition dump and on into Riethorst, which they cleared by 1530 hours, killing a German colonel along the way and taking eight prisoners. An hour later, after having positioned his platoon to defend Riethorst, Weinberg received word that one of his outposts was engaging a large enemy force approaching from the southeast. Sergeant Frederick Gaugler, in command at the outpost, opened up on the Germans with everything he had; at one point his troopers were firing so furiously that their machine guns overheated, so the gunners continued the fight with their .45s. Despite mortar rounds landing right on their position, Gaugler and his troopers held against repeated assaults until the Germans withdrew. Meanwhile, because Riethorst was key terrain—it sat on some high ground that commanded Mook and the surrounding area—Major Long reinforced Weinberg with First Platoon of C Company under Lieutenant Harold L. Gensemer. It was a propitious move, for the Germans, too, knew Riethorst was key terrain and in the next several days would try desperately to take it back.[49]

The First and Third Platoons of B Company, moving on the Mook railroad bridge, were not as successful. Not long after moving out they ran into a German platoon. The ensuing firefight did not last long, and the German defenders were anything but resolute—all thirty-three eventually surrendered—but taking the bridge depended on speed and surprise, both of which were now compromised. Still the two platoons continued their advance until, some four hundred yards from the bridge, they encountered a second group of more determined defenders. Fighting their way through the German positions, the troopers got all the way to the bridge before it blew in their faces, killing two troopers and wounding three others. With no bridge to take, the platoons returned to the drop zone, albeit with seventeen more prisoners (B Company took Mook the next day).[50]

At 2000 hours Colonel Ekman reported that he could account for more than 95 percent of his regiment and that his defensive sector was manned. Given the length of the area the 505th had to cover, "manned" really meant a loose cordon of strongpoints and roadblocks that described a rough semicircle that began southwest of Groesbeek and ran south, east, and northeast of the town. Though frequent patrols ranged the area between the strongpoints and roadblocks, the line was, to say the least, porous. Fortunately for the 505th, its first night in Holland was relatively quiet. But it would not remain so for long.[51]

Following the 505th's serials were the planes carrying the 504th headed for drop zone "O" (with the exception of those carrying the company that was to drop on "Special DZ"). They came "right in on the button."[52] "If ever we made a perfect jump," said Captain T. Moffatt Burriss, "this was it. . . . None of our practice jumps had ever gone so well."[53] Indeed, 90 percent of the regiment landed exactly where it was supposed to; the rest landed less than a mile away.[54] And although resistance on the drop zone was slight, the jump did claim the life of one man: Corporal Curtis Morris of E Company, whose parachute malfunctioned when he collided with an equipment bundle in midair. "Dutch farmers came out to assist him as we had to move forward," recalled Morris's company commander, Captain Walter S. VanPoyck. "The next day, in the town of Grave, the farmers delivered his body to us, in a casket, draped in his chute and covered with flowers."[55] Only forty-four others were injured.[56] One of these was Captain Louis A. Hauptfleisch, who landed on top of a building. "I crashed through the tiled roof top and suffered leg injuries as a result, but managed to carry out my assigned duties in the days following."[57]

It was fortunate that the 504th's drop went so well, for Gavin had assigned it not only the most difficult but more assault objectives than any other regiment, a direct reflection of the confidence he had in Tucker and his troopers. These were to seize the 640-foot bridge over the Maas at Grave, clear the town of Grave, secure the Maas-Waal Canal bridges at Heumen and Blankenberg, and clear the area between the Maas-Waal Canal and the Maas River, after which it was to tie in with the 505th on its left and the 508th on its right and defend until relieved by XXX Corps.[58]

The first of Tucker's contingent to drop was Major Willard E. Harrison's 1/504th, which was to secure the canal bridges at Heumen and Blankenberg.[59] Harrison assigned the Heumen Bridge, the southernmost of the Maas-Waal Canal bridges, to B Company and the Blankenberg Bridge, a little more than a mile north of the Heumen Bridge, to C Company; A Company was to take up a supporting position between the two bridges and be prepared to reinforce the attack on either. Because his objectives were so widely dispersed, Harrison instituted an unusual assembly procedure. Instead of assembling in a battalion mass, Harrison instructed his troopers that once they were on the ground, they were to move to a windmill he had identified from aerial photographs where they would check in, drop their excess gear, and then move to link up with their companies as the companies moved toward their respective objectives. In this manner, he hoped to leverage the surprise and shock of the airborne assault to get the bridges before they could be destroyed.[60]

As it turned out the attack on the Blankenberg Bridge was unsuccessful. The Germans blew it just as some troopers were charging onto the bridge's roadway, destroying it beyond repair. The attack on the Heumen Bridge, on the other hand, though prolonged, was ultimately successful.

Taking a cue from his battalion commander, Captain Thomas B. Helgeson's plan for taking the Heumen Bridge was also predicated on shock and surprise. For this reason, instead of leading B Company stealthily cross-country to the bridge, he lined it up on a road and ran straight at it. Amazingly, B Company got to within two hundred yards of the bridge before it was stopped by fire from a blockhouse on an island just north of the bridge, and although several troopers were able to get across the span, they were too few and too exposed to be of any use. Realizing that without the blockhouse in hand the bridge would be impassable and fearing that the Germans inside were waiting, detonator in hand, to blow the bridge when they next saw American soldiers on it, Helgeson tried several assaults on the island, all of which were unsuccessful. The standoff persisted until nightfall when Helgeson infiltrated half his force across the canal and then assaulted the island from both shores. It was over in minutes. At the cost of six dead and one wounded, the island, the blockhouse, and the bridge were firmly in American hands (whether the detonator was in the blockhouse is uncertain, and although the bridge was rigged for demolition, why it was not blown remains a mystery). The 82nd had its first bridge over the Maas-Waal Canal. It would have been for naught, however, had the Grave Bridge not been secured. But it was, and by the time the Heumen Bridge fell, it had been for several hours.[61]

Taking the Grave Bridge and, on order, the city of Grave fell to Major Edward N. Wellems's 2/504th, the second of Tucker's battalions to drop. The plan was for Captain VanPoyck's E Company, dropping on "Special DZ," to assault the west end of the bridge while the rest of the 2/504th, dropping on drop zone "O," assaulted its east end.[62] Like Harrison, Wellems ordered his troopers to assemble on the move, although Wellems went one step further by emphasizing "that if the landing was hampered, all [2/504th troopers] would fight their way to the Grave bridge without organizing tactically."[63] As it turned out, this is exactly what happened.

The first to reach the Grave Bridge were fifteen E Company troopers led by Lieutenant John S. Thompson. The fifteen, all from the same plane, overshot "Special DZ" by several hundred yards because Thompson delayed their exit for a few seconds after the green light flashed on in order to avoid parachuting onto some buildings. This landed them much closer to Grave Bridge than the rest of E Company, but Thompson, in accordance with Wellems's orders, gathered his troopers and moved on the bridge without waiting for the rest of E Company to catch up. Leading Thompson's group was Sergeant Roy E. Tidd, who, not long after moving out, found himself about to get run over by a German column consisting of two motorcycles, two trucks, and two half-tracks that was headed straight for him. Tidd opened up, killed the driver of the lead truck, and, with the exception of the two motorcyclists who sped past him, stopped the column in its tracks. This allowed Thompson and the other troopers to take to some water-filled ditches on either side of the road, which they used for cover to move alongside the stalled column. Then, standing in water that at places was neck deep, the troopers ambushed the column along its length. The Germans, despite their advantage of higher and drier ground, fled.

The fight on the road lasted no more than fifteen minutes, but fearful that word would get back to the bridge that American paratroopers were headed that way, Thompson and his troopers made for the objective with even greater haste. Upon approaching the bridge they saw German soldiers, carrying mysterious bundles, running to and from the bridge and a power plant abutting the bridge's western end. Assuming that the bundles contained explosives and that what they were witnessing was the last-minute preparation of the bridge for demolition, Thompson and his waterlogged troopers attacked, in the process cutting every wire they could find. Within minutes both the power plant and the west end of the Grave Bridge were theirs, as once again the Germans opted to flee rather than resist (it was discovered that the mysterious bundles contained nothing deadlier than underwear, shoes, and toiletries).

With the west end of the bridge in hand, Thompson made his way to the top of the power plant to take a look around. It was there that he discovered the reason for this success, for "evidently there was nobody in command [of the German forces] and there was therefore much confusion."[64] As if to underscore this point, two military sedans suddenly appeared on the road approaching the west end of the bridge. A trooper armed with a BAR took them out, killing the Germans inside to a man. Meanwhile, Private Robert McGraw silenced the last pocket of enemy resistance, an antiaircraft gun atop a tower on the bridge itself, with two rounds from his bazooka.

At about 1500 hours, Thompson was joined by a twelve-man squad led by Staff Sergeant Alek Misseres that, like Thompson's group, had moved on the bridge without waiting for the rest of E Company. With two squads in hand Thompson set about organizing roadblocks, ambush positions, and vantage points. He also fired a green signal flare to denote mission accomplished, and despite some sporadic contact, to include a clash with a German tank that his troopers mistakenly took for a XXX Corps tank before driving it away with bazooka fire, the west end of the bridge remained under his control. Captain VanPoyck, meanwhile, moved with the rest of E Company to a position south of Grave, where it could block attempts to break through to the bridge from that direction.[65]

It was not long after Thompson sent his green flare skyward that the east end of Grave Bridge was likewise secured, in large part by troopers that also missed their drop zone. Lieutenant Martin E. Middleton, F Company's First Platoon leader, was in one of the few planes that missed drop zone "O," landing several hundred yards short of it but several hundred yards closer to the east end of Grave Bridge. As instructed, Middleton set out for the bridge, collecting about twenty troopers along the way, when a member of the Dutch Resistance appeared and told him that he had been sent out to help guide paratroopers to the battalion assembly area. Although clearly a contravention of Wellems's order, for some reason Middleton followed the guide and met up with Wellems, who immediately sent him back toward the bridge with an additional fifteen troopers. Moving along a dike that ran in the direction of the bridge, Middleton next encountered his company commander, Captain Beverly T. Richardson, who told Middleton to continue on while he gathered the rest of F Company and followed. Working their way forward using the ditches and the few houses in the area as cover, Middleton's troopers secured the east end of the bridge without a loss, taking thirteen prisoners and killing five of the enemy in the process. He was joined shortly thereafter by Richardson, Wellems, Tucker, and the rest of F Company.

With such a large force gathered in one place, the Germans were sure to notice, and when they did they turned the fire of several nearby antiaircraft guns on the bridge and the paratroopers at its east end. Unwilling to deplete his force at the bridge for fear that a German counterattack may be coming, Richardson instead dispatched several two- and three-man patrols to silence the guns. They were wildly successful. One patrol took out an entrenched 20mm gun by crawling several hundred yards through water-filled ditches and a fusillade of enemy hand grenades that wounded Private First Class Willard G. Tess thirty-two times. Tess refused evacuation and assaulted and silenced the gun alongside his mates. Another patrol took out three German positions. Led by Lieutenant John E. Schaeffer, who "dashed over open terrain in the face of heavy small arms fire and charged a machine[-]gun position and two protecting riflemen, wounding several enemy soldiers and capturing six," the patrol went on to assault a 20mm gun emplacement, during which Schaeffer single-handedly killed another enemy soldier and took two more prisoner, and then used the captured 20mm gun to kill a German mortar crew.[66] Taking out the last of the German antiaircraft guns was the work of Captain Fordyce Gorham, Tucker's intelligence officer, who rushed one emplacement, killed the crew, and, like Schaeffer, used the captured gun to take out other guns nearby.

Meanwhile, Richardson sent Lieutenant Stuart McCash and one other trooper across the bridge to see who, if anyone, was still there (in all probability Richardson saw Thompson's signal flare, but since Thompson had no radio with him Richardson was uncertain about how things had progressed since then). Braving considerable enemy fire, McCash and the trooper dashed across the bridge, found Thompson, and then dashed back across the bridge with news that Thompson was firmly in command of the west end. Thus, by about 1700 hours, when the last of the German resistance around the east end of the bridge was overcome, Tucker reported that the most critical of the division's D-day bridges was secure. With it and the Heumen Bridge in hand, and the ground between the two cleared of the enemy (a task accomplished by the 3/504th), the vitally important road link necessary to pass XXX Corps on to Nijmegen was established. Tucker and his paratroopers, about 95 percent of whom were accounted for by nightfall, had then but to man the western portion of the division's perimeter and wait for Horrocks's tanks to arrive.[67]

Gavin was pleased with the 504th's performance, especially the 2/504th's action at the Grave Bridge, calling it "one of the best planned and executed operations of its type in the war" because it conformed exactly to certain principles he and his commanders had emphasized time and again in training.[68] The first was that, if possible, a bridge should be attacked from both ends. Second was that when approaching a bridge, leaders should concentrate sniper and small arms fire on its approaches and across the span to deter enemy efforts to emplace demolitions (as had Thompson's group). Third was that all wires leading to the bridge should be cut (troopers at both ends of the bridge did this, using specially issued switchblade knives).[69] Fourth, once the span was in hand, troopers were to "destroy all enemy around the bridge and allow no prisoners to loiter near[by]." And finally, once in control of the bridge and its environs, then and only then should any demolitions be removed.[70] Given these parameters, the taking of the Grave Bridge was both exemplary and a testament to the troopers' training; it would not be the last time they would be called upon to put that training to the test.

Following Tucker's 504th was the seventh serial containing companies B, C, and D of the 307th Airborne Engineer Battalion, thirty-four members of the division artillery headquarters element, and a small advance party from the 456th Parachute Field Artillery Battalion. Dropping on drop zone "N" slightly ahead of schedule, they assembled without incident and set about accomplishing their tasks. For the engineers, this was providing security for the division command post. The artillerymen, meanwhile, reconnoitered positions for the guns scheduled to arrive with the last parachute serial of the day.[71]

Serials eight, nine, and ten contained Lindquist's 508th along with forty pathfinders from the 325th who were to prepare the landing zones for the gliders soon to follow. Flying into the target area, Corporal Edward N. "Toby" Bailey of the 3/508th recalled waiting nervously for the green jump light to flash on when another trooper on his plane shouted, "Stand on your tip-toes boys[,] this is as near to heaven as you will ever get." Somewhat less effusive was Bailey's battalion commander, Lieutenant Colonel Louis Mendez who, before leaving England, gathered the pilots who would be flying his troopers to Holland and put a challenge to them: "Gentlemen . . . my officers know this map of Holland and the drop zones by heart and we're ready to go. When I brought my battalion to the briefing prior to Normandy, I had the finest combat-ready force of its size that will ever be known. By the time I gathered them together in Normandy, half were gone. I charge you: put us down in Holland or put us down in hell, but put us all down together in one place."[72]

Despite receiving heavier fire than any of the preceding serials—twenty-five 508th troopers were injured or wounded before exiting and returned to England, the most of any regiment—the pilots flying the 508th for the most part met Mendez's challenge. The regimental headquarters and most of the 1/508th and 2/508th landed accurately on drop zone "T," which was also ringed with antiaircraft guns. Yet just as had occurred when the 2/505th dropped, as soon as the 508th troopers began descending, most of the enemy abandoned their positions and fled. The pilots of the tenth serial, carrying Mendez's 3/508th, missed their target entirely but, as requested, dropped the battalion all in one place, albeit several hundred yards southeast of the drop zone. All told, of the 132 aircraft carrying the 508th only 6 or 7 missed the drop zone badly. Four or 5 dropped their troopers well short of the drop zone, although in two cases it was because the planes had been hit and were about to crash, while the other premature drops were chalked up to overeagerness on the part of the paratroopers. Two aircraft of the lead serial made an egregious navigational error and dropped twenty-five troopers from A Company, 1/508th, about 2,500 yards east of drop zone "T," which put them just across the international border, near the German town of Wyler. Assembling under the command of Lieutenant Rex Combs, who had been wounded before exiting, the troopers fought their way back to the division area. Along the way they destroyed four German antiaircraft guns and took twenty-three prisoners without losing a man.[73]

The 508th's D-day missions were to seize a series of objectives in the northern portion of the division's defensive area and establish roadblocks on several major roads, especially those that led up to the Groesbeek Heights. It was also to clear and secure the landing zone for the gliders. Finally, in accordance with the verbal instructions Lindquist received from Gavin just before takeoff, if all went well the 508th was to attempt to seize the highway bridge in Nijmegen by coup de main.

The first of Lindquist's battalions to drop was Lieutenant Colonel Shields Warren Jr.'s 1/508th, which was responsible for securing the center of the regimental front, just outside Nijmegen's southern outskirts. Of special import was the Nijmegen-Groesbeek highway, which, if left unguarded, offered untrammeled access to the division's rear. To guard against this, thirty minutes after landing Warren sent a platoon ahead to establish a roadblock on the highway while he gathered the rest of his battalion and followed. It was, said Warren, "a routine cross-country movement . . . enlivened only by the capture of four German labor troopers who surrendered without ado."[74]

The battalion also had with it one unexpected addition, picked up by Lieutenant Woodrow Millsaps, the B Company commander. According to Millsaps, upon landing he was "running all over the place, directing men to the assembl[y] area, sending radio calls, etc.," but eventually noticed that he was being shadowed by a soldier he did not recognize. Several times Millsaps confronted the soldier and told him to go join his platoon, but it was to no avail, as the soldier continued to dog Millsaps everywhere he went. Finally

Millsaps lost his temper, turned on the soldier and told him "for the last time to go to his platoon. He told me he didn't have a platoon. It was then I discovered he was wearing a strange uniform so I asked him what kind of damn dress was that. He told me it was the Air Corps uniform, that he was a member of the crew on one of the planes, and since the plane was on fire and the troopers were jumping he thought it best to go along and jump, too."[75] By 1830 hours, Warren's battalion, plus one man, was in place and digging in.[76]

Major Otho E. Holmes's 2/508th was the next to drop. Its mission was to occupy the sector between the left flank of the 1/508th and the Maas-Waal Canal, a distance of some 3,000 yards, and it was to do this with only two companies; D Company was to remain behind to clear and secure the glider landing zone. Meeting somewhat stiffer opposition that did Warren's battalion—except from a group of Germans who were taken prisoner while playing games on bicycles with their rifles slung over their backs—the rump of Holmes's battalion was in place and digging in by 2000 hours. An attempt that afternoon by Second Platoon of E Company to take the Hatert Bridge over the Maas-Waal Canal (a little more than two miles north of the blown Blankenberg Bridge) was to no avail. When the troopers got to the bridge, they found that it had already been blown.[77]

Mendez's 3/508th was to secure the regiment's right flank by occupying the northern portion of the Groesbeek Heights around the town of Berg en Dal. Assembling quickly, the battalion moved out against almost no opposition and by 1830 hours had secured its objective. Once Berg en Dal was in hand, however, things went awry. Running through Mendez's sector was the international highway linking Nijmegen with Wyler, Germany. Its interdiction was, obviously, critical, so after securing Berg en Dal, Mendez dispatched combat patrols to set up a series of roadblocks along the highway. Two of those patrols never got to the highway. The first, led by Sergeant Henry McLean of H Company, got caught up in Dutch celebrations. McLean admitted making the mistake of walking into a Dutch café in Berg en Dal and being enticed to linger by the offer of beer. A lieutenant eventually found him there and, according to McLean, "raised hell with me for not carrying out my orders," but either because McLean was too drunk or because it was too late in the day, the lieutenant ordered McLean and his troopers back to their platoon instead of on to their roadblock position.[78] A second patrol, comprising an entire platoon from I Company, was to set up a much larger roadblock near the small town of Beek, which was about a mile northeast of Berg en Dal and just on the Dutch side of the international border. It, too, never got into position, a failure Mendez attributed to an uncharacteristic lack of aggressiveness on the part of the officers leading the platoon.[79] The 508th would pay dearly for these mistakes in the days to follow.

The final parachute serial of the day consisted of forty-eight planes carrying the 376th Parachute Field Artillery Battalion to drop zone "N." Although it dropped on target, for some reason the 376th sustained quite a few jump injuries, twenty-four in all, including the battalion commander, Lieutenant Colonel Wilbur Griffith, who, though hobbled, commanded his battalion from a wheelbarrow.[80] Nevertheless, within twenty minutes of landing the artillerymen had one of their 75mm howitzers assembled and ready to fire; by 1700 hours eight guns were ready.[81]

Less than ten minutes after the 376th's drop the 82nd's only D-day glider lift arrived. It started off in England in fifty Waco gliders carrying 216 troopers from A Battery, 80th Airborne Antiaircraft Battalion and sundry headquarters, signal, reconnaissance, and air control personnel as well as twenty-seven jeeps, eight antitank guns, and several trailers loaded with supplies and ammunition. Shortly after takeoff three of the fifty gliders had to abort, two because their tow ropes broke and the third because its load shifted. All three landed safely in England, hooked up again, and subsequently flew to Holland on their own. A fourth glider started breaking up over the sea, was released, and ditched safely. A fifth was hit by antiaircraft fire and, along with its tug, went down just off the coast of Schouwen Island with all hands lost. For the remaining forty-five gliders it was a fairly uneventful flight to landing zone "N"; it is a bit surprising, therefore, that only six actually landed on it. The rest (with the exception of one glider that inexplicably landed eighty-five miles to the southwest) were released about a mile short of the planned release point—probably because by doing so the tugs could make their turn for home before flying over the Reichswald—yet managed to land within a mile of the intended landing zone. All told, 209 troopers, twenty-four jeeps, seven trailers, and, most important, all of the antitank guns made it to the target area safely. Only 7 troopers were injured in the landings.[82]

Following the 82nd's insertions the last Nijmegen-bound serial of the day arrived with Browning's corps command post. Bound for landing zone "N," it took off in thirty-two Horsa and six Waco gliders aboard which were only 105 men but "great quantities of equipment."[83] Brigadier General Floyd Parks visited Browning at the departure airfield to wish him luck and was astounded by the quantity of materiel the corps commander felt he needed. "I took a look in General Browning's glider . . . and I have never seen so much junk. It looked like a gypsy caravan. There were bicycles, bazookas, bedding rolls, radios, and all sorts of stuff he planned to use for his Command Post." Piloting Browning's glider was Colonel George Chatterton, the commander of the British Glider Pilot Regiment. He was not as impressed with the corps commander's stuff as he was with the corps commander himself: "Browning came to the glider immaculately dressed in a barathea battle-dress with a highly polished Sam Browne belt, knife-edge trousers, leather revolver holster, all gleaming like glass, a swagger cane in one hand and wearing kid gloves. He was in tremendous form because he realised that he had reached one of the climaxes of his career."[84] Of the thirty-eight gliders that took off, one Horsa aborted over England, a second over the sea, and a third broke loose over Holland well before the target area. The remaining thirty-five landed safely in the 82nd's area, twenty-eight right on landing zone "N," shortly after 1400 hours. Ninety minutes later Browning's I Airborne Corps command post, all its stuff, and all its men were gathered and in operation on the wooded slopes of the Groesbeek Heights.[85]

By day's end IX Troop Carrier Command had delivered by parachute and glider 7,444 82nd troopers to the Nijmegen area along with twelve artillery pieces, eight antitank guns, twenty-four jeeps, and more than 250 tons of supplies. Only 46 troopers failed to make it to the target area, and of those that did, only 130 sustained landing injuries.[86]

All told 335 British and 1,044 U.S. transports delivered 431 gliders and more than 19,000 troopers to the three MARKET objective areas on D day, and as at Nijmegen, the drops and glider insertions around Eindhoven and Arnhem were generally right on target.[87] Moreover, both the U.S. 101st and the British 1st Airborne Divisions also appeared to be well on their way to securing their portions of the airborne corridor. South of Nijmegen, the 101st took all its bridges intact, save one. The exception was the bridge over the Wilhelmina Canal, which was blown before it could be seized, but by last light on D day a plank bridge had been constructed on its pillars and 101st troopers were advancing southward toward XXX Corps. North of Nijmegen, the British 1st Airborne Division secured its drop and landing zones and was pushing toward the highway bridge in Arnhem, where a spearhead consisting mainly of Lieutenant Colonel John D. Frost's 2nd Parachute Battalion was already ensconced at the bridge's north end.[88]

At 1435 hours, coincident with the last airborne insertions, Horrocks's XXX Corps jumped off following a thirty-five-minute preparatory barrage fired by some 350 guns supported by 100 tank-busting RAF Typhoons. Leading the XXX Corps advance was Lieutenant Colonel J. O. E. Vandeleur's 3rd Battalion, Irish Guards, which, despite the barrage, ran into stiff enemy resistance from the outset. "The leading squadron crossed the Dutch border when, suddenly, nine tanks were knocked out, one after another. We got savage at this and put down yellow smoke wherever we thought the Germans could possibly be. The 'Tiffies' [Typhoons] came cutting in from every angle at zero feet, shooting everything to hell. It was all very thrilling, particularly as the German bazooka boys and [German] parachutists were hopping round the hedge all around us." By day's end Vandeleur's Guards had advanced but eight miles to the town of Valkenswaard, about six miles south of Eindhoven, where it laagered for the night. Montgomery had instructed Horrocks that his advance must be "rapid and violent, and without regard to what is happening on the flanks."[89] Yet for all the combat power Horrocks commanded, achieving any appreciable speed was almost impossible given that all of XXX Corps was constrained to one elevated road that, in many places, was one-tank wide and upon which vehicles appeared to German gunners as perfectly silhouetted targets. Hence, by nightfall, 17 September, the GARDEN portion of MARKET-GARDEN was already behind schedule.[90]

CHAPTER 17

THE GERMANS WERE EVERYWHERE

A well planned and executed airborne operation, like a surprise river crossing or beach landing, is likely to meet light resistance at first, but to have its most difficult fighting later, after the enemy has had a chance to recover from the initial shock and to organize his forces for counterattacks. The critical time for Operation Market would come after D Day.

—JAMES A. HUSTON, *OUT OF THE BLUE: U.S. ARMY AIRBORNE OPERATIONS IN WORLD WAR II*

"**THE ALLIED AIRBORNE** landing was a terrible shock—even to my paratroopers. For at least one or two hours we were not far from a panic"—Oberstleutnant Friedrich-August Freiherr von der Heydte, commander, *6th Parachute Regiment.*[1]

"As the troops were moving off to their quarters and the officers and myself were making for the officers' mess for lunch, we saw the first British parachutes in the sky over Arnhem. . . . It could not be deduced at this stage that a large-scale operation was under-way and we sat down quietly to lunch"—SS-Obersturmbannführer Walther Harzer, commander, *9th SS Panzer Division.*[2]

"The airborne operation came as a complete surprise, hitting [*First Parachute Army*] in the center and splitting it in halves. Actually, it was really obvious to use airborne troops in this situation in order to gain possession of bridges before their demolition. However, both the command and the troops, particularly I and my staff, were all so overtaxed and under such severe strain in the face of our difficult and many-sided mission that we thought only in terms of ground operations"—Generaloberst Kurt Student, commanding general, *First Parachute Army*.[3]

So ran German reactions when thousands of American and British parachute and glider troopers descended on them on 17 September 1944. They knew about First Allied Airborne Army—it had been highly touted in the press—and had been predicting when and where it would be used, but they were wildly inaccurate. For example, on 6 September an *Army Group B* intelligence summary posited that "a large-scale airborne landing by the First Allied Airborne Army north of the Lippe River in the area south of Muenster [approximately fifty miles east of the Rhine] is planned." Model, on the other hand, was certain the Allies would use their airborne army in another NEPTUNE-like assault and consequently ordered *Armed Forces Command Netherlands* to deploy its disparate forces along the Dutch coast.[4] And even after the drops in Holland a megalomaniacal Hitler dismissed them as unimportant, speculating that the real threat the Allied airborne army posed was as a raiding force against his headquarters in East Prussia: "We have to keep in mind—we don't want to be careless anymore—the possibility that they might make a similar mess here. . . . This thing is so dangerous that we have to be clear: if a disaster happens here—here I am, here is my entire Supreme Command, here is the Reichsmarshal, the Army High Command is here, the Reichsführer SS is here, and here is the Reich Foreign Minister! So that's the most valuable catch—that's clear. I would risk two parachute divisions without hesitation if I could get the entire Russian command in one stroke."[5] (Interestingly, Model, whose headquarters was near Arnhem, had a similar reaction to the Allied landings, thinking at first that the whole purpose of the operation was to capture him.)[6]

Such faulty analysis was, in large part, the reason the Allies were able to capture so many bridges intact, for though the Germans expected a major offensive involving First Allied Airborne Army, they did not expect it in Holland. Consequently, they were ill-prepared to counter an airborne assault, especially around Nijmegen and Eindhoven, a point underscored by Oberstleutnant Fritz Fullriede, a regimental commander in the *Hermann Göring Division*, who inspected Nijmegen's defenses just four days before the Allied offensive (the *Hermann Göring Division* had training establishments in Holland, which explains Fullriede's presence in the area). "Drive between Ede-Arnhem and Nijmegen etc. 21st NCO Anw. Company [probably an NCO training school] are securing the bridges at Nijmegen and Grave with totally inadequate forces. The bridges have not even been correctly prepared for demolition. It's criminal."[7]

Besides the flawed intelligence and inadequate preparation were the shock and confusion that gripped German commanders who suddenly found themselves and their units cut off from friendly communications and surrounded by hundreds of Allied airborne troopers. As a result, many simply did nothing, waiting on orders that never came, leaving plenty of time for the airborne troopers to accomplish their D-day missions. In sum, the airborne assault achieved almost complete tactical surprise. But surprise is fleeting.

Gavin was pleased with the results of the first day's fighting, despite being almost crippled or killed. He landed hard in Holland and cracked several vertebrae, although he was not aware of the severity of his injury until much later. Ignoring the pain, he ran off the drop zone into a nearby wood and right into the sights of a German machine gun. Fortunately, his Dutch liaison officer, Captain Arie Dirk Bestebreurtje, was with him and got off a snap shot that hit the enemy gunner square in the forehead. "Whatever your role in this division," commented Gavin as the two stood over the dead German, "you're a mighty handy man to have around."[8] Handy he was. A few minutes later Bestebreurtje spied another German attempting to flee on a bicycle. Again he brought down his target, only to discover that his second victim had with him a briefcase containing the phone numbers and addresses of Germans in the area, many of whom were subsequently rounded up by the Dutch Resistance. Finally, to complete his D-day trifecta, when Bestebreurtje got to Groesbeek he picked up a phone and called trusted agents in both Nijmegen and Arnhem to get a feel for how things were proceeding. The reports were encouraging. This news, on top of the favorable reports received from the regimental commanders during the day, boded well for the operation as a whole.[9]

Ironically, the success enjoyed by the airborne divisions on D day undermined continued success for the next few days. Unlike in Sicily and Normandy, where the scattered drops disguised the intent, the precision with which the British and Americans were dropped in Holland provided a pattern from which MARKET-GARDEN's objectives could be easily discerned, a pattern that became even clearer as the troopers seized their assault objectives. Once cognizant of this, German commanders, at least those at the highest levels, did not hesitate to enact vigorous countermeasures.

One of the first to react was SS-Obergruppenführer Wilhelm Bittrich who minutes after the landings issued a warning order to his units: "Enemy landings. Main point of effort identified around Arnhem and Nijmegen." Accordingly, he ordered the *9th SS Panzer Division* to reconnoiter Arnhem and Nijmegen, take the former, and outpost the bridges with "strong security forces." The *10th SS Panzer Division*, which was in the process of entraining for Germany, was to turn around and "move to Nijmegen and firmly occupy the main bridges, and defend the Nijmegen bridgehead."[10]

Shortly thereafter, Model arrived at *II SS Panzer Corps* headquarters and built upon Bittrich's orders to fashion a plan for the entire battle area. First, he divided it into thirds—Student's *First Parachute Army* was to defend in the south against XXX Corps and the 101st around Eindhoven; the center sector around Nijmegen became the responsibility of *Wehrkreis VI*, which had under its command the *406th Division* and *Corps Feldt*; and the British at Arnhem were to be contained by *Armed Forces Command Netherlands*—and stressed that area commanders were to prevent the Allied forces from linking up with one another. Next he told Bittrich that instead of defending, *II SS Panzer Corps* was to attack to destroy the Allied forces at Arnhem and Nijmegen.[11]

Notwithstanding the speed with which Model and Bittrich responded to the Allied assault, it took some time for their orders to be translated into action. Meanwhile, many German contingents were more intent on escape than with counterattack or defense. Such was the case at Grave.

After securing the Grave Bridge, Major Edward Wellems moved the 2/504th west of the Maas River and repositioned it in a loose cordon around Grave where, for the rest of the afternoon and early evening, his troopers made sporadic contact with small groups of Germans and Dutch Nazis trying to escape. Then, at around 2200 hours, Wellems received a call from Captain VanPoyck, whose E Company was west of Grave. VanPoyck could hear a lot of noise inside Grave, although he could not identify the sounds. Fearing that the Germans were preparing a counterattack, Wellems ordered VanPoyck to investigate. VanPoyck, in turn, told Lieutenant William Sharp to take some troopers with him to find out what was going on.

Sharp led his troopers all the way into Grave before he discovered the source of the noise. It was Dutch civilians, who were parading through the streets celebrating their impending liberation with drink and song. Conversely, the Germans Sharp observed were hurriedly burning papers and packing to leave. In fact, reported Sharp, so intent were the Germans on escaping that although he was certain he had been spotted, he encountered no resistance (Sharp also reported that there were about six hundred German paratroopers in Grave, but this was a mistake, for there were nowhere near that many German *paratroopers* in the area at the time).[12]

Based on Sharp's report, Wellems attacked into Grave with his entire battalion. Resistance was light. Some Gestapo personnel were taken prisoner along with other German stragglers at the cost of a few U.S. casualties. At 0315 hours, 18 September, Wellems radioed Tucker: "Grave buttoned up."[13] The first Dutch city of any appreciable size was in Allied hands.[14]

When the 2/504th entered Grave, the troopers witnessed scenes that would fast become commonplace: Dutch civilians, giddy about their liberation, demonstrating a great capacity for warmth toward the Allies while, at the same time, giving vent to their pent-up hatred of Germans and traitors.

The first civilians Captain VanPoyck encountered when he entered Grave, for example, were the Dutch farmers reverently bearing Curtis Morris's coffin. They were followed by another Dutch delegation composed of "local Boy Scouts [who] conducted a short parade to the town hall, escorting several female collaborators, whose heads had been shaven and marked in pitch with a swastika." According to Captain Robert "Doc" Franco, the 2/505th battalion surgeon, the Dutch could be both "warm & generous, [yet] sound almost vicious when talking about the Germans."[15]

Yet despite the vehemence with which the Dutch dealt with Germans and collaborators, virtually every trooper who fought in Holland remembered the country and its people fondly. Sergeant Earl Boling of the 2/505th remembered the Netherlands as "a beautiful country and the people seemed really happy to see us make the invasion. They were all friendly, wheras [*sic*] in France the people seemed withdrawn awaiting the outcome of the invasion before showing any friendship." "I remember initially how neat, tidy and clean looking the villages, town and countryside were—a distinct contrast to France," recalled Lieutenant Jack Tallerday of the 1/505th. "Many Dutch youths as well as their elders seemed willing to take unnecessary chances or risks to help us." Staff Sergeant Richard Paul Wagner of the 2/325th arrived in Holland several days into the operation by glider and became an immediate witness to Dutch intrepidity. "As soon as we landed and I started to get out of the glider," recalled Wagner, "I was met at the door by members of the underground. One of them asked me in perfect english [*sic*] if there was anything they could do for us or show us."[16] Corporal Charles Fergie of the 505th recalled an incident during which one Dutch family displayed both gratefulness and courage:

> We were fighting for the railroad and I was pinned down in the street in Nijmegen. For a while I thought I couldn't get out without being hit. Finally I got to one of the buildings. There was a Hollander standing there, and he pushed me against the building using himself to protect me. . . . There was a lot of fighting going on, and we were looking for cover. We broke into a house and there was a family there; mother, father and a son and daughter. They were so scared because they thought we were Germans. When they saw that we were American, they were so happy and kissed and hugged us. We stayed there about 24 hours. There was nothing there for them to eat except potatoes, but they cooked up a pot of them and shared them with us. It was the only solid food we had had in a long time. Nothing was too good for us. They were so relieved that we weren't Germans, and that we were going to help liberate their country, they marked the day [on] the calendar in their kitchen.[17]

Indeed, the Dutch helped in any way they could: caring for the wounded, sharing their food, recovering supplies after glider landings or parachute drops, providing intelligence, and taking up arms and fighting alongside the Americans. Captain Bestebreurtje was instrumental in organizing these efforts and eventually had some six hundred Dutch civilians working for him, many of whom were armed with the weapons of troopers who had been killed or wounded.[18] The Dutch, recalled Gavin, "organized and fought as units with us with no protection under the Geneva Convention. They fought in civilian clothes knowing they would be killed if they were captured by the Germans. But they were very courageous people and went right to work with us. They apparently had a very deep hatred for the Germans that came from the occupation as well as their association with the Germans in the past. They fought, and fought well."[19] The aid, assistance, and, most especially, the intelligence the Dutch provided enabled the division to capitalize on the surprise and attendant confusion in the German ranks. In one instance, however, it was the Americans who were taken by surprise, not because of any Dutch perfidy but because, like the airborne assault, it was an event wholly unanticipated.

Running south from Nijmegen to Groesbeek and, from there, east toward Kleve, Germany, was a railroad line that, although clearly marked on the 82nd's maps, seems to have escaped scrutiny. At approximately 2200 hours, 17 September, a trained filled with German soldiers left Nijmegen and passed completely through the 82nd's lines totally unhindered. Major McIlvoy, who was setting up a medical aid station in a girls' school in Groesbeek, remembered the incident vividly:

> About one-half mile from this girl's school there was a railroad crossing with the customary continental pole that comes down when a train passes, etc. Within a matter of short time, less than an hour after moving into this girl's school the gate came down and a train passed. In the car's [*sic*] open doors there were German troops. We waved, they waved back. As it later turned out, this was a train full of German soldiers that had escaped from Nijmegen by simply starting up and driving through our whole troop concentrations, no one stopping to think that this might very well be an enemy train getting out of the area.[20]

The train exited the division's lines through G Company, 3/505th's sector. According to Captain Jack Roger Isaacs, the G Company commander, when his troopers heard the distant rumbling of the train, they thought it was German tanks and prepared for an armor assault. They had, after all, been warned that the Reichswald contained a sizable armor force. No one expected a train, and so stunned were the troopers when one appeared that no one got a shot off.[21]

Gavin was livid, so to prevent a repeat performance he placed Vandervoort's 2/505th in several ambush positions along the tracks. When a second train appeared a short time later Vandervoort's troopers blew the tracks and derailed it, although to make sure it stopped one trooper fired a bazooka round into the locomotive's boiler, while other troopers raked the cars with machine-gun and small arms fire. Most of the Germans inside were either killed or captured. After the firing died down Sergeant Paul D. Nunan of D Company inspected the train to find that it was loaded with "civilian furniture, chinaware, glassware, and other loot," but what really interested him "was a supply of bread, cheese and wine to supplement our 'K' rations." The 2/505th also captured a German officer "resplendent in a dress uniform with much gold trim and impressive insignia." Vandervoort's train robbers were certain they had at least a full colonel on their hands; they were disappointed to discover that their nattily attired prisoner was but a quartermaster lieutenant.[22]

While Germans inside Nijmegen were boarding trains to leave, Lindquist's paratroopers were moving into the city. In accordance with Gavin's instructions to secure the bridge "immediately if this was practicable" once the 508th seized its other assault objectives, Lindquist sent Lieutenant Robert Weaver's Third Platoon of C Company, 1/508th, into the city on a reconnaissance mission.[23] Weaver and Lieutenant Lionel O. Frigo, the battalion intelligence officer who accompanied the platoon, were to "investigate resistance in and around the bridge, and radio back on the strength of the bridge defenses" and "if the bridge was undefended, or lightly defended, to secure it, and immediately radio battalion."[24] They never accomplished their mission.

Weaver's platoon "lost its bearings" shortly after entering Nijmegen and, "after cutting through backyards for a half hour, . . . stopped for orientation." The orientation stop lasted several hours, during which the troopers holed up in a Dutch home while Weaver and Frigo scoured the neighborhood for anyone willing to lead them to their objective. Starting out again at about 2130 hours, this time with a guide, the platoon did not get far before it was ambushed and pinned down on an open street. Within minutes fifteen troopers were wounded, so the platoon withdrew into a warren of side streets, regrouped, cared for the wounded, and then set off again, only to stumble upon another group of paratroopers engaged in a firefight around a traffic circle. Seeing there was no way he would make it to the bridge, Weaver aborted his reconnaissance mission to fight alongside his comrades.[25]

The paratroopers Weaver's platoon stumbled upon were from A and B Companies of the 1/508th. Lindquist sent them into the city to secure the highway bridge after Geert van Hees, a member of the Dutch Resistance, walked into Lindquist's command post shortly after Weaver departed to report that the bridge was lightly defended and ripe for the taking.[26] (Why Lindquist did not communicate this to Weaver is unknown, although it may be that he tried and could not get through because radio performance was notoriously bad in cities, a problem that would bedevil the division throughout its fight in Nijmegen.) Based on Hees's information, Lindquist told Lieutenant Colonel Shields Warren, whose 1/508th was closest to Nijmegen, to assemble A and B Companies, his battalion mortars, and some additional machine guns and make for the bridge under Hees's direction.[27]

While waiting for his companies to gather, Warren and Hees discussed the best route to take. Warren wanted to take the most direct route, but Hees convinced him that a more circuitous route would be better. Warren's route, explained Hees, would necessitate moving through narrow streets where even a few enemy soldiers could hold them up. Moreover, there was at least one German 88mm gun along the direct route that Warren would have to take out before he could get anywhere near the bridge. Instead, Hees recommended that they approach the bridge from the southwest. By following this route they would travel over wide boulevards, thereby retaining their freedom of maneuver. According to Warren, Hees also "stated that the Headquarters of the Dutch resistance movement was in the vicinity of [the Keizer Karel Plein, Nijmegen's main traffic circle, some 700 yards southwest of the bridge]. . . . He reasoned that information re[ference] current German strengths at the bridge would be available there, and of value to my operation. Since this traffic circle was not that great a distance from the bridge, and he knew the city and its people better than I did, I agreed to his plan."[28] Another factor that swayed Warren to Hees's recommendation was that Weaver's platoon had taken the most direct route (or so Warren thought; neither he nor Lindquist knew of Weaver's travails). Sending a second element along the same route would be tempting fate. For some reason, no thought at all was given to the route Gavin recommended, that being through the flatlands east of Nijmegen, which would avoid moving through the city altogether.[29]

The first company to arrive at the rendezvous point Warren had established was Captain Jonathan E. Adams Jr.'s A Company. Anxious to be on his way, at 2030 hours Warren told Adams to move out even though B Company had not yet arrived. Warren and his battalion headquarters element followed. Leading the way was Hees on his bicycle, who rode ahead of the Americans, checked each intersection for signs of the enemy, and then cycled back to give the all clear to the lead scout, Private Walter Dikoon.

At first, the only resistance was from joyous Dutch civilians who plied the paratroopers with sandwiches and cookies.[30] Pushing through the crowds,

Warren's column got all the way to an intersection just south of the Keizer Karel Plein where Hees told Adams to hold up while he rode forward to check in at Resistance headquarters. That was the last the Americans saw of him; Hees was subsequently taken prisoner by SS soldiers who, at that moment, were jumping off trucks and taking up defensive positions around the northern edge of the Keizer Karel Plein.

The SS soldiers were most likely from the *9th SS Panzer Division*'s reconnaissance battalion. Though Bittrich had earlier told the *9th SS* to counterattack at Arnhem, he also tasked it to send an element to cover Nijmegen until the *10th SS* could get turned around. When the *9th SS* soldiers arrived in Nijmegen they found that an Oberst Henke had already organized a defensive scheme centered on the city's two main traffic circles, the Keizer Karel Plein and the Keizer Lodewijk Plein (a smaller traffic circle directly adjacent to the southern end of the highway bridge). Integrating themselves into Henke's defenses, the SS troopers arrived at the north edge of the Keizer Karel Plein at about the same time Adams's company arrived at its southern edge. By that time it was dark, the streets were "pitch black," and neither side knew the other was anywhere near.[31]

When Hees did not return Dikoon and his platoon leader, Lieutenant Fred H. Layman, inched forward to see what was going on. As they approached the Keizer Karel Plein, "a sharp 'Halt,' unmistakeably [*sic*] in German, came through the dark, followed by a prolonged burst of fire from a Schmeiser [*sic*] machine pistol" that killed Dikoon and wounded Layman (the fire most likely came from a German sentry posted at the southern edge of the traffic circle). Intent on getting to the bridge and avoid being pinned down by what might be nothing more than a small patrol, Warren ordered Adams to attack.[32]

With Layman down, whose First Platoon was in the lead, Adams passed Lieutenant George D. Lamm's Second Platoon through the First. "This move was ticklish business," remembered Lamm. "However, the darkness, which contributed to the confusion, also assisted us in reorganizing." Creeping forward to the southern edge of the traffic circle, Lamm saw the unmistakable silhouette of a German antiaircraft gun near its center. Lamm knew it had to be taken out quickly and quietly lest it open up on his troopers with devastating effect. "Instructions were passed along to units: 'Fire only on orders or eyeball to eyeball defense! Use trench knife or bayonet when possible!'"[33]

Advancing shoulder-to-shoulder—"It was so dark, contact was maintained by touch"—Lamm's troopers captured the gun and took its crew prisoner.[34] Other German soldiers were either bayoneted or knifed, some while still in their foxholes. Then, when the Germans on the north side of the traffic circle started firing blindly into the night, Lamm led his platoon in a rush through "fierce fire" and "a hail of grenades" to the far side of the circle, chased away the defenders, and occupied their positions.[35] The rest of A Company, following behind, extended the defensive line left and right. Fifteen minutes later Lieutenant Woodrow Millsaps's B Company also arrived at the traffic circle and occupied its southern edge.[36]

Once in control of the Keizer Karel Plein, and with the enemy having faded into the night, Warren told Adams to find the Dutch Resistance headquarters Hees said was nearby. Adams again called on Lieutenant Lamm. Accompanied by a handful of troopers Lamm found the Dutch headquarters right where Hees said it would be but no one was there, so he returned to the traffic circle only to be sent out again, this time with his entire platoon, to find a post office that intelligence reports indicted housed the demolition controls for the bridge.

With Private First Class William E. Hanft on point (Hanft spoke fluent German and passable Dutch), Lamm's troopers moved stealthily through yards and alleys, silently dispatching several German sentries with their trench knives, and got to the post office without firing a shot. Clearly visible inside the post office were several German soldiers so Captain Adams, who accompanied the platoon, organized a hasty assault. Placing the bulk of the platoon in covering positions, Adams, Lamm, and a small assault team crept toward the post office, blew open the doors with Gammon grenades, and rushed inside, guns blazing. Taken by surprise, the Germans inside the building used every means available to get outside before being cut down.

Meanwhile, a fierce fight erupted outside the post office when nearby German forces, alerted by the explosions, rushed into the streets only to be taken under fire by the Second Platoon covering force. Led by two intrepid sergeants, the covering force held off the Germans long enough for Adams's assault team to complete its mission. One of those sergeants was Charles Gushue, who single-handedly took out a machine-gun position with grenades and a bayonet. The other was Alvin Henderson. Charging into the fray, Henderson killed two Germans in hand-to-hand combat, bayoneted four others, and then personally silenced four enemy machine guns, the last of which he turned on the enemy before he was killed.[37]

Inside the post office, Adams found what he believed was the control mechanism for the bridge demolitions and smashed it (as it turned out, this was not the control mechanism). With his mission (seemingly) accomplished, Adams led his assault team back to the covering force and then led the whole of Second Platoon in a fighting withdrawal back to the Keizer Karel Plein. By that time, however, the traffic circle was being swarmed by enemy forces that blocked all routes back to Warren's position, so with daylight minutes away, Adams moved the platoon into hiding in a nearby barn. With the help of Dutch civilians who supplied them with food and frustrated German attempts to find them, Adams, Lamm, and the troopers of Second Platoon, A Company, 1/508th, remained safely hidden until 20 September when another, much larger, Anglo-American force making yet another assault on the Nijmegen highway bridge rescued them.[38]

The mass of Germans Second Platoon ran into while trying to get back to the traffic circle were there as a result of Model's and Bittrich's earlier orders, which quickly and dramatically changed the size and makeup of German defenses in Nijmegen. On 17 September, before the *9th SS* reconnaissance battalion arrived, Oberst Henke had but two improvised battalions with which to defend Nijmegen. By the evening of 18 September there were thirteen to fourteen German battalions in the city. By 19 September there were more than fifteen German battalions defending Nijmegen, many of which were composed of SS soldiers and German paratroopers. By 20 September—the day the battle for Nijmegen was ultimately decided—the combat ratio in and around the city was two to one in favor of the Germans.[39]

Some of the German forces that arrived in Nijmegen the first night were held in reserve and set to preparing defensive positions adjacent to the city's two bridges—it should be noted at this point that there were two bridges over the Waal at Nijmegen, the highway bridge, which was the 82nd's main focus, and a railroad bridge, which was 1,000 yards downstream (west) of the highway bridge—but the bulk were rushed to the Keizer Karel Plein, where Warren had the equivalent of about four infantry platoons. The Germans attacked shortly after Second Platoon departed for the post office. Hitting what remained of A Company, which, with Adams gone, was under Lieutenant John P. Foley's command, they overran some outposts, regained a foothold along the edge of the traffic circle, and were close to breaking through A Company's lines when Warren committed his reserve, a platoon from B Company, which stopped the Germans long enough for Warren to effect a fighting withdrawal to the southern edge of the circle. Certain that it was just a matter of time before the Germans continued their attack, yet unwilling to quit his ground before Second Platoon returned, Warren opted for the unexpected—he counterattacked.

While Millsaps's B Company attacked directly to its front, Warren slipped the rump of A Company around his right flank in the direction of the bridge, hoping that by doing so he would regain contact with Second Platoon and perhaps even break through to the bridge. The attack caught the Germans flatfooted; B Company held the enemy in place while Foley and his troopers slipped through a gap in the enemy lines and fought their way to within 400 yards of the highway bridge. But it was too little, too late. Eventually, Foley's force ran into an even larger German force set up around the immediate approaches to the bridge. With nothing left with which to reinforce Foley, Warren broke off the attack and withdrew everyone back to the south edge of the traffic circle. He was in the process of organizing yet another counterattack when General Gavin drove up in a jeep and told him to hold. Thus ended the first attempt to take Nijmegen's highway bridge.[40]

Gavin later wrote that "it should have been obvious that Tucker's 504th was much better prepared to spare a battalion to go to the Nijmegen bridge that night."[41] This is not entirely accurate. On the evening of 17 September, Tucker's 504th was clashing with Germans and Dutch Nazis outside of Grave, had no solid information about what was inside Grave, and had not yet taken the Heumen Bridge over the Maas-Waal Canal. Lindquist's 508th, on the other hand, had seen relatively little action that day and was much closer to the bridge than was the 504th. In fact, had the 504th been sent to the bridge, it would have had to pass through the 508th's lines to get there. Gavin's statement, therefore, was perhaps less his second-guessing of his plan and more a muted observation on the relative fighting qualities of two of his regimental commanders. Gavin had unbounded confidence in Tucker, who had trained his regiment to be as aggressive and ferocious as he was. Gavin thought Lindquist, on the other hand, to be competent but lacking the killer instinct.[42] Yet it was to Lindquist that Gavin gave the authority to decide whether to go for the highway bridge, and, in the final analysis, the possibility of taking it on the first night, regardless of who commanded the operation, was something that "could only be determined after attempting it."[43]

Surprisingly, Gavin did not know that Lindquist had tried for the highway bridge until he visited the 508th's command post early on the morning of the 18th. "My heart sank," he recalled. "If he [Lindquist] thought he could go through the city to get the bridge, despite the warnings that I gave him, he was in very deep trouble; so was the division."[44] But with no time to waste bemoaning what could not be changed, Gavin audibled. If Warren could hold the enemy's attention at the Keizer Karel Plein, perhaps he could slip a force through to the bridge from another direction. And due to the initiative of Lieutenant Colonel Louis Mendez, the 3/508th commander, a force was poised to do just that.[45]

Before leaving England, Lindquist told Mendez to be prepared to move on Nijmegen's highway bridge. To this end Mendez sent a reconnaissance patrol into the city shortly after assembling his battalion so that, were he ordered to take the bridge, he would not have to make the move blindly. Subsequently, because resistance had been so light on D day, Mendez upped the ante by ordering Lieutenant Russell C. Wilde's G Company to "advance as far as possible towards the bridge."[46] Starting out after dark, Wilde led G Company to a patch of high ground on Nijmegen's southeastern outskirts, where he linked up with the reconnaissance patrol. There were no enemy anywhere, but since Wilde had not received the word to advance on the bridge, he set his company down for the night.[47]

Gavin was obviously apprised of Mendez's move and Wilde's situation when he visited Lindquist's command post on the 18th. "From intelligence reports we had just received," recalled Gavin, slipping G Company through to the highway bridge "appeared practicable, and although it would normally be well beyond the capabilities of a company, the Battalion Commander of the [T]hird [B]attalion, 508th Parachute Infantry, Colonel Mendez, was an especially fine combat leader and 'G' Company was an unusually good parachute company" (obviously Gavin's reservations about Lindquist did not apply to the 508th's leadership as a whole).[48] On Gavin's orders, at about 0745 hours, 18 September, Lindquist radioed Mendez and told him to launch G Company.

At first it appeared the stratagem would succeed. Marching swiftly in column the only thing Wilde's troopers encountered was celebrating Dutch, some still in their nightclothes. At approximately 1000 hours, when the head of the column reached a point just short of the Keizer Lodewijk Plein—the traffic circle abutting the southern end of the highway bridge—everything changed. German machine-gun and small arms fire from positions along the northern edge of the circle dispersed the civilians and forced G Company to deploy from march to attack formation. Maneuvering forward through fire that grew in intensity the closer they got to the traffic circle, the troopers gained its southern edge only to discover that besides machine guns and small arms, the Germans also had several 20mm, 47mm, and 88mm guns in the area.

"The fighting within two blocks of the bridge was fierce," remembered Private Angel Romero. "I don't think there was a house in the area that wasn't hit by artillery, rifle and machine[-]gun fire. . . . The Germans were everywhere, and we still held our own."[49] Lieutenants Ralph E. De Weese and Kenneth A. Covey, the First and Second Platoon leaders, respectively, gathered their troopers and rushed the German positions, but the enemy fire was too intense and they were driven back. Another group of troopers, guided by Agardus "Gas" Leegsma, a member of the Dutch Resistance, made it all the way to the riverbank next to the bridge before they, too, were driven back.

At 1400 hours, Mendez arrived to see how the attack was progressing. By that time G Company was barricaded inside several buildings along the southern edge of the traffic circle and had many casualties. Mendez could see that it was simply not strong enough to overcome the German force guarding the bridge, so he ordered Wilde to withdraw. Thus ended the second attempt to take the Nijmegen highway bridge. And with the Germans now fully alert and firmly entrenched along the approaches to the bridge, it was obvious that any subsequent attempt to take it would require much greater firepower—firepower only XXX Corps could provide.[50]

The 82nd did take a bridge on 18 September, a bridge over the Maas-Waal Canal at Honinghutie, which lay on the most direct route from Grave to Nijmegen and therefore was the most valuable of the canal bridges (there were two bridges at Honinghutie, a railroad bridge and a road bridge, standing side by side, but the latter was the primary target). Of course, this begs the question; if so important, why not take it on D day? The answer is unclear. There was, and still is, confusion about whether Honinghutie was a D-day objective. In addition, there was and is confusion about whose responsibility it was, the 504th's or the 508th's. Given the force array, it would seem that Honinghutie was Lindquist's responsibility and that he delayed his attack there in favor of sending Warren into Nijmegen.[51]

Whatever the reason, it was not until the morning of 18 September that Lindquist radioed Major Otho Holmes, his 2/508th commander, and told him to take Honinghutie. Holmes gave the mission to one of his most experienced officers, Lieutenant Lloyd Polette of First Platoon, F Company. Approaching from the southeast, Polette and his troopers were about 300 yards from Honinghutie when the Germans there opened up and forced the troopers to ground. "It was just breaking day and the light was in our favor," thought Polette, so he roused his troopers for a rush to the objective before they lost their advantage.[52] But the German fire was too intense, and within minutes twelve paratroopers lay dead or wounded.

Stalled some 150 yards short of Honinghutie, Polette could clearly see Germans emplacing demolitions on the bridges. Positioning his remaining troopers so that they could keep the Germans under fire, Polette then sent a runner back for help. Shortly thereafter Lieutenant Thomas Tomlinson and Second Platoon of E Company arrived and added its fire to that of Polette's platoon. For about an hour the Germans and Americans traded small arms and machine-gun fire, each side stalemating the other, until, at 1030 hours, two explosions rent the air. The Germans had detonated their charges, but when the smoke cleared it was revealed that the highway bridge, though damaged, was still standing (the railroad bridge was completely destroyed). Before the Germans had time to complete their work, Polette and Tomlinson led their troopers in a charge while a section of 81mm mortars that had just come up covered them (the mortars arrived on the backs of several cows that some enterprising troopers had pressed into service as beasts of burden). By 1200 hours the Honinghutie road bridge was in American hands.[53]

With a second bridge over the Maas-Waal Canal in hand, the 82nd solidified its control of the area between Grave and Nijmegen. All that remained was seizing the Nijmegen bridges, but with the German presence in the area steadily increasing, the division was stretched too thin to make a third go for them. The only thing Gavin could do was defend what he had and wait for XXX Corps, which was already twenty-four hours behind schedule. In the meantime, Arie Bestebreurtje, who had become the de facto commander of the local Dutch Resistance, infiltrated scores of fighters into the city to keep the bridges under surveillance, hamper German efforts to prepare them for demolition, and destroy anything that even remotely resembled demolition wires or control mechanisms.[54]

Despite assurances to the contrary, Gavin had always been skeptical about XXX Corps's ability to fight its way up the narrow corridor with anything like the speed that had been promised (Eindhoven in two to three hours, Arnhem in two to three days).[55] Accordingly, he fashioned a ground tactical plan to "conduct a good fight, well in hand, for at least three days, and almost certainly well beyond this time, if need be."[56] By the morning of 18 September he had accomplished the first part of his plan: the seizure of a perimeter south-southeast of Nijmegen, including the Groesbeek Heights, and the taking of sufficient bridges to link Nijmegen with Grave. To bolster the division's ability to defend this perimeter against inevitable counterattacks, Gavin's plan next called for the glider insertion of the bulk of the 82nd's artillery complement: 1,899 troopers, 206 jeeps, 123 trailers, and 60 guns.[57] Originally scheduled to arrive at landing zones "N" and "T" at 1000 hours on the 18th, Brereton had postponed the drop until 1400 hours because fog had closed many of the departure airfields.[58] This turned out to be a blessing in disguise, for at 1000 hours, 18 September, a large portion of both landing zones was in enemy hands.

At 0630 hours, 18 September, 3,400 German soldiers organized in four *Kampfgruppen* supported by mortars, armored cars, and half-tracks stormed across the German-Dutch border to take back the Groesbeek Heights.[59] It was the first large-scale German counterattack in the Nijmegen sector, and it hit the division where it was weakest, along a fifteen-mile-long arc that described the eastern and southeastern edges of the 82nd's perimeter. If successful, the attack would not only give the Germans possession of the Groesbeek Heights, but also put both landing zones squarely behind enemy lines. Defending the eastern portion of the arc and landing zone "T" was D Company, 2/508th. The southeastern portion of the perimeter and landing zone "N" was the responsibility of I Company, 3/505th. Both companies occupied a string of strongpoints, generally focused on key crossroads. Neither was strong enough to beat back the German onslaught.

The attack hit D and I Companies simultaneously. Faced with overwhelming numbers, the paratroopers' only recourse was to fight a delaying action, judiciously trading space to gain the time needed for reinforcements to be rushed forward. But delaying actions require centralized control, and given that the squads and platoons were so widely scattered, this was impossible. Hence, the battle devolved into a mélange of discrete small-unit actions that hinged on the skill and courage of junior leaders. Staff Sergeant Clarence Praeger of I Company was one such leader who, in an attempt to blunt the German advance in his sector, mounted a one-man counterattack; his body was later found well forward of his original position.[60] Yet despite actions like Praeger's, by 1100 hours the German attackers had either pushed back, bypassed, or overrun both parachute companies; were in possession of large portions of both landings zones; and were poised to assault the Groesbeek Heights. They had also seized the 508th's regimental ammunition dump. "The seriousness of the situation," ran one 508th report with incredible understatement, "necessitated prompt and forceful action."[61]

With a huge hole rent in his perimeter, gliders inbound to landing zones that were in enemy hands, and the key to his entire defensive plan threatened, Gavin did the only thing he could—he counterattacked. Lindquist and Ekman, attacking from the north and south, respectively, were to hit the German flanks, roll up their lines, and restore the perimeter. But getting the attacks organized would take time. Something had to be done to buy that time. For that, Gavin turned to his engineers. Placing himself in the van, Gavin led D Company, 307th Airborne Engineers, into a gap that had opened between the 508th and 505th during the melee on the landing zones. Standing firm, the engineers, in concert with elements from D Company, 2/508th, repulsed two companies of German infantry at the cost of one engineer killed and three wounded, one of whom was the engineer platoon leader, a Lieutenant Hendrix, who, though shot in the head, remained in the fight.[62]

Meanwhile, the 508th effected a maneuver against the Germans' northern flank that "could have been executed only by extremely capable troops and unusual combat leadership" and for which there existed "few parallels" (it most likely served to get Lindquist out of the Gavin's doghouse as well).[63] First, Lindquist had his reserve, C Company, 1/508th, secure a line of departure in a wooded area just north of landing zone "T." He then ordered Warren—who was still clinging to the southern edge of the Keizer Karel Plein with most of B Company and the rump of A Company—to break contact and move with all haste to the line of departure, where he was to link up with C Company and be prepared to attack on order. Fighting free of the traffic circle by leapfrogging units to the rear and then, once clear of the Germans, moving at the double, Warren and his troopers arrived at the line of departure at around noon. Thirty minutes later, Lindquist gave the order to attack.

"The attack was carried out at the double time, by troops that had fought all night long in NIJMEGEN, and was a howling success," wrote Warren afterward. "The line of departure was on the right [northern] flank of the German attack on the [landing zone], and rolled them up like a piece of tape, capturing 149 prisoners and killing approximately 50, and knocking out 16 dual 20mm [antiaircraft] guns." First Sergeant Leonard Funk led a contingent of C Company troopers that, alone, silenced seven antiaircraft guns, while, on another part of the landing zone, Sergeant Jim Kurz led some B Company troopers against several enemy machine guns that threatened to hold up the paratroopers' attack. By 1400 hours, Warren's troopers had taken back landing zone "T." They were just in time. "Just as we reached the far side of the field, the first gliders came in," recalled Kurz. "The glider troops had seen the last of the attack and cheered us as they arrived. We sat down and thanked God we had cleared the field in time."[64]

Unlike Lindquist, Ekman had only one company with which to drive the Germans from landing zone "N," and it was a partial company at that. Captain Anthony M. Stefanich, the C Company, 1/505th, commander, had but two platoons available when Ekman told him to prepare to counterattack into the landing zone (his third platoon had already been committed to the defense of Riethorst, farther south). Given such a small force, correctly timing the counterattack was critical. "I carefully guarded against pre-commitment," said Ekman, "with the pre-planned intention of launching a rapid initial attack which would disconcert the enemy and force him to fall back, with the attack so timed that the landing zones [*sic*] would be cleared . . . before [a] possible enemy counter-attack in force." Staying his hand as long as possible, it was 1330 hours when Ekman finally unleashed C Company. When he did, Stefanich's troopers rose from their concealed positions and, advancing almost shoulder-to-shoulder, swept across the landing zone while firing from the hip. "The C Company troopers were firing and the Germans were running away from us," recalled Lieutenant Jack Tallerday. "It looked like a line of hunters in a rabbit drive and the Germans looked like rabbits running in no particular pattern." Ekman's timing was perfect; just minutes after clearing landing zone "N" the first gliders appeared overhead. Success, however, came at a high cost, for C Company lost its commander to a sniper. Tallerday and a company medic worked frantically to save their captain, who was still alive when they reached him. They were too late. Mortally wounded and lying in Tallerday's arms, Stefanich told his friend to "take care of my troopers and the Company; we've come a long way together" and then passed away. "Most of us cried when we heard the news," recalled Private Arthur B. "Dutch" Schultz, who stood over Stefanich while Tallerday and the medic worked on him, whispering the Hail Mary. "It is difficult to put into words the love we felt for this man. In one sense 'he was the old man,' and in another sense we all felt obliged to sort of 'look out for him.' He was not only a symbol of leadership, he was also a model of innocence" (Stefanich did not smoke, drink, or carouse for women and when in garrison attended mass daily).[65]

MARKET-GARDEN's second great air armada, consisting of 1,336 U.S. C-47s, 340 RAF transports, and 1,205 gliders, took off from England shortly after 1100 hours. As they had the day before, Spitfires, Tempests, Thunderbolts, and Mustangs from the Air Defense of Great Britain and the U.S. Eighth and Ninth Air Forces flew escort. This time, the Luftwaffe showed up as well. At both Arnhem and Eindhoven, German fighters tried breaking through to the transports. In every instance they were unsuccessful, losing 29 planes in the process (Allied losses were 5 fighters). The escorts were not as successful at suppressing German antiaircraft batteries, however. Hampered by a light haze that reduced visibility and ordered not to fire unless fired upon to ensure against fratricide, the escorts were, in several instances, too late to silence German antiaircraft guns, which had also changed tactics, holding their fire until after the rocket-firing Thunderbolts had passed and then targeting the rear of the transport columns. As a result 21 tugs and gliders were lost to enemy flak.[66]

The 82nd's D+1 glider contingent consisted of 454 C-47 transports (arranged in eleven serials), each towing one Waco in which were the troopers, equipment, and ammunition of the division's Artillery Headquarters, the 456th Parachute Field Artillery Battalion, the 319th and 320th Glider Field Artillery Battalions, B Battery of the 80th Airborne Antitank Battalion, and sundry other division troops. Four gliders were lost before reaching the Continent—2 ditched in the Channel when their tow cables snapped, 1 returned to base when it began disintegrating in the air, and the fourth aborted when a crazed trooper pulled the tow-rope release handle. In each case the passengers either landed safely or were rescued. Eleven gliders released well short of the objective area when their tugs were hit by antiaircraft fire; the troopers of 7 of the 11 later made their way back to friendly lines with Dutch help, 6 of them with all their equipment. The remaining 439 gliders and tugs remained on course and in formation despite the heavier-than-expected flak, and at approximately 1431 hours the lead glider of the first serial cut loose over landing zone "N."[67]

Watching from the ground was Colonel George Chatterton, who piloted Browning's glider into the target area the day before. "It was a fantastic sight," wrote Chatterton. "The Germans were even more staggered than we were and all firing ceased."[68] But not for long. Although there were no longer German soldiers on the landing zones, German guns to the east and southeast could still range the area—those in the Reichswald were particularly troublesome—and the large, slow tugs and the ungainly gliders made tempting targets. To make matters worse, the Germans started shelling the landing zones. Flying through the maelstrom, 8 more C-47s were shot down, and more than 100 others were damaged. Yet, remarkably, not one glider was destroyed in the air, and 385 managed to land within the 82nd's lines. The insertions on landing zone "N" were especially accurate; all but a handful of gliders landed within a mile and a half of the target. Those headed for landing zone "T," where German fire was much heavier, were not as fortunate: Only 90 gliders landed on target; another 71 released early and landed about a mile short of the landing zone, although still within the 82nd's perimeter; several badly discomfited pilots, however, released their gliders wherever they could with devastating results.[69]

For some reason, most of the errant gliders were from the eighth and ninth serials carrying the 320th. Eight tug pilots from the eighth serial released their gliders about twelve miles southeast of landing zone "T." The troopers inside the gliders, artillerymen from B Battery, 320th, were never heard from again. Inexplicably, 9 other tug pilots from the same serial *overshot* the landing zone and released their gliders around Wyler, the German town near which Lieutenant Rex Combs and some troopers from A Company, 1/508th, landed the day before. Inside these gliders was the rest of B Battery, which, with the exception of two officers, assembled on the commander and fought its way back to division lines, albeit without any of its equipment. Some 24 to 30 tug pilots of the ninth serial also released early; these gliders landed in the no-man's-land between friendly and enemy lines three to five miles southeast of landing zone "T." The troopers, also from the 320th, assembled in some fifty-four separate groups, defended in place until nightfall, and then infiltrated to division lines. Eventually, 160 troopers from this serial made their way to safety, bringing with them 22 glider pilots, ten jeeps, and two howitzers (only 4 troopers and 9 glider pilots went missing). The only other tug pilots to miss landing zone "T" were from a flight of 8 planes in the third serial. They, too, overshot the landing zone and put their gliders down around Wyler as well. On board were 7 officers and 42 troopers from the 319th, only 4 of whom made their way back to friendly lines.[70]

Despite the mishaps and enemy fire, by nightfall 18 September the division had assembled thirty-one additional howitzers, thirteen antitank guns, 177 jeeps, 106 trailers, and approximately 211 tons of supplies. More than 1,600 troopers had also arrived to man the guns and fill out the division perimeter. Surprisingly, only 3 troopers were killed and 42 wounded during the landings.[71] This is especially noteworthy given that most of the gliders had only a single trained pilot; because of a glider pilot shortage, the copilot seats were occupied by the ranking trooper on board who received some quick instruction on how to fly and land a glider in a pinch. According to Sergeant Tom Sharkey of the 456th, "The pilot said that if anything happened to him, all I had to do was to cut loose and keep the air speed at 45 mph and we wouldn't get hurt *too* badly!" Sergeant Vernon "Mike" Aubin, also of the 456th, did "a lot of praying on the way over" after he was drafted as copilot.[72] Captain John W. Connelly, copiloting one of the gliders that came down near Wyler, successfully landed his aircraft after his pilot was killed by flak.[73]

Twenty minutes behind the gliders were approximately 130 B-24 bombers from the U.S. Eighth Air Force that had been pressed into service to deliver supplies by parachute. Each bomber carried about 2 tons of supplies that they were to drop through the bomb bays, waist, and belly of the aircraft. Wholly new to this type of mission, the bomber pilots were unsure of the tactics but finally decided to fly in 1,500 feet, descend to 300 feet for the drop, and then make a climbing turn back to 1,500 feet for the return home. Most of the bombers arrived on time and in formation. Once over the target area, however, they seem to have been unnerved by the density of the flak and subsequently delivered their loads as much as five miles off target. In all, 4 B-24s were shot down and another 38 damaged. Ultimately, the division recovered 80 percent of its expected 258 tons of supplies, although it took some time to do so since the bundles were so widely scattered. Still, it was a much-needed shot in the arm for the hard-pressed troopers on the ground who were running short of food, water, medical supplies, and, most important, ammunition.[74]

The night of 18–19 September passed in relative quiet around Nijmegen. It was as if both sides were resting, like prizefighters between rounds. There were some clashes—the troopers endured intermittent artillery and mortar barrages and repulsed German probes—but neither side mounted a significant attack. Moreover, with much more artillery available to help break up the German probes and cover the gaps in the lines, the physical and psychological strain on the troopers manning the widely spaced outposts that loosely defined the 82nd's perimeter lessened. Furthermore, to facilitate responsiveness Colonel Andy March, the division's artillery commander, placed one artillery battalion in direct support of each of the parachute regiments—the 319th to the 508th, the 456th to the 505th, and the 376th to the 504th—and kept one, the 320th, in general support. In the southwest, where the 505th was short one battalion (Vandervoort's 2/505th was being held in division reserve), Colonel Ekman had his dedicated artillery battalion do double duty. Not only did it provide supporting fires to the regiment, but Ekman positioned it so far forward that he was able to integrate the 456th's security outposts into his defensive line.[75]

Thirty miles south of Nijmegen, Royal Engineers spent the night constructing a Bailey bridge over the Wilhelmina Canal to replace the one bridge the 101st did not take on D day. Queued up for miles behind them was XXX Corps. At 0615 hours, 19 September, after ten and a half hours of grueling, nonstop work, the bridge opened for heavy traffic. Within minutes armored cars of the 2nd Household Cavalry crossed the canal and resumed the dash northward. They were followed by the whole of the Guards Armored Division. The race was back on; it was time to make up for lost time.[76]

The drive from the Wilhelmina Canal to Grave went without incident. Horrocks's XXX Corps was finally advancing with the speed Montgomery expected, its only impediment the throngs of Dutch civilians lining the roads to cheer the Tommies on their way, and at approximately 0830 hours, 19 September, the 2nd Household Cavalry linked up with Tucker's troopers south of Grave.[77] "I knew we had reached them," stated Corporal William Chennell of the Household Cavalry, "because the Americans, taking no chances, halted us with warning fire."[78] After identifying themselves as friendly, the cavalrymen passed through the 504th's lines, crossed the Grave Bridge, and sped north along the most direct route to Nijmegen, which was by way of Honinghutie. They got there just in time to warn the Guards Armored Division following behind that the Honinghutie Bridge was unsafe for anything larger than a jeep and that the best route to Nijmegen, therefore, was via the Heumen Bridge, thus preventing another traffic jam.[79]

Leading the Guards Armored Division was the 5th Guards Armored Brigade with the 1st Battalion (Motor), Grenadier Guards, and the 2nd Battalion (Armored), Grenadier Guards, in the van. When they reached the Grave Bridge, sometime around 1000 hours, both battalion commanders—Lieutenant Colonels Edward Goulburn of the 1st Grenadier Guards and N. R. "Rodney" Moore of the 2nd Grenadier Guards—were whisked away to Overasselt, a small village on the road to Heumen where Browning and Gavin were waiting. Browning, himself a Grenadier Guardsman, was proud to see his regimental kinsmen leading the way and was anxious to get them in the fight. Gavin was both thrilled and relieved that XXX Corps had finally arrived: "It is difficult to describe my feeling of elation at that moment. So far, we had been spared a major German armored attack, but now, with the availability of British armor, we felt equal to anything that could happen, so we wanted to get armor into our area as fast as it could be poured over the [Heumen] bridge and moved northward."[80] The four were soon joined by Major General Allan H. S. Adair, the Guards Armored Division commander, and Brigadier Norman W. Gwatkin, commander of the 5th Guards Armored Brigade. Browning and Gavin provided the Guardsmen an overview of the situation around Nijmegen and discussed plans for another attack on Nijmegen's bridges later that day. The meeting was over almost as soon as it began. Adair and Gwatkin returned to the vicinity of Grave to hurry their forces along, while Browning, Gavin, Goulburn and Moore proceeded to the 82nd's command post to finalize the attack plans.[81]

With no time for rehearsals or detailed coordination, the plan of attack was kept simple. Two columns would enter the city simultaneously, one aimed at the railroad bridge, the other at the highway bridge, which would be the main effort. Each column would comprise a mix of British tanks, British motorized infantry, and American paratroopers. The forces would assemble at the Sionshof, a roadside restaurant-hotel just south of Nijmegen, break into their respective columns, and jump off at 1530 hours. Each column would be led by Dutch guides who optimistically reported that "the town was not strongly held and . . . a display of force in the shape of Tanks would probably cause the enemy to withdraw." Colonel Moore was less sanguine. "It was fully realized," he later wrote, "that it might be a difficult operation, but it was thought worth the gamble."[82]

Browning thought so too. That morning, before XXX Corps arrived, he told Gavin, "The Nijmegen bridge must be taken today. At the latest tomorrow." The British 1st Airborne Division at Arnhem was being savaged, and it was not certain how much longer it could hold out. "The capture of the Nijmegen bridge was squarely on my shoulders," recalled Gavin. "This I knew."[83]

By that time Gavin also knew that the 325th's glider insertion, scheduled for 1000 hours that day, had been postponed until 1500 hours because of fog in England. This put Gavin in a difficult situation. The British tanks would need infantry support to fight through the city streets to the bridges. Gavin had planned to use the 325th for this, but there was no way it would be ready to attack by 1530 even if it did arrive on time (as it turned out the fog did not lift, and the glider insertion was postponed until D+3).[84] Waiting for XXX Corps to bring up more infantry was unsatisfactory; it would take hours to arrive since it would have to wend its way forward via the single road over which the entire corps was passing. Hence, infantry support for the attack would have to come from the 82nd, but Gavin was reluctant to pull any from his perimeter, especially in light of the German counterattack the day before. This meant he would have to use his reserve. Although only a single battalion, it was all he could spare. But it was Ben Vandervoort's battalion. "Ever since I spent a night and a day behind German-Italian lines in Sicily July 9–10, '43 with Vandervoort I had the utmost confidence in him," wrote Gavin. "He was a rare fighting man, brave, dependable, hard as nails with the troops & they loved him. As soon as the link-up occurred with the British I sent him after the bridge."[85]

Notwithstanding the haste with which the plan was put together, the columns jumped off only thirty minutes behind schedule. As had been the case when the 508th entered Nijmegen two days before, "the townspeople were out in force to welcome us," recalled Lieutenant William J. Meddaugh of E Company, 2/505th. Lieutenant James J. Coyle, also of E Company, likened the move through the suburbs to a victory parade. "The Dutch people lined the roads in crowds and cheered us on our way." One Dutchman, Cor Kleijwegt, was stunned when he encountered the paratroopers treading silently along in their rubber-soled boots, a marked contrast to the sound of German hobnails to which he had become accustomed after almost four years of occupation: "I will never forget the emotion that ran like a flame through me when a helmeted paratrooper—gun at the ready—walked past us and apparently unmoved said: 'You are free.' As I walked back almost drunk-like, I kept repeating 'you are free' as if I wanted to keep his softly spoken words like a relic."[86]

Guards Captain John Neville commanded the column making the supporting attack on Nijmegen's railroad bridge. His force consisted of five tanks from the 2nd Grenadier Guards, a platoon of mounted infantry from the 1st Grenadier Guards, and Captain Taylor Smith's D Company, 2/505th. Following their guide, Neville's column traveled a route that was about a mile west of that taken by the highway bridge column.

After moving without incident through the southern part of Nijmegen, Neville's column ran into a German force of some 750 to 1,000 men armed with machine guns and *panzerfausts* (shoulder-fired antitank weapons similar to but more powerful than American bazookas) backed by two 20mm antiaircraft guns, an antitank gun, and at least one tank that had turned a marshaling yard at the southern approach to the railroad bridge into a strongpoint. Furthermore, surrounding the marshaling yard was a high embankment too steep for tanks to negotiate. Figuring that a determined attack could break through the strongpoint and gain the southern terminus of the railroad bridge, Neville sent his infantry up and over the embankment while his tanks charged through a nearby tunnel. It was a short-lived assault. Neville's two lead tanks were destroyed as soon as they emerged on the German side of the tunnel while his infantrymen ran into a hornet's nest of small arms and automatic weapons fire. "The entire park seemed filled with tracer slugs," recalled Sergeant Paul Nunan. "My first reaction was that a German tank had moved in on us. I remember thinking that if they had infantry with them it was going to be a very tough day." Seeing that he was both outgunned and outnumbered, Neville ordered a withdrawal to a small church the column had passed along the way. Sometime during the withdrawal Lieutenant Waverly Wray, the hero of Ste.-Mère-Église, was shot and killed by a sniper while covering his company's movement to the rear. "The last I saw of him," related one trooper, "he was headed for the Germans with a grenade in one hand and a tommy gun in the other."[87]

As the main effort, the attack on the highway bridge involved a much larger force: twenty to thirty tanks (some accounts put the figure as high as forty tanks) from the 2nd Grenadier Guards, a mounted infantry company from the

1st Grenadier Guards, and the rest of Vandervoort's 2/505th. Lieutenant Colonel Goulburn commanded the British contingent, working in tandem with Vandervoort, who controlled the paratroopers. Both men, in turn, relied heavily on their subordinates.[88] Vandervoort later wrote that his battalion

> had fought with tanks before, but never in such lavish quantities. . . . It required an intuitive sense of balance not to exploit the tanks as protection for the infantry nor to preoccupy the infantry with screening the tanks. That depended on a lot of individual initiative, not play-by-play command control. Colonel Goulburn, a perceptive commander, more or less turned individual tanks loose and let them go—up the alleys and through the yards with the infantry. The spearhead of the British column, which included the paratroopers, blasted its way up the avenue and into the side streets as required by the enemy dispositions. Oversimplified, all the following column had to do was duck random shells, wait until the ruckus died down up ahead, then move up another block.[89]

En route to the highway bridge a troop of four tanks, two platoons of motorized infantry, and a platoon of paratroopers led by Guards Major George Thorne veered off for the post office, the same building assaulted two days before by Captain Adams and Second Platoon of A Company, 1/508th. Since no one from Adams's group made it back to friendly lines—it was still holed up behind enemy lines somewhere near the highway bridge—the thought persisted that the post office housed the demolition controls for the bridge. Blasting its way through the narrow streets, overrunning at least one German antitank gun along the way, Thorne's force recaptured the post office. Inside were a handful of Dutch civilians; no Germans and, more important, no demolition controls were found anywhere. Then, instead of returning to the main column, Thorne tried taking the highway bridge on his own. Advancing with two tanks and a platoon of infantry in the van, Thorne's force got as far as the Keizer Lodewijk Plein before it was ambushed. With no room to maneuver in the narrow streets and having sustained several casualties, Thorne withdrew to the post office to await further orders.[90]

The Germans that repelled Thorne and Neville were from a conglomeration of units that had been scratched together and formed into ad hoc *Kampfgruppen*, although in the two days since the 508th's attempts on the highway bridge German paratroopers and SS soldiers from the *10th SS Panzer Division* had filtered into the area in significant numbers. Moreover, command of the *Kampfgruppen* had passed to the SS and German paratroop commanders whose combat experience, along with the battlefield prowess of their soldiers, stiffened the German defenses. Neville's column had run into the Germans' rightmost position protecting the railroad bridge. Thorne's column was repulsed by forces manning the center of gravity of the German defenses in Nijmegen, a wooded area directly adjacent to the Keizer Lodewijk Plein called Hunner Park.[91]

Concealed in Hunner Park was a force several hundred strong, the core of which was a battalion from the *10th SS* backed by self-propelled, antitank, and antiaircraft guns (including several of the feared 88s that, although positioned across the river, had clear lines of fire into the traffic circle) concealed in houses and basements with lines of fire that crisscrossed the approaches to the bridge. An attack on the highway bridge, therefore, would mean first fighting through a series of combat outposts, then advancing across the open space of the Keizer Lodewijk Plein, which the Germans had turned into a kill zone, and then clearing Hunner Park. Only then could an attacker gain a clear shot at the highway bridge itself, which had its own defenses that would also have to be neutralized. The column under Goulburn and Vandervoort hit this defensive system head-on.[92]

Goulburn's column advanced quickly at first, eschewing security in favor of speed and surprise. "Speed seemed essential," remembered Goulburn, "and a rush with tanks through the town however unorthodox it might be, had an obvious chance of success." Nearer the traffic circle German resistance intensified and the pace slowed, yet the British tankers and American paratroopers pressed on. "For soldiers of different allied armies, it was amazing how beautifully the tankers and troopers teamed together," observed Vandervoort. "It was testimony to their combat acumen as seasoned veterans—both Yanks and Tommies." To avoid getting bogged down in the streets, Vandervoort's troopers took to the rooftops to cover the tanks from above. From Goulburn's vantage point in the streets below, it appeared that "the AMERICANS seemed to thoroughly enjoy the game." But a game it was not. It took three hours of intense fighting—"confusing face-to-face, kill or be killed show downs between small momentarily isolated groups and individuals"—for the paratroopers to gain a foothold in a row of houses bordering the Keizer Lodewijk Plein. It was then that the drive was stopped. Two tanks, attempting a rush through the traffic circle, were destroyed by antitank fire from Hunner Park. Lieutenant Coyle, whose platoon was occupying one of the buildings fronting the traffic circle, saw the remaining tanks back up: "I went storming back to the third tank shouting at the commander to get back with us. He said he was hit—I told him he was not hit as I could not see a mark on the tank. A British sergeant jumped out of the tank and said, 'What's that then, Mate?' pointing to a large hole on the other side of the turret which I had not seen. I felt about two feet tall. I don't know how the tank took that hit without suffering any wounded or catching fire." Vandervoort, too, wanted to continue the attack.

His plan was to blanket both sides of the bridge with mortar and artillery fire and, under covering fire from his paratroopers, have the tanks make another run at the highway bridge. But whenever his paratroopers opened fire, the Germans blasted them with their heavier guns. As Corporal Earl Boling saw things, with no British tanks to occupy them the Germans used their 88s to systematically demolish the buildings in which the paratroopers were seeking cover. To add to the chaos, German artillery observers had zeroed in on the Allied positions, and anything that moved attracted an immediate barrage. Faced with such withering enemy fire, and with night fast approaching (it was about 1900 hours when the column reached the traffic circle), Goulburn "decided that it was useless to continue . . . and that a much more carefully laid on plan should be made." Vandervoort was dismayed: "Our ammunition was plentiful with the exception of 60mm mortar rounds. All battalion communications—radio and telephone—were tied in 'Five by Five'—better than 'Ma Bell.' A dozen or more Sherman tanks, motors idling, were ready to roll when ordered. . . . In short, the battalion and the tanks were on the Line of Departure ready for a joint infantry/tank assault to put the armor over the river. There was time to establish a bridgehead north of the Waal before dark if the bridge wasn't demolished." Vandervoort insisted that his troopers could take Hunner Park. But "the generals," remarked Vandervoort, halted the column nonetheless, likely on the advice of Goulburn, who wanted to consolidate his position and wait until reinforcements could be brought forward.[93]

The generals to whom Vandervoort referred were Browning and Horrocks, who had come forward "to smell the battlefield." As equals in rank and longtime friends, Horrocks and Browning exercised joint command of the operation and "took all the major decisions together without any semblance of friction."[94] So when Goulburn counseled halt and Vandervoort wanted to attack, it was natural they would defer to their countryman, whose desire for "a much more carefully laid on plan" fitted well with the British predilection for set-piece battles, the finest practitioner of which was a man to whom they all deferred, Field Marshal Montgomery.

Later that evening Horrocks, Browning, and Adair were sequestered in a school classroom they had turned into a command post, discussing their "much more carefully laid on plan." "Suddenly the door opened and in came a tall, good-looking American General," who, in Horrocks's mind, "was as unlike the popular cartoon conception of the loud-voiced, boastful, cigar-chewing American as it would be possible to imagine."[95] It was Jim Gavin. He had a plan, too.

From left to right, Lieutenant General George S. Patton, U.S. 7th Army commander; Major General Omar N. Bradley, U.S. II Corps commander; Major General Matthew B. Ridgway, 82nd Airborne Division commander; Brigadier General Charles L. "Bull" Keerans (partially obscured), the 82nd's assistant division commander; and Brigadier General Maxwell D. Taylor, the 82nd's artillery commander, at Oujda, French Morocco, sometime before the invasion of Sicily. *U.S. Army photo*

82nd Airborne Division troopers loading a "para-rack" on the belly of a C-47 transport before the jump into Sicily, July 1943. *Photo courtesy of Starlyn Jorgensen*

A bearded John H. "Beaver" Thompson, war correspondent from the *Chicago Tribune*, talks with Colonel James M. Gavin, the 505th Regimental Combat Team commander in Sicily, July 1943. *U.S. Army photo*

504th Regimental Combat Team moving toward the Mussolini Canal in the Anzio beachhead, 24 January 1944. *U.S. Army photo*

Lieutenant General Mark W. Clark, U.S. Fifth Army commander, awarding the Silver Star to Captain (Chaplain) Delbert Kuehl, 8 April 1944, Naples, Italy. *Photo courtesy of Starlyn Jorgensen*

Unidentified officer and Colonel George V. Millett (right), the 507th Parachute Infantry Regiment commander, preparing for the jump into Normandy. Millett and some 200 of his troopers were taken prisoner shortly after D-Day. *Photo courtesy of Mike Bigalke*

Colonel William Ekman interrogating German prisoners, Normandy, France. *Photo courtesy of Mike Bigalke*

Colonel William Ekman, the 505th Parachute Infantry Regiment commander, addressing his troopers in Normandy, France, June 1944. *Photo courtesy of Al Larson*

A "stick" of paratroopers from B Company, 1/505th just before loading for the drop into Holland, 17 September 1944. *Photo courtesy of Al Larson*

376th Parachute Field Artillerymen ready themselves for the drop into Holland, September 1944. *Photo courtesy of Starlyn Jorgensen*

82nd troopers take one last look at the map before loading up for the drop into Holland, 17 September 1944. *Photo courtesy of Starlyn Jorgensen*

82nd's drop into Holland as seen from the air, 17 September 1944. *U.S. Army photo*

82nd Airborne Division dropping into Holland, 17 September 1944. *Photo courtesy of Al Larson*

82nd Airborne Division officers conferring on drop zone "N" outside Nijmegen, Holland, 17 September 1944. *Photo courtesy of Al Larson*

Colonel William Ekman (facing camera) talking with Lieutenant Colonel Edward "Cannonball" Krause somewhere in Holland, September 1944. *Photo courtesy of Mike Bigalke*

German prisoners taken during Operation Market-Garden being escorted to the rear by 82nd troopers, September 1944. *Photo courtesy of Al Larson*

King George VI (back to camera) reviews the 82nd's principle commanders in Holland. Others in the photo are, from left to right, Lieutenant General Brian Horrocks, XXX Corps commander; Brigadier General James Gavin, 82nd commander; Colonel Andy March, the 82nd's artillery commander; Colonel Roy Lindquist, the 508th commander; Colonel Reuben Tucker, the 504th commander; Colonel William Ekman, the 505th commander; and Lieutenant Colonel Charles Billingslea, the 325th commander. *Photo courtesy of Barbara Gavin Fauntleroy*

82nd Airborne Division troopers en route to Werbomont, Belgium, during Battle of the Bulge, 18 December 1944. *Photo courtesy of Al Larson*

82nd Airborne Division troopers en route to Werbomont, Belgium, 18 December 1944. Note the uncovered tractor trailers in which they were traveling. *Photo courtesy of Al Larson*

German dead left in the Ardennes by B Company, 1/505th, December 1944. *Photo courtesy of Al Larson*

Captain Harold Miller, B Company, 1/505th commander, assembles his troopers outside Rochelinval, Belgium, along the Salm River line, December 1944. *Photo courtesy of Al Larson*

German Mk V (Panther) tank destroyed by 82nd troopers outside Goronne, Belgium, January 1945. *Photo courtesy of Al Larson*

82nd Airborne Division parachute artillerymen manning a 75mm Pack Howitzer outside Wallerode, Belgium, at start of Bradley's "hurry up" offensive, January 1945. *Photo courtesy of Doug Bekke*

82nd Airborne Division troopers moving up to attack positions in preparation for Bradley's "hurry up" offensive, January 1945. *Photo courtesy of Doug Bekke*

Abandoned German 75mm gun being inspected by 82nd Airborne Division troopers outside Holzheim, Germany, February 1945. *Photo courtesy of Doug Bekke*

Major General Gavin leading the 82nd Airborne Division up New York City's Fifth Avenue during the Victory Parade, 12 January 1946. *Photo courtesy of Barbara Gavin Fauntleroy*

CHAPTER 18

THE FINEST DIVISION IN THE WORLD TODAY

September 20th was certainly a wild day.

—JAMES M. GAVIN TO CORNELIUS RYAN, 13 JULY 1973

GAVIN'S PLAN WAS unbelievably bold—renew the attacks against the southern ends of the bridges and launch an assault river crossing to seize the northern ends. He taught his troopers that the best way to take a bridge was to attack both ends simultaneously, *if possible.* He could make it possible if he had some boats. He had already sent his engineers in search of some but to no avail.[1] "I asked General Horrocks about it, and he said he thought they had some boats well down the road in the train [the rear of the column] somewhere. The discussion on this point quickly spread among the staff. They finally agreed that they should have about twenty-eight folding canvas boats in trucks somewhere farther to the rear."[2] Gavin promised that if Horrocks could get the boats, his paratroopers would make the crossing. In fact, said Gavin, he had already instructed Tucker to move the bulk of his regiment nearer Nijmegen just in case.[3]

Horrocks and Browning accepted Gavin's proposal. Given the time constraints under which they were operating, it was the best available option. At this, Gavin departed. There was much yet to do.[4]

Gavin's first order of business was to select a crossing site. The most obvious location, and the one Gavin chose, was the point where the Maas-Waal Canal intersected the Waal River. Although a considerable distance from both bridges—it was 1,500 yards downstream of the railroad bridge and

2,500 yards downstream of the highway bridge—the location offered two advantages: It would allow the troopers to load the boats under cover in the canal, and it would provide them the opportunity to get familiar with handling the boats before proceeding out into the river, which was some 300 yards wide at the site.[5] Obviously, the crossing site would also have to be cleared of the enemy. Normally, this would be problematic, but Gavin "was sure that, once released, Tucker's 504th could clear all the Germans up to the riverbank with little difficulty."[6]

Supporting fires had also to be arranged. To that end Gavin moved the 376th Parachute Field Artillery Battalion and the regiment's 81mm mortars to positions from which their guns could range the far bank. He also obtained from the Guards Armored Division a battalion—twenty-four tubes—of self-propelled "Sexton" 25-pounder howitzers. For direct fire support, Gavin gave Tucker two antitank guns from the 80th Airborne Antiaircraft Battalion, but to bolster that support Adair lent Gavin the 2nd Battalion, Irish Guards. As at La Fière, Gavin wanted to use the Guards' Sherman tanks like a Napoleonic *grande batterie*, lining them track-to-track along the near bank so they could target enemy positions with high-explosive shells. All told, approximately one hundred tubes would be supporting the river crossing.[7]

But before anything Gavin had to get the boats. This worried him for two reasons. First, time was running short for General Urquhart and his paras at Arnhem. They were surrounded, critically short of supplies, and hanging on by a thread. Second, because time was of the essence, Gavin wanted to conduct the river crossing as soon as the boats arrived, whatever the time of day. He preferred to go at night, but there was almost no chance the boats would arrive in time for a crossing that night (19–20 September). Next best would be a dawn crossing, when the light was too poor for accurate long-range fire but good enough to maneuver the boats across the river. When Gavin asked Horrocks about this possibility, Horrocks simply echoed his staff's response: "that they had the boats and that they would get them up as quickly as they could." What Gavin wanted to avoid was a daytime crossing. "It was a risky tactic," wrote Gavin, "but something had to be done. I could not conceive of sitting on the southern bank with a regiment of infantry and the Guards Armored Division while Urquhart was destroyed eleven miles away."[8] It was all dependent on the arrival of the boats.

At about 2300 hours, 19 September, Gavin sent for Tucker, who, as ordered, had assembled his regiment in a wooded area just outside Nijmegen (less three companies that were guarding the Grave, Heumen, and Honinghutie bridges). It was time to tell Tucker what he had in mind. Characteristically, Tucker was with his troopers when the call came, so his executive officer, Lieutenant Colonel Warren R. Williams, reported to Gavin in his stead. After outlining the situation, Gavin told Williams that the 504th would be conducting an assault river crossing. At the time, there was still a chance that the boats would arrive before dawn, but it was "a very iffy situation," admitted Gavin. "If the boats arrived, and if the Germans were cleared as far as the riverbank, and if everything could be organized—all this during darkness—we could get off shortly after daybreak."[9] Sometime later that night, word reached the 82nd command post that the boats would not arrive before noon on the 20th.[10] It would be a daytime crossing, the worst possible option.[11]

Tucker's troopers were flabbergasted when told what was expected of them. Lieutenant John Holabird of the 307th Engineers recalled that "at first, when we were briefed for the assault crossing, we took it as a joke. We couldn't believe anyone could be serious about it." But when told that the engineers would be manning the assault boats, Holabird's sentiments changed: "I can remember being flattered they were considering using the engineers. We were always somewhat of a joke; effete and a little precious. We usually followed people around, not led them. It was flattering—and at the same time a little fantastic—that we were to lead this flotilla across." But flattery was soon tempered by reality. "Suddenly, it came across that this was not a joke; . . . at that moment, I would have liked to have been anyplace [*sic*] in the world except there. We lived on hope, though, and I am sure I still hoped—or believed—the mission would be called off before we left; that we would wait around there until dark and then be sent back." Lieutenant Allen McClain of the 3/504th felt likewise: "If ever I had wanted to be somewhere else at a given time it would have been then!" Major Julian Cook, the 3/504th commander, "was dumbfounded." His operations officer, Captain Henry B. Keep, thought "the odds were very much against us."[12]

There was one positive aspect of the delay; it gave Tucker more time to prepare and his troopers time to rest. At 0600 hours, 20 September, Tucker issued his orders. The 2/504th, which at the time consisted of but D Company and Headquarters Company (E and F Companies were guarding bridges), would lead the way to the crossing site, clear it, and then support the crossing by fire. The 3/504th would spearhead the crossing. The 1/504th would follow the 3/504th across. Engineers from C Company, 307th Airborne Engineer Battalion, would man the boats.[13]

The 504th moved out to the crossing site at 0730 hours, with D Company, 2/504th, in the lead. Moving slowly—Tucker told D Company to avoid enemy contact and find a way to the crossing site without drawing attention to the buildup near the river—D Company gained the line of the Waal by noon, cleared out some snipers and a small group of Germans in the area, and set up security.[14] The rest of the regiment moved to the crossing site without incident. Once there the troopers settled down to wait for the boats in some low ground that was shielded from enemy observation by a dike and some large factory buildings.[15]

Meanwhile, Captain Wesley D. Harris, the C Company, 307th, commander, went forward to take a look at the launch site. When he returned, he reported that at the point where the canal flowed into the river the current was so swift that he felt it would propel the boats too far downstream. He suggested therefore that the troopers prepare the boats in their hide position, carry them up and over the dike to their front, and then launch the boats directly onto the Waal. In this manner, though still affected by the current, the boats would not drift as much, and the troopers would be closer to their objectives once they reached the far shore. But this meant that the troopers would be launching the boats in full view of the enemy. Tucker and Cook accepted Harris's recommendation, trusting that the promised fire support would provide enough cover to mitigate the risk.[16]

While Harris was conducting his reconnaissance, Cook, Keep, and the 3/504th's company commanders climbed a nearby power station to conduct one of their own. "Everyone gasped when they saw the width of the river and the lack of protection," remembered Captain Keep, adding, "This is absolutely impossible—the last evening of our lives."[17] What Keep and the others saw was, in fact, quite frightening. Not only was the river wide, but after making landfall on the far shore the troopers would be on a flat, coverless river plain some eight hundred yards deep bounded by a dike approximately thirty feet tall behind which they could clearly see Germans. Furthermore, northeast of the landing site was Hof van Holland, a huge nineteenth-century fortress that dominated the north shore and at which was located a battery of 20mm antiaircraft guns.[18] "It looked like a suicide mission," thought Captain T. Moffatt Burriss, the I Company commander.[19] To add to their concern, while Cook and his officers were scanning the river they got a taste of enemy firepower on the other side when some aircraft bound for Arnhem flew overhead. "A veritable wall of small arms and flak greeted them from the area north of the Waal," recalled Captain Carl W. Kappel, the H Company commander.[20] In a letter to his mother he wrote sometime later, Captain Keep described the impact the scene had on him and his comrades: "As we wound our way down the twisting stairs of the tower, no one said a word but from ensuing conversations I have learned that all our thoughts were identical. How could this operation succeed[?] At least ¾'s of the Battalion would be killed and the rest would drift downstream. It was a humanly impossible undertaking. However, it had to be done and quickly: the bridge must be taken: the road to [Arnhem] must be opened up."[21]

Sometime thereafter, Tucker, Lieutenant Colonel Giles A. M. Vandeleur (the commander of the 2nd Irish Guards), Browning, Horrocks, and Gavin arrived at the crossing site as well. Using the power station as a forward command post, they finalized the assault plan and fire scheme and set 1500 hours as H hour, although this was contingent upon the boats. Nevertheless, at 1445 hours a flight of Typhoons, a late yet welcome addition to the list of supporting assets, would bomb and strafe the far bank. Simultaneously, artillery and mortars would soften the landing site with high explosives until H-5 minutes and then switch to smoke between H-5 and H+5 minutes. Thereafter, indirect fires would be on call and fired only at the express request of troopers on the far shore. Complementing the indirect fires would be direct fire from the 80th's two antitank guns and twenty-four of Vandeleur's tanks, which were to fire at any targets they could clearly identify. If needed, the tanks were also to use smoke shells to cover gaps in the artillery smoke screen. Vandeleur told his tankers that "we knew it [the far shore] was heavily defended, but that we had nothing in detail about the defenses. I remember telling them also what one American company commander, I believe, told me: 'Just keep firing. If you're too close we'll let you know by firing one of our Verey lights.'"[22]

Also present at this meeting was the observant Colonel Chatterton, who was struck by the differences between the Guards and paratroopers. "One [British] brigadier wore suede shoes and sat on a shooting stick," he recalled, while three other Guards officers "had on rather worn corduroy trousers, chukka boots and old school scarves." They stood in stark contrast to Tucker, who "was wearing a helmet that almost covered his face. His pistol was in a holster under his left arm, and he had a knife strapped to his thigh." Furthermore, continued Chatteron, "Tucker occasionally removed his cigar long enough to spit and every time he did faint looks of surprise flickered over the faces of the Guards' officers."[23]

The plan for the far bank was predicated on speed and aggressiveness and focused on one overriding concern—get to the bridges. Given the number of boats that had been promised there was room for only two companies to cross in the first wave. For this dubious honor, Cook selected Kappel's H Company and Burriss's I Company. Attacking on the right, H Company was to hit the far shore and strike out immediately for Hof van Holland, silence its guns, and then move on the highway bridge. Attacking on the left, I Company was to charge the dike, wipe out the resistance there, form a defensive line to protect against counterattacks from the north, and take the north end of the railroad bridge. The rest of the battalion would cross in the second wave and follow H Company. Once the 3/504th was across, the 1/504th would follow and reinforce I Company along the dike.[24]

"There was practically no talking while we waited to cross the river," recalled Keep. According to Lieutenant Megellas of H Company, "As we waited for the boats to arrive, some of the men gathered in small groups; others did what a combat soldier does when waiting: take off his pack, assume the prone position, and catch a few winks." When Horrocks noticed this he turned to Tucker and exclaimed, "My God look at 'em. They make an assault river crossing in a very short time. They'll get killed or wounded and face intense fire but here they lay some of 'em fast asleep! . . . What wonderful troops." Many of the troopers were, in fact, simply resigned to their fate. The 504th's chaplain, Delbert Kuehl, recognized this and decided to go over with the first wave, "thinking to myself that if there ever was a time that the men may need a chaplain it was now." Megellas asked his good friend and fellow H Company platoon leader, Richard "Rivers" LaRiviere, "to contact my mother if he survived and I did not. His request to me was similar."[25]

Besides fear and anxiety, the troopers had also to deal with the slow death of Lieutenant Edward T. "Polack" Wisniewski, a popular D Company platoon leader, who was wounded while clearing the area. Wisniewski was lying in full view of German snipers. "We tried to get some medics out there," remembered Lieutenant Hanz Karl Druener, another D Company platoon leader, "but every time they moved, the Germans would either hit one of them or they couldn't make it out there." "Hearing of his fate and his patrol had a chilling effect on us," wrote Megellas, "but it prepared us for the worst."[26] Wisniewski bled out and died before anyone could get to him.

The boats arrived at about 1440 hours, twenty minutes before H hour. Each was nineteen feet long, blunt on both ends, constructed of green canvas sides, and had reinforced plywood bottoms. The sides folded flat like an accordion; when extended they were thirty inches from deck to gunwale and held in place by wooden struts. Each boat weighed three to four hundred pounds and was allotted eight paddles, although not all boats had that many. Thirty-three boats had been promised, but one of the trucks bringing them forward had been destroyed by artillery fire. The engineers had already organized the battalions into boatloads, assuming approximately ten men per boat (the rated carrying capacity) plus two to three engineers. When only twenty-six boats arrived, the loads were hastily rearranged, resulting in as many as sixteen to eighteen troopers per boat.[27]

As they unloaded and assembled the boats and saw the state of their flotilla, the troopers reacted with grim humor. "Where are the Boy Scouts to go with these toys?" quipped one trooper. "You mean I'm trusting my life to that thing?" asked another.[28] As he watched his platoon assemble its boats, Lieutenant Megellas thought back to his days of fishing the lakes of Wisconsin:

> The boat I was accustomed to was only a few feet shorter than these boats but was sturdy, wooden, and seaworthy and had a gas-powered outboard motor.

> Only three people could fish out of it; four was somewhat crowded and five or more made it overcrowded. Yet here we were, thirteen paratroopers with our individual weapons, crew-served weapons, ammunition, and packs, along with two engineers . . . preparing to squeeze into a nineteen-foot canvas boat propelled by an armful of paddles. . . . I wondered if we could stay afloat even without enemy resistance.[29]

Adding to the troopers' consternation was the absence of life vests. But every man would go, regardless of his ability to swim; it was thought that, weighted down with so much equipment, there was little chance of survival anyway if someone were to fall overboard.

The arrival of the boats and the attendant activity of unloading and assembling them attracted the attention of the enemy, who started targeting the area with artillery, but the fire did little damage beyond adding to the fear felt throughout the ranks as the troopers queued up, waiting for the signal to go. First, however, they had to await the preassault bombardment. At 1445 hours, right on schedule, the Typhoons appeared overhead, dropped their loads, and strafed the far bank. Simultaneously, the howitzers, mortars, and tanks opened up while the troopers of D Company, 2/504th, started firing so furiously that they burned out several machine-gun barrels.[30] Finally, at 1500 hours, Major Cook raised a whistle to his lips and blew.

On Cook's signal the troopers grabbed their boats by the gunwales, hoisted them on their shoulders, and set out for the riverbank some 150 yards away. It was hardly an exercise in precision. "The boats were heavy and clumsy and it was a hot day," recalled Lieutenant Holabird. "There was the usual groaning and grumbling and slipping and everybody snapping at everybody else." Moreover, with all the ammunition, equipment, and weaponry piled inside, the weight of the boats had doubled, and getting to the riverbank meant carrying them through loose sand up the near side of the dike and then down the far side through ankle-deep mud. A wire fence about halfway down the far side of the dike further slowed progress. Yet everything seemed to be going well. "We must have caught the Krauts by surprise," wrote Captain Keep, "because for the first 100 yds there wasn't a round fired from the enemy side of the river."[31]

Then, as Tucker, Keep, and Megellas described it, "all hell broke loose." "They opened up with everything they had," continued Megellas. "Small arms, machine guns, 20mm flak wagons, mortars, and artillery. As we frantically scurried for the river's edge, chaos and confusion reigned. With shells exploding all around us, we kept charging forward. At that point we were all driven by instinct and running on adrenaline with but a single purpose: to get our boats in the water and across the river."[32]

The riverbank quickly became "a scene of mass confusion," remembered Captain Kappel. In a rush to get under way several boats bottomed out in the shallow water and mud at the river's edge, forcing the troopers to scramble out, push the boats into deeper water, and then attempt to clamber back aboard. In the process several troopers lost their footing. Some swam back to shore. Most made it. Captain Kappel spotted one trooper, a nonswimmer, foundering in the swift current. Kappel dove in after him, helped the trooper back to shallow water, forced his way onto another boat, and made it to the far side with the first wave, albeit without a weapon or combat harness, having discarded them before his swim. "I think he [Kappel] was just about the bravest man that ever was," said Sergeant Albert Tarbell, who witnessed his commander's lifesaving feat. Captain Keep recalled that by the time his boatload got to the river, "the situation was horrible. The automatic and flat trajectory fire had increased and the artillery was deadly. Men were falling right and left. In everyone's ears was the constant roar of bursting artillery shells, the dull wham of a 20mm, or the disconcerting ping of rifle fire." Captain Burriss wrote, "Finally, God only knows how, we got everybody on boats and started paddling across the river." Watching from the power station, Browning turned to Tucker and said, "What magnificent troopers to move forward like that. Any nation should be proud of 'em."[33]

The sand, mud, and wire on the near bank and the confusion at the water's edge upset the timing of the attack, so "by the time [the troopers] got the boats in the water and were starting across holes began to appear in the smoke." In fact, so thin was the smoke screen that many troopers reported afterward that there was virtually nothing shielding them from enemy observation. According to Chaplain Kuehl, "By the time we reached the riverbank with the boats, the smoke was gone." Captain Keep thought the smoke screen "completely ineffective." Captain Burriss recalled that when he got to the riverbank, "The wind had already blown away the smoke, and our position was completely exposed." Vandeleur ordered his tanks to fire all the smoke they had: "Normally, we would have about 15 rounds per tank. I don't know what we had that day, but I do know that not only was it not as effective as that laid down by the big guns, there was not enough of it. By the time the airborne troops were about halfway across, huge gaps had begun to appear and the Germans were beginning to shoot them up. We had kept our smoke going for about 10 minutes before it ran out."[34]

With little or no smoke to cover them, the boats were sitting ducks. Ordnance of every shape and caliber churned the water around them. By far the deadliest fire came from the railroad bridge, an excellent vantage point from which to take the flotilla in enfilade (the next day Private Joseph A. Dickson of the engineers counted thirty-four machine guns, two 20mm guns, and one

88mm gun on that one bridge alone).[35] Lieutenant Patrick Mulloy, a veteran of the Italian campaign, likened the fire to "the worst we ever took at Anzio." Sergeant Tarbell wrote that "it looked like it was raining from the way the bullets were hitting the water." The same metaphor came to Captain Burriss: "The surface of the water looked like it was in the middle of a sudden rainstorm, the sky actually hailing bullets." To Private First Class Everett S. Trefetheren it looked like "a school of mackerel on the feed."[36]

"Lead was flying at us from all directions," recalled Lieutenant Megellas, opening "gaping holes in the canvas sides." Those not paddling "were frantically trying to keep their boats afloat, bailing with their helmets." A trooper sitting next to Chaplain Kuehl in Major Cook's boat was hit in the head by a 20mm shell. "The top of his head was sheared off and you could see inside his skull." Kuehl also recalled hearing the devout Cook chanting in a loud voice, "Hail, Mary, full of grace. Hail, Mary, full of grace." Paddling nearby, Kuehl timed his strokes with "Lord, thy will be done. Lord, thy will be done."[37] Watching from the power station, Vandeleur was "almost trying to will them on faster. It was obvious they were inexperienced in handling assault boats, which are not the easiest of things to maneuver even in the best of conditions." Doubtless, one of the boats Vandeleur spied was Staff Sergeant Clark H. Fuller's. According to Fuller, "There were only two oars, and in the excitement the men on the oars worked against each other, resulting in our boat going around in circles." Sergeant Tarbell, also in Fuller's boat, yelled at the oarsmen to pull together. "I was so scared I almost felt paralyzed," thought Fuller, thankful that someone had taken charge to get the boat headed in the right direction. Captain Burriss was in another boat that, for a time, also circled aimlessly in the middle of the river. An engineer in the stern was hit and killed, and the upper half of his torso fell into the water and acted as a rudder, forcing the boat into a constant turn. Burriss disentangled the engineer's lifeless legs from the impedimenta piled in the boat, pushed the corpse overboard, and then watched dumbstruck as "the red blood [streamed] from what was left of his head." Captain Keep, who had rowed competitively in college, "had a rather incongruous vision—of our coxswain at Princeton on Lake Carnegie pounding rhythmically on the sides of the flimsy shell and of our rowing in unison pulling to the time of his beats. And so I started to count 1, 2, 3, 4 and then repeat. All at once for no apparent reason I found myself yelling 9 in a stentorian voice. Feeling rather silly I stopped; anyway I was out of breath."[38]

It took the boats fifteen to twenty-five minutes to cross the river, although to Chaplain Kuehl "it seemed like ages."[39] Along the way more than half were either sunk or so riddled with holes that they were abandoned on the north shore. Casualties were heavy, and although no one is certain how many of the approximately three hundred troopers in the initial wave were lost, the 3/504th's casualties for the day were twenty-eight killed, one missing, and seventy-eight wounded, while C Company, 307th Engineers, lost eight killed and twenty-six wounded.[40] Lieutenant Megellas lost half his platoon in mid-stream when its boat capsized and sank after an enemy shell exploded nearby. He looked on helplessly as fifteen paratroopers "splashed frantically to keep from submerging or being swept downstream. There was nothing we could do to help them; the strong current made it impossible to maneuver our boat toward them, and there were no other boats near enough to provide aid."[41]

Because of the strong current the boats made landfall on the north bank three to five hundred yards farther downstream than anticipated. "We climbed over the wounded and dead in the bottom of the boat and up to our knees in water waded to shore where behind a small embankment we flopped down gasping for breath, safe for the moment from the incessant firing," wrote Captain Keep. Captain Kappel did not wait for his boat to beach before exiting. With only three men aboard still capable of paddling, Kappel again jumped overboard about thirty yards from shore and pushed it in the rest of the way. "The boat was half-filled with water," he recalled. "Most of it was blood." The troopers in Lieutenant Ernest Patrick Murphy's boat also disembarked early, although not of their own accord; they were thrown overboard about twenty yards from shore when a shell exploded nearby and capsized their craft. After scrambling ashore, Murphy counted his men. He could account for all save one: Private Joseph Jedlicka. Then Murphy's eyes fastened on a disturbance in the water. Major Cook saw the same thing: "I was just getting ready to get out of my boat when I saw a bubble of air come up out of the water. I hesitated a moment and looked further. I saw [a] 'bulge' in the water & kept on looking as I saw it move to the shore. My sensation was one of confusion by this thing in the water. Rapidly, the 'bulge' emerged from the water—all ashen gray just the color of the disturbed water." Carrying a BAR and two cans of ammunition, Jedlicka, a nonswimmer, used the weight as ballast to keep him on the bottom so he could walk to shore.[42]

Once ashore the troopers sought cover so they could catch their breath, gather their nerves, and prepare themselves for the assault inland. Many were so overcome with fear and exhaustion that they vomited. Yet two intrepid souls remained at the water's edge, fully exposed to enemy fire: Captain Hyman D. Shapiro, the 3/504th's assistant medical officer, and Chaplain Kuehl, who assisted Shapiro in his ministrations. The duo performed what first aid they could, administered morphine where needed, and trundled the seriously wounded into the remaining boats for transport back to the south shore. And though their courage was engraved forever in the memories of those they saved that day, both men downplayed their contributions.[43] According to Shapiro, "The role of a parachute doctor was basically a first aid man. What impressed me was that we might not really do much good as doctors. Our worth, it sometimes seemed, came from just being there, giving moral support. This contribution was our most important role." Kuehl, who was himself wounded in the process, was likewise dismissive of his actions, remembering instead the heroism of the men with whom he served: "While I was leaning over a trooper who had three bullet holes in his stomach, a mortar shell exploded behind me. I was hit by shrapnel, which hit my back, knocking me down. Despite being seriously wounded, the man cried out: 'Chaplain, they got you, too?' That was the kind of men we had."[44]

All semblance of unit cohesion had been lost in the maelstrom of the crossing. Consequently, the surviving troopers assembled around the nearest officers and sergeants, cleared their weapons, gathered their ammunition, and steeled themselves for the assault against the dike eight hundred yards away. Moreover, their blood was up. Gripped by an atavistic passion to wreak havoc and exact revenge, they were transformed from hapless sailors into rampaging soldiers of destruction. "When we finally got to the opposite shore, [wrote Sergeant Fuller,] I experienced a feeling I never felt before. All fear of the past 15 or 20 minutes that it took for the crossing seemed to leave me, to be replaced by a surge of reckless abandon that threw caution to the winds. I felt as though I could lick the whole German Army if they [*sic*] were in front of me at that moment." When Captain Burriss gave the order to charge, "Without hesitation, every single man, including several who were wounded, jumped from the embankment and started running forward and firing furiously at the machine guns on the back side of the dike." "It was kill or be killed," remembered Lieutenant Megellas. "Men driven by rage were cursing the Germans as they charged forward, running low and firing their weapons as they advanced."[45] Hyperbole aside, Captain Keep described eloquently what occurred that day on the north bank of the Waal:

> Many times I have seen troops who are driven to a fever pitch—troops who for a brief interval of combat are lifted out of themselves—fanatics rendered crazy by rage and the lust for killing—men who forget temporarily the meaning of fear. It is then that the great military feats of history occur which are commemorated so gloriously in our text books. It is an awe-inspiring sight but not a pretty one. However, I had never witnessed this human metamorphosis so acutely displayed as on this day. The men were beside themselves. They continued to plow across that field in spite of all the Kraut could do, cursing savagely, their guns spitting fire.[46]

Although not in accordance with the original plan, troopers from both companies charged across the open ground toward the dike. They were in no mind for quarter. Along the way they overran German outposts and bayoneted their occupants mercilessly.[47] Once at the dike they counted their numbers, caught their breath, and resumed their charge up and over to get at the enemy on the other side. A few Germans stood in their holes and offered their surrender. It was too late. "Our men, in a frenzy over the wholesale slaughter of their buddies, continued to fire until every German on the dike lay dead or dying," said Burriss. Captain Kappel's troopers were also gripped by bloodlust. In response to some chiding by a fellow officer about the few prisoners H Company took that day, Kappel replied, "You captured yours. We shot ours."[48]

On the other side of the dike the attack devolved into a miscellany of small-unit clashes as groups of anywhere from five to twenty paratroopers set out to "hunt Germans." Some troopers took to the trenches, clearing them with grenades. Others sought out machine-gun crews. But anywhere a German raised his head, or his hands, he was killed. "The Germans had blown their opportunity to stop us when they had us in their crosshairs on the Waal," wrote Megellas. Once over the dike, "We were no longer sitting ducks but moving targets coming at them."[49]

The fight at the dike was over by about 1545 hours, after which Burriss set most of I Company in defensive positions while he and a small contingent made for the railroad bridge. Simultaneously, H Company made for the highway bridge. Lieutenant Megellas and eleven H Company troopers went after Hof van Holland, which, despite the Typhoon attack and a steady rain of Allied artillery, was still spewing fire from four 20mm guns and countless machine guns.[50]

Megellas and his troopers came at the fort from the north. As they got closer they could see that it "resembled an inverted bowl, with sides sloping at about a forty-five-degree incline from the edge of [a water-filled] moat to the top of the fort, a distance of about fifty feet. The sloping sides were earthen and sodded. There was a parapet ringing the top from where the Germans had been firing at us."[51] Concentrating his troopers' fire along the parapet to drive the Germans to cover, Megellas then led a charge to the edge of the moat, where Sergeant Leroy Richmond stripped off his combat harness, jumped into the moat, swam across, gained the fort's wall, and crawled up the inclined face to take a look inside. From his vantage point, Richmond saw a drawbridge on the opposite side of the fort and yelled back to Megellas to try an attack from there. Circling around to the south side of the fort, where he linked up with a few more H Company troopers, Megellas first sent two troopers across the drawbridge to test the German fire. When they were driven back Megellas led another charge across the drawbridge and up the fort's wall to the parapet, where he and his troopers destroyed the enemy guns and drove the defenders into hiding in the structures below. With Hof van Holland's guns silenced and the Germans bottled up inside, Megellas and his troopers made for the bridges, save for a machine-gun crew that he left at the head of the drawbridge to keep the Germans bottled up inside the fort.[52]

Several hundred yards east of Hof van Holland was a raised embankment, running generally north-south, atop which were the railroad tracks that emanated from the north end of Nijmegen's railroad bridge. Many of the Germans that had escaped the slaughter at the dike retreated to this embankment, where they joined others already there who were forming up behind it with the intent of holding off the paratroopers until reinforcements arrived.

The first groups of paratroopers to reach the railroad embankment tried fighting their way through narrow underpasses that punctuated its length at several places. They were repulsed by German machine guns that turned the underpasses into death traps. Other troopers tried charging up and over, but this too, proved costly. With neither side strong enough to force the other to withdraw, a stalemate developed, with German and American soldiers holding positions on either side of the embankment, separated by but a few yards, periodically exchanging grenades and rifle shots. It was "jack-in-the-box shooting," said Sergeant Theodore Finkbeiner, as paratroopers on one side and Germans on the other intermittently popped up, fired a few rounds, and then quickly ducked for cover.[53]

Inexplicably, the weakest point of the German defenses along the railroad embankment was at its juncture with the railroad bridge. The first to reach that juncture were five troopers led by Lieutenant LaRiviere. Crawling through some ditches near the riverbank, LaRiviere and his troopers sneaked around the embankment, stormed the northern end of the bridge, killed fourteen Germans, and took twenty prisoners. Following a quick search for demolition wires, LaRiviere positioned his small band to defend the north end of the bridge and waited for reinforcements. By that time it was about 1700 hours; the first of the 3/504th's primary missions had been accomplished.[54]

It was not long before LaRiviere's ranks swelled as other paratroopers filtered into the area. Unable to breach the German defenses along the railroad embankment, the troopers simply headed south and followed it to the railroad bridge. Lieutenant Edward J. Sims, another H Company platoon leader, was among the first to arrive, followed shortly by Captain Burriss with twenty troopers in tow. Burriss did not tarry long, however. When he saw that the north end of the railroad bridge was in hand, he and LaRiviere set off for the highway bridge, leaving Sims in command at the railroad bridge. Soon after

Burriss departed, Major Cook and Captain Kappel arrived with approximately three platoons and solidified the hold on the railroad bridge by capturing a concrete and steel bunker that had been constructed beside the tracks.[55]

At 1740 hours, Major Cook radioed the 504th's command post to report: "Have guns and Dyke, Request Tanks to move across the bridge to help them out." Five minutes later Lieutenant Colonel Williams radioed back, "Your request is being carried out" (by that time Tucker was on the north bank of the river, having crossed over with the 1/504th).[56] But despite Williams's assurance, no tanks came. Instead, there emerged from the smoke and haze that blanketed the railroad bridge—the result of the Germans having set fire to whole city blocks to aid them in their defense—more than 300 SS soldiers hell bent on escaping Nijmegen, apparently unaware that their route was barred by American paratroopers. According to Lieutenant Sims, "We let them come within range and then opened fire." Firing two captured machine guns down the long axis of the bridge, Sims's troopers rent the enemy formation, while Captain Kappel, who had taken up position inside the captured bunker, threw Gammon grenades into their midst as fast as they were passed to him. "At the time, my men and I were tense and angry because of the strenuous fighting and loss of many of our own men during the crossing," recalled Sims. "We had little concern about destroying the large enemy force opposing us." After beating back the attack, Kappel sent a prisoner to the middle of the bridge to convince the survivors to surrender. The SS soldiers shot him down. Their mercy rejected, the paratroopers opened up a second time to finish the job. Quite a few Germans tried escaping the carnage by leaping into the Waal. When the firing stopped, 267 Germans lay dead on the bridge. Scores more were wounded.[57]

Meanwhile Burriss, LaRiviere, and a scratch group of approximately twenty troopers made for the highway bridge. Apparently, they were traveling quite close to the river because German fire from the south bank scattered their force and drove most of the group back to the railroad bridge. Burriss and LaRiviere, who were in the lead, gathered the few troopers they had remaining and continued on.

Clustered around the northern end of the highway bridge was a sizable suburb that slowed the paratroopers' movement considerably as they moved through the streets in a deadly game of hide-and-seek. But with scores of enemy soldiers traversing the area contact was inevitable. Burriss entered a house and stumbled on some German soldiers who, despite the din of battle, were sleeping. "I stepped on the porch . . . and opened the door. More than a dozen German soldiers were sleeping on the floor. One of them, a grizzled veteran, rolled over, opened one eye, saw me, and grabbed for his rifle. When he did, I tossed a Gammon grenade in the middle of the sleeping pile and dived off the porch. . . . The ensuing blast blew out the windows and the door. . . . There were no survivors." Elsewhere the group ambushed a German sedan, in the process causing it to flip over. When it did Dutch money poured out a broken window. "All of us grabbed handfuls of bills, stuffed them in our pockets and shirts, and continued toward the bridge," said Burriss.[58] Twice they found their way blocked by 88mm gun emplacements. Twice they knocked out the guns without losing a man. Finally, two hours after starting out this small band, which somewhere along the way was rejoined by the troopers that were earlier driven back, reached the highway bridge. It was 1900 hours.[59]

Although Burriss, LaRiviere, and their troopers could clearly hear the sounds of battle raging near the bridge's southern exit, the area around the northern exit was strangely quiet and deserted. Amazingly, the only person anywhere near the bridge was a lone German sentry who, when confronted by the two paratroop officers, "was so surprised to see us that he dropped his rifle, held up his arms, and immediately surrendered." With that the northern end of the highway bridge was in American hands. The next task was to keep it.[60]

Burriss's primary concern, of course, was that the Germans would blow the bridge. Although his troopers cut every wire they came across, there was no way to tell if any of them led to the demolition charges. Furthermore, he did not know where the detonating mechanism was, and dispersing his small band in a fruitless search could spell disaster if the Germans counterattacked. The only thing to do, then, was to find the explosives themselves, which he assumed were located near the center of the span where they could do the most damage, and cut the wires there. Turning to LaRiviere, Burriss told him to take two men and move out. Private James Musa was one of the troopers LaRiviere selected:

> The Germans were firing at us from the girders and there were more on the bridge. Some Germans tried to escape the advance of the Allied Forces on the south and ran toward us. We held our fire until they were within close range and then opened fire. Some turned around and started back towards the south end trying to surrender. Other Germans were still holding out in the girders on the bridge. We called for them to come down and surrender. I remember one of our men climbing a girder when an SS officer shot him in the chest. We retaliated with a hail of bullets, knocking him out of the girder and into the river below.[61]

LaRiviere and his men never got to the center of the bridge. It was not, however, the snipers that stopped them. Rather, it was the looming silhouettes of tanks approaching from the south end. Certain that this was the vanguard of a German counterattack, LaRiviere and his troopers retreated back to the northern end of the bridge and took cover beside the roadway with the rest of their group. In the failing light and swirling smoke it was difficult to tell what sort of tanks were approaching, but taking no chances as soon as they were within range the troopers let fly with two Gammon grenades. Luckily, their aim was off; the tanks were British Shermans. When the paratroopers realized this, they swarmed the tanks and their crews. According to Burriss, LaRiviere was so overjoyed he climbed aboard the lead tank and gave its commander a kiss. The time was 1915 hours.[62]

The tanks, two in number, were from the 2nd Grenadier Guards under the command of Sergeant Peter Robinson. It was Robinson's second attempt at crossing the bridge that day. The first, undertaken at around 1800 hours (the result of the misinterpretation of Cook's radio message to send tanks "across the bridge"; Cook meant the railroad, not the highway, bridge) ran into a fusillade of antitank fire from a gun on the far bank and had to be abandoned. The second, mounted twenty minutes later, resulted from a radio call from Lieutenant Colonel Moore ordering Robinson to take the bridge at all cost. Roaring forward with hatches closed and machine guns blazing, Robinson's tankers had not only to brave the same antitank fire that halted their first attempt, they also had to run a gauntlet of *panzerfausts* and grenades that were fired or dropped on them by Germans secreted in the bridge's girders. Robinson started the charge with four tanks. The two in the rear were knocked out before getting across, but Robinson's Sherman and one other made it all the way, literally skidding to a halt past some concrete barricades just shy of the bridge's northern exit ramp, where Robinson's gunner sighted the antitank gun that had earlier thwarted them. A snap shot dazed the German crew, and before they could recover, Robinson had his driver charge the emplacement, crushing both men and metal beneath the treads. Continuing off the ramp, the two Shermans destroyed a second antitank gun and annihilated a large party of German infantry before linking up with Burriss's group.[63]

The meeting of British tanks and American paratroopers at the northern end of the highway bridge has been cast as the fitting finale to the coordinated attack on Nijmegen's bridges that Gavin forwarded earlier. Yet this was not the case. Although it is true that Robinson's mad dash was the culmination of a renewed attack by Goulburn's Grenadier Guards and Vandervoort's paratroopers on the southern end of the highway bridge, and that this attack was undertaken at approximately the same time as the river crossing, a close reading of the contemporaneous records shows that, ironically, the attack through the city *was conceived and executed under the premise that there would be no river crossing*. Moreover, for most of the day Goulburn and, one may assume, Vandervoort *were wholly unaware that a river crossing had even taken place*. Hence, what looked like and has since been characterized as a finely synchronized operation was, in reality, the coincidental convergence of two separate attacks, albeit two attacks with the same objective.

When Goulburn returned to his command post after calling off his attack on 19 September, he found waiting for him a message to report to Brigadier Gwatkin to receive his orders for the next day. After first checking on the disposition of his task force, which was no mean feat given its dispersion throughout the city, it was quite late when Goulburn arrived at Gwatkin's command post to learn that he was to renew his attack the next day. American paratroopers would be crossing the river west of the city, said Gwatkin, and Goulburn was to mount a coordinated attack to support them. However, whereas Gavin envisaged (and so briefed Tucker) that *both* bridges would be attacked, Gwatkin's orders were that Goulburn *was only to renew the attack on the highway bridge*. Captain Neville's column near the railroad bridge was to hold in place to protect the flank of Vandeleur's 2nd Irish Guards as it moved through the western part of Nijmegen to the river crossing site. (It was only when checking on his forces before reporting to Gwatkin that Goulburn learned that Neville and Smith had failed to take the railroad bridge "but had done a lot of destruction amongst the BOSCH and had got safely tucked away for the night in a block of buildings South of the bridge." Given their location and strength, Goulburn felt that Neville's Guardsmen and Smith's paratroopers "would be well able to look after themselves" and were therefore well positioned and in sufficient strength to carry out Gwatkin's orders.)[64] Then, just before leaving Gwatkin's command post, Goulburn overheard a staff officer say that Vandeleur's tanks would not be required at 0800, a remark that stemmed no doubt from the delays associated with getting the boats forward. Goulburn, however, "left with the impression that that operation in the West of the town was postponed and would probably not take place at all."[65]

Goulburn next went to see Vandervoort. "I wondered if [Vandervoort] would agree to the plan I had in the back of my mind," recalled Goulburn, "[but] I had no cause to worry as he was most anxious to do whatever we thought best." Proceeding from the mistaken impression that the river crossing had been canceled and that, therefore, it was up to him and Vandervoort to take the highway bridge, Goulburn proposed throwing everything they had at it. But he also wanted to avoid another bloody frontal assault. Hence, he wanted to reposition his column so that it could attack the German defenses at the south end of the highway bridge from multiple directions simultaneously, which would mean "moving through a good portion of the town which we did not hold, and about which we knew nothing." To facilitate this repositioning, Goulburn told Nevillle that instead of guarding Vandeleur's flank, which Goulburn assumed was no longer necessary since he thought there would be no river crossing, Neville was to protect his flanks while he repositioned his column. Nevertheless, the outcome was the same—there would be no attack on the southern approaches to the railroad bridge.[66]

Even with Neville's column protecting its flanks, repositioning the rest of the task force for an attack on the highway bridge would be tricky. Goulburn's intent was to send three mechanized infantry companies, each of which he reinforced with a troop of tanks, on a wheeling movement through the city streets. Major Harry F. Stanley's No. 4 Company, 1st Grenadier Guards, which was in position around the post office—Goulburn sent it there sometime on 19 September to reinforce Major Thorne—was to jump off first and take up positions to the left of and at an approximate right angle to Vandervoort's positions at the southern edge of the Keizer Lodewijk Plein. Thereafter, No. 2 Company would follow and fall in on No. 4 Company's left to be followed by King's Company, which would fall in on No. 2 Company's left. If all went according to plan, the Goulburn-Vandervoort force would be arrayed in an *L* to the front of and on the right (western) flank of the Germans defending the highway bridge. Once everyone was in position, Goulburn would attack from all points simultaneously, thereby compelling the Germans to defend in two directions at once. "The operation looked none too easy," he recalled, "and I think most of us felt it was scarcely the orthodox role for our very mobile [battalion] and that we might lose a good proportion of it." But it was better than trying another deadly dash across the traffic circle, and, with luck, the enemy would break somewhere. Jump-off time for the repositioning movement was set for 0815 hours, 20 September.[67]

Vandervoort's troopers spent the evening of 19–20 September shoring up their positions, probing for gaps in the German defenses, and defending against enemy patrols. Periodically, the boom of a tank or self-propelled gun would rend the night, but since any muzzle flash attracted an almost immediate response, this was kept to a minimum. Somewhat more frequent were mortar and artillery exchanges, but with the combatants in such close proximity to each other this, too, was minimal. Hence, most of the fighting that night was between small groups of soldiers that bumped into one another in streets, yards, hallways, and, at times, in the same room. "German patrols . . . tried to enter the houses we occupied," wrote Vandervoort. "They were gunned down through the lace curtained front doors and windows."[68] Moreover, the glow from burning buildings and the almost constant canopy of flares played tricks on the eyes. Troopers from E Company, 2/505th, for example, moved into what they thought were some abandoned foxholes only to discover that Germans were still there. In the ensuing melee, fought with bayonets and trench knives, the paratroopers expelled the occupants only to be exposed, minutes later, to a withering artillery barrage.[69] In another instance, Corporal Earl Boling was on the ground floor of a house bordering the traffic circle when he heard the distinctive sound of hobnailed boots on the pavement outside. Since both the Germans and the British wore hobnails, Boling had his men hold their fire until he could identify the approaching forms. The distinctive cut of the helmets told the tale; it was a five-man German patrol headed right at them. Boling told one of his men to throw a grenade. This scattered the Germans, although three of them came running straight at the window where Boling and Private George Wood were keeping station. Boling dropped two of the three with his BAR, but the third kept coming. Attempting to reload, Boling got so nervous that he dropped his magazine, so he reached for the trench knife in his boot. By that time the German was at the window with his Luger drawn, but before Boling could make his lunge, Private Wood shot the German five times in the face from point-blank range. "We could see the German's head bounce with each impact," recalled Boling, "but he did not release the window sill and drop until the fifth shot." One of the few division troopers who had fought in every one of the 82nd's campaigns, Boling called that night in Nijmegen "probably the longest night of the war."[70]

By about midafternoon, "it really looked as if our plan was going to succeed," wrote Goulburn. "We had cleared a considerable portion of the town with very few casualties and everyone began to get very excited." But before ordering the assault Goulburn had to make some last-minute adjustments. Rubble from bombed-out buildings had closed off several streets leading to the traffic circle, so Goulburn could not bring all three mechanized companies on line as planned. He decided, therefore, to divide up No. 2 Company's assets between King's Company and No. 4 Company. He then directed King's Company to assault the Valkhof, a large wooded mound that was the highest point in Nijmegen, atop which stood the ruins of an ancient citadel and throughout which ran a maze of subterranean tunnels. No. 4 Company he directed toward a group of buildings that separated the Valkhof from Hunner Park.[71]

While the British were repositioning, Vandervoort's troopers kept a close eye on the German positions, dodged German artillery and mortar fire, and used everything from rifle grenades to bazookas to kill enemy snipers who had infiltrated behind their positions.[72] By far the most active of Vandervoort's force in the hours before the attack was his 81mm mortar platoon, which was dug in in a nearby cemetery, trading fire with their German opposites (in two days the platoon fired 1,650 rounds) as well as insults from passing Tommies who "thought the layout was hilarious" and accused their American brethren of being "fornicating Yank grave-robbers."[73] Otherwise, "the atmosphere of the day was like being in the eye of a hurricane. . . . We knew the storm would be back soon but not when."[74]

Before kicking off, Goulburn visited Vandervoort to finalize the assault plan. Both agreed that Hunner Park "was the place [where] the great bridge would be won or lost," and it was straight into the teeth of the German defenses there that the 2/505th was to mount its charge, traversing an area that was about a quarter mile deep, not much wider, and almost devoid of cover. It was "a bare-assed prospect," said one trooper, but there was no time for anything more elaborate. Goulburn set jump-off time for 1530 hours.[75]

The 2/505th assaulted with four platoons abreast, two each from E Company and F Company on the right and left, respectively. The rest of the battalion provided covering fire from the rooftops.[76] The several hundred Germans defending Hunner Park were commanded by SS-Hauptsturmführer Karl Heinz Euling and included, besides a hodgepodge of German army, police, and Luftwaffe troops, a battalion of SS soldiers. Moreover, the self-propelled guns and 20mm cannon that had wreaked havoc the day before were as yet unscathed, and the 88mm guns across the river targeted anything that moved across the traffic circle.[77] When the paratroopers emerged from their hiding positions they met a withering fusillade. Sergeant Spencer F. Wurst of F Company called it "the hottest, heaviest fire" he had ever encountered. "It appeared to me," Wurst continued, "that I could reach out and grab the bullets as they flew."[78] Yet the Americans gave as good as they got, advancing with bayonets fixed while firing from the hip.[79] Sergeant Wurst fired, reloaded, and fired again so quickly that his rifle barrel overheated and literally boiled the oil residue out of his wooden gun stock. According to Vandervoort, "The air in Hun[n]er Park [turned] blue with hand grenade, cannon, rifle and gun-smoke [*sic*] generated by the hundreds of combatants."[80]

American casualties were heavy, especially among the 2/505th's officers, who, as expected, led from the front. Wurst's platoon leader, Lieutenant Jack Carroll, was wounded by shell fragments. Captain Robert H. Rosen, the F Company commander, was killed while manning a machine gun atop a British tank. Lieutenant Joseph W. Holcomb, who took command of the company after Rosen was killed, was himself wounded shortly thereafter. Charging at the head of his platoon, Lieutenant John Dodd was hit in the torso by an exploding 20mm shell, a wound that should have killed him instantly. But Dodd was "a hard[-]dying young man," so the platoon medic, "with tears in his eyes, gave his dying lieutenant an overdose of morphine to ease his pain."[81] And in the midst of it all was Vandervoort, at one point directing covering fire from the rooftops, at another advancing with the assault element. Sergeant Wurst yelled at Vandervoort to get down, but the 2/505th commander ignored him and, in a calm voice, suggested that Wurst see if he could get a nearby tank into the fight.[82] He was the "best battalion commander I ever had," recalled Wurst. Captain "Doc" Franco, one of the 505th's regimental surgeons, "idolized" Vandervoort. According to Franco, John Wayne, who played Vandervoort in the movie *The Longest Day*, "was a pipsqueak compared to Vandervoort."[83]

The tide began turning in the Allies' favor when No. 4 Company broke through to the traffic circle, although this was not the original plan. Major Stanley was to have assaulted several buildings overlooking Hunner Park and from there taken up firing positions to support Vandervoort's attack, but, as he later wrote, "from the first five minutes the fighting did not conform in the slightest to my original plan." When Stanley's company jumped off it lost four tanks in quick succession to antitank fire, and its infantry was stopped cold by machine-gun and small arms fire. Withdrawing to his start point, Stanley talked things over with Goulburn, who was observing nearby. They agreed to shift the direction of No. 4 Company's assault slightly right so that it could tie in with the 2/505th. This was just what the paratroopers needed. "The British Shermans," recalled Vandervoort, "gave the troopers the cumulative edge" so that "position by position, the tank/trooper collaboration closed down on Hun[n]er Park."[84]

Meanwhile, King's Company found an unguarded spot in a barbed-wire fence, cut its way through, and then stormed "the labyrinth of buildings, trenches, deep shelters and pillboxes which the [Valkhof] consisted of." Opposed by two companies of SS engineers, the fighting was hand-to-hand. Both sides sustained significant casualties, but eventually the weight of the British attack forced the Germans to quit the Valkhof and with it the heights upon which it stood, giving King's Company clear lines of sight to the highway bridge.[85]

The last significant German strongpoint south of the highway bridge was the Haus Robert Janssen, a large building at the foot of the Valkhof Heights that was also SS-Hauptsturmführer Euling's headquarters. It was assaulted by a platoon from No. 4 Company under Lieutenant Adrian Slob who, rather than clear the building room by room, burned the defenders out with phosphorous grenades. Of the approximately 150 Germans inside, some 89 were either killed or captured, while 60, including Euling, somehow escaped and made their way to the north bank. When the Haus Robert Janssen fell, German resistance south of the highway bridge collapsed.[86]

It was at this point that Sergeant Robinson's tank platoon made its mad dash across the highway bridge (Euling recalled that what convinced him to quit the Haus Robert Janssen was seeing Robinson's tanks crossing the bridge).[87] Horrocks "could hardly bear to watch," expecting "the bridge to be blown sky-high at any moment." Also watching was SS-Standartenführer

Heinz Harmel, the *10th SS Panzer Division* commander. Harmel was in a bunker near the small town of Lent on the opposite bank and, though he had no authority to do so, was going to blow the bridge when Robinson's tanks were halfway across, but when he ordered a nearby engineer to detonate the charges, nothing happened. Again and again the engineer depressed the plunger on the detonating mechanism with no results. "I was waiting to see the bridge collapse and the tanks plunge into the river," recalled Harmel. "Instead, they moved forward relentlessly, getting bigger and bigger, closer and closer."[88] With little time to spare before the tanks were on him, Harmel left the bunker for his command post in Bemmel, just north of Lent, where he learned that the railroad bridge, too, was in Allied hands. After ordering every available antitank gun and artillery piece to assemble on the roads leading north from Nijmegen, he put a call through to *II SS Panzer Corps* headquarters.[89] "Tell Bittrich," reported Harmel tersely, that "they're over the Waal."[90]

No one has satisfactorily resolved the mystery of why the highway bridge failed to blow. Harmel offhandedly posited that the wires leading to the explosives were "probably" cut by artillery fire. Captain Burriss, on the other hand, was convinced that his small band of paratroopers cut the wires: "As soon as [Lieutenant LaRiviere] and I reached the bridge, we instructed every man to search and cut every wire he could find. I am firmly convinced that the wires we cut were the demolition wires. Until reading [Cornelius] Ryan's book [*A Bridge Too Far*], it never occurred to me there was any mystery about the wires. To me, it was part of the mission and I thought nothing about it."[91] Yet the most persistent explanation is that a twenty-two-year-old Dutch student saved the bridge. According to this version, the source of which was most likely a local newspaper story published in July 1945, sometime on 18 September Jan van Hoof, a member of the Dutch Resistance, sneaked onto the span and cut the wires connecting the explosive charges to the detonating device. The claim rests on two pieces of evidence. The first was a comment—"The bridge is safe"—van Hoof was said to have made to his sister on the evening of 18 September. The second was the discovery of insulated pliers in van Hoof's overalls. Unfortunately, van Hoof could not corroborate the story himself since he was killed the next day.[92]

The van Hoof story gained official sanction in September 1945 when a stone relief depicting him cutting the wires was unveiled near one of the northern bridge piers. This was followed in July 1946 with the posthumous award of the Dutch military's highest medal, the Militaire Willemsorde. Yet many remained skeptical, and so the Dutch government commissioned a board of inquiry to look into the affair. Following a two-year investigation (1949–1951) the board concluded that although there is a chance that van Hoof cut some wires on 18 September, it is also probable that the Germans discovered the break and repaired the sabotage. However, the board offered no explanation for the failure of the bridge to blow.[93]

Anton Timmers, a Jesuit priest and local historian, disputed the board's tepid findings. According to Timmers, a close analysis of van Hoof's whereabouts on 18 September revealed that there were only two hours during that day—1300–1500 hours—that cannot be accounted for. Hence, if van Hoof cut the wires, it would have to have been during those two hours. However, the heavy fighting going on south of the bridge during that time, the fact that the bridge was heavily guarded, and time-distance calculations that demonstrate it would have been virtually impossible for van Hoof to have gotten to and from the bridge in two hours' time convinced Timmers that there was no way that van Hoof could have sneaked onto the bridge and cut any wires. Furthermore, contended Timmers, had van Hoof cut the wires, he would surely have reported this to Arie Bestebreurtje during a meeting between the two held just prior to Goulburn's task force making its push into Nijmegen. According to Timmers, who interviewed others who were present at the meeting, van Hoof "was urged to tell all he knew about the bridge" and "did so without reserve," but he said nothing about having cut any wires and, in fact, repeated the erroneous information about the detonator being in the post office. "That he could have remained silent on the subject [of having cut the wires] was out of the question and he knew moreover that it was an offense by the Underground code to withold [*sic*] information on such a critical issue." In a postwar interview, Arie Bestebreurtje confirmed having met van Hoof just before Goulburn's attack into Nijmegen. According to Bestebreurtje, van Hoof was "very young," "very nervous," and "highly excited," so excited that Bestebreurtje "did not think he was the right kind of person to guide troops into the city," although he reluctantly agreed to allow van Hoof to accompany a British scout car (during which he was subsequently killed). But Bestebreurtje would not say that van Hoof saved the bridge, although he felt that no one knew the real truth.[94]

So what did happen? According to Timmers, who claimed he gleaned his information from persons with detailed knowledge of the means by which the bridge was to be destroyed, all of the bridge's explosives and fuses were never even emplaced because the procedure the Germans had devised to prepare it for demolition broke down in the chaos and confusion of battle. First of all, explained Timmers, the bridge was not rigged with permanently emplaced explosives. Instead, the Germans devised a procedure whereby, on command, approximately 1,000 kilograms of explosives in blocks of various shapes and sizes that were stored in a storage bunker near the northern end of the bridge were to be hustled to a designated location on the span and laid in a predesignated pattern on both the road surface and some scaffolding beneath the bridge while each of the individual detonating fuses was connected to a master detonating wire. German army engineers were primarily responsible for this mission, but as a fallback some Germans living in Nijmegen were trained to back them up and even rehearsed the procedure several times "in order to learn how to set [the charges] in the shortest possible time."[95]

According to Timmers's sources, the scaffolding charges were emplaced on 8 September 1944. This was a precautionary move, enacted at a time when German forces in Holland were retreating, but with plans in train to stem the rearward tide and stabilize the front south of Nijmegen, the highway bridge had to remain clear of obstacles so that reinforcements could be rushed forward. Hence, the roadbed charges and the fuses remained in the ammunition bunker (in order to achieve the desired effect, the scaffolding and roadbed charges had to be detonated simultaneously; otherwise, the bridge would be damaged, but not destroyed). Then, in the confusion following the Allied landings the German army engineers got cut off from Nijmegen, leaving the task of completing the preparations necessary to destroy the bridge to the German civilians. Most of the civilians, however, were summarily seconded for other duties, leaving only two who were familiar with the procedures to carry out their charge. And, in fact, these two made it to the storage bunker on the evening of 17 September, but rather than waiting around they decided instead to abandon their post and "withdrew from the service." Thus, no one with any knowledge of how to prepare the bridge for destruction was present during the critical days of 19 and 20 September, and, it appears, no one else took the initiative to ensure that the charges and fuses were emplaced. That the explosives were not emplaced was substantiated by refugees who fled the fighting in Nijmegen by crossing over the bridge, none of whom recalled seeing any explosives. Furthermore, Timmers cites evidence from a Dutch policeman who was familiar with the procedure for emplacing the explosives who stated categorically that the bridge was not prepared for demolition on 20 September. And finally, according to Lieutenant Tony Jones, a British engineer officer who followed Robinson's tanks across the bridge, only the scaffolding charges were in place.[96]

Given the above, Timmers concluded that "the fact that the bridge fell undamaged into Allied hands is attributable primarily to the courage and intrepidity of the paratroopers of the 504th U.S. Parachute Regiment."[97] But the river crossing alone would not have been enough to secure the bridge, for had not Goulburn's Guardsmen and Vandervoort's paratroopers overcome the German defenses at the south end of the bridge, Tucker's troopers north of the river, and especially the small band with Burriss at the northern end of the highway bridge, would have been easy prey for a German counterattack.

If anything, it was the shock and surprise of the Allied attack that underscored success, so discomfiting the Germans that their system for destroying the bridge was thrown into disarray.

Vandervoort called the fight for the south end of the highway bridge a "gladiatorial test of wills," a characterization apropos for the battle on both sides of the Waal River on 20 September 1944. "No quarter combat became the order of the day," he continued. "The fighting was so close individual Germans were either too brave or too scared to surrender. Probably both. The Germans seemed indifferent to death. The paratroopers retaliated with ice[-]cold ruthlessness." As might be expected in the aftermath of such vicious combat, each side accused the other of brutality. Oberstleutnant Fullriede interviewed German survivors of the battle and wrote that "the Americans behaved as they always do, throwing our wounded from the bridge into the Waal, and shooting the few prisoners among the army reservists." An SS-Hauptsturmführer Schwappacher, commander of the German contingent defending the dike that Cook's 3/504th assaulted, recalled seeing "shameful mutilations [that] had been committed against the wounded." On the other side of the ledger, Vandervoort recalled witnessing a "crazed Kraut [charge] from a deep air-raid shelter to knife a paratroop aide man tending a wounded German."[98] Lieutenant Peter G. A. Prescott, a tank platoon commander in Major Stanley's No. 4 Company, wrote of an American medic being targeted by German snipers while he was rendering aid to a wounded Guardsman.[99] Sergeant Finkbeiner encountered some Germans who used a white flag of surrender to lure Americans from behind cover only to open fire once their would-be captors showed themselves.[100]

Such accounting provides little in the way of determining the relative chivalry of either side. Rather, it is a testament to the ferocity of the fight, a fight during which both sides bled profusely. Although no accurate casualty figures exist, the official U.S. Army history puts total losses for the two battalions from the 504th that crossed the Waal and Vandervoort's battalion in Nijmegen at around 200.[101] Goulburn put British casualties at just under 100.[102] German casualties must have been significantly higher. In addition to the 267 Germans killed at the railroad bridge, several hundred more bodies were found in the small area south of the highway bridge alone (according to 82nd intelligence reports, there were some 500 German defenders in the vicinity of Hunner Park; only 60 were left alive at the conclusion of the fighting).[103] And no one knows how many Germans Cook's rampaging troopers or the troopers from the 1/504th who followed them across the river killed.[104]

Bill Downs, a CBS war correspondent who witnessed the river crossing, described what he saw in terms reminiscent of romantic histories of bygone eras: "A single isolated battle that ranks in magnificence and courage with Guam, Tarawa, Omaha Beach. A story that should be told to the blowing of bugles and the beating of drums for the men whose bravery made the capture of this crossing over the Waal . . . [p]ossible." Lieutenant General Horrocks called the crossing "one of the finest attacks ever carried out during [World War II]." As for the Nijmegen fight as a whole, Horrocks wrote, "I don't believe that any other troops in the world could possibly have fought better than the Guards and the 82nd U.S. Airborne Division when they captured the bridges at Nijmegen." And although justifiably proud of the performance put in by his Guardsmen, in private Horrocks was clear about who he felt truly carried the day. In a letter to Gavin not meant for public consumption ("Please treat this in confidence," he wrote), Horrocks was much more open in his assessment of the battle: "As I think you know, I always regarded your Division (the 82nd) as the best I ever came across in the last war. All your men were tough individuals and very quick into battle—far quicker than was the case with our troops."[105] Horrocks was not alone in his opinion of the 82nd Airborne Division. Shortly after Nijmegen's bridges had been secured, "Doc" Franco was in the 2/505th command post when in walked General Browning. Franco witnessed Browning seize Vandervoort by the hand and declare, "Congratulations, Colonel, you've shown me the best infantry I've ever seen." And when Lieutenant General Sir Miles C. Dempsey, the British Second Army commander, visited the 82nd command post a few days later, he greeted Gavin with the statement: "I'm proud to meet the Commanding General of the finest division in the world today."[106]

It is hard to argue with the observations of Downs, Horrocks, and Dempsey. In one of the hardest-fought battles of the war the troopers of the 82nd Airborne Division proved their mettle. And were it the only battle in which the division ever fought, it would suffice to secure for it a place in the annals of the U.S. Army. But it was not the division's only battle. Even more astonishingly, it was not even the only battle in which the 82nd was engaged that day.

CHAPTER 19

EVEN THE GODS WERE WEEPING

I don't think there was another day like it in the war.

—JAMES M. GAVIN TO CORNELIUS RYAN, 13 JULY 1973

AT 1330 HOURS, 20 September, Gavin was calmly sitting with his back to a tree near the crossing site waiting for the boats to arrive, a calm that belied his deep concern that Tucker was preparing to make an assault that "should have required at least a division in any Command and General Staff School exercise."[1] Gavin tried never to assign his troopers "missions that are beyond the possibility of their achievement," and though he had demanded much of them in the past, an assault river crossing, during daylight, into the teeth of prepared enemy defenses, was something he could not possibly have imagined.[2] Yet he had ordered it done—it was, in fact, his idea—and two battalions were all he could spare; there was no time to wait for reinforcements. So he wanted to be there when the troopers shoved off. But it was not to be.[3]

There was an urgent call from his chief of staff, Lieutenant Colonel Bob Wienecke. The news was bad. A massive German attack had hit the eastern and southern sides of the division perimeter. The key towns of Beek and Mook were in danger of being overrun, and the 508th (at Beek) and 505th (at Mook) were barely holding on. The Groesbeek Heights were also threatened, as was the division command post atop the heights. According to Gavin, "What Wienecke, in effect, said was that if I were going to have any Division Command Post left, I better get back and straighten the thing out."[4] More important, were the heights to fall, the Germans would command the surrounding lowlands, which, in turn, would discomfit the division's defenses and undermine the attack to seize Nijmegen's bridges. Finally, the German attack in the south was threatening the Heumen Bridge, the only trafficable bridge over the Maas-Waal Canal. Were it to be captured or destroyed, the lifeline of the British and American troops in Nijmegen would be severed.[5]

"I had to make a difficult decision right then," Gavin later wrote. "Since the river crossing was going to be extremely difficult, I should have stayed; on the other hand, Tucker was a very competent battle commander and I knew there was a real likelihood of losing Mook and the only bridge over the Maas-Waal Canal at [Heumen] and also losing Beek and the high ground at Berg en Dal. There seemed to be no question that my proper place was back where the decisive fighting was then taking place."[6] Consequently Gavin, Wood, and his aide, Captain Hugo Olson, jumped in a jeep and sped back to the division command post. According to Wienecke, Gavin "came into the C.P.—was briefed on the situation; called Lindquist—gave him his 'company' [most likely H Company, 3/508th] held by Div[ision] and said, in effect—'O.K. now kick 'em out'—called Ekman, said—I'll meet you at—(I don't remember where) I am *not* repeat *not* giving you the Div[ision] Reserve—And off he went." Gavin then sped off toward Mook, "which seemed to be the more dangerous situation," again with Wood and Olson in tow (along with a trooper named Landrum, who was driving).[7]

This second German attack was much larger than that of 18 September. It was also more stalwart, for in the interim hundreds of German paratroopers had arrived to reinforce *Corps Feldt*, the unit that the 82nd repulsed two days before. The goal of the attack remained the same, to drive the Americans from the Groesbeek Heights, but the reinforcements made possible a larger concentric attack from four directions—north, northeast, southeast, and south—that, unlike the broad, sweeping attack of the 18th, was concentrated on several specific objectives. By massing against each objective, the Germans exploited the distended American defenses—Gavin had but five battalions to cover fourteen miles of front—and achieved local superiority everywhere. Nowhere did they encounter anything larger than two understrength platoons.[8]

Attacking from the north and northeast, respectively, were *Kampfgruppe Becker* and *Kampfgruppe von Fürstenberg* (as was their standard procedure, the Germans named each *Kampfgruppe* after its commanding officer). The former comprised some seven hundred paratroopers and five assault guns. The latter numbered five hundred men from a tank replacement and training unit and had with it armored reconnaissance vehicles, half-tracks, and antitank guns. They hit the towns of Wyler and Beek in the 508th sector. Attacking from the southeast directly against the Groesbeek Heights was *Kampfgruppe*

Greschick with four to five hundred regular infantry along with fourteen 20mm cannon. Finally, attacking from the south was *Kampfgruppe Herrmann*, which numbered five to six hundred paratroopers reinforced with 88mm and 20mm guns as well as a battery of artillery. Backing up the renewed attack were the remnants of *Corps Feldt*, which had at its disposal tanks and assault guns that it fed into the battle at various stages.[9]

Gavin's first stop after leaving the division command post was a railroad overpass approximately 700 yards northwest of Mook, where a paved two-lane road passed under the railroad and ran right toward the Heumen Bridge, which was only 2,000 yards farther north. Defending the road were either one or two 505th troopers (accounts vary) who were dug in about 25 yards north (on the Heumen side) of the overpass and a lone British tank on the south (Mook) side of the overpass. When Gavin arrived it appeared that Mook had been overrun and that the Germans were headed their way. "The small arms fire was intense," he recalled. "Leaves, branches of trees and bits of masonry were flying about from the impacts. A cow walked up on the bank of the river 50 yards to the right of the overpass and shuddered and slowly went down under the impact of many hits." To make matters worse, for some reason the British tank commander put his tank in reverse and backed over a mine that blew off a track. Unharmed but in no mood to fight from an immobilized tank, the Brits dismounted and fled to the rear. With his firepower significantly diminished and no one else in the area, Gavin posted Wood and Olson along the railroad embankment and told them "to fire at the oncoming Germans as fast as [they] could."[10] He then reversed his earlier decision ("I am *not* repeat *not* giving you the Div[ision] Reserve") and sent his driver to retrieve a battalion from the Coldstream Guards. (The 1st and 5th Battalions, Coldstream Guards, had been attached to the 82nd the day before; the former was an armor battalion, the latter an infantry battalion.) Finally, he radioed Ekman, who told him yes, Mook had fallen, but he was going to take it back.[11]

Ekman had known that something was afoot in his sector for several days. Ever since taking Riethorst and Mook on the 17th and 18th, respectively, there had been a lot of activity to his front. For example, on 19 September his troopers expelled fifty to sixty Germans who had infiltrated back into Mook the night before, while his outpost at Riethorst reported German "troops in groups of 30 or 40 . . . observed 600 yards south of Riethorst moving toward Mook. . . . Some of the troops were towing guns."[12] When Ekman went to Riethorst to get a look for himself, he observed approximately "500 German foot troops . . . moving toward RIETHORST." Surely, thought Ekman, the Germans were massing for an attack, and when German patrols probed Riethorst and Mook on the night of 19–20 September, he knew it would not be long in coming.[13]

Ekman was right. At about 0900 hours, 20 September, the Germans opened their attack on the 505th's lines—which at the time were manned by only two battalions since Vandervoort's 2/505th was fighting in Nijmegen—with attacks by *Kampfgruppe Greschick* against the Groesbeek Heights and *Kampfgruppe Herrmann* at Riethorst and Mook. Defending the heights was Major James Kaiser's 3/505th. Arrayed in a string of strongpoints and outposts over an extended front, it was only a matter of time before *Kampfgruppe Greschick* broke through Kaiser's lines, but Kaiser counterattacked with his battalion reserve and, backed by fires from the 456th, regained his positions by noon, thereby ending the threat against the Groesbeek Heights. The attack by *Kampfgruppe Herrmann*, however, was not as easily repulsed.[14]

Sometime during the night of 19–20 September, the two platoons Ekman had outposted at Riethorst—Second Platoon of B Company and First Platoon of C Company, 1/505th—withdrew to a hill just north of the village, which afforded them an excellent observation point from which to direct artillery fire. Realizing this, *Kampfgruppe Herrmann* opened its attack with a prolonged artillery barrage on that hill while it moved into position for an attack on Mook. Atop the hill, the American paratroopers hunkered down, endured the bombardment, and responded in the only way they could, by calling in answering fire from the 456th. Then, at 1430 hours, coincident with the assault on Mook, a company of German paratroopers assaulted the hill at Riethorst. The American paratroopers, refusing to quit their ground, fought back with small arms and grenades, but, supported by fire from three tanks, the German paratroopers pressed on until they eventually overran the summit. Rather than withdraw, however, the troopers called the 456th for one more fire mission, this one right on top of their positions, which annihilated the German paratroopers and forced them back down the hill. After that, a stalemate developed with German paratroopers dug in at the base of the hill and American paratroopers holding its summit.[15]

Kampfgruppe Herrmann's attack on Mook opened in a similar vein—with a three-hour mortar, artillery, and *nebelwerfer* barrage behind which several tanks moved up to add their fire to the mix. Defending Mook were First and Third Platoons of B Company, 1/505th, which, like the platoons on the hill north of Riethorst, dug in, endured the bombardment, and waited for the inevitable ground assault. At about 1400 hours, the assault materialized in the form of a battalion of German paratroopers. Approaching Mook from the southeast, they were met by a fortified outpost under the command of Lieutenant William J. "Buck" Riordan who had with him eleven troopers, two antitank guns, and two machine guns, paltry firepower when compared to what the Germans brought to bear. Riordan and his troopers, like their brothers at

Riethorst, maintained their post until they were overrun. Six troopers were captured, but Riordan and five others took refuge in the cellars of some nearby buildings and spent the rest of the fight sniping at the Germans above. With Riordan's outpost gone, *Kampfgruppe Herrmann* rolled on unabated and by 1500 hours had retaken Mook.[16]

Since Mook provided *Kampfgruppe Herrmann* a good jumping-off point for an attack on the Heumen Bridge, and with little between Mook and the bridge to stop it, it was critical that Ekman do something quickly. He had already disregarded Gavin's earlier message about not releasing the division reserve and called for tank support from the Coldstream Guards.[17] He also called up his reserve, A Company, 1/505th, while Major Talton Long, the 1/505th commander, rallied B Company outside of Mook. Within forty-five minutes of being kicked out of Mook, therefore, Ekman counterattacked to take back the town with an improvised tank-infantry force composed of a squadron of tanks from the 1st Battalion, Coldstream Guards, and B Company (A Company later joined the attack as well). After several hours of house-to-house fighting Mook was again in American hands. Moreover, the Germans were on the run, so Ekman pressed the attack toward Riethorst and his two platoons on their hilltop bastion. He did not get there that night—he had to stop because his troopers ran out of ammunition—but renewed the attack the next day and achieved his end, thus ending the fight in the south.[18]

The situation at Mook had been "nip and tuck." So bad were things that Ekman formed a backup position above Mook with some three hundred glider pilots who were bivouacked nearby awaiting transport to the rear. Woefully underequipped—most had no compasses, maps, or firearms larger than a pistol—they took up their positions and remained in place until 23 September. Although Ekman did not consider them "an effective reserve for use in counter[-]attacking due to lack of organization," were the situation at Mook to deteriorate, he admitted that he would have used them "as a last resort."[19]

Gavin also thought the situation at Mook "seriously in doubt," so he remained in the area long enough to see the counterattack underway. He was heartened, however, by the resilience of the B Company troopers who, though beaten once, were anxious to get back in the fight and reclaim the town. Just before the attack kicked off, Gavin came upon Lieutenant James Morris Irvin, the B Company commander. Gavin asked, "Good fight Jim?" Morris replied, "Good fight Jim," and then led his troopers forward.[20]

Underscoring the ferocity of the 1/505th's fight was the human cost. The battalion lost twenty dead, fifty-four wounded, and seven missing at Mook, while the two platoons at Riethorst lost a further thirteen dead and twenty-two wounded. German casualties are unknown. What is known, however, is that the stand at Riethorst and counterattack at Mook broke the back of *Kampfgruppe Herrmann*, and neither Mook, Riethorst, nor the Heumen Bridge was ever in danger again.[21]

Once the counterattack into Mook got under way, Gavin left to see what was developing in the 508th sector. Like Ekman, Colonel Lindquist was covering a front well in excess of that normally required of an infantry regiment, and, also like Ekman, he did so by outposting key terrain features. Of particular import was the international highway that ran from the town of Wyler, just inside the German border, northwestward through Beek and then on to Nijmegen, where it crossed the Waal by means of the Nijmegen highway bridge. On D day, Lindquist had dispatched patrols to key spots from which they could overlook this highway, but, as we have seen, several of the patrols never got into position, leaving him blind to what may be developing along this critical avenue of approach. To correct this, Lindquist sent out much larger patrols on 19 September with orders to interdict the highway in four places: Wyler, Beek, Berg en Dal, and Hill 75.9, or "Devil's Hill."

Since it was within Germany proper, Lindquist gave the Wyler mission to one of his most experienced company commanders, Lieutenant Woodrow Millsaps, who, along with his B Company, 1/508th, troopers, took the town from a superior force of German infantry and armor. They did so by employing one of the division's favorite tactics, attacking to Wyler's central square and then splitting up into smaller assault groups and fanning out in all directions to chase the disorganized enemy out of town. By evening of 19 September, Millsaps had Wyler firmly in hand.[22]

That same day, in a stunning display of junior leadership, Corporal Robert Chisholm led I Company, 3/508th, and D Company, 307th Airborne Engineers, in a successful attack against Beek. Chisholm was in charge because the rest of I Company's officers and noncommissioned officer were casualties. Meanwhile, F Company, 2/508th, moved on to Berg en Dal, a piece of high ground west of Beek that dominated Beek and its approaches. Two antitank guns from the 80th Airborne Antiaircraft Battalion were added to the defenses at each location.[23]

Finally, Lindquist charged Lieutenant John Foley and the rump of A Company, 1/508th, at the time but forty-four men strong, to take Hill 75.9, which was known locally as *Duivelsberg*, or "Devil's Hill," a piece of high ground about two hundred yards long, fifty to seventy-five feet wide, and some three hundred yards above sea level, situated just south the highway about midway between Wyler and Beek.[24] A platoon from G Company, 3/508th, had already made several unsuccessful attacks on the hill. Foley took this platoon under wing and, guided by a Dutch farmer, led his force to the base of the hill where he told his troopers that, when he gave the word, they were to attack up the hill on the run, firing as fast as they could while yelling at the top of their lungs to give the impression of a much larger force. Foley's ruse worked. German paratroopers atop the hill "were literally yelled out of their holes."[25] "We attacked on the run over the hill and down the northeast side of the hill," recalled Sergeant Bob White. "The Germans on that side of the hill had their backs to us. The ones we did not kill ran down the hill to the woods." Foley's troopers then manned the German defenses and repelled several counterattacks. When the fighting finally died down, German dead "littered the hillside," as did several motorcycles, trucks, staff cars, and two 20mm cannon. Foley's force atop the hill had also been hit hard; seventeen troopers were down, including ten dead, but Devil's Hill was in American hands.[26]

Taking Wyler, Beek, Berg en Dal, and Devil's Hill gave Lindquist control of the international highway. It also placed the troopers at each location in the crosshairs of *Kampfgruppe Becker* and *Kampfgruppe von Fürstenberg* which attacked on 20 September to regain control of the highway in order to pave the way for a much larger armored thrust into Nijmegen. Predictably, the attack opened with an assault on Millsaps's B Company at Wyler.

At about 0845 hours, three infantry companies supported by tanks and flak wagons from *Kampfgruppe Becker* and *Kampfgruppe von Fürstenberg* converged on Wyler from three directions. Outgunned and outnumbered, Millsaps's troopers held out for six hours, aided in no small measure by fire from the 319th Glider Field Artillery Battalion, but eventually the weight of the German attack began to tell, so, at about 1500 hours, low on ammunition and almost wholly surrounded, Millsaps ordered a withdrawal to a farming village south of town to regroup. Certain that the Germans would pursue him, but unwilling to withdraw any farther, Millsaps called for reinforcements and prepared his troopers to defend. He could not have been more stunned when what emerged from Wyler was not an attacking force but a column of about seventy-five German soldiers marching toward the farming village behind one of their number bearing a large flag on which was emblazoned a red cross. Assuming they were intent either on surrender or the evacuation of their wounded, Millsaps had his troopers hold their fire. At about a hundred yards from the farming village, however, the column dispersed into attack formation, precipitating another firefight (although the flagman inexplicably continued marching toward the village and was taken prisoner). Running dangerously low on ammunition, it looked as though Millsaps would have to withdraw again when there appeared to his rear several British tanks. Unfortunately, the tanks mistook Millsaps's troopers for the enemy and started shelling the American positions until, for some reason, they withdrew. By this time it was early evening. Millsaps's force contained more casualties than not, he was almost out of ammunition, and it did not appear he was going to be reinforced, so he requested and received permission to return to friendly lines. Hounded by roving bands of German soldiers and slowed by wounded that he refused to leave behind, Millsaps led his troopers in a running gunfight back to friendly lines, which he and his troopers reentered at dawn, 21 September.[27]

The reason Millsaps had not been attacked by a larger German force at the farming village is because the main body of *Kampfgruppe Becker* and *Kampfgruppe von Fürstenberg* rolled through Wyler to Beek, several miles to the northwest. About four hundred German paratroopers, advancing behind a rolling artillery barrage, hit the town at midafternoon. Corporal Chisholm and his force of D Company engineers and I Company paratroopers held them off until several German half-tracks added their 20mm guns to the fight, after which Chisholm, too, ordered a withdrawal.[28]

Chisholm withdrew toward the Berg en Dal high ground, and it must have been about this time that Gavin arrived at Berg en Dal from the opposite direction.

> As we went up the road enroute [*sic*] to Beek, we came to the road crossing near the de Groot Hotel in Berg-en-dahl [*sic*]. . . . [I]t was on a high ridge, heavily wooded. From there the road down to Beek was steep and curved in several places. As we reached the top of the ridge the entire place was under very heavy fire. . . . I remember very well crawling across the road on my stomach to the woods on the far side. About fifty yards inside the woods I [Gavin] ran into members of the 508th digging in.[29]

Gavin could see that Chisholm's troopers were reeling from their near escape from Beek, though they had some fight left. During their withdrawal they knocked out a German half-track in an S-turn farther down Berg en Dal's slope, thereby precluding other enemy vehicles from negotiating the steep, winding road to the summit and negating, at least temporarily, the enemy armor threat. But even with no enemy armor to worry about, Lieutenant Colonel Louis Mendez, the 3/508th commander and the man responsible for defending Berg en Dal, told Gavin that he would be hard pressed to do so.[30]

"As I understood the situation then, it was seriously in doubt," Gavin later admitted, for were Berg en Dal to fall, the Germans "could have walked into the outskirts of Nijmegen almost unmolested, our forces on that front were so thin."[31] Gavin told Mendez that he would get all the artillery support he needed and that, if he could hold the night, he would be reinforced with more infantry. But in reality Gavin had nothing left. All of his infantry battalions were already committed, the promised arrival of the 325th was soon dashed, and three of the division's artillery battalions were supporting fights elsewhere, leaving only the 319th available to support Mendez and the rest of the 508th. Moreover, artillery ammunition was running low. Hence, after reconsidering the situation, Gavin decided there was but one thing to do—counterattack.[32]

Gavin knew his enemy. He knew that the Germans did not like to fight at night, and therefore, if Mendez could hold on until then, he was "hopeful that the Germans, as they often did, would stop their attack at darkness."[33] This would give him time to send a force around the Germans fronting Berg en Dal with the aim of retaking Beek. Even if the attack was unsuccessful, Gavin was certain that by merely threatening Beek he would discomfit the German attack at Berg en Dal by forcing the Germans to withhold forces to defend Beek that they otherwise would have used to attack Berg en Dal. He would be proved right on all points.

At 1900 hours, 20 September, Lieutenant Louis G. Toth, the H Company, 3/508th, commander, received a warning order to take Beek, drive through it, and set up a defensive line 1,000 yards northeast of the town. He was also told that Beek was lightly defended, but two antitank gunners from the 80th Airborne Antiaircraft Battalion who had been with Chisholm's force told Toth this was not so, contending instead that there were at least four hundred Germans in the town along with half-tracks and other armored vehicles. With the two antitank gunners as guides, Toth led his force to Beek expecting a fight, but when he arrived at its outskirts undetected and with no sign of the enemy, he could not help but be confused. When he sent his First Platoon into Beek to take a look around, his confusion vanished. German machine guns lying in ambush opened up, killed the platoon leader, and pinned the rest of the platoon down. Lieutenant Vernon Thomas, the assistant platoon leader, took charge and, fighting house-to-house, led First Platoon to a churchyard to regroup. Toth then sent his Second Platoon under Lieutenant Bruce B. Van to get First Platoon out, but it, too, got pinned down. Rather than risk his Third Platoon, Toth, ordered a withdrawal, designating some high ground south of town as the company rendezvous point. Lieutenant Van could not make it. Second Platoon had many casualties, and he refused to leave them behind. Lieutenant Thomas and First Platoon, however, were able to break out of the churchyard and arrived at the rendezvous point around midnight.[34]

With only two platoons at his disposal, Toth knew there was no way he was going to take Beek, much less sweep through it. But he also knew Gavin's intent—to force the Germans to defend Beek—so he renewed his attack at daybreak, 21 September. This, too, was repulsed, but Toth kept at it. He was reinforced twice, by a platoon each from F and G Companies, and mounted three separate assaults on Beek, none of which were stout enough to break through the German defenses. Finally, at around 1700 hours, while preparing his fourth assault of the day Toth got word that the Germans inside the town were withdrawing. Following up quickly, Toth and his conglomerate force of F, G, and H Company troopers had Beek in hand by 1800 hours.[35]

It is difficult to determine the cause of the Germans' abrupt withdrawal. Assuredly, they had suffered casualties, although to what extent is uncertain, yet they were well ensconced inside Beek, and it would have taken a much larger force than Toth had at his disposal to dislodge them. What is certain is that by tying down the Germans at Beek, Toth and his troopers undermined the attack on Berg en Dal. As a result, Mendez was able to the hold Berg en Dal, which, in turn, quashed all German hopes of breaking through to Nijmegen on 20 September, and by 21 September, with the Nijmegen bridges in Allied hands, it was too late. Gavin's gambit had paid off, but it was a costly one; H Company lost seventy troopers, and even after being reinforced, Toth entered Beek with fewer than fifty troopers on the evening of 21 September.[36]

Coincident with the attacks on Wyler, Beek, and Berg en Dal, a third prong from *Kampfgruppe Becker* and *Kampfgruppe von Fürstenberg* attacked Devil's Hill, touching off the most prolonged, if not the most ferocious, fight along the division perimeter. Preceded by an artillery and mortar barrage, two companies of German paratroopers stormed the hill where Lieutenant Foley and his A and G Company troopers were dug in. Advancing to within point-blank range, the German paratroopers fought their American opposites hole-to-hole but were repulsed. The Germans then withdrew and sent forward a "well-dressed German officer" who called on the Americans to surrender. A combative Foley responded, "If you want me, come and get me!"[37] Elsewhere, the Germans attempted a ruse similar to the one they had tried outside of Wyler. Corporal James Blue and Private First Class Don Johnson were manning an outpost when two German soldiers with their hands in the air advanced toward them. "At a distance of about fifty yards we could see that one of them had something on his back. Shortly he fell forward, and the second soldier attempted to fire the machine gun that was attached to his comrade's back. We had our sights on them; they were riddled with gunfire."[38] The fight at Devil's Hill continued for four days. Foley and his troopers stubbornly refused to quit its summit. They were reinforced once, on 21 September, by Captain Adams (who was suffering from two wounds but refused to abandon his men), Lieutenant Lamm, and Second Platoon of A Company who joined them after being liberated from their hiding place inside Nijmegen. The rest of the time they were virtually cut off. Ammunition ran low, down to five rounds per man, until an ammunition detail slipped through German lines with a resupply. Sleep was another problem. The almost incessant shelling and ferocious assaults forced the troopers to take unusual steps to remain alert—at night, the men strung bandoleers from foxhole to foxhole that they tied to their bodies so that they could shake one another awake in the event of an attack. Faced with such an obstinate foe, their attacks in other sectors long since over, the Germans finally abandoned their assault on Devil's Hill on the evening of 23 September and withdrew. The weary American paratroopers on its summit simply watched them go, save eleven of their number who had lost their lives in its defense.[39]

The fight along the division perimeter had been a near-run thing. The 505th and 508th held despite being everywhere outnumbered and outgunned because of the toughness, tenacity, initiative, and leadership of the troopers, noncommissioned officers, and officers at all levels, traits that Gavin had done much to imbue through the sheer force of his personal example. He was justifiably proud of what the 82nd accomplished on 20 September, "a day unprecedented in the division's combat history." It is surprising, then, that a little more than two weeks later he penned the following to Matthew Ridgway: "I believe it to be in the best interest of all concerned that I be relieved of command of this Division" and "that when I am relieved steps be taken to relieve me from assignment to the XVIII Airborne Corps. It is understood that this will undoubtedly involve a reduction in grade."[40]

Gavin's piquant request was in response to a letter he received from Ridgway titled "Military Courtesy." The letter was provoked by an incident that occurred on 20 September at the division command post, an incident Ridgway thought a "flagrant breach of military courtesy." In essence, Ridgway wanted Gavin to explain why, when Gavin arrived at the division command post following Wienecke's frantic call and found Ridgway there, he made "no apparent effort . . . to contact your Corps Commander, nor in any way to acknowledge his presence [in the command post], which was completely ignored."[41]

Gavin explained that he was surprised to find Ridgway in the command post. He did not know he was coming, nor that he had arrived, and when Gavin walked in, Ridgway was huddled with some staff officers, and, as he explained in his reply, he "weighed carefully in [his] own mind whether to interrupt your discussion or go to MOOK as quickly as possible and then return." Since the situation at Mook "appeared none too good" and Gavin was certain that Ridgway would "want the correct picture when I talked to you," he elected to leave for Mook, intending to return as soon as he could. Furthermore, continued Gavin, "knowing your usual understanding and appreciation of such combat conditions and, in addition, taking the liberty of assuming that a more friendly understanding existed between us than apparently actually did exist, I asked my Chief of Staff to extend to you my apologies for having to rush off and explain that I would return in a matter of minutes." Gavin also emphasized that he was not at the command post for "more than several minutes" and that "the distance separating us was beyond ordinary speaking distance." Hence, when he returned to the command post to find Ridgway gone, Gavin carried on with his duties, though he attempted on succeeding days to contact Ridgway, but to no avail. Gavin ended his letter by stating that since "the welfare of the Division should come above all else" and it was obvious that "my relations with your headquarters are not entirely compatible, and that my behavior has been such as to warrant the basic communication," he asked to be relieved.[42]

But it was not military courtesy that engendered Ridgway's letter to Gavin and there was no way that Ridgway was going to relieve his most experienced combat commander, the man he had personally recommended to take command of his beloved 82nd.[43] A few days later, in fact, Ridgway explained to Wienecke, who was in England to consult with the XVIII Airborne Corps staff, that he had sent the letter "in a moment of hasty judgement [*sic*] . . . and that the whole affairs [*sic*] was to be regretted." Years later Ridgway would admit that "Gavin, as fine a combat commander as any in our service in WW II—as he amply demonstrated—was facing a critical operation . . . [and] had plenty of justification for his brusqueness toward me" on 20 September. What had really spurred Ridgway's letter was two things: the fact that he still "harbored a sense of deep disappointment, if not of resentment, that command of the operation . . . had been given to General Browning" and his dissatisfaction "with the apathy and . . . lack of aggressiveness of the British forces" through which he had passed en route to the 82nd command post.[44]

One incident in particular underscored for Ridgway the latter sentiment. During his journey to the front, Ridgway's party was halted by a junior British officer who told them they could not proceed because the road ahead was under small arms fire. With no way of knowing what the immediate situation really was, Ridgway did as the officer requested, but after forty minutes of waiting, during which he witnessed no action on the part of the British to open the road, he grew impatient. Leaving his jeep and driver in place, Ridgway set out on foot with his aide and bodyguard and walked all the way to the 101st Division command post, one and a half miles away up the supposedly fire-swept road, without a shot being fired.[45]

Consequently, it was Ridgway's pique at being passed up for command combined with his disgust at the lack of aggressiveness of the British that landed him in a foul mood when he arrived at the 82nd command post. He knew he could have, and would have, done it better. "I always felt, and I still feel," he wrote years later, "that the sluggish actions of the ground armies in that campaign were inexcusable. A more vigorous command supervision from the top could have driven the armored force on through." Furthermore,

Ridgway had been told "to be ready to mount an airborne operation with the units retrieved from the battlefield at the earliest possible moment after 1 October."[46] But with XXX Corps listlessly making its way toward Arnhem, he knew there was no way that Montgomery would soon release the American airborne divisions, and the longer the two divisions stayed in Holland, the more casualties they would sustain and the longer it would take for them to ready themselves for another operation.

Ridgway was not alone in bemoaning British sluggishness. When Gavin crossed Nijmegen's highway bridge at dawn on 21 September to see how the 504th was faring, he found Tucker "so irate that he was almost unable to speak." Tucker's troopers had expanded their foothold on the northern bank of the Waal to a depth of about 1,000 yards in the expectation that XXX Corps would use the space to organize a dash to Arnhem. Instead, the British sat and waited. "We've got the road ahead cleared for about [a] quarter of a mile," said Lieutenant Ernest Murphy to a British tanker. "Now it is up to you to rescue your comrades." But the tankers refused to budge without additional armor and infantry, which had yet to come up. Captain Burriss and Lieutenant LaRiviere were apoplectic. Sergeant Jimmy Shields overheard LaRiviere tell "the lead British tanker to get going or 'I'll blow your head off and take the tanks myself.'" Burriss went even further. Climbing aboard Captain Lord Peter Carrington's tank—Carrington was second in command of No. 1 Squadron, 2nd Grenadier Guards (the unit from which Robinson's tanks had come), and had crossed the highway bridge in his tank to take charge of the British contingent on the northern bank—Burriss cocked his Thompson submachine gun, put it to Carrington's head, and shouted, "You get this tank moving, or I'll blow your damn head off." Fortunately, Carrington ducked into his tank and locked the hatch before Burriss could carry out his threat.[47]

It cannot be argued that the terrain between Nijmegen and Arnhem was good tank country. The area was rife with dikes and marshlands that hampered off-road movement, large open fields that offered excellent observation for antitank gunners, and numerous orchards and villages in which those gunners could hide. Additionally, the main road connecting Nijmegen with Arnhem was, as was usual in Holland, atop a raised embankment three to six feet high and bordered on either side by deep drainage ditches that tanks could not cross.[48] "It was perfect defensive country in which the anti-tank gun hidden in the orchards was always master of the tank silhouetted against the sky-line," remembered Horrocks. Lieutenant Colonel Giles Vandeleur called it "a ridiculous place to operate tanks." Giles's cousin, Lieutenant Colonel J. O. E. "Joe" Vandeleur, commander of 3rd Battalion, Irish Guards, recalled that when he went forward to take a look at the terrain with his second in command, the latter remarked, "We're never going to get a yard up this bloody road."[49]

Yet the entire operation was predicated on a swift advance up that road. What Tucker's troopers expected, therefore, was a full-throated attack toward Arnhem immediately following their capture of Nijmegen's bridges. Instead, they met with what to them seemed undue caution, an attitude that did not sit well with troopers who had just completed an assault river crossing. Furthermore, notwithstanding British claims that they needed more tanks and infantry before jumping off, they were slow to bring them forward. Some seventeen hours after Sergeant Peter Robinson's two tanks charged across the highway bridge, there were only four tanks north of the Waal—three of them from Robinson's platoon (one of Robinson's tanks that had been knocked out during the charge was later found to be in working condition and moved forward to join the other two north of the Waal) and the fourth Lord Carrington's—and two companies of infantry. Neither the tanks, which were laagered at Lent, a suburb just north of the highway bridge, nor the infantry, which was posted at the north end of the highway bridge, was in any position to continue the advance.[50]

The reason for the delay was that Horrocks and Adair had decided to lead the advance with the Vandeleurs' relatively fresh Irish Guards. This meant passing them through the bloodied Grenadier Guards, which took time. Horrocks and Adair made this decision because they expected they would have to fight their way to Arnhem, an expectation based on a report from a troop of armored cars from the 2nd Household Cavalry that had, in fact, pushed beyond Tucker's lines the night of 20–21 September. The report stated that the Germans were dug in at a crossroads some two miles north of the highway bridge.[51]

Although Horrocks and Adair had no way of knowing this, the report was misleading. Following the fall of the highway bridge SS-Standartenführer Heinz Harmel hastily patched together a thin infantry screen north of Nijmegen, but it was incapable of sustained defense against even a modest armored thrust. "The English drank too much tea," scoffed Harmel. "The four panzers who crossed the bridge made a mistake when they stayed in Lent. If they had carried on their advance, it would have been all over for us."[52] The delay allowed Harmel time to rush reinforcements south from Arnhem, so that when the British finally did kick off their advance, the German defenses were more robust, counting two battalions of infantry; sixteen tanks, including several Panthers and at least one Tiger; two batteries of 88mm guns; at least one battery of 75mm antiaircraft guns; and some twenty 20mm cannon.[53]

It took until 1230 hours, 21 September, for the Irish Guards to get into position for the advance on Arnhem. In the van, lined up bumper-to-bumper on the Nijmegen-Arnhem road, were Giles Vandeleur's tanks. Riding atop the tanks were his cousin Joe's infantrymen. "I remember quite well my orders were simply to get through to Arnhem," recalled Giles Vandeleur. "Our advance, funnily enough, was based on a time program, as though we were on a peacetime march. We were to advance at a normal speed of an approach march, 15 miles in two hours."[54]

The lead tank moved out at 1330 hours. At 1340 hours it was a burning hulk, as were the two tanks behind it, victims of German antitank fire. The fourth tank in line, unable to maneuver off the raised road, simply stopped, the entire column held up behind. As soon as the Germans opened fire, the infantrymen atop the tanks took cover in the roadside ditches, where they were promptly pinned down by machine-gun fire. Speeding forward in his scout car to get a better look at the conflagration that had engulfed the head of the column, Giles Vandeleur came upon the commander of the lead squadron, whose tank was idling near a farmhouse. Both men jumped off their vehicles to confer but were quickly chased to cover behind the farmhouse by enemy fire.

> Amusingly [recalled Giles Vandeleur], although I wasn't amused at the time, I couldn't get to my scout car. It was a Humber armor[ed] car with two entrances: A lid on the top or a trap door on the side. I couldn't get to it with the German machine gun firing across the field, so I shouted to Goldman [the driver] to try and tell him to back the car up to the corner, so we could get in. Everytime [*sic*] I shouted, Goldman lifted the lid and the Germans poured a burst of fire over his head. Immediately, he would duck and slam the lid down, only to peer out cautiously when I called him again. This was followed by another burst of fire and down went the lid. We must have done this three or four times and finally I became exasperated and crawled back to Joe along a ditch.[55]

"It was a bloody mess," recalled Joe Vandeleur. "I ordered we try to slip the tanks off the road, but we couldn't get them off." He then tried passing some tanks and infantry around the German left flank via a nearby railroad line, but they, too, got pinned down. The obvious recourse was to blast the German positions with close air support, artillery fire, or both, but the radio link with the circling Typhoon fighter-bombers was down and the pilots were under strict orders not to attack without an express request from the ground commander; they eventually returned to base fully loaded. Artillery support was to be provided by the 153rd Field Regiment (Leicestershire Yeomanry), but because of a coordination failure, two of the regiment's three batteries were on the move when the attack began, leaving only one battery of eight guns available to respond, and it "was bloody slow registering on its targets."[56] As a result it took three and a half hours before the Irish Guards' calls for artillery support were answered. With no hope of breaking through the stout German defenses, at 1900 hours the attack up the Nijmegen-Arnhem road was called off.[57]

Following behind the Irish Guards were the Welsh Guards, whose task it was to cross the highway bridge, turn left at Lent, and then attempt to break through to Arnhem along secondary roads. It was 1700 hours before the Welsh Guards got moving, having spent some four hours stalled on the highway bridge when the Irish Guards ahead of them were held up. The prescribed route would take the Welsh Guards through Oosterhout, a small town just beyond the westernmost point of the 504th's perimeter that was being held by C Company, 1/504th, and where, earlier in the day, Private John R. Towle earned the Medal of Honor.

The C Company troopers were told that the Germans had abandoned Oosterhout. They were surprised, therefore, when two tanks, a half-track, and about a hundred infantrymen rolled out of Oosterhout headed straight for them. "We were conjecturing whether the Krautheads would wipe us all out or give us a chance to surrender," wrote Sergeant Ross S. Carter, but then Private Towle, the only remaining bazooka gunner in the company showed up. Towle "climbed up the bank, took a quick peep at the tanks, then slid down and got his bazooka."[58] He then rushed forward some 200 yards in order to get a clear shot at the tanks, fired several rounds, and drove them off. He then turned his bazooka on a nearby house, killing nine Germans who had taken up position inside. Finally, he moved another 125 yards through enemy fire to a third position and was taking aim at the German half-track when he was mortally wounded.

Towle almost single-handedly blunted the German attack. Had the Welsh Guards been ready, a counterattack might well have broken through Oosterhout and found its way clear to Arnhem. But it was several hours before the Welsh Guards arrived, and by that time the Germans had reinforced Oosterhout. Subsequently, the Germans easily blunted the Welsh Guards' belated attack, after which the Guards moved back to the highway bridge, thus ending the last attempt to get through to Arnhem on 21 September.[59]

When the Irish and Welsh Guards aborted their advances on Arnhem, they withdrew into the bridgehead north of the Waal that was still being held by Tucker's 504th. Tucker had been told that he was to be relieved by the 43rd (Wessex) Division.[60] This is normally accomplished by the relieving unit moving forward to occupy the positions of the unit being relieved. However, when the 43rd arrived in Nijmegen at noon on 21 September, its commander, Major General Sir Ivor Thomas, ordered his two lead brigades to advance no farther than the north end of the railroad and highway bridges. At first it appeared that Thomas was waiting for the Irish and Welsh Guards to clear the way before moving forward, but when later in the day both Guards units retired, Thomas inexplicably remained in place. This meant that in order to execute the relief, Tucker's troopers would have to conduct two very difficult and dangerous tactical maneuvers: a withdrawal under pressure and a rearward passage of lines. Furthermore, with the relief scheduled for the early morning hours of 22 September, both would have to be done at night, when it was difficult to discern friend from foe, over approximately 1,000 yards of terrain that was still infested with German stragglers. "It was a ticklish situation," wrote Captain Henry Keep. "We were to withdraw from our present position with the Nazis hot on our tail as soon as they realized what was going on. Could our companies get back to the security of the bridge without being cut off by the Krauts? We were to receive no assistance or cover from anyone."[61]

The withdrawal began at 0500 hours, 22 September, under tight control by Tucker, Major Julian Cook, the 3/504th commander, and Major Willard Harrison, the 1/504th commander, who carefully leapfrogged companies back to the highway bridge (for some reason the railroad bridge was not used). "It was a very skillfully directed maneuver," wrote Keep. "To make a long story short our troops eventually reached the security of the close-in defense of the bridge by the British, and we moved across this huge structure still littered with the dead we had killed what seemed eons ago but what in reality was barely 2 days." "When we got to the bridge entrance, we saw some British troops there," recalled Sergeant Albert Tarbell. "They did not seem too concerned about the situation and we remarked to them why it was they were still milling around. . . . We let them know our feelings, that we would not leave our men stranded like that. It was not a very cordial meeting." By midmorning the bridgehead north of the Waal, albeit significantly smaller, was in British hands.[62]

Tarbell's remarks were likely engendered by his knowledge that the situation at Arnhem was desperate. The only element of the British 1st Airborne Division to reach the Arnhem highway bridge, a disparate force of paratroopers composed mostly of troopers from the 2nd Battalion, 1st Parachute Regiment, under Lieutenant Colonel John Frost, had been overrun. Most of Frost's men were either killed or taken prisoner. The last holdouts surrendered at 0500 hours, 21 September. The rest of the 1st Airborne Division had been driven into Oosterbeek, Arnhem's western suburb. Clinging tenuously to a thumb-shaped perimeter, the base of which was anchored on the north bank of the Neder Rijn, besieged by an overwhelming force of German armor, and running seriously low on ammunition, medical supplies, food, and water, the 1st Airborne Division was barely hanging on. A glimmer of hope arrived in the form of Major General Stanislaw Sosabowski's Polish Parachute Brigade, which dropped on the south side of the Neder Rijn on 21 September. But with no means to cross the river and lacking the firepower to fight through the German defenses posted at the Arnhem highway bridge, the Poles, too, had to await XXX Corps.[63]

The first XXX Corps units to get anywhere near Arnhem were two troops from the Household Cavalry that slipped through the German lines during the night of 21–22 September and, by following separate and circuitous routes over secondary roads, managed to link up with Sosabowski's Poles at Driel, a village on the south bank of the Neder Rijn that was roughly opposite the 1st Airborne Division's perimeter on the north bank. Also at Driel were Lieutenant Colonels Charles Mackenzie and Eddie Myers, two staff officers that General Urquhart, the 1st Airborne Division commander, sent across the river in a rubber dinghy with a message for Horrocks (compounding British difficulties at Arnhem was a near-total breakdown of its radio communications). Using a radio on one of the Household Cavalry's scout cars, Mackenzie informed the XXX Corps commander: "We are short of food, ammunition, and medical supplies. We cannot hold out for more than 24 hours. All we can do is wait and pray."[64]

Yet despite Mackenzie's pleas and an order from XXX Corps to take "all risks," the 43rd Division, which was now the corps's lead element, continued its plodding pace.[65] An attack up the main Nijmegen-Arnhem road by the division's 129th Brigade ground to a halt shortly after jumping off, stymied by the same defenses that the Irish Guards ran into the day before. Only slightly more successful was a concurrent attack by Brigadier Hubert Essame's 214th Brigade at Oosterhout, the same route tried by the Welsh Guards, which spent most of 22 September fighting street-to-street through Oosterhout until finally, with daylight lapsing, a frustrated Essame threw Lieutenant Colonel George Taylor's 5th Duke of Cornwall's Light Infantry (DCLI) Battalion into the mix with orders to bust through the German defenses at all costs. Jumping off at 1850 hours, the 5th DCLI broke out of Oosterhout and less than an hour later was with Sosabowski's paratroopers at Driel.[66]

With the 5th DCLI and the two Household Cavalry troops on hand, Sosabowski turned his attention to the problem of getting across the Neder Rijn and into the 1st Airborne's perimeter. One solution was to use some DUKWs (amphibious trucks) the 5th DCLI had brought forward, but for several reasons—the steep banks, the swift current, the noise—Sosabowski decided not to use them. A second solution presented itself in the form of a makeshift ferry his troopers had fashioned from dinghies and improvised rafts. Though of limited carrying capacity, the ferry offered Sosabowski a means to get fresh troops, their equipment, and needed supplies across the river without arousing German attention. Shortly after nightfall on 22 September Sosabowski put the ferry into operation. He had shuttled but 52 of his Poles across the river when German sentries discovered the ferry and brought machine guns and mortars to bear to sink every dinghy and raft.[67]

When Horrocks learned that the 5th DCLI had linked up with Sosabowski, he still thought that "there was every chance that the airborne division, replenished with stores and reinforced by the Poles and British infantry, might well be able to hold out."[68] But when Sosabowski's attempt to ferry his Poles across the river failed, he was not so sure. Adding to his concern were reports that the Germans had cut the main highway in the 101st's sector—a situation that was not rectified until 26 September—which stopped the flow of supplies, most critically ammunition, fuel, and assault boats, to the forces in and around Nijmegen fighting to break through to Arnhem.[69]

Yet Horrocks and Browning were determined to save the 1st Airborne, so, despite the paucity of supplies, they ordered General Thomas to renew his attack northward. Jumping off on the morning of 23 September the 43rd's third brigade, the 130th, finally broke through the German defenses north of Nijmegen and made it to Driel later that afternoon. This prompted Sosabowski to try a second river crossing with some assault boats the 130th brought with it. Although more successful than the previous night's attempt—some 250 Poles got across the river before German fire made additional crossings untenable—it was too little, too late, especially in that only about 150 of the Poles that made it across got through to the 1st Airborne. The remainder were either killed or captured.[70] Urquhart's situation report that evening read:

> Many attacks during the day by small parties, SP guns and tanks including flame-thrower tks. Each attack accompanied by very heavy mortaring and shelling within Div perimeter. . . . Physical contact not yet made with those on SOUTH Bank of river. Resup[ply] a flop, small quantities of amn only gathered in. Still no food and all ranks extremely dirty owing to shortage of water. Morale still adequate, but continued heavy mortaring and shelling is having obvious effects. We shall hold but at the same time hope for a brighter 24 hours ahead.[71]

The next day, 24 September, Horrocks and Browning went to Driel to get a feel for the situation themselves. Climbing to the top of a Driel church, Horrocks, Browning, Sosabowski, Thomas, and Lieutenant Colonel Taylor of the 5th DCLI surveyed the far bank. Fearing that Urquhart's troopers might be cut off from the river altogether, Horrocks ordered yet another river crossing. The plan was to cross Sosabowski's Poles and a battalion from the 43rd Division, the 4th Dorsets, at a point just west of the 1st Airborne perimeter where it was thought there was a smaller, weaker German presence. At a conference later in the day during which the details of the plan were finalized, Sosabowski protested and urged that the crossing be made even farther downstream in order to completely avoid German defenses on the north bank. The discussion became heated when, his suggestion having been rejected, Sosabowski interjected, "I am General Sosabowski. I command the Polish Para Brigade. I do as I like." Taken aback by this affront, Horrocks countered, "You are under my command. You will do as I bloody well tell you." "All right," responded Sosabowski. "I command the Polish Para Brigade and I do as you bloody well say."[72] As it turned out, Sosabowski was right. The first wave of approximately 315 troopers from the 4th Dorsets piled into nine assault boats and paddled right into the teeth of German defenders on the north bank. Fewer than half made it across, and most of those who did were killed or captured.[73]

The next morning, 25 September, Urquhart sent Browning the following:

> Must warn you that unless physical contact in some strength is made with us early 25 Sep consider it unlikely that we can hold out any longer. All ranks are now completely exhausted as the result of 8 days continuous effort. Lack of food and water and deficiency in arms combined with high officer casualties [*sic*] rate has had its effect. Even comparatively minor enemy offensive action may cause complete disintegration. Should this become apparent all will be told to break towards the bridgehead if any rather than surrender. Controlled movement from present position in face of enemy is out of the question now. We have done our best and will continue to do so as long as possible.[74]

"General Browning and I," wrote Horrocks, "came to the conclusion that there was nothing for it but to withdraw the 1st British Airborne Division over the river."[75] That night, 25–26 September, 2,163 troopers from the 1st Airborne Division and the Glider Pilot Regiment, 160 Poles, and 75 4th Dorset soldiers were either ferried or swam across the Neder Rijn. A driving rain covered their withdrawal. At least 300 more hid or escaped by other means; of these, approximately 140 crossed the river later, thanks in large part to the Dutch. A further 1,485 British and Polish troopers perished in the fighting around Arnhem; 6,525 were taken prisoner.[76] "It was a tragic scene," summed up Horrocks. "As the exhausted paratroopers swam or were ferried across the river in torrential rain, it seemed that even the gods were weeping at this grievous end to a gallant enterprise."[77]

The withdrawal of the 1st Airborne Division brought MARKET-GARDEN to a close. Montgomery's bid to leap the Rhine, bust into the Ruhr, and end the war in 1944 had come to naught. Yet MARKET-GARDEN added an additional 130 miles to 21st Army Group's front, almost double the size of its front before the operation. Holding that front required the one thing that Montgomery had in short supply: infantry.[78] Ironically, although MARKET-GARDEN had been predicated on the "intention that as soon as the ground forces have joined up with the airborne troops the two United States divisions [would] be withdrawn," the situation that emerged as a result of the operation dictated otherwise.[79] For the 82nd and 101st, this spelled several more weeks of combat.

By the time the 504th withdrew from north of the Waal, the 82nd had already suffered 649 casualties, including more than 150 killed.[80] In addition, like the rest of the Allied force around Nijmegen, it was also short on supplies, especially ammunition. A resupply drop on the afternoon of 19 September had been "decidedly unsatisfactory." Only 32 of 167 aircraft that were to deliver 265 tons of supplies got through to the drop zone (the rest were either grounded in England by bad weather or turned back by heavy fog over Belgium), and those that did scattered their delivery over such a wide area, much of it outside Allied lines, that only 20 percent of what was dropped was recovered.[81] A drop the next day helped alleviate the situation. Flying out of southern England where the skies were clear, 310 planes carrying 441 tons of supplies made their way to Nijmegen. Like the drop the day before, the loads were scattered, but with a massive assist from the Dutch, who gathered most of the loads and brought them to division supply points, somewhere between 60 and 80 percent of the tonnage was recovered. This was the division's last large parachute mission in Holland, and although it solved the division's critical supply shortages, at least temporarily, a far more pressing problem was the continual postponement of the 325th lift.[82]

Given the breadth of the area the Allies controlled around Nijmegen through Driel, the dearth of infantry was especially acute. Fortunately, except for isolated clashes, enemy pressure was light in the 82nd's sector on 21 and 22 September. This allowed commanders to adjust their lines, reorganize their forces, and rest their troopers. Yet the division was overextended, so it was with some relief that Gavin received word on 23 September that his glider troopers were finally inbound.

The stranded glider troopers were also relieved that the wait was over. Every day since 19 September, the planned insertion date, they had marched to their assigned gliders, anticipating a break in the weather. Four times they readied to go, and four times they experienced that strange blend of relief and dread that accompanied postponement. Even the normally staid unit journals reflected the effect this had on the troopers:

> September 19, 1944—Today was supposed to have been the big day for us in this operation. . . . Troops all took stations . . . weather was quite hazy and foggy . . . flight was postponed for 24 hours.
>
> September 20, 1944—Everyone out bright and early this morning. . . . Weather quite foggy this AM but the sun is trying to come out and maybe it will be alright for a take off today. Weather did not clear. . . . [Troops] move back to their tents to sweat tomorrow.
>
> September 21, 1944—Still at the airfields. [T]he takeoff was postponed for another 24 hours. . . . This is getting a little monotonous now. The boys are all set to go but they dont [*sic*] like the idea of sweating the ride out from day to day. Most of the men were in on the ride to France and know what a glider ride can be.
>
> September 22, 1944—Bad weather seems to be all we are running into now. If it isn't on this side of the [C]hannel its [*sic*] on the other. The past few days have been a little trying on the nerves.[83]

Finally, on 23 September, D+6, "the weather broke nice and clear," and within hours the 82nd's glider echelon—all three battalions of the 325th; C, D, E, and F Batteries, 80th Airborne Antiaircraft Battalion; A Company, 307th Airborne Engineer Battalion; and other division troops—some 3,385 troopers along with 104 jeeps, 59 trailers, and 25 artillery pieces were aboard their gliders and ready to go.[84] Takeoff commenced shortly after noon. Including the aircraft bound for the 101st, British 1st Airborne, and Sosabowski's Poles, the sky train comprised 490 gliders and 655 tug or drop planes (three gliders aborted; one cut loose over England, and the other two turned back because of mechanical problems). Accompanied by another impressive array of airpower—thirteen groups and twenty-two separate squadrons of Spitfires and Mustangs along with eighty-eight rocket firing planes—the transports flew via the Southern Route in order to minimize the time spent over enemy-held territory. Along the way the escorts destroyed 18 German gun positions, damaged 17 more, and shot down 26 German aircraft at a cost of 6 Allied planes.[85]

Yet despite the precautions and heavy escort, transports and gliders were lost, mostly around Veghel, a town about halfway between Eindhoven and Nijmegen where the Germans were still present in strength. In the words of Lieutenant Colonel Teddy Sanford, the 1/325th commander, it was near Veghel that "hell turned out to celebrate." He continued, "I saw one of my gliders containing a trailer loaded with anti-tank mines and three men, explode. It almost knocked down two more gliders. A spray of machine gun bullets came up through the floor of my glider and a 20mm shell hit our left wing, but no one was hurt." Private First Class James H. Newcomer of the 2/325th, a replacement who was entering combat for the first time, was looking out his glider's port window when suddenly the glider next to his got hit and "in an instant . . . blew apart." Corporal Raymond T. Burchell, a veteran in the 1/325th, was sitting next to another replacement on the ride in. When something hit the outside of the glider, the replacement made a remark about hail. "I said, 'Hail, your ass! Those are bullets.' He turned whiter than a ghost." Sergeant Aaron Gelber's glider was flying low enough for him to get a good look at the cause of the trouble: "I looked down and saw a large group of German troops below running around, shooting at us. We were able to see the bastards laughing and pointing while they were shooting. Looking ahead, I was able to see two tow planes going down flying at four hundred to five hundred feet." In all, 9 planes were shot down and 96 damaged. Hardest hit were the first and fourth serials. The former, comprising 49 tugs and tows, lost 3 C-47s from enemy ground fire and released 21 of its gliders early, most of which landed in areas under friendly control, so the troopers inside were able to assemble and make it to their units on foot. Colonel Charles Billingslea, the 325th commander, was among this group. When he finally arrived at the 82nd's command post, he "took quite a kidding from his old parachute friends about not understanding the idea of riding the glider all the way to the objective instead of getting out part way."[86] The fourth serial was not as fortunate. When the squadron leader released his glider because he was about to crash, 17 others did so as well. Six of the gliders landed in enemy territory; its occupants were never heard from again.[87]

All told 348 gliders made it to the 82nd's area, with the first arriving at 1602 hours. The majority, 210 gliders, landed within an oval a mile across and a mile and a half long that was roughly contiguous with drop zone "O"—designated landing zone "O"—which was being used because landing zones "N" and "T" were thought to be too vulnerable to enemy fire. Another 100 landed along the Maas River opposite Grave, while the rest were within a half mile of either of the two main concentrations.

Although landing zone "O" had originally been ruled out as an area suitable for gliders because of its small, narrow fields and the herds of livestock that grazed there, the glider pilots proved their mettle, and the Wacos their robust construction, by bringing their loads safely to ground. Still there were some hair-raising landings. Lieutenant Edgar L. Cook of the 2/325th saw a glider to his left smash "through a brick wall and except for its wings being sheared off, it stood up well," while a glider to Cook's right encountered a more intransigent obstacle. "I looked out as we were gliding in and saw a bull standing right in the path of a glider on our right," said Cook. "He just stood there, pawing at the ground, refusing to budge. The nose of that glider caught him right in the center of the forehead and it looked like an acre of hamburg[er]." Private First Class Joseph J. Oberkrieser's glider smashed through "a heavy wire fence with thick posts like short telephone poles," which knocked the wheels off the glider, causing it to slide on its skids through a furrowed field before coming to rest. "I was holding my rifle across my legs and the bouncing of the glider across the rough terrain caused me to continually rap my knees with it. To my surprise, the machine remained essentially intact and nothing inside, including us had been damaged." Private First Class Raymond E. Fary was in a glider loaded with an antitank gun and a trailer. "We had a hard landing due to the weight. . . . The landing gear collapsed and the wing snapped, but we had no casualties." Notwithstanding the difficult delivery, of the twenty-four guns, eighty-two jeeps, and forty-seven trailers that put down on landing zone "O," only one jeep was destroyed. Moreover, of the more than 2,900 troopers that landed there, all but 10 were ready for duty—late, but welcome reinforcements to the hard-pressed paratroopers. "I'm sure glad you bastards are here," quipped a 505th officer to Lieutenant Cook when he and his glider troopers went into the line later on that night.[88]

By 1800 hours, less than an hour after the last glider landed, the 325th was at 75 percent strength and ready to move out. Its orders were to relieve the 505th around Mook and Riethorst. By 0500 hours, 24 September, the 325th was in position.[89]

The most dangerous part of the 325th's sector was just north of Riethorst where a salient extended several hundred yards into the American lines. Inside the salient was the Kiekberg Wood, "a veritable jungle about 1200 yards wide and more than 1700 yards long," an excellent staging area for an enemy attack.[90] To forestall this, Billingslea positioned the 2/325th along its northern edge, while the 1/325th took position along its southern and western edges. That there were at least some Germans in the Kiekberg became evident at 0900 hours, 24 September, only four hours after the 325th arrived in the area, when E Company, 2/325th, traded fire with some Germans inside the wood. Later that night, E Company sent a patrol into the Kiekberg to try to get a fix on the size and type of enemy force it had encountered. It was to no avail. The patrol leader, Lieutenant John Yarborough, returned five and a half hours after departing to report he had advanced only two to three hundred yards inside the wood because "the terrain was rough and that control was difficult due to thick undergrowth."[91]

The next morning E Company's Private First Class Frank A. Plebanek "was awakened by the sound of very heavy rifle and machine pistol firing right outside my foxhole. The Germans had broken through our lines and were spraying our holes with machine pistol fire."[92] The Germans were also using flamethrowers, a weapon that so unnerved some E Company troopers that they shed their equipment and quit their positions in disarray. Backing up E Company, however, were paratroopers from B Company, 1/505th, who held off the German attack long enough for Lieutenant Robert Worley to get the glider troopers turned around. Then, while brandishing a bazooka, Worley took out a German flamethrower, drove off an accompanying flak wagon, and led E Company in a counterattack that regained the lost positions around the Kiekberg by nightfall.[93]

That night, 25–26 September, Lieutenant Yarborough led a second, much larger, patrol into the Kiekberg. This time he got no farther than a hundred yards inside the wood before withdrawing, turned back not by the undergrowth but by heavy small arms and machine-gun fire. It was by now patently obvious that there was a sizable enemy force concealed in the Kiekberg, and intelligence gleaned from other sources indicated that additional German forces were headed that way. Gavin ordered Billingslea to clear the wood before they got there. Billingslea's plan was to attack the morning of 27 September against the northern edge of the Kiekberg with F and G Companies, 2/325th, while E Company made a diversionary attack against the wood's western edge. A seven-minute artillery barrage was to start things off.[94]

The attack jumped off at 0537 hours, 27 September. High explosive rounds from the 319th and 320th Glider Field Artillery Battalions and several batteries of XXX Corps artillery slammed into the Kiekberg, while F and G Company moved "hand tip to hand tip at a fast walk" across the last bit of open ground before entering the wood.[95] Once inside the wood, however, the tight attack formation began breaking apart; squads lost contact with their platoons, platoons with their companies, and the companies with each other. Still the troopers pressed on until, deeper in the wood, they were ambushed by thirty cleverly concealed machine guns that forced the troopers to ground and completed the disintegration of the attack formation. Had it not been for the combined efforts of Major Charles W. "Tad" Major (the 2/325th commander), Lieutenant George M. Cockle (the G Company commander), and Captain Junior Woodruff (the F Company commander), disintegration may have turned to disaster. Rushing about without regard for their safety, Cockle and Woodruff re-formed their companies, while Major led forward B Company, 1/325th, to serve as a rallying point around which to assemble. By about 1000 hours, Major, Cockle, and Woodruff had reestablished control, but all thought of continuing the attack had been abandoned. Instead, Major had his troopers dig in to secure what they had gained, a wedge inside the Kiekberg about five hundred yards deep and eight hundred yards wide. Prisoner interrogations later ascertained that two German infantry battalions had been staging in the Kiekberg, preparing to spearhead another attempt to break through the 82nd's lines. As intended, the 2/325th's attack spoiled these plans, but having sustained some sixty casualties, it was unable to clear the wood entirely.[96]

The next two days saw stalemate in the Kiekberg. The 2/325th defended its foothold against several large counterattacks, but was likewise thwarted when it tried to attack. Even small patrols dispatched to find gaps in the German defenses were unable to advance very far before overwhelming fire from well-camouflaged German positions drove them back.[97] But Billingslea was not content with simply holding a portion of the Kiekberg; he wanted it all, for by clearing the wood he could reduce the salient in which it was contained and thereby concentrate his forces along a shorter, more easily defensible line. In so doing, he would also deny the Germans a position in which they could assemble free from interdiction by Allied artillery and air power. At first he tried breaking the stalemate through sheer force of will, constantly moving among his troopers to encourage them to hang on while chiding them to be on the lookout for an opening or weakness in the enemy lines that they could exploit. At one juncture, he rushed to a point in the perimeter where some troopers thought they heard the clank of tank treads, told them, "It's all right, you guys, we're going to push them back," and then led the counterattack himself.[98] But the German defenses were too stout for one chewed-up battalion, much less one man, to break. So at 1600 hours, 29 September, Billingslea withdrew Major's 2/325th from the Kiekberg. But he had not given up. For his next act, he would attack with two battalions.[99]

Billingslea's plan was straightforward: Four companies aligned along the north face of the Kiekberg would conduct a coordinated attack in company columns. On the right E and G Companies, 2/325th, were to attack in a southwesterly direction, while on the left, F and G Companies, 2/401st, attacked in a southeasterly direction. As before, a seven-minute artillery barrage would cover the troopers' advance into the wood.[100]

Scheduled to jump off at 0800 hours, 30 September, the 2/325th's attack ran into trouble even before it began. A heavy artillery concentration, no one was sure whether it was from friendly or enemy guns, caught G Company, 2/325th, in the open as it was leading the battalion to the line of departure. Wounded in the barrage were Major Major, and his executive officer, Captain Dave Stokely. Then a German counterattack against G Company's flank brought it and the rest of the 2/325th to a halt. To get the battalion back on track Billingslea grabbed the 2/401st's executive officer, Captain Samuel Ogden, and put him in command of the 2/325th. But the newly appointed Ogden could not get the battalion moving. Lieutenant Cockle's G Company already had four dead and twelve wounded, was pinned down by a German machine gun on its flank, and was still under artillery fire. "This is murder," was Cockle's reply when Ogden told him to press on. The other company commanders agreed, so Ogden suspended the 2/325th's attack and withdrew.[101]

The 2/401st's attack also jumped off as planned, with F and G Companies advancing on the left and right, respectively. Major Osmond Leahy, the battalion commander, had deliberately positioned his companies this way in order to enhance command and control; he wanted the "stable and deliberate" G Company commander, Captain John B. Sauls, to set the pace, while F Company, led by the "dashing" Captain James M. Harney, guided off of it. As was the case with the 2/325th, the 2/401st received incoming artillery fire as soon as it started, but Sauls and Harney kept their troopers moving forward. Once they got into the wood, however, enemy resistance stiffened, and the inevitable occurred—troopers went to ground—and when they did, command and control broke down. Things went from bad to worse when Sauls reported that a fairly large German force was massing to his front, while Harney's F Company was nowhere to be found and Harney, who had been shot in the thigh and was out of action, did not answer his radio. Fearing the worst, Leahy and his command group rushed forward only to stumble upon a scene that "shocked us into disbelief!" American and German soldiers were "standing a few feet apart with their weapons still in their hand[s]," seemingly taking a time-out from the war, a time-out that neither side appeared particularly anxious to have end.[102]

It was approximately 1100 hours when Leahy came upon this surreal interlude. The informal truce had been going on for about thirty minutes. It had been initiated by Lieutenant Clarence H. Knutson, G Company's First Platoon leader, and two German sergeants. Knutson and the twenty troopers with him were low on ammunition and had been cut off from G Company for several hours yet continued moving forward and must have been well ahead of the rest of the battalion when Knutson and his point man, Sergeant Marvin Watts, flushed fifteen Germans from their hiding place, all of whom immediately threw up their hands to surrender. Knutson had set his troopers to disarming the prisoners when there suddenly appeared a second, larger, group of Germans who were not interested in surrendering. Instead, the two sergeants in command of the second group demanded that Knutson surrender to them. When Knutson refused there ensued an impromptu parley, with each side trying to convince the other to lay down its arms. Meanwhile, the soldiers intermingled, exchanged cigarettes, showed one another pictures of loved ones, and passed around a bottle of cognac one of the Germans proffered. Knutson could clearly see that he was outnumbered by about three to one and that the Germans were heavily armed and, unlike his force, had ample ammunition, so it was in his best interest to remain calm and keep the Germans talking for as long as possible. Things began looking up when Lieutenant Lee Travelstead arrived on the scene with news that Major Leahy and reinforcements were on the way. When Knutson told the German sergeants this, they changed tack. They were willing to surrender but could do so only if a German officer gave them permission. Seeing a means out of his precarious predicament, Knutson struck a strange bargain, what amounted to a temporary exchange of hostages. His men would take the two German sergeants to meet Major Leahy in order to arrange the terms of surrender, while he and one other man proceeded under escort to treat with a German officer.

Incredibly, Knutson's gamble paid off. While making their way to the German rear—during which, for some reason, they were not blindfolded—Knutson and his fellow hostage, Sergeant Richard Richardson, counted more than three hundred heavily armed and amply supplied German soldiers. Sauls's report to Leahy had been accurate; the Germans were massing, and had it not been for Knutson's bravado, which temporarily stayed what appeared to be an imminent counterattack, the disorganized Americans may well have been overrun. Eventually, Knutson and Richardson were brought before a German lieutenant who, unwilling to grant the surrender Knutson demanded, dispatched a runner to find the battalion commander. Shortly thereafter, a second German lieutenant arrived who engaged his counterpart in a heated argument. Although neither Knutson nor Richardson understood what was being said, it was apparent that the second lieutenant was angry because the counterattack had been stalled, and in what appeared to be an attempt to prove a point about the relative weakness of the American force, he abruptly turned on Knutson and, in English, demanded to know, "How many men have you?" Nonplussed, Knutson replied, "Is that a fair question?" Taken aback by Knutson's arrogance, the lieutenant blustered on about his strength, adding, "We have many tanks in the Reichswald," to which Knutson responded dryly that tanks were not much use in a forest. Fed up with Knutson's impudence, the German lieutenant ordered that Knutson and Richardson be returned to their unit, this time blindfolded. Arriving back at the site where their strange odyssey began, and where against all reason the truce was still holding firm, Knutson and Richardson met Major Leahy and told him all they had witnessed.[103]

While moving forward Leahy obtained a clear sense of his situation. It was not good. He found F Company, but it was so far behind it was almost out of the action, and G Company, though farther advanced, had sustained considerable casualties and was disorganized. Continuing the attack was out of the question, especially given Knutson's estimate of the enemy strength. Moreover, Leahy's operations sergeant, who was fluent in German, told him that one of the Germans mentioned that they were combat veterans recently transferred from the Eastern Front whose mission it was to break through to the Groesbeek Heights. Leahy's overriding concern, therefore, was to gain time so he could regain control of his battalion, organize it to defend, and warn the rest of the division about what was coming. The best way to do this was to continue Knutson's ruse.[104]

Following the return of Knutson and Richardson to the clearing, a German major appeared and, in perfect English, demanded Leahy's surrender on the grounds that the Americans were hopelessly outnumbered. Although, based on Knutson's report, Leahy knew this to be true, he refused, countering that it was the Germans who were outnumbered and should, therefore, surrender. Visibly perturbed, the German major persisted and, when firing broke out at some distance to the east, insisted that Leahy order his men to cease firing while they were negotiating. Leahy replied that the units they heard firing were not under his command—although they most assuredly were—thereby inferring that there were many more Americans in the Kiekberg than was the case. Playing on the German major's distress, Leahy then offered him safe passage through the American lines if he and his soldiers agreed to lay down their arms and come peaceably. "We are fighting on the border of the [Reich] to the last man," came the major's reply.[105] Having reached an impasse, Leahy and the major finally agreed to an hour's truce, after which each side would be free to do what it would. The German major saluted smartly and left. The bluff had worked.[106]

Concerned that in its present state his battalion would not be able to hold against a German attack, which he was certain would come once the truce expired, Leahy immediately set about regaining control of his companies. He did this by establishing one of the few easily recognizable trails in the Kiekberg as a rally point and passed the word that every American in the wood was to converge on the trail where he and his junior leaders sorted them out and put them in position. Billingslea also gave Leahy control of the 2/325th, which he moved forward to help bolster the line. By nightfall, Leahy had elements of four companies dug in along the trail, and when the Germans did attack, shortly after midnight on 1 October, the line held and proved such a strong defensive position that it was continuously manned by a succession of Allied units until April 1945, when British and Canadian forces used it as their start point for the final drive into Germany.[107]

When asked about the Kiekberg truce, Leahy surmised that it happened because "the sudden close contact brought a very human factor to realization. The situation became too personal and the fighting spirit was lost."[108] Unofficial battlefield truces are unusual, although not unknown, occurrences; they were not uncommon, for example, during the American Civil War and on the Western Front during World War I. What set the Kiekberg truce apart was, unlike the others, it was also a bold ruse that precluded what might have been a slaughter. Leahy's battalion, disorganized and short one company, had already suffered significant casualties. Harney's F Company could muster but seventy troopers, whereas Sauls's G Company had only forty-three troopers still capable of fighting.[109] Had the German force that Knutson and Richardson counted attacked before Leahy was able to organize a defensive line, the casualty rolls could have been much higher.

The fight in the Kiekberg had taken a toll on the 325th, but Billingslea's troopers were not done. Shortly after it repelled the German attack along the Kiekberg trail, Gavin appeared at the 325th's command post with another mission. The British were bringing another corps, VIII Corps, into the battle area. To facilitate the move, British engineers had to build more bridges, two of which were to span the Maas River opposite Mook. The British were also "anxious that no identification of that group [VIII Corps] be obtained on that front until the bridging operations were well under way."[110] Billingslea, therefore, was to hand over the Kiekberg to the 505th, move all three of his battalions to Mook, and attack to clear the area southeast of Mook for a distance of approximately 3,500 yards. This would allow the engineers to build the bridges free of observed artillery fire and defeat German attempts to determine the Allies' order of battle. The attack was to begin on 2 October.[111]

Billingslea's plan was to advance with two battalions abreast—the 2/401st on the right and the 1/325th on the left, each of which would advance with two companies abreast—while the 2/325th followed in reserve. To facilitate control the lead battalions were to cross the line of departure at precisely 0530 hours, 2 October. Furthermore, during the advance the 1/325th was to keep alignment with the 2/401st to its right, which, in turn, would set the pace and direction of the advance by guiding along the Maas River to its right. To achieve surprise Billingslea elected to forego a preparatory artillery barrage.[112]

Jumping off five minutes behind schedule because some units got lost en route to Mook, the troopers advanced slowly yet steadily through a thick ground fog. By 0930 hours they were 1,100 yards beyond the line of departure, having stopped twice to clear enemy outposts that each time compelled the entire line to halt, but the fog was beginning to clear, which exposed the troopers to increasingly accurate enemy fire. Moreover, their ability to return fire was hampered by a logistical error. For some reason the troopers had been supplied with British rifle cartridges that, although the same caliber, were slightly longer and caused their rifles to jam. By about noon, therefore, the attack line began to waver and break apart. The attack frontage, initially 400 yards, more than doubled, and there were large gaps between companies. To cover the gaps, Billingslea committed his reserve, the 2/235th, and called on the British for armor and artillery support. Fifteen tanks and seventy-six artillery tubes responded. Working in tandem with the artillery and armor, the troopers reinvigorated the advance, busted through the enemy to their front, and took scores of prisoners. Continuing forward under a steady hail of enemy artillery and mortar fire, Billingslea's troopers eventually gained their objective, a dike road, by 0100 hours, 3 October, and dug in. There they remained until the following night, covering the last of the bridge building effort, after which they were ordered to fall back to Mook.[113]

The attack on the Mook Plain had been costly; the 325th lost 9 officers and 280 enlisted men. Yet the regiment retained its fighting trim, which it demonstrated during a German counterattack that hit the 325th as it was pulling back from the dike road. The withdrawal commenced at about 2000 hours, 3 October, and was well under way when there suddenly emerged from the enemy side of the dike an entire infantry company supported by two self-propelled guns. Hitting at the juncture of the 1/325th and 2/325th, the attack created a great deal of confusion and may have resulted in a precipitous rout had it not been for junior leaders who quickly got their troopers in hand, turned them around, and organized a hasty defense. Meanwhile, the rightmost company on the line, E Company, 2/401st, counterattacked into the German flank. Led by troopers like Private First Class Edward C. Kuzio, a BAR gunner who took up position amid the enemy and, in less than an hour, fired twenty-four magazines into the German main body, E Company routed the attackers, restored the original defensive line, and stayed in place until the withdrawal was complete.[114]

Thus ended the division's last significant action of the campaign. Yet it would be more than a month before the 82nd's troopers saw the last of Holland. Because of Montgomery's infantry shortage, the division was kept in place guarding 21st Army Group's lines of communication from positions along the German border. In one sense, it was routine duty, an "'eight to five' war," in the words of Sergeant "Dutch" Schultz.[115] But it was much more insidious than that. Captain Keep perhaps described it best:

> The most wearing, nerve-racking part of a campaign is the period of holding static front-line positions when both sides sit across from "No Man's Land" and stare at each other awaiting the build-up which will mark the eventual big push. For this military treading water is noted for terrifying and deadly artillery duels almost constantly in progress when after a certain period of time men involuntarily duck and cringe at the slightest sound of shellfire. Local skirmishes and the dreaded constant night-patrols are also prevalent at such a time. It is a period of forever being cold and dirty and damp, of living in fox-holes half filled with water, of eating unheated "C" rations because you don't dare light a fire, of constantly being shelled, and of dreading the

> dangerous patrol you must of necessity go out on that night. All that is part of "holding the line." And forever is the whole atmosphere redolent with the wildest of rumors. "We are being relieved tomorrow" etc.[116]

It was classic static warfare, a mission for which the airborne divisions were ill-suited. By 28 September the 82nd had already lost 102 officers and 1,567 enlisted men killed, wounded, or missing in action, approximately 14 percent of its ground strength in Holland.[117] Hundreds more would be added to the rolls before the division was finally relieved and sent back to the rear to rest, recuperate, and reorganize. But eventually respite did come; it would, however, be short-lived.

CHAPTER 20

YOU ARE LOOKING AT THE SURVIVORS

It was quite a normal occurrence for all hell to break out suddenly on the 82nd U.S. Airborne front—shelling, mortaring, machine-gun fire, the lot. Whenever I rang up Jim Gavin to find out what was going on he gave me the same answer: "We're just having a bit of a patrol." I usually discovered that his "bit of a patrol" had consisted of at least a hundred U.S. paratroopers carrying out a large-scale raid on the German positions. Like all first-class troops these two divisions [the 82nd and 101st] were never content to sit quiet; they were always hitting back at the Germans. And under their deceptively gentle exterior both Maxwell Taylor and Gavin were very tough characters indeed. They had to be, because the men they commanded were some of the toughest troops I have ever come across in my life.

—BRIAN HORROCKS, *ESCAPE TO ACTION*

THE 82ND'S EXTENDED Dutch sojourn was the predictable result of MARKET-GARDEN's failure.

Montgomery had posited that MARKET-GARDEN would open the port at Antwerp, thereby solving the Allies' parlous supply situation. This would be accomplished by cutting the German *Fifteenth Army*'s lines of communication, which would force it to withdraw from the Scheldt Estuary lest it be destroyed. Eisenhower was intrigued, and although the prudent course of action would have been to clear the Scheldt *before* undertaking another major combat operation, he approved MARKET-GARDEN.[1] It was a gamble, and when it failed, Antwerp assumed even greater importance.

Montgomery's offensive had sapped almost all available supplies, and with winter fast approaching it was imperative that Antwerp be opened lest the Allies be brought to a complete halt. But the Canadian First Army, to which Montgomery assigned the task of clearing the Scheldt, made little headway, and Montgomery's other army, the British Second, was decisively engaged holding the rest of 21st Army Group's overextended front. "I underestimated the difficulties of opening up the approaches to Antwerp," admitted Montgomery later. "I reckoned that the Canadian Army could do it *while* we were going for the Ruhr. I was wrong."[2] The cascading effect was that Montgomery could not release the American airborne divisions because he had nothing left with which to replace them, so on 18 October, over strident complaints by Brereton, Eisenhower gave tacit approval for 21st Army Group to retain both American airborne divisions until the Scheldt was cleared.[3]

For the troopers of the 82nd, this meant manning a defensive line east and southeast of Nijmegen that began just south of the Waal and ran generally south along the eastern face of the Groesbeek Heights to the Maas. "I do not recall anything drastic happening during that period," wrote Lieutenant Chester A. Garrison of the 2/504th. "But that does not mean that we had a happy time. Quite the opposite. Being subject to enemy fire for two months without a break had its toll. There were patrols, rumors, wounds, deaths, and occasional encounters with the enemy. We were constantly alerted to the possibility of enemy build-up and an all-out attack. All of this was psychologically wearing, and the oncoming winter was physically testing."[4]

When on the line—units were periodically rotated to Grave or Nijmegen, for rest, hot food, and showers—the troopers lived a subterranean existence in foxholes covered with stout logs that provided protection against artillery and mortar fire. "The closest thing to a foxhole is a grave," recalled Sergeant John McKenzie. "Living in a hole like a rabbit, no matter how well it was improved, was damp, confining, and extremely claustrophobic." Nonetheless, some troopers went to great lengths to make their holes livable. Private Norb Studelska of the 508th had a foxhole that "was a model of comfort. I took great pride in making my home the best on the block. It was chest deep, long enough to lie flat when I slept and narrow at the top. To keep things neat and clean, as my mother had taught me, I completely lined the hole with the canopy of a main chute. . . . I had a built-in shelf for my personal gear and a picture of my childhood sweetheart, Elaine Olsen, whom I married after the war." Private Steve Schmelick, one of the 508th's communication linemen, wired several foxholes in the regimental headquarters area with headsets so the occupants could listen to the radio, while Privates Matthew Bellucci and Dick Nelson, also of the 508th, had a light in their foxhole that was powered by a nearby generator.[5] At echelons well above foxhole level, meanwhile, changes were afoot that would directly impact the troopers' quality of life.

On 9 October, Browning's I Airborne Corps headquarters was relieved and sent back to the United Kingdom, there being no need for what by that time were four corps in the Eindhoven-Nijmegen area (the others were the British Second Army's VIII, XII, and XXX Corps), and the 82nd and 101st thereupon fell under Horrocks's XXX Corps for both operational and logistical matters.[6] Horrocks was elated to have them. "I never heard an Englishman as enthusiastic as General Horrocks was when he began extolling the 82nd and 101st," reported General Floyd Parks to General Brereton. As Horrocks put it, "As this difficult battle progressed I became more and more impressed with the fighting qualities of the 82nd and 101st U.S. Airborne Divisions. . . . What impressed me so much about them was their quickness into action; they were great individualists. They were also commanded by two outstanding men . . . [who] were quiet, sensitive men of great charm, with an almost British passion for understatement."[7] Horrocks, of course, witnessed firsthand the 82nd's conduct on 20 September when it simultaneously crossed the Waal, fought through Nijmegen, and countered large-scale attacks along its perimeter, to say nothing of the equally ferocious battles the 101st waged in its sector. It is understandable, therefore, that he would be so enamored of the fighting prowess of "his" American airborne divisions. Interestingly, Browning was not as captivated by Gavin's "individualists." A protégé of Field Marshal Alan Brooke who, like Montgomery, epitomized the British penchant for deliberately planned and executed set-piece battles, Browning was uncomfortable with the way Gavin delegated authority to his subordinates. During a cocktail party held in Nijmegen prior to his departure, Browning gently chastised Gavin for this. As the party was coming to an end, remembered Gavin, Browning

> walked me through the garden and allowed as how I gave too much freedom of action to my subordinates. I couldn't believe it. Freedom of action! The Germans had us outnumbered in each of the tactical fights we got into, when we were scrambling for our lives, and we won all of our engagements. That has always stuck in the back of my mind, for I couldn't understand it by American standards at all. We give our subordinates, and that includes division and corps commanders, as well as small unit leaders, a great deal of freedom of action so that they can take advantage of unexpected surprises that arise from time to time.[8]

Browning's admonition also revealed the difference between being an airborne theorist, which is how Gavin saw Browning, and an airborne commander. Holland was Gavin's third airborne battle and Browning's first. The detailed planning with which Browning was comfortable was certainly necessary beforehand, and Gavin was a stickler about addressing every contingency that might occur during rehearsals, but Gavin knew that no plan survives first contact with the enemy. Once battle was joined, the most effective way to accomplish the mission was to trust your subordinates who, knowing the intent of an operation, took matters in their own hands to realize that intent.

But Gavin's methods required subordinates who were capable, subordinates who were aggressive and tough and would show the initiative and leadership required to accomplish the mission despite changed circumstances. Subordinates like this were the product of standards that demanded and rewarded these attributes. Ridgway established the standards; Gavin honed them to a fine edge. The end result was an airborne ethos that infused the ranks and set the 82nd apart, even from the 101st. It was this ethos that had impressed Horrocks and worried Browning.

What made this ethos so powerful and effective in the 82nd was its many exemplars—Tucker, Billingslea, Ekman, Warren, Vandervoort, Cook, Mendez, and so many others were revered because they epitomized the tough, aggressive combat leader who underwrote the division's success in combat. The paradigm, however, was Gavin. Stories of his battlefield exploits were legendary. Sergeant Robert M. Murphy related a story reminiscent of so many others. "I was in an outpost in Holland when this lone guy in a jeep came out of the German lines," recalled Murphy. "I figured it was an enemy soldier in a captured vehicle, and I got him in my rifle sights. Then I saw the two stars on his helmet. Gavin, by God! Here we were supposedly the advanced guard, and he's ahead of us."[9] Corporal John Leh II of the 80th Airborne Antiaircraft Battalion had a similar experience. Leh's antitank gun had been put out of action during the German counterattack near Wyler.

> Just after daylight, I saw a tall erect soldier with an M1 slung over his shoulder walking along the edge of the woods. He peered down at our damaged AT gun. . . . [A] shell had landed between the trails in our ammo dump, and our "Betsy" was no longer useable. "Doesn't that nut know he's right on the front lines?" I thought to myself. "He should be more careful." I looked. . . . I looked again. . . . It was Slim Jim Gavin himself. Well, if he could walk around like that, I guessed that I could get out of my foxhole. What a guy . . . to be up here with us!!!![10]

Captain Hugo Olson, Gavin's aide, who perhaps knew the general better than anyone, characterized his boss as a man of great calm whom the troopers revered because he was always up front with them instead of in some warm, dry, relatively safe rear headquarters. General Gary E. Luck, a longtime paratrooper and onetime commander of XVIII Airborne Corps, recounted a story about his father-in-law, Private First Class H. R. Patrick, a World War II veteran who served with the 82nd, that captures the feeling many in the ranks had for Gavin. Luck was going through his father-in-law's personal possessions when he came across an Army-issue Bible. In the middle of the Bible was a section for unit information.

> One spot asked for the company clerk's name. My father-in-law listed (I believe) a Technical Sergeant Hill. It then asked for his commander's name, which clearly meant his *company* commander. However, PFC Patrick had penned in "Gen. Gavin." Think about that. This means a soldier at the bottom of the 82nd's organization felt a direct connection to his division commander. I am told that the entire division felt General Gavin was their "personal" commander, such was his leadership style, and such was their trust and confidence in him.[11]

According to Olson, Gavin's battlefield wandering resulted from his fervent belief in the value of personal reconnaissance. Gavin was never content to hear about what was going on; he wanted to see it. Moreover, Gavin "seemed to know instinctively where he should be and where he should make a reconnaissance. He knew instinctively where a counterattack would come from and where to put his defenses." Olson called this Gavin's "sixth sense." Carl von Clausewitz called it *coup d'oeil,* the "inward eye" that allows a great captain to make a "sound decision in the midst of action."[12]

If there was one thing Gavin would have liked more control over once the 82nd was attached to XXX Corps, it was chow. "Coming under XXX Corps hardly caused a ripple in our ranks," recalled Lieutenant Megellas, "except when we received British rations." According to Sergeant McKenzie, eating British rations "brought many Americans very close to mutiny." All the British ration items "were canned and among them were steak and kidney pie, mutton stew, scrambled eggs, kippered herring, plum pudding, and something called treacle pudding. Besides our unfamiliarity with these dishes, the main differences between British and American rations were the quality of the ingredients and the seasoning. Many British meat-based items had a rank taste and smell and seemed spoiled, whereas American rations seemed fresher and were of much higher quality." Private Allen Langdon remembered that British rations were so difficult for Americans to stomach, many "Dutch cows, pigs, chickens, and rabbits suffered accordingly as a means of filling GI stomachs at least once a day." But it was not all bad. The rations were slightly modified to account for American tastes—the troopers got U.S. coffee instead of tea and U.S. cigarettes instead of the "mouth-burning" English variety.[13] And there was also a rum ration. This made the division supply officer, Major Albert Marin, an instant hero. Soon after XXX Corps assumed control of the 82nd, Marin went to see his British counterpart to make the necessary logistical arrangements. When asked if he had received his rum ration yet, the perplexed Marin replied that he had not.

> So they got a couple of trucks and they got this ration of rum (Hudson's Bay) which was passed out to the troops on a per capita basis and everybody had a nice binge. It came in at least an inch high on a canteen cup—180 proof, that's a lot of good liquor. And Al was back a week later at 30 Corps and they said did he need any more rum. And he said "well, what we have is pretty well gone." So they got some more. And the third time he was back and they asked this question they said "really, old boy, has the fighting been that heavy?" and he said "No, its [*sic*] been pretty quiet as a matter of fact." Then it came out that the rules of the British Army under which the rum was being rationed was that all hands got a drink only when a brigadier or better said "well done." And of course the Americans were just dishing it out with the food.[14]

For the most part Marin's characterization of operations during this period of static warfare as "pretty quiet" was correct, but only when compared with the ferocious fighting that had come before. Still, there were sections of the division front that were almost dormant. According to Staff Sergeant James E. Jones, the river plain just south of the Waal was blissfully serene: "The Germans had accordions and no fighting was taking place at that time at all and we would call over and ask them to sing a particular song and if they knew it, in just a little while we would hear the accordion start and we would get our song played for us. In some cases, we would holler across 'Hello Jerry' and we would get an answer. To my knowledge no one at that time fired any shots at either side to disrupt the nice relationship we had." At times it seemed that both sides were simply too exhausted to fight. Sergeant Stanley Kass, who headed the 508th's demolition section, took a patrol out one night and destroyed a German artillery piece that had been bombarding the 508th's lines. For some reason the gun was unguarded, or at least Kass thought so. Later, he learned from a friend in the intelligence section that two Germans had had Kass and his patrol in their sights the entire time. These two Germans, who had subsequently been taken prisoner, insisted they could have killed everyone in the patrol had they wanted. When asked why they did not, they replied, "We wanted a good night's sleep!"[15]

Yet it was not all peace and quiet everywhere all the time. Intelligence estimated that the Germans had 150–200 tubes in the area opposite the 82nd's lines, and they used them to great effect; it was fire from these guns that accounted for most of the division's casualties during the latter part of its stay in Holland. Particularly troublesome were the *nebelwerfers*, which could be manhandled into position, set up quickly to launch a barrage of shells in just seconds, and then broken down and moved before an effective response could be mounted. The Germans were also experts at artillery raids—short, concentrated bombardments on a specific point fired without prior registration or adjustment—a technique they had perfected in the waning months of World War I.[16]

The Allies fought fire with fire, using their own quite plentiful artillery complement to target German gun positions, break up suspected enemy troop concentrations, knock out command posts, and interdict lines of communication. By the end of the campaign, the 82nd's four artillery battalions had fired a total of 125,874 rounds, an average of more than 2,200 rounds per day. Hence, even when relatively quiescent, the front was hardly quiet.[17]

There was one fairly significant fight during this period of static warfare. It occurred in the Den Heuvel, "a finger of trees projecting into an open field" located at the approximate center of the division line. At first it was thought that the wood was free of enemy, so it was to positions fronting the Den Heuvel that the 3/504th was sent after it was relieved from its positions north of the Waal. Captain Burriss, the I Company commander, was not so sure. Neither was Major Cook. "If the Krauts held these woods, they would be able to observe our every move, so Major Cook decided we should seize and hold it."[18]

Tucker was also uncomfortable about the Den Heuvel, but he was chary of sending Cook's battalion into the wood without first discerning what, if anything, was in there, so on the night of 24–25 September, Tucker sent several patrols into the wood to take a look around. They returned and reported no sign of the enemy, but Tucker was unconvinced, so the next night he sent out two more patrols. They, too, saw nothing, giving rise to the hopeful notion that perhaps the Den Heuvel was unoccupied after all. This hope was dashed when at 0130 hours, 26 September, an enemy patrol emerged from the wood, hit H Company's sector, threw some grenades that killed one trooper and wounded a second, and withdrew without a trace, thereby precipitating a back-and-forth battle that would steadily increase in intensity and eventually involve elements of both the 504th and the 508th before it was over.[19]

Immediately following the German raid Lieutenant Don Graebner of G Company gathered twenty-one troopers and headed out in search of the perpetrators, but to no avail. The Germans had disappeared, leaving no spoor, so to forestall future raids Graebner established a combat outpost inside the wood where the thick undergrowth provided excellent concealment. Were the Germans to attempt another raid, thought Graebner, his troopers might be able to ambush them. At the very least, they would provide early warning.

The thick wood hid Graebner's troopers so well that the Germans were oblivious to their presence. Just before dawn, a German walked into the area and, thinking that one of Graebner's troopers was a comrade, engaged him in conversation. The trooper, Sergeant Henry Hoffman, was digging a foxhole and calmly "continued to dig with his left hand, pulled out his .45 with his right and killed the German." The shot alerted other Germans hidden nearby, and a close-range firefight broke out. Graebner's troopers held their ground, but in the process Graebner and two other troopers were wounded. Moreover, Cook learned that an even larger German force was gathering in the wood, so he sent Lieutenant Bernard Karnap with his I Company platoon and three tanks to extract Graebner's troopers before they were overrun. By noon, 26 September, the extraction was complete.[20]

But Karnap was not done. Nicknamed "Babyface" because of his "cherubic look" and "because, like the gangster Babyface Nelson, he loved to kill, even if it meant exposing himself to danger," after extracting Graebner's platoon Karnap grabbed five troopers and led them back into the wood.[21] In the ensuing action Karnap, who was described as both "brave" and "vicious," proved both appellations true.[22] With his five troopers in tow, Karnap destroyed two German strongpoints and killed ten Germans. He then called his platoon and Graebner's platoon forward and positioned them at the edge of the wood to wait for what he was sure would be a counterattack. (Karnap also reportedly ordered ten of nineteen prisoners he had taken killed "because there were not enough men to handle them and hold the wood at the same time.")[23] When the counterattack hit, Karnap became a one-man mortar section. Moving from point to point with an 81mm mortar tube that he used by wedging it against a tree, he led the effort to drive off the attackers.[24]

The "shellacking" Karnap and his troopers gave the Germans had obviously "alerted and angered them," recalled Burriss.[25] It was also obvious that they were preparing another sizable counterattack to drive Karnap and his two platoons out of the Den Heuvel. To preclude this, Burriss led the rest of I Company to Karnap's position and took command.

The counterattack Burriss foretold opened at precisely 0500 hours, 28 September, with "the damnedest artillery barrage." Within thirty minutes, some 2,000 rounds fell in an area approximately one hundred yards square. According to Burriss, "The treetops burst into flames all around us and the ground shook like an earthquake." Under cover of the barrage a battalion of German infantry infiltrated all around the American positions, and once the barrage lifted they came "swarming shoulder to shoulder in mass formation."

Three German tanks entered the fray as well, firing point-blank into individual foxholes. One intrepid bazooka gunner tried to take one of them out, but his rounds bounced off the armor "like a tennis ball," while "the tank continued forward and ran over him." By about 0600 hours Burriss could see that he was in danger of being overrun. When he reported this to Cook, he was told to withdraw. According to Burriss, "By this time, the Krauts had overrun our position; as we withdrew, they were running side by side with my men, both sides shooting at each other."[26] Less than half of the troopers who made it back were still combat effective. American losses were seven killed, twenty-two missing, and twenty wounded. Burriss, who spearheaded the assault crossing of the Waal, called the fight in the Den Heuvel the worst he ever experienced.[27]

On 29 September, Major Otho Holmes's 2/508th relieved the hard-hit 3/504th opposite the Den Heuvel. Later that night Holmes dispatched two combat patrols of his own to investigate the wood. One of the patrols stumbled upon a string of enemy foxholes and fought the Germans "hole to hole" before withdrawing in the face of heavy fire from at least eight machine guns and one 20mm cannon. Having established that the Germans were still present in strength inside the Den Heuvel and that it would be too costly to force them out, the decision was made to simply keep them there. So for the next three days Holmes and his troopers remained in their holes and kept a watchful eye on the wood, all the while enduring heavy shelling. Then, at around midnight, 1 October, the Germans attacked again. Advancing behind a rolling barrage, a battalion of panzer grenadiers supported by tanks, engineers, half-tracks, and assault guns hit the 2/508th's line in the E Company sector. The weight of the attack drove one platoon back, but before the Germans could exploit their breakthrough, Holmes threw his F Company into the fray, which hit the panzer grenadiers in the flank and restored the original line. Retreating back to the protection of the wood, the Germans left behind twenty-eight prisoners and several destroyed half-tracks and self-propelled guns. The 2/508th sustained nine killed and wounded. It was the last significant action in the area around the Den Heuvel.[28]

During the attack two D Company troopers, Frank Haddy and Luis Arellano, also bagged a Panther tank that was headed straight at them. "The barrel on that tank seemed a mile long," recalled Haddy, but the two waited until the tank was almost on top of them before firing their bazooka. "At about ten yards we let her fly. The tank exploded and lit up the area like daylight." Private Bill McClure was in a nearby foxhole watching Haddy and Arellano, awed by their cool and then stunned when Haddy "stood on the road bank next to the burning tank, and while tracer bullets were flying in all directions, . . . put one foot on the tank's track, beat on his chest and yelled like Tarzan." Yanked back to reality when a second tank arrived, Haddy and Arellano reloaded, fired, and forced it to withdraw.[29]

The Den Heuvel fight was an anomaly. For the most part, the most significant combat activity in which the troopers engaged during the latter phase of their stay in Holland was patrolling, the majority of which were launched to gather intelligence. The best way to gain that intelligence was by interrogating prisoners, which meant moving cautiously into enemy territory, avoiding sentries, quietly subduing a German soldier, and then escorting him back to friendly lines. Usually these missions occurred at night, but not always. Captain Arthur W. Ferguson of the 3/504th witnessed one trooper, fortified by his British rum ration, capture some prisoners in broad daylight. According to Ferguson, it had been several days since any prisoners had been taken, so the division offered enticements—trips to Antwerp or Paris and even back to England—to anyone who could take one. Shortly thereafter, Ferguson was standing in an observation post with General Gavin when they spied a trooper to their front get out of his foxhole, grab his rifle, cock his helmet back on his head, and, before anyone could stop him, start walking across a flat flood plain toward the German positions 300 yards away.

> Every one [*sic*] watched in amazement, including General Gavin, as this trooper walked across this open space in full view of the enemy (if they had been watching) up to a culvert and called for the "Krauts" to come out with their hands up. The surprised Germans, three or four, meekly came out, and with a little urging from the trooper, turned and made their way to our lines, followed by the trooper. General Gavin met the trooper, still rather tipsy, and pinned the Silver Star on him.[30]

Private Bennie J. Siemanowicz of the 505th accomplished a similar feat. For ten days Siemanowicz watched from his observation post as two Germans directly opposite him constructed a luxurious fighting position, complete with sheet-metal roofing. On the day they completed their task Siemanowicz left his post and ran across a mined bridge and then along a dike to reach the prize foxhole in full view of soldiers on both sides. Lieutenant Colonel Warren Williams was watching. According to Williams, Siemanowicz approached the foxhole, shouted something, and then fired into the hole, after which the two Germans crawled out with their hands up, one of them obviously wounded. Siemanowicz then made the healthy German pick up his comrade and herded both of them back to friendly lines, alternating between firing at nearby positions to keep other Germans' heads down and kicking the healthy prisoner in the buttocks whenever he slowed. When Siemanowicz reached U.S. lines unharmed, Williams and an officer from London who was visiting the front rushed down to talk with him. "We . . . asked him why he had walked out in the exposed area and taken such a risk. His reply was, 'Aw, I heard the division had been yelling for some prisoners, so I thought I would get a couple.' The next question was what had he been drinking. To this, he replied, 'Oh, a couple bottles of vino.' He was actually quite inebriated."[31]

Of course, not all prisoner snatches were motivated by liquid courage, nor were they as easily accomplished. Lieutenant Megellas led one such patrol. Megellas had a well-deserved reputation as a hard-nosed, tactically proficient leader, so when Tucker wanted prisoners he turned to Megellas. Getting one would be challenging, however. German defenses in the area consisted of a string of fortified blockhouses atop an embankment that was 1,000 yards away and across a large bog spanned by a single footbridge. Assuming that the footbridge was seeded with mines and barbed wire and under observation from enemy outposts, Megellas moved out at night with his entire platoon in case he had to fight his way into or out of enemy lines. At the friendly side of the footbridge he halted his platoon and crawled forward alone to check for mines. Along the way he got noisily entangled in some barbed wire, which alerted some Germans in a nearby foxhole, but Megellas kept his head, freed himself from the wire, and then crawled to the foxhole and demanded that its occupants surrender. When no one answered he tossed a grenade inside and crawled to a second foxhole. Again he demanded surrender. Again he received no answer. Again he finished off the occupants with a grenade. He then crawled to a third foxhole and killed its occupants with his carbine. All told Megellas killed four Germans, wounded several more, and knocked out a machine-gun nest before coming upon an enemy soldier who was willing to surrender. But Megellas was not content with one prisoner, so he asked his captive how many more of his comrades were nearby. When the German replied in broken English that he did not understand, Megellas hit him in the mouth, knocked him to the ground, and started choking him until the startled German sputtered that there were ten others in the vicinity. Megellas then had his captive call out and demand their surrender. When only one came forward Megellas called his platoon forward and led it in a raid that killed six more Germans and resulted in four more prisoners. Still Megellas was not satisfied, so he sent the prisoners back with two of his troopers and led the rest in a raid on the embankment, during which they killed eleven more Germans at the cost of only one man wounded, whom Megellas slung over his shoulder and carried back to friendly lines, followed by the rest of his platoon and two more prisoners.[32]

As Megellas's patrol indicates, as time went by and the Germans fortified their defenses, prisoners became harder to come by. When one was taken, therefore, they were quickly and carefully shepherded back to friendly lines in hopes that this would curtail, at least temporarily, the need for additional patrols. Inevitably, however, higher headquarters' appetite for intelligence would generate a demand for more prisoners. Captain Adam Komosa, the 2/504th's assistant operations officer, recalled that when no prisoners were taken, the pressure to get one increased commensurately. Colonel Tucker grew especially impatient and put out the word that if sections could not take a prisoner, then a squad would be sent out the next night. If the squad failed to return with a prisoner, a platoon would go the following night, and so on. It finally got to the point that an entire company was sent out on a mission. The task fell to F Company, 2/504th. Komosa moved forward to an observation post to watch.

> Soon the troopers entered into the wooded area, and there was hell to pay. Angry exchanges of machine gun and small arms fire now took place. Much shouting, some screaming, and a hell of a lot of swearing was heard. In a little while it was all over. The shooting stopped, and the troopers started coming back out of the woods. I heard some swearing about that time. It sounded as though there was an argument between several troopers themselves. I heard one say, "Let me throw my bayonet through that son of a bitch." About that time one of the non-coms—I believe it was First Sergeant Bishop—stepped in and barked in his usually commanding manner, "Look you stupid ass! If we don't bring this dried up little bastard back to the C.P. alive, we'll have to come out here tomorrow night and do this all over again." From that moment on, and until they returned to the C.P., they guarded their prisoner with unusual caution.[33]

One of the most intrepid of the division's patrol leaders was the 504th's Ted Bachenheimer, who continued the same behind-the-lines heroics he had conducted at Anzio. According to Private Matthew W. Kantala Jr., Bachenheimer "was a boy that the officers didn't push around. He could get away with most anything." Captain Louis Hauptfleisch wrote that Gavin was not certain if he should court-martial or promote Bachenheimer.[34] He ultimately decided on the latter and awarded him a battlefield commission. According to Private First Class Willard "Bill" Strunk:

> Ted was one of the finest soldiers any country would ever want. Ted Bachenheimer was a very calm man in any circumstances. At night Bachenheimer would organize patrols and go behind German lines to gain information on German positions. He would speak German fluently. Many times on patrols he would talk to the Germans. The combat patrol would then take them

> prisoners. He was very serious about his work. He would sit and discuss ideas on how to get information from the Germans.[35]

Shortly before the 82nd left Holland, Bachenheimer left on a patrol, some say dressed in a German uniform, and was never heard from again. It was a tremendous loss for the division.[36]

The 82nd was finally pulled off the line on 11 November, replaced by the 3rd Canadian Division, which had just completed the fight to clear the Scheldt Estuary. The troopers assembled in Nijmegen to prepare for movement to the rear, which they hoped meant the English bases from which they had deployed. But it was not to be. Instead, they moved into two French army cantonments near Rheims, France—Camps Suippes and Sissonne. They arrived in their new home less 4,297 of their number missing, wounded, injured, or dead, about 30 percent of the total that deployed to Holland.[37] Projections were that it would take until mid-January 1945 to get the division combat ready.[38]

Notwithstanding the cost, few questioned the success of MARKET, the airborne portion of the operation.[39] In his after-action report, Gavin opined that MARKET "served to emphasize the value of lessons learned in past airborne operations" and validated the principles enumerated in Training Circular No. 113.[40] Ridgway echoed Gavin's assessment, writing in his own after-action review that "the experience of Operation MARKET has produced no basic alteration of accepted principles respecting the employment of airborne forces" and that it had, "in fact, further strengthened my conviction that our principles are sound and, if accorded due consideration in the planning and execution of airborne operations, will offer the maximum prospect of success."[41] General Brereton felt that "despite the failure of the [British] 2nd Army to get through to Arnhem and establish a permanent bridgehead over the Lower Rhine, Operation MARKET was a brilliant success." The airborne troops, he continued, "accomplished what was expected of them. It was the breakdown of 2nd Army's timetable on the first day—their failure to reach Eindhoven in 6 to 8 hours as planned—that caused the delay in the taking of the Nijmegen bridge and the failure at Arnhem."[42] General Arnold also pronounced MARKET a success. "I am pleased with the success of your initial operation," he wrote in a personal letter to Brereton.

> There had been discussion among American commentators about the failure to obtain the full possible measure of success at Arnhem. To meet this point there was presented at an off-the-record background Press Conference, now being held in the Air Staff weekly, a detailed map showing our front-line

> position after your retirement south of the [unintelligible—presumably Neder Rijn]. The hypothetical question was asked as to whether that indicated military failure or military success. In sending my commendatory message to you I stated my pleasure at your success and I meant success.[43]

Eisenhower and Marshall were also pleased with the performance of the First Allied Airborne Army. Two days after the initial drops, Eisenhower sent a message to Brereton in which he wrote, "The initial major operation of the Allied Airborne Army has already proceeded sufficiently far to confirm the wisdom of the decision to organize all our airborne divisions under [a] single command." Marshall likewise sent Brereton a message in which he praised Brereton, the First Airborne Army staff, and the pilots, crews, and airborne forces "for the courageous and determined manner in which they have carried out their duties." Even after the war, when emotions had cooled, a board of general officers convened to look at the conduct of airborne operations in the context of the war as a whole was effusive in its praise of Operation MARKET. "This was the largest airborne operation in history, was a daylight operation, surprise was complete, the operation was successful and if success seemed easy it was only because of the skill with which it was executed."[44]

Despite the praise heaped on the airborne divisions after MARKET, or perhaps because of it, both Gavin and Ridgway harbored concerns about what this could portend. What especially bothered Gavin was the "practice of assigning an airborne Division frontage far in excess of that normally given a ground Division." This "must be weighed very carefully and full consideration given to the probable enemy reaction." In Holland, there were wide gaps in the division's lines that "a vigorous, alert enemy, with the proper means at his disposal, could have capitalized on . . . to seriously jeopardize the integrity of our defense set-up."[45] Ridgway seized on Gavin's assessment and developed it further, writing, "There is a point here of such vital importance to future airborne operations in this theater in this war, that I wish to emphasize it in the strongest possible manner." When MARKET-GARDEN was conceived the Germans were conducting "a hasty and somewhat disorganized withdrawal under powerful Allied pressure." The enemy's "command had been badly shattered, and his control severely crippled." But since that time, the situation on the Western Front had changed. "Now we face a different foe. His precipitated [*sic*] retreat has ended, his command has been restored and invigorated, his control reestablished, and he fights with the aid of strong ground defenses, closer to his sources of supply." What two airborne divisions accomplished in MARKET-GARDEN, he warned, "is no indication of what we may expect to accomplish in certain situations now." If thrown against a well-prepared, well-entrenched, well-supplied enemy determined to fight vigorously in defense of his homeland, "these magnificent divisions [might] be assigned a task wholly beyond their strength."[46]

Ridgway's warning applied universally to Allied forces on the Western Front in the autumn of 1944. The Germans were everywhere waging a spirited defense, and although they were still falling back, it was upon the prepared, albeit somewhat decrepit, defenses of the Siegfried Line. Meanwhile, the Ruhr industrial area, MARKET-GARDEN's ultimate goal, was still pumping out war materiel—ball-bearing production was up, fighter production was up, and the numbers for tank and truck production were still high.[47] Meanwhile, the Allies' lines of communication were getting ever longer (especially without Antwerp in hand), as the Germans were falling back on theirs. As a result, the Allied armies had slowed to a crawl. Even Patton, a man defined by his lightning thrusts, was stuck in the Saar Valley, his Third Army engaged in a slogging match for Metz. Eisenhower had risked everything on Montgomery, and Montgomery had failed—there was no bridgehead over the Rhine, no destruction of the Ruhr, no clearing of the Scheldt (until much later). It was not just airborne divisions that would have a tough go of it under these conditions. The same applied to all Allied divisions, regardless of their makeup.

Yet Montgomery remained MARKET-GARDEN's "unrepentant advocate," contending that "if the operation had been properly backed from its inception, and given the aircraft, ground forces, and administrative resources necessary for the job—it would have succeeded *in spite of* my mistakes, or the adverse weather, or the presence of the 2nd S.S. Panzer Corps in the Arnhem area." On the other hand, General Bradley thought the operation "a massive assault *in the wrong direction* at what was probably the most crucial moment on the German front," adding that "in permitting Monty to launch Market-Garden, Ike committed his greatest tactical error of the war."[48]

Faced as he was with a struggle among his subordinates and a determined enemy, Eisenhower decided to resume his broad-front approach, a decision he announced during a 5 October conference at his headquarters in Versailles. According to Field Marshal Brooke, Ike's future strategy "consisted of the capture of Antwerp, an advance to the Rhine in the north and south, forcing the Rhine north and south of the Ruhr, capture of [the] Ruhr followed by an advance on Berlin either from [the] Ruhr or from Frankfurt depending on which was most promising. Meanwhile [U.S. Lieutenant General Jacob L.] Devers [the 6th Army Group commander] in the south to threaten Munich as a cover plan." According to Stephen Ambrose, Ike's decision was "the safe, cautious route." He continued, "Under his directives no army would take heavy casualties, no general would lose his reputation, credit for the victory could be shared by all, and there was no chance of the Germans reversing the situation by surrounding and destroying an advanced force. Eisenhower's policy would surely lead to victory. The only trouble was that if the Germans decided to fight on it would take time."[49] No one expected the Germans to roll over. It was expected, rather, that they would take advantage of the benefits of waging a defensive fight from prepared positions with shortened lines of communication, to say nothing of the psychological boost accrued from fighting on the borders of the Fatherland. Furthermore, with Rundstedt back in command of the Western Front (he returned to command in September), predictions were that the Germans would conduct "a textbook defense," falling back from position to position, trading space for time, and conducting nothing larger than limited counterattacks.[50] What the Allies did not know, and never considered, was that Rundstedt no longer had any control over strategy. Nor did any other German army officer. Despite their training, experience, and pedigree, they had become mere ciphers, the last vestige of their influence having disappeared with the smoke that, for a brief moment on 20 July 1944, engulfed Hitler's conference room.[51]

When he emerged, shaken but alive from the debris of the wooden hut that exploded around him during the failed attempt on his life on 20 July, Hitler was certain of two things: that he had been saved for some higher purpose and that vengeance would be swift, hard, and his alone. His survival, he said later on that night in a radio broadcast, was "confirmation of the task imposed upon me by Providence," and he pledged that he would get even with the conspirators "in the way that we National Socialists are accustomed."[52] Several of the conspirators, including Oberst Count Claus Schenk Graf von Stauffenberg, the plot's leader and the man who set the bomb, had already been executed. Others were rounded up, tortured, ridiculed, and paraded in front of a sham People's Court before being ignominiously hanged by wire nooses from meat hooks. Nearly 250 persons were executed and thousands more thrown into concentration camps during the blood orgy that followed the failed plot.[53]

But blood alone would not suffice. Hitler's messianic self-image required something more. It required complete sublimation. In this Germany's generals acquiesced.

Because the plot's leaders were mostly high-ranking Army officers, counting in its ranks at least two field marshals (including Rommel) and sixteen generals, it was left to those who remained to demonstrate beyond doubt their loyalty and the loyalty of the Army. Hence, three days after the attempt Generaloberst Heinz Guderian, acting chief of staff of the Army, issued a general order in which he pledged the devotion of all German soldiers to the Führer and German people, stating that "the only road open to an honest soldier" was "the road of duty and honour." The next day, as a result of Göring's toadyism, the Nazi salute was made the only mode of salutation for all branches of the service (in place of the hand salute), a further "indication of the unshakeable loyalty to the Führer and of the close bonds of comradeship between Wehrmacht and Party." Then, as if to one-up Göring, on 29 July Guderian issued a second general order demanding that "every General Staff officer must be a National Socialist officer-leader, that is, not only by his knowledge of tactics and strategy, but also by his model attitude to political questions, and by actively cooperating in the political indoctrination of younger commanders in accordance with the tenets of the Führer."[54] With this diktat all those who wore the wine-red stripe that marked them as the elite of the German officer corps "submissively . . . accepted the status of a puppet and the mission to preach National Socialism. None resigned, none resisted."[55] Yet the debasement of the Army by those in its highest echelons seemingly knew no bounds. On 14 August, the Army's cowed leaders requested that the Führer cleanse its ranks of the plotters so that they could be turned over to the German people for justice. To this end Hitler appointed a Court of Honor, composed of high-profile officers, including Keitel, Guderian, and Rundstedt, the court's president. It was this court that conducted the investigations against the alleged conspirators and turned over those they found complicit in the plot to the bestial Gestapo. "There was no courage of Opposition left," wrote one historian of the affair, "let along the courage of Resistance."

> All that remained was a numbed sense of continuing duty, a duty which all now saw with nightmare clarity was leading swiftly and inevitably to disaster. Yet of all those who realized this truth, so great was the impact of the aftermath of July 20, with its trials and its hangings and its general horror, that none could be found even to raise a voice in respectful criticism of the *Führer*'s genius. Indeed the reverse was true. All who could do so vied with one another in reaffirming their loyalty and allegiance, blind and abject, before their *Führer*.[56]

While bringing the Army to heel, Hitler turned also to the total mobilization of the German nation. He was abetted in this by the reaction of the majority of Germans who were appalled by the assassination attempt, relieved that their Führer was still alive, and approved of the purging of those complicit in the plot. Some measures had been in train before 20 July, most significantly those enacted by Armaments Minister Albert Speer that made more efficient use of resources and hundreds of thousands of impressed foreign laborers. After 20 July, Hitler ratcheted up the mobilization of the home front. Led by Joseph Goebbels, a massive forced induction of Germany's remaining manpower freed up a million men for military service who, by

December 1944, were subsequently formed into twenty-five *Volks Grenadier* (People's Grenadier) divisions, numerous artillery and rocket units, and a home guard, the *Volkssturm*.[57]

So the stage was set. Hitler, the unassailable warlord—surrounded by sycophants, unopposed by a supine officer corps, and buttressed by statistics that, on paper at least, indicated that there yet existed enough men and materiel for one last major effort—was set to fulfill his destiny. The task before him—to win the war and save Germany and the West from Bolshevism—was one that Hitler believed only he had the will to carry out. "This war must be won by us," he told his secretaries. "Otherwise Europe will be lost to Bolshevism. . . . I am the only one who knows the danger, and the only one who can prevent it."[58] It but remained to determine the path by which victory would be achieved.

On 16 September, Hitler had a revelation that, he insisted, illuminated that path. During that day's situation briefing the normally listless Führer suddenly became animated; pounding the map in front of him, he startled everyone with his announcement: "Führer decision . . . Counterattack out of the Ardennes . . . Target Antwerp . . . Cut the joint between the English and Americans . . . a new Dunkirk!"[59]

The idea of a counteroffensive in the west had been fomenting in Hitler's mind for some time, but nothing concrete was done to bring it to fruition until, following his 16 September announcement, Hitler tasked Jodl to come up with some alternatives. Secrecy was to be maintained at all costs; commanders were not to be informed until the last minute (the 20 July plot convinced Hitler that there was a hidden fifth column in the officer corps that was passing secrets to the Russians).[60] By October Jodl had come up with five courses of action. Hitler selected two for further development. By 21 October, the plan had been finalized. The next day Hitler summoned General der Kavallerie Siegfried Westphal, chief of staff of *OB West*, and General der Infanterie Hans Krebs, chief of staff of *Army Group B*, to the *Wolfsschanz* to receive their orders.[61]

Hitler briefed the plan himself. The aim of the offensive, code-named *Wacht am Rhein* (Watch on the Rhine), "was, by cutting off the British Army from its bases of supply, to force it to evacuate the Continent."[62] With that accomplished Hitler surmised that the Americans, who he believed had no stomach for the war, would quit the European struggle, thereby freeing the Wehrmacht to turn and finish off the Russians. As he explained to Speer: "A single breakthrough on the western front! You will see! That will lead to a collapse and panic among the Americans. We'll drive through in the middle and take Antwerp. With that, they'll have lost their supply harbour. And there'll be a huge encirclement of the entire English army with hundreds of thousands of prisoners. Like it was in Russia!" Furthermore, as Jodl later explained, "The Russians had so many troops even if we had succeeded in destroying thirty divisions it would have made no difference. On the other hand, if we destroyed thirty divisions in the West, it would amount to more than one third of the whole invasion army."[63] Moreover, the final objective—Antwerp—was little more than a hundred miles away, a not unreasonable distance for armored and mechanized forces.[64]

Wacht am Rhein was to proceed in two phases. Phase one would see three armies of *Army Group B*—the *5th Panzer Army*, the *6th Panzer Army*, and the *7th Army*—attack through the Ardennes to seize bridgeheads over the Meuse River. Phase two would be a continuation of the advance, culminating in the capture of Antwerp. Hitler told his generals that they could count on thirty divisions for the offensive, including three paratroop and twelve panzer or panzer grenadier divisions. Additionally, twelve *Volks* artillery corps, ten *werfer* (rocket launcher) brigades, and a host of other support troops would be available. The Luftwaffe, too, would weigh in with some 1,500 fighters, 100 of which would be jets. Finally, more than four million gallons of fuel and some fifty trainloads of ammunition would be stockpiled for the offensive. A target date of 25 November was set. Meteorologists predicted that there would be at least ten days of overcast skies during this time, thereby negating Allied air superiority (despite Göring's promises, Hitler did not have much faith in the Luftwaffe). It was also a new moon phase, further limiting visibility and in so doing abetting the element of surprise.[65]

When Westphal and Krebs returned to their respective commands and briefed their commanders, there was shock all around. "This plan hasn't got a damned leg to stand on," commented Generalfeldmarschall Model, the *Army Group B* commander. Rundstedt felt likewise: "When I received this plan early in November [*sic*] I was staggered. Hitler had not troubled to consult me about its possibilities. It was obvious to me that the available forces were far too small for such an extremely ambitious plan. . . . In fact, no soldier believed that the aim of reaching Antwerp was really practicable. But I knew by now it was useless to protest to Hitler about the *possibility* of anything."[66] Rundstedt was correct. There was no talking Hitler out of his grandiose plan. When Rundstedt forwarded his doubts about the plan, Hitler ignored them, and when Rundstedt and Model together tried selling Hitler on a less ambitious scheme, Hitler tersely replied, "Preparations for an improvisation will not be made." Finally, in a last-ditch effort to forestall what they were certain was a flawed operation, the field marshals enlisted the support of two of Hitler's favorites—General der Panzertruppen Hasso-Eccard von Manteuffel of the *5th Panzer Army* and SS-Oberstgruppenführer Josef "Sepp" Dietrich of the *6th Panzer Army*—both of whom also opposed

Wacht am Rhein. This, too, proved fruitless.[67] "I have had to make hard—infinitely hard—decisions in my life," explained Hitler to an assemblage of senior officers a few days before the invasion, adding that, for Germany, "in the coming ten, twenty, thirty, maybe fifty years, no man would come with more authority, more possibilities to influence the nation, and more decisiveness, than myself." Wars are won, he continued, by making an opponent recognize that he cannot win anymore. "Thus, the most important task is to bring the enemy to this realization." Waging a defensive war would not do this. Nor, presumably, would a limited offensive.[68]

Sometime after 23 November the attack was postponed, first to 10 December and ultimately to 16 December, yet Hitler's enthusiasm remained undiminished.[69] On 11 December he moved into the *Adlerhorst* (Eagle's Eyrie), his headquarters at Ziegenberg, near Bad Nauheim, to be closer to what he had come to regard as the decisive theater of operations, seeking a repeat of the stunning victory German forces had gained over the same ground in May 1940.[70]

During their prewar preparations the French viewed the Ardennes—a triangle-shaped area whose eighty-mile-wide base generally defined the German frontier from Eupen, Belgium, in the north to Luxembourg City in the south and then extended westward to the Meuse River—as impassable to armored or mechanized forces. It was, they believed, too heavily forested to accommodate large numbers of tanks and trucks that would, in any event, have a difficult time negotiating the region's twisting, narrow roads and meandering rivers and streams. They were of course wrong, for it was through this seemingly impenetrable maze that, in May 1940, German panzers moved with amazing speed, stopping only when they reached the French coast at Abbeville.[71]

In December 1944, the Allies were equally blind to the possibility of a strike through the Ardennes. Located in the southern part of the U.S. First Army zone, the Ardennes was an economy-of-force sector where units could be rested, reequipped, reorganized, and, for those new to the front, acclimated to combat. Lieutenant General Courtney H. Hodges, the First Army commander, assigned responsibility for the sector to Major General Troy H. Middleton's U.S. VIII Corps. With three infantry divisions under his command—the U.S. 106th, 28th, and 4th—Middleton was charged with defending a front that was three times larger than that normally assigned to a corps. Moreover, the 106th Infantry Division, the northernmost unit in the corps zone, was new to combat, while the 28th and 4th Infantry Divisions, which held the central and southern sections of the corps front, respectively, had recently returned from bloody combat in the Hürtgen Forest, where they had lost a combined total of more than 9,000 men.[72] Writing after the war, Eisenhower claimed that he was fully aware that he was "running a definite risk" in the Ardennes, but felt justified in doing so in order to maintain the momentum of attacks elsewhere.[73] Bradley, too, felt justified in manning the Ardennes with such a weak force because he was certain that were the Germans to attack there, they could be easily interdicted by Allied air power.[74]

Allied perceptions about the improbability of a major German attack in the Ardennes were underscored by intelligence summaries at every level of the chain of command. On 9 December, VIII Corps intelligence surmised that "the enemy's present practice of bringing new divisions to this sector to receive front line experience and then relieving them out for commitment elsewhere indicates his desire to have this sector of the front remain quiet and inactive." Colonel Benjamin A. "Monk" Dickson, the First Army intelligence chief, echoed this sentiment: "During the last month there has been a definite pattern for the seasoning of newly-formed divisions in the comparatively quiet sector opposite VIII Corps prior to their dispatch to [a] more active front." Bradley's intelligence chief, Brigadier General Edwin L. Sibert, took an even more expansive view of the enemy situation, reporting that "it is near certain that attrition is steadily sapping the strength of the German forces on the Western Front and that the crust of defenses is thinner, more brittle and more vulnerable than it appears in our G-2 maps or to the troops in the line." In light of his analysis, Sibert predicted that "with continued Allied pressure in the south and in the north, the breaking point may develop suddenly and without warning."[75] The attrition of which Sibert wrote was based on casualty figures disseminated by SHAEF, which estimated that the Germans were losing approximately 9,000 men a day or about five divisions per week.[76]

The likelihood of a German attack was discounted at lower levels as well. Private First Class John Marshall's tank company was attached to the 28th Infantry Division. Marshall recalled that being in the Ardennes "was like a holiday, as though we'd never fight again." Captain Charles B. MacDonald, a company commander in the 2nd Infantry Division, recalled that though it was cold and wet in the Ardennes, "Life became routine in the relative comfort and quiet of our new location." Lieutenant George Wilson, a company commander in the 4th Infantry Division, also remembered the "unaccustomed luxury" of life on the front line in the VIII Corps area, although he worried about the large sector his company had to defend. "All I could do was shake my head at the futility of ever having to defend our positions against serious attack, should it come to that."[77] But the prevailing attitude was that the odds of a German attack in the Ardennes were practically nil. "Take it easy, General," was Major General Walter M. Robertson's advice to his counterpart, Major General Alan W. Jones, whose green 106th Infantry Division relieved Robertson's veteran 2nd Infantry Division in the northern part of the VIII Corps sector. "The Krauts won't attack even if they were ordered to."[78]

Myriad commentators have since debated the insouciance with which the Allies discounted the possibility of a German counteroffensive in the Ardennes in December 1944. Some, like Bradley, have argued that the Allies were fooled because of their overreliance on ULTRA intercepts that had all but dried up in the weeks preceding the German offensive because of Hitler's ban on the use of radios.[79] Others have argued that ULTRA did, in fact, reveal certain key pieces of information that, had they been properly interpreted, would have painted a vastly different picture.[80] A third group has posited that it was not Allied intelligence that failed; rather, it was the effectiveness of the German deception plan that was designed to make the Allies think that units were being emplaced not for a major counteroffensive but rather as fire brigades for use against Allied breakthroughs.[81] This debate, much like the debate over the supposed failure of intelligence that preceded the Japanese attack on Pearl Harbor, is one that will never be resolved. However, as Stephen Ambrose wrote, "Intelligence makes no decisions."[82] It is, instead, the mind-set of the people who make predictions based on the intelligence they receive, much of which is oftentimes contradictory, that is the decisive element, and in December 1944, virtually no one expected that the Germans would, or could, make a large-scale attack through the Ardennes.

Allied commanders made one other significant miscalculation in the fall of 1944: They put two U.S. airborne divisions fresh from combat in the middle of the French champagne region.

The 82nd arrived at Camps Suippes and Sissonne in mid-November. After settling into their new homes, the troopers set about completing the standard postcombat tasks of accounting for and cleaning equipment and turning in weapons for maintenance. Mundane work to be sure, but the troopers were thankful for the roofs over their heads, warm beds, and three hot meals a day, to say nothing of having survived another campaign. What they really looked forward to, however, was their first weekend pass. And when that weekend arrived, the majority of the division went to nearby Rheims. The ensuing mayhem was colossal. Fights with rear-echelon soldiers were rampant, an impetus fueled, in part, by the presence of American soldiers from some all-black service and supply units. And despite the arrests and disciplinary measures taken against the malefactors, the same thing occurred the next weekend, so at the request of the local rear-area commander, Gavin placed strict controls on the number of passes that would be granted for subsequent weekends, which meant that the vast majority of the division's troopers spent the remainder of their time in France restricted to post. "There were two problems," wrote Sergeant William H. Tucker. "One was that we had been in the field too long and were ready to let loose. Another was that none of us had any experience drinking champagne. We did not understand that such a light, apparently frivolous drink made a person drunk inside an hour and a half."[83] Gavin put it a bit differently: "The trouble seems to center in three things. There is no way to get a girl of easy virtue, all houses are off limits and guarded, food cannot be bought in town anywhere, champagne can be bought by the bottle anywhere anytime."[84]

To offset the strict rationing of passes, attempts were made to bring entertainment to the troopers. One of the most memorable came about through the efforts of Sergeant McKenzie of the 456th, who procured the services of a French entertainment troupe for a hundred dollars, eight cartons of cigarettes, and ten pounds of coffee. The troupe consisted of a magician, jugglers, and some mimes, but the real stars were the "statuesque dancers," two very well-built young women who struck a series of poses in the nude. The troupe stayed in camp for a few nights and put on several shows. "The [armed] guard detail on their rooms had to be doubled," recalled McKenzie.[85] The Thanksgiving meal was also a big hit as the cooks went all out to serve a traditional feast, and in early December some Major League ballplayers, including Frankie Frisch, Mel Ott, Dutch Leonard, and Bucky Walters, stopped by the camps to spend time with the troopers. The division also formed a football team and began practicing for a much-ballyhooed New Year's Day game against the 101st. Eventually, several weeks' mail also caught up with the troopers, but this proved a double-edged sword, for every delivery contained one or two "Dear John" letters.[86]

The few troopers fortunate enough to get a pass went to Brussels, Paris, or the French Riviera. A favorable exchange rate, about fifty French francs to the dollar, ensured that they had plenty of money, with a room in Paris going for twenty francs and a meal for ten. Moreover, these troopers generally comported themselves well, no doubt motivated by fear of what would happen if reports were otherwise. No less an authority than Lieutenant General John Clifford Hodges Lee, the commanding general of the European communications zone, who stopped by the 82nd's base camps to see his son (who was a captain in the division), regaled Gavin with "the excellent appearance and behavior of our lads in Paris." Lee also told Gavin about a conversation he had had with another general officer during which he commented on how sharp and alert the 82nd troopers looked, to which the other general replied, "Alert, youre [*sic*] damn right they look alert. Hell, you are looking at the survivors."[87]

While in camp the bulk of the troopers' time, especially in the first several weeks, was devoted to rest, repairing weapons and equipment, and receiving and integrating replacements. No serious combat training was conducted, the only collective endeavors being physical fitness and some close order drill. Yet

Gavin looked forward to instituting a rigorous training program, and the area around Sissonne was an especially attractive location for doing so. The Germans had used it during the occupation, and "the remains of their training arrangements show[ed] evidences of lots of work." He also counted on having that most important resource—time. "I am counting on three months," he wrote in his diary not long after arriving at Sissonne. A few days later he predicted an even longer stay. "It promises to be a long stretch here, I wouldn't be surprised if we were here in May. It is difficult to see how the United Nations can mount a large[-]scale effective attack before spring. Any immediate show will no doubt be done by the 17th [Airborne Division], later the 13th [Airborne Division] will be available."[88]

Hence, the most rigorous physical activity the troopers engaged in during the first several weeks of their stay at Suippes and Sissonne was the fighting in the streets and bars of Rheims. That was a good thing. "We can use a few months of rest and recreation as well as reorganization and training," wrote Gavin.[89] More important, it would help dispel a dread in the ranks that had been brought to his attention by the division's chaplains. "The four jump people are sweating out any more jumps feeling that they have used up about all their luck," confided Gavin to his diary.

> I understand exactly how they feel, I feel the same way myself. They have always done a fine job but now their ranks are thinning, many of them are banged up from combat and hardly fit mentally or physically for further parachute operations yet they have no other prospects. It hardly seems right, there should be some way out other than being killed or wounded. There is no other now. Some day there is going to be a hell of a mess when complete units refuse to jump in combat again. There should be some relief for them or some promise of relief.[90]

But all such hopes and promises vanished in the early-morning hours of 16 December, swept away by a furious artillery, rocket, and mortar barrage announcing Hitler's last gasp for victory.

CHAPTER 21

TO TURN THE TIDE

In brief, the 82d Airborne Division, still awaiting reinforcements and much re-supply at its base camps in the general area of RHEIMS, FRANCE, moved 150 miles with its first combat elements going into position in less than 24 hours and the entire Division closing in a new combat area in less than 40 hours from the time of the initial alert. It fought, stopped, and held against the best Divisions the German leader, Field Marshal VON RUNSTEDT [sic], could pit against it, protecting the North shoulder of the Allied line, preventing the GERMAN break-through from turning North to LIEGE, BELGIUM, and providing a safe area through which trapped Allied units could withdraw from the break-through area.

—JAMES M. GAVIN, *THE STORY OF THE 82D AIRBORNE DIVISION IN THE BATTLE OF THE BELGIAN BULGE IN THE SIEGFRIED LINE AND ON THE ROER RIVER*

THE VOICE ON the other end of the phone was "almost so panicky that I didn't understand initially what he was talking about, but he said something about the Krauts breaking through all over the place," recalled Lieutenant Rufus K. Broadaway, Gavin's junior aide-de-camp.[1] It was Sunday evening, 17 December 1944. Gavin, his staff, and two guests—Colonel Rupert Graves and Lieutenant Colonel Melvin Zais, the commander and executive officer of the independent 517th Parachute Infantry Regiment—were having dinner. As the junior man present it fell to Broadaway to answer the phone. The panicked voice on the other end was that of Colonel "Doc" Eaton, the XVIII

Airborne Corps chief of staff who, after his initial outburst, told Broadaway to put Gavin on the line.

Eaton told Gavin that "he had just received a call from SHAEF to the effect that the situation at the front to the east appeared to be critical; that the airborne divisions were to be prepared to move 24 hours after daylight the following day; [and] that the Corps Commander, General Ridgway, was in England and could not be contacted immediately."[2] Gavin took the message and returned to his guests. "There was no change in his expression," remembered Zais. "He smiled and said, 'Let's get on with dinner.' I recall relaxing with relief, because I was enjoying this visit and I did not want it interrupted." It was only after dessert that Gavin's "expression and attitude suddenly reflected a complete reversal." Looking around the table, he announced: "Gentlemen, we've got work to do. That call was from Doc Eaton. The Germans have counter attacked [*sic*] and broken through in the Ardennes. The situation is critical. General Ridgway . . . is in England. General Taylor . . . is in the States. I am the acting Corps Commander. We must move out with both divisions within twenty four [*sic*] hours. The 82d Airborne Division will move first."[3] With this announcement "everyone sprang to action." There was no panic. Though spurred with urgency, everything, and everyone, was "controlled and soft as velvet." Gavin and his staff had been through this before; they knew what to do and could do it well. According to Zais, "It was . . . a vivid example of a leader who could keep his cool, hide his emotions, organize his thoughts, and, at the appropriate time, turn on the heat."[4]

Gavin had already told Eaton to tell Brigadier General Anthony C. McAuliffe, the 101st's artillery commander who, in Taylor's absence, was the acting division commander, to prepare the 101st for an immediate move. Gavin sent the same message to his artillery commander, Brigadier General Andy March, who was in Suippes with the other half of the 82nd. Around 2130 hours Eaton called back with an update. Both airborne divisions were to "move without delay in the direction of Bastogne, [Belgium,] where further orders would be received," and XVIII Airborne Corps had been placed under the operational control of U.S. First Army. Gavin and his staff sketched out a hasty movement plan: The 82nd would move first, approximately an hour after daylight on 18 December; the 101st would follow with a tentative departure time of 1400 hours, 18 December.[5]

The calm with which Gavin and his staff went about their duties, and that had so impressed Lieutenant Colonel Zais, was not replicated elsewhere in the division that night. There was much to do and little time in which to get it done. Equipment and weapons turned in for maintenance had to be retrieved, regardless of their state of repair. Supplies had to be scrounged. Somehow transportation to get the division to Belgium had to be procured. Plans had to be issued. Inspections conducted. Orders disseminated. Ammunition distributed. The first priority, however, was assembling the troopers.

Fortunately, most troopers were in camp, a direct result of past indiscretions. The 505th's troopers were in a theater at Camp Suippes watching a performance of the Ballet Russe de Monte Carlo when a call went out for all staff officers to report to the regimental command post.[6] "They started calling for the highest ranking officers," recalled Sergeant William L. Blank, and "the calls kept coming on down the ranks." Blank and his buddies joked that they would be calling out the sergeants next. They were right.[7] The 325th's officers had been invited to a dance at a nearby field hospital. No sooner had they arrived when word came to "return immediately to camp, regiment is on alert!"[8] The 325th's troopers, meanwhile, were watching a movie in Camp Sissonne's theater. Suddenly, the film stopped, the lights came on, and an announcement was made that everyone was to return to their barracks immediately.[9] The troopers of the 456th were already in their barracks; they were in the midst of a champagne party made possible by the resourceful Sergeant McKenzie who had procured fifty cases of champagne. McKenzie recalled little of that night, having drunk himself into unconsciousness. He awoke in the back of a weapons carrier headed for the front, fully outfitted in his combat gear.[10] Some 250 replacements bound for the 504th had perhaps the most abrupt evening of all. They had just disembarked at a railroad station outside of Camp Sissonne when an officer walked up and welcomed them with the news that they were moving out in the morning.[11]

The fortunate few who were on pass had them immediately rescinded. Getting the troopers back to camp was the work of the military police who, knowing their prey, scoured bars and brothels as far away as Paris. Troopers already in military police custody got a reprieve. When Colonel Robert Wienecke, the division chief of staff, called the commander of the 82nd's Military Police Platoon to alert him to what was occurring, he was told, "Colonel, I'm up to my ears in wild troopers, and the jails are filled." "Sheriff," replied Wienecke, "cut everyone loose. Mark them for duty, and get the hell over here." Even troopers as far away as the United Kingdom got the call. Staff Sergeant Wheatley "Chris" Christiansen was in England recovering from wounds he received in Holland. He had just been released from the hospital and was awaiting transport back to France. "Sunday afternoon on the 17th, I had gone into town and was in my favorite pub when a 505 officer came in and said all passes had been cancelled. We were to report back to camp, as we were pulling out that night. That evening about fifty of us, plus about the same amount of rear-echelon service troops, were taken down to Southampton and loaded on a LCT and from there over to France." No one had to tell Private First Class Jack Hillman to get back to his unit. Recovering from his second combat-related injury, Hillman was tired of being shuttled from hospital to hospital, so he went AWOL and made his way back to Camp Suippes "just in the nick of time to enjoy a winter vacation in the Bulge."[12]

In his after-action review Gavin wrote, "The division was ready for a move, since, because of our past and usual[ly] quick commitments, we [had] maintained a high degree of readiness as a standard operating procedure."[13] There is much to indicate, however, that this was not universally the case. According to Colonel William Ekman and his operations officer, Major William J. Harris, the 505th's "equipment situation was bad. Many of the weapons were in ordnance, there were shortages in food and ammunition, all requests for such items had not been completely filled, clothing was in the laundry, equipment was stored, [and] winter clothing had not been issued to the regiment."[14] Major J. W. Medusky, the 508th's operations officer, confirmed that his regiment, too, had to move out "on such short notice that it was impossible to recover many of the mortars, BARs, and light machine guns which were still in ordnance; nor were there basic loads of ammunition immediately available."[15] Major John C. H. Lee Jr., the division's assistant operations officer, noted that not only did the 307th Airborne Engineer Battalion deploy without all of its weapons, but it was also short explosives and mines, critical items for defending against an armored or mechanized enemy. He also highlighted another critical shortage: maps. Ekman, Harris, and Medusky underscored this shortage, noting that the only thing the convoy commanders had to guide them during the move to Belgium were mimeographed strip maps.[16]

Weapons shortages were critical, of course, but even more critical was the lack of warm clothing. After Normandy, the division had been issued heavier jumpsuits.[17] This provided the troopers some protection from the cold, but alone it was not enough. Lieutenant Rusty Hays was one of the few whose kit was anywhere near adequate for the weather. He deployed with cotton underwear, long underwear, wool pants, a wool shirt, a medium-weight field jacket, his combat pants and blouse, a wool overcoat, combat boots (jump boots fitted too snug and did not provide protection against the cold), wool gloves, a wool knit cap, a cocoon sleeping bag, two wool blankets, and a shelter half. "I was lucky," he recalled. "There were some men who, for one reason or another, did not have many of these items and had to leave for combat without them." Sergeant Spencer Wurst was one of those men; his only over garment was a field jacket.[18]

The night of 17–18 December in Camps Suippes and Sissonne was, as one trooper characterized it, a "well-organized scramble."[19] Yet eventually order emerged from the chaos. Trucks of all types arrived at the camps, having been diverted from all over northwestern Europe. Much to the chagrin of the troopers most of the trucks were ten-ton tractor-trailer rigs, the trailers being nothing more than uncovered flatbeds with panel sides. There were also too few of them, so to make room the troopers had to stand. It was going to be a long, cold ride. And then a light rain began to fall.[20] Private First Class Malcolm Neel was one of the fortunate few who found a place in a covered truck. Sitting near the tailgate, he overheard "one of our guys, looking out at a group of cold, wet paratroopers standing packed in an open semi-trailer, say, 'Boy, I feel sorry for the first Germans those guys get hold of.'"[21]

The 82nd's hurried departure was the result of the Allied high command's blindness to the possibility of a German counteroffensive, a blindness underscored by the actions that day of the two highest-ranking commanders responsible for the Belgian front. On 16 December, several hours *after* German shells had pummeled the VIII Corps's forward positions and *after* German ground elements had overrun American positions, a wholly unaware General Bradley awoke in his headquarters in the Hôtel Alfa in Luxembourg City, dressed, breakfasted, and then departed by car for Eisenhower's headquarters at Versailles. Stopping en route for a leisurely lunch at the Ritz in Paris, Bradley arrived at Versailles shortly after noon. He had come to see Eisenhower to discuss replacements, but found that his meeting was postponed because Eisenhower's orderly, Sergeant Mickey McKeough, was marrying Pearlie Hargreaves, a SHAEF staff secretary, and the Supreme Commander was hosting the event in the chapel of Louis XIV. Hence, it was not until 1600 hours that the two generals met. When they did, both were still oblivious to events in the Ardennes. Their first inkling that something was amiss occurred an hour later when Major General Strong, the SHAEF intelligence chief, interrupted them to report that the Germans had broken through in the VIII Corps sector. Strong intimated that something big was afoot, but Bradley disagreed. "My initial reaction to these fragmentary and unclear reports was that von Rundstedt had launched a limited spoiling attack. . . . I was not overly concerned."[22] Additionally, since the reports were "fragmentary and unclear," and it is a widely held military axiom that in a crisis first reports are generally much worse than the situation truly warrants, the two decided that there was little they could do until they got more information. Moreover, there was another pressing social engagement—the wedding reception—at which Eisenhower's presence had been requested, so the meeting broke up with no action taken. Later that evening Eisenhower and Bradley met for dinner, during which they broke open some champagne to celebrate the news that President Roosevelt had nominated Eisenhower for a fifth star. After dinner they played bridge.[23]

As the evening wore on a clearer picture of what was happening emerged. First reports, it turned out in very unaxiomatic fashion, were correct. Eisenhower and Bradley suspended their bridge game and repaired to the SHAEF war room. "Ike sensed it before I did," wrote Bradley. "This was no spoiling attack."[24] This was corroborated the next morning when the most recent batch of ULTRA intercepts arrived, one of which was Rundstedt's exhortation to the "Soldiers of the Western Front":

> Your great hour has come. Large attacking armies have started against the Anglo-Americans. I do not have to tell you more than that. You feel it yourself. *We gamble everything!*
>
> You carry with you the holy obligation to give all to achieve superhuman objectives for our Fatherland and Führer![25]

In response to the German breakthrough, Bradley and Eisenhower fashioned a plan that was right out of doctrine. According to doctrine, defeating an enemy penetration required, first, building up the shoulders of the salient to keep the attack frontage from widening and eventuating a wholesale collapse. Second, in order to hinder the enemy advance important road junctions had to be held and a solid defensive wall formed along some easily defensible terrain feature. Finally, a counterattack force had to be readied to hit the enemy in the flank so that he could be cut off and destroyed. Orders to this effect went out the night of the 16th and were confirmed and amplified the next morning. Securing the shoulders fell to the U.S. 7th and 10th Armored Divisions in the north and south, respectively. Hodges was to construct a blocking position along the Meuse, drawing the forces to do so from elsewhere in First Army. Patton was to ready the counterattack force. Middleton's VIII Corps was to secure vital road hubs.[26]

But the situation at the front developed more quickly than anticipated and threatened to spiral out of control. Two green divisions, the U.S. 99th Infantry (the southernmost division in the U.S. V Corps sector, just north of Middleton's VIII Corps sector) and 106th Infantry, had been hit hard, the latter having all but disintegrated. The undermanned U.S. 28th and 4th Infantry Divisions were also falling back. By evening of 17 December the lead element of the German main attack, *Kampfgruppe Peiper* of the *1st SS Panzer Division*, was just forty-two miles from the Meuse. Middleton had already committed most of his forces (he had but one engineer combat battalion left as a reserve) with little discernible effect on the German advance. Furthermore, his VIII Corps headquarters at Bastogne was in danger of being overrun. Hodges, likewise, had little left, having sent his reserves to fortify the Meuse. Bradley had nothing.[27]

There had been quite a lot of talk at SHAEF for some time about forming a theater reserve force. Eisenhower wanted one so he would have something on hand to exploit operational success or, if needed, counter an enemy breakthrough, but once the Anglo-American armies broke out of Normandy, divisions were fed into the line as quickly as they arrived on the Continent. In early December, with the Allies halted along the entire front, Eisenhower revived the idea, and on 14 December the SHAEF operations section submitted a staff estimate for a theater reserve force of at least three divisions. When the Germans attacked two days later, this idea had yet to come to fruition. So, when Hodges called Bradley on 17 December and told him that he needed the SHAEF reserve, he was, in a sense, talking about nothing more than a concept.[28]

Eisenhower did, however, have something of a reserve force, although not one in the same sense as had been outlined in the staff estimate. Instead, the reserve force Eisenhower had at hand could be called one only inasmuch as it comprised combat units that were not engaged. This was the 82nd and 101st Airborne Divisions, but when Bradley communicated Hodges's request to SHAEF, Eisenhower was chary of releasing them. Not only were they all he had left, but they were also far from combat ready. Yet he eventually acceded, "albeit reluctantly," and thereby set in motion the chain of events that resulted in the troopers of both divisions riding in open trailers in the dead of winter for hundreds of miles to defeat an enemy that was long thought dead.[29]

Leading the way was Jim Gavin. After issuing his orders—orders that, because of a paucity of intelligence, were simply to mount up and move toward Bastogne—Gavin left Camp Sissonne at 2300 hours, 17 December, to find out what was going on.[30] Traveling with him were Lieutenant Colonel Al Ireland, Captain Hugo Olson, and a driver. Their destination was U.S. First Army's command post at Spa, Belgium, more than one hundred miles away. "It was a wickedly miserable night," Gavin wrote. "There was a steady light rain, considerable fog, and quite a few bridges were out." Driving under blackout conditions made the trip even more difficult, so Gavin and his party did not reach Spa until 0900 hours, 18 December. Gavin went immediately to the First Army war room to report to General Hodges, who "seemed a bit weary," and Hodges's chief of staff and G-3, Major General William B. Kean and Brigadier General Truman C. "Tubby" Thorson.[31] The three told Gavin that although the situation at the front was still vague, one clear and immediate threat had been identified: *Kampfgruppe Peiper*. To stop it, Gavin was to divert one of the airborne divisions to a small hill mass around the crossroads at Werbomont, Belgium. Which of the two airborne divisions to divert was a foregone conclusion. The 82nd was already on the road leading the massive two-division convoy. Moreover, its camps around Rheims were much closer to Werbomont than were the 101st's. Gavin sent word back, therefore, that the 82nd was to divert to Werbomont while the 101st was to remain on course for Bastogne. Furthermore, to facilitate command and control, Gavin temporarily attached the 82nd to the U.S. V Corps, then holding the northern portion of the salient, while the 101st was to be under the operational control of VIII Corps (although Gavin was also the acting XVIII Airborne Corps commander at the time, it was decided that standing up the corps headquarters would wait until General Ridgway arrived, who at the time was en route to the Continent). Then, with nothing more to do at Spa, Gavin jumped in his jeep and left for Werbomont.[32]

Gavin and his party reached Werbomont around midafternoon to find that the area "offered excellent defensive possibilities, being the dominant terrain for many miles."[33] Gavin then ventured a little more than a mile east to the village of Habiemont, which was situated on a slight rise overlooking the north-south Lienne Creek. Like almost all waterways in the Ardennes, the Lienne, though narrow, had steep banks and was, therefore, an effective vehicular obstacle. To Gavin's surprise, also at Habiemont was a detachment of engineers under the command of Lieutenant Alvin Edelstein.[34] They had been there for about an hour rigging the heavy masonry bridge over the Lienne at Habiemont for demolition. Gavin no doubt informed Edelstein that the 82nd would arrive shortly. Whether it would be on time was another matter, for while they were conversing they were accosted by civilians who told them that they had come from Trois Ponts, a village seven miles to the east, where there were many Germans who seemed hell bent on taking the Habiemont Bridge. There was little, however, that Gavin and his small party could add to the defense, so rather than tarry Gavin continued with his reconnaissance. Driving north along the Lienne, Gavin found a second bridge at the minuscule hamlet of Forges, about a mile north of Habiemont, although this bridge "did not appear to be strong enough to take heavy tanks."[35] Content that he had a good feel for the terrain, Gavin returned to Habiemont, informed Lieutenant Edelstein of the Forges Bridge (Edelstein told Gavin there was nothing he could do about the Forges Bridge; he needed all the explosives he had to properly prepare the heavier Habiemont Bridge for demolition), and then left with his party for Bastogne in order to coordinate with VIII Corps and General McAuliffe.[36]

Reaching Bastogne at about 1730 hours, Gavin found there "considerable confusion. Vehicles were being loaded, and members of the [VIII Corps] staff seemed to be hurrying away."[37] Things were not much better in the VIII Corps command post, where Gavin met with Middleton and the corps staff, none of whom had "solid information except that the situation was quite fluid and that they were leaving."[38] Present also were several officers from the U.S. 28th Infantry Division, who "seemed to feel that their division had been overrun, although they were uncertain of its whereabouts."[39] Finally, Gavin met with McAuliffe and told him to place himself and the 101st under VIII

Corps, organize an all-around defense, and hold until relieved. Gavin then departed for Werbomont to await the arrival of his troopers.[40]

Gavin and his party were back at Werbomont by about 2000 hours. Minutes later the first trucks carrying 82nd troopers drove up. With little time to spare the troopers were hustled into position around the village, a scene repeated all night long as truck after truck found its way to Werbomont. By daylight, 19 December, the crossroads was secure, completely enclosed within the division's perimeter.[41]

For the troopers the ride to Werbomont had been tortuous. "Progress was painfully slow," recorded a 504th report, "with the convoy seldom attaining a speed in excess of fifteen miles per hour."[42] Driving at night under blackout conditions over slick, unfamiliar roads contributed to the snail-like pace, but nearer the front the main cause for the holdup was traffic snarls. Hundreds of refugees and soldiers from broken units cluttered the roads trying to escape the onrushing Germans. "As the trucks neared their destination, roads became congested and traffic so snarled that the column did not move for hours," recorded a 325th narrative.[43] According to a 505th report, "All the way up [the 505th serials] encountered convoys of retreating troops and guns."[44] According to Private First Class Virgil Goodwin, "When we got closer to the front we made several stops because the roads were jammed with civilians and soldiers coming from the way we were going. Some of the retreating soldiers wanted to know if we thought we could turn the tide. We told them that was what we intended to do." Sergeant Wurst recalled a similar scene: "The closer we got to the front, the worse the panic became. Riding in the open cattle trucks, we saw it all. The sides were three or four feet high, and there was no top or covering. We leaned out and hollered at the retreating men, 'Hey, you guys are going in the wrong direction.' They would look back at us and earnestly say, 'Oh no, *you* guys are going in the wrong direction.'"[45]

But not every American unit had cut and run. Unbeknownst to the cold, weary troopers disembarking at Werbomont, their reception would have been much hotter had it not been for the intrepid stand of Lieutenant Edelstein's engineers and a battalion of straight-leg infantry from the U.S. 30th Infantry Division.[46]

A full hour before anyone was in Werbomont, several tanks leading a subsidiary column from *Kampfgruppe Peiper* came crashing out of the darkness straight toward Habiemont and its bridge. Huddled in his foxhole on the west side of Lienne Creek was Corporal Fred Chapin, who had with him the detonator for the demolition charges. Chapin's orders were to wait until Lieutenant Edelstein gave him the signal to blow the bridge. But Chapin was nervous. The tanks were getting close. Suddenly, while still some two hundred yards short of the bridge the lead tank fired its main gun. The explosion threw Chapin to the bottom of his hole. Scrambling to his feet, Chapin looked toward Edelstein's foxhole. At first there was no sign of the lieutenant. Then, through the still descending debris Chapin spied Edelstein frantically waving at him. Chapin needed nothing more. With a turn of a key the bridge erupted in a flash of light, dust, stone, and mortar. The only bridge over the Lienne capable of handling heavy armor was no more. Frustrated by those "damned engineers," SS-Obersturmbannführer Joachim Peiper, the *Kampfgruppe* commander, ordered his men to fan out in search of other crossings. Eventually, they found the smaller, less robust bridge at Forges, so later that night Peiper sent some half-tracks and self-propelled guns across it in an attempt to get behind the American defenses along the Lienne. They did not get far. Elements of the 2nd Battalion, 119th Infantry, from the 30th Infantry Division, lying in wait, cut them to pieces.[47]

The next morning, with no news about *Kampfgruppe Peiper*'s whereabouts, Gavin went forward on another reconnaissance mission. Only then did he learn that the Habiemont Bridge had been blown. He also came across the remnants of the German detachment that the 2/119th Infantry encountered. "I visited the locality at daylight . . . and found about five armored vehicles, armored cars and [self-propelled guns], knocked out, with several German dead lying about the road."[48] Lieutenant Edward Arn's F Company, 2/119th, had participated in the fight, and Arn was still in the area when Gavin drove up.

> Just as I was preparing to move into Chevron [a small village near where the German column had been ambushed] with the rest of the company, I heard a jeep coming down the highway behind me. I nearly fell down into the [Amblève] River [*sic*, Chevron was quite a ways south of the Amblève; Arn must have meant the Lienne Creek] when it pulled up and a tall, lean paratroop officer leaped out with two stars on his battered helmet.
>
> "Who's in command here?"
>
> "I am, sir, Lt. Arn, F Company of the 119th Regiment, 30th Division . . . at your service."
>
> "I'm Jim Gavin of the 82nd Airborne Division," he waved away my salute with a grin. "Looks to me, Lt., that you've had quite a night of it up here."

Arn was "dumbfounded" at the sight of a major general so far out in front of his division with only a driver as an escort. He was even more dumbfounded when Gavin asked if it would be all right if he went forward to take a look around. Arn, of course, consented, but obviously failed to notify the rest of his company, for minutes later, one of his platoon leaders called back in alarm. "Sir, I wish to suggest that you have me relieved. I'm going nuts. There's a two-star general in a jeep coming into town. I can't believe it."[49]

Meanwhile, Ridgway and several members of his XVIII Airborne Corps staff arrived at Werbomont. They had hurriedly flown to the Continent from England, landing near Rheims at 1030 hours, 18 December. From there Ridgway and his aide, Captain Don Faith, and the corps's intelligence and operations officers, Lieutenant Colonels Whitfield Jack and Alexander Day Surles, and a driver piled into an "ancient" military sedan and sped toward Bastogne, where Ridgway expected to find both of his airborne divisions. "The fog was thick as heavy smoke, [and] a cold drizzling rain was falling," recalled Ridgway, who added that although he was not usually "a nervous man in an automobile," he got "pretty jumpy" when, for the sixth time, his driver narrowly missed crashing into the back of one of the many trucks traveling the same road. When asked what was wrong the driver said he could not see very well, so Ridgway took the wheel and drove the rest of the way.[50] Arriving at Bastogne at about 2030 hours, Ridgway went immediately to the VIII Corps command post.

> The gloom inside [VIII Corps] headquarters was thicker than the fog outside. This atmosphere of uncertainty was in no way the fault of General Middleton, a magnificent soldier with a wonderful combat record in two wars. But the most disquieting thing in any war is to be in a completely unknown situation. General Middleton knew that some of his units had been overrun. He knew the German attack had opened a great gap in his lines. But nearly all his communications with his forward elements were out, and he had no knowledge of where his forces were, nor where the Germans were, nor where they might strike next.[51]

While at Bastogne, Ridgway learned that the 101st had been attached to VIII Corps and that his XVIII Airborne Corps, comprising the 82nd, a portion of the U.S. 3rd Armored Division, and the U.S. 30th Infantry Division, was to take command of the sector around Werbomont. Moreover, he was to report to First Army headquarters as soon as possible to receive more detailed orders, but since it was already dark, Ridgway elected to stay the night rather than risk getting lost or, worse, bumping into the Germans. Middleton's VIII Corps, meanwhile, left for its new location at Neufchâteau, about eighteen miles southwest of Bastogne. The next morning, as soon as it was light enough to travel, Ridgway too departed, leaving McAuliffe in command at Bastogne. "I felt a keen regret, and I think Tony did, too," recalled Ridgway, for "the 82nd and the 101st were brothers in the blood. They had fought side by side in Normandy, and they knew and trusted each other. Now they were to be separated." Though there was little he could do to aid McAuliffe and his troopers, he took solace in the knowledge that, were the enemy to make it that far, "paratroopers were accustomed to fight[ing] surrounded."[52]

It was about 1030 hours, 19 December, when Ridgway and his staff drove into Werbomont. Gavin, who was "delighted to see General Matthew Ridgway and his Corps back in action," cut short his reconnaissance and returned to town to give him an update. Ridgway then continued on to First Army headquarters, which, by that time, had displaced to Chaudfontaine, a small town on the outskirts of Liège.[53]

When Ridgway got to Chaudfontaine, Hodges told him that his primary mission was to find *Kampfgruppe Peiper* and stop its westward advance. But in addition, XVIII Airborne Corps was to fill the gap between V Corps in the north and VIII Corps in the south. At the time First Army headquarters was rife with reports of enemy penetrations. Several indicated that the Germans had cut the main north-south thoroughfare, Highway N15, connecting Bastogne with Liège near Houffalize, about eighteen miles southeast of Werbomont, and that enemy spearheads were as far west as Hotton, about thirteen miles southwest of Werbomont. As it turned out the reports of enemy forces in Hotton were incorrect (German spearheads did not reach that point until 21 December), although First Army did not discover this until much later. However, reconnaissance elements from the *Fifth Panzer Army* had found an undefended gap in the U.S. lines just south of Houffalize. Were the main body of *Fifth Panzer Army* to follow, the already considerable breach between V and VIII Corps that Ridgway's XVIII Airborne Corps was to fill would be torn wide open. Ridgway thus returned to Werbomont with a formidable task list: get his corps headquarters up and running; gain control of his divisions; find and stop *Kampfgruppe Peiper*, which was somewhere north of Werbomont; shore up the southern part of the corps zone to contain the reported penetrations there; and defend against additional German advances emanating from the east.[54]

During his stopover in Werbomont before leaving for First Army, Ridgway approved Gavin's plan to relieve the 2/119th and expand the division perimeter eastward across the Lienne. In fact, Tucker's 504th and Ekman's 505th were already moving in that direction when the two generals talked, and by early afternoon of 19 December both regiments were occupying defensive positions well east of Lienne Creek with the 504th in the north and the 505th in the south. Gavin also had Lindquist move his 508th to Chevron (where Gavin had earlier met Lieutenant Arn), where he was to establish a blocking position behind the 504th and 505th.[55] When Ridgway returned to Werbomont, he told Gavin to expand the division perimeter even farther in order to protect the corps's southern flank. Although both men recognized the potentially dangerous ramifications of splitting the 82nd into so many smaller parts out of supporting range of one another, there was no one else to whom Ridgway could turn; he had yet to gain control of the 30th Infantry Division and those elements of the 3rd Armored Division that, on paper at least, were to fall under XVIII Airborne Corps. Gavin assigned the southern flank mission to Billingslea's 325th, which was still in position around Werbomont. Billingslea, in turn, sent the 2/401st to Barvaux, an important road junction and river-crossing site approximately eight miles southwest of Werbomont, and F Company, 2/325th, to the Manhay-Grandménil area, approximately six miles due south of Werbomont. The rest of the 325th remained in Werbomont, constituting both the corps and the division reserve. Finally, in order to establish a linkage between his elements on either side of the Lienne, Gavin told Lindquist to occupy Villetes and Bra, two villages east and west of the creek, respectively, about five miles southeast of Werbomont. Lindquist sent H Company, 3/508th. By nightfall, 19 December, all movements were complete.[56]

Consequently, when day broke on the twentieth, the 82nd's small defensive perimeter around Werbomont of twenty-four hours earlier had become a semicircular defensive trace approximately fourteen miles wide (north to south) and eight miles deep (east to west). Despite this expansion nowhere did the division make enemy contact. *Fifth Panzer Army*'s spearheads around Houffalize had stalled well south of the division's area and *Kampfgruppe Peiper* had mysteriously disappeared. Yet in spite of its strange absence or, more likely, because of it, *Kampfgruppe Peiper* still constituted the greatest threat both to XVIII Airborne Corps and First Army, and it was, therefore, on finding, fixing, and finishing Peiper that Ridgway concentrated on 20 December.[57]

Recoiling from the bloody nose delivered by Edelstein's engineers and the 2/119th, *Kampfgruppe Peiper* had doubled back and concentrated along the line of the Amblève, several miles north of the 82nd's positions. Comprising the bulk of the combat power of the *1st SS Panzer Division*, *Kampfgruppe Peiper* was cut off from the rest of its division and strung out in a sausage-shaped perimeter about four miles long on a winding road that paralleled the north bank of the Amblève. To its west, north, and east were disparate elements of the 30th Infantry Division and Combat Command B of the U.S. 3rd Armored Division.[58] Its only remaining outlet was via a bridgehead it had established south of the Amblève near the village of Cheneux. With but a vague idea of *Kampfgruppe Peiper*'s whereabouts, Ridgway's scheme was to find and then crush it between Combat Command B and the 30th Infantry Division attacking from the north and west and the 82nd attacking from the south.[59]

Gavin learned that there were Germans in Cheneux early on the morning of 20 December, independent of any information from XVIII Airborne

Corps. While visiting Tucker's command post in the hamlet of Rahier, a little more than a mile southwest of Cheneux, Tucker informed him that "he had just received intelligence from civilians to the effect that approximately 125 vehicles, including approximately 30 tanks, had moved through [Rahier] the afternoon before, moving in the direction of Cheneux." The information, wrote Gavin, "appeared to be reliable" and posed "some interesting problems." Gavin surmised that the Germans had "given up hope of crossing the [Lienne] creek obstacle at Habiemont . . . and had turned to the main road [north of the Amblève]," and, if that were the case, "the seizure of the bridge over the Amblève River at Cheneux was imperative if their further movement was to be blocked."[60] But what of the German armor? According to Gavin, "Any ordinary infantry regiment would want at least a battalion of tanks in support before it attacked, but Tucker's idea was to attack the Germans and take their armor away from them. He figured he would then have his own." This was no mere bravado. The 504th had acquired a truckload of *panzerfausts* in Holland, a much more effective antitank weapon than the American bazooka, and so armed felt equal to the task.[61]

Tucker was "anxious to go after them without delay," so he assigned the mission to his regimental reserve, Lieutenant Colonel Willard E. Harrison's 1/504th, which was also in Rahier, despite the fact that it had only two of its three rifle companies present (the third, A Company, had earlier been sent on a mission elsewhere).[62] Spurred by Tucker's impatience, Harrison simply moved up the Rahier-Cheneux road in attack formation with B Company in the lead while the rest of the battalion followed. Jumping off at 1300 hours, Harrison's troopers had not gone far when they ran into a German reconnaissance element moving straight at them from the opposite direction. Immediately, Captain Thomas Helgeson, the B Company commander, slipped a platoon around the German right flank while several troopers from the 80th Airborne Antiaircraft Battalion provided covering fire using a 77mm gun mounted in a captured German half-track. At first it looked as though Helgeson's flanking attack would work, but once his troopers got within a hundred yards of Cheneux, large-caliber fire emanating from inside the town made it obvious that the Germans "apparently had more armor than originally estimated."[63] At 1700 hours, unable to move forward, Helgeson withdrew B Company to the cover of a nearby wood to regroup.[64]

Following B Company's withdrawal, Tucker gathered Harrison and his commanders to discuss plans for continuing the attack after dark. Attacking at night would negate the Germans' firepower advantage, but it would also make control more difficult. To mitigate the latter, Harrison elected to advance with two companies abreast, with B Company moving up the right side of the road to Cheneux while C Company moved up the left side. Using the road in this manner, the companies could stay oriented on the objective and keep from inadvertently crossing paths in the dark. Additionally, because the ground outside Cheneux was flat and strewn with barbed wire, Harrison had his company commanders organize their companies into four assault waves that were to advance at fifty-yard intervals in order to ensure than an entire company did not get pinned down at once. Two tank destroyers that had wandered into the division area during the day were also brought forward with orders to move up the road itself to provide heavy fire support. Jump-off time was set at 1930 hours following a ten-minute artillery barrage.[65]

The attack jumped off right on schedule and almost immediately ran into trouble. The troopers in the first two waves got hung up in the wire-strewn fields and, so immobilized, were easy targets for German guns. "The men were falling like flies," recalled Staff Sergeant James M. Boyd of B Company. Meanwhile, the tank destroyers, chary of venturing too far forward lest they be targeted by antitank weapons, stayed in the rear and never got in the fight. Without heavy fire support, the attack stalled all along the line. It was Staff Sergeant George Walsh of B Company who supplied the spark that reignited the advance. Walsh and his troopers were pinned down by fire from a fortified roadblock to their front. With no way around the enemy position, Walsh finally stood up, yelled "Let's get the sons of bitches!" and charged. Followed by several nearby troopers, Walsh and his men "fired until their ammunition was exhausted; then they used their rifles as clubs and drew trench knives as they converged on the roadblock and engaged the enemy in close-in fighting." But Walsh was not done. Crawling under fire to an enemy 20mm gun, Walsh pulled out a grenade with which he intended to kill the gun's crew only to find that he could not pull the pin because he had been shot through the wrist. Undeterred, Walsh crawled to another trooper, had him pull the pin, and then crawled back to the German position and silenced the gun. Walsh's charge seemed to unhinge the German defenses. The American line started moving forward, albeit with no dearth of Walsh-like heroics elsewhere. A Private Barkley in C Company, for example, silenced a second 20mm cannon by stealthily crawling alongside it and then jumping aboard and slitting the gunner's throat. Led by men like these, Harrison's troopers eventually gained a foothold inside Cheneux, where they barricaded themselves inside some buildings and waited for reinforcement.[66]

Reinforcements arrived in the form of G Company, 3/504th, which Tucker sent forward later. Tucker realized, however, that Harrison was too weak to finish the Germans who still held most of Cheneux. The next morning, therefore, he and Lieutenant Colonel Julian Cook led the rest of the 3/504th on a wide flanking march to the east. Tucker's intent was to get behind Cheneux and attack the town from the north while G Company and the remnants of Harrison's 1/504th attacked through the town from the south. But before attacking Cheneux, Tucker and Cook had also to seize and clear the area between it and the Amblève (which was actually a few hundred yards northeast of the town). This took them all day, hampered as they were by the rough terrain and several German outposts. Yet by 1900 hours Cheneux was in American hands, and the last of *Kampfgruppe Peiper* south of the Amblève either had been destroyed or had retreated back across the river.[67]

Cheneux cost the 504th dearly. Before the battle C Company counted 8 officers and 119 men. By the evening of 21 December, only 3 officers and 38 troopers were still standing. But it was B Company that was hardest hit; only 18 troopers remained in its ranks when the smoke cleared. The 1/504th and 3/504th combined suffered 225 casualties, including 23 killed. *Kampfgruppe Peiper* also suffered considerably, especially in terms of materiel, having lost fourteen 20mm flak wagons, six half-tracks, four trucks, four 105mm howitzers, and one Tiger tank. In addition, 31 SS soldiers were taken prisoner, half of whom were wounded. The remainder were either killed or managed to escape. As he had boasted, Tucker incorporated the functioning enemy vehicles into his regiment. "When I went over the battlefield with them the next day," wrote Gavin, "they pointed out that they were now the 504th Parachute Armored Regiment."[68]

By securing Cheneux and clearing the south bank of the Amblève, the 504th denied *Kampfgruppe Peiper* its last escape route from the perimeter in which it found itself, a perimeter that, by nightfall on 21 December, was much more constricted due to concentric attacks by the 30th Infantry Division and Combat Command B of the 3rd Armored Division. Yet Peiper remained a dangerous threat, especially since no one seemed to know where he would attack next. "They are trying to get out forward or backward or something," reported Major General Leland S. Hobbs, the 30th Infantry Division commander. But unbeknownst to Hobbs, or anyone else in the U.S. chain of command, Peiper was low on ammunition and fuel. Several attempts to break through to him by the main body of the *1st SS Panzer Division* had been aborted. Peiper had little choice, therefore, but to stay put and await succor.[69]

Meanwhile, the Germans were again threatening the southern part of XVIII Airborne Corps's defensive front, which, with the exception of that portion occupied by the 82nd, was still being formed. On 20 December the *116th Panzer* and *560th Volks Grenadier Divisions* crashed into an area that contained nothing more than a scattering of rear-echelon units and a weak force from the 3rd Armored Division, which had yet to move forward into position on the corps (and 82nd) right. To make matters worse, the *116th Panzer* seized an American depot containing some 25,000 gallons of fuel and 15,000 rations. Beyond supplying the German panzers a windfall of fuel, the loss of the depot had a significant secondary effect, for the captured supplies belonged to the U.S. 7th Armored Division, which, at the time, was in danger of being completely cut off and destroyed at St. Vith.[70]

Located approximately twenty-seven miles northeast of Bastogne, St. Vith was another critical crossroads, so when an advance party from the 7th Armored Division arrived at his VIII Corps command post in Bastogne on 16 December, Middleton ordered the division to continue on to St. Vith to link up with the 106th Infantry Division already there. When the 7th's lead echelons arrived at St. Vith the following day they found that the 106th was almost combat ineffective. In addition, the next few days saw the area around St. Vith get increasingly crowded when the rest of the 7th Armored arrived along with scores more American units, many of which had barely escaped the onrushing panzers and were in no state to add measurably to the defense of the crossroads. By 20 December, the Americans in and around St. Vith were almost wholly cut off from friendly lines as German units to the north, south, and east attacked and probed constantly in an effort to seize the crossroads. When Brigadier General Robert W. Hasbrouck, the 7th Armored Division commander, sent a message to First Army on 20 December, he summed up the situation succinctly: "I am out of touch with VIII Corps," he began, and were he to hold St. Vith he needed help.[71] Hodges radioed back that help was on the way: "Ridgway with armor and infantry is moving from west to gain contact with you. When communication is established you come under command of Ridgway."[72]

Ridgway's plan to relieve St. Vith was bold. Issued at 1600 hours, 20 December, it called for an advance by three divisions abreast—from left to right, the 30th Infantry Division, the 82nd, and the 3rd Armored Division—with the intent to "destroy or drive back all enemy forces in zone," reestablish contact with the 7th Armored and 106th Infantry Divisions, and "be prepared for further offensive action."[73] The last phrase is telling. Ridgway did not see this as a rescue mission; rather, he wanted to initiate a general advance that would sweep through St. Vith and, with the added combat power of the 7th and 106th, continue attacking into the flank of the German forces around Bastogne. But it was not to be. Attempts by the 30th Infantry Division and Combat Command B of the 3rd Armored Division to reduce Peiper's forces north of the Amblève came to naught, and the rest of the 3rd Armored Division, which was to form up on the 82nd's right, was unable to do so because of the attacks by the *116th Panzer* and *560th Volks Grenadier Divisions.*

As a result, the only division that could advance was the 82nd, which, within hours of receiving its mission, was moving by truck and forced march, expanding its perimeter even farther to the east, southeast, and south. By daybreak on 21 December, the division's new perimeter resembled a giant horseshoe with the open end in the west. Arrayed along the top of the horseshoe was the 504th, left in place along the south bank of the Amblève to keep *Kampfgruppe Peiper* bottled up. The middle portion of the horseshoe paralleled the Salm River, which was guarded in the north by the 505th and in the south by one battalion of the 508th. Located at the horseshoe's lower bend was Salmchâteau, also defended by the 508th, as was a portion of the horseshoe's bottom rung, which paralleled one of the few high-speed east-west thoroughfares in the Ardennes, Highway N28. Finally, arrayed along the outer portion of the bottom rung of the horseshoe was the 325th, with two of its battalions on line, while the third was held back as the division reserve. Save for the 504th, none of the regiments had yet made enemy contact.[74]

The inability of the 30th Infantry and 3rd Armored Divisions to advance compelled Ridgway to shelve his plan to sweep through St. Vith and attack into the German flank. But even had Ridgway been able to organize the advance he envisioned, it is questionable whether he could have continued it beyond St. Vith given the condition of the American forces there. On 21 December, Hasbrouck reported that the previous day's attacks against the pocket had been repulsed but noted the Germans "will be back stronger today." "My reserve is small," Hasbrouck continued, "and comprises a tank battalion, less one medium company, two platoons of infantry, one [tank destroyer] Company and a hodgepodge of remnants of the 14th Cav. Group which are perhaps more of a liability than an asset." In addition, he noted that since arriving at St. Vith he had collected all manner of units, "some legal [attached by order] and some we just found and appropriated." Finally, Hasbrouck intimated that there were problems in the 106th. One was that though it was the second-largest force at St. Vith, the 106th's strength, "as nearly as I can find out, comprises one [regimental combat team] and some service troops," not nearly enough to cover its sector of the pocket. A second problem was the 106th's commander, Major General Alan Jones. Hasbrouck suggested there was something seriously wrong with him. "He is a Major General, and I am a Brigadier so it is probably not legal to attach him to me," wrote Hasbrouck, but "I most definitely do *not* want to be attached to him and suggest he be directed to cooperate with me in holding our present positions which I know he will do." Gavin had a similar opinion of Jones: "On 21 December I visited the Command Post of the U.S. 106th Infantry Division at Renceveaux, a small town just west of Vielsalm. General Alan W. Jones was the division commander, and as I entered his Command Post, he was the picture of dejection. I felt sorry for him. . . . General Jones was depressed by the loss of two of his infantry regiments. They had been overrun several days before."[75]

A second report from Hasbrouck at 2237 hours 21 December brought more bad news: St. Vith was in German hands.[76] "I seriously doubt his ability and that of his teammates [the 106th Infantry] to hold," reported Ridgway in a phone conversation with Major General Kean of First Army later that night. "I would like to authorize their withdrawal back to the 82d area tonight," he continued, adding, "I think it can be made in orderly fashion." Kean approved Ridgway's plan, stating that "the last instructions [First] ARMY had sent to 7th Armd made it clear that he [Hasbrouck] was not expected to sacrifice his Command out there."[77] Ridgway ordered the withdrawal that night. But it was not to be a complete withdrawal. Under the overall command of General Jones—Ridgway was anxious to clear up the command difficulties and, absent his personal observation of Jones's demeanor, placed the senior officer in charge of the operation—the 7th Armored, 106th Infantry, and its various hangers-on were to fall back to the Salm and form a fortified "goose egg" on the east side of the river, anchored on the critical crossing sites of Salmchâteau and Vielsalm, a small village on the Salm about two miles north of Salmchâteau.[78]

The drastically changed situation east of the Salm forced a concomitant change in the 82nd's mission. As Gavin pointed out, "Only the narrow neck of land from Vielsalm to Salmchâteau, held by the 82d Airborne Division, connected the St. Vith forces with remaining forces of the First Army. Its retention would be decisive." The 82nd, therefore, had to defend the Salm and keep open the links with the American forces east of the river at all costs. Failure to do so would spell the final destruction of the 7th Armored, 106th Infantry, and their myriad hangers-on. Fortunately, the terrain around Vielsalm and Salmchâteau, according to Major Medusky, was so favorable to the defense that he believed that the 508th "could have held out there for a month if necessary."[79] But retaining Vielsalm and Salmchâteau required that the whole of the division horseshoe be defended, for a breakthrough anywhere along the line could turn the Salm River from a protective barrier into an anvil on which the 82nd could be hammered into oblivion. The first test against this barrier came in the 505th's sector near the confluence of the Amblève and Salm Rivers at the pinprick hamlet of Trois Ponts.

Even before receiving orders to expand the perimeter eastward, Gavin sent reconnaissance patrols east, south, and west. A patrol from the 3/505th, advancing toward the Salm, came upon Trois Ponts and, much to its surprise, discovered there more engineers. According to Lieutenant Colonel James Kaiser, the 3/505th commander, making contact with a friendly element at Trois Ponts "was revealing to say the least. There had been no intelligence reports on this particular area and least of all, the 3rd [Battalion] had not expected to contact American troops in this spot." Equally surprised were the engineers at Trois Ponts, who fired on the 3/505th patrol, inflicted one casualty, and took the others prisoner "because they would not believe at first their story that the 82d Airborne Division was in the area."[80]

Major Robert W. Yates was in command at Trois Ponts. He had been there since 17 December with 120 men and an arsenal that included eight bazookas, four machine guns, and one antitank gun and its crew that he commandeered when they passed through Trois Ponts looking for their parent unit. His mission was to prepare the bridges in the area—one at Trois Ponts over the Salm and two just north of Trois Ponts over the Amblève—for demolition. On 18 December, a column of tanks from *Kampfgruppe Peiper*, moving westward along the north bank of the Amblève, ran into Yates's engineers. "We proceeded at top speed towards Trois Ponts in an effort to seize the bridge there," recalled Peiper. "If we had captured the bridge at Trois Ponts intact and had had enough fuel, it would have been a simple matter to drive through to the Meuse River early that day."[81] But as Peiper's lead tank approached one of the Amblève River bridges, the antitank gun crew went into action and knocked off one of its treads. There then occurred a lopsided exchange of fire, during which the other tanks in the column destroyed the American antitank gun and killed its crew, but not before the engineers blew the Amblève River bridges, thereby thwarting Peiper's plan to pass through Trois Ponts, forcing him to instead proceed along the north bank of the river. Yates, meanwhile, withdrew his force to Trois Ponts, which was on the west bank of the Salm, and blew the bridge there as well. Barricaded inside Trois Ponts, Yates and his men kept watch as German patrols made several attempts to wade the Salm, all of which were discovered and cut down before they could reach the west bank.[82]

When the 3/505th patrol discovered them, Yates and his men were still holed up inside Trois Ponts. Ekman immediately rushed several bazooka teams forward to reinforce this "gallant group who had held of[f] enemy armored columns for three days with their bazookas and mine detectors."[83] Later on that evening, he also sent Lieutenant Colonel Ben Vandervoort's 2/505th to Trois Ponts to take over the defense there. Vandervoort and his troopers were in position ready to defend by early morning on the twenty-first.[84]

Some three miles southeast of Trois Ponts, at the village of Wanne, SS-Oberführer Wilhelm Mohnke was preparing the main body of his *1st SS Panzer Division* to break through to *Kampfgruppe Peiper*. The plan had been for *Kampfgruppe Peiper* to push forward without regard for its flanks or rear, while the rest of the *1st SS Panzer Division* followed in its wake. By day two of the offensive, however, Mohnke had lost contact with Peiper, and the rest of his division was strung out and straggling. But he had gathered the equivalent of an armored infantry regiment at Wanne by 21 December and, after trying unsuccessfully to cross to the north bank of the Amblève, was preparing to move against the Salm to look for crossings there. If he could get across the

Salm, he could, he thought, link up with Peiper and revitalize the counteroffensive's spearhead. He made Trois Ponts his primary point of aim.[85]

To get across the Salm, Mohnke would have to fight through Ekman's 505th. Starting at Trois Ponts, where Vandervoort's 2/505th was concentrated, the 505th's lines stretched south along the river for some 8,000 yards. South of the 2/505th was the 3/505th, guarding subsidiary Salm River crossings at La Neuville and Grand Halleux. South of the 3/505th was the 1/505th, which was tied in with the 508th to its south. Gavin's instructions were to defend the river from the west bank, place only minimal forces on the east bank, and keep the enemy from crossing the river at all costs.[86]

In accordance with Gavin's instructions, Ekman told Vandervoort to put no more than a company on the east side of the river at Trois Ponts. Vandervoort sent Lieutenant William J. Meddaugh's E Company. Crossing over the Salm River Bridge at Trois Ponts, which Yates's engineers had repaired, Meddaugh deployed E Company inside a wood on a bluff overlooking the river and astride a winding road leading to the bridge. "It was an excellent position for an ambush," wrote Vandervoort, "but inherently a weak one to defend against armor accompanied by infantry. But up on the bluff, it was the best position available." To bolster their defense, Meddaugh's troopers sprinkled antitank mines across their front and brought an antitank gun with them. Meddaugh also deployed bazooka teams in forward ambush positions in order to add some depth to his position.[87]

Backing up Meddaugh was F Company, Headquarters Company, and Yates's engineers positioned in buildings along the west bank of the river, covering the bridge that they had also rewired for demolition with machine guns. Vandervoort placed his last company, D Company, at a small crossing site south of Trois Ponts. With their preparations complete, Vandervoort's troopers "settled down to wait in the bitter cold. No fires. No lights. No smoking."[88]

Not long after they were in place, Meddaugh's troopers "bushwacked" a lone half-track that ran right up to their positions, oblivious to their presence. Less than an hour later a second German vehicle appeared. It was destroyed by an antitank mine. Both were patrols Mohnke had sent to probe toward the Salm. When the second vehicle did not return, Mohnke launched an all-out assault.[89]

At about 0945 hours, 21 December, approximately eight hundred SS soldiers hit E Company. Supporting the attack were several Tigers, Panthers, and self-propelled guns. Fortunately for Meddaugh's troopers, the winding roads, damp ground, and constricted terrain limited off-road mobility, and when two of the vehicles ventured forward, the antitank gun crew knocked them out, which kept the others temporarily at bay. Meanwhile, E Company, supported by the battalion's 81mm mortars and the 456th's howitzers, held off the German infantry. Yet despite horrendous losses, the SS soldiers kept coming. Later, some prisoners taken during the fight were asked why they employed such unimaginative tactics. They replied that "that was what they had been doing ever since the start of their offensive, and up to now everybody had run away or surrendered."[90]

But Meddaugh's troopers did not run. According to Vandervoort, they "were proud, tough, battle-seasoned soldiers" with orders "to stay and to try to hold the Germans east of Trois Ponts. Unless ordered off of the position, confronted with being surrounded and captured, they probably would have gone down fighting under the treads of the Tiger tanks." Vandervoort, however, was not prepared to sacrifice E Company, and since they were too heavily engaged to withdraw, he sent a platoon from F Company over as reinforcement. But Mohnke was also throwing in more soldiers, who knocked out the antitank gun and freed the tanks to move forward and engage the paratroopers in their foxholes. "The Germans were all over the landscape," went one report. "Everywhere one looked, small groups of them were engaging [Meddaugh's] troops in firefights."[91]

Vandervoort responded by sending the rest of F Company across the river. Still the SS soldiers came. Shortly thereafter, a message arrived from Ekman: Relinquish the bridgehead, "as it was costing more than it was worth." By that time the Germans were almost on top of the American lines. There was no way his paratroopers could disengage and withdraw, so Vandervoort told D Company to cross from its position to the south and hit the Germans in their flank. Only after Colonel Ira P. Swift, Gavin's newly assigned assistant division commander, arrived at Trois Ponts and reiterated Ekman's order did Vandervoort acquiesce. Rushing forward into the battle area, Vandervoort "issued the classic tactical order, 'Let's get the hell out of here.'" With the Germans close on their heels, his paratroopers "intuitively improvised 'walking fire' in reverse. Moving backward and using the trees for cover, they simply outshot any pursuer who crowded them too closely."[92] When they got to the river, some escaped over the bridge; others jumped from the cliffs into the river and swam across. Miraculously, most of D and F Companies got back relatively unscathed, but E Company left almost half its strength on the east bank and could count only forty to fifty troopers still standing at the end of the day.[93]

Later that night Mohnke tried seizing the Salm River Bridge at Le Neuville in the 3/505th's area. Self-propelled guns loaded with infantry appeared out of nowhere and raced toward the bridge, their advance covered by a sudden artillery barrage. A platoon of paratroopers guarding the bridge's east end withdrew just in time, and then, "as a German soldier was waving the first vehicle onto the bridge, it was blown out from under his feet."[94]

The next day, 22 December, Mohnke threw his SS soldiers against several points along the Salm. Near Trois Ponts, thirty to forty SS soldiers waded the river in an attempt to infiltrate the village. Vandervoort's troopers waited until they were in midstream and then opened up. Most of the Germans were killed in the water; none reached the west bank.[95] Toward evening Mohnke threw a battalion against the bridge at Grand Halleux. The SS soldiers approached "screaming at the top of their voices," but the platoon from the 3/505th outposted on the east bank held them off long enough to withdraw across the bridge and blow it before any Germans could get to it.[96] Elements of the same battalion also hit A Company, 1/505th, farther south. They, too, advanced with yells and screams. Unfazed, the A Company troopers held their ground and unleashed a withering fusillade. According to Ekman, who witnessed the carnage, the Germans "dashed down the bank into the river and in the river they still are."[97] Thus ended Mohnke's last attempt at crossing the Salm. Two days of bludgeoning his *1st SS Panzer Division* against the 505th's lines left him with little remaining combat power.[98] *Kampfgruppe Peiper* was on its own.

For the 505th, the stand along the Salm had been a near-run thing. Although aided by the terrain and the river to its front, covering such a wide area stretched the regiment to the limit. At one point, so desperate was Ekman for riflemen that he improvised a company from truck drivers and cooks to fill gaps in his line.[99] By that time, however, the threat against the Salm River had subsided. But another emerged in the south, where there was no river behind which to defend.

CHAPTER 22

SINGING THE BLUES ABOUT THE RIGHT FLANK

In the aftermath of the Battle of the Bulge, the tenacious and heroic stand of Tony McAuliffe and the 101st Airborne Division at Bastogne would capture the public imagination. Less well known, but no less important, was a similar tenacious and heroic stand of the American forces at St. Vith. . . . Some historians—and senior German commanders—believe the American stand at St. Vith was more important than the stand in Bastogne.

—CLAY BLAIR, *RIDGWAY'S PARATROOPERS: THE AMERICAN AIRBORNE IN WORLD WAR II*

FOR THE BATTALIONS on the southern portion of the division's horseshoe-shaped perimeter—from west to east the 2/401st, 1/325th, and 3/508th—21 December passed in relative calm. There was some desultory artillery fire, but no direct enemy contact. Yet Billingslea and Gavin were uneasy. The 3rd Armored Division was supposed to tie in with the 82nd at the southern rung of the horseshoe but had not done so. "The non-appearance of the 3rd Armored was a source of worry to everyone concerned," recalled Colonel Charles Billingslea, but especially for him since it was his regiment's flank that was exposed.[1] In addition, Billingslea was stretched thin. With only two of his three battalions forward—the 2/325th was being held in division reserve—he had extended his right flank as far as he could, which left huge gaps in his line.

Adding to Billingslea's unease were reports from civilians passing through the lines that German forces were massing to the south, although when

Billingslea sent out patrols to check out the reports, they found no sign of the enemy. What they did discover, much to their surprise, was a mishmash of American rear-echelon units. Since there had been nothing to indicate that there were any friendly units in the area, the thought was that the civilians had mistaken Americans for Germans. The only certainty, it seemed, was uncertainty. As Lieutenant Colonel Osmond Leahy, the 2/401st commander put it, "Everything was very confused and everybody was asking, 'Is it safe to go this way?'"[2]

By the afternoon of the twenty-second, confusion gave way to dread. An outpost sighted a column of approximately one hundred unidentified vehicles moving north toward the division's lines. Any doubt that the unidentified vehicles were German was erased when a jeep-mounted patrol from the 1/325th ran head-on into the vehicular column. German fire blew the rear wheel off the lead jeep, but the occupants, unharmed, piled in a second jeep and sped back to friendly lines. Then a second outpost sighted an infantry column moving north along a parallel route. The most comprehensive information on the trouble brewing in the south, however, came from one man, Corporal Robert G. Mangers of the 3/508th, whom fate deposited at a perfect, though precarious, vantage point.[3]

Mangers and four other troopers left friendly lines on a reconnaissance patrol on 21 December. Somewhere along their route the jeep in which they were riding broke down. Mangers and three of his troopers continued the reconnaissance on foot, but returned to the jeep before dark since its radio was their only means of communication. The next day, while working on their jeep, they spotted an enemy patrol. Mangers called the sighting in and then ordered the other troopers to return to friendly lines; he would stay with the jeep alone and continue to observe and report. For the next twenty hours, Mangers rendered incredibly accurate reports of enemy dispositions, including detailed information about numbers and types of vehicles and unit insignia. Mangers also called in artillery fire on enemy formations. Finally, when told to return to friendly lines, that he had done enough, Mangers replied that he could not; the enemy was too close, so he remained in position and continued sending reports until 0900 hours, 23 December, when he sent his last report, destroyed his radio, and tried making his way back to friendly lines. He never got there (nor did the other members of his patrol) and was subsequently listed as missing in action. In fact, however, he was taken prisoner and spent the rest of the war in a prisoner-of-war camp.[4]

Despite the reports of German units headed their way, Billingslea's troopers were denied permission to use artillery against them. At 0200 hours, 22 December, Ridgway had ordered the limited withdrawal of units from the St. Vith pocket, and the staff officers who held rein on the guns were worried that the troopers might be mistaking American vehicles making for safety for German vehicles on the attack.[5] Not until Captain Lee Travelstead, the F Company, 2/401st, commander, made his way forward and sneaked close enough to the enemy vehicles to describe their markings and muzzle brakes were the artillery officers convinced that, in fact, it was Germans they were being asked to fire on.[6]

What Travelstead saw were vehicles from the *2nd SS Panzer Division*'s reconnaissance battalion, which along with the *116th Panzer* and *560th Volks Grenadier Divisions* was massing "for an attack to push through the XVIII Airborne Corps in a climactic, dramatic bid for Spa and Liège." Inexplicably, the battalion was snarled in a traffic jam of its own making inside two small villages, Ottre and Joubiéval, just a few hundred yards south of the 2/401st's lines—perfect targets. Finally convinced by Travelstead's descriptions, the artillery officers released the 320th Glider Field Artillery and the 254th Field Artillery (155mm howitzers supporting the 82nd) Battalions to fire. German forces at both locations were mauled. According to Lieutenant Colonel Leahy, who observed the barrage at Ottre, the vehicle column "was in wild disorder and burning practically from beginning to end."[7] After falling back in disarray, the Germans reorganized and advanced a second time. Again the artillery fired. Again the Germans fell back. A third advance was also repulsed with artillery fire, but by the afternoon of 22 December it was clear that a major attack was brewing and that it would take more than artillery to hold it off.[8]

The appearance of the *2nd SS Panzer Division* made the 82nd's exposed right flank an even more acute concern. Were the *2nd SS* to either break through or slip by the flank altogether, it would have a clear and wholly undefended line of march northward to *Kampfgruppe Peiper*, and it would also be loose in the division rear. With no help forthcoming from First Army, Ridgway, Gavin, and Billingslea traveled to the 3rd Armored's command post at Manhay for a face-to-face talk with the division commander, Major General Maurice Rose. A gap some four miles wide separated the two divisions. Through the gap ran Highway N15, the north-south Bastogne-Liège road, a high-speed motorway that ran straight toward the Meuse. But Rose told them there was nothing he could do, that "he was covering a concentration of other forces and that his front was so extended that he could not occupy and hold in strength the terrain [between him and the 82nd's flank]."[9]

Gavin was in a fix. An enemy thrust up Highway N15 would be disastrous. The doctrinal solution was to withdraw, shorten the length of the defensive front, and cover the exposed flank. But by the afternoon of 22 December Ridgway's order for a limited withdrawal of forces from around St. Vith had become an order for their complete withdrawal.[10] Rescuing the 7th Armored and 106th Infantry Divisions and their multitudinous hangers-on was predicated on the 82nd holding its positions. Hence, for the 82nd, withdrawal was not an option. The division would have to stay and fight it out.

Billingslea, too, knew the score, so even before leaving Rose's command post he asked Gavin to give him the 2/325th. Gavin assented. Although one battalion would hardly suffice to fill the gap between the two divisions, with the 2/325th in hand Billingslea could at least reinforce a key crossroads in the gap at a place called Baraque de Fraiture. Assuredly, one battalion could not completely halt the *2nd SS Panzer Division*'s drive up Highway N15, but it might slow it long enough to get the St. Vith forces safely withdrawn and for Ridgway to conjure up some reinforcements.[11]

About the only thing Gavin and his lightly armed troopers had going for them was the terrain, which, if used correctly, could turn the enemy's greatest strength—its armor—into a weakness. Encumbered by heavy tanks, self-propelled guns, and half-tracks, the *2nd SS* was reliant on the few roads in the area that could support such a force. Although smaller German vehicles and dismounted infantry could take to the back roads and trails to find ways through or around the American lines, they eventually had to return to the main roads and clear them so that the heavier vehicles could pass. By focusing his defenses on the main roads, crossroads, and the adjacent key terrain, and counting on the tenacity of his troopers, Gavin hoped to hold back the German armor and, if he could do that, though porous, his lines would hold, at least long enough to evacuate the St. Vith forces.

Another enemy weakness Gavin sought to exploit was their reliance on bridges, especially those robust enough to support tanks. Based on a map study, his engineers determined that "the Germans would have to use a small road over a bridge near the town of Petite-Langlir [about six miles south of the division's lines] in the middle of the sector of the 325th if they were going to use armor against the 325th."[12] Were that bridge to be blown or damaged, the *2nd SS* would be unable to bring its combat power to bear against the center of the 325th's line, thereby reducing the risk Gavin was taking by stretching Billingslea's regiment over such a long front, for even with the 2/325th Billingslea's frontage measured some 10,000 yards, with gaps of up to 2,100 yards between units.[13]

Major John Lee volunteered to lead a patrol to take out the Petite-Langlir Bridge. Lee and eight engineers from A Company, 307th Engineers, departed friendly lines around midnight, 22 December. Their route, a purposefully circuitous one designed to avoid enemy troop concentrations, brought them to a point about 600 yards short of the bridge where Lee placed the troopers in a hide position and then crawled forward with a sergeant to get a better look at their objective. The map study had been correct. The bridge was a sturdy, wooden pile structure about sixty-five feet long traversing a stream about forty feet wide. German vehicles, including tanks, were crossing it and moving north toward the 325th's lines, but Lee could see that were the bridge destroyed the stream's steep and soggy banks, swift current, and the large rocks in its bed would force them to find someplace else to cross. The trick was to rig the bridge with enough explosives to destroy it or at least make it unusable for tanks without being discovered. Taking all eight men with him would assuredly alert the sentries patrolling the bridge's span, so instead Lee, the sergeant, and one other man emplaced the explosives while the rest of the patrol covered them. This meant several hours of standing in freezing water, but finally, at 0600 hours, 23 December, the three lit the fuses and crept away. Six minutes later the explosives blew and completely destroyed the bridge. Making their way back to friendly lines, Lee and his troopers caught a ride part of the way from a passing vehicle, although they were so cold and wet that "from time to time . . . the demolition party would dismount and run behind the weapons carrier to get warm and keep [their] feet from freezing." The mission against the Petite-Langlir Bridge was, observed Gavin, a "display of unusual gallantry and perseverance."[14] Moreover, its destruction eliminated the threat of an armored thrust against the center of Billingslea's lines.

Baraque de Fraiture, the crossroads for which Billingslea requested the return of the 2/325th, was at first glance nothing special—a small clearing containing a handful of buildings surrounded by thick woods. But Baraque de Fraiture was unique; not only was it one of the highest points in the Ardennes, it also straddled the intersection of two of the region's most important roads: the north-south Highway N15 and the east-west Highway N28. The Germans needed the crossroads so they could move on to the Meuse. For the Americans, its loss would threaten not only the existence of the 3rd Armored, the 82nd, and the St. Vith forces, but also unhinge all of XVIII Airborne Corps and expose the flank of the entire U.S. First Army. Possession of Baraque de Fraiture, therefore, could very well spell victory or defeat for either side.[15]

Because Rose had been unable to muster a force of any strength to send to Baraque de Fraiture, the defense of this critical point had been "on a strictly catch-as-catch-can basis" since 19 December, the day that Major Arthur C. Parker III, the executive officer of the 589th Field Artillery Battalion, pulled into the clearing with three 105mm howitzers, several other vehicles, and approximately 110 men.[16] Ignoring orders to withdraw, Parker set his artillerymen to defending what he could clearly see was key terrain and in subsequent days commandeered other stray units as they, too, stumbled upon the crossroads. By 22 December, the force at Baraque de Fraiture included, besides the

589th's artillery, four half-tracks mounting multiple .50-caliber machine guns and a 37mm antitank gun from the 7th Armored Division; several tanks, also from the 7th Armored; additional tanks, tank destroyers, and self-propelled guns from the 3rd Armored; and an understrength company from the independent 509th Parachute Infantry Battalion (the 509th had also been in bivouac near Rheims and was subsequently rushed forward to reinforce the 3rd Armored on Ridgway's order).[17] Dug in behind a minefield, this hodgepodge collection of units had already blunted several probing attacks by elements of the *560th Volks Grenadier Division*, but pressure against the crossroads was mounting. It was with an eye toward alleviating some of that pressure that Billingslea sent Major Richard M. Gibson's 2/325th to Fraiture, a village of some thirty closely spaced buildings on a ridge about three-quarters of a mile northeast of the crossroads.[18]

Gibson's orders were to defend the Fraiture ridge so as to lend support to the defenders at Baraque de Fraiture while adding some depth to the American defenses along Highway N15. To this end, Gibson emplaced G and E Companies on the ridge south and southwest of Fraiture so that they could overlook the crossroads and sent Captain Junior Woodruff's F Company to Baraque de Fraiture to help out there. Backing up his defenders from inside Fraiture were his headquarters troops, his battalion's 81mm mortars, and two American armored cars that were in the village when Gibson arrived.[19]

Gibson's troopers were in place by 1100 hours, 22 December. They spent the rest of the day improving their positions under a constant rain of artillery fire, a certain sign that an attack was in the offing. At Baraque de Fraiture, the F Company troopers also received quick lessons on how to operate the antiaircraft guns and tanks beside which they would be fighting, just in case. But against all expectations the attack did not come that day.[20]

The *2nd SS Panzer Division*, hidden in a wood to the south, had run out of gas, at least temporarily. In anticipation of renewing the advance, however, large groups of dismounted panzer grenadiers infiltrated into attack positions all around Baraque de Fraiture. One group even ambushed and captured a platoon of tank destroyers that someone had sent to reinforce the crossroads. Eventually, the crossroads was completely surrounded.[21]

Unexpectedly, when the Germans renewed their attack to open Highway N15 at dawn on 23 December they bypassed Baraque de Fraiture and instead assaulted Fraiture ridge. This took Gibson by surprise. Because of the intense cold he had manned the ridge with a skeleton force that he constantly rotated so the majority of his troopers could stay warm inside Fraiture's buildings. But it was so cold that when the Germans struck and the sentries tried opening up, they found that the bolts of their weapons were frozen shut. Virtually unopposed, a battalion of panzer grenadiers from the *2nd SS Panzer Divi-*

sion's 4th Panzer Grenadier Regiment swept through Gibson's sentry line and into Fraiture. Roused by the few shots their sentries got off, the troopers inside the village scrambled for their guns, tumbled out into the streets, and literally met the enemy face-to-face. Gibson, meanwhile, led his mortar platoon in a counterattack, driving it straight through the center of Fraiture with orders to fire on anyone who did not immediately identify himself as an American, while Lieutenant George Cockle, the G Company commander, led one of his rifle platoons in a flanking attack against the German left rear. Faced with stout resistance to their front and flank, the panzer grenadiers broke off the attack and retreated back to the safety of the wood from which they had emerged.[22]

The fight cost Gibson thirty-three casualties, a heavy toll (German losses are unknown), but with Fraiture ridge still in American hands, there remained the possibility that it would compel the Germans to divert combat power from an attack on Baraque de Fraiture and thereby heighten the chances of the defenders there. So Gibson restored his lines, now fully manned, and kept cold watch for another attack. But none came. Instead, the Germans pasted Fraiture with artillery and mortar fire and turned their attention to the crossroads below.[23]

While attacking Fraiture ridge, the Germans kept the defenders at Baraque de Fraiture at bay with a heavy artillery barrage, which took a toll on the Americans who had already been there for several days. Moreover, when Captain Woodruff arrived at the crossroads he discovered that the defenders were seriously short of ammunition, food, and batteries for their radios. A Lieutenant Kotary, the 2/325th's supply officer, had managed to infiltrate some supplies into Baraque de Fraiture, but it was not enough, so when at 1600 hours the intensity of the bombardment on the crossroads increased, Woodruff radioed Gibson that the "forces at the cross-roads were disintegrating" and requested permission to withdraw.[24] The request was denied. Regardless of what the other American forces did, F Company was to hold Baraque de Fraiture at all costs.[25]

At 1630 hours the bombardment of Baraque de Fraiture lifted. Peering over the lip of their foxholes, the troopers beheld a harrowing sight—Panthers and Tigers were bearing down on the crossroads from three sides. Following behind was the entire *4th Panzer Grenadier Regiment*. Using their 88mm guns like sniper rifles, the Tigers commenced a systematic destruction of everything at the crossroads: Buildings, tanks, antiaircraft guns, trucks, jeeps, and individual fighting positions were reduced in a matter of minutes. Several American tank crews abandoned their vehicles. Employing the scant knowledge they had obtained the day before about operating a Sherman, some of Woodruff's troopers scrambled aboard the abandoned tanks and attempted to return fire.

But a Sherman's gun was no match for a Tiger's. By 1700 hours every American tank and tank destroyer at Baraque de Fraiture was a burning hulk. With nothing to deter them, the Germans drove onto the crossroads to claim their prize. Woodruff radioed again: "Position was hopeless . . . overrun by enemy 'Tiger' tanks . . . [request] permission to withdraw."[26] This time his request was accepted. There was nothing more F Company could do. The hulks of ten Sherman tanks, three howitzers, four half-tracks, four tank destroyers, and eight trucks cluttered the small Belgian Alamo. Every other American soldier at Baraque de Fraiture that had not been killed or wounded had already fled.[27]

The brief stand at Baraque de Fraiture cost F Company dearly. Nineteen troopers, including Woodruff, hid out all night in the wood before making it the three-quarters of a mile back to their battalion at Fraiture. Another 25 straggled into friendly lines over the next few days. On its march into Baraque de Fraiture, F Company counted 116 troopers. Now it was 44 strong. But the sacrifice had not been in vain. While Woodruff, his troopers, and the other unlucky souls at Baraque de Fraiture were battling Tigers and Panthers, some 15,000 survivors of the equally horrendous fight at St. Vith, as well as a hundred tanks, were evacuated to safety.[28]

With the fall of Baraque de Fraiture, Billingslea "started singing the Blues about my right flank where the 3rd Armored was supposed to be in strength."[29] Gavin, too, was concerned. During the fight for the crossroads Gavin traveled to Gibson's command post and, from there, tried to make his way on foot to Baraque de Fraiture, only to be turned back by overwhelming numbers of the enemy (Gibson, too, tried to get through to Woodruff and, like Gavin, was unsuccessful).[30] Gavin, therefore, saw firsthand what the Germans had in the area. Moreover, he knew how paltry his own defenses were. "On the afternoon of December 23, at about 1700 hours, I checked the dispositions along the Fraiture ridge. At this time riflemen were scattered 100 to 200 yards apart. There was a little antitank defense, and the possibility of defending the ridge against a major German attack appeared nothing less than fantastic."[31] Gavin had already reported this parlous state of affairs to XVIII Airborne Corps to no avail; the corps had nothing to send him.[32] Consequently, Gavin told Tucker to free up a battalion for use on the southern front. Tucker sent Lieutenant Colonel Edward Wellems's 2/504th.[33] Initially positioned behind the center of the 325th's front to serve as a blocking force, when Baraque de Fraiture fell, Gavin ordered Wellems to counterattack to restore the position. But when Wellems moved to Gibson's command post at Fraiture to get a look at his objective, he had second thoughts. Gibson told Wellems, "I would not attack the damned place with a Regiment not to mind a Battalion."[34] It appears Gavin, too, thought better of committing the 2/504th against the German armor massed at the crossroads and called the counterattack off, electing instead to position it just north of the 2/325th's position as a backstop.[35]

With Baraque de Fraiture in enemy hands, "there was nothing to prevent the German forces from entering the rear of the Division area." Frantically looking for something with which he could at least delay a German rush up Highway N15, Gavin again made his way to the 3rd Armored command post at Manhay, only to find that it had pulled out. "I found one MP on duty and the town completely abandoned."[36] He then went to the corps command post where he met "Doc" Eaton. "I said, you've got to give me orders, I've got to have something to do. I can't sit there and let the Germans come around behind me and cut me off. And no one's telling me what to do. I don't think anyone knows the situation. We've got a bad layout down there. . . . Eaton looked at me, listened to it all, wouldn't say a goddamned word. He didn't say Jim, withdraw your right flank, he didn't do a thing, he didn't say a thing. He didn't know what to say, he couldn't say anything."[37] Gavin left the corps command post with "a profound sense of foreboding." He was certain that the Germans would attack up Highway N15; Gibson's battered 2/325th at Fraiture could do little more than watch. Rose's 3rd Armored Division, which had responsibility for the highway, "had disappeared into thin air." The 82nd's defensive line was already twenty-five miles long. Everywhere there were huge gaps, to say nothing of the exposed right flank in the south. Gavin had already accepted considerable risk when he denuded Tucker's front to send the 2/504th to aid Billingslea, but when he returned empty-handed from corps, Gavin called Tucker again: Be prepared to send a second battalion to the threatened flank; contain the still dangerous *Kampfgruppe Peiper* with what was left.[38] Finally, not long after returning to his own command post, he received word that Manhay had fallen, although "there seemed to be some doubt about this, however, and due to the darkness and confusion it was impossible to determine exactly where anyone was" (the reports were, in fact, wrong; Manhay did not fall until evening on the twenty-fourth).[39] Things could not have been any more dismal.

Were the worst to happen—were the Germans to mount an all-out drive up Highway N15 toward Liège—Gavin decided that he would hurl whatever he could at them and conduct a fighting withdrawal. Although using a lightly armed and equipped airborne division to fight a retrograde action against an SS panzer division was a seemingly suicidal task, Gavin's only concern was that he would be unable to slow the Germans sufficiently to gain the time needed to keep the Germans from crossing the Meuse. "If somehow I could get my hands on some armor," he mused, "we would be in pretty good shape for some time, since we never had trouble with the German infantry." That evening his wish was answered. Most likely as a result of his earlier remonstrance at the corps command post, Ridgway gave Gavin Brigadier General William M. Hoge's Combat Command B of the U.S. 9th Armored Division. Hoge's command had just escaped from St. Vith and was "practically exhausted from the past week's fighting. They were very short of infantry, and in the opinion of General Hoge Combat Command B was incapable of a sustained defense or offense."[40] But they were all Gavin had, and Hoge's armor, combined with Gavin's infantry, might be enough to hold. Gavin posted Hoge's force astride Highway N15.[41]

The German plan for 24 December was exactly as Gavin envisioned: a headlong rush up Highway N15 toward Liège. The fall of Baraque de Fraiture and St. Vith had opened the way for the concentration of the entire *II SS Panzer Corps*, the same corps, under the same commander, Wilhelm Bittrich, that the 82nd had fought in the streets of Nijmegen, only this time consisting of the *2nd SS* and *9th SS Panzer Divisions*. Furthermore, Bittrich had control of the *Führer Begleit Brigade*, an independent formation composed of three panzer grenadier battalions, a panzer regiment, an artillery battalion, and an antiaircraft battalion, and it had been promised two additional divisions, the *12th SS Panzer* and *3rd Panzer Grenadier*, as soon as they could be pushed forward.[42] With that much combat power there was a real chance that Bittrich could effect the breakthrough upon which the entire German campaign plan was predicated. There were but two challenges he had to overcome before unleashing his panzers: a straitened fuel supply and some recalcitrant Americans on either side of Highway N15 that were denying him the maneuver room his force required. The first could be solved through improvisation, prioritization, and forcible appropriation. The second required further attacks on either side of N15. The task of clearing the area east of the highway—ground still held by the 325th—Bittrich assigned to the *Führer Begleit Brigade* and the *2nd SS Panzer Division*.

The twenty-fourth opened with an attack by the *Führer Begleit Brigade* on Regné, a village about 2,000 yards east of Fraiture. Posted there was a platoon from F Company, 2/401st, supported by two antitank guns. Under cover of the morning mist eight tanks and at least two platoons of panzer grenadiers shot their way into Regné, destroyed one antitank gun, machine-gunned its crew, and wiped out a third of the platoon. In the melee, some troopers took to the cellars and hid out. The rest broke contact and were making their way north when they met Lieutenant Colonel Leahy, who had procured several tank destroyers, most likely the remnants of the forces evacuated from St. Vith, which he pushed forward astride the road running north from Regné. As soon as the first German tank appeared, they let loose a volley and destroyed it. The rest retreated. It seemed a short respite had been won.[43]

The Germans next turned their attention to Fraiture. The fall of Regné cleared the way for the *Führer Begleit Brigade* to move on Fraiture from the east, while the *4th Panzer Grenadier Regiment* of the *2nd SS Panzer Division* attacked from the south. Billingslea could see this too, so, since he had nothing left to send Gibson, he ordered him to withdraw to a position closer to the 2/401st. The order came just in time. The Germans struck just as the last trooper cleared Fraiture, and American dive-bombers—where they came from and how they got there are mysteries—held up the Germans long enough for Gibson's troopers to get away. Another German force, however, caught the 2/325th as it was passing through a ravine, but Gibson's troopers had had enough. They fought back ferociously and, though fighting from low ground, exacted a terrible revenge for the beating they had taken the past couple of days. When the smoke cleared the Germans quit the field and left behind fifty dead and twenty-six prisoners. American casualties numbered six. Gibson and his troopers made it the rest of the way to their new position around Lierneux without incident.[44]

The withdrawal from Fraiture made Leahy's 2/401st, entrenched on commanding terrain above Regné, the outermost unit on the division flank. Hence, when Billingslea ordered Leahy to counterattack to retake Regné, Leahy demurred. Abandoning his strong position to attack an armored enemy force did not seem prudent. On further consideration Billingslea agreed, yet it was important that Regné be retaken. Its possession gave the enemy command over several miles of Highway N28, the east-west lateral that intersected Highway N15 at Baraque de Fraiture, and thus sufficient maneuver room to bring up additional armor and mechanized units with which to attack northward. Conversely, without Regné, Bittrich would have to launch his attack on a more constricted front.[45]

Regné's importance was not lost on Gavin either, and because of this he gave Billingslea use of a valuable commodity to get it back: a company of Shermans from Combat Command B, 9th Armored Division, part of the same element plugging the gap through which ran Highway N15. Using the Shermans in combination with B Company, 1/325th, Billingslea improvised a counterattack. The plan was for his troopers to ride the tanks until they reached some high ground north of Regné. At that point the troopers would dismount and, in coordination with one of the tank platoons, advance on the town under cover of a rolling artillery barrage while the other two tank platoons took up blocking positions south and west of Regné to mop up any enemy attempting to escape.[46]

The attack went off without a hitch. At 1400 hours artillery began plastering Regné; in twenty minutes 113 high explosive shells hit the village.

When the barrage lifted the B Company troopers and their supporting tanks shot their way the last few yards into town and, working in tandem and displaying "unusual gallantry and élan," set about chasing the Germans out.[47] By 1500 hours, Regné was back in American hands.[48]

Losing Regné had serious consequences for the impending German attack up Highway N15. Without access to the terrain around the village, Bittrich was forced to assemble his attack echelons in a much more constricted area. With barely enough maneuver room for the *2nd SS Panzer Division* there was no way he could squeeze the *9th SS Panzer Division* into the front lines as well. He therefore had to scrap his plan to attack with two divisions abreast. Instead, the *2nd SS* would lead the attack with the *9th SS* following. But this, too, was complicated by the ripple effect the loss of Regné had on Bittrich's lines of communication. Keeping an armor division supplied with ammunition and fuel required unfettered access to an adequate road net, but with the *9th SS* jammed in behind the *2nd SS*, supply trucks from the latter had to share the road with the tanks, half-tracks, and self-propelled guns of the former as it attempted to move forward. Immense traffic jams resulted, and to make matters worse Allied fighter-bombers ranging the skies above forced the Germans to move only at night or risk destruction. As a result the *9th SS* fell behind schedule, and when it finally did attack, it did so on its own, its actions separate from and uncoordinated with those of the *2nd SS*.[49]

Taking back Regné not only denied Bittrich the opportunity to mount a massed armor attack, it also provided the Allies valuable intelligence. Sometime after the Americans regained control of Regné, an officer from the *2nd SS Panzer Division* wandered into the town and was taken prisoner. He had with him a complete set of orders outlining Bittrich's scheme of maneuver. "They proved of great value," wrote Gavin later, "since they gave us definite information of the enemy's intentions for the following several days."[50] Those intentions were to take Manhay and from there continue the advance up Highway N15 through Werbomont on to Liège.[51]

The plans also underscored the significance of the 325th's defense of the division's southwest flank. Though stretched over a frontage doctrine dictated should be assigned to nothing smaller than a division, Billingslea's regiment had not only held on long enough to allow the evacuation of the St. Vith forces, but also frustrated Bittrich's attempts to position the entire *II SS Panzer Corps* for an attack up Highway N15. Yet the 82nd was still in a precarious position. Having saved the St. Vith forces, it was now time for the 82nd to be saved lest it be encircled as well.

CHAPTER 23

MAKING MONKEYS OUT OF THE GERMANS

Unfortunately, I couldn't tell you the name of the town, but it was out in the Battle of the Bulge. Somewhere near St. Vith. And I had my squad; actually, my section was out there with their 81mm mortars set up. About two foot of snow all around us out in a field and of course you couldn't see anything. Suddenly, this jeep drove up and put on his brakes and stopped and he said to the driver . . . I didn't hear him, but he must have said to the driver, "take this box and come on with me." Immediately . . . one of my men, I guess, alerted me that this was the general. And I thought, "Oh, my God. What's General Gavin . . . what's he coming here for? Is he going to ask me some technical questions or some . . . quill me on my fight orders or, you know, the routine we had and what have you?" And I had not even thought about it being Christmas because on the field of battle we don't have holidays. Anyway, the driver came up with this box. . . . And General Gavin came and said, "Hey, fellas, Merry Christmas." And got down in the hole with us . . . said, "I just come to spend a little time with you." So the driver opened up the box and passed them out. It was fried chicken. Well, I'll tell you the honest truth, I don't know I got a piece of chicken or not out of the box because I was so nervous with him being present. But, anyway, the rest of them gnawed on their chicken and remarked what a hell of a time . . . and then he said, "Well fellas, I got a long way to go and a lot of ground to cover." And he said to the driver, "Come on, let's go." And he left the box of chicken there. And he said once again, "Merry Christmas." I was a nervous wreck.

—Paul Stephenson Jr., interview by the author, 11 April 2002[1]

On the morning of 24 December, there arrived at the XVIII Airborne Corps command post at Werbomont an incongruous figure: Field Marshal Bernard Law Montgomery. It was time, he announced, to "tidy up the battlefield."[2]

Montgomery's visit would doubtless have surprised the thousands of soldiers then fighting under XVIII Airborne Corps command. What would have surprised them even more would have been the knowledge that their divisions, the corps, and the entire U.S. First Army had been under Montgomery's control for four days already because of a decision by the Supreme Commander as he, in his own way, sought to tidy up the battlefield as well.

Eisenhower's decision resulted from several considerations. By 19 December, intelligence reports indicated that the German main effort had developed a distinctly westward orientation. In the eyes of Major General Strong, the SHAEF intelligence chief, and Major General J. F. M. Whiteley, SHAEF's deputy chief of staff for operations, the orientation of the German thrust brought with it the danger that Bradley's 12th Army Group would be split and Bradley, whose command post was well to the south of the Bulge in Luxembourg City, would be unable to control his forces fighting along the northern face of the Bulge, in particular Hodges's First Army. Yet Bradley refused to reposition his headquarters. When Eisenhower suggested he do so, Bradley stated flatly that he would "never move backwards with a headquarters" because "too much prestige was at stake."[3] Strong and Whiteley, both British officers, had a solution, albeit one they knew would stir up a hornet's nest: Army group boundaries should be redrawn, with Montgomery taking charge of the northern face of the Bulge while Bradley retained responsibility for the southern face. Doing so, however, would mean that two of the three American armies in 12th Army Group—Hodges's First Army and Lieutenant General William H. Simpson's U.S. Ninth Army (which was on line north of First Army)—would be placed under Montgomery, leaving Bradley with but one army, Patton's Third. Before going to Eisenhower, Strong and Whitely floated their idea by the SHAEF chief of staff, "Beetle" Smith, who "reacted negatively and with considerable heat, [but] then cooled off and admitted the logic of the proposal."[4] When Smith, in turn, presented the idea to Eisenhower, the Supreme Commander called Bradley to ask what he thought. Bradley insisted that there was no need to redraw any boundaries, that he had good communications with Hodges and Simpson and that he was having auxiliary telephone lines laid to ensure this would continue. But when Smith interjected with a pointed question—whether the move would make sense were Montgomery an American—Bradley admitted that it would. That sealed the deal, so on the morning of 20 December, Eisenhower redrew the army group boundaries, which gave Montgomery temporary command of the First and Ninth Armies.[5]

Montgomery had already taken measures to secure his rear area and right flank, which, in essence, meant securing the line of the Meuse River. Working in concert with Lieutenant General J. C. H. Lee, the communications zone commander, Montgomery cobbled together a Meuse River guard force from rear-echelon personnel, tank replacement center troops, and British Special Air Service Commandos and placed them in defensive positions around every crossing site in the path of the German advance. Additionally, he directed Lieutenant General Brian Horrocks to countermarch XXX Corps and move south immediately to take over the defense of the Meuse.[6]

With his flank and rear secured—no doubt in anticipation of taking command of the forces in the northern half of the Bulge—Montgomery was primed to sweep into First Army and take control.[7] Arriving at Hodges's headquarters just ninety minutes after Eisenhower called him about the new command arrangement—like "Christ come to cleanse the Temple"—Montgomery immediately set about exerting order on what he considered a chaotic situation.[8] "The first thing to do was to see the battle on the northern flank *as one whole*," he explained.[9] What this meant was arraying the forces along the northern face of the Bulge on a continuous line. This he did in two phases. The first was the withdrawal of the St. Vith forces.[10] When that was complete he turned to the salient being held by the 82nd. It was with that in mind that he visited Ridgway's command post on 24 December.

Montgomery's first act upon arriving at XVIII Airborne Corps was to commend Ridgway "on the conduct of his command during the initial operation," but then wasted no time in getting to what he had really come for—since "the Corps had fought with distinction, [it] could withdraw with honor to itself and its units." This contradicted an order Ridgway issued earlier that day in which he exhorted his division commanders to hold their positions. "In my opinion this is the last dying gasp of the German Army. He is putting everything he has into this fight. We are going to smash that final drive here today in this Corps Zone. This command is the command that will smash the German offensive spirit for this war. Impress every man in your division with that spirit. We are going to lick the German here today." After several hours with Montgomery, however, Ridgway changed his mind. Admitting that he had had "an entirely contrary view" earlier that morning, he telephoned First Army headquarters to report that Montgomery was headed that way "with a very important suggestion, which originated with him, and which, in view of the picture he gave me, I entirely agree with."[11] The suggestion was that the 82nd should withdraw.

"I was greatly concerned with the attitude of the troops toward the withdrawal," wrote Gavin in his after-action review, "the Division having never made a withdrawal in its combat history."[12] Many troopers felt likewise. "The withdrawal order did not set well with my platoon or me," remembered Lieutenant Megellas of the 504th. According to Sergeant Bill Lord of the 508th, the withdrawal order "was a shock to everyone. The 82nd Airborne Division, which had prided itself on its record 'no ground gained ever relinquished,' was moving back!" Sergeant Ray Burchell of the 1/325th agreed. "It was not like us to retreat. We had been fighting SS troops and had badly beaten them." Private Allen Langdon concurred, convinced that he and his fellow 505th troopers could have "held the Salm River line until hell froze over because, for defense, it may well have been the best position the regiment held during the whole war." But Colonel Charles Billingslea, whose glider troopers had been fighting on the division's exposed flank, was not as quick to question the decision. "The losses of the Regiment up to this point had been very heavy and [he was] of the opinion that if it had stayed there [in the south], its losses would have been heavier." In his memoirs Gavin concurred with Billingslea, backing off what he had penned in his after-action report. Acknowledging that the "troopers did not like to withdraw in front of the Germans" and would have "much preferred to attack" since "they knew they had beaten the Germans in every tactical engagement so far," hindsight brought a greater appreciation of the larger "tactical situation confronting XVIII Corps" and compelled him to conclude that "a withdrawal was very much in order."[13]

Gavin issued his withdrawal order on the afternoon of 24 December. He had, in fact, selected the withdrawal positions several days earlier as a result of an order from Ridgway to identify "a suitable defensive position that would tie in with the divisions on my right and left" following the extrication of the forces from St. Vith.[14] The position he selected "shortened the sector allocated to the 82nd by about 50 per cent," was "far superior in terms of fields of fire and cover for the defenders," and placed the division "in a much better position to launch a counterattack when the moment for that came."[15] The bulk of the division was to start pulling back to the new position at about 2100 hours. A covering force of one platoon per company was to stay behind until 0400 hours, 25 December, when it too was to pull back. The 307th Engineers were to support the withdrawal by blowing bridges and culverts, laying minefields, and blockading roads with felled trees.[16]

The night of 24–25 December was clear and cold. The clouds had cleared two days before, ushering in much colder temperatures and snow. "Thereafter the snow and cold became as great a factor in the battle as the enemy, and on the occasions when the temperature fell to below zero, it was a constant struggle to keep hands, feet, and ears from freezing."[17] Illumination was about 70 percent, "with brilliant moonlight shimmering on the sparkling blanket of snow that covered the countryside," which aided the troopers greatly as they made their way to their new positions.[18]

For the most part the withdrawal went exactly as planned. According to Gavin, "In all of the operations in which we have participated in our two years of combat and they have been many of multitudinous types, I have never seen a better executed operation than the withdrawal on Christmas Eve."[19] There was one exception. The exception occurred along the 505th's line of march where, in an incident that could only have taken place on a battlefield as confused and chaotic as that of the Bulge, two enemy forces withdrawing in opposite directions crossed paths.

By 23 December, the ring around *Kampfgruppe Peiper*, which was still holding out along the north bank of the Amblève, had grown tight. Peiper and his SS soldiers were being pummeled by artillery, had few supplies, and had no hope of succor.[20] Peiper's only option, if he were to save something of his force, was to infiltrate what he could back east. SS-Oberführer Mohnke granted this permission on the afternoon of 23 December. Leaving behind some 300 of his number, almost all of whom were wounded, as well as approximately 170 American prisoners, twenty-eight tanks, seventy half-tracks, and twenty-five artillery pieces, Peiper led about 800 of his men in a breakout attempt starting at 0100 hours, 24 December. At daybreak on the twenty-fourth they took cover in a dense wood near Trois Ponts. As soon as it was dark again they continued their eastward trek with an eye to crossing the Salm and rejoining the rest of the *1st SS Panzer Division*. It was then that they crossed paths with Ekman's troopers moving to their new positions.[21]

Gavin and Ekman were well aware that Peiper was attempting a withdrawal of his own, and Ekman had received numerous reports about unidentified soldiers in his rear.[22] One was from Vandervoort and his operations officer, Captain Charles E. Sammon, who were spooked while conducting a reconnaissance of the withdrawal route. Sensing movement in some bushes, they issued the challenge, got no reply, and then sprayed the area with their Thompsons before hightailing it out of there.[23] Another was from a supply detail that reported a platoon of soldiers wearing hobnailed boots and full field gear headed eastward along a road. When challenged, the unidentified platoon took cover.[24] Major Daniel McIlvoy, the regimental surgeon, was making his way to the new defensive position when he had his driver stop their jeep to let a column of what they assumed were German prisoners cross in front of them. "They were crossing in columns of two's. After they crossed, we drove on, but suddenly realized that they had their guns and no troopers were with them."[25]

Ekman was in a quandary. Should he stop and fight, or should he continue with his assigned mission? According to Gavin:

> [Ekman] knew that at daylight [on 25 December] he had to be fitted into the divisional defensive front, wired in and mined, prepared for a strong German attack if it came. His inclinations were to stop all movement and fight the Germans wherever he found them that night. He asked me to

> consider further my decision to carry out the withdrawal. It was an interesting problem, but from the viewpoint of Corps and Army, and even Division, for that matter, it would have been inexcusable to be caught at daylight with one regiment Kraut-hunting through the woods all over a gap of several miles wide. There was only one thing to do and that was to carry out the assigned mission to withdraw and organize along the new front west from [Trois Ponts]. This, I told him to do. His fighting, therefore, was to be limited to that which was necessary to get on his objective and get it organized.[26]

Consequently, Ekman told his subordinates "to skirt enemy resistance and continue on mission which was to withdraw and be in new position by dawn."[27]

The 1/505th and 2/505th made it to the new position without making contact. The 3/505th was not as lucky, for *Kampfgruppe Peiper* made the area occupied by the 3/505th its point of aim. This became clear just before the 3/505th's main body started pulling back. Some 120 SS soldiers trying to get to the Salm stumbled into I Company's assembly area. According to Sergeant Bill Dunfee, I Company's troopers "were all packed up awaiting orders to move out. . . . We were lying back on our packs dozing, when all hell broke loose. The Germans came from our rear, shooting and yelling like a bunch of Indians. I didn't have to see them to know who it was; the rapid rate of the German machine guns, the pink tracers told me. They wanted to go home for Christmas, too." Dunfee and his mates tumbled into their foxholes and returned fire. In the ensuing fight they killed or wounded approximately 80 Germans before they reached the river, and many of those that did make it to the Salm were cut down by I Company's machine gunners when they emerged on the opposite bank. A second clash with Peiper's men occurred at approximately 2330 hours. Lieutenant Colonel James Kaiser, the 3/505th commander, was in an armored car driving toward the spot he had selected for his battalion command post. Along the way he came upon American engineers putting in a roadblock who told Kaiser that they had received small arms fire from a nearby wood. After a few bursts from the armored car's .50-caliber machine gun, "moaning and confused shouting could be heard from the woods." Kaiser called on the Germans to surrender; when a few started to do so, "a sharp German command halted the movement and the Germans replied with [small arms] fire."[28] Following a short firefight, Kaiser and the engineers withdrew. A third clash with *Kampfgruppe Peiper* occurred at approximately 0320 hours, 25 December. Again it was I Company that was involved. Because of its earlier fight I Company's main body did not pull out of its positions along the Salm until about 0245 hours, 25 December. Traveling in column along a dirt road, I Company ran into a sizable German column moving in the opposite direction. The two point elements exchanged fire at close range, about fifteen to twenty yards. Both were pinned down, but the Americans acted first, blanketing the road ahead with 60mm mortar fire. They also pushed up two squads on either side of the road to take the German column in the flank. Eventually, each side broke contact. While regrouping the Americans found they had two additions to their ranks, Lieutenant William Cameron and Staff Sergeant Russell H. Burton, forward observers from the 456th Parachute Field Artillery Battalion. They had been captured earlier and used the confusion of the firefight to make their escape.[29] Later on that night, I Company picked up a third American straggler, Major Hal D. McCown, commander of the 2/119th Infantry Battalion. "He stated that he had just escaped from the Germans and that he had valuable information to get through to higher headquarters."[30] McCown accompanied I Company to the 82nd's new positions and from there was shuttled off to higher headquarters. His reports substantiated that it was, in fact, the remnants of *Kampfgruppe Peiper* that had crossed paths with the 3/505th.[31]

Incredibly, the 505th suffered only 4 casualties during the withdrawal, all wounded. In return Ekman's troopers inflicted at least 100 casualties on the enemy.[32] Gavin later noted that "Peiper always considered it quite a feat of daring to have withdrawn through the 504th and 505th." But what Peiper did not realize, he continued, was that "the 504th had mostly pulled out and that the 505th was [also] withdrawing the night he went through." "By an act of God, it was one night in the entire war when such a thing could have been accomplished because we had to let them do it. With the facts as [Ekman] saw them and as I saw them, if he had attempted to escape the night before, he would have been surrounded and destroyed as much of his forces were earlier when he tried to cross the river near Stoumont [when Peiper's men ran into Tucker's 504th at Cheneux]."[33] As it was, by savaging *Kampfgruppe Peiper* at Cheneux and then again during its withdrawal, and then beating the *1st SS Panzer Division* along the Salm, the 82nd ensured that "that elite unit could no longer be considered an armored division."[34]

While the main body of the division pulled back, the covering force was to maintain the illusion that the 82nd was still in position.[35] "To fully appreciate the position of the men assigned to cover the withdrawal," wrote Sergeant Bill Lord of the 508th, "it must be realized that they were holding in heavily wooded, mountainous country, and even with a full-strength regiment on line it had been very difficult to maintain contact with units on the left and right. Now that less than one-third of the Regiment was holding the same ground, contact was nearly impossible."[36] Given this situation, commanders positioned their covering forces along likely avenues of approach with orders to remain in place until 0400 hours, 25 December, after which they were to quietly slip away. If at any time their ruse was discovered, they were to hold as long as possible in order to gain time for the main body to get in position. It was a dangerous mission, and commanders selected only their toughest and most tactically savvy leaders to carry it out. In the A Company, 1/508th, sector, the task fell to Lieutenant George Lamm.

Lamm was no stranger to difficult missions. It was his platoon that had been cut off for several days behind German lines in Nijmegen. And already in the Bulge, while covering the withdrawal of American forces out of the St. Vith pocket, he and his platoon "became engaged in one of the most colorful fights of the 'Bulge' campaign," a fight that would earn Lamm the Distinguished Service Cross (though he had been put in for the Medal of Honor).[37]

It was the evening before the withdrawal. Lamm and eight of his troopers were outposted on the east side of the Salm in Vielsalm. The remainder of A Company occupied covering positions on the west bank. Things had been quiet in the 508th's sector along the Salm; the St. Vith pocket had been directly to the regiment's front, and it was on that pocket that the Germans had concentrated their effort. But once the last of the St. Vith forces withdrew, there was nothing between the 508th and the enemy. This became the case at 1900 hours, 23 December, when word was passed that "all known vehicles and remaining troops" had crossing into friendly lines. But General Hasbrouck, who was in Vielsalm counting his units back to safety, was not so sure so he asked Captain Jonathan Adams, the A Company commander, if he could keep the Vielsalm bridges open and intact until midnight. Since this was against Adams's orders, he called higher headquarters for approval, which was granted. It was a gamble worth taking if it saved a few more Americans from death or capture. Besides, both Ridgway and Gavin, on whose shoulders ultimately rested the decision to keep the bridges intact, had the utmost faith in the ability of the men guarding them. A few hours later that faith was tested and not found wanting.[38]

Sometime around 2230 hours, Lamm spied figures approaching from the east. In the dark he could not tell if they were friendly or enemy, but since the only reason he and his troopers were still on the east bank of the river was to guard the bridges in the event American stragglers appeared, he held his fire. The figures were about ten yards away when he finally got a good look. They were Germans, about a platoon's worth, and they were headed right toward him. He opened fire at point-blank range, killed some, scattered the rest, and then gave the signal to withdraw, a sharp blast on his whistle, and fell back to the railroad bridge—there were two bridges remaining at Vielsalm, a railroad bridge and a road bridge—to count his men over and cover them as they crossed. When his last man passed Lamm followed and gave another blast on his whistle to signal the demolition team to ignite the fuses attached to explosives on each of the bridges. But nothing happened. For some reason the demolition team was out of position. Someone was going to have to go back onto each of the bridges, find the fuses, and pull the ignition rings. But by that time the Germans had recovered and were moving on both bridges. Furthermore, their strength had grown to about company size, and, to make matters worse, they had a tank with them that was systematically blasting houses on the west side of the Salm. Yet the bridges had to be blown. So Lamm organized his troopers into something of a flying wedge. The idea was that the wedge, with Lamm on point, would advance back onto the bridges with the troopers firing from the hip while the demolition team followed behind, found the fuses, pulled the rings, and then gave the signal to withdraw, at which time the wedge would reverse course. Lamm's aggressiveness seems to have taken the Germans by surprise, for despite the disparity in numbers the tactic worked, aided in great measure by covering fire from the rest of the company that was so heavy that Germans caught in the open on the far bank bounced "like so many rubber balls" off of doors and walls.[39] When the fuses on both bridges were relit, Lamm and his men again fell back to cover and waited. Thirty seconds later there was an explosion, but only one. The railroad bridge had been completely destroyed but the road bridge was still standing, its fuse having fizzled out. So, for a second time, Lamm employed his wedge tactics. For a second time it worked. And, for a second time, the fuse failed. There would have to be a third attempt to destroy the road bridge. This time, either out of frustration or because the demolition team was out of fuses, Lamm single-handedly lugged a box of Composition C-2 to the approximate middle of the span, ran back to cover, and then had a bazooka gunner fire a rocket into the box. The subsequent explosion destroyed the flooring of the bridge, but the hoped-for sympathetic detonation of the explosives packed around the bridge's abutment did not occur. Since the flooring could be easily replaced, Lamm counterattacked a fourth time, driving the Germans from the bridge long enough for the demolition team to jerry-rig a detonating device that would complete the destruction of the bridge. This time they were successful.[40]

The next day, when word came down that the division was withdrawing and that each company was to provide a platoon for the covering force, Lamm and his Second Platoon got the call. At first, it looked as though the previous night's battle for the bridges had taken all the fight out of the Germans, for things were relatively quiet along the 508th's front after the main body departed. Then, at about 2300 hours, artillery began falling in the A and B Company sectors. The troopers hunkered in their foxholes, not sure what this might portend, but when the Germans switched to smoke rounds, blanketing both banks of the Salm in a thick cloud, they knew and prepared themselves for a ground assault.

It is likely that the troopers heard the attacking Germans before they actually saw them, for once again it was SS soldiers, this time from *19th Panzer Grenadier Regiment* of the *9th SS Panzer Division* who ran forward yelling and screaming. The B Company platoon "split the enemy formation with deadly bands of steel, and the troopers held." Lamm's platoon, positioned much closer to the river, was overrun. Keeping his head, Lamm improvised on his wedge tactics, formed his troopers into a tight phalanx, and shot his way out of trouble. Eventually, they linked up with the regimental covering force that, under the overall command of Lieutenant Colonel Thomas Shanley, the regimental executive officer, fought a delaying action for most of the seven miles back to the new positions, "one of the best pieces of fighting in the 508th's history." This compelled the *19th Panzer Grenadier Regiment* to break off its pursuit, and by 0800 hours, Christmas Day, the covering force had rejoined the main body at the new defensive line and the division could report "all regiments were on their positions, mining and wiring were under way and all troops were dug in."[41]

The withdrawal erased a dangerously exposed salient, brought the 82nd on line with the other divisions in XVIII Airborne Corps, and placated Montgomery's penchant for tidiness. It also shortened considerably the frontage for which XVIII Airborne Corps and its constituent divisions were responsible. With the 30th Infantry Division on its left and the remnants of the 7th Armored Division on its right, the 82nd's new defensive array faced south and ran along a generally straight line from Trois Ponts southwest to a point just short of Manhay.[42]

With a much shorter line to defend, Gavin planned to cover the front with his three parachute regiments—from left to right the 505th, 508th, and 504th—and place the 325th in division reserve. Intelligence indicated that the Germans were preparing another major attack toward Liège and the Meuse, so it would be handy to have an entire regiment available to commit as either a stopgap or a counterattacking force. It was a luxury to which Gavin was unaccustomed. It was a luxury that he would never get to experience.[43]

Not long after the 325th settled into its reserve location, Captain Olson, Gavin's senior aide, "burst into the [325th's] C.P. with the news that the Germans had driven the 3rd Armored out of [Tri-le-Cheslaing]," a hamlet about 2,000 yards east of Manhay.[44] Clearly, there was some confusion about boundaries and units. Tri-le-Cheslaing was well inside in the 7th Armored's defensive sector, and the 3rd Armored Division was not even in XVIII Airborne Corps anymore. Regardless, Billingslea dispatched the 1/325th to Tri-le-Cheslaing with orders to retake the town and hold it until further notice. Once again Billingslea's glider troopers would be guarding the division's right flank.[45]

The 1/325th got to Tri-le-Cheslaing sometime late in the morning of 25 December. There was no sign of the enemy, but since Billingslea's orders were to hold the position until relieved, Lieutenant Colonel Richard E. Gerard, the battalion commander, organized a defensive ring around the hamlet. Things remained quiet until 2200 hours when a German tank pulled out of the wood south of Tri-le-Cheslaing and began systematically bombarding it. Gerard had with him two tank destroyers and a Sherman tank, but he had them hold their fire and lay low; sensing that the bombardment was but prelude to a more significant attack, Gerard did not want reveal that he, too, had heavy firepower until he absolutely had to. The German tank fired twelve shots and retired. Gerard was correct, though—the bombardment was a precursor to something more. At 0600 hours the next morning a battalion of panzer grenadiers from the 325th's familiar nemesis, the *4th Panzer Grenadier Regiment* of the *2nd SS Panzer Division*, hit Gerard's C Company dug in on the south side of town and punched a hole in its line by concentrating their entire force on a narrow front. Some panzer grenadiers even succeeded in infiltrating beyond the C Company positions into Tri-le-Cheslaing itself; 10 of them attacked Gerard's command post, but while the headquarters personnel fought them off, A and B Companies counterattacked, swept the hamlet clean of the enemy, restored C Company's lines, and inflicted heavy casualties on the attackers. Gerard's hidden armor added to the carnage. The fight lasted for approximately forty-five minutes. By the time the firing died down Gerard's troopers had chased the attackers back into the wood south of town, which Gerard then blanketed with artillery. A second attack never came. A patrol sent later in the day to take a look around the wood reported that "there were [G]erman dead all over the woods. They saw no live [G]ermans."[46] This ended the last attempt by the *II SS Panzer Corps* to break through to the Meuse. At 2000 hours, an armored infantry battalion from the 7th Armored relieved the 1/325th at Tri-le-Cheslaing, but rather than return to reserve, the 1/325th, shifted slightly east and remained on line, providing the link between the 82nd, to its left, and the 7th Armored, to its right.[47]

The 82nd's withdrawal opened the way for other German units to enter the battle, most notably the *9th SS Panzer Division* and the *62nd Volks Grenadier Division*, both of which moved into the voided salient. But the 82nd's engineers had done a masterful job of covering the withdrawal, felling countless trees and laying hundreds of mines, which slowed the German advance and gained time the troopers needed to prepare their new defensive positions. And though many had had reservations about the decision to withdraw, Gavin's troopers remained undaunted. Typical of their attitude was that displayed by

Staff Sergeant Frank L. Sirovica of the 3/508th, who, upon reaching the new defensive line, implored his platoon to "dig in, and dig in good! We have to stop the Germans here! We are not going to give up any more ground!" Private Angel Romero, one of those in Sirovica's charge, was more than happy to dig, for though "the ground was frozen hard as stone," the digging "helped keep us from freezing to death."[48]

The *9th SS* and *62nd* first made their presence felt along the new line on 26 December with probing attacks against the center of the division line. The *62nd*, wrote Gavin, "proved to be of very poor quality and not well trained. They consistently lost patrols by having them destroyed by our outposts and they appeared to be very vulnerable to our own patrols."[49] The *9th SS* was another matter. On 28 December it mounted a vicious assault on two villages, Erria and Villettes. Defending was Lieutenant Colonel Louis Mendez's 3/508th.

Erria, in the east, and Villettes, in the west, anchored the left and right flanks of the 3/508th. The battalion's mission—to defend the high ground north of the east-west road connecting the two villages—was fairly standard, so Mendez employed a standard defensive scheme, posting G Company on his left at Erria and H Company on his right at Villettes, while keeping I Company in reserve, which had only 38 effectives and could not have covered much ground anyway.

Just after midnight on 27 December, Villettes was hit with a concentration of high-explosive and smoke shells. The H Company troopers huddled in their foxholes and peered into the darkness, searching for the silhouette of enemy infantry or, worse, tanks. They saw nothing.

Suddenly, Mendez received a call from his G Company commander at Erria, Captain Russell C. Wilde. His outposts had been driven back. A few minutes later Wilde called again. He was in a fight with the *19th Panzer Grenadier Regiment* of the *9th SS*. One of his platoons had been overrun, although the troopers remained in their holes and fired into the German rear, and the weight of the German attack forced G Company out of Erria. Wilde responded with artillery and mortar fire (some 1,200 artillery rounds and 660 mortar rounds were fired that night) to isolate the German spearhead in Erria and keep it from being reinforced from follow-on echelons, some of which tried slipping to the east to find another way through the American wall of steel. When they did so, they ran in F Company, 2/508th, in particular Private Warren Zuelke, who repositioned his machine gun so that he could fire into the German flank. His fire was devastating. "It was a sin, and I'm not proud of it . . . ," recalled Zuelke, "to have murdered as we did that night, both Germans and cows."[50]

"The battle for Erria was the most aggressive German attack I experienced during the whole war," recalled Private Marvin Risnes of G Company. "We lost a few men but those SS troopers, Hitler's best, lost many more." (G Company losses were ten dead and thirteen wounded.) According to Private Romero, "The Germans were yelling, calling the roll, and cursing Roosevelt," but "their yells turned into screams as our machine guns opened up on them."[51] Once the advance had been contained, Mendez called on Colonel Roy Lindquist for help to push the Germans out of Erria; his 38 I Company troopers were simply not enough to do the work. Lindquist loaned him the regimental reserve, which, together with Mendez's troopers, attacked from north to south through the town. By 0355 hours, 28 December, the village had been cleared and the lines restored.[52]

Surveying the scene at daybreak, Mendez's troopers counted 127 dead Germans. Another 50 were found in front of H Company. It had been a slaughter. Belgian civilians living south of Erria "reported that for three days after the attempt German ambulances were streaming through the village with wounded from the battle."[53]

The fights at Tri-le-Cheslaing and Erria were the most significant the 82nd had in its new defensive position. Those fights and the division's aggressive combat patrols seriously eroded the combat power of the *2nd SS*, *9th SS*, and *62nd Volks Grenadier Divisions*, all of which suspended offensive operations. In fact, so ruthless were some troopers on patrol that Lindquist enjoined his 508th to "save a few [Germans] for identification purposes." Gavin too was impressed with his troopers' performance, especially given his misgivings about the effect the withdrawal would have on their morale. "This has been an experience the like of which I hope I never have again," he wrote in his diary on the last day of 1944. "Our army has a hell of a lot to learn but at present these airborne troopers of this division are making monkeys out of the [G]ermans opposing them. They are better trained and far superior combat soldiers."[54]

The 82nd's stand at Tri-le-Cheslaing and Erria, when combined with the fights at Cheneux, Trois Ponts, the Salm River, Fraiture, Baraque de Fraiture, and Regné contributed significantly to the ruination of Hitler's scheme to break through to the Meuse. With his last remaining mobile formations, or what was left of them, caught in a salient of their own making, the prudent course of action would have been to withdraw. This is what Hitler's generals advised. It was not, however, what Hitler ordered. Instead, he ordered his forces to dig in and wage a battle of attrition.[55]

Having stopped the German drive, the Allies had to decide whether to conduct a full-throated counteroffensive or a more limited counterattack.

Eisenhower and Bradley wanted the former—a massive, coordinated undertaking that would cut off and destroy the Germans in the Ardennes. To this end Bradley forwarded a plan by which Patton's Third Army, staging out of Bastogne (which it relieved on 26 December) would drive north while Hodges's First Army drove south. The aim was to cut the salient at its waist and surround the enemy's mobile formations, most of which were in the western portion of the salient. The German head was in the noose; it was now but a matter of cinching it tight.[56]

The only problem with Bradley's plan was that he did not own First Army; it was still under Montgomery's control, and Montgomery was more interested in stabilizing the Ardennes front so that he could resume his drive north to the Ruhr. Hence, while Eisenhower and Bradley were talking counteroffensive, Montgomery was talking counterattack. The First Army had suffered "severe losses," claimed Montgomery, and therefore it was "useless to pretend that we were going to turn this failure into a great victory."[57] Moreover, Montgomery's reading of ULTRA intercepts led him to believe that the Germans were planning another major push against First Army, and he insisted that it would be better to absorb the blow rather than counterattack. Eisenhower and Bradley, of course, read the same intercepts, and although they acceded that the Germans were *considering* an offensive in the north, all indications were that they lacked the combat power to do so. On 28 December, Eisenhower traveled to 21st Army Group headquarters to get Montgomery to come around. After several hours of discussion, Montgomery finally agreed that if an enemy attack did not materialize by 1 January, he would launch an offensive into the northern half of the Bulge.[58]

Ridgway agreed with Eisenhower and Bradley and sent messages to First Army and 21st Army Group stating that XVIII Airborne Corps "would be prepared to launch a general attack by daylight 31 December 1944, and recommended this action."[59] He could attack with his entire corps, which at the time consisted of the 7th Armored, 82nd Airborne, 30th Infantry, and 75th Infantry Divisions, toward St. Vith. His aim was to regain the ground lost in the withdrawal, secure the St. Vith crossroads, and place the corps in a position from which it could develop the situation southward. When his message met with silence, Ridgway pressed his ideas in face-to-face meetings with Hodges and Montgomery on each of the last four days of 1944. He was continually rebuffed.[60]

Eventually, when the German thrust he predicted did not occur, Montgomery was forced to honor his promise. But he did so halfheartedly. First, he obtained from Eisenhower permission to postpone his attack until 3 January. Then, since Eisenhower had not dictated the specifics of the promised offensive, Montgomery disingenuously issued an attack plan that was limited in scope. Rather than unleashing the Americans under his command in an all-out offensive so they could link up with Patton's Third Army advancing from the south (which had jumped off on 30 December) Montgomery opted for a less ambitious attack. Major General J. Lawton Collins's VII Corps, with two armored and two infantry divisions, was to attack the tip of the salient, advancing west to east while pushing the Germans before it. Ridgway's XVIII Airborne Corps was to advance in a southeasterly direction to protect VII Corps's northern flank, but it was to attack with only one division, the 82nd. Ridgway's other units, the 30th Infantry and 7th Armored, were to remain in place (Montgomery also stripped XVIII Airborne Corps of the 75th Infantry Division, transferring it to VII Corps for the offensive). Finally, to ensure he could exercise tight control over his headstrong, offensively minded American subordinates, Montgomery established a series of phase lines that he used to monitor and manage their rate of advance. Gavin found these control measures "frustrating, indeed infuriating" because Montgomery's frequent orders to halt once a phase line was reached undermined the momentum of the attack and allowed the Germans time to stop, regroup, and dig in.[61] But annihilating the Germans forces in the salient was not on Montgomery's agenda. He sought, instead, to simply usher them out of Belgium, and thereby limit his commitment to the Ardennes so that he could concentrate on his drive to the Ruhr. As Collins likened it, Montgomery was "emptying the sack by pushing from the bottom."[62]

Given the constraints under which he was forced to operate, Gavin's attack plan resembled "a huge stable door . . . being closed." Hinged at Trois Ponts in the east, Gavin's "door" would swing south and east over the same ground from which the 82nd withdrew with an intended end state of the division occupying roughly the same positions it left on Christmas Eve. For the attack Gavin was given a tank and tank destroyer battalion, but the terrain ahead was "definitely . . . infantry country and poor infantry country at that."[63] For this reason he led with three regiments on line—from east to west the 517th, which had been attached to the 82nd for the attack (and to which the independent 551st Parachute Infantry Battalion was further attached), the 505th, and the 325th—with two regiments, the 504th and 508th, following in support while the tanks and tank destroyers were integrated to provide close-in heavy fire support as needed.[64]

The attack jumped off at 0830 hours, 3 January, a cold, foggy day that portended even worse weather ahead. It had been expected that the division would be able to advance to and occupy its former positions in twenty-four hours. It took more than four days. There were three reasons for this:

weather, the frequent phase-line halts, and an enemy that, because of the halts, was time and again afforded the opportunity to fight from behind prepared defenses. It turned out to be one of the 82nd's most difficult attacks of the war.

"It took us 5 days [*sic*] through the worst winter I ever was [in] to gain back that 7 miles," wrote the 325th's Lieutenant Colonel Teddy Sanford to his wife. Advancing in subzero temperatures up and down densely forested hills while wading through snow that in places drifted twelve to fifteen feet deep was exhausting, especially for men who had already endured more than two weeks of winter weather without benefit of warm clothes, shelter, sleep, and food. To ease movement and facilitate control in these conditions, units advanced in columns, the troopers on point breaking trail for those following (point men were generally rotated every thirty minutes, about the longest anyone could bear). "I felt more like a snowplow than a scout," recalled Fred Gladstone of the 3/508th.[65] Furthermore, the troopers carried only what they needed—weapons, ammunition, some rations stuffed in their pockets, and water. Everything else was left behind. The plan was to bring up the gear over one main supply artery, located in the center of the zone of advance, off of which would branch smaller supply lines to the units on the flanks. It fell to Lieutenant Colonel Edwin A. Bedell as commander of the 307th Airborne Engineer Battalion to keep the artery and its branches open. It was a Herculean undertaking, for it was no mere matter of keeping the roads plowed; mines had to be removed, bridges and culverts repaired, and obstacles and debris cleared away and rendered safe from booby traps. The 307th's after-action review supplied some sense of the immensity of this job:

> The existing trails consisted of two ruts down a fire break. These trails were first checked for mines. Next, the trail was cleared of debris and snow by bulldozer. The ruts were filled using picks and shovels. For most of each trail this was sufficient, the ground was frozen. However, springs dotted the hillsides pouring water out at about 50° F. This comparatively warm water kept the ground in the vicinity from freezing causing "soft spots." A log "corduroy" matting was built over these soft spots and on the matting was placed [fabricated metal] matting. These frozen trails, matted when necessary, took all loads including tank destroyers and tanks. The snow on the roads [however,] was creating a problem in the rear areas. The narrow winding road to the division clearing station was becoming impassable. The high crown and the iced top combined threw vehicles off the road into the ditches.[66]

The result was that "all traffic for the three units [in the van] came down . . . one passable road, creating traffic congestion known only to Times Square on Saturday night."[67] Even the rugged four-wheel-drive jeeps could not get through. About the only thing that could negotiate the trails were the new "weasels" that had been loaned the division—small, tracked vehicles with limited cargo space—but there were few of these, and, as always, priority going forward was to ammunition, medical supplies, and water. Anything else, including the packs containing warm and dry clothes, did not get forward until 7 or 8 January, after the division occupied its final objective line. It all added up to one thing for the troopers—misery.[68]

"More than one 'old man' would have given his right arm to have been back in the blistering heat of Oujda," wrote Private Langdon of the first night of the advance, "a night which few of the men would ever forget."[69] Private First Class Virgil M. Goodwin of the 1/505th seconded Langdon:

> I was miserable, cold, and hungry, with feet that had no feeling in them. It was one of the most miserable nights I have ever spent. I dug out the snow and put some pine boughs down. I tried to sleep on that, but it was so cold, you were afraid to go to sleep because you would never wake up. I spent most of the night leaning up against a tree, standing on pine boughs. When you started to go to sleep you would start to fall and wake up; then jog in place to try to get the circulation going in your feet.[70]

Sergeant Albert Tarbell of the 3/504th employed a similar technique. "I found a small tree that I could put my hands on and started to walk around it to keep from freezing during the night. A person can sleep and walk like that."[71]

Given the conditions, evacuating the wounded took on added urgency, for the extreme cold exacerbated the effects of shock and blood loss. Here the 82nd's medics again proved their mettle, taking whatever measures were necessary to get the wounded to ambulances and the ambulances to aid stations. During an attack on a ridgeline up which no vehicles could travel, Private Zeke Zuccala and his fellow medics "formed a daisy chain . . . and passed the wounded from man to man down the hill to the ambulances." Private Romero, wounded during this attack, was wandering in the rear with another wounded trooper looking for help. They came upon some medics using a "weasel" to evacuate people. "These medics were exhausted to the point that I thought they needed to be tended to more than we did. The bottom part of their legs were covered with ice and they were half frozen themselves, but they let us ride while they pushed and pulled." "The medics could never be given enough credit for the job they did," wrote Lieutenant Dick Durkee of the 551st. "They were always on the spot as soon as a man was wounded, regardless of all danger to themselves."[72]

Since their attack at Erria, the Germans fronting the 82nd's lines had been on the defensive, building extensive fortifications that integrated obstacles, wire, mines, and interlocking fields of fire. Although they had redeployed their best troops, those of the *9th SS*, and what remained was "a heterogeneous mass of second rate troops . . . raw, ill-trained recruits, satellite troops and impressed Russians" of the *62nd Volks Grenadier Division,* they were ensconced in well-prepared positions that afforded cover, concealment, and, in most cases, a modicum of warmth and comfort that they defended fiercely.[73] Accordingly, some of the stoutest enemy resistance encountered during the attack occurred on the first day.

The 505th, attacking in the center to take the towns of Fosse (3/505th) and Reharmont (1/505th) and a large farm complex at Noirfontaine (2/505th), met the stiffest resistance. Patrols sent out in advance of the attack reported that none of the objectives were occupied by anything larger than a platoon. Although true for Noirfontaine, reinforced companies backed by plenty of artillery and mortars defended both Fosse and Reharmont, and as a result the 505th suffered "more casualties . . . than in any other single day in its combat history."[74]

Lieutenant Colonel Kaiser's plan for taking Fosse was for G and H Companies to bypass the town and take up positions on high ground to the southwest from which they could provide supporting fire while I Company attacked into the town from the north. All was going well until I Company, led by Captain Archibald A. McPheeters, emerged from a wood two hundred yards from Fosse's outskirts and got pinned down by small arms, machinegun, and artillery fire. McPheeters was killed instantly, as was the only other officer in the company, Lieutenant Richard A. Degenhardt. In response, Kaiser diverted G Company to go to I Company's aid, but before it could get there it too was chewed up by "the most fierce [*sic*] artillery barrage encountered by the 3rd Bn. in this campaign." Meanwhile, H Company's supporting fire from the heights above the town proved ineffective. Fosse had a great many stone buildings that the Germans had turned into strongpoints. Reducing them required tank support, but the only available tanks were with the 1/505th at Reharmont, a little more than a mile to the west, and until Reharmont was taken, no tanks could get through to Fosse. So Kaiser pulled his companies back and waited.[75]

When Reharmont fell around 1100 hours, Ekman sent some tanks to the high ground above Fosse, where they laid down a direct-fire barrage that turned the enemy strongpoints to rubble. Kaiser then ordered an all-out attack. Converging on Fosse from the north and southwest, the 3/505th troopers shot their way into town, firing from the hip, machine gunners cradling their guns in their arms, ammunition belts draped over their shoulders. The attack put the German defenders to rout and precipitated a wholesale collapse. According to Kaiser, everywhere he went in the town "ten or twenty Germans would come out of hiding and surrender." By 1735 hours, Fosse was in American hands. The 3/505th took 150 prisoners, including a battalion commander."[76] But the price had been high. "When the day was finished, so was 'I' Company. Every officer was either dead or wounded and two-thirds of the men were casualties. Sergeant William H. Tucker, waiting at the Regimental Aid Station for his turn to get patched up, saw Colonel Krause [the regimental executive officer] pacing up and down and said to him, 'Well, Colonel, a lot of old boys got it today.' The Colonel never said a word. As he looked at Tucker his eyes filled with tears and he turned away."[77]

The 1/505th's fight for Reharmont had been equally devastating. To get to the town the troopers had first to cross a stream and then climb a forested hill while enduring a rain of German artillery and mortar shells. Furthermore, in the middle of the wood was a crossroad on which were zeroed four 88mm guns. In order to get to the wood on the other side the troopers had to chance their luck and quickness by timing the fire from the guns and then rushing across before the gunners could reload. Private First Class Joseph Tallett of C Company recalled that the volume of fire from the German guns was so heavy that "three or four hours later, when we finally got out of there, it looked like someone had taken a lawn mower and just mowed the trees down. All that was left were tree stumps." On the other side of the crossroads the wood continued for another three hundred yards and then ended abruptly, leaving about a hundred yards of open space between the edge of the wood and Reharmont. Major Talton Long, the battalion commander, ordered C Company to try a quick assault, but every trooper who emerged from the wood was either killed or wounded. Two lieutenants, Walter Haupt and Wilbert H. Robbins, were among the former. A third lieutenant, Edwin H. Barker, who stepped forward to lead C Company once the other officers went down, was shot through with "so many bullet holes in him no one thought he could possibly live [although he did]."[78]

As at Fosse, what was needed was tank support, but the creek's banks were too steep for any vehicle to attempt a crossing, and the only bridge in the area had been partially destroyed. So while Long's troopers held up inside the wood line, engineers worked frantically to shore up the damaged bridge so that it could support the weight of the tanks waiting nearby. Working in freezing water while being pounded by enemy artillery and mortar fire, the engineers finally got the bridge back in commission. Private Tallett, who could see the bridge from his position, remembered that the engineers received some high-level help: "General James M. Gavin . . . was in the water up to his chest assisting the combat engineers to get that bridge back together so the tanks could cross. That was a sight as far as leadership goes. You had to say this was a good place to be with men like Gavin."[79] Once the tanks moved forward to provide direct-fire support, the troopers rushed the town from three sides. Not long thereafter Reharmont belonged to the 1/505th, as did another 120 prisoners. But like its sister battalion at Fosse, the 1/505th suffered grievously, with the heaviest toll being that sustained by C Company, which was down to half strength.[80]

The 325th, attacking on the 505th's right and the 517th, attacking on its left, also had to fight their way forward on the first day. While attacking near Trois Ponts on the extreme left of the division's zone the 2/517th ran into an artillery barrage that killed 14 and wounded another 93 troopers, yet it continued forward and secured its objectives and 137 prisoners by nightfall.[81] The 325th, meanwhile, advanced on the villages of Ancomont and Odrimont, took the high ground above each in turn, and bagged another 233 prisoners while killing an estimated 250 of the enemy.[82]

On day two of the attack, the 82nd consolidated its gains but had to limit its offensive thrusts "pending further advance by VII Corps" on its left.[83] For the 325th this meant taking Ancomont and Odrimont and a third village, Heirlot, all of which fell with relative ease.[84] The most significant action of the second day occurred in the 505th's sector. Sometime that afternoon a German officer inadvertently drove into the 1/505th's lines and was either killed or captured (accounts vary). He had with him orders indicating that an entire battalion was passing near Reharmont, so Major Long organized a counterattack force consisting of his headquarters personnel and one of the accompanying tanks, but the attack stalled when the Germans took out the tank with a *panzerfaust* and withdrew to some high ground to dig in. Returning to Reharmont, Long organized a second counterattack force, this time consisting of three squads and two tanks. Moving up a firebreak that led to the German position, the tanks on the trail and the troopers in skirmish lines to the left and right, this second force fought its way into the midst of the German battalion and precipitated a rout. Private Tallett and his squad were at the edge of the wood, picking off fleeing Germans as they emerged. "It was a turkey shoot," recalled Tallett, "like crushing roaches." All told, Long and his troopers killed or captured 315 Germans without losing a man.[85]

On 5 January the 82nd continued its creeping advance to the southeast, took more prisoners, and gained the high ground overlooking the Salm. The next day, however, it was again halted in place to allow VII Corps to catch up. Finally, at 0630 hours, 7 January, the 82nd kicked off its last attack of the advance, one that would bring it onto and through the last of the positions from which it had withdrawn on Christmas Eve. Gavin committed the entire division.[86]

One of the toughest attacks of the day was by Lieutenant Colonel Mendez's 3/508th on a portion of the long ridge north of Highway N28 known as Thier du Mont. Mendez got the mission because his battalion had occupied this sector before the withdrawal. His plan was to hit the ridgeline at its westernmost point and then swing east to take the German defenses atop it in flank. He had a platoon each of tanks and tank destroyers for the attack, but the terrain was such that he had to lead with infantry. Advancing in column with G Company in the lead, Mendez's troopers were traversing several hundred yards of open ground toward the base of the ridge when the Germans hit them with a devastating artillery and mortar barrage; "observers on the hill were so alert that 3–4 shells were pumped in every time a man in G Co. would move."[87] Mendez pushed his tanks and tank destroyers forward to lend some weight to the attack, but as soon as they appeared, 88s on the ridge above destroyed four of them, and the rest withdrew. The 88s then turned their fire on G Company.

"Those 88s were firing point blank on our men as we advanced," recalled Sergeant Risnes. "I saw a machine gunner whose head was blown off by a direct hit. With his head gone, he took three or four more steps with the gun still on his shoulder, before dropping in the snow."[88] Yet G Company pressed on, urged forward by its commander, Captain Wilde. As the troopers neared the base of the ridge the Germans laid down a smoke screen to hide their positions, but rather than shielding the German positions the wind carried the smoke into the open ground, providing cover for G Company. Captain Wilde seized the opportunity and ordered a charge. Staff Sergeant Frank Sirovica's platoon led the way, taking out three 88s and three machine-gun nests while Sirovica took out a fourth gun by himself.

With G Company amid the German positions, Mendez led his other two companies forward and swept over the ridge. The haul was eight artillery pieces and seventy-five prisoners. But, again, the cost was high, especially in G Company, which started the day with one hundred men but had only thirty-three remaining at day's end. "Tell Lou Mendez and those men that this is the best job I've ever had done for me," Gavin told the 3/508th's executive officer. Mendez, still hurting from his losses, replied that he didn't do it for Gavin, or for the division; he did it for his men.[89]

Attacking on the 3/508th's right was the 2/325th and 2/401st against another ridge, Thier del Preux, which was just west of Thier du Mont. Both battalions got onto the ridge with relative ease, but when two companies from the 2/401st continued the attack down the opposite slope toward the town of Grand Sart, German Panthers, self-propelled guns, and a battalion of infantry ambushed them in a draw. Several nearby Shermans came to their rescue and drove off the German armor, which allowed the 2/401st troopers to regroup and counterattack, during which they took some three hundred prisoners. This cleared the way for elements of 3rd Armored Division to take Grand Sart later that night.[90]

Elsewhere the 504th and 505th closed on the west bank of the Salm. The enemy there was not nearly as numerous as at Thier du Mont and Thier del Preux, although at places the fight was just as tough. One of those places was the village of Mont where Second Platoon, D Company, 2/504th, was "to go as far as possible, occupy the enemy and 'raise as much hell' as possible." On point was Private First Class William Landsedeal. A better man could not have been selected. Just outside Mont, the platoon ran into a German machine-gun nest. Crawling forward under fire, Landsedeal coolly sighted in and killed the gunner. At Mont's outskirts, the platoon was pinned down by snipers. Again Landsedeal crawled forward, got in behind the snipers, and killed them. Further into Mont, the platoon ran into a second machine-gun nest. This time Landsedeal used grenades to silence the gun and then led Second Platoon through Mont, fighting house-to-house all the way. Hit while clearing the last of the buildings, Landsedeal got up and continued his one-man assault until he was hit again, this time in the head, and killed. He was the only man Second Platoon lost that day.[91]

The 3/504th, attacking Petit Halleux, also ran into stout resistance. Here, the role of Landsedeal was played by Lieutenant Ernest Murphy of H Company. About eight hundred yards outside the town, one of two supporting tank destroyers hit a mine and exploded. Six troopers were killed or wounded in the blast. "At this point, enemy machine guns opened up on us and we were pinned to the ground," recalled Technical Sergeant Eddie C. Heibert. "I saw Lieutenant Murphy crawl forward for about 50 yards under a curtain of murderous machine gun fire and call for the remaining TD [tank destroyer] to come up to him. The TD silenced two of the enemy machine guns." Having silenced the enemy guns, Murphy rushed back to the company, grabbed two squads, and led the attack into town. "When we reached the town," recalled Private First Class David E. Ward Jr., "Lieutenant Murphy ran from house to house under heavy enemy fire, firing his Thompson submachine gun and throwing hand grenades, forcing many of the enemy to surrender."[92] Spurred by Murphy's assault, H Company moved into town behind him, cleared it, and took some two hundred prisoners.

The hardest fight in the 505th's zone that day was outside of Goronne, the 2/505th's objective. In the lead was Lieutenant Joe Meyers's D Company. Moving out while it was still quite dark, Meyers led his troopers across an open valley and then uphill through a forest without incident. About halfway through the forest his scouts found some communication wire. Using the wire as a guide, D Company moved another several hundred yards when, suddenly, the scouts ordered a halt and called Meyers forward. The communication wire had led Meyers and his men right into the middle of a German defensive position, but the Germans were all asleep, and were it not for the snoring, the scouts might never have discovered this. Quickly, Meyers organized two teams that he had move from foxhole to foxhole, quietly awakening the Germans, disarming them, and then passing them to the rear. This took some time, but it was better than a fight. Then, explained Meyers, "One of our men was about half asleep on his feet. He looked up, saw a German POW and in his confusion shot him. All hell broke loose."

For the next several hours, Meyers and his troopers fought it out at close range with Germans all around them. To make matters worse, Meyers's radio was not working, so he had no idea where the rest of the battalion was or if help was on the way—that is, until Lieutenant Henry G. Coustillac of the 80th Airborne Antiaircraft Battalion somehow infiltrated through German lines and slipped into D Company's perimeter. Coustillac told Meyers that two Tiger tanks had pinned down the rest of the 2/505th in the valley and had already destroyed several Shermans. But, continued Coustillac, he had brought with him an antitank gun and crew. If Meyers could help get the gun into position for a flank or rear shot at the Tigers, perhaps they could at least scare them off. Minutes later, Meyers saw another "slim figure . . . crawling up the firebreak" to his position. It was Vandervoort. Meyers briefed him on the plan. In order to get the antitank gun to a position from which it would have a shot at the Tigers, D Company would have to gain a point higher up the hill. Vandervoort agreed, adding that he would assist by attacking the Germans fronting D Company in the flank with his battalion staff.

The attack went off as planned, although Coustillac was killed and several others were wounded by a mortar barrage that hit just as D Company gained the high ground. Before Meyers could put the antitank gun into operation, however, he received a call telling him to hold fire because a tank destroyer was en route to his location (apparently, gaining the high ground also enhanced Meyers's radio reception). When it arrived, the captain in command of the tank destroyer was understandably uneasy about his task. The only way to take on a Tiger was from the flank or rear, and then only if you had numbers on your side and you could hit it with several volleys simultaneously. But there was only one tank destroyer and one antitank gun at hand. So the tank destroyer captain organized an unusual attack. First he placed the tank destroyer and the antitank gun in positions from which they both had clear shots at the nearest Tiger. Next he bore-sighted each of the guns to ensure their aim was true. Then he put one man in charge of the antitank gun and took position inside the tank destroyer himself. On his order, the tank destroyer and the antitank fired simultaneously, disabling the nearest Tiger and driving the other away. With the Tigers gone, the German infantry melted away, and Meyers led the battalion into Goronne with nary a fight.[93]

The mortar barrage that killed Coustillac and wounded several D Company troopers also felled one of the division's stalwarts—Ben Vandervoort—who was seriously wounded in the face and upper torso. When Gavin was told, he rushed to the aid station. "When I got there, he was on a stretcher in an ambulance. He had been hit in the eye by a shell fragment and apparently had lost one eye. I felt very bad about it, because just a day or two earlier we had been talking about bringing Vandervoort to division headquarters. He had been commanding a company and then a battalion since Sicily, and the veterans among us believed that the chances of his luck running out were quite high and that we should make a change."[94] "During my thirty years of service," said Meyers years later, "I hope I was able to instill in the young officers who served under me some of the outstanding traits of character and leadership I observed in Colonel Vandervoort. He was a true warrior."[95]

Having regained the positions from which it had withdrawn on Christmas Eve, the division settled into the defense. On 10 January, the green 75th Infantry Division moved up to replace the 82nd (during which time the 517th was detached from the 82nd and attached to the 75th). The relief was completed the next day. Gavin recalled the scene years later:

> And then this poor 75th came up. And that poor division w[a]s green as grass. They were pulling little orange crates and boxes on icy roads in which they had the heavy equipment, cause they got tired of carrying it. And they were all wearing long overcoats, black overshoes. The perfect picture of a you[n]g trainee coming out of Fort Benning and doing things exactly like they're supposed to do. In the meantime, the 82nd was wearing their jump suits, no black over[sh]oes that they should have worn—they wouldn't put them on unless they had to put them on. All carrying their weapons. Tucker, by that time, killed people in long overcoats because the Germans always wore long overcoats. The reason they were pulling their equipment was that the manual says you shouldn't bring troops up under artillery fire in trucks. So that meant within ten miles of the front, there was artillery fire and everybody walk[s]. Christ, by the time they got to their posts, they were dead. They didn't know when to take a chance and when not to. What you do in a situation like that is scoot the trucks up one at a time. In a random pattern. If you lose one, th[a]t's better then having all your men walking ten miles.[96]

During the attack to regain its positions the 82nd captured 2,571 Germans (including 5 battalion commanders) and killed an estimated 2,250 more.[97] The *62nd Volks Grenadier Division* was totally destroyed. But the

82nd also suffered. All told, the Battle of the Bulge cost 255 troopers killed, 1,735 wounded, and 274 missing, while an additional 1,697 troopers incurred some sort of nonbattle casualty, mostly trench foot, frostbite, and other weather-related injuries.[98] Since few replacements had been received since leaving Camps Suippes and Sissonne, many rifle companies were down to half strength or less. Many old-timers were also lost. Besides Vandervoort, Landsedeal, McPheeters, and the others mentioned above, the division's casualty list included the 3/504th's Captain Kappel, who had led his company on the Waal River crossing in Holland—wounded; Captains White and Ogden of the 2/401st—killed (Ogden was awarded the Distinguished Service Cross posthumously for his actions during the advance); Lieutenant Colonel Major and Major Gibson, the commander and executive officer of the 2/325th—wounded; and Captain Olson and Sergeant Wood, Gavin's longtime aide and orderly—wounded.[99] "I lost some very fine officers," mused Gavin in his diary. "There is little doubt in view of our losses of the past few weeks that continued attacks will do the division irreparable harm as an airborne division." Relief, therefore, had come at a propitious time. But it was a relief that, though "almost idyllic," was way too short.[100]

CHAPTER 24

ANOTHER NASTY JOB

The spread of this "easy-end-to-the-war" disease meant that elite units like the airborne divisions—which were willing, able, and trained to fight—would be called on for greater effort and even more suffering. Because of their willingness to fight, these high-quality fighting divisions could be expected to carry the fight to the end. Perhaps the most dangerous period of the war lay ahead for the 82d Airborne Division.

—JOHN D. MCKENZIE, *ON TIME, ON TARGET: THE WORLD WAR II MEMOIR OF A PARATROOPER IN THE 82D AIRBORNE*

"ONE OF THE best places the regiment was ever situated in a combat area" was how almost every trooper described the Belgian village in which he was housed after the division was relieved at the front in early January 1945.[1] Although not really a rest break—the 82nd remained in reserve—the troopers took this opportunity to relax, thaw out, and get clean and healthy.[2]

They spent the first few days off the line cleaning and repairing weapons and equipment, exchanging worn combat uniforms for new ones, and taking long, heated showers in mobile showering tents. Replacements were also brought forward and integrated into the ranks. Yet many units remained seriously short, especially the infantry regiments. Losses had simply been too high. Private First Class "Dutch" Schultz of C Company, 1/505th, had been evacuated early in the campaign because of a respiratory infection. When he reported back to duty it was "to a company that was virtually wiped out. The officers were all gone and we had about thirty men left." Staff Sergeant Chris

Christiansen recalled that when G Company, 3/505th, left the front "we were down to less than fifty percent strength. In the past, we had lost more men killed, but no other place took quite a toll as the Ardennes." Most telling was the loss of so many veterans, men whose battlefield experience had proved invaluable in the past. To make up for this commanders commuted the sentences of troopers in the guardhouse "because it was well known that some of the . . . worst garrison soldiers were also some of [the] best combat men." Yet even with the replacements, jailhouse returnees, and troopers returned from the hospital, some units remained at less than half strength.[3]

Once units were reorganized Gavin instituted a training program that emphasized calisthenics, zeroing weapons, tank-infantry coordination, and methods for taking out pillboxes.[4] The training was none too difficult, however. Physical and mental recuperation was the primary goal. According to a 2/505th report, "The entire battalion did nothing but enjoy themselves for the first time since leaving Camp Sissone and Camp Suippes on the 18th of December."[5] And although there was some recreation available, including movies, band concerts, and Red Cross vans that served coffee and doughnuts, what really reinvigorated the troopers was the welcoming attitude of the Belgian people among whom they lived.[6]

For the first time while in a rear area many troopers lived in private homes, a circumstance prompted by the villagers themselves. Corporal George D. Graves Jr. of the 504th wrote in his journal that "the townspeople were exceptionally cooperative and eager to help; as one housewife put it, 'All Our Doors Are Open to you.'"[7] In Pepinster, Belgium, two battalions of the 325th were, at first, quartered in a textile factory while the third occupied a school. "The buildings were unheated. At the textile factory some of the men immediately gathered up anything made of wood and started a fire on the concrete floor. This filled the building with heavy smoke, making life more miserable. The people of Pepinster began to gather at the entrance to the building and by primitive communications, invited twos, threes and fours of the 325 men to stay in their homes. Gathering up their packs, the men left the building in droves."[8] In return the troopers shared what they could with their hosts. Gifts of canned fruit and coffee obtained from mess halls were the most common offerings. "They hadn't seen real coffee in years," recalled Private Al Langdon, and such gifts "led to many a pleasant evening spent in cozy kitchens, drinking coffee and eating fruit tarts, rice pies, or other delicacies which the womenfolk made." Inevitably, the villagers and their hard-bitten guests grew quite close. "Most of the GIs became so attached to the family they stayed with that they started calling them 'Mama' and 'Papa,'" remembered Captain Wayne Pierce.[9] According to Corporal Graves:

> Before long the Belgian housewives were caring for the men as they would have their own boys. There were few families who didn't have a son who was a prisoner in Germany or who had been killed or wounded in the early part of the war. The mothers took to sewing and mending clothes, making linings for jackets and sleeping bags and all sorts of little helpful things for the men. Some insisted on sharing their food with the men. They went to our movies and entertainments with us and shared our Christmas packages from home. Everyone was so appreciative of the fact that they were out of the snow and cold with a roof over their heads that there was no disciplinary problem whatsoever.[10]

According to Sergeant Albert Tarbell of the 504th, when it was time to return to the front, "the whole family lined up to bid us goodbye. It was a tearful farewell, because I guessed they figured we would never meet again." Just before the 505th left Theux, where it had been quartered, the mayor presented Colonel Ekman with a proclamation: "During their stay in Theux, . . . the soldiers of the 505th Parachute Infantry Regiment, under the command of Colonel William E. Ekman, made the best impression on the inhabitants with whom they were billeted, their behavior being perfect in every way. While they were with us, we got to know them as fine fighting men, whose one wish was to beat and annihilate the Germans, who held us under bondage for four years."[11]

"The rest and recreation afforded the troops at this time did much to bolster their physical and mental well being," recorded a division medical report.[12] But there remained a war to be won and a dangerous enemy that, though rebuffed in the Ardennes, had yet to collapse. It was in how that collapse would be brought about—a debate that consumed the highest reaches of the Allied command—that were sewn the seeds that terminated the 82nd's Belgian idyll.

"The clash," as Air Chief Marshal Tedder characterized the debate, "was between those who favored a continuance of the Ardennes offensive, which Bradley described as a going concern, with great possibilities, and the preparations of a heavy all-out assault in the north."[13] As Bradley saw things, once First and Third Armies linked up, which they did on 16 January, and he regained control of First Army, which occurred the next day, he would be in position to pursue the broken foe all the way to the Rhine. Bradley's concept, which he called his "hurry up" offensive, would ensure "constant and mounting pressure" on the Germans, avoid an operational pause, exploit German expectations that the Allies would reinvigorate Montgomery's Ruhr offensive as their main effort, and put 12th Army Group in a position to unhinge the

German forces facing Montgomery, thereby clearing the way for the overly deliberate field marshal once he did mount his drive. It would also restore American prestige lost in the wake of the Bulge debacle.[14]

Montgomery, on the other hand, was convinced that First and Third Armies were nowhere near strong enough to carry out Bradley's plan. He contended that once the Bulge had been reduced, resources should be directed to his army group so it could close on and cross the Rhine farther north. To this end he presented Eisenhower a two-phased plan, code-named VERITABLE-GRENADE, to be carried out by the Canadian First Army, the British Second Army, and the U.S. Ninth Army (which remained in 21st Army Group's control).[15]

Characteristically, Eisenhower split the difference. Since it would take time for Montgomery to organize VERITABLE-GRENADE, Eisenhower gave Bradley the go-ahead to launch his "hurry up" offensive, with the caveat that if it did not achieve "decisive success," defined as "a quick, broad penetration of the West Wall [Siegfried Line]," he would stop it.[16]

Bradley's scheme of maneuver was to launch First and Third Armies, which were already massed along a twenty-five-mile section of the front that ran through the Ardennes and Eifel (another heavily forested region south of the Ardennes), in a northeasterly direction toward the strategic road center of Euskirchen, Germany, about thirty miles away. This would put them behind the Roer River defenses and across the Erft River, the last major water obstacle before the Rhine. To get there, however, Bradley's forces would first have to breach the Siegfried Line.[17]

The Siegfried Line was a fortified belt counting some 3,000 mutually supporting pillboxes that extended almost the entire length of Germany's western frontier. Touted in Nazi propaganda as impregnable, by 1945 the fortifications were in disrepair, although there were stretches that had been maintained better than others. The area through which Bradley proposed to advance was just such a stretch, consisting of two bands of pillboxes about five miles apart situated behind natural or man-made antitank obstacles, the latter generally being rows of "dragon's teeth," which were "pyramid-shaped reinforced concrete projections" that ranged in height from two and a half feet to almost five feet high. Though in no sense impregnable, the Siegfried Line added significantly to the "defensive potentiality of the terrain along the German border" in that "steel and concrete can lend backbone to a defense, even if the fortifications are outmoded and even if the defenders are old men and cripples."[18]

Since Hodges's First Army was closest to Euskirchen, Bradley made its attack the main effort. Patton's Third Army, positioned farther south, would mount a supporting drive. Hodges, in turn, elected to advance with V Corps on the left (north) and XVIII Airborne Corps on the right while VII Corps followed. Of the two lead corps, Hodges designated XVIII Airborne Corps his main effort.[19]

Because of the heavily forested hills in his attack zone Ridgway asked Hodges for four infantry divisions: the U.S. 1st, 30th, 84th, and 82nd Airborne. "I didn't see much use for an armored division," Ridgway said, "so I begged them [First Army] to give me a fourth infantry division [the 84th] in exchange for the armored division [the 7th], because I had the four [independent] tank battalions, which is all I need in this kind of thing."[20] He would attack with two divisions up front, the 1st in the north and 82nd in the south, while the other divisions followed.[21]

> I led off with the 1st Division and the 82nd, and I don't think any commander ever had such a magnificent experience as to see those two splendid divisions, both veteran outfits at their highest state of combat effectiveness, attacking side by side. It was a joy to see. It was like watching two great racehorses, driving head and head to the finish line. All I had to do was give them their head and then help them with all means at the Corps's disposal, and with everything that I could get from [First] Army.[22]

Although colorful, Ridgway's simile belied the true nature of the advance. Unusually low temperatures and heavy snowfall slowed progress considerably. It took the divisions four days to move the eight to twelve miles that separated their lines of departure from the Siegfried Line, at which point they were still another twenty miles from Euskirchen. Gavin called the advance "the most arduous in the Division's history and, at its end, probably the most bitterly fought."[23]

Gavin had mixed feelings about the advance. "The fact that we were again going to attack I found rather pleasant," he confided to his diary. "The troops are ready also. Sitting around gets rather tiresome. . . . If the war must be finished why then lets [*sic*] at it." But he was also wary of Ridgway's motives. Commanding his first corps in combat, Gavin felt that his boss was "most anxious to committ [*sic*] us," for it would "undoubtedly make his attack a success." He continued, "Ridgway is very ambitious . . . and it is unlikely that he will ever command a ground corps again, at least it doesn't happen every day. I do not believe that he would hesitate to exploit the 82nd to the utmost regardless of the long[-]range harm it may do."[24]

By "long-range harm" Gavin meant the possibility of using the 82nd in another airborne operation. He knew that General Brereton recently told SHAEF that if the airborne divisions were brought up to strength, First Allied Airborne Army could mount four airborne operations in the next eight months. Obviously, this implied refitting the airborne divisions in a rear area, thus making them unavailable for Bradley's offensive. When Brereton proposed this to Hodges and Ridgway, the latter heartily disagreed on the grounds that there was not enough time to plan for another airborne operation, much less four, and a winter airborne assault was simply out of the question anyway.[25] Of course, MARKET-GARDEN proved that it did not take weeks or months to plan for an airborne operation, and there was no reason that one could not be mounted in winter. Gavin knew what was going on but chose to steer clear of the "complexities of ambition and subterfuge involved," yet in the privacy of his diary he railed against Ridgway's machinations: "Ridgway . . . is hell bent on keeping us in his corps and he will never let us go without a direct order from SHAEF. It is all most unfortunate from an A/B [airborne] viewpoint. I believe that SHAEF would promptly act on his recommendation to send us back for A/B preparation if he would so recommend. This he will never do until he is ordered to command an A/B operation."[26]

Despite his facile argument against Brereton's plan, Ridgway did have a valid reason for keeping the 82nd in the fight: specifically, the unsatisfactory performance of other American infantry divisions. The 75th Infantry Division was a case in point. Two days after relieving the 82nd, Ridgway ordered the 75th to attack to complete the destruction of several German divisions around St. Vith, but its attack was so tentative that two German divisions escaped. Ridgway subsequently relieved both the division commander and the division artillery commander.[27] Gavin was disgusted:

> If our infantry would fight this war would be over by now. . . . We all know it and admit it and yet nothing is being done about it. American infantry just simply will not fight. No one wants to get killed, not that anyone else does but at least others will take a chance now and then. Our artillery is wonderful and our air corps not bad. But the regular infantry, terrible. Everyone wants to live to a ripe old age. The sight of a few [G]ermans drives them to their holes. Instead of being imbued with an overwhelming desire to get close to the [G]erman and get him by the throat they want to avoid him if the artillery has not already knocked him flat. This is the fault of our training.[28]

Ridgway's fight to keep the 82nd and Gavin's private doubts about Ridgway's motivations for doing so brings to fine relief a deeper issue—the different manner in which each man approached the war. For Ridgway, it was personal. For Gavin, it was a chance to prove the efficacy of a new way of waging war.

Ridgway always aspired to be, above all else, a combat leader. "The whole training of an officer seeks to accomplish one purpose," he wrote, "to instill in him the ability to take over in battle in a time of crisis." Before the war he had been embarrassed by the great "blot" on his record, "or rather . . . that blank on my record where it said, 'Combat service—None.'" When America entered the war, he set out with single-minded determination to erase that blot. Escaping his War Department posting for the 82nd Infantry Division "meant combat" and "everything I had ever dreamed of since I first stepped out before my company as a scared shavetail down on the Mexican border."[29] When he replaced Bradley as commander of the 82nd, he worked his War Department contacts, including his close personal relationship with General Marshall, to get into the fight as soon as possible, using as ammunition the unique capabilities his newly formed 82nd Airborne Division offered. This remained his modus operandi throughout his tenure with the division. The fact that the 82nd represented a revolutionary means of waging war was of secondary importance to Ridgway; rather, it was exploiting the division's uniqueness to get it and him to the forefront of major combat operations that remained his primary focus. This focus remained the same when he was elevated to corps command, but after MARKET-GARDEN his emphasis shifted. Since it did not appear likely that another large-scale airborne operation would be mounted anytime soon, he set out to establish XVIII Airborne Corps as the preeminent ground combat corps in the theater. To make that happen he needed subordinate units that would attack with élan and aggressiveness. Keeping the 82nd under his command was important, therefore, not because there might be another airborne operation, but because the 82nd's proven battlefield prowess was something that would make XVIII Airborne Corps a favorite of army commanders. Ridgway laid the groundwork for this shift in November 1944 when, in a letter to the War Department, he proposed that "an Airborne Division should fight in the line as an Infantry Combat Division when not being employed as an Airborne Unit" and then went on to propose organizational changes that would give airborne divisions the robustness to act in that capacity.[30]

Though every bit the combat soldier as was Ridgway, Gavin was more fixated on the potentialities of airborne warfare.[31] Like Ridgway, he had railed against his prewar posting at West Point when America entered the war and lobbied aggressively to get into a combat unit. But unlike Ridgway, just any combat unit would not do. Gavin set his sights on the Army's nascent parachute force, the development of which he had been following closely. "The whole concept of vertical envelopment was an exciting one," he declared, offering a "new dimension of tactics" that could revolutionize warfare.[32] And once he was accepted into the airborne fraternity Gavin took up the cause with a vengeance. It was Gavin who was the brains behind the doctrinal publications that guided the use of American airborne units throughout the war, and it was because of him that the 82nd forged new ways to better its performance, experimenting with pathfinders, navigational aids, new parachutes, new ways to insert gliders, and even with dropping mules to use as prime movers for howitzers and mortars. His diaries are replete with passages about new tactics, techniques, and procedures that caught his eye, adopting those that worked and discarding those that proved ineffectual, but never shying from the effort. "Working with a new weapon as we are we are certain to make mistakes and many of them. When the time comes in this airborne effort that we are not making mistakes then the time has come when we are ceasing to improve and grow. We should always be overreaching and extending, probing into the future, groping into the black uncertain beyond. Only so do we grow." Gavin never lost the "lasting and firm faith in the efficacy of airborne troops as a means of waging war."[33] Just as Heinz Guderian, Erwin Rommel, and George Patton had demonstrated the deadly potentialities of armored warfare, so did Gavin see in airborne units a means to bring decisiveness to the battlefield.

Both men, of course, shared a determination to defeat the enemy. But while Gavin felt that using airborne troops in the manner for which they were designed was the best way to bring this about—a few weeks later, while the 82nd was being used as standard infantry he would write, "the [G]erman army is ripe for airborne attack. They could be taken apart now"—Ridgway maintained that the division was too good a fighting unit to be taken out of the line to prepare for an eventuality that might not occur.[34] Ultimately, Ridgway's view prevailed, so on 26 and 27 January Gavin's troopers left the comfort of their Belgian homes and trucked to attack positions just northeast of St. Vith.[35]

The XVIII Airborne Corps jumped off in the early morning hours of 28 January. Mirroring Ridgway's scheme of maneuver, Gavin attacked with two regiments abreast—the 325th on the left (north) and the 504th on the right—with the 505th and 508th following each, respectively. In order to gain surprise, Ridgway ordered that the attack commence without a preparatory artillery barrage. His ploy was wildly successful. "The 1st Infantry Division ran over German positions where individuals were found asleep," recorded a Corps report, "and the 82d Airborne Division caught the enemy at breakfast." The result was that "despite the cold and waist[-]deep snow, which necessitated changing the lead man every forty (40) to fifty (50) yards, the initial assault proceeded rapidly."[36]

Rapidly would not have been the adverb that came most readily to mind for the troopers conducting the attack. True, the temperature was cold and the snow deep, and point men had to be rotated lest they keel over from exhaustion from breaking trail, but the sterile language of the corps report does not do justice to the difficulties encountered during Bradley's "hurry up" offensive. "The weather was a more severe handicap than the enemy during the initial stages of the attack," remembered Ekman. Tucker called it "the most back[-]breaking trek" ever, a serious statement from a man who had experienced combat in the mountains of Italy. Lieutenant Virgil Carmichael of the 3/504th said it was so cold that water froze solid in canteens. According to Gavin, the 325th's advance "was the most difficult task ever accomplished by the regiment." The terrain, wrote Sergeant Bill Lord, was "about the toughest to be found anywhere."[37]

Given the conditions, it was fortunate that the German defenses fronting the 82nd were, at first, more a muddle of scattered strongpoints than an organized defensive line. In fact, so muddled and scattered were the defenses that Colonel Charles Billingslea's 325th troopers surprised several isolated pockets of Germans even before the regiment got to its start point. The prisoners, who were both relieved at being out of the war and disgruntled over their superiors' lack of concern for their welfare, repaid their former masters by suggesting several attack routes that would avoid the German defenses. Billingslea adjusted his line of march accordingly, and the prisoners' suggestions proved true. Following the new routes, by nightfall the 325th advanced approximately five miles to some high ground just above the town of Wereth, Belgium, without significant enemy contact (the 325th took the town the next day).[38]

The 504th's attack on the first day was equally uneventful, at least until the very end. Moving in column with the 3/504th in the lead, it took Tucker's troopers twelve hours to advance approximately six miles to a wooded ridge just north of Herresbach, Belgium. Along the way contact had been light. Once on the ridge Tucker's plan was to consolidate for the night, bring up the 2/504th to a position west of Herresbach, and then attack the town from two directions the next morning. The weather forced a change of plan. According to Lieutenant Carmichael, "[Lieutenant Colonel] Cook ordered the companies to set up a defensive position. Some of the officers came to the CP and a general discussion followed to the effect that there was a town down there—*with houses*—and here we were freezing our asses off in the woods." So Cook radioed Tucker and asked permission to have a go at Herresbach. Tucker agreed. Cook then turned to Lieutenant Jim Megellas of H Company and ordered him to "take those two cans [either tanks or tank destroyers that were supporting the 3/504th; accounts differ] and get into that town."[39]

A road ran from the top of the ridge and then across seven hundred yards of treeless plain straight into Herresbach. With Megellas's platoon leading in skirmish formation on either side of the road, Lieutenant "Rivers" LaRiviere's platoon following, and the two armored vehicles driving straight down the road (which for some reason had been plowed), H Company moved out just after dark. About three hundred yards from the edge of town they ran into

German infantry marching in the middle of the road in the opposite direction. Following Megellas's lead the H Company troopers waded into the German column, firing from the hip at point-blank range.[40] The two armored vehicles fired their machine guns so furiously into the enemy mass, they turned "red hot—glowing in the semi-darkness." "It was a killing frenzy unlike any other I experienced in the war," recalled Megellas. "We were shooting everything in sight."[41] Ten minutes later the fight was over. An entire infantry battalion had been destroyed, more than 100 enemy dead were later found in the field, and another 180 were taken prisoner. Not a single American was hit. It was, said Lieutenant Colonel Edward Wellems, "the perfect battle."[42]

Yet it was not over. Herresbach still had to be taken. Leaving the slaughtered remnants of the German column on the road for the rest of the battalion to mop up, Megellas led his troopers to the edge of town and regrouped. Suddenly, a Panther tank emerged from the center of town headed straight at them. Since none of the supporting American armored vehicles were yet in position to fire on the Panther, Megellas charged the tank, disabled it with a Gammon grenade, and then climbed on top and finished the crew with a fragmentation grenade down the top hatch. With the Panther out of commission, Megellas orchestrated an attack through the rest of Herresbach, using his armor (which had belatedly arrived on the scene) as heavy direct-fire support.[43] The German defenders were so stunned by the swiftness of the American assault that they surrendered in droves. Sergeant H. Donald Zimmerman recalled that it was as if "every man was fighting his own war [by] rounding up prisoners going house to house." Privates Harold Sullivan and Rufus Sampson, acting together, rounded up 25 Germans in one building alone.[44]

With Herresbach firmly in hand by 1900 hours, along with 100 or so prisoners, Tucker moved up his other two battalions and enclosed the town in regimental-size perimeter. Shortly thereafter, the Germans counterattacked. They made three separate attempts to take back Herresbach and were repulsed each time. The next morning, with help from some tanks that had come up, Tucker moved to strengthen his position by clearing the high ground to the south. Again it fell to H Company to lead the way, only this time it was Lieutenant LaRiviere's platoon in the van while Megellas's platoon followed. Better prepared than were their comrades the night before, the German defenders put up more of a fight, but LaRiviere and Megellas pressed the attack and eventually cleared the high ground, adding another 76 prisoners to the 504th's haul at a cost of 12 casualties.[45]

On day two of the advance, Gavin passed the 505th and 508th through the 325th and 504th, respectively. The 505th's objective was a north-south road some three miles northeast of Wereth. Despite scant resistance, it took Ekman's troopers all day to get there. According to Major William Carpenter, who took command of the 2/505th after Vandervoort's wounding, his troopers, who were leading the advance, "were now beginning to feel the lack of rations and the crudeness of the roads" and were exhausted. "By this time the entire Bn. was out on their feet [because of] the continuous marching and state of mental alertness that had to be maintained," added Lieutenant Colonel James Kaiser. With no clear idea about where they were in the trackless forests, the troopers simply followed a route of march selected for them by spotter aircraft flying overhead. These small, highly maneuverable two-seaters buzzed the regimental column and dropped yellow streamers to which notes were attached with instructions like "I will fly in the direction you will find Germans."[46] In this manner the 505th reached its objective just before dark, took another 50 prisoners, and suffered no casualties.[47]

Meanwhile, the 508th attacked in two separate battalion columns to take the towns of Medendorf (2/508th) and Holzheim (1/508th), some two to two and a half miles northeast of Herresbach. The former fell against light resistance by noon.[48] Holzheim, which housed a much larger enemy garrison, was not as easily taken. Advancing on the town from two directions simultaneously, the 1/508th troopers faced concentrated small arms and machine-gun fire from Germans defending from inside. Lieutenant Colonel Shields Warren countered with artillery and mortar fire, hoping to drive the defenders from their guns long enough for his troopers to close with and destroy them. Under the conditions, this was unusual. "An interesting characteristic of the winter war [was that] neither side wanted to destroy the villages with artillery fire, since invariably they used them for shelter. They would encircle them, dig out the occupants with rifles and bayonets, and do everything they could to rout out the enemy so as to have the houses for their own use later."[49] Perhaps because the Germans did not expect it either, Warren's barrage worked, and within minutes Holzheim, some 90 prisoners, and five artillery pieces were his.[50]

Clearing Holzheim meant, among other things, evacuating the prisoners to the rear, most of which were captured by Sergeant Bill Traband and two other troopers from C Company. Traband turned the prisoners over to Private Merrel Arthur and his squad whose job it was to escort them to the rear. "We proceeded to march the prisoners out of town for about 300 yards or so when we came upon [First Sergeant Leonard] Funk and [Headquarters] platoon of about 3 or 4 men," recounted Arthur.

> Here we stopped and made the prisoners sit on the ground out of observation of the Germans, who were shelling us at the time. After sitting on the ground for awhile, all of a sudden the prisoners jumped up, threw their arms in the air and said, "Heil Hitler." I poked one with my bayonet and said "Sit down." He replied "Nein." I stepped around the column and looked down

> the row to see what the commotion was all about. I saw men dressed in snowcapes [*sic*] talking and yelling to our guards there [both sides were wearing snow capes, some of which had been improvised from white sheets, making identification of friend and foe difficult]. The impression I had was that it was some Belgium [*sic*] resistance fighters giving us a hard time on what to do with the prisoners, but instead they were trying to make our guards surrender.[51]

What happened was that another group of Germans was escorting American prisoners back to their rear area and, thinking that Holzheim was still in German hands, made their way there. When they came upon German prisoners under American guard, the officer in charge of the German escorts, speaking perfect English and outfitted in a snow cape that masked his identify, bluffed his way past the American guards, disarmed them, and was in the process of rearming his comrades when Funk arrived on the scene. "My first thought," recalled Arthur, "was, mess with Funk fellow and you're dead, and how true it was."[52]

Having heard the commotion, Funk was walking over to investigate when he rounded a building and found himself face-to-face with the German officer, who stuck his Luger in Funk's belly and demanded that he surrender. "I've got to admit that German had 'balls' and big ones," wrote Arthur, "but they weren't big enough when he met Funk." According to Funk, "When the German officer stuck that Luger in my belly, the thought flashed through my mind that I had always told the troops that I would never surrender as long as I had a functioning weapon and trigger finger. As I started to take the sub-Thompson [*sic*] off my shoulder, the German relaxed the pistol against my belly and reached out his other hand to take my weapon. At that moment, I went into fast action, whipped that gun around and cut him down before he could react."[53] After killing the officer, Funk reloaded and took on the rest of the armed Germans. Other members of the headquarters section also came running up, and within minutes Funk and his troopers had the situation under control. About twenty-one Germans were killed, many more were wounded, and the rest were rounded up. None escaped. For his actions, Leonard Funk was awarded the Medal of Honor, making him the most highly decorated 82nd Airborne Division trooper of the war (he had already received the Silver Star for actions in Normandy and the Distinguished Service Cross for his heroism in Holland).[54]

It took the division two more days to close on the Siegfried Line, hampered more by the snow and weather than by German resistance. The 508th, which remained in the van in the southern part of the division zone, advanced two miles and took Lanzerath and some high ground northeast of the town on 30 January. On 31 January it pushed on to another piece of high ground overlooking the town of Losheim, about a mile due east of Lanzerath, where it overran a company of infantry in a railroad defile. By the end of the day Lindquist's troopers were settled into defensive positions overlooking the westernmost outposts of the Siegfried Line.[55]

In the north, the 325th leapfrogged past the 505th to attack a second railroad defile some three to four miles to the northeast. It reached its objective by midafternoon on 30 January against practically no resistance. Despite the snow it had been able to advance swiftly, so swiftly in fact that E Company, 2/325th, almost captured the *5th Parachute Regiment*'s command group, overrunning the site just fifteen minutes after the commander and his staff departed.[56]

On 31 January, it was the 505th's turn to spearhead the advance in the north, so it passed through the 325th en route to its objective, the town of Losheimergraben, a major road and railroad junction about a mile beyond the 325th's positions. Forced to leave the supporting armor behind because it could not cross over the railroad defile the 325th had taken the day before, the 505th advanced in column with the 1/505th in the lead. All went well until the outskirts of Losheimergraben, where a force of about a hundred Germans supported by self-propelled guns took the 1/505th under fire. Lieutenant Colonel Talton Long, the 1/505th commander, immediately deployed the battalion into attack formation and charged Losheimergraben with all three companies. Following a short yet sharp firefight, the town was Long's. Fifty enemy dead were counted. Fifty more were made prisoner. Friendly casualties were relatively light, except in A Company, which had attacked the town head-on.

Following behind the 1/505th, the 2/505th skirted the northern edge of Losheimergraben to take a road intersection 4,000 yards to the northeast. It, too, met stiff resistance from infantry and self-propelled guns, but swept through the Germans with the help of some tanks that finally found a way across the defile. By morning, 1 February, the 505th had consolidated its positions and tied in with the 1st Infantry Division to its north and the 508th to its south. Occupying the most advanced positions in the 82nd's zone, it was firmly entrenched inside Germany and squarely abutting the Siegfried Line, although this seems to have escaped the Germans manning the defenses. "The fact that the presence of the battalion was unknown was confirmed . . . when the sentries on the Siegfried Line never looked in their direction."[57]

The first of February was a day of decision. Although the 1st Infantry and 82nd Airborne Divisions had closed to positions overlooking the Siegfried Line, and had arguably advanced as fast as possible under the conditions, they had not attained the "quick, broad penetration of the West Wall" by which Eisenhower defined "decisive success," so, as he said he would, Eisenhower canceled Bradley's drive and ordered him to start shifting troops to Simpson's Ninth Army in preparation for VERITABLE-GRENADE. Bradley's 12th Army Group, meanwhile, was to assume an "aggressive defense."[58]

When he canceled Bradley's offensive Eisenhower clearly indicated that VERITABLE-GRENADE was to be the main effort, but Bradley was not content to sit back and watch. In his mind, "aggressive defense" could mean just about anything "short of another major offensive," and Bradley chose to interpret it "as an order to 'keep moving' toward the Rhine with a low profile." For XVIII Airborne Corps and the 1st Infantry and 82nd Airborne Divisions, this portended an attack into "the densest concentration of pillboxes in this part of the West Wall" that, though limited in intent, was anything but limited in effect.[59] For the 82nd, it turned out to be one of the most costly attacks of the advance.[60]

Knowing what he was up against, Gavin sought to mitigate the tactical advantages that accrued to the Germans defending from within their fortifications by concentrating his attack on a narrow front, using mass to overcome the power of the defensive. To do this, he would first concentrate three of his regiments—the 325th, 504th, and 505th—opposite a five-mile section of the Siegfried Line. He would then attack with all three regiments simultaneously, jumping off in the early morning when it was hoped the enemy would be least alert. If all went well, a weak spot would be found and exploited before the Germans could plug the hole.

Although simple in concept, attacking with three regiments through such a narrow corridor was a tricky proposition. The first step, of course, was to move each regiment to its respective attack position without alerting the enemy. This was accomplished on 1 February. With the 505th and 508th manning the division's forwardmost positions providing a shield, Gavin moved the 325th and 504th to their attack positions directly behind the 505th. Step two was implementing a scheme of maneuver that would keep the attacking regiments from tripping over one another. Gavin did this by assigning each regiment a slightly different direction of attack (the 508th and an attached cavalry squadron were to remain on the defensive in the southern part of the 82nd's zone). The 505th, already up front, was to attack in a southeasterly direction. The 504th was to follow the 505th and attack due east into the Gerolstein Forest. Following the 504th, the 325th was to attack in a northeasterly direction to seize the towns of Neuhof and Udenbreth. Jump-off time was 0400 hours, 2 February.[61] "I prayed that it would not be as rough as we all knew it would be," wrote Corporal Graves.[62] His prayers were not answered.

Of the three attacking regiments, the 505th had the easiest time taking its objectives, though not without a fight. Colonel Ekman's plan was to advance with two battalions abreast—the 1/505th on the right and 3/505th on the left—while the 2/505th followed, but congestion at the line of departure delayed the 3/505th and forced Ekman to modify his plan: Instead of advancing abreast, the two lead battalions advanced in echelon with the 1/505th to the right front and the 3/505th to the left rear. Moreover, although it jumped off several hours after the 1/505th, because of the southeasterly orientation of the attack, the 3/505th was actually closer to the Siegfried Line and thus made first contact when G Company stumbled upon a nest of pillboxes. Quick thinking by Lieutenant Colonel Kaiser, who led I Company on a flanking attack, unhinged the German defenses, which in turn freed up both G and I Companies to fight through and clear the pillboxes. By midafternoon, the 3/505th could account for six pillboxes destroyed and sixty prisoners. Meanwhile, the 1/505th's advance had been relatively uneventful, and by day's end Ekman's troopers were consolidated and dug in some 4,000 yards into the Siegfried Line.[63]

Attacking due east into the "somber, forbidding shadows of Forst Gerolstein," Tucker's 504th encountered much stiffer resistance than did Ekman's 505th.[64] Jumping off at dawn with the 2/504th in the van, the regiment made good progress until about 0930 hours when Captain Herbert H. Norman's E Company, 2/504th, which was leading the column, got pinned down in an open field by fire from several camouflaged pillboxes. Moving forward to assess the situation, Lieutenant Colonel Warren saw that extracting E Company was going to be difficult. The textbook response was to call in artillery and withdraw under cover of the barrage, but with only a few score yards separating the German pillboxes from the exposed E Company troopers, this was not an option; an errant artillery round would do more harm than good. So instead, Warren called forward all his bazooka gunners (many of whom were armed with *panzerfausts*), machine gunners, and mortar crews with the intent of having them provide suppressive fire to keep the enemy's head down long enough to get E Company off the deadly field. Time was of the essence; E Company was steadily taking casualties, including Captain Norman, who was fatally wounded.

With Norman down, Lieutenant John Thompson took over E Company. His first act in command was to request mine detectors, for in addition to being pinned down E Company was stuck in a minefield. Colonel Tucker denied Thompson's request. There was no time to wait for the mine detectors to come forward, Tucker countered, and the deep snow should cushion most of the mines anyway. (According to a regimental report, "Mines and booby traps were encountered by the thousands, yet [fortunately] only a small percentage of those actually disturbed were detonated" because of corrosion caused by prolonged exposure to the elements.)[65] Meanwhile, Lieutenant William J. Sweet's F Company had come forward, and with the situation critical—the

Germans were by that time plastering the entire column with artillery—Warren told Sweet to find some way to get among the pillboxes to clear them out. Sweet, in turn, asked one of his most experienced platoon leaders, Stuart McCash, for ideas.

Surveying the situation, McCash came up with a bold plan. He would lead his Second Platoon forward in a charge through the heavily mined open area toward a draw that, he believed, would put him and his troopers under the guns in the pillboxes. Covering Second Platoon would be the bazookas, machine guns, and mortars Warren had assembled that were to concentrate their fire on the pillboxes fronting the area over which McCash and his troopers would charge. Timing was critical. Since there was little room to maneuver, Warren would have to cease the suppressive fire before McCash could charge. If timed right, McCash and Second Platoon would be in the draw before the Germans could recover. If the timing was off, McCash and his troopers might very well suffer the same fate as E Company. But there were no other options.

For twenty minutes Warren's bazookas, machine guns, and mortars peppered the designated pillboxes. Then, as suddenly as it started, the firing ceased. Immediately, McCash and his troopers charged across the open field, oblivious to the mines and through a hail of enemy fire that Wellems thought was "the best he had seen since entering France and the Continent." But the tactic worked. McCash and most of his men got to the draw and were under the enemy guns. Moving carefully, for the draw, too, was mined, McCash's troopers took out two pillboxes in an assault that "was S.O.P. out of the Infantry Journal."[66] With that the enemy fire slackened, and Thompson led what remained of E Company into the breach created by McCash's platoon. Warren followed with the rest of the battalion. Once in the midst of the German defenses the troopers fanned out. Four more pillboxes fell, after which the remaining Germans surrendered. The 2/504th lost seven officers and thirty-eighty troopers either dead or wounded, and the final objective was still about a mile away.[67]

Still in the lead, the 2/504th plunged deeper into the Gerolstein Forest. By midafternoon it was atop some high ground just south of its objective when it ran into two German infantry battalions moving forward to plug the gap the 2/504th just created. Lieutenant Martin Middleton, the lead platoon leader, halted his troopers, pulled in his flanks, and formed a defensive glacis in the Germans' path. The rest of the battalion, falling in on Middleton's left and right, extended and bolstered the line. For three hours the Germans tried battering their way through the 2/504th until, spent, they withdrew into the forest. During the fight Lieutenant Middleton was "wounded so many times he looked like a sieve" but remained at his post until, wounded a fifth time, he was evacuated.[68]

Following the German withdrawal Warren resumed his advance and secured his objective, a piece of high ground overlooking one of several small rivers inside the Gerolstein Forest. Tucker then hurried forward his other two battalions, swinging the 1/504th slightly south to tie in with the 2/504th's right flank while the 3/504th took up position to its north. By nightfall the regiment was dug in, ready to defend.

The 504th had torn a hole 6,000 yards deep and 2,000 to 3,000 yards wide in the West Wall and was farther east than any other unit in First Army, which made it the focal point of fierce counterattacks for several days. Again and again the Germans hurled themselves at Tucker's paratroopers, yet the 504th held, aided in no small measure by the 376th Parachute Field Artillery Battalion, which fired more than 2,000 rounds in support.[69] During one attack, an enemy battalion wandered blindly into the 2/504th's positions. Warren's troopers let it get "dangerously close and then opened up with artillery, 81mm and 60mm mortars, small arms and bazookas" and wiped it out.[70] Only once did the Germans penetrate Tucker's defenses. On the morning of 4 February, they launched an unusually heavy attack against the 1/504th and drove it back, but it was a short-lived gain. Lieutenant Colonel Willard Harrison rallied his troopers, counterattacked, and restored the original line. Thus ended the last significant fight in the forest, and from the appearance of the enemy prisoners, "a shivering, miserable looking lot," Germany was on its last legs.[71] Yet when fighting from prepared positions, they could still be a daunting foe, as the 325th found out during its attack to the north.[72]

Irrespective of the quality of the defenders, the 325th's mission had the makings of a nightmare. Not only would it have to smash through the Siegfried Line, but it also had to clear the towns of Neuhof and Udenbreth, both of which lay squarely *within* the Siegfried Line defenses, and then continue its advance to a piece of high ground several hundred yards farther east. To accomplish this mission, Billingslea planned to mass his regiment against one of the towns, seize and clear it, and then use the first town as a base from which to attack the second. Once the second town was in hand, he would then move on the high ground. Attacking both towns simultaneously was out of the question. The 325th was seriously under strength, and Billingslea could not risk attenuating what little combat power he could muster.

The regiment would attack in a column. Lieutenant Colonel Gerard's 1/325th would lead and take the smaller town of Neuhof. Lieutenant Colonel Leahy's 2/401st would follow, pass through Neuhof, and then turn north to take Udenbreth. Lieutenant Colonel Ostberg's 2/325th would be Billingslea's reserve. Accompanying the infantry would be engineers from B Company, 307th Engineers, who would be responsible for reducing any obstacles. Billingslea also had attached an entire tank battalion and a company of tank destroyers for the attack. Jump-off time was set for 0400 hours, 2 February, following a ten-minute artillery bombardment.[73]

There was no doubt that the 325th had drawn the toughest assignment, yet no one was quite sure how strong the defenses around Neuhof and Udenbreth were. Reports were conflicting. According to Lieutenant Colonel Gerard, for example, reconnaissance patrols "reported no enemy in pillboxes in the vicinity of Neuhof." Lieutenant Colonel Leahy recalled much the same thing: "On the 1st [of] February, the Battalion sent patrols into the Siegfried Line which was reported to be lightly held." However, the regimental after-action report intimated that the patrol reports painted an inaccurate picture of the German defenses in the area through which the 325th would be attacking because none of the patrols got any closer to the objective area than "the southern edge of Neuhof."[74] Moreover, pillboxes and what appeared to be connecting trenches were clearly visible outside of Neuhof from the 1/325th's attack position, which was in a wood about 1,000 yards away. Doubtless because his battalion was to lead the attack, Gerard opted to probe the German defenses to see what, if anything, they held, so, on the afternoon of 1 February, he sent Lieutenant Harry Teras's Third Platoon, C Company, 1/325th, forward to find out.

To get to the pillboxes, Teras's platoon had to cross a treeless meadow that sloped down from the battalion attack position and then rose up to the outskirts of the village. At the bottom of the meadow was an intermittent stream. Just beyond the stream were rows of dragon's teeth behind which were pillboxes. Jumping off following a short artillery barrage, Teras and his troopers got no farther than the meadow when, according to Private First Class Raymon Hook, another C Company trooper who was watching from inside the wood, they discovered that "the Germans were there." "They waited until the patrol was well out in the open. They let loose with such a withering fire that many men were wounded and one killed. . . . There was no cover out there, only a few sparse and dry bushes without leaves. Some men got back to the woods, but others lay in the snow, not moving until darkness fell, and then they crawled back to the woods, if their wounds permitted. The able bodied of the 3rd Platoon went back out after dark to bring in the seriously wounded." As Gerard remarked dryly, "Obviously the pillboxes on the [G]erman positions were occupied and Neuhof was strongly defended." Raymon Hook was not as blithe. "The regimental staff had gotten their answer! The Siegfried Line was indeed manned and fully alert to our presence." The cost of the probe was one killed and four wounded, including Lieutenant Teras. It was obvious that "the next day's operation would be a difficult and hazardous one."[75]

Given what he learned from Teras's probe, Gerard's plan was to advance in attack formation—two companies forward and one in reserve—on either side of a dirt road that, in the dark, would help guide the battalion to its objective since it ran due east from the attack position across the meadow and into the southern edge of Neuhof. To mitigate the effect of enemy fire from the pillboxes the two lead companies—A Company to the left of the road and B Company to the right—were to advance in dispersed skirmish formation. Arrayed at the edge of the wood to provide supporting fire were a company of tanks and F Battery, 80th Airborne Antiaircraft Battalion's .50-caliber machine guns. Indirect fire support would be provided by the battalion's mortars. Finally, the tank destroyers were to be ready to rush forward in the event any German tanks made an appearance.[76]

At 0350 hours, 2 February, the 320th Glider Field Artillery Battalion commenced firing a high-explosive barrage on the German defenses outside Neuhof. Although an impressive sight, not everyone was heartened by the spectacle. "Of course, we alerted every German within twenty miles with a terrific barrage, which was only a waste of ammunition, because none of those shells could penetrate one of those pillboxes," recalled Captain James Helmer, commander of A Company, 1/325th. Ten minutes later the attack jumped off. It took about thirty minutes for the troopers to traverse the meadow and cross the stream, which was done without a shot being fired. Once across the stream and into the dragon's teeth on the upward slope they started receiving fire from pillboxes at the edge of town, but return fire from the supporting tanks and heavy machine guns silenced them. Continuing on, the troopers picked their way through the dragon's teeth, carefully avoiding the many mines (according to Gerard, "the [G]ermans had neglected to activate much of the AP [antipersonnel] minefield," but it is more likely the mines failed because of corrosion).[77] At 0455 hours, Captain Helmer's A Company, which appears to have been advancing faster than B Company, captured a pillbox. Inside were four Germans, all of whom were taken prisoner. Fifteen minutes later, all hell broke loose.[78]

"At 0510 the attacking companies were hit by a tremendous volume of small arms, mortar, SP [self-propelled gun] and artillery fire," remembered Gerard. "White phosphorus shells from enemy weapons illuminated the battle scene. The volume of fire pinned most of the elements of the attacking companies in the dragons [*sic*] teeth and on the open slopes of the hill." Immediately, the troopers went to ground. Those lucky enough to survive the opening fusillade continued the attack on their bellies. "We crawled and crawled most of the morning," recalled Private First Class Clinton Riddle of

B Company. "Many of our men had been killed or wounded. They were being hit all around me."[79] Having had more than enough time to verify their kill zones, clear their fields of fire, and zero their weapons, the Germans delivered devastatingly accurate fire that hit the companies from the front and both flanks.[80] "The sound of German machine guns seemed to be everywhere," thought Private First Class Leonard T. O'Brien of C Company, who, along with the rest of his company, was still inside the wood and could not see what was going on in the meadow. "Men and tanks kept pouring down the road . . . and still the fighting did not seem to diminish or move farther away. What was happening up ahead?"[81]

With dawn approaching it was imperative that something be done lest A and B Companies be caught in the open in the light of day and annihilated. Taking a chance that the Germans had no antitank weapons in the area, Gerard ordered a platoon of tanks forward to take out the strongpoints that had his troopers pinned down. Moving rapidly while firing at everything in sight, the tanks forced the Germans' heads down long enough for A Company to take out two more pillboxes and get into the German trench line. Other troopers used a bazooka to destroy a large iron gate barring the road so that the tanks could continue past the dragon's teeth, but no sooner had the lead tank moved past the gate when it was hit by three antitank rounds. Seeing this, the other tanks withdrew. "The sight of the tanks pulling back had a definite lowering effect on the infantry morale," recalled Gerard, who ordered one of the tank company commanders to move the rest of his company forward "regardless of loss." Gerard also sent forward a platoon from C Company. So reinforced, A and B Companies got through the dragon's teeth, the trench line, and the pillboxes and gained a toehold in the southern part of Neuhof.[82]

Despite having made it to Neuhof, A and B Companies were in a fix. The ground between the town and the wood was still under heavy fire, effectively isolating them from the rest of the regiment. In addition, their flanks were exposed and their ranks depleted. "When we moved out of our forest that morning to begin the attack," recalled Captain Helmer, "Company A had a total of one hundred one officers and men. When we finally regrouped [in Neuhof] we had thirty-three men left." Even harder hit was B Company, which arrived in Neuhof with but seventeen effectives.[83]

To protect the exposed flank, Gerard moved the rest of C Company forward. Private O'Brien entered the meadow and was met with "an awesome sight. . . . The road was being covered by at least two Jerry machine guns. The road was strewn with bodies of both Americans and Germans in all manner of dismemberment. Some had been run over by tanks." According to Private

First Class Hook, "When we, as the reserve, moved up into the town at last, there was still much fighting. On our way down the same road . . . I saw many casualties. One was a lieutenant who had been hit directly on the lieutenant's bar on the front of his helmet. A shocking sight, as was the high number of dead along this road." Billingslea, who along with Gavin was with the 1/325th at Neuhof, positioned C Company in some pillboxes with orders to guard the flank and "not let the Krauts get back in."[84]

Billingslea next ordered Leahy's 2/401st forward so that it could leapfrog through the 1/325th and attack Udenbreth. Billingslea had hoped to do this while it was still dark, but it had taken the 1/325th more than two hours to fight its way into Neuhof, and a breakdown in communications delayed further the commitment of the 2/401st. This meant that Leahy's troopers would have to traverse the deadly meadow in daylight. Charging across the meadow followed by another tank company that was "blasting everything and anything they saw," the 2/401st got to Neuhof only to discover that the northern half of town was still in enemy hands and would have to be cleared before it could move on Udenbreth.[85] This was a "critical moment" because "it was apparent that the side that could bring up supporting fire would gain the advantage."[86] Were the Germans to react first, they could seal off Neuhof and contain the breach in the Siegfried Line. To prevent this, Billingslea called forward his last battalion and all his tanks and tank destroyers.

Advancing across the exposed meadow, the 2/325th troopers moved through the same heavy fire that those before them experienced. Sometime during the move the battalion commander, Lieutenant Colonel Ostberg, climbed aboard a tank to direct its fire. A German round decapitated him. Major Richard M. Gibson, the executive officer, took over and led the battalion to the southwestern edge of Neuhof where it was ordered to wait until the rest of the town was cleared. The day before the attack Lieutenant Walter G. Frauenheim had taken command of F Company, 2/325th, from the respected Junior Woodruff, who had rotated back to the States. Frauenheim had just ordered his troopers to take cover when he spied Gavin. "The general spotted me in the ditch and I rather reluctantly, to say the least, got my posterior out of that ditch and met him. He said, 'Son, it's too hot up there for you right now. What's your name?' I told him and as he departed he said, 'Good luck, son,' in a rather serious tone. Things got better, but at that time things didn't look very promising.'"[87]

Neuhof was finally cleared by about 1030 hours. Leahy was ready to go for Udenbreth, but Billingslea held him back. Neuhof had been a hard fight. Udenbreth was larger and the 2/401st had already taken significant losses so Billingslea wanted to throw tanks and tank destroyers into the attack, but when he called for them he discovered that many had returned to the rear to rearm and refuel. It was, therefore, another hour and a half before the attack on Udenbreth jumped off.

When it did, the 2/401st attacked on a line parallel to and contiguous with the Siegfried Line, which required the troopers to pick their way through pillboxes and trenches while dodging enemy artillery and small arms fire. They also encountered something new—underground bunkers—which were given away by smokestacks coming out of the ground. "We didn't understand this," recalled Private First Class Robert Eschbaugh, so "I decided to see what a hand grenade would do. I pulled the pin and dropped it down the pipe. In a little while, a bunch of Germans came out [of their underground bunker] off to the right."[88]

Meanwhile, things had turned dire back at Neuhof. Three German tanks, including one Tiger, several self-propelled guns, half-tracks, and about seventy infantrymen supported by mortars hit the southeastern edge of town at 1400 hours. Within minutes eight American tanks and two tank destroyers were burning hulks while German infantry penetrated the town and threatened to overrun the 1/325th's command post. Hurriedly, Billingslea grabbed the 2/325th and led it in a counterattack. He also directed the fire of the remaining American tanks against the German armor. Corporal Lloyd Crick, a forward observer for the 1/325th, was nearby when Billingslea met with one of the tank commanders. "After looking at the Tiger tanks [*sic*], I heard the tank commander say to Colonel Billingslea, 'I can shoot at them, but I can't knock them out.' All that Colonel Billingslea said was, 'Shoot at them.'" Orchestrating danger-close artillery fire, tank fire, and his 2/325th, Billingslea successfully drove off the German armor and cleared Neuhof of German infantry by 1530 hours.[89]

Thirty minutes later, Leahy reported that Udenbreth had also fallen, except for three pillboxes at the northern edge of town that were firing "on anything and everything that moved." Having already taken some seventy casualties that day, Leahy opted to seal off the area around the pillboxes and reorganize his battalion to hold the rest of the town rather than attempt another assault. Later that night the Germans slipped out of their pillboxes, leaving Udenbreth to the 2/401st.[90]

With both Neuhof and Udenbreth in hand, Billingslea pulled the hard-hit 1/325th back into reserve, kept the 2/325th in Neuhof and the 2/401st in Udenbreth, tied in the flanks, registered heavy concentrations of artillery in front of his positions, and cleared his fields of fire. Gavin left Billingslea with one order: "Hold the two towns."[91] This Billingslea and his troopers did, using the artillery to break up several counterattacks later in the afternoon and early evening. All thoughts of continuing the attack onto the high ground to the east were forgotten.[92]

The fight for Neuhof and Udenbreth had been bloody for both sides. German losses, at least those that could be counted, were 275 prisoners, 44 killed, and eight armored vehicles destroyed. The 325th lost 50 dead and 175 wounded, while the tank battalion and tank destroyer company were both reduced to about 50 percent strength.[93] According to medic Edwin Lainhart, in some places the bodies were "so thick you had to go around or walk on them."[94]

On 3 February, Gavin penned some telling thoughts in his diary. It was nine days since his last entry, the one in which he wrote of feeling pleased about moving into the attack. "About six days ago we jumped off . . . with the mission of punching the Seigfried [*sic*] line near Udenbreath [*sic*] and Neuhof. Yesterday we seized that portion of the line within our sector and it was a very rough deal. Five days of attacking thru country entirely devoid of raods [*sic*] and even in many cases trails. Deep snow hampered all movement throughout and the krauts resisted quite bitterly." His troopers had prevailed, he continued, because "after the first day we had [the enemy] on his ass and it was simply a case of going fast enough to keep him there." This, for Gavin, was the key to success. "Nowadays one must move fast both to stay alive and to kill. If considerable confusion and chaos results [*sic*] that is to be accepted as a normal component of such an operation."[95] Yet despite moving fast, or at least as fast as possible given the conditions, the enemy was not yet beaten. This Gavin attributed to another cause, the sluggishness of higher headquarters.

Gavin railed about higher headquarters several times in his diary. "It seems very clear to me that our higher headquarters take entirely too much time to put plans and orders into effect." "If all is orderly and well conducted speed is sacrificed." "To take 24 to 48 hrs to get a division rolling in the attack is r[i]diculous." "We must learn to move more quickly or we will be beaten." This stodginess he laid at the feet of "older officers" who "get ideas that stay with them that they can neither rid themselves of nor do they desire to rid themselves of." The solution, he felt, "would appear [to be] to get younger officers in some of the higher commands or on the higher staffs." In the meantime, it portended for the 82nd continued employment wherever speed, shock, and aggressiveness were required, although the costs of employing lightly armed airborne troopers in sustained ground combat haunted him as evidenced by a non sequitur he inserted in the midst of his private discourse: "Ed Ostberg was hit and killed yesterday. Like most paratroop officers he was hit exposing himself when he should have been using cover."[96]

Gavin's next diary entry was seven days later. By that time things had changed dramatically, although not at all to Gavin's liking. "To our dismay and disbelief the penetration into the Seigfried [*sic*] line at Udenbreth was not exploited." Instead, the U.S. 99th Infantry Division was to relieve the 1st Infantry and 82nd Airborne Division and conduct a holding action. "Thus the build-up is to be abandoned and much of our sweating and losses was in vain. Difficult to explain this sort of thing to the troops." Yet there remained, as Gavin put it, another "nasty job and one that could have been done by anyone."[97] Just as Gavin foretold, the division was to be shipped elsewhere because others were too slow or too tentative in the attack.

The changes resulted from the priority Eisenhower had assigned to VERITABLE-GRENADE. Montgomery sold VERITABLE and GRENADE as complementary drives by the Canadian First and American Ninth Armies, respectively. VERITABLE was an attack by the Canadian First Army from its positions around Nijmegen in a southeasterly direction along the west bank of the Rhine River. Its scheduled jump-off date was 8 February. Two days later GRENADE was to kick off with an assault by the U.S. Ninth Army across the Roer River and a subsequent drive to the northeast to link up with the Canadians. Then, having cleared the west bank of the Rhine, Montgomery would send his remaining army, the British Second, across the Rhine and on into the Ruhr.[98]

Ironically, though Montgomery touted his plan as the most efficacious way to bring about the collapse of Nazi Germany, its success depended upon the actions of two of his foremost critics: Omar Bradley and Courtney Hodges. To set the stage for VERITABLE-GRENADE, Bradley and Hodges had to accomplish three critical tasks. First, Bradley had to transfer eight of his divisions to Simpson's Ninth Army to ensure Simpson was strong enough to undertake GRENADE. Second, Bradley had to shift the First Army's northern boundary, which abutted the Ninth Army's southern boundary, farther north so that Simpson could attack on a concentrated front. Finally, and most important, Hodges was to take the Roer River dams—in particular the Urft and Schwammenauel dams—in order to keep the Germans from destroying them and flooding the Roer River Valley. "Until we seized those dams," wrote Bradley, "the Germans could flood Simpson's [Ninth Army] sector and stop his advance."[99] This last task Hodges assigned to Major General C. Ralph Huebner's V Corps.[100]

The reassignment of divisions and the shifting of army boundaries were in large part accomplished by 5 February. The task of taking of the Roer River dams was halfway complete; on 4 February, the U.S. 9th Infantry Division took the Urft dam largely intact against little opposition. What remained was to take the Schwammenauel dam, a task Huebner assigned to the U.S. 78th Infantry Division.[101]

Taking the Schwammenauel dam meant first taking the town of Schmidt, Germany, an important crossroads about two miles northeast of the dam atop one of the highest ridgelines west of the Roer.[102] And getting to Schmidt meant traversing the Hürtgen Forest, already the scene of four unsuccessful and exceedingly bloody Allied attacks.[103] Sitting at the northernmost tip of the Ardennes, the Hürtgen was a high bog heavily forested and carved by numerous rivers and streams. Upon entering the Hürtgen, "a man might experience for the first time the stifling embrace of the kind of forests he had heard or read about in old German folk tales. Like Hansel and Gretel, he might be inclined to drop things behind him to mark his path."[104]

Jumping off on the morning of 5 February, the 78th made good progress at first but then got slowed by minefields. An impatient Huebner took control of the battle from the 78th's commander and proceeded to issue a stream of conflicting orders that served only to slow progress further. Moreover, fully alert to Huebner's intent, German resistance stiffened. As a result, by nightfall on 7 February Schmidt was still in enemy hands (except for two small footholds on its outskirts elements of the 78th had taken) as was the Schwammenauel dam, and the start of GRENADE was less than sixty hours away.[105]

When the attack on Schmidt failed, the call went out for help. Something somewhere had to be found that could get the attack moving again. It was a "nasty job," and on the evening of 6 February it became Gavin's nasty job. What followed constituted the last act of the 82nd in the fight begun by the German attack into Belgium. During this time Gavin and his troopers saw very little fighting, but what they did see made a lasting impression on them and brought to stark and bloody clarity the very things Gavin wrote about in his diary.[106]

The events of this last act can be summarized briefly. When Gavin received the call for help, the only thing readily available was Ekman's 505th, which had been pulled off the front on 3 February and sent to a rest area near Vielsalm, but it was only at about 33 percent strength. The remainder of the division was in the process of being relieved. But there was no time to wait for the entire division to assemble before moving north, so instead Gavin's staff issued a string of orders that introduced the 82nd into the new battle area in stages.

First, in order to get something to the hard-pressed 78th immediately, a task force was improvised—Task Force A—composed of the 505th and the peripatetic 517th under the command of the assistant division commander, Colonel Ira Swift. Forming up on the move, by 7 February Task Force A had passed to V Corps control and was in position three to four miles north of Schmidt, where it dug in and sent out patrols to probe enemy positions. The next morning, Swift sent the 2/505th forward to relieve one of the 78th's regiments so that it, in turn, could help clear Schmidt. That day, 8 February, also saw the opening of the 82nd's command post in the area (absorbing Task Force A) as well as the arrival of the 508th, which relieved the 517th so that it could join its parent organization, the U.S. 13th Airborne Division, newly arrived on the Continent. By 9 February, the entire 82nd Airborne Division was closed along the new front and on 10 February attacked eastward with two regiments—the 505th and 508th—both of which gained their objectives, a stretch of high ground on the west bank of the Roer River, by morning. There the 82nd remained, its positions relatively unchanged, until it was relieved on 18 February and sent back to France.[107]

As it turned out the alacrity with which the 82nd responded to the call for help was for naught. Due in large part to Huebner's meddling the 78th did not take the Schwammenauel dam until 10 February, and when it did it discovered that Allied assumptions about German intentions were incorrect. The Germans never intended to destroy the dam. Instead, by sabotaging the dam's power plant and discharge valves, they unleashed a steady flow of water calculated to create a long-lasting flood in the Roer River Valley. In this they succeeded, and GRENADE was postponed to 23 February.[108]

No one was more pleased to return to France than Gavin. Operating under V Corps had been difficult and eerily reflective of the thoughts he penned in his diary. "They take forever to plan and stage a show and then they get nowhere after they start. The analogy of hitching a racehorse [the 82nd] to a plow [V Corps] is no fallacy." But not only was V Corps slow. Gavin doubted the tactical acumen and leadership abilities of Huebner and his staff, especially after visiting the 78th's command post where he found Huebner and the 78th's commander bent over a map. "The Corps Commander occasionally drew a short line, a quarter to a half an inch, with a blue grease pencil. It represented an infantry battalion, and he was suggesting to the Division Commander a tactical scheme by moving battalions about. I had the strangest feeling when I realized how remote they were from the realities, from what it was like up where the battalions were."[109] Conversely, the first thing Gavin did when he arrived in the new battle area was conduct a personal reconnaissance, during which he discovered that the route V Corps had assigned the 82nd was nothing more than a cart path that intersected the steep Kall River Valley in the heart of the Hürtgen. "I proceeded down the trail on foot," wrote Gavin.

> It was obviously impassable for a jeep; it was a shambles of wrecked vehicles and abandoned tanks. The first tanks that attempted to go down the trail

> had evidently slid off and thrown their tracks. In some cases the tanks had been pushed off the trail and toppled down the gorge among the trees. Between where the trail begins . . . and the bottom of the canyon, there were four abandoned tank destroyers and five disabled and abandoned tanks. In addition, all along the sides of the trails there were many, many dead bodies, cadavers that had just emerged from the winter snow.[110]

The bodies were all wearing the insignia of the U.S. 28th Infantry Division, a red keystone signifying the unit's Pennsylvania roots, but because of the beating it took in the Hürtgen, its soldiers coined another name for the patch—the bloody bucket.

Continuing down the valley, Gavin crossed the Kall River by negotiating planks that had been thrown across the arches of a long-since demolished bridge and then started up the other side, where he came upon more dead American soldiers. "Nearby were dozens of litter cases, the bodies long dead. Apparently an aid station had been established near the creek, and in the midst of the fighting it had been abandoned, many of the men dying on their stretchers." Ascending the opposite side of the valley, Gavin saw more of the same—the debris of war and bodies, both American and German, that marked the ebb and flow of battle in the Hürtgen. Eventually, he emerged into a clearing, across which he could see Kommerscheidt, a small village just north of Schmidt. He had seen no Germans, at least none that were still alive, but he was uneasy. Darkness was approaching, and he wanted to get back to friendly lines, which meant retracing his path through the Kall River Valley, and he did not want to get stuck there in the dark. It was, he remembered, "like something from the lower levels of Dante's *Inferno*."[111]

When Gavin returned from his reconnaissance he called the V Corps chief of staff. There was no way, Gavin explained, to sustain an attack over the trail he just traversed, so he suggested an alternate route. "He [the V Corps chief of staff] listened to my story, then laughed and asked, 'Have you tried pack mules?'" Such blithe indifference infuriated Gavin. "There is nothing that angers a combat soldier more than a higher headquarters staff officer belittling the problems of the combat infantryman."[112] Undeterred, Gavin visited V Corps, confronted the staff face-to-face, and forced them to adjust their plan. As a result only one regiment, the 505th, had to advance through the hellish Kall River Valley. The rest of the division took Gavin's alternate route. Maneuvering in this manner, it took the 82nd one day to accomplish a task that had eluded the Allies for six months, the seizure of the west bank of the Roer River.[113]

Writing after the war, Gavin compared the Battle of the Hürtgen Forest to Passchendaele, the World War I battle in which the British Army lost some

240,000 soldiers. The similarities between the two are striking. Both were fought in seas of mud, both raged on inconclusively for several months, and both resulted in little tactical or strategic effect. But to Gavin, the strongest similarity between the two battles was the manner by which they were conceived, that being by château generals with little conception of what they were demanding of their soldiers. In his history of the First World War, published in 1930, British military historian and commentator B. H. Liddell Hart related the tale of a British staff officer who came to the front after the fighting at Passchendaele had died down to view the reality of what to him had theretofore been known only through reports and lines drawn on maps. Stepping from his car, he took one look at the mud and muttered to himself, "My God, did we send men to advance in that?" He then broke down and had to be led from the scene by his escort. Although perhaps apocryphal, the tale is illustrative of how Gavin felt about the Hürtgen fight. American senior officers, he wrote, "frequently lacked the firsthand knowledge of the conditions under which the troops were being compelled to fight. They had fought the battle on maps. And battles are not won on maps."[114]

Although not privy to the high-level failures that stirred Gavin's ire, the division's troopers did share one impression with their commander. As soon as they arrived in the area they knew they were in the midst of something the likes of which they had never before witnessed. "The towns that the convoy passed through, going north, did not appear badly damaged as a result of the war. Some gave no evidence of even a shot being fired into them—that is, until we reached Hurtgen [*sic*]," wrote the 505th's scribe in the regimental after-action review. The town of Hürtgen and the other towns and villages in the area "were absolutely leveled. Through Sicily, Italy, Normandy, and Holland this unit has seen the devastation of war, but never anything to compare with this. Had the houses not had cellars the troops would have found absolutely no cover at all." "When daylight came, it was a discouraging sight," recalled Sergeant Spencer Wurst of the 2/505th. "Only one house [in a village Wurst passed through] had been left standing, and it was a skeleton. Every other wall in town had been blown down. The tallest structures were a foot or a foot and a half high, and even they were few and far between." As had Gavin, Private Langdon compared the area to "a scene out of World War I trench warfare." He continued, "This area had been the arena of a gigantic struggle since the fall before and it looked the part. There was hardly a spot that hadn't been churned up by artillery or bombs. The few towns had been absolutely leveled, and stubs of trees here and there were the only evidence that anything had ever lived in this hell-hole. To compound the dismal scene, the snow had mostly melted in this area and it was a vast sea of mud as far as the eye could see." Sergeant McKenzie of the 456th remembered the Hürtgen as "a huge graveyard of unburied corpses" and the Kall River Valley as "something out of mankind's worst nightmare." When the 2/505th passed through the valley en route to Schmidt, "one was able to count more dead lying there than one could count in the battalion." Ridgway, who made his own reconnaissance of the Hürtgen, described it as "a graveyard of war, a no man's land populated by ghosts." So appalling was the scene that one of his subordinate commanders suggested that under no circumstances should a green unit, unfamiliar with the sights and smells of a battlefield be made to operate there.[115] But the Hürtgen was no ordinary battlefield. It was a massacre.

So it was with great relief that Gavin and his troopers boarded trucks and trains for the trip back to their old base camps around Rheims, France, where, in the words of an unknown 504th scribe, "Life, molded and compressed to the limitations of a garrison existence, [had] once again, and happily, become GI as hell."[116]

CHAPTER 25

PRESENT AT THE END

*During this attack, a tank commander who had joined the Battalion at Duren [*sic*] in March, and who had not worked with the 82nd Airborne Division, called back to Captain Wright on his radio and asked whether the troops he could see out in front of him were enemy or friendly forces. Captain Wright assured him that they were our own paratroopers. The Sergeant was amazed that they were up abreast and even in front of our tanks, spread out in a wide attack. During his experience he had always had to look back to the rear to find the infantrymen. He radioed back to Captain Wright that he sure wished he could have had soldiers like these with him all the time. A few minutes later I heard him call Captain Wright again on the radio and say, "Believe it or not, Captain, four paratroopers on bicycles just passed my tank and are now spearheading. More power to them." A few minutes later he radioed, "Good Lord, here comes a horse and buggy loaded with about eight paratroopers—they are now passing me." Just a little later he again called and said, "Captain, this is the damndest thing I ever saw; look over there to the left; there's about twenty men riding horses, they are paratroopers and they are rounding up Jerries."*

—GEORGE K. RUBEL, QUOTED IN DAWSON, *SAGA OF THE ALL AMERICAN*

THE 82ND RETURNED to Camps Suippes and Sissone on 20–21 February. Much had changed. Most notably two hospitals had taken over the barracks, relegating the troopers to pyramidal tents (with the exception of the 504th, which moved to a new camp near Laon). But the weather was pleasant, making the conditions somewhat tolerable, and since the hospitals came "with their quota of about 190 nurses they [were] rather welcome."[1] Moreover, once settled the division instituted a liberal leave policy. Most troopers got three-day passes to Paris, Brussels, London, and the Riviera. A lucky few received thirty-day furloughs to the United States. Meanwhile, replacements arrived to fill out the ranks, including former members of the independent 509th and 551st Parachute Infantry Battalions, both of which were disbanded because of the heavy losses they sustained in the Ardennes. Within a few weeks the division was at full strength.[2]

With many of the veterans on pass or furlough, training for the first few weeks consisted mainly of physical training and organized athletics. After about the third week it got more rigorous. For those who needed it there was a parachute qualification course or glider orientation flights. Weapons and tactical training also began in earnest, as did parachute and glider assault training.[3] During one airborne exercise tragedy struck when a plane lost its propeller and plunged through the descending paratroopers. Yet Gavin pressed on, allaying fears by always being the first man to jump.[4]

The reason for the emphasis on airborne operations was that the 82nd was earmarked for several that were still being considered. One was Operation CHOKER II, a drop to support the U.S. Seventh Army's bid to cross the Rhine at Worms. A second, Operation ARENA, called for a massive drop one hundred miles beyond the Rhine with the purpose of establishing "a 'fortress' area from which a decisive offensive could be launched at the east end of the Ruhr, to seize the high ground east of Paderborn [Germany] in order to deny to the enemy this defensive position, and to provide an airhead toward which the Southern Group of armies [i.e., Bradley's army group] could advance."[5] A third plan under consideration, and one that trumped all others, was Operation ECLIPSE, an airborne assault into the very heart of Nazi Germany—Berlin.[6]

ECLIPSE had been on First Allied Airborne Army's drawing board since before MARKET-GARDEN (under the code name TALISMAN). In November 1944 SHAEF assigned it a higher priority and renamed it. The plan envisioned dropping two U.S. airborne divisions and a British airborne brigade onto airfields in and around Berlin "in the event of a sudden collapse of German resistance," after which the troopers would race to the city, take control of the government, capture high government officials, seize documents, take over communications, and wait for linkup with ground forces.[7]

Gavin got word to prepare for ECLIPSE around 5 March, although he also received conflicting signals about whether there was any chance that the operation would come off.[8] Two days later, for example, Gavin attended a dinner for all the American airborne commanders in theater at SHAEF headquarters during which Eisenhower downplayed the strategic importance of Berlin, stating that "the capture of Berlin in itself would not lead to a general collapse of the Nazi regime." Conversely, continued Eisenhower, seizing the Ruhr "would have more serious repercussions on the Germans' will to resist, because of its far-greater effect on Germany's capacity to continue the war." Reflecting on the conversation in his diary Gavin wrote that he felt that the chances of jumping on Berlin were slim. "Eclipse probably would never come off because the Russians would be there first. . . . How in the world can it be arranged for the Russia[n]s to wait at one street while we load up and jump a week later. Even now they are close to Berlin."[9] Yet five days after the dinner "Doc" Eaton assured Gavin that "the whole thing is firm politically and that it would go." In fact, XVIII Airborne Corps's planning for ECLIPSE was so advanced that Ridgway was considering such weighty matters as the troopers' decorum once they took control of the German capital. "It is believed that the reaction of the German mind will be tremendously influenced by the personal appearance of individual soldiers who participate in Operation ECLIPSE," wrote Ridgway in a memorandum to First Allied Airborne Army, and therefore, "it is the intention of this headquarters to take into ECLIPSE a dress as well as a field uniform." General Brereton and his staff also remained enamored of ECLIPSE. The operation "is definitely not abandoned," wrote Brereton in his diary. "Even if the Russians capture Berlin, the plan would be shifted to Munich or whatever city the German government moved to."[10]

Faced with this ambiguity, Gavin prepared the 82nd as if ECLIPSE were a definite go. Training jumps and rehearsals were held on a nearby abandoned airfield so the troopers could familiarize themselves with the tasks that would be required of them were ECLIPSE to happen. Although billed as routine training, the specificity with which it was staged fueled rampant rumors; the division's veterans had seen this before and knew something big was in the wind. Gavin added to the rumormongering when, during a speech before the entire division, he mentioned the possibility of a Berlin drop, albeit while also suggesting several other potential missions, including eventual deployment to the Pacific, a comment for which he had no basis of support beyond conjecture.[11]

Feelings about a drop on Berlin were mixed. The troopers followed closely the progress of the war, hoping that it would end before the 82nd was again called to action while at the same time harboring a desire to be in at the kill.[12] Gavin reflected this duality. "I'd sure like to live through combat jump number five," he confided to his diary. "I believe that five are as many as one man should be given. Beyond that is too much. We all realize it now. There is a drain on the courage of a man that cannot be replaced." (The idea that men have a limited supply of courage is one that Gavin returned to often in his writings. In this he was influenced by Lord Moran's book *The Anatomy of Courage*, published in early 1945. "Courage is will-power, whereof no man has an unlimited stock; and when in war it is used up, he is finished," wrote

Moran. "A man's courage is his capital and he is always spending.")[13] A drop on Berlin would sorely test the courage of many. "It was a sobering prospect, especially for the veterans with four parachute combat jumps," recalled Gavin. "But at the same time it *was* exciting. This was to be the final battle, and to be in at the finish, after the long road from North Africa, was very much to our liking."[14]

But on the very evening that Gavin dined with the Supreme Commander an event occurred that altered drastically the final form of the Anglo-American drive in Europe and, in so doing, affected the 82nd's future employment.

While the U.S. Ninth Army waited for the Roer River flood to abate so that it could launch GRENADE, Bradley, Hodges, and Patton posited a plan that, if successful, would destroy all German forces west of the Rhine in the 12th Army Group's sector, advance the U.S. First and Third Armies to the west bank of the river, and position the army group to envelop the Ruhr from the south. Eisenhower approved the plan, code-named Operation LUMBERJACK, on 20 February. It was launched on 3 March.

Executed "with drill-hall precision," LUMBERJACK so discomfited German defenses that elements of the U.S. 9th Armored Division were able to capture the 1,069-foot Ludendorff railroad bridge over the Rhine at Remagen, Germany, virtually intact.[15] News of this coup passed quickly up the chain of command. Eventually, it got to SHAEF, where Eisenhower, in the midst of dinner with his airborne commanders, was called away to take an urgent call from Bradley. "When he reported that we had a permanent bridge across the Rhine I could scarcely believe my ears," Eisenhower wrote. "He and I [Bradley] had frequently discussed such a development as a remote possibility but never as a well-founded hope."[16] Immediately, Eisenhower approved Bradley's decision to push four to five divisions across as fast as possible.[17]

"Fortuitous events have a way sometimes of altering the most meticulous of plans," wrote Charles MacDonald in the U.S. Army's official history of the campaign.[18] Since the Normandy landings Montgomery had maintained a steadfast focus on driving to the Ruhr and from there on to Berlin, arguing with a vehemence that at times approached insubordination that all other operations in Western Europe should be secondary to his drive and that were this to be done, the war would be brought to a quick end. Although reluctant to give Montgomery the carte blanche he wanted, for the most part Eisenhower had supported the irascible field marshal. But the capture of the Ludendorff Bridge gave Eisenhower cause to reconsider. Although the unexpected capture of the Ludendorff Bridge did not conform with SHAEF's blueprint for advancing into Germany because it was too far south (when faced with this logic by SHAEF's chief planner, an apoplectic Bradley countered, "What in the hell do you want us to do, pull back and blow it up?"),

Eisenhower realized that by taking the bridge Bradley's army group was suddenly better positioned than Montgomery's to finish off the Germans.[19] Exploiting Bradley's bridgehead, however, would necessitate a reorientation of the Anglo-American drives and a reprioritization of effort. Based on this calculus, three weeks after the fall of the Ludendorff Bridge Eisenhower altered his strategy. It would be Bradley, not Montgomery, who would thenceforward orchestrate the main effort. It would be Bradley, not Montgomery, who would encircle and reduce the Ruhr (with Simpson's U.S. Ninth Army returned to him so he could do so). And it would be the Elbe River, not Berlin, that would define the limit of the Anglo-American advance from the west.[20]

Eisenhower's decisions made moot many of the airborne plans under consideration. The first to go was Operation ECLIPSE. With Berlin no longer the Anglo-American point of aim there was no reason to continue planning for this contingency, and Brereton's notion that the operation could be switched to wherever the Nazi leadership fled was likewise nullified when it became clear that Hitler had no intention of leaving the German capital. Second to go was CHOKER II, the airborne drop in support of the U.S. Seventh Army's attempt to cross the Rhine.[21] That left ARENA, the massive drop east of the Ruhr in the vicinity of Paderborn. Although in Ridgway's estimation ARENA was both strategically and tactically sound—an estimation influenced, no doubt, because it also called for the employment of XVIII Airborne Corps—he predicted that the plan would "stand or fall upon the hard facts of the ability and willingness of SHAEF to provide the aircraft and air fields in the quantities and for the periods of time which represent minimum essential needs." He was right. On 26 March SHAEF canceled ARENA because it could be launched only "at extreme expense of other air efforts, particularly as regards strategic air forces in their overall role. . . . The cost of launching the operation is a large one—chiefly in weakening the air support of the main operation [Bradley's drive east of the Rhine], and diversion of strategic bombing."[22]

The Allies did stage one final large-scale airborne operation in Europe, however—Operation VARSITY, a two-division drop to support Montgomery's belated Rhine River crossing in the north. The concept was to cover the British Second Army as it crossed by dropping the U.S. 17th Airborne and British 6th Airborne Divisions under XVIII Airborne Corps control adjacent to the Diersfordter Wald, an elevated wood some three to five miles east of the Rhine, to deny its use to enemy observers and neutralize the large concentration of German artillery and support elements that intelligence indicated was hiding in the wood. The drop, which was hugely successful, occurred just days before Eisenhower announced his decision to switch the

Allied main effort to Bradley's army group. In light of this switch, many questioned the commitment of so many paratroopers, gliders, glider troopers, and transport planes, especially given the minimal tactical benefit gained by VARSITY. But since he was about to relegate Montgomery's army group to a supporting role, Eisenhower was chary of denying his volatile subordinate the assets required for a last big show.[23]

VARSITY occurred on 24 March 1945. Watching as the troop transports flew over their base camps, many an 82nd trooper felt a sense of relief.[24] Captain Wayne Pierce of the 325th recalled thinking "maybe the war would end without the need for the 325/82 Airborne again." Private First Class Lane Lewis of the 3/508th felt likewise. "We were only too happy not to be going along. The war against Germany was coming to a close." Yet others were anxious to get back in the fight. In a letter to his sister, Lieutenant James Megellas wrote, "Things are awful quiet and unexciting here. When coming back from the front, a warm, dry place to sleep and eating warm food again seems heavenly but after a month or so I find myself becoming restless." Sergeant John McKenzie of the 456th felt similarly. "All the rumors and doing nothing had sapped our energy, and we looked forward to doing something useful again."[25]

One other significant event occurred during the few weeks the division was back in France. Orders from the War Department arrived prescribing organizational changes that were to take effect on 1 March 1945. One of the changes was that glider regiments were to have three infantry battalions. This meant that the 2/401st ceased being an attachment and became instead an assigned element of the 325th and was redesignated the 3/325th. The order also mandated that airborne divisions were to have no more than two parachute regiments, which meant the 82nd had to release the 508th. Gavin was not pleased. "Based on our experiences in Normandy and, especially, in Holland, I strongly feel that there is a real necessity to have available three [parachute] regiments as the initial balanced striking force for an airborne division," wrote Gavin to Ridgway. "In both those battles, especially in Holland, the late arrival of the glider forces was rather costly." Furthermore, noted Gavin, a "strong personal friendship [had] grown between us and the troops of that fine regiment." Yet as Ridgway pointed out, it was difficult to take issue with the 508th's detachment given the new mission for which it had been earmarked, Operation JUBILANT, an on-call operation to liberate Allied prisoner-of-war camps in the event the Nazis started murdering prisoners in a last act of malevolent defiance. "With respect to the 508th," counseled Ridgway, "its contemplated employment leaves little basis on which to lodge an objection. The rescuing and safeguarding of our prisoners in German hands well merits our utmost efforts."[26]

The 82nd and 508th parted ways on 2 April when the division moved out for another mission and Colonel Roy Lindquist and his troopers remained behind. Two days later the 508th moved to airfields near Chartres, France, and was put on forty-eight-hour alert for JUBILANT. Fortunately, JUBILANT never had to be carried out, so the 508th saw no further action in the war. Instead, the regiment remained at Chartres until late May 1945, when it briefly returned to Camp Sissonne before moving to Frankfurt, Germany, for occupation duty, with its primary mission being the provision of security and an honor guard for Eisenhower's postwar headquarters. Finally, after approximately eighteen months of occupation duty, the 508th returned to the United States where, on 24 November 1946, it was deactivated.[27]

When the 82nd left its camps around Rheims, it was for a mission that arose as a result of Eisenhower's change in strategy. Because Eisenhower had shifted the priority of effort to Bradley's army group, it was on the cusp of destroying Generalfeldmarschall Model's *Army Group B* and more than 300,000 German soldiers in what became known as the Ruhr Pocket. The U.S. First and Ninth Armies had linked up at Lippstadt, Germany, east of the Ruhr, on 1 April, after which Bradley assumed control of the battle and turned both armies inward to squeeze Model from the north, south, and east. To complete the job, Bradley needed a force to keep the Germans in the pocket from escaping back across the Rhine to the west. This became the mission of the newly formed U.S. Fifteenth Army under Major General Leonard T. Gerow. On 30 March, Gavin received word that, effective the next day, the 82nd would be attached to Gerow's command and be under the immediate control of Major General Ernest N. Harmon's U.S. XXII Corps. Its mission was to defend that portion of XXII Corps's sector along the Rhine centered on Cologne, Germany.[28]

While in camp around Rheims rumors about what the future held for the 82nd were rampant. They came to a crescendo following VARSITY. Many of these "latrine communiqués" held that the 82nd was going home. Others posited that the division would again be committed to combat, although "no one knew where."[29] One especially persistent rumor combined elements of both: The division was to return to the States and the troopers given furloughs after which they would regroup and prepare for a drop on Japan.[30] "They are straining at the leash," observed Captain Harry Butcher when he had dinner with the airborne commanders at Eisenhower's headquarters, "never knowing from day to day what their next show will be." It was thus with both relief and resignation that the troopers received word to pack up and move out—relief that they would not be mounting another airborne operation, resignation that they were again being committed to action. Even Colonel Reuben Tucker's hyperaggressive troopers were somewhat muted when word reached them that they would be moving forward. According to a regimental report, "The end of the war seemed near and according to General Gavin in his talk to the 504th, 'We want to be in on the finish.' How enthusiastically the fighting men endorsed this sentiment could not readily be determined."[31]

Gavin, for one, was more than ready to get back into the fray. "Six weeks out of the line is plenty although I appreciated the opportunity to absorb and train the reinforcements." Hence, as soon as he issued movement orders to his subordinate commanders he left for the front. His first stop was Fifteenth Army headquarters where he met Gerow for the first time. "He told me that he wanted us to be aggressive," recalled Gavin, "to seek contacts with the Germans across the river, and to identify the formations opposing us. I assured him that we would."[32] Gavin then went to meet the commander and staff of the U.S. 86th Infantry Division, whose sector the 82nd was to take over, to coordinate the relief in place and conduct a reconnaissance of his new area.[33]

Moving out by train and truck beginning 2 April, the 82nd relieved the 86th Infantry Division in stages, taking sole possession of its assigned area along the Rhine on 4 April. Given the width of the division's frontage, Gavin arrayed all three of his infantry regiments along the river: the 504th in the north, the 325th (less the 3/325th, which was held in reserve) in the center, and the 505th in the south. He also inaugurated an artillery assault on anything even remotely suspected of being a military target. On the day the 82nd took control of the sector the division's artillerymen pumped 478 rounds of high explosive across the Rhine into the Ruhr Pocket. They more than quadrupled this the next day, firing a total of 2,215 rounds in 104 separate fire missions.[34] They kept up this pace for ten days at the end of which the division's organic artillery battalions, reinforced by several attached artillery formations, fired 729 missions and delivered more than 13,000 rounds onto known and suspected enemy positions.[35]

The artillery attacks, while aggressive, did not fulfill Gerow's requirement to make contact with and identify the enemy formations on the other side of the Rhine. That could be done only by sending troops across the river, and to that end General Harmon ordered that units in XXII Corps were to conduct "not less than one patrol per front line battalion per night." Gavin upped the ante, directing that "within the discretion of the Regimental Commander, up to one rifle company may be left on the far bank of the RHINE RIVER to screen, observe, and report on enemy activity."[36]

The 82nd sent its first patrols out on the night of 4–5 April, all of which were ferried across the river in a variety of boats scrounged and crewed by engineers from the 307th Engineers. Several of the patrols made contact, and at least one trooper was killed and three wounded, but only one prisoner was brought back. It was an inauspicious start and one that the ever-aggressive Tucker sought to rectify.[37]

Tucker reasoned that squad-size patrols might be annihilated if they ran into a large enemy force since, with a river to their back, they could not easily withdraw to friendly lines. Taking full advantage of the leeway Gavin granted in his patrol order, Tucker elected to send an entire company across the Rhine to seize and hold a foothold that could be used as a base of operations from which to conduct patrols. Furthermore, reasoned Tucker, given the size of the force he was sending across the river, the Germans might be fooled into thinking that the Americans were establishing another bridgehead across the Rhine and commit "disproportionate forces" to repel it.[38] Of course, any enemy forces committed against Tucker's troopers would be unavailable for use elsewhere in the Ruhr Pocket, thus easing Bradley's task of reducing the pocket. And finally, given the massive artillery contingent backing the division, it was a shared belief that a company could hold off just about anything the enemy could throw at it.[39]

The mission fell to Captain John N. Pease's A Company, 1/504th. The objective was Hitdorf, a small village along the eastern bank of the Rhine just north of Cologne. Pushing off from the west bank at approximately 0230 hours, 6 April, Pease led the first wave of A Company troopers across the river in an uneventful crossing. But as soon as they landed on the east bank they started receiving fire. To make matters worse, they discovered that they had landed in a minefield. Since withdrawal was not an option—the boats had returned to the west bank to pick up the second wave—the troopers pushed inland in two groups, knocked out several machine-gun nests, and eventually made their way to the objective. Meanwhile, successive waves of A Company troopers crossed the river, encountered more enemy fire, and, like the first wave, fought through it. By 0830 hours Hitdorf was in American hands, as were sixty-eight prisoners. Although several troopers had been killed and wounded, Pease felt he was still strong enough to hold, and despite the initial heavy resistance the situation appeared to be well in hand.[40]

But the peace was short-lived. At 0845 hours the Germans counterattacked in company strength, drove in the A Company outposts, and were within 150 yards of Pease's main line of defense before his paratroopers turned them back. Thirty-three more prisoners were taken, "while the remainder of the attacking force was believed to be either killed or wounded, as none were observed to leave the area." By now Pease had almost as many prisoners as paratroopers, so he had his executive officer, Lieutenant Reneau Breard, take them under guard to the crossing site so they could be ferried across the river. According to Breard, "About noon we put the prisoners in the boats and sent them back across. And then, we didn't have any boats to get back. If we had any wounded, we couldn't send them back."[41] Meanwhile, the Germans started pounding Hitdorf with artillery, which cut all wire communications from the company command post to the defending platoons and from the company to the battalion command post across the river. The 376th Parachute Field Artillery Battalion responded in kind, but its effectiveness was significantly curtailed when a German 88 took out A Company's artillery observation post, which had been located in Hitdorf's church steeple.[42]

The German barrage lasted two hours, but A Company took few casualties and hung on. Then, at about 1530 hours, a second company-size counterattack emerged from behind a smoke screen at the southeastern edge of Hitdorf. Supporting the attack were two tanks. Lieutenant Rex E. Hazen, a forward observer from the 376th, called in artillery and momentarily stopped the attack, but the Germans regrouped and hit the town again. Defending was Pease's Third Platoon. The Third Platoon leader, a Lieutenant Hallock, sent a runner to the company command post requesting *panzerfausts*, but before Pease could react, the platoon was overrun and neither Hallock nor his troopers were heard from again. Then another enemy force numbering approximately 200 infantry hit Second Platoon's sector in the north. Outgunned and outnumbered, Pease orchestrated a fighting withdrawal back to the river where he formed a horseshoe-shaped perimeter with the open end facing the water. During the withdrawal Lieutenant James A. Kiernan, the Second Platoon leader, single-handedly kept the Germans at bay until being badly wounded by a grenade. He was "just perforated all over his body," recalled Lieutenant Breard, who helped the wounded Kiernan get back to the west bank.[43]

With their backs to the river, Pease and his troopers fought it out at point-blank range with German infantry and armor while Tucker sent help. At 0130 hours, 7 April, Captain T. Moffatt Burriss's I Company, 3/504th, pushed off from the west bank in nine metal boats. Halfway across they were pinpointed by spotlights and targeted by small arms and machine-gun fire. Eight of the boats made it through the fire to the far bank; the ninth, containing Burriss, capsized, and its occupants swam back to the near shore. Landing at a point just south of Hitdorf, I Company regrouped under Lieutenant Bernard "Babyface" Karnap who led it north to counterattack the Germans surrounding A Company. Fighting their way through the German lines, I Company linked up with Pease's A Company and covered its withdrawal across the river. By 0230 hours, A Company, its wounded, and its prisoners had been safely evacuated. I Company followed shortly thereafter.[44]

Tucker's Hitdorf gambit was costly; A Company lost 9 killed, 24 wounded, and 74 missing, while I Company suffered another 4 wounded. German losses, besides the approximately 85 prisoners A Company captured, were estimated at upwards of 350 killed and wounded.[45] Although the tally favored the 504th, the after-action review was not as sanguine:

> In reality, the number of KIAs is greatly in excess of the figure 9. However, darkness and the inherent [confusion] of 24 hours of continuous fighting, precluded the possibility of ascertaining the death of every man who fell. In view of the excessively high casualties, it is difficult to say that the mission was a success. From the view point of those GIs involved, the operation was a miniature "Dunkirk" with at most, a hollow satisfaction achieved. Fighting men don't believe in moral [victories]. Whether or not "A" Company served its purpose in diverting enemy troops from a more important sector is [impossible] to say. In any case, "A" was hit and hit hard by at least a battalion of troops, plus a platoon of tanks supported by a battalion or more of artillery.[46]

General Harmon was also displeased. Sometime while A Company was still on the east bank he and Gavin "had quite a fight" on the phone about what Tucker was trying to accomplish. Gavin argued that sending small patrols across the river every night was just as dangerous. "The krauts wait until the boat is just about ready to touch down on the far shore and then they blast it out of the water," he told Harmon. "No future in that."[47] But Harmon was having none of it. He ordered Gavin to withdraw the company immediately and desist from similar forays in the future.

Gavin brooded about Harmon's upbraiding for days. He was galled by the strictures Harmon placed on his freedom of maneuver, strictures that did not conform to what the Fifteenth Army commander told him. Besides, German resistance in the Ruhr Pocket was collapsing fast. Once the pocket was reduced, the 82nd would be pinched out of the fight. Gavin did everything he could to avoid this. He pleaded with Ridgway, whose XVIII Airborne Corps was fighting along the southern edge of the Ruhr Pocket, to get the division transferred back to the corps but to no avail. "I have asked and shall continue to ask on every appropriate occasion for your reassignment," replied Ridgway to one of Gavin's requests. "I was informed that the decision, however, was made by the Supreme Commander himself, so that until I can see General Bradley in person there is little I can do." When Ridgway talked to Bradley he received the same reply. "I made every possible effort to get you, being supported by General Hodges in full," wrote Ridgway a few days later. "I think General Bradley, too, was entirely sympathetic, but the decision came from still higher up." Certain that the division would see no more action against Germans, Gavin turned his attention to the Japanese. "I want to get to the Pacific. As this thing approaches a wind-up I realize that I will have a frightful time adapting myself to the years of peace and ways of peace. Fighting and excitement have become my daily sustenance, I miss [them] after awhile."[48]

Ironically, it was a possible deployment to the Pacific that caused Harmon to react so heatedly when he learned about Hitdorf. Bradley had told Harmon that the "airborne divisions were destined for transfer fairly soon to the Pacific theater. Consequently he ordered us to limit our forays across the Rhine to forces of platoon size and smaller; this would ensure that our casualty figures were kept low," but Harmon did not relay this to Gavin until *ten days after* the fight at Hitdorf.[49] "Gen[eral] Harmon told me yesterday [16 April] that he had it from a very high level that we are on a high priority for shipment to the Pacific," recorded Gavin in his diary. "I have also had it from another source that we are on a very high priority for shipment to the states. So far everything fits into the picture. We are being held back for ready preparation and shipment to the states and then to be refitted and shipped to the Pacific."[50] Yet this, too, was not to be. A week later Ridgway told Gavin that "there is little chance of us going to the Pacific after this winds up. This was a shock. We have our hearts set on it."[51]

After Hitdorf, Gavin curtailed cross-river operations markedly; patrols were limited to no more than four per night, all had to be of platoon size or less, and all had to return before daybreak. Still the division sustained casualties, as Gavin had warned, when several patrols were shot up in midriver. Within limits, Gavin maintained his artillery attacks, but the frequency of these, too, gradually decreased as friendly units on the far bank closed in on the Germans surrounded in the Ruhr Pocket.[52]

Despite Hitdorf, the dangerous cross-river patrols, and the constant boom of artillery, many troopers, especially the veterans, viewed their stay along the Rhine as "more of a rest cure than a battle." According to a 325th report, "For the first time, . . . veteran glidermen tasted some of the sweetness of war. The so-called living in the field was more comfortable than the tent camp left behind in France." Most troopers, in fact, did not live "in the field" but lived in buildings and private homes from which they evicted their former occupants and augmented their diets with fresh food and liquor scrounged from local sources. There were even band concerts and movies. About the only thing missing was female companionship. Eisenhower had promulgated a nonfraternization order that caused a good deal of grumbling in the ranks. "Higher headquarters was adamant on the point of no association between the troops and the Germans," recalled Gavin, but "after the long trek all the way from North Africa, some of the frauleins looked quite attractive." Gavin dutifully passed on Eisenhower's order, but did not expend a lot of energy enforcing it. The great fear was that the troopers would be "politically contaminated," but as Gavin told General Patton, "The GIs reasoned that as long as they kept on their airborne caps and their jump boots, as tokens of their patriotism, they should be allowed to do anything, or almost anything."[53]

With German resistance in the Ruhr Pocket crumbling, it was "a quite unlikely possibility" that any enemy forces would attempt a breakout through the division's lines.[54] Gavin, therefore, focused on other tasks, the most significant of which was assisting occupation authorities with searches and seizures; apprehending Wehrmacht deserters, Nazi officials, and designated war criminals; collecting weapons, ammunition, and other implements of war; and enforcing laws and ordinances and the general supervision of German civil administrators. On 15 April, when the division was pinched out of the fight by friendly units moving up the east side of the Rhine from the south, these tasks became the division's full-time job. Ultimately, the 82nd assumed responsibility for 650 square miles of occupied Germany and apprehended 653 deserters, Nazis, and war criminals. Yet by far the most difficult of the division's occupation tasks was supervising several displaced persons camps containing more than 25,000 souls.

There were three displaced persons camps in the 82nd's area: one for Westerners, one for Russians, and one for Poles. "The displaced persons, slaves really, are quite a problem . . . ," wrote Gavin, "especially the russians [*sic*] who love nothing more than to beat up or rape a german [*sic*]. Next to burning his home to the ground or robbing and looting they like this best." Gavin assigned oversight of the camps to the 3/325th, although it was augmented by individuals from other units. One augmentee was Sergeant McKenzie of the 456th, who seconded Gavin's observations about the Russians. "They believed . . . that they had earned a right to raid German cities, steal whatever they could, and rape the women," he recalled. "They hated the Germans with a passion."[55] And it was the Russian camp, the largest of the three with more than 10,000 persons, that caused the most problems.

Although highly organized and comparatively well disciplined, the Russian internees could not understand why they had not been released. This placed their American guards in an intolerable quandary. "We did not want to waste time guarding our allies," recalled Sergeant McKenzie, but on the other hand there was no way the Russians would be left to roam free and wreak havoc.[56] Eventually, tempers came to a head, and a near riot broke out. Called to the scene in the dead of night, Gavin drove his jeep into the middle of the Russian compound, climbed atop the hood, and harangued the angry crowd for about an hour, "trying to explain . . . why we were doing what we were doing, and why it was in the common good to bring the war to an end quickly with no rioting and confusion in the rear areas."[57] With that, tempers cooled and the riot was averted. Yet it was an uneasy peace, and one the troopers did not feel particularly well suited to enforce. "It was a job," recalled Lieutenant Megellas, "to which [even] combat-hardened paratroopers were unaccustomed."[58]

The troopers were also unaccustomed to being so near the front without participating in the fight. While they were conducting occupation duties, on 18 April the rest of Bradley's 12th Army Group completed the reduction of the Ruhr Pocket.[59] Watching from the sidelines made Gavin uneasy. "We continue in our present occupational role and in SHAEF reserve," he confided to his diary. "We all feel a terrible let down." What truly concerned him was what he saw happening as the Army began preparing for occupation duty. Units that had been trained for combat were being transitioned into contingents of prison guards, policemen, sanitation workers, and food and welfare providers. The 417th Field Artillery Group, which supported the 82nd during its watch on the Rhine, was a particularly poignant example: "My 417th FA group just off the boats has been given a definite occupational assignment. Their guns are to be put in cosmoline for long storage and they are to start guard duties of the occupied areas. It kills them."[60]

For the man who had literally conceived the idea of an American airborne division—who had argued that such a thing was not only possible but necessary and who then rose to command one that had more combat jumps and more combat time than any other—the very thought of breaking up the 82nd was anathema. Nevertheless, the destruction of *Army Group B* portended a quick end to the war in Europe, as did events on the Eastern Front where the Red Army had already commenced the final bombardment of Berlin. There was little fighting left to be done, and, as General J. C. H. Lee characterized it, it was not "worthy of the 82nd."[61] But unbeknownst to Gavin, measures were in train that would require of him and his troopers one last advance and bring about a fitting denouement to the 82nd's wartime adventure.

Ever since Eisenhower designated 12th Army Group as the main effort, it had advanced with audacity that had been absent since Patton's breakout from Normandy. Even before completing the reduction of the Ruhr Pocket, Bradley launched elements of three armies—the Ninth, First, and Third—headlong toward the Elbe and Mulde Rivers, the tentative line of demarcation between the converging Anglo-American and Soviet forces, with orders to get there ahead of the Red Army.[62] This they did. The Ninth Army reached the Elbe on 11 April, and both the First and Third Armies followed suit nine days later; the Russians arrived on 25 April. In the north, however, the 21st Army Group lagged far behind.

In a fit of pique about being relegated to a supporting role, Montgomery was advancing slowly even by his standards. His mission was to take Lübeck on the Baltic. Doing so would secure Bradley's northern flank, cut off any Wehrmacht remnants still in Denmark, and, most important, interpose 21st Army Group between Denmark and the onrushing Red Army. "Manifestly, . . . we must do everything possible to push across the Elbe without delay, drive to the coast at Lubeck [*sic*] and seal off the Danish peninsula," wrote Eisenhower to his recalcitrant subordinate on 31 March.[63] When Montgomery failed to quicken his pace, Eisenhower wrote him again to remind him of the urgency of his mission and offer him whatever he needed, within reason, to get going. A morose Montgomery replied that the only thing he required was for Bradley to extend his left flank. Bradley did this and Montgomery still dallied. Exasperated by Montgomery's foot-dragging, Eisenhower flew to 21st Army Group headquarters on 20 April for a face-to-face meeting. This time Montgomery requested two things from the Supreme Commander: the use of a railroad bridge, which Eisenhower promptly granted, and an American corps. Eisenhower had been anticipating this and had secretly earmarked Ridgway's XVIII Airborne Corps, which would comprise the U.S. 7th Armored, 8th Infantry, and 82nd Airborne Divisions, for just this purpose. Although Bradley was none too happy about lending Montgomery his best corps, he acquiesced, hoping that it would compel Montgomery to move faster. Besides, recalled Bradley, "No one could build a fire under Monty better than Ridgway."[64]

Bradley informed Ridgway of his new assignment on 21 April. Ridgway reported to Montgomery's headquarters the next day and learned that XVIII Airborne Corps would be inserted between the British Second Army (in the north) and the U.S. Ninth Army (in the south), that it would be under the operational control of Second Army, and that its mission was to protect the right flank of Second Army as it crossed the Elbe and advanced toward the Baltic. Montgomery left it to Ridgway and General Sir Miles Dempsey, the British Second Army commander, to work out the details. "You'll find Dempsey down the road," Montgomery told Ridgway. "You two have worked together before [during Operation VARSITY]. Go down there and fix it up between you."[65]

As ordered, Ridgway immediately made his way to Second Army headquarters, where Dempsey outlined for him the details of his plan, which was, to say the least, complex. The advance on Lübeck was to begin with an assault river crossing of the Elbe near Lauenburg on 1 May by British VIII Corps. Once a bridgehead was secured, engineers would construct a bridge over the Elbe over which would then pass, in order, the remainder of VIII Corps, British XII Corps, and two divisions of Ridgway's XVIII Airborne Corps (the U.S. 8th Infantry Division, which was already assembling near Lauenburg, and the British 6th Airborne Division, control of which would pass to Ridgway after it crossed the Elbe). Once assembled east of the Elbe,

XII Corps was to turn left toward Hamburg while the two divisions of XVIII Airborne Corps turned right, advancing up the Elbe some ten to fifteen miles to uncover two additional bridging sites where Ridgway was to build his own bridges in order to cross the remainder of his corps. Then, once all of XVIII Airborne Corps was across the Elbe, Ridgway was to move north to protect VIII Corps's right flank as it drove on the Baltic while simultaneously driving east, where it was to seek contact with the Red Army. Orchestrating the flow of forces across the single bridge at Lauenburg would take some time, added Dempsey, who estimated that Ridgway's forces would not be able to begin crossing any earlier than 6 or 7 May.[66]

Ridgway was aware that he was to "build a fire" under Montgomery, but the ponderous scheme of maneuver that Dempsey outlined made this impossible. Something had to be done to force the pace. While conducting a reconnaissance of the Elbe near Bleckede, one of the sites where Dempsey wanted XVIII Airborne Corps to build a bridge, Ridgway hit upon a solution. "I went down to the river bank to take a look," he later explained. "I exposed myself as much as I thought necessary, but drew no fire. Across the wide river all was silent." The silence compelled "some hard, fast thinking. It seemed to me we had an opportunity here to get a jump on the German, to seize a bridgehead across the twelve-hundred-foot river before he had a chance to reorganize."[67] Based on his reconnaissance, Ridgway presented Dempsey a modified plan that would get XVIII Airborne Corps across the Elbe quicker. Instead of waiting to cross the Elbe at Lauenburg, Ridgway proposed conducting his own river crossing at Bleckede, where he would seize a bridgehead, build a bridge, and then cross his forces as they came available. He would then expand his bridgehead outward, build a second bridge at Darchau (about twelve miles upriver from Bleckede), and then rush all his forces across the Elbe so that he could attack toward the Baltic. Dempsey accepted Ridgway's plan with one condition—Ridgway would have to implement it sooner than anticipated, for as a result of Eisenhower's prodding, Montgomery had advanced his timetable by two days. British VIII Corps was going to cross the Elbe on 29 April; Ridgway would have to conduct his operation as soon as possible thereafter. Ridgway agreed and the race was on.[68]

At the time Ridgway had only two regiments anywhere near Bleckede. Both were from the 8th Infantry Division, but they were in position behind British VIII Corps, preparing to cross at Lauenburg, as envisaged in Dempsey's original plan. The 7th Armored Division was still assembling and was not, in any case, the type of unit Ridgway could call upon to conduct a hasty river crossing. That left the 82nd, which was still in position around Cologne, about 250 miles away, but it had one assault river crossing under its belt (over the Waal at Nijmegen) and had twice demonstrated (at Salerno and in the Bulge) its ability to move fast and attack with little or no preparation. Hence, much "to the dismay of my Staff," wrote Ridgway, "I ordered [Gavin] to cross the Elbe . . . and attack, without awaiting the arrival of reinforcing units." And although his reconnaissance indicated that the far bank was seemingly devoid of enemy soldiers, were some to appear, Ridgway was confident that his old division could make the crossing, seize a bridgehead, and hold. It was a risky decision, but one for which Ridgway "had no cause to regret."[69]

For some reason, Gavin never got word that Ridgway's plans had changed until sometime on the evening of 28 April. Up until then he was under the impression that the 82nd would be participating in nothing more than "the severance and clearing up of Denmark," which was not expected to commence until sometime after 30 April.[70] It was with no great haste, therefore, that the division trekked north; it took two full days to turn over the Cologne area to other units and an additional two days to make the journey to Bleckede, although the latter was more the result of transportation difficulties and traffic jams than a lack of urgency.[71] Within the ranks, the leisurely pace reinforced hopes that the fighting was over. "Most people just assumed that the regiment would occupy a little more German territory while the British Army went on about its business and the war came to an end," recalled Private Allen Langdon of the 505th. Captain Charles Sammon of the 2/505th remembered being under the "impression that we were coming north to be placed in Corps reserve, some 50 miles behind the lines." Even Gavin was a bit melancholy about the 82nd's new assignment. "It cannot amount to much," he predicted, "except considerable discomfort and very little fighting."[72]

It was not until he arrived in the vicinity of Bleckede that Gavin learned the plan had changed.

> General Dempsey asked when I could cross the river. I told him that I should have most of the Division closed up in 24 hours and could cross it tomorrow night [the night of 30 April–1 May]. He said it wouldn't do; he was anxious that we cross the Elbe, confront the Russians, and block them from moving into Denmark. General Ridgway told me that he could let me have two battalions of the 8th Infantry Division, which was going to come in on the left. It seemed a bit risky, but since the war was coming to an end, it was a risk worth taking.[73]

Quite a risk it was. The only divisional units anywhere near Bleckede at the time were the 82nd's Reconnaissance Platoon and the 307th Airborne Engineer Battalion. The rest of the division was strung out for more than 200 miles between Cologne and Bleckede on trucks and trains, with the first elements not scheduled to arrive until 0455 hours, 29 April. Furthermore, since

Ridgway had set H hour for the crossing at 0100 hours, 30 April, Gavin and his staff would have to cobble together a plan on the fly, feeding units into the fight as they arrived. There would be no time to complete the myriad preparations that normally precede an assault river crossing—even the Waal River assault had been undertaken with more time to prepare—so Gavin and his staff concentrated on only the most essential tasks: procuring boats, finding suitable launching sites, and conducting a limited reconnaissance of the far shore.[74]

Finding boats and determining the best locations from which to launch the crossing was a job for the division's engineers, who set about their tasks with a fury. In less than twenty-four hours they not only identified suitable crossing points, but also procured 116 canvas assaults boats, 34 motorized metal boats, 7 large motorized rafts, more than 2,000 life vests, and 300 paddles. They also coordinated with a nearby British armored division for the use of 30 "Buffalos," tracked amphibious vehicles that could ferry follow-on echelons across the Elbe once a bridgehead on the far shore had been established.[75]

Ridgway's assessment notwithstanding, it was also imperative to get a feel for the enemy situation on the far bank. To that end Gavin sent four squad-size reconnaissance patrols across the Elbe on the night of 28–29 April. Three of the four got over and back without incident and brought back nine prisoners. The fourth was within fifteen yards of the far shore when it was taken under fire by heavy automatic weapons fire that sank its boat. Two of the eight troopers in the patrol swam back to the near shore. The others went missing. What the patrols uncovered was that the 82nd was facing a hodgepodge of German units, including policemen, sailors, and school troops that had been hurriedly pressed into service. Obviously, a few were capable of resistance, but it was believed that in the face of a determined attack, they would collapse.[76]

The 1/505th and 2/505th were the first of the division's main body to arrive at Bleckede, the troopers marching into town around 0400 hours, 29 April, "happily unaware that they had an assault crossing to make." Still under the impression that they would be doing nothing strenuous or, for that matter, dangerous, the troopers set to making themselves comfortable in abandoned homes and replicating the living conditions they had enjoyed along the Rhine. Their spirits were dashed when they learned they were going to make a river crossing. "Of all the operations undertaken by the 505 in World War II," recalled Private Langdon, "probably no operation was 'sweat out' by the 'old men' more than this one." With the war coming to an end, no one wanted his name to be the last one added to the casualty list, especially those who had been with the 82nd since North Africa. The fact that they were being called upon to conduct a high-risk operation with little time to prepare added to their unease. No sooner had the troopers billeted themselves in Bleckede's deserted homes than they were rousted outside, put in formation, and marched to their respective crossing sites. But there was one sop. The Germans had left behind a "bountiful supply of vintage booze" that the troopers liberated, so "it was not exactly a sober group of 505ers who formed up that evening to move out to the crossing site."[77]

Three factors made planning for the crossing complicated: the terrain, the troops available, and the accelerated time schedule. The engineers had identified four good crossing sites in the vicinity of Bleckede, where the Elbe takes a pronounced U-shaped turn with the open portion facing east (Bleckede is on the western side of the river just outside the base of the U). Two of the sites were along the upper (northern) arm of the U, one in the base, and the fourth along the lower (southern) arm of the U. Which and how many of the crossing sites to use was a conundrum. Based on what his reconnaissance patrols found, Gavin knew the Germans were defending along the east bank of the river, which put them inside its U-shaped bend. Were he to cross at all four sites simultaneously, it might be possible to envelop them and tear a huge hole in their defenses. But at H hour, the only troops available for the crossing would be the 1/505th, the 2/505th, the engineers, and his reconnaissance platoon; the rest of the division would not arrive until well after the appointed jump-off time. Spreading such a small force among four sites was risky, and although there was plenty of artillery available to cover them—the division artillery officer, General Andy March, and his staff had done yeoman work coordinating for fire from six artillery battalions in the area, including one battalion each of 8-inch and 155mm guns—synchronizing the fire from so many guns would be extremely difficult given that, once the forces were on the far shore, they would be attacking *toward* one another. A safer bet would be to use only two sites so that he could mass what little force he had and use his artillery freely, but this would cost him the chance of enveloping the enemy. What decided the issue was Gavin's confidence in his troopers (although assuredly he did not know their state of sobriety at the moment). He would cross at all four sites simultaneously, pitting Colonel William Ekman's 505th against what was, at best, a pickup team of Germans.[78]

The final plan was relatively straightforward. The 2/505th would cross at the two northern sites, and the 1/505th would cross at the base of the U and the southern site. At H hour, each battalion was to send one rifle company across. For the 2/505th, companies D and E were in the van while companies A and C were to lead the 1/505th's assault. After seizing footholds on the far shore into which the remainder of each battalion could be inserted, the troopers were to clear the far bank, link up, and then continue their attack inland, their movements coordinated by a series of five phase lines. The rest of the division's infantry elements would be ferried across the Elbe as they arrived. Finally, Ridgway wanted to begin constructing his bridge as soon as practicable. Normally, this would not occur until after the assaulting infantry had pushed enemy artillery out of range of the bridging site, but given Ridgway's focus on getting the rest of XVIII Airborne Corps across the Elbe as quickly as possible, he had two engineer combat groups standing by ready to construct the bridge as soon as the far shore was cleared. It was, Gavin thought, "a feasible undertaking, although a bit marginal."[79]

Ultimately, success hinged on Ekman's troopers attacking with their usual aggressiveness and élan. According to the division's after-action review, that was exactly what occurred. "By nightfall, April 30, 1945, the 82d Airborne Division had established a small bridgehead East of the ELBE River in the vicinity of BLECKEDE, GERMANY. This bridgehead had been established by the 505th Parachute Infantry in a splendid example of coordination and river crossing technique by a veteran regiment." But as Private Langdon recollected, the "operation was the most screwed up, fouled up affair that I ever saw in my time in the war. That we came through it practically unscathed had to have been Divine Intervention." Near chaos reigned at the crossing sites, fueled in no small measure by alcohol. According to Captain Thomas M. Furey, the 1/505th troopers arrived at their crossing sites "filled with a new spirit, having obtained a store of cognac in Bleckede." A 307th report stated that "at one crossing site the passengers were unusually noisy" and that the semi-intoxicated troopers "sang and made ribald comments between boats" while getting under way. So loud, in fact, was the commotion that it forced a last-minute change in plans. "Everything had been arranged with the basic idea that there would be no preparatory artillery fires; that the element of surprise would be employed for what it was worth," remembered Captain Furey. "But with the confusion of getting the boats off the trucks and into the water and with the loud whisperings of last minute orders, it was felt that the element of surprise was lost."[80] Hence, "it was thought better to take advantage of the shock action of the artillery," so a ten-minute preparatory barrage was hastily arranged.[81] This, too, proved disruptive. Several rounds fell near the crossing site from which C Company, 1/505th, was embarking, and although it resulted in no casualties, it did create "a state of disorganization which required a few minutes to settle."[82] A second change of plan occurred when the 2/505th arrived at its two crossing sites only to find that there were no boats there. The coordinated crossing Gavin envisaged thus became a staggered crossing, with the 1/505th shoving off on schedule and the 2/505th crossing an hour and forty-five minutes later.[83]

The trip across the Elbe, which was more than 1,000 feet wide at each crossing site, took approximately thirty minutes. But for three of the four companies in the first wave it took a bit longer because of unexpected stops along the way. Both C Company, 1/505th, and E Company, 2/505th, hit sand bars. Mistaking the sand bars for the far shore, the troopers disembarked, fanned out, and assaulted, only to find they were still only about halfway to the far shore, whereupon they returned to their boats and pushed off again for the last leg of their crossing. The troopers of A Company, 1/505th, launched their boats in a small stream that emptied into the Elbe, the intent being to launch out of sight of the far shore and allow the troopers to become familiar with their craft before heading across the river. Apparently, "some of the men were imbued with the idea that the stream in which the boats were being launched was the Elbe River," and at least two boats paddled across the stream and launched an assault on a spit of land that separated the stream from the Elbe River proper. These troopers, too, eventually discovered their mistake, reembarked, and paddled to the far shore. Of the four companies in the first wave, only D Company, 2/505th, got across without detouring.[84]

Fortunately for the troopers in the first wave, it started snowing just before H hour, which served to cover their crossing and muffle their noisy approach. As a result, not a shot was fired during the crossing, and by 0300 hours, 30 April, all four companies of the first wave were across the river and firmly planted on its far bank, where they found enemy resistance negligible. Most of the Germans were dug in along a dike that bounded the east bank of the Elbe, but rather than fight, the defenders opted to hide. According to Captain Furey, "It required a hand grenade to properly induce them out, and they emerged, one by one, each a screaming mass of blood."[85]

Once the dike was cleared, the troopers pushed inland against spotty resistance, mostly from isolated strongpoints built around machine guns or 20mm antiaircraft guns, which the Germans had in abundance. In almost every case the defenders surrendered once the paratroopers returned fire. Typical was the experience of D Company, 1/505th, which ran into a German antiaircraft unit. "They showed signs of resistance," recalled Captain Sammon, but then "Company D fired four rounds of [high explosive] with a recoilless 57mm gun and the entire unit surrendered" (the 82nd received these new guns just before departing for the Rhine). Once in captivity, the German commander said that it was his intention to hold out until he received artillery fire so that he could surrender honorably. "He was mighty surprised when he saw the gun that fired the artillery," added Sammon wryly.[86]

Ironically, it was one of the follow-on units that encountered the most determined resistance of the day. Arriving shortly after H hour, the 3/505th crossed the Elbe in the British "Buffalos" and, once on the far bank, attacked in a southeasterly direction toward the second bridging site near Darchau.

Along the way it ran into stiff resistance at the small town of Stiepelse, which cost the 3/505th 8 killed and 43 wounded and fell only after being plastered by artillery. But the fight at Stiepelse was an anomaly (the 1/505th and 2/505th, for example, each lost only a single man wounded that day), and by nightfall the 505th was entrenched along phase line five. More telling was the prisoner haul: 588 Germans passed into the division's prisoner-of-war enclosures that day, portending what would become, in the next several days, a deluge.[87]

Less than two hours after Ekman's first wave hit the far shore, Ridgway put his bridge builders to work. Standing in freezing water and enduring what both Gavin and Ridgway agreed was one of the heaviest artillery barrages either had experienced—Gavin thought the Germans were simply expending the last of their artillery ammunition—it took them just under fifteen hours to build a 1,200-foot span.[88]

Meanwhile, Tucker's troopers arrived, were hustled off the trains that brought them to Bleckede, and "immediately entrucked and taken into the bridgehead. Then, after being briefed and issued ammunition, they were committed to the attack."[89] Taking position behind the 3/505th at Stiepelse, the 504th spent the night preparing to continue the advance to Darchau in the morning.

The 505th's attack on 30 April had "broken the crust, the outer defenses," recalled Captain David L. Hollingsworth of the XVIII Airborne Corps intelligence section, and with that "the entire enemy resistance collapsed."[90] "It was obvious that the German was disintegrating rapidly," echoed the 82nd's report, "and it was of the utmost importance that regardless of the physical condition of our troops, the momentum of our drive be maintained until the enemy was completely destroyed or overrun." Since the 325th was still en route, in order to maintain that momentum Ridgway attached the 8th Infantry Division's 121st Infantry Regiment to the 82nd. It, too, was ferried across the river that night and took up position on the 505th's northern flank.[91]

The attack began anew at 0500 hours, 1 May, with the 504th passing through the 3/505th to advance on Darchau. Twenty minutes later the rest of the 505th recommenced its attack to the east, and at 0600 hours the 121st attacked northward. Tanks and tank destroyers were rushed over the recently completed bridge to reinforce the infantrymen, but found there was little German armor with which to contend. Everywhere the attackers moved with surprising speed, oftentimes outrunning their artillery support. According to the 319th Glider Field Artillery Battalion's report, the infantry was "advancing so rapidly that the battalion had done no firing since their [*sic*] registration" on 29 April and had to move forward in order to keep pace with the infantry it was supporting.[92] The 376th Parachute Field Artillery Battalion had much the same experience; it moved three times on 1 May so that it could keep Tucker's 504th within range.[93] In order to maintain its support of the 505th, the 456th Parachute Field Artillery Battalion had to move even before the bulk of its artillerymen had arrived, making do by manning the guns with supply sergeants and drivers.[94] By day's end the 504th had advanced twelve miles to the southeast, the 505th had pushed a farther nine miles due east, and to the north the 121st had carved out enough room for Ridgway to insert a second division east of the Elbe, turning over that sector to the 8th Infantry Division (and returning the 121st to the 8th's control). Ridgway also got control of a third division east of the Elbe, the British 6th Airborne (which crossed the Elbe via the Lauenburg Bridge), when it linked up with the 121st Infantry Regiment in the north.[95] To top off the day's achievements, after the 504th uncovered Darchau, Ridgway's engineers repeated their bridge-building feat by constructing a second bridge over the Elbe, this one 852 feet long, in six hours and fifteen minutes.[96]

As had been the case on 30 April, German resistance on 1 May was scant. "Resistance to our advance was negligible," recorded the 504th's report, "as those German troops which the Regiment was able to make contact with surrendered en masse almost without resistance." The same was true in the 505th's sector. According to Private Langdon, "The only Krauts we saw had their hands in the air." Indeed, about the only danger the troopers encountered on 1 May was from a new type of mine the Germans had strewn liberally along the roads. Fabricated from a 500-pound bomb, the mine had a magnetic detector that allowed a preset number of vehicles to pass before detonating. The resulting explosion "left a huge crater in the road large enough to accommodate a small house," recalled Lieutenant Megellas. Lieutenant Edward Sims saw one go off. "The explosion lifted one of our tanks about 30 feet in the air, killing the entire crew."[97] To counter this new threat, the 307th Engineers enlisted the help of technical experts from XVIII Airborne Corps as well as captured German military engineers. Working together, by day's end they devised a means to both locate and defuse the mines. Thereafter, mine-clearing parties composed of both Germans and Americans fanned out and cleared the roads, doubtless saving scores of unnecessary deaths, military and civilian, Axis and Allied.[98] And there was a growing pool of captured German manpower from which to choose, for on 1 May an additional 696 Germans surrendered to the 82nd.[99] "We were absolutely inundated with prisoners and [displaced persons]," recalled Langdon. "We stopped in a small town and set up a road block and thereafter processed prisoners that were just streaming in."[100] So anxious were the Germans to surrender to Americans (and thereby escape the Red Army closing from the east) that whole units would give up to anyone wearing a U.S. uniform. The 82nd's Reconnaissance Platoon, ranging far ahead of the main body, took approximately 470 prisoners alone, a figure that exceeded the platoon's strength fifteen times.[101]

During the night of 1–2 May Ridgway pushed as much of XVIII Airborne Corps over the Elbe as possible, for at daybreak he intended to unleash an attack that would gain for the corps and 21st Army Group its final objectives and achieve contact with the Red Army. His plan was to have the 8th Infantry Division attack in the center of the corps zone along a northeasterly axis toward Schwerin and then (if practicable) on to Wismar on the Baltic, thereby sealing off the Jutland Peninsula and Denmark from the onrushing Soviets, while the 82nd continued its attack to the east and southeast and the British 6th Airborne conducted a limited attack to the north. The bulk of the 7th Armored would be kept in reserve, ready to rush through the 8th Infantry and on to Wismar if required. Ridgway was going to push his troops hard; the enemy was showing signs of collapse and was to be given no time to organize a last-ditch line of defense.[102]

Gavin's plan was to pass Colonel Billingslea's 325th, which had come up during the night, through Ekman's 505th and continue attacking east to the fairly large town of Ludwigslust while Tucker's 504th continued its attack to the southeast. Reinforcing each regiment were tanks and tank destroyers from the 7th Armored Division. With their final objectives some twenty-five miles away, both Billingslea and Tucker spearheaded their attacks with a battalion of infantry mounted on tanks and tank destroyers. *Speed* was the watchword. Enemy resistance was insignificant. All indications were that the end was near.[103]

The second of May dawned "a lovely spring morning. The fields were freshly green, and flowers and chestnut trees along the road were in full bloom." It was also strangely quiet; "not even an occasional round of friendly or enemy fire could be heard." Jumping off at 0500 hours, the troopers moved through a landscape seemingly devoid of humanity, at least German humanity. As the 325th's Captain Pierce remembered it, the attack seemed more like a training exercise. "The only shot fired that morning was at a deer," he recalled. "The deer was not hit." Gavin, who was up before dawn "in anticipation of something unusual happening," rode forward in a jeep with Colonel Billingslea over streets and roads that were completely deserted. It was some time before they saw their first German, a lone soldier on a motorcycle, whom they chased down and took prisoner. "He was the last German in the war we were to see running away," noted Gavin.[104]

Around midmorning, things began to change. The German collapse had begun. Both Billingslea's and Tucker's lead elements were "overrunning groups of bewildered enemy with hardly any will to resist, who thought [the 82nd was] still at the Elbe while they were fighting what appeared to be a retrograde action with the Russians." Other groups of Germans, bypassed by the advance, made their way to the nearest Americans and surrendered (waiting, no doubt, until daylight when they would not be mistaken for raiding parties). One group approached the 319th's command post and "requested to be directed to the Prisoner of War Inclosure [*sic*]."[105] Another German commander chose a more expeditious manner of ending his wartime service: He surrendered himself and his entire unit to an American sergeant he had captured the day before.[106]

Eventually, the troopers encountered ever-larger groups of Germans. "They seemed to be milling about indecisively and to be not particularly desirous to fight," remembered Gavin. "It was an eerie sight for those of us who had fought for more than three years all the way from Africa, for the mere sight of that bucket helmet meant certain death unless one reacted instantly and instinctively, taking cover and firing. So, taking our lives in our hands, we drove right up to them. They wanted to surrender."[107] Everywhere resistance was practically nonexistent. The 82nd lost but one tank to a *panzerfaust*, and there were a few scattered firefights, but overwhelmingly the Germans were bent on surrendering.[108] And whereas the day began with no sign of a German, by late morning the troopers "were engulfed by an endless stream of German soldiers, German civilians and displaced personnel, fleeing in panic before the Russian drive, hoping to get across the Elbe into American areas." Fighting through the mass of humanity clogging the roads, the 325th and 504th took their respective objectives by noon. The troopers of the 2/325th, riding aboard tanks and tank destroyers, entered Ludwigslust to find the town "packed with German soldiers desirous of getting away from the Russian army."[109] Corporal Leonard Linton of the division's civil-military affairs section was up front with them:

> We kept on rushing on that road [to Ludwisglust] until we no longer saw any of our men but increasing numbers of all types of German Army vehicles ranging from horsecarts [*sic*] to rows of Tiger tanks and their prime movers, as well as large numbers of Hussars of Hungarian horse-mounted cavalry in parade-like close-order which seemed unreal at the time. Most units' disorder or disarray was indescribable; none of them was firing or threatening. Every now and then a neat disciplined unit would appear to the credit of some unknown commander. Periodically I would stop the jeep at the level of some German command car and yell in German that they are all prisoners of the 82nd ABN of the US Army and to order their men to disarm themselves and throw the bolts and breach blocks of their weapons into the ditch.[110]

In the 504th's zone it was the same story. "Germans in all town[s] offer no resistance and seem to be waiting for us so they can surrender," ran the noon entry in the 3/504th's combat journal. By 1540 hours, the journal noted: "Roads congested with Germans or D.P.'s [displaced persons]. All weapons from PW's collected and put in piles along road."[111] The commander of the *5th Jäger Division*, in order to ensure the smooth movement of his unit into American prisoner-of-war camps, had even posted guides along the way. Like many German formations the 82nd captured that day, "They had their tanks, artillery pieces, supply trains with them. All were armed, but had no intention of shooting. They were permitted to keep their tanks and vehicles for pulling supply trailers. If they had run out of gas, as many of them had, captured gasoline was obtained for them."[112] As the 82nd's after-action review noted: "After more than two years of intense and, at times, very costly fighting with the German Army, the spectacle that began to unfold itself was an unbelievable one."[113] But the day was not over.

At about 1415 hours, a delegation of German officers entered the 325th's lines. The general in charge of the group announced that they represented the commanding general of the *Twenty-first Army* and that they had come to arrange for its surrender. Private Shirley R. Gossett of the 1/325th was one of the first to meet the group. "Since our only officer was a [second lieutenant] he wanted to see a much more higher officer to surrender to. We took his caravan to Division Headquarters as he requested." By that time, the division headquarters had been established in the palace of the grand duke of Mecklenburg in Ludwigslust. When the group arrived, Gavin was standing outside near the intersection of the town's two main thoroughfares, "looking like any other GI in the 82nd," except for the two stars on his collar and helmet.[114] According to Gavin:

> An American GI came up to me and said that there was a German general looking for the American general who was in charge. I told him to send him over. He arrived, rather haughtily, I thought, and a bit threadbare, but otherwise impeccably attired in the field gray uniform of the Wehrmacht. It was set off by the red collar tabs and insignia of a general, and an Iron Cross dangled at his throat. When told that I was the American general, he looked at me with some disdain, saying that I couldn't be; I was too young and did not look like a general to him. It took only a moment to change his mind.[115]

The German general asked Gavin if he could arrange for the surrender of his wounded and Allied prisoners. Gavin replied that he "would accept the surrender of his complete army only and on unconditional terms." The general stated that he would carry this message to his commander, and the two arranged a second meeting for 2000 hours that night at the palace.[116]

At the prescribed time General der Infanterie Kurt von Tippelskirch, commander of the *Twenty-first Army*, arrived at the palace with several members of his staff. Tippelskirch tried to convince Gavin that he would surrender *only* to Gavin, and because of that the 82nd should "move out and accept the surrender of his army where it stood," an obvious ploy to use the 82nd as cover to ensure his soldiers ended up in American and not Russian prisoner-of-war camps. Gavin demurred. "I told him that the Russians were our allies and that I proposed to move against him and destroy his army in conjunction with them if he did not surrender." Out of options, Tippelskirch accepted, and at 2120 hours the two commanders signed a surrender document. Tippelskirch agreed to "unconditionally surrender the 21st German Army, all of its attachments, and equipment and appurtenances thereto, to the Commanding General of the 82d Airborne Division, United States Army." Furthermore, the document stipulated that the unconditional surrender was "valid only for those troops of the 21st Army which pass through American lines," thereby avoiding any hint of German-American collusion against the Russians.[117]

Over the next several days some 144,000 German soldiers walked or rode into captivity through the 82nd's lines (conversely, the Elbe River campaign cost the 82nd 21 troopers killed, 122 wounded, and 11 missing). Since there was no way the division could process that many prisoners, the vast majority were simply disarmed and herded to the rear in captured vehicles. For two days following the surrender there was "an apparently endless stream" of these vehicles moving "bumper to bumper" over the bridge at Bleckede, all "loaded to overflowing with the bedraggled remnants of the German Army." The division's troopers acted as road guides and column guards; provided medical care for those who needed it; issued rations; set up a military government in their zone; screened the prisoners, displaced persons, and civilian population for Nazis and SS officials; and collected all the captured war materiel in several salvage yards, a haul that included almost 2,000 trucks and cars, 81 half-tracks, 11 tanks, 21 flak wagons, 35 artillery pieces, approximately 1,000 antiaircraft guns, 655 antitank guns, and tens of thousands of rounds of ammunition of all calibers.[118]

"There will never be a day like this again nor a week for that matter," recorded Gavin in his diary the day after accepting Tippelskirch's surrender. Spearheading what Bradley called a "little-known but astonishingly effective drive," the 82nd not only compelled the surrender of one of the few German armies still capable of organized resistance, but also opened the way for the rest of the corps to rush across the Elbe to seize its final objectives three days ahead of schedule.[119] Despite violating one of the most sacrosanct of military dictums—to never commit units piecemeal, especially in the presence of a much larger enemy—Ridgway's decision to hurl the 82nd across the Elbe and feed in the rest of the division as it arrived was, in Gavin's estimation, "one of the best decisions of the war."[120] It also had tremendous postwar consequences, particularly when viewed in light of the Cold War, for it allowed Ridgway to speed the advance on Wismar, which the British 6th Airborne Division took on 2 May, just two hours before the Red Army arrived.[121] "If you had not ordered us across," wrote Gavin to Ridgway in 1979, "the Russians would be in Denmark today, and the whole situation in Scandinavia and the Baltic would be different than it is today." Of course, Ridgway's gamble would not have paid such dividends had he not had a unit on which he could rely to react with speed and aggressiveness, but as he wrote in his memoirs, the 82nd "was accustomed to move fast."[122]

In his last report of the war Lieutenant Colonel Robert H. Neptune, commander of the 376th Parachute Field Artillery Battalion, wrote, "The once great German Army had collapsed before our eyes and after two long years which saw us in Africa, Sicily, Italy, England, Holland, France, Belgium, Luxemburg, and finally only 132 kilometers from Berlin, Germany, we had been present at the end. It was hard for many of us to realize just what was happening."[123] Ironically, it was a similar sense of not fully realizing "just what was happening" that pervaded the 82nd's ranks when it was first committed to combat in Sicily twenty-one months before. They quickly discovered, however, that speed, aggressiveness, daring, and initiative were uncertainty's antidotes and displayed these attributes through some of the toughest fights of the European war. Now they stood on the outskirts of Berlin as uncertain as when they began. There was one thing, however, about which the troopers who wore the "AA" of the 82nd Airborne Division were definitely certain—that they were members of a "proven outfit where reputations are made and fame is everywhere."[124]

EPILOGUE

SOLDIERS RECENTLY ENGAGED IN WAR

In these days, when men and officers seem to have turned their thoughts exclusively to getting home, I want you to know that there are a great number of us who realize that the past few years have been climactic in our lives. Nothing we, personally, can ever do can recreate the atmosphere of the great airborne D-days. . . . Now the exaltation which was once part of our daily lives as sky-borne soldiers has subsided and we walk silently into the future remembering that once our comrades lent fire and a touch of greatness to the American cause. . . .

And so, for myself as well as all those others in the Division who remember the roar of planes at night; the white-hot instant when the warning light flashes on; and the magnificence of night skies full of swaying chutes, I want to say this:

"We hope, with all our hearts, that your wish will be fulfilled, and that somewhere, somehow, there will always be an 82nd. If we can know that somewhere your men will dare the challenge to 'stand up and hook up,' and know the moment of pride and strength which is its reward, then a little part of us will always be alive, free and invincible."

—A LIEUTENANT OF THE 82ND AIRBORNE DIVISION
(JOHN V. MCNALLY) TO JAMES M. GAVIN, 19 OCTOBER 1945

FOLLOWING THE SURRENDER of the *Twenty-first Army*, the 82nd turned its attention to processing the thousands of persons passing through its lines—Wehrmacht and SS soldiers, German civilians fleeing the Russians, displaced persons from almost every country in Europe, and Allied prisoners of war who simply started walking west when their guards abandoned them. Combat operations were suspended. For the troopers of the 82nd Airborne Division, the war had come to an end.[1] But there was yet one last fight to wage, this one for the division's very existence.

Within days of Germany's surrender the War Department ordered that all those eligible for release from the service be returned to the United States and discharged.[2] Planning for this eventuality had been ongoing for more than two years. The initial plan was to demobilize by unit, but at the behest of the National Resources Planning Board the plan was changed; instead, the Army would demobilize by individual. To facilitate this, a scoring system was enacted that awarded soldiers a certain number of points for time in service, time overseas, time in combat, number of wounds, and the number of children he had. Those with the most points, the "high-point" men, would be the first to return to the United States and their civilian lives.[3]

The 82nd sent home 647 high-point troopers in the three weeks it spent at Ludwigslust before moving back to France. Although certainly a welcome release for those going home, having its ranks depleted so suddenly was an unsettling portent for those concerned with the postwar life of the 82nd. This was because the War Department announced that only three of the Army's five airborne divisions would be retained in the peacetime establishment. (By the end of the war the United States had formed five airborne divisions, four of which, the 13th, 17th, 82nd, and 101st, were in Europe under XVIII Airborne Corps control. The fifth airborne division, the 11th, served in the Pacific under MacArthur.) Obviously, the most expeditious manner of paring down would be to disband the airborne divisions with the most high-point men, and since the 82nd had more combat time than any other airborne division, it naturally had the most high-point men, some 6,000 in all, well more than half its authorized strength.[4]

Ridgway learned of the plans for the postwar airborne force in late April 1945. What he did not know was which of his four airborne divisions would be preserved, so he sent his corps artillery commander, Brigadier General Lemuel Mathewson, to General Bradley's headquarters to find out. Mathewson's report back to Ridgway was ominous. According to Mathewson, although General Bradley "would dislike as much as anyone to see a fine fighting organization such as the 82nd broken up," he did not appear to be particularly engaged with the issue and seemed to have accepted the War Department's position that it was all about individuals and numbers and not about "salvaging any particular unit, regardless of its traditional background or military achievements."[5]

Bradley's unsatisfactory reply—which must have come as something of a surprise since he had commanded the 82nd—spurred Ridgway to action.

Since the final decision had not been made about which airborne divisions would remain and unwilling to let 12th Army Group, SHAEF, or the War Department decide the issue for him, Ridgway instructed his staff to come up with a concept that would both meet the War Department's demand for rapid demobilization and preserve the 82nd. The resultant concept was summarized in a memorandum by Ridgway's chief of staff, "Doc" Eaton.

The concept was based on the assumption that two of the four European-based airborne divisions would be retained on the active rolls and took into consideration the combat experience of the leadership of each of the divisions. Given those criteria, it called for the retention of the 82nd and 101st and the early return to the United States and subsequent disbandment of the 13th and 17th Airborne Divisions (the 13th Airborne Division never saw a day of combat, while the 17th Airborne Division did not enter the fight until the Bulge). In order to meet War Department guidance for the rapid demobilization of veterans, the high-point men would be transferred to the 13th and 17th Airborne Divisions before those divisions returned to the United States (in turn, low-point men would be transferred into the 82nd and 101st to fill their slots). This concept, wrote Eaton in summary, was based on "a weighing of administrative and morale factors as well as probable employment in combat," and presented a cogent and justifiable rationale for retaining the two airborne divisions with the most seasoned leadership and proven combat records.[6]

Four days after submitting his memorandum, Eaton learned that morale, proven leadership, and combat performance counted for little to those in the higher echelons. On 30 May, he received a call from Eisenhower's operations officer, Major General Harold R. "Pinky" Bull, during which Bull told him that the War Department had earmarked the 82nd and 17th for disbandment, leaving the 13th and 101st as the two European airborne divisions that would remain on the active rolls. Eaton was incredulous. Ridgway, said Eaton, was adamant about keeping the 82nd alive, but this made little headway with Bull. "He told me that it didn't seem to make any difference on the future war standing whether the 82d was disbanded or not, because it could be reactivated from the 13th at a later date," reported Eaton to his boss. Bull did, however, offer a means to forestall the decision. At the time the U.S. 2nd Armored Division was on occupation duty in Berlin, and SHAEF was shopping around for a replacement. Eaton jumped at the idea. "I told him that we would do everything to save the 82d, and therefore the 82d would certainly be acceptable as a substitute for the 2d Armored." Bull told Eaton that he would have to get permission from the War Department first.[7] By mid-June, that permission was granted, and the 82nd, then in base camps in France, began preparing for its new mission.[8]

The 82nd assumed its role as the American contingent to the Berlin occupation force in August. Two months later it again received word that it was to be deactivated. The final shape of the postwar Army had finally been approved, and it envisaged not three but two airborne divisions. Adding insult to injury, it was also announced that the 101st had been selected to march in America's victory parade down New York City's Fifth Avenue, tentatively scheduled for January 1946. Gavin laid this feat of legerdemain squarely at the feet of Major General Maxwell Taylor, who had just given up command of the 101st: "We knew that the commanding general of the 101st had been ordered to the Military Academy at West Point to be superintendent when the war came to an end. He took that position in early September, 1945. We all assumed therefore that on his return he called on the Department of the Army to plead the case of the 101st, and thus have it kept on active duty while the 82nd was inactivated."[9]

Upon receiving the news, Gavin thought long and hard about making a trip to Washington to plead the 82nd's case, but his duties in Berlin precluded that possibility. Furthermore, unlike Taylor he did not have a personal relationship with General Marshall, nor was he savvy in the ways of War Department politics (Taylor, on the other hand, had served in Marshall's secretariat for a year prior to his transfer to the 82nd in July 1942). But Gavin refused to go down without a fight. Engaging in what he called his "hardest battle of the war," Gavin worked both official and unofficial channels to mount a massive public relations and information campaign to save the 82nd Airborne Division.[10] His first action, of course, was an appeal to Ridgway, who at the time was temporarily (and fortuitously) attached to the War Department General Staff in Washington. Ridgway did not disappoint.[11]

After hearing from Gavin, Ridgway sent a memorandum to Marshall in which he compared the records of the 82nd and 101st. The 82nd fought in two wars, he noted, the 101st in only one. In fact, he reminded Marshall, the 82nd spawned the 101st by halving its strength. Enumerating the combat action of the two divisions, Ridgway noted that the 82nd had two more campaign credits than the 101st, that it had suffered more casualties in the course of the war, and that during the Battle of the Bulge, which earned the 101st national recognition as a result of its stand at Bastogne, the 82nd "engaged in at least equally severe combat, [and] suffered greater battle losses." "Both divisions have splendid records," he admitted, "but the facts show a much longer and at least equally brilliant battle record in the case of the 82nd." And in a veiled reference to the relationship he knew Marshall had with Taylor, he wrote that "personalities of former and present commanders should not be factors in arriving at a decision, which should be based solely on record, in and out of combat." Then, in a flourish that was typical Ridgway, he framed the decision as one with moral and transcendent implications: "Retention of the 82nd will be accepted by the Army as a just and proper recognition of its service. Inactivation of this Division and retention of any other Airborne Division will be viewed as a grave injustice to the many thousands of living and dead who contributed to its achievements. The United States Army will not wish to perpetuate such feelings."[12]

Ridgway sent a copy of his memorandum to Eisenhower, who was still in Europe, and whose opinion he knew would carry great weight, especially since it was common knowledge that Eisenhower would be replacing the soon-to-retire Marshall as Army chief of staff. Eisenhower agreed with Ridgway's recommendation. In a supporting memorandum that he cabled to the War Department Eisenhower wrote, "I concur fully in the presentation made by General Ridgway. . . . In spite of my admiration for the 101st, if a choice must be made I am quite certain that the 82nd should be the one to be retained."[13]

Not one to trust wholly in War Department officialdom—it was, after all, composed of the same people who had made the decision to inactivate the 82nd in the first place—Gavin turned to a coterie of unofficial, albeit well-placed, allies for assistance: the press. This was not a difficult task. According to Colonel Barney Oldfield, the First Allied Airborne Army's public relations officer (and a former member of the 505th), "The decision [to inactivate the 82nd] fell almost as hard on a militant section of the press corps which was high on the Eighty Second." These militants included Bill Walton from *Time*, who had jumped with the 82nd into Normandy; John "Beaver" Thompson of the *Chicago Tribune*, who made the drop into Sicily; Martha Gellhorn of *Collier's*, who took up the division's cause "like a suffragette"; Charles Collingswood of CBS; and Judy Barden of the *New York Post*. Led by Oldfield, these and other members of the press used their newspapers, magazines, and microphones to let out "a steady stream of comment questioning the wisdom of letting the celebrated Eighty-second go down the military drain when its great record would be such an inspiration to the peacetime Army." "The men of the Eighty-second Airborne Division . . . are going home soon with mixed emotions," ran one representative communiqué in the 15 October 1945 issue of the *New York Times*. "Theirs is one of the proudest divisions in the United States Army and to the men who helped to build its traditions and fame it seems that the logic behind the decision to send its battle colors into the limbo of a museum while the names of other less famous fighting units are perpetuated is debatable."[14]

Gavin's two-pronged campaign worked with surprising speed. Whether due to the hue and cry of the press or the memoranda from Ridgway and Eisenhower or both, in early November the War Department reversed its decision. The 101st would be deactivated and the 82nd retained.[15] Later that month Gavin received another heartening message—the 82nd Airborne Division would lead the victory parade.[16]

So it was that at precisely 1300 hours, 12 January 1946, Gavin stepped off at the head of 8,800 82nd Airborne Division troopers from beneath New York City's Washington Arch and headed up Fifth Avenue. Overhead were forty C-47s, each towing a glider, a fitting aerial complement. It was an overcast day, threatening rain, with temperatures in the forties. When asked about the chance of rain, Gavin promised to go, regardless of the conditions. "It's one of those things you dream about," Gavin answered. "We'd all say: 'When we get back we'll all parade up Fifth Avenue.' It was just like our saying we'd parachute down on Berlin. We never thought it would happen."[17] Some two to four million people lined the parade route, cheering, crying, waving, and throwing confetti, but Gavin and his troopers kept eyes front and marched in silent, disciplined tribute to all those who never made it back. Columnist Ed Bliss was one of those millions watching the 82nd stride by that day. In a piece he wrote to commemorate Gavin's death in February 1990, he recalled vividly what he saw and felt:

> There was no sun. It was dark, befitting men who had come back from death. It was all dark: the sky, the street, the helmets, the rifles, the battle dress. Although CBS and NBC had brought out their large parabolic microphones to pick up the martial music, I remember only two bands. For long stretches the only sound you heard was the tread of thousands of pairs of boots, an unforgettable haunting sound. You felt pride—and pain. As they passed, and kept passing, and kept passing, the tears came. Out of this many, so many must be missing. It almost seemed these were the missing. There was no glamor [*sic*] in this parade. These were soldiers recently engaged in war.[18]

So ended the 82nd Airborne Division's World War II odyssey, during which it spent 422 days in combat in five separate campaigns, earned fifteen Presidential Unit Citations, and three foreign awards (the Belgian Fourragere, the French Fourragere, and the Dutch Military Order of Willems). Its bloody laurels counted more than 181,000 enemy prisoners of war and innumerable more killed and wounded. Three 82nd troopers won the Medal of Honor (DeGlopper, Funk, and Towle), 79 earned a Distinguished Service Cross, and almost 900 were awarded Silver Stars. But it had all come at significant cost. All told, the 82nd suffered 19,586 casualties during the war (more than two times the division's authorized strength), including 2,665 killed in action (with another 1,600 missing as of October 1945).[19] Time and again it was savaged only to come back fighting, and it never failed to accomplish any mission it was assigned, despite almost always being outnumbered and outgunned.

There are myriad reasons for its success. Foremost was leadership. Ridgway and Gavin epitomized the up-front leadership by example that was demanded of every commissioned and noncommissioned officer who wore the 82nd patch. There were a few who did not live up to this high standard, but the vast majority did. Hence, instead of being *sent* into battle, the troopers of the 82nd Airborne Division were *led* into battle. And there was also the ethos of toughness, aggressiveness, and initiative that permeated the division, traits that were pounded into the troopers during training and expected of them in combat. According to Lieutenant Colonel George K. Rubel, whose 740th Tank Battalion was often attached to the 82nd, "These were truly fighting men. A squad of the 82d Airborne Division will take on a company of the German Army, an 82d Airborne Division Company will take on a German Battalion, and to assign any unit of the 82d Airborne Division an objective is to know that the objective will be taken and held."[20]

In the midst of the Battle of the Bulge, there occurred one exchange that, perhaps more than any other, exemplifies the attitude of the troopers of the 82nd Airborne Division. It was 22 December 1944. The U.S. First Army was still in headlong retreat from the onrushing panzers that were seemingly everywhere. A column of American tanks came upon a lone bazooka gunner in a snow-covered bunker. The lead tank commander leaned down from his hatch to ask the lone trooper where the American lines were. The bazooka gunner, a private from the 325th Glider Infantry Regiment, replied, "You've just arrived at the American front lines, pal. Now you just pull your tank up behind me. I'm the 82nd Airborne Division, and this is as far as the bastards are going."[21]

NOTES

INTRODUCTION

1. Transcript of comments by Stephen Ambrose in Steven Weingartner, ed., *The Greatest Thing We Have Ever Attempted: Historical Perspectives on the Normandy Campaign*, 16.

2. S[amuel] L[yman] A[twood] Marshall, *Men Against Fire: The Problem of Battle Command in Future War*, 27 (quote), 50. Marshall's claims about the number of men who fired their weapon have since been proved false. Marshall had no statistics to back up his assertion, and even his primary assistant claimed that he could not recall Marshall ever asking soldiers about firing their weapons. However, this point was not discovered and made public until 1988. See Frederic Smoler, "The Secret of the Soldiers Who Didn't Shoot."

3. Marshall, *Men Against Fire*, 43, 156.

4. Edward A. Shils and Morris Janowitz, "Cohesion and Disintegration in the Wehrmacht in World War II," 178 (emphasis in original). This article was originally published in *Public Opinion Quarterly* in 1948.

5. Charles Horton Cooley, *Social Organization* (New York: n.p., 1909), 23, as quoted in ibid., 218n3.

6. Dennis Showalter provided the author with a draft copy of a book foreword in which he made this comment. This foreword was subsequently published in Russell A. Hart's *Clash of Arms: How the Allies Won in Normandy* (Boulder: Lynne Rienner, 2001). Others who have contributed to this view of German combat superiority include Paul L. Savage and Richard A. Gabriel, "Cohesion and Disintegration in the American Army" and *Crisis in Command: Mismanagement in the Army*; Trevor N. Dupuy, *A Genius for War: The German Army and General Staff, 1807–1945* and *Numbers, Predictions, and War: Using History to Evaluate Combat Factors and Predict the Outcome of Battle*; and Martin van Creveld, *Fighting Power: German and U.S. Army Performance, 1939–1945*.

7. John Keegan, *Six Armies in Normandy: From D-Day to the Liberation of Paris*, 320; Russell F. Weigley, *Eisenhower's Lieutenants: The Campaign of France and Germany, 1944–1945*, 729–730.

8. Omer Bartov, *The Eastern Front, 1941–45: German Troops and the Barbarisation of Warfare*, 36, 38, 69.

9. Omer Bartov, *Hitler's Army: Soldiers, Nazis, and War in the Third Reich*, 6, 166, 169.

10. H. P. Willmott, *The Great Crusade: A New Complete History of the Second World War*, xi.

11. Richard Overy, *Why the Allies Won*, 2, 6 (emphasis in the original).

12. Michael D. Doubler, *Closing with the Enemy: How GIs Fought the War in Europe, 1944–1945*, 2, 7; Peter R. Mansoor, *The GI Offensive in Europe: The Triumph of American Infantry Divisions, 1941–1945*, 4.

13. See Mark S. Watson, *Chief of Staff: Prewar Plans and Preparations*, 16; and John T. Ellis Jr., *The Airborne Command and Center*, 3.

CHAPTER 1: OUR WHOLE FUTURE IS IN THE AIR

1. Harry C. Butcher, *My Three Years with Eisenhower: The Personal Diary of Captain Harry C. Butcher, USNR, Naval Aide to General Eisenhower, 1942 to 1945*, 827.

2. Headquarters, 319th Glider Field Artillery Battalion, 82nd Airborne Division, "The Unit History of the 319th Glider Field Artillery Battalion (from May 1, 1945 to June 3, 1945 Incl.)," n.d., pp. 2–3, 382-FA(319)-0.3, Box 12435, Record Group 407, National Archives and Records Administration II, Modern Military Reference Branch, College Park, Maryland (hereafter NARA II).

3. William Mitchell, *Memoirs of World War I: "From Start to Finish of Our Greatest War,"* 268.

4. William B. Breuer, *Geronimo! American Paratroopers in World War II*, 7.

5. James A. Huston, *Out of the Blue: U.S. Army Airborne Operations in World War II*, 47–48.

6. James E. Mrazek, *The Glider War*, 53; Gerard M. Devlin, *Silent Wings: The Saga of U.S. Army and Marine Combat Glider Pilots During World War II*, 17–27.

7. John W. Morgan, "Airborne Field Artillery," 55.

8. J. T. Ellis, *Airborne Command and Center*, 1; William C. Lee, "Air Infantry," 16.

9. J. T. Ellis, *Airborne Command and Center*, 1; Maurice A. J. Tugwell, "Day of the Paratroops," 42.

10. Articles 198–202 of the Versailles Treaty dictated that Germany surrender its aviation materiel, including 17,000 planes and engines. Besides being permanently prohibited from maintaining any military or naval air force, the German aviation industry was completely shut down for six months following the signing of the treaty. After that time, severe restrictions were imposed on the performance criteria for German aircraft, limiting their range, speed, and power. Finally, German airspace was to be controlled by the Allied powers for several years. See James S. Corum, *The Luftwaffe: Creating the Operational Air War, 1918–1940*, 49.

11. Göring quoted in Edward V. Rickenbacker, *Seven Came Through*, 104 (emphasis in original).

12. Mrazek, *The Glider War*, 27–28.

13. Devlin, *Silent Wings*, 29, 31.

14. James E. Mrazek, *The Fall of Eben Emael: Prelude to Dunkerque*, 37–38.

15. David M. Glantz, *The Soviet Airborne Experience*, 4–11, 14 (quote).

16. Mrazek, *The Glider War*, 230–233; Devlin, *Silent Wings*, 28–29.

17. James M. Gavin, *On to Berlin: Battles of an Airborne Commander, 1943–1946*, xiv. One reason the Soviets may not have been able to make sense of all those men and airplanes is, perhaps, the purges that emasculated the Red Army in the 1930s, to include the purging of the most innovative and brilliant of the interwar reformers, Tukhachevsky.

18. Wavell quoted in Glantz, *Soviet Airborne Experience*, 11–13; see also 4–11. An airhead, much like a beachhead, is an area seized and controlled by airborne forces (either parachutists or glidermen) during an airborne assault.

19. Breuer, *Geronimo!* 3; James Lucas, *Storming Eagles: German Airborne Forces in World War Two*, 8–9.

20. See also John Hackett, "Student," 464–466; and Lucas, *Storming Eagles*, 172–176. The German parachute forces, unlike those of any other major belligerent of World War II, were air force organizations, a result, no doubt, of Hermann Göring's influence. It should also be noted that the Germans did not have separate glider and parachute units. German paratroopers were also trained in glider operations. As will be seen, this was not the case with the American airborne divisions, which were composed of separate parachute and glider units. Because of his efforts in raising this force, Student is universally regarded as the father of Germany's airborne force.

21. J. T. Ellis, *Airborne Command and Center*, 5.

22. Jack G. Cornett, "Development of Airborne Forces," 26.

23. James M. Gavin, "Beyond the Stars," 61, 67, James M. Gavin Papers, Box 2, Folder "Chapter 2: Autobiography," United States Army Military History Institute, Carlisle Barracks, Pennsylvania (hereafter USAMHI).

24. Lee, "Air Infantry," 14; William C. Lee, "Air-Landing Divisions," 20.

25. J. T. Ellis, *Airborne Command and Center*, 3.

26. Gavin, "Beyond the Stars," 61.

27. Cornett, "Development of Airborne Forces," 26.

CHAPTER 2: A BREED APART

1. This memorandum to Lynch is reproduced in Gerard M. Devlin, *Paratrooper! The Saga of U.S. Army and Marine Parachute and Glider Combat Troops During World War II*, 35.

2. Ibid., 36.

3. Ridgely Gaither to Dr. Randolph Doffermyre, 17 May 1957, copy of letter in possession of the author. In 1940, Captain Gaither was Lee's assistant.

4. J. T. Ellis, *Airborne Command and Center*, 15.

5. James M. Gavin, transcript of interview, 1 April 1983, Clay and Joan Blair Collection, Box 53, Folder "Gavin, James M.," USAMHI.

6. J. T. Ellis, *Airborne Command and Center*, 2–4.

7. Ibid., 2.

8. This memorandum from the Adjutant General's Office, dated 25 June 1940, subject: Organization of Test Platoon, Parachute Troops and Air Infantry, is reproduced in appendix no. 2 of ibid., 84.

9. This memorandum from the Office of the Infantry School, Fort Benning, Georgia, dated 1 July 1940, subject: Parachute Troops and Air Infantry, is reproduced in appendix no. 3 of ibid., 85–87.

10. Devlin, *Paratrooper!* 50–55.

11. Thad P. Selman, interview by the author, Atlanta, Georgia, 13 April 2002.

12. Ibid. During the interview, Selman was insistent that the plane from which they jumped was a C-33 transport and not a B-18 bomber, despite the existence of a plaque at Lawson Field that states that it was the latter aircraft that carried the first Army paratroopers aloft.

13. Devlin, *Paratrooper!* 71–75; J. T. Ellis, *Airborne Command and Center*, 5.

14. This memorandum from the War Department Adjutant General's Office, Washington, D.C., dated 16 September 1940, subject: Constitution of the 1st Parachute Battalion, is reproduced in appendix 4 of J. T. Ellis, *Airborne Command and Center*, 88.

15. Devlin, *Paratrooper!* 82–85.

16. William P. Yarborough, interview by John R. Meese and H. P. Houser III, 28 March 1975, William P. Yarborough Papers, Box "Oral Interview," Folder "Section One (Duplicate)," USAMHI; Omar N. Bradley and Clay Blair, *A General's Life*, 101.

17. The term *straight leg* or *leg* was (and still is) a derisive term that paratroopers called nonjumping soldiers. It was a reference to the dress uniform trousers worn by nonparatroopers, which had a straight, sharp crease extending from the soldier's waist to the top of his low quarter shoes.

18. Devlin, *Paratrooper!* 91–93. Yarborough not only designed the Army's airborne wings but also played a significant part in designing the jump boots.

19. Breuer, *Geronimo!* 26.

20. John D. McKenzie, *On Time, On Target: The World War II Memoir of a Paratrooper in the 82d Airborne*, 46; Richard Mott Janney, *Richard Mott Janney, 1st Lt. 505 Reg. 82 A.B. Div. Killed in Action Villa Literno, Italy, October 5, 1943*, 60; hardbound memorial booklet found in World War II Veterans Survey Project, Box "505th PIR (1)," Folder "Janney, Richard Mott, 505th Regt.," USAMHI.

21. William L. Blank, personal history narrative, World War II Veterans Survey Project, Box "82nd Airborne Division. 505th PIR 1," Folder "Blank, William L. S/SGT, 505 Parachute Inf., 82nd Airborne Div.," USAMHI.

22. Matthew B. Ridgway to George C. Marshall, 12 June 1944, in *The Papers of George C. Marshall: Selected Correspondence*, microfilm.

23. Kent Roberts Greenfield, Robert R. Palmer, and Bell I. Wiley, *The Organization of Ground Combat Troops*, 94

24. Devlin, *Paratrooper!* 90–96.

25. McKearney quoted in Gerald Astor, ed., *June 6, 1944: The Voices of D-Day*, 52; Joe Stolmeier, interview by the author, Atlanta, Georgia, 13 April 2002; McKenzie, *On Time, On Target*, 50.

26. Stolmeier, interview, 13 April 2002.

27. James A. Huston, "Thoughts on the American Airborne Effort in World War II," 5.

28. Melvin Zais, interview by William L. Golden and Richard C. Rice, 20 January 1977, Melvin Zais Papers, Box "Oral History," USAMHI; Bradley and Blair, *A General's Life*, 101–102; J. T. Ellis, *Airborne Command and Center*, 11.

29. Twaddle quoted in Greenfield, Palmer, and Wiley, *Organization of Ground Combat Troops*, 97. The maneuvers to which Twaddle referred were the large-scale Louisiana and Carolina maneuvers held in September and November 1941. Only one company of paratroopers participated in the former. The latter included the entire 502nd Parachute Infantry Battalion. Neither "provided a realistic tactical test of airborne warfare in that none of the . . . drops were of sufficient scale to have much impact on the greater scheme of the [simulated] battle at hand." Christopher R. Gabel, *The U.S. Army GHQ Maneuvers of 1941*, 190–191.

30. Greenfield, Palmer, and Wiley, *Organization of Ground Combat Troops*, 97–98.

31. E. G. Chapman, "American Divisions Take to the Air," 11; J. T. Ellis, *Airborne Command and Center*, 15–16. E. G. Chapman was the first chief of staff of Airborne Command, later assumed command of the unit, and then moved from that assignment to command the 13th Airborne Division. Airborne Command was originally constituted under Colonel Lee at Benning but shortly thereafter moved to Fort Bragg, and then, in April 1943, to Camp Mackall, North Carolina.

32. Quoted in J. T. Ellis, *Airborne Command and Center*, 5–7, 48–49 (quote).

33. Arnold quoted in Devlin, *Silent Wings*, 38.

34. Mrazek, *The Glider War*, 129–134.

35. Ronald M. Buffkin, "Assault Gliders: A World War II Phenomenon," 80; Mrazek, *The Glider War*, 58.

36. Devlin, *Paratrooper!* 119–120. The 550th Airborne Infantry Battalion was also, eventually, expanded and transformed into a glider unit, the 550th Glider Infantry Regiment.

37. Ibid., 119.

38. War Department Adjutant General, Message to Commanding General, Fifth Army and Commanding General, 1st Armored Corps, 23 June 1943, Matthew B. Ridgway Papers, Box 2a, Folder "Matthew B. Ridgway, Personal File, 1942–1943," USAMHI (capitalization in the original). In *Bitter Victory: The Battle for Sicily, July–August 1943*, Carlo D'Este wrote, "One disgruntled gliderman was heard to rage, 'I would give a year's pay if the desk-bound son of a bitch in Washington who decided crash-landing in one of these canvas coffins isn't hazardous duty would go up with us just once'" (249).

39. Ross S. Carter, *Those Devils in Baggy Pants*, viii; William C. Ryder to James M. Gavin, 17 May 1941, Gavin Papers, Box 7, Folder "West Point Records Parachute Training Transfer Records," USAMHI.

40. Endorsement to Gavin's request for parachute duty, Ryder to Gavin, 17 May 1941.

41. James M. Gavin, *War and Peace in the Space Age*, 45–46.

42. Jonathan M. Soffer, *General Matthew B. Ridgway: From Progressivism to Reaganism, 1895–1993*, 42.

43. An example of this departure from accepted modes of military conduct is related in Bradley Biggs, *Gavin: A Biography of General James M. Gavin*, 34. During a 1972 interview with Biggs, Gavin told the following story, which occurred while he was commanding the 505th Parachute Infantry Regiment at Fort Benning, Georgia: "The Regimental Adjutant of the 505th came into my office and told me that one of our troopers had been arrested for having sexual intercourse with a young lady on the lawn of the Courthouse in Phenix City [Alabama, a town right near Fort Benning]. The question he was asked from the Post Headquarters was 'What am I going to do about it?' referring to me. 'Well,' I replied, 'in view of the fact that the young man will be asked to give his life for his country in the next few months, I suggest we give him a medal.' I heard nothing further of it."

44. Gavin, *On to Berlin*, 2; Gavin, "Beyond the Stars," 75 (see chap. 1, n. 23).

45. James M. Gavin, interview by Clay Blair, 28 September 1982, Blair Collection, Box 53, Folder "Gavin, James M.," USAMHI.

CHAPTER 3: MEN OF A PARTICULARLY HIGH ORDER

1. Marvin A. Kreidberg and Merton G. Henry, *History of Military Mobilization in the United States Army, 1775–1945*, 597.

2. Charles E. Kirkpatrick, *An Unknown Future and a Doubtful Present: Writing the Victory Plan of 1941*, 125 (quote), 100. The Victory Plan did not ignore the Japanese threat. Rather, it was based on a planning assumption that Germany was the more menacing and immediate threat and that, if the United States were to enter the war, it would concentrate its resources to bring about the defeat of Germany and its allies first while maintaining a strategic defensive in the Pacific. At the conclusion of the European war, the resources of both the United States and the United Kingdom would be concentrated in the Pacific for the fight against Japan.

3. Kreidberg and Henry, *History of Military Mobilization*, 597; Russell F. Weigley, *History of the United States Army*, 435.

4. Weigley, *History of the United States Army*, 436.

5. Headquarters, 82d Infantry Division, General Order No. 1, 25 March 1942, 382–1.13, Box 12351, Record Group 407, NARA II.

6. James J. Cooke, *The All-Americans at War: The 82nd Division in the Great War, 1917–1918*, 3; G. Edward Buxton Jr., ed., *Official History of the 82nd Division: American Expeditionary Forces "All American" Division, 1917–1919*, 2. When the War Department began organizing divisions for service in World War I, it adopted a system that reserved the numerical designations 1 through 25 for Regular Army divisions, 26 through 75 for National Guard divisions, and 76 and higher for National Army divisions, with the members of each type division wearing distinctive "US," "NG," or "NA" collar insignia as appropriate. The intent was that Regular Army divisions would comprise mostly regulars and volunteers, National Guard divisions would comprise mostly guardsmen, and National Army divisions would be formed primarily from draftees. Within a year these distinctions became meaningless because personnel turbulence was so pronounced that eventually all divisions were composed of significant numbers of all three types of soldiers. Therefore, in August 1918, Major General Peyton C. March, the chief of

staff of the Army, ordered the elimination of all distinctions among the three components. See Leonard P. Ayres, *The War with Germany: A Statistical Summary*, 26; and Edward M. Coffman, *The War to End All Wars: The American Military Experience in World War I*, 61–62.

7. Cooke, *All-Americans at War*, 27.

8. American Battle Monuments Commission, *American Armies and Battlefields in Europe: A History, Guide, and Reference Book*, 328; Buxton, *Official History of the 82nd Division*, 29.

9. Cooke, *All-Americans at War*, 125; American Battle Monuments Commission, *82d Division: Summary of Operations in the World War*, 53.

10. Alvin C. York, *Sergeant York: His Own Life Story and War Diary*, 188.

11. Clay Blair, *Ridgway's Paratroopers: The American Airborne in World War II*, 15.

12. Walter V. Bingham and James Rorty, "How the Army Sorts Its Man Power," 28.

13. Greenfield, Palmer, and Wiley, *Organization of Ground Combat Troops*, 199–200; Blair, *Ridgway's Paratroopers*, 21.

14. Bradley and Blair, *A General's Life*, 105–106.

15. Ibid., 106.

16. Ibid.; Wayne Pierce, *Let's Go!* 5; Bradley and Blair, *A General's Life*, 106–107.

17. Clark quoted in Blair, *Ridgway's Paratroopers*, 22; Bradley and Blair, *A General's Life*, 106.

18. Bradley and Blair, *A General's Life*, 107–108; Blair, *Ridgway's Paratroopers*, 23.

19. Blair, *Ridgway's Paratroopers*, 3–14.

20. Bradley and Blair, *A General's Life*, 104; Matthew B. Ridgway, interview by Colonel John M. Blair, 15 December 1971, Ridgway Papers, Box 51, Folder "Interview by John M. Blair, volume I," USAMHI; Bradley and Blair, *A General's Life*, 108.

21. John S. D. Eisenhower, *The Bitter Woods*, 299; Duane A. Lempke, "Ridgway's Leadership Legacy," 71; Wayne Pierce to Clay Blair, 24 August 1983, Blair Collection, Box 51, Folder "Pierce, Wayne," USAMHI.

22. James A. Casey, taped statement transcript, 1 November 1983, Blair Collection, Box 53, Folder "Casey, James A.," USAMHI.

23. Blair, *Ridgway's Paratroopers*, 4.

24. Matthew B. Ridgway and Harold H. Martin, *Soldier: The Memoirs of Matthew B. Ridgway*, 22 (quotes), 23.

25. Soffer, *Ridgway*, 6.

26. Rupert D. Graves to Clay and Joan Blair, 14 November 1983, Blair Collection, Box 53, Folder "Graves, Rupert D.," USAMHI.

27. Soffer, *Ridgway*, 4–5 (emphasis in original); Matthew B. Ridgway, "Morale-Discipline-Leadership (Outline of a 30 Minute Talk for Chaplains)," n.d., Ridgway Papers, Box 4, Folder "Matthew B. Ridgway, Speeches to His Troops, 1942–1944," USAMHI.

28. Soffer, *Ridgway*, 8.

29. Matthew B. Ridgway, interview by Lieutenant Colonel Robert M. Elton and Major Matthew P. Caulfield, 29 August 1969, Ridgway Papers, Box 51, Folder

"Ridgway Interview Robert M. Elton and M. P. Caulfield Covering His Whole Career but Focusing on Korea," USAMHI.

30. Ibid.

31. Ridgway, "Morale-Discipline-Leadership."

32. Ridgway and Martin, *Soldier*, 27.

33. Memorandum by C. L. Patrick, "Re General Ridgeway [*sic*]," 19 September 1983, Blair Collection, Box 54, Folder "Patrick C. L.," USAMHI; Maxwell D. Taylor, *Swords and Plowshares*, 44.

34. Robert L. Dickerson to Clay Blair, 20 September 1983, Blair Collection, Box 53, Folder "Dickerson, Robert L.," USAMHI.

35. Louis A. Hauptfleisch to Clay Blair, 6 March 1984, Blair Collection, Box 53, Folder "Hauptfleisch, Louis 504," USAMHI.

36. Matthew B. Ridgway, "Notes on ARMY Comdr's Training Comments," 7 May 1942, Ridgway Papers, Box 4, Folder "Matthew B. Ridgway: Excerpts from His Notebook on Training, 1942," USAMHI; Memorandum, Headquarters, 82d Airborne Division, "Training," 31 August 1942, Ridgway Papers, Box 4, Folder "Matthew B. Ridgway, Memoranda on Training, 1942," USAMHI.

37. Louis Morton, "Germany First: The Basic Concept of Allied Strategy in World War II," 44.

38. Maurice Matloff and Edwin M. Snell, *Strategic Planning for Coalition Warfare, 1941–1942*, 183–186.

39. As a result of a reorganization of the War Department in March 1942, General Headquarters, U.S. Army, was closed. Its operational functions were subsumed by what would later be known as the Operations Division of the War Department. Its training and organizing functions were taken over by a new organization, Army Ground Forces, which General McNair commanded. See Greenfield, Palmer, and Wiley, *Organization of Ground Combat Troops*, 154–155.

40. Ibid., 273.

41. Huston, *Out of the Blue*, 72.

42. Lee quoted in Jerry Autry, *General William C. Lee, Father of the Airborne: Just Plain Bill*, 126; this memorandum from McNair to George C. Marshall, dated 19 June 1942, is reproduced in appendix 1 of Huston, *Out of the Blue*, 257–258.

43. Gavin, *On to Berlin*, 3.

44. J. T. Ellis, *Airborne Command and Center*, 53; memorandum, McNair to Marshall, 19 June 1942, in appendix 1 of Huston, *Out of the Blue*, 257–258.

45. J. T. Ellis, *Airborne Command and Center*, 53.

46. Ridgway and Martin, *Soldier*, 54.

47. Matthew B. Ridgway and Walter F. Winton Jr., seminar transcript, "Troop Leadership at the Operational Level: The Eighth Army in Korea," Ridgway Papers, Box 51, unmarked folder, USAMHI.

48. Pierce, *Let's Go!* 9; Blair, *Ridgway's Paratroopers*, 38.

49. Anonymous witness quoted in Blair, *Ridgway's Paratroopers*, 38 (emphasis in original). This witness also told Blair that the day after Ridgway's announcement, 4,500 men went absent without leave (AWOL) from the 82nd. Ridgway called the witness in and asked what had gone wrong. The witness replied, "You scared the pants off 'em"; that many did not want to be glider troopers, and many others did

not want to transfer out of the 82nd. He also assured Ridgway, however, that in a few days most would be back, which also held true.

50. Pierce, *Let's Go!* 10.

51. Headquarters, 82d Infantry Division, General Order No. 24, "Reorganization of the 82d Infantry Division into the 82d Airborne Division, and the 101st Airborne Division," 15 August 1942, 382-1.13, Box 12351, Record Group 407, NARA II.

52. Pierce, *Let's Go!* 10; Huston, *Out of the Blue*, 247.

53. J. T. Ellis, *Airborne Command and Center*, 53.

54. Huston, *Out of the Blue*, 246.

55. Chapman, "American Divisions Take to the Air," 11.

56. Pierce, *Let's Go!* 10; Huston, *Out of the Blue*, 247.

57. Joe Stolmeier, one the members of the original test battery (the artillery equivalent of the parachute test platoon), told the following story about his first contact with the idea of parachute artillery: "Well, this little . . . second lieutenant came and give us a talk just after retreat one day, and he made a plea to get some of us experienced artillerymen to come into the parachute troops he was going to form. He and some other officers were going to form a parachute troop artillery company that were going to drop from airplanes with artillery and support the infantry. And of course we made fun of him. All of us made fun of him. We asked him questions. Asked him questions about the jackasses, if they were going to drop those jackasses to pull the pack . . . it's a mountain gun and all. And he said no, he didn't think so, 'cause he thought it would break their legs." Stolmeier, interview, 13 April 2002 (see chap. 2, n. 25).

58. Blair, *Ridgway's Paratroopers*, 40; J. T. Ellis, *Airborne Command and Center*, 53; Huston, *Out of the Blue*, 247; John Whiteclay Chambers II et al., eds., *The Oxford Companion to American Military History*, s.v. "Artillery." The range of a 75mm howitzer was 9,475 yards, 12,500 yards for a 105mm, and 16,300 for a 155mm. According to Blair, one of the glider artillery battalions had twelve snub-nosed M-3 105mm howitzers instead of the 75mm pack howitzers. Although it is true that as the war progressed the airborne artillerymen did acquire 105mm howitzers, both snub-nosed and standard, these were not authorized until December 1944. See Greenfield, Palmer, and Wiley, *Organization of Ground Combat Troops*, 349; and John B. Wilson, *Maneuver and Firepower: The Evolution of Divisions and Separate Brigades*, 194–196.

59. General Board Report, United States Forces, European Theater, Study No. 16, "Organization, Equipment, and Tactical Employment of the Airborne Division," pp. 6–7, 17 June 1945, Ridgway Papers, Box "World War II Lessons Learned," Folder "Report of the General Board United States Forces, European Theater: Organization, Equipment, and Tactical Employment of the Airborne Division," USAMHI.

60. Letter to Commanding General, Army Ground Forces, Subject: Improvement of Pers. of 82d and 101st A/B Div., dated 28 August 1942, quoted in J. T. Ellis, *Airborne Command and Center*, 39.

61. Robert R. Palmer, Bell I. Wiley, and William R. Keast, *The Procurement and Training of Ground Combat Troops*, 5–9. The AGCT was a cognitive instrument

"designed to measure [a soldier's] ability to learn." Numerical scores on the AGCT were grouped into five categories, I through V. Enlisted men selected for Officer Candidate School had to fall into Category I or II, with the latter category being the main source of quality noncommissioned officers as well.

62. Ibid., 50.

63. This memorandum from Headquarters, Army Ground Forces, dated 18 September 1942, subject: Improvement of Personnel in Airborne Divisions, is reproduced in appendix 20 of J. T. Ellis, *Airborne Command and Center*, 124–125.

64. Palmer, Wiley, and Keast, *Procurement and Training of Ground Combat Troops*, 20; Ridgway and Martin, *Soldier*, 58.

65. Charles W. Mason, "The 82d Under Ridgway," chap. 2, p. 1, n.d., Ridgway Papers, Box 5, Folder "Charles W. Mason, *The 82d Under Ridgway*," USAMHI.

66. Blair, *Ridgway's Paratroopers*, 33–40.

67. Ridgway, interview, 15 December 1971.

68. Blair, *Ridgway's Paratroopers*, 42–43.

69. Gerald M. Cummings to Clay Blair, 20 October 1983, Blair Collection, Box 53, Folder "Cummings, Gerald M.," USAMHI; Osmond Leahy to Clay Blair, 16 May 1983, Blair Collection, Box 54, Folder "Leahy, Osmond A.," USAMHI; Wayne Pierce to Clay Blair, 4 October 1983, Blair Collection, Box 51, Folder "Pierce, Wayne," USAMHI; Arthur G. Kroos Jr. to Clay Blair, 17 June 1983, attached taped statement transcript, Blair Collection, Box 54, Folder "Kroos, Art," USAMHI; Ridgway, interview, 15 December 1971.

70. Blair, *Ridgway's Paratroopers*, 36.

71. Matthew B. Ridgway to Brigadier General A. R. Bolling, Assistant Chief of Staff, G-1, Army Ground Forces, 26 March 1943, Ridgway Papers, Box 2a, Folder "Matthew B. Ridgway, Personal File, 1942–1943," USAMHI.

72. Devlin, *Silent Wings*, 78.

73. Huston, *Out of the Blue*, 104.

74. Headquarters, Airborne Command, General Order No. 5, 10 February 1943, 382-1.13, Box 12350, Record Group 407, NARA II. As a result of this reorganization, other elements of the division were also reorganized. For example, the 82nd's engineer unit, the 307th Airborne Engineer Battalion, converted one of its glider companies into a parachute company, giving it two parachute and one glider company. See also Blair, *Ridgway's Paratroopers*, 519; and Stuart Cutler to Clay Blair, 20 February 1984, Blair Collection, Box 53, Folder "Cutler, Stuart," USAMHI.

75. Blair, *Ridgway's Paratroopers*, 61–63; Ridgway and Martin, *Soldier*, 58–59.

CHAPTER 4: A WHOLE NEW DIMENSION TO SOLDIERING

1. James M. Gavin, interview by Lieutenant Colonel Donald G. Andrews and Lieutenant Colonel Charles H. Ferguson, 16 April 1975, Gavin Papers, Box "Oral History," USAMHI; Yarborough, interview, 28 March 1975 (see chap. 2, n. 16). Interestingly, the Soviet manuals Yarborough obtained were translated by his father, a Russian linguist who had served in the U.S. 31st Infantry Regiment in Siberia during the First World War.

2. War Department, FM 31-30, *Tactics and Technique of Air-Borne Troops*, 31–33.

3. Mark Clark quoted in Huston, *Out of the Blue*, 61–62. See also Devlin, *Paratrooper!* 138. Clark made this statement in a letter to Bill Lee.

4. Ridgway and Martin, *Soldier*, 53.

5. John Norton, interview by the author, Washington, D.C., 22 February 2001. Norton remained with the 82nd throughout the war, serving first as a company commander in the 505th, then successively as a battalion executive officer, a regimental plans officer, and, once Gavin took command of the division, the division plans officer.

6. Allen Langdon, *"Ready": The History of the 505th Parachute Infantry Regiment, 82nd Airborne Division, World War II*, 1.

7. Gavin, interview, 16 April 1975.

8. Memorandum from Lee to the Army Chief of Staff, dated 2 July 1942, Subject: Policy Regarding Tng. of A/B Tr., quoted in J. T. Ellis, *Airborne Command and Center*, 52; Pierce, *Let's Go!* 15–19 (quote on 15).

9. Melvin Zais, interview by Colonel William L. Golden and Colonel Richard C. Rice, 20 January 1977, Zais Papers, Box "Oral History," USAMHI. Melvin Zais went on to earn four stars and command of the 101st Airborne Division in Vietnam.

10. Pierce, *Let's Go!* 11, 14–15.

11. Huston, *Out of the Blue*, 118. The question of what to do with glider pilots once they were on the ground generated a great deal of discussion in the Anglo-American airborne community. The British formed their glider pilots into a regiment and trained them to fight as infantry once they had delivered their loads. The Americans, on the other hand, viewed glider pilots as too valuable to risk in direct combat and therefore sought to evacuate them to the rear as soon as possible after a glider insertion. Gavin, for one, disagreed with the American position and said so forcefully. He was overruled by Ridgway and others. This became an especially contentious issue during the drop into Holland.

12. Memorandum from Ridgway to the Assistant Chief of Staff, Operations Division, War Department General Staff, "Airborne Troops," 2 December 1943, Ridgway Papers, Box 2a, Folder "Matthew B. Ridgway, Personal File, 1942–1943," USAMHI.

13. Pierce, *Let's Go!* 21; Blair, *Ridgway's Paratroopers*, 52.

14. Poster reproduced in appendix 22 of J. T. Ellis, *Airborne Command and Center*, 130.

15. Ridgway's first glider flight ended ingloriously. Shortly after being told that the 82nd was to become an airborne division Ridgway traveled to Wright Field, Ohio, to get checked out in the glider. The glider he was in was an experimental model outfitted with both wheels and landing skids. The wheels were used for takeoff and were supposed to drop off during flight so the glider could land on its skids. But there was a malfunction on Ridgway's glider; the wheels remained attached, so when the glider landed, instead of skidding to a stop, it continued rolling at high speed and there were no brakes. The glider was headed right for an idling bomber, so Ridgway and his artillery commander, Brigadier General Joe

Swing, leaped from the aircraft. As Ridgway described the incident, "Our dry dive onto the concrete proved to have been premature. Some quick-thinking airmen, at considerable risk to themselves, grabbed the wing of the glider as it whizzed past them and diverted it from the runway well short of the bomber." See Ridgway and Martin, *Soldier*, 56–57.

16. Kroos to Blair, 17 June 1983 (see chap. 3, n. 69). One reason Ridgway held himself so erect was because of a severe back injury he sustained when he fell off a horse while a cadet at West Point, which bothered him throughout his life. Ridgway was ever fearful that this injury would end his career. See Ridgway and Martin, *Soldier*, 24–26.

17. Benjamin H. Vandervoort to Clay Blair, 12 June 1983, Blair Collection, Box 55, Folder "Vandervoort, Benjamin," USAMHI. Vandervoort was an original member of Gavin's 505th Parachute Infantry Regiment and became one of the division's best battalion commanders before being returned to the United States as a result of a severe wound he sustained in Belgium. It is Vandervoort whom John Wayne plays in the movie *The Longest Day*.

18. Alfred Ireland to Clay Blair, 20 February 1984, Blair Collection, Box 53, Folder "Ireland, Alfred W.," USAMHI.

19. Bob Piper, telephone interview by the author, 16 June 2001; Gavin, interview, 1 April 1983 (see chap. 2, n. 5).

20. Gavin, *On to Berlin*, 143.

21. Soffer, *Ridgway*, 3, 63; Gavin, interview, 16 April 1975. In the same interview, Gavin highlighted an interesting by-product of encouraging this attitude, that being unusual discipline problems that required special handling. In Gavin's words, "First of all, when they went into combat, they were told if they wanted blankets or any other refinements, kill a German and take his; and if you need a truck, take a German truck. Well, of course, it wasn't long in combat and they began taking trucks from the 1st Infantry Division and anybody else's they could get their hands on. . . . Yet, it was better to learn to tolerate a certain amount of misbehavior but have guys who were really capable fighters and confident and proud."

22. Gavin, interview, 28 September 1982 (see chap. 2, n. 45); Taylor, *Swords and Plowshares*, 47.

23. Ridgway and Martin, *Soldier*, 59–60; Matthew B. Ridgway to Elbridge G. Chapman, 12 April 1943, Ridgway Papers, Box 2a, Folder "Matthew B. Ridgway, Personal File, 1942–1943," USAMHI. See also Blair, *Ridgway's Paratroopers*, 69; Pierce, *Let's Go!* 23; and Ridgway and Martin, *Soldier*, 59–60.

24. Norton, interview, 22 February 2001.

25. Langdon, *"Ready,"* 8.

26. James M. Gavin, Personal Diary, 8 April 1943, Gavin Papers, Box 8, Folder "Diary Passages: April–Dec, Fort Bragg, North Africa, and Sicily," USAMHI.

27. Mason, "The 82d Under Ridgway," chap. 2, p. 2 (see chap. 3, n. 65).

28. Langdon, *"Ready,"* 8; Pierce, *Let's Go!* 28.

29. Gavin, Personal Diary, 24 April 1943; Langdon, *"Ready,"* 8; Pierce, *Let's Go!* 25–29.

30. Ridgway and Martin, *Soldier*, 62; Gavin, Personal Diary, 8, 17 April 1943.

CHAPTER 5: A SMALL PHALANX IN A VAST, STRANGE LAND

1. Albert N. Garland and Howard McGaw Smyth, *Sicily and the Surrender of Italy*, 4 (quote), 6. Churchill estimated that the Germans would likely move four to six divisions into Italy at the mere threat of continued Allied operations in the Mediterranean.

2. Ibid., 11 (quote), 8.

3. Arthur Bryant, *The Turn of the Tide: A History of the War Years Based on the Diaries of Field-Marshal Lord Alanbrooke, Chief of the Imperial General Staff*, 449.

4. Garland and Smyth, *Sicily and the Surrender of Italy*, 10. The American focus on the primacy of shipping tonnage was underscored by Lieutenant General Brehon B. Somervell, the commanding general, Army Services of Supply, who "estimated that once the Mediterranean was cleared of enemy forces the Allies would save 1,825,000 tons of shipping in the first five months." To the Americans, this was much more important than eliminating Italy from the war. Ibid., 8.

5. Brooke, diary entry, 22 January 1943, in Bryant, *Turn of the Tide*, 457.

6. Ibid., 454–455.

7. Eisenhower was somewhat put out with having been saddled with the British committee system of command and drafted a memo to Marshall "demanding a continuation of the centralization of command in his own person" with which he was familiar and which he thought had worked so well during Operation TORCH. His chief of staff, Major General Walter Bedell "Beetle" Smith, persuaded him not to send the memo, and thenceforward Eisenhower begrudgingly accepted the command arrangement in the interests of Anglo-American unity. Garland and Smyth, *Sicily and the Surrender of Italy*, 10–11.

8. Ibid., 56.

9. D'Este, *Bitter Victory*, 87.

10. Garland and Smyth, *Sicily and the Surrender of Italy*, 52–53.

11. Headquarters, U.S. Seventh Army, "Report of Operations," 1 October 1943, p. a3–a4, copy in the Department of History Library, U.S. Military Academy, West Point, NY; D'Este, *Bitter Victory*, 75–79; Garland and Smyth, *Sicily and the Surrender of Italy*, 58. Force 141's initial plan was based on a concept that had been forwarded by the British Joint Planning Staff of the Imperial General Staff and approved by the Combined Chiefs of Staff at Casablanca. The timing of the landings changed as the plan evolved, but the concept of sequential landings remained until Montgomery's intercession.

12. Montgomery quoted in D'Este, *Bitter Victory*, 79, 82.

13. Montgomery quoted in Garland and Smyth, *Sicily and the Surrender of Italy*, 61. According to D'Este, Montgomery "considered Alexander's role was to meet his logistical requirements, to act as a buffer with those who would otherwise distract his attention, and to command with the very loosest rein, all of which Alexander obligingly did." D'Este, *Bitter Victory*, 100.

14. Martin Blumenson, ed., *The Patton Papers, 1940–1945*, 235. These quotes are from a transcript of a 29 April 1943 meeting attended by Alexander, Patton, Tedder, and Cunningham. Montgomery was too busy to attend, so he sent Lieutenant

General Sir Oliver Leese, his XXX Corps commander, in his stead. Leese presented Montgomery's plan to the group.

15. Gavin, *On to Berlin*, 6. Browning had commanded the British 1st Airborne Division, which was slated to support Montgomery's Eighth Army during Operation HUSKY, a point not lost on Ridgway.

16. Ridgway and Martin, *Soldier*, 66–67.

17. Headquarters, U.S. Seventh Army, "Report of Operations," a3.

18. Ridgway and Martin, *Soldier*, 67.

19. Garland and Smyth, *Sicily and the Surrender of Italy*, 115.

20. On 22 May 1943, Patton wrote in his diary that in his role as Eisenhower's principal airborne adviser, Browning was "trying to get control of the paratroops." Patton, diary entry, 22 May 1943, in Blumenson, *Patton Papers*, 254.

21. Blair, *Ridgway's Paratroopers*, 65; Breuer, *Geronimo!* 58.

22. Headquarters, U.S. Seventh Army, "Report of Operations," d1.

23. Garland and Smyth, *Sicily and the Surrender of Italy*, 105–108.

24. Headquarters, U.S. Seventh Army, "Report of Operations," d1.

25. Garland and Smyth, *Sicily and the Surrender of Italy*, 115; Samuel Eliot Morison, *The Two-Ocean War: A Short History of the United States Navy in the Second World War*, 248. The aircraft figures would change slightly up until D day because of maintenance schedules and the arrival of additional or replacement aircraft in theater. According to Morison, 580 ships of various types supported Patton's Seventh Army for the initial landings; Montgomery was supported by 795 ships.

26. Ernest F. Fisher, "Evolution of US Airborne Doctrine," 71.

27. See also John C. Warren, *Airborne Missions in the Mediterranean, 1942–1945*, 26–27, 41–48.

28. Matthew B. Ridgway to Maxwell Taylor, 22 April 1943, Blair Collection, Box 48, Folder "Chrono File: Sicily," USAMHI.

29. Garland and Smyth, *Sicily and the Surrender of Italy*, 88–89.

30. Ibid., 91–92; Warren, *Airborne Missions in the Mediterranean*, 41–48.

31. Garland and Smyth, *Sicily and the Surrender of Italy*, 91–105.

32. *82d Airborne Division in Sicily and Italy*, n.d., p. 5, Folder "82nd Airborne Division—WWII After Action Report: Sicily," 82nd Airborne Division Museum, Fort Bragg, NC.

33. Pierce, *Let's Go!* 29.

34. Gavin, Personal Diary, 29 April 1943 (see chap. 4, n. 26).

35. Pierce, *Let's Go!* 28–32; Langdon, *"Ready,"* 8–9.

36. Ridgway and Martin, *Soldier*, 63.

37. Pierce, *Let's Go!* 33; Langdon, *"Ready,"* 9. The *Jean Bart* was destroyed by the U.S. battleship *Massachusetts* in the initial hours of the invasion of North Africa the previous November.

38. Margaret Bierbaum, ed., *As Ever, John: The Letters of Col. John V. McNally to His Sister, Margaret McNally Bierbaum, 1941–1946*, 13.

39. Langdon, *"Ready,"* 9.

40. See also Bierbaum, *As Ever, John*, 13–16.

41. Starlyn R. Jorgensen, *History of the 456th Parachute Field Artillery Battalion*, 48. In *Ridgway's Paratroopers*, Blair reports a similar incident as related to him by

"Doc" Eaton. Eaton told Blair that while settling into his tent that night, he turned on the radio and heard Axis Sally proclaim, "Welcome to Africa, Matt Ridgway and your bad boys." See Blair, *Ridgway's Paratroopers*, 71.

42. Blair, *Ridgway's Paratroopers*, 65; Pierce, *Let's Go!* 38–42. The 80th Airborne Antiaircraft Battalion comprised six firing batteries, three of which had 37mm antitank guns and three of which had .50-caliber machine guns.

43. Blair, *Ridgway's Paratroopers*, 71; Langdon, *"Ready,"* 9; Pierce, *Let's Go!* 36. A "forty and eight" was a French railcar designed to hold either forty men or eight horses.

44. Langdon, *"Ready,"* 9. Wayne Pierce relates a very similar story about an encounter between German POWs and 325th troopers in *Let's Go!* 38.

45. Pierce, *Let's Go!* 38; Buck Dawson, ed., *Saga of the All American*, n.p.

46. Langdon, *"Ready,"* 12.

47. Kroos to Blair, 17 June 1983 (see chap. 3, n. 69); Shaker quoted in Breuer, *Geronimo!* 61; Janney, *Richard Mott Janney*, 69.

48. James A. Gray to Clay Blair, 8 August 1984, Blair Collection, Box 53, Folder "Gray, James A.," USAMHI. Gray commanded the 1/505th when it arrived in North Africa, but was relieved of command before the Sicily jump for going absent without leave.

49. Kroos to Blair, 17 June 1983; Langdon, *"Ready,"* 12; Gavin, Personal Diary, 18 June 1943.

50. Dan McIlvoy, "Medical Detachment, 505th Parachute Infantry, 82nd Airborne Division in World War II," World War II Veterans Survey Project, Box "82d Airborne Division, 505th PIR (2)," Folder "McIlvoy, Dan (M.D.) 505th Parachute Infantry Med. Det.," USAMHI.

51. Information on the training conducted in North Africa from Memorandum, Headquarters, Fifth Army Airborne Training Center, "Report of Airborne Operations, 'Husky' and 'Bigot,'" 15 August 1943, pp. 3–4, Gavin Papers, Box 11, Folder "Invasion of Sicily, Intelligence Reports, Organizational and Operation Plans, After Action Report + Inquiry of Friendly Fire Losses, Maps," USAMHI. This report was written by Lieutenant Colonel Charles Billingslea, who was assigned to Mark Clark's Fifth Army Headquarters as an airborne observer. He later transferred to the 82nd and served as commander of the 325th Glider Infantry Regiment. His comments about the field artillery stemmed from his observation that "the artillery range was not altogether satisfactory it being too restricted" and was not attributed to the failure of the division's artillerymen themselves (3). See also James P. McGinity Diary, 382-INF(505)-0.3.0, "Exec's Diary—1st BN, 505th Para. Inf., 17 May–9 July 43," Box 12459, Record Group 407, NARA II.

52. Ridgway and Martin, *Soldier*, 65.

53. McGinity Diary, 3 and 5 June 1943; Langdon; *"Ready,"* 13; Gavin, Personal Diary, 9 June 1943.

54. Gavin, Personal Diary, 9 June 1943. The 82nd sustained two nonhuman jump injuries while in North Africa as well. Major Mark J. Alexander was given the task of determining if mules could be safely dropped by parachute so that, once in Sicily, the division's artillerymen could use them to transport their howitzers and ammunition. After purchasing two mules from a local Arab, Alexander

and his "test board" fitted them with forty-eight-foot parachutes, coaxed them aboard a plane, and took off. Once they were at the right drop altitude the mules were blindfolded and pushed out the door. Unfortunately, the experiment proved unsuccessful; both mules broke their legs upon landing and had to be destroyed. Six weeks later, the troopers "would learn firsthand that Sicily had more mules per square foot than nearly any other country in the world." William B. Breuer, *Drop Zone Sicily: Allied Airborne Strike, July 1943*, 7. Information on the mule drop is also contained in Langdon, *"Ready,"* 13–14; and Ridgway and Martin, *Soldier*, 66.

55. Warren, *Airborne Missions in the Mediterranean*, 28.

56. Headquarters, U.S. Fifth Army Airborne Training Center, "Report of Airborne Operations," 3.

57. Gavin, Personal Diary, 29 May 1943.

58. Langdon, *"Ready,"* 12.

59. Gavin, *On to Berlin*, 8–9; McGinity Diary, 19, 20, 24, 29 May, 3 June 1943. So real did the Allies perceive the threat from Spanish Morocco that Clark's Fifth Army drew up a contingency plan, Operation BACKBONE II, that called for the seizure of that portion of Spanish Morocco adjacent to the Straits of Gibraltar as well as key terrain in eastern Spanish Morocco to deny the enemy access to Allied lines of communication. The concept of the operation called for the 82nd Airborne Division to seize several targets, to include the cities of Tanger and Melilla. See Memorandum, Headquarters U.S. Fifth Army, "Mission for 82nd Airborne Division," 11 May 1943, Ridgway Papers, Box 2a, Folder "Matthew B. Ridgway, Personal File, 1942–1943," USAMHI.

60. Warren, *Airborne Missions in the Mediterranean*, 28.

61. Gavin, Personal Diary, 16 May 1943. A regimental combat team was a combined arms unit formed around a combat regiment, usually an infantry regiment or, in the case of airborne divisions, a parachute or glider regiment. It was generally composed of anywhere from two to four infantry battalions, an artillery battalion, and other supporting assets such as engineers, signal, and medical units.

62. Ridgway, interview, 15 December 1971 (see chap. 3, n. 20). Gavin was four years older than Tucker and had assumed command of the 505th about four months earlier than Tucker did. When Tucker took command of the 504th he was thirty-one years old, perhaps the youngest regimental commander in the Army at the time.

63. Melvin Zais, "Glimpses of Gavin," Zais Papers, Box "Family Papers, Correspondence, Including Barrie Zais, Mitchell Zais, LTG James Gavin," Folder "Glimpses of Gavin," USAMHI; Kroos to Blair, 17 June 1983; Zais, "Glimpses of Gavin."

64. H. L. Covington, *A Fighting Heart: An Unofficial Story of the 82nd Airborne Division*, 31.

65. Edwin Sayre to James M. Gavin, 15 September 1970, Gavin Papers, Box 11, Folder "Letters to & from Col. Edward [*sic*] Sayre, Remembering Sicily Operations, File Page Including # of Planes (C-47) for Operation Husky," USAMHI.

66. *82d Airborne Division in Sicily and Italy*, 5. In addition to the 3/504th and the 456th Parachute Field Artillery Battalion, Gavin's combat team also contained B Company, 307th Airborne Engineer Battalion; detachments from the 82nd Sig-

nal Company and the 307th Airborne Medical Company; and an air support party and prisoner of war interrogation teams.

67. Headquarters, 82nd Airborne Division, Field Order No. 1, 23 June 1943, 382-0.3, "82nd A/B Div., Synopsis of Opns. in Sicilian Campaign," Box 12345, Record Group 407, NARA II (capitalization in original).

68. The official designation of this unit changed several times. Originally the 504th Parachute Infantry Battalion, it later became the 2nd Battalion, 503rd Parachute Infantry Regiment, and finally the 509th Parachute Infantry Battalion. See Devlin, *Paratrooper!* 678n2. The three jumps included a botched attempt to seize Tafaraoui airfield, just south of Oran, Algeria, on D day of Operation TORCH; a second, uncontested, jump onto Youk les Bains airfield near the Tunisian border; and a small three-plane jump during which thirty men attempted, unsuccessfully, to blow a railroad bridge near El Djem, Tunisia.

69. Edson D. Raff, *We Jumped to Fight*, 18.

70. Matthew B. Ridgway to Major General Geoffrey Keyes, 25 May 1943, Ridgway Papers, Box 2a, Folder "Matthew B. Ridgway, Personal File, 1942–1943," USAMHI. General Keyes led the planning effort for Operation HUSKY for Patton.

71. Browning's letter to Yardley is reproduced in William P. Yarborough, *Bail Out over North Africa: America's First Combat Parachute Missions, 1942*, 150.

72. Garland and Smyth, *Sicily and the Surrender of Italy*, 34, 33.

73. The deception measures included Operation MINCEMEAT, a ruse made famous in the book *The Man Who Never Was* and a subsequent movie of the same name. While working for MI 5's XX Committee, Ewen Montagu, the book's author, devised a scheme whereby a corpse dressed as a Royal Marine officer carrying top-secret dispatches to Alexander washed ashore in Spain. The dispatches, opened and passed from Spanish to German authorities before being returned to the British, ostensibly unopened, pointed to Allied landings in Sardinia and Greece. A more recent book on this scheme is *Operation Mincemeat: How a Dead Man and a Bizarre Plan Fooled the Nazis and Assured an Allied Victory*, by Ben Macintyre.

74. Garland and Smyth, *Sicily and the Surrender of Italy*, 77. Interestingly, Guzzoni had never even visited Sicily before assuming command of its defense.

75. Ibid., 46–47, 82–83.

76. Frido von Senger und Etterlin, *Neither Fear nor Hope: The Wartime Career of General Frido von Senger und Etterlin, Defender of Cassino*, 128. See also Garland and Smyth, *Sicily and the Surrender of Italy*, 46–47, 82–83.

77. Garland and Smyth, *Sicily and the Surrender of Italy*, 80–81.

78. Ibid., 81.

79. Ibid., 86–87.

80. Senger und Etterlin, *Neither Fear nor Hope*, 132–133; Albert Kesselring, *The Memoirs of Field-Marshal Kesselring*, 161.

81. Garland and Smyth, *Sicily and the Surrender of Italy*, 87.

82. Kesselring, *Memoirs*, 161.

83. Warren, *Airborne Missions in the Mediterranean*, 28.

84. Headquarters, Fifth Army Airborne Training Center, "Report of Airborne Operations," 5.

85. Ridgway and Martin, *Soldier*, 60–61.

86. Pierce, *Let's Go!* 51.

87. William D. Mandle and David H. Whittier, *Combat Record of the 504th Parachute Infantry Regiment: April 1943–July 1945*, n.p.

88. Ridgway and Martin, *Soldier*, 66; Gavin, Personal Diary, 6 June 1943.

89. Bierbaum, *As Ever, John*, 37.

CHAPTER 6: A SELF-ADJUSTING FOUL-UP

1. See Edwin M. Sayre, *The Operations of Company "A" 505th Parachute Infantry (82d Airborne Division), Airborne Landings in Sicily 9–24 July 1943 (Sicily Campaign) (Personal Experience of a Company Commander)*, 10 November 1947, p. 8, Donovan Research Library, Fort Benning, GA; Langdon, *"Ready,"* 17; and Robert M. Piper, *The Operation of the 505th Parachute Infantry Regimental Combat Team (82d Airborne Division) in the Airborne Landings on Sicily, 9–11 July 1943 (Sicilian Campaign) (Personal Experience of Assistant Regimental Adjutant)*, n.d., pp. 12–13, Donovan Research Library, Fort Benning, GA; Headquarters, Fifth Army Airborne Training Center, "Report of Airborne Operations," 6 (see chap. 5, n. 51).

2. Gavin, *War and Peace in the Space Age*, 53 (capitalization in original).

3. Gavin, Personal Diary, 10 April 1943 (see chap. 4, n. 26).

4. Ibid., 22 June 1943. The metallic crickets Gavin wrote of here were the same crickets used by the 101st Airborne Division during the invasion of Normandy and made famous in the movie *The Longest Day*. In a letter to author Clay Blair after the war, Gavin wrote, "Most of us who tried [the crickets] in Sicily wanted no part of them [in Normandy]. They were just a nuisance. They started, for example, teaching people to use one click for a challenge, expecting two [clicks] in response. That didn't work, because once you made one click, if you thoughtlessly released it, it clicked itself again. In the second place some of the troopers lost them when they dropped out of their pockets when they jumped. They always had their voices. . . . I think that the 101st used them [in Normandy], but to the veterans of the 82nd, they seemed pretty silly. You couldn't find them in your pockets when you needed them and you couldn't walk around all night holding a cricket in your hand." James M. Gavin to Clay Blair, 19 July 1983, Blair Collection, Box 53, Folder "Gavin, James M.," USAMHI.

5. Gavin, Personal Diary, 26 June 1943.

6. Ibid., 30 June 1943. Alfred W. Ireland, Gavin's regimental S-1 (personnel officer) at the time, was the one responsible for coming up with the nicknames of the regimental leadership. In an oral interview after the war, Ireland stated, "Back in '42 we received word that the Japanese would trick our guys by calling out names of the different individuals, major this, colonel that, and captain this. So headquarters wanted nicknames put on every officer in the whole regiment. At that time Gavin said, 'Al, I want you to nickname every field officer and all the key people.' So I had to sit down and come up with names for everyone. That's how Slim Jim [Colonel Gavin] got his nickname. I nicknamed him Slim Jim because at the time there was a pretzel called Slim Jim Pretzels and he was a tall slim guy and

I said, 'I hope you don't mind, but I'm nicknaming you "Slim Jim."' He laughed and said, 'That's fine.' I nicknamed Gorham 'Hard Nose' because that's just exactly as I saw him. He was a tough, hard-nosed soldier. He was the kind of guy who would do it all himself." Patrick K. O'Donnell, *Beyond Valor: World War II's Rangers and Airborne Veterans Reveal the Heart of Combat*, 43.

7. Gavin, Personal Diary, 7 July 1943.

8. Headquarters, 82nd Airborne Division, "Index Outline to G-3 Operational History of 82d A/B Division July 9–August 21, 1943 (Sicilian Campaign)," 31 August 1943, Gavin Papers, Box 11, Folder "Invasion of Sicily, Intelligence Reports, Organizational and Operation Plans, After Action Report + Inquiry on Friendly Fire Losses, Maps," USAMHI; Garland and Smyth, *Sicily and the Surrender of Italy*, 89.

9. Blumenson, *Patton Papers*, 274. A significant portion of the American invasion force, including the whole of the U.S. 45th and 1st Infantry Divisions, had already set sail on 4 and 5 July, respectively. See also Garland and Smyth, *Sicily and the Surrender of Italy*, 108.

10. Headquarters, Fifth Army Airborne Training Center, "Report of Airborne Operations," 6. When outfitted, each paratrooper carried his individual weapon with bayonet, a secondary weapon, a trench knife, an entrenching tool, 168 rounds of ammunition, one "Hawkins" antitank mine, four fragmentation grenades, rations, a gas mask, a first-aid kit, an escape kit, a blanket, rope, extra socks, underwear, and personal hygiene items. See Sayre, *Operations of Company "A,"* 8.

11. Warren, *Airborne Missions in the Mediterranean*, 29.

12. Headquarters, Fifth Army Airborne Training Center, "Report of Airborne Operations," 6.

13. See Robert Goralski, ed., *World War II Almanac, 1931–1945: A Political and Military Record*, 442; Huston, *Out of the Blue*, 84; Warren, *Airborne Missions in the Mediterranean*, 2; Piper, *Operation of the 505th Parachute Infantry Regimental Combat Team*, 14. For all its ruggedness, the C-47 did have two significant weaknesses: It lacked self-sealing tanks and had an unarmored crew compartment. These would remain major points of contention between the airborne and troop carrier pilots, on one side, and the bomber and fighter pilots, on the other, for the remainder of the war.

14. *82d Airborne Division in Sicily and Italy*, 6 (see chap. 5, n. 32).

15. Gavin, *On to Berlin*, 19–20.

16. Warren, *Airborne Missions in the Mediterranean*, 29–33.

17. Memorandum, Headquarters, 82d Airborne Division, "Reported Loss of Transport Planes and Personnel Due to Friendly Fire," 2 August 1943, Gavin Papers, Box 11, Folder "Invasion of Sicily, Intelligence Reports, Organizational and Operation Plans, After Action Report + Inquiry of Friendly Fire Losses, Maps," USAMHI.

18. Matthew B. Ridgway to Chet Hanson, 5 April 1949, Blair Collection, Box 48, Folder "Chrono File: Sicily," USAMHI (capitalization in original).

19. Warren, *Airborne Missions in the Mediterranean*, 33.

20. The 64th Troop Carrier Group was on loan from the 51st Troop Carrier Wing, then carrying elements of the British 1st Airborne Division to its D-day

objectives. After D day, the 64th returned to its parent headquarters. See Headquarters, North African Air Force Troop Carrier Command (Provisional), "Report on Operations and Activities Troop Carrier Command (Prov.) Including Operation HUSKY 18 May, 1943 to 31 July, 1943," n.d., pt. 1, ser. A, in *Records of the War Department's Operations Division, 1942–1945*, p. 2, reel 5.

21. Warren, *Airborne Missions in the Mediterranean*, 34.

22. Ibid., 34–35.

23. Sayre, *Operations of Company "A,"* 9 (capitalization in original).

24. Warren, *Airborne Missions in the Mediterranean*, 35.

25. Sayre, *Operations of Company "A,"* 9.

26. Warren, *Airborne Missions in the Mediterranean*, 35.

27. James M. Gavin, *Airborne Warfare*, 8–9.

28. Ibid., 9.

29. Mark Alexander, telephone interview by the author, 16 June 2001.

30. Warren, *Airborne Missions in the Mediterranean*, 36.

31. Quoted in Jorgensen, *History of the 456th Parachute Field Artillery Battalion*, 62 (capitalization in original).

32. Ireland quoted in O'Donnell, *Beyond Valor*, 44; Thompson quoted in Breuer, *Geronimo!* 71. Thompson had also jumped into North Africa with the 509th.

33. Warren, *Airborne Missions in the Mediterranean*, 33–34.

34. *82d Airborne Division in Sicily and Italy*, 6–7; Garland and Smyth, *Sicily and the Surrender of Italy*, 117. All fifty men who did not drop were cleared of any responsibility for their actions and participated in the second drop.

35. Gavin, *Airborne Warfare*, 16.

36. T. Moffatt Burriss, *Strike and Hold: A Memoir of the 82d Airborne in World War II*, 50–51.

37. D'Este, *Bitter Victory*, 253, 244.

38. Ibid., 245. See also Breuer, *Drop Zone Sicily*, 75–82. Upon being evacuated after the fight for Avola, one American paratrooper, Lieutenant Thomas W. Graham, came face-to-face with the British Eighth Army commander. "We American paratroopers moved toward the British landing beach for eventual evacuation back to North Africa. For transportation, we had mules and carts. I was riding a bicycle with no tires—not an easy task. On the way, we passed General [Bernard] Montgomery, beret and all, standing at an intersection and waving his troops inland. He seemed exasperated over our ragtag group cluttering up the narrow road." Breuer, *Geronimo!* 82–83.

39. Piper, *Operation of the 505th Parachute Infantry Regimental Combat Team*, 19.

40. Breuer, *Drop Zone Sicily*, 65; Gavin, *Airborne Warfare*, 14; Piper, *Operation of the 505th Parachute Infantry Regimental Combat Team*, 24–25.

41. *82d Airborne Division in Sicily and Italy*, 35–36; Breuer, *Drop Zone Sicily*, 109–110; D'Este, *Bitter Victory*, 246; Piper, *Operation of the 505th Parachute Infantry Regimental Combat Team*, 18–19. There are conflicting reports about the makeup of the enemy battalion Eaton's group destroyed. Breuer and D'Este contend it was a German battalion, while all other reports contend it was Italian. Given the confusion in the Axis ranks, it could have been either. After driving off the column, Eaton withdrew his force to the south, fearing a more coordinated

counterattack by much larger numbers. Eaton and his men eventually linked up with elements from the 180th Infantry Regiment of the 45th Infantry Division and continued to fight with them until 12 July, when they finally returned to 82nd control.

42. Memorandum, Headquarters, 307th Airborne Engineer Battalion, "Report After Action Against Enemy as Required by AR 345-105," 21 August 1943, Box "82nd Airborne Division—WWII, 307th Eng. Bn., Unit History, Incident Reports," Folder "307th Abn. Eng. Bn. AAR—Sicily," 82nd Airborne Division Museum, Fort Bragg, NC. Elements of the B Company, 307th Airborne Engineer Battalion, fought with Swingler's force during this time. See also Garland and Smyth, *Sicily and the Surrender of Italy*, 119; and Piper, *Operation of the 505th Parachute Infantry Regimental Combat Team*, 26–27.

43. For actions at Marina di Ragusa, see Alexander, interview, 16 June 2001.

44. Except where noted, see Breuer, *Drop Zone Sicily*, 115–118; Devlin, *Paratrooper!* 230; Garland and Smyth, *Sicily and the Surrender of Italy*, 156; Langdon, *"Ready,"* 21–22; Gavin, *Airborne Warfare*, 14–15 and *On to Berlin*, 22–23; Piper, *Operation of the 505th Parachute Infantry Regimental Combat Team*, 23–24; and Sayre, *Operations of Company "A,"* 19.

45. Garland and Smyth, *Sicily and the Surrender of Italy*, 109–111, 119–120, 147.

46. Ibid., 119–120, 147, 148.

47. Ibid., 148–149.

48. Except where noted, the following account of the fight led by Captain Sayre and Lieutenant Colonel Gorham is from Sayre's personal reminiscence of the events in Sayre, *Operations of Company "A,"* 10–18.

49. Ibid., 10.

50. From a report of the incident written by Jack "Beaver" Thompson contained in *82d Airborne Division in Sicily and Italy*, 11.

51. In some accounts of this fight, the Axis column is identified as the western half of Conrath's division, but this is not possible, for at this time it had still not reached its attack positions, which were north of Casa del Priolo. Italian *Mobile Group E*, which had started its movement from an area just west of Niscemi, had also been divided into two columns for movement, and it was the eastern column of *Mobile Group E* that Sayre's paratroopers encountered during this fight. See Garland and Smyth, *Sicily and the Surrender of Italy*, 149–150.

52. Edwin M. Sayre, interview by the author, Atlanta, GA, 13 April 2002.

53. Breuer, *Drop Zone Sicily*, 104–105; Langdon, *"Ready,"* 24; Sayre, *Operations of Company "A,"* 13.

54. Sayre, *Operations of Company "A,"* 14.

55. Garland and Smyth, *Sicily and the Surrender of Italy*, 152.

56. Ibid., 154.

57. Ibid., 154–155.

58. Ibid., 159–160, 161. A report by a naval transport commander who had been dispatched to the beaches by Admiral Hewitt estimated that 150–200 landing craft were stranded on the 45th Division beaches alone.

59. Ibid., 163–164.

60. Ibid., 165.

61. Sayre, *Operations of Company "A,"* 14. Unless otherwise noted, the account of this action is taken from this source.

62. Sayre, interview, 13 April 2002. Sayre noted that the only reason he started shooting with both .45s was because he just happened to have them both in his hands when the Germans entered the streambed. He explained that he was examining them to ensure there was no dirt in the barrels. Still, the legend of his two-handed shooting persisted. According to Sayre, "That's when I got my reputation for being the fast draw from Texas. You can draw pretty fast when you already have your guns in your hands."

63. Garland and Smyth, *Sicily and the Surrender of Italy*, 165–167; and Sayre, *Operations of Company "A,"* 15.

64. Quotes are from Sayre, *Operations of Company "A,"* 15–16. See also Garland and Smyth, *Sicily and the Surrender of Italy*, 168, 170–171. It took the combined efforts of the 32nd Field Artillery Battalion (the guns of which were being employed as direct-fire weapons), the 16th Infantry Cannon Company, and elements of the 18th Infantry and 41st Armored Infantry Regiments supported by four Sherman tanks to stop the German advance. Sixteen German tanks were destroyed on the plain before the Germans withdrew.

65. Gavin, *On to Berlin*, 24.

66. Ireland quoted in O'Donnell, *Beyond Valor*, 45.

67. Gavin, *On to Berlin*, 25. Gavin noted that "we had heard that the Germans had scared the wits out of the natives with their stories about the atrocities committed by American parachutists. They spread the news that we were long-term convicts who had been granted our freedom in exchange for becoming paratroopers. This was given credence by the practice in many parachute units of having all the men shave their heads. After the battle of Sicily was over, the Sicilians told us the shaved heads were one of the things that had convinced them that the Germans were right." In his book, Breuer substantiated Gavin's claim by quoting a German officer who told a gathering of Sicilians in Vittoria that "American paratroopers are cutthroats. You had better beware of them if they should land. All of the paratroopers are former convicts of the worst type—murderers, rapists and thugs. They were released from prison to join the paratroops." Breuer, *Drop Zone Sicily*, 23.

68. Gavin, *On to Berlin*, 25, 26.

69. Ireland quoted in O'Donnell, *Beyond Valor*, 45.

70. Garland and Smyth, *Sicily and the Surrender of Italy*, 169; Gavin, *On to Berlin*, 27–28; Langdon, *"Ready,"* 26; O'Donnell, *Beyond Valor*, 45; Piper, *Operation of the 505th Parachute Infantry Regimental Combat Team*, 27.

71. Gavin, *On to Berlin*, 28.

72. James M. Gavin to Mark Alexander, 23 August 1978, Gavin Papers, Box 12, Folder "Letters to and from 82nd Vets on Airborne Operations in Holland, September 1944," USAMHI.

73. Like Gavin, Wechsler's group had been dropped well away from their intended drop zone. Landing approximately three kilometers south of Comiso, Wechsler and his engineers had been marching to the sound of the guns and had traveled some twenty miles when Gavin found them. See Memorandum, Head-

quarters, 307th Airborne Engineer Battalion, "Report After Action Against Enemy as Required by AR 345-105."

74. Memorandum, Headquarters, 505th Parachute Infantry Regiment, "Airborne Assault Operations," 14 August 1943, 382-INF(505)-0.3, Box 12455, Record Group 407, NARA II.

75. Gavin, "Beyond the Stars," 78 (see chap. 1, n. 23).

76. Gavin, *On to Berlin*, 28.

77. Ireland quoted in O'Donnell, *Beyond Valor*, 46.

78. Gavin, *On to Berlin*, 29.

79. James M. Gavin to Clay Blair, 5 April 1983, Blair Collection, Box 53, Folder "Gavin, James M.," USAMHI.

80. Gavin, *On to Berlin*, 30.

81. Ibid., 31.

82. Jorgensen, *History of the 456th Parachute Field Artillery Battalion*, 71.

83. Gavin, *On to Berlin*, 32. The driver of the Italian personnel carrier, Captain Lewis Baldwin of C Battery, 456th Parachute Field Artillery Battalion, was posthumously awarded the Distinguished Service Cross for this action. See Jorgensen, *History of the 456th Parachute Field Artillery Battalion*, 72; and Murray Goldman letter, May 1945, http://www.ww2-airborne.us/units/505/505_memories.html.

84. Gavin, *On to Berlin*, 30.

85. Vandervoort quoted in D'Este, *Bitter Victory*, 294; Gavin quoted in O'Donnell, *Beyond Valor*, 46.

86. Ireland quoted in O'Donnell, *Beyond Valor*, 46; Gavin, *On to Berlin*, 33. In a document in which he commented on Clay Blair's draft of *Ridgway's Paratroopers*, 82nd veteran and historian Allen Langdon disputed Gavin's version of this incident as quoted here. Langdon wrote, "Where Gavin states . . . 'he [Krause] went to the rear,' it should be said that he 'went to the rear to have a small wound he had sustained treated.' This latter is corroborated by Dr. Daniel McIlvoy, the Bn. Surgeon, who had no love for Krause. To not state this leaves Gavin vulnerable because if Krause 'went to the rear' without any excuse, Gavin was derelict in his duty by not relieving him on the spot. To not state why Krause went to the rear is assassination of character by omission." See Allen Langdon to Clay Blair, n.d., Blair Collection, Box 54, Folder "Langdon, Allen," USAMHI. In describing the same incident in his book *"Ready,"* Langdon wrote, "At about this time, Major Krause, who had been lightly wounded and was on his way to the aid station to get bandaged, came over the ridge and told Gavin that the 3rd Battalion's losses were considerable and those who were still effective were pinned down" (26). Blair gave both versions of the event in *Ridgway's Paratroopers* but added comments from an anonymous "senior 505 officer, who shared Gavin's misgivings about Krause," who recalled that after the battle, "Gavin came across Krause sitting on a roadside curb, head down and sobbing. Krause said, in essence, his troopers would never be as brave again as they had been that day. Krause himself had been brave. He went down into the vineyard in front of the ridge and bounced 2.36-inch bazooka shells off a German tank. There was no effect on the tank and every German gun in the area fired at the spot where they saw the bazooka blast. It was our

first real hard-fought battle—with the issue in doubt all afternoon. We were all affected to some degree by first-battle trauma. Somehow, relieving Krause didn't seem the right thing . . . to do at that moment" (99). Krause was an enigma and was both brave and vexing that day. If it is true that Krause went to the rear because he was "lightly wounded," the question remains: Why didn't he return to the fight after he was treated?

87. Janney, *Richard Mott Janney*, 80.

88. Action described by Ireland in O'Donnell, *Beyond Valor*, 47–48; Ireland quoted in Breuer, *Geronimo!* 87.

89. Gavin, *On to Berlin*, 33–34; Langdon, *"Ready,"* 27; Headquarters, 505th Parachute Infantry Regiment, "Airborne Assault Operations."

90. Piper, *Operation of the 505th Parachute Infantry Regimental Combat Team*, 18. This is substantiated in *82d Airborne Division in Sicily and Italy*, 12.

91. The *Livorno Division*, the best-equipped Italian division on the island, attacked Gela at the same time but sustained such heavy casualties at the hands of U.S. Army Rangers that it ceased to be an effective fighting force. See Garland and Smyth, *Sicily and the Surrender of Italy*, 169–170.

92. Ibid., 171–173. Though Guzzoni nominally commanded Conrath and the *Hermann Göring Division*, the Germans were wary of Italian war weariness. Hence, they maintained a separate chain of command and were not above countermanding orders or acting independently if they felt that by doing so they would serve German interests.

93. Foreword by Gavin in Langdon, *"Ready,"* xiii. See also D'Este, *Bitter Victory*, 246–247. D'Este explains that the reason Gavin had not been told about the presence of German armor on Sicily was because this information had been gleaned from ULTRA intercepts, the highly secret Allied code-breaking effort. It was feared that if the Germans were to discover that the Allies knew of the presence of their armor on the island, they would also discover that the Allies were intercepting and reading their radio transmissions that they believed to be unbreakable.

94. Gavin, *On to Berlin*, 43.

95. See *82d Airborne Division in Sicily and Italy*, 11; Garland and Smyth, *Sicily and the Surrender of Italy*, 187–188; and Gavin, *On to Berlin*, 41. Carlo D'Este disputes the fact that Gorham was killed by a Tiger tank but mistakenly confuses the date of Gorham's death (*Bitter Victory*, 300). D'Este writes that Gorham was killed on 11 July, and on that date the only Tiger tanks present were fighting at Biazzo Ridge. While this is correct, Gorham was killed on 12 July, and during that action, fought on the Niscemi–Piano Lupo road, Tiger tanks were present. For his gallantry during the period 10–12 July, Gorham was posthumously awarded two Distinguished Service Crosses. In a letter to Clay Blair, Gavin wrote that "Art Gorham, as you must know, [was] a highly respected, gutsy, fighter. If he lived, he would have commanded the 505 right after Sicily." See Gavin to Blair, 5 April 1983.

96. Garland and Smyth, *Sicily and the Surrender of Italy*, 175.

CHAPTER 7: A VERY RUGGED DELIVERY

1. Captain Faith served as Ridgway's aide throughout World War II and remained in the Army afterward, rising to the rank of lieutenant colonel and command of a battalion in the 7th Infantry Division. He was killed during the Korean War while leading a breakout attempt through Chinese Communist forces that had surrounded the division at the Changjin (Chosin) Reservoir. For his actions Lieutenant Colonel Faith was posthumously awarded the Medal of Honor. See Billy C. Mossman, *Ebb and Flow, November 1950–July 1951*, 132–136.

2. Ridgway and Martin, *Soldier*, 71. Allen's report, of course, was not correct. There were some paratroopers to his front, most notably the group under Lieutenant Colonel Gorham and Captain Sayre. But according to the plan, Gavin's *entire* regimental combat team should have been to Allen's front, and this certainly was not the case.

3. Ibid., 71–73. According to the original plan for the drop, Follmer's company was to knock out an Italian strongpoint near Lake Biviere and then light huge bonfires to serve as guideposts for the seaborne elements of the 1st Infantry Division. Though not able to do this himself because of his broken ankle, Follmer's platoon leaders accomplished both missions. See Breuer, *Drop Zone Sicily*, 84–87. After Sicily, Follmer remained with the 82nd but had the most unfortunate luck on airborne operations. During the jump into Normandy, Follmer broke his right hip and was invalided out of the Army. Normandy was Follmer's third combat jump and Ridgway's first. Strangely, after Ridgway climbed out of his parachute harness in Normandy, the first person he met was Bill Follmer, lying on his back. When Ridgway approached him and asked what was wrong, Follmer commented that he thought he had broken his back, to which Ridgway replied, "Well . . . I guess you hope to god you never see *me* again." See Ridgway and Martin, *Soldier*, 6; and letter from Willard B. Follmer to Clay Blair, 5 February 1984, Blair Collection, Box 53, Folder "Follmer, Willard R." USAMHI.

4. Blair, *Ridgway's Paratroopers*, 92; Ridgway and Martin, *Soldier*, 73; Warren, *Airborne Missions in the Mediterranean*, 39.

5. See Memorandum, "Follow-up Lift 82nd Airborne Division," n.d., signed by A. S. Nevins for Eisenhower; Headquarters, 82nd Airborne Division "Plan for CT 504 (less 3d Bn.)," 29 June 1943; Memorandum, Headquarters, 82nd Airborne Division, "Red, White, Blue, Green, Purple, and Brown Messages," 30 June 1943; and copy of actual message sent by Ridgway on 11 July. All the above are exhibits in H. A. Craig et al., *Proceeding of Board of Officers Considering Airborne Operations*, 23 July 1943, pt. 1, ser. A, in *Records of the War Department's Operations Division*, reel 4.

6. Garland and Smyth, *Sicily and the Surrender of Italy*, 175.

7. Breuer, *Drop Zone Sicily*, 139; Huston, *Out of the Blue*, 159; Warren, *Airborne Missions in the Mediterranean*, 37.

8. Warren, *Airborne Missions in the Mediterranean*, 39. For the second drop, the planes also employed a new tactic, flying in a "stepped-down" attitude wherein the trailing planes in each V flew at a slightly lower altitude, which made it easier to see the silhouette of the lead plane against the sky.

9. Garland and Smyth, *Sicily and the Surrender of Italy*, 176; Warren, *Airborne Missions in the Mediterranean*, 39.

10. Delbert Kuehl quoted in O'Donnell, *Beyond Valor*, 52.

11. Gavin, *On to Berlin*, 74.

12. James M. Gavin, interview, 4 January 1983, Blair Collection, Box 53, Folder "Gavin, James M.," USAMHI. Tucker finally got his star after the war and ended his military career as the commandant of cadets at the Citadel.

13. Headquarters, 82d Airborne Division, "Reported Loss of Transport Planes and Personnel." Some of the others Ridgway had enlisted to his cause were Major General Browning; Major General Geoffrey Keyes, Patton's deputy commander; and Major General Joseph M. Swing, Eisenhower's American airborne adviser. These three had been instrumental in getting the naval planners to agree that if the aircraft followed certain prescribed routes, they would be safe from friendly fire. But designing aerial routes that avoided the convoys was one thing; ensuring that the ships did not fire on the aircraft required positive fire-control measures from both the naval and the ground force commanders.

14. Message, 5 July 1943, Ridgway Papers, Box 2a, Folder "Matthew B. Ridgway, Personal File, 1942–1943," USAMHI (capitalization in original).

15. Message, 6 July 1943, ibid. See also Blumenson, *Patton Papers*, 281. A notation at the bottom of the message indicates that Patton's G-3 passed this message to Vice Admiral Henry K. Hewitt that same day. Hewitt was the commander of the naval task force charged with transporting Patton's Seventh Army to Sicily.

16. Headquarters, 82d Airborne Division, "Reported Loss of Transport Planes and Personnel."

17. Garland and Smyth, *Sicily and the Surrender of Italy*, 177.

18. Morison, *Two-Ocean War*, 259.

19. Patton diary entry for 11 July 1943 in Blumenson, *Patton Papers*, 280.

20. Warren, *Airborne Missions in the Mediterranean*, 39.

21. Harrison's testimony on the fratricide is paraphrased in Headquarters, 82d Airborne Division, "Reported Loss of Transport Planes and Personnel."

22. From after-action report quoted in Warren, *Airborne Missions in the Mediterranean*, 39. Each plane had flares that they were to fire to ensure recognition by friendly forces, but in the heat of battle, and mixed with the hundreds of tracers and airburst antiaircraft shells, these were futile.

23. Garland and Smyth, *Sicily and the Surrender of Italy*, 177–181; Warren, *Airborne Missions in the Mediterranean*, 40. Another six of the 316th's planes turned back without dropping because the fire was too intense. All told, eight planes returned to North Africa with full loads. Aboard were a total of 104 paratroopers, many of whom were wounded.

24. *82d Airborne Division in Sicily and Italy*, 7–8 (see chap. 5, n. 32).

25. Warren, *Airborne Missions in the Mediterranean*, 40.

26. Joint interview of Flight Officer Anderson and Lieutenant Harpster, pilot and copilot of aircraft No. 505, 45th Troop Carrier Squadron, 316th Troop Carrier Group, included in report from Headquarters, 52nd Troop Carrier Wing, 12 July 1943, exhibit in Craig et al., *Proceeding of Board of Officers* (capitalization in original); Warren, *Airborne Missions in the Mediterranean*, 40.

27. O'Malley quoted in Breuer, *Geronimo!* 92. Surprisingly, not all the men aboard the six planes that crashed were killed.

28. Komosa quoted in Garland and Smyth, *Sicily and the Surrender of Italy*, 180; Kuehl quoted in O'Donnell, *Beyond Valor*, 53; Warren, *Airborne Missions in the Mediterranean*, 40.

29. Statement by Charles A. Drew, n.d., Gavin Papers, Box 11, Folder "Invasion of Sicily, Intelligence Reports, Organizational and Operation Plans, After Action Report + Inquiry on Friendly Fire Losses, Maps," USAMHI.

30. Headquarters, 82d Airborne Division, "Reported Loss of Transport Planes and Personnel." There is much confusion about what the correct sign-countersign was that night. Lieutenant Charles Drew stated he was told it was "George—Marshall" and that he later found out it was, ironically, "Think—Quickly." See statement by Charles A. Drew.

31. Garland and Smyth, *Sicily and the Surrender of Italy*, 182.

32. Ibid.

33. Quoted in Taylor, *Swords and Plowshares*, 50.

34. See Breuer, *Geronimo!* 93–94; Nelson Mayhew, "The Yacht Club: The Sixty-second Troop Carrier Squadron and the Evolution of Combat Airdrop Operations During World War II," 12. In *Geronimo!* Breuer writes that Sergeant Fielding Armstrong, the crew chief aboard the plane on which Keerans was riding, saw Keerans on Sicily the next morning. Their plane had been shot down during the run in to Sicily and ditched about four hundred yards from the coast. Most of the crew and some paratroopers struggled free of the wreckage and made it to shore. While Armstrong was searching for his pilot and copilot, he encountered Keerans standing near the beach. Keerans asked Armstrong if he would accompany him inland. Armstrong declined, saying he wanted to return to his unit in North Africa. Mayhew substantiates this story in "Yacht Club." Gavin saw Keerans as "a problem boy" who "liked to go on a [drinking] spree every now and then. 3 and 4 days." Keerans was on Gavin's boat during the voyage to North Africa, and, though the senior army officer aboard, Keerans "was drunk most of the time . . . and he'd have us do crazy things and it'd just drive you bananas." Ridgway thought about relieving him, but Keerans "was one of those guys that everybody in the U.S. Army knew he drank and they all took care of him and protected him." That was why Keerans was told he could not go on the mission to Sicily. See Gavin, interview, 4 January 1983. In an 8 May 1943 diary entry, made while sailing for North Africa, Gavin noted, "Gen[eral] K[eerans] back to normal after a three or four day drunk. I dislike that in anyone. . . . I thought that he had given up those habits. I never want to serve in his division if he gets one. . . . With no one to whom he would be accountable it is probable that he would be drunk most of the time. . . . Even when he is sober his judgement [*sic*] is not entirely sound. I am tired of tolerating his drunk[en]ness for days at a time and then defending my policies the remainder of the time." See Gavin, Personal Diary, 8 May 1943 (see chap. 4, n. 26). Apparently, Keerans's reputation had spread to the lower ranks as well. When learning that Keerans had been shot down (and presumably killed) during the 504th drop, an unknown historian of C Company, 1st Battalion, 325th Glider Infantry Regiment, which was still in North Africa, wrote, "I don't believe we can get anyone worse

(than Keerans) as CO of our combat team. The Army and the 'cause' didn't lose a helluva lot when they lost him." See Pierce, *Let's Go!* 56.

35. Warren, *Airborne Missions in the Mediterranean*, 40.

36. Bradley and Blair, *A General's Life*, 188. See also *82d Airborne Division in Sicily and Italy*, 9, 13; and Chester Garrison and Lewis P. Fern, "Unit Journal of the 2nd Battalion 504th Parachute Infantry 82nd Airborne Division," unmarked box, Folder "*S-1 Journal—Sicily, Salerno, Anzio (2/504th)," in an unmarked box from the 82nd Airborne Division Museum, Fort Bragg, NC.

37. Patton diary entry for 13 July 1943 in Blumenson, *Patton Papers*, 285–286. In *A General's Life*, Bradley contended that Patton accepted Alexander's plan because he was fearful of being relieved. According to Bradley, "In Tunisia [Eisenhower] had sharply warned him to curb his rampant Anglophobia and 'to respond to General Alexander's orders exactly as if they were issued by me.' Only the day before, Ike had landed on him hard in person. Ike's accusatory cable about the paratrooper disaster had arrived just that morning, and Patton already felt the blame must rest on him" (188). It is true that in his 13 July diary entry, Patton wrote of the disaster and Eisenhower's subsequent cable, saying, "Perhaps Ike is looking for an excuse to relieve me." Blumenson, *Patton Papers*, 283.

38. Lucian K. Truscott Jr., *Command Mission: A Personal Story*, 222.

39. Garland and Smyth, *Sicily and the Surrender of Italy*, 230–231.

40. *82d Airborne Division in Sicily and Italy*, 14.

41. Garland and Smyth, *Sicily and the Surrender of Italy*, 245, 249.

42. *82d Airborne Division in Sicily and Italy*, 14. See also 15, 21. The division's total prisoner count on day one of the advance was 848, at a cost of only 7 wounded.

43. Gavin, Personal Diary, 31 July 1943.

44. *82d Airborne Division in Sicily and Italy*, 15–16, 20–21.

45. Garland and Smyth, *Sicily and the Surrender of Italy*, 245, 252.

46. Gavin, Personal Diary, 31 July 1943.

47. Mandle and Whittier, *Combat Record of the 504th Parachute Infantry Regiment*, n.p.

48. See *82d Airborne Division in Sicily and Italy*, 16; Garrison and Fern, "Unit Journal of the 2nd Battalion 504th Parachute Infantry"; Gavin, Personal Diary, 31 July 1943; John P. O'Malley to William P. Yarborough, 20 January 1980, Blair Collection, Box 48, Folder "Chrono File: Sicily," USAMHI; Yarborough, interview, 28 March 1975 (see chap. 2, n. 16).

49. Quoted in *82d Airborne Division in Sicily and Italy*, 16–17 (capitalization in original).

50. Edward C. Krause, "Extracts from Battalion Journal of 23 July 1943, Montevago, Sicily," n.d., 382-INF(505)-0.3, Box 12455, Record Group 407, NARA II.

51. *82d Airborne Division in Sicily and Italy*, 17.

52. Ibid., 17–18.

53. Map overlay, "Sicilian Campaign, 82d A/B Div. Operations, 162400–292400 July," n.d., 382–0.3, Box 12345, Record Group 407, NARA II.

54. Warren, *Airborne Missions in the Mediterranean*, 47–52.

55. Report from Headquarters, 52nd Troop Carrier Wing, 12 July 1943, exhibit in Craig et al., *Proceeding of Board of Officers.* Because he believed that his pilots had dropped Tucker's men on the Gela-Farello landing area, Clark concluded that the "mission was successful as far as dropping equipment and personnel was concerned," although "it was disastrous so far as losses to this Wing are concerned."

56. Memorandum, Headquarters, North Africa Air Force Troop Carrier Command (Prov.), "Operation—HUSKY (Subsequent Missions 52nd TC Wing and American 82nd Airborne Division)," 13 July 1943, exhibit in Craig et al., *Proceeding of Board of Officers.* Like Clark, Williams also insisted that though the mission was costly for the air force, the pilots successfully delivered their paratroopers where designated.

57. Patton diary entry of 13 July 1943 in Blumenson, *Patton Papers,* 283; Memorandum from Joseph M. Swing, "Comments on Night Operation, 82d Airborne Division Night D Plus 1/D plus 2," 16 July 1943, reproduced as appendix 11 in Huston, *Out of the Blue,* 273.

58. Dwight D. Eisenhower to George C. Marshall, 17 July 1943, in *The Papers of Dwight David Eisenhower: The War Years, II,* ed. Alfred D. Chandler, 1259.

59. Cable from Cunningham to Eisenhower, 23 July 1943, exhibit in Craig et al., *Proceeding of Board of Officers.*

60. Craig et al., *Proceeding of Board of Officers.*

61. Harry Lewis, "Reactions to Airborne Operations Conference Held NATOUSA, 241430 July 43," Blair Collection, Box 48, Folder "Chrono File: Sicily," USAMHI. See also Craig et al., *Proceeding of Board of Officers.*

62. Craig et al., *Proceeding of Board of Officers.*

63. Allied Force Headquarters, Training Memorandum Number 43, *Employment of Airborne Forces,* 2 August 1943, pt. 1, ser. A, in *Records of the War Department's Operations Division,* reel 8.

64. Headquarters, 82d Airborne Division, "Reported Loss of Transport Planes and Personnel."

65. Gavin, *Airborne Warfare,* 1.

66. Quoted in Huston, *Out of the Blue,* 166; Gavin, *On to Berlin,* 52–53; Patton quoted in ibid., 164; Bradley quoted in Bradley and Blair, *A General's Life,* 184. Bradley also wrote that the resistance that had grown up against the airborne forces ran much deeper than the desire to disband airborne divisions in that many wanted to do away with the concept of military parachutists altogether. According to Bradley, many of his "infantry cohorts declared the paratroopers a dead dodo. There was soon a strong move in Washington to abolish the force" (184). Interestingly, in light of the experience of the Sicily campaign, Generals Ridgway and Taylor also questioned the usefulness of airborne divisions as then organized. On 29 July, Taylor submitted a memorandum to Ridgway in which he observed that "as the 82nd Airborne Division has no immediate chance for use in combat as an Airborne Division, it is exposed to deterioration thru idleness unless given a new mission." He recommended, therefore, that the parachute troops be formed into separate regiments and divorced from the 82nd, which should then be organized as an "Air Ranger" division capable of movement by glider, plane, or assault boat to conduct air or amphibious

landing operations and "Ranger type of missions." See Memorandum, Maxwell D. Taylor to Matthew B. Ridgway, "Airborne Operations," 29 July 1943, Ridgway Papers, Box 2a, Folder "Matthew B. Ridgway, Personal File, 1942–1943," USAMHI. Two days after receiving Taylor's memorandum, Ridgway drafted one of his own in which he maintained that airborne divisions should be employed as divisions and not piecemeal. Like Taylor, he also stated that if they are not used, they would deteriorate and that "therefore if appropriate opportunities do not appear imminent, or if sufficient aircraft to permit employment of the division as a whole are not available, the division should be unhesitatingly employed, as a whole, as a light infantry combat division, with missions appropriate to its fire power and combat strength." He went on to say that the division's "parachute elements should be withdrawn and incorporated in separate parachute regiments" and that the division be reconstituted as an air-landing division for movement by glider or plane. See Memorandum, Headquarters, 82nd Airborne Division, "Airborne [Troops] Divisions," 31 July 1943, Ridgway Papers, Box 2a, Folder "Matthew B. Ridgway, Personal File, 1942–1943," USAMHI. There is no evidence to indicate that either of these memoranda, the second of which exists only in draft with Ridgway's editing scrawled in the borders, ever got any further than Ridgway's desk. What these documents do demonstrate, however, is the frustration both men felt with having to rely on the untrained and insufficiently equipped Troop Carrier Command to supply them with a means to get to the battlefield.

67. Dwight D. Eisenhower to George C. Marshall, 20 September 1943, *The Papers of Dwight David Eisenhower: The War Years, III*, ed. Alfred D. Chandler, 1440 (italics in original).

68. Pierson quoted in E. M. Flanagan Jr., *The Angels: A History of the 11th Airborne Division*, 49.

69. Quoted in Huston, *Out of the Blue*, 167.

70. Training Circular 113, excerpted in ibid., 264.

71. Flanagan, *Angels*, 55.

72. McNair to Swing, 16 December 1943, quoted in Devlin, *Silent Wings*, 132.

73. Remarkably, despite all the boards, reports, and exercises that resulted from the Sicily fratricide, War Department censors kept the incident quiet until April 1944. In a diary entry for 4 April 1944, Eisenhower's naval aide, Captain Harry Butcher, wrote, "The unfortunate loss of twenty-three transport aircraft in the Sicilian operation by our own naval gunfire eventually reached the press." He continued, "There has been considerable hue and cry at home. As a matter of fact, the story could have been released months ago, but with action developing so fast in the Mediterranean and other problems pressing for attention, this affair was more forgotten than purposely hidden." See Butcher, *My Three Years with Eisenhower*, 511–512.

74. Gavin, *On to Berlin*, 51.

75. Memorandum, Headquarters, 505th Parachute Infantry Regiment, 26 July 1943, Gavin Papers, Box 11, Folder "Personal Records to James Gavin, Memo to Ridgway, Orders 505th Parachute Regimental Combat Team," USAMHI. In this same memo, Gavin also noted that the bazooka had to be modified in length to permit it to be jumped on the individual. To recognize the courage bazooka gunners

had to display in order to kill a tank, having to maneuver to the side or rear of the tank where the armor was thinner, and by so doing increasing the chances of being killed, Gavin arranged that a special insignia be designed for them. As he explained it, "Near Trapani are an old convent and monastery on the very high mountain of Erice. I arranged for the nuns there to embroider an insignia to be worn over the left breast of the jumpsuit for the bazooka carriers. It consisted of crossed bazookas and a bolt of lightning in the regimental colors, red and blue. We issued them to all the bazooka men as soon as we got back to Africa a few weeks later. There was no authority in regulations for it, but it seemed like a good idea, and the bazooka men were proud to wear them." Gavin, *On to Berlin*, 45.

76. Memorandum, Headquarters, 505th Parachute Infantry Regiment, 26 July 1943.

77. Gavin, *On to Berlin*, 52.

78. James M. Gavin, "Airborne Plans and Operations in the Mediterranean Theater," 22.

79. Memorandum, Headquarters, 505th Parachute Infantry Regiment, 26 July 1943.

80. Memorandum, Headquarters 82nd Airborne Division, "Analysis of Methods of Employment of 82d Airborne Division, NORTHWEST AFRICAN THEATER, Summer of 1943," 26 July 1943, Ridgway Papers, Box 2a, Folder "Matthew B. Ridgway, Personal File, 1942–1943," USAMHI.

81. See Gavin, *On to Berlin*, 50; and Michael A. Chester to James M. Gavin, 30 March 1959, Gavin Papers, Box 11, Folder "Letters to Gavin, Comments, and Inquiries about D-Day mentioned from *Longest Day*," USAMHI.

82. Gavin, *Airborne Warfare*, 17.

83. Gavin, Personal Diary, 10 August and 31 July 1943.

84. Transcript of seminar by Matthew B. Ridgway and Walter F. Winton, "Troop Leadership at the Operational Level: The Eighth Army in Korea," 9 May 1984, Fort Leavenworth, Kansas, Ridgway Papers, Box 51, unmarked folder, USAMHI.

85. Gavin, interview, 28 September 1982 (see chap. 2, n. 45).

86. Gavin, interview, 4 January 1983.

87. Gavin, interview, 28 September 1982.

88. Memorandum, "Award of Distinguished Service Cross," 2 August 1943, Gavin Papers, Box 7, Folder "Records for Receiving Citations and Awards of Valor: Distinguished Service Cross Silver Star," USAMHI.

89. Stephen E. Ambrose, *Citizen Soldiers: The US Army from the Normandy Beaches to the Bulge and the Surrender of Germany, June 7, 1944–May 7, 1945*, 121.

90. Kesselring's comments in Helmuth Reinhardt et al., *Airborne Operations: A German Appraisal*, 25 (emphasis added); Student quoted in Dawson, *Saga of the All American*, n.p.

CHAPTER 8: TAKING OFF FOR THE GATES OF HELL

1. Maurice Matloff, *Strategic Planning for Coalition Warfare, 1943–1944*, 106–108. According to Arthur Bryant, Alan Brooke's biographer, "The British took to

the [Casablanca] conference an elaborate staff, cipher and planning organisation, with the technical mechanism for presenting every quantitative calculation that might be called for. They sent it out in advance to Casablanca in a six-thousand-ton liner equipped . . . as a headquarters and communications vessel, thus temporarily transferring Great George Street [the site of British Imperial Headquarters] to Morocco." Quoting Brigadier Sir Ian Jacob, a member of Churchill's War Cabinet Secretariat, who kept a diary during the conference, "What was completely lacking in the American party was any kind of staff who could tackle the problems that were bound to arise in the course of the conversations, and to produce detailed solutions for the Chiefs of Staff. When the U.S. Chiefs saw how the land lay and the size of our party, they suddenly woke up to the fact that they had left most of their clubs behind." Bryant, *Turn of the Tide*, 443.

2. Matloff, *Strategic Planning for Coalition Warfare*, 123–124 (capitalization in original); Winston S. Churchill, *The Hinge of Fate*, 793.

3. Forrest C. Pogue, *George C. Marshall: Organizer of Victory*, 205.

4. Matloff, *Strategic Planning for Coalition Warfare*, 152–153. Also present at the Algiers conference were Alexander, Montgomery, and Tedder. Besides Marshall and Eisenhower, the other Americans present were Major General "Beetle" Smith; Major General Lowell W. Rooks, Eisenhower's G-3; and Major General Thomas T. Handy, chief of the War Department's Operations Division.

5. Butcher, *My Three Years with Eisenhower*, 318, diary entry for 30 May 1943.

6. Martin Blumenson, *Salerno to Cassino*, 10–12.

7. Matloff, *Strategic Planning for Coalition Warfare*, 157–158 (capitalization in original). Secretary of War Henry L. Stimson was with Churchill in London when the latter received news of Marshall's suggestion to go for Naples. Based on Churchill's reaction, Stimson got the impression that the prime minister thought that Marshall had finally come around to the British way of thinking. To clarify the situation, Stimson called Marshall to confirm that Marshall only meant this as a means to exploit Italian weakness and gain position in Italy in the cheapest possible manner and did not represent a wholesale abandonment of the agreed-upon 1 May 1944 date for OVERLORD. Marshall confirmed Stimson's thoughts, telling him, "You are absolutely correct. This is exactly what we are after" (158).

8. Blumenson, *Salerno to Cassino*, 16–17.

9. Garland and Smyth, *Sicily and the Surrender of Italy*, 260.

10. Blumenson, *Salerno to Cassino*, 19–20; Garland and Smyth, *Sicily and the Surrender of Italy*, 261–262; Matloff, *Strategic Planning for Coalition Warfare*, 158–159.

11. Blumenson, *Salerno to Cassino*, 18–21, 30; Garland and Smyth, *Sicily and the Surrender of Italy*, 269; Matloff, *Strategic Planning for Coalition Warfare*, 160.

12. Blumenson, *Salerno to Cassino*, 26.

13. Ibid.

14. Eisenhower and Major General Lucas quoted in ibid., 30.

15. Ibid., 43.

16. Memorandum, Headquarters, 82nd Airborne Division, "Lessons of Airborne Operation in ITALY," 25 October 1943, p. 2, 382-0.4, Box 12348, Record Group 407, NARA II.

17. The division had sustained 964 casualties during the Sicilian campaign. Unit breakouts were as follows: The 504th, 388 casualties; the 505th, 424 casualties; the 307th Airborne Engineer Battalion, 39 casualties; the 376th Parachute Field Artillery Battalion, 57 casualties; the 456th Parachute Field Artillery Battalion, 55 casualties; and the Division Headquarters, 1 casualty. *82d Airborne Division in Sicily and Italy*, 39–40 (see chap. 5, n. 32).

18. Ridgway and Martin, *Soldier*, 29. About the various schemes for which the 82nd was considered and against which he fought, Ridgway wrote, "I knew the airborne's limitations, as well as I knew its magnificent capabilities. I fought against these foolhardy schemes as stubbornly as I could, and I am convinced that on several occasions I saved the 82nd, or large elements of it, from being dropped into situations where it would have been destroyed as a fighting force" (29).

19. Mason, "The 82d Under Ridgway," chap. 4, p. 1 (see chap. 3, n. 65).

20. Gavin, *On to Berlin*, 55.

21. Matthew B. Ridgway to Maxwell D. Taylor, 8 August 1943, Ridgway Papers, Box 2a, Folder "Matthew B. Ridgway, Personal File, 1942–1943," USAMHI.

22. Mark Clark, *Calculated Risk*, 179. According to the calculations of the air planners, the air currents and mountainous terrain would force the troop transport pilots to drop the paratroopers from altitudes of from 1,500 to 2,000 feet, and glider release would have to be made at altitudes between 4,500 and 6,000 feet. Both would have not only scattered the parachute and glider forces but also exposed them for a prolonged period of time to enemy ground fire. See Memorandum, Headquarters, 82nd Airborne Division, "Lessons of Airborne Operation in ITALY," 3–4. In an article published after the war, Gavin wrote, "On thinking back now to the situation at the time, it seems to me that this first plan contemplated the use of our airborne units merely to gain a temporary tactical advantage. Their use in the manner planned would hardly have had a decisive bearing on the outcome of the operation as a whole. It was a good thing that the decision was made to drop the plan." Gavin, "Airborne Plans and Operations," 24.

23. See *82d Airborne Division in Sicily and Italy*, 41–42; and Headquarters, 82nd Airborne Division, "Lessons of Airborne Operation in ITALY," 3–4.

24. *82d Airborne Division in Sicily and Italy*, 51–52 (capitalization in original).

25. At the time of the Salerno landings only six of the fifteen German divisions in Italy were south of Rome, with two more in the vicinity of Rome itself. See Vincent J. Esposito, ed., *The West Point Atlas of American Wars, 1900–1953*, sec. 2, map 94; and Ralph S. Mavrogordato, "Hitler's Decision on the Defense of Italy," 311–312.

26. See Blumenson, *Salerno to Cassino*, 44; Gavin, "Airborne Plans and Operations," 24–26; Warren, *Airborne Missions in the Mediterranean*, 57; and Headquarters, 82nd Airborne Division, "Lessons of Airborne Operation in ITALY," 4–7.

27. Headquarters, 82nd Airborne Division, "Lessons of Airborne Operation in ITALY," 2.

28. Patrick D. Mulcahy, "Airborne Activities in the Avalanche Operation, Preliminary Report by Major Patrick D. Mulcahy, AFHQ, Observer," 22 September 1943, pp. 1–2, 382-1, Box 12348, Records Group 407, NARA II.

29. See Mandle and Whittier, *Combat Record of the 504th Parachute Infantry Regiment*, n.p.; *82d Airborne Division in Sicily and Italy*, 43–46; Mulcahy, "Airborne

Activities in the Avalanche Operation," 2; Ralph P. Eaton, "Contact Imminent: A Narrative of the Pre-campaign Activities of the 82nd Airborne Division, July–September 1943, Prepared by the 82nd Airborne General Staff," 26 December 1943, p. 5, Ralph P. Eaton Papers, Folder "'Contact Imminent' July to September 1943," USAMHI.

30. Headquarters, 82nd Airborne Division, "Lessons of Airborne Operation in ITALY," 7; Headquarters, 82nd Airborne Division, "Development of Operation GIANT," 9 September 1943, pp. 1–2, Blair Collection, Box 48, Folder "Chrono File: Anzio," USAMHI.

31. Butcher, *My Three Years with Eisenhower*, 404, diary entry for 2 September 1943.

32. Except where noted, see Garland and Smyth, *Sicily and the Surrender of Italy*, 441–485.

33. Lyman L. Lemnitzer, "Directive to the Commanding General, 82nd Airborne Division," 3 September 1943, Arthur S. Nevins Papers, Box 2, Folder "Personal File—Mediterranean, esp. Sicily + Southern Italy," USAMHI. Brigadier General Nevins was Alexander's operations officer. Mark Clark was also present at Alexander's headquarters on 3 September where he was told that the 82nd was no longer available for his use. According to Carlo D'Este, when Clark learned of this, he told Eisenhower, "No! That's my division! . . . Taking away the Eighty-Second just as the fighting starts is like cutting off my left arm." Carlo D'Este, *Fatal Decision: Anzio and the Battle for Rome*, 35. See also Clark, *Calculated Risk*, 180.

34. See Garland and Smyth, *Sicily and the Surrender of Italy*, 485–489; Headquarters, 82nd Airborne Division, "Lessons of Airborne Operation in ITALY," 7–10; Headquarters, 82nd Airborne Division, "Development of Operation GIANT," 3–4.

35. Garland and Smyth, *Sicily and the Surrender of Italy*, 488; Ridgway and Martin, *Soldier*, 80; Headquarters, 82nd Airborne Division, "Lessons of Airborne Operation in ITALY," 7–10; Headquarters, 82nd Airborne Division, "Development of Operation GIANT," 4.

36. Headquarters, 82nd Airborne Division, "Development of Operation GIANT," 5 (capitalization in original).

37. Ibid., 5–6.

38. Headquarters, 82nd Airborne Division, "Lessons of Airborne Operation in ITALY," 7–10; Headquarters, 82nd Airborne Division, "Development of Operation GIANT," 6.

39. Ridgway and Winton, "Troop Leadership at the Operational Level" (see chap. 7, n. 84). Gardiner was a fifty-three-year-old pilot who was also the former governor of Maine.

40. Except where noted, see Ridgway and Martin, *Soldier*, 81–82; and Headquarters, 82nd Airborne Division, "Development of Operation GIANT," 7.

41. Gardiner quoted in Richard Tregaskis, *Invasion Diary*, 105. Unless otherwise noted, the account of the Taylor-Gardiner mission to Rome is taken from Maxwell D. Taylor and William T. Gardiner, "Mission to ROME," 9 September 1943, reproduced in *82d Airborne Division in Sicily and Italy*, 56–59.

42. Ibid.

43. Ibid., 56. According to Gardiner, Carboni stated, "The Germans are suspicious. They had cut off the Italians' gasoline supply and some of their ammunition. There were only twenty rounds for some of the pieces. When I asked Carboni about getting more ammunition, his only reply was that we had destroyed the largest factory. He said that he had the facilities for only a few hours' fighting; that if he moved his armored units more than thirty miles, they would be immobilized." Tregaskis, *Invasion Diary,* 105–106.

44. Taylor and Gardiner, "Mission to ROME," reproduced in *82d Airborne Division in Sicily and Italy*, 56–57.

45. Ibid., 57, 58–59. According to Gardiner, both Carboni and Badoglio attempted to maneuver Taylor into canceling GIANT II on his authority. At one point, "Gen[eral] Carboni . . . asked Gen[eral] Taylor to concur in recommending that the airborne mission to Rome should be cancelled. But this, Taylor said, could not be done: the Italians must assume responsibility for adopting a position and he would report it. Gen[eral] Taylor handled that very well. The Italians were evidently trying to jockey us into a position where we should make that decision." Tregaskis, *Invasion Diary*, 106.

46. Taylor and Gardiner, "Mission to ROME," reproduced in *82d Airborne Division in Sicily and Italy*, 57–59. Taylor sent a fourth message to Allied Force Headquarters before leaving Rome, requesting permission to return with the deputy chief of *Comando Supremo*, Generale di Corpo d'Armata Carlo Rossi, and an interpreter, in order that Rossi might represent the changed Italian position. Although a response to this message was never received, Taylor and Gardiner returned with Rossi and his interpreter anyway.

47. Headquarters, 82nd Airborne Division, "Development of Operation GIANT," 9. There is some confusion about whether GIANT II was canceled on 8 September, postponed indefinitely on 8 September, or postponed on 8 September and canceled on 9 September. Regardless, once Taylor and Gardiner returned, with Rossi in tow, there was no further thought of conducting a drop on Rome.

48. Sayre, interview, 13 April 2002 (see chap. 6, n. 52).

49. Taylor, *Swords and Plowshares*, 64.

50. Gavin, *On to Berlin*, 62–63.

51. James M. Gavin to Joseph I. Greene, 29 March 1946, Gavin Papers, Box 10, Folder "General Ridgway, Matthew B., Letters on Insignia, 504th Regt. Combat Team, 505th at Nijmegen + 82nd Airborne Division," USAMHI.

52. Ridgway and Martin, *Soldier*, 82. According to Eisenhower biographer Merle Miller, Eisenhower never lost "his enthusiasm for GIANT II. After the war, in an interview with an Army historian, he said, 'I wanted very much to make the air drop in Rome, and we were all ready to execute that plan. . . . I was anxious to get in there.'" According to Miller, Brigadier Kenneth Strong was also disappointed when GIANT II was canceled. Miller wrote, "In a similar interview with an army historian in 1947, [Strong] said, 'My opinion is that the cancellation of GIANT II was a great mistake. If the airborne division had been sent . . . the Italians would have welcomed us, and they would have held the airfields for us.'" Strong was, according to Miller, "sparing in his approval of Taylor. He said that the paratroop officer had learned nothing in Rome that he had not been told before undertaking

the risky mission; nevertheless, he advised against it." Merle Miller, *Ike the Soldier: As They Knew Him*, 550. This is not entirely true. Taylor did not know that the Italian forces had been starved of ammunition and gasoline, both critical commodities on which the operation depended. He learned this while in Rome. Moreover, Castellano had promised the Allies an impressive list of aid. Taylor discovered that much of what Castellano promised was simply not available. Regardless, it was the Italians who would have been most responsible for supplying that aid, Carboni and Badoglio, who directed that the drop be canceled, not Taylor.

53. Blumenson, *Salerno to Cassino*, 122.

54. *82d Airborne Division in Sicily and Italy*, 46–47.

55. Gavin, Personal Diary, 11 September 1943 (see chap. 4, n. 26).

56. See *82d Airborne Division in Sicily and Italy*, 47–48; Headquarters, 319th Glider Field Artillery Battalion, "Report of Action During Month of September, 1943," 10 October 1943, p. 6, 382-FA(319)-0.3, Box 12434, Record Group 407, NARA II; "Airborne Operations, July–September 1943," n.d., Gavin Papers, Box 11, Folder "Invasion of Sicily, Intelligence Reports, Organizational and Operation Plans, After Action Report + Inquiry of Friendly Fire Losses, Maps," USAMHI; Eaton, "Contact Imminent," 8–9.

57. Blumenson, *Salerno to Cassino*, 122.

58. Ridgway selected Lewis's glider troops and the 3/504th for this mission because both had already undergone extensive amphibious training in preparation for GIANT I. See "The 325th Glider Infantry in Action," 19 October 1943, 382-INF(325)-0.3, Box 12448. Record Group 407, NARA II; *82d Airborne Division in Sicily and Italy*, 74; "Airborne Operations, July–September 1943," 8.

59. In a handwritten note to Montgomery, Alexander spelled out his subordinate's mission quite clearly. He was to secure the Messina Strait and to follow the enemy "with such force as you can make available, bearing in mind that the greater the extent to which you can engage enemy forces in the southern tip of Italy, the more assistance you will be giving to AVALANCHE." This note is reproduced in Bernard Law Montgomery, *The Memoirs of Field-Marshal the Viscount Montgomery of Alamein*, 175 (capitalization in original).

60. Anonymous soldier quoted in Charles B. MacDonald, *The Mighty Endeavor: The American War in Europe*, 207.

61. Blumenson, *Salerno to Cassino*, 79, 90–91.

62. The German evacuation of Sicily was complete by 17 August. In all, they succeeded in evacuating more than 39,000 men, more than 9,000 vehicles, 94 guns, 47 tanks, 1,100 tons of ammunitions, 970 tons of fuel, and 15,700 tons of miscellaneous equipment and supplies. Both the *Hermann Göring* and the *15th Panzer Grenadier Divisions* were reconstituted in Italy. See Garland and Smyth, *Sicily and the Surrender of Italy*, 416.

63. MacDonald, *Mighty Endeavor*, 202.

64. Shelford Bidwell, "Kesselring," 279–280. In a cable to his *Tenth Army* commander sent following Eisenhower's announcement, Kesselring said, "If we retain our fighting spirit and remain dead calm, I am confident that we will continue to perform the tasks entrusted to us by the Fuehrer. Italian troops will be asked to continue the fight on our side by appeals to their honor. Those who refuse are to be

ruthlessly disarmed. No mercy must be shown the traitors. Long live the Fuehrer." Blumenson, *Salerno to Cassino*, 69.

65. General der Panzertruppen Heinrich von Vietinghoff quoted in Blumenson, *Salerno to Cassino*, 64.

66. Information on German plans and dispositions is from the following sources: Blumenson, *Salerno to Cassino*, 78–79; Mavrogordato, "Hitler's Decision on the Defense of Italy," 314; and Walter Warlimont, *Inside Hitler's Headquarters, 1939–45*, 318.

67. Blumenson, *Salerno to Cassino*, 97–98.

68. Ibid., 107–110.

69. Ibid., 76, 112–115.

70. Ibid., 117 (quote), 116.

71. Ibid., 118–119.

72. Ibid., 119–120.

73. Ibid., 120–122; Yarborough, interview, 28 March 1975 (see chap. 2, n. 16). Yarborough had been the 2/504th's commander during the Sicily campaign but was relieved while the division was on occupation duty in western Sicily because he had challenged both Ridgway and Tucker. Having parachuted into North Africa with Edson Raff, Yarborough thought his experience earned for him the right to question authority. In addition, he thought that his experience was not being sufficiently recognized. According to Yarborough, "I went up to Palermo and then I got orders to . . . come back and see Ruben [*sic*] Tucker and also go and see Ridgway, who said, 'Your services are no longer required. You're a pain in our ass, excuse me, but you go back to Mark Clark and tell him that he should find another job for you.' So, I went back to Mark Clark and Mark Clark said to me, he said, 'You know, knowing your personality and that of General Ridgway,' he said, 'I never should have assigned you or allowed you to be assigned to that outfit in the first place.' He said, 'Now you . . . you come back here with me and in due course, I'll see that you get a . . . you get another command.' But in the meantime, I wanted to die. I felt like a . . . I felt that if I could only get into combat someplace and get an honorable slug or whatever, that I would have paid the price for my high spirited stupidity, you see. Challenging . . . challenging authority in a way that . . . no outfit can work on that basis. You just can't have that kind of thing and I recognized where the deficiency lay. It was with me and not with Ridgway or with Tucker. So, this was how I then got back in the parachute planning business for the invasion of . . . of Italy."

74. Quoted in Clark, *Calculated Risk*, 199, 203. Afraid of a repeat of the Sicily friendly-fire incident, Ridgway insisted that "rigid control of antiaircraft fire is absolutely essential." In response, Clark called his naval and ground force commanders and ordered them to hold all antiaircraft fire and to bring down all barrage balloons beginning at 2100 hours, 13 September, and that they were not to act otherwise until they received word to free their guns and balloons from him personally. See Warren, *Airborne Missions in the Mediterranean*, 61.

75. Warren, *Airborne Missions in the Mediterranean*, 61–62; Yarborough, interview, 28 March 1975; Memorandum, Headquarters, 82nd Airborne Division, "Report of Arrival of Units in ITALY," 22 October 1943, Ridgway Papers, Box 2a, Folder "Matthew B. Ridgway, Personal File, 1942–1943," USAMHI.

76. Mulcahy, "Airborne Activities in the Avalanche Operation," 6; Joe Watts quoted in O'Donnell, *Beyond Valor*, 67; Tucker quoted in Devlin, *Paratrooper!* 301.

77. Warren, *Airborne Missions in the Mediterranean*, 61–62, 65; Reuben H. Tucker, "504th Parachute Infantry Action in Italy," n.d., 382-INF(504)-0.3, Box 12451, Record Group 407, NARA II. "Eureka" was the code name for the transmitting device that the division's pathfinders set up on the ground to help guide the transport planes to the drop zones. "Rebecca" was the code name for the receiver on board the transport aircraft. Only a select few transport aircraft were outfitted with Rebecca, usually those flown by flight commanders.

78. "Airborne Operations, July–September 1943," 8; Tucker, "504th Parachute Infantry Action in Italy."

79. Warren, *Airborne Missions in the Mediterranean*, 65–66; Headquarters, 82nd Airborne Division, "Report of Arrival of Units in ITALY." A total of 130 planes took off. Five turned back because of mechanical difficulties. Of the remaining 125, 2 planes were wildly off course. One dropped its stick of paratroopers well behind enemy lines at Eboli. The other strayed over the Allied fleet in the Gulf of Salerno, where, despite Clark's stern orders about holding all fire, some itchy-fingered gunners opened up and set the port engine on fire. The paratroopers aboard jumped as soon as they were over land, wandered for a few days in no-man's-land, and then fought for several more days alongside the British. Led by Lieutenant Jack Tallerday of the 1/505th, this small band finally made its way to Salerno, where Tallerday went in search of a truck that could transport them back to his regiment. Before he left, Tallerday pointed to a house where he told his men to rest until he returned. "Unknown to the Lieutenant, of course, the house was one of ill repute, well stocked with occupants and refreshments, and so it was a happy, but reluctant to leave, group of warriors that Tallerday found when he returned later in the day with a British truck." Langdon, *"Ready,"* 31.

80. Mission statement quoted in Gavin, *Airborne Warfare*, 31.

81. Yarborough, interview, 28 March 1975.

82. Except where noted, information on the Avellino drop taken from Gavin, *Airborne Warfare*, 31–32; Huston, *Out of the Blue*, 169; and Warren, *Airborne Mission in the Mediterranean*, 68–69. Ironically, Yarborough took command of the 509th once it was reassembled at Naples.

83. Gavin, "Airborne Plans and Operations," 28; Clark, *Calculated Risk*, 206.

84. Journal, 14–28 September 1943, 2nd and 3rd Sticks, 1st Platoon, C Company, 307th Airborne Engineer Battalion, attachment to Memorandum, Headquarters, 307th Airborne Engineer Battalion, "History of 307th A/B Engr. Bn. 82nd A/B Div., from 22 Sept. 1943 to 30 Sept. 1943," 18 October 1943, Box "82d Airborne Division—WWII—307th Eng. Bn.—Unit History—Incident Reports," 82nd Airborne Division Museum, Fort Bragg, NC. First Lieutenant William C. Kellogg led the group of twenty-seven men from the 307th Airborne Engineer Battalion who destroyed this bridge. They wandered the hills causing what destruction they could and hiding from the Germans for thirteen days. They inflicted twenty-four German casualties and destroyed one small German armored vehicle, two personnel carriers, and sixty-seven telephone poles before linking up

with British patrols. They also rescued one downed aviator. For his actions, Lieutenant Kellogg was awarded the Distinguished Service Cross.

85. Blumenson, *Salerno to Cassino*, 132.

86. Quoted in Warren, *Airborne Missions in the Mediterranean*, 69.

87. Mandle and Whittier, *Combat Record of the 504th Parachute Infantry Regiment*, n.p.; Gavin, *Airborne Warfare*, 31; Blumenson, *Salerno to Cassino*, 145.

88. Blumenson, *Salerno to Cassino*, 129–131; Mandle and Whittier, *Combat Record of the 504th Parachute Infantry Regiment*, n.p.; Headquarters, 504th Parachute Infantry, "S-2 Journal, September 1943," 20 October 1943, 382-INF(504)-0.3, Box 12451, Record Group 407, NARA II.

89. Blumenson, *Salerno to Cassino*, 134.

90. Tregaskis, *Invasion Diary*, 114. Tregaskis accompanied Tucker's men on this attack.

91. Journal, 13–29 September 1943, C Company, 307th Airborne Engineer Battalion, attachment to Memorandum, Headquarters, 307th Airborne Engineer Battalion, "History of 307th A/B Engr. Bn. 82nd A/B Div., from 22 Sept. 1943 to 30 Sept. 1943." Captain Wight was the company commander.

92. Blumenson, *Salerno to Cassino*, 135. Since Ridgway's division had been parceled out to other units, the position of deputy corps commander also gave him some modicum of control over his regiments.

93. Mandle and Whittier, *Combat Record of the 504th Parachute Infantry Regiment*, n.p.

94. Blumenson, *Salerno to Cassino*, 136. Ross Carter told an amusing story of the taking of Altavilla in his book. At one point, Tucker turned to one of his troopers, a Greek American named Perici, and told him to "take six men and go into [Altavilla] and find out how many Krautheads are in it." At first, Perici refused. When Tucker, on the edge of rage, asked why, Perici responded, "Sir, . . . I've been in this army for four years. I done learned that I can't go to town without a pass. The MP's would get me as shore [*sic*] as hell is red-hot." Tucker thus wrote out a pass for Perici to enter Altavilla with his six-man patrol. Perici conducted his reconnaissance during which his patrol ran into stiff German resistance. Returning to Tucker, Perici reported, "Sir, they's MP's in that damn town with tanks and half tracks. A rough bunch, sir!" Carter, *Devils in Baggy Pants*, 54–55.

95. Carter, *Devils in Baggy Pants*, 47. For their leadership in the fight Tucker, Major Robert B. Acheson, and Major Don B. Dunham were awarded Distinguished Service Crosses. Dunham's was a posthumous award. Blumenson, *Salerno to Cassino*, 135.

96. Gavin, *On to Berlin*, 69.

CHAPTER 9: A FORCE UPON WHICH THE FIFTH ARMY COULD DEPEND

1. Blumenson, *Salerno to Cassino*, 154–155.

2. Headquarters, 82nd Airborne Division, "Report of Arrival of Units in ITALY" (see chap. 8, n. 75); William O. Darby and William H. Baumer, *Darby's Rangers: We Led the Way*, 116.

3. Darby and Baumer, *Darby's Rangers*, 116; Pierce, *Let's Go!* 69–74.

4. For their actions Meintzer and Private First Class Robert Cooper, one of E Company's intrepid machine gunners, were awarded the Silver Star. See Pierce, *Let's Go!* 69–74; Memorandum, Headquarters, 82nd Airborne Division, "Award of Silver Star Medal," 23 October 1943, Box "82nd Airborne Division WWII 325th GIR *Personal Papers," Folder "Personal Papers—Meintzer, Wade M. (E Co., 325th GIR)," 82nd Airborne Division Museum, Fort Bragg, NC; and Headquarters, 325th Glider Infantry Regiment, "The 325th Glider Infantry in Action," 19 October 1943, 382-INF(325)-0.3, Box 12448, Record Group 407, NARA II. Meintzer's platoon was often referred to as the 2/325th's "Ranger" platoon, but it should not be confused with the Army Rangers with which the glider troopers were fighting at the time. Meintzer's men were selected from within the 2/325th to serve as the battalion's reconnaissance force, and although they had undergone "Ranger-like" training, they were not Army Rangers.

5. Memorandum, Headquarters, 82nd Airborne Division, "Commendation of Company 'E,' 325th Glider Infantry," 23 October 1943, Box "82nd Airborne Division WWII 325th GIR *Personal Papers," Folder "Personal Papers—Meintzer, Wade M. (E Co., 325th GIR)," 82nd Airborne Division Museum, Fort Bragg, NC. Dickerson, the E Company commander, later wrote that he often observed Ridgway well forward, inspecting the front, ensuring weapons were sighted correctly and that defensive lines were tactically sound. During one such visit while E Company was defending Monte San Angelo, Ridgway questioned Dickerson about his appearance. "We were very short of ammunition, food, and water. The weather was very warm. I had not shaved in about ten days because of the water shortage and did not insist that my men do so. Early on a sunny morning, who appears from the valley below but General Ridgway. His first question was 'Why aren't you shaved?' He would not accept the excuse about water, but pointed out that I was the senior office on that mountain, and expected to set the example and that I should dry shave immediately then require my men to do so. Then he asked how many casualties we had suffered, complimented me on the performance of Company E, and approved all my weapons and troop dispositions. His last words were, 'You and your soldiers have done a fine job.'" Dickerson to Blair, 20 September 1983 (see chap. 3, n. 34).

6. Blumenson, *Salerno to Cassino*, 155–156.

7. Ibid., 157, 163. It is a remarkable testament to Darby's leadership that he was only a lieutenant colonel yet put in command of such a large force. Ridgway likewise saw in Darby unusual talent, as his subsequent actions would show.

8. Ibid., 164. When he assumed command of the forces on the Sorrento Peninsula, Ridgway finally regained control of all major elements of the 82nd save two. One of the exceptions was G Company, 2/325th, which Clark had earlier sent to occupy the island of Ischia, just outside the Gulf of Naples, where it remained until 23 October. The other was the 456th Parachute Field Artillery Battalion, which was still in Sicily. See Headquarters, 82nd Airborne Division, "Report of Arrival of Units in ITALY"; Headquarters, 325th Glider Infantry Regiment, "Activities of the 325th Glider Infantry During October, 1943," n.d., 382-INF(325)-0.3, Box 12448, Record Group 407, NARA II; and Headquarters, 325th Glider Infantry Regiment,

"The 325th Glider Infantry in Action," 19 October 1943, 382-INF(325)-0.3, Box 12448, Record Group 407, NARA II.

9. Memorandum by Matthew B. Ridgway, "Operations," 26 September 1943, 382-INF(505)-0.1, Box 12455, Record Group 407, NARA II.

10. *82d Airborne Division in Sicily and Italy*, 72 (see chap. 5, n. 32).

11. Blumenson, *Salerno to Cassino*, 165.

12. Headquarters, 505th Parachute Infantry Regiment, "Historical Record for the Month of October 1943," 4 November 1943, 382-INF(505)-0.3, Box 12455, Record Group 407, NARA II.

13. Gavin, *On to Berlin*, 71.

14. Blumenson, *Salerno to Cassino*, 165.

15. Gavin, *On to Berlin*, 71.

16. Norton, interview, 22 February 2001 (see chap. 4, n. 5).

17. Gavin, *On to Berlin*, 72; Norton, interview, 22 February 2001.

18. Gavin, *On to Berlin*, 72.

19. Norton, interview, 22 February 2001; Ridgway and Martin, *Soldier*, 88; Gavin, *On to Berlin*, 73. According to Ridgway, the reason there were no crowds is because he had summoned the city's chief of police and ordered him to clear the streets. "I gave him explicit instructions," wrote Ridgway. "I told him I wanted the streets of Naples cleared completely, because when we came in we were coming fast, and anybody in our path, either German or Italian, was going to get hurt. We gave him time to get back to town and carry out his order, and then we went in." See Ridgway and Martin, *Soldier*, 88. See also Matthew B. Ridgway to his wife, 7 October 1943, Ridgway Papers, Box 2a, Folder "Matthew B. Ridgway, Personal File, 1942, 1943," USAMHI.

20. Norton, interview, 22 February 2001.

21. Gavin, Personal Diary, 19 October 1943 (see chap. 4, n. 26). See also Norton, interview, 22 February 2001; and Memorandum, Headquarters, 82nd Airborne Division, "Restoration and Maintenance of Order in the City of NAPLES," 18 November 1943, Ridgway Papers, Box 2a, Folder, "Matthew B. Ridgway, Personal File, 1942–1943," USAMHI.

22. Ridgway and Martin, *Soldier*, 88.

23. Gavin, *On to Berlin*, 73.

24. Blumenson, *Salerno to Cassino*, 168.

25. "Company 'B,' 307th Airborne Engineer Battalion, Station and Record of Events, from Jan. 1/43 to Jan. 1/44," n.d., Box "82nd Airborne Division, WWII, 307th Eng. Bn., Unit History Incident Report," Folder "307th Abn. Eng. Bn. History 1943," 82nd Airborne Division Museum, Fort Bragg, NC. Some thought that the explosion was caused by B Company's own explosives, but this was never proved, and the prevailing mind-set, given the other explosions throughout the city, was that it was a German booby trap. See Ridgway and Martin, *Soldier*, 89–90.

26. Blumenson, *Salerno to Cassino*, 168–169.

27. Ibid., 192–193, 203–204.

28. According to Alexander, the reason he moved so fast was because one of the many airborne plans Fifth Army had thought up for the 82nd in support of AVALANCHE called for the 2/505th to drop on Arnone and Cancello to seize

the bridge there. Thus, planning for that drop resulted in his battalion being "well prepared for the later mission in support of the 23rd Armored Brigade, inasmuch as . . . we had carefully studie[d] aerial photos of the Arnone area, we knew the exact location of pillboxes, buildings, etc., exactly as depicted in the previous photographic studies." Mark Alexander to William E. Ekman, 5 October 1978, Gavin Papers, Box 10, Folder "82nd Airborne Division, Personal Letters w/ Veterans on Historical Events (WWII), Postcard of Ste. Mere–Eglise w/ 82nd Memorial Window," USAMHI.

29. Ibid.

30. Except where noted see Langdon, *"Ready,"* 33–34; and Headquarters, 505th Parachute Infantry Regiment, "Historical Record for the Month of October 1943."

31. See Langdon, *"Ready,"* 33–34; Tregaskis, *Invasion Diary*, 165; Norton, interview, 22 February 2001; and Headquarters, 505th Parachute Infantry Regiment, "Historical Record for the Month of October 1943."

32. Maxwell Taylor had unofficially assumed this position following Keerans's death, but he was away from the division most of the time as a member of the Allied liaison group to the Italian government. According to Taylor, "Apparently I qualified for membership on the basis of having become an Italian expert after some twenty-four hours in Rome." Quoted in Blair, *Ridgway's Paratroopers*, 156.

33. Gavin, *On to Berlin*, 73–74.

34. Gavin, Personal Diary, 19 October 1943. Batchellor was later relieved of command while the 82nd was in England preparing for the Normandy invasion. A married man, Batchellor "fell in love with an Irish lass where we were training and he neglected the regiment to be with her almost every afternoon." Mark Alexander quoted in Blair, *Ridgway's Paratroopers*, 193. According to Gavin, Batchellor "really wasn't a good regimental commander," but "it was hard to find regimental commanders of parachute regiments at that time, with the limited experience we had. You had to have someone with combat experience." Batchellor had fought with the 505th in Sicily and Italy and as regimental executive officer was first in line to take the regiment when Gavin left. After being relieved of regimental command, Batchellor was given command of a parachute battalion, the 1st Battalion, 508th Parachute Infantry Regiment, which jumped into Normandy as part of the 82nd. It was while commanding the 1/508th that Batchellor was subsequently killed in Normandy. The fact that he was reported killed as a member of the 508th and not the 505th was a difficult thing to explain to his widow and something Gavin tried to avoid for the rest of his life. See Gavin, interview, 4 January 1983.

35. Langdon, *"Ready,"* 34.

36. According to Blair, Ridgway, Taylor, and Taylor's executive officer, Colonel Francis A. "Andy" March, had all soured on the 456th after having relieved its commander, Lieutenant Colonel Harrison B. Harden Jr., for what they felt was poor performance in Sicily. The battalion would later be split to form a second parachute field artillery battalion, the 463rd, which fought in Italy and southern France while the rump rejoined the 82nd in England, where it retained the 456th designa-

tion and regained the confidence of Ridgway. See Blair, *Ridgway's Paratroopers*, 160; and Jorgensen, *History of the 456th Parachute Field Artillery Battalion*, 84–88.

37. Headquarters, 505th Parachute Infantry Regiment, "Historical Record for the Month of October 1943."

38. Norton, interview, 22 February 2001.

39. Ridgway and Martin, *Soldier*, 93.

40. Warren, *Airborne Missions in the Mediterranean*, 70.

41. Gavin, Personal Diary, 23 October 1943.

42. Dwight D. Eisenhower to Walter Bedell Smith, "Notes for Chief of Staff," 2 October 1943, in *Papers of Eisenhower: The War Years, III*, ed. Chandler, 1481.

43. Ibid.

44. Matthew B. Ridgway to Alfred M. Gruenther, "Suggested for Inclusion in Personal Letter to General EISENHOWER from General CLARK," 14 October 1943, Blair Collection, Box 48, Folder "Chrono File: Anzio," USAMHI. Gruenther was Clark's chief of staff at Fifth Army.

45. Matthew B. Ridgway to Paul L. Williams, 6 November 1943, Ridgway Papers, Box 2a, Folder "Matthew B. Ridgway, Personal File, 1942–1943," USAMHI.

46. Headquarters, 82nd Airborne Division, "Airborne Training," 6 November 1943, Ridgway Papers, Box 2a, Folder "Matthew B. Ridgway, Personal File, 1942–1943," USAMHI (emphasis in original).

47. Marshall quoted in Huston, *Out of the Blue*, 51.

48. Dwight D. Eisenhower to Harold Rupert Leofric Alexander, 29 December 1943, *Papers of Eisenhower: The War Years, III*, ed. Chandler, 1634. Even Butcher noted a change in Eisenhower after the announcement, writing in his diary that Eisenhower stated one morning at breakfast that he did not want to hang around in the Mediterranean and "wait until Rome is taken because once [the] decision had been taken to change your job, everyone has 'ants in his pants' to get on with the new one and inevitably loses interest in the old." Butcher, *My Three Years with Eisenhower*, 456.

49. Ralph Bennett, *Ultra and Mediterranean Strategy*, 251; Blumenson, *Salerno to Cassino*, 207–245; John Ellis, *Cassino: The Hollow Victory*, 27.

50. Quote from Blumenson, *Salerno to Cassino*, 220. See also Mandle and Whittier, *Combat Record of the 504th Parachute Infantry Regiment*, n.p.; and Mason, "The 82d Under Ridgway," chap. 4, p. 4 (see chap. 3, n. 65).

51. Journal, 27 October 1943–23 April 1944, C Company, 307th Airborne Engineer Battalion, attachment to Memorandum, Headquarters, 307th Airborne Engineer Battalion, "Unit History," 1 August 1944, Box "82nd Airborne Division, WWII, 307th Eng. Bn., Unit History, Incident Reports," Folder "307th Abn. Eng. Bn. C Co. Sicily/Italy Sep. 43–Apr. 44," 82nd Airborne Division Museum, Fort Bragg, NC.

52. Gavin, Personal Diary, 13 November 1943.

53. Devlin, *Paratrooper!* 337.

54. Martin Blumenson, *Mark Clark*, 143.

55. Matthew B. Ridgway to Mark Clark, 10 November 1943, Blair Collection, Box 48, Folder "Chrono File: Anzio," USAMHI (capitalization in original).

56. Mark Clark to Matthew B. Ridgway, 12 November 1943, ibid. Reminiscing after the war, Clark wrote, "It was a sad day for me when Ridgway departed. He was an outstanding battle soldier, brilliant, fearless and loyal, and he had trained and produced one of the finest Fifth Army outfits." Clark, *Calculated Risk*, 236. Notwithstanding his affection for and trust in Clark, one of Ridgway's last acts before leaving Italy was to ensure that Maxwell Taylor, who also remained behind as a member of the Allied liaison team to the Italian government, would be well positioned to watch over Tucker and his troopers. To this end Ridgway requested that when Taylor's liaison duties were over, he "report to and assume command of C[ombat] T[eam] 504, and when released from [the Mediterranean] Theater to bring it on to rejoin the Division." Ridgway also received assurance from "Beetle" Smith that Taylor would, in fact, return to the 82nd and not be assigned elsewhere. True to his charter, Taylor reported to Fifth Army headquarters in December and kept pressure on Clark to release Tucker's combat team as soon as possible. But other events, to include Taylor's reassignment to command of the 101st Airborne Division, intervened, and so the 504th remained stranded in Italy. Although it did eventually return to 82nd control before the Normandy invasion, it was both too late and too bloodied to take part. For the quote, see Matthew B. Ridgway to Maxwell D. Taylor, 7 November 1943, Ridgway Papers, Box 2a, Folder "Matthew B. Ridgway, Personal File, 1942–1943," USAMHI. See also Blair, *Ridgway's Paratroopers*, 171.

57. Pierce, *Let's Go!* 89; Mason, "The 82d Under Ridgway," chap. 4, page 4.

58. Collectively, the units sailing for the United Kingdom had sustained 78 killed and 263 wounded and listed 15 troopers as missing or prisoners of war. Some of the heaviest fighting in Italy was yet to come. See *82d Airborne Division in Sicily and Italy*, 96–98.

59. See Pierce, *Let's Go!* 89–90. It was not uncommon for 82nd troopers to go AWOL from the hospital in order to remain with the division. Bradley wrote that as early as the invasion of Sicily, 82nd troopers would leave the hospital in an attempt to keep up with their peripatetic division. In one instance, Bradley was well to the east on Sicily when he came across an American paratrooper hitching a ride. When Bradley asked him where he came from, the trooper replied, "The hospital, sir. I'm AWOL from the hospital but I had to bust out before they ran me through that repple-depple [replacement detachment] routine. Otherwise I would never had gotten back to my old outfit." Bradley turned the matter over to his G-1 who ensured the man returned to the 82nd. See Omar N. Bradley, *A Soldier's Story*, 141. Other division troopers too sick or too injured to move received Ridgway's personal assurance that "within regulations and policies of the Commanding General of this Theater, the 82d Airborne Division, to which you have given your best efforts, will use its utmost endeavors to secure your return to your own Company or Battery, and as quickly as possible." Headquarters, 82nd Airborne Division, 9 November 1943, Ridgway Papers, Box 3, Folder "World War II, Personal Files, Matthew B. Ridgway, Correspondence, January 1942–November 1943," USAMHI. In the upper-left-hand corner of the letter contained in the file, Ridgway penned, "a copy to go by name to every member of the Division left in hospital." Anecdotal evi-

dence indicates that Ridgway remained true to his word. Captain Edwin Sayre, for example, who was wounded during the fight at Arnone, spent many months in the hospital but returned to the division before war's end. See Sayre, interview, 13 April 2002 (see chap. 6, n. 52).

60. Pierce, *Let's Go!* 92.

61. Gavin, *Airborne Warfare*, 39.

62. Mandle and Whittier, *Combat Record of the 504th Parachute Infantry Regiment*, n.p.; Journal, 27 October 1943–23 April 1944, C Company, 307th Airborne Engineer Battalion, attachment to Headquarters, 307th Airborne Engineer Battalion, "Unit History."

63. Blumenson, *Salerno to Cassino*, 257.

64. Ibid., 251–159, 270–277. Although the area's real name is Monte Sambucaro, Fifth Army maps referred to this high ground as Monte Sammucro, a name that will be retained here. See Blumenson, *Salerno to Cassino*, 208.

65. James Megellas, *All the Way to Berlin: A Paratrooper at War in Europe*, 29–30. Megellas joined the 504th on Thanksgiving Day, 1943. He remained with the regiment throughout the war, becoming one of the division's most decorated officers.

66. Carter, *Devils in Baggy Pants*, 136, 108.

67. Mandle and Whittier, *Combat Record of the 504th Parachute Infantry Regiment*, n.p.

68. Garrison and Fern, "Unit Journal of the 2nd Battalion, 504th Parachute Infantry" (see chap. 7, n. 36).

69. Megellas, *All the Way to Berlin*, 30–41; Mandle and Whittier, *Combat Record of the 504th Parachute Infantry Regiment*, n.p.; Garrison and Fern, "Unit Journal of the 2nd Battalion, 504th Parachute Infantry."

70. Garrison and Fern, "Unit Journal of the 2nd Battalion, 504th Parachute Infantry."

71. Carter, *Devils in Baggy Pants*, 133–134.

72. Incident related by the C Company commander, Captain A. E. "Ernie" Milloy, in Breuer, *Geronimo!* 157; Kuehl quoted in Megellas, *All the Way to Berlin*, 33.

73. Megellas, *All the Way to Berlin*, 41; Mandle and Whittier, *Combat Record of the 504th Parachute Infantry Regiment*, n.p.

74. Headquarters, 504th Parachute Infantry, "Narrative of Events of the 504th Parachute Infantry Combat Team on the Anzio Beachhead," 21 June 1945, 382-INF(504)-1.6, Box 12454, Record Group 407, NARA II.

75. Blumenson, *Salerno to Cassino*, 257.

76. Martin Blumenson, "General Lucas at Anzio," 325.

77. See Blumenson, *Salerno to Cassino*, 293; and Blumenson, "General Lucas at Anzio," 325.

78. Blumenson, *Salerno to Cassino*, 293–294.

79. Stalin quoted in Matloff, *Strategic Planning for Coalition Warfare*, 363; Winston S. Churchill, *Closing the Ring*, 420–421; Telegram from Churchill to British Chiefs of Staff, 19 December 1943, quoted in ibid., 429.

80. Except where noted, see Churchill, *Closing the Ring*, 428–441; Blumenson, *Salerno to Cassino*, 296–298; and Blumenson, "General Lucas at Anzio," 327–328.

81. Blumenson, "General Lucas at Anzio," 330–331. Lucas's troop list was later increased to include another infantry regiment, most of the U.S. 1st Armored Division, and additional artillery.

82. Warren, *Airborne Missions in the Mediterranean*, 71. Warren contended that all the fears that brought about the cancellation of SUN ASSAULT were unfounded and in retrospect wrote, "Suggestions that the 504th might have swept up the unguarded road to Rome can be discounted, not only because of the suicidal nature of such a dash, but also because a parachute regiment, almost devoid of vehicles, could not race 30 miles in a day. What the paratroops could have done within the limits of their mission and capabilities would have been to reconnoiter, to inform the commanders on the beaches that the way was clear, and to advance through Carroceto to the strategically valuable junction of Campoleone, about seven miles away. Campoleone was a natural bastion for the northern end of the Anzio beachhead. The Allies later paid heavily in vain attempts to take it after the Germans had established themselves there. If SUN ASSAULT had been carried out, Campoleone could have been occupied safely and cheaply." Warren, *Airborne Missions in the Mediterranean*, 72. Writing after the war, Gavin concurred, although he maintained that "if the capabilities of the 504th in this situation can be gauged by its performance in combat throughout Italy, it would almost certainly have entered Rome." Gavin, "Airborne Plans and Operations," 29.

83. Headquarters, 504th Parachute Infantry, "Narrative of Events of the 504th Parachute Infantry Combat Team on the Anzio Beachhead."

84. War Department Historical Division, *Anzio Beachhead: 22 January–25 May 1944*, 6, 14.

85. Canaris and Westphal quoted in Blumenson, *Salerno to Cassino*, 319.

86. Ibid., 318–319.

87. War Department Historical Division, *Anzio Beachhead*, 18.

88. Headquarters, 504th Parachute Infantry, "Narrative of Events of the 504th Parachute Infantry Combat Team on the Anzio Beachhead."

89. Megellas, *All the Way to Berlin*, 50.

90. Headquarters, 504th Combat Team, "S-3 Operations Summary," 5 February 1944, p. 1, 382-INF(504)-0.3, Box 12451, Record Group 407, NARA II.

91. D'Este, *Fatal Decision*, 137–138.

92. Headquarters, 504th Parachute Infantry, "Narrative of Events of the 504th Parachute Infantry Combat Team on the Anzio Beachhead."

93. See also Headquarters, 504th Combat Team, "S-3 Operations Summary," 1; and Headquarters, 504th Parachute Infantry, "Narrative of Events of the 504th Parachute Infantry Combat Team on the Anzio Beachhead."

94. Westphal quoted in Blumenson, "General Lucas at Anzio," 350 (quote), 340.

95. Blumenson, *Salerno to Cassino*, 361–362.

96. Baldino quoted in Breuer, *Geronimo!* 164–165.

97. Headquarters, 504th Parachute Infantry, "Narrative of Events of the 504th Parachute Infantry Combat Team on the Anzio Beachhead."

98. Carter, *Devils in Baggy Pants*, 166–167.

99. Headquarters, 504th Parachute Infantry, "Narrative of Events of the 504th Parachute Infantry Combat Team on the Anzio Beachhead."

100. Gavin, *On to Berlin*, 75.

101. Williams quoted in Breuer, *Geronimo!* 171.

102. Headquarters, 504th Parachute Infantry, "Narrative of Events of the 504th Parachute Infantry Combat Team on the Anzio Beachhead."

103. Garrison and Fern, "Unit Journal of the 2nd Battalion, 504th Parachute Infantry." The "screaming mimis" referred to were most likely German *Nebelwerfer*, multibarrel mortars that threw salvos of 150mm, 210mm, or 300mm projectiles fitted with sirens that caused them to wail as they flew through the air. See Max Hastings, *Overlord: D-Day and the Battle for Normandy*, 188.

104. War Department Historical Division, *Anzio Beachhead*, 22; Headquarters, 504th Combat Team, "S-3 Operations Summary," 2.

105. Headquarters, 504th Combat Team, "S-3 Operations Summary," 2; Garrison and Fern, "Unit Journal of the 2nd Battalion, 504th Parachute Infantry"; Headquarters, 504th Parachute Infantry, "Narrative of Events of the 504th Parachute Infantry Combat Team on the Anzio Beachhead."

106. Blumenson, *Salerno to Cassino*, 390. Elements of the 3rd Infantry Division's 7th and 15th Infantry Regiments were also to make infiltration attacks in support of the attack on Cisterna in order to cut the roads north and south of the town.

107. Headquarters, 504th Combat Team, "S-3 Operations Summary," 2; Headquarters, 504th Parachute Infantry, "Narrative of Events of the 504th Parachute Infantry Combat Team on the Anzio Beachhead."

108. For the attack in support of the Cisterna operation, see War Department Historical Division, *Anzio Beachhead*, 30–31; Headquarters, 504th Combat Team, "S-3 Operations Summary," 2–3; Headquarters, 504th Parachute Infantry, "Narrative of Events of the 504th Parachute Infantry Combat Team on the Anzio Beachhead"; and Garrison and Fern, "Unit Journal of the 2nd Battalion, 504th Parachute Infantry."

109. Headquarters, 504th Parachute Infantry, "Narrative of Events of the 504th Parachute Infantry Combat Team on the Anzio Beachhead."

110. Blumenson, *Salerno to Cassino*, 390–391; Headquarters, 3rd Battalion, 504th Parachute Infantry Regiment, "The Anzio Beachhead, Italy," n.d., untitled box, Folder "*Histories—Anzio (3/504th)," 82nd Airborne Division Museum, Fort Bragg, NC.

111. Blumenson, *Salerno to Cassino*, 364–365.

112. War Department Historical Division, *Anzio Beachhead*, 44–46.

113. See ibid.; Blumenson, "General Lucas at Anzio," 345; Bennett, *Ultra and Mediterranean Strategy*, 267.

114. War Department Historical Division, *Anzio Beachhead*, 55.

115. Ibid., 54–55.

116. Ibid., 55.

117. Headquarters, 3rd Battalion, 504th Parachute Infantry Regiment, "The Anzio Beachhead, Italy."

118. Megellas, *All the Way to Berlin*, 60 (quote), 62–63.

119. Granado quoted in ibid., 67. Granado was liberated in May 1945 and was awarded the Distinguished Service Cross for his actions at the embankment.

120. Headquarters, 3rd Battalion, 504th Parachute Infantry Regiment, "The Anzio Beachhead, Italy."

121. Burriss, *Strike and Hold*, 95.

122. Headquarters, 3rd Battalion, 504th Parachute Infantry Regiment, "The Anzio Beachhead, Italy"; and War Department Historical Division, *Anzio Beachhead*, 61.

123. Headquarters, 3rd Battalion, 504th Parachute Infantry Regiment, "The Anzio Beachhead, Italy"; War Department Historical Division, *Anzio Beachhead*, 62; Blumenson, *Salerno to Cassino*, 423.

124. Memorandum, Headquarters, Fifth Army, "Citation of Unit," n.d., untitled box, Folder "*Unit Awards—3/504th PUC," 82nd Airborne Division Museum, Fort Bragg, NC.

125. Megellas, *All the Way to Berlin*, 76; Headquarters, 504th Parachute Infantry, "Narrative of Events of the 504th Parachute Infantry Combat Team on the Anzio Beachhead."

126. Robert Kinney quoted in O'Donnell, *Beyond Valor*, 88.

127. Megellas, *All the Way to Berlin*, 77.

128. One Combat Team veteran, Captain Louis Hauptfleisch, railed against the 504th's being left out of the Normandy invasion: "True, the 504th [including the 376th Parachute Field Artillery Battalion and C Company of the 307th Airborne Engineers] was short of officers and enlisted men. But how often had we enjoyed the luxury of having our ranks filled during our overseas actions? That should not have been construed as an impediment . . . since, at that time, the majority of Os and EMs in the 504th Combat Team represented a valuable base of combat-experienced troops. Replacements were flowing in regularly, so the 504th seemed to be adequate and ready." Quoted in Breuer, *Geronimo!* 189. Another veteran, Private Al Langdon of the 505th, disagreed. "For what it is worth," wrote Langdon, "I agree with Ridgway that the 504 was in no condition to go into Normandy. I was on the detail that readied their camp near Leicester and I saw them when they arrived. I have never seen a more beat-up bunch of men." Allen Langdon to Clay Blair, n.d., Blair Collection, Box 54, Folder "Langdon, Allen," USAMHI.

129. Carter, *Devils in Baggy Pants*, 197. Not everyone was enamored of the 504th's character, especially Ridgway, and hence it was perhaps fortuitous that it remained in Italy. Ridgway had become increasingly exasperated with Tucker's indifference to administrative matters, an attitude that permeated the regiment, and was close to firing Tucker. Before leaving for Britain, Gavin had a talk with Tucker about this. "Tucker does not realize, or if he does he has at last gotten fed up with the pressure, but his situation is critical," penned Gavin in his diary. When the 504th again entered combat with the division, Gavin was the division commander, and he was much more forgiving of Tucker's attitude. See Gavin, Personal Diary, 31 October 1943. Lieutenant Colonel Charles "Chuck" Billingslea took over as executive officer during the Salerno fight when Leslie Freeman was wounded (Freeman, of course, recovered and led the 3/504 brilliantly during Anzio and the fight in the Campoleone salient). A colleague recalled that Billingslea was "cold, brilliant, and fearless. He also had a well organized mind. Tucker was very, very weak in administration—paperwork, detailed planning, and so on—so Billingslea became an extremely strong addition to the 504's leadership." Quoted in Blair, *Ridgway's Paratroopers*, 160. Billingslea went on to take command of the 325th after Normandy.

CHAPTER 10: A TERRIBLE AND HANDSOME SIGHT

1. Blair, *Ridgway's Paratroopers*, 170–173.

2. Memorandum, Headquarters, 82nd Airborne Division, "Summary of Principles Covering Use of the Airborne Division," 27 November 1943, Ridgway Papers, Box 2a, Folder "Matthew B. Ridgway, Personal File, 1942–1943," USAMHI. In his memorandum, Ridgway acknowledged that occasions may arise when the resources required to commit an entire airborne division might not be available. In those instances, "the Division should be unhesitatingly employed as a whole as a light infantry combat division with missions appropriate to its fire power and combat strength." The main thrust of the memorandum, however, was that airborne divisions afforded commanders a capability with which they could attain operational or strategic objectives and should not be frittered away against minor tactical gains.

3. Memorandum, Matthew B. Ridgway to the Assistant Chief of Staff, Operations Division, War Department General Staff, "Pay Status, Airborne Troops," 2 December 1943, Ridgway Papers, Box 2a, Folder "Matthew B. Ridgway, Personal File, 1942–1943," USAMHI.

4. Memorandum, Headquarters, 82nd Airborne Division, "Changes in Tables of Organization Airborne Divisions," 15 November 1943, Ridgway Papers, Box 2a, Folder "Matthew B. Ridgway, Personal File, 1942–1943," USAMHI.

5. This was part of Marshall's overall effort to obtain for all infantrymen extra pay and recognition based on statistics that showed their casualty rates were "seventy to eighty percent of the total figure." See George C. Marshall to Matthew B. Ridgway, 16 March 1944, Ridgway Papers, Box 3, Folder "Personal File Jan.–Jul. 44," USAMHI; and Palmer, Wiley, and Keast, *Procurement and Training of Ground Combat Troops*, 58–59, 62.

6. Message from Office of the Chief of Staff, War Department to Dwight D. Eisenhower, 25 October 1943, *Papers of Marshall*, microfilm, reel 31 (capitalization in original); Matthew B. Ridgway to George C. Marshall, 1 November 1943, ibid., reel 31; Gavin, Personal Diary, 19 November 1943 (see chap. 4, n. 26).

7. Directive from the Combined Chiefs of Staff to COSSAC, 23 April 1943, quoted in Gordon A. Harrison, *Cross-Channel Attack*, 49. Initially, COSSAC was also to plan small-scale raids and prepare several contingencies to jump Allied forces across the Channel in the event of a German collapse. By April 1943, however, COSSAC's planning focus had evolved into a singular concentration on a large-scale cross-Channel invasion.

8. Gavin, *On to Berlin*, 83.

9. Gavin, Personal Diary, 19 November 1943; Gavin, *On to Berlin*, 84. In this work, Gavin wrote that he visited Morgan first, but his diary clearly shows that Bradley's headquarters was his first stop and that he did not meet with Morgan until the next day.

10. Gavin, Personal Diary, 20 November 1943. When Gavin departed he ran into Major General Ray Barker, Morgan's American deputy chief of staff. When Gavin told him that he had just talked with Browning, Barker replied, "Oh yes, he is an empire builder."

11. Ibid., 17 November 1943.

12. Lewis H. Brereton, *The Brereton Diaries: The War in the Air in the Pacific, Middle East, and Europe, 3 October 1941–8 May 1945*, 223; Gavin, Personal Diary, 20 November 1943.

13. Gavin, Personal Diary, 23 November 1943.

14. Frederick Morgan, *Overture to Overlord*, 76. Morgan also wrote that the system did, indeed, have its merits, not least of which was that matters of vital importance regarding crucial aspects of an operation were referred to all concerned. The system's success, however, was contingent upon "the adroit selection" of committee chairmen "who will reduce chatter to a minimum" and of efficient committee secretaries "who can write the minutes beforehand to ensure that the proceedings keep to the proper course." F. Morgan, *Overture to Overlord*, 76.

15. Gavin, Personal Diary, 12 December 1943.

16. Ibid., 17 December 1943.

17. Gavin, *On to Berlin*, 90.

18. Memorandum, Supreme Headquarters, Allied Expeditionary Force, "Employment of Airborne Forces," 19 January 1944, Ridgway Papers, Box 3, Folder "World War II—Personal Files, August 1942–May 1943," USAMHI.

19. F. Morgan, *Overture to Overlord*, 152.

20. "Digest of Operation 'Overlord,'" appendix A of Harrison, *Cross-Channel Attack*, 452–454.

21. John C. Warren, *Airborne Operations in World War II, European Theater*, 2–4, 8.

22. Ed Cray, *General of the Army: George C. Marshall, Soldier and Statesman*, 13. Eisenhower got the job because, according to Roosevelt, he would not be able to sleep at night were General Marshall away from Washington.

23. Montgomery, *Memoirs*, 191. Except where noted, see Stephen E. Ambrose, *The Supreme Commander: The War Years of General Dwight D. Eisenhower*, 335; David Eisenhower, *Eisenhower at War, 1943–1945*, 120; and Warren, *Airborne Operations in World War II*, 7.

24. See Butcher, *My Three Years with Eisenhower*, 475; D. Eisenhower, *Eisenhower at War*, 120–123; and Warren, *Airborne Operations in World War II*, 7. Eisenhower had, of course, to refer these recommendations to the Combined Chiefs of Staff as well as to Roosevelt and Churchill. All were accepted.

25. Ray S. Cline, *Washington Command Post: The Operations Division*, 209.

26. Harrison, *Cross-Channel Attack*, 182–183; Warren, *Airborne Operations in World War II*, 7.

27. Harrison, *Cross-Channel Attack*, 184; Warren, *Airborne Operations in World War II*, 8–9.

28. Bradley, *A Soldier's Story*, 232.

29. Except where noted, see Harrison, *Cross-Channel Attack*, 184–185; and Warren, *Airborne Operations in World War II*, 8–9.

30. Roger Hand, "Overlord and Operational Art," 88–89; Morgan, *Overture to Overlord*, 203–205; Warren, *Airborne Operations in World War II*, 5–6. Marshall and Arnold had already tried once to get Plan C accepted. Following the QUADRANT Conference, where they heard Morgan's COSSAC plan for the first time, they invited Morgan to Washington for more detailed discussions, during which

they proposed their Orléans Gap scheme. Morgan, who was out of his element discussing airborne operations, asked Leigh-Mallory to fly to Washington to hear the proposal. Arriving in Washington at the end of October 1943, Leigh-Mallory rejected the proposal out of hand, asserting that airborne forces were too lightly armed to take on German armor, which he was certain would counterattack; that it was impractical to keep such a large force supplied by air; and that the Luftwaffe and German antiaircraft defenses were much too stout to ensure its success. Undeterred, Marshall and Arnold shelved their plan until such time as a Supreme Commander was named.

31. Huston, *Out of the Blue*, 171.

32. Reproduced in appendix XII of ibid., 274–275.

33. Interestingly, Leigh-Mallory was not included, perhaps because he had heard this all before and either he or Eisenhower felt he did not require a second rendition or perhaps because Eisenhower desired a fresh, unbiased look at the proposal.

34. Memorandum from Brigadier General Frederick W. Evans and Colonel Bruce W. Bidwell to George C. Marshall, 1 March 1944, in *Papers of Marshall*, reel 22 (emphasis in original).

35. Dwight D. Eisenhower to George C. Marshall, 19 February 1944, in ibid., reel 15 (emphasis in original). Writing to Clay Blair after the war, Gavin commented, "Actually, Marshall had good grounds for observing that we were beginning to use airborne troops in pennypackets, as we used armor in World War I. Only when we made a mass out of the armor did it become truly effective as we demonstrated in World War II. The problem was that we really had no effective antitank weapons for the paratroops. . . . So, we could see the Orleans [*sic*] Gap chewed to pieces by German panzers long before linkup could occur. Marshall and Arnold had an interesting idea, which, unfortunately, was not valid with the state of the antitank art then in being." Gavin to Blair, 19 July 1983, Blair Collection, Box 53, Folder "Gavin, James M.," USAMHI.

36. Warren, *Airborne Operations in World War II*, 9–10.

37. Ibid.

38. To be "bigoted" was to be privy to the specifics of the overarching plan. This group was kept as small as possible for reasons of security. Although all plans were classified, those that addressed when and where the invasion were to occur were marked "Top Secret—Bigot."

39. See Harrison, *Cross-Channel Attack*, 158; and Robert W. Coakley and Richard M. Leighton, *Global Logistics and Strategy, 1943–1945*, 353.

40. Gavin, Personal Diary, 24 and 25 November 1943.

41. Except where noted, see Langdon, *"Ready,"* 35–36; Pierce, *Let's Go!* 92–93; *Operation Neptune, Normandy, 6 June–8 July 1944*, n.d., p. 1, unmarked box, Folder "82d Airborne Division, WWII After Action Reports: Normandy," 82nd Airborne Divisions Museum, Fort Bragg, NC.

42. One means by which this integration was facilitated was by having the division's combat veterans live with the new troopers for a short time. Bill Lord was with the 508th when it joined the 82nd in England. According to Lord, "If any man who was with the Regiment in Ireland were questioned on what was the most valuable training he got there, he would undoubtedly answer that it was knowledge

and confidence acquired from the battle veterans of the 82nd Airborne Division. Men of the 505th Parachute Infantry, veterans of the Sicily and Italy jumps, lived with each company of the 508th for about a week. They explained what they knew of war and gave many helpful hints about fighting the Germans. Credit must be given to those who selected these visitors, for they were all very sincere in their efforts to help, and no line was handed out for the untested soldiers to swallow." William G. Lord II, *History of the 508th Parachute Infantry*, 13.

43. Gavin, Personal Diary, 17 December 1943.

44. See Blair, *Ridgway's Paratroopers*, 191; Devlin, *Paratrooper!* 332; Huston, *Out of the Blue*, 173–174; Pierce, *Let's Go!* 98; and *Operation Neptune*, 1.

45. See Blair, *Ridgway's Paratroopers*, 192–193; Huston, *Out of the Blue*, 73; and Jorgensen, *History of the 456th Parachute Field Artillery Battalion*, 97–100.

46. The British Horsa was substantially larger than the American Waco. Made of plywood, it was sixty-eight feet long and almost twenty feet high and had a wingspan of eighty-eight feet. It had a payload of 7,000 pounds, which equated to twenty-eight fully equipped soldiers or a howitzer, a jeep and trailer, or an antitank gun. Britain produced more than 5,000 Horsas during the war. See Charles J. Masters, *Glidermen of Neptune: The American D-Day Glider Attack*, 9.

47. See also reminiscence of Adolph "Bud" Warnecke in Astor, *June 6, 1944*, 58; and *Operation Neptune*, 1.

48. Gavin, Personal Diary, 19 March and 4 June 1944.

49. Ibid., 23 February 1944.

50. Memorandum, Headquarters, 82nd Airborne Division, "Tactical Exercise," 14 March 1944, Blair Collection, Box 51, Folder "Pierce, Wayne," USAMHI.

51. Brereton, *Brereton Diaries*, 262–263.

52. Jorgensen, *History of the 456th Parachute Field Artillery Battalion*, 101–102.

53. Brereton, *Brereton Diaries*, 267; Gavin, Personal Diary, 16 May 1944.

54. See also Brereton, *Brereton Diaries*, 263–264; and Warren, *Airborne Operations in World War II*, 25–26.

55. The term *OB West* refers both to the headquarters in overall command of German defenses in the West as well as to the person occupying the position of commander in chief in the West, in this case Rundstedt. Despite the grandiose title, Hitler sharply curtailed the authority of *OB West*. For example, Rundstedt had no command authority over Luftwaffe air or antiaircraft units, Kriegsmarine sea or coast artillery units, or any of the military governors of the occupied countries. He had but tactical control of the Waffen SS, which for all other matters reported to Heinrich Himmler. He also had very limited control over his panzer reserves, having to obtain approval from Hitler before employing them. Finally, Rommel, because of his rank as a field marshal, had the right of direct access to Hitler despite commanding an army group subordinate to Rundstedt. See Harrison, *Cross-Channel Attack*, 128, 243–248.

56. Generalleutnant Hans Speidel, quoted in Robert J. Kershaw, *D-Day: Piercing the Atlantic Wall*, 24. Speidel was Rommel's chief of staff when the latter took command of *Army Group B*.

57. See Harrison, *Cross-Channel Attacks*, 146–149, 237–238, 242–248; Max Pemsel, *Report of the German Seventh Army Chief of Staff (June 1942–5 June 1944)*,

p. 23, Cornelius Ryan Collection, Box 27, Folder 3 "Pemsel, Lt. Gen. Max," Ohio University, Athens (hereafter OU); "Anti-Invasion: The Normandy Battles from the Enemy Side," *R.A.C. Journal* 4, no. 1, Ryan Collection, Box 3, Folder 1 "Anti-Invasion—the Normandy Battles from the Enemy Side—R.A.C. Journal," OU.

58. From Führer Directive No. 51 as translated and contained in appendix D to Harrison, *Cross-Channel Attack*, 464.

59. Stephen E. Ambrose, *D-Day, June 6, 1944: The Climactic Battle of World War II*, 29.

60. From Führer Directive No. 51 contained in Harrison, *Cross-Channel Attack*, 464.

61. Ibid., 149, 246.

62. Ibid., 138–140; David Irving, *The Trail of the Fox: The Search for the True Field Marshal Rommel*, 313; Samuel W. Mitcham Jr., *The Desert Fox in Normandy: Rommel's Defense of Fortress Europe*, 5. Hitler's order to build an Atlantic Wall resulted from the abortive Allied raid on the French port of Dieppe, France, in August 1942. Staged by a mixed force of approximately 5,000 Canadians and 1,000 British Commandos (accompanied by a small party of American Rangers), its aim was to test the proposition that an amphibious assault could be conducted directly into a port city. It was a disaster. The Allies sustained 3,369 casualties against negligible German losses. See Elizabeth-Anne Wheal, Stephen Pope, and James Taylor, eds., *The Meridian Encyclopedia of the Second World War*, s.v. "Dieppe Raid."

63. Rommel quoted in Cornelius Ryan, *The Longest Day, June 6, 1944*, 24.

64. Except where noted, see Harrison, *Cross-Channel Attack*, 137–138; and Mitcham, *Desert Fox in Normandy*, 7.

65. Mitcham, *Desert Fox in Normandy*, 20–21.

66. Devlin, *Silent Wings*, 174.

67. Pemsel, *Report of the German Seventh Army Chief of Staff*, 20.

68. Blumentritt in Günther Blumentritt et al., *Fighting the Invasion: The German Army at D-Day*, 26.

69. Harrison, *Cross-Channel Attack*, 259.

70. Irving, *Trail of the Fox*, 332–333.

71. Harrison, *Cross-Channel Attack*, 260.

72. See Bradley, *A Soldier's Story*, 235; Harrison, *Cross-Channel Attack*, 186; Warren, *Airborne Operations in World War II*, 10–11; and *Operation Neptune*, 2. The only change made to the 101st Airborne Division's scheme of maneuver was to relieve it of responsibility for capturing Ste.-Mère-Église. This was originally the mission of the 101st's 501st Parachute Infantry Regiment, but when the 82nd assumed this mission, the 501st was shifted south and given responsibility for protecting the southern flank of the 101st's airhead. Warren, *Airborne Operations in World War II*, 11.

73. *Operation Neptune*, 2–4, 6, 10, annex 3.

74. Dwight D. Eisenhower, *Crusade in Europe*, 246; D. Eisenhower, *Eisenhower at War*, 241.

75. Dwight D. Eisenhower, Memorandum for Diary, 22 May 1944, *Papers of Eisenhower: The War Years, III*, ed. Chandler, 1881.

76. Leigh-Mallory quoted in D. Eisenhower, *Eisenhower at War*, 241 (quote), 242.

77. Dwight D. Eisenhower to Trafford Leigh-Malory, 30 May 1944, *Papers of Eisenhower: The War Years, III*, ed. Chandler, 1894–1895. Four years later, after Eisenhower had retired from the Army, a reporter asked him what he considered the high point of his military career. Hesitating for a moment, Eisenhower replied that the obvious thing to say would be the surrender of Germany, but that had been anticipated for so long that it was somewhat anticlimactic when it finally did occur. He then said that his greatest moment was when he got word that the 82nd and 101st Airborne Divisions had landed and were in action on the Cotentin Peninsula the morning of D-Day. "Had it failed, he went on, he would have gone to his grave haunted by the thought that he had killed 20,000 young Americans stupidly." See Leonard Rapport and Arthur Northwood Jr., *Rendezvous with Destiny: A History of the 101st Airborne Division*, 56–57.

78. McKenzie, *On Time, On Target*, 11; *Operation Neptune*, annex 3.

79. Bill Walton, interview by Cornelius Ryan, 18 March 1958, Ryan Collection, Box 9, Folder 4 "Walton, Bill," OU. When conducting research for his books *The Longest Day* and *A Bridge Too Far*, Cornelius Ryan and his research assistants sent out hundreds of questionnaires to surviving participants on both sides. The answers to these questionnaires, along with a vast store of letters, diaries, orders, and other material, are at the Alden Library at Ohio University, Athens.

80. McKenzie, *On Time, On Target*, 19; James J. Coyle questionnaire, Ryan Collection, Box 7, Folder 50 "Coyle, James J.," OU.

81. Dunfee quoted in Astor, *June 6, 1944*, 2; Walton, interview, 18 March 1958.

82. Pierce, *Let's Go!* 104.

83. Walton, interview, 18 March 1958; Hubert S. Bass to Cornelius Ryan, 20 March 1959, Ryan Collection, Box 7, Folder 37, "Bass, Hubert," OU; Dan McIlvoy, "Medical Detachment, 505th Parachute Infantry, 82nd Airborne Division in World War II," World War II Veterans Survey Project, Box "82nd Airborne Division, 505th PIR (2)," Folder "McIlvoy, Dan (M.D.) 505th Parachute Infantry Med. Det.," USAMHI.

84. Bierbaum, *As Ever, John*, 41–42.

85. Harrison, *Cross-Channel Attack*, 269.

86. Robert L. Bearden questionnaire, Ryan Collection, Box 7, Folder 38 "Bearden, Robert L.," OU; Ben F. Pearson questionnaire, Ryan Collection, Box 8, Folder 28 "Pearson, Ben F.," OU.

87. Anthony "Tony" Joseph DeMayo questionnaire, Ryan Collection, Box 7, Folder 51 "DeMayo, Anthony J.," OU. Mildred Gillars was an aspiring actress who dropped out of Ohio Wesleyan University and subsequently went to Germany in the 1920s to study music. When the war broke out she was teaching English in Berlin and had fallen in love with a Nazi Foreign Ministry official who convinced her to broadcast propaganda. Supplied with information from German intelligence sources, her broadcasts were often remarkably accurate, even about matters that were supposedly secret. After the war she was convicted of treason and spent twelve years in a U.S. federal prison for women. After her release she taught language and music at a Catholic convent in Columbus, Ohio, but subsequently returned to Ohio Wesleyan, where, at the age of seventy-two, she finally earned her bachelor's

degree in speech. She died in Columbus, Ohio, in 1988. See Mark M. Boatner, *Biographical Dictionary of World War II*, s.v. "Gillars, Mildred Elizabeth."

88. Harrison, *Cross-Channel Attack*, 272–274.

89. Walton, interview, 18 March 1958.

90. Eisenhower's message is reproduced in D. Eisenhower, *Eisenhower at War*, 256–257; Krause quoted in Devlin, *Paratrooper!* 376; Jones quoted in Astor, *June 6, 1944*, 3; Lord quoted in ibid., 1, 58.

91. See Warren, *Airborne Operations in World War II*, 13–14, 48, 224; and *Operation Neptune*, 4, annex 1c. The one plane that failed to take off was destroyed on the airstrip when a trooper's grenade accidentally detonated. Three troopers were killed and nine wounded as a result of the explosion. Devlin, *Paratrooper!* 378–379.

92. Bierbaum, *As Ever, John*, 42; Martha Gellhorn, "Stand Up and Hook Up!" n.p.

CHAPTER 11: *ALLES KAPUTT!* THE AMERICANS ARE KILLING EVERYBODY!

1. Harrison, *Cross-Channel Attack*, 276. The Germans also lacked weather stations any farther west than the Channel Islands, and it was from the west that the weather came. Hence, the predictive ability of German meteorologists was severely hampered. In his work Robert Kershaw quoted a Dr. Müller, who was the chief meteorologist for *OB West*. Müller contended that he had, in fact, predicted the same break in the weather that compelled Eisenhower to risk a 6 June invasion. However, the Germans were making their calculations based on the weather in the Pas de Calais, not Normandy. See R. Kershaw, *Piercing the Atlantic Wall*, 53.

2. Kurt Assman, "Normandy 1944," *Forces Magazine*, March 1955, 5, copy contained in Ryan Collection, Box 3, Folder 2, OU.

3. D. Eisenhower, *Eisenhower at War*, 261.

4. See also testimony by Blumentritt in Blumentritt et al., *Fighting the Invasion*, 171; Harrison, *Cross-Channel Attack*, 275; translated copy of German *Fifteenth Army Kriegstagebuch* (War Diary), entry for 5 June 1944, Ryan Collection, Box 27, Folder 22, OU. All times given are in Double British Summer Time (DBST), which was one hour ahead of German clocks set at Central European time. There is some controversy about whether or not *Fifteenth Army*, whose area of operations began just east of Caen, was, in fact, placed in a higher state of alert once its listening post intercepted the BBC messages. Most contend that it was; however, the War Diary clearly states that this did not occur until 0230 hours on 6 June and only *after* the headquarters had received reports of paratroopers having landed in its rear area. The confusion is perhaps the result of the wording used in the diary. The entry for 2233 (2333 DBST) hours, 5 June, states that corps and army headquarters were alerted—in the sense that they were informed—that a message had been intercepted. The entry for 0130 (0230 DBST) hours, 6 June, clearly indicated that *Fifteenth Army* was placed on Alert II, the highest level of alert.

5. Anonymous pathfinder quoted in Ryan, *Longest Day*, 95. See also Devlin, *Paratrooper!* 685–686; Warren, *Airborne Operations in World War II*, 33, 48, 53,

55; and Chester to Gavin, 30 March 1959 (see chap. 7, n. 81). To bolster the green 507th and 508th pathfinder teams, their security detachments were composed of volunteers from the veteran 504th.

6. See Warren, *Airborne Operations in World War II*, 33, 48, 53, 55; Chester to Gavin, 30 March 1959; and Combat Interview "507-2 on D-Day and Immediately After," n.d., CI-170 "82nd Airborne Div. Operation 'Neptune' June 1944," Box 24057, Record Group 407, NARA II. The 505th pathfinders were accompanied by a stowaway who jumped in with them. According to Gavin this was "an Air Force colonel of World War I, Lafayette Escadrille, vintage" named Bagby. "For the deed he received the Silver Star and a verbal reprimand." See James M. Gavin to Cornelius Ryan, 3 April 1959, Ryan Collection, Box 8, Folder 21, OU. Backing up Gavin's assertion is an interview conducted after the war with 505th pathfinder Clarence Ollom, who said, "Something sticks in my mind that some high-ranking officer was on the plane with me." See interview of Clarence Ollom in Steve Anderson and Louis Eschle, "From Sicily to the Siegfried Line," 54. Chester also confirmed that this unknown colonel flew in with the 505th pathfinders.

7. Warren, *Airborne Operations in World War II*, 11–12, 14–15. The route taken by the 101st was exactly the same until HOBOKEN. At that point the 101st aircraft deviated to a point farther south on the west coast of the Cotentin (MULESHOE), followed a route south of and parallel to that taken by the 82nd, and dropped on three drop zones south and east of the 82nd's. In order to avoid congestion, the 101st also departed first and dropped a few minutes before the 82nd. The British 6th Airborne Division, dropping at the opposite end of the Allied invasion beachhead, flew its own separate route to Normandy. The Allies also mounted several ancillary operations designed to either blind or deceive the German defenders while troop transports were in the air. One such operation involved a force of British and American aircraft that jammed every German radar and fighter control station in Normandy and the Channel Islands. Simultaneously, a force of British Stirling bombers dropped dummy parachutists and "Window" (strips of aluminum that, when dropped, simulated a large number of aircraft) along the coastal area of France north of the Seine, while another group of Stirlings dropped "Window" in the southwest portion of the Cotentin.

8. Ibid., 48.

9. Lyle Britain Putnam questionnaire, Ryan Collection, Box 8, Folder 31, OU; Ambrose, *D-Day*, 198; DeMayo questionnaire (see chap. 10, n. 87); Robert Martin Piper questionnaire, Ryan Collection, Box 8, Folder 30, OU; Putnam questionnaire; Burns quoted in Ambrose, *D-Day*, 198.

10. Jack P. Nix, *505th Parachute Infantry Regiment (A Legacy of Lessons)*, 5. In preparing this paper, Nix interviewed several officers who had served in the 505th under Gavin. It was Brigadier General Walter F. Winton who recalled that when he reported into the 505th as a lieutenant he knocked on Gavin's door, received permission to enter, and saluted. Winton recalled that before returning the salute and without even looking up from his desk, Gavin told him, "Lieutenant, in this outfit you'll jump first and eat last."

11. Bierbaum, *As Ever, John*, 41.

12. Kroos to Blair, 17 June 1983 (see chap. 3, n. 69).

13. Gavin, *On to Berlin*, 83.

14. Kroos to Blair, 17 June 1983. According to Kroos, Ridgway was also concerned about injuring his back during the jump, especially since he suffered from chronic back problems. The last thing he wanted was to be incapacitated in Normandy. Hence, instead of selecting his chute on the flight line like the rest of his troopers, Ridgway had Kroos select a parachute for him ahead of time so that in the privacy of Ridgway's quarters they could adjust it so that it fitted perfectly.

15. Mark Alexander, "Thirty Four Days in Normandy in 1944." This is a personal reminiscence of his experiences in Normandy written by Alexander for his son, in possession of the author.

16. "Debriefing Conference—Operation Neptune," 13 August 1944, Gavin Papers, Box 11, Folder "Debriefing Conference—Airborne Operations on D-Day by 82nd Airborne Division, Interviews w/ Battalion and Regimental Commanders on Problems and Other Complications from Invasion," USAMHI. On 13 August 1944, the 82nd held a debriefing conference at the Glebe Mount House in Leicester, England. Each commander of a unit of battalion size or larger spoke freely about his experience and his impressions and recommendations. Their statements were transcribed as near to verbatim as possible.

17. Ridgway, interview, 29 August 1969 (see chap. 3, n. 29). See also Warren, *Airborne Operations in World War II*, 48–50.

18. See Warren, *Airborne Operations in World War II*, 53–55; and "Debriefing Conference—Operation Neptune."

19. See also Warren, *Airborne Operations in World War II*, 55–58; and "Debriefing Conference—Operation Neptune."

20. See Warren, *Airborne Operations in World War II, European Theater*, 48–58; and *Operation Neptune*, annex D-1 (see chap. 10, n. 41). According to one glider pilot, seeing what had become of the disciplined formations of C-47s that had left England just hours before was a chilling precursor of what they were about to endure. "As soon as we saw them come back straggling in one by one with no sort of a formation at all . . . we knew that something had gone terribly wrong. They circled the field once, and from several of the planes red flares were fired, indicating that there were wounded aboard. They were all strung out at different altitudes, and we could tell from the absence of the bluish exhaust flames that several of them were on single engine. I remember that no one said a word, we were so scared. We just stood there on the edge of the field counting them as they came in on their approach. It took over an hour before the last plane landed. Something had gone terribly wrong." Quoted in Milton Dank, *The Glider Gang: An Eyewitness History of World War II Glider Combat*, 110.

21. Excerpt from Friedrich Hayn, *Die Invasion*, 6, copy contained in Ryan Collection, Box 26, Folder 18, OU. Hayn also offers an interesting perspective on the makeup of the 82nd, a perspective that reveals much about the German mind-set vis-à-vis the importance of race. "A significant episode was the arrival of the first prisoners at Corps Headquarters. All of them belonged to the 82nd U.S. Airborne Division and had 'dropped from the sky.' They were robust men and excellently equipped. . . . Already the first four of them were a good example of the racial composition of their unit. There was an officer of Anglo-Saxon descent with reddish

hair. . . . The next was a Pole with closely cropped hair and fanatical features. . . . [The third was a] half-breed from California with a mongolian sprinkling. . . . Finally there was a certain Braun, born 1913 in Stuttgart. . . . So the 82nd U.S. Division really deserved its nickname of 'All American.' America, the great melting pot of races!" (11).

22. Seventh Army Telephone Log, Ryan Collection, Box 26, Folder 6, OU. According to this log, at 0300 hours (0400 hours DBST) the *LXXXIV Corps* chief of staff called his counterpart at *Seventh Army* to report that the Allied airborne attacks were concentrated in two spots: one in the *716th Division* area, where the British 6th Airborne had landed, and one in the *91st Division* area, where the 82nd and 101st had landed. Two hours later, he called back to refine his estimate, correctly citing Ste.-Mère-Église as the focus of the U.S. airborne effort on the Cotentin.

23. See statements by Günther Keil, commander of the *91st Division*'s *1058th Infantry Regiment*, and Friedrich von Criegern, the *LXXXIV Corps* assistant chief of staff, in Blumentritt et al., *Fighting the Invasion*, 180–186.

24. See Devlin, *Paratrooper!* 388–389; and James M. Gavin to Frank McKee, 25 October 1979, Gavin Papers, Box 11, Folder "82nd Airborne Division, 508th Parachute Infantry Regiment, Letters About D-Day Invasion," USAMHI.

25. Friedrich von Criegern in Blumentritt et al., *Fighting the Invasion*, 185.

26. Ambrose, *Citizen Soldiers*, 34. In 1944, there were, on average, fourteen hedgerows per kilometer.

27. Gavin has insisted that the 82nd did not use the famous metallic crickets used by the 101st on D-Day to aid assembly. In an article written just after the war, he stated categorically that "Sicily and Italy had taught us that it was undesirable to blacken our faces or use crickets as signals. We decided to rely solely on oral challenge and response, and a quick response it had better be." James M. Gavin, "Back Door to Normandy: Airborne Plans and Counter Plans for the Invasion of Europe," 12. However, it appears that some of the division's troopers did get their hands on the crickets. James Eads recalled getting out of his harness and, after hearing a sound behind him, "dropped flat and tried to see what or who was there. Taking a chance on a hunch, I snapped my cricket, and an answering two clicks came back." Ronald J. Drez, ed., *The Voices of D-Day: The Story of the Allied Invasion Told by Those Who Were There*, 135. Chaplain George Wood of the 505th also remembered being "alone in a field surrounded by hedgerows, snapping my cricket, when [another paratroop officer] came up behind me & said, 'Stop that damn noise.'" George B. Wood questionnaire, Ryan Collection, Box 9, Folder 5, OU. With or without crickets, the hedgerows made assembly exceedingly difficult.

28. Morgan, *Overture to Overlord*, 157. Much has been written concerning the apparent ignorance of the Allies about the *bocage* and the effect it had on tactical operations in Normandy. Stephen Ambrose wrote, "The great failure on the part of the Allied intelligence community was that it did not anticipate the problems of fighting on the offensive in the hedgerow country." He attributed this ignorance to the fact that the Allies were so narrowly focused on getting ashore and staying ashore, "they hadn't studied the hedgerow country or worked out techniques for fighting in that difficult terrain." Ambrose in Weingartner, *Greatest Thing We Have Ever Attempted*, 9. According to Morgan, however, COSSAC "had studied and

restudied all sources of information on the point and had argued that over and above all its manifest disadvantages the existence of the bocage country in this particular relationship to the beaches could be entered on both sides of the balance sheet. In our favour was the possibility that the enemy would regard it as unlikely that we should deliberately commit ourselves to the passage of such an obstacle immediately on landing. Also we had in mind the defensive-offensive nature of the operation in prospect." Morgan, *Overture to Overlord,* 157. A review of Annex 1c (tactical terrain study) to the 82nd's field order for the operation shows that, at least in one division, there was an awareness of the physical dimensions of the hedgerows. However, nowhere in this annex is there any mention of the difficulty it would cause to those in the attack. Field Order No. 6, 1 May 1944, Annex 1c, Tactical Terrain Study, 382-ART-0.3, Box 12429, Record Group 407, NARA II.

29. Extracts from the 505th Regimental S-2 briefing that was presented to every man in the division. Contained in Benjamin H. Vandervoort, "505th Normandy Campaign," n.d., p. 4, Ryan Collection, Box 9, Folder 1, OU.

30. Combat Interview "Statement of Brig. Gen. James M. Gavin," n.d., CI-170 "82nd Airborne Div. Operation 'Neptune' June 1944," Box 24057, Record Group 407, NARA II (capitalization in original).

31. Combat Interview "508 Regiment After the Drop," n.d., CI-170 "82nd Airborne Div. Operation 'Neptune' June 1944," Box 24057, Record Group 407, NARA II.

32. Amorose quoted in Breuer, *Geronimo!* 224–225.

33. See Combat Interview by R. H. Wienecke, n.d., CI-170 "82nd Airborne Operation 'Neptune' June 1944," Box 24057, Record Group 407, NARA II; and Langdon, *"Ready,"* 53–54.

34. See Wienecke Combat Interview; Langdon, *"Ready,"* 53–54; and "Request for a French Decoration for the Two Battalions of Parachutists Which Landed at Sainte Mere-Eglise," n.d., Ridgway Papers, Box 3, Folder "Personal File Jan.–Jul. 44," USAMHI. This letter, written by the mayor of Ste.-Mère-Église, was addressed to Charles de Gaulle.

35. Anderson and Eschle, "From Sicily to the Siegfried Line," 55; Wood questionnaire.

36. Fitzgerald quoted in Ambrose, *D-Day,* 314.

37. See Wienecke Combat Interview; Langdon, *"Ready,"* 53–54; and Thomas A Donahue interview synopsis, n.d., Ryan Collection, Box 7, Folder 53, OU.

38. Mace quoted in Ambrose, *D-Day,* 237; "Request for a French Decoration for the Two Battalions of Parachutists Which Landed at Sainte Mere-Eglise."

39. Gavin quoted in Breuer, *Geronimo!* 249.

40. One of the two gliders that landed in Ste.-Mère-Église crashed into the roof of a two-story building at the western edge of the town that had been set up as an aid station. The townspeople had already donated large quantities of food and drink, much of which was stored in the aid station for use as needed. According to Captain Putnam, the 2/505th's surgeon, the glider fell through the roof, and all its contents, a jeep, ammunition, and some troopers, landed right on top of the stockpiled food. "In the midst of all this, I saw my sergeant (a huge specimen of muscle and generally impassive efficiency) throw his helmet down, sit in the middle of ruined food and

drink, and combine profuse tears with abundant profanity and a dissertation of Fate." Putnam questionnaire.

41. DeMayo questionnaire; Jack Tallerday questionnaire, Ryan Collection, Box 8, Folder 46, OU; Charles W. Mason questionnaire, Ryan Collection, Box 8, Folder 19, OU.

42. For the DETROIT glider mission, see also Warren, *Airborne Operations in World War II*, 61, 64–65.

43. Allen Langdon to Clay Blair, 17 October 1983, Joan Blair Collection, Box 54, Folder "Langdon, Allen," USAMHI; Mark Alexander to Clay Blair, 9 June 1983, Blair Collection, Box 53, Folder "Alexander, Mark J.," USAMHI; William E. Ekman questionnaire, Ryan Collection, Box 8, Folder 1, OU.

44. Wienecke Combat Interview. Although he assumed command of the battalion while still in Italy, Vandervoort remained a major until the day of the jump into Normandy. He was promoted to lieutenant colonel on the flight line.

45. Ridgway and Martin, *Soldier*, 7.

46. Putnam questionnaire.

47. Langdon, *"Ready,"* 56–57; Benjamin H. Vandervoort questionnaire and attached untitled manuscript, Ryan Collection, Box 9, Folder 1, OU. Vandervoort succeeded the popular Mark Alexander as commander of the 2/505th and began his tenure trying too hard to impress others. He was "a very proud individual, with the ambition to do a good job," recalled Captain Putnam, but he quickly earned a reputation as "anxious, indecisive, and with too much desire to gain personally with no regard to cost of trouble to others." Putnam questionnaire. As a result, morale in the battalion plummeted and the AWOL rate skyrocketed. Ridgway sent Gavin to investigate. What Gavin found was that Vandervoort had turned into a martinet, had subsequently lost control of the battalion, and was using mass punishment in hopes of regaining control. Gavin, Personal Diary, 11 February 1944 (see chap. 4, n. 26). Gavin set things straight and two months later recorded that Vandervoort was "a good soldier" whose "battalion will do well in its next fight." Ibid., 13 April 1944.

48. Langdon, *"Ready,"* 56–57; Vandervoort questionnaire and attached untitled manuscript.

49. Ibid.; Combat Interview "Neuville-au-Plain," n.d., CI-170 "82nd Airborne Div. Operation 'Neptune' June 1944," Box 24057, Record Group 407, NARA II.

50. See statement by Keil in Blumentritt et al., *Fighting the Invasion*, 181–182.

51. Vandervoort untitled manuscript; Theodore L. Peterson to Cornelius Ryan, 22 March 1959, Ryan Collection, Box 8, Folder 29, OU.

52. Vandervoort untitled manuscript.

53. According to Stephen Ambrose, Niland's brother, a lieutenant in the 4th Infantry Division, was killed that same morning on UTAH beach, and a second brother was killed that same week in Burma. The fourth Niland brother, Fritz, was in the 101st and subsequently "snatched out of the front line by the Army." Hence, the basis for the movie *Saving Private Ryan*. Ambrose, *D-Day*, 316–317.

54. Vandervoort untitled manuscript; Peterson to Ryan, 22 March 1959; Combat Interview "Neuville-au-Plain." Sebastian, Smitson, and Kelly were eventually captured. In his letter to Ryan, Peterson also recalled seeing Vandervoort in the area.

Having obviously returned to the scene of the fight after ordering Peterson's platoon forward, Vandervoort was sitting in a jeep "just as calm as you [can] be talking on his radio" and directing the fire of the antitank gun and a nearby machine gun.

55. Wienecke Combat Interview.

56. Sergeant Bill Dunfee quoted in Astor, *June 6, 1944*, 118.

57. For the I Company fight, see Wienecke Combat Interview; and Combat Interview "Attack on Hill 20 by 'I' Company," n.d., CI-170 "82nd Airborne Operation 'Neptune' June 1944," Box 24057, Record Group 407, NARA II.

58. See Pierce, *Let's Go!* 109–110; Edson D. Raff questionnaire, Ryan Collection, Box 8, Folder 32, OU; and Combat Interview "South of Ste. Mere Eglise," n.d., CI-170 "82nd Airborne Div. Operation 'Neptune' June 1944," Box 24057, Record Group 407, NARA II.

59. Warren, *Airborne Operations in World War II*, 66.

60. Ibid., 67; Combat Interview "South of Ste. Mere Eglise."

61. Raff questionnaire.

62. Warren, *Airborne Operations in World War II*, 68.

63. Combat Interview "South of Ste. Mere Eglise."

64. Memorandum, Headquarters, 82nd Airborne Division, "History of Division Headquarters and Headquarters Company in Operation 'NEPTUNE,'" 31 July 1944, 382-HQ-0.3, Box 12447, Record Group 407, NARA II.

65. Warren, *Airborne Operations in World War II*, 68–69. In a combat interview conducted soon after the battle, Raff stated that after the insertion of the first echelon he called the commanding general of the 4th Infantry Division and asked him to send a message to the rear stating that no more glider missions should come in on landing zone "W." Combat Interview "South of Ste. Mere Eglise."

66. Warren, *Airborne Operations in World War II*, 68–69; "Narrative Report," n.d., 382-FA(320), Box 12436, Record Group 407, NARA II; Memorandum, Headquarters, 319th Glider Field Artillery Battalion, "Historical Record 319th Glider FA Bn. for June, 1944," n.d., 382-FA(319)-0.3, Box 12434, Record Group 407, NARA II.

67. Warren, *Airborne Operations in World War II*, 69–70.

68. Richard Brigham Johnson, "RBJ's Adventures in Normandy, June, 1944: Written by RBJ December 1976, at the Request of His Children," December 1976, Gavin Papers, Box 11, Folder "D-Day Story by an R. B. J. (Richard) Letter to Richard by Dick," USAMHI.

69. Warren, *Airborne Operations in World War II*, 70–71. After HACKENSACK there were several other small-scale glider and parachute insertions, all into landing zone "W," which by that time had been totally secured. On 9 June two gliders with badly needed signal equipment arrived. On 10 June, six Wacos carrying jeeps and more than six tons of equipment made another successful landing. On 12 June, five Wacos landed and were immediately followed by one stick of fifteen paratroopers. Finally, on 13 June, eleven Wacos with ammunition and equipment were flown in. See ibid., 78.

70. Jones quoted in Ambrose, *D-Day*, 220; Ernest Leffel Gee questionnaire, Ryan Collection, Box 8, Folder 5, OU.

71. Melvin quoted in Drez, *Voices of D-Day*, 146.

72. *Operation Neptune*, annex D, appendix 1.

73. Memorandum, Headquarters 82nd Airborne Division, 28 July 1944, Ridgway Papers, Box 3, Folder "Personal File Jan.–Jul. 44," USAMHI. Ridgway spoke for both divisions in his capacity as the ranking American airborne officer in theater.

74. See Pierce, *Let's Go!* 189; Coyle questionnaire (see chap. 10, n. 80); and Reminiscence of Clinton Riddle in O'Donnell, *Beyond Valor*, 154. By act of Congress, glider troopers were to be awarded glider flight pay on par with paratrooper jump pay. According to Pierce, the troopers received word of this award in late June 1944. Pierce, *Let's Go!* 186.

75. Harrison, *Cross-Channel Attack*, 342.

76. Ibid.

77. Vandervoort untitled manuscript.

78. Benjamin H. Vandervoort, "Waverly W. Wray, Ste Mère Eglise, Normandy, June 7, 1944," n.d., Blair Collection, Box 55, Folder "Vandervoort, Benjamin," USAMHI.

79. For Wray's attack, except where noted, see also Vandervoort untitled manuscript and "Waverly W. Wray." For his actions that day, Wray was awarded the Distinguished Service Cross.

80. Vandervoort untitled manuscript.

81. Putnam questionnaire; Ekman questionnaire.

82. Harrison, *Cross-Channel Attack*, 342.

83. Bass to Ryan, 20 March 1959.

84. Otis L. Sampson, "Destination," n.d., p. 17, Gavin Papers, Box 11, Folder "Letters to Gavin, Comments, and Inquiries about D-Day Mentioned from *Longest Day*," USAMHI.

85. Except where noted, see Combat Interview "Concluding Actions at Ste. Mere Eglise," n.d., CI-170 "82nd Airborne Div. Operation 'Neptune' June 1944," Box 24057, Record Group 407, NARA II; Vandervoort untitled manuscript; and Coyle questionnaire.

86. Sampson, "Destination," 18.

87. Vandervoort untitled manuscript; Gavin quoted in Langdon, *"Ready,"* 64.

88. Weigley, *Eisenhower's Lieutenants*, 93.

CHAPTER 12: YOU CROSSED THAT CAUSEWAY

1. Vandervoort, "505th Normandy Campaign."

2. Langdon, *"Ready,"* 66; John J. Dolan to James M. Gavin, 23 March 1959, Collection, Box 7, Folder 52, OU.

3. Except where noted, see Langdon, *"Ready,"* 66–68; Robert M. Murphy, *No Better Place to Die*, 22–23; and Combat Interview "Concluding Actions at Ste. Mere Eglise" (see chap. 11, n. 85).

4. Langdon, *"Ready,"* 66–68; Murphy, *No Better Place to Die*, 22–23; Dolan to Gavin, 23 March 1959; Combat Interview "Concluding Actions at Ste. Mere Eglise."

5. Ibid.

6. Langdon, *"Ready,"* 68–70; Combat Interview "Movements on East Bank at Merderet Crossing," n.d., CI-170 "82nd Airborne Div. Operation 'Neptune' June

1944," Box 24057, Record Group 407, NARA II; Combat Interview "508 Regiment After the Drop" (see chap. 11, n. 31).

7. Langdon, *"Ready,"* 69–70; reminiscences of Homer Jones and Jim Kurz in Astor, *June 6, 1944*, 246–248; Combat Interview "Movements on East Bank at Merderet Crossing"; Combat Interview "508 Regiment After the Drop."

8. Langdon, *"Ready,"* 69; Dolan to Gavin, 23 March 1959; Combat Interview "Statement of Brig. Gen. James M. Gavin" (see chap. 11, n. 30).

9. Walton, interview, 18 March 1958 (see chap. 10, n. 79).

10. Except where noted, see Combat Interview "Statement of Brig. Gen. James M. Gavin."

11. Graham quoted in Astor, *June 6, 1944*, 140.

12. For Gavin's march from the railroad to Chef du Pont, see Langdon, *"Ready,"* 69; Dolan to Gavin, 23 March 1959; Combat Interview "Statement of Brig. Gen. James M. Gavin"; and Combat Interview "Operation of 507th Regiment Following Drop," n.d., CI-170, "82nd Airborne Div. Operation 'Neptune' June 1944," Box 24057, Record Group 407, USAMHI.

13. See Combat Interview "Statement of Brig. Gen. James M. Gavin"; and Combat Interview "Operation of 507th Regiment Following Drop."

14. Roy E. Creek, interview, n.d., n.p., World War II Oral History Project, Eisenhower Center, University of New Orleans.

15. Except where noted, see Combat Interview "Statement of Brig. Gen. James M. Gavin"; and Combat Interview "Operation of 507th Regiment Following Drop."

16. For Creek's fight at Chef du Pont, see Murphy, *No Better Place to Die*, 48–50; Combat Interview "Statement of Brig. Gen. James M. Gavin"; Combat Interview "Operation of 507th Regiment Following Drop"; and Lew Milkovics, "A Day by Day Account of the 508 P.I.R. in Normandy," n.d, World War II Veterans Survey Project, Box "82nd Airborne Division, 507th PIR, 508th PIR," Folder "Milkovics, Lew, Hq. Co. 508th PIR," USAMHI.

17. James M. Gavin to Arthur A. Maloney, 4 March 1959, Gavin Papers, Box 11, Folder "Letters to Gavin, Comments, and Inquiries about D-Day Mentioned from *Longest Day*," USAMHI.

18. For the fight at Cauquigny, see Combat Interview "Levy's Group," n.d, CI-170 "82nd Airborne Div. Operation 'Neptune' June 1944," Box 24057, Record Group 407, NARA II; Charles J. Timmes to Richard Brigham Johnson, 12 April 1977, Gavin Papers, Box 11, Folder "82nd Airborne Division, 508th Parachute Infantry Regiment, Letters About D-Day Invasion," USAMHI; Combat Interview "507-2 on D-Day and Immediately After"; reminiscences of Bill Dean, Homer Jones, and Jim Kurz in Astor, *June 6, 1944*, 246–248. Much has been written about the decisions made that day at La Fière bridge, especially in light of the ferocious fight that subsequently erupted across its span. Schwartzwalder's actions appear questionable, but it should be remembered that when Schwartzwalder arrived at Cauquigny, nothing was happening. Hence, his logical course of action was to move to link up with his regiment, which he knew, from talking with Levy, was in large part gathered at Timmes's orchard. Others have questioned Kellam's actions, particularly his failure to reinforce the far bank. Since Kellam had with him almost his entire battalion, sending a company to the far shore would have been a sound

tactical move. But from Kellam's perspective, the far bank was secured. He could not have missed seeing Schwartzwalder's large column moving over the bridge, and the conversation he had with Levy must have left him with the impression that he did not have to send a company to the far side since there already was a company over there. Finally, the time interval between Schwartzwalder's departure and the German attack was simply too short for Kellam to react, even if he had known that Schwartzwalder had continued on to Timmes's location. Both men made decisions based on what they saw and what they knew they had to do. Neither had the luxury of hindsight with which their critics have, since that day, questioned their actions.

19. Langdon, *"Ready,"* 69–70.

20. Ibid., 70; Murphy, *No Better Place to Die*, 41; Dolan to Gavin, 23 March 1959.

21. Murphy, *No Better Place to Die*, 42–43. All four bazooka team members were subsequently awarded the Distinguished Service Cross.

22. Except where noted, see Dolan to Gavin, 23 March 1959; and Combat Interview "Concluding Actions at Ste. Mere Eglise." The German tanks were actually captured French Renault tanks. It was not uncommon for German forces in France to use captured enemy equipment.

23. James M. Gavin to Cornelius Ryan, 23 March 1959, Ryan Collection, Box 8, Folder 27, OU; William Dale Owens, "'D Day' June 6th 1944," n.d., Ryan Collection, Box 8, Folder 27, OU.

24. Alexander, "Thirty Four Days in Normandy."

25. Langdon, "*Ready*," 71; Owens, "D Day."

26. Gavin to Ryan, 23 March 1959; Owens, "D Day."

27. Walton, interview, 18 March 1958; Owens and Dolan quoted in Murphy, *No Better Place to Die*, 61.

28. Except where noted, see Langdon, "*Ready*," 71–72; Murphy, *No Better Place to Die*, 56–61; Combat Interview "Statement of Brig. Gen. James M. Gavin"; Combat Interview "Concluding Actions at Ste. Mere Eglise"; Dolan to Gavin, 23 March 1959; and Combat Interview "508 Regiment After the Drop."

29. See Gavin, *On to Berlin*, 110; Lord, *History of the 508th Parachute Infantry*, 20–21; Combat Interview "Statement of Brig. Gen. James M. Gavin"; Combat Interview "508 Regiment After the Drop"; and Milkovics, "A Day by Day Account of the 508 P.I.R. in Normandy."

30. For Lindquist at Chef du Pont, see Lord, *History of the 508th Parachute Infantry*, 20–21; Combat Interview "Statement of Brig. Gen. James M. Gavin"; Milkovics, "A Day by Day Account of the 508 P. I. R. in Normandy"; and Combat Interview "508 Regiment After the Drop." Gavin later upbraided Lindquist for his decision, but given what Lindquist knew, or thought he knew, at the time, it is easy to understand why he made it. Had Lindquist followed Gavin's orders and moved across the river and on to Cauquigny, he would have left both his rear and Chef du Pont exposed to attack from the German force to the south.

31. For the fight at the Chef du Pont causeway, see Combat Interview "Statement of Brig. Gen. James M. Gavin"; Milkovics, "A Day by Day Account of the 508 P. I. R. in Normandy"; and Combat Interview "508 Regiment After the Drop."

32. Gavin, Personal Diary, 24 March 1944 (see chap. 4, n. 26).

33. Except where noted, see Combat Interview "Colonel Millett's Group," n.d., CI-170 "82nd Airborne Div. Operation 'Neptune' June 1944," Box 24057, Record Group 407, NARA II; and Combat Interview "Initial Operations of 325th Glider Infantry," CI-170 "82nd Airborne Div. Operation 'Neptune' June 1944," Box 24057, Record Group 407, NARA II.

34. See also Murphy, *No Better Place to Die*, 68; Combat Interview "507-2 on D-Day and Immediately After"; and Combat Interview "Initial Operations of 325th Glider Infantry."

35. Medal of Honor Citation for Charles N. DeGlopper, Box "82nd Airborne Division, WWII, 325th GIR, *Personal Papers," Folder "*Personal Papers—DeGlopper, Charles N. (C Co., 325th GIR)," 82nd Airborne Division Museum, Fort Bragg, NC.

36. Except where noted, see Murphy, *No Better Place to Die*, 68, 91–92; Pierce, *Let's Go!* 133–136; Combat Interview "507–2 on D-Day and Immediately After"; and Combat Interview "Initial Operations of 325th Glider Infantry."

37. Combat Interview "Colonel Millett's Group."

38. Gavin, interview, 4 January 1983 (see chap. 7, n. 12).

39. Lee C. Travelstead untitled manuscript, n.d., Blair Collection, Box 55, Folder "Travelstead, Lee C.," USAMHI.

40. Except where noted, see Combat Interview "Initial Operations of 325th Glider Infantry" and Combat Interview "Statement of Brig. Gen. James M. Gavin."

41. Gavin, interview, 4 January 1983.

42. Johnson, "RBJ's Adventures in Normandy" (see chap. 11, n. 68).

43. Except where noted, see Murphy, *No Better Place to Die*, 71; and Combat Interview "Crossing of Merderet by 325-3," n.d., CI-170 "82nd Airborne Div. Operation 'Neptune' June 1944," Box 24057, Record Group 407, NARA II.

44. Pierce, *Let's Go!* 143.

45. Combat Interview "Crossing of Merderet by 325-3."

46. Johnson, "RBJ's Adventures in Normandy."

47. Pierce, *Let's Go!* 144.

48. Matthew B. Ridgway, interview by John M. Blair, 24 November 1971, Ridgway Papers, Box 51, Folder "Interview by John M. Blair, Volume I," USAMHI.

49. Except where noted, see Combat Interview "Crossing of Merderet by 325-3."

50. See Murphy, *No Better Place to Die*, 72; and Combat Interview "Crossing of Merderet by 325-3."

51. James M. Gavin interview, 28 September 1982, Blair Collection, Box 53, Folder "Gavin, James M.," USAMHI.

52. Gavin, interview, 16 April 1975 (see chap. 4, n. 1).

53. Except where noted, see Combat Interview "Composite Force Under Captain Rae at Merderet Crossing," n.d., CI-170 "82nd Airborne Div. Operation 'Neptune' June 1944," Box 24057, Record Group 407, NARA II; and Combat Interview "Statement of Brig. Gen. James M. Gavin."

54. Breuer, *Geronimo!* 257.

55. Combat Interview "Composite Force Under Captain Rae at Merderet Crossing."

56. Gavin, *On to Berlin*, 252; Ridgway and Winton, "Troop Leadership at the Operational Level" (see chap. 7, n. 84); Ridgway, interview, 24 November 1971.

57. Quoted in Murphy, *No Better Place to Die*, 77–78; Johnson, "RBJ's Adventures in Normandy."

58. See Combat Interview "Initial Operations of 325th Glider Infantry" and "Regimental History, 325th Glider Infantry, *The Normandy Campaign*, 6 Jun. 44–14 Jul. 44," n. d., 382-INF(325)-0.3, Box 12448, Record Group 407, NARA II.

59. Combat Interview "Crossing of Merderet by 325-3."

60. See ibid. and Combat Interview "Initial Operations of 325th Glider Infantry."

61. "Regimental History, 325th Glider Infantry, *The Normandy Campaign*"; Combat Interview "Continuation of Merderet Crossing," n.d., CI-170, "82nd Airborne Div. Operation 'Neptune' June 1944," Box 24057, Record Group 407, NARA II.

62. According to Lieutenant Vernon L. Wyant Jr., a 325th officer on liaison duty with the division headquarters, Lewis was so distraught over what befell his troopers on the bridge that he had to be sedated. It took him three days to recover. Lewis displayed as much personal courage as anyone during the attack on the bridge and was, according to Wyant, too keyed up to rest following the attack and "constantly paced up and down the room [of his regimental command post]. His grief at having to order the causeway attack and the fact that so many men were killed, was overwhelming. He constantly mumbled seemingly without any coherent meaning." After observing Lewis in this state for about twenty minutes Wyant decided to contact the regimental surgeon. "Dr. Johnson came into the room, tried to talk with the Colonel, observed his pacing and tried to get him to relax and rest. He was not successful so the two of us retired from the room. Dr. Johnson advised me that Col. Lewis should be moved to the Division Aid Station for rest and observation. The problem was how to accomplish this as Col. Lewis would be very much against it. Dr. Johnson decided that the best plan would be for him to approach Lewis with the idea of giving him a sedative to relax him. . . . Dr. Johnson's plan was to give Lewis a strong sedative. This would put him in a position where he could be moved to the division aid station by way of a jeep and stretcher. Col. Lewis agreed to what he thought was a mild sedative and just as darkness closed in, he was taken by jeep to the Division Aid Station. The troops of the regiment, including most of the officers, had no knowledge of this incident at the time." Three days later Lewis returned to duty and led the regiment for the rest of its time in Normandy. One of his first acts after returning, however, was to give Johnson and Wyant "the worst dressing down either of us had experienced in our Army Service!" He then shook both men's hands, and nothing more was ever said of the matter. Lewis was an old man by airborne standards, but he was a tough old man. What occurred with Lewis has often been ascribed to battle fatigue. This is not entirely true. What no one knew at the time is that Lewis was suffering from cancer, which would hospitalize him upon the division's return to England and kill him in less than a year. Wyant's reminiscence reproduced in Jerry L. Richlak Sr., ed., *Glide to Glory*, 230–231.

63. Gavin, *On to Berlin*, 118; Combat Interview "Composite Force Under Captain Rae at Merderet Crossing." For the attack on Le Motey, see also Gavin, *On to Berlin*, 118–119; Combat Interview "Composite Force Under Captain Rae at Merderet Crossing"; Statements on Fighting at La Fière by Gavin and Willard E.

Harrison, n.d., Gavin Papers, Box 12, Folder "Letters to and from 82nd Vets on Airborne Operations in Holland, September 1944," USAMHI; and Combat Interview "Continuation of Merderet Crossing."

64. Harrison, *Cross-Channel Attack*, 401; "Regimental History, 325th Glider Infantry, *The Normandy Campaign*."

65. "Regimental History, 325th Glider Infantry, *The Normandy Campaign*."

66. Ridgway and Martin, *Soldier*, 14; James M. Gavin to Richard Brigham Johnson, 7 March 1977, Gavin Papers, Box 11, Folder "82nd Airborne Division, 508th Parachute Infantry Regiment, Letters About D-Day Invasion," USAMHI.

67. Johnson, "RBJ's Adventures in Normandy."

CHAPTER 13: CAN'T ANYTHING STOP THOSE MEN?

1. See Devlin, *Paratrooper!* 412.

2. Matthew B. Ridgway, "Resume of Service of Pvt. John J. Van Valkenburg," n.d., Ridgway Papers, Box 3, Folder "Personal File Jan.–Jul. 44," USAMHI; Combat Interview "Colonel Millett's Group" (see chap. 12, n. 33); Combat Interview "Within the Perimeter," n.d., CI-170 "82nd Airborne Div. Operation 'Neptune' June 1944," Box 24057, Record Group 407, NARA II.

3. See Memorandum, Headquarters, 307th Airborne Engineer Battalion, "Engineer Operations Report," 9 July 1944, Box "82nd Airborne Division—WWII—307th Eng. Bn.—Unit History—Incident Reports," Folder "307th Abn. Eng. Bn.—Reports June–Jul. 44," 82nd Airborne Division Museum, Fort Bragg, NC; and Headquarters, 319th Glider Field Artillery Battalion, "Historical Record 319th Glider FA Bn. for June, 1944."

4. Wood questionnaire (see chap. 11, n. 27).

5. Walton, interview, 18 March 1958 (see chap. 10, n. 79).

6. See "Status of Personnel, Operation Neptune, 82d Airborne Division," 26 July 1944, 382-0.3, Box 12345, Record Group 407, NARA II; and "Operation Neptune, 82d Airborne Division, Analysis of Officer Casualties" 26 July 1944, 382-0.3, Box 12345, Record Group 407, NARA II.

7. "Regimental History, 325th Glider Infantry, *The Normandy Campaign*" (see chap. 12, n. 58).

8. "Status of Personnel, Operation Neptune, 82d Airborne Division." All told, the division sustained a casualty rate of 46 percent.

9. Pierce, *Let's Go!* 191; J. Wilson, *Maneuver and Firepower*, 168.

10. "Sworn Statement of Technical Sergeant Edward William Shimko with Reference Glider Landing in Vicinity of Caen, France on 7 June 1944," n.d., CI-170 "82nd Airborne Div. Operation 'Neptune' June 1944," Box 24057, Record Group 407, NARA II. For Shimko and his men, even the trip to France was unusual. Ten to twelve minutes into the flight the latches that secured the glider's nose broke (the noses were designed to swing up and away to facilitate loading and unloading), exposing a gap more than two feet wide. Shimko and his men grabbed the nose, pulled it closed, and attempted to secure it shut, but when it came undone again, the tug and glider returned to the departure airfield. There the latches on the swing-away nose were wired shut, and the tug and glider took off a second time.

11. See Breuer, *Geronimo!* 271–282; reminiscence of Frank E. Naughton in O'Donnell, *Beyond Valor*, 157–162; "Statement of Captain Frank Brummett, S-3, 3rd Bn. 507th Prcht. Regt.," n.d., 382-0.3.0, Box 12346, Record Group 407, NARA II. The Germans also razed a large portion of Graignes, to include blowing the edifice off a twelfth-century Roman Catholic church.

12. Funk quoted in Breuer, *Geronimo!* 223.

13. Langdon, *"Ready,"* 72–73; Harrison, *Cross-Channel Attack*, 386–387; Combat Interview "Continuation of Command Narrative," n.d., CI-170 "82nd Airborne Div. Operation 'Neptune' June 1944," Box 24057, Record Group 407, NARA II; Combat Interview "Advance on Le Ham," n.d., CI-170 "82nd Airborne Div. Operation 'Neptune' June 1944," Box 24057, Record Group 407, NARA II.

14. Ekman questionnaire (see chap. 11, n. 43).

15. Vandervoort questionnaire (see chap. 11, n. 47).

16. Harrison, *Cross-Channel Attack*, 386–387.

17. Ibid.; Langdon, *"Ready,"* 74; 505th Combat Journal, n.d., 382-INF(505)-0.3, Box 12456, Record Group 407, NARA II; Combat Interview "Advance on Le Ham"; *Operation Neptune*, 9 (see chap. 10, n. 41).

18. Harrison, *Cross-Channel Attack*, 387–388; Langdon, *"Ready,"* 74; Combat Interview "Advance on Le Ham."

19. Langdon, *"Ready,"* 74–76; 505th Combat Journal; Combat Interview "Advance on Le Ham."

20. Ibid.; "Regimental History, 325th Glider Infantry, *The Normandy Campaign*"; Headquarters, 82nd Airborne Division Artillery, "Unit History," 9 September 1944, 382-ART-0.3, Box 12429, Record Group 407, NARA II.

21. Swenson quoted in Pierce, *Let's Go!* 172–173.

22. Except where noted, see Langdon, *"Ready,"* 76; Harrison, *Cross-Channel Attack*, 388; Pierce, *Let's Go!*, 172–174; 505th Combat Journal; Combat Interview "Advance on Le Ham"; and Memorandum, Headquarters, 456th Parachute Field Artillery Battalion, "Narrative History of the 456th Parachute Field Artillery Battalion During the Period 20 February–15 July 1944, and C and D Battery from 14 November 1943 to 19 February 1944," 9 August 1944, 382-FA(456)-0.3, Box 12442, Record Group 407, NARA II.

23. Pierce, *Let's Go!* 174; Wilson, *Maneuver and Firepower*, 168; 505th Combat Journal.

24. For background on the attack to Baupte, see Bradley and Blair, *A General's Life*, 256; Harrison, *Cross-Channel Attack*, 352, 364, 402–403; Lord, *History of the 508th Parachute Infantry*, 27; Milkovics, "A Day by Day Account of the 508th P.I.R. in Normandy" (see chap. 12, n. 16); Headquarters, 82nd Airborne Division Artillery, "Unit History"; and *Operation Neptune*, 14.

25. Giegold quoted in Zig Boroughs, *The Devil's Tale: Stories of the RED DEVILS of the 508 Parachute Infantry Regiment, 82nd Airborne Division, in World War Two*, 90 (capitalization in original); Headquarters, 307th Airborne Engineer Battalion, "Unit History," 10 August 1944, 382-ENG-0.3, Box 12433, Record Group 407, NARA II.

26. Chatoian quoted in Boroughs, *Devil's Tale*, 91, 92.

27. Except where noted, see Lord, *History of the 508th Parachute Infantry*, 27; Milkovics, "A Day by Day Account of the 508th P.I.R. in Normandy"; Headquarters, 82nd Airborne Division Artillery, "Unit History"; and *Operation Neptune*, 14.

28. Harrison, *Cross-Channel Attack*, 402.

29. For the 508th's advance south of the Douve, see also Lord, *History of the 508th Parachute Infantry*, 27–29; and Milkovics, "A Day by Day Account of the 508th P.I.R. in Normandy."

30. For the German attack on Baupte, see Harrison, *Cross-Channel Attack*, 402; Lord, *History of the 508th Parachute Infantry*, 30; Milkovics, "A Day by Day Account of the 508th P.I.R. in Normandy"; and Headquarters, 82nd Airborne Division Artillery, "Unit History."

31. Martin Blumenson, *Breakout and Pursuit*, 204; Harrison, *Cross-Channel Attack*, 401–403; Weigley, *Eisenhower's Lieutenants*, 98–99. One 82nd veteran, Richard Brigham Johnson, related after the war that Gavin had told him that the soldiers of the 90th, "mostly from Texas and Oklahoma, who called themselves Tough 'Ombres,' and wore a 'TO' shoulder patch, were so demoralized by the sight of our dead and wounded [presumably as they passed through the 82nd's lines at La Fière and Chef du Pont] that they were unable to . . . continue the attack." Johnson, "RBJ's Adventures in Normandy" (see chap. 11, n. 68).

32. Harrison, *Cross-Channel Attack*, 403; Pierce, *Let's Go!* 181–182; "Regimental History, 325th Glider Infantry, *The Normandy Campaign*"; 505th Combat Journal; *Operation Neptune*, 15; Combat Interview "Operation of the 325th Glider Infantry 2d Phase," n.d., CI-170 "82nd Airborne Div. Operation 'Neptune,' June 1944," Box 24057, Record Group 407, NARA II.

33. Blair, *Ridgway's Paratroopers*, 512; Harrison, *Cross-Channel Attack*, 404; "Regimental History, 325th Glider Infantry, *The Normandy Campaign*"; 505th Combat Journal; *Operation Neptune*, 16–17; Combat Interview "Operation of the 325th Glider Infantry 2d Phase."

34. Vandervoort quoted in 505th Combat Journal.

35. Langdon, *"Ready,"* 79, 80.

36. Except where noted, see Harrison, *Cross-Channel Attack*, 404–408; Langdon, *"Ready,"* 80; "Regimental History, 325th Glider Infantry, *The Normandy Campaign*"; 505th Combat Journal; *Operation Neptune*, 18–19; Combat Interview "Operation of the 325th Glider Infantry 2d Phase"; and Milkovics, "A Day by Day Account of the 508th P.I.R. in Normandy."

37. Harrison, *Cross-Channel Attack*, 415.

38. Except where noted, see Harrison, *Cross-Channel Attack*, 417; Langdon, *"Ready,"* 80; Weigley, *Eisenhower's Lieutenants*, 101, 106; and *Operation Neptune*, 19–20.

39. Blumenson, *Breakout and Pursuit*, 37; Harrison, *Cross-Channel Attack*, 415–416; *Operation Neptune*, 21.

40. For the attack across the Douve, see Blair, *Ridgway's Paratroopers*, 509; *Operation Neptune*, 21; "Regimental History, 325th Glider Infantry, *The Normandy Campaign*"; Combat Interview "Operation of the 325th Glider Infantry 2d Phase"; "Notes on the 325th Narrative," n.d., "82nd Airborne Div. Operation 'Neptune,'

June 1944," Box 24057, Record Group 407, NARA II; Headquarters, 307th Airborne Engineer Battalion, "Unit History."

41. Harrison, *Cross-Channel Attack*, 423–426; *Operation Neptune*, 22–24.

42. Blair, *Ridgway's Paratroopers*, 287; Blumenson, *Breakout and Pursuit*, 44; Alexander, "Thirty Four Days in Normandy."

43. Shields Warren to Clay Blair, 24 October 1983, Blair Collection, Box 55, Folder "Warren, Shields (508)," USAMHI.

44. Langdon, *"Ready,"* 82.

45. Blumenson, *Breakout and Pursuit*, 37–38, 53.

46. Ibid., 53–58.

47. Ibid., 56–60.

48. Blumenson, *Breakout and Pursuit*, 60–61; *Operation Neptune*, 26–27.

49. Langdon, *"Ready,"* 82; Lord, *History of the 508th Parachute Infantry*, 34; *Operation Neptune*, 23.

50. Lord, *History of the 508th Parachute Infantry*, 33.

51. Langdon, *"Ready,"* 83; Lord, *History of the 508th Parachute Infantry*, 34; *Operation Neptune*, 26–27.

52. Blumenson, *Breakout and Pursuit*, 61; Langdon, *"Ready,"* 82–83.

53. Blumenson, *Breakout and Pursuit*, 61–62; Pierce, *Let's Go!* 187; *Operation Neptune*, 26; "Regimental History, 325th Glider Infantry, *The Normandy Campaign*"; Combat Interview "Continuing the 325th Narrative," n.d., CI-170 "82nd Airborne Div. Operation 'Neptune' June 1944," Box 24057, Record Group 407, NARA II.

54. Blumenson, *Breakout and Pursuit*, 62; Langdon, *"Ready,"* 83–84; Lord, *History of the 508th Parachute Infantry*, 34–36; *Operation Neptune*, 27–28; Milkovics, "A Day by Day Account of the 508th P.I.R. in Normandy."

55. Blumenson, *Breakout and Pursuit*, 62–63; Langdon, *"Ready,"* 84; Lord, *History of the 508th Parachute Infantry*, 37; *Operation Neptune*, 27–28; Milkovics, "A Day by Day Account of the 508th P.I.R. in Normandy"; "Regimental History, 325th Glider Infantry, *The Normandy Campaign*."

56. Blumenson, *Breakout and Pursuit*, 62–63; Langdon, *"Ready,"* 84; Lord, *History of the 508th Parachute Infantry*, 37; *Operation Neptune*, 27–29; Milkovics, "A Day by Day Account of the 508th P.I.R. in Normandy."

57. Blumenson, *Breakout and Pursuit*, 63.

58. For the statistics on the attack on La Poterie Ridge and Geach's attack, see Pierce, *Let's Go!* 188; and Headquarters, First United States Army, General Orders No. 45, 9 August 1944, Box "82nd Airborne Division WWII 325th GIR *Personal Papers," Folder "Personal Papers—Geach, James L. (HHC, 1/325th GIR)," 82nd Airborne Division Museum, Fort Bragg, NC.

59. Langdon, *"Ready,"* 84; Lord, *History of the 508th Parachute Infantry*, 37–38; Pierce, *Let's Go!* 189; Milkovics, "A Day by Day Account of the 508th P.I.R. in Normandy"; "Regimental History, 325th Glider Infantry, *The Normandy Campaign*"; Headquarters, 82nd Airborne Division Artillery, "Unit History"; *Operation Neptune*, 29–30.

60. *Operation Neptune*, annex 1D(2); and "Status of Personnel, Operation Neptune, 82d Airborne Division." There exists no definitive accounting of the costs in

Normandy. The figures given here are based primarily on the former source, which, in turn, was based on the latter, although updated to include discoveries occurring after 26 July 1944.

61. 505th Combat Journal; Eichen quoted in Ambrose, *Citizen Soldiers*, 60.

CHAPTER 14: A LASTING AND FIRM FAITH IN THE AIRBORNE

1. Blair, *Ridgway's Paratroopers*. "The Stuff of Instant Legend" was the title Blair gave to his section on Normandy.

2. Moon quoted in Richlak, *Glide to Glory*, 269–270.

3. Pierce, *Let's Go!* 199.

4. Memorandum, Headquarters, 82nd Airborne Division, "Training for Future Airborne Operations," 30 June 1944, Ridgway Papers, Box 3, Folder "Personal File, Jan.–Jul. 44," USAMHI.

5. McKenzie, *On Time, On Target*, 38.

6. Except where noted, see Jorgensen, *History of the 456th Parachute Field Artillery Battalion*, 133; Langdon, *"Ready,"* 86; and Megellas, *All the Way to Berlin*, 82.

7. Lord, *History of the 508th Parachute Infantry*, 38; Langdon, *"Ready,"* 86.

8. Brigadier General Pleas B. Rogers to Major General Maxwell D. Taylor, 24 July 1944, Ridgway Papers, Box 3, Folder "Personal File, Jan.–Jul. 44," USAMHI.

9. Ridgway and Martin, *Soldier*, 105; Gellhorn, "Stand Up and Hook Up!" n.p. According to Ross Carter, when the 504th troopers returned from Italy they, too, went wild on furloughs. His explanation for this behavior closely parallels that given by Gellhorn: "The truth of the matter is that we conducted ourselves like uncouth barbarians. Africa, plus the campaigns in Sicily and Italy, had dissolved most of the thin veneer that civilization spreads over the instincts. The boys simply went wild in England and didn't give two hoots in hell what they said or did." Carter, *Devils in Baggy Pants*, 202.

10. Ridgway and Martin, *Soldier*, 105.

11. McKenzie, *On Time, On Target*, 38.

12. Langdon, *"Ready,"* 86.

13. *Operation Neptune*, annex 1 D (2) (see chap. 10, n. 41). Figures are as of December 1944.

14. See Blumenson, *Breakout and Pursuit*, 344; and Warren, *Airborne Operations in World War II*, 85.

15. Soffer, *Ridgway*, 64.

16. Karel Margry, ed., *Operation Market-Garden: Then and Now*, 1:18.

17. Omar N. Bradley to Commanding General, U.S. Forces, European Theater, 25 July 1945, General Board Report, United States Forces, European Theater, Study No. 16, "Organization, Equipment, and Tactical Employment of the Airborne Division," appendix 6 (see chap. 3, n. 59). In fairness, it should be noted that Leigh-Mallory was the first to admit that he was wrong. In his diary entry for 6 June 1944, Eisenhower's naval aide Harry Butcher wrote, "In typical British sporting fashion, Air Chief Marshal Leigh-Mallory has written General Ike to admit that he was wrong about the airborne operation. The Marshal frankly said that it is sometimes difficult in this life to admit that one was wrong, but he has never

had a greater pleasure than in doing so on this occasion." Butcher, *My Three Years with Eisenhower*, 570.

18. Eisenhower, *Crusade in Europe*, 260; Bidwell's report quoted in Huston, *Out of the Blue*, 186.

19. See Carter, *Devils in Baggy Pants*, 206–207; and Megellas, *All the Way to Berlin*, 84.

20. Carter, *Devils in Baggy Pants*, 207; Megellas, *All the Way to Berlin*, 85.

21. Memorandum, Headquarters, 82nd Airborne Division, "82d Airborne Division—Operation NEPTUNE," 25 July 1944, Ridgway Papers, Box 3, Folder "Personal File, Jan.–Jul. 44," USAMHI (capitalization in original).

22. Memorandum, Headquarters, 82nd Airborne Division, "Organization of Airborne Division," 10 July 1944, Ridgway Papers, Box 3, Folder "Personal File, Jan.–Jul. 44," USAMHI (capitalization in original).

23. Blair, *Ridgway's Paratroopers*, 516–518; Huston, *Out of the Blue*, 75.

24. Chester B. McCoid to Clay Blair, 16 January 1984, Blair Collection, Box 54, Folder "McCoid, C. (Chester) B, 507 Co. Cmdr.," USAMHI.

25. James M. Gavin to Clay Blair, 21 November 1983, Blair Collection, Box 53, Folder "Gavin, James M.," USAMHI.

26. Edson Raff, untitled narrative, n.d., pp. 3 (quote), 11, 12, Blair Collection, Box 54, Folder "Raff, Edson D.," USAMHI.

27. Ibid., 37 (quote), 12, 14.

28. Ibid., 24. That it was Raff who requested that the 507th be transferred to the 17th Airborne Division is borne out by one of the 507th's best battalion commanders, Charles Timmes, who wrote, "Raff volunteered the Regt to go to the 17th AB Div," adding it was "a decision we in the 507th deplored." See Charles J. Timmes to Clay Blair, 16 June 1983, Blair Collection, Box 55, Folder "Timmes, Charles J.," USAMHI.

29. McCoid to Blair, 16 January 1984 (emphasis in original). Charles Timmes seconded McCoid's characterization of Raff, labeling him "an outstanding combat cmdr." See Timmes to Blair, 16 June 1983.

30. Ridgway and Martin, *Soldier*, 31.

31. Matthew B. Ridgway to Clay Blair, 6 August 1984, Blair Collection, Box 54, Folder "Ridgway Correspondence," USAMHI. That Ridgway knew of the personal attacks Raff made and continued to make on him is confirmed by a letter from Blair to Ridgway in which the former cites a manuscript Raff was preparing for publication. "Based on the Raff ms I would say (privately to you only) that Raff is your bitterest critic. I am certain his ms will never be published. It is a scurrilous, nearly-hysterical attack on you for every conceivable . . . reason." See Clay Blair to Matthew B. Ridgway, 14 August 1984, Blair Collection, Box 54, Folder "Ridgway Correspondence," USAMHI.

32. Cummings to Blair, 20 October 1983 (see chap. 3, n. 69); Pierce to Blair, 4 October 1983, Blair Collection, Box 51, Folder "Pierce, Wayne," USAMHI.

33. Gavin, Personal Diary, 19 July 1944 (see chap. 4, n. 26).

34. Warren, *Airborne Operations in World War II*, 81.

35. Huston, *Out of the Blue*, 78.

36. Brereton, *Brereton Diaries*, 228.

37. Dwight D. Eisenhower to George C. Marshall, 8 July 1944, *Papers of Eisenhower: The War Years, III,* 1988. Eisenhower sent the 8 July cable to "clearly" explain his ideas about the new airborne command, something he mentioned to Marshall in a previous cable sent 20 June.

38. Dwight D. Eisenhower to Henry H. Arnold, 13 July 1944, in ibid., 2001–2002.

39. Dwight D. Eisenhower to George C. Marshall, 15 July 1944, in ibid., 2008.

40. See Boatner, *Biographical Dictionary of World War II,* s.v. "Brereton, Lewis Hyde"; Brereton, *Brereton Diaries,* 167–213; Devlin, *Silent Wings,* 231; Goralski, *World War II Almanac,* 274.

41. Brereton, *Brereton Diaries,* 308. In their book *Paratrooper: The Life of Gen. James M. Gavin,* T. Michael Booth and Duncan Spencer maintained that Brereton got the job because Bradley, who was incensed over the disastrous D-Day drops, was convinced that this had occurred because Brereton was too fixated on strategic bombing and not enough on improving the performance of his transport pilots. Reasoning that if the bombers were taken away from Brereton (Ninth Air Force comprised the IX Troop Carrier Command, the IX Bomber Command, and the IX Tactical Command), he would pay more attention to his troop transports, and that subsequently drop accuracy would improve, Bradley presented his case to Eisenhower, who accepted it without question (205). Clay Blair makes a similar case in *Ridgway's Paratroopers,* 299.

42. Dwight D. Eisenhower to Walter Bedell Smith, 1 August 1944, *Papers of Eisenhower: The War Year, III,* 2053.

43. Warren, *Airborne Operations in World War II,* 81. Eisenhower also tried to acquire for Brereton's staff either of two very highly thought of officers then serving in the Mediterranean: Field Marshal Alexander's American deputy, Major General Lyman L. Lemnitzer, or Clark's Fifth Army chief of staff, Major General Alfred M. Gruenther. Both requests were denied. See Dwight D. Eisenhower to George C. Marshall, 17 July 1944, *Papers of Eisenhower: The War Years, III,* 2013–2014. That Arnold was able to provide three general officers so quickly was the result of his personal interest in the project as well as the fact that he was not hamstrung by a hidebound personnel management system, as were his ground force compatriots. Though officially still a part of the Army, the U.S. Army Air Force was, for all practical purposes, a separate service, and it was clear that after the war this would become a reality. Because of this, promotions within the Army Air Force were achieved at a much faster pace than they were in the ground army, and there was much more flexibility in the management of officers. Finally, there may have been one other reason behind Arnold's alacrity in providing Brereton three Army Air Force officers—he had, since the formation of parachute forces, been quietly angling for the Army Air Force to have its own Marine Corps–like ground combat arm and doubtless thought that the First Allied Airborne Army would provide an example of how this could be accomplished.

44. Huston, *Out of the Blue,* 81. See also Warren, *Airborne Operations in World War II,* 82.

45. Ridgway and Martin, *Soldier,* 18.

46. Blair, *Ridgway's Paratroopers,* 303.

47. James M. Gavin, interview by Lieutenant Colonel Donald G. Andrews and Lieutenant Colonel Charles H. Ferguson, 29 May 1975, Gavin Papers, Box "Oral History," USAMHI.

48. Blair, *Ridgway's Paratroopers*, 303; "World War II Casualties, Decorations, Citations (Also Miscellaneous Information)," unmarked box, Folder "82nd Airborne Division—WWII Casualties and Awards," 82nd Airborne Division Museum, Fort Bragg, NC.

49. Taylor quoted in Blair, *Ridgway's Paratroopers*, 544. See also 191.

50. Gavin, interview, 28 September 1982 (see chap. 2, n. 45), 29 May 1975. See also Blair, *Ridgway's Paratroopers*, 301; Floyd Lavinius Parks, Diary of the Chief of Staff, First Allied Airborne Army (entry for 4 September 1944), Floyd Lavinius Parks Papers, Box 2, USAMHI; and Gavin, Personal Diary, 24 July 1944.

51. Gavin, Personal Diary, 16 August 1944.

CHAPTER 15: WE'LL NEED TWO DIVISIONS TO DO THAT

1. Harrison, *Cross-Channel Attack*, 457. The entire "Directive to Supreme Commander, Allied Expeditionary Force" is reproduced in appendix B of Harrison's work, 457–458.

2. Department of the Army, *The Army Almanac*, 491.

3. Blumenson, *Breakout and Pursuit*, 657.

4. Roland G. Ruppenthal, "Logistics and the Broad-Front Strategy," 420–421.

5. Hitler quoted in Matthew Cooper, *The German Army, 1933–1945: Its Political and Military Failure*, 505.

6. Hitler quoted in Blumenson, *Breakout and Pursuit*, 340. As a result of this last order, some 180,000 to 280,000 German troops and their equipment were lost, although several of these fortress towns along the Channel coast held out until the end of the war.

7. Ibid., 457.

8. Ibid., 555–558.

9. Cooper, *German Army*, 512.

10. Eisenhower quoted in Ambrose, *Supreme Commander*, 492; Weigley, *Eisenhower's Lieutenants*, 253.

11. Ambrose, *Supreme Commander*, 492; Ruppenthal, "Logistics and the Broad-Front Strategy," 422.

12. Ambrose, *Supreme Commander*, 494–495; Ruppenthal, "Logistics and the Broad-Front Strategy," 421–422.

13. Montgomery, *Memoirs*, 243.

14. For contending points of view, see Bradley and Blair, *A General's Life*, 313; and Montgomery, *Memoirs*, 243.

15. Montgomery, *Memoirs*, 246, 249.

16. Eisenhower cable to Marshall, 24 August 1944, quoted in Blumenson, *Breakout and Pursuit*, 659.

17. Bradley and Blair, *A General's Life*, 331.

18. Brereton, *Brereton Diaries*, 334.

19. Margry, *Operation Market-Garden*, 1:18.

20. Blumenson, *Breakout and Pursuit*, 615–618, 686.

21. Huston, "Thoughts on the American Airborne Effort," 8. In the same article, Huston wrote, "Though the opportunity certainly presented itself several times in Europe, airborne troops never were used to block retreating enemy forces until the main ground forces could destroy them. It is possible that the drop of two or three airborne divisions between Falaise and Argentan, about 12 August 1944, could have closed the escape route of the Germans in the pocket there and so brought about their annihilation" (6).

22. Memorandum from General Henry H. Arnold to the Commanding General of the U.S. Command and General Staff School, "Narrative of MARKET Operation," 4 November 1944, Gavin Papers, Box 12, Folder "Military Documents Outlining Market (Airborne) Operation, Copies to Command General + Staff, Gen. H. Arnold, 18th Airborne Corps," USAMHI.

23. Eisenhower, *Crusade in Europe*, 303.

24. SHAEF intelligence summary dated 2 September 1944, quoted in Blumenson, *Breakout and Pursuit*, 685.

25. Except where noted, see Ambrose, *Supreme Commander*, 493; Blumenson, *Breakout and Pursuit*, 689–690; Charles B. MacDonald, *The Siegfried Line Campaign*, 12–13; and Warren, *Airborne Operations in World War II, European Theater*, 85–86.

26. Weigley, *Eisenhower's Lieutenants*, 260.

27. Brian Horrocks, Eversley Belfield, and H. Essame, *Corps Commander*, 80.

28. For Operation COMET, see Margry, *Operation Market-Garden*, 1:18; and Warren, *Airborne Operations in World War II*, 87–88.

29. Brereton, *Brereton Diaries*, 340.

30. Bradley quoted in Ryan, *A Bridge Too Far*, 112; Bradley and Blair, *A General's Life*, 327; Horrocks, Belfield, and Essame, *Corps Commander*, 56.

31. See Bradley and Blair, *A General's Life*, 326; and Montgomery, *Memoirs*, 251.

32. MacDonald, *The Siegfried Line Campaign*, 119.

33. Bradley and Blair, *A General's Life*, 328.

34. Montgomery, *Memoirs*, 250.

35. The meeting took place aboard the plane because Eisenhower had wrenched his knee and was all but immobile. On 2 September, while flying back from a meeting with Bradley and Patton, Eisenhower's C-47 was grounded at Chartres with a broken muffler. Captain Dick Underwood, Eisenhower's personal pilot, commandeered a small two-seat L-5 liaison plane, and the two took off for SHAEF forward headquarters at Granville. Meeting increasingly high headwinds, the L-5 soon ran low on fuel. Looking for a place to land, Underwood made for a strip of beach close to Granville. Though the landing was successful, Underwood and Eisenhower were wary of German mines; neither could recall if the area had yet been cleared. Inching his way carefully over the sand, Eisenhower slipped and hurt his knee. Underwood subsequently helped the Supreme Commander to the coastal road where they flagged down a jeep for the final leg of their journey to Granville. Eisenhower's doctor ordered a knee brace and bed rest. D. Eisenhower, *Eisenhower at War*, 439–440.

36. Eisenhower quoted in Ambrose, *Supreme Commander*, 515.

37. Montgomery, *Memoirs*, 252.

38. Eisenhower quoted in Ryan, *A Bridge Too Far*, 85, 88.

39. Letter from Patton to his wife dated 3 September 1944 in Blumenson, *Patton Papers*, 538. See also diary entry for the same day on "rock soup" strategy (538).

40. Montgomery, *Memoirs*, 251; Parks, Diary, 4 September 1944 (see chap. 14, n. 50).

41. Parks, Diary, 10 September 1944; Warren, *Airborne Operations in World War II*, 89.

42. Brereton, *Brereton Diaries*, 337–338.

43. Ibid., 338.

44. Ridgway and Martin, *Soldier*, 108.

45. Gavin quoted in Ryan, *A Bridge Too Far*, 478. For the incident involving Brereton and Browning, see also Brereton, *Brereton Diaries*, 336–341; Soffer, *Ridgway*, 65; and Parks, Diary, 3, 4, 5, 6, 10 September 1944.

46. Gavin, *On to Berlin*, 143; Huston, *Out of the Blue*, 12–13; Minutes for the 10 September Sunninghill Park Conference in Parks, Diary, 10 September 1944.

47. Gavin, *Airborne Warfare*, 74; Margry, *Operation Market-Garden*, 1:24; Warren, *Airborne Operations in World War II*, 88; Minutes for the 10 September Sunninghill Park Conference in Parks, Diary, 10 September 1944.

48. Margry, *Operation Market-Garden*, 1:18; Warren, *Airborne Operations in World War II*, 89.

49. First Allied Airborne Army, *Operations in Holland, September–November 1944*, n.d., p. 11, Ryan Collection, Box 95, Folder 6, OU.

50. Warren, *Airborne Operations in World War II*, 89–90.

51. Gavin, *On to Berlin*, 145.

52. Ibid., 148. See also Memorandum, Headquarters, 82nd Airborne Division, 23 October 1945, Ryan Collection, Box 100, Folder 3, OU; James M. Gavin to Cornelius Ryan, 18 November 1966, Ryan Collection, Box 101, Folder 9, OU.

53. Memorandum, Headquarters, 82nd Airborne Division, 23 October 1945. Browning's concept for the 101st drop around Eindhoven envisioned a "kite string" of drop zones stretching for some thirty miles north and south of the city. Taylor objected to this scheme, contending that a concentrated drop would be more effective. With Brereton's backing, Taylor flew to British Second Army headquarters for a meeting with Montgomery and Lieutenant General Miles C. Dempsey, the Second Army commander (and XXX Corps's parent headquarters). After a somewhat heated exchange, Montgomery agreed to allow Dempsey and Taylor to settle the matter between them. As a result, the 101st's thirty-mile airborne corridor was reduced to sixteen miles. Warren, *Airborne Operations in World War II*, 89.

54. James A. Huston, "The Air Invasion of Holland," 38.

55. Gavin, *On to Berlin*, 143; Memorandum, Headquarters, 82nd Airborne Division, 5 October 1945, Ryan Collection, Box 100, Folder 3, OU (capitalization in original).

56. Memorandum, Headquarters 82nd Airborne Division, "Lessons of Operation Market," 3 December 1944, Ryan Collection, Box 100, Folder 3, OU; Memorandum, Headquarters, 82nd Airborne Division, 23 October 1945.

57. Warren, *Airborne Operations in World War II*, 89.

58. First Allied Airborne Army, *Operations in Holland*, 13.

59. Ibid., 12.

60. Memorandum, Headquarters, 82nd Airborne Division, 23 October 1945 (capitalization in original).

61. James M. Gavin to John G. Westover, 25 July 1945, Gavin Papers, Box 12, Folder "Recollections of Market-Garden Operations w/ Friends in the '50s," USAMHI.

62. Gavin to Westover, 25 July 1945.

63. Office of Assistant Chief of Air Staff, Intelligence, *Airborne Assault on Holland: An Interim Report*, 12.

64. For the timing and composition of the insertions, see also Huston, *Out of the Blue*, 20; MacDonald, *The Siegfried Line Campaign*, 132–133; and Weigley, *Eisenhower's Lieutenants*, 296.

65. Warren, *Airborne Operations in World War II*, 90 (capitalization in original), 91.

66. Ibid., 95–96.

67. Memorandum, Headquarters, 82nd Airborne Division, 23 October 1945.

68. Except where noted, see Warren, *Airborne Operations in World War II*, 96, 100; and Office of Assistant Chief of Air Staff, Intelligence, *Airborne Assault on Holland*, 12–14.

69. Gavin, *On to Berlin*, 151; Margry, *Operation Market-Garden*, 1:132; Memorandum, Headquarters, 82nd Airborne Division, 23 October 1945.

70. Gavin, *Airborne Warfare*, 90 (emphasis in original).

71. Huston, *Out of the Blue*, 21–22; Warren, *Airborne Operations in World War II*, 94.

72. Warren, *Airborne Operations in World War II*, 96.

73. Gavin, *On to Berlin*, 151. See also Gavin to Blair, 21 November 1983 (see chap. 14, n. 25).

74. Gavin to Ryan, 18 November 1966.

75. Gavin, *Airborne Warfare*, 103–104.

76. For the D-day drops and glider insertions, see Devlin, *Silent Wings*, 242; Huston, "The Air Invasion of Holland," 46, 52–56; Huston, *Out of the Blue*, 7–8; Margry, *Operation Market-Garden*, 1:132; and Warren, *Airborne Operations in World War II*, 109–112.

77. Devlin, *Silent Wings*, 256; Margry, *Operation Market-Garden*, 1:276.

78. Devlin, *Silent Wings*, 242; Huston, "The Air Invasion of Holland," 46–47; Margry, *Operation Market-Garden*, 2:603.

79. Gavin, *On to Berlin*, 146–147.

80. Quoted in Ryan, *A Bridge Too* Far, 135.

81. Gavin, *On to Berlin*, 151–152.

82. Philip H. Nadler questionnaire, Ryan Collection, Box 103, Folder 12, OU.

83. Huston, "The Air Invasion of Holland," 51.

84. Message, First Allied Airborne Army, 16 September 1944, Ryan Collection, Box 95, Folder 9, OU (capitalization in original).

CHAPTER 16: A SUNDAY DRIVE IN AN AIRPLANE

1. Kurt Student, "Arnheim—Last German Victory," *Der Frontsoldat erzählt*, no. 5 (1953): 3, copy in Ryan Collection, Box 131, Folder 7, OU. Depending on the source, Student's command has been called the *First Airborne Army*, *First Paratroop Army*, or *First Parachute Army*. The latter will be used here.

2. Jodl quoted in R. Kershaw, *"It Never Snows in September,"* 21.

3. For the German situation, see ibid., 14; MacDonald, *The Siegfried Line Campaign*, 125–126; and Weigley, *Eisenhower's Lieutenants*, 255.

4. See A. Korthals Altes et al., *September 1944: Operation Market Garden*, 10; and Ryan, *A Bridge Too Far*, 18–23.

5. Dombrowski quoted in R. Kershaw, *"It Never Snows in September,"* 20; Hensel quoted in ibid., 24.

6. Quoted in Ambrose, *Supreme Commander*, 496.

7. British I Airborne Corps, "Allied Airborne Operation in Holland," n.d., p. 1, 101-(A/B)-0.3.0, Box 2008, Record Group 407, NARA II (capitalization in original).

8. MacDonald, *The Siegfried Line Campaign*, 121.

9. Margry, *Operation Market-Garden*, 1:79, 82.

10. Koch quoted in Ambrose, *Supreme Commander*, 496.

11. Smith quoted in MacDonald, *The Siegfried Line Campaign*, 122.

12. Urquhart quoted in Margry, *Operation Market-Garden*, 1:80.

13. Ibid.

14. Horrocks, Belfield, and Essame, *Corps Commander*, 82–84.

15. MacDonald, *The Siegfried Line Campaign*, 123–124.

16. Except where noted, see R. Kershaw, *"It Never Snows in September,"* 22; MacDonald, *The Siegfried Line Campaign*, 123–124; and Office of the Chief Historian, Operational (German Branch), Manuscript B-717, General Student's Post-War Interrogation Report, 22 December 1947, pp. 3–9, Ryan Collection, Box 131, Folder 7, OU.

17. R. Kershaw, *"It Never Snows in September,"* 23; MacDonald, *The Siegfried Line Campaign*, 124–125; Office of the Chief Historian, Operational (German Branch), Manuscript B-717, Student's Post-War Interrogation Report, 3–9.

18. Weigley, *Eisenhower's Lieutenants*, 293.

19. MacDonald, *The Siegfried Line Campaign*, 125. Model did not remove all his forces from around the Scheldt Estuary. He, too, knew the importance of Antwerp to the Allies, and therefore he kept just enough forces in place around the estuary to ensure Antwerp remained closed to Allied ships.

20. Ibid., 126–127.

21. Bittrich quoted in Ryan, *A Bridge Too Far*, 116. Since the war several authors have posited that the plans for MARKET-GARDEN had been compromised and this is what led Model to position the *II SS Panzer Corps* near Arnhem. The most persistent myth is that Christiaan Lindemans, a onetime Dutch Resistance fighter who had been turned by German intelligence and was generally know by his nickname, "King Kong," because of his huge size, revealed to the Germans the entire

outline of MARKET-GARDEN. However, although it may be true that Lindemans knew something of MARKET-GARDEN, he was not in a position to relay this information to his German handlers until sometime on 15 September, eleven days *after* Model ordered the *9th* and *10th SS Panzer Divisions* to Arnhem. Additionally, according to reports rendered by the German intelligence officers who debriefed Lindemans, the only thing he knew was that the British were preparing a huge attack with the object of occupying Eindhoven, news of no great account since Eindhoven was a logical objective for a continued British advance. Nothing was said about Arnhem. Yet in 1952, Oreste Pinto, a former Dutch colonel who had worked on the SHAEF staff as an interrogator, stated in his memoirs that Lindemans had given the MARKET-GARDEN plans to the Germans. Not longer thereafter, Pinto's assertions were refuted by another retired Dutch officer, Theodoor Boeree, but the rumor persisted, abetted by the fact that Lindemans, who had committed suicide while awaiting trial after the war, had had some dealings with the Dutch royal family. Hence, in 1980 a Dutch historian, Louis de Jong, again asserted that Lindemans had betrayed the plan, although with the caveat that the Germans failed to act on the information. Then in 1986, charges that Lindemans had been liquidated in order to keep quiet information that would embarrass the Dutch royals led to his body's being exhumed to see if, in fact, the body in the grave was that of Lindemans. Examination of the body revealed it to be his. Still, an official inquiry that same year resulted in the opening of the Dutch secret service files on Lindemans, which proved little. Finally, in 1997, Lindemans's suicide note surfaced and has, to date, provided satisfactory evidence that Lindemans took his own life. See Margry, *Operation Market-Garden*, 1:86; and Theodoor Boeree to James M. Gavin, 8 September 1953, Ryan Collection, Box 101, Folder 9, OU.

22. Office of Assistant Chief of Staff, G-2, Supreme Headquarters Allied Expeditionary Force, *Weekly Intelligence Summary*, 16 September 1944, p. 7, Gavin Papers, Box 12, Folder "Military Documents and Maps for Operation 'Market,' Readiness Reports of Airborne Divisions," USAMHI (capitalization in original).

23. Urquhart quoted in Margry, *Operation Market-Garden*, 1:80; Montgomery, *Memoirs*, 273.

24. Horrocks, Belfield, and Essame, *Corps Commander*, 93. Horrocks also wrote, "In the course of the war, I had received many orders and instructions from Montgomery, but this was the first time that he, the master of the tactical battle, completely underestimated the enemy strength. I had no idea whatever that the 9th [SS] and 10th [SS] Panzer Divisions were refitting just north-east of Arnhem, nor had Dempsey [the British Second Army commander] so far as I know" (93).

25. Adam Anthony Komosa, "Invasion of Holland, 'Market,'" 12 January 1968, p. 6, Ryan Collection, Box 103, Folder 5, OU; Office of Assistant Chief of Air Staff, Intelligence, *Airborne Assault on Holland*, 12; Warren, *Airborne Operations in World War II*, 102.

26. Megellas, *All the Way to Berlin*, 92. See also Komosa, "Invasion of Holland," 6.

27. Megellas, *All the Way to Berlin*, 93; Donald Douglas Lassen questionnaire, Ryan Collection, Box 104, Folder 57, OU; Jack Roger Isaacs questionnaire, Ryan Collection, Box 104, Folder 47, OU; James Emory Baugh questionnaire, Ryan

Collection, Box 106, Folder 2, OU; Jack Tallerday questionnaire, Ryan Collection, Box 105, Folder 9, OU; Hanz Karl Druener questionnaire, Ryan Collection, Box 102, Folder 21, OU.

28. Komosa, "Invasion of Holland," 6; Megellas, *All the Way to Berlin*, 104–105; Carl W. Kappel, "The Operations of Company 'H,' 504th Parachute Infantry (82nd Airborne Division) in the Invasion of Holland, 17–21 September 1944," n.d., p. 12, Ryan Collection, Box 103, Folder 1, OU.

29. British I Airborne Corps, "Allied Airborne Operation in Holland," 3; Office of Assistant Chief of Air Staff, Intelligence, *Airborne Assault on Holland*, 12; Warren, *Airborne Operations in World War II*, 101–114.

30. Gellhorn, "Rough and Tumble," n.p.

31. Office of Assistant Chief of Air Staff, Intelligence, *Airborne Assault on Holland*, 14.

32. Hugo V. Olson, interview by Frederic Kelly, 24 January 1967, Ryan Collection, Box 102, Folder 2, OU; Young quoted in Dank, *Glider Gang*, 173; Albert A. Tarbell questionnaire, Ryan Collection, Box 103, Folder 21, OU; Hugo V. Olson, interview, 24 January 1967; John Augur Holabird Jr., interview, 27 February 1969, Ryan Collection, Box 106, Folder 10, OU.

33. Warren, *Airborne Operations in World War II*, 102.

34. British I Airborne Corps, "Allied Airborne Operation in Holland," 6–8.

35. Warren, *Airborne Operations in World War II*, 107.

36. Carmichael quoted in Megellas, *All the Way to Berlin*, 96; Allen French McClain III questionnaire, Ryan Collection, Box 103, Folder 9, OU.

37. Warren, *Airborne Operations in World War II*, 107–109.

38. Orcutt quoted in Breuer, *Geronimo!* 330.

39. Office of Assistant Chief of Air Staff, Intelligence, *Airborne Assault on Holland*, 8.

40. Warren, *Airborne Operations in World War II*, 101.

41. Earl W. Boling questionnaire, Ryan Collection, Box 104, Folder 9, OU.

42. Lassen questionnaire.

43. Robert L. Machol, "The Story of the 82nd Airborne Division," n.d., p.1, Ryan Collection, Box 104, Folder 60, OU.

44. Gavin, *On to Berlin*, 159–160; Piper quoted in Michel De Trez, ed., *The Way We Were: Col. Robert N. Piper, "Bob,"* 33.

45. Quoted in Langdon, *"Ready,"* 95 (see also 93); Huston, "Air Invasion of Holland," 56; Warren, *Airborne Operations in World War II*, 109. According to Gavin, "After Sicily we were told time and again that parachute operations might succeed at night and under conditions where antiaircraft could not engage the air transports, but if they dared to fly over German antiaircraft guns in any numbers, they would be totally blown from the skies." Gavin, *On to Berlin*, 160. The 2/505th's drop put lie to this notion and vindicated a position that Gavin had long been preaching, that airborne forces could, in fact, conduct a parachute assault on prepared enemy positions.

46. Daniel B. McIlvoy to Clarence F. Montgomery, 31 October 1960, Ryan Collection, Box 104, Folder 66, OU; Daniel B. McIlvoy to Cornelius Ryan, 6 October 1967, Ryan Collection, Box 104, Folder 66, OU.

47. For the 3/505th's actions after the drop, see Langdon, *"Ready,"* 93–95; Warren, *Airborne Operations in World War II*, 109; Memorandum, Headquarters, 505th Parachute Infantry Regiment, "Invasion of Holland," 27 October 1944, Box 12456, no folder, Record Group 407, NARA II.

48. En route to the drop zone, the pilots carrying the 1/505th had somehow veered so far south that they ran into a serial dropping the 101st near Eindhoven; following some hasty navigational adjustments, they got back on track to make their drop on time and on target. See Langdon, *"Ready,"* 95; Warren, *Airborne Operations in World War II*, 109; Combat Interview "1st Bn., 505th Para. Inf., 82d Abn. Div. *Mook and Riethorst* (Major Talton W. Long)," n.d., CI-171 "82nd Airborne Division Holland, 17–26 Sep 44," Box 24057, Record Group 407, NARA II; and Combat Interview "Company B, 505th Prcht. Regt., 82d Abn. Div. (Lt. Harold E. Miller, CO)," n.d., CI-171 "82nd Airborne Division Holland, 17–26 Sep. 44," Box 24057, Record Group 407, NARA II.

49. Langdon, *"Ready,"* 95; Combat Interview "Company B, 505th Prcht. Regt., 82d Abn. Div. (Lt. Harold E. Miller, CO),"; Combat Interview "Co. B, 1st Bn., 505th Prcht. Inf., 82d Abn. Div.," n.d., CI-171 "82nd Airborne Division Holland, 17–26 Sep. 44," Box 24057, Record Group 407, NARA II; Combat Interview "1st Bn., 505th Para. Inf., 82d Abn. Div. *Mook and Riethorst* (Major Talton W. Long)."

50. Combat Interview "1st Bn., 505th Para. Inf., 82d Abn. Div. *Mook and Riethorst* (Major Talton W. Long)"; Combat Interview "Company B, 505th Prcht. Regt., 82d Abn. Div. (Lt. Harold E. Miller, CO)."

51. Warren, *Airborne Operations in World War II*, 110.

52. Combat Interview "Colonel Reuben H. Tucker, CO 504th Regt., 82d Abn. Div.," n.d., CI-171 "82nd Airborne Division Holland, 17–26 Sep. 44," Box 24057, Record Group 407, NARA II.

53. Burriss, *Strike and Hold*, 106.

54. Warren, *Airborne Operations in World War II*, 110.

55. Walter S. VanPoyck questionnaire, Ryan Collection, Box 103, Folder 24, OU. In his questionnaire VanPoyck incorrectly identified this trooper as Corporal Jon Morris. After the war, however, some of the Dutchmen who were involved with the burial turned over personal effects that clearly identified the trooper as Curtis Morris. Corporal Jon Morris was, in turn, subsequently killed a few days later. Starlyn Jorgensen, telephone interview by the author, 4 June 2001.

56. Combat Interview "Colonel Reuben H. Tucker, CO 504th Regt., 82d Abn. Div."

57. Louis A. Hauptfleisch questionnaire, Ryan Collection, Box 102, Folder 29, OU.

58. Combat Interview "82d Airborne Division," n.d., CI-171 "82nd Airborne Division Holland, 17–26 Sep. 44," Box 24057, Record Group 407, NARA II.

59. The Maas-Waal Canal was about eight miles long and was spanned by five bridges, only four of which were of immediate concern to the 82nd. These four bridges, from south to north, were located near the towns of Heumen, Blankenberg, Hatert, and Honinghutie and were designated, in order, bridges 7, 8, 9, and 10. From a tactical standpoint the most important bridges were, in relative order, 10 (Honinghutie), 7 (Heumen), 8 (Blankenberg), and then 9 (Hatert). Bridge 10

held primacy of place because it lay directly on the six-mile stretch of paved road that connected Grave with Nijmegen. Bridge 7 was next in order of importance because it connected another high-speed highway from Grave, through Malden, and then on to Nijmegen. The fifth bridge across the canal was located near Weurt, just below where the canal intersects with the Waal River west of Nijmegen and was too far north to be of any tactical significance. See "Operation Market," p. bridges 21, 382-0, Box 12344, Record Group 407, NARA II.

60. Combat Interview "1st Battalion, 504th Para. Inf., 82d Abn. Div.," n.d., CI-171 "82nd Airborne Division Holland, 17–26 Sep. 44," Box 24057, Record Group 407, NARA II.

61. For 1/504th's assault on the canal bridges, see Combat Interview "1st Battalion, 504th Para. Inf., 82d Abn. Div."; Combat Interview "Company A, 1st Bn., 504th Para. Inf., 82d Abn. Div.," n.d., CI-171 "82nd Airborne Division Holland, 17–26 Sep. 44," Box 24057, Record Group 407, NARA II; Combat Interview "Company C, 1st Bn., 504th Prcht. Regt., 82d Abn. Div.," n.d., CI-171 "82nd Airborne Division Holland, 17–26 Sep. 44," Box 24057, Record Group 407, NARA II; and "Operation Market," pp. bridges 24–29.

62. According to VanPoyck, his company was selected for this mission as a result of his losing a drawing of lots. See VanPoyck questionnaire.

63. Combat Interview "Major Edward N. Wellems, CO 2d Bn., 504th Para. Inf., 82d Abn. Div.," n.d., CI-171 "82nd Airborne Division Holland, 17–26 Sep. 44," Box 24057, Record Group 407, NARA II.

64. Combat Interview "Company E, 504th Prcht. Regt., 82d Abn. Div.," n.d., CI-171 "82nd Airborne Division Holland, 17–26 Sep. 44," Box 24057, Record Group 407, NARA II.

65. For Thompson's fight at the west end of the Grave Bridge, see, except where noted, Ryan, *A Bridge Too Far*, 240; Combat Interview "Company E, 504th Prcht. Regt., 82d Abn. Div."; Statement by John S. Thompson, "The Holland Jump," n.d., Gavin Papers, Box 12, Folder "Recollections of 504th and 508th P.I.R. Personnel on Combat Operations in Holland," USAMHI; and "Operation Market," pp. bridges 3–13.

66. Memorandum, Headquarters, 82nd Airborne Division, "Award of the Silver Star Medal," 14 September 1945, Ryan Collection, Box 103, Folder 16, OU.

67. For the taking of the east end of the Grave Bridge, except where noted, see Combat Interview "Colonel Reuben H. Tucker, CO 504th Regt., 82d Abn. Div."; Combat Interview "Company F, 2d Battalion, 504th Para. Inf. Regt.—82d A/B Division," n.d., CI-171 "82nd Airborne Division Holland, 17–26 Sep. 44," Box 24057, Record Group 407, NARA II; Combat Interview "Major Edward N. Wellems, CO 2d Bn., 504th Para. Inf., 82d Abn. Div."; "Operation Market," pp. bridges 13–17; and Warren, *Airborne Operations in World War II*, 110.

68. James M. Gavin to Major General A. C. Smith, 17 January 1954, Gavin Papers, Box 12, Folder "Recollection of Holland Operation by Gen. Gavin to Gen. Smith, Commanding General," USAMHI.

69. James M. Gavin to Cornelius Ryan, 2 October 1973, Ryan Collection, Box 101, Folder 9, OU. See also Gavin to Smith, 17 January 1954. So zealous were

82nd troopers about cutting wires that, at times, it worked against them. Soon after assembling his company on 17 September, Captain T. Moffatt Burriss, the I Company 3/504th commander, was approached by one of his troopers and asked about a large cable that "resembled the expanded torso of a giant black snake" the trooper had come across while digging a foxhole. "Cut it," came Burriss's reply. The next day Burriss got an angry phone call from Colonel Tucker, who told Burriss that the trooper had cut the international telephone cable that the division and British I Airborne Corps had planned to use for their communications back to England. "Two days later, when I Company left that position," wrote Burriss, "the linemen were still splicing wires and talking in what sounded like several languages." Burriss, *Strike and Hold*, 107–108.

70. Gavin to Smith, 17 January 1954.

71. Warren, *Airborne Operations in World War II*, 110; 82nd Airborne Division, Division Artillery After Action Review, "Unit History, Operation Market," 382-ART-0.3, Box 12429, Record Group 407, NARA II; Headquarters, 307th Airborne Engineer Battalion, "Historical Narrative," 16 October 1944, 382-ENG-0.3, Box 12433, Record Group 407, NARA II; Memorandum, Headquarters, 456th Parachute Field Artillery Battalion, "Unit History of the 456th Parachute Field Artillery Battalion from 17 September 1944 to 16 October 1944," 26 October 1944, 382-FA(456)-0.3, Box 12444, Record Group 407, NARA II.

72. Edward N. Bailey questionnaire, Ryan Collection, Box 102, Folder 10, OU; Mendez quoted in Ryan, *A Bridge Too Far*, 175.

73. Except where noted, see Warren, *Airborne Operations in World War II*, 111; Memorandum, Headquarters, 508th Parachute Infantry Regiment, "57 Days in Holland and Germany with the 508th Parachute Infantry," 7 December 1944, Ryan Collection, Box 100, Folder 3, OU; Louis G. Mendez Jr. to James M. Gavin, 8 November 1945, Ryan Collection, Box 101, Folder 9, OU; and Statement by Shields Warren Jr., n.d., Gavin Papers, Box 12, Folder "Recollections of 504th and 508th P.I.R. Personnel on Combat Operations in Holland," USAMHI.

74. Warren statement.

75. Woodrow Wilson Millsaps to Heather Chapman, 27 July 1967, Ryan Collection, Box 105, Folder 34, OU.

76. For the 1/508th jump, except where noted, see Lord, *History of the 508th Parachute Infantry*, 41–42; and Memorandum, Headquarters, 508th Parachute Infantry Regiment, "57 Days in Holland and Germany with the 508th Parachute Infantry."

77. Memorandum, Headquarters, 508th Parachute Infantry Regiment, "57 Days in Holland and Germany with the 508th Parachute Infantry"; "Operation Market," pp. bridges 32–33.

78. McLean's story from Boroughs, *Devil's Tale*, 153–155.

79. Mendez to Gavin, 8 November 1945. One of the few casualties suffered by the 3/508th on D day was the mortal wounding of the I Company commander, Lieutenant Robert Mitchell. This may have contributed to the unit's lack of aggressiveness.

80. Margry, *Operation Market-Garden*, 1:166; 82nd Airborne Division, Division Artillery After Action Review, "Unit History, Operation Market."

81. Margry, *Operation Market-Garden*, 1:166; 82nd Airborne Division, Division Artillery After Action Review, "Unit History, Operation Market."

82. Devlin, *Silent Wings*, 246, 250–251; Huston, "The Air Invasion of Holland," 56; Warren, *Airborne Operations in World War II*, 111–112.

83. Warren, *Airborne Operations in World War II*, 112.

84. Parks and Chatterton quoted in Margry, *Operation Market-Garden*, 1:170.

85. Warren, *Airborne Operations in World War II*, 112.

86. Ibid., 226–227.

87. Warren, *Airborne Operations in World War II*, 226–227; Office of Assistant Chief of Air Staff, Intelligence, *Airborne Assault on Holland*, 14.

88. Except where noted, see British I Airborne Corps, "Allied Airborne Operation in Holland," 6–8.

89. Vandeleur quoted in Margry, *Operation Market-Garden*, 1:218; Montgomery quoted in Weigley, *Eisenhower's Lieutenants*, 292–293.

90. For XXX Corps's advance, except where noted, see British I Airborne Corps, "Allied Airborne Operation in Holland," 6–8.

CHAPTER 17: THE GERMANS WERE EVERYWHERE

1. Friedrich-August Freiherr von der Heydte to James M. Gavin, 30 January 1954, Ryan Collection, Box 2, Folder 2, OU.

2. Harzer quoted in R. Kershaw, *"It Never Snows in September,"* 65–66.

3. Office of the Chief Historian, Operational (German Branch), Manuscript B-717, Student's Post-War Interrogation Report, 9 (see chap. 16, n. 16). Besides surprise, Student also experienced a sense of awe: "At noontime I suddenly was startled at my desk [by] a rushing sound which became louder and louder [Student was at his headquarters in a small cottage south of Vught, about twenty miles northwest of Eindhoven]. I stepped out onto the balcony. Everywhere I looked I saw airplanes—troop transporters and freight gliders—which flew in loose formation or one by one and very low. New units kept appearing and disappearing in the distance. I was deeply impressed by this mighty spectacle so suddenly offered to me. In this moment I didn't think of the danger of our position but I thought instead full of reflection and longing of our own earlier airborne operations. Sunk in thought, I commented to my chief of staff . . . who had hurried out onto the balcony, 'If ever I had had such mighty means at my disposal!'" See Student, "Arnheim—Last German Victory," 5 (see chap. 16, n. 1).

4. Army Group B intelligence report quoted in MacDonald, *The Siegfried Line Campaign*, 135.

5. Helmut Heiber and David M. Glantz, eds., *Hitler and His Generals, Military Conferences, 1942–1945: The First Complete Stenographic Record of the Military Situation Conferences, from Stalingrad to Berlin*, 498–499. Transcript of conference conducted 17 September 1944.

6. R. Kershaw, *"It Never Snows in September,"* 68.

7. Fullriede diary excerpted in ibid., 37.

8. Arie D. Bestebreurtje, interview by Frederick Kelly, 28–30 November 1966, Ryan Collection, Box 101, Folder 7, OU.

9. Gavin, *On to Berlin*, 153–155; Bestebreurtje, interview, 28–30 November 1966; James M. Gavin to Arie D. Bestebreurtje, 9 July 1973, Ryan Collection, Box 101, Folder 9, OU. For some reason it was several days before the Germans cut the Dutch phone system, an asset that the Americans, at least, used to their benefit with the aid of the Dutch Resistance. "It was an odd situation," wrote Gavin, "and a very amusing one and it went on for several days before the Germans took over control of the commercial telephone system. Calls were placed to Arnhem and inquiries made of the success of the landings of the British Division and calls were made to Nijmegen and other near-by towns. In fact, someone on the staff wanted to know why we didn't call Berlin and talk to Adolf Hitler. I suppose that we could have in the first twenty-four hours but there were other far more important things to do." James M. Gavin, "Airborne Army's First Test," 41–42.

10. Bittrich's order is reproduced in full in R. Kershaw, *"It Never Snows in September,"* 321.

11. See ibid., 76–78; and MacDonald, *The Siegfried Line Campaign*, 142. Much has been made about some lost orders that fell into Student's hands soon after the drop that supposedly helped the Germans divine Allied intentions and organize their countermeasures. During a postwar interrogation, Student claimed that two hours after the initial landings, "the enemy attack order for the airborne operation was in my possession at my command post. It had been captured on one of the gliders near Vught. . . . The capture of this extremely valuable document . . . greatly facilitated and speeded up the initiation and execution of all counter measures. The German command now clearly visualized the intentions as well as the forces employed in this giant airborne operation." See Office of the Chief Historian, Operational (German Branch), Manuscript B-717, Student's Post-War Interrogation Report, 10–11. The impact of this captured order, however, was minimal, and, despite Student's recollection, what was revealed was not the entire plan for Operation MARKET but only the operations order for the 101st. The glider in question was a Horsa from Browning's Corps Headquarters element, and it did not go down near Vught, but rather much farther away, near Dongen, some sixteen miles to the southwest. The glider contained a Phantom signals detachment (a special signal unit devoted to the passing of intelligence between headquarters) of eight men who, along with their two pilots, fought off the Germans for as long as they could before surrendering. In the process they also attempted to destroy their documents but apparently overlooked the 101st order. For the most detailed explanation of this incident, see Margry, *Operation Market-Garden*, 1:173. Regardless, Bittrich's warning order demonstrates that once the landings occurred, there was really no secret to what was being attempted. Furthermore, Bittrich claimed that "I never realized until after the war . . . that the Market-Garden plans had fallen into our hands. I have no idea why Model did not tell me. In any case, the plans would simply have confirmed my own opinion that the important thing to do was prevent the link-up between the airborne troops and the British Second Army—and for that, they certainly needed the bridges." Ryan, *A Bridge Too Far*, 284.

12. Walter S. VanPoyck, interview, 27 January 1988, Ryan Collection, Box 103, Folder 24, OU.

13. Entry for 0315 hours, 18 September 1944, in Headquarters, 504th Parachute Infantry Combat Team, Unit Journal, Ryan Collection, Box 103, Folder 23, OU.

14. For the taking of Grave, except where noted, see Combat Interview "Major Edward N. Wellems, CO 2d Bn., 504th Para. Inf., 82d Abn. Div."; Combat Interview "Company E, 504th Prchut. Regt., 82d Abn. Div." (see chap. 16, n. 64); Combat Interview "Company D, 2d Bn., 504th Regiment–82d A/B Div.," n.d., CI-171 "82nd Airborne Division Holland, 17–26 Sep. 44," Box 24057, Record Group 407, NARA II; and Combat Interview "Companies D and F, 2d Bn., 504th Para. Inf., 82d Abn. Div.," n.d., CI-171 "82nd Airborne Division Holland, 17–26 Sep. 44," Box 24057, Record Group 407, NARA II.

15. VanPoyck questionnaire; Robert Franco questionnaire, Ryan Collection, Box 104, Folder 33, OU.

16. Earl W. Boling questionnaire, Ryan Collection, Box 104, Folder 9, OU; Tallerday questionnaire (see chap. 16, n. 27); Richard Paul Wagner questionnaire, Ryan Collection, Box 106, Folder 34, OU.

17. Questionnaire answer by Charles Fergie, Ryan Collection, Box 104, Folder 30, OU.

18. James M. Gavin to Cornelius Ryan, 19 May 1975, Ryan Collection, Box 2, Folder 2, OU; Gavin to Smith, 17 January 1954 (see chap. 16, n. 68).

19. James M. Gavin, interview by James Blue, n.d., tape provided to author by Starlyn Jorgensen.

20. McIlvoy to Ryan, 6 October 1967 (see chap. 16, n. 46).

21. Isaacs questionnaire (see chap. 16, n. 27). Isaacs recalled that his troopers had mined the tracks, but for some reason they had been told to keep the safety pins in the mines; hence, the train passed over the mines without detonating them.

22. Paul D. Nunan questionnaire, Ryan Collection, Box 104, Folder 72, OU. See also Gavin, *On to Berlin*, 161; Langdon, *"Ready,"* 95; Donald William McKeage questionnaire, Ryan Collection, Box 104, Folder 67, OU; Tallerday questionnaire; Memorandum, Headquarters, 505th Parachute Infantry Regiment, "Invasion of Holland" (see chap. 16, n. 47); and Gavin to Smith, 17 January 1954.

23. Gavin to Westover, 25 July 1945 (see chap. 15, n. 61).

24. Warren statement.

25. "Operation Market," pp. bridges 41–42 (see chap. 16, n. 59). Interestingly, one group of soldiers from Weaver's platoon did make it to the bridge and found it almost wholly undefended. According to Private Joe Atkins, who was the point man for the platoon, as soon as they entered the city, "a crowd of people gathered around us, and we had to push our way through." Atkins and two other troopers at the head of the formation became separated from the main body but pushed on to the bridge. There they found "a few German soldiers . . . standing around a small artillery weapon." While his mates covered him, Atkins jumped into the open with his Thompson submachine gun in hand and yelled for the Germans to surrender. "The Germans were so surprised," recalled Atkins, "the six or seven defenders of the bridge gave up without resisting." The three paratroopers remained at the bridge for about an hour, guarding their prisoners and awaiting the rest of their platoon. Once darkness set in, however, and with no other friendly troops in sight, they decided to pull back, "knowing we could not hold off a German attack." They left their prisoners behind, despite entreaties by the Germans to be

taken along. "As we were leaving," added Atkins, "we could hear heavy equipment approaching the bridge." Atkins quoted in Boroughs, *Devil's Tale*, 157–158.

26. Warren statement.

27. Except where noted, see Margry, *Operation Market-Garden*, 1:164; "Operation Market," pp. bridges 39; and Memorandum, Headquarters, First Battalion, 508th Parachute Infantry, "Holland Operation," 2 November 1945, Gavin Papers, Box 12, Folder "Recollections of 504th and 508th P.I.R. Personnel on Combat Operations in Holland," USAMHI.

28. Shields Warren Jr. to Clay Blair, 3 December 1983, Blair Collection, Box 55, Folder "Warren, Shields (508)," USAMHI.

29. Except where noted, see Margry, *Operation Market-Garden*, 1:164; and Warren statement.

30. Boroughs, *Devil's Tale*, 158; Lord, *History of the 508th Parachute Infantry*, 43.

31. See also R. Kershaw, *"It Never Snows in September,"* 99–101; Boroughs, *Devil's Tale*, 159; and Margry, *Operation Market-Garden*, 1:164. It is unclear exactly what German units were at the traffic circle when A Company arrived, but the evidence suggests that there was a mixture of Waffen SS and soldiers from Henke's improvised task force. Several A Company troopers clearly remember there being SS soldiers present, who were easily identified by the twin silver runes on their collar tabs. These could only have been from the *9th SS Panzer Division*'s reconnaissance battalion since, at the time, the *10th SS Panzer Division* was still north and east of Arnhem. Additionally, that Henke's soldiers were already at the Keizer Karel Plein when the SS arrived is underscored by the fact that, during the fight for the traffic circle, American troopers engaged enemy soldiers who were fighting from foxholes that could only have been prepared by soldiers at the site long before the SS arrived. The only soldiers in Nijmegen who could have done this were those Henke had gathered under his command.

32. Warren statement.

33. Lamm quoted in Boroughs, *Devil's Tale*, 160.

34. Lamm quoted in ibid.

35. Warren statement.

36. For the fight at the traffic circle, except where noted, see Memorandum, Headquarters, First Battalion, 508th Parachute Infantry, "Holland Operation"; and "Operation Market," pp. bridges 38–39.

37. Both Gushue and Henderson were awarded the Distinguished Service Cross, Henderson's posthumously. In a unit rife with legendary characters, Alvin Henderson stood out as a man of extraordinary courage and toughness. In Normandy, Henderson found himself with some troopers who had been dropped far off course. Prowling behind enemy lines, creating as much havoc as possible, Henderson displayed an unusual talent for silencing German sentries with his knife, although eventually his luck ran out and he was taken prisoner. Not one to be deterred by such a setback, Henderson waited and, when the time was right, overpowered his guards and escaped. He then made his way to the Channel, where he stole a boat, sailed back to England, and then bummed rides to the 508th base camp; he reported present for duty about a week before the Holland drop. Boroughs, *Devil's Tale*, 162.

38. For the fight at the post office, except where noted, see Boroughs, *Devil's Tale*, 161–166; Lord, *History of the 508th Parachute Infantry*, 44–45; Warren statement; Memorandum, Headquarters, First Battalion, 508th Parachute Infantry, "Holland Operation"; "Operation Market," pp. bridges 40–41; and Shields Warren Jr. to James M. Gavin, 13 January 1954, Gavin Papers, Box 12, Folder "82nd Division's Narrative Report, Operation 'Market' for Adjutant General's Records Branch," USAMHI.

39. R. Kershaw, *"It Never Snows in September,"* 305.

40. For Warren's fight at the traffic circle, see Warren statement; "Operation Market," pp. bridges 39–41; Gavin to Westover, 25 July 1945; and Gavin, "Airborne Army's First Test," 43.

41. Gavin, *On to Berlin*, 162.

42. James M. Gavin, interview by Frederic Kelly, 20 January 1967, Ryan Collection, Box 101, Folder 10, OU.

43. Gavin to Westover, 25 July 1945.

44. Gavin to Blair, 21 November 1983 (see chap. 14, n. 25).

45. Except where noted, see Gavin to Westover, 25 July 1945; and Gavin to Smith, 17 January 1954.

46. Louis G. Mendez Jr. to James M. Gavin, 8 November 1945, Ryan Collection, Box 101, Folder 9, OU.

47. See Lord, *History of the 508th Parachute Infantry*, 46; Statement by Howard A. Greenawalt, n.d., Gavin Papers, Box 12, Folder "Recollections of Market-Garden Operations w/ Friends in the 50s," USAMHI; Mendez to Gavin, 8 November 1945; and "Operation Market," pp. bridges 42–44.

48. Gavin to Westover, 25 July 1945.

49. Romero quoted in Boroughs, *Devil's Tale*, 179.

50. For G Company's attack on the highway bridge, except where noted, see Lord, *History of the 508th Parachute Infantry*, 46; Statement by Howard A. Greenawalt; Mendez to Gavin, 8 November 1945; and "Operation Market," pp. bridges 42–44. "Gas" Leegsma, the Dutch Resistance fighter who joined G Company in the fight, has an interesting history. He remained with the company after the fight. His detailed knowledge of the area and of German dispositions proved invaluable, and eventually the G Company troopers became so enamored of him they outfitted Leegsma with an American uniform and smuggled him back to their base camp once they were withdrawn from Holland. "Gas" subsequently fought alongside G Company during most of the Battle of the Bulge before he was found out and shipped home. For his efforts, however, he was recognized by Prince Bernhard of the Netherlands and awarded with the opportunity to attend the British Royal Military College at Sandhurst. He then served in the Dutch army until 1962, attaining the rank of captain before finally returning to civilian life. See Boroughs, *Devil's Tale*, 178–179.

51. Although silent on the matter in his published works *On to Berlin* and *Airborne Warfare*, in a letter to the authors of the Army's official history of the campaign Gavin maintained that Tucker, whose regiment was southwest of Honinghutie, was to have sent a patrol up the road linking the Grave and Honinghutie Bridges on D day, while Lindquist was to have taken the bridge by attacking from

the east. Yet the division order and after-action report are both silent on the matter, although the latter does state categorically that "all initial missions of 508 were accomplished by 2030 [hours, 17 September]." See Division After Action Review, Market-Garden, n.d., 382-0.3.0, Box 12346, Record Group 407, NARA II. Moreover, in his after-action review Lindquist maintained that "the capture of Bridge #10 (Honinghutie) was not specifically prescribed as a mission for this Regiment." See Memorandum, Headquarters, 508 Parachute Infantry, "Capture of Bridge #10," 19 October 1944, Ryan Collection, Box 101, Folder 9, OU. Still, given the respective areas of responsibility, logic would dictate that Lindquist would have been given the Honinghutie mission since his regiment was much closer and much less engaged on D day.

52. Sworn Statement by Lloyd L. Polette, 16 October 1944, Ryan Collection, Box 101, Folder 9, OU.

53. For the attack on Honinghutie, see also Boroughs, *Devil's Tale*, 170–173; Lord, *History of the 508th Parachute Infantry*, 46–47; Margry, *Operation Market-Garden*, 1:289; "Operation Market," pp. bridges 33–35; Memorandum, Headquarters, 508 Parachute Infantry, "Capture of Bridge #10," 19 October 1944; and Memorandum, Headquarters 508th Parachute Infantry, "57 Days in Holland and Germany with the 508th Parachute Infantry" (see chap. 16, n. 73). Not only was there controversy about whose responsibility it was to take the Honinghutie Bridge, but there was also controversy about which regiment ultimately took it. Some have claimed a platoon from C Company, 1/504th, actually took the bridge, but evidence proves that this platoon arrived after Polette and Tomlinson were already in possession of the bridge. See Combat Interview "Company C, 1st Bn., 504th Regt.—82d A/B Division," n.d., CI-171 "82nd Airborne Division Holland, 17–16 Sep. 44," Box 24057, Record Group 407, NARA II. For his actions at Honinghutie, Polette was awarded the Distinguished Service Cross.

54. Gavin to Ryan, 2 October 1973 (see chap. 16, n. 69); Gavin, interview by James Blue.

55. MacDonald, *The Siegfried Line Campaign*, 133–134.

56. Gavin to Smith, 17 January 1954.

57. Warren, *Airborne Operations in World War II*, 121.

58. Brereton made this decision at 1800 hours on 17 September based on weather predictions from his staff meteorologists. Gavin received word that the glider flight had been postponed at 0840 hours, 18 September. The morning of 18 September, Brereton made additional changes, ordering all transports to fly the Northern Route due to low-lying clouds over the Continent that would have made navigating the Southern Route difficult. See Warren, ibid., 117–118, 120.

59. R. Kershaw, *"It Never Snows in September,"* 121–122.

60. Langdon, *"Ready,"* 96. Clarence Praeger was posthumously awarded the Distinguished Service Cross.

61. Memorandum, Headquarters 508th Parachute Infantry, "57 Days in Holland and Germany with the 508th Parachute Infantry." See also Langdon, *"Ready,"* 96; Lord, *History of the 508th Parachute Infantry*, 47; and Margry, *Operation Market-Garden*, 1:276.

62. Gavin to Smith, 17 January 1954; Memorandum, Headquarters, 307th Airborne Engineer Battalion, "Engineer Report," 19 September 1944, 382-ENG-0.3, Box 12433, Record Group 407, NARA II. Most accounts of this action have Gavin employing two engineer companies as his stopgap, but contemporaneous records clearly show that it was D Company, 307th Airborne Engineer Battalion, alone that served in this role.

63. Gavin to Westover, 25 July 1945.

64. Warren to Blair, 3 December 1983 (capitalization in original); Kurz quoted in Boroughs, *Devil's Tale*, 184. Warren validates Kurz's recollection: "As the last dual 20mm gun was knocked out, the first glider was released over the LZ." Warren to Blair, 3 December 1983. For the 1/508th attack on the landing zone, see also Devlin, *Paratrooper!* 501; Lord, *History of the 508th Parachute Infantry*, 47–48; Memorandum, Headquarters 508th Parachute Infantry, "57 Days in Holland and Germany with the 508th Parachute Infantry"; and Warren statement. For their actions on the landing zone, Kurz was awarded the Silver Star and Funk the Distinguished Service Cross.

65. William E. Ekman to James M. Gavin, 22 January 1954, Gavin Papers, Box 12, Folder "82nd Division's Narrative Report, Operation 'Market' for Adjutant General's Records Branch," USAMHI; Tallerday questionnaire; Arthur B. Schultz to Cornelius Ryan, 28 October 1966, Ryan Collection, Box 105, Folder 2, OU. For the C Company attack on the landing zone, see also Ambrose, *Citizen Soldiers*, 123; Langdon, *"Ready,"* 96; and Richard H. Brownlee questionnaire, Ryan Collection, Box 104, Folder 12, OU.

66. Warren, *Airborne Operations in World War II*, 118, 120–121; Office of Assistant Chief of Air Staff, Intelligence, *Airborne Assault on Holland*, 16.

67. Devlin, *Silent Wings*, 256–257; Warren, *Airborne Operations in World War II*, 118, 120–122; Office of Assistant Chief of Air Staff, Intelligence, *Airborne Assault on Holland*, 16.

68. Chatterton quoted in Dank, *Glider Gang*, 176.

69. Except where noted, see Warren, *Airborne Operations in World War II*, 122.

70. Ibid., 122–123; Devlin, *Silent Wings*, 259; Memorandum, Headquarters, 320th Glider Field Artillery Battalion, "Narrative Report," 26 October 1944, 382-FA(320)-0.3, Box 12436, Record Group 407, NARA II; After Action Report, "The History of the 319th Glider Field Artillery Battalion," n.d., Ryan Collection, Box 101, Folder 4, OU.

71. Warren, *Airborne Operations in World War II*, 122, 226; Division Artillery After Action Review, "Unit History, Operation Market" (see chap. 16, n. 71).

72. Sharkey and Aubin quoted in Jorgensen, *History of the 456th Parachute Field Artillery Battalion*, 160 (emphasis in original).

73. After Action Report, "The History of the 319th Glider Field Artillery Battalion."

74. Warren, *Airborne Operations in World War II*, 123–124; James Edward Duke Jr. questionnaire, Ryan Collection, Box 107, Folder 9, OU.

75. 82nd Airborne Division, Division Artillery After Action Review; Memorandum, Headquarters, 456th Parachute Field Artillery Battalion, "Unit History of the 456th Parachute Field Artillery Battalion from 17 September 1944 to 16 Octo-

ber 1944," 26 October 1944, 382-FA(456)-0, Box 12444, Record Group 407, NARA II.

76. Margry, *Operation Market-Garden*, 2:330–331.

77. Brian Horrocks, *Escape to Action*, 217; Margry, *Operation Market-Garden*, 2:340; Ryan, *A Bridge Too Far*, 411; Division After Action Review, Market-Garden.

78. Chennell quoted in Ryan, *A Bridge Too Far*, 411.

79. Altes et al., *September 1944*, 64; Margry, *Operation Market-Garden*, 2:343; Combat Interview "Colonel Reuben H. Tucker, CO 504th Regt, 82d Abn. Div." (see chap. 16, n. 52).

80. Gavin, *On to Berlin*, 169.

81. Margry, *Operation Market-Garden*, 2:345, 348.

82. Edward Goulburn, "Battle of Nijmegen," n.d., p. 1, Ryan Collection, Box 102, Folder 17, OU (capitalization in original); Moore quoted in Margry, *Operation Market-Garden*, 2:349. See also Langdon, *"Ready,"* 97; and Division After Action Review, Market-Garden.

83. Gavin, *On to Berlin*, 170.

84. Warren, *Airborne Operations in World War II*, 127–128, 131.

85. James M. Gavin to Cornelius Ryan, 13 July 1973, Ryan Collection, Box 101, Folder 9, OU.

86. Meddaugh quoted in George R. Jacobus, ed., *Echoes of the Warrior: Personal Experiences of the Enlisted Men and Officers of E Company of the 505th Parachute Infantry Regiment, 82nd Airborne, in World War II*, 369; Coyle quoted in Deryk Wills, ed., *Put on Your Boots and Parachutes*, 141; Kleijwegt quoted in Margry, *Operation Market-Garden*, 2:352.

87. Nunan questionnaire; unnamed trooper in Ambrose, *Citizen Soldiers*, 125. For Neville's attack on the railroad bridge, see also Langdon, *"Ready,"* 97–98. and Margry, *Operation Market-Garden*, 2:362.

88. Langdon, *"Ready,"* 97; Margry, *Operation Market-Garden*, 2:350.

89. Benjamin H. Vandervoort, "Nijmegen Bridge, Holland—September 1944," n.d., pp. 4–5, Gavin Papers, Box 12, Folder "82nd Division's Narrative Report, Operation 'Market' for Adjutant General's Records Branch," USAMHI.

90. Margry, *Operation Market-Garden*, 2:361; Goulburn, "Battle of Nijmegen," 4–5.

91. R. Kershaw, *"It Never Snows in September,"* 139–141; Margry, *Operation Market-Garden*, 2:358–359.

92. Ibid.

93. Goulburn, "Battle of Nijmegen," 2; Vandervoort, "Nijmegen Bridge," 4; Goulburn, "Battle of Nijmegen," 4 (capitalization in original); Vandervoort, "Nijmegen Bridge," 5–6; Coyle quoted in Wills, *Put on Your Boots and Parachutes*, 141; Goulburn, "Battle of Nijmegen," 5; Vandervoort, "Nijmegen Bridge," 8. See also William J. Meddaugh and Sam Appleby, "Attack on the Nijmegen Bridge," n.d., Ryan Collection, Box 104, Folder 4, OU; James J. Coyle questionnaire, Ryan Collection, Box 104, Folder 21, OU; Margry, *Operation Market-Garden*, 2:360; and Recollection of Earl Boling in Jacobus, *Echoes of the Warrior*, 134–139. Gavin was also disappointed with the decision and recalled later that it was his "personal belief [that the 2/505th] would have captured the south end of the Nijmegen [highway]

bridge without additional support from 30 Corps." Gavin to Smith, 17 January 1954.

94. Horrocks, Belfield, and Essame, *Corps Commander*, 109–110.

95. Ibid., 110.

CHAPTER 18: THE FINEST DIVISION IN THE WORLD TODAY

1. Memorandum, Headquarters, 307th Airborne Engineer Battalion, "Engineer Situation Report from 181800 Sept. to 191800 Sept. 1944," 19 September 1944, Box "82nd Airborne Divisions—WWII—307th Eng. Bn.—Unit History—Incident Reports," Folder "307th Abn. Eng. Bn. Reports Sept.–Nov. 44," 82nd Airborne Division Museum, Fort Bragg, NC; Memorandum, Headquarters, 307th Airborne Engineer Battalion, "Engineer Situation Report from 191800 Sept. to 201800 Sept. 1944," 20 September 1944, Box "82nd Airborne Divisions—WWII—307th Eng. Bn.—Unit History—Incident Reports," Folder "307th Abn. Eng. Bn. Reports Sept.–Nov. 44," 82nd Airborne Division Museum, Fort Bragg, NC.

2. Gavin, *On to Berlin*, 171. See also Gavin to Smith, 17 January 1954 (see chap. 16, n. 68).

3. See various entries on 19 September 1944 in Headquarters, 504th Parachute Infantry Combat Team, Unit Journal (see chap. 17, n. 13); and Combat Interview "Colonel Reuben H. Tucker, CO 504th Regt., 82d Abn. Div." (see chap. 16, n. 52).

4. Gavin, *On to Berlin*, 171. In his memoirs, Horrocks maintained that it was he and Browning who first thought of the idea of a river crossing: "We suggested to Gavin that there was only one solution—to cross the River Waal by assault boats just west of the town, while maintaining the pressure on the road bridge, and thus to capture first the railway bridge and secondly the road bridge from the rear. It is to Jim Gavin's eternal credit that he agreed at once to this apparently suicidal river crossing in the flimsy British assault boats which the U.S. troops had never even seen, let alone handled, in the swiftly running river." Horrocks, Belfield, and Essame, *Corps Commander*, 111. The evidence suggests, however, that it was Gavin who had the idea. The fact that he had his engineers looking for boats and ordered Tucker to move up to the river *before* the meeting at the schoolhouse underscores this.

5. Gavin, *On to Berlin*, 171–172; Margry, *Operation Market-Garden*, 2:490.

6. Gavin, *On to Berlin*, 170.

7. Ibid.; Margry, *Operation Market-Garden*, 2:489–490.

8. Gavin, *On to Berlin*, 171, 172.

9. Ibid., 172.

10. Gavin to Smith, 17 January 1954.

11. See also James M. Gavin to Hugo V. Olson, 18 April 1968, Ryan Collection, Box 102, Folder 17, OU; and various entries for 19 September 1944 in Headquarters, 504th Parachute Infantry Combat Team, Unit Journal.

12. Holabird, interview, 27 February 1969 (see chap. 16, n. 32); McClain questionnaire (see chap. 16, n. 36); Julian Cook, interview by Cornelius Ryan, 25 February 1968, Ryan Collection, Box 102, Folder 17, OU; Henry B. Keep, interview by Frederick Kelly, 5 December 1967, Ryan Collection, Box 103, Folder 2, OU.

13. Combat Interview "Colonel Reuben H. Tucker, CO 504th Regt., 82d Abn. Div."

14. Entry for 20 September 1944 from Chester Garrison, "Unit Journal of the 2nd Battalion 504th Parachute Infantry, 82nd Airborne Division [Holland]," unmarked box, Folder "*S-1 Journal—Holland (2/504th)," 82nd Airborne Division Museum, Fort Bragg, NC; Combat Interview "Major Edward N. Wellems, CO 2d Bn., 504th Para. Inf., 82d Abn. Div." (see chap. 16, n. 63); Combat Interview "Colonel Reuben H. Tucker, CO 504th Regt., 82d Abn. Div."

15. Margry, *Operation Market-Garden*, 2:490; Combat Interview "3d Bn., 504th Para. Inf., 82d Abn. Div.," n.d., CI-171 "82nd Airborne Division Holland, 17–26 Sep. 44," Box 24057, Record Group 407, NARA II; Combat Interview "1st Battalion, 504th Para. Inf., 82d Abn. Div." (see chap. 16, n. 60).

16. Memorandum, Headquarters, 307th Airborne Engineer Battalion, "Report of Action, 307 A/B Engr. Bn. (less 'A' and 'H&S' Cos.)," 25 September 1944, Box "82nd Airborne Division—WWII—307th Eng. Bn.—Unit History—Incident Reports," Folder "307 Eng. History Sep. to Nov. 44," 82nd Airborne Division Museum, Fort Bragg, NC; Combat Interview "3d Bn., 504th Para. Inf., 82d Abn. Div."; Combat Interview "Colonel Reuben H. Tucker, CO 504th Regt., 82d Abn. Div."

17. Keep, interview, 5 December 1967.

18. Margry, *Operation Market-Garden*, 2:490; Cook, interview, 25 February 1968; Combat Interview "3d Bn., 504th Para. Inf., 82d Abn. Div."

19. T. Moffatt Burriss, interview, 11 December 1967, Ryan Collection, Box 102, Folder 14, OU.

20. Kappel, "The Operations of Company 'H,'" 25 (see chap. 16, n. 28).

21. Henry B. Keep to his mother, 20 November 1944, Ryan Collection, Box 103, Folder 2, OU.

22. Giles A. M. Vandeleur, interview, 10 August 1967, Ryan Collection, Box 103, Folder 2, OU.

23. Chatterton quoted in Ryan, *A Bridge Too Far*, 432–433. In his book Ryan places this meeting as having occurred earlier, but that could not have been correct. The only time Gavin, Tucker, Browning, and Horrocks were present at the same place and time was at the power station right before the assault was launched.

24. See Megellas, *All the Way to Berlin*, 116; Combat Interview "3d Bn., 504th Para. Inf., 82d Abn. Div."; and Combat Interview "1st Battalion, 504th Para. Inf., 82d Abn. Div."

25. Keep, interview, 5 December 1967; Megellas, *All the Way to Berlin*, 114; Horrocks quoted in Reuben H. Tucker, untitled manuscript on Waal River crossing, n.d., Ryan Collection, Box 103, Folder 23, OU. See also Combat Interview "3d Bn., 504th Para. Inf., 82d Abn. Div." Kuehl quoted in O'Donnell, *Beyond Valor*, 114; Megellas, *All the Way to Berlin*, 114.

26. Hanz Karl Druener, interview, 5 March 1968, Ryan Collection, Box 102, Folder 21, OU; Megellas, *All the Way to Berlin*, 115.

27. Margry, *Operation Market-Garden*, 2:491; "Operation Market," p. bridges 62 (see chap. 16, n. 59).

28. Quoted in Burriss, *Strike and Hold*, 112.

29. Megellas, *All the Way to Berlin*, 116.

30. Combat Interview "Major Edward N. Wellems, CO 2d Bn., 504th Para. Inf., 82d Abn. Div."; "Operation Market," p. bridges 63; Combat Interview "Colonel Reuben H. Tucker, CO 504th Regt., 82d Abn. Div."

31. Holabird, interview, 27 February 1968; Keep to his mother, 20 November 1944.

32. Megellas, *All the Way to Berlin*, 117. See also Keep to his mother, 20 November 1944; and Combat Interview "Colonel Reuben H. Tucker, CO 504th Regt., 82d Abn. Div."

33. Carl W. Kappel, interview by Frederick Kelly, 27 February 1968, Ryan Collection, Box 103, Folder 1, OU; Albert A. Tarbell, interview, 27 February 1968, Ryan Collection, Box 103, Folder 21, OU; Keep to his mother, 20 November 1944; Burriss, *Strike and Hold*, 113; Browning quoted in Tucker, untitled manuscript on Waal River crossing. See also Kappel, "The Operations of H," 28; and "Operation Market," pp. bridges 65–66.

34. Vandeleur, interview, 10 August 1967; Kuehl quoted in O'Donnell, *Beyond Valor*, 216; Keep to his mother, 20 November 1944; Burriss, *Strike and Hold*, 112–113; Vandeleur, interview, 10 August 1967.

35. "Operation Market," p. bridges 66.

36. Mulloy quoted in Ryan, *A Bridge Too Far*, 462; Tarbell questionnaire (see chap. 16, n. 32); Burriss, *Strike and Hold*, 113; Trefetheren quoted in Combat Interview "3d Bn., 504th Para. Inf., 82d Abn. Div."

37. Megellas, *All the Way to Berlin*, 123; Kuehl in O'Donnelll, *Beyond Valor*, 217. As Cook remembered he, too, was using the prayer to time his strokes: "Being a Catholic I began to pray 'Hail Mary' (one stroke) 'Full of Grace' (2nd stroke) but since 'the Lord is with thee' is too long I kept repeating 'Hail Mary' one stroke 'full of grace' on the next stroke." See Julian Aaron Cook questionnaire, Ryan Collection, Box 102, Folder 17, OU.

38. Vandeleur, interview, 10 August 1967; Clark H. Fuller questionnaire, Ryan Collection, Box 102, Folder 25, OU; Burriss, *Strike and Hold*, 114; Keep to his mother, 20 November 1944.

39. Kuehl quoted in O'Donnell, *Beyond Valor*, 217. See also "Operation Market," pp. bridges 66.

40. See Margry, *Operation Market-Garden*, 2:491; "Operation Market," pp. bridges 71; Combat Interview "3d Bn., 504th Para. Inf., 82d Abn. Div."; and Memorandum, Headquarters, 307th Airborne Engineer Battalion, "Report of Action, 307 A/B Engr. Bn. (less 'A' and 'H&S' Cos.)," 25 September 1944, Box "82nd Airborne Division—WWII—307th Eng. Bn.—Unit History—Incident Reports," Folder "307 Eng. History Sep. to Nov. 44," 82nd Airborne Division Museum, Fort Bragg, NC. According to some accounts, thirteen boats were lost during the initial crossing attempt and another two were sunk as the engineers ferried them back across the river to pick up the second wave. However, the engineer report, probably the most reliable of the sources, stated that only ten boats returned to the south shore after taking the first wave over.

41. Megellas, *All the Way to Berlin*, 123.

42. Keep to his mother, 20 November 1944; Kappel, interview, 27 February 1968; Cook questionnaire. For the Jedlicka story, see also Ernest Patrick Murphy

questionnaire, Ryan Collection, Box 103, Folder 11, OU; and "Operation Market," pp. bridges 66.

43. See, for example, Burriss, *Strike and Hold*, 115; and Megellas, *All the Way to Berlin*, 124.

44. Hyman D. Shapiro, interview by Frederick Kelly, 10 March 1968, Ryan Collection, Box 106, Folder 52, OU; Kuehl quoted in O'Donnell, *Beyond Valor*, 217.

45. Fuller questionnaire; Burriss, *Strike and Hold*, 114; Megellas, *All the Way to Berlin*, 125.

46. Keep to his mother, 20 November 1944.

47. Kuehl in O'Donnell, *Beyond Valor*, 217.

48. Burriss, *Strike and Hold*, 115; Kappel, interview, 27 February 1968. The carnage did not stop with the troopers in the first wave. Corporal Jack Louis Bommer of the 504th's Headquarters Company crossed with the second wave and recalled, "Surrenders—I saw few of, there was not time. I did see old German men grab our M-1s and beg for mercy—they were shot point blank. Such is war." See Jack Louis Bommer questionnaire, Ryan Collection, Box 102, Folder 12, OU.

49. Megellas, *All the Way to Berlin*, 127.

50. Entry for 1545 hours, 20 September 1944, in Headquarters, 504th Parachute Infantry Combat Team, Unit Journal, and entry for 1545 hours, 20 September 1944, in Headquarters, Third Battalion, 504th Parachute Infantry, Unit Journal, "*Holland Campaign*, 17 Sept. 1944–15 Nov. 1944," Ryan Collection, Box 103, Folder 1, OU.

51. Megellas, *All the Way to Berlin*, 128.

52. See ibid., 129–130; Combat Interview "Company H, 504th Prcht. Regt., 82d Abn. Div." n.d., CI-171 "82nd Airborne Division Holland, 17–26 Sep. 44," Box 24057, Record Group 407, NARA II; "Operation Market," pp. bridges 69–70; and Combat Interview "3d Bn., 504th Para. Inf., 82d Abn. Div."

53. Theodore Finkbeiner to Heather Chapman, 12 March 1968, Ryan Collection, Box 102, Folder 24, OU. Finkbeiner was almost killed when he tried to peek over the embankment. When he did so, he found himself peering into the working end of a machine gun. Fortunately, Finkbeiner's reflexes were fast, but only barely so, for when he ducked, the muzzle blast from the machine gun knocked the wool cap he was wearing off his head.

54. See Combat Interview "Company H, 504th Prcht. Regt., 82d Abn. Div."; "Operation Market," p. bridges 70; and Combat Interview "3d Bn., 504th Para. Inf., 82d Abn. Div."

55. See Burriss, *Strike and Hold*, 120–121; Combat Interview "Company H, 504th Prcht. Regt., 82d Abn. Div."; "Operation Market," p. bridges 70; Combat Interview "3d Bn., 504th Para. Inf., 82d Abn. Div."; and Kappel, "The Operations of H," 32–33.

56. Entries for 1740 and 1745 hours, 20 September 1944, in Headquarters, 504th Parachute Infantry Combat Team, Unit Journal.

57. Sims quoted in Megellas, *All the Way to Berlin*, 132. See also Kappel, "The Operations of H," 32–34; Tarbell, interview, 27 February 1968; and McClain questionnaire.

58. Burriss, *Strike and Hold*, 121, 122. According to Burriss, other units following behind did the same: "Some weeks later," he continued, "when we moved to

the rear for a rest, I saw some of the most incredibly high stakes in poker games that I had ever witnessed. The only money used was Dutch guilders."

59. See also "Operation Market," pp. bridges 72–73; Combat Interview "3d Bn., 504th Para. Inf., 82d Abn. Div."; and Richard G. LaRiviere, Michael Kogut, and Irwin Soper, group interview, 23 March 1968, Ryan Collection, Box 103, Folder 7, OU.

60. Burriss, *Strike and Hold*, 122. See also "Operation Market," pp. bridges 72–73; and Combat Interview "3d Bn., 504th Para. Inf., 82d Abn. Div."

61. Musa quoted in Megellas, *All the Way to Berlin*, 134.

62. Breuer, *Geronimo!* 358; Burriss, *Strike and Hold*, 122–123; Margry, *Operation Market-Garden*, 2:500; La Riviere, Kogut, and Soper, interview, 23 March 1968; "Operation Market," p. bridges 73; T. Moffatt Burriss to James M. Gavin, 8 February 1979, Gavin Papers, Box 12, Folder "Letters to and from 82nd Vets on Airborne Operations in Holland, September, 1944," USAMHI.

63. Margry, *Operation Market-Garden*, 2:500–503; Goulburn, "Battle of Nijmegen," 10 (see chap. 17, n. 82). Every member, save one, of the tanks that were knocked out was taken prisoner. The one was Lance-Sergeant "Rocky" Knight, who had been wounded and left for dead by the Germans. When he recovered, he found that one of the two tanks was still in working order—it had been hit by a *panzerfaust* but had not caught fire—so he climbed aboard and drove it to join Robinson at the far end. Once there, he obtained a crew of paratroopers and spent the remainder of the night defending the shallow bridgehead. See Margry, *Operation Market-Garden*, 2:503.

64. Goulburn, "Battle of Nijmegen," 5 (capitalization in original). Captain Neville was not as sanguine about his position. After evacuating his wounded, Neville placed his three remaining tanks in locations from which they could defend along the likely avenues of approach for German armor and then placed his infantry in buildings from which they could defend the tanks. He asked Captain Smith to do the same. "The American commander, who was otherwise a most-cooperative man," wrote Neville, "refused at this stage to have anything to do with sentries on the grounds that his men need 'a good night's sleep.' Despite some forceful words from me, he remained adamant. To protect themselves against surprise attack, their so-called 'sentries' slept behind the doors, so that any intruder would have to wake them up before getting in. My own expectation was that we would be rushed during the night; and at frequent intervals we could hear the Germans moving around us." Neville quoted in Margry, *Operation Market-Garden*, 2:362.

65. Goulburn, "Battle of Nijmegen," 5. Why Goulburn did not clarify this is hard to tell. In his account of the battle, he admits to being not only tired but very sick as well. "I had a shocking cough and I [don't] think I stopped coughing for more than 30 seconds at a time" (5).

66. Ibid., 6.

67. Ibid. See also Margry, *Operation Market-Garden*, 2:496; and H. F. Stanley, "One Aspect of the Battle of Nijmegen Bridge, Tues.–Wed. 19/20 Sep. 1944," n.d., p. 2, Ryan Collection, Box 102, Folder 17, OU.

68. Vandervoort, "Nijmegen Bridge," 9.

69. Memorandum, Company "E" 505th Infantry, 12 October 1944, "Attack of the Nijmegen Bridge," reproduced in Jacobus, *Echoes of the Warrior*, 349–351.

70. Boling questionnaire (see chap. 16, n. 41).

71. Goulburn, "Battle of Nijmegen," 7. See also Margry, *Operation Market-Garden*, 2:496; Stanley, "One Aspect of the Battle of Nijmegen Bridge," 3; and R. Kershaw, *"It Never Snows in September,"* 141.

72. Meddaugh and Appleby, "Attack on the Nijmegen Bridge" (see chap. 17, n. 93); Recollection of Earl Boling in Jacobus, *Echoes of the Warrior*, 134–139.

73. Vandervoort, "Nijmegen Bridge," 11. See also Margry, *Operation Market-Garden*, 2:495.

74. Vandervoort, "Nijmegen Bridge," 10.

75. Ibid., 11; Goulburn, "Battle of Nijmegen," 8.

76. Vandervoort, "Nijmegen Bridge," 11; Langdon, *"Ready,"* 99.

77. R. Kershaw, *"It Never Snows in September,"* 99, 139–141.

78. Spencer F. Wurst, "Against All Possible Fire," 30.

79. Meddaugh and Appleby, "Attack on the Nijmegen Bridge."

80. Wurst, "Against All Possible Fire," 30; Vandervoort, "Nijmegen Bridge," 12.

81. Vandervoort, "Nijmegen Bridge," 12. See also Langdon, *"Ready,"* 99; and Wurst, "Against All Possible Fire," 28.

82. Wurst, "Against All Possible Fire," 31; Coyle in Wills, *Put on Your Boots and Parachutes*, 145.

83. Spencer F. Wurst, interview by the author, 12 September 2004; Robert Franco, interview by the author, 13 September 2004.

84. Stanley, "One Aspect of the Battle of Nijmegen Bridge," 3; Vandervoort, "Nijmegen Bridge," 13. See also Margry, *Operation Market-Garden*, 2:498; and Goulburn, "Battle of Nijmegen," 8–9.

85. Goulburn, "Battle of Nijmegen," 9.

86. Stanley, "One Aspect of the Battle of Nijmegen Bridge," 4; R. Kershaw, *"It Never Snows in September,"* 140–141, 201; Margry, *Operation Market-Garden*, 2:499.

87. R. Kershaw, *"It Never Snows in September,"* 201.

88. Horrocks, Belfield, and Essame, *Corps Commander*, 117; Harmel quoted in Ryan, *A Bridge Too Far*, 473.

89. Ryan, *A Bridge Too Far*, 473–474; R. Kershaw, *"It Never Snows in September,"* 215.

90. Harmel quoted in Ryan, *A Bridge Too Far*, 474.

91. Harmel quoted in R. Kershaw, *"It Never Snows in September,"* 201; Burris to Gavin, 8 February 1979.

92. According to reports, van Hoof was sitting atop a half-track when it was ambushed and set afire. Wounded, though not seriously, van Hoof tried limping away from the wreckage but was overtaken by a group of Germans who came running up with guns drawn. When asked who he was, van Hoof declared himself a "Dutchman, Free Netherlands." He was then searched, and, finding nothing of any importance besides his wallet, the Germans beat him prostrate. They then shot him. Van Hoof's body was found just three hundred yards from the bridge he was reputed to have saved. See Margry, *Operation Market-Garden*, 2:363; and Anton

Timmers, "The Battle for the Waalbridge at Nijmegen," 13 March 1949, pp. 10, 12–13, Ryan Collection, Box 102, Folder 17, OU.

93. See Margry, *Operation Market-Garden*, 2:363; and Timmers, "The Battle for the Waalbridge," 10.

94. Timmers, "The Battle for the Waalbridge," 12; Bestebreurtje, interview, 28–30 November 1966 (see chap. 17, n. 8). That the van Hoof story had gained so much traction Bestebreurtje attributed to officials at the Catholic university the youth attended before his death, and named them as the agents principally responsible for generating and perpetuating the story.

95. Timmers, "The Battle for the Waalbridge," 5, 15–16.

96. Ibid., 18, 20 (quote), 21. See Jones's statement in Margry, *Operation Market-Garden*, 2:505–506. Interestingly, although much of the information surrounding the failure to destroy the highway bridge is contained in Cornelius Ryan's papers, Ryan decided not to bring it to light when writing *A Bridge Too Far*. Instead, Ryan acknowledges in a footnote that "the failure of the demolition charge remains a mystery to this day," and that "although the evidence is against [van Hoof], personally I would like to believe that the young Dutchman, who was shot by the Germans for his role in the underground during the battle, was indeed responsible." Ryan, *A Bridge Too Far*, 474.

97. Timmers, "The Battle for the Waalbridge," 22.

98. Vandervoort, "Nijmegen Bridge," 12; Fullriede and Schwappacher quoted in R. Kershaw, *"It Never Snows in September,"* 212; Vandervoort, "Nijmegen Bridge," 14. In his memoir, John McKenzie related a very similar incident that occurred sometime later in the campaign. According to McKenzie, a German paratroop major who had been taken prisoner was being treated for some slight wounds when he pulled a knife and killed the attending doctor. He was then shot and killed by four nearby troopers. "This and similar incidents made the fighting between the 82d and the SS paratroopers [*sic*] a no-holds-barred, to-the-death struggle. Shooting helpless prisoners was against the rules of war and most soldiers considered it reprehensible. Nevertheless, after the doctor died, both sides began to kill prisoners without mercy. After two weeks of this pointless killing, both sides informally stopped it." McKenzie, *On Time, On Target*, 75.

99. Margry, *Operation Market-Garden*, 2:497.

100. Megellas, *All the Way to Berlin*, 131.

101. MacDonald, *The Siegfried Line Campaign*, 182.

102. Goulburn, "Battle of Nijmegen," 14.

103. See R. Kershaw, *"It Never Snows in September,"* 194; and Vandervoort, "Nijmegen Bridge," 14.

104. Once the bridges were secured and the fighting had momentarily died down, the Allies set about mopping up and consolidating their gains. This lasted well into the night. During this time, in spite of the ferocity of the battle just concluded (and counter to German assertions to the contrary), several hundred German prisoners were taken. For example, while they were checking the bridge for explosives, Lieutenant Tony Jones's sappers took eighty-one Germans prisoner, all of whom were hiding in various compartments on the bridge itself. Later on that night, Private Fred Toenjost, a 3/504th trooper who spoke excellent German, con-

vinced another 115 Germans hiding in the bottomlands to give up. And while mopping up the area south of the railroad bridge, a thirteen-man patrol from F Company, 2/504, picked up another 217 prisoners. See Margry, *Operation Market-Garden*, 2:506; Virgil F. Carmichael questionnaire, Ryan Collection, Box 102, Folder 16, OU; and Combat Interview "Major Edward N. Wellems, CO 2d Bn., 504th Para. Inf., 82d Abn. Div."

105. Downs quoted in Dawson, *Saga of the All American*, n.p.; Horrocks, *Escape to Action*, 219, 231; Brian Horrocks to James M. Gavin, 3 August 1975, Ryan Collection, Box 2, Folder 2, OU. Interestingly, engaging in a bit of counterfactual history, Horrocks also stated, "Finally, I do hope that whoever makes this film [*A Bridge Too Far*, based on Cornelius Ryan's book of the same name] about Arnhem will be careful, because there is still a lot of bitterness about this particular operation, and one doesn't want to hurt the relatives of people who were killed if this can be avoided. I will not be critical, but I know very well that if the 82nd had been given the role of the 1st British Airborne Division, the Battle would have been won, and we should have got our bridgehead over the Rhine at Arnhem."

106. Franco questionnaire (see chap. 17, n. 15); Dempsey quoted in Gavin, *On to Berlin*, 185.

CHAPTER 19: EVEN THE GODS WERE WEEPING

1. Gavin to Ryan, 13 July 1973 (see chap. 17, n. 85).

2. Gavin, *On to Berlin*, 252.

3. See also Gavin to Olson, 18 April 1968 (see chap. 18, n. 11).

4. Gavin to Ryan, 2 October 1973 (see chap. 16, n. 69).

5. See also Robert H. Wienecke to Cornelius Ryan, 14 May 1968, Ryan Collection, Box 102, Folder 6, OU.

6. Gavin, *On to Berlin*, 175. The bridge at Heumen was also called the Molenhoek Bridge in some accounts. Reflecting on this incident during an interview years later, Gavin said, "I would have been better off in Holland if I'd had an assistant division commander, particularly when I got involved on two different fronts; first crossing the Rhine River [*sic*, Gavin obviously meant the Waal River] which was a major battle in itself, and then fighting for the defense of [Molenhoek] and [Beek], which was a tremendous battle all in itself." Furthermore, Gavin was of the opinion that "you can't make a decision off of a map ten miles from the battle. You really have to get out there where you smell it, taste it, and talk to people. Lots of times they are yelling for help they don't need, and sometimes they need help and don't even know it." Gavin, interview, 29 May 1975 (see chap. 14, n. 47).

7. Wienecke to Ryan, 14 May 1968 (emphasis in original); Gavin, *On to Berlin*, 175.

8. MacDonald, *The Siegfried Line Campaign*, 177; Margry, *Operation Market-Garden*, 2:508.

9. R. Kershaw, *"It Never Snows in September,"* 189–190; Margry, *Operation Market-Garden*, 1:285; Margry, *Operation Market-Garden*, 2:508.

10. Gavin to Smith, 17 January 1954 (see chap. 16, n. 68); Gavin to Olson, 18 April 1968.

11. See also Gavin, *On to Berlin*, 175–176; Gavin, interview, 16 April 1975 (see chap. 4, n. 1); and Division After Action Review, Market-Garden (see chap. 17, n. 51).

12. Combat Interview "Co. B, 1st Bn., 505th Prcht. Inf., 82d Abn. Div." (see chap. 16, n. 49).

13. 505th Regimental S-3 Journal, entry for 1005, 19 September 1944, Ryan Collection, Box 101, Folder 4, OU (capitalization in original). See also Combat Interview "1st Bn., 505th Para. Inf., 82d Abn. Div., *Mook and Riethorst* (Major Talton W. Long)" (see chap. 16, n. 48); Combat Interview "Company B, 505th Prcht. Regt., 82d Abn. Div. (Lt. Harold E. Miller, CO)" (see chap. 16, n. 48).

14. See Memorandum, Headquarters, 456th Parachute Field Artillery Battalion, "Unit History of the 456th Parachute Field Artillery Battalion from 17 September 1944 to 16 October 1944," 26 October 1944 (see chap. 16, n. 71); and Memorandum, Headquarters, 505th Parachute Infantry, "Invasion of Holland," 27 October 1944, Ryan Collection, Box 101, Folder 4, OU.

15. Combat Interview "Co. B, 1st Bn., 505th Prcht. Inf., 82d Abn. Div."; Memorandum, Headquarters, 456th Parachute Field Artillery Battalion, "Unit History of the 456th Parachute Field Artillery Battalion from 17 September 1944 to 16 October 1944," 26 October 1944.

16. See Langdon, *"Ready,"* 98–99; Combat Interview "1st Bn., 505th Para. Inf., 82d Abn. Div. *Mook and Riethorst* (Major Talton W. Long)"; Combat Interview "Company B, 505th Prcht. Regt., 82d Abn. Div. (Lt. Harold E. Miller, CO)"; "Operation Market," pp. flanks 23–24 (se chap. 16, n. 77).

17. According to the 505th's operations journal, the British tanks reached the railroad underpass at 1440 hours. The troop commander obviously left one tank behind to provide rear security and then proceeded on toward Mook. When Gavin arrived at the underpass he saw the lone tank and reported a great deal of firing coming from Mook. Hence, it is obvious that Gavin arrived at the underpass sometime after 1440 hours, by which time Ekman already set in train plans for a counterattack. The fact that Gavin felt assured that Ekman did, in fact, have things in hand bears this out. See 505th Regimental S-3 Journal, entry for 1440, 20 September.

18. See also See Langdon, *"Ready,"* 98–99; Margry, *Operation Market-Garden*, 2:510; Ekman to Gavin, 22 January 1954 (see chap. 17, n. 65); Combat Interview "1st Bn., 505th Para. Inf., 82d Abn. Div. *Mook and Riethorst* (Major Talton W. Long)"; Combat Interview "Company B, 505th Prcht. Regt., 82d Abn. Div. (Lt. Harold E. Miller, CO)"; Combat Interview "Co. B, 1st Bn., 505th Prcht. Inf., 82d Abn. Div."; "Operation Market," pp. flanks 23–24.

19. Ekman to Gavin, 22 January 1954. See also Devlin, *Silent Wings*, 269, 280; Langdon, *"Ready,"* 99; and Margry, *Operation Market-Garden*, 2:510. A few days after the fight at Mook, Gavin wrote General Paul Williams, commander of the IX Troop Carrier Command, about glider pilots on the battlefield. "In looking back over the past weeks' operation," he wrote, "one of the outstanding things, in my opinion, and one thing in most urgent need of correction, is the method of handling our glider pilots. I do not believe there is anyone in the combat area more eager and anxious to do the correct thing and yet so completely, individually and collectively,

incapable of doing it, than the glider pilots." Though willing to help, Gavin felt that the glider pilots were a definite liability since they arrived without the proper equipment, arms, training, and organization. Furthermore, they had a tendency to wander about the battlefield and thereby "became involved in small unit actions to the extent that satisfied their passing curiosity." Gavin recommended that the pilots "should be assigned to airborne units, take training with the units and have a certain number of hours allocated periodically for flight training." Gavin was obviously influenced by the British system wherein the glider pilots formed a separate regiment and were fully trained and equipped as infantry. Gavin's recommendation came to naught, vetoed by Ridgway, who maintained that since the primary duty of glider pilots was to fly, they would stay assigned to IX Troop Carrier Command. See Gavin's letter to General Williams reproduced in Devlin, *Silent Wings*, 279.

20. Gavin to Smith, 17 January 1954; James Morris Irvin questionnaire, Ryan Collection, Box 104, Folder 46, OU.

21. See also Langdon, *"Ready,"* 98–99; Margry, *Operation Market-Garden*, 2:510; Ekman to Gavin, 22 January 1954; Combat Interview "1st Bn., 505th Para. Inf., 82d Abn. Div. *Mook and Riethorst* (Major Talton W. Long)"; Combat Interview "Company B, 505th Prcht. Regt., 82d Abn. Div. (Lt. Harold E. Miller, CO)"; Combat Interview "Co. B, 1st Bn., 505th Prcht. Inf., 82d Abn. Div."; and "Operation Market," pp. flanks 23–24.

22. See "Operation Market," pp. flanks 16–18; and Memorandum, Headquarters, 508th Parachute Infantry Regiment, "57 Days in Holland and Germany with the 508th Parachute Infantry," 7 December 1944 (see chap. 16, n. 73).

23. Lord, *History of the 508th Parachute Infantry*, 48–50; Memorandum, Headquarters, 508th Parachute Infantry Regiment, "57 Days in Holland and Germany with the 508th Parachute Infantry," 7 December 1944; Memorandum, Headquarters 307th Airborne Engineer Battalion, "Subject: Report of Action, 307 A/B Engr. Bn. (less 'A' and 'H&S' Cos.)," 25 September 1944, 382-ENG-0.3, Box 12433, Record Group 407, NARA II.

24. Because the 508th Parachute Infantry Regiment's nickname was the Red Devils, many have incorrectly assumed that this hill, which would see a good deal of fighting, was named after the regiment.

25. Memorandum, Headquarters, 508th Parachute Infantry Regiment, "57 Days in Holland and Germany with the 508th Parachute Infantry," 7 December 1944.

26. Bob White quoted in Boroughs, *Devil's Tale*, 194 (quote), 191–195. See also Lord, *History of the 508th Parachute Infantry*, 48–49; and "Operation Market," pp. flanks 14–15.

27. R. Kershaw, *"It Never Snows in September,"* 191; Margry, *Operation Market-Garden*, 2:511; Millsaps to Chapman, 27 July 1967 (see chap. 16, n. 75); "Operation Market," pp. flanks 16–18; Memorandum, Headquarters, 508th Parachute Infantry Regiment, "57 Days in Holland and Germany with the 508th Parachute Infantry," 7 December 1944; After Action Report, "The History of the 319th Glider Field Artillery Battalion" (see chap. 17, n. 70).

28. Lord, *History of the 508th Parachute Infantry*, 51; Gavin, interview, 16 April 1975; Memorandum, Headquarters, 508th Parachute Infantry Regiment, "57 Days in Holland and Germany with the 508th Parachute Infantry," 7 December

1944; Memorandum, Headquarters, 307th Airborne Engineer Battalion, "Historical Narrative," 16 October 1944 (see chap. 16, n. 71).

29. Gavin to Olson, 18 April 1968.

30. See also Gavin, *On to Berlin*, 176–177; R. Kershaw, *"It Never Snows in September,"* 192; Gavin, interview, 16 April 1975; Gavin to Smith, 17 January 1954.

31. Gavin to Smith, 17 January 1954.

32. See also 82nd Airborne Division, Division Artillery After Action Review, "Unit History, Operation Market" (see chap. 16, n. 71).

33. Gavin, *On to Berlin*, 177.

34. Lord, *History of the 508th Parachute Infantry*, 51; "Operation Market," pp. flanks 2–5.

35. Gavin, *On to Berlin*, 177; Lord, *History of the 508th Parachute Infantry*, 51; "Operation Market," pp. flanks 5–7.

36. Lord, *History of the 508th Parachute Infantry*, 51; "Operation Market," pp. flanks 7.

37. Memorandum, Headquarters, 508th Parachute Infantry Regiment, "57 Days in Holland and Germany with the 508th Parachute Infantry," 7 December 1944.

38. Blue quoted in Boroughs, *Devil's Tale*, 196.

39. See also ibid. 191–201; and Memorandum, Headquarters, 508th Parachute Infantry Regiment, "57 Days in Holland and Germany with the 508th Parachute Infantry," 7 December 1944.

40. Gavin, *On to Berlin*, 177; Endorsement letter from Headquarters, 82nd Airborne Division to C[ommanding] G[eneral], XVIII Corps (Airborne), 6 October 1944, Gavin Papers, Box 10, Folder "General Ridgway, Matthew B., Letters on Insignia, 504th Regt. Combat Team, 505th at Nijmegen + 82nd Airborne Division," USAMHI.

41. Memorandum, Headquarters, XVIII Corps Airborne to Brigadier General James M. Gavin, "Military Courtesy," 5 October 1944, Gavin Papers, Box 10, Folder "General Ridgway, Matthew B., Letters on Insignia, 504th Regt. Combat Team, 505th at Nijmegen + 82nd Airborne Division," USAMHI.

42. Endorsement letter from Headquarters, 82nd Airborne Division to C[ommanding] G[eneral], XVIII Corps (Airborne), 6 October 1944 (capitalization in original). In *On to Berlin*, Gavin wrote that he did, in fact, speak briefly with Ridgway before departing. "I told him that I had a very difficult situation on my hands and that I would have to move on." But as the following account drawn from contemporaneous sources indicates, the two did not communicate with one another at all. Gavin, *On to Berlin*, 175.

43. Jonathan Soffer wrote that Ridgway hated giving up the 82nd, and according to Maxwell Taylor, Ridgway "never really cut his emotional cord to the division" and "was bound to over-supervise its commander." According to Taylor, he "used to thank god that I didn't get the 82d. . . . I'd have been fired." See Soffer, *Ridgway*, 64.

44. Gavin, Personal Diary, 16 October 1944 (see chap. 4, n. 26); Matthew B. Ridgway to Cornelius Ryan, 24 June 1973, Ridgway Papers, Box 6, Folder "Matthew B. Ridgway, Cornelius Ryan, James Gavin, Correspondence, June–July 1973, Concerning Operation Market Garden, September, 1944," USAMHI.

45. Ridgway and Martin, *Soldier*, 110–111. Ridgway and his party began their journey to the battle area with General Lewis Brereton and select members of the First Allied Airborne Army staff. Bad weather had scotched their plans on 18 September, but the next day they flew to the Continent and landed at Antwerp, despite the airfield's being under German artillery fire. They then procured a truck and drove to Montgomery's headquarters in Brussels, where General "Freddie" de Guingand, the 21st Army Group chief of staff, lent them some jeeps that they used to drive on to the XXX Corps area, where traffic snarls slowed their progress significantly. Finally arriving at Eindhoven's center square at dusk, they found it "jammed with vehicles of all kinds—gasoline trucks, ammunition trucks, and troop transports." Suddenly, a single plane buzzed overhead and dropped two flares. "Lewis, I don't like the looks of this," said Ridgway. "Let's get the hell out of here." The two parties jumped in their jeeps and sped to a nearby park. "We'd gone about two blocks when the whole world exploded." Approximately 120 German Stukas and JU-88 bombers proceeded to tear Eindhoven apart, their task facilitated by the combustible mass of flammable and explosive-bearing vehicles in the town center. "We leaped from the jeeps and hit the ground . . . Lewis in his nice uniform scrambling for the pistol he had dropped." There they remained, "flat on our stomachs for about an hour," while Eindhoven exploded around them. When the aerial attack subsided, Ridgway could not find Brereton, so he decided to try to continue on to the 101st headquarters, a few miles north of the city. But the devastation was so widespread, with fires raging throughout the city, that there was no way that Ridgway was going to make it out that night, so he finally ordered his driver to pull off to the side of the road where he and his companions spent the night sleeping in a ditch. Brereton, meanwhile, opted to turn around and spent the night in a British military police headquarters three miles south of Eindhoven. The next morning, 20 September, Ridgway set out again, arriving at the 82nd headquarters coincident with the German attacks along the perimeter. See Brereton, *Brereton Diaries*, 349–350; and Ridgway and Martin, *Soldier*, 109–110.

46. Ridgway and Martin, *Soldier*, 111; Brereton, *Brereton Diaries*, 349.

47. Gavin quoted in Ryan, *A Bridge Too Far*, 478; Murphy and Shields quoted in Megellas, *All the Way to Berlin*, 135, 137; Burriss, *Strike and Hold*, 124.

48. Margry, *Operation Market-Garden*, 2:577.

49. Horrocks, *Escape to Action*, 221; G. Vandeleur, interview, 10 August 1967 (see chap. 18, n. 22); J. O. E. Vandeleur, interview, 18 April 1967, Ryan Collection, Box 102, Folder 17, OU.

50. Margry, *Operation Market-Garden*, 2:504.

51. Ibid., 577–580.

52. Harmel quoted in R. Kershaw, *"It Never Snows in September,"* 215.

53. Ibid., 125–126, 221; MacDonald, *The Siegfried Line Campaign*, 185.

54. G. Vandeleur, interview, 10 August 1967. See also Margry, *Operation Market-Garden*, 2:578–580.

55. G. Vandeleur, interview, 10 August 1967.

56. J. Vandeleur, interview, 18 April 1967.

57. See also Margry, *Operation Market-Garden*, 2:578–580.

58. Carter, *Devils in Baggy Pants*, 35.

59. For the actions at Oosterhout, see also Margry, *Operation Market-Garden*, 2:581–583; War Department, General Order No. 18, 15 March 1945, citation for Private John R. Towle, Company C, 504th Parachute Infantry, the 82nd Airborne Division Museum, Box "504th PIR—WWII Personal Papers," Folder "*Personal Papers—Towle, John R. (C Co., 1/504th)," Fort Bragg, NC; Combat Interview "Company C, 1st Bn., 504th Prcht. Regt., 82d Abn. Div.," n.d., CI-171 "82nd Airborne Division Holland, 17–26 Sep. 44," Box 24057, Record Group 407, NARA II; and Combat Interview "Company C, 1st Bn., 504th Regt.—82d A/B Division."

60. 505th Regimental S-3 Journal, entry for 1025, 21 September 1944. On 19 September, the 43rd Division was still in its assembly area in Belgium when it received word to move forward. Though quick to respond, the 43rd spent most of the next morning strung out on the road south of Eindhoven, held up while the 101st fended off several attacks north of the city. It took the 101st and elements of XXX Corps seven hours to push the Germans out of range of the main road, at which time the 43rd sped northward, reaching Grave by nightfall, 20 September. Curiously, instead of maintaining the momentum of the advance by moving straight into Nijmegen and across the Waal as rapidly as possible, Major General Thomas opted to employ his lead brigade, the 130th, against three subsidiary missions: taking over guard missions at the Grave Bridge and Bridge 10 (Honinghutie) and clearing Nijmegen of German stragglers. Using the lead brigade in this manner (as opposed to one of the following brigades) imposed a further delay on the brigades following, the 214th and 129th, which subsequently were not in position to renew the attack on Arnhem until the morning of 22 September. See Margry, *Operation Market-Garden*, 2:520–531.

61. Keep to his mother, 20 November 1944 (see chap. 18, n. 21).

62. Ibid.; Tarbell quoted in Megellas, *All the Way to Berlin*, 137. See also Margry, *Operation Market-Garden*, 2:521–525; "Operation Market," pp. bridges 76 and 81; Combat Interview "1st Battalion, 504th Para. Inf., 82d Abn. Div." (see chap. 16, n. 60); and Combat Interview "Colonel Reuben H. Tucker, CO 504th Regt, 82d Abn. Div." (see chap. 16, n. 52).

63. Margry, *Operation Market-Garden*, 2:460–483, 584, 610.

64. Mackenzie quoted in Margry, *Operation Market-Garden*, 2:593; First Allied Airborne Army, "Report on Operations 'Market' and 'Garden,'" n.d., pp. 14–15, 101—(A/B)—0.3.0, Box 2008, Record Group 407, NARA II.

65. First Allied Airborne Army, "Report on Operations 'Market' and 'Garden,'" n.d., 14.

66. See also Horrocks, *Escape to Action*, 224–225; Margry, *Operation Market-Garden*, 2:592–594; and First Allied Airborne Army, "Report on Operations 'Market' and 'Garden,'" n.d., 14–15.

67. Horrocks, *Escape to Action*, 228; Margry, *Operation Market-Garden*, 2:596; First Allied Airborne Army, "Report on Operations 'Market' and 'Garden,'" n.d., 15.

68. Horrocks, *Escape to Action*, 228.

69. Margry, *Operation Market-Garden*, 2:542–552.

70. Ibid., 597; First Allied Airborne Army, "Report on Operations 'Market' and 'Garden,'" n.d., 15–16.

71. 1st Airborne Division War Diary reproduced in *Operation Market-Garden*, 2:677 (capitalization in original).

72. Sosabowski and Horrocks quoted in Margry, *Operation Market-Garden*, 2:599.

73. See also Horrocks, *Escape to Action*, 229–230; Margry, *Operation Market-Garden*, 2:601; and First Allied Airborne Army, "Report on Operations 'Market' and 'Garden,'" n.d., 17.

74. Urquhart's message is reproduced in Margry, *Operation Market-Garden*, 2:682.

75. Horrocks, *Escape to Action*, 230.

76. Margry, *Operation Market-Garden*, 2:683; First Allied Airborne Army, "Report on Operations 'Market' and 'Garden,'" n.d., 18.

77. Horrocks, *Escape to Action*, 230.

78. MacDonald, *The Siegfried Line Campaign*, 204–205.

79. Administrative Instruction No. 1, Headquarters, British Airborne Troops, 12 September 1944, reproduced in Huston, "Air Invasion of Holland," 42.

80. Memorandum, Headquarters 307th A/B Medical Company, "Report of Unit Operations in Holland (September 17, 1944 to October 16, 1944)," 6 November 1944, 382-MED-0.3, Box 14713, Record Group 407, NARA II.

81. Warren, *Airborne Operations in World War II*, 131.

82. Ibid., 134–135. In addition to the parachute drops, one Waco glider loaded with one and a half tons of supplies was also delivered.

83. S-1 Journal, 325th Glider Infantry, Ryan Collection, Box 106, Folder 62, OU.

84. Ibid. See also Margry, *Operation Market-Garden*, 2:603; and Warren, *Airborne Operations in World War II*, 142.

85. Warren, *Airborne Operations in World War II*, 141–142.

86. Sanford quoted in Richlak, *Glide to Glory*, 280–281; Newcomer, Burchell, and Gelber quoted in Phil Nordyke, *All American All the Way*, 566–567; Warren R. Williams Jr. questionnaire, Ryan Collection, Box 103, Folder 26, OU.

87. See also Warren, *Airborne Operations in World War II*, 143; and Margry, *Operation Market-Garden*, 2:603.

88. Edgar L. Cook, interview, 27 January 1967, Ryan Collection, Box 106, Folder 23, OU; Oberkrieser and Fary quoted in Nordyke, *All American*, 567; Cook, interview, 27 January 1967. For the 325th's insertion, see also Warren, *Airborne Operations in World War II*, 143–144.

89. Warren, *Airborne Operations in World War II*, 144; "325th Glider Plays Important Role in Historic Operation," n.d., 382-INF(325)-0.3, Box 12448, Record Group 407, NARA II; Combat Interview "325th Glider Infantry Regiment," n.d., CI-171 "82nd Airborne Division Holland, 17–26 Sep. 44," Box 24057, Record Group 407, NARA II.

90. "325th Glider Plays Important Role in Historic Operation."

91. Combat Interview "The Attack on the Kiekberg Woods," n.d., CI-171 "82nd Airborne Division Holland, 17–26 Sep. 44," Box 24057, Record Group 407, NARA II.

92. Plebanek quoted in Nordyke, *All American*, 568.

93. See also Richlak, *Glide to Glory*, 278–279; Combat Interview "Co. B, 1st Bn., 505th Prcht. Inf., 82d Abn. Div."; 82nd Airborne Division, Division Artillery After Action Review, "Unit History, Operation Market"; and Memorandum, Headquarters, 320th Glider Field Artillery Battalion, "Narrative Report," 26 October 1944 (see chap. 17, n. 70).

94. Combat Interview "The Attack on the Kiekberg Woods"; 82nd Airborne Division, Division Artillery After Action Review, "Unit History, Operation Market"; "325th Glider Plays Important Role in Historic Operation." Fifteen British tanks were to support the main attack as well, but they never got into the fight.

95. Combat Interview "The Attack on the Kiekberg Woods."

96. See ibid. and "325th Glider Plays Important Role in Historic Operation."

97. Combat Interview "The Attack on the Kiekberg Woods."

98. Cook, interview, 27 January 1967.

99. See also Combat Interview "The Attack on the Kiekberg Woods."

100. Ibid.

101. Except where noted, see Combat Interview "The Second Attack on the Kiekberg Woods," n.d., CI-171 "82nd Airborne Division Holland, 17–26 Sep. 44," Box 24057, Record Group 407, NARA II.

102. See Leahy's account of the battle in Richlak, *Glide to Glory*, 286. See also Combat Interview "The Second Attack on the Kiekberg Woods."

103. Combat Interview "The Second Attack on the Kiekberg Woods."

104. See Leahy's account of the battle in Richlak, *Glide to Glory*, 287; and Combat Interview "The Second Attack on the Kiekberg Woods."

105. Quoted in Leahy's account of the battle in Richlak, *Glide to Glory*, 287.

106. See also Combat Interview "The Second Attack on the Kiekberg Woods."

107. See Leahy's account of the battle in Richlak, *Glide to Glory*, 287; Pierce, *Let's Go!* 212–213; and Combat Interview "The Second Attack on the Kiekberg Woods."

108. See Leahy's account of the battle in Richlak, *Glide to Glory*, 287.

109. Combat Interview "The Second Attack on the Kiekberg Woods."

110. James M. Gavin to Matthew B. Ridgway, 3 October 1944, Ridgway Papers, box 3, Folder "Matthew B. Ridgway: World War II—Personal, August to December 1944," USAMHI.

111. Except where noted, see Pierce, *Let's Go!* 213; "325th Glider Plays Important Role in Historic Operation"; Combat Interview "The Attack on the Mook Plains," n.d., CI-171 "82nd Airborne Division Holland, 17–26 Sep. 44," Box 24057, Record Group 407, NARA II; and Combat Interview "325 Glider Infantry Regiment," n.d., CI-171 "82nd Airborne Division Holland, 17-26 Sep. 44, Box 24057, Record Group 407, NARA II.

112. Combat Interview "The Attack on the Mook Plains"; Combat Interview "325 Glider Infantry Regiment."

113. Pierce, *Let's Go!* 213–215; Combat Interview "The Attack on the Mook Plains"; Combat Interview "325 Glider Infantry Regiment."

114. See Combat Interview "The Attack on the Mook Plains"; Combat Interview "325 Glider Infantry Regiment"; and "325th Glider Plays Important Role in Historic Operation."

115. Schultz to Ryan, 28 October 1966 (see chap. 17, n. 65).

116. Keep to his mother, 20 November 1944.

117. Brereton, *Brereton Diaries*, 358. Although exact figures are impossible to come by, a good estimate is that by 28 September approximately 12,100 division troopers had been delivered to the 82nd either by parachute, glider, or ground transportation. See Warren, *Airborne Operations in World War II*, 226.

CHAPTER 20: YOU ARE LOOKING AT THE SURVIVORS

1. As Eisenhower later explained, "The attractive possibility of quickly turning the German north flank led me to approve [MARKET-GARDEN and] the temporary delay in freeing the vital port of Antwerp." See *Report by the Supreme Commander to the Combined Chiefs of Staff* quoted in MacDonald, *The Siegfried Line Campaign*, 209. Yet even Field Marshal Brooke, Montgomery's avid champion, criticized his protégé's decision to move on Arnhem before clearing the approaches to Antwerp. Writing in his diary following a high-level conference chaired by Eisenhower at his Versailles headquarters, Brooke stated, "During the whole discussion one fact stood out clearly, that Antwerp must be captured with the least possible delay. I feel that Monty's strategy for once is at fault, instead of carrying out the advance on Arnhem he ought to have made certain of Antwerp in the first place. [Admiral Sir Bertram H.] Ramsay [Eisenhower's naval commander] brought this out well in discussion and criticized Monty freely. Ike nobly took all blame on himself as he had approved Monty's suggestion to operate on Arnhem." Alex Danchev and Daniel Todman, eds., *War Diaries, 1939–1945, Field Marshal Lord Alanbrooke*, 600.

2. Montgomery, *Memoirs*, 273 (emphasis in original).

3. See MacDonald, *The Siegfried Line Campaign*, 198–229. General Brereton expressed concern about Montgomery's refusal to release the 82nd and 101st as early as 5 October 1944. "The delay in the withdrawal of the 82nd and 101st Divisions from Holland is giving me grave concern. . . . 21st Army Group is resisting efforts to have them withdrawn, claiming that insufficient troops are available because of the [Scheldt] estuary operation." Brereton, *Brereton Diaries*, 361.

4. Chester A. Garrison, Unit Journal of the 2nd Battalion 504th Parachute Infantry, Gavin Papers, Box 12, Folder "Letters to and from 82nd Vets on Airborne Operations in Holland, September 1944," USAMHI.

5. McKenzie, *On Time, On Target*, 81; Boroughs, *Devil's Tale*, 205 (Studelska quote), 211–212.

6. MacDonald, *The Siegfried Line Campaign*, 199; Headquarters, First Allied Airborne Army, "First Allied Airborne Army Operations in Holland, September–November 1944," 101-A/B-0.3.0, Box 2008, Record Group 407, NARA II.

7. Brereton, *Brereton Diaries*, 363; Horrocks, *Escape to Action*, 228–229. Horrocks maintained his support of American airborne division troopers even if it meant arguing with the Supreme Commander. Sometime after the 82nd and 101st had been pulled out of Holland, Horrocks happened to meet Eisenhower at Lieutenant General William H. Simpson's U.S. Ninth Army headquarters. "Eisenhower was, I remember, very angry just then with the 82nd and 101st U.S. Airborne

Divisions which had been under my command during the Arnhem battle. After being pulled back into reserve they had apparently behaved badly and caused quite a lot of trouble in the rear area." According to Horrocks, Eisenhower muttered, "They are a disgrace to the American Army." "This was more than I could stand, because they were both magnificent divisions in battle. I leapt to their defence and suggested that it was a pity the whole American Army did not consist of similar 'disgraces.'" On hearing this Eisenhower's chief of staff, "Beetle" Smith, let out a roar. "Well, well," he said, "I never thought to hear a Britisher standing up for U.S. troops against an American general!" Horrocks, *Escape to Action*, 234–235.

8. James M. Gavin to Carlo D'Este, 2 September 1980, quoted in Carlo D'Este, *Decision in Normandy*, 288. Shortly after returning to England, Browning left First Allied Airborne Army to become chief of staff for Lord Louis Mountbatten's Southeast Asia Command, a post in which he served for the remainder of the war. Boatner, *Biographical Dictionary of World War II*, s.v. "Browning."

9. Murphy quoted in "Gen. Gavin: Guts, Glory, and Rare Modesty," *Boston Globe*, 26 February 1990, Gavin Papers, Box 7, from pamphlet titled "Lt. Gen. James. M. Gavin 82d Airborne Division," USAMHI. Gavin was promoted to major general on 20 October 1944. See "Military History of James Maurice Gavin, 017676," Gavin Papers, Box 7, Folder "Collection of Short Bibliographies of General Gavin on Military Service," USAMHI.

10. John Leh II personal history narrative, World War II Veterans Survey Project, Box "WWII Veterans Survey 82nd Airborne Division Other than Parachute Infantry Regiment," Folder "Leh, John II 80th Airborne Antiaircraft Batt.," USAMHI.

11. Foreword by General Gary E. Luck in Tom Clancy, *Airborne: A Guided Tour of an Airborne Task Force*, xiv (emphasis in original).

12. Olson, interview, 24 January 1967 (see chap. 16, n. 32); Carl von Clausewitz, *On War*, 102.

13. Megellas, *All the Way to Berlin*, 165; McKenzie, *On Time, On Target*, 73; Langdon, *"Ready,"* 102.

14. John C. H. Lee Jr., interview, n.d., Ryan Collection, Box 106, Folder 12, OU. Interestingly, Captain Lee's father was Lieutenant General John C. H. Lee, the Allied communications zone commander and, as such, the man responsible for overseeing logistics for the entire theater. General Lee was almost universally reviled by front-line commanders like Gavin, Ridgway, and Patton, who detested his imperiousness, religious zealotry (in reference to his initials, he was often mockingly called General "Jesus Christ Himself" Lee), and luxurious Parisian lifestyle.

15. James Elmo Jones questionnaire, Ryan Collection, Box 104, folder 50, OU; Boroughs, *Devil's Tale*, 212.

16. See Bruce I. Gudmundsson, *Stormtroop Tactics: Innovation in the German Army, 1914–1918*; and Timothy T. Lupfer, *The Dynamics of Doctrine: The Changes in German Tactical Doctrine During the First World War*, for two excellent discussions of the development of this technique.

17. For use of artillery, see also Memorandum, 82nd Airborne Division Artillery, "Narrative History," n.d., 382-ART-0.3, Box 12429, Record Group 407, NARA II.

18. Burriss, *Strike and Hold*, 147.

19. Combat Interview "Company I, 3d Bn., 504th Para. Regt., 82d Abn. Div.," n.d., CI-171 "82nd Airborne Division Holland, 17–26 Sep. 44," Box 24057, Record Group 407, NARA II.

20. Ibid.

21. Burriss, *Strike and Hold*, 147–148. See also Combat Interview "Company I, 3d Bn., 504th Para. Regt., 82d Abn. Div."

22. Burriss, interview, 11 December 1967 (see chap. 18, n. 19). See also Nordyke, *All American*, 571.

23. Combat Interview "Company I, 3d Bn., 504th Para. Regt., 82d Abn. Div."

24. Burriss, interview, 11 December 1967.

25. Burriss, *Strike and Hold*, 148.

26. Ibid., 148, 149.

27. Burriss, interview, 11 December 1967; Combat Interview "Company I, 3d Bn., 504th Para. Regt., 82d Abn. Div."

28. Memorandum, Headquarters, 508th Parachute Infantry Regiment, "57 Days in Holland and Germany with the 508th Parachute Infantry," 7 December 1944 (see chap. 16, n. 73). See also Lord, *History of the 508th Parachute Infantry*, 55.

29. Account from Boroughs, *Devil's Tale*, 208. Haddy earned the Silver Star for this action.

30. Arthur William Ferguson questionnaire, Ryan Collection, Box 102, Folder 23, OU. Ferguson could not recall if the trooper got his trip to the rear.

31. Williams questionnaire (see chap. 19, n. 86). See also Leonard Machol's monograph "The Story of the 82nd Airborne Division," 9 (see chap. 16, n. 43).

32. Megellas, *All the Way to Berlin*, 153–161. For his actions that night Megellas was awarded the Distinguished Service Cross.

33. Komosa, "Invasion of Holland, 'Market,'" 22–25 (see chap. 16, n. 25). It was fortunate that the first sergeant stepped in when he did. According to Komosa, "The prisoner was just a little squirt who probably didn't weigh over 90 pounds soaken [*sic*] wet. He looked and shaked [*sic*] like a starved chicken that had been abandoned in the slush for some time. But it turned out that he carried very impressive credentials. He was a pilot, a paratrooper, and a graduate of a number of schools of higher learning, including a school of the Nazi party. Why he was an ordinary soldier, I'll never know."

34. Matthew Kantala, interview, 28 February 1968, Ryan Collection, Box 102, Folder 30, OU; Hauptfleisch questionnaire (see chap. 16, n. 57).

35. Willard M. Strunk questionnaire, Ryan Collection, Box 103, Folder 18, OU.

36. See also John Richard Duncan questionnaire, Ryan Collection, Box 102, Folder 22, OU. The rumor was that Bachenheimer was captured and shot while attempting to escape, but if he was caught in German uniform, it is likely that he was shot immediately.

37. See Gavin, *On to Berlin*, 190; Headquarters, 307th Airborne Engineer Battalion, "Historical Narrative," 7 December 1944, Box "82nd Airborne Division—WWII—307th Eng. Bn.—Unit History—Incident Reports," Folder "307th Eng. History Sep. to Nov. 44," 82nd Airborne Division Museum, Fort Bragg, NC; Document titled "82nd Airborne Division—WWII Casualties and Awards," unmarked

box, 82nd Airborne Division Museum, Fort Bragg, NC. The casualty figures given are as of 12 December 1944 and break out as follows: missing in action—622; wounded in action, not returned to duty—1,796; wounded in action, returned to duty—821; injured in action, not returned to duty—327; injured in action, returned to duty—196; killed in action or died of wounds—535. Most of the casualties were sustained during the "quiet" phase of the operation, that following 28 September.

38. Hugh M. Cole, *The Ardennes: Battle of the Bulge*, 305.

39. The 101st, which was not pulled out of Holland until 27 November 1944, sustained 3,792 casualties during MARKET-GARDEN. Hardest hit of all, of course, was the British 1st Airborne Division, which sustained 6,462 casualties and was all but destroyed as a fighting force. See MacDonald, *The Siegfried Line Campaign*, 199, 205–206.

40. Headquarters, 82nd Airborne Division, "Lessons of Operation Market," 3 December 1944 (see chap. 15, n. 56).

41. Headquarters, XVIII Airborne Corps, "Operation MARKET, Airborne Phase, D to D Plus Ten, Inclusive," 4 December 1944, Gavin Papers, Box 12, Folder "Military Documents Outlining Market (Airborne) Operation, Copies to Commanding General + Staff, Gen. H. Arnold, 18th Airborne Corps," USAMHI (capitalization in original).

42. Brereton, *Brereton Diaries*, 360–361 (capitalization in original).

43. H. H. Arnold to Lewis Brereton, 13 October 1944, Gavin Papers, Box 12, Folder "Military Documents Outlining Market (Airborne) Operation, Copies to Commanding General + Staff, Gen. H. Arnold, 18th Airborne Corps," USAMHI.

44. Eisenhower and Marshall quoted in Office of the Assistant Chief of Air Staff, Intelligence, *Airborne Assault on Holland*, 44; General Board Report, United States Forces, European Theater, Study No. 16, "Organization, Equipment, and Tactical Employment of the Airborne Division," 5 (see chap. 3, n. 59).

45. Headquarters, 82nd Airborne Division, "Lessons of Operation Market," 3 December 1944.

46. Headquarters, XVIII Airborne Corps, "Operation MARKET, Airborne Phase, D to D Plus Ten, Inclusive," 4 December 1944.

47. Cole, *Ardennes*, 4–5. So optimistic were reports of German production that a few weeks before MARKET-GARDEN was launched, Reich Minister Albert Speer told Hitler that German war stocks could be expected to last through 1945.

48. Montgomery, *Memoirs*, 273 (emphasis in original); Bradley and Blair, *A General's Life*, 333 (emphasis in original).

49. Danchev and Todman, *War Diaries*, 600; Ambrose, *Supreme Commander*, 530.

50. Bradley and Blair, *A General's Life*, 350.

51. See also Cole, *Ardennes*, 9; and D. Eisenhower, *Eisenhower at War*, 534.

52. Hitler quoted in Cooper, *German Army*, 534.

53. See also Ian Kershaw, *Hitler, 1936–45: Nemesis*, 687–728; and J. W. Wheeler-Bennett, *The Nemesis of Power: The German Army in Politics, 1918–1945*, 635–689.

54. Guderian's order of the day, Göring, and Guderian's general orders quoted in Cooper, *German Army*, 535.

55. Wheeler-Bennett, *Nemesis of Power*, 679.

56. Ibid., 695–696.

57. See I. Kershaw, *Hitler*, 689, 708, 713; Gerhard L. Weinberg, *A World at Arms: A Global History of World War II*, 754–755; Charles V. P. von Luttichaur, "The German Counteroffensive in the Ardennes," 448.

58. Hitler quoted in I. Kershaw, *Hitler*, 695.

59. Excerpt from General der Flieger Werner Kriepe's diary quoted in Charles Whiting, *Ghost Front: The Ardennes Before the Battle of the Bulge*, 54. See also Cole, *Ardennes*, 1–2; and I. Kershaw, *Hitler*, 726–728.

60. During a meeting with Jodl and other staff officers eleven days after the assassination attempt, Hitler mused aloud about traitors in the ranks. "So we only have to ask ourselves today—or rather, we don't have to ask ourselves anymore: how does the enemy learn about our thinking? Why are so many things neutralized? Why does he react to everything so quickly? [—] It's probably not the perception of the Russians at all, but permanent treason, constantly being carried out by some damned little clique." Heiber and Glantz, *Hitler and His Generals*, 447. Transcript of 31 July 1944 meeting at the *Wolfsschanze* in East Prussia. All officers who were privy to the plan were vetted by Hitler personally. All were made to sign an oath of secrecy. Anyone who violated this oath faced immediate death. Once the plan was finalized and disseminated to the field for execution, the use of teletype, telephone, or radio to discuss the plan was prohibited, and all lines and radio nets were monitored to ensure compliance. The only approved method for exchanging information was by courier, all of whom were closely watched by the Gestapo and other security agents. This heightened level of operational security contributed significantly to the ability of the Germans to achieve the surprise they did. See Cole, *The Ardennes*, 49.

61. Cole, *Ardennes*, 19–21; Charles B. MacDonald, *A Time for Trumpets: The Untold Story of the Battle of the Bulge*, 32.

62. Quote by General der Panzertruppen Hasso-Eccard von Manteuffel, the *5th Panzer Army* commander, in B. H. Liddell Hart, *The German Generals Talk*, 275. The original code name for the operation was also chosen with an eye toward deception, selected so as to lead anyone hearing it to think that it referred to the German plan of defense along the Rhine River. The code name was later changed to Operation *Herbstnebel* (Autumn Mist). See Cole, *Ardennes*, 21; and Warlimont, *Inside Hitler's Headquarters*, 490.

63. Speer quoted in I. Kershaw, *Hitler*, 731; Jodl quoted in Luttichaur, "The German Counteroffensive in the Ardennes," 452. According to Luttichaur, Jodl underestimated his effect—the destruction of thirty Allied divisions would amount to almost half those on the Continent at the time.

64. See also Cole, *Ardennes*, 21; D. Eisenhower, *Eisenhower at War*, 513; MacDonald, *Time for Trumpets*, 23. According to Gerhard Weinberg, "Hitler's view of the Americans as incapable of fighting effectively and of the American home front as likely to crack under a heavy blow at the front reflected his long-held perception

of the United States. There is no evidence that Hitler realized or that a single one of his military advisors pointed out to him that, of all the major belligerents, the United States was the one which up to this point had been *least* damaged by the war and had by far the greatest recuperative powers, so that even a really major defeat was less likely to have a serious impact on its war effort." Weinberg, *A World at Arms*, 765–766 (emphasis in original).

65. Cole, *Ardennes*, 22; Liddell Hart, *The German Generals Talk*, 275.

66. Model quoted in Cole, *Ardennes*, 26; Rundstedt quoted in Liddell Hart, *The German Generals Talk*, 275 (emphasis in original). Liddell Hart gleaned these comments from various German generals after the war, and though there is an element of truth in what they had to say, there is also some self-serving. For example, other sources have quoted Rundstedt as saying, "The operational idea as such can almost be called a stroke of genius." See, for example, Cole, *Ardennes*, 20.

67. Cole, *Ardennes*, 28–32.

68. Helmut Heiber and Glantz, *Hitler and His Generals*, 536, 539, transcript of speech to senior army leaders given at the *Adlerhorst*, 12 December 1944.

69. Cole, *Ardennes*, 39; I. Kershaw, *Hitler*, 742.

70. I. Kershaw, *Hitler*, 742.

71. See Robert Alan Doughty, *The Breaking Point: Sedan and the Fall of France, 1940*, 11; MacDonald, *Time for Trumpets*, 25; and Earl F. Ziemke, "Rundstedt," 191.

72. The 28th Infantry Division arrived in the Ardennes on 19 November. It had sustained nearly 5,000 casualties during the Hürtgen fight, some of which were made up with 3,400 replacements that arrived on 1 December. The 4th Infantry Division arrived in the Ardennes on 7 December, having lost 25 percent of its strength in the Hürtgen. Replacements for the 4th had not yet arrived when the Germans launched their counteroffensive. See Whiting, *Ghost Front*, 172.

73. D. Eisenhower, *Crusade in Europe*, 338.

74. Bradley and Blair, *A Generals' Life*, 354. See also Cole, *Ardennes*, 55–56. This is not to say that Bradley did not warn Middleton to take precautions. He did tell Middleton to be prepared to conduct a fighting withdrawal in the event of a German attack and that he was to furthermore ensure than nothing of importance, especially fuel and ammunition, was in the withdrawal area. Bradley did not, however, anticipate that Middleton would be hit with a major counteroffensive and forced to withdraw as far as he ultimately had to.

75. VIII Corps intelligence and Dickson quoted in Ambrose, *Supreme Command*, 554; Sibert quoted in Bradley and Blair, *A General's Life*, 347.

76. Bradley and Blair, *A General's Life*, 349. Noel Annan, at the time a member of the SHAEF intelligence staff, made an interesting observation about the role of intelligence in Eisenhower's headquarters that sheds some light on the manner with which enemy casualty figures were ballyhooed. "Intelligence at SHAEF was governed by what one might call the 'Happy Hypothesis.' This was that the German Army had been so shattered in Normandy and battered in Russia that it was only a matter of two or three months before the war would end. When I arrived at SHAEF, I formed the impression that the intelligence appreciations were tuned to justify Eisenhower's policy to attack all along the line. This policy required intelli-

gence to report the German Army as being incapable of mounting an offensive." Annan quoted in Whiting, *Ghost Front*, 163.

77. Marshall quoted in ibid., 173; Charles B. MacDonald, *Company Commander*, 97–102; George Wilson, *If You Survive*, 188–190. Wilson wrote that his understrength company had to cover a sector more than a mile long, and one observation post was more than five miles from the company command post.

78. Quoted in Whiting, *Ghost Front*, 189–190.

79. Bradley and Blair, *A General's Life*, 351.

80. With regard to this contention two pieces of information are generally cited. The first concerns ULTRA intercepts of German state railway communications that revealed a massive movement of troops and supplies westward, along with Luftwaffe intercepts that called for the provision of local air cover over vital river crossings. The second concerns a series of coded messages sent by Baron Hiroshi Oshima, the Japanese ambassador to Germany, who summarized his meetings with German officials for his superiors in Tokyo. Those messages, which also spoke of a coming German offensive, were likewise intercepted and decoded. See MacDonald, *Time for Trumpets*, 48–49; and Whiting, *Ghost Front*, 124–126, 131–135.

81. See especially Cole, *Ardennes*, 50.

82. Ambrose, *Citizen Soldiers*, 181.

83. Gavin, Personal Diary, 28 November 1944 (see chap. 4, n. 26); William H. Tucker, *Parachute Soldier*, 107. See also Pierce, *Let's Go!* 227; Langdon, *"Ready,"* 105; and McKenzie, *On Time, On Target*, 86.

84. Gavin, Personal Diary, 28 November 1944.

85. McKenzie, *On Time, On Target*, 87.

86. See also Pierce, *Let's Go!* 227–228; and Lord, *History of the 508th Parachute Infantry*, 60.

87. Gavin, Personal Diary, 14 December 1944. See also Pierce, *Let's Go!* 227–229; Langdon, *"Ready,"* 105; Spencer F. Wurst and Gayle Wurst, *Descending from the Clouds: A Memoir of Combat in the 505 Parachute Infantry Regiment, 82d Airborne Division*, 213; Lord, *History of the 508th Parachute Infantry*, 60.

88. Gavin, Personal Diary, 15, 21 November 1944.

89. Ibid., 21 November 1944.

90. Ibid., 18 November 1944.

CHAPTER 21: TO TURN THE TIDE

1. Rufus K. Broadaway, interview by the author, 3 December 2005.

2. After Action Report, *The Story of the 82d Airborne Division in the Battle of the Belgian Bulge in the Siegfried Line and on the Roer River*, n.d., Ridgway Papers, Box 5, USAMHI.

3. Zais, "Glimpses of Gavin." See also Zais, interview, 20 January 1977 (see chap. 2, n. 28). General Ridgway was in England overseeing readiness tests for the U.S. 17th Airborne Division. General Taylor was in Washington. Ridgway sent him there in another attempt to convince the War Department that the table of organization and equipment for airborne divisions had to be increased. Other senior

leaders were in England conducting a critique of MARKET-GARDEN. See Blair, *Ridgway's Paratroopers*, 361.

4. Zais, "Glimpses of Gavin." See also Zais, interview, 20 January 1977.

5. After Action Report, *The Story of the 82d Airborne Division in the Battle of the Belgian Bulge in the Siegfried Line and on the Roer River*, n.d.

6. Headquarters, 505th Parachute Infantry, "History of Operations of the 505th Parachute Infantry Regiment in the Belgian Campaign, Part I," n.d., 382-INF(505)-0.3, Box 12460, Record Group 407, NARA II.

7. Blank narrative (see chap. 2, n. 21).

8. Pierce, *Let's Go!* 229–230.

9. Richlak, *Glide to Glory*, 305.

10. McKenzie, *On Time, On Target*, 89–92.

11. Megellas, *All the Way to Berlin*, 177–178. The 505th also had to hurriedly integrate replacements, approximately two hundred, that arrived just hours before the regiment left Camp Suippes. See Combat Interview "German Breakthrough," interview with Colonel William L. [*sic*] Ekman and Major William J. Harris, 17 February 1945, p. 1, CI-173 "82nd Airborne Div. Ardennes, 18 Dec. 44–9 Feb. 45, Box 24058, Record Group 407, NARA II.

12. Wienecke quoted in Tucker, *Parachute Soldier*, 112; Christiansen and Hillman quoted in Nordyke, *All American*, 587–588.

13. After Action Report, *The Story of the 82d Airborne Division in the Battle of the Belgian Bulge in the Siegfried Line and on the Roer River*, n.d.

14. Combat Interview "German Breakthrough," interview with Colonel William L. [*sic*] Ekman and Major William J. Harris, 17 February 1945. To illustrate the shortages in key weapons, Ekman and Harris noted that "the 505th went into battle with only 3 81mm mortars and 7 or 8 60mm mortars for the entire regiment." The authorized complement for a parachute regiment was twelve 81mm mortars and twenty-seven 60mm mortars. See General Board Report, "Organization, Equipment, and Tactical Employment of the Airborne Division," 9 (see chap. 3, n. 59).

15. Combat Interview "German Breakthrough," interview with Major J. W. Medusky, 15 February 1945, p. 1, CI-172 "82nd Airborne Div. Ardennes, 18 Dec. 44–9 Feb. 45, Box 24058, Record Group 407, NARA II. Interestingly, Medusky also pointed out that when the 508th deployed, it was about 430 troopers short of its authorized strength, the largest deficit of any of the infantry regiments. Why this was so can only be conjectured, but it may have been the result of the fact that, officially, the 508th was not part of the 82nd. Although both Ridgway and Gavin treated the 508th as an inherent part of the division, its official status was *an independent parachute regiment attached* to the 82nd. It is likely that the 508th's independent status affected its priority for replacements, personnel officers being more likely to fill larger units first. This lower priority may have also extended to replacing materiel. Years later Lieutenant Colonel Zais recalled that when he and Graves got back to their base camp, they received a call from the 508th's supply officer. "He wanted to borrow or draw from us a certain number of mortars, a certain number of rifles, light machine guns, and a variety of other things, because they had not yet reconstituted their basic load or replenished all of the weapons that they had lost in their engagement in Holland, even though they had had more time to do it than we had."

Zais talked this over with Graves, who "said that since they were in fact, going, and we didn't know whether we were going or not, that he felt we had to support them." This caused problems later on when the 517th was alerted for the Bulge as well. "We immediately began scrambling very, very hard, and sent trucks to Paris to pick up weapons to replace what we had given to the 508th. This may sound overly dramatic, but it's absolutely true; I can still see vividly, big barrels of gasoline setting out near where we were loading the trucks, and we were dipping rifles covered with cosmoline into those barrels of gasoline and handing the dripping weapons to soldiers in the trucks who were busy wiping them down with oily rags as the trucks were pulling out." Despite this last-minute scramble, Zais said that the 517th was in good shape when it got to Belgium. See Zais, interview, 20 January 1977.

16. See Combat Interview with Major John C. H. Lee Jr., 28 March 1945, p. 1, CI-173 "82nd Airborne Div. Ardennes, 18 Dec. 44–9 Feb. 45, Box 24058, Record Group 407, NARA II; Combat Interview "German Breakthrough," interview with Colonel William L. [*sic*] Ekman and Major William J. Harris, 17 February 1945; Combat Interview "German Breakthrough," interview with Major J. W. Medusky, 15 February 1945.

17. Langdon, *"Ready,"* 108.

18. Hays quoted in Nordyke, *All American*, 588; Wurst and Wurst, *Descending from the Clouds*, 215.

19. Langdon, *"Ready,"* 108.

20. Almost every 82nd trooper who participated in the Battle of the Bulge recalled the cattle trucks and the miserably long drive to the front. See, for example, Burriss, *Strike and Hold*, 165; Langdon, *"Ready,"* 108; Lord, *History of the 508th Parachute Infantry*, 60; Pierce, *Let's Go!* 230; and Wurst and Wurst, *Descending from the Clouds*, 216.

21. Neel quoted in Nordyke, *All American*, 589.

22. Bradley and Blair, *A General's Life*, 355–356.

23. See also Butcher, *My Three Years with Eisenhower*, 722; D. Eisenhower, *Eisenhower at War*, 555–557; and MacDonald, *Time for Trumpets*, 184–185.

24. Bradley and Blair, *A General's Life*, 356.

25. Reproduced in Whiting, *Ghost Front*, 196 (emphasis in original). Bradley confirmed that although he and Eisenhower looked to ULTRA intercepts in an attempt to gain a clearer picture of what was occurring, it was not until receiving this message on the morning of 17 December that their fears of a German counteroffensive were corroborated. Once the import of Rundstedt's message set in, Eisenhower's chief of staff, General Smith, turned to Bradley and said, "Well, Brad, you've been wishing for a counterattack. Now it looks as though you've got it." Bradley responded, "A counterattack, yes. But I'll be damned if I wanted one this big." Smith was referring to some statements Bradley made weeks earlier about wanting the Germans to come out to fight so he could get at them. See Bradley and Blair, *A General's Life*, 356.

26. Except where noted, see Bradley and Blair, *A General's Life*, 356–257; and D. Eisenhower, *Eisenhower at War*, 558. That this was, in fact, the U.S. Army doctrinal solution to a breakthrough, see Cole, *Ardennes*, 334.

27. See Bradley and Blair, *A General's Life*, 357; Cole, *Ardennes*, 266, 305, 312–313.

28. Cole, *Ardennes,* 332–333.

29. Ibid., 305.

30. It seems that it was "Beetle" Smith, Eisenhower's chief of staff, who chose Bastogne as the initial rendezvous point for the airborne divisions based simply on a map study of the area. Ibid., 306–307.

31. Gavin, *On to Berlin,* 205.

32. Except where noted, see Cole, *Ardennes,* 336; Gavin, *On to Berlin,* 205–206, 216–217; MacDonald, *Time for Trumpets,* 432; After Action Report, *The Story of the 82d Airborne Division in the Battle of the Belgian Bulge in the Siegfried Line and on the Roer River,* n.d.; and Ridgway's Official Diary, 18 December 1944, Ridgway Papers, Box 5a, Folder "Historical Record: Ardennes, December 17, 1944 to February 14, 1945," USAMHI.

33. After Action Report, *The Story of the 82d Airborne Division in the Battle of the Belgian Bulge in the Siegfried Line and on the Roer River,* n.d.

34. The engineers were from A Company, 291st Engineer Combat Battalion. The 291st was part of the 1111th Engineer Combat Group, which was responsible for operating sawmills and conducting road repairs throughout the Ardennes. A Company had been posted in Werbomont. When the call came to take care of the bridge at Habiemont, it could muster only fifteen engineers because the rest of the company had already been sent elsewhere. Lieutenant Edelstein, an A Company officer, was actually with the 1111th headquarters at the time, but when it fell back through Habiemont, he posted himself with the engineers at the bridge and took command there. MacDonald, *Time for Trumpets,* 243.

35. Gavin, *On to Berlin,* 216.

36. See also Cole, *Ardennes,* 343; MacDonald, *Time for Trumpets,* 242–244; and After Action Report, *The Story of the 82d Airborne Division in the Battle of the Belgian Bulge in the Siegfried Line and on the Roer River,* n.d.

37. Gavin, *On to Berlin,* 216. Hodges had ordered Middleton to evacuate his command post to Neufchâteau, Belgium, about eighteen miles southwest of Bastogne. By the time Gavin and McAuliffe arrived, most of the VIII Corps staff was already gone. Middleton and a few others had remained behind to brief the airborne commanders personally before pulling out. Cole, *Ardennes,* 315.

38. Gavin, *On to Berlin,* 216.

39. After Action Report, *The Story of the 82d Airborne Division in the Battle of the Belgian Bulge in the Siegfried Line and on the Roer River,* n.d.

40. Gavin, *On to Berlin,* 216–217; After Action Report, *The Story of the 82d Airborne Division in the Battle of the Belgian Bulge in the Siegfried Line and on the Roer River,* n.d. The flow of events and orders that resulted in the 82nd being deployed to Werbomont and the 101st to Bastogne was not as smooth and clear-cut as described here. As can be imagined, the shock and speed of the German onslaught created a great deal of confusion and chaos. For example, when he left Spa it was clear to Gavin that his division was to be diverted to Werbomont and the 101st was to continue on to Bastogne, as he had originally ordered. For some reason, however, McAuliffe believed that it was the 101st that was to head for Werbomont. How or why he got that impression is uncertain. McAuliffe, it seems, learned that the 101st was to assemble at Bastogne only when he made a detour there to speak with Mid-

dleton (McAuliffe, like Gavin, had departed ahead of the main body of the 101st). Consequently, it was Colonel Thomas L. Sherburne, the 101st's acting artillery commander at the head of the column, who diverted the 101st to Bastogne after he learned from some military policemen that McAuliffe's jeep had gone there. Finally, though he was certain that the 101st was to assemble at Bastogne, Middleton also believed that the 82nd was to assemble at Houffalize, a major road junction about ten miles northeast of Bastogne. See Cole, *Ardennes*, 307; and MacDonald, *Time for Trumpets*, 291.

41. Cole, *Ardennes*, 268; Gavin, *On to Berlin*, 217–218; MacDonald, *Time for Trumpets*, 242–244; After Action Report, *The Story of the 82d Airborne Division in the Battle of the Belgian Bulge in the Siegfried Line and on the Roer River*, n.d.

42. "History 504th Parachute Infantry, 18 December 1944–11 January 1945," n.d., p.1, 382-INF(504)-0.3, Box 12453, Record Group 407, NARA II.

43. Headquarters, 325th Glider Infantry, "The 325th Glider Infantry in the Bulge," 14 January 1945, 382-INF(325)-0.3, Box 12448, Record Group 407, NARA II.

44. Combat Interview "German Breakthrough," interview with Colonel William L. [*sic*] Ekman and Major William J. Harris, 17 February 1945.

45. Goodwin quoted in Nordyke, *All American*, 590; Wurst and Wurst, *Descending from the Clouds*, 218 (emphasis in original).

46. Cole, *Ardennes*, 268; Gavin, *On to Berlin*, 217–218; MacDonald, *A Time for Trumpets*, 242–244; After Action Report, *The Story of the 82d Airborne Division in the Battle of the Belgian Bulge in the Siegfried Line and on the Roer River*, n.d.

47. Cole, *Ardennes*, 268; Gavin, *On to Berlin*, 217–218, MacDonald, *Time for Trumpets*, 243–244; After Action Report, *The Story of the 82d Airborne Division in the Battle of the Belgian Bulge in the Siegfried Line and on the Roer River*, n.d.

48. After Action Report, *The Story of the 82d Airborne Division in the Battle of the Belgian Bulge in the Siegfried Line and on the Roer River*, n.d.

49. Edward Arn, untitled manuscript, n.d., 88, Gavin Papers, Box 12, Folder "Letters to and from 82nd Vets on Airborne Operations in Holland, September 1944," USAMHI (appears to have been misfiled).

50. Ridgway and Martin, *Soldier*, 113.

51. Ibid.,114.

52. Ridgway and Martin, *Soldier*, 144. See also Cole, *Ardennes*, 344–345; and Ridgway's Official Diary, 18, 19 December 1944.

53. Gavin, *On to Berlin*, 221.

54. See Cole, *Ardennes*, 317, 344–345; After Action Report, *The Story of the 82d Airborne Division in the Battle of the Belgian Bulge in the Siegfried Line and on the Roer River*, n.d.; Ridgway's Official Diary, 18 and 19 December 1944.

55. See Cole, *Ardennes*, 343, 345; and After Action Report, *The Story of the 82d Airborne Division in the Battle of the Belgian Bulge in the Siegfried Line and on the Roer River*, n.d.

56. See Cole, *Ardennes*, 317, 345; After Action Report, *The Story of the 82d Airborne Division in the Battle of the Belgian Bulge in the Siegfried Line and on the Roer River*, n.d.; and Combat Interview "German Breakthrough," interview with Major J. W. Medusky, 15 February 1945.

57. Cole, *Ardennes*, 268–269, 347–348.

58. *Kampfgruppe Peiper* was named after its commander, the twenty-nine-year-old SS-Obersturmbannführer Joachim Peiper. Built around Peiper's *1st SS Panzer Regiment*, the *Kampfgruppe* comprised approximately 4,000 Waffen SS soldiers, seventy-two medium tanks about evenly split between Mk IVs and Mk Vs (Panthers), a light antiaircraft battalion outfitted with 20mm self-propelled guns, twenty-five assault guns/tank destroyers, an artillery battalion of towed 105mm howitzers, a battalion of SS panzer grenadiers in eighty half-tracks, and two SS engineer companies. In addition, it had as an attachment the *501st SS Heavy Panzer Battalion* and its thirty Mk VI (Tiger) tanks. Peiper was a tall, well-educated man, fluent in both English and French, who had already acquired considerable combat experience on the Eastern Front, where his bravery earned for him Nazi Germany's highest award for valor, the Knight's Cross of the Iron Cross. He was also incredibly ruthless, with a reputation for burning down entire Russian villages and taking very few prisoners. He continued his ways during the Battle of the Bulge, and by 20 December 1944, his *Kampfgruppe* had already murdered approximately 350 American prisoners and at least 100 unarmed Belgian civilians. Included in these figures are approximately 80 Americans his Waffen SS soldiers gunned down near Malmédy. After the war an Allied tribunal found him guilty of war crimes and sentenced him to death, but due in large part to the machinations of Senator Joseph McCarthy, his sentence was eventually commuted and subsequently reduced. In all, he spent thirteen years in jail. See Boatner, *Biographical Dictionary*, s.v. "Peiper, Joachim"; Cole, *Ardennes*, 261–262; and MacDonald, *Time for Trumpets*, 197–198.

59. Cole, *Ardennes*, 268–269, 348–351; Headquarters, XVIII Corps (Airborne), "Operation Report, Ardennes, 19 December 1944 to 13 February 1945," 1 March 1945, Blair Collection, Box 48, Folder "Chrono File: Bulge," USAMHI.

60. After Action Report, *The Story of the 82d Airborne Division in the Battle of the Belgian Bulge in the Siegfried Line and on the Roer River*, n.d.

61. Gavin, *On to Berlin*, 222–223.

62. Ibid.

63. Combat Interview "504th Parachute Infantry Regt. 82nd A/B Division," CI-173 "82nd Airborne Div. Ardennes, 18 Dec. 44–9 Feb. 45," Box 24058, Record Group 407, NARA II.

64. See also Combat Interview "1st Bn., 504th Para. Inf. Regt., 82nd Inf. Div.," CI-173 "82nd Airborne Div. Ardennes, 18 Dec. 44–9 Feb. 45," Box 24058, Record Group 407, NARA II; and Reuben Tucker, interview by J. F. O'Sullivan, 28 March 1945, CI-173 "82nd Airborne Div. Ardennes, 18 Dec. 44–9 Feb. 45," Box 24058, Record Group 407, NARA II.

65. Combat Interview "1st Bn., 504th Para. Inf. Regt., 82nd Inf. Div."

66. Ibid.

67. See Combat Interview "3rd Bn., 504th Para. Inf. Regt., 82nd AB Inf. Div.," Box 24508, Folder CI-173 "82nd Airborne Div. Ardennes," 18 Dec. 44–9 Feb. 45, Record Group 407, NARA II; and Tucker, interview, 28 March 1945.

68. Gavin, *On to Berlin*, 225. See also "History 504th Parachute Infantry, 18 December 1944–11 January 1945," n.d.; Combat Interview "504th Parachute In-

fantry Regt. 82nd A/B Division"; Combat Interview "1st Bn., 504th Para. Inf. Regt., 82nd Inf. Div."; Combat Interview "3rd Bn., 504th Para. Inf. Regt., 82nd AB Inf. Div."; Tucker, interview, 28 March 1945. In *A Time for Trumpets*, Charles MacDonald took issue with the attack on Cheneux. "The story of the attack of those two companies was another of those incredibly heroic actions. But however courageous, the unsupported infantry attack across open fields laced with barbed-wire fences was as ill-conceived and senseless as many of the herdlike German assaults. . . . Afforded time to mount an attack with accurate artillery support—or even with the support of just the two tank destroyers—those companies could have taken Cheneux at far less cost and with no great forfeiture of time" (449). In one sense MacDonald is correct. With more artillery support and more time to prepare, it is possible that Tucker could have taken Cheneux at far less cost. The fact is, however, that the 504th *was* provided artillery support during the attack. On 20 December, the 376th Parachute Field Artillery Battalion fired some 120 rounds in support of the night assault by B and C Companies, and the next day fired an additional 72 rounds at specific targets in and around Cheneux. The rest of the divisional artillery, meanwhile, was supporting the other regiments in the 82nd's area of responsibility. Moreover, the plan of attack *did* call for the use of the tank destroyers, but fear of heavier German armor in the town made them ineffective. And, finally, time was something that neither Gavin nor Tucker felt they had a lot of. As Gavin pointed out in his after-action review, "It was imperative that the bridge [just north of Cheneux] be seized," and although the bridge was not seized in the traditional sense of the word (i.e., both ends were not in U.S. hands), the fact that the 504th controlled its southern exit was crucial. Had the attack been unsuccessful or delayed until a more substantial force could be brought to bear (where that force would come from is something MacDonald does not address) and the outlet to the south bank of the Amblève remained in German hands, the chance to bottle up *Kampfgruppe Peiper* might not have been realized. Furthermore, if afforded the opportunity to mass south of the river, *Kampfgruppe Peiper* could have completely overrun the 82nd, thereby tearing a huge hole in the still-forming XVIII Airborne Corps defensive line. See After Action Report, *The Story of the 82d Airborne Division in the Battle of the Belgian Bulge in the Siegfried Line and on the Roer River*, n.d., pp.2–3; Gorman S. Oswell, 376th Parachute Field Artillery Battalion S-2, "Notes on German Breakthrough History," CI-173 "82nd Airborne Div. Ardennes, 18 Dec. 44–9 Feb. 45," Box 24058, Record Group 407, NARA II; and Headquarters, 82nd Airborne Division Artillery, "Narrative History," n.d., 382-ART-0.3, Box 12429, Record Group 407, NARA II.

69. Hobbs quoted in Cole, *Ardennes*, 363–364, 348–366.

70. Ibid., 257–259.

71. Hasbrouck quoted in ibid., 393–395.

72. Hodges quoted in ibid., 395. See also 274–276.

73. XVIII Airborne Corps Diary, 20 December 1944, Ridgway Papers, Box 5a, Folder "Historical Record: Ardennes, December 17, 1944 to February 14, 1945," USAMHI.

74. After Action Report, *The Story of the 82d Airborne Division in the Battle of the Belgian Bulge in the Siegfried Line and on the Roer River*, n.d.

75. Robert W. Hasbrouck to Matthew B. Ridgway, 21 December 1944, Ridgway Papers, Box 5a, Folder "Historical Record: Ardennes, December 17, 1944 to February 14, 1945," USAMHI (emphasis in original); Gavin, *On to Berlin*, 229.

76. XVIII Airborne Corps Diary, 2237 hours, 21 December 1944.

77. XVIII Airborne Corps Diary, Record of General Ridgway's Side of Conversation with General Kean, 2350 hours, 21 December 1944 (capitalization in original).

78. Cole, *Ardennes*, 406–407. The whole issue of command of the forces in the St. Vith pocket stirred up quite a bit of controversy after the war. Several historians mistakenly wrote that Ridgway relieved Hasbrouck. Gavin, too, was under that impression. In *On to Berlin* he wrote, "General Bob Hasbrouck's handling of the 7th Armored Division was one of the great actions in the Battle of the Bulge. Yet, strangely, because of his evaluation of the division's predicament and its need to be reinforced or withdrawn, he was relieved of command by his Corps Commander [Ridgway] early in the morning of December 22. More interesting, however, is the fact that when the situation became clearer to Corps he was restored late in the afternoon of the same day" (232). In fact, it was not Hasbrouck that Ridgway relieved but General Jones. In a letter to Clay Blair, Ridgway wrote "in part this [misunderstanding] arose from the fact initially—and before I had had time to reach the CP of General Jones—I had directed that the 7th Armd Div be placed under General Jones' command, as I wanted a single commander in control on the spot in the critical situation existing in the ST VITH pocket, and Jones was senior." Continuing, Ridgway asserted that "not once did I even entertain any thought of relieving General Hasbrouck of his command." However, "as soon as I reached the CP of General Jones and observed his condition, I at once recognized that he was physically incapable of exercising command, even of his own Division, much less of the combined forces in the ST VITH pocket." Ridgway cleared the room of everyone except himself, Jones, and Colonel James B. Quill, his liaison officer to the 106th Division, and dictated an order relieving Jones of his command. See Matthew Ridgway to Clay Blair, 11 January 1984, Ridgway Papers, Box 3, Folder "World War II: Personal Files—Matthew B. Ridgway, Correspondence with James M. Gavin, September–October 1978, Concerning General Gavin's Book *On to Berlin* Covering Operations in the Mediterranean and European Theaters, 1943–1944," USAMHI. Colonel Quill's handwritten order, as dictated by Ridgway, is still extant. After being relieved, Jones was temporarily made assistant commanding general of the XVIII Airborne Corps, a sinecure in which he exercised no command responsibilities. Meanwhile, all of Jones's forces were assigned to the 7th Armored Division. See handwritten note, Headquarters, XVIII Corps, 22 December 1944, Ridgway Papers, Box 3, Folder "Matthew B. Ridgway: World War II—Personal, August to December 1944," USAMHI.

79. After Action Report, *The Story of the 82d Airborne Division in the Battle of the Belgian Bulge in the Siegfried Line and on the Roer River*, n.d.; Combat Interview "German Breakthrough," interview with Major J. W. Medusky.

80. Combat Interview "Battle of the Bulge," interview with Lieutenant Colonel James P. Kaiser, 26 March 1945, p. 2, CI-173 "82nd Airborne Div. Ardennes, 18 Dec. 44–9 Feb. 45," Box 24058, Record Group 407, NARA II; Combat Interview "German Breakthrough," interview with Colonel William L. [*sic*] Ekman and Ma-

jor William J. Harris, 17 February 1945. The engineers were from C Company, 51st Engineer Combat Battalion.

81. Peiper quoted in Cole, *Ardennes*, 267.

82. See also Combat Interview "Defense at Trois Ponts," interview with Major Robert Yates, 17 February 1945, p. 2, CI-172 "82nd Airborne Div. Ardennes, 18 Dec. 44–9 Feb. 45, Box 24058, Record Group 407, NARA II.

83. Ekman quoted in Combat Interview "German Breakthrough," interview with Colonel William L. [*sic*] Ekman and Major William J. Harris.

84. For C Company, 51st Engineer Combat Battalion's actions at Trois Pont, see Cole, *Ardennes*, 267–268; and Combat Interview "Defense at Trois Ponts," interview with Major Robert Yates, 17 February 1945. For movement of 2/505th into Trois Ponts, see Combat Interview "German Breakthrough," interview with Colonel William L. [*sic*] Ekman and Major William J. Harris, 17 February 1945.

85. Cole, *Ardennes*, 368–371.

86. Combat Interview with Colonel William Ekman, 22 March 1945, p. 3, CI-173 "82nd Airborne Div. Ardennes, 18 Dec. 44–9 Feb. 45, Box 24058, Record Group 407, NARA II; Combat Interview "German Breakthrough," interview with Colonel William L. [*sic*] Ekman and Major William J. Harris, 17 February 1945; Benjamin H. Vandervoort, "The Battle of the Bulge: Trois Ponts," n.d., manuscript in possession of the author.

87. Vandervoort, "The Battle of the Bulge: Trois Ponts," n.d. See also Combat Interview "German Breakthrough," interview with Colonel William L. [*sic*] Ekman and Major William J. Harris, 17 February 1945.

88. Vandervoort, "The Battle of the Bulge: Trois Ponts," n.d.

89. Ibid.

90. Lieutenant Eugene Doerfler quoted in Gavin, *On to Berlin*, 227. See also Jorgensen, *History of the 456th Parachute Field Artillery Battalion*, 219–220.

91. Vandervoort, "The Battle of the Bulge: Trois Ponts," n.d.; Combat Interview "Battle of the Bulge," interview with Major William Carpenter and Captain Charles E. Sammon, 27 March 1945, p. 3, CI-173 "82nd Airborne Div. Ardennes, 18 Dec. 44–9 Feb. 45, Box 24058, Record Group 407, NARA II.

92. Combat Interview "Battle of the Bulge," interview with Major William Carpenter and Captain Charles E. Sammon, 27 March 1945, p. 3, CI-173 "82nd Airborne Div. Ardennes, 18 Dec. 44–9 Feb. 45, Box 24058, Record Group 407, NARA II; Gavin, *On to Berlin*, 228; Vandervoort, "The Battle of the Bulge: Trois Ponts," n.d.

93. Combat Interview "Battle of the Bulge," interview with Major William Carpenter and Captain Charles E. Sammon, 27 March 1945.

94. Combat Interview "Battle of the Bulge," interview with Lieutenant Colonel James P. Kaiser, 26 March 1945.

95. Combat Interview "Battle of the Bulge," interview with Major William Carpenter and Captain Charles E. Sammon, 27 March 1945.

96. Combat Interview "Battle of the Bulge," interview with Lieutenant Colonel James P. Kaiser, 26 March 1945.

97. Ekman quoted in Combat Interview "German Breakthrough," interview with Colonel William L. [*sic*] Ekman and Major William J. Harris, 17 February

1945. See also Combat Interview "1st Battalion, 505th Parachute Infantry," interview with Lieutenant Colonel Talton W. Long, Captain Charles Paterson, and Staff Sergeant D. Curtis Raleigh, 26 March 1945, p. 4, CI-173 "82nd Airborne Div. Ardennes, 18 Dec. 44–9 Feb. 45, Box 24058, Record Group 407, NARA II.

98. Cole, *Ardennes*, 374.

99. Combat Interview "German Breakthrough," interview with Colonel William L. [*sic*] Ekman and Major William J. Harris, 17 February 1945.

CHAPTER 22: SINGING THE BLUES ABOUT THE RIGHT FLANK

1. Combat Interview "325th Glider Infantry Regiment," interview with Colonel George [*sic*] Billingslea, 24 March 1945, CI-172 "82nd Airborne Div. Ardennes, 18 Dec. 44–9 Feb. 45, Box 24058, Record Group 407, NARA II.

2. Combat Interview, "3rd Battalion—325th Glider Infantry," interview with Lieutenant Colonel Osmond A. Leahy, 25 March 1945, CI-172 "82nd Airborne Div. Ardennes, 18 Dec. 44–9 Feb. 45, Box 24058, Record Group 407, NARA II. See also Combat Interview, interview with Lieutenant Colonel Richard E. Gerard, 26 March 1945, CI-172 "82nd Airborne Div. Ardennes, 18 Dec. 44–9 Feb. 45, Box 24058, Record Group 407, NARA II; and Headquarters, 325th Glider Infantry, "The 325th Glider Infantry in the Bulge," 14 January 1945 (see chap. 21, n. 43).

3. Combat Interview, interview with Lieutenant Colonel Richard E. Gerard, 26 March 1945; Combat Interview, "3rd Battalion—325th Glider Infantry," interview with Lieutenant Colonel Osmond A. Leahy, 25 March 1945.

4. Apparently, Mangers thought that instead of trying to hide from the innumerable German infantry, armor, and mechanized columns moving northward, his best bet for getting back to friendly lines would be to join them. Wrapped in a Germany army snow cape, Mangers waited until dark and then slipped from his hiding place and took position at the rear of a passing German infantry column. Knowing but one word of German—*Ja*—Mangers affected the guise of a disgruntled, slightly off-kilter private by muttering incessantly (and incoherently) under his breath and answering all queries put to him with the one word of German he knew. This worked well for a time, until an inquisitive German sergeant asked him something for which *Ja* was an inappropriate reply, and he was discovered and taken prisoner. For the Mangers story, see Lord, *History of the 508th Parachute Infantry*, 62; and Combat Interview "German Breakthrough," interview with Major J. W. Medusky, 15 February 1945 (see chap. 21, n. 15).

5. Cole, *Ardennes*, 406–407; XVIII Airborne Corps Diary, 1400 hours, 22 December 1944 (see chap. 21, n. 73).

6. Combat Interview, interview with Lieutenant Colonel Richard E. Gerard, 26 March 1945; Headquarters, 325th Glider Infantry, "The 325th Glider Infantry in the Bulge," 14 January 1945.

7. Cole, *Ardennes*, 385; Combat Interview, "3rd Battalion—325th Glider Infantry," interview with Lieutenant Colonel Osmond A. Leahy, 25 March 1945.

8. See Cole, *Ardennes*, 420–421; Combat Interview "German Breakthrough," interview with Lieutenant Colonel Paul E. Wright, 17 February 1945, CI-172

"82nd Airborne Div. Ardennes, 18 Dec. 44–9 Feb. 45, Box 24058, Record Group 407, NARA II; Combat Interview, interview with Major V. R. Butz, 20 February 1945, CI-172 "82nd Airborne Div. Ardennes, 18 Dec. 44–9 Feb. 45, Box 24058, Record Group 407, NARA II; Combat Interview, "3rd Battalion—325th Glider Infantry," interview with Lieutenant Colonel Osmond A. Leahy, 25 March 1945; Combat Interview "325th Glider Infantry Regiment," interview with Colonel George [*sic*] Billingslea, 24 March 1945.

9. After Action Report, *The Story of the 82d Airborne Division in the Battle of the Belgian Bulge in the Siegfried Line and on the Roer River*, n.d. (see chap. 21, n. 2). See also Combat Interview "325th Glider Infantry Regiment," interview with Colonel George [*sic*] Billingslea, 24 March 1945. Both Gavin and Billingslea wrote afterward that this meeting occurred sometime on 22 December, although both were silent about the exact time. Given the timing of subsequent events, it is probable that this meeting occurred either very late on 21 December or very early on 22 December.

10. After Action Report, *The Story of the 82d Airborne Division in the Battle of the Belgian Bulge in the Siegfried Line and on the Roer River*, n.d.; Cole, *Ardennes*, 412.

11. Combat Interview "325th Glider Infantry Regiment," interview with Colonel George [*sic*] Billingslea, 24 March 1945.

12. Gavin, *On to Berlin*, 231.

13. See also After Action Report, *The Story of the 82d Airborne Division in the Battle of the Belgian Bulge in the Siegfried Line and on the Roer River*, n.d.; Combat Interview "325th Glider Infantry Regiment," interview with Colonel George [*sic*] Billingslea, 24 March 1945; Combat Interview with Lieutenant Colonel Charles W. Major and Captain Herbert L. Little, 25 March 1945, CI-172 "82nd Airborne Div. Ardennes, 18 Dec. 44–9 Feb. 45, Box 24058, Record Group 407, NARA II.

14. Memorandum, Headquarters, 307th Airborne Engineer Battalion, "Report of Demolition Party," 23 December 1944, Gavin Papers, Box 12, Folder "Letters to and from 82nd Vets on Airborne Operations in Holland, September, 1944," USAMHI; After Action Report, *The Story of the 82d Airborne Division in the Battle of the Belgian Bulge in the Siegfried Line and on the Roer River*, n.d.

15. See Cole, *Ardennes*, 388–389; R. Ernest Dupuy, "Parker's Crossroads," 14.

16. The rest of the 589th had been ambushed and destroyed during the retreat. Cole, *Ardennes*, 389. In some accounts of the fighting at Baraque de Fraiture, the crossroads is called "Parker's Crossroads." However, sometime before 22 December Parker was wounded, and command of the forces at Baraque de Fraiture passed to Major Elliott Goldstein.

17. Combat Interview "509 Para. Inf.," n.d., CI-173 "82nd Airborne Div. Ardennes, 18 Dec. 44–9 Feb. 45, Box 24058, Record Group 407, NARA II.

18. See also Cole, *Ardennes*, 389–390; and Dupuy, "Parker's Crossroads," 14–15.

19. See Cole, *Ardennes*, 390; Combat Interview with Lieutenant Colonel Charles W. Major and Captain Herbert L. Little, 25 March 1945; Combat Interview "325th Glider Infantry Regiment," interview with Colonel George [*sic*] Billingslea, 24 March 1945; and Headquarters, 325th Glider Infantry, "The 325th Glider Infantry in the Bulge," 14 January 1945.

20. See Cole, *Ardennes*, 390; Combat Interview with Lieutenant Colonel Charles W. Major and Captain Herbert L. Little, 25 March 1945; Combat Interview "325th Glider Infantry Regiment," interview with Colonel George [*sic*] Billingslea, 24 March 1945; Headquarters, 325th Glider Infantry, "The 325th Glider Infantry in the Bulge," 14 January 1945.

21. See Cole, *Ardennes*, 390; Combat Interview with Lieutenant Colonel Charles W. Major and Captain Herbert L. Little, 25 March 1945; Combat Interview "325 Glider Inf.—2nd Bn.," n.d., CI-173 "82nd Airborne Div. Ardennes, 18 Dec. 44–9 Feb. 45, Box 24058, Record Group 407, NARA II.

22. See Cole, *Ardennes*, 390–391; Combat Interview with Lieutenant Colonel Charles W. Major and Captain Herbert L. Little, 25 March 1945I; Combat Interview "325th Glider Infantry Regiment," interview with Colonel George [*sic*] Billingslea, 24 March 1945.

23. See Cole, *Ardennes*, 390–391; Combat Interview with Lieutenant Colonel Charles W. Major and Captain Herbert L. Little, 25 March 1945; Combat Interview "325th Glider Infantry Regiment," interview with Colonel George [*sic*] Billingslea, 24 March 1945.

24. Combat Interview "325th Glider Infantry Regiment," interview with Colonel George [*sic*] Billingslea, 24 March 1945.

25. See Cole, *Ardennes*, 390–391; Combat Interview with Lieutenant Colonel Charles W. Major and Captain Herbert L. Little, 25 March 1945; Combat Interview "325th Glider Infantry Regiment," interview with Colonel George [*sic*] Billingslea, 24 March 1945.

26. Combat Interview "325th Glider Infantry Regiment," interview with Colonel George [*sic*] Billingslea, 24 March 1945.

27. See Cole, *Ardennes*, 391; Combat Interview "325th Glider Infantry Regiment," interview with Colonel George [*sic*] Billingslea, 24 March 1945; and Headquarters, 325th Glider Infantry, "The 325th Glider Infantry in the Bulge," 14 January 1945.

28. See Combat Interview "325th Glider Infantry Regiment," interview with Colonel George [*sic*] Billingslea, 24 March 1945; and Headquarters, XVIII Airborne Corps, "Summary of Operations: 18 December 1944 to 13 February 1945," 1 March 1945, Blair Collection, Box 48, Folder "Chrono File: Bulge," USAMHI.

29. Combat Interview "325th Glider Infantry Regiment," interview with Colonel George [*sic*] Billingslea, 24 March 1945.

30. Combat Interview with Lieutenant Colonel Charles W. Major and Captain Herbert L. Little, 25 March 1945.

31. After Action Report, *The Story of the 82d Airborne Division in the Battle of the Belgian Bulge in the Siegfried Line and on the Roer River*, n.d.

32. See XVIII Airborne Corps Diary, 1812 hours, 22 December 1944, which reads: "General GAVIN called at 1812 and stated that he was a little perturbed over the situation on the south in front of Billingsly [*sic*]. He felt that there might be considerable force behind the enemy that appeared this afternoon."

33. Tucker, interview, 28 March 1945 (see chap. 21, n. 64); Combat Interview "2nd Bn., 504th Para. Inf. Regt., 82nd Inf. Division," n.d., CI-173 "82nd Airborne Div. Ardennes, 18 Dec. 44–9 Feb. 45, Box 24058, Record Group 407, NARA II.

34. Gibson quoted in Combat Interview "325th Glider Infantry Regiment," interview with Colonel George [*sic*] Billingslea, 24 March 1945.

35. See also Edward N. Wellems to James M. Gavin, 13 March 1959, Gavin Papers, Box 11, Folder "Letters to Gavin, Comments, and Inquiries About D-Day Mentioned from *Longest Day*," USAMHI.

36. After Action Report, *The Story of the 82d Airborne Division in the Battle of the Belgian Bulge in the Siegfried Line and on the Roer River*, n.d.

37. James M. Gavin, interview, 4 January 1983, Blair Collection, Box 53, Folder "Gavin, James M.," USAMHI.

38. Gavin, *On to Berlin*, 235–236.

39. After Action Report, *The Story of the 82d Airborne Division in the Battle of the Belgian Bulge in the Siegfried Line and on the Roer River*, n.d. See also Cole, *Ardennes*, 589.

40. Gavin, *On to Berlin*, 236; After Action Report, *The Story of the 82d Airborne Division in the Battle of the Belgian Bulge in the Siegfried Line and on the Roer River*, n.d.

41. Cole, *Ardennes*, 392.

42. Ibid., 174, 580.

43. See ibid., 584–585; Combat Interview "325th Glider Infantry Regiment," interview with Colonel George [*sic*] Billingslea, 24 March 1945; Headquarters, 325th Glider Infantry, "The 325th Glider Infantry in the Bulge," 14 January 1945; Combat Interview "325 Glider Infantry—3rd Bn.," n.d., CI-173 "82nd Airborne Div. Ardennes, 18 Dec. 44–9 Feb. 45, Box 24058, Record Group 407, NARA II; and Combat Interview, "3rd Battalion—325th Glider Infantry," interview with Lieutenant Colonel Osmond A. Leahy, 25 March 1945.

44. Cole, *Ardennes*, 585; Combat Interview "325th Glider Infantry Regiment," interview with Colonel George [*sic*] Billingslea, 24 March 1945; Headquarters, 325th Glider Infantry, "The 325th Glider Infantry in the Bulge," 14 January 1945; Combat Interview with Lieutenant Colonel Charles W. Major and Captain Herbert L. Little, 25 March 1945.

45. Combat Interview "325th Glider Infantry Regiment," interview with Colonel George [*sic*] Billingslea, 24 March 1945; Combat Interview, "3rd Battalion—325th Glider Infantry," interview with Lieutenant Colonel Osmond A. Leahy, 25 March 1945.

46. Combat Interview "325th Glider Infantry Regiment," interview with Colonel George [*sic*] Billingslea, 24 March 1945; Combat Interview, "3rd Battalion—325th Glider Infantry," interview with Lieutenant Colonel Osmond A. Leahy, 25 March 1945; Headquarters, 325th Glider Infantry, "The 325th Glider Infantry in the Bulge," 14 January 1945.

47. After Action Report, *The Story of the 82d Airborne Division in the Battle of the Belgian Bulge in the Siegfried Line and on the Roer River*.

48. See also Combat Interview "325th Glider Infantry Regiment," interview with Colonel George [*sic*] Billingslea, 24 March 1945; Combat Interview, "3rd Battalion—325th Glider Infantry," interview with Lieutenant Colonel Osmond A. Leahy, 25 March 1945; Headquarters, 325th Glider Infantry, "The 325th Glider Infantry in the

Bulge," 14 January 1945; Combat Interview, interview with Major V. R. Butz, 20 February 1945.

49. Cole, *Ardennes*, 595.

50. After Action Report, *The Story of the 82d Airborne Division in the Battle of the Belgian Bulge in the Siegfried Line and on the Roer River*, n.d.

51. See also Gavin, *On to Berlin*, 231.

CHAPTER 23: MAKING MONKEYS OUT OF THE GERMANS

1. Stephenson never forgot this moment. When the war was over, he named his first-born son James Gavin Stephenson.

2. Ridgway, interview, 15 December 1971 (see chap. 3, n. 20).

3. Bradley quoted in D. Eisenhower, *Eisenhower at War*, 562.

4. Cole, *Ardennes*, 423.

5. See also ibid., 423–425; D. Eisenhower, *Eisenhower at War*, 561–576; Bradley and Blair, *A General's Life*, 361–364; MacDonald, *Time for Trumpets*, 549–550; and D. Eisenhower, *Crusade in Europe*, 355. Strong and Whiteley were correct—the decision did cause considerable controversy, much of which continued to rankle after the war. For his part, Eisenhower tried to paper over the animosity, writing in *Crusade in Europe* that "the depth of the German advances on the eighteenth and nineteenth had broken all normal communications between Bradley's headquarters at Luxembourg and the headquarters of the Ninth and First Armies. For this reason it was completely impossible for Bradley to give to the attack on the southern shoulder the attention that I desired and at the same time keep properly in touch with the troops in the north who were called upon to meet the heaviest German blows." Given the situation, he continued, "only one solution seemed applicable," and then tactfully, if somewhat disingenuously wrote, "Because of my faith in the soundness of the teamwork that we had built up, I had no hesitancy in adopting this solution." D. Eisenhower, *Crusade in Europe*, 355. Bradley remained bitter about the decision until his death. In *A General's Life* he wrote that the Battle of the Bulge gave the British "a potent new excuse to fault U.S. leadership and strategy and advance their own ideas. They did not hesitate to use it. Montgomery, Alan Brooke and Churchill all came to us like sharks at a shipwreck. Montgomery was the first to scent blood and attack. He led the pack. He would continue to be the most vicious and ravenous" (361). He went on to say that by knuckling under to Eisenhower's decisions, he made "one of my biggest mistakes of the war" (363). Montgomery was uncharacteristically mute on the subject, writing, "I think the less one says about this battle the better, for I fancy that whatever I do say will almost certainly be resented." Montgomery, *Memoirs*, 281.

6. Cole, *Ardennes*, 557.

7. Montgomery was actually actively campaigning for the redrawing of the army group boundaries, as Alan Brooke made clear in his diary entry for 20 December 1944: "Received telegram from Monty which showed clearly that the situation in France was serious. American front penetrated, Germans advancing on Namur with little in front of them, north flank of First American Army in state of

flux and disorganization, etc etc. Also suggested that he should be given command of all forces north of the penetration." Alan Brooke goes on to write that he gave Montgomery's cable to Churchill, who then called Eisenhower to suggest Montgomery's proposed course of action. Eisenhower told Churchill that he had already issued orders to that effect. Danchev and Todman, *War Diaries*, 637.

8. Anonymous staff officer quoted in D. Eisenhower, *Eisenhower at War*, 576.

9. Montgomery, *Memoirs*, 283 (emphasis in original).

10. For his part, Hasbrouck welcomed Montgomery's decision to evacuate the last of the St. Vith forces still inside Ridgway's "goose egg." Writing after the war, Hasbrouck praised Ridgway as "a very courageous man with great determination and drive." But, he continued, "his command sense and good judegment [*sic*] were not always the best. Notably poor was his decision to leave the 7th Armored and its many attached troops to be surrounded in a heavily wooded area just east of Vielsalm. He wanted this as an island for him to fight back to. Fortunately, Field Marshal Montgomery cancelled Ridgway's orders soon after being apprised of them." Robert Hasbrouck to Clay Blair, n.d., Blair Collection, Box 53, Folder "Hasbrouck, Robert W.," USAMHI.

11. Headquarters, XVIII Corps (Airborne), "Operation Report, Ardennes, 19 December 1944 to 13 February 1945," 1 March 1945 (see chap. 21, n. 59); Ridgway's Official Diary, 0645 hours, 1300 hours 24 December 1944 (see chap. 21, n. 32).

12. After Action Report, *The Story of the 82d Airborne Division in the Battle of the Belgian Bulge in the Siegfried Line and on the Roer River*, n.d. (see chap. 21, n. 2). Another of Gavin's concerns was the rumors of German soldiers running around the First Army's rear area dressed as Americans. In his after-action report he wrote that "the German was using every artifice conceivable to create doubt and confusion in the minds of American fighting units. He was using our arms, equipment and vehicles, frequently leaving their own abandoned and disabled at bottlenecks on the roads. False messages were being used and Germans in American officers' uniforms were known to be in the rear areas" (7). Though wildly overblown, there was some truth to the rumors. One of Hitler's favorites, SS-Obersturmbannführer Otto Skorzeny, the same man who had engineered Mussolini's dramatic escape from captivity following his overthrow, had organized a special unit, *Panzer Brigade 150* (also called the *Brandenburger Brigade*), that consisted of approximately 2,000 men, 150 of whom spoke English, who were outfitted with American uniforms, equipment, and identification papers. Their mission was to infiltrate behind U.S. lines, seize key bridges, and sew confusion in the rear areas through sabotage. In addition, approximately 1,000 German paratroopers under the command of Oberst Friedrich A. Freiherr von der Heydte parachuted behind American lines early in the morning on 17 December in order to seize some key roads (these men were in German uniforms). The operation, code-named *Greif* (Condor), met with varying degrees of success. Heydte's paratroopers were widely scattered, many were taken prisoner, and failed completely in their mission. Skorzeny's saboteurs, on the other hand, did cause some chaos in the American rear. The net result was that American soldiers were suspect of anyone they did not immediately recognize as friendly, especially when word got out that one of the chief missions of the paratroopers/saboteurs was to assassinate Eisenhower, the result of wild stories told by those who were taken

prisoner. According to Hugh Cole, "The American officer who had the misfortune to appear on the heels of the most recent rumor in some headquarters where he was unknown stood a good chance of being welcomed with a cocked pistol leveled at his belt buckle." Cole, *Ardennes*, 559. To prove their bona fides, soldiers were asked to name state capitals, recount baseball trivia, and sing nonsensical nursery rhymes. In his after-action report Gavin wrote that one 82nd trooper liberated from German captivity during the battle said that he was taken prisoner by Germans wearing American uniforms (7). He must also have been aware of an incident that occurred in the 3/508th's sector on the day of the withdrawal. According to Lieutenant Colonel Otho Holmes, the 3/508th's commander, one of his patrols killed a German officer and sergeant whom they ambushed riding in an American jeep. When they were searched, it was found that both were wearing American uniforms under their German kits, and the officer was wearing a brand-new pair of U.S. jump boots. Combat Interview with Lieutenant Colonel Otho Holmes, 28 March 1945, CI-172 "82nd Airborne Div. Ardennes, 18 Dec. 44–9 Feb. 45, Box 24058, Record Group 407, NARA II. See also Cole, *Ardennes*, 269–271, 558–559.

13. Megellas, *All the Way to Berlin*, 196; Lord, *History of the 508th Parachute Infantry*, 63; Burchell quoted in Nordyke, *All American*, 639; Langdon, *"Ready,"* 111; Combat Interview "325th Glider Infantry Regiment," interview with Colonel George [*sic*] Billingslea, 24 March 1945 (see chap. 22, n. 1); Gavin, *On to Berlin*, 238–239.

14. After Action Report, *The Story of the 82d Airborne Division in the Battle of the Belgian Bulge in the Siegfried Line and on the Roer River*, n.d.

15. Gavin, *On to Berlin*, 238.

16. See ibid., 238–239; Lord, *History of the 508th Parachute Infantry*, 63; and After Action Report, *The Story of the 82d Airborne Division in the Battle of the Belgian Bulge in the Siegfried Line and on the Roer River*, n.d.

17. Langdon, *"Ready,"* 110–111. Langdon commented, however, that as cold as it was during the withdrawal, it "was like Indian Summer" compared to what the troopers would endure in the future.

18. Lord, *History of the 508th Parachute Infantry*, 63.

19. After Action Report, *The Story of the 82d Airborne Division in the Battle of the Belgian Bulge in the Siegfried Line and on the Roer River*, n.d.

20. The Allies used proximity fuses, also known as POZIT or VT fuses, for the first time in ground combat against *Kampfgruppe Peiper,* thus underscoring the gravity with which the Allies viewed the thrust by Peiper. The fuse, "a tightly guarded American secret design for detonating projectiles by external influence in the close vicinity of a target, without explosion by contact," had been around for a while, but fears that a dud might land in enemy hands had limited its use to fire over water or in an antiaircraft mode. Though a lethal weapon that, postwar, would become the weapon of choice against infantry in the open, according to Hugh Cole claims "as to the value of the much touted VT fuse in halting the German advance are grossly exaggerated." Cole, *Ardennes*, 655.

21. See also Cole, *Ardennes*, 369, 374–377.

22. Memorandum, Headquarters, 505th Parachute Infantry Regiment, 18 January 1945, "Report on Enemy Contact by 505 During Withdrawal Dec. 24–25, 1944," 382-0.3, Box 12345, Record Group 407, NARA II.

23. Combat Interview "Battle of the Bulge," interview with Major William Carpenter and Captain Charles E. Sammon, 27 March 1945 (see chap. 21, n. 91).

24. Memorandum, Headquarters, 505th Parachute Infantry Regiment, 18 January 1945, "Report on Enemy Contact by 505 During Withdrawal Dec. 24–25, 1944."

25. McIlvoy, "Medical Detachment, 505th Parachute Infantry, 82nd Airborne Division in World War II" (see chap. 5, n. 50).

26. James M. Gavin to John Toland, 4 March 1959, Gavin Papers, Box 11, Folder "Letters to Gavin, Comments, and Inquiries About D-Day Mentioned from *Longest Day*," USAMHI.

27. Memorandum, Headquarters, 505th Parachute Infantry Regiment, 18 January 1945, "Report on Enemy Contact by 505 During Withdrawal Dec. 24–25, 1944."

28. Dunfee quoted in Nordyke, *All American*, 640; Memorandum, Headquarters, 505th Parachute Infantry Regiment, 18 January 1945, "Report on Enemy Contact by 505 During Withdrawal Dec. 24–25, 1944."

29. Jorgensen, *History of the 456th Parachute Field Artillery*, 232–233.

30. Memorandum, Headquarters, 505th Parachute Infantry Regiment, 18 January 1945, "Report on Enemy Contact by 505 During Withdrawal Dec. 24–25, 1944."

31. Ibid.; Combat Interview "Battle of the Bulge," interview with Lieutenant Colonel James P. Kaiser, 26 March 1945 (see chap. 21, n. 80).

32. Memorandum, Headquarters, 505th Parachute Infantry Regiment, 18 January 1945, "Report on Enemy Contact by 505 During Withdrawal Dec. 24–25, 1944."

33. James M. Gavin to Edward N. Wellems, 4 March 1959, Gavin Papers, Box 11, Folder "Letters to Gavin, Comments, and Inquiries About D-Day Mentioned from *Longest Day*," USAMHI; Gavin to Toland, 4 March 1959.

34. Cole, *Ardennes*, 377.

35. After Action Report, *The Story of the 82d Airborne Division in the Battle of the Belgian Bulge in the Siegfried Line and on the Roer River*, n.d.

36. Lord, *History of the 508th Parachute Infantry*, 63.

37. Combat Interview with Major Benjamin F. Delamater III and First Lieutenant Ernest J. Hager, 28 March 1945, CI-172 "82nd Airborne Div. Ardennes, 18 Dec. 44–9 Feb. 45, Box 24058, Record Group 407, NARA II.

38. Ibid.; Adams's Combat Interview reproduced in Nordyke, *All American*, 634–636.

39. Lamm quoted in Combat Interview "German Breakthrough," interview with Major J. W. Medusky, 15 February 1945 (see chap. 21, n. 15).

40. Except where noted, see Adams interview in Nordyke, *All American*, 634–636; and Combat Interview with Major Benjamin F. Delamater III and First Lieutenant Ernest J. Hager, 28 March 1945.

41. Lord, *History of the 508th Parachute Infantry*, 63, 65; After Action Report, *The Story of the 82d Airborne Division in the Battle of the Belgian Bulge in the Siegfried Line and on the Roer River*, n.d.

42. Cole, *Ardennes*, 587, map 8.

43. See ibid., map 8; After Action Report, *The Story of the 82d Airborne Division in the Battle of the Belgian Bulge in the Siegfried Line and on the Roer River*, n.d.; and Combat Interview "325th Glider Infantry Regiment," interview with Colonel George [*sic*] Billingslea, 24 March 1945.

44. Cole, *Ardennes*, 590; Combat Interview "325th Glider Infantry Regiment," interview with Colonel George [*sic*] Billingslea, 24 March 1945.

45. See also Cole, *Ardennes*, 590; Combat Interview, interview with Lieutenant Colonel Richard E. Gerard, 26 March 1945 (see chap. 22, n. 2).

46. Ibid.

47. See also Cole, *Ardennes*, 595–596; Combat Interview, interview with Lieutenant Colonel Richard E. Gerard, 26 March 1945; Combat Interview "325th Glider Infantry Regiment," interview with Colonel George [*sic*] Billingslea, 24 March 1945; Headquarters, 325th Glider Infantry, "The 325th Glider Infantry in the Bulge," 14 January 1945 (see chap. 21, n. 43); and Combat Interview, interview with Major V. R. Butz, 20 February 1945 (see chap. 22, n. 8).

48. Sirovica and Romero quoted in Boroughs, *Devil's Tale*, 242.

49. After Action Report, *The Story of the 82d Airborne Division in the Battle of the Belgian Bulge in the Siegfried Line and on the Roer River*, n.d.

50. Zuelke quoted in Boroughs, *Devil's Tale*, 245. For the German attack on Erria, see also Cole, *Ardennes*, 600–601; Lord, *History of the 508th Parachute Infantry*, 66–67; and Combat Interview with Lieutenant Colonel Louis G. Mendez Jr. and First Lieutenant John T. Little, 28 March 1945, CI-172 "82nd Airborne Div. Ardennes, 18 Dec. 44–9 Feb. 45, Box 24058, Record Group 407, NARA II.

51. Risnes quoted in Boroughs, *Devil's Tale*, 249–250; Combat Interview with Lieutenant Colonel Louis G. Mendez Jr. and First Lieutenant John T. Little, 28 March 1945; Romero quoted in Boroughs, *Devil's Tale*, 245–246.

52. Except where noted, see also Combat Interview with Lieutenant Colonel Louis G. Mendez Jr. and First Lieutenant John T. Little, 28 March 1945; and Combat Interview with Lieutenant Colonel Otho Holmes, 28 March 1945.

53. Combat Interview "German Breakthrough," interview with Major J. W. Medusky, 15 February 1945. See also Combat Interview with Lieutenant Colonel Louis G. Mendez Jr. and First Lieutenant John T. Little, 28 March 1945.

54. Combat Interview "German Breakthrough," interview with Major J. W. Medusky, 15 February 1945; Gavin, Personal Diary, 31 December 1944 (see chap. 4, n. 26).

55. Blair, *Ridgway's Paratroopers*, 410.

56. Cole, *Ardennes*, 555; Blair, *Ridgway's Paratroopers*, 409; Weigley, *Eisenhower's Lieutenants*, 545.

57. Montgomery quoted in D. Eisenhower, *Eisenhower at War*, 594.

58. For the Allies' differing views, see also Blair, *Ridgway's Paratroopers*, 409; Weigley, *Eisenhower's Lieutenants*, 544–545; and Bradley and Blair, *A General's Life*, 374.

59. Headquarters, XVIII Corps (Airborne), "Operation Report, Ardennes, 19 December 1944 to 13 February 1945," 1 March 1945 (see chap. 21, n. 59).

60. See also Blair, *Ridgway's Paratroopers*, 416.

61. Gavin, *On to Berlin*, 249.
62. Quoted in Blair, *Ridgway's Paratroopers*, 416. For the plan for the attack, see also Weigley, *Eisenhower's Lieutenants*, 546; and Headquarters, XVIII Corps (Airborne), "Operation Report, Ardennes, 19 December 1944 to 13 February 1945," 1 March 1945.
63. Gavin, *On to Berlin*, 249; Ridgway's Official Diary, Notes from Corps Commander's Conference, 31 December 1944.
64. See also After Action Report, *The Story of the 82d Airborne Division in the Battle of the Belgian Bulge in the Siegfried Line and on the Roer River*, n.d.
65. Sanford quoted in Richlak, *Glide to Glory*, 313; Gladstone quoted in Boroughs, *Devil's Tale*, 256.
66. Memorandum, 307th Airborne Engineer Battalion, "Historical Narrative 1 January 1945–22 February 1945," n.d., 382-ENG-0.3, Box 12433, Record Group 407, NARA II.
67. Combat Interview "Battle of the Bulge," interview with Major William Carpenter and Captain Charles E. Sammon, 27 March 1945.
68. See also Langdon, *"Ready,"* 114; Megellas, *All the Way to Berlin*, 208; Combat Interview "Battle of the Bulge," interview with Major William Carpenter and Captain Charles E. Sammon, 27 March 1945; and Combat Interview with Colonel William Ekman, 22 March 1945 (see chap. 21, n. 86).
69. Langdon, *"Ready,"* 114.
70. Goodwin quoted in Nordyke, *All American*, 671.
71. Tarbell quoted in Megellas, *All the Way to Berlin*, 209.
72. Zuccala and Romero quoted in Boroughs, *Devil's Tale*, 252, 253; Durkee quoted in Nordyke, *All American*, 675.
73. "History 504th Parachute Infantry, 18 December 1944–11 January 1945," n.d. (see chap. 21, n. 42).
74. Langdon, *"Ready,"* 112. See also After Action Report, *The Story of the 82d Airborne Division in the Battle of the Belgian Bulge in the Siegfried Line and on the Roer River*, n.d.
75. Combat Interview "Battle of the Bulge," interview with Lieutenant Colonel James P. Kaiser, 26 March 1945.
76. Ibid.
77. Langdon, *"Ready,"* 113.
78. Tallett quoted in O'Donnell, *Beyond Valor*, 261; Langdon, *"Ready,"* 113.
79. Tallett quoted in O'Donnell, *Beyond Valor*, 261.
80. Langdon, *"Ready,"* 114.
81. Combat Interview "Battle of the Bulge," interview with Lieutenant Colonel James P. Kaiser, 26 March 1945.
82. Headquarters, 325th Glider Infantry, "The 325th Glider Infantry in the Bulge," 14 January 1945.
83. After Action Report, *The Story of the 82d Airborne Division in the Battle of the Belgian Bulge in the Siegfried Line and on the Roer River.*
84. Headquarters, 325th Glider Infantry, "The 325th Glider Infantry in the Bulge," 14 January 1945.

85. Tallett quoted in ibid., 261; Langdon, *"Ready,"* 114–115; Combat Interview with Lieutenant Colonel Talton W. Long, Captain Charles Paterson, and Staff Sergeant D. Curtis Raleigh, 26 March 1945, CI-173 "82nd Airborne Div. Ardennes, 18 Dec. 44–9 Feb. 45, Box 24058, Record Group 407, NARA II.

86. After Action Report, *The Story of the 82d Airborne Division in the Battle of the Belgian Bulge in the Siegfried Line and on the Roer River*, n.d.

87. Combat Interview "German Breakthrough," interview with Major J. W. Medusky, 15 February 1945.

88. Risnes quoted in Boroughs, *Devil's Tale*, 251.

89. Gavin quoted in Lord, *History of the 508th Parachute Infantry Regiment*, 71. Mendez's comments related to the author by Starlyn Jorgensen, who spoke with Mendez about the attack years afterward. For the attack on Thier du Mont, see also Lord, *History of the 508th Parachute Infantry Regiment*, 68–71; Combat Interview with Lieutenant Colonel Louis G. Mendez Jr. and First Lieutenant John T. Little, 28 March 1945; and Combat Interview "German Breakthrough," interview with Major J. W. Medusky, 15 February 1945. For his actions during the fight Staff Sergeant Sirovica was awarded the Distinguished Service Cross.

90. Pierce, *Let's Go!* 255–257; Headquarters, 325th Glider Infantry, "The 325th Glider Infantry in the Bulge," 14 January 1945; Combat Interview with Lieutenant Colonel Charles W. Major and Captain Herbert L. Little, 25 March 1945; Combat Interview "325th Glider Infantry Regiment," interview with Colonel George [*sic*] Billingslea, 24 March 1945.

91. Combat Interview "2nd Bn., 504th Para. Inf. Regt., 82nd Inf. Division," n.d., Box 24508, Folder CI-173 "82nd Airborne Div. Ardennes," 18 Dec. 44–9 Feb. 45, Record Group 407, NARA II.

92. Heibert and Ward quoted in Megellas, *All the Way to Berlin*, 211–212.

93. For the fight at Goronne, see Meyers's narrative in Nordyke, *All American*, 680–682.

94. Gavin, *On to Berlin*, 253. Vandervoort did lose an eye and as a result was medically retired from active duty. But being on the division staff was no sure means to avoid injury. The very next day, while out with Gavin at the front, Captain Olson, his longtime aide, was wounded in the legs by shrapnel. Olson was out of commission for about a month before returning to the 82nd. Gavin, *On to Berlin*, 254.

95. Meyers quoted in Nordyke, *All American*, 681.

96. Gavin, interview, 4 January 1983

97. After Action Report, *The Story of the 82d Airborne Division in the Battle of the Belgian Bulge in the Siegfried Line and on the Roer River*, n.d.

98. Brereton, *The Brereton Diaries*, 392.

99. See Gavin, *On to Berlin*, 254; Megellas, *All the Way to Berlin*, 210; Pierce, *Let's Go!* 253; Combat Interview with Lieutenant Colonel Charles W. Major and Captain Herbert L. Little, 25 March 1945; Combat Interview, "3rd Battalion—325th Glider Infantry," interview with Lieutenant Colonel Osmond A. Leahy, 25 March 1945 (see chap. 22, n. 2); Gavin, Personal Diary, 14 January 1945.

100. Gavin, Personal Diary, 14 January 1945; McKenzie, *On Time, On Target*, 126.

CHAPTER 24: ANOTHER NASTY JOB

1. Langdon, *"Ready,"* 117.

2. See also Headquarters, XVIII Corps (Airborne), "Operation Report, Ardennes, 19 December 1944 to 13 February 1945," 1 March 1945 (see chap. 21, n. 59).

3. Schultz and Christiansen quoted in Nordyke, *All American*, 695; Langdon, *"Ready,"* 117.

4. See Langdon, *"Ready,"* 117; Pierce, *Let's Go!* 267; After Action Report, *The Story of the 82d Airborne Division in the Battle of the Belgian Bulge in the Siegfried Line and on the Roer River*, n.d. (see chap. 21, n. 2); and Memorandum, Headquarters, 320th Glider Field Artillery Battalion, "Narrative Report of Action Against the Enemy, January 1–31 1945," n.d., 382-FA(320)-0.3, Box 12437, Record Group 407, NARA II.

5. Combat Interview "Battle of the Bulge," interview with Major William Carpenter and Captain Charles E. Sammon, 27 March 1945 (see chap. 21, n. 91).

6. Memorandum, Headquarters, 320th Glider Field Artillery Battalion, "Narrative Report of Action Against the Enemy, January 1–31, 1945," n.d.

7. George D. Graves Jr. personal journal, entry for 9 January 1945, William B. Breuer Collection, Box 2, Folder "Correspondence with Veterans of the 504th Parachute Infantry Regiment," USAMHI.

8. Pierce, *Let's Go!* 265.

9. Langdon, *"Ready,"* 117; Pierce, *Let's Go!* 267.

10. Graves journal, entry entitled "Respite at Remouchamps."

11. Tarbell quoted in Megellas, *All the Way to Berlin*, 216; Proclamation reproduced in Langdon, *"Ready,"* 117.

12. Memorandum, Headquarters, 307th Airborne Medical Company, "Unit Operations, January 1, 1945 to January 31, 1945," 13 February 1945, Box 14713, Folder 382-MED-0.3 "307th A/B Med. CO—Rpt. of Unit Opns., Holland," 17 Sep.–16 Oct. 44, Record Group 407, NARA II.

13. Tedder quoted in D. Eisenhower, *Eisenhower at War*, 622.

14. MacDonald, *The Last Offensive*, 57; Bradley and Blair, *A General's Life*, 386.

15. D. Eisenhower, *Eisenhower at War*, 622–623; Arthur Bryant, *Triumph in the West: A History of the War Years Based on the Diaries of Field-Marshal Lord Alanbrooke, Chief of the Imperial General Staff*, 291.

16. MacDonald, *The Last Offensive*, 57.

17. Ibid.; Bradley and Blair, *A General's Life*, 390.

18. MacDonald, *The Siegfried Line Campaign*, 34, 35. See also 30–34 for a fuller discussion of the Siegfried Line.

19. Blair, *Ridgway's Paratroopers*, 426; MacDonald, *The Last Offensive*, 60.

20. Ridgway's Official Diary, Report of Division Commander's Conference, 26 January 1945 (see chap. 21, n. 32).

21. Headquarters, XVIII Corps (Airborne), "Operation Report, Ardennes, 19 December 1944 to 13 February 1945," 1 March 1945.

22. Ridgway and Martin, *Soldier*, 127–128.

23. After Action Report, *The Story of the 82d Airborne Division in the Battle of the Belgian Bulge in the Siegfried Line and on the Roer River*, n.d. See also MacDonald, *The Last Offensive*, 63; and Blair, *Ridgway's Paratroopers*, 429.

24. Gavin, Personal Diary, 24 and 14 January 1945 (see chap. 4, n. 26).

25. Ridgway's Official Diary, 20 January 1945.

26. Gavin, Personal Diary, 24 January 1945.

27. See Blair, *Ridgway's Paratroopers*, 421–422; and MacDonald, *The Last Offensive*, 43.

28. Gavin, Personal Diary, 18 January 1945.

29. Ridgway and Martin, *Soldier*, 199, 49, 50.

30. Memorandum, Organization and Training Division, G-3, War Department, "Reorganization of the Airborne Division," 8 November 1944, in *The Papers of George C. Marshall: Selected World War II Correspondence*, Reel 31 of 40.

31. Gavin's battlefield exploits have, to a great extent, overshadowed his powerful intellect. But those who knew him well knew how intelligent he was. John Norton called him "America's outstanding thinker, believer and architect of mobile warfare in our time." Melvin Zais, who eventually rose to four-star rank himself, thought Gavin "brilliant." Always the student of war and warriors, Gavin's papers are filled with references to great thinkers. For example, Gavin's wartime diary at the U.S. Military History Institute at Carlisle Barracks, Pennsylvania, contains a green notebook in which are included quotes from Voltaire, Nietzsche, Suvorov, Ardant du Picq, Alexis de Tocqueville, and Socrates, to name a few. After the war, as director of U.S. Army research and development, he championed the military use of helicopters and satellite communications and predicted well before it happened that rocket technology would allow man to walk on the moon. See Gavin, Personal Diary; John Norton, Memorial Service Speech, "A Tribute to General James M. Gavin," 6 March 1990, given to the author by General Norton; Zais, "Glimpses of Gavin" (see chap. 5, n. 63); and Boatner, *Biographical Dictionary of World War II*, s.v. "Gavin."

32. Gavin, *On to Berlin*, 2.

33. Gavin, Personal Diary, 5 November 1943 and 16 August 1944.

34. Ibid., 15 February 1944.

35. After Action Report, *The Story of the 82d Airborne Division in the Battle of the Belgian Bulge in the Siegfried Line and on the Roer River*, n.d. The 508th Regimental Combat Team (the 508th Parachute Infantry Regiment plus the 319th Glider Field Artillery Battalion; D Company, 307th Airborne Engineers; and B Company, 80th Airborne Antiaircraft Battalion) had been temporarily detached from the division for four days (21 to 24 January) and placed in a relatively quiet part of the 7th Armored Division's defensive lines where it saw very little action. It was then returned to division control and moved with the division to the new assembly areas on 26–27 January. See After Action Report, *The Story of the 82d Airborne Division in the Battle of the Belgian Bulge in the Siegfried Line and on the Roer River*, n.d; and Lord, *History of the 508th Parachute Infantry*, 73–75.

36. Headquarters, XVIII Corps (Airborne), "Operation Report, Ardennes, 19 December 1944 to 13 February 1945," 1 March 1945; After Action Report, *The*

Story of the 82d Airborne Division in the Battle of the Belgian Bulge in the Siegfried Line and on the Roer River, n.d.

37. Combat Interview with Colonel William Ekman, 22 March 1945 (see chap. 21, n. 86); Tucker, interview, 28 March 1945 (see chap. 21, n. 64); Virgil Carmichael's account of the Battle for Herresbach, Breuer Collection, Box 2, Folder "Correspondence with Veterans of the 504th Parachute Infantry Regiment," USAMHI; Headquarters, 325th Glider Infantry, "12 Miles into the Siegfried Line," 8 February 1945, 382-INF(325)-0.3, Box 12448, Record Group 407, NARA II; Lord, *History of the 508th Parachute Infantry*, 75.

38. Combat Interview, interview with Lieutenant Colonel Richard E. Gerard, 26 March 1945 (see chap. 22, n. 2); Combat Interview "325th Glider Infantry Regiment," interview with Colonel George [*sic*] Billingslea, 24 March 1945 (see chap. 21, n. 43); Headquarters, 325th Glider Infantry, "12 Miles into the Siegfried Line," 8 February 1945.

39. Virgil Carmichael's account of the Battle for Herresbach (emphasis in original); Cook quoted in Megellas, *All the Way to Berlin*, 224. See also Tucker, interview, 28 March 1945; and Combat Interview "504th Parachute Infantry Regt. 82nd A/B Division" (see chap. 21, n. 63).

40. Tucker, interview, 28 March 1945.

41. Virgil Carmichael's account of the Battle for Herresbach; Megellas, *All the Way to Berlin*, 225.

42. Ralph R. Larkin to James M. Gavin, 21 January 1980, Gavin Papers, Box 12, Folder "Letters to and from 82nd Vets on Airborne Operations in Holland, September, 1944," USAMHI. See also Mandle and Whittier, *Combat Record of the 504th Parachute Infantry Regimen*t, n.p; and Combat Interview with Captain Henry B. Keep and First Lieutenant James Megellas, 29 March 1945, CI-173 "82nd Airborne Div. Ardennes, 18 Dec. 44–9 Feb. 45," Box 24058, Record Group 407, NARA II.

43. Megellas, *All the Way to Berlin*, 227; "History, 504th Parachute Infantry, 30 December, 1944–31 January, 1945," n.d., 382-INF(504)-0.3, Box 12453, Record Group 407, NARA II; Headquarters, 82nd Airborne Division, "Award of Silver Star Medal," 10 March 1945, Box "504th PIR—WWII Personal Papers," Folder "*Personal Papers—Megellas, James (H Co., 3/504th)," 82nd Airborne Division Museum, Fort Bragg, NC.

44. Zimmerman quoted in Megellas, *All the Way to Berlin,* 228.

45. Ibid., 229–234; Combat Interview with Captain Henry B. Keep and First Lieutenant James Megellas, 29 March 1945; "History, 504th Parachute Infantry, 30 December 1944–31 January 1945," n.d.

46. Combat Interview "Battle of the Bulge," interview with Major William Carpenter and Captain Charles E. Sammon, 27 March 1945; Combat Interview "Battle of the Bulge," interview with Lieutenant Colonel James P. Kaiser, 26 March 1945 (see chap. 21, n. 80); Combat Interview "Battle of the Bulge," interview with Major William Carpenter and Captain Charles E. Sammon, 27 March 1945.

47. See also Langdon, *"Ready,"* 119; and Headquarters, 325th Glider Infantry, "12 Miles into the Siegfried Line," 8 February 1945.

48. One measure of the terribly cold weather in which the troopers were operating was related by Lieutenant George E. Miles, the E Company commander, who found that both his Thompson submachine gun and pistol were frozen when he tried to use them against a sniper in Medendorf. When he asked his executive officer, Lieutenant Dave Liebman, for his pistol, "He handed it to me then swore as his helmet was knocked off his head. He finally killed the young sniper and proceeded to a barn to rest. I thanked him for the .45 and he replied, 'Good you didn't have to use it—there were no bullets in it.'" See Nordyke, *All American*, 707–708.

49. Gavin, *On to Berlin*, 255. The official historian of this campaign wrote similarly about the value of the villages to the soldiers on both sides. "The state of the weather gave the little Ardennes towns an added dimension as prizes of war. Not only did the towns control the roads needed for tanks and trucks but they also afforded shelter, a chance for the men to thaw out and dry out, to get a night's sleep under cover." MacDonald, *The Last Offensive*, 46.

50. See also Lord, *History of the 508th Parachute Infantry*, 77–78; and Combat Interview with Major Benjamin F. Delamater III and First Lieutenant Ernest J. Hager, 28 March 1945; Combat Interview with Lieutenant Colonel Otho Holmes, 28 March 1945 (see chap. 23, n. 12).

51. Arthur quoted in Lewis Milkovics, ed., *"The Devils Have Landed,"* 168.

52. Arthur quoted in ibid.

53. Arthur quoted in ibid., 169; Funk quoted in Boroughs, *Devil's Tale*, 276.

54. For Funk's actions at Holzheim, see also Lord, *History of the 508th Parachute Infantry*, 77–78; Nordyke, *All American*, 706–707; and Combat Interview with Major Benjamin F. Delamater III and First Lieutenant Ernest J. Hager, 28 March 1945. During the firefight Funk's closest friend, Staff Sergeant Edward W. Wild, was killed, possibly by fire from Funk's gun. The death hit Funk hard. According to John Hardie, another of Funk's company mates, "At a time when courage was commonplace and prevalent, [Funk] had a brand of unique courage beyond that of the rest of the men. In trying to understand Funk's enormous capability in combat, I have come to convince myself that it was his upbeat attitude to go ahead, his instantaneous capacity to decide to act upon those decisions which readily turned potential defeat into triumph. That German officer who had accosted him in Holzheim felt confident there was no way he could lose when he had his machine pistol in Funk's chest. But he did, and those who were with Funk cannot really explain how it was possible. But that was Leonard's capacity." John Hardie, Speech at Leonard Funk Memorial Dedication Ceremony, 19 June 1999, Camp Blanding, Florida, copy in possession of the author. The citation for Funk's Medal of Honor is reproduced in Milkovics, *"The Devils Have Landed,"* 169–170.

55. See Lord, *History of the 508th Parachute Infantry*, 79–81; Combat Interview with Lieutenant Colonel Otho Holmes, 28 March 1945; Combat Interview with Major Benjamin F. Delamater III and First Lieutenant Ernest J. Hager, 28 March 1945; Combat Interview with Lieutenant Colonel Louis G. Mendez Jr. and First Lieutenant John T. Little, 28 March 1945 (see chap. 23, n. 50); After Action Report, *The Story of the 82d Airborne Division in the Battle of the Belgian Bulge in the Siegfried Line and on the Roer River*, n.d.

56. Headquarters, 325th Glider Infantry, "12 Miles into the Siegfried Line," 8 February 1945; Combat Interview "325th Glider Infantry Regiment," interview with Colonel George [*sic*] Billingslea, 24 March 1945; Combat Interview with Lieutenant Colonel Charles W. Major and Captain Herbert L. Little, 25 March 1945 (see chap. 23, n. 90); After Action Report, *The Story of the 82d Airborne Division in the Battle of the Belgian Bulge in the Siegfried Line and on the Roer River*, n.d.

57. Combat Interview "Battle of the Bulge," interview with Major William Carpenter and Captain Charles E. Sammon, 27 March 1945. For the 505th's attacks around Losheimergraben, see also Langdon, *"Ready,"* 119; Combat Interview with Colonel William Ekman, 22 March 1945; and After Action Report, *The Story of the 82d Airborne Division in the Battle of the Belgian Bulge in the Siegfried Line and on the Roer River*, n.d.

58. Bradley and Blair, *A General's Life*, 392; MacDonald, *The Last Offensive*, 67, 69–70; Blair, *Ridgway's Paratroopers*, 428–430; Weigley, *Eisenhower's Lieutenants*, 581–583.

59. Bradley and Blair, *A General's Life*, 392; MacDonald, *The Last Offensive*, 68.

60. See Bradley and Blair, *A General's Life*, 392; MacDonald, *The Last Offensive*, 67, 69–70; Blair, *Ridgway's Paratroopers*, 428–430; and Weigley, *Eisenhower's Lieutenants*, 581–583.

61. After Action Report, *The Story of the 82d Airborne Division in the Battle of the Belgian Bulge in the Siegfried Line and on the Roer River*, n.d; History, 504th Parachute Infantry, 1 February 1945–11 March 1945, n.d., 382-INF(504)-0.3, Box 12453, Record Group 407, NARA II; Langdon, *"Ready,"* 119; Headquarters, 325th Glider Infantry, "12 Miles into the Siegfried Line," 8 February 1945.

62. Graves, Personal Diary, 1 February 1945.

63. Combat Interview "Battle of the Bulge," interview with Major William Carpenter and Captain Charles E. Sammon, 27 March 1945; Combat Interview "Battle of the Bulge," interview with Lieutenant Colonel James P. Kaiser, 26 March 1945; Langdon, *"Ready,"* 119; Combat Interview with Lieutenant Colonel Talton W. Long, Captain Charles Paterson, and Staff Sergeant D. Curtis Raleigh, 26 March 1945 (see chap. 23, n. 85); After Action Report, *The Story of the 82d Airborne Division in the Battle of the Belgian Bulge in the Siegfried Line and on the Roer River*, n.d.

64. History, 504th Parachute Infantry, 1 February 1945–11 March 1945, n.d.

65. Ibid.

66. Wellems quoted in Combat Interview "Cracking the Siegfried Line," interview with Lieutenant Colonel Edward N. Wellems and Captain Victor W. Campana, 29 March 1945, CI-173 "82nd Airborne Div. Ardennes, 18 Dec. 44–9 Feb. 45, Box 24058, Record Group 407, NARA II.

67. For the 2/504th's fight, see also Combat Interview "German Breakthrough," interview with Colonel William L. [*sic*] Ekman and Major William J. Harris, 17 February 1945; History, 504th Parachute Infantry, 1 February 1945–11 March 1945, n.d.; Tucker, interview, 28 March 1945; Megellas, *All the Way to Berlin*, 235; and Combat Interview with First Lieutenant James E. Dunn, Staff Sergeant Edgar L. Lauritsen, and Staff Sergeant Sam D'Crenzo, 29 March 1945, CI-173 "82nd Airborne Div. Ardennes, 18 Dec. 44–9 Feb. 45, Box 24058, Record Group 407, NARA II.

68. Graves, Personal Diary, 2 February 1945.

69. Headquarters, 376th Parachute Field Artillery Battalion, "Narrative History—Period 1 February to 28 February 1945," n.d., 382-FA(376)-0.3, Box 12440, Record Group 407, NARA II.

70. Combat Interview "Cracking the Siegfried Line," interview with Lieutenant Colonel Edward N. Wellems and Captain Victor W. Campana, 29 March 1945.

71. Graves, Personal Diary, 3 February 1945.

72. For the fight in the Gerolstein Forest, see also History, 504th Parachute Infantry, 1 February 1945–11 March 1945, n.d.; and After Action Report, *The Story of the 82d Airborne Division in the Battle of the Belgian Bulge in the Siegfried Line and on the Roer River*, n.d.

73. Combat Interview "325th Glider Infantry Regiment," interview with Colonel George [*sic*] Billingslea, 24 March 1945; Headquarters, 325th Glider Infantry, "12 Miles into the Siegfried Line," 8 February 1945.

74. Combat Interview, interview with Lieutenant Colonel Richard E. Gerard, 26 March 1945; Combat Interview, "3rd Battalion—325th Glider Infantry," interview with Lieutenant Colonel Osmond A. Leahy, 25 March 1945 (see chap. 22, n. 2); Headquarters, 325th Glider Infantry, "12 Miles into the Siegfried Line," 8 February 1945.

75. Hook quoted in Nordyke, *All American*, 715; Combat Interview, interview with Lieutenant Colonel Richard E. Gerard, 26 March 1945; Hook quoted in Nordyke, *All American*, 715; Headquarters, 325th Glider Infantry, "12 Miles into the Siegfried Line," 8 February 1945. For Lieutenant Teras's probe, see also Combat Interview, interview with Lieutenant Colonel Richard E. Gerard, 26 March 1945.

76. Nordyke, *All American*, 718; Combat Interview, interview with Lieutenant Colonel Richard E. Gerard, 26 March 1945; Headquarters, 325th Glider Infantry, "12 Miles into the Siegfried Line," 8 February 1945.

77. Helmer quoted in Nordyke, *All American*, 718. See also 82nd Airborne Division Artillery, "Narrative History 1 February 1945 to 19 February 1945," n.d., 382-ART-0.3, Box 12430, Record Group 407, NARA II; Combat Interview, interview with Lieutenant Colonel Richard E. Gerard, 26 March 1945.

78. See also Headquarters, 325th Glider Infantry, "12 Miles into the Siegfried Line," 8 February 1945; and Nordyke, *All American*, 718.

79. Combat Interview, interview with Lieutenant Colonel Richard E. Gerard, 26 March 1945; Riddle quoted in Nordyke, *All American*, 718.

80. Combat Interview, interview with Lieutenant Colonel Richard E. Gerard, 26 March 1945.

81. O'Brien quoted in Nordyke, *All American*, 718–719.

82. Combat Interview, interview with Lieutenant Colonel Richard E. Gerard, 26 March 1945; Headquarters, 325th Glider Infantry, "12 Miles into the Siegfried Line," 8 February 1945.

83. Helmer quoted in Nordyke, *All American*, 725; Combat Interview, interview with Lieutenant Colonel Richard E. Gerard, 26 March 1945.

84. O'Brien and Hook quoted in Nordyke, *All American*, 721–722.

85. Combat Interview "325th Glider Infantry Regiment," interview with Colonel George [*sic*] Billingslea, 24 March 1945.

86. Headquarters, 325th Glider Infantry, "12 Miles into the Siegfried Line," 8 February 1945.

87. Frauenheim quoted in Nordyke, *All American*, 724. For the 2/401st's advance, see also Combat Interview with Lieutenant Colonel Charles W. Major and Captain Herbert L. Little, 25 March 1945; Combat Interview, "3rd Battalion—325th Glider Infantry," interview with Lieutenant Colonel Osmond A. Leahy, 25 March 1945; Pierce, *Let's Go!* 278.

88. Eschbaugh quoted in Nordyke, *All American*, 720. See also Pierce, *Let's Go!* 276.

89. Crick quoted in Nordyke, *All American*, 722. See also Combat Interview "325th Glider Infantry Regiment," interview with Colonel George [*sic*] Billingslea, 24 March 1945; Combat Interview with Lieutenant Colonel Charles W. Major and Captain Herbert L. Little, 25 March 1945; Combat Interview, interview with Lieutenant Colonel Richard E. Gerard, 26 March 1945; and Headquarters, 325th Glider Infantry, "12 Miles into the Siegfried Line," 8 February 1945.

90. Combat Interview, "3rd Battalion—325th Glider Infantry," interview with Lieutenant Colonel Osmond A. Leahy, 25 March 1945.

91. Gavin quoted in Headquarters, 325th Glider Infantry, "12 Miles into the Siegfried Line," 8 February 1945.

92. Combat Interview with Lieutenant Colonel Charles W. Major and Captain Herbert L. Little, 25 March 1945.

93. Headquarters, 325th Glider Infantry, "12 Miles into the Siegfried Line," 8 February 1945; Combat Interview, "3rd Battalion—325th Glider Infantry," interview with Lieutenant Colonel Osmond A. Leahy, 25 March 1945.

94. Lainhart quoted in Nordyke, *All American*, 724.

95. Gavin, Personal Diary, 3 February 1945.

96. Ibid.

97. Ibid., 10 February 1945.

98. MacDonald, *The Last Offensive*, 135; Montgomery, *Memoirs*, 295.

99. Bradley and Blair, *A General's Life*, 392.

100. MacDonald, *The Last Offensive*, 69; Headquarters, XVIII Corps (Airborne), "Operation Report, Ardennes, 19 December 1944 to 13 February 1945," 1 March 1945.

101. MacDonald, *The Last Offensive*, 135–136, 73–75.

102. Charles B. MacDonald, *The Battle of the Huertgen Forest*, 39.

103. From September through mid-November 1944 Hodges's First Army launched three separate one-division attacks through the Hürtgen Forest. Though all were aimed in the general direction of the dams, taking them was not, at the time, their primary purpose, and all were stopped well short of the dams in any event. A fourth assault, this time by two infantry divisions reinforced with an armored combat command, was tried in December 1944. The express aim of this fourth assault was to get to the dams, but it was cut short by the German Ardennes offensive. MacDonald, *The Last Offensive*, 70. For a detailed account of the fighting in the Hürtgen prior to February 1945, see MacDonald, *Battle of the Huertgen Forest.*

104. MacDonald, *Battle of the Huertgen Forest*, 5.

105. MacDonald, *The Last Offensive*, 75–80.

106. See After Action Report, *The Story of the 82d Airborne Division in the Battle of the Belgian Bulge in the Siegfried Line and on the Roer River*, n.d.; and Headquarters, 505th Parachute Infantry, "History of Operations of the 505th Parachute Infantry Regiment in the Belgium Campaign, Part III," n.d., 382-INF(505)-0.3, Box 12458, Record Group 407, NARA II.

107. See Blair, *Ridgway's Paratroopers*, 431–432; Langdon, *"Ready,"* 119–121; Lord, *History of the 508th Parachute Infantry*, 81–82; After Action Report, *The Story of the 82d Airborne Division in the Battle of the Belgian Bulge in the Siegfried Line and on the Roer River*, n.d.; Headquarters, 505th Parachute Infantry, "History of Operations of the 505th Parachute Infantry Regiment in the Belgium Campaign, Part III," n.d.; and Headquarters, 325th Glider Infantry, "325th Narrative—February 1–20, 1945," 6 March 1945, 382-INF(325)-0.3, Box 12448, Record Group 407, NARA II.

108. MacDonald, *The Last Offensive*, 81–82.

109. Gavin, Personal Diary, 17 February 1945; Gavin, *On to Berlin*, 265–266.

110. Gavin, *On to Berlin*, 261.

111. Ibid., 261–263.

112. Ibid., 264.

113. Ibid., 265–266; Blair, *Ridgway's Paratroopers*, 432

114. Gavin, *On to Berlin*, 268. See also John Keegan, *The First World War*, 358–369; and James L. Stokesbury, *A Short History of World War I*, 239–242. In *On to Berlin*, Gavin wrote, "Looking back on the winter war, I realize that one battle made an indelible impression on my mind. It was the battle for Schmidt beyond the Huertgen [*sic*] Forest." And, in fact, although the 82nd played a relatively minor role in this fight, Gavin devoted eight pages to discussing and analyzing it. In one of the book's few footnotes, he also made the point that when he visited the Army's Command and General Staff College in the mid-1970s, he saw that the faculty there used the battle for Schmidt as a case study "to drive home [to the students] the need for senior commanders to learn firsthand the battlefield conditions under which their troops might fight." Gavin, *On to Berlin*, 267–268.

115. Headquarters, 505th Parachute Infantry, "History of Operations of the 505th Parachute Infantry Regiment in the Belgium Campaign, Part III," n.d.; Wurst and Wurst, *Descending from the Clouds*, 238–239; Langdon, *"Ready,"* 120; McKenzie quoted in Jorgensen, *History of the 456th Parachute Field Artillery Battalion*, 243; Combat Interview "Battle of the Bulge," interview with Major William Carpenter and Captain Charles E. Sammon, 27 March 1945; Ridgway and Martin, *Soldier*, 132.

116. History, 504th Parachute Infantry, 1 February 1945–11 March 1945, n.d. See also After Action Report, *The Story of the 82d Airborne Division in the Battle of the Belgian Bulge in the Siegfried Line and on the Roer River*, n.d.

CHAPTER 25: PRESENT AT THE END

1. Gavin, Personal Diary, 26 February 1945 (see chap. 4, n. 26). See also Pierce, *Let's Go!* 280–281; Lord, *History of the 508th Parachute Infantry*, 82, 84; Langdon, *"Ready,"* 122; Megellas, *All the Way to Berlin*, 237; and After Action Re-

port, *The Story of the 82d Airborne Division in the Battle of the Belgian Bulge in the Siegfried Line and on the Roer River*, n.d. (see chap. 21, n. 2).

2. Gavin, *On to Berlin*, 268; Langdon, *"Ready,"* 122; Lord, *History of the 508th Parachute Infantry*, 84, 86; Pierce, *Let's Go!* 280–282.

3. The division was also introduced to the C-46, the C-47's larger twin that could carry twice as many paratroopers, thirty-six as opposed to eighteen, and which could disgorge jumpers from its two aft paratroop doors simultaneously. Gavin was one of the first in the division to jump from a C-46, and they were used during several of the training jumps. See Gavin, Personal Diary, entries for 12 and 18 March 1945; and Blair, *Ridgway's Paratroopers*, 440.

4. See also Gavin, *On to Berlin*, 269–279; Lord, *History of the 508th Parachute Infantry*, 84, 86; Megellas, *All the Way to Berlin*, 239; and Pierce, *Let's Go!* 281.

5. Huston, *Out of the Blue*, 217. ARENA called for the insertion of four to six airborne divisions to seize several airfields into which four conventional infantry divisions could be flown. Then, while the airborne divisions defended the airfields, the heavier infantry divisions would conduct offensive operations in the enemy's rear, thereby cutting German lines of communication to the front and easing the way for the eventual crossing of the Rhine. Overall command of ARENA would fall to Brereton's First Allied Airborne Army and would involve XVIII Airborne Corps and the British I Airborne Corps. Maneuver units earmarked for ARENA included the U.S. 13th, 17th, 82nd, and 101st Airborne Divisions; the British 1st and 6th Airborne Divisions; and the U.S. 2nd, 84th, and 103rd Infantry Divisions. A fourth U.S. infantry division and a third U.S. corps headquarters element would round out the troop list. See Huston, *Out of the Blue*, 217; and Blair, *Ridgway's Paratroopers*, 445–447. ARENA was the direct result of General Marshall's insistence that airborne units in Europe were not being used to their full potential. In December 1944, while in Washington to discuss plans for the reorganization of airborne divisions with the War Department staff, Maxwell Taylor also had an office call with Marshall. "Everyone in Washington appeared pleased over the conduct of Airborne troops in battle," Taylor reported. "However, General Marshall is emphatic in speaking about the 'timidity' of our planning. His idea of the proper Airborne operation is to seize an air head and then pour in large quantities of troops. . . . I pointed out some of the difficulties in such an operation in Europe, but I am not sure he was listening. He damned without stint Montgomery['s] 'Carpet' in Holland." Maxwell Taylor to Matthew B. Ridgway, 17 January 1945, Ridgway Papers, Box 3, Folder "Matthew B. Ridgway: World War II—Personal, January to February 1945," USAMHI.

6. See also Blair, *Ridgway's Paratroopers*, 436, 445–447.

7. Brereton, *Brereton Diaries*, 370.

8. Gavin, Personal Diary, 12 March 1945.

9. Butcher, *My Three Years with Eisenhower*, 768; Gavin, Personal Diary, 12 March 1945. At the time Gavin wrote this entry Soviet armies were arrayed along the Oder and Neisse Rivers, less than fifty miles east of Berlin. See Peter Young, ed., *Atlas of the Second World War*, 219.

10. Gavin, Personal Diary, 12 March 1945; Ridgway's memorandum of 8 March 1945 to First Allied Airborne Army quoted in Gavin, *On to Berlin*, 270 (capitalization in original); Brereton, *Brereton Diaries*, 398.

11. Gavin, *On to Berlin*, 269–271; McKenzie, *On Time, On Target*, 156; Pierce, *Let's Go!* 282; Megellas, *All the Way to Berlin*, 241.

12. See McKenzie, *On Time, On Target*, 157; Pierce, *Let's Go!* 282: Megellas, *All the Way to Berlin*, 239–241.

13. Gavin, Personal Diary, 12 March 1945; Charles McMoran Wilson [Lord Moran], *The Anatomy of Courage*, xvi. Perhaps no better illustration of Moran's concept occurred in the 456th Parachute Field Artillery Battalion. During one of the training jumps for ECLIPSE, Corporal Jim Hancock, a veteran with service stretching back to Sicily who had already earned a Silver Star and Purple Heart, refused to jump. Hancock's uncharacteristic action sent a shock wave through the battalion. Certain that Hancock had simply suffered from a temporary case of nerves, the 456th's officers arranged that he be given a second chance. Again Hancock refused to exit the plane. Unwilling to give up on a man who had already survived so much, a third jump was arranged. This time Hancock did not even get on the plane. While waiting to board, he hit the quick release on this parachute harness, dropped it on the tarmac, and walked away. According to his commander, Captain Herman Alley, Hancock "was found in the billets that evening and told us that he had lost his nerve and didn't care what happened." Alley quoted in Jorgensen, *History of the 456th Parachute Field Artillery Battalion*, 250. Hancock was eventually court-martialed, sentenced to two years' hard labor (of which he served only six months), and dishonorably discharged. Undoubtedly, Gavin was apprised of the situation. See also McKenzie, *On Time, On Target*, 157–161.

14. Gavin, *On to Berlin*, 269 (emphasis in original).

15. Bradley and Blair, *A General's Life*, 401.

16. D. Eisenhower, *Crusade in Europe*, 379.

17. For LUMBERJACK and the capture of the Remagen Bridge, see also Bradley and Blair, *A General's Life*, 400–407; Weigley, *Eisenhower's Lieutenants*, 617–628; and MacDonald, *The Last Offensive*, 208–235.

18. MacDonald, *The Last Offensive*, 208.

19. Quoted in Bradley and Blair, *A General's Life*, 407.

20. See also Weigley, *Eisenhower's Lieutenants*; MacDonald, *The Last Offensive*, 339–343; and Stephen E. Ambrose, *Eisenhower and Berlin, 1945: The Decision to Halt at the Elbe*, 17–98.

21. MacDonald, *The Last Offensive*, 278.

22. Ridgway quoted in Huston, *Out of the Blue*, 218. See also Blair, *Ridgway's Paratroopers*, 448.

23. See Warren, *Airborne Operations in the European Theater*, 156–193; and MacDonald, *The Last Offensive*, 296–314. Unlike the other airborne operations to date, the VARSITY drop came twelve hours *after* the commencement of the ground assault. This sequencing, suggested by General Dempsey, the commander of the British Second Army, was necessitated because of the need to deconflict the airspace over the drop zones and to ensure that Allied artillery rounds and Allied transport planes and gliders were not flying through the same piece of sky at the same time, a recipe for disaster. Gavin, who had never witnessed an airborne operation in which he was not participating, flew up from Sissonne and observed the drop from a transport plane flying well above the troop carrier formation. It was

"quite a sight" and "appeared a bit dangerous," he later wrote, unusual comments from a man who had already survived four combat jumps. Gavin, Personal Diary, 25 March 1945.

24. "The Unit History of the 319th Glider Field Artillery Battalion (from April 1, 1945 to April 30, 1945, Incl.)," n.d., 382-FA(319)-0.3, Box 12435, Record Group 407, NARA II.

25. Pierce, *Let's Go!* 282; Lewis quoted in Nordyke, *All American*, 734; Megellas, *All the Way to Berlin*, 239; McKenzie, *On Time, On Target*, 161.

26. James M. Gavin to Matthew B. Ridgway, 9 April 1945, Ridgway Papers, Box 3, Folder "Matthew B. Ridgway, Personal File, February to April 1945," USAMHI; Matthew B. Ridgway to James M. Gavin, 8 April 1945, Ridgway Papers, Box 3, Folder "Matthew B. Ridgway, Personal File, February to April 1945," USAMHI. See also Lord, *History of the 508th Parachute Infantry*, 86–100; Brereton, *Brereton Diaries*, 415; Blair, *Ridgway's Paratroopers*, 439; and Pierce, *Let's Go!* 282.

27. Lord, *History of the 508th Parachute Infantry*, 100.

28. See Weigley, *Eisenhower's Lieutenants*, 677; MacDonald, *The Last Offensive*, 323; Gavin, *On to Berlin*, 278; 82nd Airborne Division, *Action in Central Europe, April–May 1945*, n.d., unmarked box, Folder "82nd Airborne Division—WWII After Action Report: Cent. Europe," 82nd Airborne Division Museum, Fort Bragg, NC; and Gavin, Personal Diary, 2 April 1945.

29. Headquarters, 504th Parachute Infantry, "History, 31 March–31 April [*sic*] 1945," n.d., 382-INF(504)-0.3, Box 12453, Record Group 407, NARA II; "Historical Narrative, 307th Airborne Engineer Battalion, April 1945," 10 May 1945, Box "82nd Airborne Division—WWII—307th Eng. Bn.—Unit History—Incident Reports," Folder "307th Hist. Apr.–Oct. 45," 82nd Airborne Division Museum, Fort Bragg, NC.

30. McKenzie, *On Time, On Target*, 155.

31. Butcher, *My Three Years with Eisenhower*, 767; Headquarters, 504th Parachute Infantry, "History, 31 March–31 April [*sic*] 1945," n.d.

32. Gavin, Personal Diary, 2 April 1945; Gavin, *On to Berlin*, 278.

33. See also 82nd Airborne Division, *Action in Central Europe, April–May 1945*, n.d.; and MacDonald, *The Last Offensive*, 367.

34. 82nd Airborne Division, *Action in Central Europe, April–May 1945*, n.d.

35. Headquarters, 82nd Airborne Division Artillery, "Narrative History, 2 April–15 April 1945, Rhine Operation," n.d., 382-ART-0.3, Box 12430, Record Group 407, NARA II. Gavin's artillery assault prompted an unusual visit from the enemy. On the second day of the bombardment Captain Burriss and his troopers were keeping watch along the river when they spied some German soldiers on the far bank maneuvering a boat into the water. Because one of the Germans was carrying a large white flag, Burriss had his men hold their fire. They then watched as the Germans rowed toward them, bemused at the sight of one of them, obviously an officer and significantly older the rest, standing in the bow like George Washington. Upon landing the older man, who turned out to be a German medical officer in the rank of colonel, demanded to see the American commander. Though infuriated by the colonel's haughtiness—according to Lieutenant Megellas, "the Colonel was an arrogant Nazi, slickly dressed, medals all over his chest and wearing a monocle,

Hollywood style"—the troopers complied with the colonel's request and sent word back that a German officer was requesting an audience with the division commander. Megellas, *All the Way to Berlin*, 250. Shortly thereafter, Gavin arrived at Burriss's command post. Speaking through an interpreter, the colonel demanded that the Americans stop firing their artillery on a German hospital. His ire up, Gavin snapped back that were the hospital properly marked, it would not have been fired upon. Chastened, the colonel produced a letter signed by his superior, General der Infanterie Friedrich Koechling, the *LXXXI Corps* commander (part of Model's force surrounded in the Ruhr Pocket), that identified the colonel as the corps surgeon. Attached to the letter was a map on which was outlined the location of the hospital and other areas where the Germans were collecting their wounded. Gavin immediately designated the areas no-fire zones. With that matter settled Gavin had then to address the question of what to do with the colonel and his party. His first impulse was to take them prisoner, but he feared that that decision might be reversed by either XXII Corps or the U.S. Fifteenth Army because of the colonel's status as a medical officer, so, after discussing the matter with General Harmon, he sent the colonel and his party back across the Rhine. In the almost twenty months since the division had first seen action, this was one of the few times that the 82nd set prisoners free, and it was most certainly the first time that one of such high rank had been let go. See also Gavin, Personal Diary, 9 April 1945; and Burriss, *Strike and Hold*, 177–178.

36. Both orders quoted in 82nd Airborne Division, *Action in Central Europe, April–May 1945*, n.d. (capitalization in original).

37. See also Burriss, *Strike and Hold*, 177; Megellas, *All the Way to Berlin*, 246–247; and 82nd Airborne Division, *Action in Central Europe, April–May 1945*, n.d.

38. 82nd Airborne Division, *Action in Central Europe, April–May 1945*, n.d.

39. See also Megellas, *All the Way to Berlin*, 247; and Headquarters, 504th Parachute Infantry, "History, 31 March–31 April [*sic*] 1945," n.d.

40. See Nordyke, *All American*, 736–737; Mandle and Whittier, *Combat Record of the 504th Parachute Infantry Regiment*, n.p.; Megellas, *All the Way to Berlin*, 248; Headquarters, 504th Parachute Infantry, "History, 31 March–31 April [*sic*] 1945," n.d.

41. Headquarters, 504th Parachute Infantry, "History, 31 March–31 April [*sic*] 1945," n.d.; Breard quoted in Nordyke, *All American*, 738.

42. See also Nordyke, *All American*, 738; and Megellas, *All the Way to Berlin*, 248.

43. Breard quoted in Nordyke, *All American*, 739. See also Megellas, *All the Way to Berlin*, 248–249; Mandle and Whittier, *Combat Record of the 504th Parachute Infantry Regiment*, n.p.; Headquarters, 376th Parachute Field Artillery Battalion, "Narrative History," 10 May 1945, 382-FA(376)-0.3, Box 12440, Record Group 407, NARA II; and Headquarters, 504th Parachute Infantry, "History, 31 March–31 April [*sic*] 1945," n.d. For his actions, Kiernan was awarded the Distinguished Service Cross.

44. Megellas, *All the Way to Berlin*, 249; Mandle and Whittier, *Combat Record of the 504th Parachute Infantry Regiment*, n.p.; Burriss, *Strike and Hold*, 178–182; Headquarters, 504th Parachute Infantry, "History, 31 March–31 April [*sic*] 1945," n.d.

45. Burriss, *Strike and Hold*, 182; "Historical Narrative, 307th Airborne Engineer Battalion, April 1945," 10 May 1945; Headquarters, 504th Parachute Infantry, "History, 31 March–31 April [*sic*] 1945," n.d.

46. Headquarters, 504th Parachute Infantry, "History, 31 March–31 April [*sic*] 1945," n.d. After the war, A Company was awarded a Presidential Unit Citation for Hitdorf. See "Award of the Presidential Unit Citation," unmarked box, Folder "*Unit Awards—A Co. PUC," 82nd Airborne Division Museum, Fort Bragg, NC.

47. Gavin, Personal Diary, 9 April 1945.

48. Matthew B. Ridgway to James M. Gavin, 5 and 8 April 1945, Ridgway Papers, Box 3, Folder "Matthew B. Ridgway, Personal File, February to April 1945," USAMHI; Gavin, Personal Diary, 13 April 1945.

49. E. N. Harmon, Milton MacKaye, and William Ross MacKaye, *Combat Commander: Autobiography of a Soldier*, 250.

50. Gavin, Personal Diary, 17 April 1945. In his autobiography, Harmon wrote that Gavin knew about the Pacific *before* the foray against Hitdorf (a battle about which Harmon gets several other facts wrong), but Gavin's diaries disprove this. The first mention Gavin makes about the possibility of the 82nd being transferred to the Pacific is in his 17 April 1945 entry. It is unlikely that, were Gavin told earlier, he would not have recorded this in his diary. Moreover, Gavin is very specific about when he was told for the first time. Harmon, MacKaye, and MacKaye, *Combat Commande*r, 250–251.

51. Gavin, Personal Diary, 25 April 1945.

52. See 82nd Airborne Division, *Action in Central Europe, April–May 1945*, n.d.; Headquarters, 82nd Airborne Division Artillery, "Narrative History, 2 April–15 April 1945, Rhine Operation," n.d; "Historical Narrative, 307th Airborne Engineer Battalion, April 1945," 10 May 1945; Headquarters, 307th Airborne Engineer Battalion, "Patrol Reports," n.d., Box "82nd Airborne Division—WWII—307th Eng. Bn.—Unit History—Incident Reports," Folder "307th Abn. Eng. Bn. Reports Apr.–May 34," 82nd Airborne Division Museum, Fort Bragg, NC; James M. Gavin to Matthew B. Ridgway, 8 April 1945, Ridgway Papers, Box 3, Folder "Matthew B. Ridgway, Personal File, February to April 1945," USAMHI.

53. "Narrative to Accompany the Unit History of the 325th Glider Infantry for the Month of April 1945," n.d., 382-INF(325)-0.3, Box 12448, Record Group 407, NARA II; Gavin, *On to Berlin*, 279. See also "Narrative to Accompany the Unit History of the 325th Glider Infantry for the Month of April 1945," n.d.; Headquarters, 82nd Airborne Division Artillery, "Narrative History, 2 April–15 April 1945, Rhine Operation," n.d.; and Langdon, *"Ready,"* 125.

54. Pierce, *Let's Go!* 283.

55. Gavin, Personal Diary, 9 April 1945; McKenzie, *On Time, On Target*, 165.

56. McKenzie, *On Time, On Target*, 165–166.

57. Gavin, *On to Berlin*, 278–279. See also "Narrative to Accompany the Unit History of the 325th Glider Infantry for the Month of April 1945," n.d.; Headquarters, 82nd Airborne Division Artillery, "Narrative History, 2 April–15 April 1945, Rhine Operation," n.d.; Gavin to Ridgway, 9 April 1945.

58. Megellas, *All the Way to Berlin*, 255. For the division's occupation tasks, see also "Narrative to Accompany the Unit History of the 325th Glider Infantry for

the Month of April 1945," n.d.; Headquarters, 82nd Airborne Division Artillery, "Narrative History, 2 April–15 April 1945, Rhine Operation," n.d.; and Gavin to Ridgway, 9 April 1945.

59. The reduction of the Ruhr Pocket was a resounding victory for the Americans. Thousands of German soldiers were killed or wounded, and another 317,000 surrendered, which was more prisoners than the Russians took at Stalingrad and more than the combined total of German and Italian prisoners bagged during the final phase of the battle for North Africa. Included in the German prisoner haul were 25 generals and 1 admiral. Generalfeldmarschall Model was not among them. He and a small group of staff officers evaded capture and fled to a small forest just north of Düsseldorf where, on 21 April, Model committed suicide. The Allies also liberated some 200,000 displaced persons and 5,639 Anglo-American prisoners of war. See MacDonald, *The Last Offensive*, 372; Weigley, *Eisenhower's Lieutenants*, 677, 680; and Max Hastings, *Armageddon: The Battle for Germany, 1944–1945*, 468.

60. Gavin, Personal Diary, 18 April 1945.

61. Ibid., 13 April 1945.

62. At the time 12th Army Group also included the U.S. Fifteenth Army, but it remained west of the Rhine and did not participate in the pursuit to the Elbe and Mulde Rivers. MacDonald, *The Last Offensive*, 379.

63. Eisenhower quoted in Weigley, *Eisenhower's Lieutenants*, 719.

64. Bradley and Blair, *A General's Life*, 427. For background on Eisenhower's decision to lend XVIII Airborne Corps to Montgomery, see also Weigley, *Eisenhower's Lieutenants*, 721–722; Blair, *Ridgway's Paratroopers*, 488; and Headquarters, XVIII Airborne Corps, "Summary of Operations, the Elbe to the Baltic, 27 April to 3 May 1945," 20 May 1945, Blair Collection, Box 48, Folder "Chrono File: Ruhr/Elbe," USAMHI.

65. Montgomery quoted in Ridgway and Martin, *Soldier*, 142

66. See Blair, *Ridgway's Paratroopers*, 490–491; Weigley, *Eisenhower's Lieutenants*, 719–722; Matthew B. Ridgway, "Summary of Operations XVIII Corps (Airborne)," 20 April 1949, Blair Collection, Box 48, Folder "Chrono File: Ruhr/Elbe," USAMHI; and Headquarters, XVIII Airborne Corps, "Summary of Operations, the Elbe to the Baltic, 27 April to 3 May 1945," 20 May 1945.

67. Ridgway and Martin, *Soldier*, 142–143.

68. Weigley, *Eisenhower's Lieutenants*, 722; Headquarters, XVIII Airborne Corps, "Summary of Operations, the Elbe to the Baltic, 27 April to 3 May 1945," 20 May 1945.

69. Matthew B. Ridgway to Cornelius Ryan, 24 June 1979, Ridgway Papers, Box 6, Folder "Matthew B. Ridgway, Cornelius Ryan, James Gavin, Correspondence, June–July 1973, Concerning Operation Market Garden, September 1944," USAMHI.

70. Gavin, Personal Diary, 25 April 1945.

71. 82nd Airborne Division, *Action in Central Europe, April–May 1945*, n.d.

72. Langdon, *"Ready,"* 126; Combat Interview, interview with Captain Charles E. Sammon, 14 May 1945, CI-361 "XVIII A/B Corps, Rhine-Ruhr-Elbe Operation," 24 Mar.–1 May 45, Box 24117, Record Group 407, NARA II; Gavin, Personal Diary, 25 April 1945.

73. Gavin, "Beyond the Stars," 93 (see chap. 1, n. 23). In this draft autobiography as well as in *On to Berlin*, Gavin incorrectly gave the date of 29 April for this meeting. According to contemporary accounts, however, which generally agree on the timing of subsequent events, this meeting could have taken place only on 28 April. See, for example, 82nd Airborne Division, *Action in Central Europe, April–May 1945*, n.d.; Combat Interview, interview with Captain Charles E. Sammon, 14 May 1945; and Combat Interview, interview with Captain Thomas M. Furey, 13 May 1945, CI-361 "XVIII A/B Corps, Rhine-Ruhr-Elbe Operation," 24 Mar.–1 May 45, Box 24117, Record Group 407, NARA II.

74. See also Gavin, *On to Berlin*, 284; Headquarters, 307th Airborne Engineer Battalion, "Historical Narrative, 307th Airborne Engineer Battalion, May 1945," 10 June 1945, Box "82nd Airborne Division—WWII—307th Eng. Bn.—Unit History—Incident Reports," Folder "307th Hist. Apr.–Oct. 45," 82nd Airborne Division Museum, Fort Bragg, NC; Reconnaissance Platoon, 82nd Airborne Division, "Record of Events for Month of April 1945, After Action Report, 1–5 May 45," 10 May 1945, 382-CAV-0.3, Box 12432, Record Group 407, NARA II; Headquarters, XVIII Airborne Corps, "Summary of Operations, the Elbe to the Baltic, 27 April to 3 May 1945," 20 May 1945.

75. Headquarters, 307th Airborne Engineer Battalion, "Historical Narrative, 307th Airborne Engineer Battalion, May 1945," 10 June 1945.

76. 82nd Airborne Division, *Action in Central Europe, April–May 1945*, n.d.; Reconnaissance Platoon, 82nd Airborne Division, "Record of Events for Month of April 1945, After Action Report, 1–5 May 45," 10 May 1945.

77. "XVIII Corps (Airborne), Elbe River to Baltic Sea, 30 April to 3 May 1945," n.d., CI-361 "XVIII A/B Corps, Rhine-Ruhr-Elbe Operation," 24 Mar.–1 May 45, Box 24117, Record Group 407, NARA II; Langdon, *"Ready,"* 126. See also Allen Langdon to Clay Blair, 3 March 1984, Blair Collection, Box 54, Folder "Langdon, Allen," USAMHI.

78. See Langdon, *"Ready,"* 127; Headquarters, 307th Airborne Engineer Battalion, "Historical Narrative, 307th Airborne Engineer Battalion, May 1945," 10 June 1945; Headquarters, 82nd Airborne Division Artillery, "Narrative History, 28 April–30 April 1945, Elbe River Crossing," n.d., 382-ART-0.3, Box 12430, Record Group 407, NARA II.

79. Gavin, *On to Berlin*, 285. See also Blair, *Ridgway's Paratroopers*, 492–493; Langdon, *"Ready,"* 126; 82nd Airborne Division, *Action in Central Europe, April–May 1945*, n.d.; Combat Interview, interview with Captain Hunter S. Marston, 11 May 1945, CI-361 "XVIII A/B Corps, Rhine-Ruhr-Elbe Operation," 24 Mar.–1 May 45, Box 24117, Record Group 407, NARA II.

80. 82nd Airborne Division, *Action in Central Europe, April–May 1945*, n.d. (capitalization in original); Langdon to Blair, 3 March 1984; Combat Interview, interview with Captain Thomas M. Furey, 13 May 1945; Headquarters, 307th Airborne Engineer Battalion, "Historical Narrative, 307th Airborne Engineer Battalion, May 1945," 10 June 1945; Combat Interview, interview with Captain Thomas M. Furey, 13 May 1945.

81. "XVIII Corps (Airborne), Elbe River to Baltic Sea, 30 April to 3 May 1945."

82. Combat Interview, interview with Captain Thomas M. Furey, 13 May 1945.

83. See "XVIII Corps (Airborne), Elbe River to Baltic Sea, 30 April to 3 May 1945," n.d.; Combat Interview, interview with Captain Charles E. Sammon, 14 May 1945.

84. See Langdon, *"Ready,"* 126–127; Headquarters, 307th Airborne Engineer Battalion, "Historical Narrative, 307th Airborne Engineer Battalion, May 1945," 10 June 1945; Combat Interview, interview with Captain Thomas M. Furey, 13 May 1945; Combat Interview, interview with Captain Charles E. Sammon, 14 May 1945; and "XVIII Corps (Airborne), Elbe River to Baltic Sea, 30 April to 3 May 1945."

85. Combat Interview, interview with Captain Thomas M. Furey, 13 May 1945.

86. Combat Interview, interview with Captain Charles E. Sammon, 14 May 1945. See also "XVIII Corps (Airborne), Elbe River to Baltic Sea, 30 April to 3 May 1945."

87. For the fight on the Elbe, see also Langdon, *"Ready,"* 127–128; 82nd Airborne Division, *Action in Central Europe, April–May 1945*, n.d.; "XVIII Corps (Airborne), Elbe River to Baltic Sea, 30 April to 3 May 1945"; Combat Interview, interview with Captain Charles E. Sammon, 14 May 1945; Combat Interview, interview with Captain Thomas M. Furey, 13 May 1945; Combat Interview, interview with Second Lieutenant William P. Ramsey, 11 May 1945, CI-361 "XVIII A/B Corps, Rhine-Ruhr-Elbe Operation," 24 Mar.–1 May 45, Box 24117, Record Group 407, NARA II; Combat Interview, interview with First Lieutenant Francis J. Myers, 14 May 1945, CI-361 "XVIII A/B Corps, Rhine-Ruhr-Elbe Operation," 24 Mar.–1 May 45, Box 24117, Record Group 407, NARA II.

88. Blair, *Ridgway's Paratroopers*, 493, Gavin, *On to Berlin*, 285; "XVIII Corps (Airborne), Elbe River to Baltic Sea, 30 April to 3 May 1945."

89. 82nd Airborne Division, *Action in Central Europe, April–May 1945*, n.d.

90. Combat Interview, interview with Captain David L. Hollingsworth, 9 May 1945, CI-361 "XVIII A/B Corps, Rhine-Ruhr-Elbe Operation," 24 Mar.–1 May 45, Box 24117, Record Group 407, NARA II.

91. 82nd Airborne Division, *Action in Central Europe, April–May 1945*, n.d.

92. "The Unit History of the 319th Glider Field Artillery Battalion (from May 1, 1945 to June 3, 1945 Incl.), n.d., 382-FA(319)-0.3, Box 12435, Record Group 407, NARA II.

93. Headquarters, 376th Parachute Field Artillery Battalion, "Narrative History," 31 May 1945, 382-FA(376)-0.3, Box 12440, Record Group 407, NARA II.

94. Headquarters, 456th Parachute Field Artillery Battalion, "Narrative History of the 456th Parachute Field Artillery Battalion for the Period of 1 April to 30 April 1945," 8 May 1945, 382-FA(456)-0.3, Box 12445, Record Group 407, NARA II.

95. The British 6th Airborne Division crossed over the Lauenburg Bridge during the night of 30 April–1 May by ruse. According to Ridgway, the British VIII Corps commander (to whom the 6th Airborne Division was attached while it was west of the Elbe) "impounded the airborne people and would not let them approach the bridgehead until the armor had crossed. This left the airborne troopers champing at the bit. Then some bright trooper figured out a ruse. The airborne wore a red beret, with a black lining, and the armored people wore a black beret. So the airborne

troopers turned their berets inside out and went across under the noses of the MP's, disguised as armored elements." Once across, the British paratroopers turned right and marched hard to link up with XVIII Airborne Corps before they were discovered. "It was a damned smart stunt," commented Ridgway, and one for which he was very grateful. Ridgway and Martin, *Soldier*, 144.

96. See also 82nd Airborne Division, *Action in Central Europe, April–May 1945*, n.d.; and "XVIII Corps (Airborne), Elbe River to Baltic Sea, 30 April to 3 May 1945."

97. Headquarters, 504th Parachute Infantry, "History, 1 May 1945–5 May 1945," n.d., 382-INF(504)-0.3, Box 12453, Record Group 407, NARA II; Langdon to Blair, 3 March 1984; Megellas, *All the Way to Berlin*, 258.

98. Headquarters, 307th Airborne Engineer Battalion, "Historical Narrative, 307th Airborne Engineer Battalion, May 1945," 10 June 1945. See also Megellas, *All the Way to Berlin*, 258.

99. 82nd Airborne Division, *Action in Central Europe, April–May 1945*, n.d.

100. Langdon to Blair, 3 March 1984.

101. Reconnaissance Platoon, 82nd Airborne Division, "Record of Events for Month of April 1945, After Action Report, 1–5 May 45," 10 May 1945.

102. "XVIII Corps (Airborne), Elbe River to Baltic Sea, 30 April to 3 May 1945."

103. Headquarters, 325th Glider Infantry, "Narrative of Operations and Activities Month of May, 1945," n.d., 382-INF(325)-0.3, Box 12448, Record Group 407, NARA II; Headquarters, 504th Parachute Infantry, "History, 1 May 1945–5 May 1945," n.d.; Combat Interview, interview with Major Fordyce Gorham, 11 May 1945, CI-361 "XVIII A/B Corps, Rhine-Ruhr-Elbe Operation," 24 Mar.–1 May 45, Box 24117, Record Group 407, NARA II.

104. Gavin, *On to Berlin*, 285; "The Unit History of the 319th Glider Field Artillery Battalion (from May 1, 1945 to June 3, 1945 Incl.), n.d.; Pierce, *Let's Go!* 288; Gavin, *On to Berlin*, 285.

105. 82nd Airborne Division, *Action in Central Europe, April–May 1945*, n.d.; "The Unit History of the 319th Glider Field Artillery Battalion (from May 1, 1945 to June 3, 1945 Incl.), n.d.

106. Headquarters, 307th Airborne Engineer Battalion, "Engineer Periodic Report From 040001 to 042400 May 45," 4 May 1945, Box "82nd Airborne Division—WWII—307th Eng. Bn.—Unit History—Incident Reports," Folder "307th Abn. Eng. Bn. Reports Apr.–May 45," 82nd Airborne Division Museum, Fort Bragg, NC.

107. Gavin, *On to Berlin*, 285–285.

108. Reconnaissance Platoon, 82nd Airborne Division, "Record of Events for Month of April 1945, After Action Report, 1–5 May 45," 10 May 1945.

109. "XVIII Corps (Airborne), Elbe River to Baltic Sea, 30 April to 3 May 1945"; Combat Interview, interview with Captain Robert Hanson and Captain Irven Bushman, 11 May 1945, CI-361 "XVIII A/B Corps, Rhine-Ruhr-Elbe Operation," 24 Mar.–1 May 45, Box 24117, Record Group 407, NARA II.

110. Leonard Linton to James M. Gavin, 4 October 1978, Gavin Papers, Box 10, Folder "Letters and Cards, to + from Gavin and 82nd Airborne Div. Veterans," USAMHI (capitalization in original).

111. 3rd Battalion, 504th Parachute Infantry Battalion Combat Journal, 1200 hours, 2 May 1945, untitled box, Folder "*Histories—Ardennes (3/504th)," 82nd Airborne Division Museum, Fort Bragg, NC; 3rd Battalion, 504th Parachute Infantry Battalion Combat Journal, 1540 hours, 2 May 1945.

112. "XVIII Corps (Airborne), Elbe River to Baltic Sea, 30 April to 3 May 1945." See also Combat Interview, interview with Major Fordyce Gorham, 11 May 1945.

113. 82nd Airborne Division, *Action in Central Europe, April–May 1945*, n.d.

114. Shirley R. Gossett to James M. Gavin, n.d., Gavin Papers, Box 10, Folder "Letters w/ Members of 505th Parachute Inf. Regiment, 82nd Division—Active and Association," USAMHI; Gavin, *On to Berlin*, 286.

115. Gavin, *On to Berlin*, 286. When asked what he said to the German general that caused him to change his mind, Gavin replied, "I simply swore at the German, loudly and somewhat gutturally. It was the sort of thing they respect more than anything else. He blanched a bit, but from there on he was very respectful." James M. Gavin to Ian S. Wilde, 25 October 1979, Gavin Papers, Box 12, Folder "Letters to and from 82nd Vets on Airborne Operations in Holland, September, 1944," USAMHI.

116. Gavin, Personal Diary, 3 May 1945; Gavin, *On to Berlin*, 286. See also Headquarters, 325th Glider Infantry, "Narrative of Operations and Activities Month of May, 1945," n.d.

117. Gavin, Personal Diary, 3 May 1945; 82nd Airborne Division, *Action in Central Europe, April–May 1945*, n.d.

118. 82nd Airborne Division, *Action in Central Europe, April–May 1945*, n.d. The war materiel figures given do not include the vehicles that passed directly through the 82nd's lines into XVIII Airborne Corps holding areas west of the Elbe.

119. Gavin, Personal Diary, 3 May 1945; Bradley and Blair, *A General's Life*, 434. Bradley added, "When I learned that an entire army group [*sic*] . . . had surrendered to Jim Gavin's 82nd Airborne Division, my old outfit, I was pleased" (434).

120. James M. Gavin to Matthew B. Ridgway, 27 June 1979, Ridgway Papers, Box 6, Folder "Matthew B. Ridgway, Cornelius Ryan, James Gavin, Correspondence, June–July 1973, Concerning Operation Market Garden, September 1944," USAMHI.

121. MacDonald, *The Last Offensive*, 464. Ridgway had not intended to take Wismar with the British 6th Airborne Division, but Dempsey had approached him requesting that British elements of XVIII Airborne Corps have the honor of being the first 21st Army Group units to make contact with the Russians. At first, Ridgway demurred. Dempsey's request would throw his attack "off stride," as he had already made plans to take Wismar with the U.S. 7th Armored Division. Getting the 6th Airborne to Wismar would mean Ridgway would have to move it diagonally across the 7th's line of attack, "which could cause all sorts of trouble on the roads." But then Ridgway reconsidered, and in deference to Dempsey, for whom he had great admiration, and the courage and sacrifice of the British people, Ridgway changed his plan and turned the 6th Airborne loose. The British paratroopers did not disappoint, making it to Wismar "with amazing rapidity." See Ridgway and Martin, *Soldier*, 145.

122. Gavin to Ridgway, 27 June 1979; Ridgway and Martin, *Soldier*, 145.

123. Headquarters, 376th Parachute Field Artillery Battalion, "Narrative History," 31 May 1945.

124. Gavin, Personal Diary, 8 May 1945.

EPILOGUE: SOLDIERS RECENTLY ENGAGED IN WAR

1. 82nd Airborne Division, *Action in Central Europe, April–May 1945*, n.d. (see chap. 25, n. 28).

2. MacDonald, *The Last Offensive*, 475. Generaloberst Alfred Jodl, representing Grossadmiral Karl Dönitz, who became the German head of state after Hitler committed suicide on 30 April 1945 in Berlin, signed a formal surrender at Eisenhower's headquarters in Rheims at 0241 hours, 7 May, to become effective 2301 hours, 8 May. The surrender ceremony was repeated the next day in Berlin for the benefit of the Russians, with Generalfeldmarschall Wilhelm Keitel standing in for Jodl.

3. See Greenfield, Palmer, and Wiley, *Organization of Ground Combat Troops*, 439–443; Matloff, *American Military History*, 530–531; and Weigley, *History of the United States Army*, 486–487, 569.

4. See Greenfield, Palmer, and Wiley, *Organization of Ground Combat Troops*, 450; 82nd Airborne Division, *Action in Central Europe, April–May 1945*, n.d.; Memorandum, Headquarters, XVIII Corps (Airborne), "Order of Airborne Divisions Returning to the United States," 26 May 1945, Ridgway Papers, Box 3, Folder "Matthew B. Ridgway: World War II—Personal—April to May 1945," USAMHI.

5. Memorandum, Headquarters, XVIII Corps Artillery (Airborne), 14 May 1945, Ridgway Papers, Box 3, Folder "Matthew B. Ridgway: World War II—Personal—April to May 1945," USAMHI.

6. See also Gavin, Personal Diary, 25 April 1945; Greenfield, Palmer, and Wiley, *Organization of Ground Combat Troops*, 450; and Memorandum, Headquarters, XVIII Corps (Airborne), "Order of Airborne Divisions Returning to the United States," 26 May 1945.

7. Memorandum, Headquarters, XVIII Corps (Airborne), 31 May 1945, Ridgway Papers, Box 3, Folder "Matthew B. Ridgway: World War II—Personal—April to May 1945," USAMHI.

8. "82d Abn. Div. Operations Report," 382-0.3, Box 12345, Record Group 407, NARA II.

9. Gavin, "Beyond the Stars," 102 (see chap. 1, n. 23).

10. Ibid., 105.

11. See also Taylor, *General Maxwell Taylor*, 36–48; Gavin, "Beyond the Stars," 104–105; and Blair, *Ridgway's Paratroopers*, 498–499. Ridgway had returned to the United States in late May 1945 for a two-week leave, during which he received word that General MacArthur's plans for the invasion of Japan called for the use of XVIII Airborne Corps. Ridgway therefore extended his stay in the United States to supervise the redeployment of the corps from Germany to Fort Campbell, Kentucky, where it was to refit before moving on to Manila, where it would stage for the invasion. Ridgway was in Manila when the Japanese surrendered, but soon returned to

the United States, where he spent some time in the War Department before assuming his postwar assignment as Commanding General, Mediterranean Theater of Operations.

12. Memorandum for the Chief of Staff, "Inactivation of Airborne Divisions," 18 October 1945, Gavin Papers, Box 10, Folder "82nd Airborne Division Inactivation Papers," USAMHI.

13. Memorandum, CG US Forces European Theater Main Frankfurt, Germany to War Department, 5 November 1945, Gavin Papers, Box 10, Folder "82nd Airborne Division Inactivation Papers," USAMHI.

14. Barney Oldfield, *Never a Shot in Anger*, 298; Gavin, "Beyond the Stars," 104–105; "Airborne Division Coming Home Soon," *New York Times*, 15 October 1945.

15. War Department Outgoing Classified Message to COMGENUSFET [Commanding General, U.S. Forces European Theater], 5 November 1945, Gavin Papers, Box 10, Folder "82nd Airborne Division Inactivation Papers," USAMHI.

16. James M. Gavin to Clay Blair, 6 March 1984, Blair Collection, Box 53, Folder "Gavin, James M.," USAMHI.

17. "82d Set to March Full Parade Route," *New York Times*, 3 January 1945.

18. Copy of Ed Bliss's column "Men of Consequence," in Gavin Papers, Box 7, bound pamphlet "Lt. Gen. James M. Gavin 82nd Airborne Division," USAMHI. See also Meyer Berger, "City Millions Hail the 82d in GI Tribute, *New York Times*, 13 January 1945; and Frederick Graham, "Mighty Air Show Leaves City Awed," *New York Times*, 13 January 1946.

19. Statistical Summary of 82nd Airborne Division in World War Two, 382-0.3.0, Box 12347, Record Group 407, NARA II.

20. Rubel quoted in ibid.

21. Quoted in Devlin, *Silent Wings*, 288.

BIBLIOGRAPHY

PRIMARY SOURCES

Interviews

Alexander, Mark
Broadaway, Rufus K.
Franco, Robert
Jorgensen, Starlyn
Norton, John
Piper, Bob
Sayre, Edwin M.
Selman, Thad P.
Stephenson, Paul Jr.
Stolmeier, Joe
Wurst, Spencer F.

Archival Sources

Athens, Ohio: Ohio University Library, the Cornelius Ryan Collection (OU)
Carlisle Barracks, Pennsylvania: United States Army Military History Institute (USAMHI)
Clay and Joan Blair Collection
William B. Breuer Collection
Ralph P. Eaton Papers
James M. Gavin Papers
Arthur S. Nevins Papers
Floyd Lavinius Parks Papers
Matthew B. Ridgway Papers
World War II Veterans Survey Project
William P. Yarborough Papers
Melvin Zais Papers

College Park, Maryland: National Archives and Records Administration II, Modern Military Reference Branch, Record Group 407 (NARA II)
Section 101: Headquarters, First Allied Airborne Army.
Section 382: 82nd Airborne Division
Combat Interview Section CI-170: 82nd Airborne Division Operation "Neptune" June 1944
Combat Interview Section CI-171: 82nd Airborne Division Holland, 17–26 Sep. 44
Combat Interview Sections CI-172 and CI 173: 82nd Airborne Division Ardennes, 18 Dec. 44–9 Feb. 45
Combat Interview Section CI-361: XVIII Airborne Corps, Rhine-Ruhr-Elbe Operations
Fort Benning, Georgia: Donovan Research Library, Student Papers of Personal Experiences During World War II
Fort Bragg, North Carolina: 82nd Airborne Division Museum, World War II Papers of the 82nd Airborne Division
New Orleans, Louisiana: Eisenhower Center, University of New Orleans, World War II Oral History Project
United States Army War College, Student Papers
West Point, New York: United States Military Academy, Department of History Library, Orders Related to the Invasion of Sicily

Microfilm

The Papers of George C. Marshall: Selected World War II Correspondence. Bethesda: University Publications of America, 1993.
Records of the War Department's Operations Division, 1942–1945. Bethesda: University Publications of America, 1993.

Newspapers

Boston Globe
New York Times

Printed Government Sources

American Battle Monuments Commission. *American Armies and Battlefields in Europe: A History, Guide, and Reference Book.* Washington, DC: Government Printing Office, 1938.
———. *82d Division: Summary of Operations in the World War.* Washington, DC: Government Printing Office, 1944.
Ayres, Leonard P. *The War with Germany: A Statistical Summary.* 2nd ed. Washington, DC: Government Printing Office, 1919.
Ellis, John T., Jr. *The Airborne Command and Center.* Army Ground Forces Historical Study, no. 2. Washington, DC: Headquarters, Army Ground Forces, 1946.

Office of Assistant Chief of Air Staff, Intelligence. *Airborne Assault on Holland: An Interim Report*. Washington, DC: Headquarters, Army Air Forces, 1945.

Reinhardt, Helmuth, et al. *Airborne Operations: A German Appraisal*. Center of Military History Publication 104-13. Facsimile ed. Washington, DC: Center of Military History, 1989.

War Department, FM 31-30. *Tactics and Technique of Air-Borne Troops*. Washington, DC: Government Printing Office, 1942.

War Department Historical Division. *Anzio Beachhead: 22 January–25 May 1944*. Washington, DC: Historical Division, War Department, 1948. Reprint, Washington, DC: Center of Military History, 1990.

Warren, John C. *Airborne Missions in the Mediterranean, 1942–1945*. U.S. Air Force Historical Study, no. 74. Maxwell Air Force Base, AL: U.S. Air Force Historical Division, Research Studies Institute, 1955.

———. *Airborne Operations in World War II, European Theater*. U.S. Air Force Historical Study, no. 97. Maxwell Air Force Base, AL: U.S. Air Force Historical Division, Research Studies Institute, 1956. Reprint, Manhattan, KS: MA/AH Publishing, Sunflower University Press, n.d.

Published Sources

Alexander, Mark. "Thirty Four Days in Normandy in 1944." N.p., 2001.

Astor, Gerald, ed. *June 6, 1944: The Voices of D-Day*. New York: St. Martin's Press, 1994.

Bierbaum, Margaret, ed. *As Ever, John: The Letters of Col. John V. McNally to His Sister, Margaret McNally Bierbaum, 1941–1946*. Fairfield, CT: Roberts Press, 1985.

Bingham, Walter V., and James Rorty. "How the Army Sorts Its Man Power." *Infantry Journal* 51, no. 4 (1942): 22–30.

Blumenson, Martin, ed. *The Patton Papers, 1940–1945*. Boston: Houghton Mifflin, 1974.

Blumentritt, Günther, et al. *Fighting the Invasion: The German Army at D-Day*. Ed. David C. Isby. Mechanicsburg, PA: Stackpole Books, 2000.

Boroughs, Zig. *The Devil's Tale: Stories of the RED DEVILS of the 508 Parachute Infantry Regiment, 82nd Airborne Division, in World War Two*. College Park, GA: Static Line Books, 1992.

Bradley, Omar N. *A Soldier's Story*. Chicago: Rand McNally, 1951.

Bradley, Omar N., and Clay Blair. *A General's Life*. New York: Simon and Schuster, 1983.

Brereton, Lewis H. *The Brereton Diaries: The War in the Air in the Pacific, Middle East, and Europe, 3 October 1941–8 May 1945*. New York: William Morrow, 1946.

Burriss, T. Moffatt. *Strike and Hold: A Memoir of the 82d Airborne in World War II*. Washington, DC: Brassey's, 2000.

Butcher, Harry C. *My Three Years with Eisenhower: The Personal Diary of Captain Harry C. Butcher, USNR, Naval Aide to General Eisenhower, 1942 to 1945*. New York: Simon and Schuster, 1946.

Carter, Ross S. *Those Devils in Baggy Pants*. New York: Appleton-Century-Crofts, 1951.
Chandler, Alfred D., ed. *The Papers of Dwight David Eisenhower: The War Years, II*. Baltimore: Johns Hopkins University Press, 1970.
———. *The Papers of Dwight David Eisenhower: The War Years, III*. Baltimore: Johns Hopkins University Press, 1970.
Chapman, E. G. "American Divisions Take to the Air." *Military Review* 23, no. 1 (1943): 11–16.
Churchill, Winston S. *Closing the Ring*. Vol. 5 of *The Second World War*. Boston: Houghton Mifflin, 1951.
———. *The Hinge of Fate*. Vol. 4 of *The Second World War*. Boston: Houghton Mifflin, 1950.
Clark, Mark. *Calculated Risk*. New York: Harper & Brothers, 1950.
Clausewitz, Carl von. *On War*. Ed. and trans. Michael Howard and Peter Paret. Princeton: Princeton University Press, 1976.
Cornett, Jack G. "Development of Airborne Forces." *Military Review* 25, no. 9 (1945): 26–36.
Covington, H. L. *A Fighting Heart: An Unofficial Story of the 82nd Airborne Division*. N.p.: Ted Davis, 1949.
Danchev, Alex, and Daniel Todman, eds. *War Diaries, 1939–1945, Field Marshal Lord Alanbrooke*. Berkeley and Los Angeles: University of California Press, 2001.
Dank, Milton. *The Glider Gang: An Eyewitness History of World War II Glider Combat*. Philadelphia: J. B. Lippincott, 1977.
Darby, William O., and William H. Baumer. *Darby's Rangers: We Led the Way*. San Rafael, CA: Presidio Press, 1980.
Dawson, Buck, ed. *Saga of the All American*. Fort Lauderdale: Hoffman Publishing, n.d.
Drez, Ronald J., ed. *The Voices of D-Day: The Story of the Allied Invasion Told by Those Who Were There*. Baton Rouge: Louisiana State University Press, 1994.
Eisenhower, Dwight D. *Crusade in Europe*. Garden City, NY: Doubleday, 1948.
Gavin, James M. "Airborne Army's First Test." Pt. 2, *Infantry Journal* 62, no. 2 (1948): 39–46.
———. "Airborne Plans and Operations in the Mediterranean Theater." *Infantry Journal* 59, no. 2 (1946): 22–29.
———. *Airborne Warfare*. Washington, DC: Infantry Journal Press, 1947.
———. "Back Door to Normandy: Airborne Plans and Counter Plans for the Invasion of Europe." *Infantry Journal* 59, no. 5 (1946): 9–19.
———. *On to Berlin: Battles of an Airborne Commander, 1943–1946*. New York: Viking Press, 1978.
———. *War and Peace in the Space Age*. New York: Harper & Brothers, 1958.
Gellhorn, Martha. "Rough and Tumble." In *Saga of the All American*, ed. Buck Dawson. Fort Lauderdale: Hoffman Publishing, n.d.
———. "Stand Up and Hook Up!" In *Saga of the All American*, ed. Buck Dawson. Fort Lauderdale: Hoffman Publishing, n.d.

Harmon, E. N., Milton MacKaye, and William Ross MacKaye. *Combat Commander: Autobiography of a Soldier*. Englewood Cliffs, NJ: Prentice-Hall, 1970.
Heiber, Helmut, and David M. Glantz, eds. *Hitler and His Generals, Military Conferences, 1942–1945: The First Complete Stenographic Record of the Military Situation Conferences, from Stalingrad to Berlin*. Trans. Roland Winter, Krista Smith, and Mary Beth Friedrich. New York: Enigma Books, 2003.
Horrocks, Brian. *Escape to Action*. New York: St. Martin's Press, 1960.
Horrocks, Brian, Eversley Belfield, and H. Essame. *Corps Commander*. New York: Charles Scribner's Sons, 1977.
Jacobus, George R., ed. *Echoes of the Warrior: Personal Experiences of the Enlisted Men and Officers of E Company of the 505th Parachute Infantry Regiment, 82nd Airborne, in World War II*. Privately published, 1992.
Janney, Richard Mott. *Richard Mott Janney, 1st Lt. 505 Reg. 82 A.B. Div., Killed in Action, Villa Literno, Italy, October 5, 1943*. Baltimore: Gilman School, n.d.
Kesselring, Albert. *The Memoirs of Field-Marshal Kesselring*. Trans. William Kimber. Novato, CA: Presidio Press, 1989.
Langdon, Allen. *"Ready": The History of the 505th Parachute Infantry Regiment, 82nd Airborne Division, World War II*. Indianapolis: Western Newspaper Publishing, 1986.
Lee, William C. "Air Infantry." *Infantry Journal* 48, no. 1 (1941): 14–16.
———. "Air-Landing Divisions." *Infantry Journal* 48, no. 4 (1941): 20–22.
Lord, William G., II. *History of the 508th Parachute Infantry*. Nashville: Battery Press, 1977.
MacDonald, Charles B. *Company Commander*. New York: Bantam Books, 1978.
McKenzie, John D. *On Time, On Target: The World War II Memoir of a Paratrooper in the 82d Airborne*. Novato, CA: Presidio Press, 2000.
Megellas, James. *All the Way to Berlin: A Paratrooper at War in Europe*. New York: Ballantine Books, 2003.
Milkovics, Lewis, ed. *"The Devils Have Landed."* Longwood, FL: Creative Printing and Publishing, 1993.
Mitchell, William. *Memoirs of World War I: "From Start to Finish of Our Greatest War."* New York: Random House, 1928.
Montgomery, Bernard Law. *The Memoirs of Field-Marshal the Viscount Montgomery of Alamein*. Cleveland: World Publishing, 1958. Reprint, New York: Signet Books, 1959.
Morgan, Frederick. *Overture to Overlord*. Garden City, NY: Doubleday, 1950.
Morgan, John W. "Airborne Field Artillery." *Military Review* 23, no. 6 (1943): 55–57.
Murphy, Robert M. *No Better Place to Die*. Croton Falls, NY: Critical Hit, 1999.
Nix, Jack P. *505th Parachute Infantry Regiment (a Legacy of Lessons)*. Carlisle Barracks, PA: Army War College Paper, 1989.
Nordyke, Phil. *All American All the Way*. St. Paul: Zenith Press, 2005.
O'Donnell, Patrick K., ed. *Beyond Valor: World War II's Rangers and Airborne Veterans Reveal the Heart of Combat*. New York: Simon & Schuster, 2001. Reprint, New York: Touchstone, 2002.

Oldfield, Barney. *Never a Shot in Anger*. Battle of Normandy Museum Edition. Santa Barbara: Capra Press, 1956.
Pierce, Wayne. *Let's Go!* Chapel Hill: Professional Press, 1997.
Raff, Edson D. *We Jumped to Fight*. New York: Eagle Books, 1944.
Richlak, Jerry L., Sr., ed. *Glide to Glory*. Chesterland, OH: Cedar House, 2002.
Rickenbacker, Edward W. *Seven Came Through*. Garden City, NY: Doubleday, Doran, 1943.
Ridgway, Matthew B., and Harold H. Martin. *Soldier: The Memoirs of Matthew B. Ridgway*. New York: Harper & Brothers, 1956.
Schweppenburg, Leo Freiherr Geyr von. "Glimpses of the US Soldier." *Military Review* 42, no. 4 (1962): 23–29.
Senger und Etterlin, Frido von. *Neither Fear nor Hope: The Wartime Career of General Frido von Senger und Etterlin, Defender of Cassino*. Trans. George Malcolm. Novato, CA: Presidio Press, 1989.
Taylor, Maxwell D. *Swords and Plowshares*. New York: W. W. Norton, 1972.
Tregaskis, Richard. *Invasion Diary*. New York: Random House, 1944.
Truscott, Lucian K. Jr. *Command Mission: A Personal Story*. New York: E. P. Dutton, 1954.
Tucker, William H. *Parachute Soldier*. Athol, MA: Haley's, 1994.
Warlimont, Walter. *Inside Hitler's Headquarters, 1939–45*. Trans. R. H. Barry. Novato, CA: Presidio Press, 1964.
Wilson, George. *If You Survive*. New York: Ivy Books, 1987.
Wurst, Spencer F. "Against All Possible Fire." *World War II* 19, no. 5 (2004): 26–31.
Wurst, Spencer F., and Gayle Wurst. *Descending from the Clouds: A Memoir of Combat in the 505 Parachute Infantry Regiment, 82d Airborne Division*. Havertown, PA: Casemate, 2004.
Yarborough, William P. *Bail Out over North Africa: America's First Combat Parachute Missions, 1942*. 2nd ed. Williamstown, NJ: Phillips Publications, 2000.
York, Alvin C. *Sergeant York: His Own Life Story and War Diary*. Ed. Tom Skeyhill. Garden City, NY: Doubleday, Doran, 1928.

SECONDARY SOURCES

Official Histories

Blumenson, Martin. *Breakout and Pursuit*. Washington, DC: Center of Military History, 1961. Reprint, Washington, DC: Center of Military History, 1993.
———. "General Lucas at Anzio." In *Command Decisions*, ed. Kent Roberts Greenfield. Washington, DC: Center of Military History, 1987.
———. *Salerno to Cassino*. Washington, DC: Government Printing Office, 1969.
Cline, Ray S. *Washington Command Post: The Operations Division*. Washington, DC: Government Printing Office, 1951. Reprint, Washington, DC: Center of Military History, 1990.
Coakley, Robert W., and Richard M. Leighton. *Global Logistics and Strategy, 1943–1945*. Washington, DC: Center of Military History, 1989.

Cole, Hugh M. *The Ardennes: Battle of the Bulge*. Washington, DC: Center of Military History, 1994.

Department of the Army. *The Army Almanac*. Washington, DC: Government Printing Office, 1950.

Gabel, Christopher R. *The U.S. Army GHQ Maneuvers of 1941*. Washington, DC: Center of Military History, 1991.

Garland, Albert N., and Howard McGaw Smyth. *Sicily and the Surrender of Italy*. Washington, DC: Government Printing Office, 1965. Reprint, Washington, DC: Center of Military History, 1993.

Greenfield, Kent Roberts, Robert R. Palmer, and Bell I. Wiley. *The Organization of Ground Combat Troops*. Washington, DC: Government Printing Office, 1947. Reprint, Washington, DC: Center of Military History, 1987.

Harrison, Gordon A. *Cross-Channel Attack*. Washington, DC: Center of Military History, 1989.

Kirkpatrick, Charles E. *An Unknown Future and a Doubtful Present: Writing the Victory Plan of 1941*. Washington, DC: Center of Military History, 1990.

Kreidberg, Marvin A., and Merton G. Henry. *History of Military Mobilization in the United States Army, 1775–1945*. Washington, DC: Department of the Army, 1955.

Luttichaur, Charles V. P. von. "The German Counteroffensive in the Ardennes." In *Command Decisions*, ed. Kent Robert Greenfield. Washington, DC: Center of Military History, 1987.

MacDonald, Charles B. *The Last Offensive*. Washington, DC: Government Printing Office, 1973. Reprint, Honolulu: University Press of the Pacific, 2005.

———. *The Siegfried Line Campaign*. Washington, DC: Center of Military History, 1963. Reprint, Washington, DC: Center of Military History, 1990.

Matloff, Maurice, ed. *American Military History*. Washington, DC: Center of Military History, 1988.

———. *Strategic Planning for Coalition Warfare, 1943–1944*. Washington, DC: U.S. Government Printing Office, 1959.

Matloff, Maurice, and Edwin M. Snell. *Strategic Planning for Coalition Warfare, 1941–1942*. Washington, DC: Government Printing Office, 1953. Reprint, Washington, DC: Center of Military History, 1990.

Mavrogordato, Ralph S. "Hitler's Decision on the Defense of Italy." In *Command Decisions*, ed. Kent Roberts Greenfield. Washington, DC: Center of Military History, 1987.

Morton, Louis. "Germany First: The Basic Concept of Allied Strategy in World War II." In *Command Decisions*, ed. Kent Roberts Greenfield. Washington, DC: Center of Military History, 1987.

Mossman, Billy C. *Ebb and Flow, November 1950–July 1951*. Washington, DC: Center of Military History, 1990.

Palmer, Robert R., Bell I. Wiley, and William R. Keast. *The Procurement and Training of Ground Combat Troops*. Washington, DC: Government Printing Office, 1948. Reprint, Washington, DC: Center of Military History, 1991.

Ruppenthal, Roland G. "Logistics and the Broad-Front Strategy." In *Command Decisions*, ed. Kent Roberts Greenfield. Washington, DC: Center of Military History, 1987.

Watson, Mark S. *Chief of Staff: Prewar Plans and Preparations*. Washington, DC: Center of Military History, 1950.

Wilson, John B. *Maneuver and Firepower: The Evolution of Divisions and Separate Brigades*. Washington, DC: Center of Military History, 1998.

Books and Articles

Altes, A. Korthals, K. Margry, G. Thuring, and R. Voskuil. *September 1944: Operation Market Garden*. Derde Druk, Netherlands: De Haan, 1987.

Ambrose, Stephen A. *Citizen Soldiers: The US Army from the Normandy Beaches to the Bulge and the Surrender of Germany, June 7, 1944–May 7, 1945*. New York: Simon & Schuster, 1997.

———. *D-Day, June 6, 1944: The Climactic Battle of World War II*. New York: Simon & Schuster, 1994.

———. *Eisenhower and Berlin, 1945: The Decision to Halt at the Elbe*. New York: W. W. Norton, 1967.

———. *The Supreme Commander: The War Years of General Dwight D. Eisenhower*. Garden City, NY: Doubleday, 1969.

Anderson, Steve, and Louis Eschle. "From Sicily to the Siegfried Line." *Military History* 20, no. 2 (2003): 50–57.

Autry, Jerry. *General William C. Lee, Father of the Airborne: Just Plain Bill*. San Francisco: Airborne Press, 1995.

Bartov, Omer. *The Eastern Front, 1941–45: German Troops and the Barbarisation of Warfare*. New York: St. Martin's Press, 1986.

———. *Hitler's Army: Soldiers, Nazis, and War in the Third Reich*. New York: Oxford University Press, 1991. Reprint, New York: Oxford University Press Paperback, 1992.

Bennett, Ralph. *Ultra and Mediterranean Strategy*. New York: William Morrow, 1989.

Bidwell, Shelford. "Kesselring." In *Hitler's Generals: Authoritative Portraits of the Men Who Waged Hitler's War*, ed. Correlli Barnett. London: George Weidenfield & Nicolson, 1989. Reprint, New York: Quill/William Morrow, 1989.

Biggs, Bradley. *Gavin: A Biography of General James M. Gavin*. Hamden, CT: Archon Books, 1980.

Blair, Clay. *Ridgway's Paratroopers: The American Airborne in World War II*. Garden City, NY: Doubleday, 1985.

Blumenson, Martin. *Mark Clark*. New York: Congdon & Weed, 1984.

Boatner, Mark M., III. *Biographical Dictionary of World War II*. Novato, CA: Presidio Press, 1996.

Booth, T. Michael, and Duncan Spencer. *Paratrooper: The Life of Gen. James M. Gavin*. New York: Simon & Schuster, 1994.

Breuer, William B. *Drop Zone Sicily: Allied Airborne Strike, July 1943*. Novato, CA: Presidio Press, 1983.

———. *Geronimo! American Paratroopers in World War II*. New York: St. Martin's Press, 1989.

Bryant, Arthur. *Triumph in the West: A History of the War Years Based on the Diaries of Field-Marshal Lord Alanbrooke, Chief of the Imperial General Staff*. Garden City, NY: Doubleday, 1959.

———. *The Turn of the Tide: A History of the War Years Based on the Diaries of Field-Marshal Lord Alanbrooke, Chief of the Imperial General Staff*. Garden City, NY: Doubleday, 1957.

Buffkin, Ronald M. "Assault Gliders: A World War II Phenomenon." *Military Review* 72, no. 7 (1992): 80–82.

Buxton, G. Edward, Jr., ed. *Official History of the 82nd Division: American Expeditionary Forces "All American" Division, 1917–1919*. Indianapolis: Bobbs-Merrill, 1919.

Chambers, John Whiteclay, II, et al., eds. *The Oxford Companion to American Military History*. Oxford: Oxford University Press, 1999.

Clancy, Tom. *Airborne: A Guided Tour of an Airborne Task Force*. New York: Berkley Books, 1997.

Coffman, Edward M. *The War to End All Wars: The American Military Experience in World War I*. Oxford: Oxford University Press, 1968. Reprint, Lexington: University Press of Kentucky, 1998.

Cooke, James J. *The All-Americans at War: The 82nd Division in the Great War, 1917–1918*. Westport, CT: Praeger, 1999.

Cooper, Matthew. *The German Army, 1933–1945: Its Political and Military Failure*. New York: Stein and Day, 1978. Reprint, Lanham, MD: Scarborough House, 1990.

Corum, James A. *The Luftwaffe: Creating the Operational Air War, 1918–1940*. Lawrence: University Press of Kansas, 1997.

Cray, Ed. *General of the Army: George C. Marshall, Soldier and Statesman*. New York: Simon & Schuster Touchstone Book, 1990.

Creveld, Martin van. *Fighting Power: German and U.S. Army Performance, 1939–1945*. Westport, CT: Greenwood Press, 1982.

D'Este, Carlo. *Bitter Victory: The Battle for Sicily, July–August 1943*. New York: HarperCollins, 1988.

———. *Decision in Normandy*. New York: Dutton, 1983.

———. *Fatal Decision: Anzio and the Battle for Rome*. New York: HarperCollins, 1991. Reprint, New York: HarperPerennial, 1992.

Devlin, Gerard M. *Paratrooper! The Saga of U.S. Army and Marine Parachute and Glider Combat Troops During World War II*. New York: St. Martin's Press, 1979.

———. *Silent Wings: The Saga of U.S. Army and Marine Combat Glider Pilots During World War II*. New York: St. Martin's Press, 1985.

Doubler, Michael D. *Closing with the Enemy: How GIs Fought the War in Europe, 1944–1945*. Lawrence: University Press of Kansas, 1994.

Doughty, Robert Alan. *The Breaking Point: Sedan and the Fall of France, 1940*. Hamden, CT: Archon Books, 1990.

Dupuy, R. Ernest. "Parker's Crossroads." *Infantry Journal* 62, no. 4 (1948): 14–16.

Dupuy, Trevor N. *A Genius for War: The German Army and General Staff, 1807–1945*. Englewood Cliffs, NJ: Prentice-Hall, 1977.

———. *Numbers, Predictions, and War: Using History to Evaluate Combat Factors and Predict the Outcome of Battle*. Indianapolis: Bobbs-Merrill, 1979.

Eisenhower, David. *Eisenhower at War, 1943–1945*. New York: Random House, 1986.

Eisenhower, John S. D. *The Bitter Woods*. New York: G. P. Putnam's Sons, 1969.

Ellis, John. *Cassino: The Hollow Victory*. New York: McGraw-Hill, 1984.

Esposito, Vincent J., ed. *The West Point Atlas of American Wars, 1900–1953*. New York: Praeger, 1959.

Fisher, Ernest F. "Evolution of US Airborne Doctrine," *Military Review* 46, no. 5 (1966): 71–77.

Flanagan, E. M., Jr. *The Angels: A History of the 11th Airborne Division*. Novato, CA: Presidio Press, 1989.

Glantz, David M. *The Soviet Airborne Experience*. Combat Studies Institute Research Survey, no. 4. Fort Leavenworth, KS: U.S. Army Command and General Staff College, 1984.

Goralski, Robert, ed. *World War II Almanac, 1931–1945: A Political and Military Record*. New York: G. P. Putnam's Sons, 1981.

Gudmundsson, Bruce I. *Stormtroop Tactics: Innovation in the German Army, 1914–1918*. New York: Praeger, 1989.

Hackett, John. "Student." In *Hitler's Generals: Authoritative Portraits of the Men Who Waged Hitler's War*, ed. Correlli Barnett. New York: George Weidenfield & Nicolson, Quill/William Morrow, 1989.

Hand, Roger. "Overlord and Operational Art." *Military Review* 75, no. 3 (1995): 86–91.

Hastings, Max. *Armageddon: The Battle for Germany, 1944–1945*. New York: Alfred A. Knopf, 2004.

———. *Overlord: D-Day and the Battle for Normandy*. New York: Simon & Schuster, 1984. Reprint, New York: Touchstone, 1985.

Huston, James A. "The Air Invasion of Holland." *Military Review* 32, no. 5 (1952): 37–57.

———.*Out of the Blue: U.S. Army Airborne Operations in World War II*. West Lafayette, IN: Purdue University Studies, 1972.

———. "Thoughts on the American Airborne Effort in World War II." *Military Review* 31, no. 1 (1951): 3–14.

Irving, David. *The Trail of the Fox: The Search for the True Field Marshal Rommel*. New York: Thomas Congdon Books, 1977.

Johnson, Samuel. *The History of Rasselas, Prince of Abissinia*. London: Penguin Classics, 1985.

Jorgensen, Starlyn R. *History of the 456th Parachute Field Artillery Battalion*. N.p., 1998.

Keegan, John. *The First World War*. New York: Alfred A. Knopf, 1999.

———. *Six Armies in Normandy from D-Day to the Liberation of Paris*. New York: Viking Press, 1982. Reprint, New York: Penguin Books, 1983.

Kershaw, Ian. *Hitler, 1936–45: Nemesis*. New York: W. W. Norton, 2000.

Kershaw, Robert J. *D-Day: Piercing the Atlantic Wall.* Annapolis, MD: Naval Institute Press, 1994.

———. *"It Never Snows in September": The German View of MARKET-GARDEN and the Battle of Arnhem, September 1944.* Hersham, England: Ian Allan Publishing, 1994.

Lempke, Duane A. "Ridgway's Leadership Legacy." *Military Review* 68, no. 11 (1988): 69–75.

Liddell Hart, B. H. *The German Generals Talk.* New York: William Morrow, 1948. Reprint, New York: Quill, 1979.

Lucas, James. *Storming Eagles: German Airborne Forces in World War Two.* London: Arms and Armour Press, 1988.

Lupfer, Timothy T. *The Dynamics of Doctrine: The Changes in German Tactical Doctrine During the First World War.* Leavenworth Paper no. 4. Fort Leavenworth, KS: Combat Studies Institute, U.S. Army Command and General Staff College, 1981.

MacDonald, Charles B. *The Battle of the Huertgen Forest.* New York: Berkley, 1963.

———. *The Mighty Endeavor: The American War in Europe.* New York: Oxford University Press, 1969. Reprint, New York: Da Capo Press, 1992.

———. *A Time for Trumpets: The Untold Story of the Battle of the Bulge.* New York: Bantam Books, 1985.

Macintyre, Ben. *Operation Mincemeat: How a Dead Man and a Bizarre Plan Fooled the Nazis and Assured an Allied Victory.* New York: Crown, 2010.

Mandle, William D., and David H. Whittier. *Combat Record of the 504th Parachute Infantry Regiment: April 1943–July 1945.* Paris: Draeger Frères, n.d.

Mansoor, Peter R. *The GI Offensive in Europe: The Triumph of American Infantry Divisions, 1941–1945.* Lawrence: University Press of Kansas, 1999.

Margry, Karel ed. *Operation Market-Garden: Then and Now.* Vol. 1. London: Battle of Britain International, 2002.

———. *Operation Market-Garden: Then and Now.* Vol. 2. London: Battle of Britain International, 2002.

Marshall, S[amuel] L[yman] A[twood]. *Men Against Fire: The Problem of Battle Command in Future War.* New York: William Morrow, 1947. Reprint, Gloucester, MA: Peter Smith, 1978.

Masters, Charles J. *Glidermen of Neptune: The American D-Day Glider Attack.* Carbondale: Southern Illinois University Press, 1995.

Mayhew, Nelson. "The Yacht Club: The Sixty-second Troop Carrier Squadron and the Evolution of Combat Airdrop Operations During World War II." Master's thesis, University of Alabama, 1992.

Miller, Merle. *Ike the Soldier: As They Knew Him.* New York: G. P. Putnam's Sons, 1987.

Mitcham, Samuel W., Jr. *The Desert Fox in Normandy: Rommel's Defense of Fortress Europe.* Westport, CT: Praeger, 1997.

Montagu, Ewen. *The Man Who Never Was.* Philadelphia: Lippincott, 1953.

Morison, Samuel Eliot. *The Two-Ocean War: A Short History of the United States Navy in the Second World War.* Boston: Little, Brown, 1963.

Mrazek, James E. *The Fall of Eben Emael: Prelude to Dunkerque*. Washington, DC: Robert B. Luce, 1970.

———. *The Glider War*. New York: St. Martin's Press, 1975.

Overy, Richard. *Why the Allies Won*. New York: W. W. Norton, 1995. Reprint, New York: W. W. Norton, 1997.

Pogue, Forrest C. *George C. Marshall: Organizer of Victory*. New York: Viking Press, 1973.

Rapport, Leonard, and Arthur Northwood Jr. *Rendezvous with Destiny: A History of the 101st Airborne Division*. Washington, DC: Infantry Journal Press, 1948.

Ryan, Cornelius. *A Bridge Too Far*. New York: Simon and Schuster, 1974.

———. *The Longest Day, June 6, 1944*. New York: Simon & Schuster, 1959. Reprint, New York: Pocket Books, 1970.

Savage, Paul L., and Richard A. Gabriel. "Cohesion and Disintegration in the American Army." In *The Military in America from the Colonial Era to the Present*, ed. Peter Karsten. New York: Free Press, 1980.

———. *Crisis in Command: Mismanagement in the Army*. New York: Hill and Wang, 1978.

Shils, Edward A., and Morris Janowitz. "Cohesion and Disintegration in the Wehrmacht in World War II." In *Military Conflict: Essays in the Institutional Analysis of War and Peace*, ed. Morris Janowitz. Beverly Hills, CA: Sage Publications, 1975.

Smoler, Frederic. "The Secret of the Soldiers Who Didn't Shoot." *American Heritage* 40, no. 2 (1989): 37–45.

Soffer, Jonathan M. *General Matthew B. Ridgway: From Progressivism to Reaganism, 1895–1993*. Westport, CT: Praeger, 1998.

Stokesbury, James L. *A Short History of World War I*. New York: William Morrow, 1981.

Taylor, John M. *General Maxwell Taylor: The Sword and the Pen*. New York: Doubleday, 1989. Reprint, New York: Bantam Books, 1991.

Trez, Michel De, ed. *The Way We Were: Col. Robert N. Piper, "Bob."* Wezembeek-Oppem, Belgium: D-Day Publishing, 2002.

Tugwell, Maurice A. J. "Day of the Paratroops." *Military Review* 57, no. 3 (1977): 40–53.

Weigley, Russell F. *Eisenhower's Lieutenants: The Campaign of France and Germany, 1944–1945*. Bloomington: Indiana University Press, 1981.

———. *History of the United States Army*. New York: Macmillan, 1967.

Weinberg, Gerhard L. *A World at Arms: A Global History of World War II*. Cambridge: Cambridge University Press, 1994.

Weingartner, Steven, ed. *The Greatest Thing We Have Ever Attempted: Historical Perspectives on the Normandy Campaign*. Wheaton, IL: Cantigny First Division Foundation, 1998.

Wheal, Elizabeth-Anne, Stephen Pope, and James Taylor, eds. *The Meridian Encyclopedia of the Second World War*. New York: Penguin Books, 1992.

Wheeler-Bennett, J. W. *The Nemesis of Power: The German Army in Politics, 1918–1945*. 2nd ed. New York: Viking Press, 1967.

Whiting, Charles. *Ghost Front: The Ardennes Before the Battle of the Bulge*. Cambridge: Da Capo Press, 2002.

Willmott, H. P. *The Great Crusade: A New Complete History of the Second World War*. New York: Macmillan, 1989. Reprint, New York: Free Press, 1991.

Wills, Deryk, ed. *Put on Your Boots and Parachutes*. Leicester, England: AB Publishers, 1992.

Wilson, Charles McMoran [Lord Moran]. *The Anatomy of Courage*. London: Constable, 1945. Reprint, Garden City Park, NY: Avery Publishing Group, 1987.

Young, Peter, ed. *Atlas of the Second World War*. New York: G. P. Putnam's Sons, 1974.

Ziemke, Earl F. "Rundstedt." In *Hitler's Generals: Authoritative Portraits of the Men Who Waged Hitler's War*, ed. Correlli Barnett. New York: George Weidenfield & Nicolson, Quill/William Morrow, 1989.

INDEX